From the Physical to the Most Ephemeral

The Object

Characteristics

Physicality

From the Physical to the Most Ephemeral

This book is about looking at and understanding sculpture. Let us begin with a work entitled *The Curved House* by Louise Bourgeois. We may have a preconceived idea of what a sculpture should look like. If so, is this a sculpture? And if so, what is the sculptor telling us? Yes, it appears to be a house, but it is far too small to be anything but a miniature doll's house. Carved from a block of marble, it is a solid mass, with no space for rooms inside. So maybe it is not meant to be a house in the normal sense. The whole form appears to be curved: was the stone malleable at one time? Fabricated not from steel nor cast in bronze, it is hewn from pink marble. Why this particular material? The artist presents the viewer with a simple opposition. Pink evokes soft flesh, but the stone has been carved into a sharp-edged geometric architectural mass – a child's drawing of a house hardened into stone. But houses are not usually curved; this curvature is an allusion to both the organic and its opposite. Look at the four windows and the door. They are recessed planes cut into each opening; they define the solid mass within and block entry. A house more for the eye and mind than for the body. Perhaps it is a symbolic house, an inaccessible container for childhood memories, or a home desired but never inhabited. How should one perceive the flesh-coloured stone? There is much more to consider but with these few questions the journey towards understanding has already begun.

What follows provides the information we need to discover the wealth of meaning contained within sculpture, introducing the fourteen Elements of Sculpture. These Elements form sculpture's visual language and an understanding of them reveals the structure and vocabulary of sculptural expression. It is difficult to imagine a single work that utilizes all fourteen Elements to the same degree, so some Elements will be primary, others secondary, while others may not be used at all.

Elements range from the most physical, Material, to the most ephemeral, Memory. The other Elements are Place, Surface, Edge, Texture, Colour, Scale, Mass, Centre of Gravity, Volume, Space, Movement and Light. Each Element is defined and illustrated by examples ranging from the early history of sculpture to the present. As we analyse and come to understand these examples, it helps us appreciate the conceptual and formal richness to be found within the long history of this art form. We see there is a greater

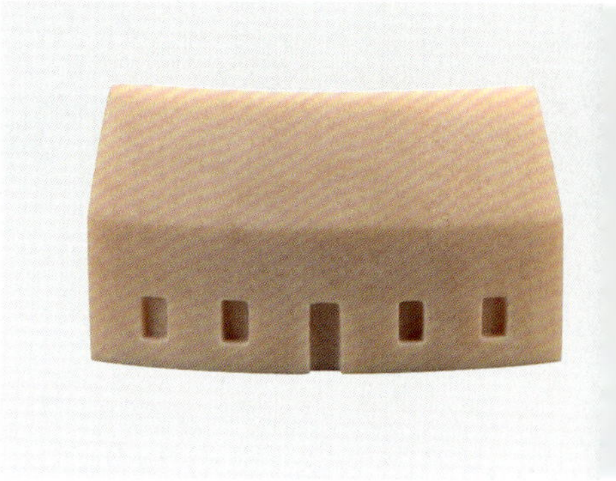

Louise Bourgeois (1911–2010)
The Curved House

2010
Pink marble
12.1 × 21 × 7 cm
(4 ¾ × 8 ¼ × 2 ¾ in)
Whitney Museum of American Art, New York
(edition of 12 with 3 APs)

commonality of sculptural concerns across time and cultures than we may first have assumed.

Although we may think of these Elements as the *facts* of all three-dimensional form, they are especially relevant to the experience of sculpture. Not only do they make up the essential vocabulary of form for the viewer, but they also provide necessary insight into the creative imagination of the artist, because the Elements constitute the sculptor's aesthetic vocabulary as well. I have chosen to construct this book around these fourteen Elements because they establish the factual basis for individual interpretation.

Experiencing the Third Dimension

Sculpture is material form in real space; this is its most basic quality. Ideally a work reveals itself slowly, unfolding as the viewer walks around it, eyes constantly moving and exploring every aspect of the form in an attempt to engage with its dimensional presence. But more often than not, when we look at a sculpture for the first time, no matter how exceptional the object might be, the mind wanders, searching for similar images. Past forms flood our consciousness and so without circling we assume we already know it.

Experiencing sculptural form demands that the viewer be not only curious, but also actively engaged in the desire to see and understand. Constantin Brancusi's *White Negress I* (overleaf) is especially interesting in this respect as it invites a radically new understanding from each vantage point.

Like a tree, a sculpture does not have a clearly defined front, back or side. We begin with what appears to be three or possibly four carved marble parts comprising a meticulous assemblage of forms. From the first view we assume that the large ovoid is a head. Full, clearly defined but slightly askew lips are topped by a prominent but off-centre chignon. These features dominate the face and add a certain lyricism to a composition that is otherwise symmetrically balanced. The 'head' is poised on a small marble cylinder that maintains the verticality of the sculpture. The pure white marble carved cylinder in turn rests in the middle of an equilateral cross.

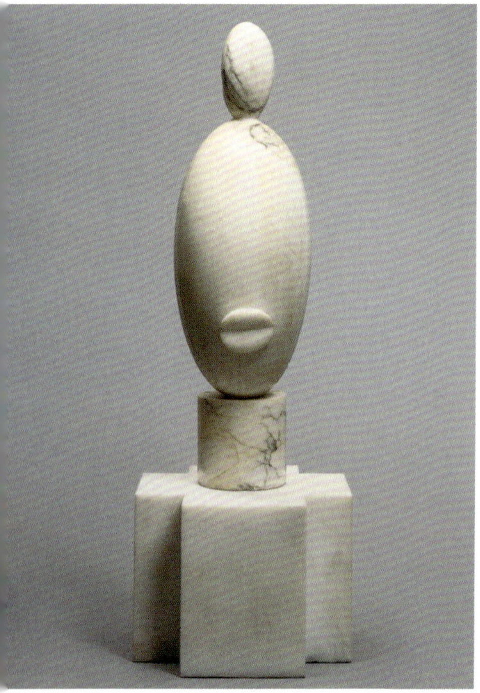

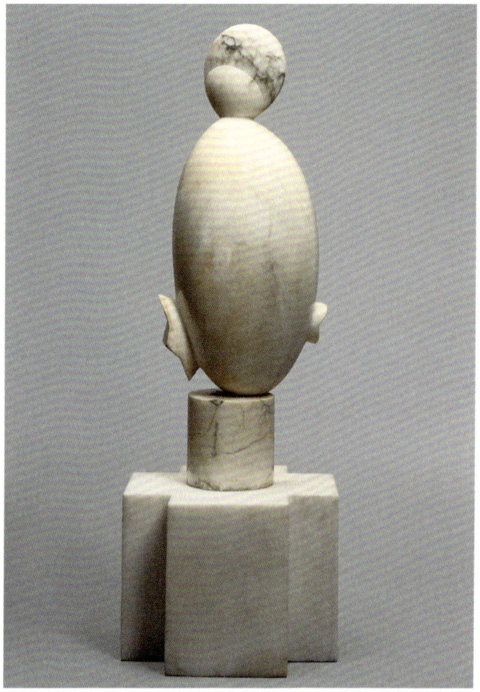

Constantin Brancusi (1876–1957)
White Negress I

1923
Veined marble, marble two-part base
38.1 × 14.3 × 17.9 cm
(15 × 5 ⅝ × 7 in)
Philadelphia Museum of Art, PA

As we move around the sculpture to the next view, a transformation takes place. What was a quite convincing 'head' now evolves into a swimming fish. The lips that previously appeared to be integrated into the surface of the head now protrude, as does the zigzag tail. The ellipse at the top, first perceived as the Negress's topknot, has now become the dorsal fin of a fish.

In the first view, the small cylinder of veined marble might have been understood as a neck, or possibly a collar on which the head is evenly balanced and centred. But from the second view we see that Brancusi has shifted the mass of the form towards the outer edge of the cylinder and by tipping the ovoid form backwards slightly, the fish is propelled forwards.

Continue around the sculpture. In the next view our literal associations having to do with head/fish disappear, and the form evolves into almost total abstraction. As we move around the work the geometric abstractions of the third view rearrange themselves back into a swimming fish. Now the sculpture

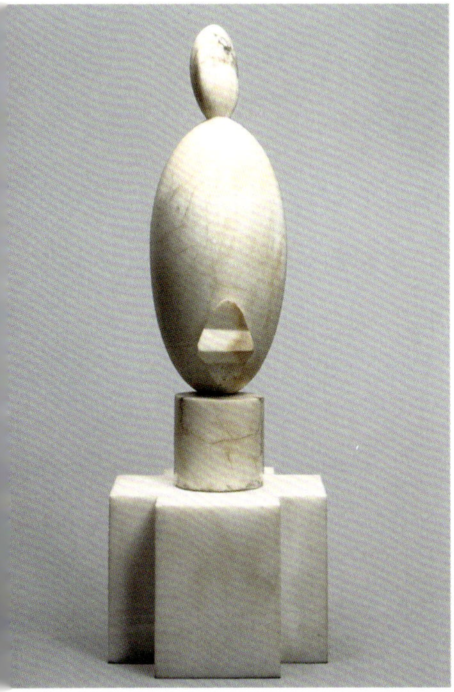

becomes a carefully considered composition of different forms fitting together, composing a visual puzzle.

Observe the white equilateral cross. It plays a critical role in the work. With its geometric repetition and symmetry, it is the only form in the composition that appears constant as we walk around the sculpture; it acts as a counterpoint to the more organic forms above it. Both literally and figuratively it supports the irony that lies at the core of this carefully composed but improbable assemblage of opposites: head/fish, land/water, white/black Negress.

Few of these possibilities could have been foreseen or imagined when viewing the work from a single vantage point. Only by moving around a sculpture can the viewer experience the multitude of surprises that lie within three-dimensional forms. Sculpture is form in space.

The Fourteen Elements of Sculpture

The Elements are the vocabulary of sculptural form. They both guide and encourage us to ask questions that may lead towards understanding a particular work. For example, how does the choice of one material over another alter the meaning of a sculpture? Such questions encourage answers that in turn may provide clues to the meaning of a work. The fourteen Elements afford a structure that will assist viewers in their attempt to discover, understand and appreciate the experience of sculpture.

Although a particular work may contain any number of Elements in any order of prominence, they are organized here into six sections. These categories gather together individual Elements that share similar characteristics. I begin with the Element, Material, as every object is made from something, and systematically progress to the least physical – Memory.

How we decide to order the Elements when looking at a specific sculpture is highly personal and subject to change. The categories, and the Elements within them, are intended as a guide for the viewer to consider, not as a dogmatic closed structure.

1

The Object

The first two Elements affirm that a sculpture is a three-dimensional object in real space. It is this thing in this place.

Material

Andy Goldsworthy

Mark di Suvero

Constantin Brancusi

Gian Lorenzo Bernini

Edgar Degas

Felix Gonzalez-Torres

Shinique Smith

Jacob Epstein

Place

Maurizio Cattelan

Bamana Culture, Mali

Robert Smithson

Auguste Rodin

Han Dynasty, China

Niccolò dell'Arca

Haida Culture, Canada

Material

The matter from which a thing is made.

Material is first, because everything is made from something. Each material contains unique characteristics. The sculptor must be aware of the numerous possibilities within a particular material. And have knowledge of the tools and techniques needed to work with it. Nothing the sculptor does to the material is neutral; every act contains meaning. Creating a sculpture is a three-way conversation between sculptor, material and viewer. Material is by necessity at the centre of that conversation, and it is as much alive as the other two. However, the ultimate aesthetic challenge for the sculptor is to create form that transcends the material from which it is made.

As the twentieth century progressed, the range of artistic materials increased exponentially, and the exploration of these new materials greatly expanded the expressive potential of modern and contemporary sculpture. That being so, when we see a contemporary work for the first time, one logical question might be: why did the sculptor choose this particular material?

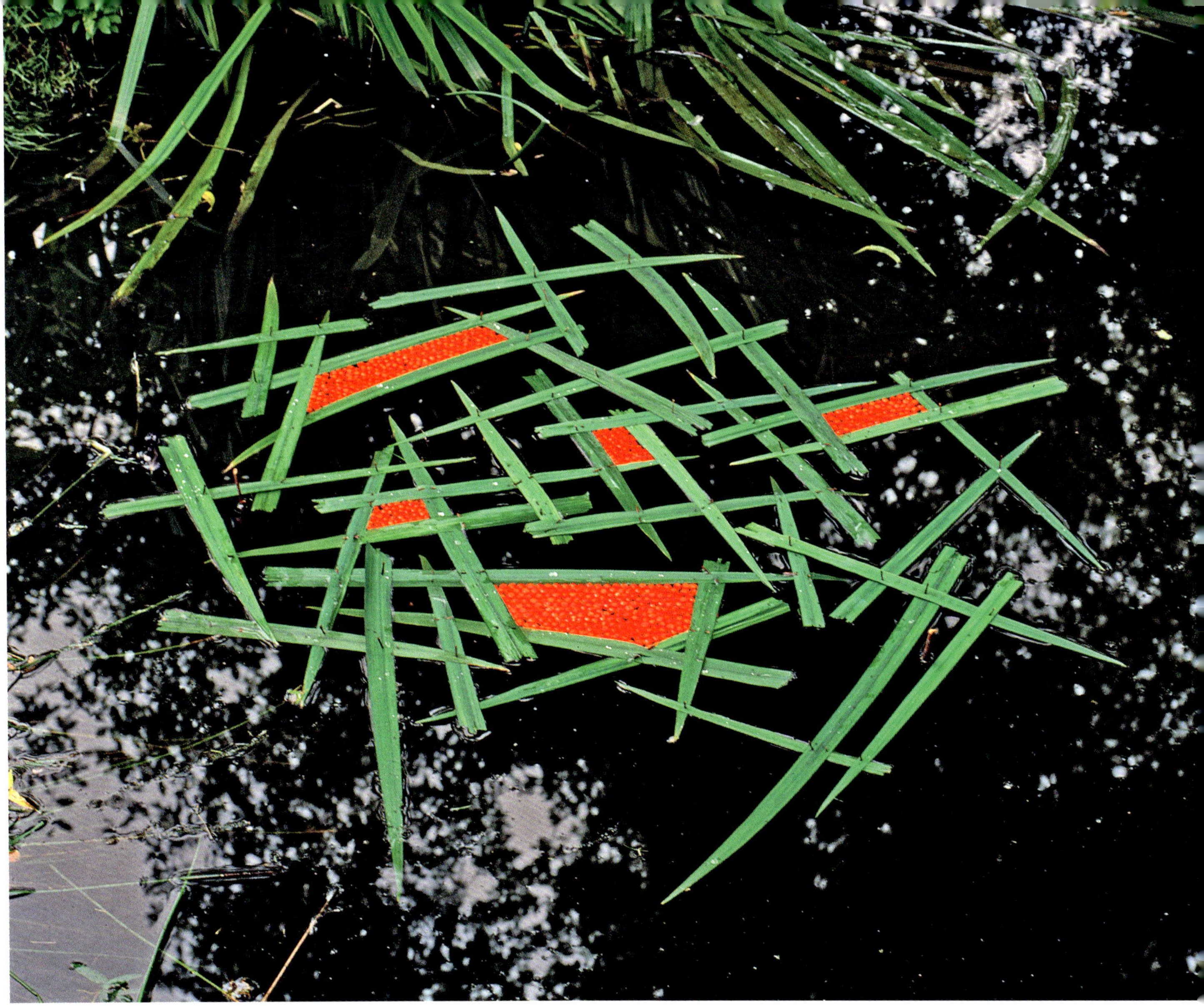

Andy Goldsworthy (b. 1956)
Iris blades pinned together with thorns
filled in five sections with rowan berries
fish attacking from below
difficult to keep all the berries in
nibbled at by ducks

1987
Iris blades, thorns, rowan berries
29.7 × 29.3 cm (11 ¾ × 11 ½ in)
Yorkshire Sculpture Park, West Bretton

Made from found natural materials, this work by Andy Goldsworthy is difficult to appreciate in a photograph. It is composed of iris leaves floating on the surface of a still pond. Enclosed within the iris leaves are five small 'rafts' of red rowan berries. As we see it here, it may appear to be more of an exercise in Sumi calligraphy using coloured ink than a sculpture of leaves and berries floating on still water. Goldsworthy has been very careful to make certain that his part in the process of making this work was at all times subservient to the natural materials he selected and to the place that he chose for its site. Moments after the photograph was taken the work may have been radically altered by a breeze, washed away by the next rain or in other ways changed. All of these exacting decisions made by the sculptor with regard to material, site and process are fundamental in determining what we see and therefore what we understand.

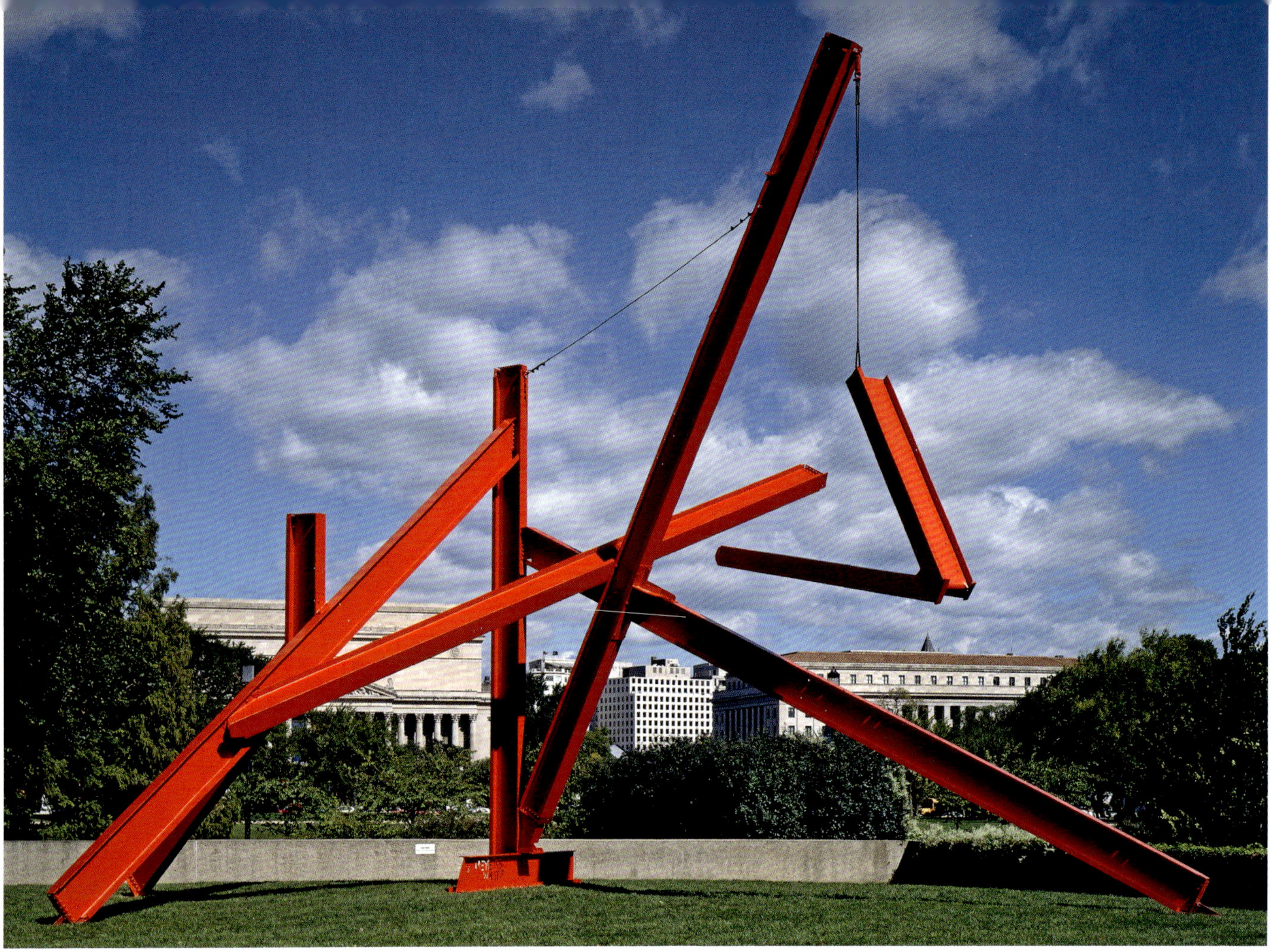

Mark di Suvero (b. 1933)
Are Years What? (for Marianne Moore)

1967
Painted steel
121.9 × 121.9 × 91.4 m
(40 × 40 × 30 ft)
Hirshhorn Museum and Sculpture Garden, Washington DC

Constructing a sculpture out of I-beams that are 60 feet long demands a very different order of thinking from that of the previous work. The sheer size and engineering confidence of this large-scale painted steel piece by Mark di Suvero are overwhelming. When one experiences the sculpture in this setting, even the trees and the buildings beyond become less important than the explosive red architectonic structural authority of the work. Like a huge crane, the central cantilever suspends a floating V-shaped I-beam structure high over the head of the viewer that can move freely in the wind. This creates a lyrical moment in an otherwise aggressive work.

The Goldsworthy and the di Suvero sculptures represent two very different aesthetic approaches and so each demands different materials and working methods. In the case of Goldsworthy, the work results from an intimate understanding of the sculptural possibilities of natural materials within a natural environment, while the di Suvero work results from a thorough knowledge of how to adapt industrial tools, materials and methods to the creation of a gigantic work of art that is able to visually compete within an urban environment.

Constantin Brancusi (1876–1957)
Torso of a Young Man

c. 1917–22
Maple, limestone base
48.3 × 31.5 × 18.5 cm (19 × 12 ⅜ × 7 ¼ in)
Philadelphia Museum of Art, PA

Constantin Brancusi
Torso of a Young Man

1917
Brass, limestone base
68.8 × 30.5 × 19.1 cm (27 × 12 × 7 ½ in)
Cleveland Museum of Art, OH

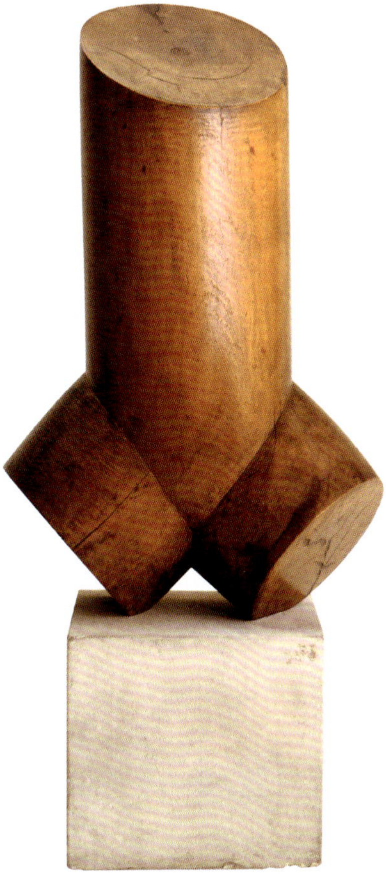

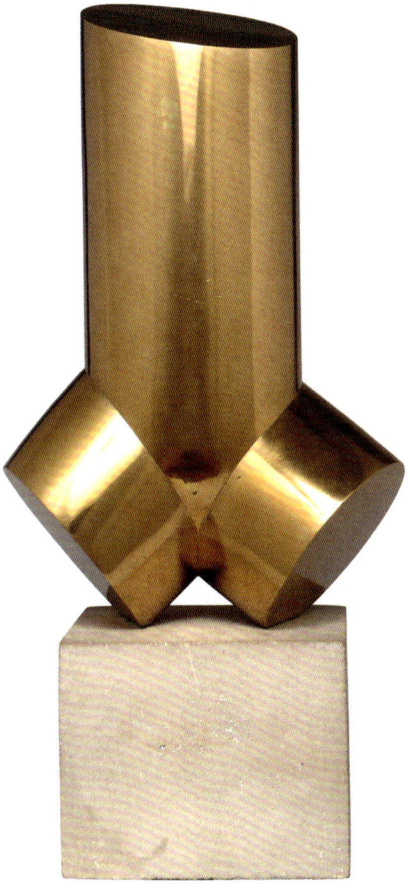

Consider now the same basic form made from two materials by the same artist, and how that change in material may make a critical difference to the work's content and our understanding of it. Both works by Constantin Brancusi are entitled *Torso of a Young Man*: one is made of bronze, the other of wood. There are numerous works by Brancusi in which the artist makes the same basic form from different materials. And with each material change the meaning of the work shifts. In this wood piece, consider how limbs grow out from the trunk of a tree forming a V, in much the same way that legs grow from the human torso. The bronze piece is the same basic form and is almost the same size as the other, but the similarities stop there. In the wooden version tool marks from the process of making have been left; also evident are the annual rings of the maple tree that it was cut from. None of these traces of process, natural or otherwise, is evident in the bronze, as it has been polished to a near perfect machine-like reflective surface. This polished surface, depending on the intensity of the light, may cause the form of the *Torso* to dissolve into its own reflected light. Not so with the wood, which absorbs light. The titles tell us that both works show a male youth, but at first glance what we see is a youthful torso without male genitalia, thus more girl than boy. However, we must look at the sculpture in total, as it is only then that what had been missing now becomes its whole form – an erect penis. One torso is a carved inverted tree trunk that grows naturally and needed limited carving – its material, process and final form are all evident. The other torso could be a metal machine part, which belies its organic reference.

Gian Lorenzo Bernini (1598–1680)
Apollo and Daphne

1623–4
Carrara marble
243 cm (96 in) high
Galleria Borghese, Rome

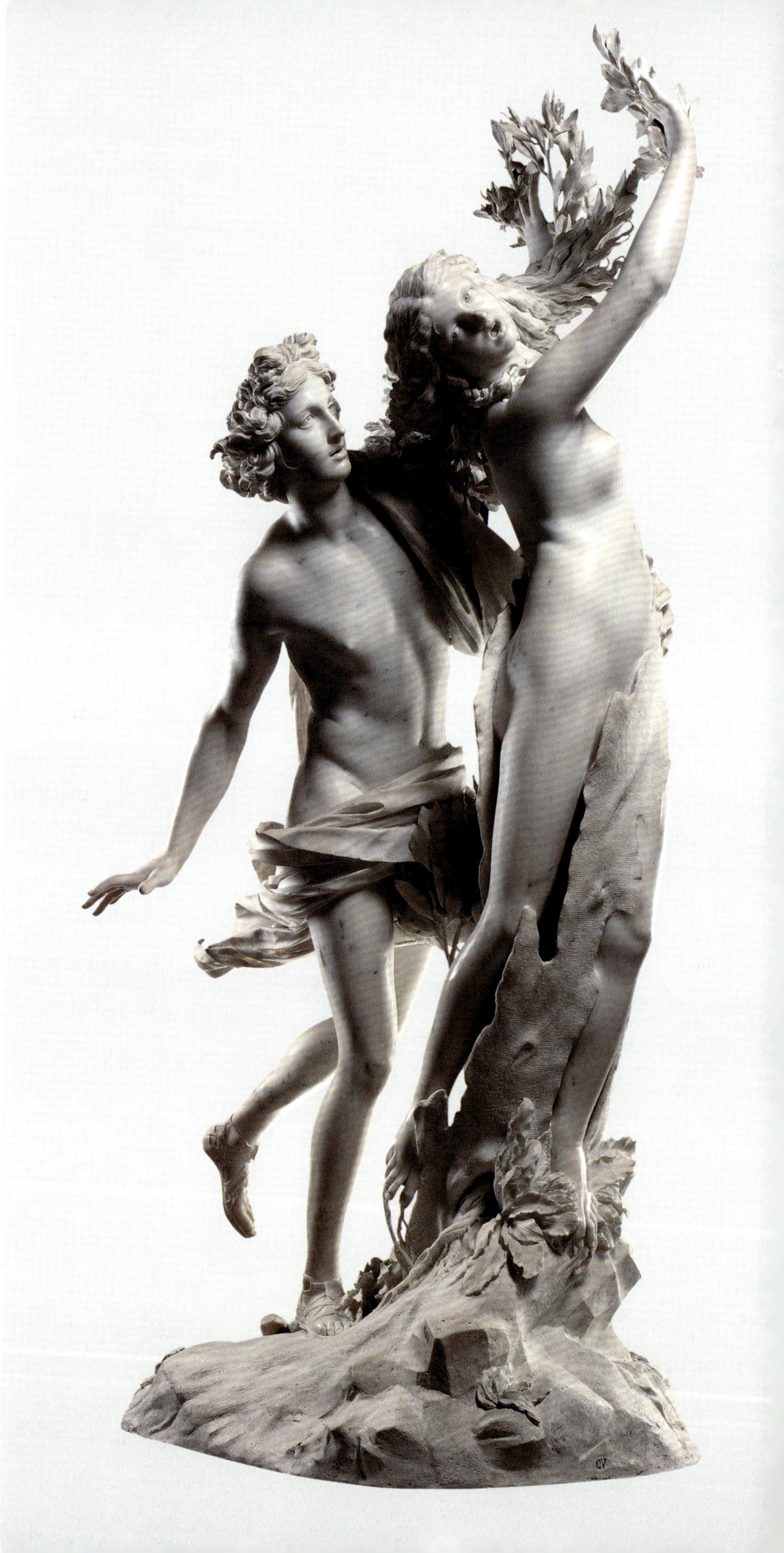

The Baroque sculptor Gian Lorenzo Bernini chose to portray the cathartic moment in classical mythology when Daphne, fleeing Apollo's desire, can only escape his lust by transforming herself into a laurel tree. Bernini, through his consummate skill as a stone carver, was able to capture this moment of transformation, ascension and unrequited desire in great detail. In the seventeenth century there were only four primary materials available to the sculptor – bronze, terracotta (fired clay), wood and stone. In this instance, white marble was the ideal choice both because it evokes the classical and because of its material translucence communicates an uncanny frozen moment in time and light.

Edgar Degas (1834–1917)
The Little Fourteen-Year-Old Dancer

Executed in wax 1878–81; cast in bronze after 1922
Bronze, tulle, silk
99.1 cm (39 in) high
Philadelphia Museum of Art, PA

l
c
fi
S.
oı
pa
to
the
wh
stoı
of tl
anti
the t
in co
a perc

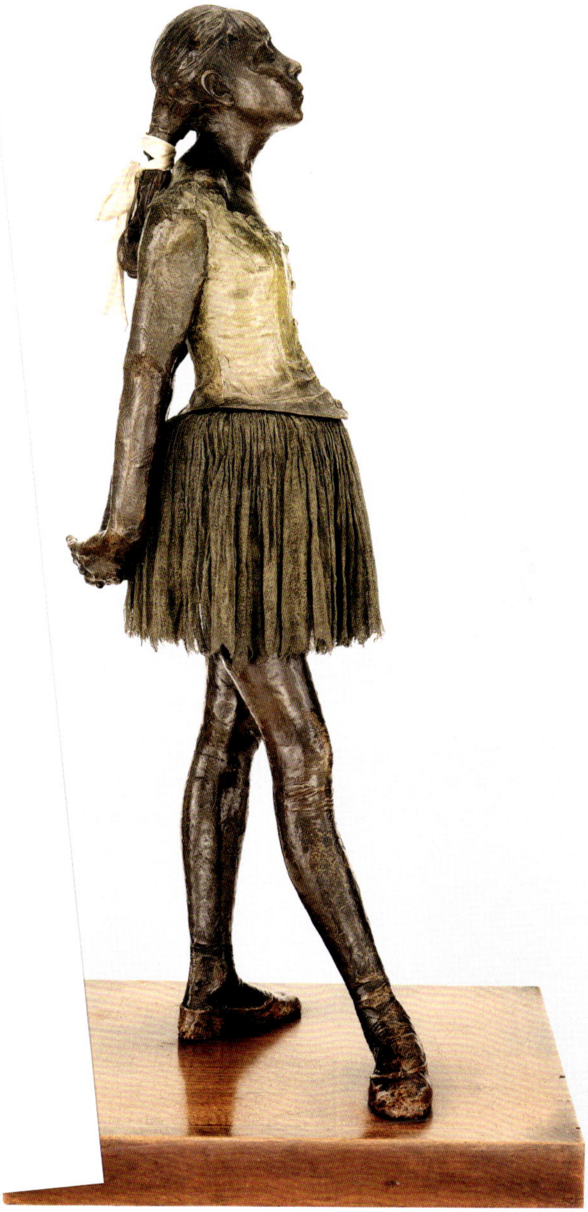

Felix Gonzalez-Torres (1957–1996)
'Untitled' (Portrait of Ross in LA)

1991
Candies individually wrapped in multicoloured cellophane, endless supply
Overall dimensions vary with each installation, ideal weight 75 kg (175 lbs)
Art Institute of Chicago, IL

In the early stages of looking at a sculpture and trying to come to tentative conclusions about it, it is important to resist one interpretation over another before we have had the opportunity to look, question and think. In this work by Felix Gonzalez-Torres, we might be tempted to take it literally: a pile of candy in the corner. However, modernism brought a freedom of choice in sculptural material – sculpture was no longer confined to being cast in bronze or carved in stone; it could be made from anything, even cellophane-wrapped candy. From the curatorial statement on the wall we learn that what first appears to be simply hundreds of multicoloured wrapped candies may be interpreted as a silent offering to the memory of the artist's lover, Ross Laycock, who died of an AIDS-related illness. As an allegorical representation, we read that the viewer is meant to take and eat the candies as a remembrance of Ross, thus granting him 'perpetual life'. As the numbers of candies diminish they may be replenished so the average weight of the work remains at about 175 pounds, which was Ross's ideal body weight.

As viewers, we frequently make two common assumptions. One has to do with the material permanence of sculpture and the other with the status of the museum as a place that protects and preserves objects. Both assumptions are thoughtfully questioned here. The work is always changing. Once candy is taken, new pieces may be added. Through this constant cycling we are reminded of the impermanence and fragility of life. But this is only one possible interpretation among others. A balance must be found between blind acceptance of what we are told and critically looking and considering the work for ourselves.

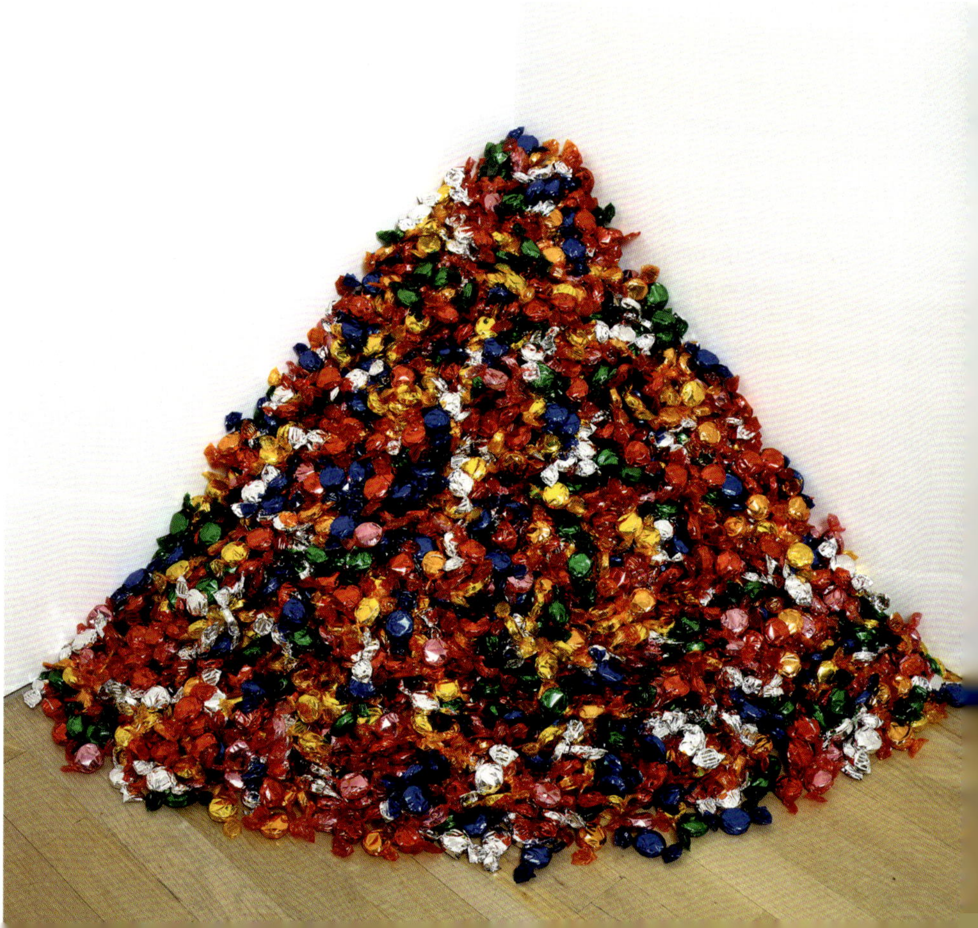

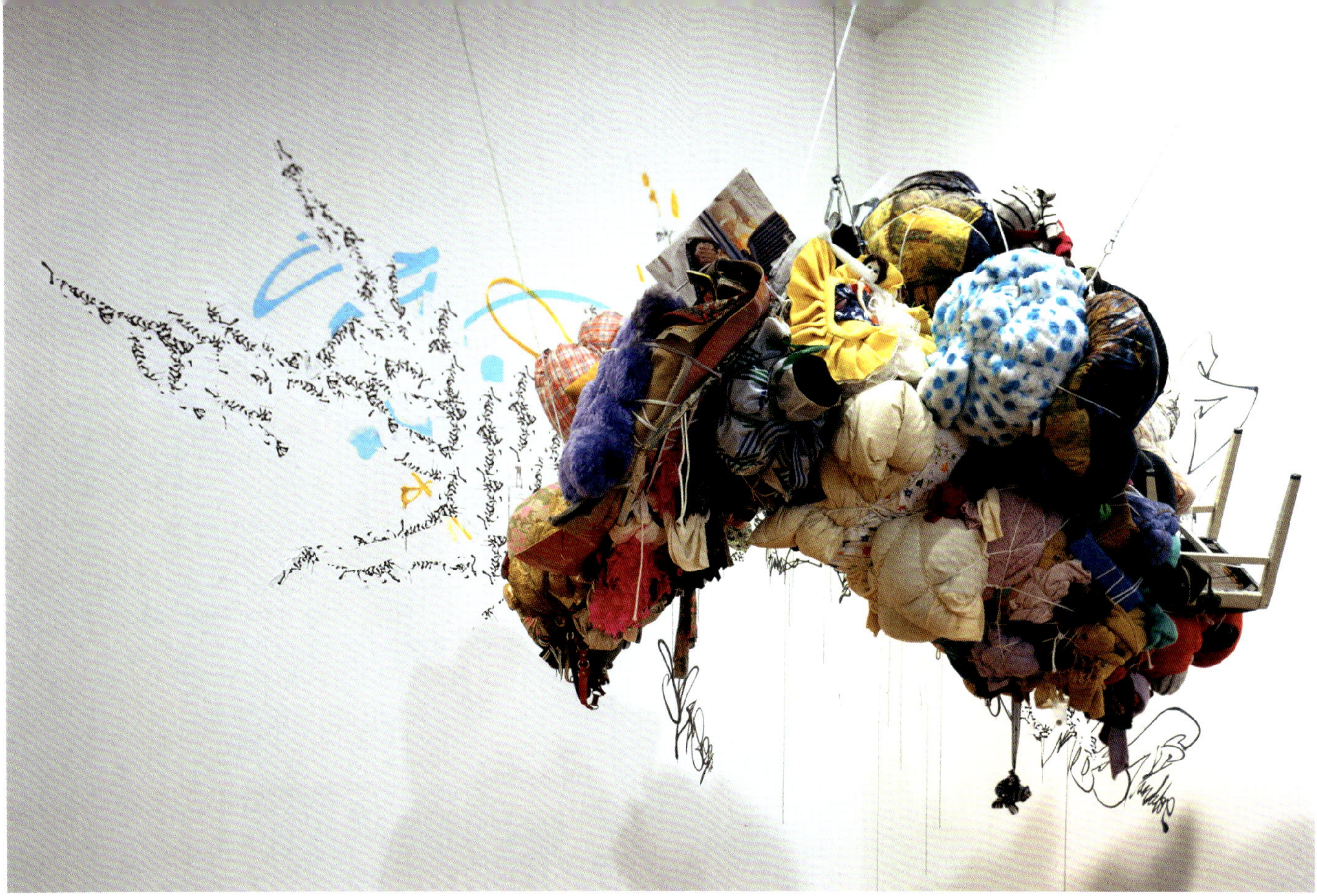

Shinique Smith (b. 1971)
Arcadian Cluster

2006
Clothing, fabric, found objects, acrylic, binding; wall drawing
Excluding wall drawing: 224 × 335 × 244 cm (96 × 132 × 96 in)
Installed at PS1 Contemporary Art Center, New York

Like the Gonzalez-Torres work opposite, this sculpture by Shinique Smith is made from found objects that would never have been considered as materials for sculpture until the early part of the twentieth century. It is composed of various man-made found household articles. We see a chair, bed coverings, a child's doll, belts and various pieces of clothing, mostly polyester, all tied together in a seemingly off-hand manner using string and rope into a free-floating mass of stuff. These objects were made in the second world, imported to the first, consumed, then exported again, to be consumed once more, by the third world. Even their material presence in this sculpture feels transitory; the form is a suspended mass of stuff in which nothing belongs, not even the graffiti on the wall behind. They are united only by their material differences.

Jacob Epstein (1880–1959)
The Rock Drill

1913–5; reconstruction 1974
Polyester resin, metal, wood
205 × 141.5 cm (80 ¾ × 55 ¾ in)
Birmingham Museum and Art Gallery

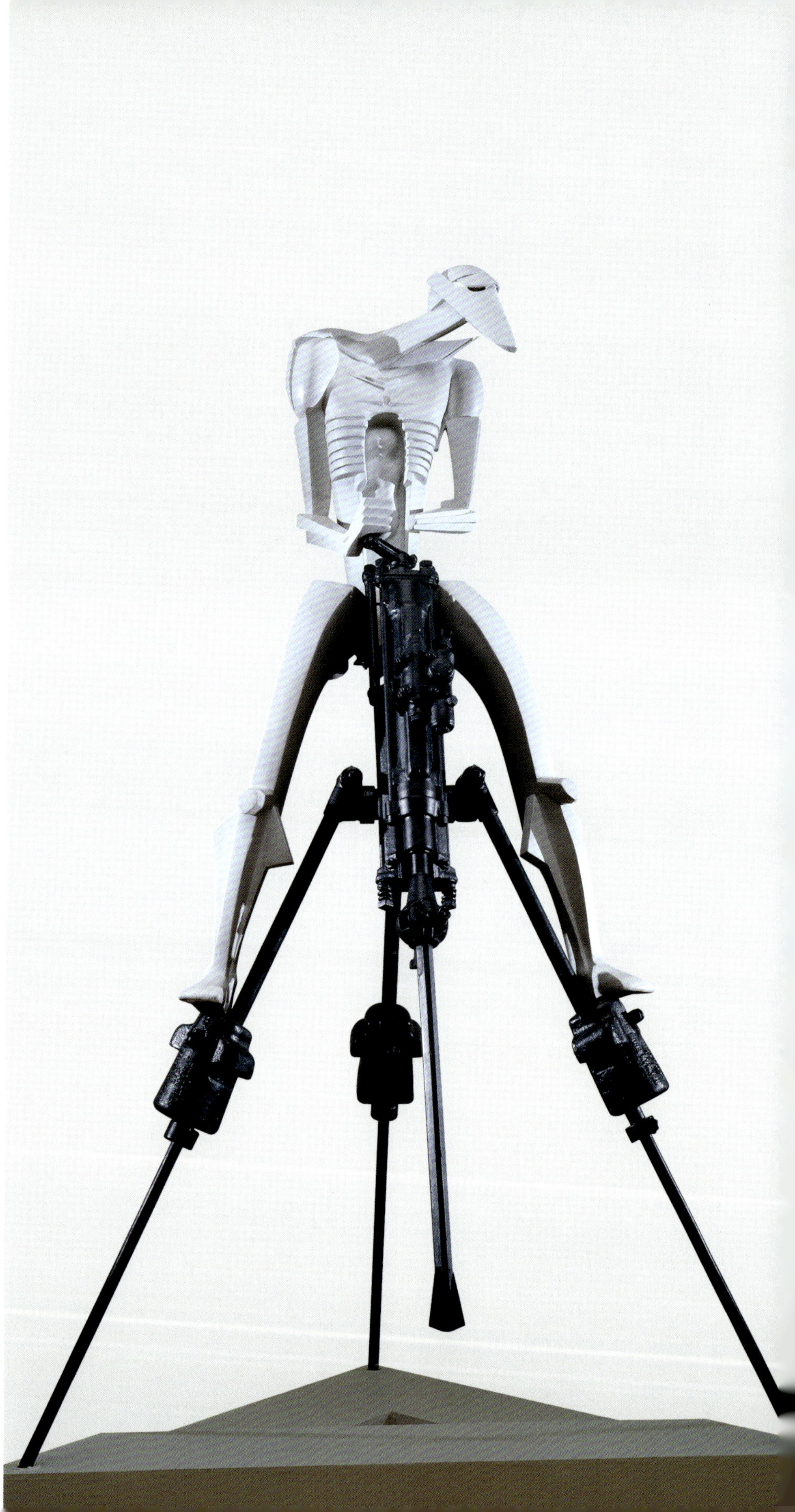

All material in sculpture is, to a greater or lesser extent, found or discovered by the sculptor. The preconceived expectation of the viewer may have a great deal to do with how a particular material choice is understood. Jacob Epstein's choice of a violent and aggressively sexual industrial machine must have had a deeply disturbing effect when first seen.

From the moment he saw it in a stone quarry, Epstein was immediately fascinated by the drill's violent mechanical power. He purchased the machine and took it to his studio. The drill remains unchanged within the total work – a found object – while the machine-like 'robot' man or driller made from plaster stands astride the device. Epstein forms the man, possibly the Minotaur, in such a way as to convey the impression that he/it too could have been made by a machine: observe the robot-like head. And although the driller straddles or rides the drill he does not dominate it. The overall impression is one of a ferocious and brutal battle between two savage forces, and this confrontation is made even more poignant by the material choice of the found rock drill.

... you cannot make what you want to make, but what the material permits you to make. You cannot make from marble what you would make out of wood, or what you would make out of stone ... Each material has its own life ... we must not try to make materials speak our language, we must go with them to the point where others understand their language.

— Constantin Brancusi

Everything is sculpture ... Any material, any idea without hindrance born into space, I consider sculpture.

— Isamu Noguchi

... challenging the material, looking at the shape and learning from things, and having the opportunity to touch all of these different things, to feel their difference – in a word to learn from them because they all have qualities, they all have something ... Material is everything to me.

— Tony Cragg

What matters for me in art is to make one forget material ... Art is invisible.

— Medardo Rosso

Place

The environment that surrounds the object.

With Place, our focus expands out from the object to the larger environment that surrounds it. The environment in which a sculpture is situated is either *active* or *passive*.

In the *active* sense the object's immediate environment plays a significant role in how we understand a particular sculpture. The two are so entwined that to remove one from the other is impossible without destroying the meaning of the total work. Sculptures in which place and object are one are often referred to as 'site-specific' works.

A *passive* environment means that the place surrounding the object is secondary to it. But it does not mean place can be separated entirely from meaning. The same sculpture seen in different environments may have its meaning altered. In an effort to negate these distractions so that the viewer's focus is directed towards the object, exhibition practices have settled on the ultimate passive environment, the white box. These well-lit immaculate spaces are found in almost every contemporary museum or gallery. But even here it is necessary to be attentive – how sculpture is exhibited will always, on some level, influence how the viewer understands it.

The relationship between location, object and meaning is complex, and the many ways in which environment can influence meaning are not fully appreciated. For example, to what degree are we able to separate the cultural status of a museum from our emotional, aesthetic response to an object seen within it? The environment surrounding a sculpture is never neutral. It contains past and present histories that in both subtle and overt ways influence meaning.

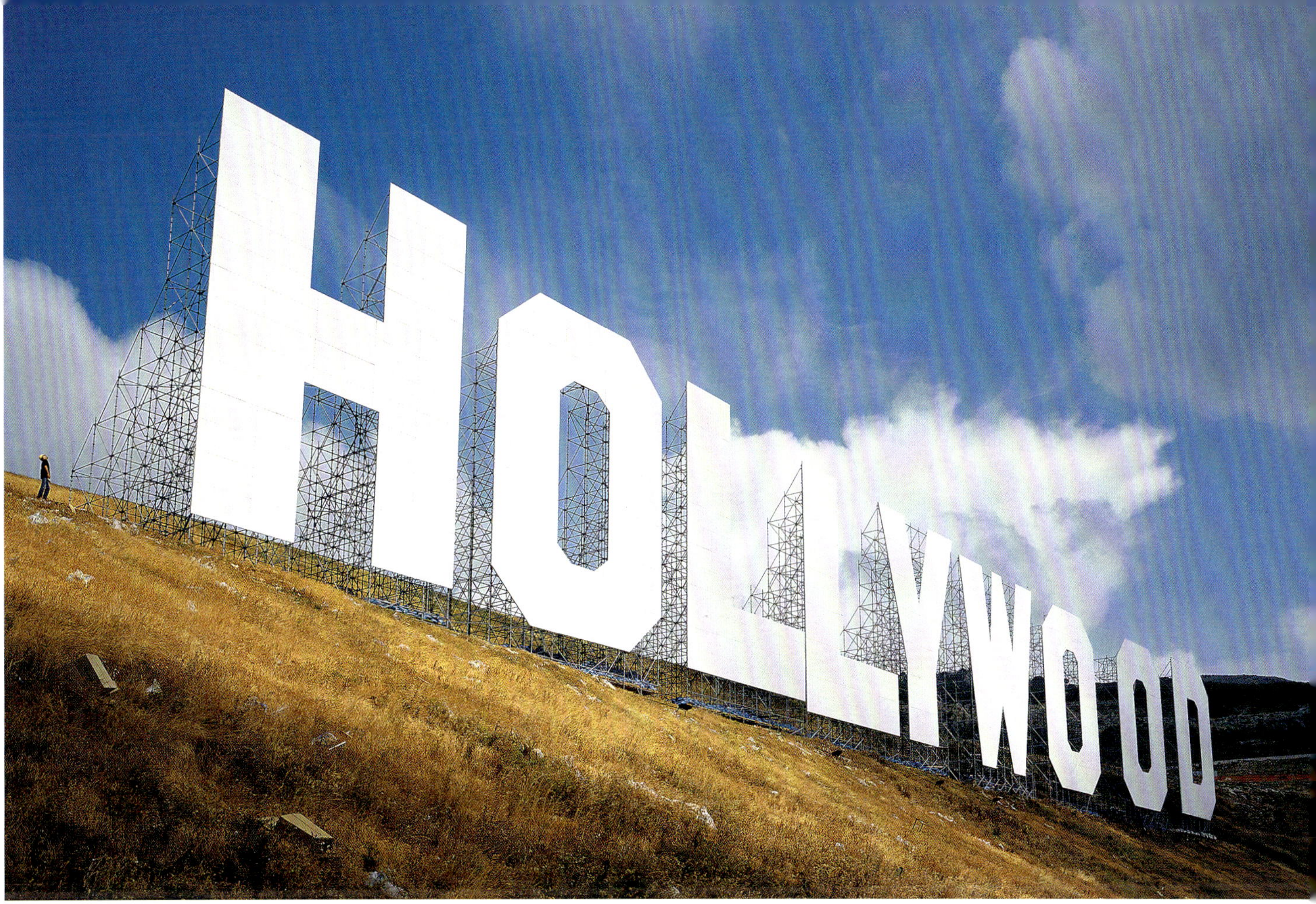

Maurizio Cattelan (b. 1960)
Hollywood

2001
Scaffolding, aluminium, halogen headlights
23.4 × 166 m (76 ft 9 in × 544 ft 7 in)
Installed at Bellolampo's landfill, Palermo, Sicily, for the 49th Venice Biennale

This large-scale site-specific piece made by Maurizio Cattelan for the 49th Venice Biennale shows Place taking an active role in the meaning of the work. The pseudo sign satirizes the real one in Los Angeles; it was constructed by the artist on top of the rubbish dump outside Palermo, Sicily. It is an example of dislocation and the subconscious emotional connections that we have to a particular place. In order for viewers to fully appreciate the work, they must be aware of the sign's original location in Hollywood, of the larger issues associated with the prominence of film in world culture, and the corrupting influence of that prominence. And, of course, the fact that *Hollywood* was located on top of a rubbish heap in Sicily, not on a hill overlooking Los Angeles.

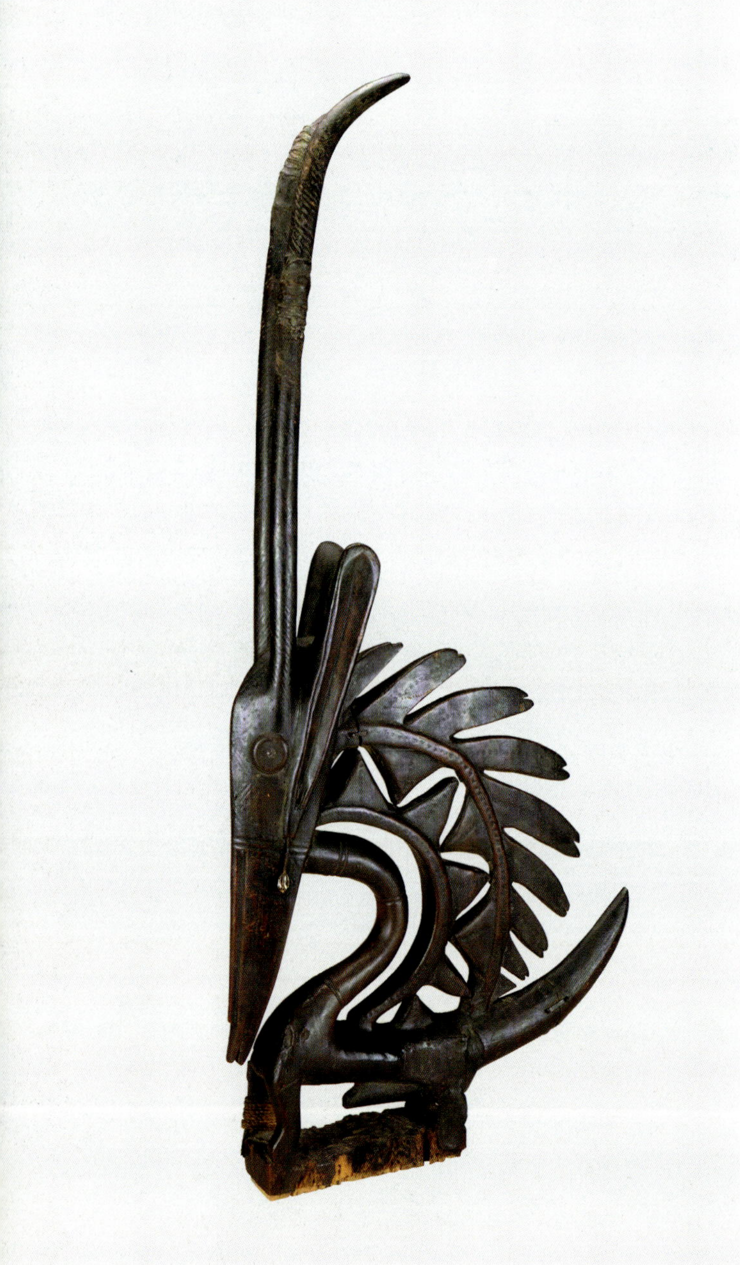

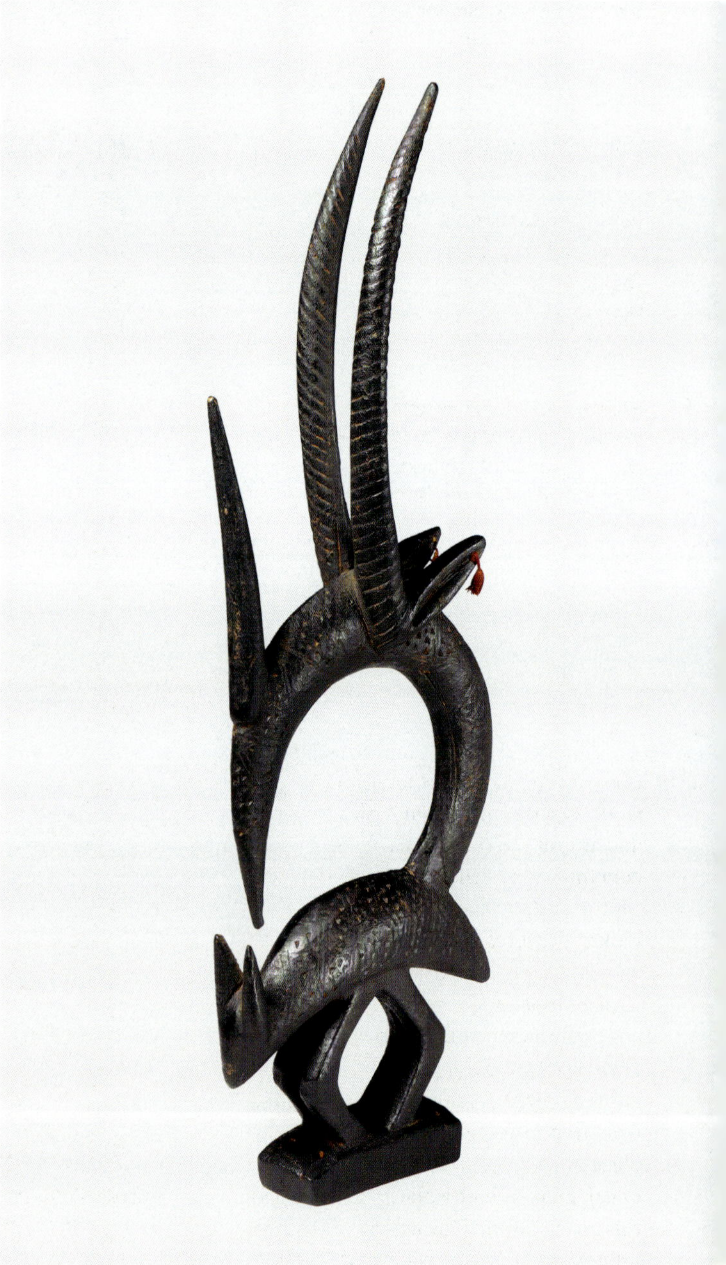

(far left) Bamana Culture, Mali
Chiwara Headdress

Early – mid 20th century
Wood, metal
100 cm (3 ft 6 ½ in) high
Smithsonian National Museum of African Art, Washington DC

(left) Bamana Culture, Mali
Chiwara Headdress

Late 19th – early 20th century
Wood
60 cm (1 ft 11 ½ in) high
Musée du Quai Branly, Paris

(right) Bamana men wearing headdresses to dance to Chiwara, the mythological half man, half antelope, who is believed to bring good luck to farmers

Mali, 1978

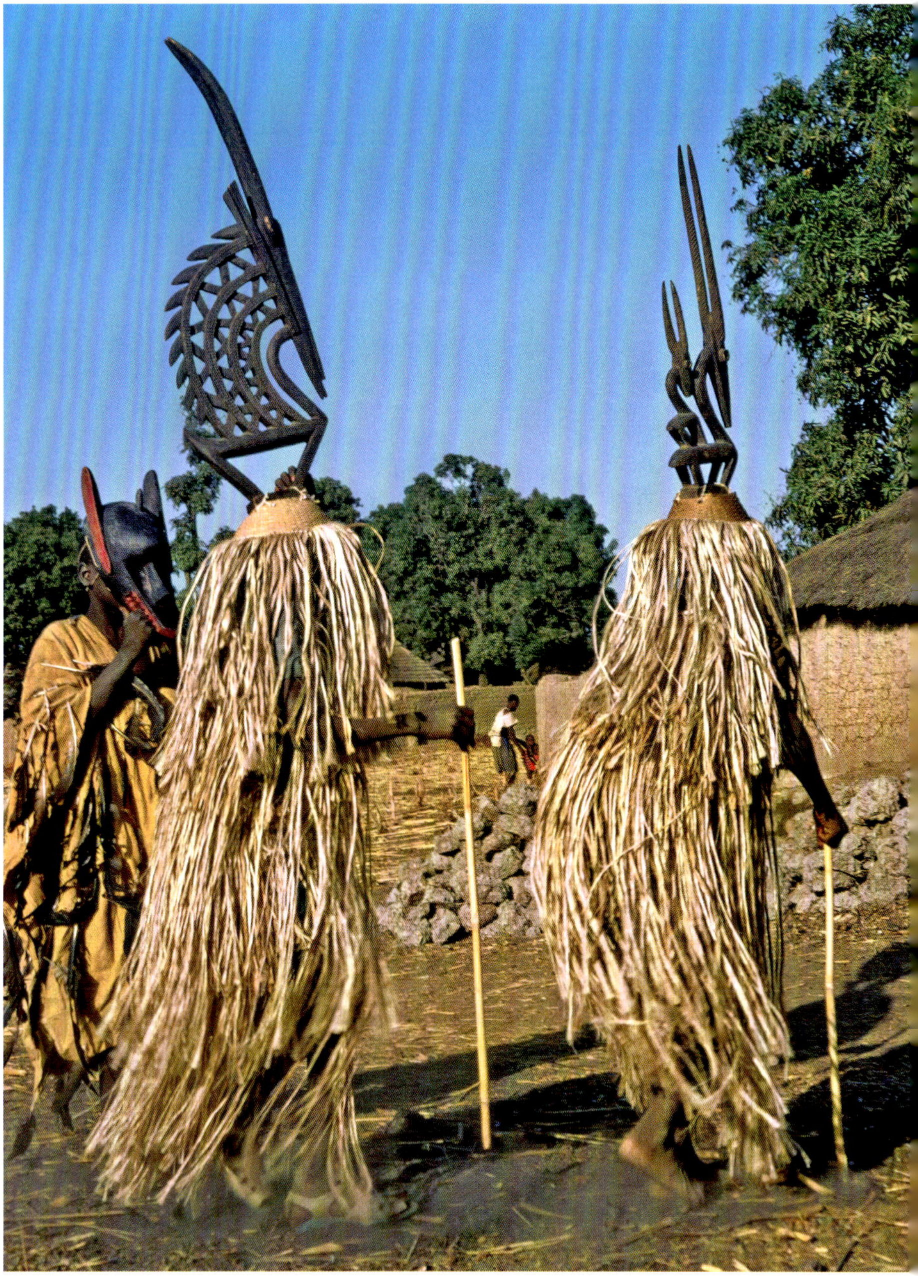

Look carefully at these male and female wooden sculptures from Mali on the left, and attempt to come to a tentative conclusion as to their original meaning for the sculptors who carved them. Now look at the photograph on the right showing dancers wearing similar objects as headdresses. Contrast your original conclusion with your present feelings. How has the meaning of these objects been altered now that they have been removed from their original cultural setting and placed in a museum? What has been lost or gained by their displacement? And is this an example of the active or passive influence of Place on their meaning?

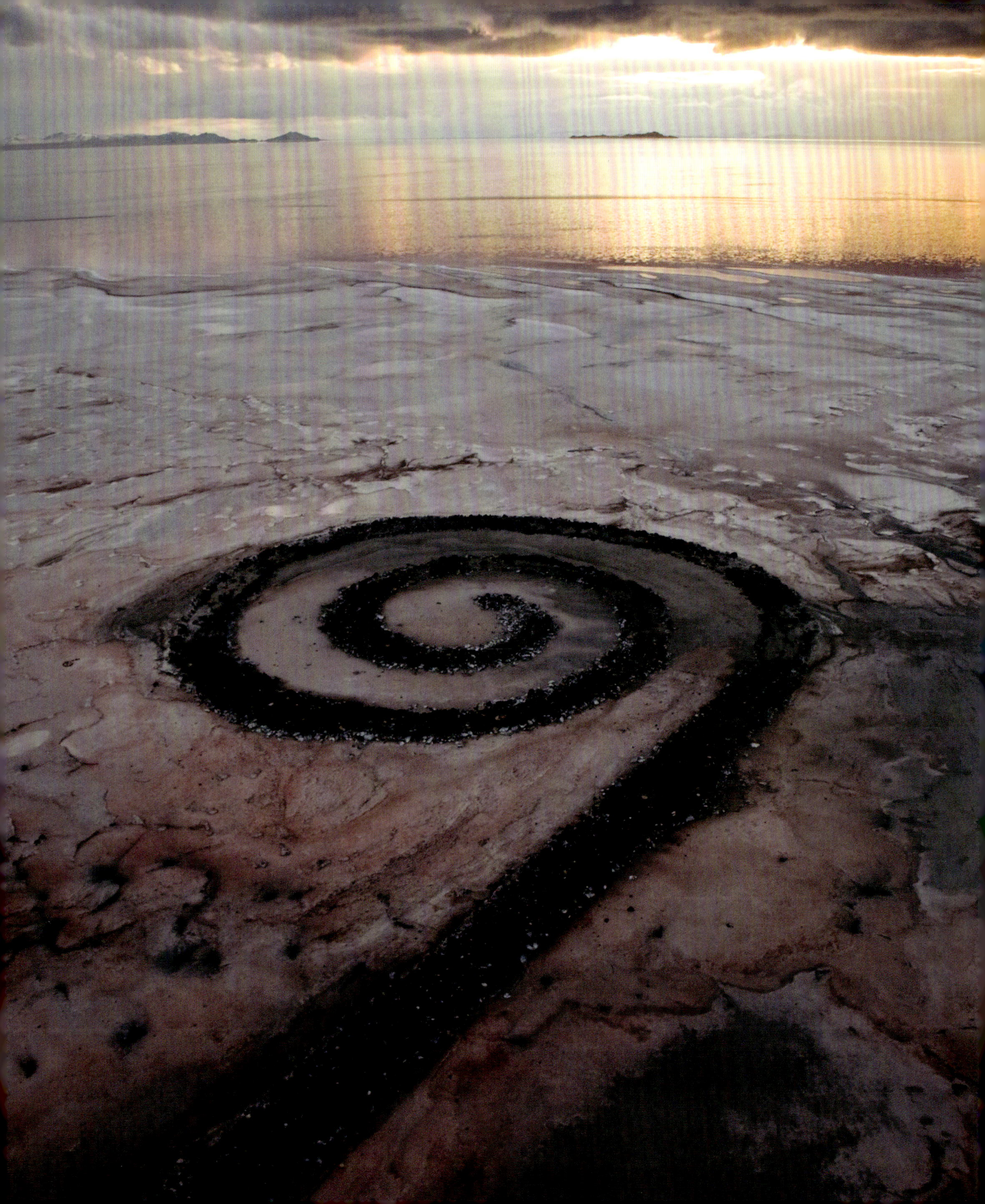

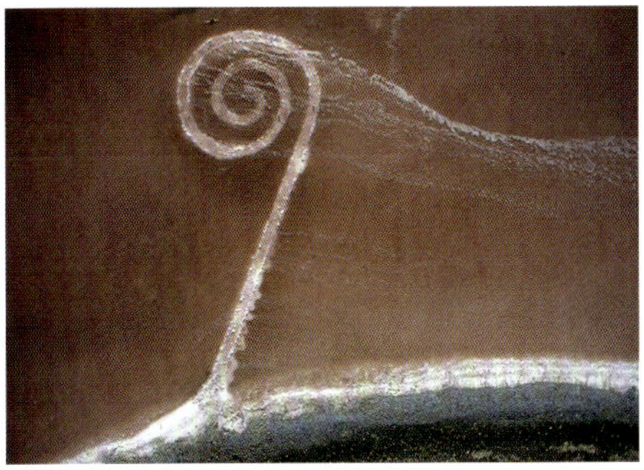

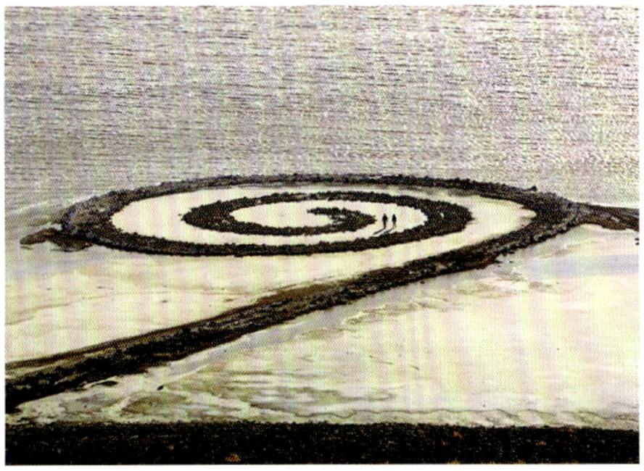

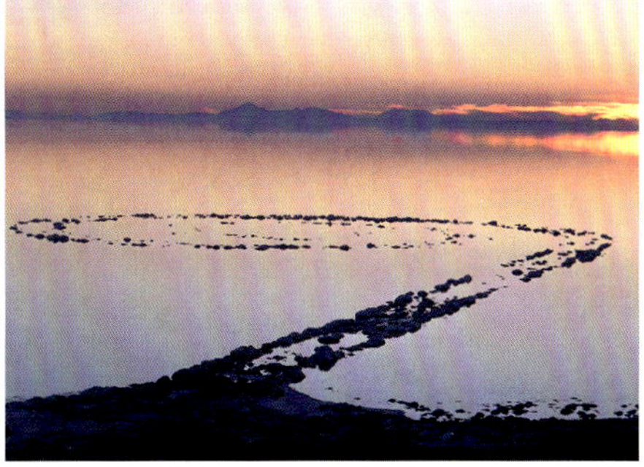

Robert Smithson (1938–1973)
Spiral Jetty

1970
Earth, rock, salt
152 × 91 m (500 × 300 ft)
Rozel Point, Great Salt Lake, UT

In 1970, Robert Smithson completed a large-scale site-specific earthwork entitled *Spiral Jetty* at the edge of the Great Salt Lake in Utah. The work extends about 500 feet from the shoreline and measures approximately 300 feet across. The road-like 'jetty' is approximately the width of the dump trucks that hauled the large boulders, smaller stones and dirt from a nearby site to form the extended spiral. In his writings, Smithson is quite explicit as to why this work needed to be constructed on this particular site. Site and jetty are united; the one cannot exist without the other. But nature is in a continual state of transformation. Smithson frequently uses the word 'entropy' to describe these changes. The photographs show how the natural environment changes the work over time, sometimes in extreme ways that may alter our aesthetic understanding of the *Jetty*.

In the photograph on the far left, the basic form of *Spiral Jetty* is clearly visible. At times, because of the variations in the weather and in the salt content of the lake, the water changes from the reflected blue of the sky to red (top left). When the lake water recedes, natural evaporation takes place and salt crystals form (top centre). But when the lake rises, the water completely submerges the jetty and it all but disappears from view, becoming visible only from the air (top right). These natural alterations occur slowly over time, while the basic stone and gravel structure of *Spiral Jetty* remains intact. It is apparent from his writings and conversations that Smithson foresaw many, though not all, of these active changes.

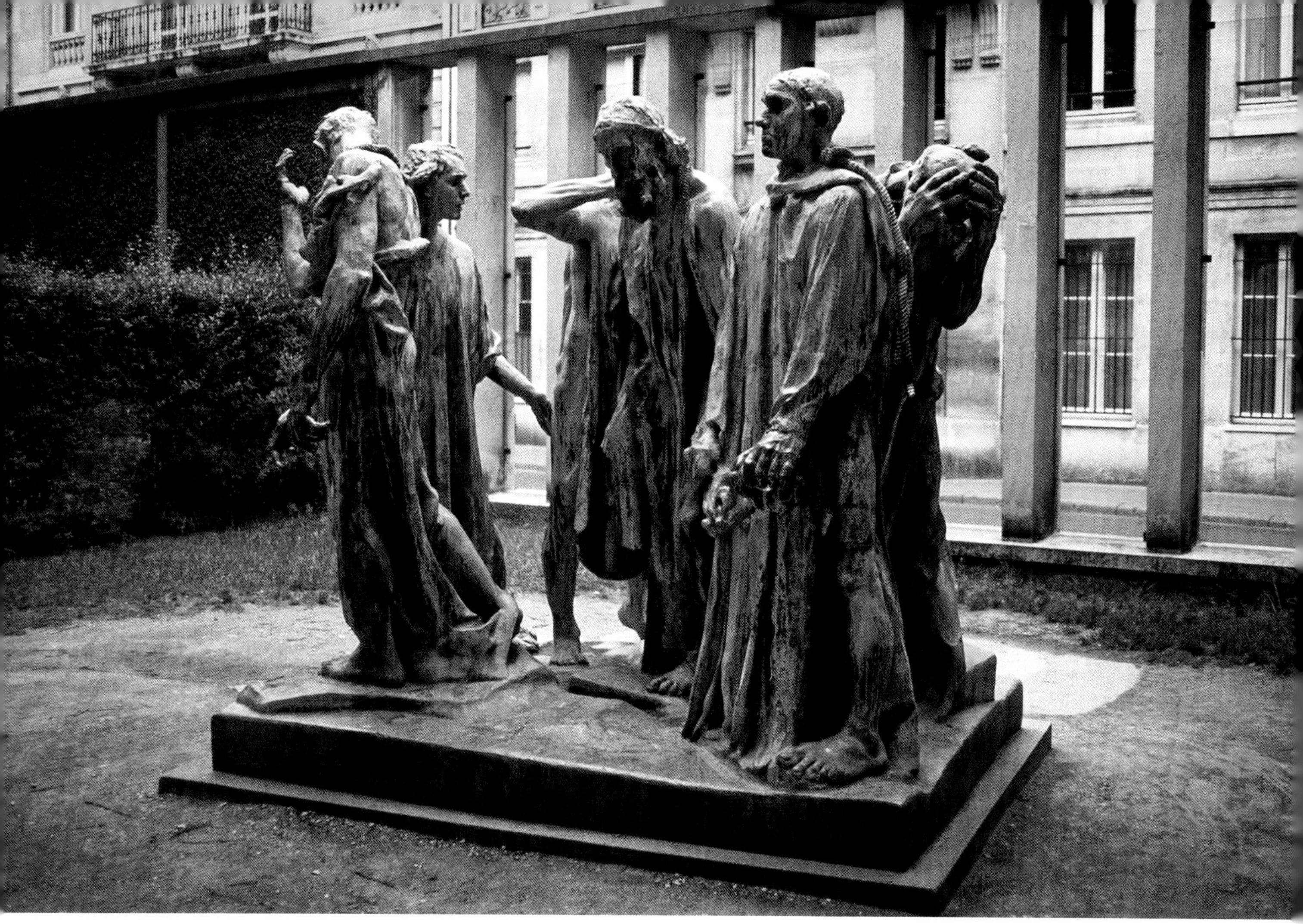

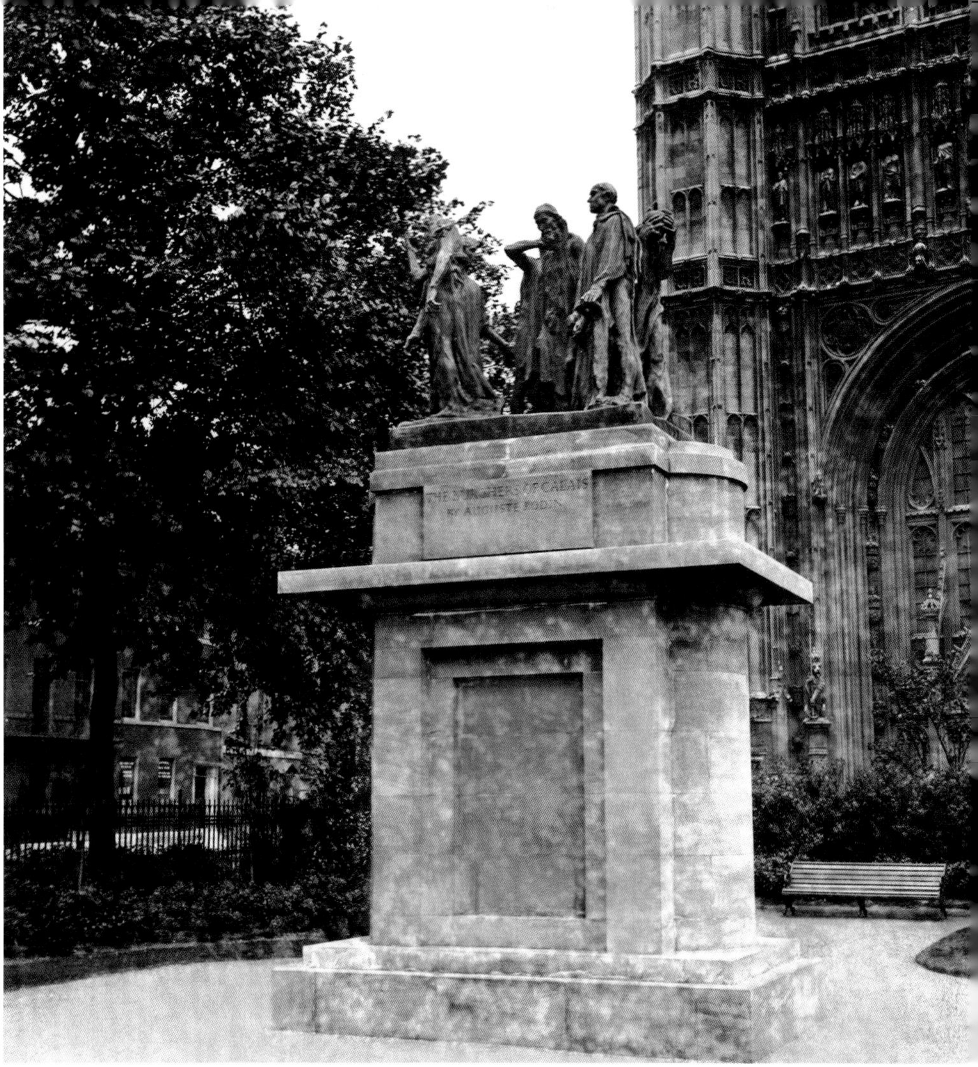

Auguste Rodin (1840–1917)
The Burghers of Calais

1884–9; photographed 1994
Bronze
Sculpture: 201.6 × 205.4 × 195.9 cm
(79 ⅓ × 80 ⅞ × 77 in);
plinth: 30.5 cm (12 in) high
Rodin Museum, Paris

Auguste Rodin
The Burghers of Calais

1884–9; photographed 1915
Bronze
Sculpture: 201.6 × 205.4 × 195.9 cm
(79 ⅓ × 80 ⅞ × 77 in);
plinth: 4.9 m (16 ft) high
Victoria Tower Gardens, London

The position of a sculpture relative to the viewer's field of vision may alter the sculpture's meaning, as well as altering its surrounding environment. There are many castings of Auguste Rodin's *The Burghers of Calais* in various locations, many of which have been installed on plinths of different height. The photograph on the left shows the work the way it is most often exhibited, on a platform that is approximately 12 inches high. The photograph above shows the same sculpture on a plinth 16 feet high, which is how it was sited, with Rodin's encouragement, from 1915 to 1956 in Victoria Tower Gardens, London.

The ground-level position seen on the left allows the viewer to visually enter into the interior of the sculpture in ways that are impossible when it is 16 feet off the ground. It allows us to experience the monumentality of these figures measured against our own bodies. Our eye can focus on a detail, then move to a whole figure, then to the composition in total. But when elevated, the six figures are reduced in size and they take on a compositional unity and ethereal remove that discourages any focus on parts or details. As the viewer moves closer to the elevated plinth, the Burghers are seen against the buildings that surround it and the sky above. The lower portion of their bodies appears to meld into a confused mass giving few clues as to the relative position of each figure's feet, preventing the viewer from understanding their movement within the composition. That said, a distinct advantage of the higher base is that the work holds its place within its immediate active architectural environment in ways that the lower one does not. The cultural importance we place upon the classical plinth may have played a part in Rodin's original request.

In part we understand our world relative to our bodies and our field of vision. Looking up is different from looking at an object at eye level. The placement of the same object on ground level or raised above us can dramatically change how we respond to a sculpture. Is this an example of the active or passive role of Place? I would suggest that it is an interesting illustration of both.

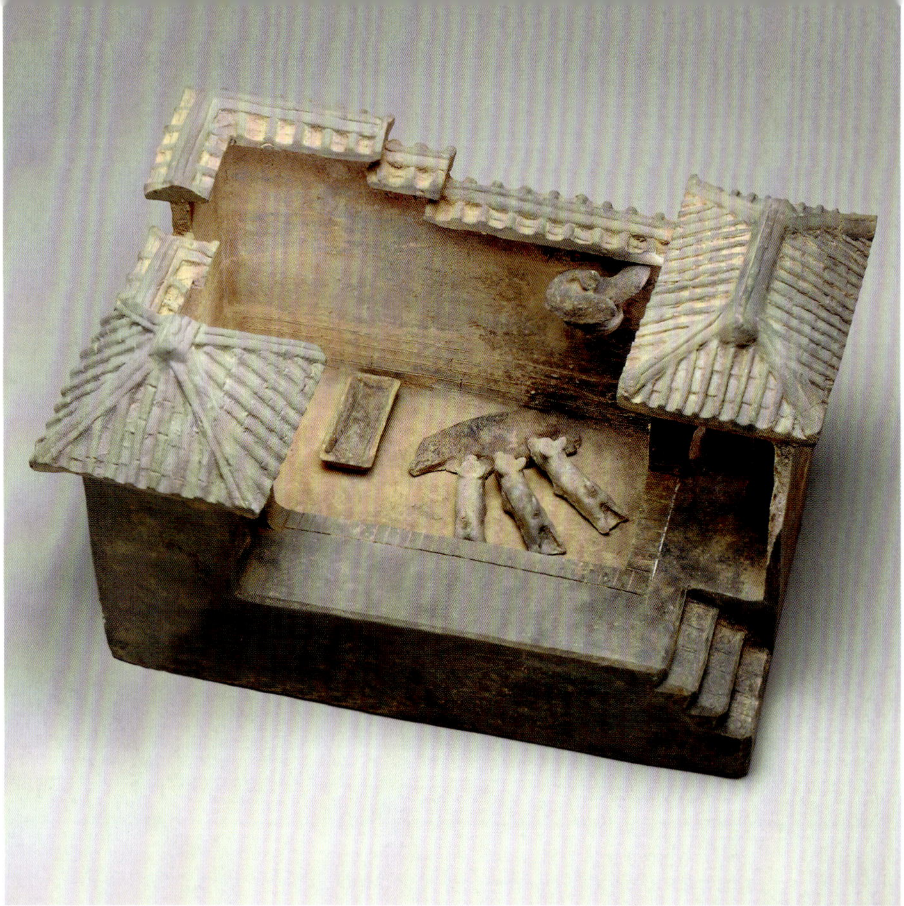

Han Dynasty, China
Funerary Model of a Pigsty

206 BC – 24 AD
Earthenware
22.9 × 39.4 × 28 cm (9 × 15 ½ × 11 in)
Minneapolis Institute of Arts, MN

This small grave object from the Han Dynasty in China is an example of a sculptural place that contains an environment – farm animals within an architectural space. The sculptor has created a work that provides an intimate insight into how humans and their animals shared a domestic rural habitat at that moment in time and place. Like an architectural model, because the object is small, it is necessary to experience it from the side rather than only looking down from the top as it is shown here. When we do, we see that walls exclude the viewer on three sides. As we move around the work, we see the stairs; we enter and move along the two elevated walkways that end with the open-doored tiled-roof latrines. At this point the sculpture remains an interesting but still mysterious architectural environment. But from the walkway when we look down into the courtyard/pigsty that contains the animals, the generalized environment changes into this specific place. A place inhabited with small suckling pigs. Lavishly detailed, this is a lowly environment, but one in which the animals, the latrines and other elements are given careful attention by the sculptor. It is a sculptural place in which the eye can move around each element, creating narratives that a single monolithic sculpture often precludes.

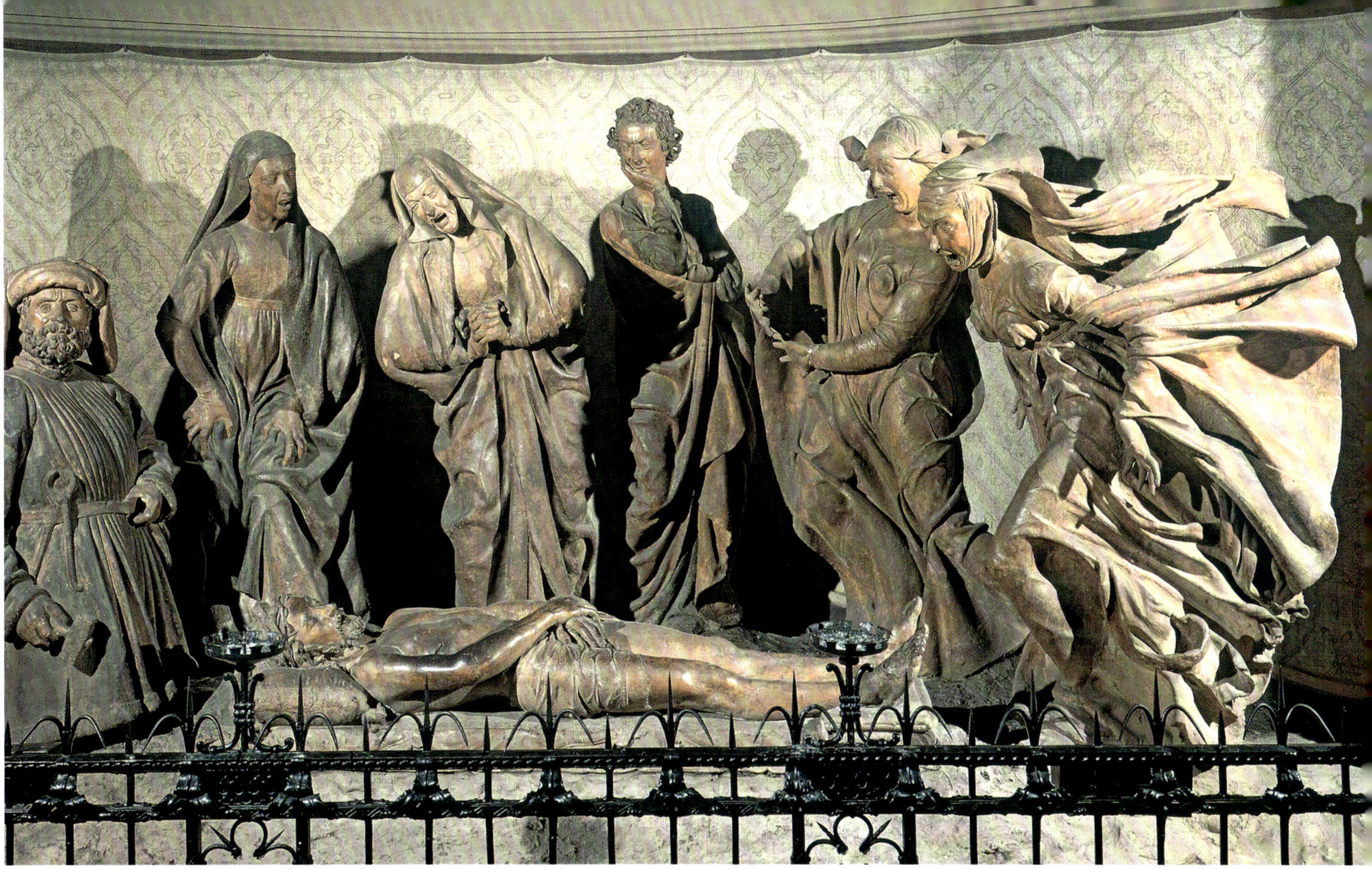

Niccolò dell'Arca (1440–1494)
Lamentation over the Dead Christ

c. 1460–90
Painted terracotta
Approx. 1.5 m (4 ft 11 in) high
Santa Maria della Vita, Bologna

In the Han Dynasty work opposite, the outer walls not only surround the work, but also exclude the animals from view and isolate the small sculpture. Not so with this work by Niccolò dell'Arca, which is also made from terracotta. The viewer shares the space with the six life-size figures that form an arc around the dead Christ. The sculptural power, presence and scale of the figures so animate the space within the chapel that the viewer feels compelled to participate; but such feelings are tenuous. Although the composition is raised slightly above the floor, the central figure of Christ has become secondary. Rather it is the chorus of the grieving mourners, each expressing their individual suffering and personal loss, that attracts and holds our attention. These biblical figures are set within a theatrical stage; their dramatic and expressive emotions create a sense of intense sorrow. Approaching, we begin to appreciate the details that dell'Arca has lavishly rendered. On the far right is Mary Magdalene. She is propelled forward towards Christ in a turbulent rush of grief and drapery. Although physically open, the tableau finally excludes the viewer because the figures are so intensely intertwined with their private sorrow and anguish. Place here is active. Initially the chapel provides a larger context, but it recedes in importance as the intense emotional environment defined by the sculpture dominates everything.

Haida Culture, Canada
Skidegate native village, Haida Gwaii, British Columbia
Canada, 1878

The location of a society may dictate the iconography that an indigenous people choose to utilize in the creation of their visual culture. This was certainly true in the case of the Haida culture located at Skidegate, Queen Charlotte Islands, British Columbia. Heavily wooded and defined by the Pacific Ocean, this is a remote but temperate place. We have all seen totem poles removed from their environment and exhibited in museums. These heraldic animal totems contain supernatural visual images that cannot easily be deciphered. The poles are composed of finely carved polychrome images of animals from the natural habitat, along with other mythological creatures invented by the culture. Made from wood taken from the forest surrounding the village, there are two basic types. The first is the frontal pole, often attached to the house and between 40 and 60 feet high. The others are monuments to the dead. These always face the water and are capped with rectangular chambers holding the body of the deceased. As in *Spiral Jetty*, site and form are one. But here precise communication is paramount. More than just an aesthetic object the pole and the images on it, living and imagined, are a manifestation of the spiritual beliefs held by both the sculptor and the community.

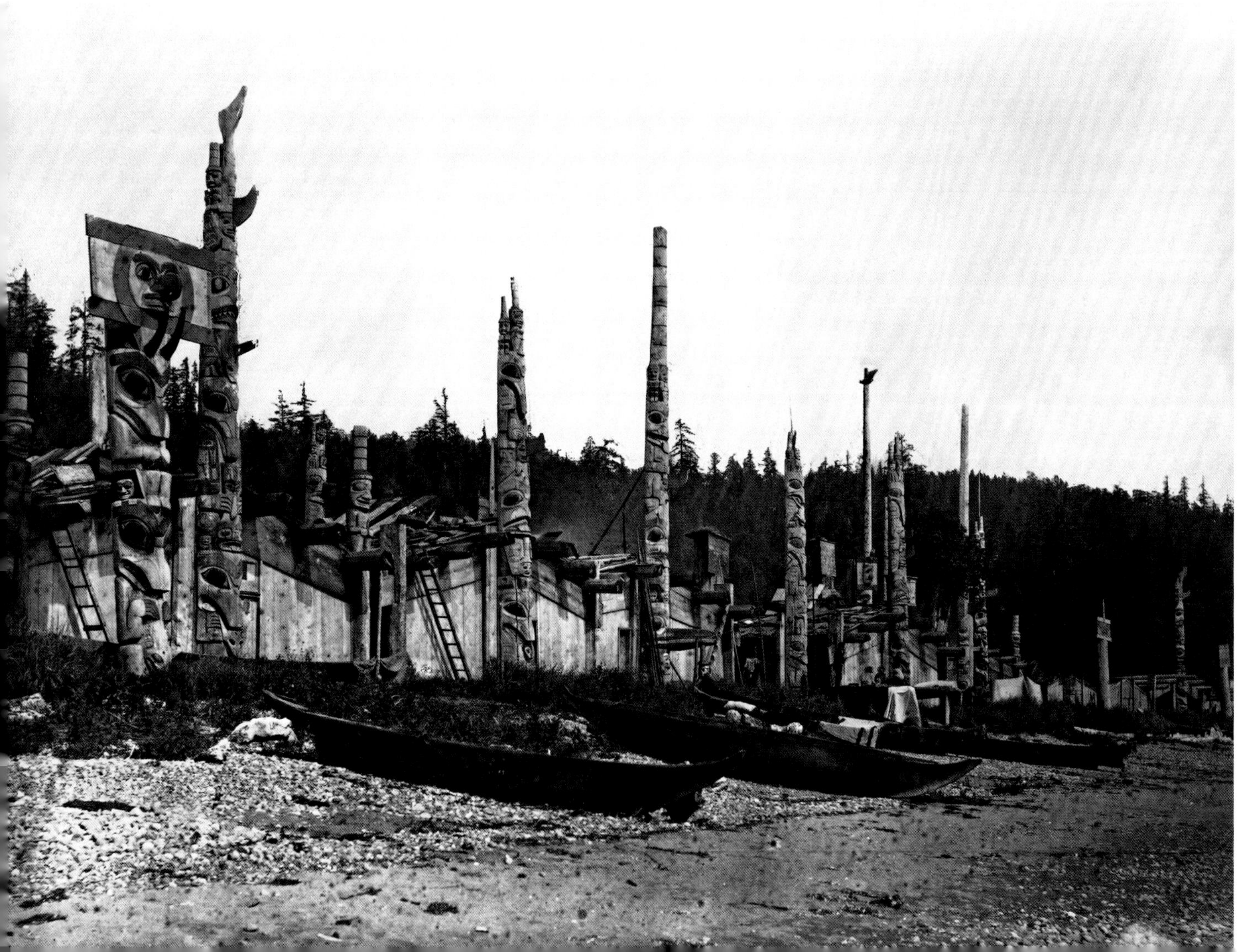

A work of art when placed in a gallery loses its charge, and becomes a portable object or surface disengaged from the outside world.

— Robert Smithson

... we can take people to places where they have never been. I don't mean physically, but mentally. We can ask hard questions, we can suggest difficult answers. All that is part of our privilege.

— Alfredo Jaar

2

Characteristics

The salient features shared by all forms; what we first notice when we look at an object. Together these elements give us important clues as to the object's form and shape – its identity.

Surface

Christo and Jeanne-Claude
Carl Andre
Max Bill
Antonio Canova
Wolfgang Laib
Anish Kapoor
Larry Bell

Edge

New Kingdom period, Egypt
Richard Deacon
Phillip King
Antoine Pevsner
Barbara Hepworth
Constantin Brancusi
Francesco Laurana

Colour

Early Classical period, Greece
Max Klinger
Pablo Picasso
Alexander Calder
Lynda Benglis
Tony Cragg
Katarzyna Kobro
Yves Klein
Katharina Fritsch

Texture

Eva Hesse
Michelangelo
Meret Oppenheim
Bena Biombo Culture, Democratic Republic of Congo
Germaine Richier
John Chamberlain
Donatello
Jean-Antoine Houdon
Jean Arp

Scale

Alberto Giacometti
Old Kingdom period, Egypt
Leonardo da Vinci
Polykleitos
Pablo Picasso
Chimu Culture, Peru
Henri Gaudier-Brzeska
Tom Friedman
Claes Oldenburg
Isamu Noguchi

Surface

The outermost covering of any object.

Our eyes comprehend the surfaces of objects in an instant. What we see is compromised by past experience, and so the sensual pleasures that these surfaces could bring are often diminished. For example, all wooden surfaces may become this tabletop; if we can name it, we wrongly believe we know it. The blind are forced to 'see' with other senses – primary among them is touch. The hand can experience form in ways that the eyes cannot. But only the hand and the eyes learning to see together can reveal, for example, the surface ambiguity of the cold, smooth, hard transparency of glass.

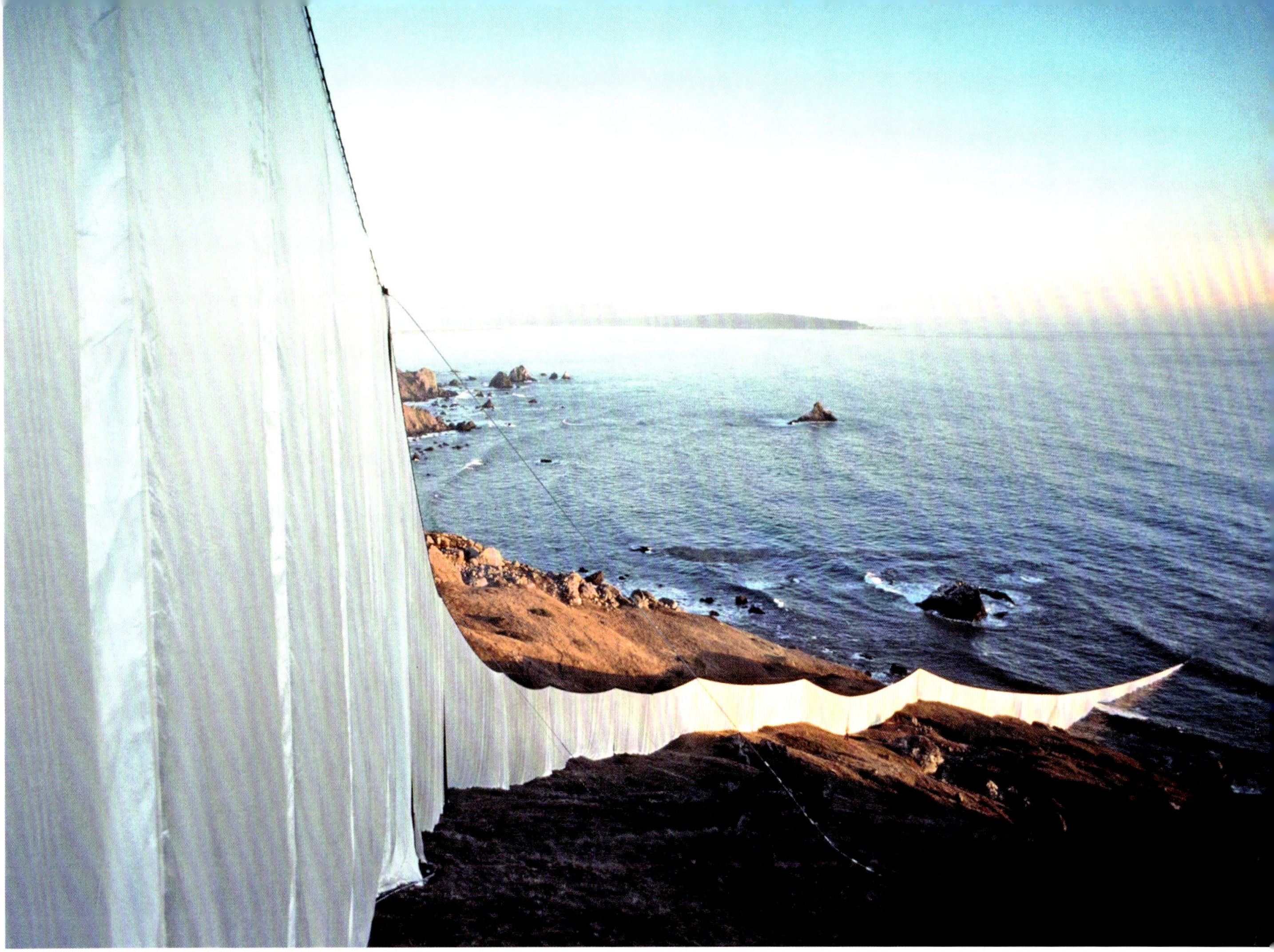

Christo and Jeanne-Claude
(b. 1935; 1935–2009)
Running Fence

1972–6
Nylon fence
5.5 m (18 ft) high; 39.4 km (24 ½ miles) long
Sonoma and Marin Counties, CA

The 24 ½-mile long *Running Fence* by Christo and Jeanne-Claude, made from translucent white nylon fabric, was completed on 10 September 1976. Rising and falling, moving and changing in the wind and light, the gossamer surface advanced from the rolling hills of the interior farmland to the Californian coast and disappeared into the Pacific Ocean. The work was two continuous surfaces merging to become a monumental diaphanous horizontal and vertical plane – not a surface in the sense of the outside of something, as it was simultaneously inside and out.

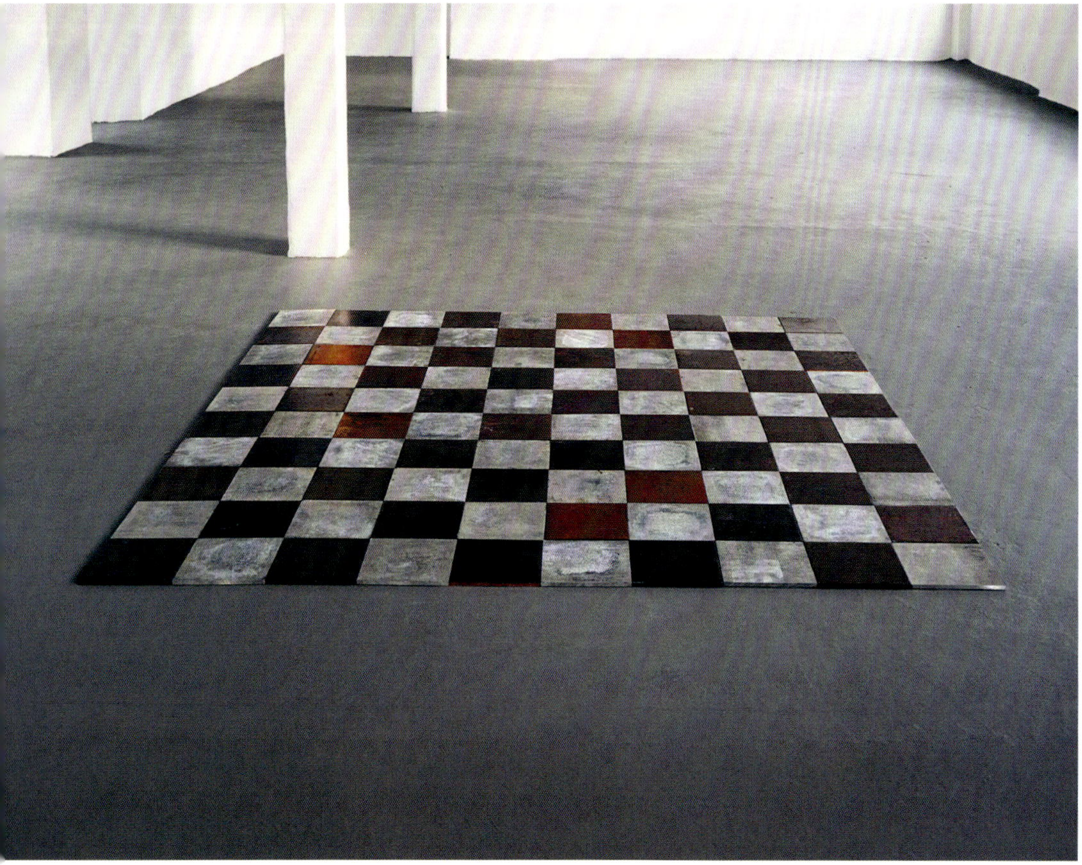

Carl Andre (b. 1935)
Copper-Magnesium Alloy Square

1969
100 copper and magnesium square plates
Overall: 1 × 200 × 200 cm (⅜ × 78 ¾ × 78 ¾ in)
Private collection, Düsseldorf

In contrast to *Running Fence*, *Copper-Magnesium Alloy Square* by Carl Andre is a visually one-sided floor-relief; a horizontal thin flat surface that builds up from the floor/ground plane and challenges the viewer's space. It is not a monolithic mass placed on a base to be venerated; rather, composed of one hundred copper and magnesium square plates, it asks to be thought of as a formalistic object that is self-referential. It is a sculpture/surface that not only expresses its materiality – copper and magnesium – but also the flatness of the floor it rests on. And like the floor, it is meant to be walked on by the viewer.

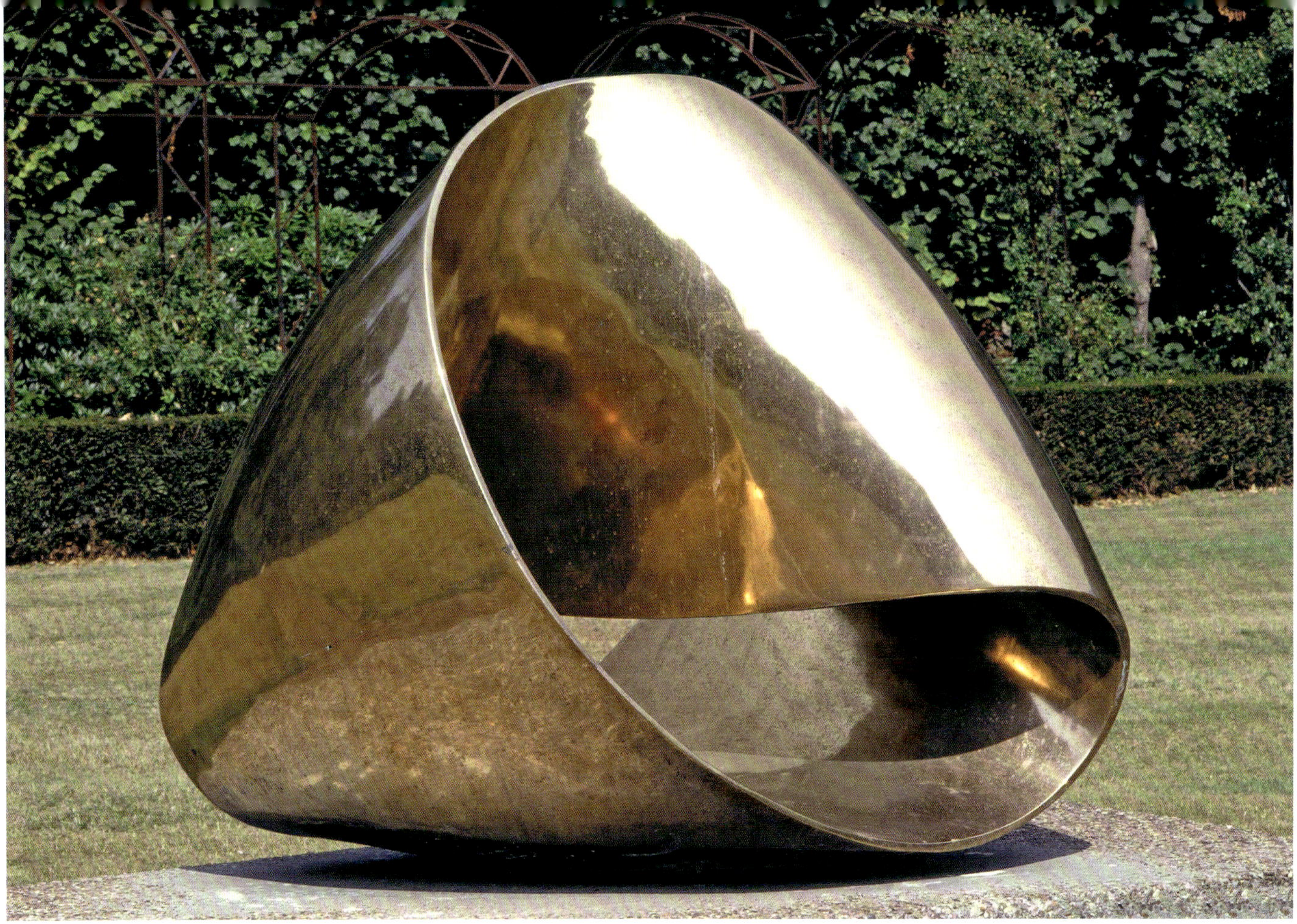

Max Bill (1908–1994)
Endless Ribbon

1953
Bronze
125 × 125 × 80 cm (49 ¼ × 49 ¼ × 31 ½ in)
Middelheim Sculpture Park, Antwerp

Endless Ribbon is one variation within a series of works by the Swiss sculptor Max Bill based upon a geometric phenomenon first discovered by the nineteenth-century German mathematician A. F. Möbius. For the sake of illustration, we could say that the form begins as a long flat strip, normally thought of as having two surfaces (top and bottom) with four edges. If we were to cut and twist the strip in opposite directions, and then join the ends together, we would have a möbius strip. By that simple act a remarkable figure emerges, one which, instead of two surfaces, has only one, and a single defining edge. This work by Bill is about surface and the expressive possibilities contained within geometry. The sculpture at first appears to be a known form having two surfaces until we test that assumption using either hand or eye.

Antonio Canova (1757–1822)
The Three Graces

1815–7
Marble
173 × 97 × 75 cm (68 × 38 × 29 ½ in)
Victoria and Albert Museum, London

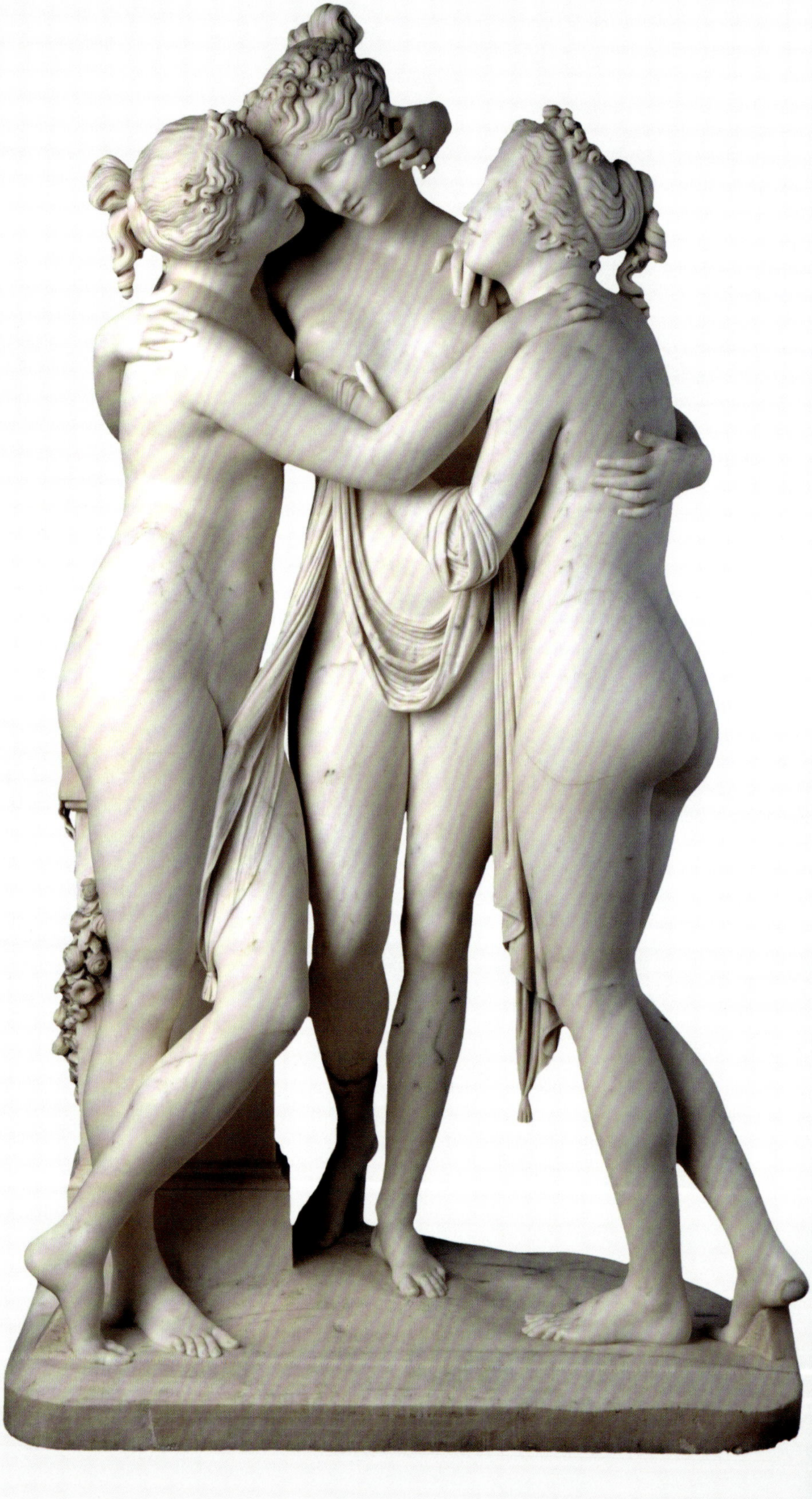

The erotic sensuality of the marble surfaces of *The Three Graces* reveals how a cold hard resistant material may be transformed into the illusion of warm flesh by the creative craft of the sculptor. When we see this work in person, it becomes very apparent how carefully Antonio Canova gives form to these surfaces using files and abrasives of varying degrees of coarseness. The sensuousness of the flesh is so beautifully articulated that light falling across the figures conveys the illusion of life. This is especially evident where the fingers of one figure press into the soft flesh of another. Observe how the folding surfaces within the long strand of drapery that appears to tie the figures together contrast with the tactile, sensual skin they lie against.

Wolfgang Laib (b. 1950)
Milkstone

1998–2001
Marble, milk
6 × 73 × 59 cm (2 ⅜ × 28 ¾ × 23 ¼ in)
Private collection

Milkstone by Wolfgang Laib is also carved from white marble, but to a very different aesthetic purpose from Canova's work. Most surfaces are the result of the sculptor's working process, but the top surface of this sculpture is made in a very different way. It is the result of the surface tension of pooled milk constrained by the slightly raised edge defining the indented white marble surface beneath. The milk swells above the stone's raised outer edges like water in a glass that is about to overflow. Because the marble is nearly the same colour as the milk, the liquid and the solid stone appear to merge. It is only when we look at the sculpture very carefully that we perceive the physical distinction between the two. The natural curvature of the surface of the milk is perfect beyond what the hand can make. Laib uses surface tension – a property of all liquids – to demonstrate that the sculptor is not limited to forming a surface with traditional tools and materials.

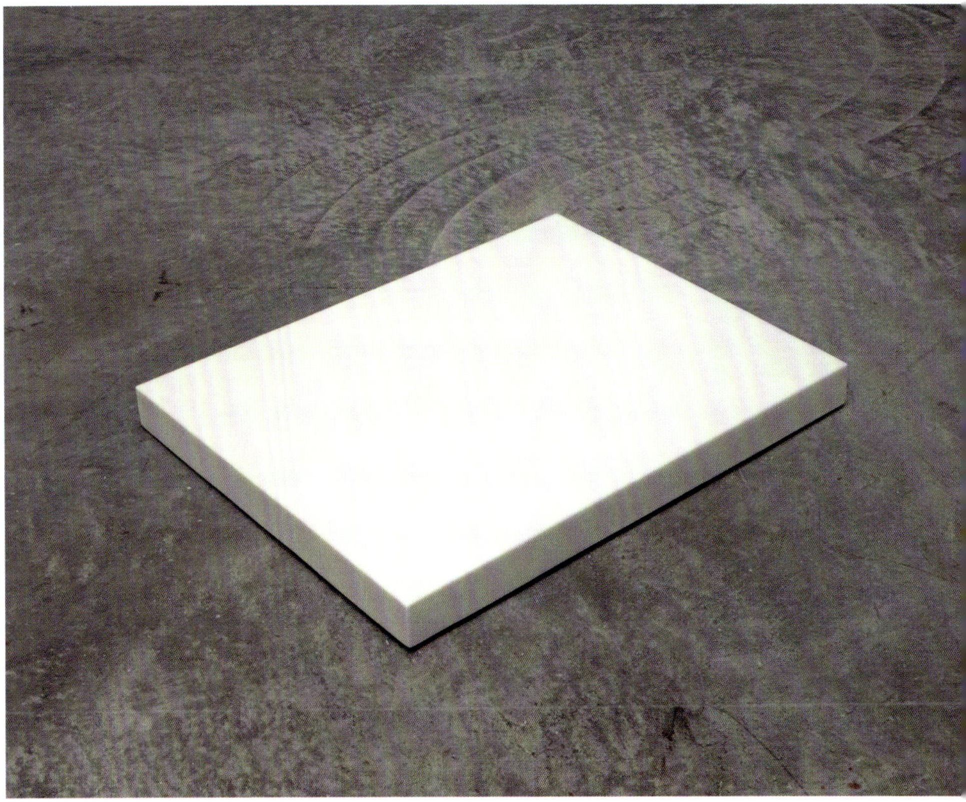

Anish Kapoor (b. 1954)
Cloud Gate

2004
Stainless steel
10 × 20 x 12.5 m (33 x 66 x 41 ft)
Millennium Park, Chicago, IL

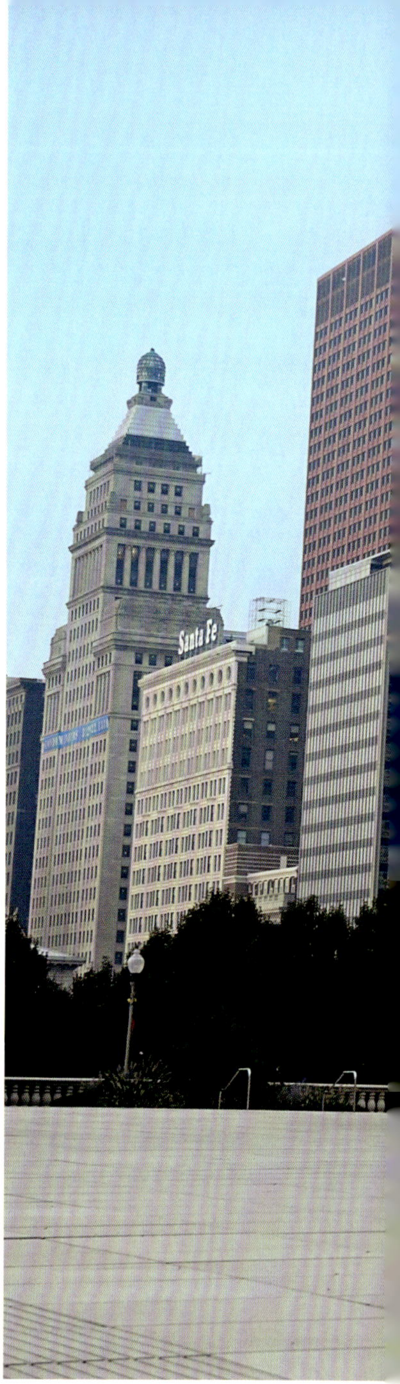

The surface of a flat mirror, as we shall see next in Larry Bell's *The Cat*, disappears into its reflected surroundings. However, when curved, that same mirrored surface becomes a distorted and refracted image of the things around it. This optical fact is seen on a monumental scale in *Cloud Gate* by Anish Kapoor. Its mirrored panoramic surface reflects the buildings along Michigan Avenue in Chicago and the sky above. As viewers approach this apparently immaterial mass of light and reflections, they may also discover their images within its seemingly endless, flexing surface.

Viewers can enter the arched concavity; there, all is reversed and images that had been stretched are now compressed. The sculpture is made of hundreds of stainless steel rectangles welded in place over an elaborate armature. Once joined, each weld was ground and the whole polished to near mirror perfection by skilled craftsmen over a two-year period. *Cloud Gate* is a gigantic buoyant apparent mass. Its mirrored stainless steel surface dissolves into the natural light and the surrounding buildings wihtout giving up the presence of its form.

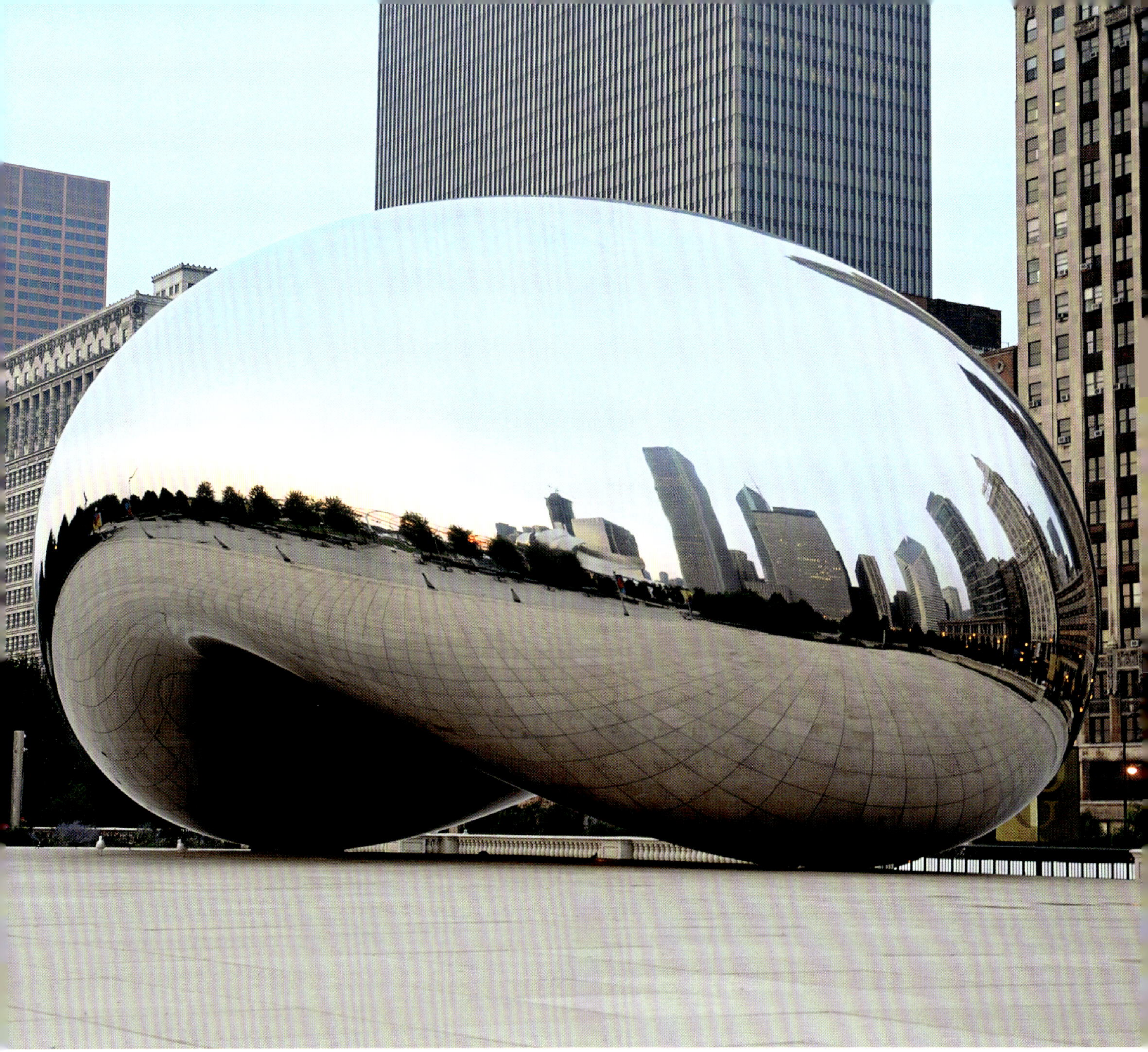

Larry Bell (1939)
The Cat

1981
4 panels float glass coated with Inconel;
8 panels triangular float glass, uncoated
4 panels: 182.9 × 243.8 × 1.3 cm (72 × 96 × ½ in);
8 panels: 182.9 × 182.9 × 1.3 cm (72 × 72 × ½ in)
Albuquerque Museum Collection, NM

Most of the previous examples of Surface have been made from opaque materials. In this work by Larry Bell we see a series of transparent glass surfaces coated with a mirror-like industrial substance called Inconel. Because of the way light reflects off the surfaces, and also because of the sensitivity of the Inconel to light and its mirroring qualities, near objects like the floor appear in sharp detail then fade, whereas distant objects disappear into a fog in the upper portions of the glass sheets. As we walk around the sculpture the surfaces are in a continual state of flux. They appear to be moving forward and back, then disappearing, top edges merging with the walls of the room, while the floor that we stand on reflects flawlessly into a mirrored surface, then vanishes into a screen of light.

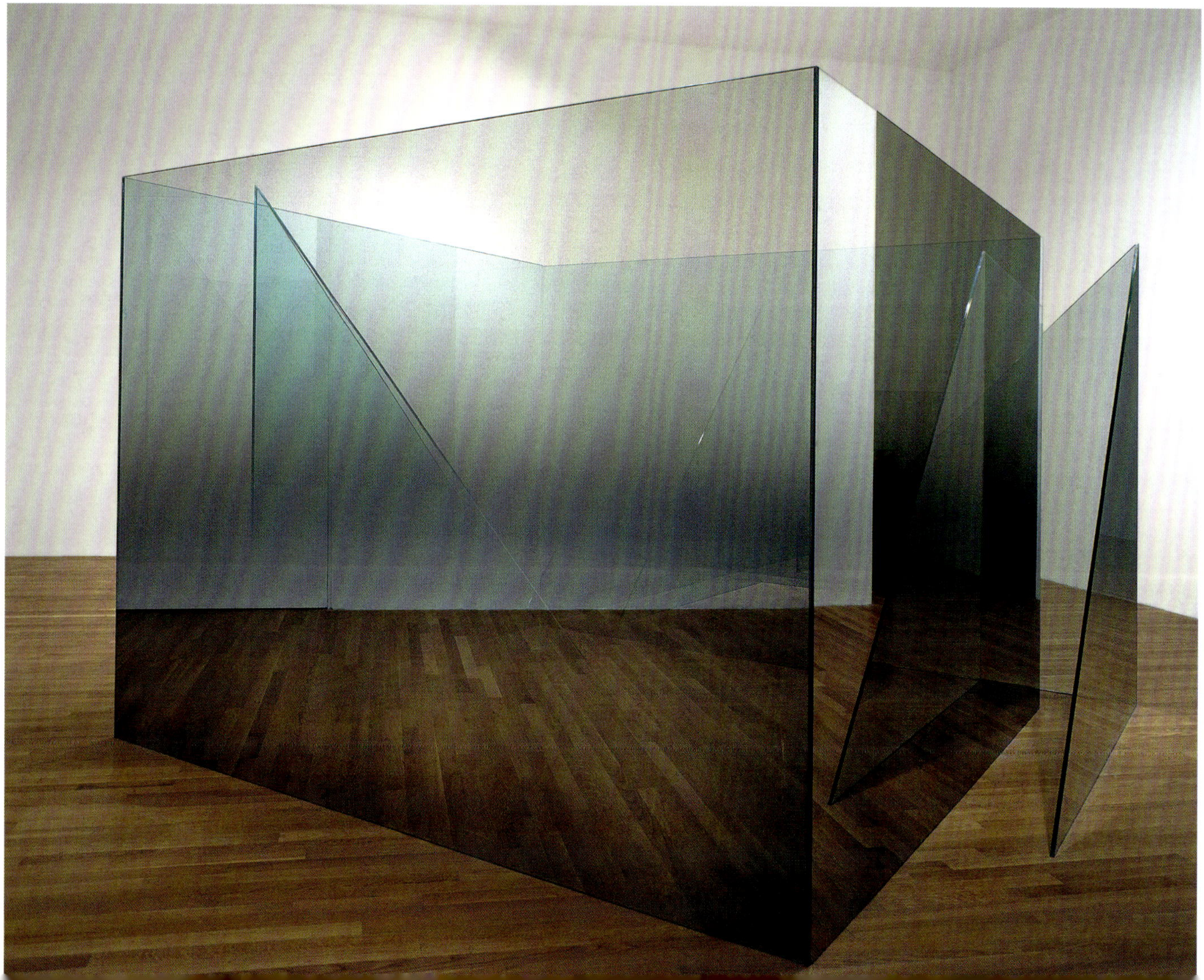

Instead of imagining the various parts of the body as more or less flat surfaces, I represented them as projections of interior volumes. I endeavoured to express in each swelling of the torso or the limbs the presence of a muscle or a bone that continued deep beneath the skin.

— Auguste Rodin

What is real is not the external form, but the essence of things ... it is impossible for anyone to express anything essentially real by imitating its exterior surface.

— Constantin Brancusi

Edge

The meeting of two surfaces.

Every object has a defining outer edge or boundary. Edge is also the meeting of two or more surfaces or planes. This page has four edges, for example. Those are its outer or defining limits, the place where material meets the surrounding space. That defining edge may also be referred to as its silhouette, border, outline, boundary perimeter or profile. The hard sharp edge of a razor that cuts, the soft edge on a shirt collar, the natural edge of an oak leaf are all examples. For the sculptor it is often this silhouette or contour that is the work's most dramatic consideration, as it becomes a constantly moving horizon over which forms appear and disappear as the sculpture turns in space.

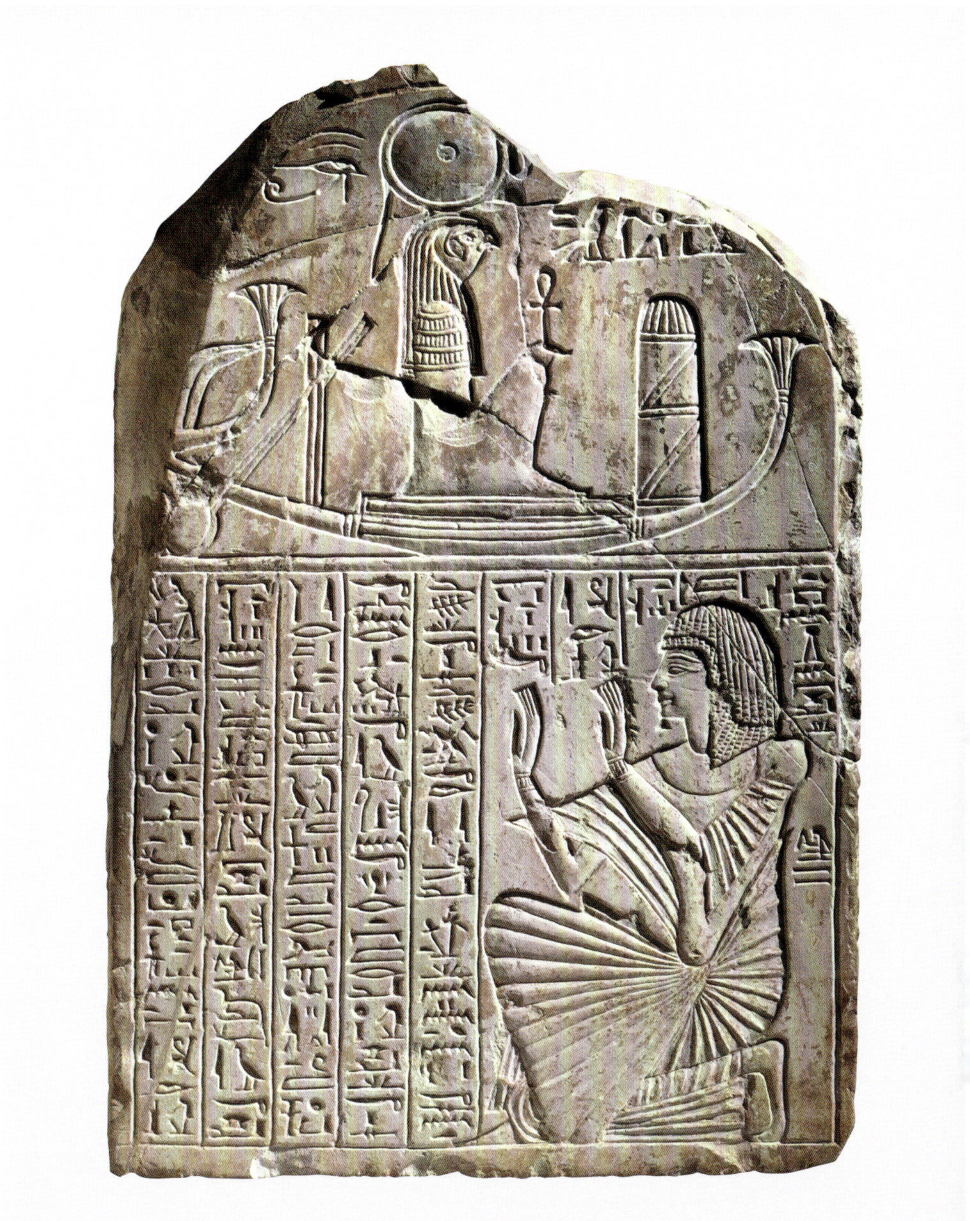

New Kingdom period, Egypt
Stela of Anhorkhawi

c. 1184–1153 BC or later
Limestone
42.8 × 30 × 7.7 cm (16 ⅞ × 11 ¾ × 3 in)
Brooklyn Museum, New York

When writing about sculpture, authors frequently use the word 'line', when what is being referred to is more correctly called an 'edge', and may be seen clearly in this Egyptian stela or grave marker. This type of relief is called 'sunken-relief' because the images have been carved into a flat ground plane. Sunken-relief is the earliest of the four types of relief – the others being *alto* or high-relief, *bas* or low-relief and floor-relief. The upper part of the stela shows the deity Re-Horakhty seated in a boat crossing to heaven. Below, the deceased, Anhorkhawi, kneels in adoration. Concentrate now on the image of Anhorkhawi: its sharp bounding edge isolates the figure. The left elbow becomes the centre of the radiating fans of folding drapery that not only define but also fully articulate the anatomy of the lower part of the figure. And this complex, exacting spatial illusion has been carved into the top half inch of the stone's surface.

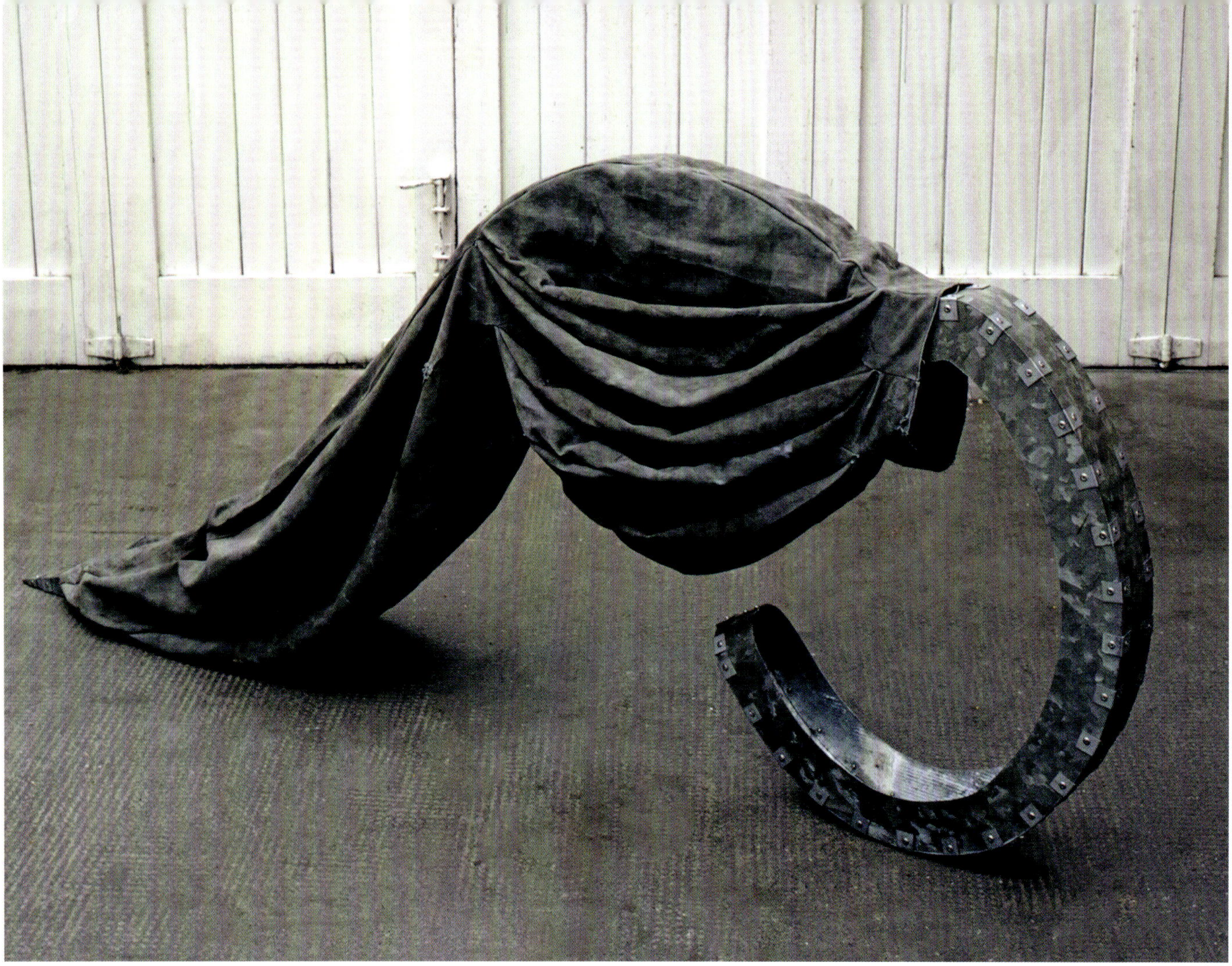

Richard Deacon (b. 1949)
On The Face Of It

1984
Galvanized steel, canvas
86 × 208 × 31 cm (33 ⅞ × 81 ⅞ × 12 ¼ in)
Private collection, on long loan to Bonnefanten Museum, Maastricht

One of the ways materials make themselves evident is through the character of their edges. Edge is a change in the direction of a surface, but it can also be more nuanced than that. In Richard Deacon's *On The Face Of It* the array of different kinds of edge is due to the way the artist has chosen to work two different materials, steel sheet and canvas. The canvas resembles at once a long flowing train and the soft scalloped edges of a theatre curtain. A slender arching steel open-box form extends out from, or into, the opening edge of the darkened canvas sleeve. Concealed within may be an invisible 'leg' that, along with the exterior hooked steel element, supports the work in its upright position. That is one possibility. Another is that the flowing drapery is the work's primary support. The inside of the thin steel appendage is defined by two curved sharp edges that propel the form back into the mysterious interior from which it emerged. Both the sheet metal form and its mysterious canvas cloak assert their individual materiality in part through the character of their distinctive edges.

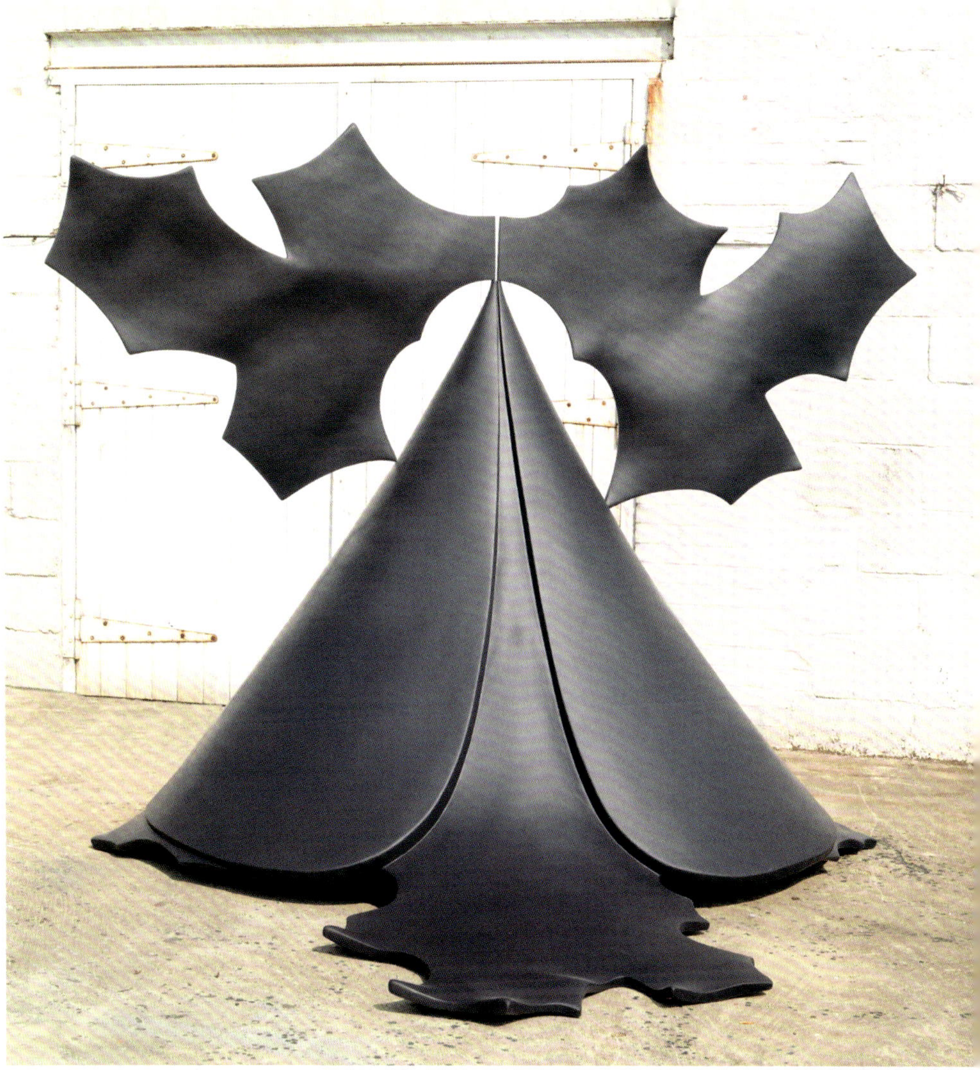

Phillip King (b. 1934)
Genghis Khan

1963
Painted fibreglass
213 × 366 × 275 cm (83 ⅞ × 144 × 108 ¼ in)
Tate, London

In 1963 Phillip King constructed a work from fibreglass entitled *Genghis Khan*. An upright split skirt-like cone drapes over and is supported by a scallop-edged under surface. Because of the cone's curtain-like opening, the under form dramatically extends its tongue from beneath the softer edges of the parted outer cone. In fact these spiky-edged under forms appear to support the whole apparent mass of the sculpture – apparent because what is inside the black conical mass is one of the mysteries of the work. The most striking and conspicuous aspect of the sculpture, its outstretched knife-edged bat-like wings, contrasts with the serenity and sedate flow of the cone. The difference between the smooth surface of the cone with its rounded edges and the flat sharp edge wings gives drama to the work. As we move around it, the cone remains the same while the wings evolve from a thin edge to a threatening outstretched black plane. The wings stand, asymmetrically poised, balancing on the cone's point. Their scalloped edges and violent points are menacing in ways that the passive cone with its rounded edges is not.

Antoine Pevsner (1884–1962)
Construction in Space in the Third and Fourth Dimension

1959
Bronze
2.4 m (8 ft) high
University of Chicago Law School, IL

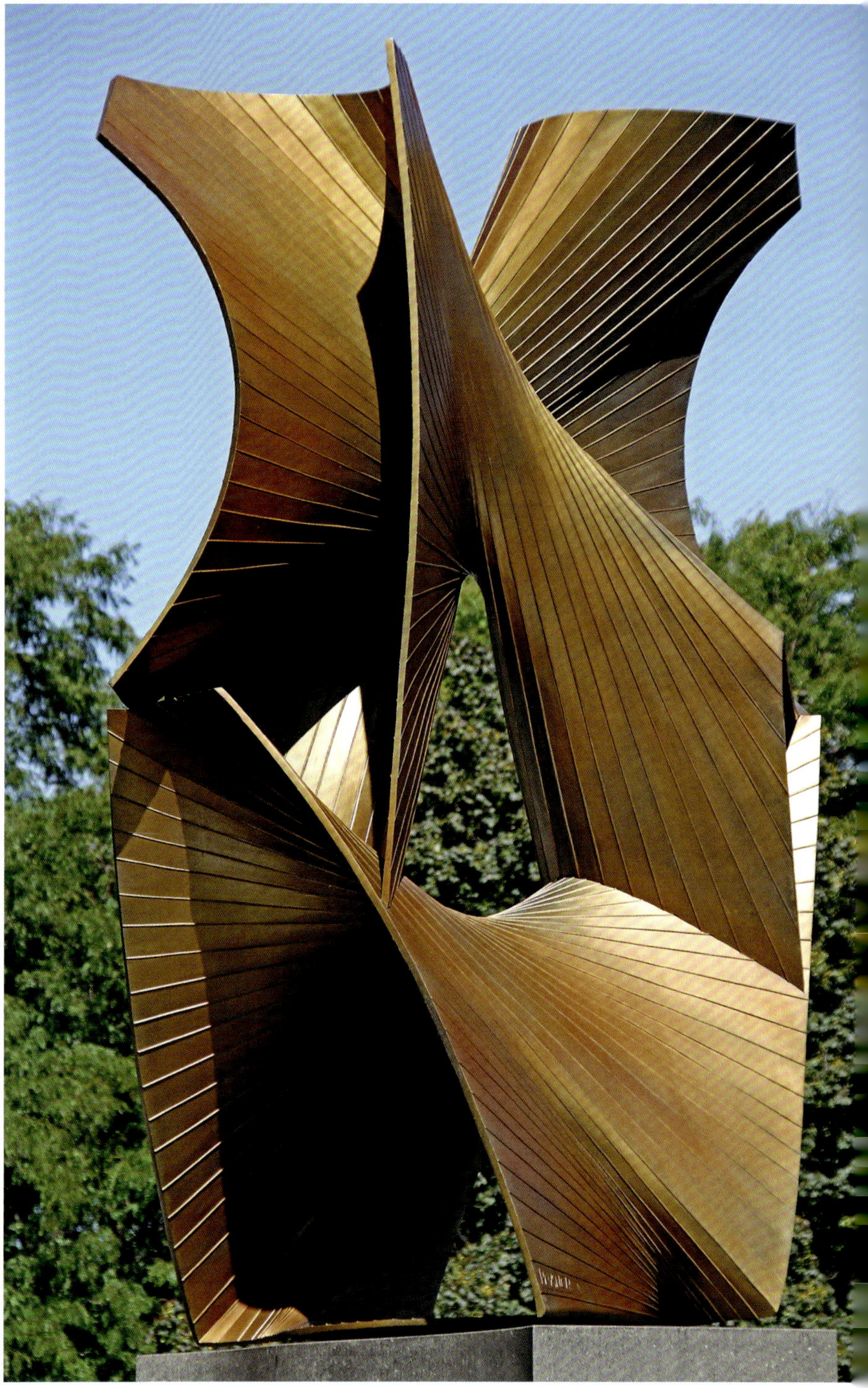

As we have seen, edges can become nuanced parts of the whole. But this is not the case with *Construction in Space in the Third and Fourth Dimension* by the Russian sculptor Antoine Pevsner. There are two parts to this complex form, one fitting within and above the other. Looked at from a distance its severe edges and starkly defined silhouette are the sculpture's most dramatic aspect. These curved outer edges and interior volumes are in continuous motion, expanding and contracting around the work's hollow core. They shape the sculpture's formal identity, which is a series of joined hyperbolic parabolas. These geometric forms are created from an array of doubly ruled saddle-shaped quadric surfaces that are generated by an arrangement of straight lines. The outer edges provide a starting point for the multitude of ruled edges seen on its bronze surfaces. These not only explain the geometry on which the sculpture is based, but they also give direction to the surfaces. In this and similar Constructivist works, geometry and mathematics become the essence of the form as its edges, surface planes and volumes open out to the infinity of space.

Barbara Hepworth (1903–1975)
Pendour

1947–8
Painted plane wood
30.6 × 74.5 × 23.8 cm (12 ⅛ × 29 ⅜ × 9 ⅜ in)
Hirshhorn Museum and Sculpture Garden, Smithsonian Institution, Washington DC

Up to this point Edge has been seen as something that could best be described as a fold or an abrupt change in the plane of a surface. In this example, Barbara Hepworth's *Pendour*, there are changes in direction, but there are also abrupt changes in colour. With such sudden shifts, not only are the edges clearly defined, but clarity is given as well to each of the two defining surfaces. Even in this small photograph it is easy to see exactly where the edge between the painted concave rough inner surfaces and the smooth wood exterior meet. It is this clarity of edge and the resulting white and blue elliptical volumes that give the work its lyrical aspect – a visual exchange between flowing surfaces and clearly defined edges.

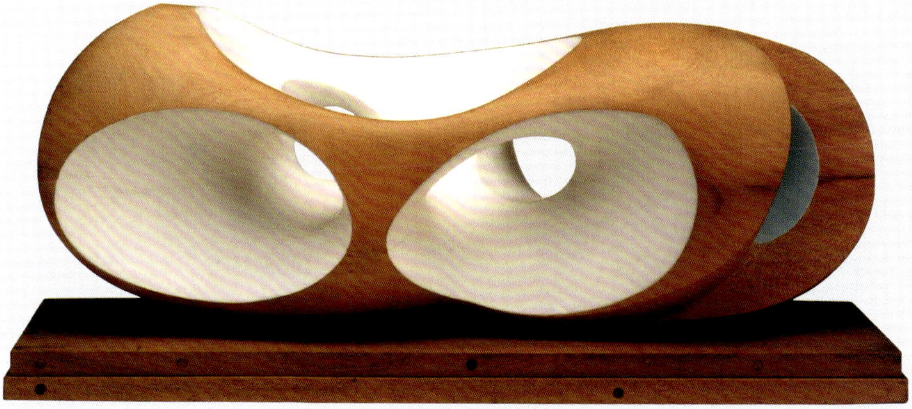

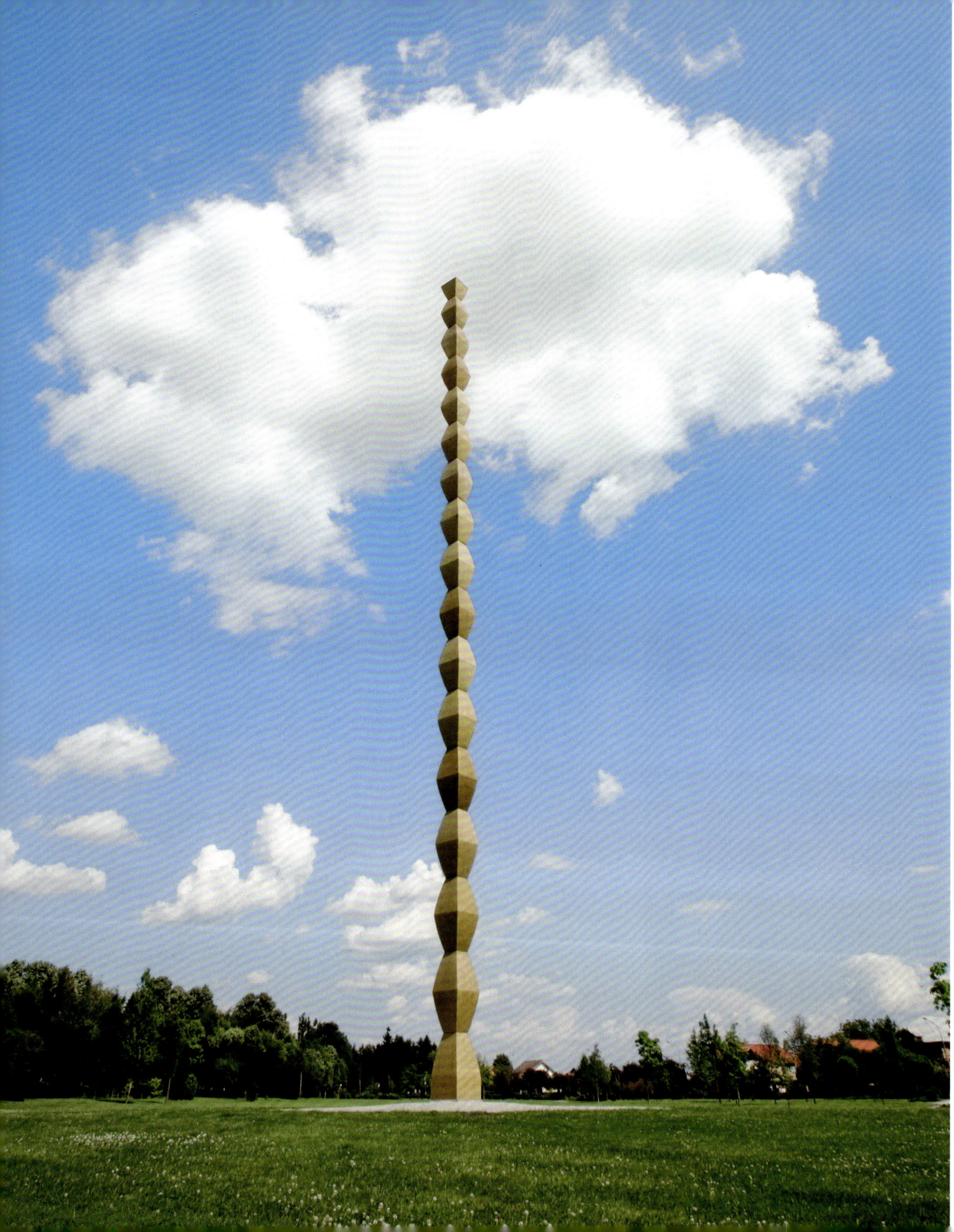

Constantin Brancusi (1876–1957)
Endless Column

1938
Cast iron with bronze metallic spray
29.3 m (96 ft) high
Târgu Jiu, Romania

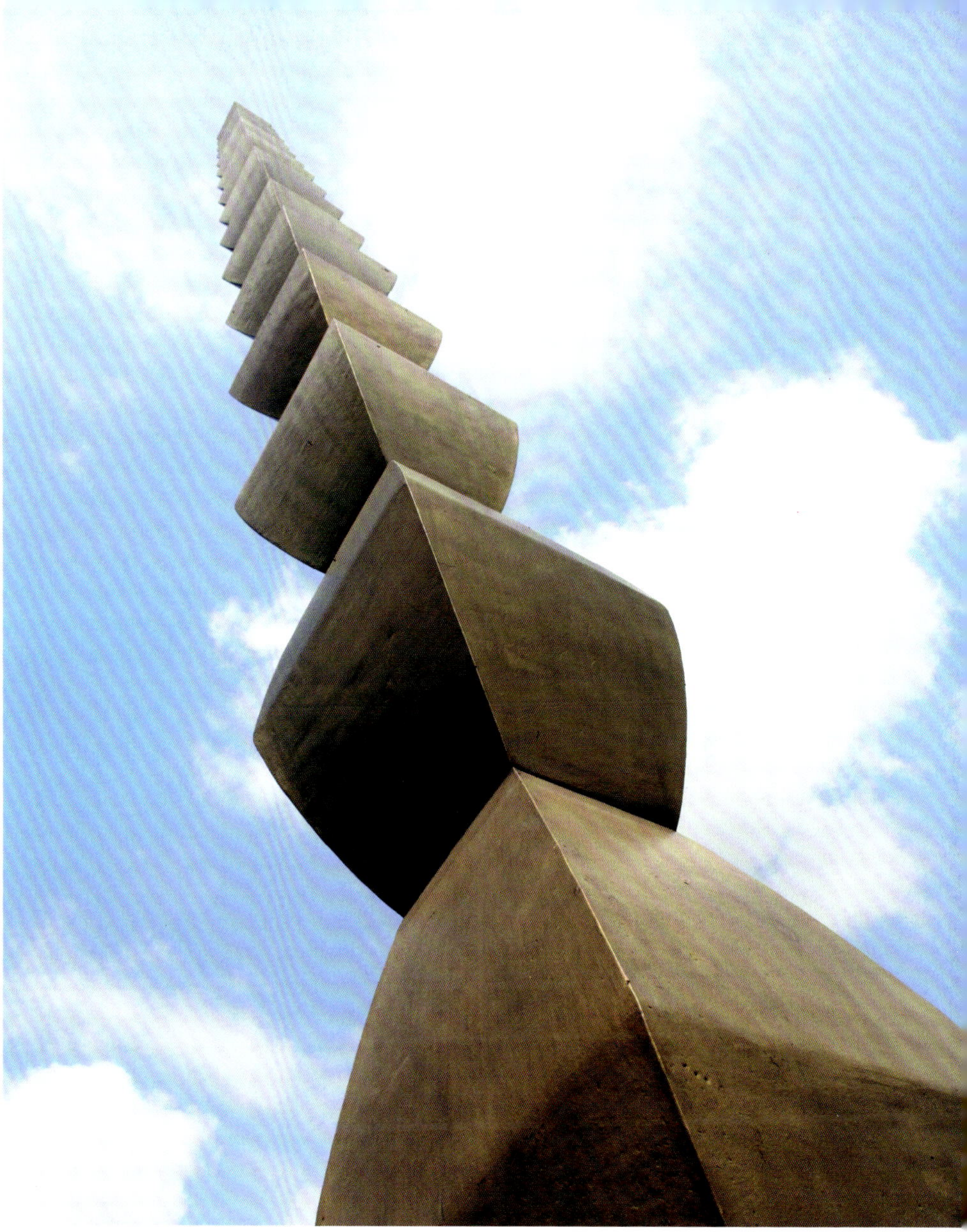

Constantin Brancusi's *Endless Column* is one of the clearest examples of a sculpture in which its presence results from the repetition of its outer edges and the simplicity of its silhouette. The work is composed of fifteen giant hollow bead-like sections, plus a half bead at the top and another half at the bottom that has been extended to form a base. When we stand nearby and gaze up at its rising pulsating form, the work seems to be an infinite repetition of planes and edges. This illusion is caused not only by its height, but also because its deceptive simplicity makes it easy for the imagination to repeat what the eye sees. The column is a paradox in that it appears to be more edge than plane, a constantly moving articulated series of edges that while rising up are simultaneously descending. Razor-sharp zigzag edges appear to cut the sky into two parts while simultaneously knitting it back together. Strangest of all is how the column contradicts the rules of one-point perspective. Visually the beads should appear to grow smaller as the column ascends, but contrary to what we see in the photograph, the beads deceptively remain the same size when we stand in front fo the actual sculpture. The *Endless Column* offers one of sculpture's best examples of the gulf that exists between what is known by the mind and what is seen by the eye.

Francesco Laurana (1430–1502)
Beatrice of Aragon

1471–4
White marble
40.6 × 40.3 × 20.3 cm (16 × 15 ⅞ × 8 in)
Frick Collection, New York

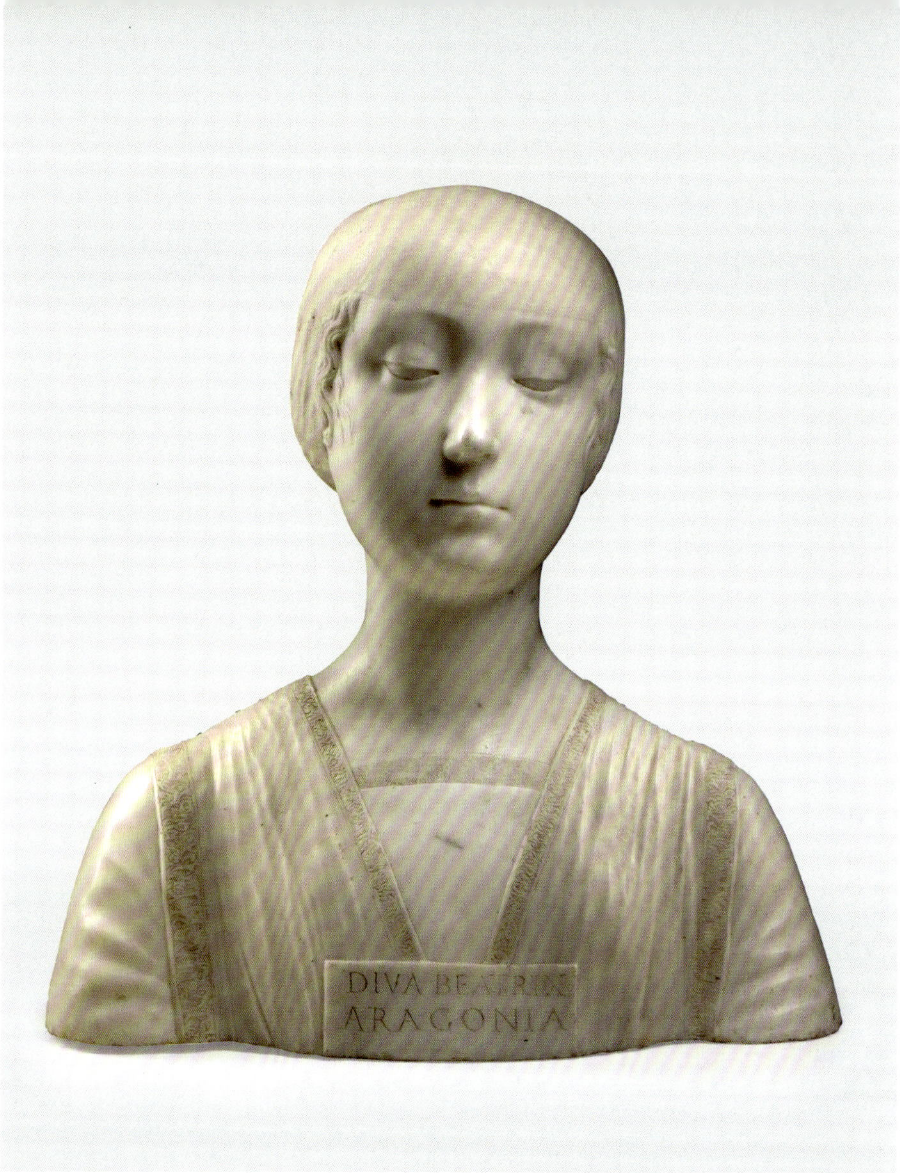

This portrait of Beatrice of Aragon is one of the most enigmatic and affecting of the Italian sculptor Francesco Laurana's portraits. Beatrice's serene white mask seems to defy all considerations having to do with Edge. But it is precisely Laurana's subtle use of this Element that provides the work with its compelling presence. Most immediately apparent are the embroidered outer edges of the dress, patterned with almost geometric simplicity; such precise details convey that the dress is made from a woven fabric. So subtly do Beatrice's clearly defined features emerge from the white facial mask that we cannot catch her gaze. We only see her partially closed eyelids and then become aware of the exquisitely carved edges that define their forms and shape her expression. As our eyes move upwards the soft edges of curled hair dissolve into her temples. And it is here that the most astonishing use of Edge appears. She wears a cap of the thinnest fabric imaginable. It lies across her forehead, so sheer that it is all but invisible. Then standing back, the whole projects an ethereal beauty, and delicacy of features that are in part due to Laurana's use of a range of finely carved edges.

The most basic and important operation in the act of visual perception is to locate the edges of things.

— Michael Baxandall

In looking at an object we reach out for it. With an invisible finger we move through the space around us, go out to the distant places where the things are found, touch them, catch them, scan their surfaces, traces their borders, explore their texture. It is an eminently active occupation.

— Rudolf Arnheim

Texture

The particular feel and character of a given surface.

The surface quality of something may be experienced by hand, eye or both. Every material has a unique texture. Touch this page, touch your sleeve. These are *actual* textures. Defying touch, the black type on this white page is an example of a *visual* texture. In this case the hand discerns no change across a surface, but the eye does. More than the other Elements, Texture is a haptic experience. But if we are asked not to touch sculpture in a museum, is there an alternative? I believe there is. We have a rich textural memory to draw on, so we can use our imaginations to call up past experiences. We do this all the time for we can never touch every object our eyes see. Through the sense or memory of touch, Texture informs sight.

Eva Hesse (1936–1970)
Accession

1968
Galvanized steel and rubber
78.1 × 78.1 × 78.1 cm (30 ¾ × 30 ¾ × 30 ¾ in)
Detroit Institute of Arts, MI

Texture is a product of Eva Hesse's working process in this sculpture and is specific to the materials used. Hundreds of pieces of rubber tubing are folded and their ends passed through the five sides of a perforated open steel cube. When we experience sculpture in person we have an intense, visceral response to its underwater sea anemone-like textural presence. The simplicity of means and the clarity of form given the materials used only add to its mystery. The extreme contrast between the visual intensity of the inside and the relative passivity of the outside holds our attention and makes it impossible not to reach out and touch its outer surface irregularities, and then reach inside and experience the hair-like tentacles within.

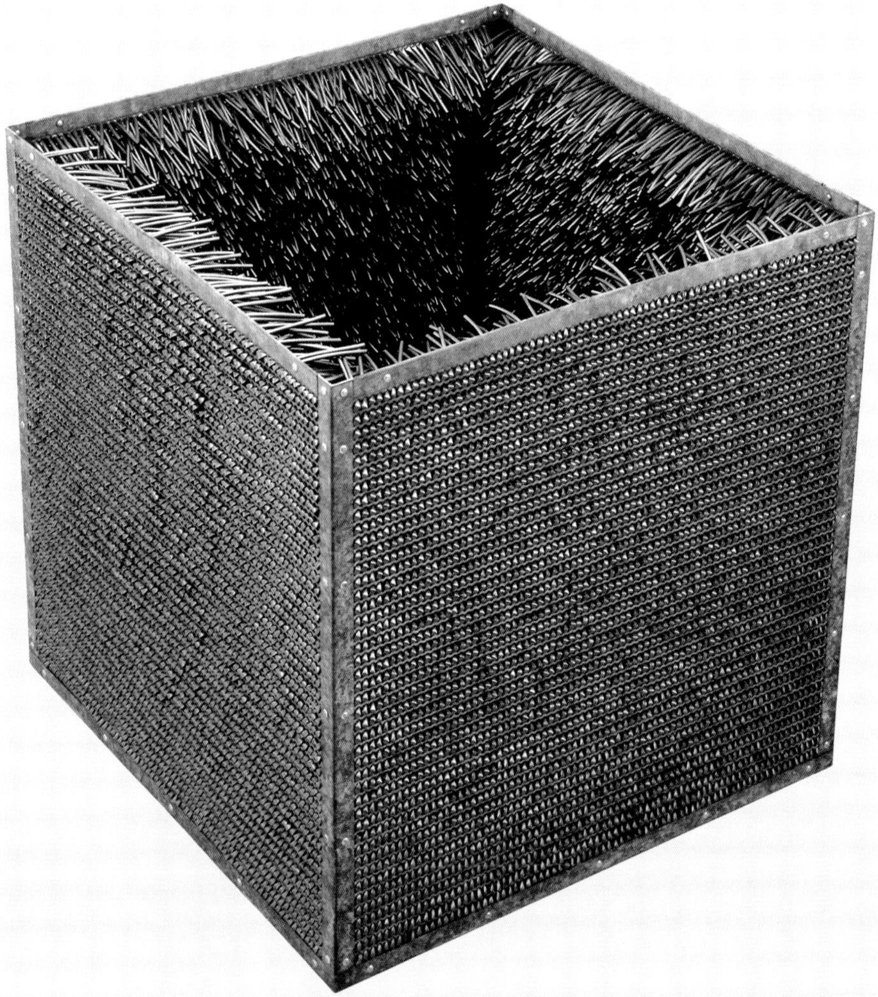

Michelangelo (1475–1564)
St Matthew

1503
Marble
271 cm (106 ¾ in) high
Galleria dell'Accademia, Florence

Perhaps more relief than sculpture in the round, this marble sculpture of St Matthew by Michelangelo clearly illustrates the visual and descriptive power of a dynamic violent texture. This variously broken surface is a result of the process of carving, and is sometimes referred to as *non finito*, which literally means not finished. These unfinished areas of rough texture may suggest forms within the stone that are struggling to emerge from the larger block. Because of this lack of resolution, parts of the figure of St Matthew are left to the imagination of the viewer to complete. Or not. Texture plays a descriptive role here. Look carefully at the difference between the left and right legs. Bent at the knee, the upper portion of the left leg is polished smooth, and projects forward. At the same time the tense right leg, present only in contour, supports the body weight and is consumed by the carved surface texture. Imagine the leg and foot within the plane of the yet-to-be resolved stone. In this and similar works by Michelangelo our preconceived thoughts about what constitutes a finished sculpture are shown to have little consequence, and so may be antithetical to a larger aesthetic vision. Here, figure, stone and process merge; the three conjoin, fully realized and elucidated by the richness of their various textures.

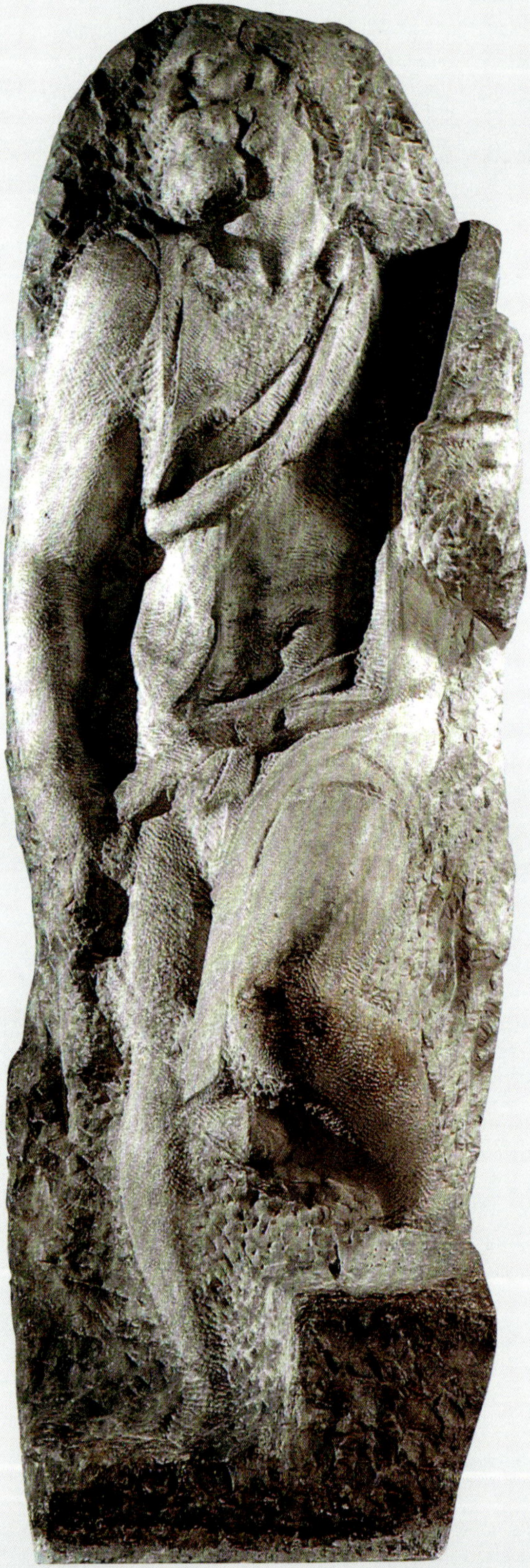

Meret Oppenheim (1913–1985)
Object

1936
Fur covered cup, saucer and spoon
7.3 cm (2 ⅞ in) high
Museum of Modern Art, New York

Even in the photograph the surrealistic teacup and spoon by Meret Oppenheim has an overwhelmingly sense-filled but paradoxical textural presence. The work has been carefully crafted from what appears to be deer hide. Because of the clarity of the forms we immediately know that these are objects that both belong in the mouth and, because they are made from fur, objects that the mouth would find impossibly repugnant. We are not only startled but also deeply repelled by this visceral absurdity. The work also gains textural poignancy and emotional tension because of our clear memory of the smooth inviting texture of a real spoon and the pleasure of a warm cup of tea.

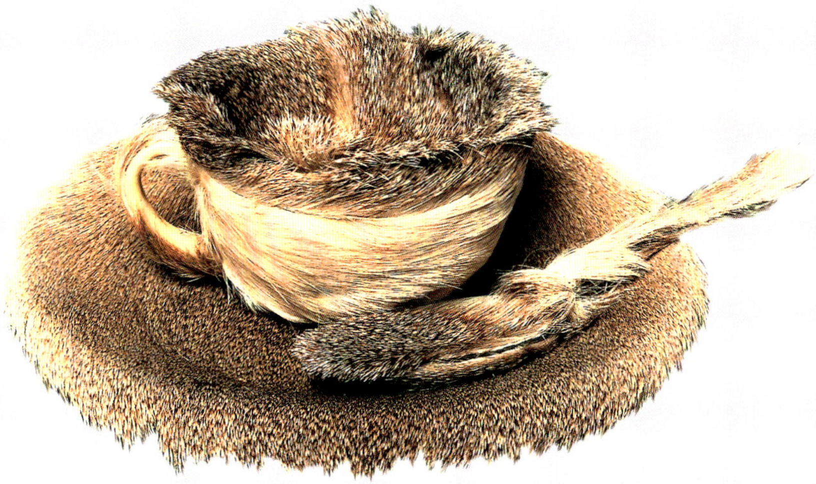

Bena Biombo Culture, Democratic Republic of Congo
Mask

Wood, metal, plant fibres
35.5 × 40 × 41 cm (14 × 15 ¾ × 16 ⅛ in)
Musée du Quai Branly, Paris

This mask is made from polychrome wood and raffia, and illustrates three different types of texture. Like the fur in the Oppenheim work above, the dried grass collar is a natural real texture that is coarse to the touch. The wood from which the mask is carved is relatively hard allowing the sculptor to create a smooth surface finish that is inviting to the touch. Perhaps the most startling areas are the four slightly raised rectangles of visual texture. These contain small intricately painted triangles that may represent scarification. Because they are painted on, their texture is more for the eye than for the hand.

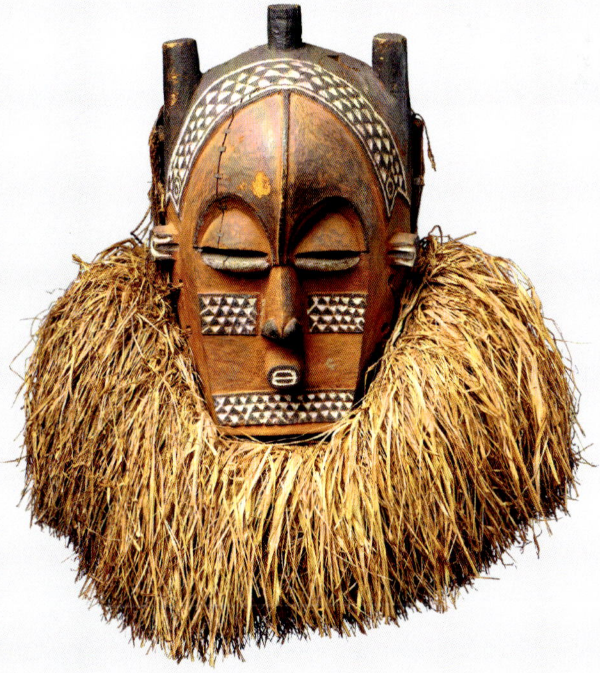

Germaine Richier (1902–1959)
The Mandoline or The Cicada

1954–5
Polished natural bronze, brass wire, stone
60 × 39 × 44 cm (23 ⅝ × 15 ⅜ × 17 ⅜ in)
Private collection

Like many European artists of her generation, Germaine Richier was deeply affected by the violence of World War II. In response, her primary focus became the animal world, particularly insects. Here Richier merges anthropomorphism with the insect, revealing a strange, barely visible, sometimes terrifying realm of creatures that can, with disconcerting ease, enter our repressed subconscious. The bronze body has been eaten away leaving a coarse turbulent surface with lace-like piercings. These openings create an unsettling visual texture that lends the work a feeling of decay. Thin brass wire extends beyond the bronze and forms the antennae, legs and head, reinforcing the insect reference. Not only does this material give a sense of frailty, but the twisting forms of the wire – like lines on paper – suggests the creation of form as we watch. Finally, there is an almost pathetic violence to the work that is intensified by the penetrating large pin that displays the sculpture like an entomologist's specimen.

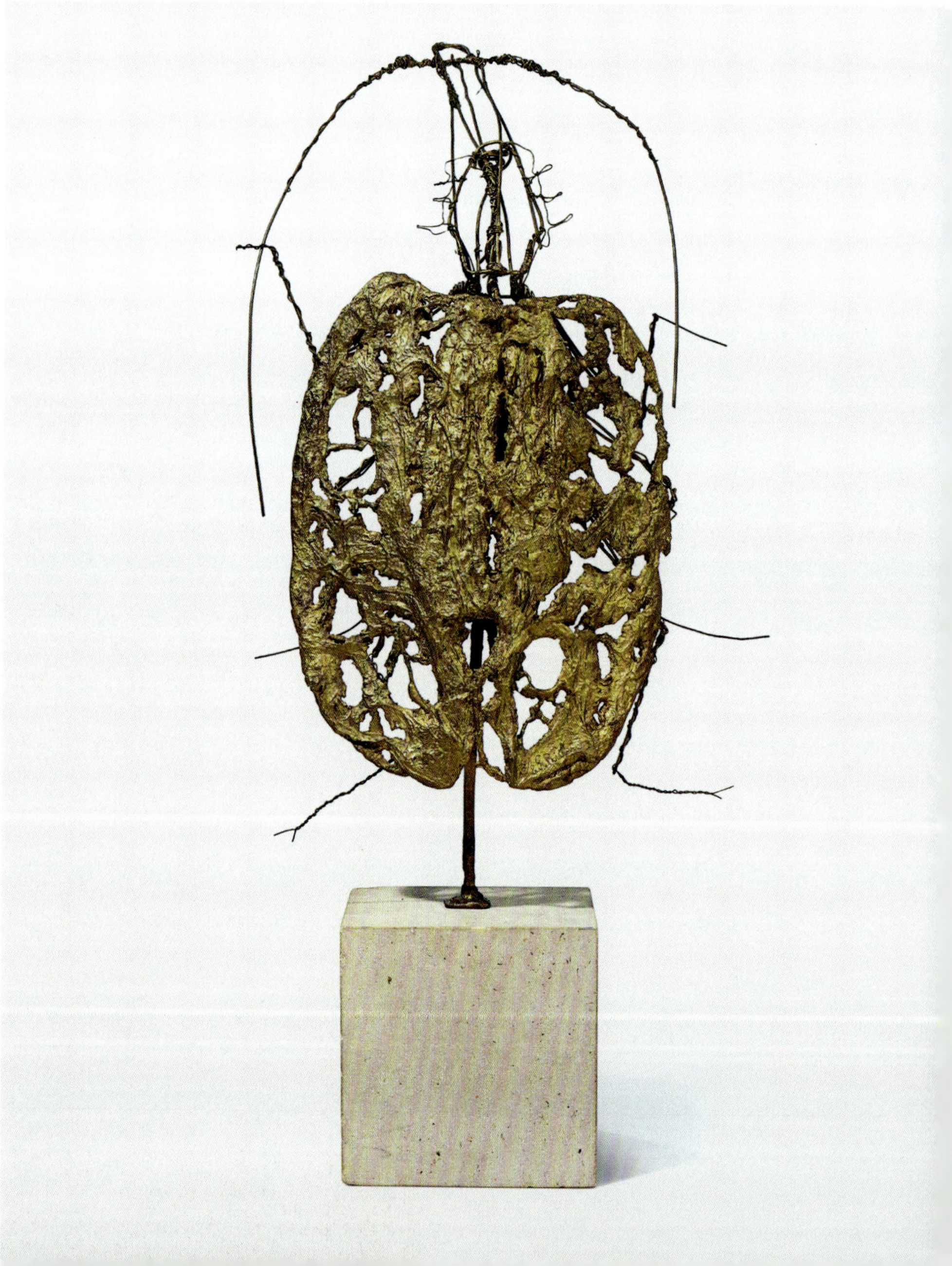

John Chamberlain (1927–2011)
Neptune's Cap

2005
Stainless steel
241.3 × 182.9 × 134.6 cm (95 × 72 × 53 in)
Ovitz Family Collection, Los Angeles

The process of making in John Chamberlain's *Neptune's Cap* is palpable and violent. He has taken pieces of shredded, bent and twisted steel and constructed a textural mass that aggressively confronts the viewer with its physicality. Nearly 8 feet high, the sculpture is the product of enormous machines that have the power to tear and shred auto and truck bumpers as if they were paper. Countless crushed and ragged ribbons have been welded together into a chrome-plated turbulent block of writhing texture that is terrifying to the touch.

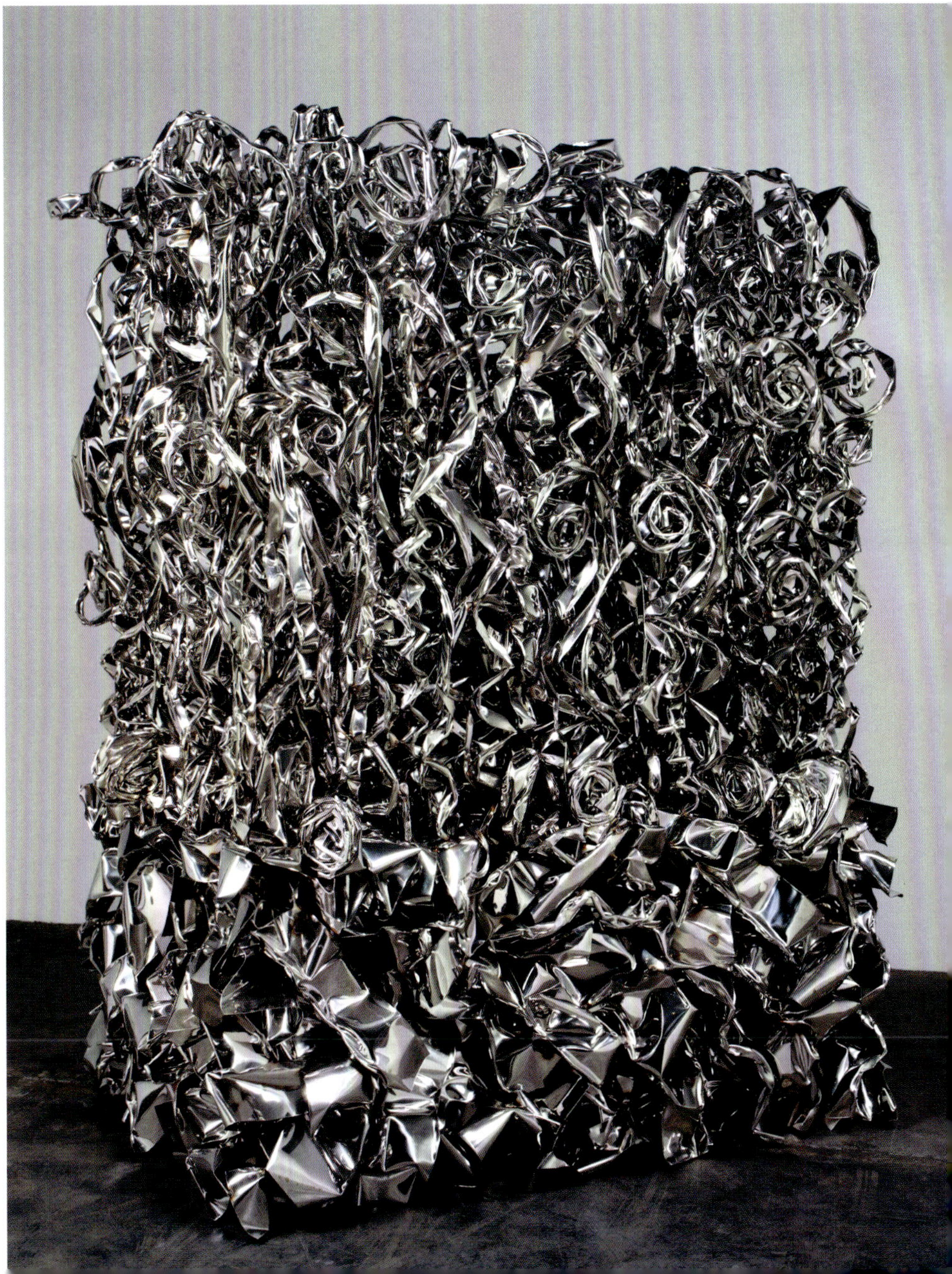

Donatello (1386–1466)
Penitent Magdalene

c. 1456–60
Wood with polychromy and gold
1.9 m (6 ft 3 in) high
Museo dell'Opera del Duomo, Florence

Approached from the back, this 6-foot-high wooden sculpture of Mary Magdalene is a puzzling abstraction. From this angle, all we recognize are her emaciated but delicately carved legs supporting what appears to be a textural cascade of filthy knotted hair, and torn and rotting fabric. Hair and clothes merge in such confusion that her body is consumed by this frenzied texture. When we walk around the sculpture, the richness of the carving becomes apparent as she hesitantly, painfully, steps into our space. Sunken blank eyes stare out and are unable to return our gaze; a pained sorrowful mouth is the only feature that animates her head. Her withered body is testament to her abstinence and deprivation. To convey her devotion, Donatello carved a figure that avoids all reference to feminine beauty. She is the essence of transcendental spiritual enlightenment. Only her prayerful nearly touching fingers and her youthful hands convey the beauty within the piety of her ardour.

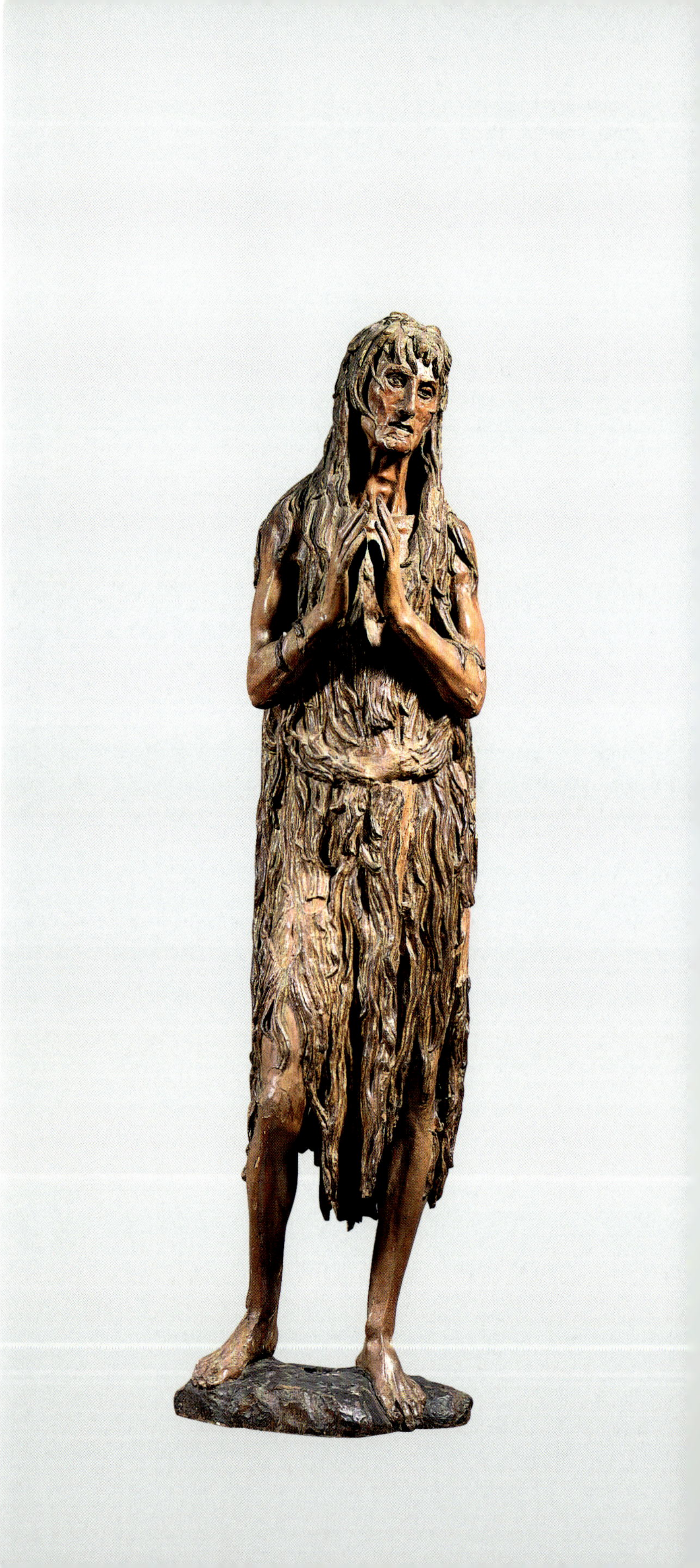

Jean-Antoine Houdon
Bust of Anne-Marie-Louise Thomas de Domangeville de Sérilly, Comtesse de Pange

1780
Marble
89.9 cm (35 ¼ in) high
Art Institute of Chicago, IL

Jean-Antoine Houdon uses subtle changes in texture to describe areas of transition in his bust of the Comtesse de Pange. Notice, for example, the carefully carved transition between the hard tight flesh of the forehead and the soft hair that grows from it. The hair is pulled back into turbulent twisting curls that eventually rest on her shoulders. Each moment is explained intricately. At her bodice the texture of lace lies softly on top of her breast. The carving of this veil of texture is so exact that it not only clarifies the fineness and precision of the lace, but also the forms beneath it. The thickness of various fabrics, the varied surfaces of flesh, the flowing twisting hair; all of these surface changes are carved in minute detail with precise attention paid to their individual textures.

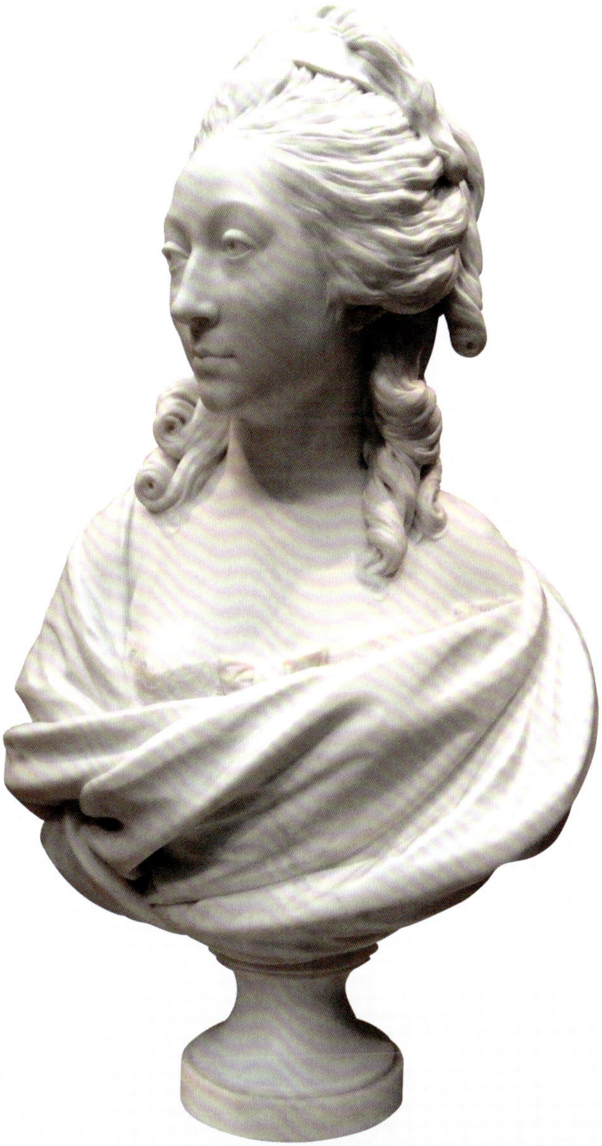

Jean Arp (1886–1966)
Demeter

1961
Bronze
104.1 × 50.5 × 41.9 cm (41 × 19 ⅞ × 16 ½ in)
Israel Museum, Jerusalem

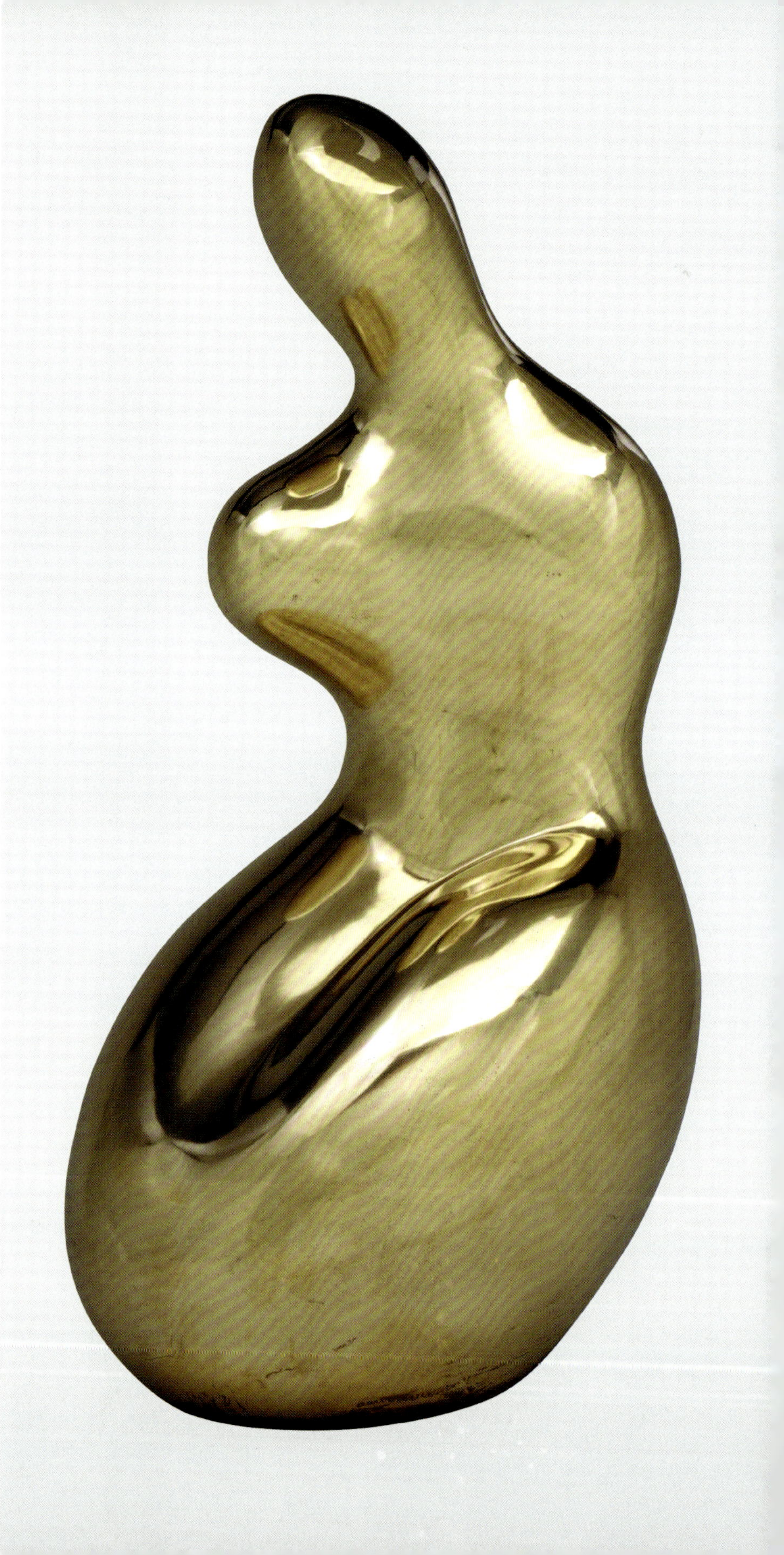

Any visual disturbance of a pristine surface may be thought of as visual texture. Visual texture is beyond touch, as demonstrated in Jean Arp's *Demeter*. The bronze is polished to a mirrored finish that results in a contrast between the smooth hard feel of the metal and the reflected images seen on its surface. It is tempting to speculate about a connection between form and title, as Demeter was the goddess of fertility and of the natural cycles of life and death. The shape of the sculpture recalls a luxuriant, regenerative female form, which is consistent with the myth. But by polishing the bronze reflective surface, Arp encourages light and the other forms that surround the sculpture to reflect, ricochet and move across its surface so that the hard materiality of the sculpture dissolves into the sum of the objects that surround it. Texture here becomes a fluid series of reflected images, light and shade, challenging the surface integrity of the sculpture.

Nature's works are three-dimensional and can be touched with the hand; painting is only an object of vision and of no other sense, while sculpture exists also in three-dimensions in which it resembles nature, and is an object not only of vision but of touch, too.

— Bronzino

Then at last I can understand sculpture; I think and compare
See with a feeling eye, feel with a seeing hand.

— Johann Wolfgang von Goethe

Colour

A visual sensation. Colour may be applied to the surface of a sculpture or inherent to the material it is made from. Hue, tint and shade are words that describe the character of colour.

Although at first colour might appear to belong more to painting than to sculpture, it plays a vital role in our understanding of sculptural form. All materials have their own distinguishing colour; I will refer to that as *inherent* colour. Any material may be painted or stained, and I will refer to that as *applied* colour. We see in colour, and those colours in turn provide us with necessary perceptual information to make sense of the multitude of forms in our visual world. Few of the Elements are so intimately linked to our emotions as Colour. Our perceptual universe is a place in which colour and form are intimately linked; retain the form and alter the colour, or vice versa, and much of the meaning of a particular object changes. A red lemon will taste different. These critical links between colour and form are made early on and are absolutely necessary for us to survive. But because the sculptor has freedom of choice, the relationship between colour and sculpture is more complex, ambiguous and far more interesting.

Early Classical period, Greece
The Archer from Temple of Aphaia, Aegina

490–480 BC
Marble
Approx. 147 cm (57 ⅞ in) high
Munich Glyptothek Museum

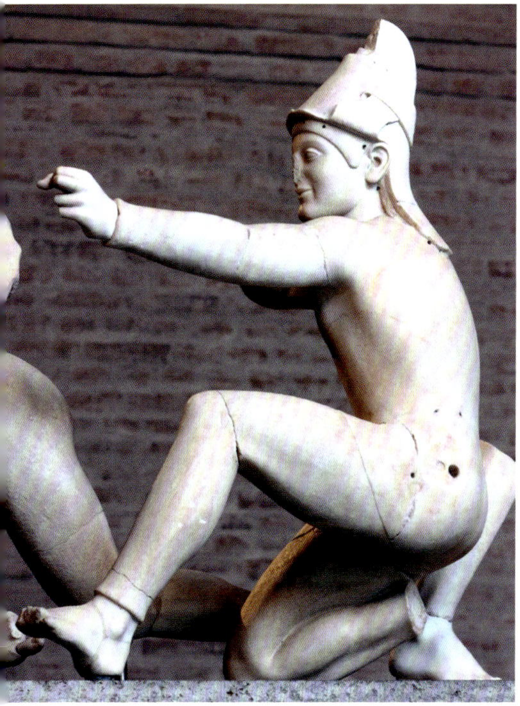

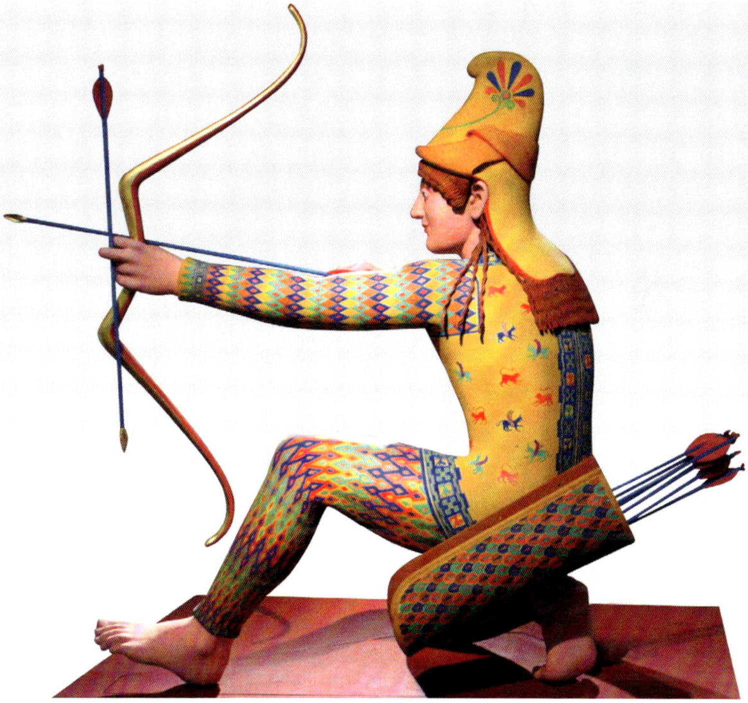

Contrary to our preconceptions, an example of applied colour can be found in classical sculpture. The thought of Greek sculpture conjures figures of utter whiteness: the gods and goddesses appear to us in a bleached remove. But while this is how we view the classical world, it was not how the Greeks understood themselves. As far as we know, most or all of the sculpture of antiquity was painted. Take, for example, the archer from the west pediment of the Temple of Aphaia in Aegina. The bleached whiteness of the archer shown here seems to confirm all of our mistaken impressions. However, as a result of years of research, most recently by curators at the Munich Glyptothek Museum, we now have a far more accurate view of the original polychrome surfaces of Greek sculpture. The image on the right is a reconstruction from a recent exhibition at the museum, which uses sculptural models, to-scale reproductions and documentation to show us how sculpture actually appeared to the classical eye. These painted sculptures transport us to a very different cultural world than we are accustomed to. Colour can change far more than just the surface of a sculpture.

Max Klinger (1857–1920)
Beethoven

1902
Marble of several colours, bronze and glass, metal, ivory and precious stone inlays
3.1 m (10 ft 2 in) high
Museum Der Bildenden Künste, Leipzig

An example of the imaginative use of the inherent colour of materials is this work by Max Klinger. The sculptor utilizes the colour within natural stone, bronze and ivory to define the various parts within his intricate work. The heroic throne of Beethoven is dark bronze, contrasting with his white marble flesh. The small heads that surround the composer are carved in part from ivory. The drapery that folds across the lower half of his body is an amber marble; projecting earth-like from under the drapery and left foot is a grey natural stone. Perched on the stone is a black granite eagle, the symbol of the German state. All rest on a plinth of reddish brown stone that raises the work above eye level. This array of colours and the use of various materials give the appearance of a bizarre sculpture that resides in a curious place somewhere between classical Greece and the European Baroque.

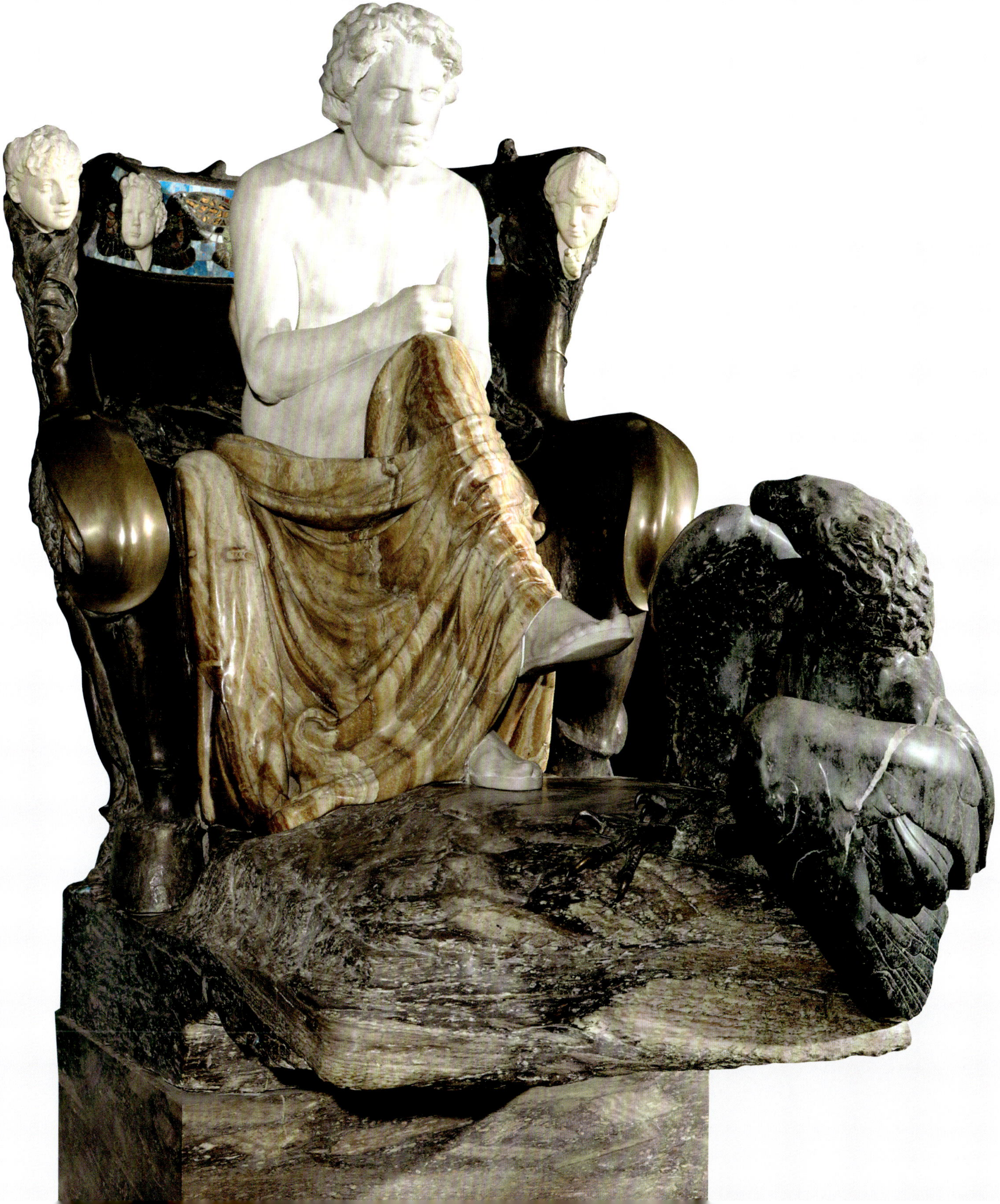

Pablo Picasso (1881–1973)
Glass of Absinthe

1914
Painted bronze, silver-plated spoon
21.5 cm (8 ½ in) high
Museum of Modern Art, New York

Pablo Picasso
Glass of Absinthe

1914
Painted bronze, sand and silver-plated spoon
21.5 cm (8 ½ in) high
Musée Picasso, Paris

Pablo Picasso
Glass of Absinthe

1914
Painted bronze, silver-plated spoon
21.5 cm (8 ½ in) high
Philadelphia Museum of Art, PA

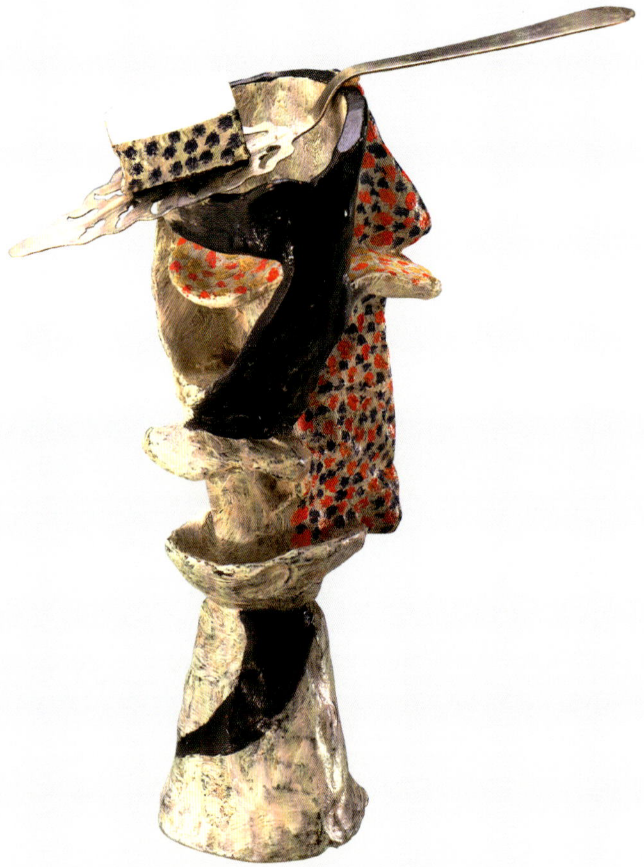

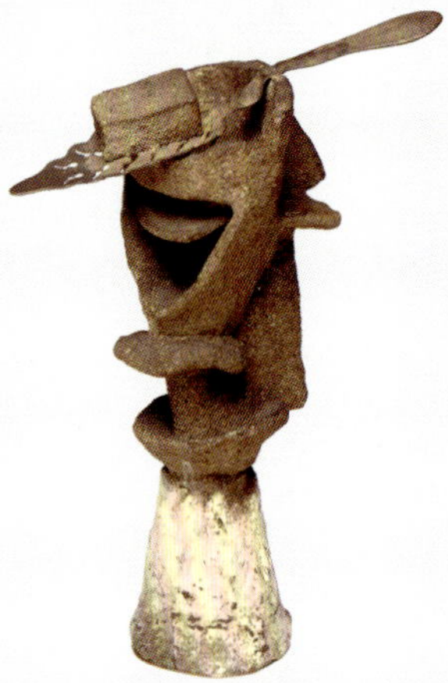

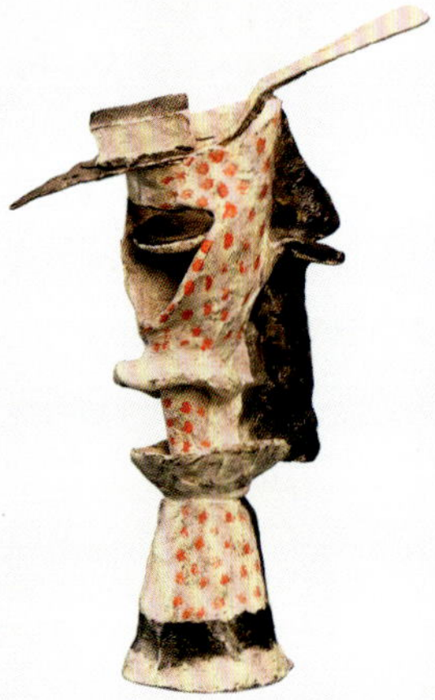

Colour is fundamental to how we respond to our sensory world, so it is difficult to imagine everyday objects in different colours. These three works are cast from the same plaster original. Pablo Picasso made several bronze castings of it, added the silver sugar server, and painted each in different colours, studying how colour affects our perception of form. The closest to the original plaster form is top right. Here, Picasso added sand to the paint, visually dividing the work in two. In the other two works, the addition of applied colour provides a visual texture, creating an ambiguous 'camouflaged' surface. In the work on the left the two black slashes appear to cut deeply into the bronze form. However, the areas with pointillist red and blue dots appear to flow together, almost merging with the sugar cube and its matching dots. In the version bottom right, the dots extend all the way down the glass to the black stripe, creating the appearance of a commonality of surfaces. The palpable aesthetic differences between these works make for a fascinating meditation on how colour may change our understanding of form. We know they have the same basic form but with the addition of colour, Picasso has altered not only the appearance of their surfaces, but also the objects' meaning.

Alexander Calder (1898–1976)
Little Face

1945
Copper wire, thread, glass objects, wood
33 cm (13 in) high
Museum of Contemporary Art Chicago, IL

Our minds have the capacity to store millions of images and frequently they are intimately linked with particular colours. This critical relationship between object and colour is one of the primary ways in which we know our world. Notice the colour of each facial feature/mobile element within this head by Alexander Calder. Out of all the colours of broken glass to be found, out of all the glass objects Calder had to choose from, he carefully selected these four: a broken red reflector for the mouth, a blue triangular shard for the nose, and two carefully balanced clear circular pieces for the eyes. Once seen and considered, Calder's decisions become obvious, but it is interesting and instructive to note that these associations between facial features and colours are not at all apparent at first sight.

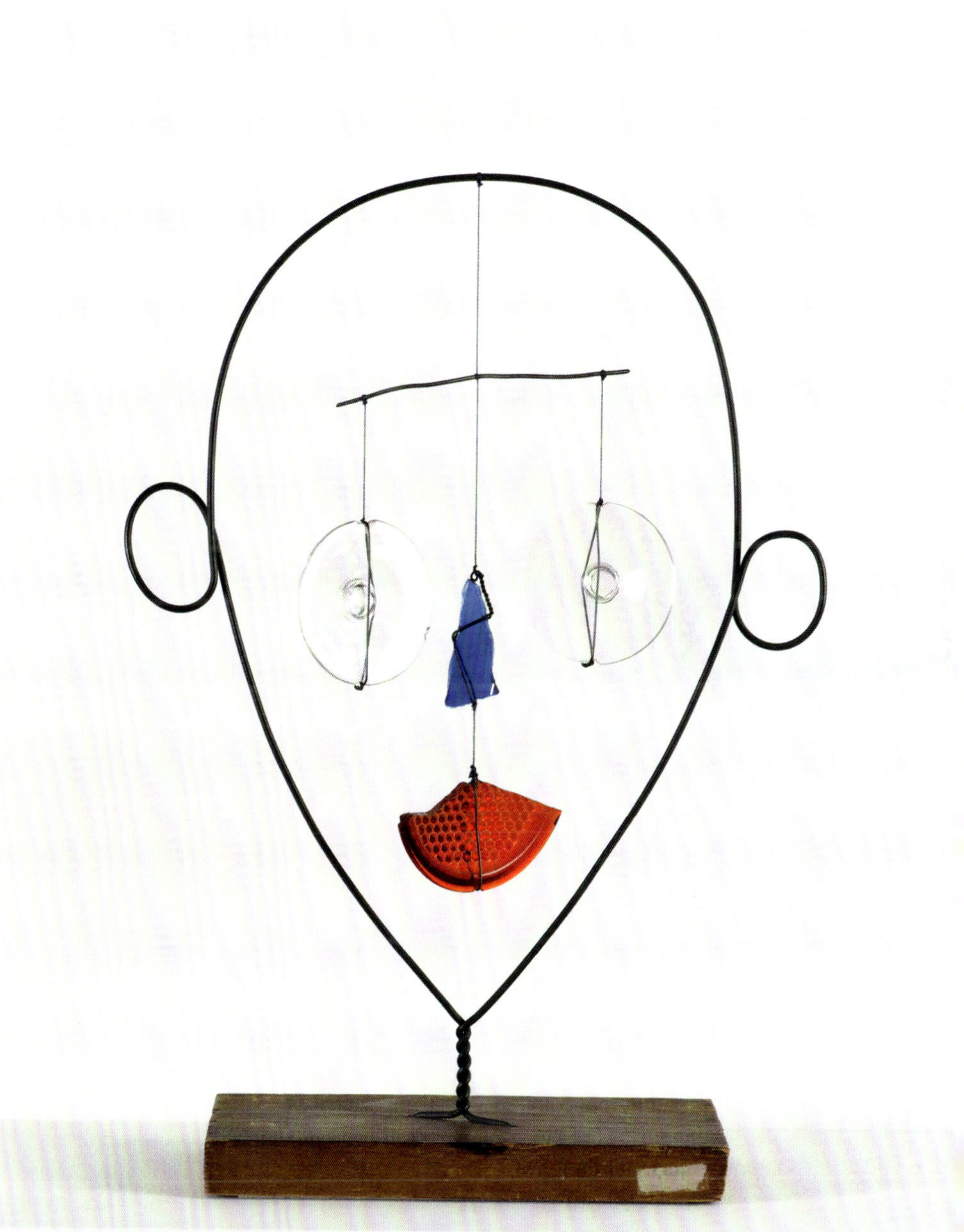

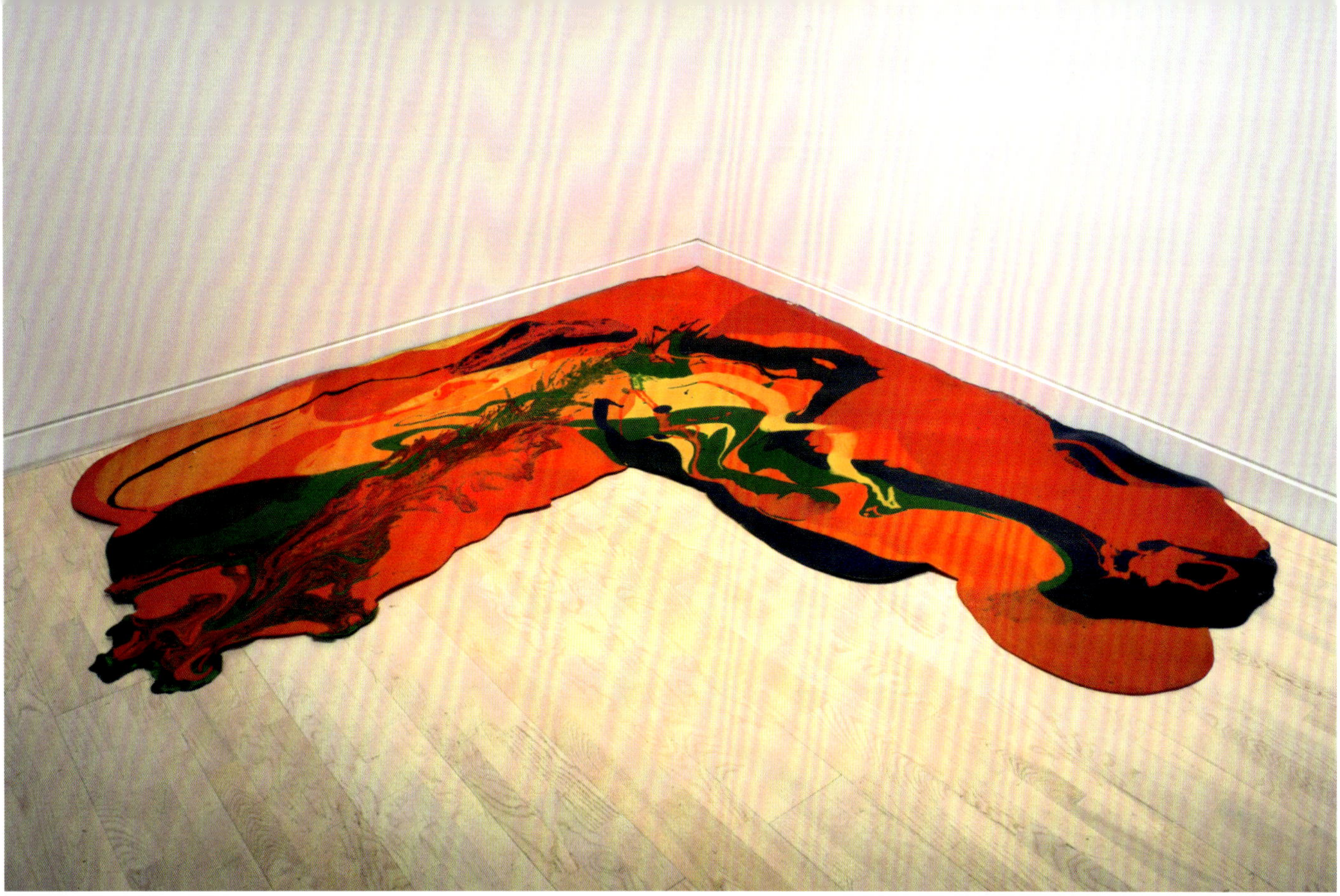

Lynda Benglis (b. 1941)
Corner Piece

1969
Poured pigment latex
2.69 × 2.74 m (8 ft 10 in × 9 ft)
Hirshhorn Museum and Sculpture Garden,
Smithsonian Institution, Washington DC

Tony Cragg (b. 1949)
Commercial Moon

1984
Found plastic fragments
2.1 m (7 ft) high
Private collection

Rivers of latex pigmented with the three primary colours plus green have been poured on the gallery floor where they form a flexible congealed 'river' of colours that appears to be in a state of unresolved ebb and flow. The colours blend together as they spill out, each attempting to maintain its individual place and hue within the thin membrane of the total surface. The rivulets of different colours reflect the process of pouring used to create the work, and together they give a sense of movement, identity and direction to this polychrome floor-relief trapped within the corner of the gallery.

Ours is a consumer society, a throwaway culture, a world in which the rubbish dump may become a source for inspiration and a storehouse for materials. Tony Cragg accomplishes some of the same things compositionally that Klinger exploits (see p. 68), namely to create a unity of form from disparate parts. In *Commercial Moon*, Cragg creates a low-relief sculpture composed of carefully selected found plastic objects that, without cutting, fit within a silhouette of the moon's first quarter. They are arranged in an abbreviated colour wheel. The plastic toys and other objects progress from red to blue, through yellow and the secondary colours of orange and green. All are ordered by form and colour. If the work were monochromatic it would lose a great deal of the lyrical tension that results from the individual identity of each object and its artificial/inherent colour.

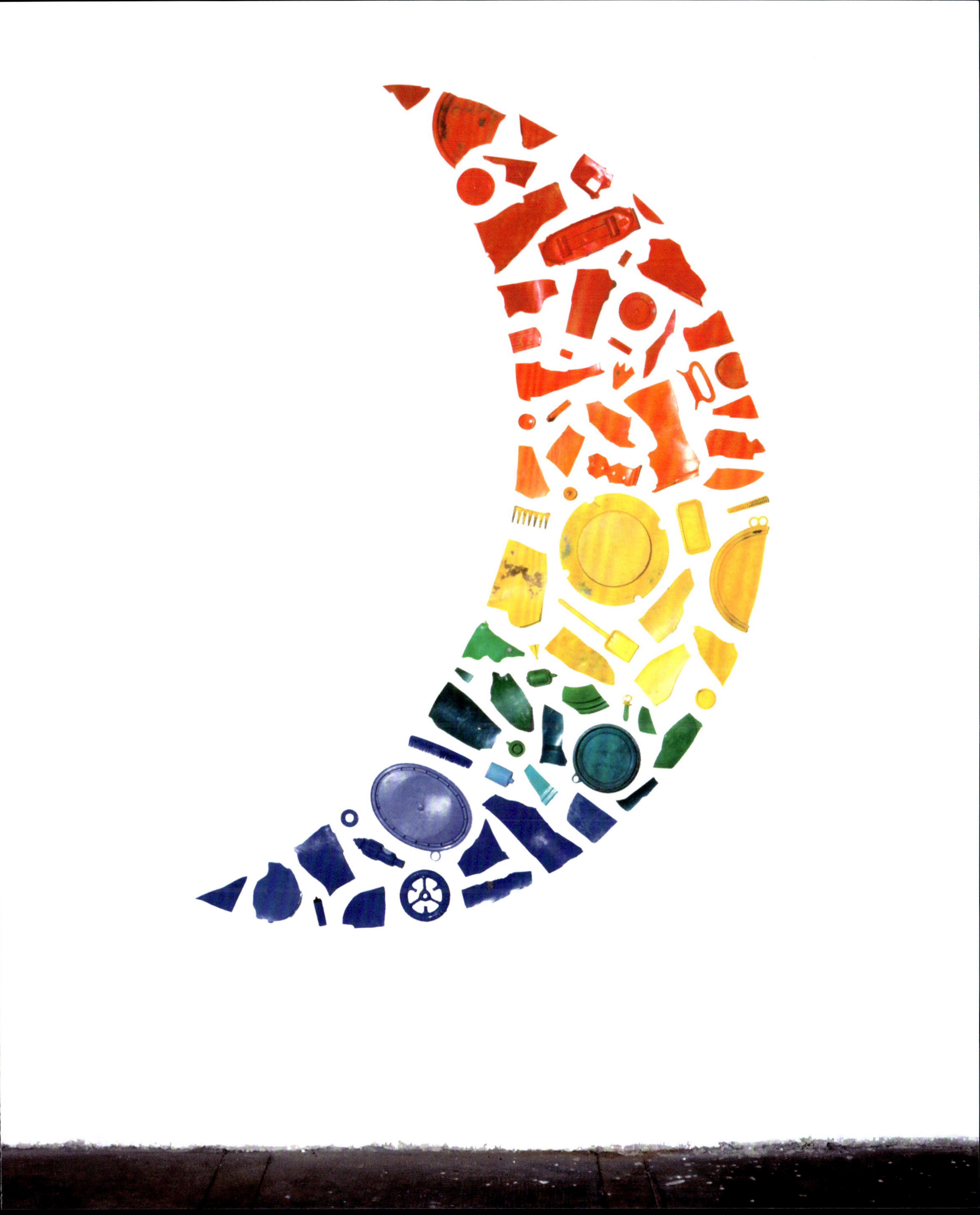

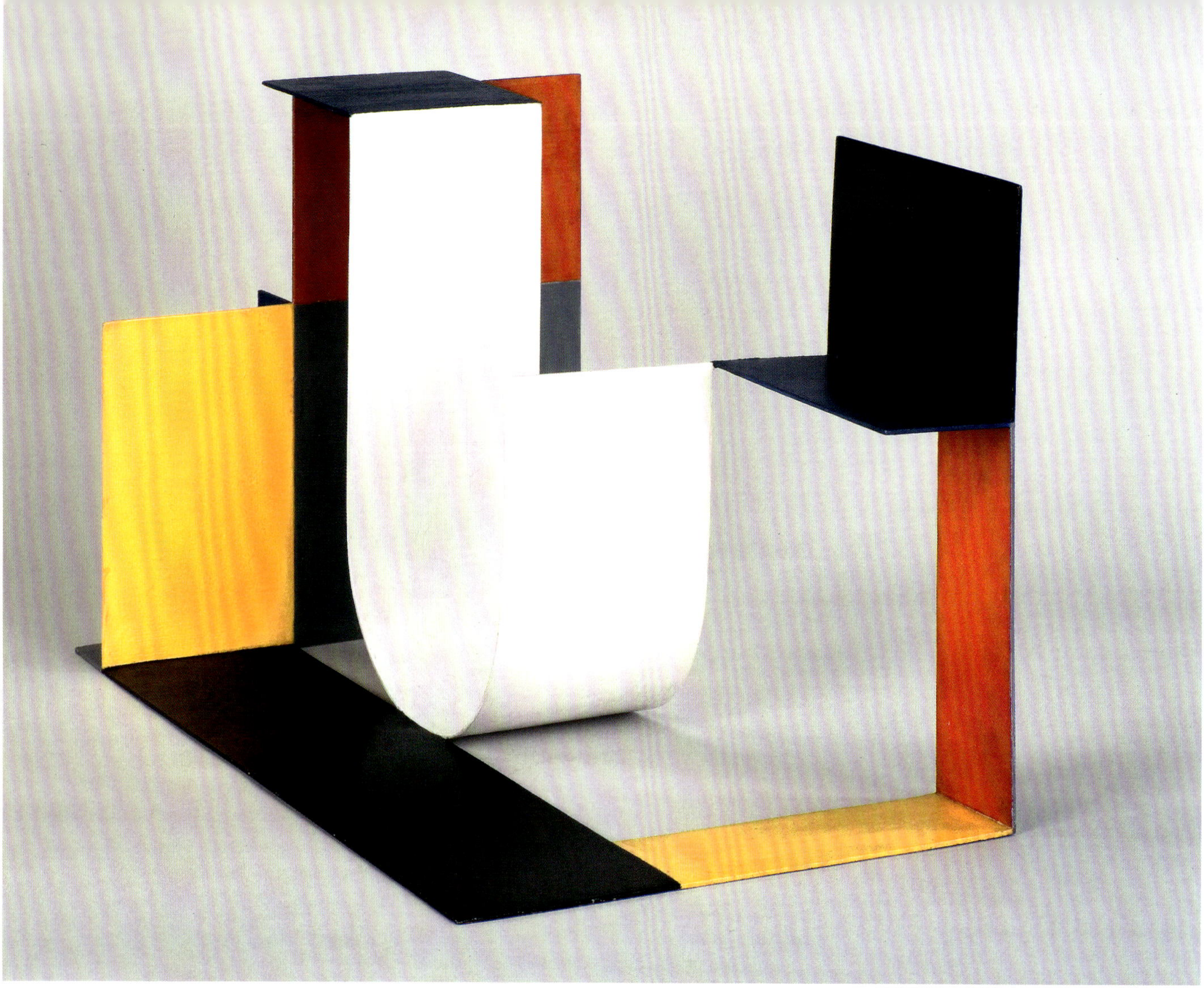

Katarzyna Kobro (1898–1951)
Spatial Composition

1929
Painted steel
40 × 60 × 40 cm (15 ¾ × 23 ⅝ × 15 ¾ in)
Muzeum Sztuki, Lodz

Colour may also be the manifestation of a sculptor's social/political ideology. In *Spatial Composition* by Katarzyna Kobro the choice of these particular colours comes directly from the artist's belief that the fundamental goal of sculpture is the expression of spatial relationships and that specific colours and their interaction may have a positive influence on our constructed world. This and similar works were painted using a palette of the three primary colours plus white, grey and black. The use of these vivid colours radically alters the relative spatial position of the planes that construct the work. Under controlled circumstances on a flat surface, warm colours tend to advance in space, while cool colours recede. But in this sculpture by Kobro, colour/space relationships are used to alter the expected spatial flow and create a tension between form and colour that keeps oscillating as we circle the piece. Many of her sculptures were based in part on a modular system that if expanded, she believed, could have a revolutionary influence on modern design and architecture. Imagine this sculpture all white; it would be a very different work, yielding a very different, in her words, 'ethical/moral' aesthetic experience.

Yves Klein (1928–1962)
Portrait Relief I: Arman

1962
Painted bronze on gilded panel
175.3 × 94 cm (69 × 37 in)
Philadelphia Museum of Art, PA

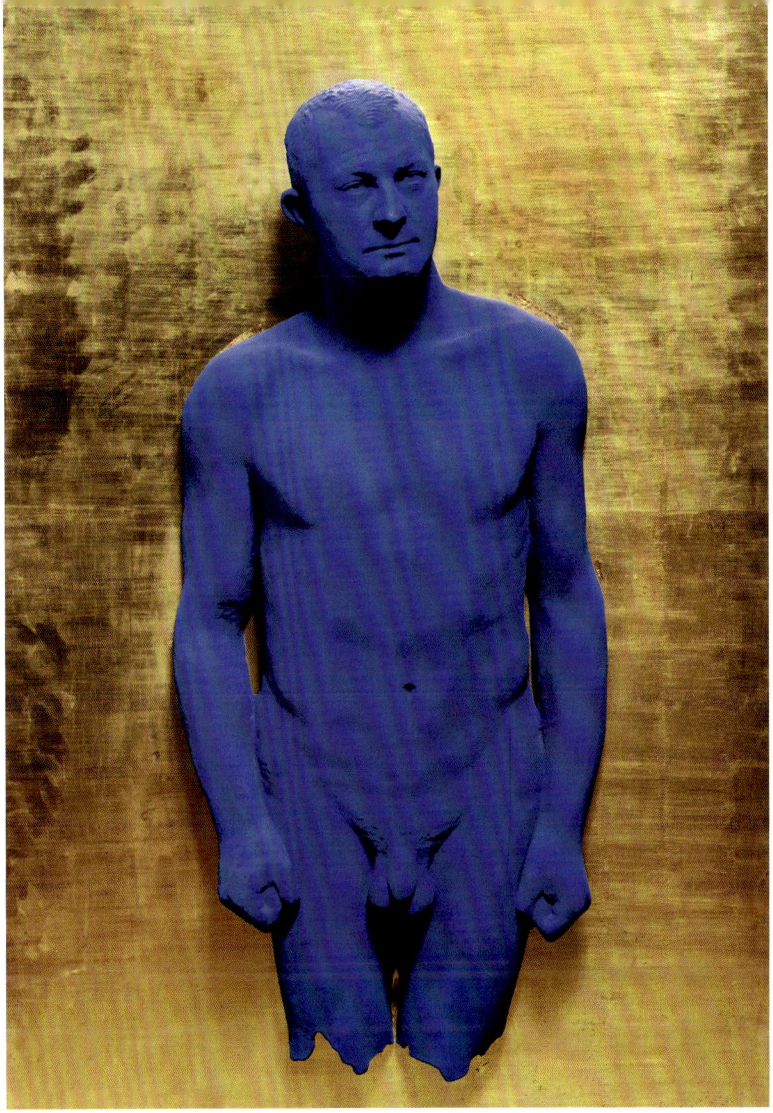

Certain colours may carry a symbolic or deeply personal meaning. For a multitude of reasons, we may have a favourite colour. Yves Klein's was ultramarine blue. This is one of a series of painted bronze sculptures cast from life and mounted on a reflective ground plane of gold leaf. Notice how the arms and other body parts pull free from the gold surface, while the back remains fully connected to the background: an example of *alto* or high-relief. The sculpture is a paradox: light reflects off the brilliant gold leaf background, but that same light is absorbed by the figure that visually recedes into its own deep blue-pigmented surface. Klein attempts to objectify the emotions that connect us to particular colours, in this case erasing from our consciousness all spectral memory, replacing it with what he might have called a heavenly blue metaphysical void. Klein went so far as to invent the precise colour for that void – 'International Klein Blue'. This was ultramarine blue pigment suspended within a clear synthetic resin that dries invisible, leaving a surface of matt pigment so blue and so matt that it absorbs almost all surface light into its porous blue depths.

Katharina Fritsch (b. 1956)
Monk

1997–9
Polyester and paint
193 × 58.4 × 43.1 cm (76 × 23 × 17 in)
Art Institute of Chicago, IL

At first glance the monochromatic black of *Monk* appears to have an aesthetic function similar to the blue in the Yves Klein work. But unlike Klein, Katharina Fritsch rarely paints two sculptures the same colour. Her highly refined and realistic human figures or animals will, given their particular aesthetic environment or solitary individuality, dictate a particular colour. This life-sized column-like figure is resolved fully in the round, and its flat black presence becomes a veil that shrouds the work. The monk appears to be projecting his religious piety inward, filtered through this film of colour. His closed eyes heighten this feeling as he stands erect in a tranquil state of deep meditation. The relative darkness of the gallery in which the work is exhibited adds to the introspective presence of the sculpture. Black is a colour that carries with it the associative power of the unknown; it is simultaneously all colours of the spectrum, and also their absence.

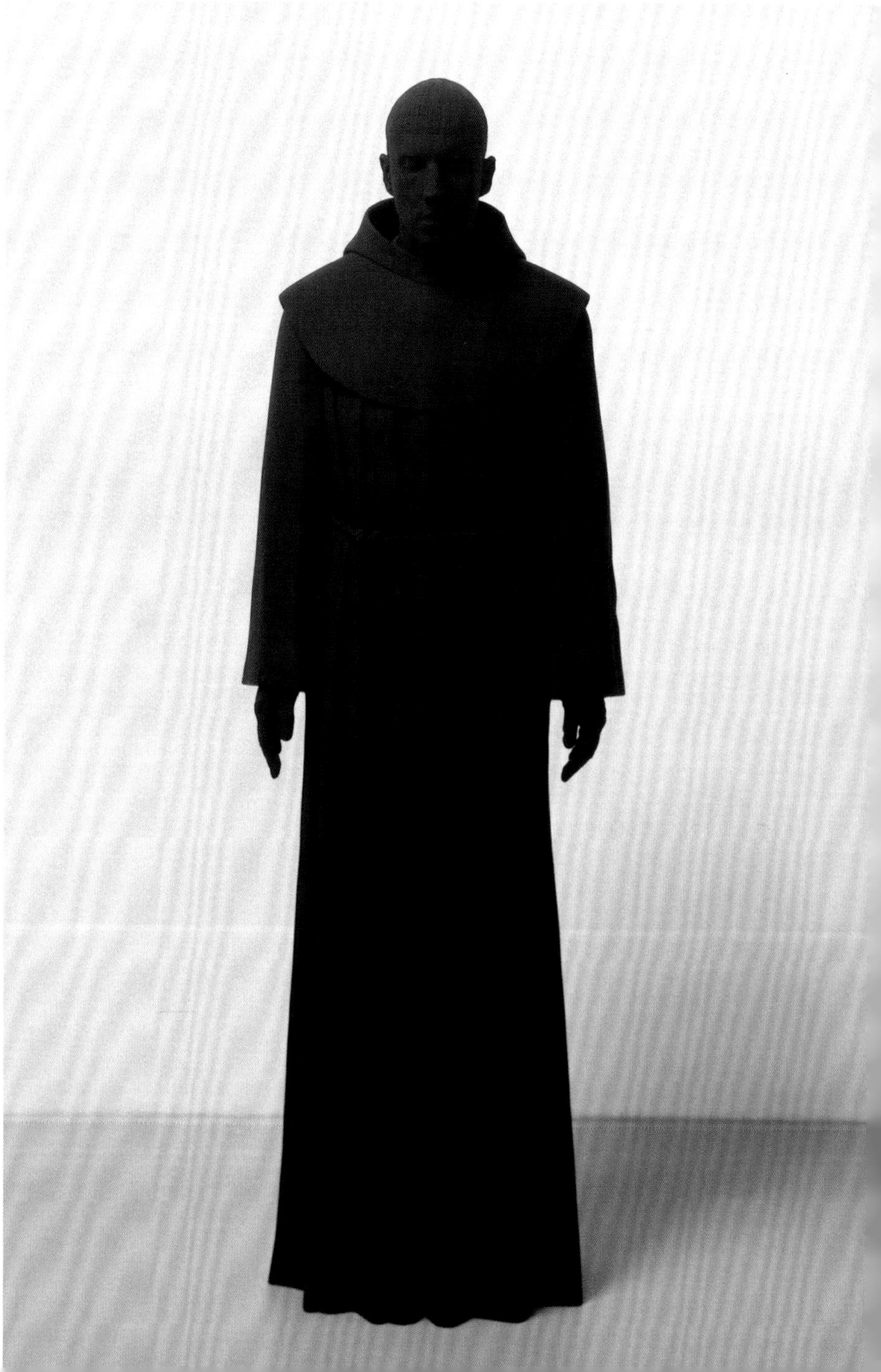

I love red so much that I almost want to paint everything red.

— Alexander Calder

Colour is this response to what we are perceiving. So there isn't something out there that we perceive; we are actually creating this vision ...

— James Turrell

Some painters transform the sun into a yellow spot; others transform a yellow spot into the sun.

— Pablo Picasso

Scale

The actual or relative dimensions of an object, or parts of an object in relation to one another.

In the vocabulary of sculpture, scale and size are not synonymous. Size is normally thought of in terms of large and small – the relative dimensions of a thing. Size can be measured in units, but scale is more ambiguous. It has to do with the perceived internal dimensions of a sculpture and how those relate to the world beyond the object. Scale has two aspects. One is the relative physicality of the whole and the way the viewer understands that physicality. This might be called monumentality, or perceived size versus real size. The other is proportion – the relative size of parts to, and within, a whole. This has to do with the internal relationships between forms within the sculpture, and/or between the sculpture and the external world in which it exists. Imagine how our perception of the Statue of Liberty would change if it were reduced to the size of a pocket trinket. Much of its meaning is communicated by way of its colossal size and that size is a result of its interior proportions. Even if we have never seen the statue on Liberty Island, knowing that it is grandiose imparts particular meaning and significance in our culture. In the first two works, actual size and relative proportions get mixed up for interesting aesthetic reasons.

Alberto Giacometti (1901–1966)
The Forest (Composition with Seven Figures and a Head

1950
Painted bronze
58.4 × 60 × 48.3 cm (23 × 23 ⅝ × 11 in)
Metropolitan Museum of Art, New York

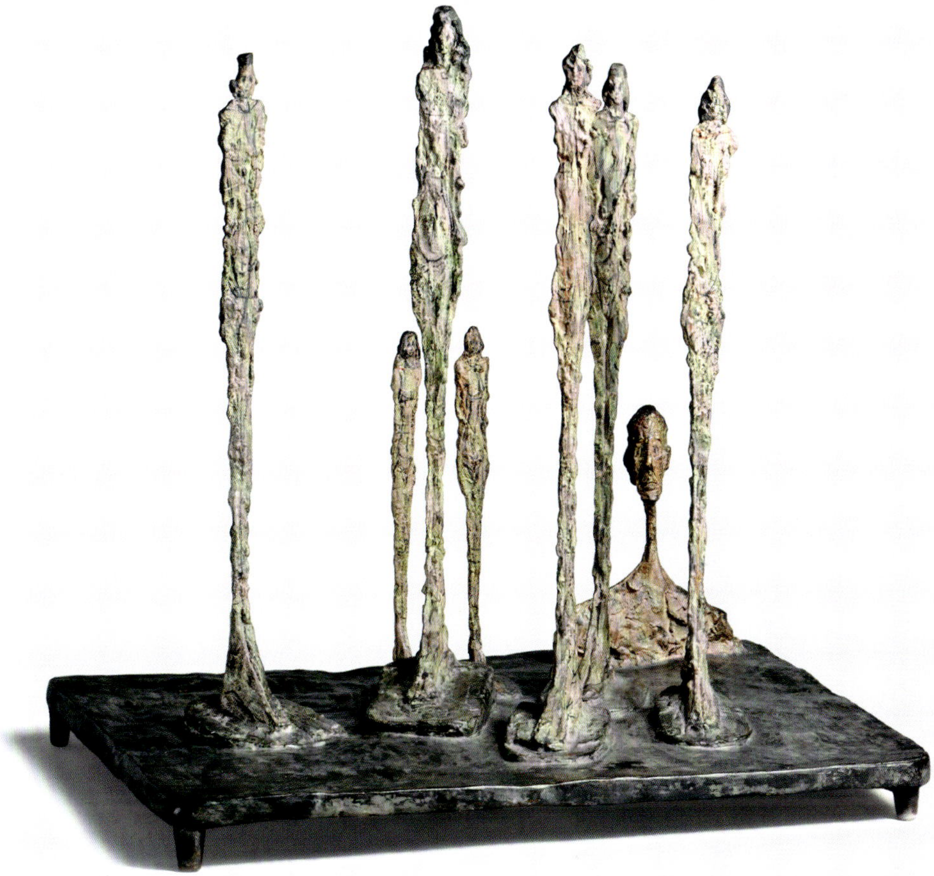

Inspired by the memory of a stand of trees on the edge of a clearing near his childhood home in Stampa, Switzerland, Alberto Giacometti created *The Forest* in 1950. But specifically, as he later wrote, this particular composition was also the result of placing sculptures on the floor to clear his worktops. So chance plays an interesting role here.

On first view, the impossibly long thin proportions of the seven figures are one of the most striking aspects of the work; their heads are too small in proportion to their elongated bodies while their feet are too large. The tallest figure is 23 inches high and they are all female. The two figures at the back are much smaller than the five at the front, creating a false perspective that visually pushes the taller five forwards. But when we consider Scale, it is the portrait head at the rear that becomes the most interesting. The figures outnumber the head and they are the 'forest' that defines half of the work's narrative. The other half, the head, interrupts their closed conversation. And it does so because of its scale. With its long neck and broad shoulders, it is proportionally much larger than the figures and, even though it is shorter, it has a more life-like presence than the figures. This discontinuity in scale, proportion and real size challenges the viewer with a seemingly impossible paradox. Both the figures and the head share the same ground plane and space, so if we accept the scale and proportions of the figures, how can we accept the presence of the bust in the same composition? Giacometti utilizes Scale here to construct a disturbing but carefully considered improbability that challenges not only our imagination but also our innate sense of the probable.

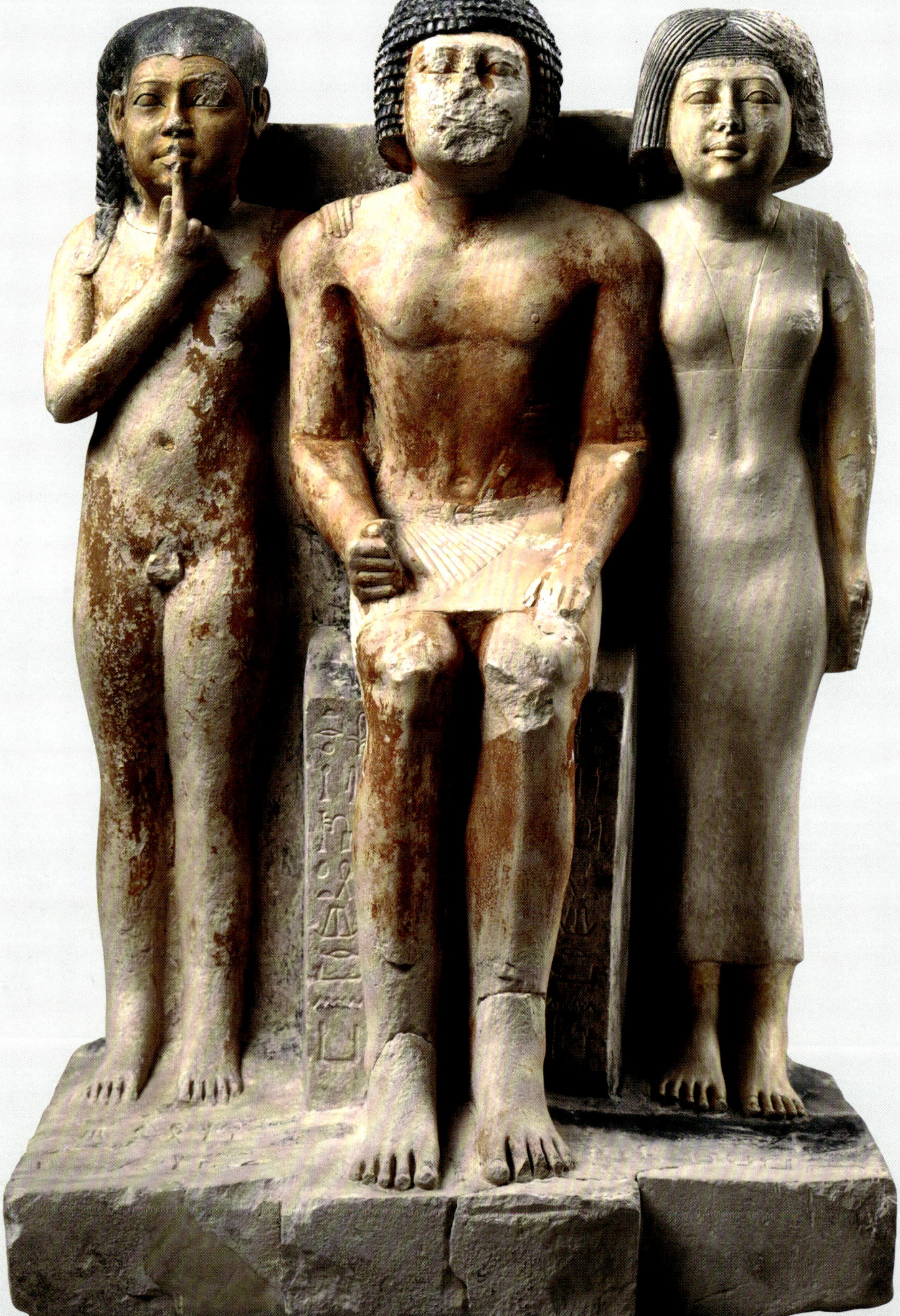

Old Kingdom period, Egypt
Statue of Nykara and his Family

2455–2350 BC
Painted limestone
57.5 × 36.8 × 272.7 cm (22 ⅝ × 14 ½ × 10 ⅞ in)
Brooklyn Museum, New York

This is a family that appears to share the commonality of scale, size and proportions that is absent in *The Forest* (see p. 79). But look and think critically about what you see here. Resist making assumptions. Because the heads of the ancient Egyptian family are in a level line we believe at first that they are, in reality, the same height. Move to the side and it becomes immediately apparent that Nykara, a scribe, is seated. If he stood up he would tower over both his wife and son, and so the dramatic tension within the composition would radically shift in ways that are both opposite and analogous to *The Forest*. But if we are able, using the sense perceptions within our own body, to enter intuitively into what is being looked at, then the essence of these two sculptures would be immediately apparent. The most important tool we possess for measuring and understanding scale, proportion and size, is our own body. However, with the solidity of the three figures, their realistic rendering and, to a certain extent, the addition of colour, the sculptor convinces us of the accuracy of his fictional scale.

Leonardo da Vinci (1452–1519)
Vitruvian Man

c. 1490
Pen and ink with wash over metalpoint on paper
34.4 × 25.5 cm (13 ½ × 10 in)
Gallerie dell'Accademia, Venice

The Greek philosopher Protagoras insisted: 'Man (not the universe) is the measure of all things'. In some important respects the history of figurative sculpture may be understood as a search for visually versus mathematically correct proportions. That is correct to the extent that the sculptural image conforms to ever-changing culturally defined ideals. Historically, however, there were cultures that believed that images of our bodies and mathematical truth could not only coexist, but the one could possibly perfect the other. Consider the *Vitruvian Man* by Leonardo da Vinci. Here, Leonardo places the idealized human figure into a geometric construct – the square and the circle. Geometry is constant, while the image of a human body is far more malleable and fluid, so Leonardo is able to alter the human form to fit within his geometry and our eyes find it to be a perfectly acceptable realistic rendering. But there are limits. In *The Forest* (see p. 79) the proportions of the seven figures and the bust as they relate to the human body are clearly incorrect and composed from a very different set of proportions to the *Vitruvian Man*. Our expectations about the visual scale of each figure have become separated from our innate sense of correct proportion.

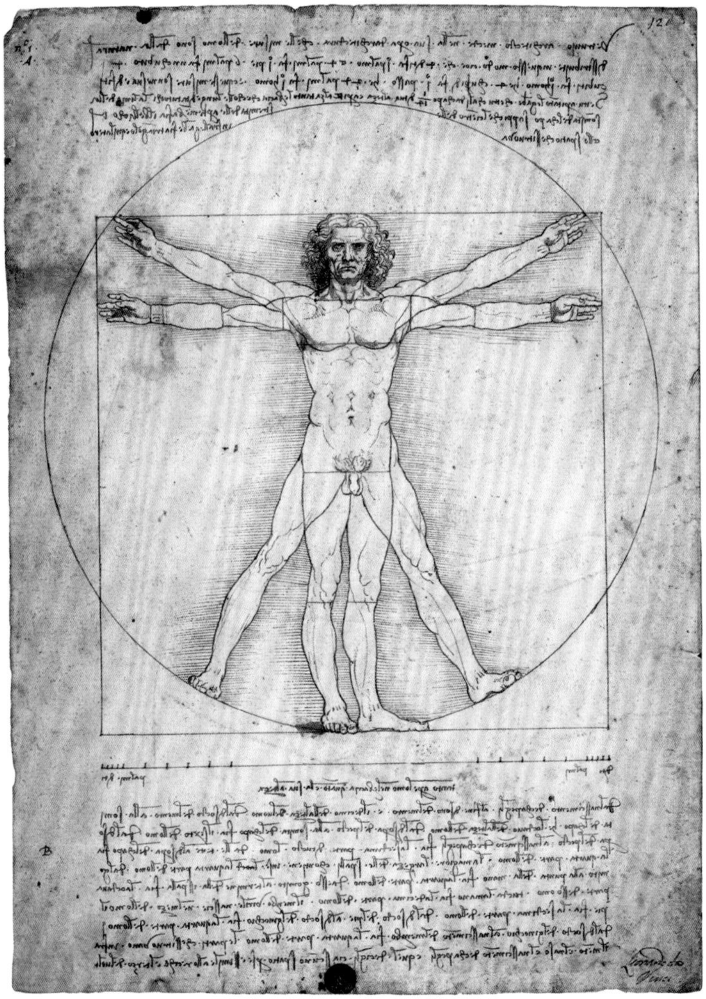

Roman copy of Polykleitos (attrib.)
Diadoumenos (Youth tying a fillet around his head)

c. 69–96 AD
Marble (Pentelic) from original bronze
185.4 cm (73 in) high
Metropolitan Museum of Art, New York

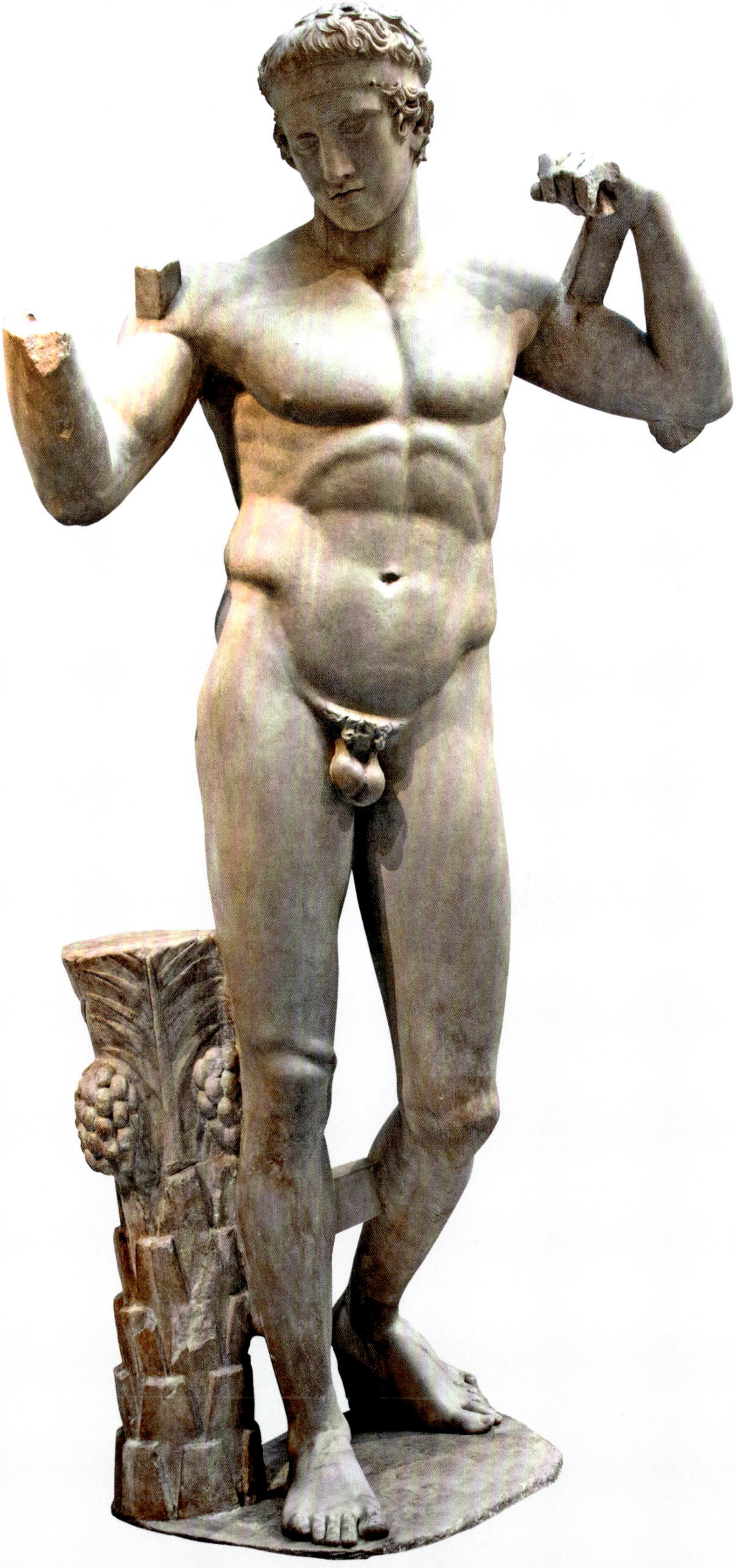

The canon of Polykleitos might thus be thought to be both qualitative and quantitative, having to do with essential life force as well as ideal physical appearance.

— David Summers

This is a Roman copy of the *Diadoumenos*, a fourth-century BC classical Greek marble sculpture by Polykleitos. The historical assumption surrounding this work is that here we may observe parts relating to the whole within a defined harmonic system of ideal human proportions – the result of mathematical ratios established by the sculptor. These still unknown relationships between parts and the whole are collectively referred to as the Canon of Proportions. In contemporary Western culture, however, we have taken the search for the ideal human body and the search for eternal beauty away from the sculptor and turned it over to the capriciousness of the media.

Passport photograph of Marie-Thérèse Walter

c. 1935

Pablo Picasso (1881–1973)
Head of a Female

1932
Bronze
128.5 × 54.5 ×62.5 cm (50 ½ × 21 ½ × 24 ½ in)
Picasso Museum, Paris

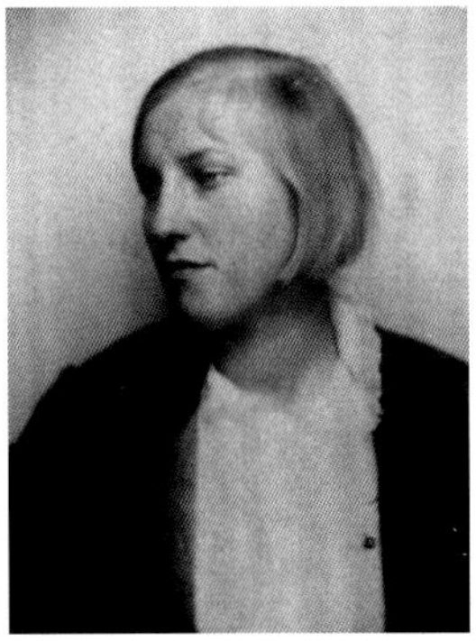

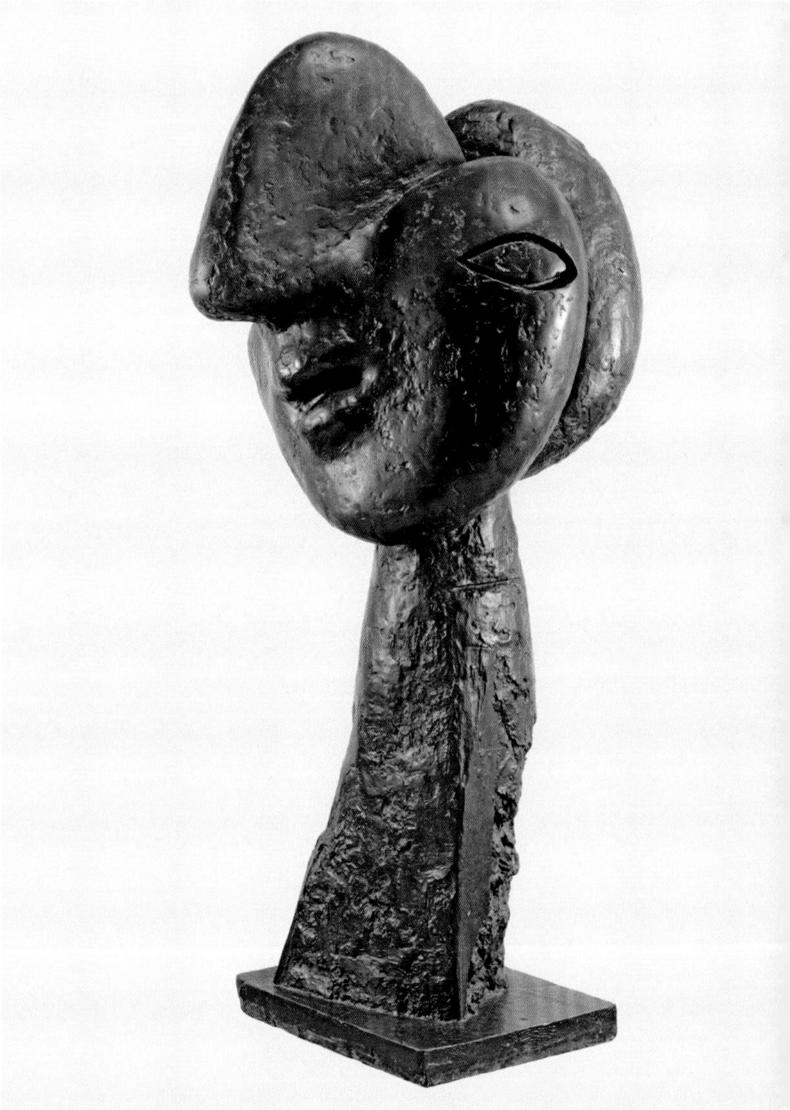

Specific features have been radically altered in scale, proportion and placement in Pablo Picasso's bronze portrait of Marie-Thérèse Walter. Looking at her passport photograph taken at a similar time, then moving to her bronze portrait, it becomes clear that in order to convey more accurately the basic shape and overall presence of Marie-Thérèse's head, Picasso has chosen to break apart and then resynthesize the various forms he saw in her face. He has enlarged the nose, shifted features and altered relative proportions, regardless of the assumed correct scale and size, and their proper placement. He has done so because there is an aesthetic 'correctness' of form within the sculpture that exceeds our perceptual habits. How things appear, and how they are, are not always the same.

Chimu Culture, Peru
Ceramic Vessel/Ritual Figure

1200–1450 AD
Ceramic and pigment
23.9 cm (9 ⅜ in) high
Art Institute of Chicago, IL

An important yet often overlooked aspect of Scale is the relative size of parts within a whole and the possible meaning of these disparities. Look at the changes in scale and proportion in this ritual vessel from the north coast of Peru. At first, we want to accept its proportions, but such acceptance relieves the tension that gives this fascinating object its peculiar animism. The swollen torso of the mother is similar in form to the ceremonial vessel that she carefully holds in place with her tiny left hand and extended arm. With her right hand she cradles her nursing child. Both child and her arm are in proportion to each other but wildly out of proportion to the vast fullness of her inflated body. Legs have been abstracted into a generalized rounded support for the whole. Minuscule feet frame and hold a tiny spout that both contrasts with the larger opening of the vessel tied to the mother's back, and recalls the small breast that the child nurses from. In total, she is a nourishing vessel. These small moments within the larger composition gain power and presence from extreme differences in scale relative to the immensity of the mother's inflated body.

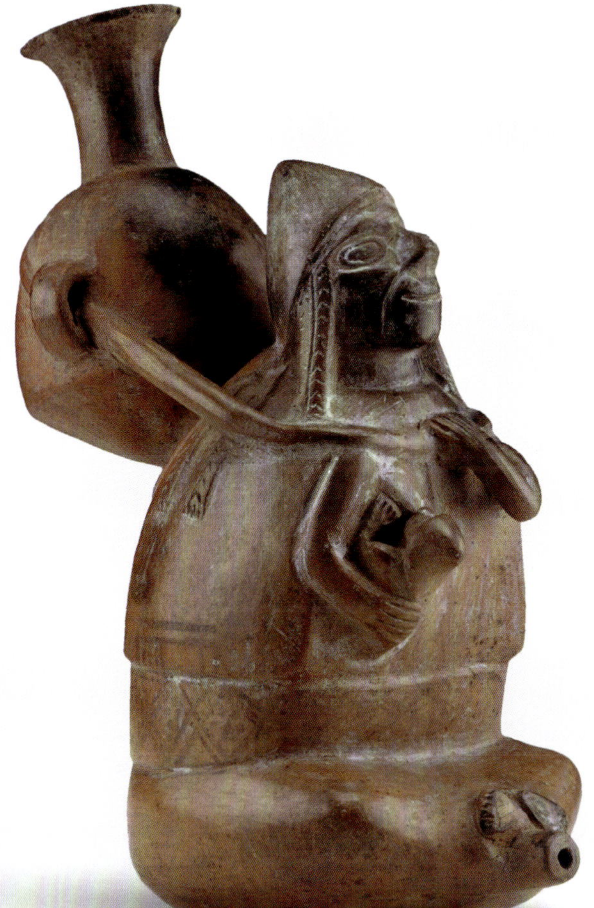

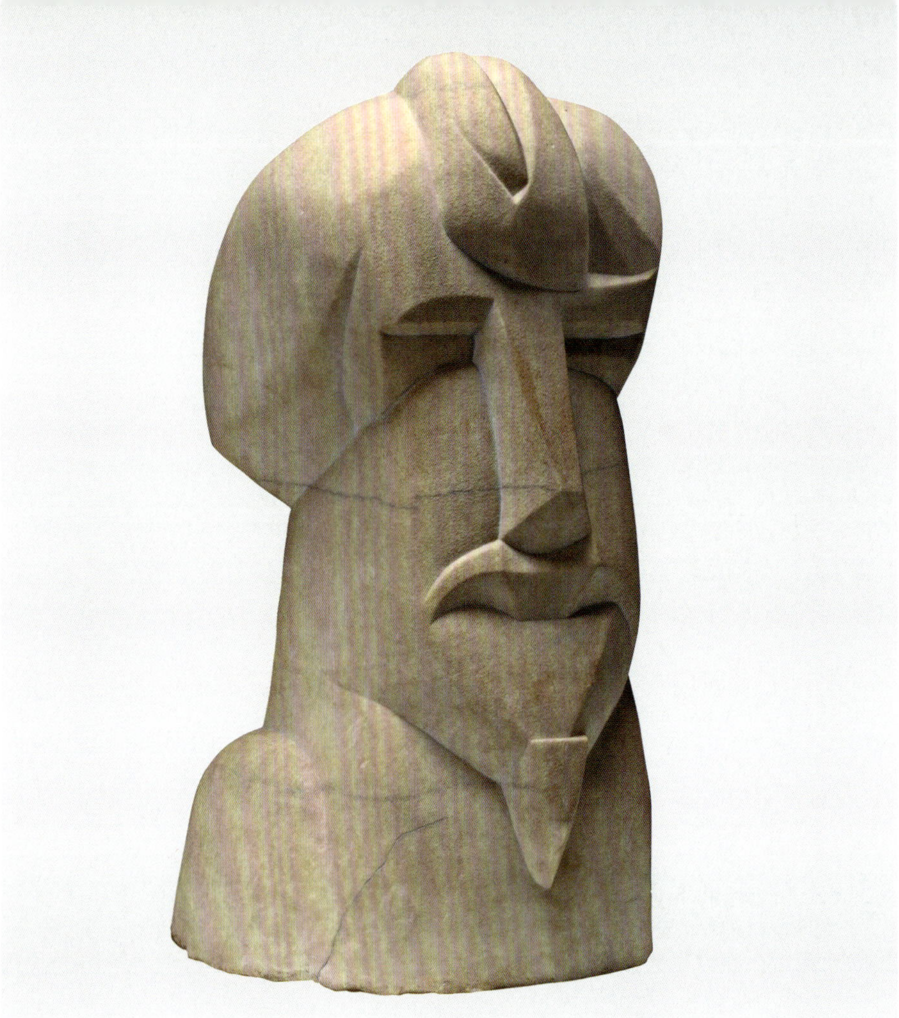

Henri Gaudier-Brzeska (1891–1915)
The Hieratic Head of Ezra Pound

1914
Marble
90.5 × 45.7 × 48.9 cm (35 ⅝ × 18 × 19 ¼ in)
National Gallery of Art, Washington DC

Although sharing the same stem, the word 'monumentality' in sculpture has a different meaning from the word 'monument'. Monumentality in sculpture is a subjective impression that may be defined as the object's perceived scale being greater than its actual size. A monument may be defined as a physical marker, and its size may be measured in feet and inches. Monumentality is something to be aspired to, as it may be understood as evidence of a life force within the sculpture. Such a work possesses a commanding presence that far exceeds its actual size. *The Hieratic Head of Ezra Pound* by Henri Gaudier-Brzeska is monumental in this sense of the word. It is about three times the size of a normal head, so although physical size plays a role in the work's monumentality, I feel size is a secondary consideration. The precisely carved planes that clearly define the most prominent of Pound's features, as well as the generalized abstraction of these features, may well be part of its mystery. These aggressive, brooding, magisterial forms appear to burst out beyond the physical confines of the stone and enter the space of the viewer. This may be because the defining facial planes, led by the sharply triangular nose, are simple convex curves. As in the Chimu vessel on the previous page, these rounded forms expand and grow out in every direction rather than compress and recede. Beyond words, this seemingly ancient head confronts the viewer with its austere monumentality.

Tom Friedman (b. 1965)
Untitled (Self-Portrait)

1994
Aspirin tablet
0.8 × 0.5 × 0.8 cm (⅜ × ¼ × ⅜ in)
Acquavella Galleries, Inc., New York

The very small object may hold greater fascination for the imagination than the very large, in part because we might wonder how such a tiny thing was made. In 1994 Tom Friedman carved *Untitled (Self-Portrait)* out of an aspirin tablet. Difficult to photograph because it is so small, it must have been many times more difficult to carve. Here size is not a search for some reconciliation between seeing and understanding. *Untitled (Self-Portrait)* is more of a purely technical challenge. It addresses the literal and symbolic fragility of self-image. When confronted by the sculpture, we strain to make sense out of the minute features and we wonder at the craft needed to carve such an impossibly small thing. Or is this meant only as a joke – aspirin equals headache?

Claes Oldenburg (b. 1929)
Clothespin

1976
Corten steel, stainless steel, aluminium and cast resin; painted with polyurethane enamel
13.7 × 3.7 × 1.4 m (45 ft × 12 ft 3 in × 4 ft 6 in)
Collection Centre Square Plaza, Fifteenth and Market Streets, Philadelphia, PA

Claes Oldenburg's *Clothespin* is a compelling example of what can occur in our perception of scale when the right choice of object combines with the abstractions of form produced by a radical change in size. Made from Corten and stainless steel, it is 45 feet high and located in Philadelphia. The height of the work was carefully scaled to the site, and although the buildings around it are much taller, they do not diminish the sculpture's presence. Oldenburg has made several significant changes to the work's proportions in relation to an actual wooden clothespin. These changes in scale and proportion provide the sculpture with a strong vertical movement. It rises from its base with a dynamic erect vitality that allows the form to compete with the buildings around it. Notice how the top of the clothespin has been detailed; do you see two heads, face to face? Then look farther down to the spring that joins the two parts together. Oldenburg chose to enlarge the spring and make it from bright stainless steel that dramatically contrasts with the dark rust of the Corten. Is it possible that the spring might also be the arms of two dancers in an embrace? Through the careful manipulation of scale, size and proportion, Oldenburg has not only enlarged a common object but has created a sculpture that simultaneously remembers its origin and becomes a new thing.

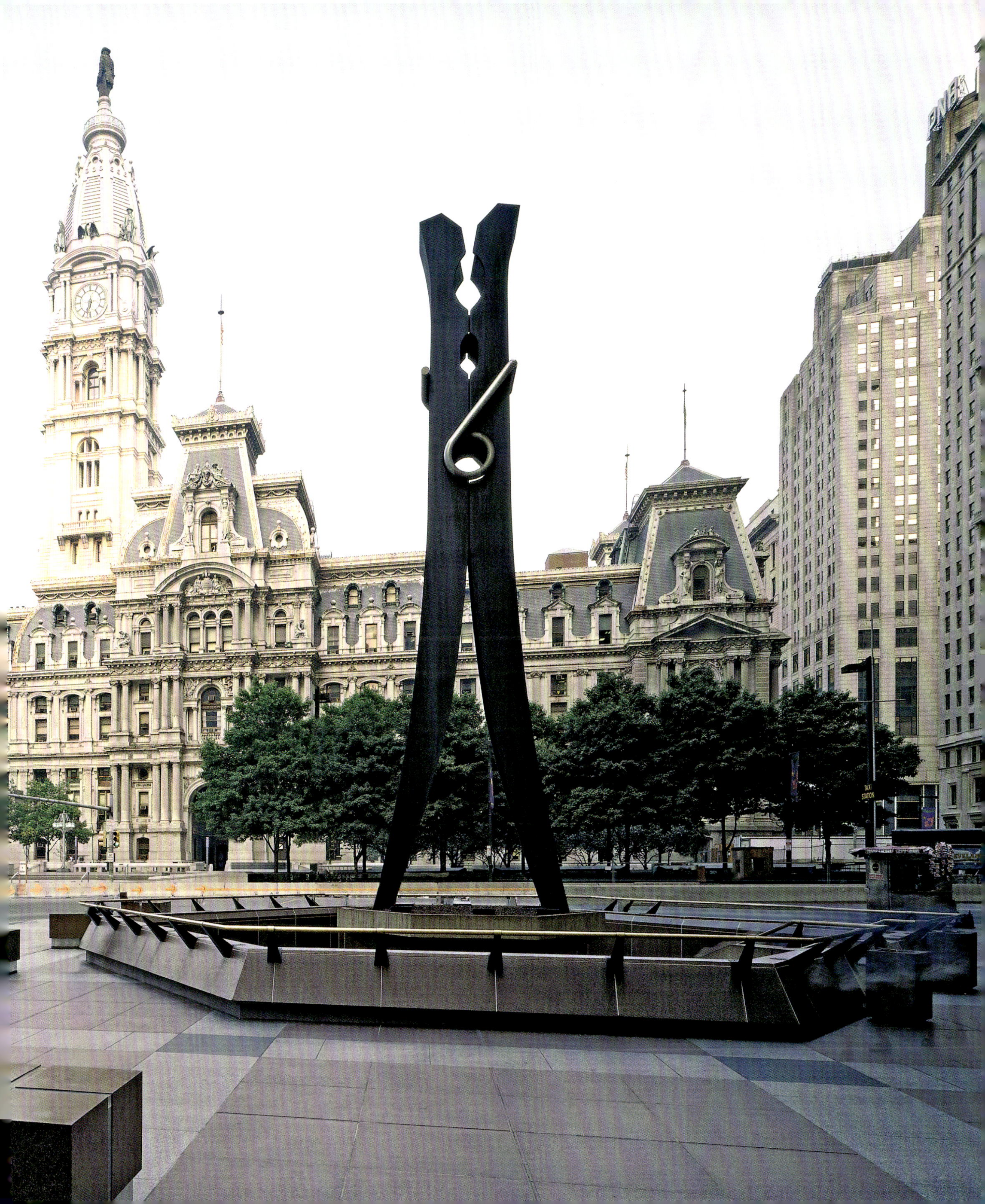

Isamu Noguchi (1904–1988)
Sun at Noon

1969
French red marble, Spanish Alicante marble, Diorite and wood base
Sculpture: 154.9 × 154.9 × 21 cm (61 × 61 × 8 ¼ in); base: 33 × 89.9 × 89.9 cm (31 × 35 ⅜ × 35 ⅜ in)
Noguchi Museum, Long Island City, NY

When we look at figurative sculpture, our bodies may be our truest measure of their relative size. But how large is a circle, a square or a triangle? Stand next to one and I'll tell you, but that answer is less than satisfying. The geometric purity of this stone 'ring' by Isamu Noguchi rephrases the question. Seen first from a distance, the viewer has few references to help calculate its actual size. By existing in the world of pure geometry the sculpture demands that we resolve these questions within the physicality of the object itself rather than in the material world of feet and inches. The dimensions, proportions and carved stone elegance of *Sun at Noon* exist within the confines of its physical presence. I am not its measure.

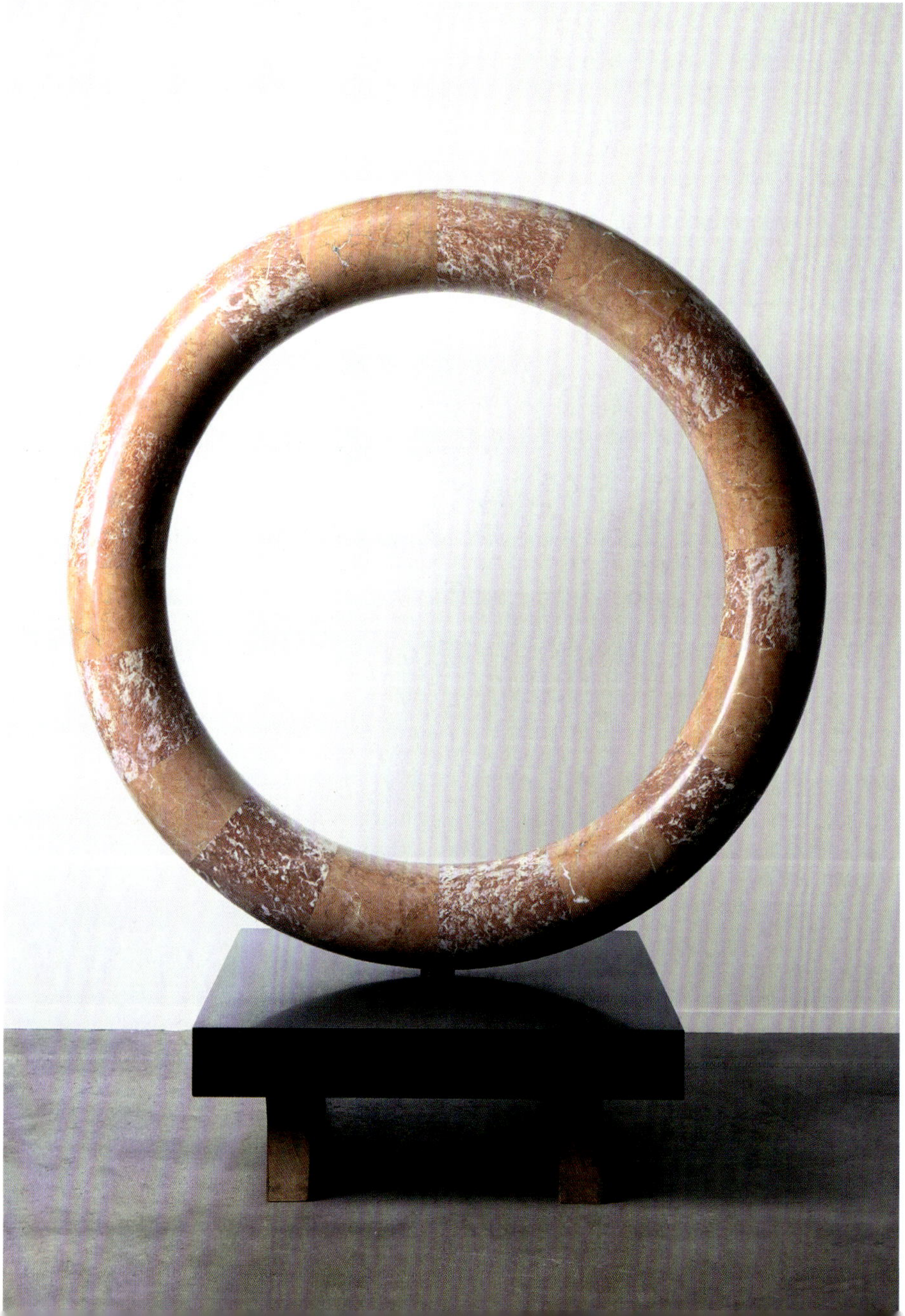

I think the sense of scale that a piece has is always a relation between your body and the object that's external to it. I mean, that is where the scale comes in, it seems to me: you relate it to yourself.

— Robert Morris

There is a right physical size for every idea.

— Henry Moore

First, when I work, it's only the abstract qualities I'm working with, which is the material, the form it's going to take, the size, the scale, the positioning, where it comes from – the ceiling or the floor. However, I don't value the totality of the image on these abstract or aesthetic points. For me it's a total image that has to do with me and life.

— Eva Hesse

3

Physicality

There is more to a particular form than its outward characteristics. These two Elements address the physicality of an object. Here aspects of a work's material substance are determined, as these provide clues to attributes of form and shape.

Mass

Gutzon Borglum

Aristide Maillol

Tony Smith

Richard Serra

Paleolithic period

Tim Hawkinson

David Mach

Nancy Rubins

Centre of Gravity

Barnett Newman

Early Classical period, Greece

Auguste Rodin

Michelangelo Pistoletto

Kenneth Snelson

Ronald Bladen

Lorado Taft

Mass

A measure of the amount of matter contained in or constituting a dense physical presence.

Mass is a primal material attribute. In physics everything that is 'real' possesses some quantifiable mass, and that includes space and light. But mass in physics is very different from mass in sculpture. In sculpture it is communicated as a function of the visual weight within a particular object. Mass is a mountain, a pile, a magnitude, an immensity. Mass is an enormous bulk. I refer to the latter as *actual* mass, but in sculpture mass may also be *apparent*, that is, the object appears to contain a great mass when in actuality it does not. And mass is also the sum of many things.

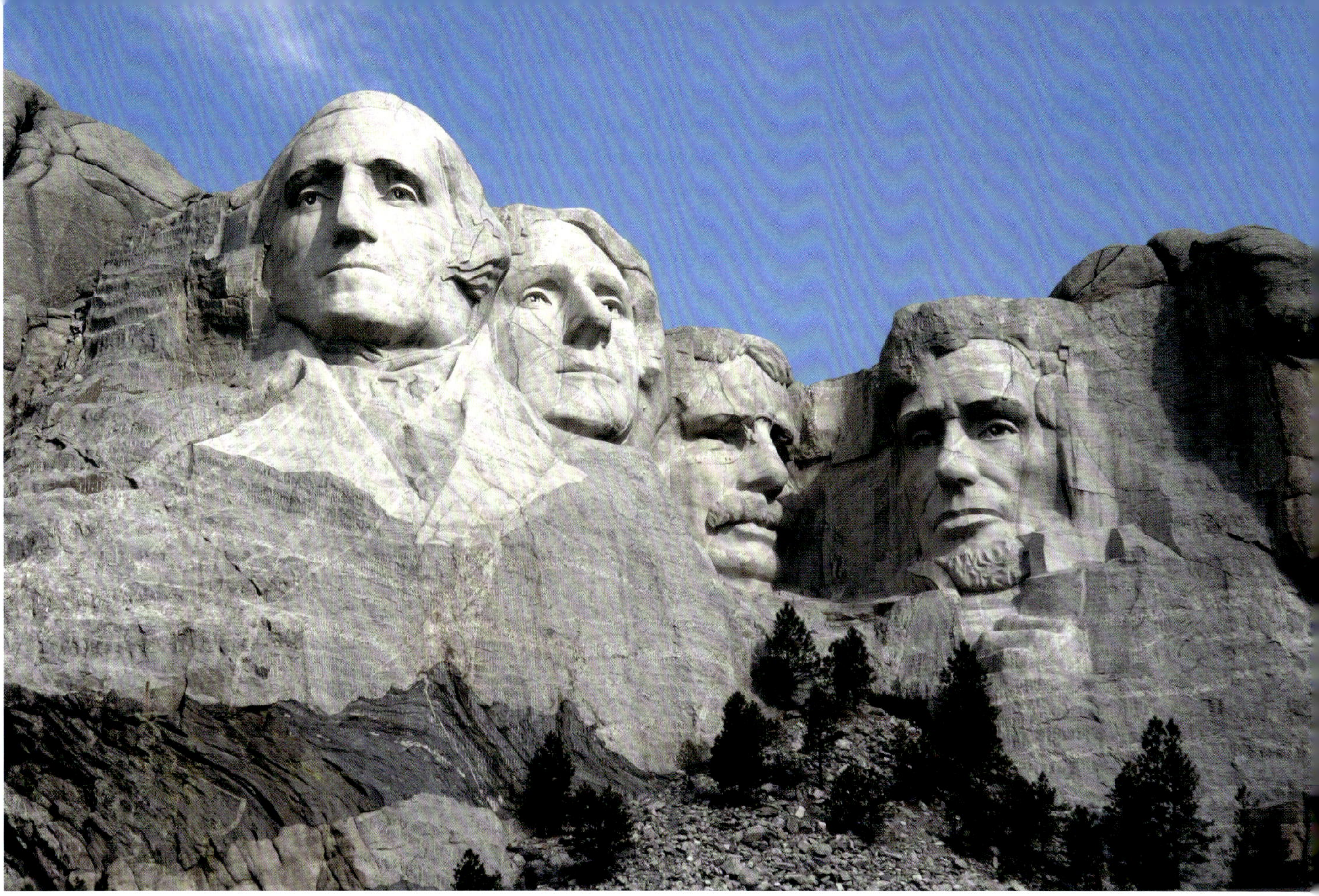

Gutzon Borglum (1867–1941)
Mount Rushmore National Memorial

1941
Granite
Approx. 30 × 60 m (100 × 200 ft)
Black Hills, SD

Along with Auguste Bartholdi's *Statue of Liberty*, the best-known sculpture in the United States is the four stone faces at Mount Rushmore. More relief than sculpture in the round, the work was blasted, not carved in the usual sense, out of a granite mountain in South Dakota. Completed in 1941, each head is approximately 60 feet high. A man can stand upright in the iris of George Washington's eye. To comprehend its mass and monumentality we must stand in front of the mountain. Although these presidential portraits emerge with an uncanny physical presence, the far larger mountains of stone that surround the work consume their sculptural power. Here in the natural world, actual mass can be experienced in its most elemental state.

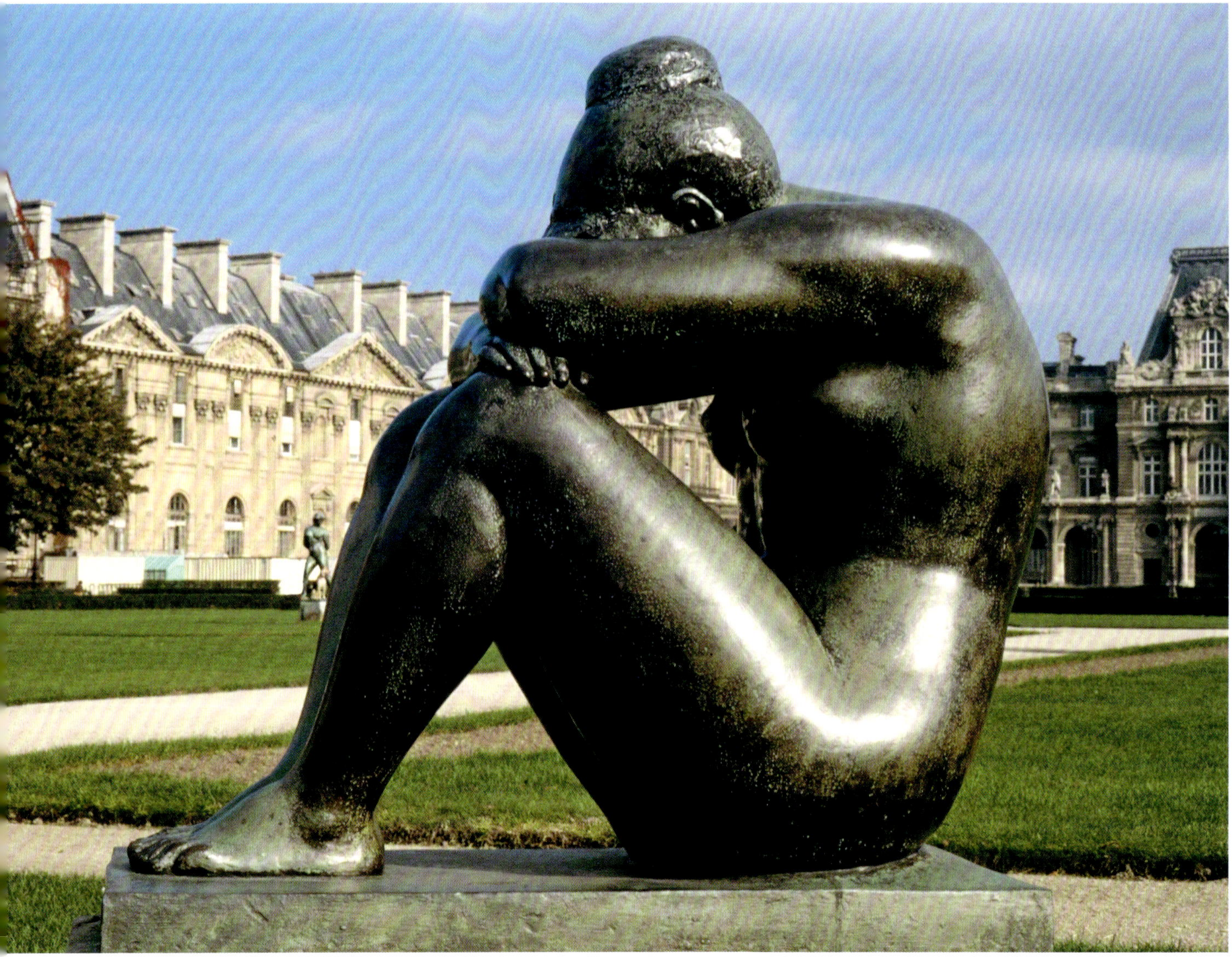

Aristide Maillol (1861–1944)
Night

1909
Bronze
110 × 60 × 105 cm (43 ⅜ × 23 ⅝ × 41 ⅜ in)
Jardin des Tuileries, Paris

Consider the possibility of what might be called an open mass as opposed to the closed mass just discussed. A good example may be found in *Night* by Aristide Maillol. Viewed from the front, we see the contours that outline the bodily mass of the seated figure along with the enclosed triangular volume of space between the sculpture's bent legs and crossed arms. The pose is one of the most massive the human body can comfortably assume. But when walking around *Night*, the sculpture, which appeared to be closed, opens and so becomes less massive. The solidity of the front view breaks into two triangles, but this time open to the space and light beyond. As we continue to walk around it, the sculpture closes again and the immense weight of the back of the seated figure becomes immediately apparent. In this view the gravitational pull on the mass of the body is experienced through its substantial bulk pressing down on the buttocks, and in the taut arch of the back bowing out and into the space of the viewer. The work produces a potent kinaesthetic response, one that gives expression to both the pose and the full weight of its open mass.

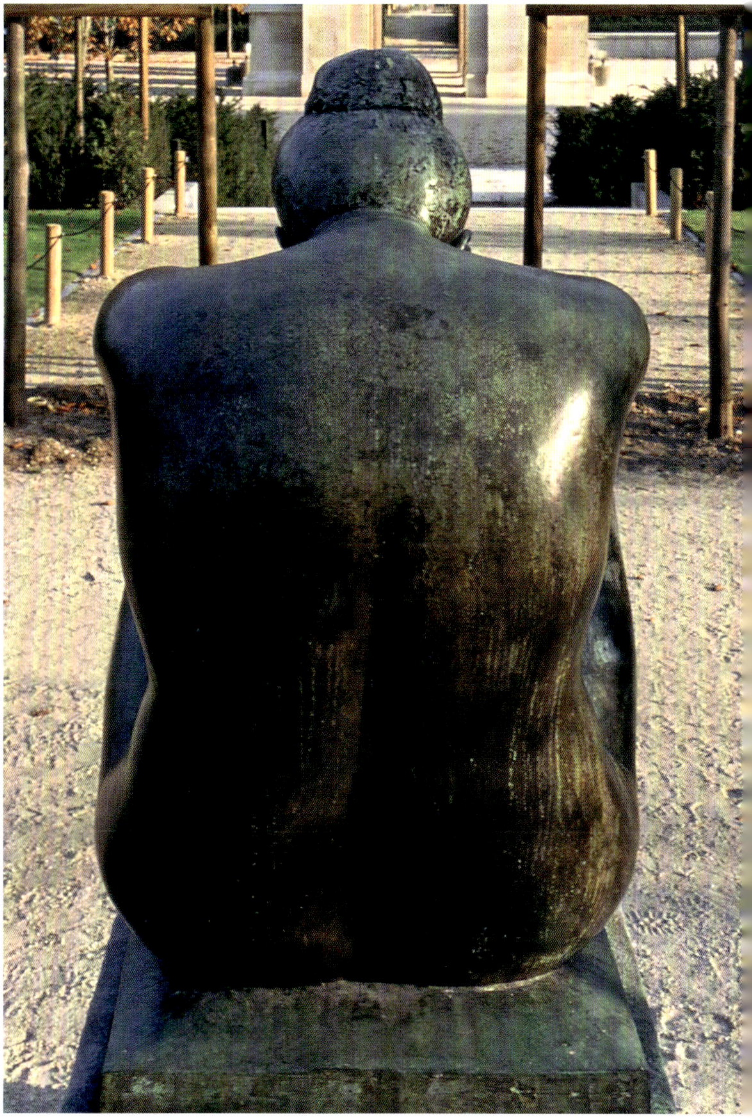

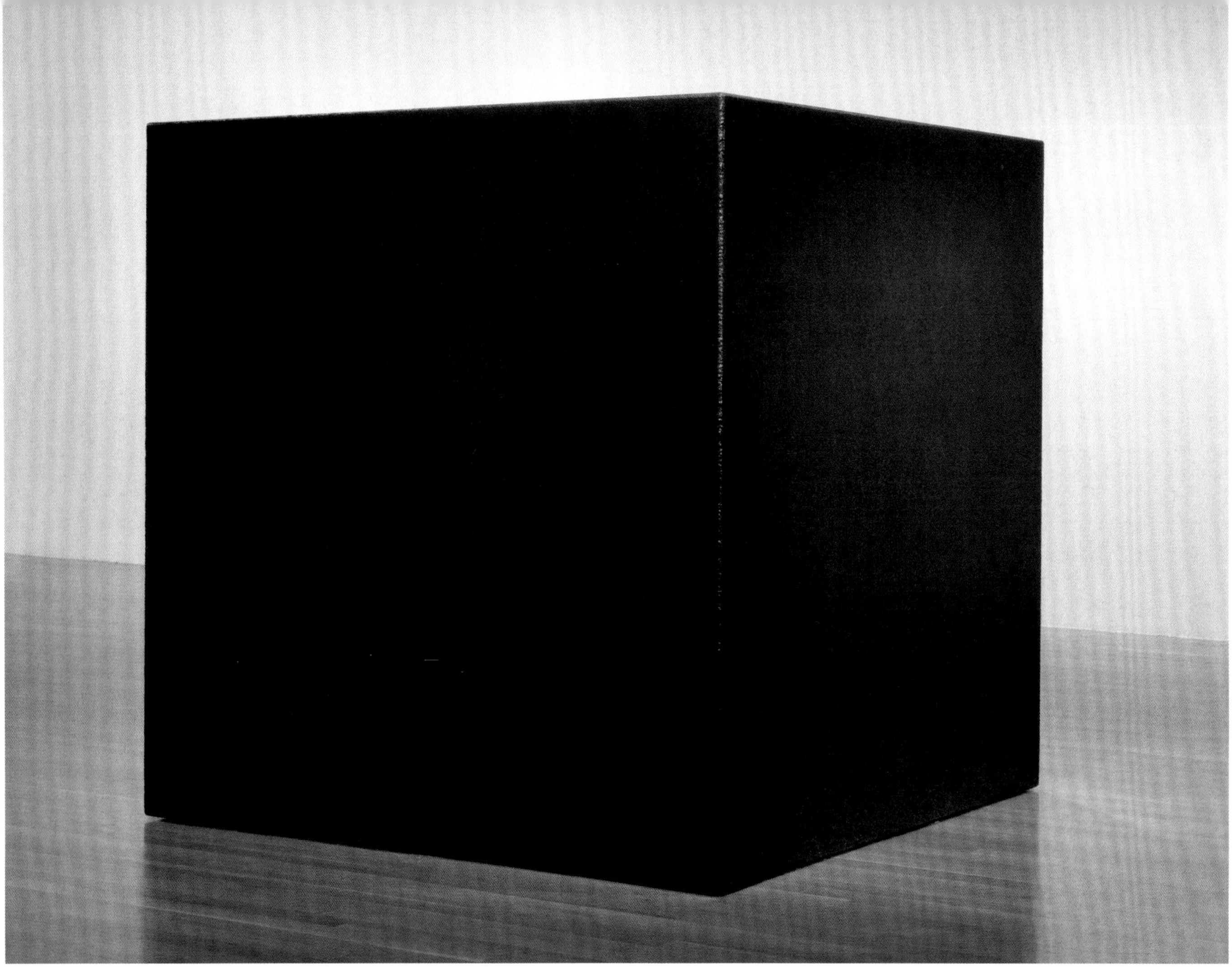

Tony Smith (1912–1980)
Die

1962; fabricated 1998
Steel
182.9 × 182.9 × 182.9 cm
(72 × 72 × 72 in)
Museum of Modern Art,
New York

Richard Serra (b. 1939)
Round

1997
Forged weatherproof steel
170.2 × 221 × 221 cm (67 × 87 × 87 in)
Collection of the artist

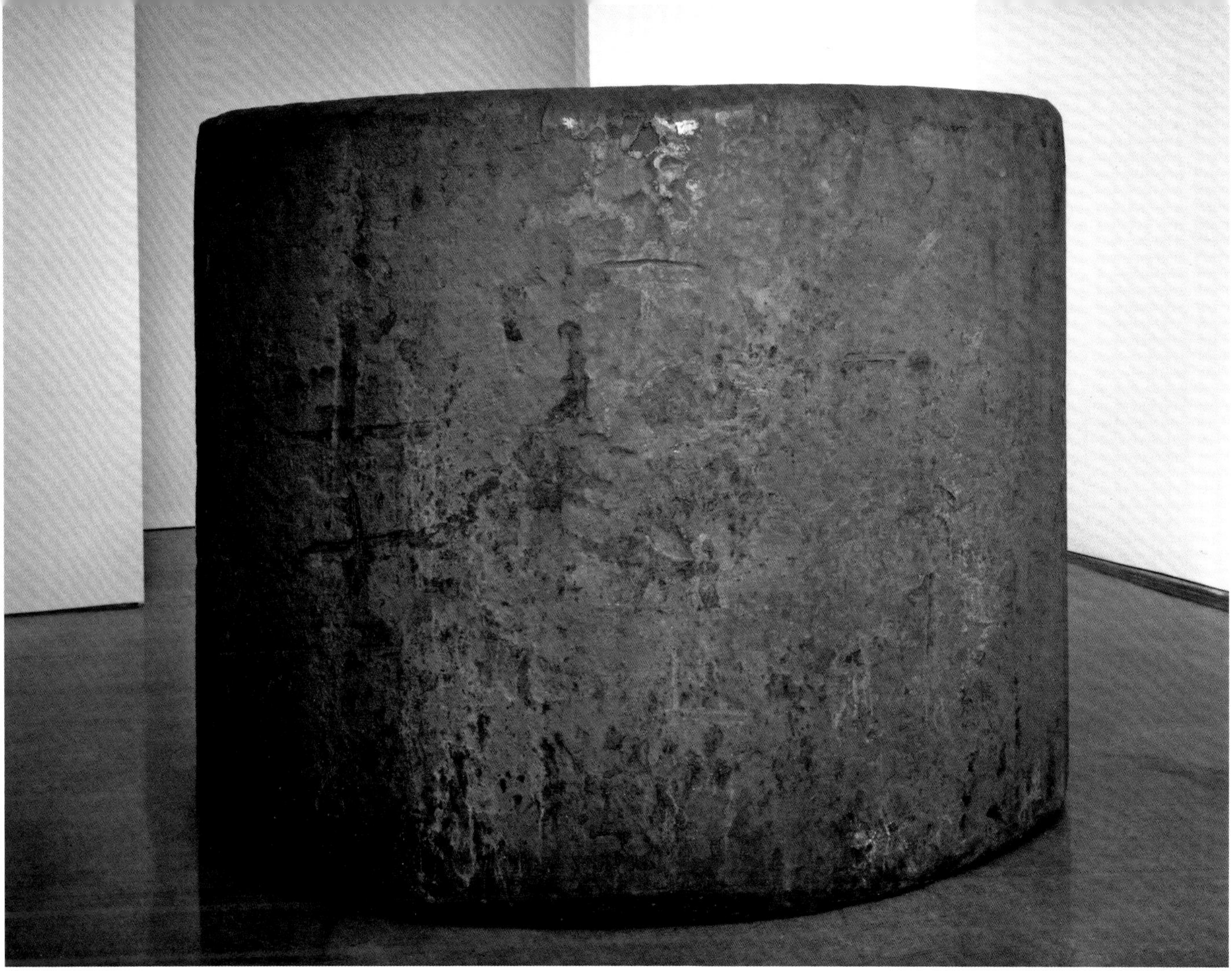

There is a gulf between our understanding of things seen and how they may actually exist in the world. A comparison of *Die* by Tony Smith and *Round* by Richard Serra addresses the contrast between actual and apparent mass. Although both appear to be cubic in the photographs, only the Smith is an actual cube, while the Serra is a cylinder. Both are made from steel; both are meant to rest on the ground; both present themselves to the viewer as massive monoliths of about the same height relative to our bodies. However, the Smith is a hollow cube, a thin steel shell. The Serra in contrast bears marks on its surface that show the process of casting and forging a large heavy steel billet. We can sense the mass and weight of the Serra immediately, a perception confirmed by the solid silence it emits when touched. A hollow drum-like echo was the reply when I touched the Smith. *Die* appears to the eye to be one thing – a large and imposing solid mass, but in reality it is something else – a hollow enclosed volume. The Serra possesses an actual physical mass, while the mass of the Smith is apparent.

Paleolithic period
Venus of Willendorf

c. 24,000 BC
Stone
11.5 cm (4 in) high
Naturhistorisches Museum, Vienna

Tim Hawkinson (b. 1960)
Bather

2009
Eggshell
17.8 × 10.2 × 8.9 cm (7 × 4 × 3 ½ in)
Private collection, Dallas

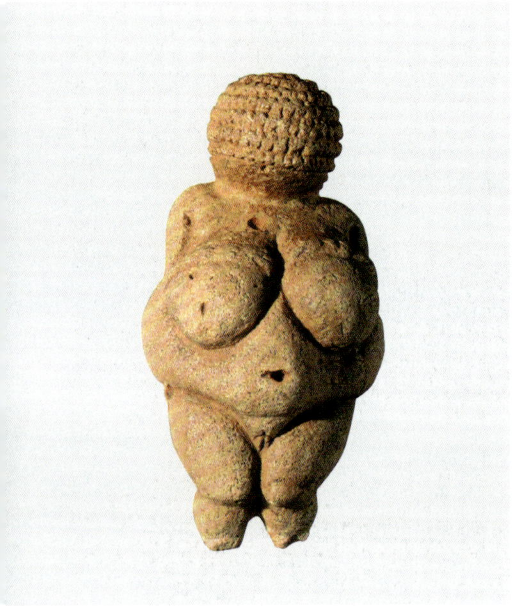

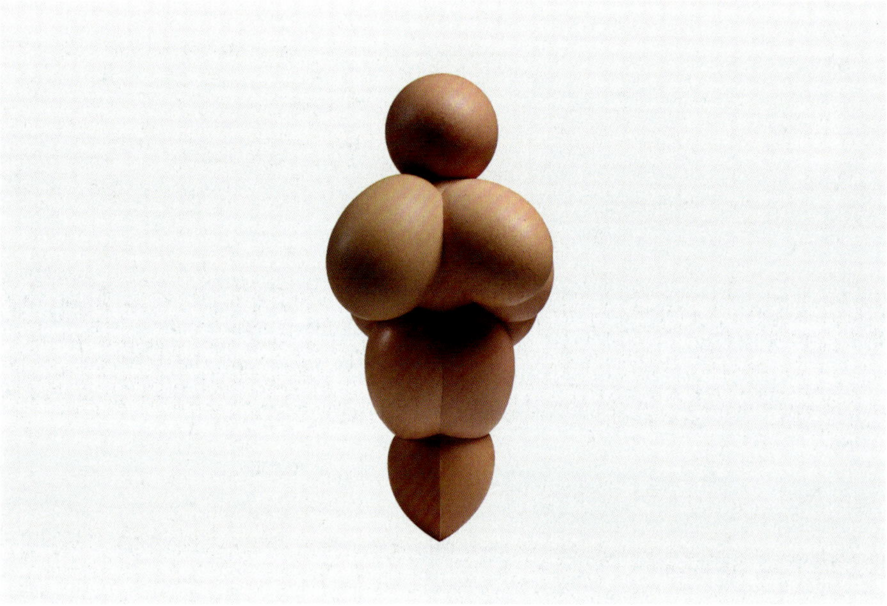

Here we see two further examples of actual versus apparent mass, but in this instance the difference between the two becomes a conscious aspect of both the form and content of the contemporary work.

One of the oldest sculptures from prehistory is the *Venus of Willendorf*. It stands 4 inches high and is carved from stone. Its small scale and the rounded fullness of its female forms suggest that this was an amulet to be carried or worn in the belief that it enhanced fertility and had life-giving powers. The sculpture possesses a massive monumentality, in part because of the stone's density and in part because of the apparent weight of its rounded fecund female forms. Also, the lush regenerative mass of the individual parts overcomes any preconceived notions to do with monumentality as a consequence of size. Defined only by hair, the anonymous nature of the head relative to the explicit carving that defines the sexual organs reinforces the possibility that there may be a subconscious relationship between the hope of fertility and full, massive forms.

In *Bather*, Tim Hawkinson has carefully constructed a convincing surrogate image of the *Venus of Willendorf*. Massive in appearance only, all notions to do with the original fall away once the viewer identifies its material as eggshells. When that moment occurs the sculpture becomes something very different – a satirically humorous object. That said, reference to the *Venus* persists, and the eggshells successfully communicate the possibility of regeneration with few of the pervasive cultural beliefs that are the essence of the original. Once I realized that these were empty eggshells my response to the sculpture was similar to the one I had when I touched *Die* (see previous page). But neither *Round* nor *Die* needs some other point of reference in the way that *Bather* does. *Bather* not only wants the *Venus* reference, but it needs it to make its satirical point. One important aspect of that point is precisely the difference between actual and apparent mass.

David Mach (b. 1956)
Polaris

1983
6,000 rubber tyres
Dimensions variable
Installed at the Southbank Centre, London

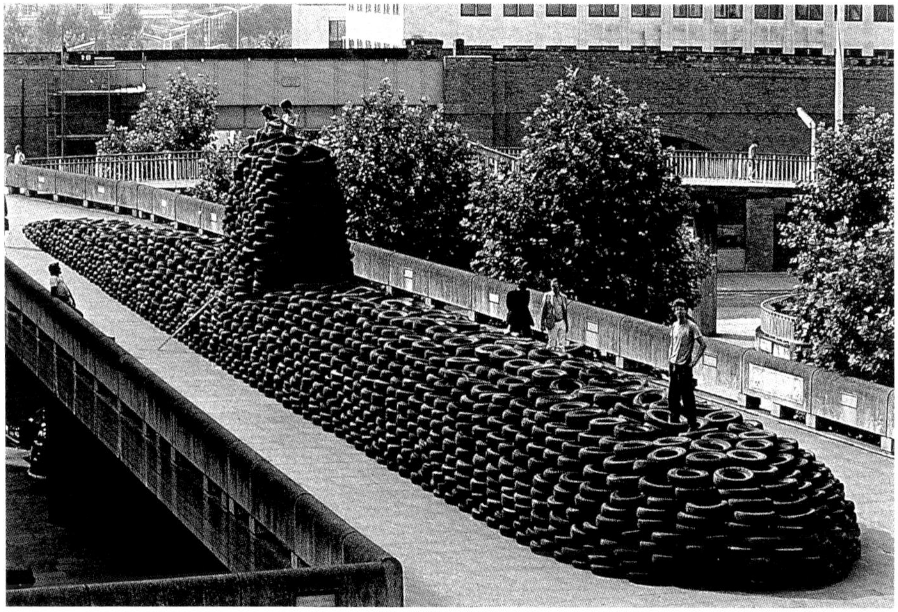

Unlike the stone faces on Mount Rushmore that opened this section, *Polaris* by David Mach is a mass that merely appears to rise up from the earth/ocean. Its mass results from numbers – an accumulation, a collection. Six thousand recycled tyres went into making this partially submerged full-scale reconstruction of a Polaris class atomic submarine. Because the basic form of the submarine spreads and expands as it lies on the concrete, its apparent mass appears to extend down below the surface. *Polaris* is visually planted in, not on, the earth. The image of a surfacing submarine is clearly and convincingly rendered in part because of the artist's choice of materials. The sinister industrialized matt black tyres are the same colour as the actual submarine; there also exists a vague memory of inflatable beach toys, inner tubes and water. Made from a massive number of tyres, the closed form and unified colour of *Polaris* convey the illusion of a great earthbound hulk.

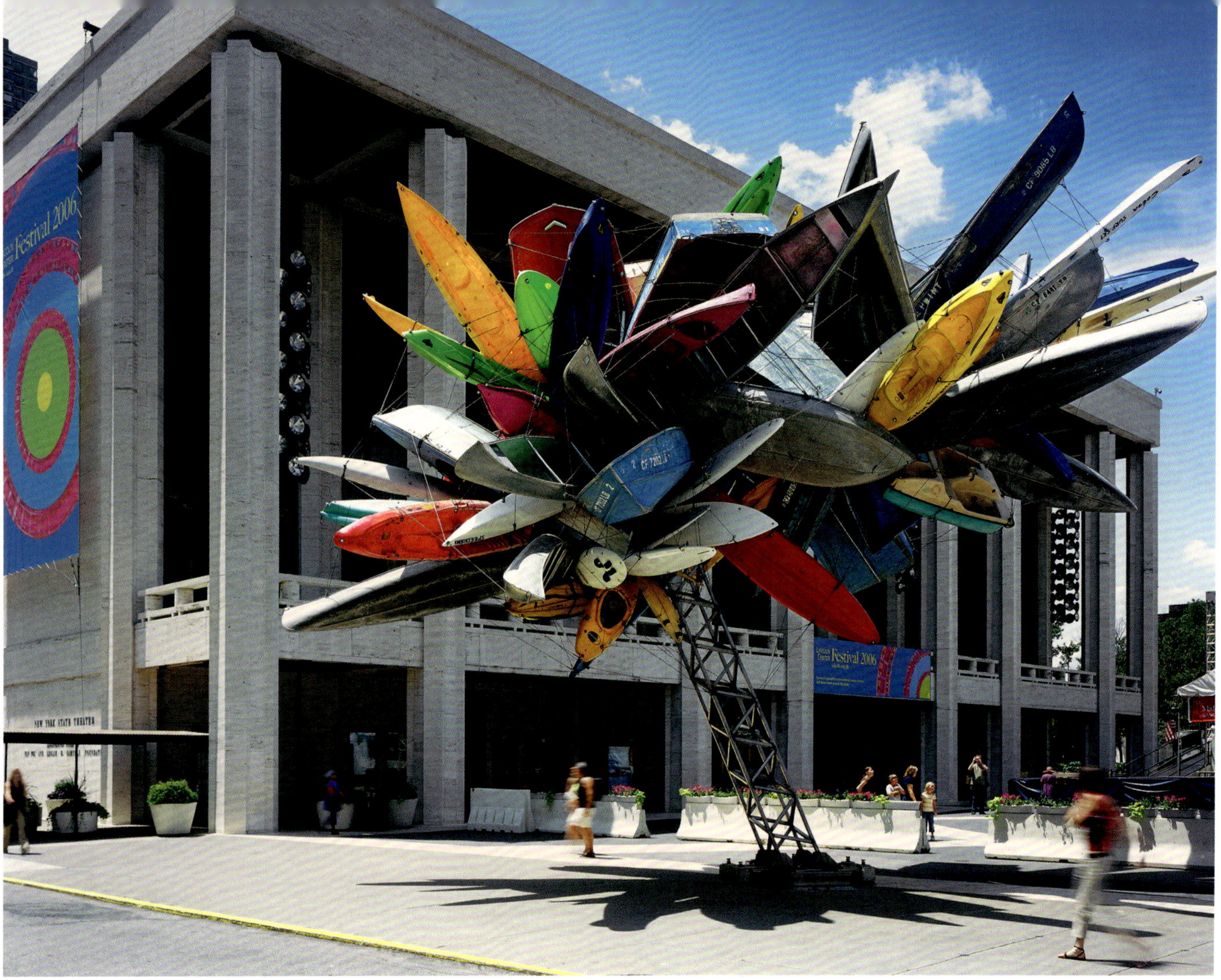

Nancy Rubins (b. 1952)
Big Pleasure Point

2006
Boats, stainless steel, stainless steel wire cable
Approx. 13.7 × 16.8 × 12.2 m (45 × 55 × 40 ft)
Installed at Josie Robertson Plaza, Lincoln Center, New York

Big Pleasure Point by Nancy Rubins is a gathering of human-powered boats. Mass here is the result of accumulation. This is not only an example of Mass by sheer numbers, but also Mass by differences in form, in colours and in types. It was located for a time at the east entry to the Lincoln Center in New York. Suspended high from an angled steel support, the work resembled a giant flower levitating over the heads of viewers. The sculpture forced us to accept the possibility that a great mass in terms of numbers could hover, no longer earthbound. Although constructed from an accumulation that defies counting, each boat was centred, radiating outward and then tied into position. But contrary to that process of gathering together, when the viewer looked at the work from a distance, it appeared to be an explosion of mass.

We have a sensation of the amount of space occupied by the object, which is the quantity of volume, or bulk. If we refer to the quality of matter the object contains, we speak of its mass.

— Herbert Read

Carving is interrelated masses conveying an emotion; a perfect relationship between the mind and colour, light and weight, which is the stone.

— Barbara Hepworth

The voids must have as much importance as the masses. Sculpture is a taking possession of space, a space limited by forms.

— Henri Laurens

Centre of Gravity

The relative alignment of mass with respect to the earth within a particular form or forms.

Gravity is the force that gives weight to objects of mass in the universe. Centre of gravity is a property of any object; it is the median location of the weight within that object – the balance point. Because sculpture is visual, this median location is frequently not quantifiable in the ways that the laws of physics are. But that does not mean the visual/weight reality of balance in sculpture is less discernible. We measure the relative centre of gravity within the objects in our world out there by the equilibrium felt in here, in the body. Every freestanding object has a centre of gravity. Sculpture may assert that fact or it may visually alter or manipulate its presence.

Barnett Newman (1905–1970)
Broken Obelisk

1963–9
Corten steel
7.7 × 3.2 × 3.2 m
(25 ft 5 in × 10 ft 6 in × 10 ft 6 in)
Rothko Chapel, Houston, TX

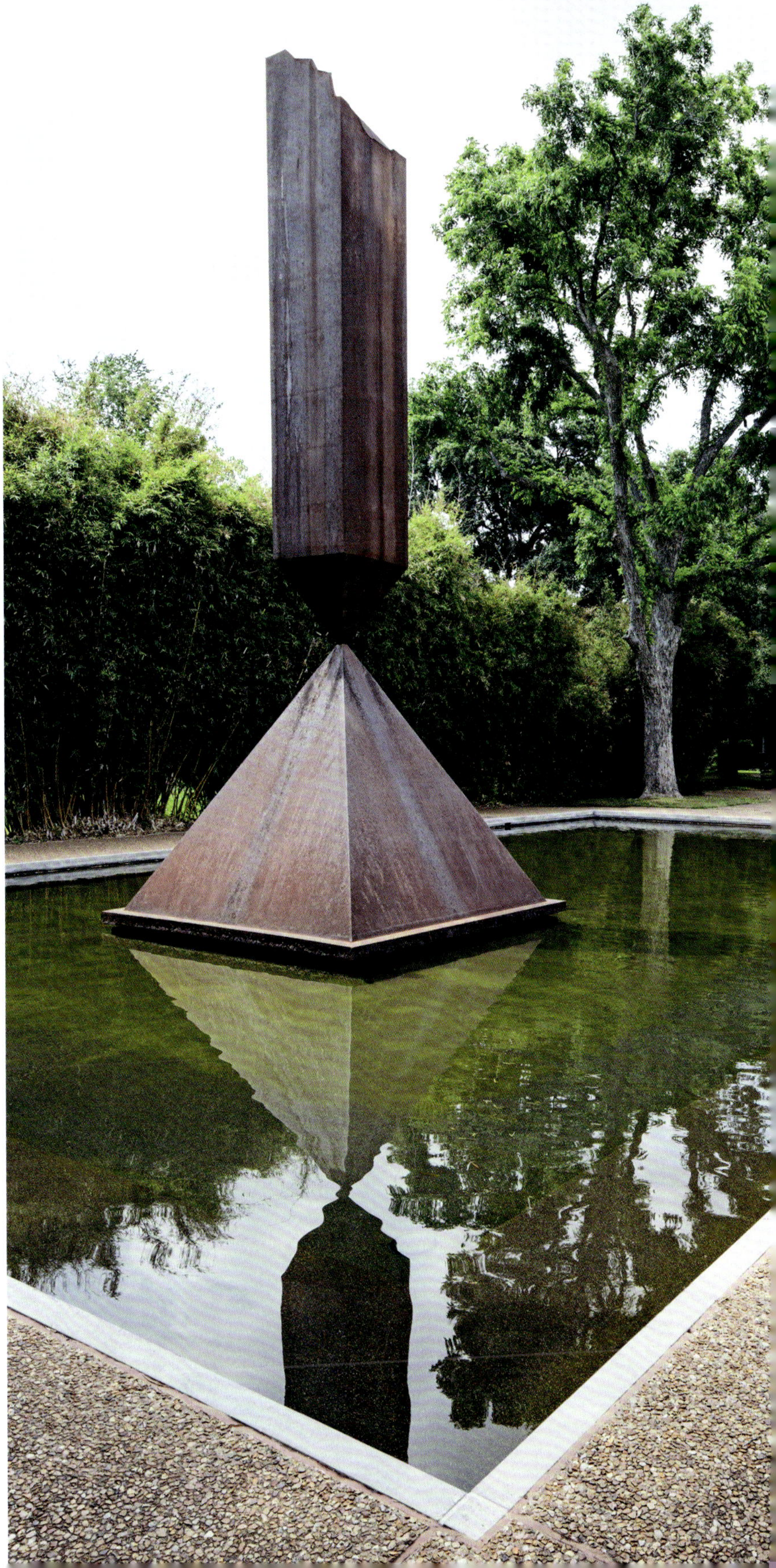

When considering Centre of Gravity, one of the first experiments that may come to mind is the difficulty of making something that is long and narrow, like a pencil, balance on its point. More tenuous is balancing a large geometric mass point to point with another similar form. Such a feat creates an obvious perceptual tension and question – when will it fall? *Broken Obelisk* by Barnett Newman balances an inverted Egyptian obelisk on the apex of a pyramid form. Made from rusted steel, the whole composition has the feel of the eternal past and the suspension of time. We look and wait, expecting the obelisk to fall, but no matter how long we wait it never does. That fact defies the laws of both gravity and reason.

Early Classical period, Greece
Charioteer of Delphi

c. 475 BC
Bronze
1.8 m (5 ft 10 ¾ in) high
Archaeological Museum, Delphi

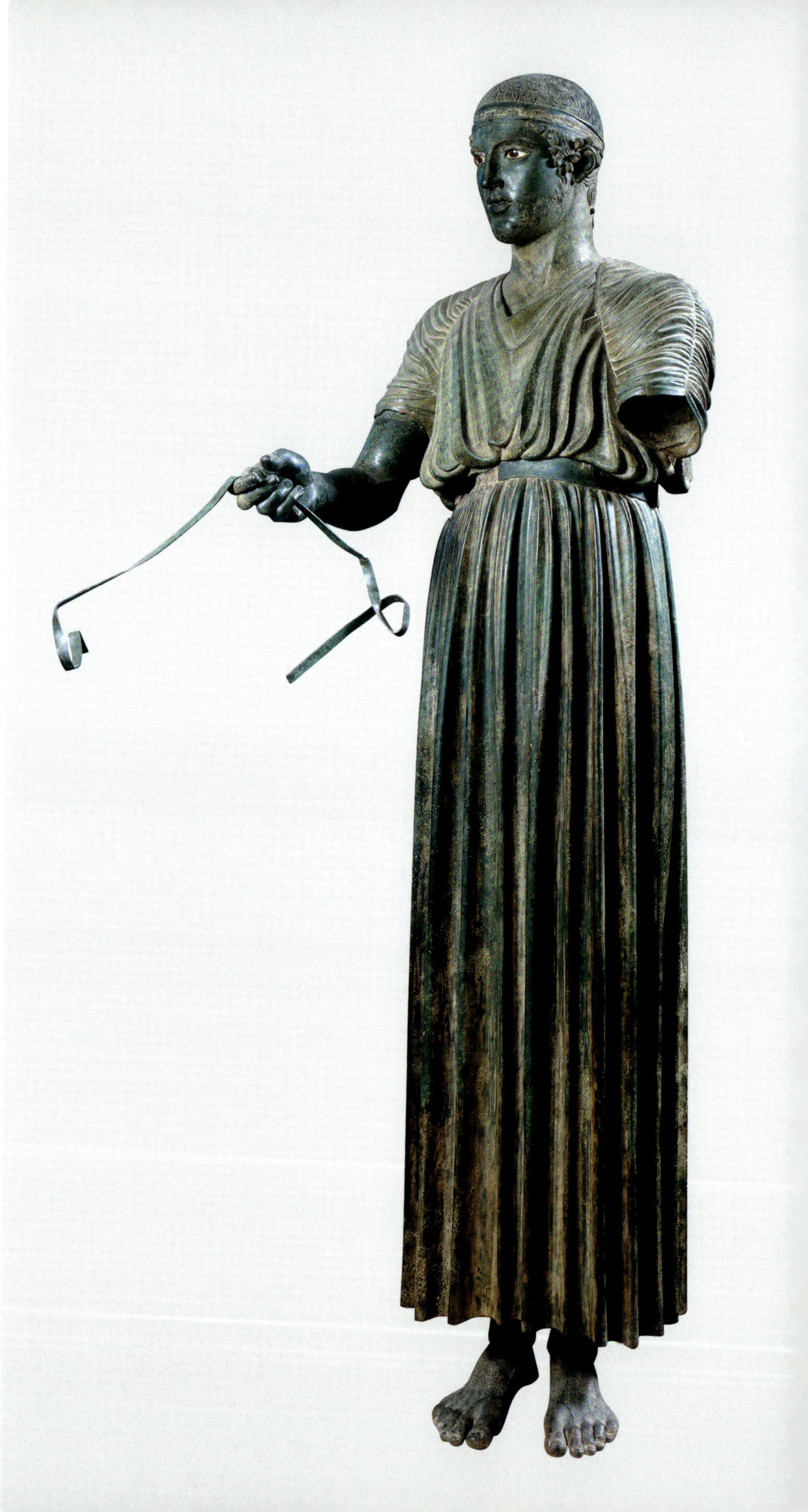

Standing tall and proud, the *Charioteer of Delphi* wears a chiton whose parallel folds resemble the vertical flutes of a stable architectonic Doric column. With only his tense arm extending, this cylindrical mass of the charioteer's chiton-robed body is carefully balanced on his feet. Here the centre of gravity, like that of the *Broken Obelisk,* is easily seen, but there is a significant difference. The *Broken Obelisk* contains a passive point-to-point structural tension and balance, whereas we know that the young man driving his chariot must maintain his equilibrium while moving at great speed. For his survival it is imperative that he maintain both a psychic and physical equilibrium. One that defies the violence of his surroundings. To project this image of internal courage the sculptor utilizes a carefully poised, balanced pillar that resists all the forces that stand against it.

Auguste Rodin (1840–1917)
Balzac

1898
Plaster
2.8 m (9 ft) high
Musée d'Orsay, Paris

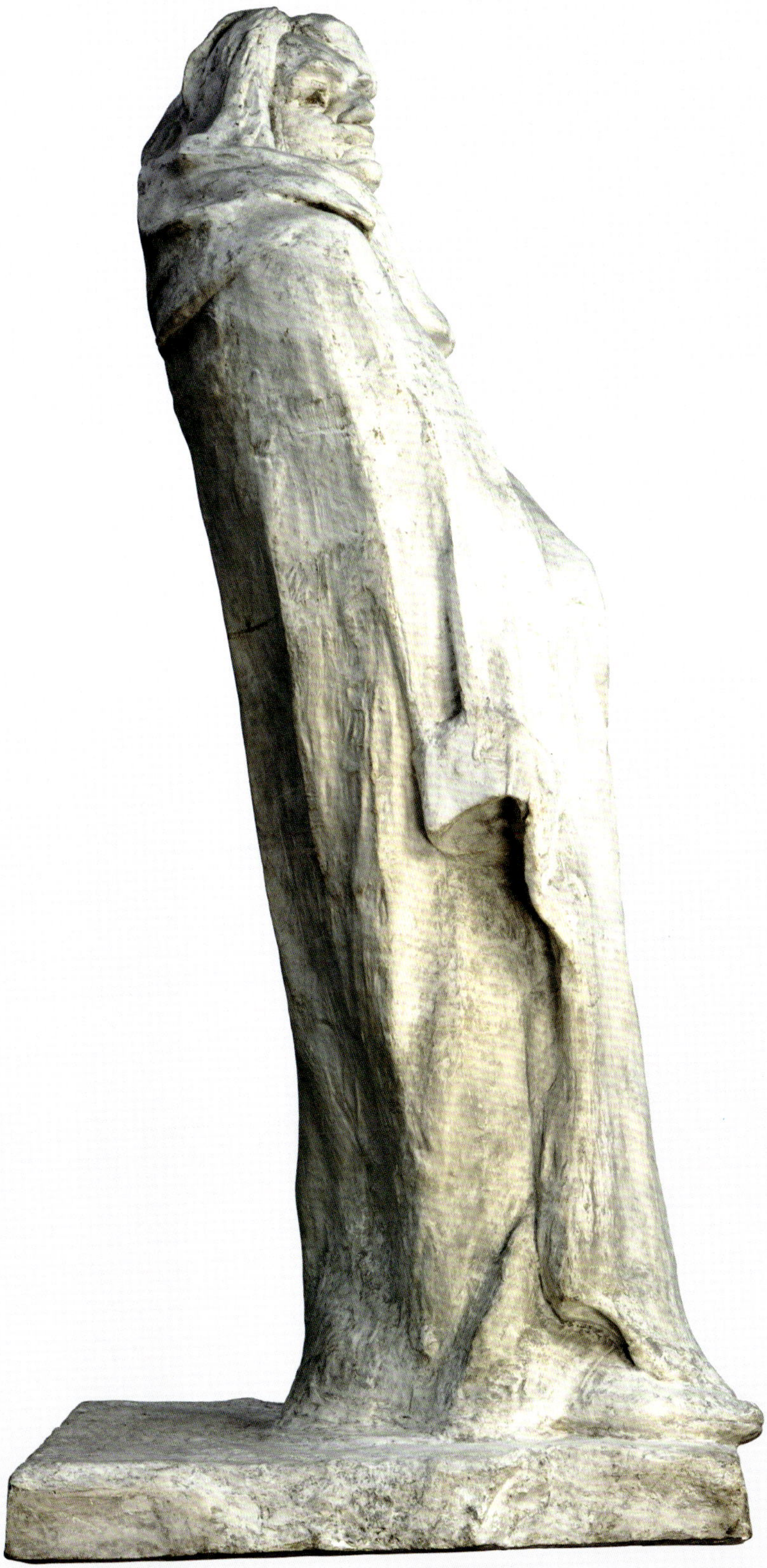

By inclining the central axis so that the centre of gravity moves away from the vertical, Auguste Rodin propels his *Balzac* both forwards and backwards through space. He begins the work's dramatic shift of mass by extending the toes of the right foot forward 4 inches beyond the front edge of the sculpture's rectangular base. By doing this, the centre of gravity is altered and the whole sculpture begins its backward-leaning ascent. The figure inclines at the precise angle necessary for the vertical mass to maintain its unsettled stasis. Our eyes move up and along the backward-leaning robed figure, until the enormous introspective head, eluding our gaze, halts our ascent.

Rodin never met the writer and there was only one daguerreotype image available that he might have seen. The sculpture is not a likeness in the usual sense, nor was it meant to be. It is, however, a depiction of the powerful influence Balzac's writings exerted over the sculptor.

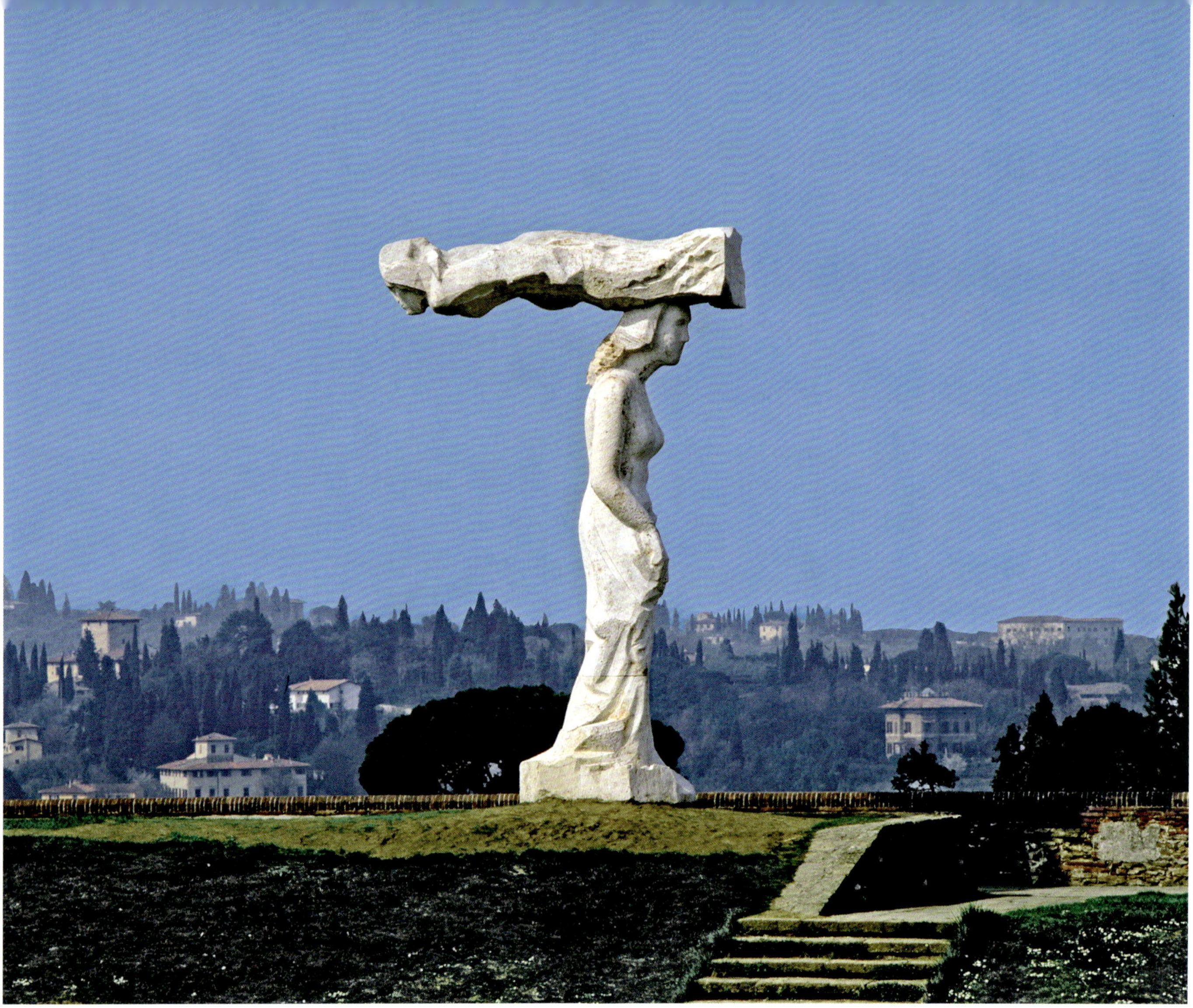

Michelangelo Pistoletto (b. 1933)
Dietofront (About-turn)

1981–4
Marble
6 × 4 × 1.8 m (19 ft 8 in × 13 ft 2 in × 5 ft 11 in)
Porta Romana, Florence

This gigantic cast marble work by Michelangelo Pistoletto stands in Florence at the Porta Romana. A startlingly cantilevered figure has miraculously attached herself at right angles to the top of a somewhat larger standing female and in doing so has drastically altered the centre of gravity and the equilibrium within both figures. The earthbound figure is now levered backward by the tense flying mass connected to her head. Her lack of any outward indication of this radical change in her centre of gravity causes an impossible tension; the top figure seems prepared to fly away as two-thirds of its cantilevered mass is now free. Precariously suspended in space, her aerodynamic pose – arms tightly drawn into her sides, head projecting forward and legs tensed – adds to the possibility of her flight. By shifting the centre of gravity within these two figures the sculptor has created a visual tension that challenges our innate perceptual equilibrium.

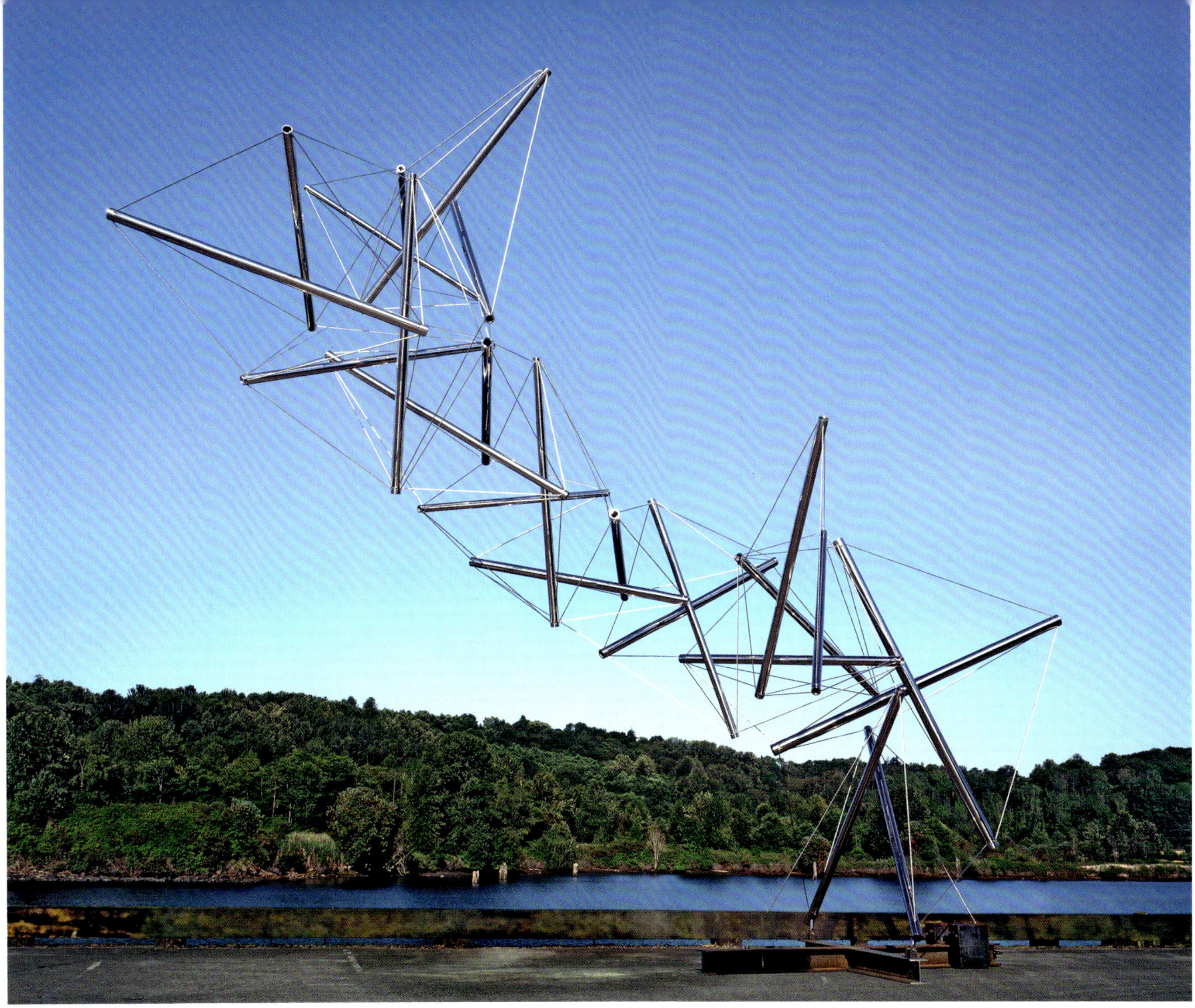

Kenneth Snelson (b. 1927)
Dragon

2000–3
Stainless steel
9.3 × 9.4 × 3.7 m (30 ft 6 in × 31 ft × 12 ft)
Installed at Pinwheel Corporation, Seattle, WA
Collection of the artist

Dragon by Kenneth Snelson is also a cantilever, but all aspects of its support are evident. It utilizes a structural system that the artist calls 'tensegrity', which allows him to build an open structure of great strength using cables and rods that are held in tension. The structure appears to resist or defy our normal assumptions about gravity, mass and structural engineering; the work thus takes on an illusory presence that borders on the dangerous. Centre of Gravity, although still present, has become a visual jumble that evades simple analysis.

Ronald Bladen
Untitled

1965
Polished aluminium
3 parts, each 284 × 122 × 53 cm
(9 ft 4 in × 4 ft × 1 ft 9 in)
Hamburger Bahnhof, Berlin

The manipulation of space, volume and mass belongs to sculpture as well as to architecture. I acutely felt this affinity between the two disciplines when I walked within *Untitled* by Ronald Bladen. The three massive, angled slabs challenged my instinctual, innate sense of verticality – *my* centre of gravity. As I approached and walked between two of the angled elements, a feeling of unease and anxiety came over me. The three slabs so disturbed my sense of equilibrium that after a time I became apprehensive just being in the gallery with them hovering above. More walls than sculpture now, I was afraid they would fall on me. The oppressive distance between them only reinforced my fears. In the previous examples, Centre of Gravity has remained somewhere within the object being looked at, but here I felt that the disequilibrium between the parts of the sculpture and the room had mysteriously shifted and were now as present in my body as they were in the sculpture.

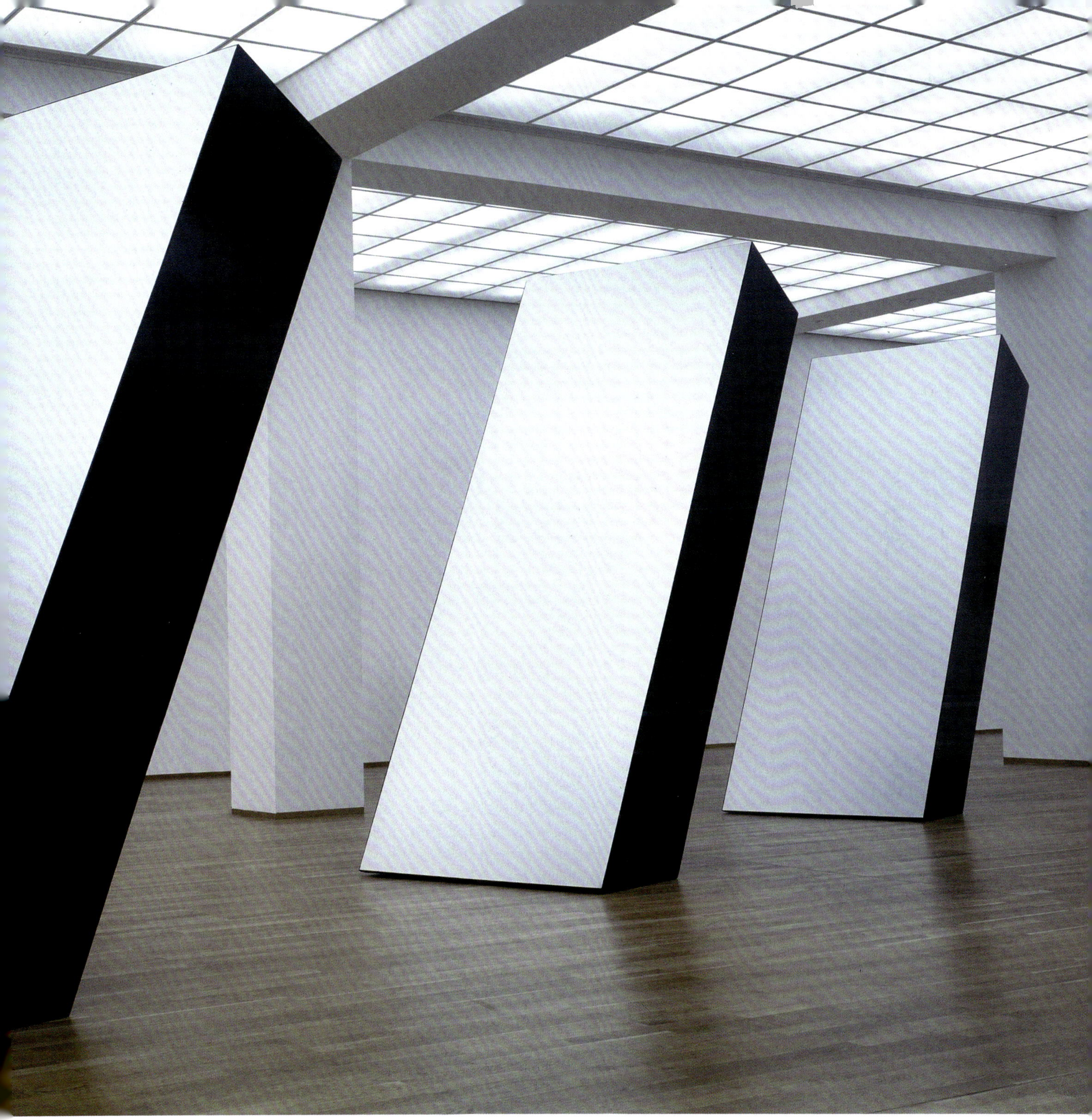

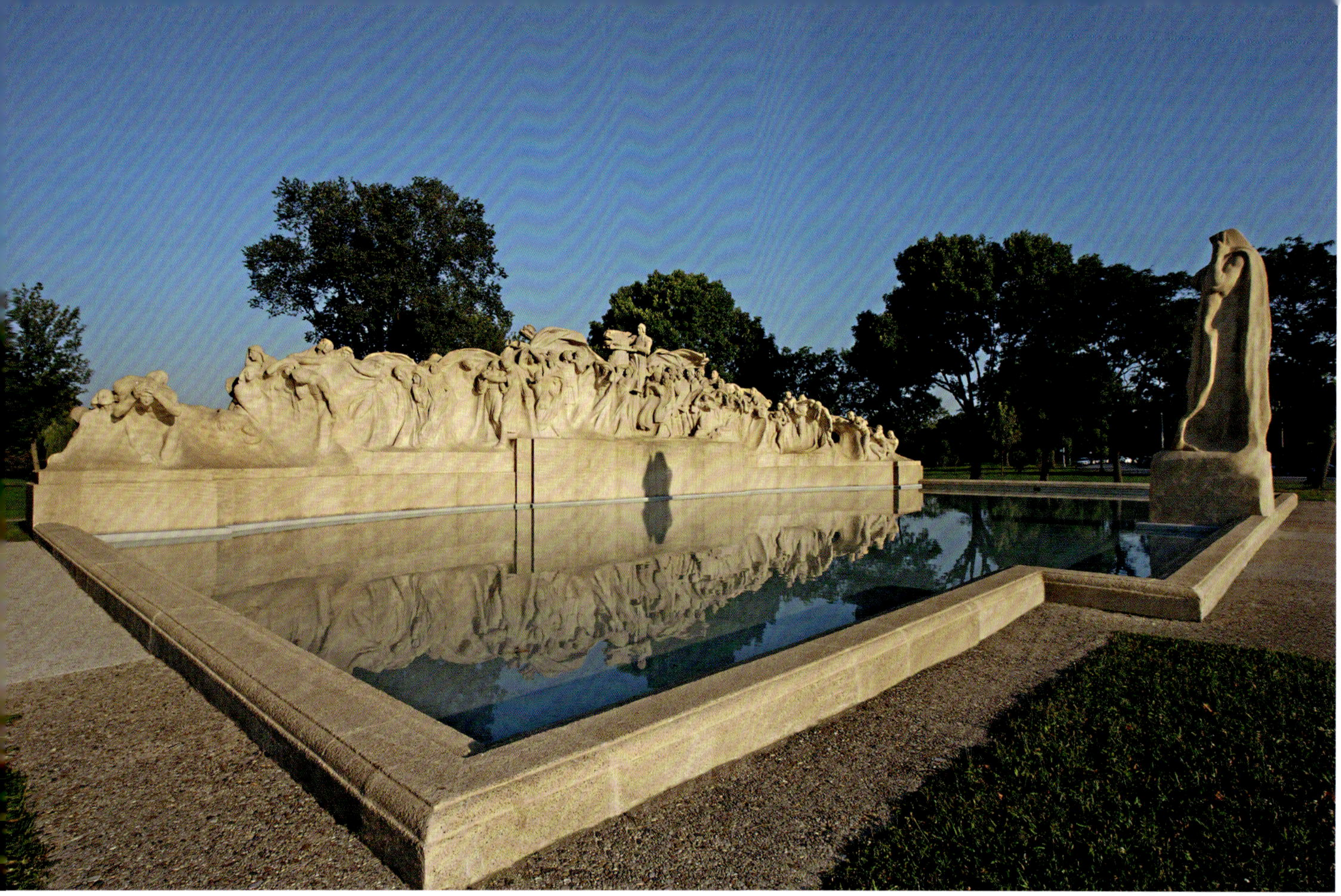

Lorado Taft (1860–1936)
The Fountain of Time

1922
Cast concrete, water
7.3 × 38.4 m (24 × 126 ft)
Washington Park, Chicago, IL

Here, Lorado Taft utilizes both a horizontal earthbound mass that reconciles itself to the forces of gravity, and an overshadowing vertical figure, to pose a question in the mind of the viewer. The horizontal wave of 102 figures is grounded in place, while the centre of gravity of the 24-foot high standing figure of Time challenges that same force. Separating the two is a pool of water. The figures progress from showing birth, on the right, to the final moments of resignation before death, on the left. Because our perceptual differences between the horizontal and the vertical are so deeply ingrained, we ignore the possibility of their larger mortal significance. Through metaphor, Taft exploits this tension between these two opposing forces. The finite gravity-bound horizontal stream of humanity is separated by a pool of water and watched over by the eternal, vertical figure of Time. The cynical clarity of the sculpture – we are finite, time is infinite, and there is no balance point, no compromise presented – challenges us to create our own resolution between these primal forces.

Gravity unites sculpture and spectator in a common dependence on the resistance to the pull of the earth.

— William Tucker

It is weight that gives meaning to weightlessness.

— Isamu Noguchi

4

Expanding the Core

All sculptures to some degree will contain many of the Elements mentioned. But now some judgement is required. Is the form open to the space that surrounds it? Or is it an enclosed mass? Is the core within the form readily apparent? Yes, a sculpture is an object surrounded by space, but how the object addresses that space through its materiality is a question that these two Elements – Volume and Space – may answer.

Volume

Bruce Nauman

Henri Matisse

Naum Gabo

Vladimir Tatlin

William Tucker

Kofun period, Japan

Donald Judd

Lara Schnitger

Rachel Whiteread

Space

Vladimir Baranoff-Rossiné

Konstantin Medunetsky

Alberto Giacometti

David Smith

Anthony Caro

Sol LeWitt

Anne Truitt

Walter De Maria

Volume

An amount of space and/or material occupied or defined by a three-dimensional object. Volumes are expressed in cubic units.

Prior to the twentieth century, the history of sculpture was the history of the figure with little consideration given to its surrounding space. Modernism opened this previously closed monolith allowing the spatial volume to enter. Volume in sculpture may be experienced in two ways, either as a visible solid presence that is sometimes difficult to differentiate from the Element, Mass, or as a quantifiable but invisible space. This defined volumetric space, although unseen in the normal sense, can take on a viscosity and specific authority that the space surrounding the sculpture does not have. This progression from mass to volume had to be visualized and understood before the revolution of space as a material in sculpture could be explored.

Bruce Nauman (b. 1941)
Untitled (Pair of Hands)
from Fifteen Pairs of Hands

1996
White bronze and painted steel base
One of 15 pairs of hands, dimensions variable
Private collection

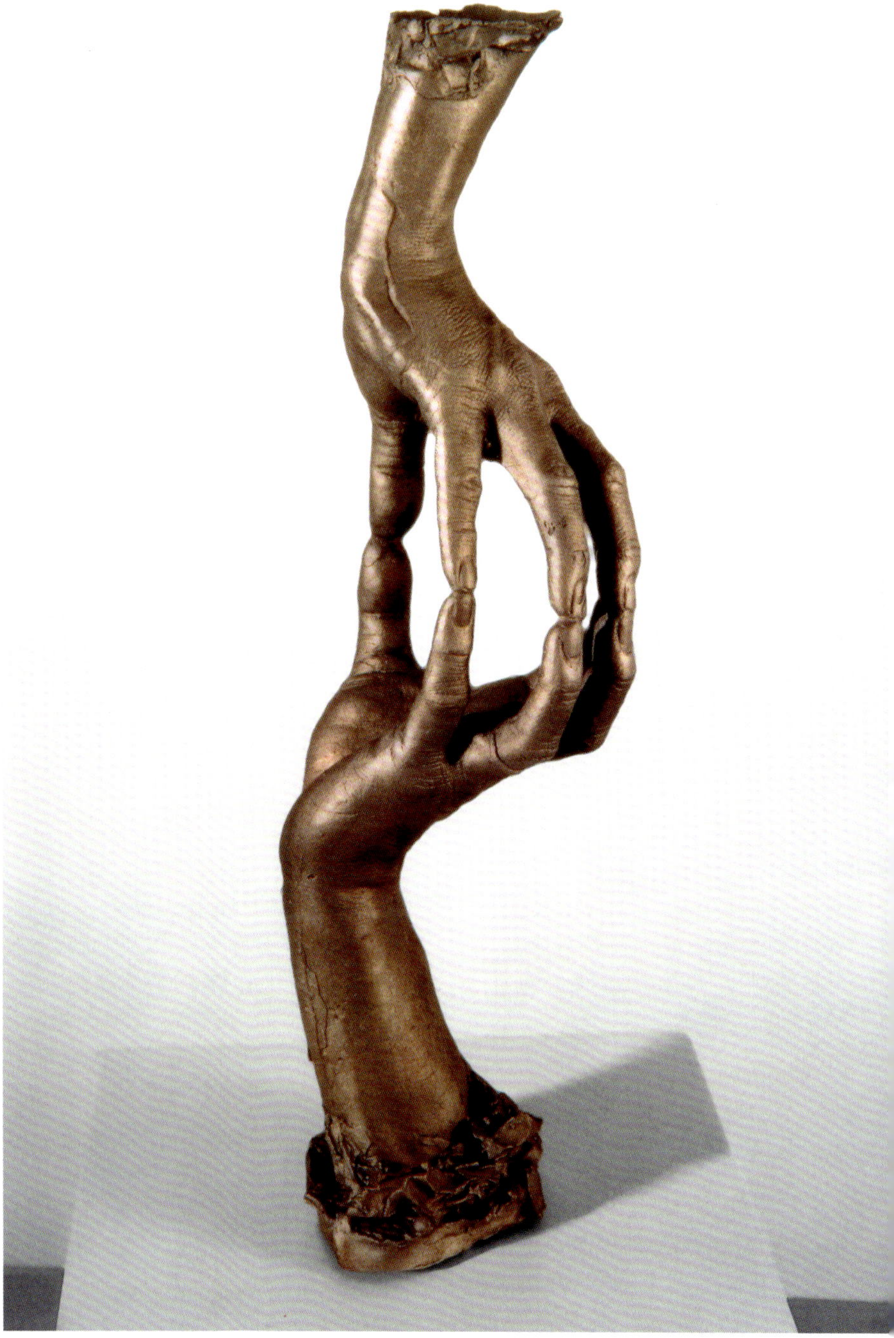

Bruce Nauman's *Untitled (Pair of Hands)* illustrates the moment when the infinity of space becomes a defined volume. Often, the phrase 'negative space' is used when describing this particular characteristic of a sculpture, when what is being referred to should be called a 'volume'.

To feel this sense of Volume, bring both arms forward, hands moving slowly together as if attempting to grasp a large ball. As you do this you are creating, from the surrounding space, an enclosed volume. Almost tactile now, the enclosed volume takes on a viscous physicality.

Henri Matisse (1869–1954)
The Serpentine

1909
Bronze
55.9 × 27.9 × 17.8 cm (22 × 11 × 7 in)
Musée Matisse de Nice

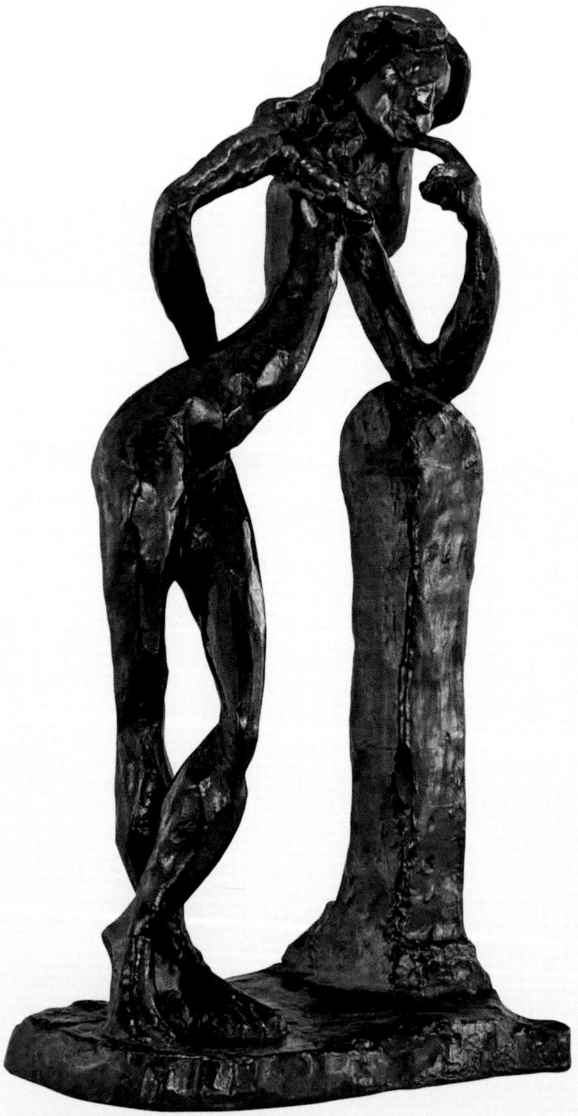

One of the earliest examples of Volume in modern sculpture is *The Serpentine* by Henri Matisse. As we walk around the piece the volumes contained within the bronze anatomical parts open, compress, twist and expand with respect to adjacent forms. The figure appears to rest on the prominent pillar-like object. But there is another possibility – the perceived density of the volumes within the composition are so palpable that they, not the pillar, appear to be supporting the weight of her body. Volume has now become material for the sculptor to form.

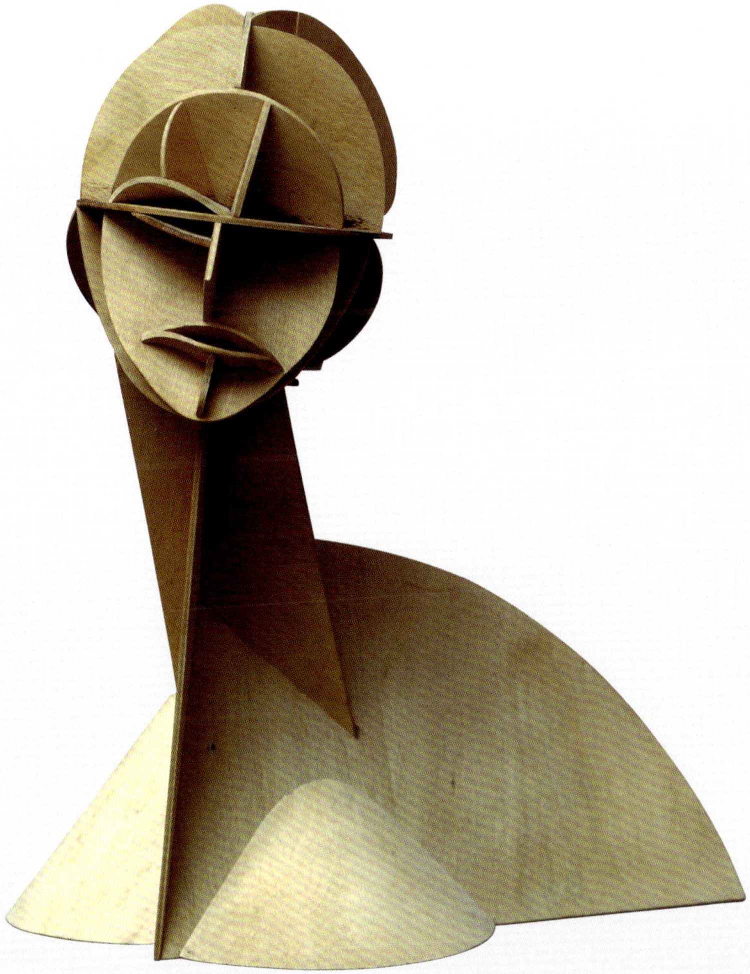

Naum Gabo (1890–1977)
Constructed Head No. 1

1915 (reassembled in 1985)
Three-layered plywood
54 cm (24 ¼ in) high
Städel Museum, Frankfurt am Maim

Converging flat planes may create a volume; Naum Gabo called this a 'stereometric construction' of volumetric space. In his *Constructed Head No. 1* we see how this new understanding of volume is utilized to form a traditional portrait head, one that might, at another time, have been made from bronze or marble. As in the Tatlin work that follows, volume displaces mass. Like Tatlin, Gabo was associated with the Constructivists at the time of the 1917 Russian Revolution – a period of social, artistic and political renewal that embraced new scientific theories and the use of industrial materials for aesthetic expression.

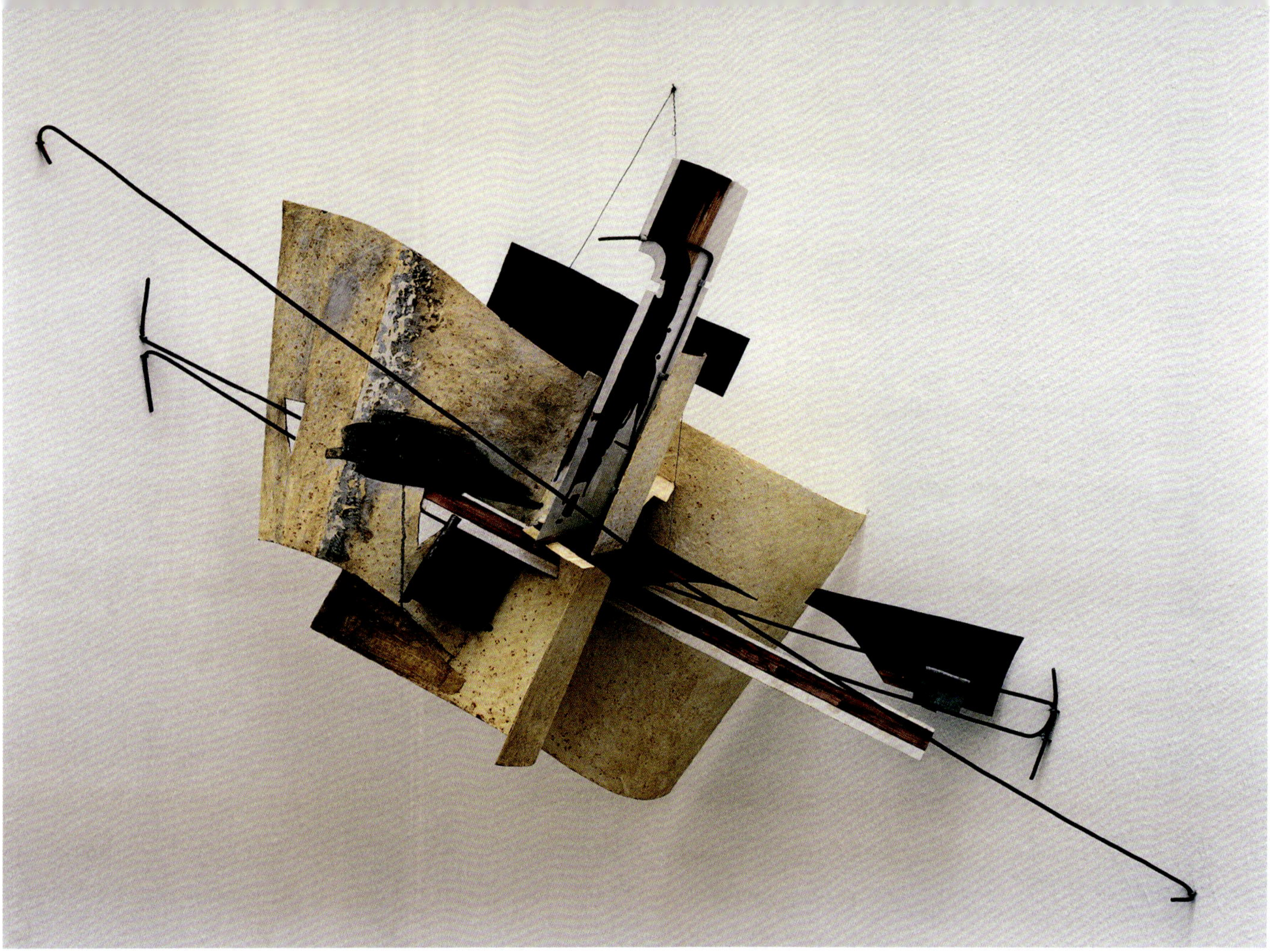

Vladimir Tatlin (1885–1953)
Corner Counter-Relief

1915
Steel, aluminium, paint
94 × 94 × 230 cm (37 × 37 × 90 ½ in)
Kunsthalle, Düsseldorf

Inspired by his journey to Picasso's studio in 1913 and the Cubist musical instrument reliefs that he saw there, Vladimir Tatlin constructed this *Corner Counter-Relief* on his return to Russia. In part this revolutionary work was inspired by traditional Russian icons, and in part by Tatlin's philosophical position – *faktura*, or 'truth to materials'. Each material contains certain unique physical characteristics, he speculated, and so each demands its own working methods. Tatlin begins with flat steel sheets that may be easily curved to enclose volumes of space. These thin sheets of steel were readily available in contrast to the more traditional materials of bronze or marble. The work contains volumes of space rather than the monolithic mass of the figure. Thus it is one of the earliest experiments in creating a non-figurative formal sculpture. We could say that there have been only two ideas in the history of art: to do, or not do the figure. *Corner Counter-Relief* by Tatlin represents one of the earliest attempts to accomplish the latter. The steel is curved and bent, constructed from back to front in opposition to the traditional relief that is carved into the stone. It is a non-representational form that explores the revolutionary possibilities found in manipulating spatial volumes and exploring new materials. And like ancient icons, Tatlin's reliefs are suspended within the converging flat planes – 'stereometric' cubic volume – of the corner of a room.

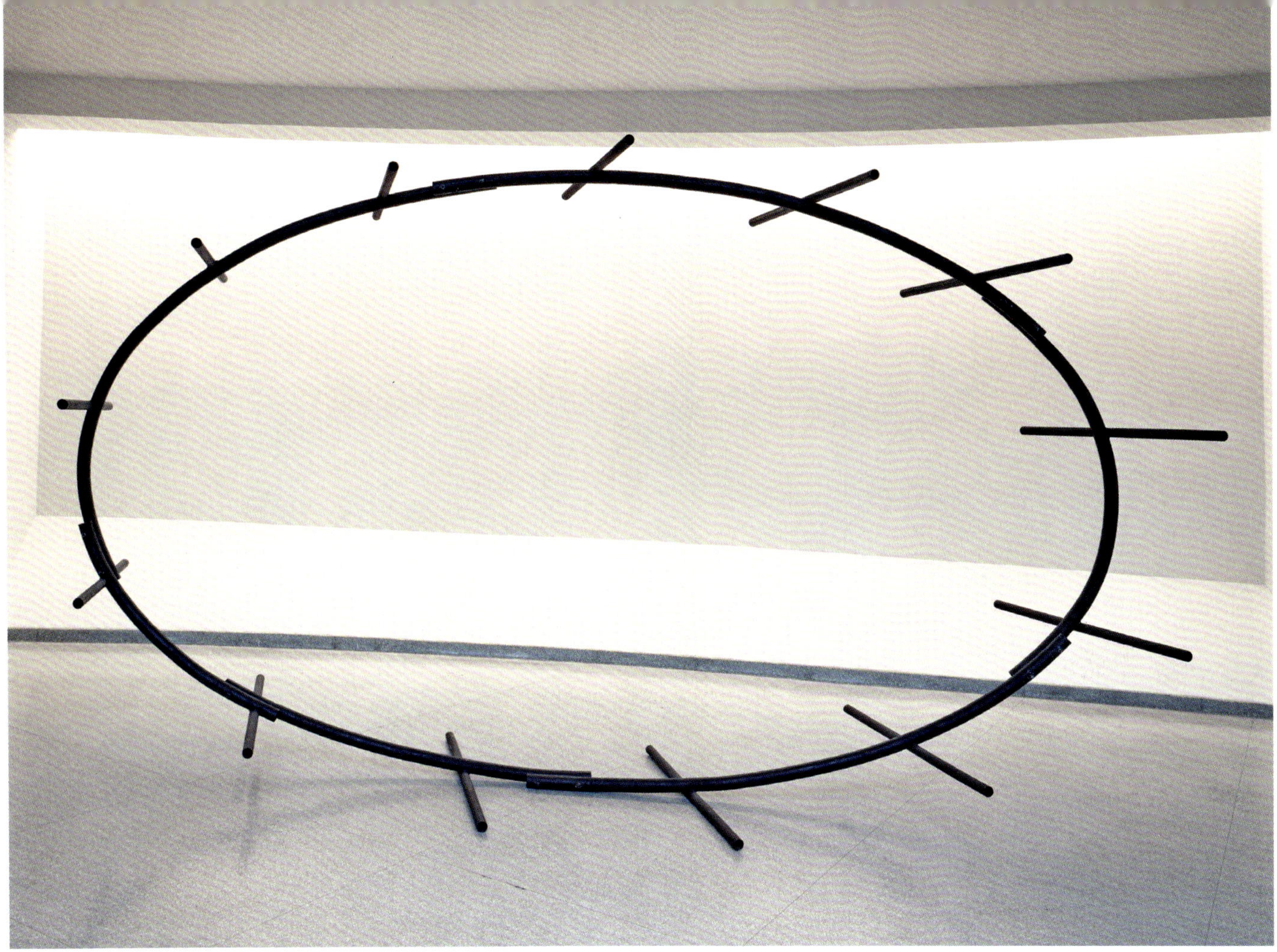

William Tucker (b. 1935)
An Ellipse

1978
Steel
274.3 × 457.2 × 127 cm (108 × 189 × 50 in)
Solomon R. Guggenheim Museum, New York

Volume is a contained space, but seldom does it extend and merge with what is sometimes referred to as 'self-space' – the psychological protective space that immediately surrounds our bodies. Yet this is precisely what occurs when the viewer enters the elastic volume of *An Ellipse* by William Tucker. The defined volume that lies within the rods attached to the plane of the ellipse takes on a palpable viscosity. I believe this physical intensification of volume is due in part to the scale of the sculpture: at 9 feet high, the work is considerably taller than the viewer and its width usually extends just beyond that of the viewer's peripheral vision. Depending upon where we stand in relation to the work, our 'self-space' is either pulled in or pushed away as if the sculpture's volume were also a magnetic field. It is this dynamic relationship between the volume of *An Ellipse* and the viewer's personal space that transmits the kinaesthetic sensation felt in the sculpture.

Kofun period, Japan
Haniwa Warrior

6th century AD
Ceramic with polychrome
135.5 × 41.9 × 27.3 cm (53 ⅜ × 16 ½ × 10 ¾ in)
Tokyo National Museum

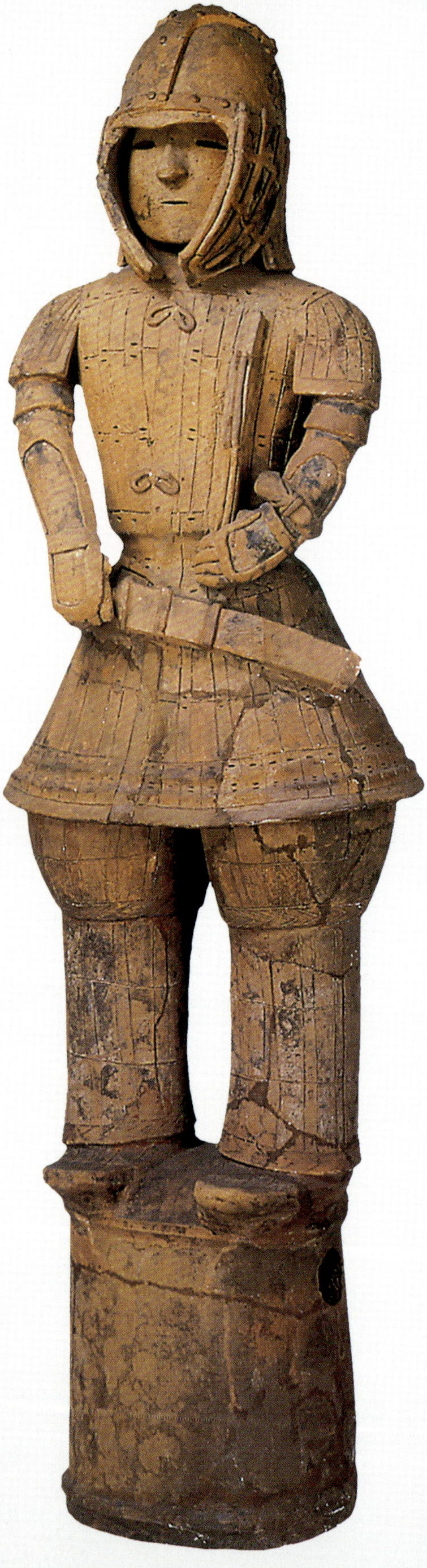

Volume may be perceptually sensed as well as seen with the eye. I often visited a *Haniwa Warrior* figure like this as a young boy. I passed time staring through the two almond-shaped eyes into the shadowed volume within, speculating as to the contents of its hollow inner core. The eyes are cut through the thin membrane of clay; they give life to the otherwise impenetrable shell and its inaccessible volume. *Haniwa* literally means 'circle of clay'. These figures are coil-built, smoothed, then fired. The swelling bulbous forms that methodically construct the sculpture, one on top of the other, are the first indications of what the eyes confirm. The warrior feels hollow not massive and his blank gaze is only one way to confirm the work's hidden volume within.

Donald Judd (1928–1994)
Untitled

1972
Copper, enamel, aluminium
91.6 × 155.5 × 178.2 cm (36 × 61 ¼ × 70 ⅛ in)
Tate, London

Donald Judd's *Untitled* is an open container made from thick copper plate. It is larger than most of his work from the same period, so large, in fact, that we can only see inside when standing very close to it. When we look inside, instead of seeing the copper volume we might expect, we are startled by a glowing cadmium red vapour, which it seems the copper walls can barely contain. Looking more closely, we realize that only the bottom surface has been painted, not the sides, and that Judd found the precise hue in relation to the colour of the copper to turn the enclosed volume into a red pulsating fog.

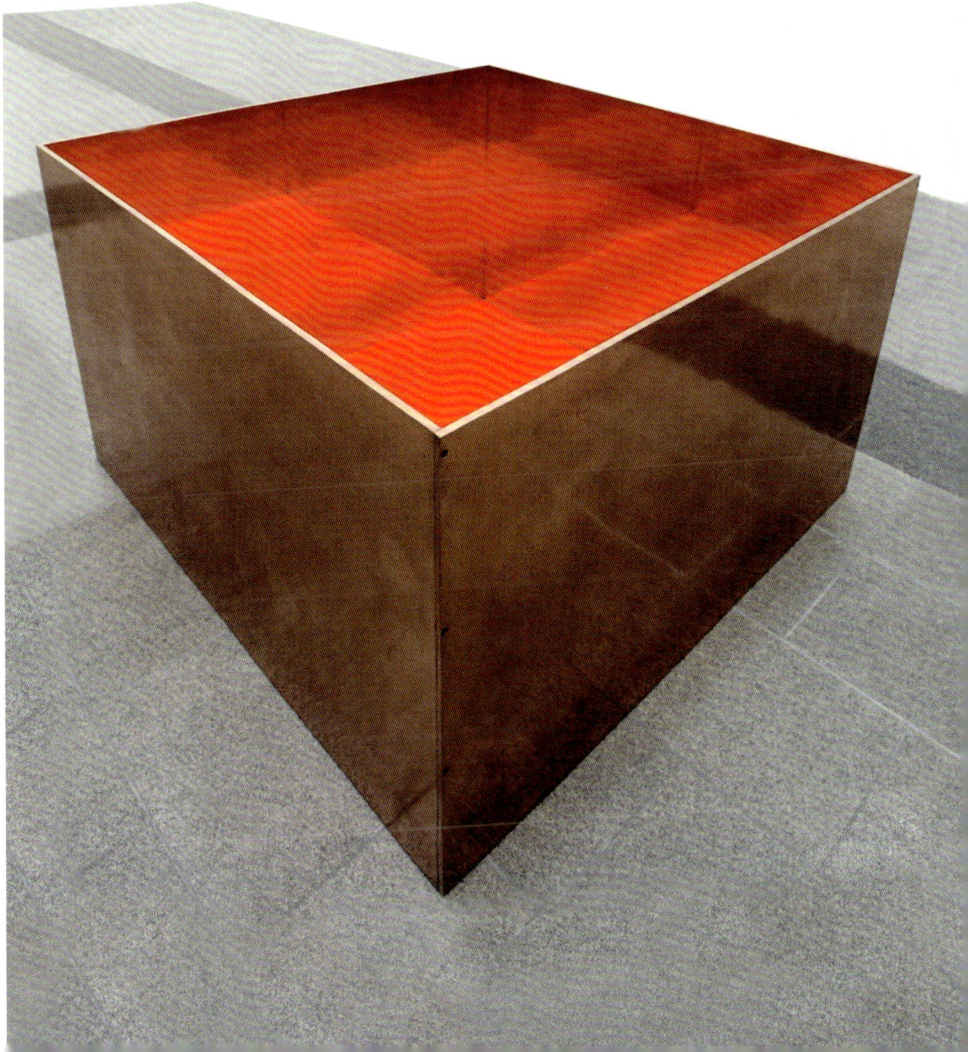

Lara Schnitger (b. 1969)
Hornament

1999
Stockings, chopsticks
Dimensions variable
Collection of the artist

One volume can be dependent on another for its form as in this work by Lara Schnitger. Because the black-veiled surface membrane of the suspended volume is made from stitched-together stockings, it is without a rigid skeletal form of its own, and so will change each time it is exhibited. The frail web-like translucency of the work with its multitude of circular openings allows the viewer not only to see every aspect of the buoyant, stretching volume within, but to measure this elastic form against the volume of the room that gives it shape. This tension between volume within and without provides a clear example of the difference between the two, which is not always as apparent as we would like to believe.

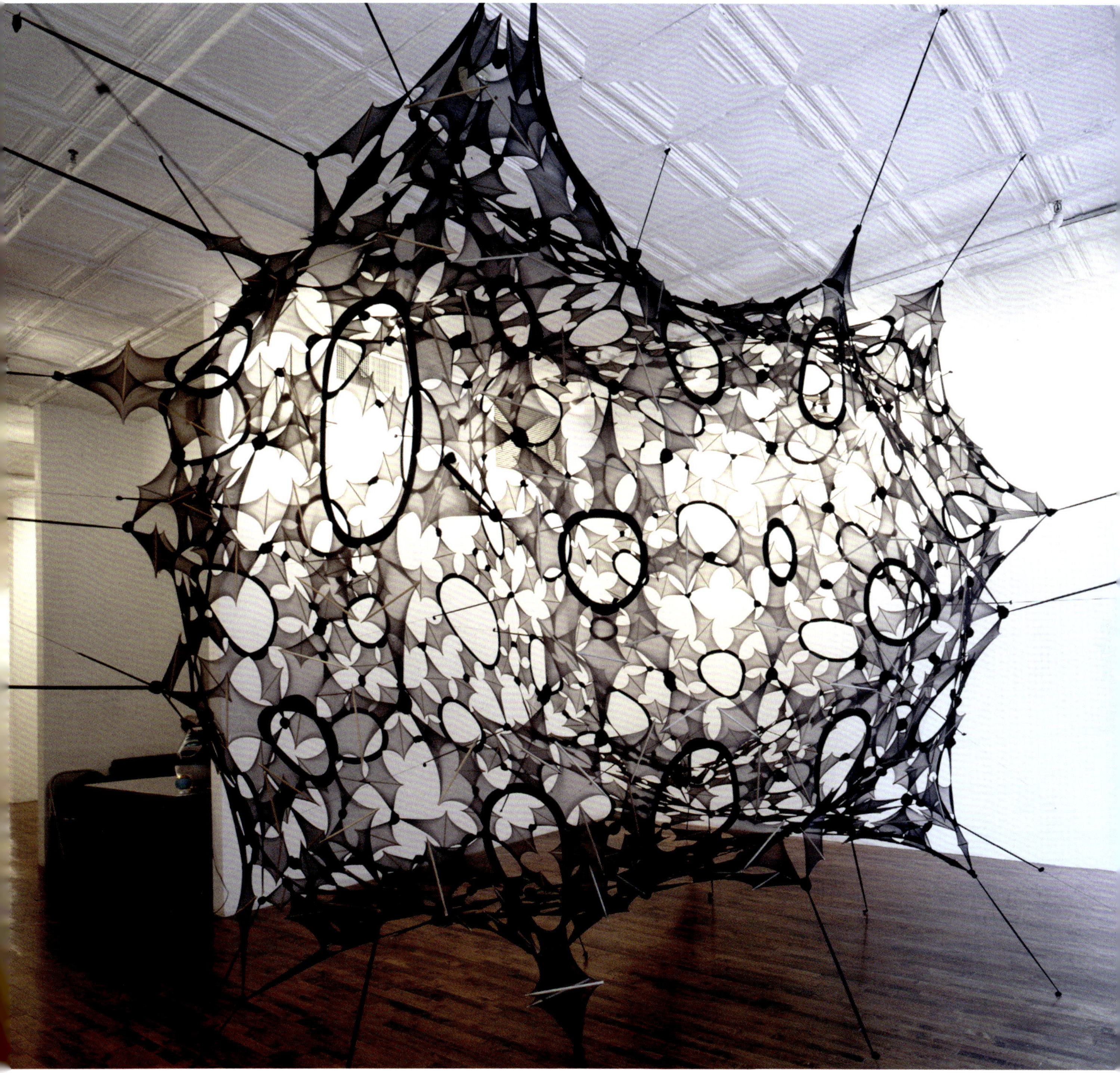

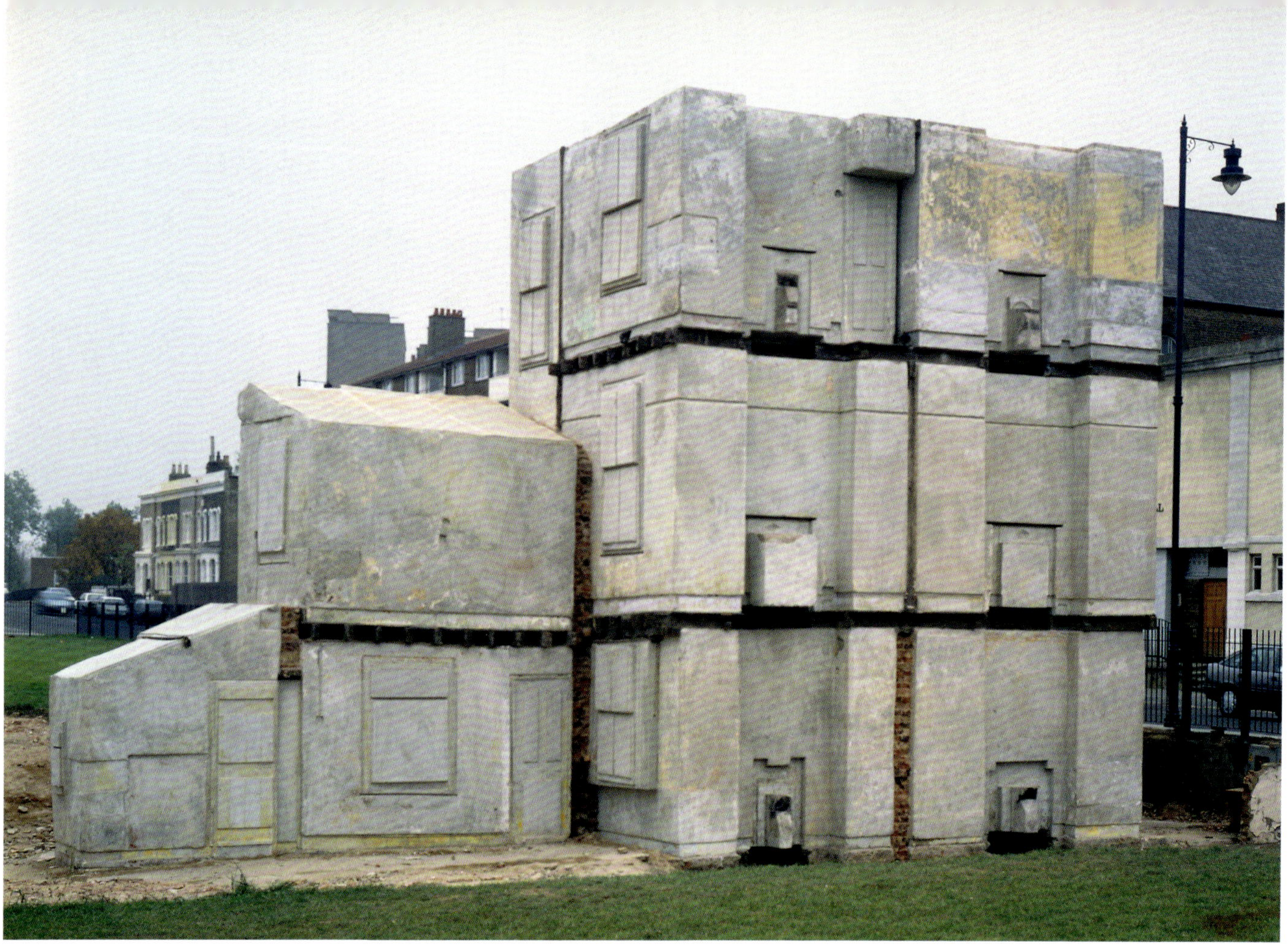

Rachel Whiteread (b. 1963)
House

1993; destroyed 1994
Concrete
Approx. 10 m (32 ft) high
Commissioned by Artangel, installed at Grove Road, London

To understand a concept fully, it is frequently helpful to consider its opposite aspect. In 1993 Rachel Whiteread cast a three-storey London townhouse in concrete, appearing to replace the volume of space within, no matter how small, with the grey liquid. After it set she stripped away the entire siding, framework, doors and windows, leaving a faithfully detailed concrete casting of the house. What had been a series of open rooms, or volumes, was now a massive three-storey concrete block. Windows extended beyond the outside walls, when previously they had projected into the rooms. Thus volume had been transformed into its mass.

We renounce in sculpture the mass as a sculptural element ... we take four planes [in space] and we construct with them the same volume as four tons of mass.

— Naum Gabo and Antoine Pevsner

Let us throw everything away and therefore proclaim the absolute and total abolition of the finite line and the closed statue. We open up the figure and lock up the environment in it.

— Umberto Boccioni

Sculpture is the art of the hole and the lump.

— Auguste Rodin

A hole in the block of a piece of sculpture is in most cases nothing but the expression of impotence and weakness.

— Fritz Wotruba

Space

The continuous expanse within which all things move or exist.
The interval between points or objects.

Space is infinite. Volume is contained. The aesthetic use of Space as a material, more than any other single Element, transformed the art of sculpture in the twentieth century. All sculpture is material in real space, but around 1914, something revolutionary occurred. Space became an expressive medium like clay, bronze and stone had been. Space is often characterized, incorrectly for our purpose here, as an empty expanse. Throughout the discussion that follows Space will be thought of in two ways. First, it is a material that can be manipulated and formed like any other sculptural material. Although invisible, its presence can be perceptually felt. Second, Space is the substance that surrounds the objects in our world. The former might be thought of as a modernist invention, while the latter may be considered to be a more established understanding of Space. Space became an aesthetic material that in time far surpassed the wildest fantasies of the early modern sculptors.

Vladimir Baranoff-Rossiné (1888–1944)
Symphony Number 1

1913
Polychrome wood, cardboard, crushed eggshells
161.1 × 72.2 × 63.4 cm (63 ¼ × 28 ½ × 25 in)
Museum of Modern Art, New York

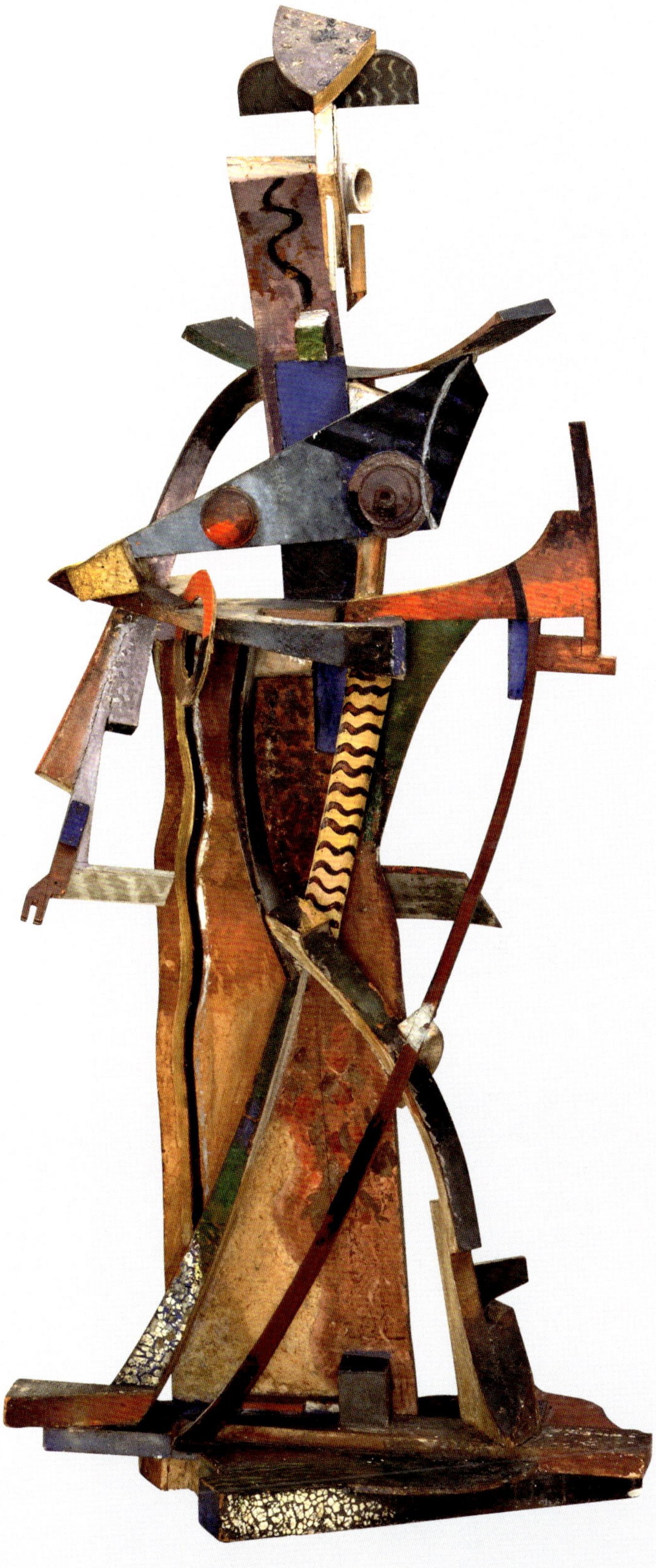

Traditionally the human figure was thought of as a unified closed form. We may see in this Cubist work by Vladimir Baranoff-Rossiné, an early attempt to challenge that assumption. *Symphony Number 1* was constructed from what, at that time, was a strange list of materials – wood, cardboard, crushed eggshells, found objects and paint. Its variously painted planes, circles and curves put the whole sculpture into a state of visual vibration. The work clearly marks the critical moment of transition when the figure opens its solid mass to the space that surrounds it. The human figure as a monolith gives way to other more formal concerns, concerns including the possibility that space may be both material and content.

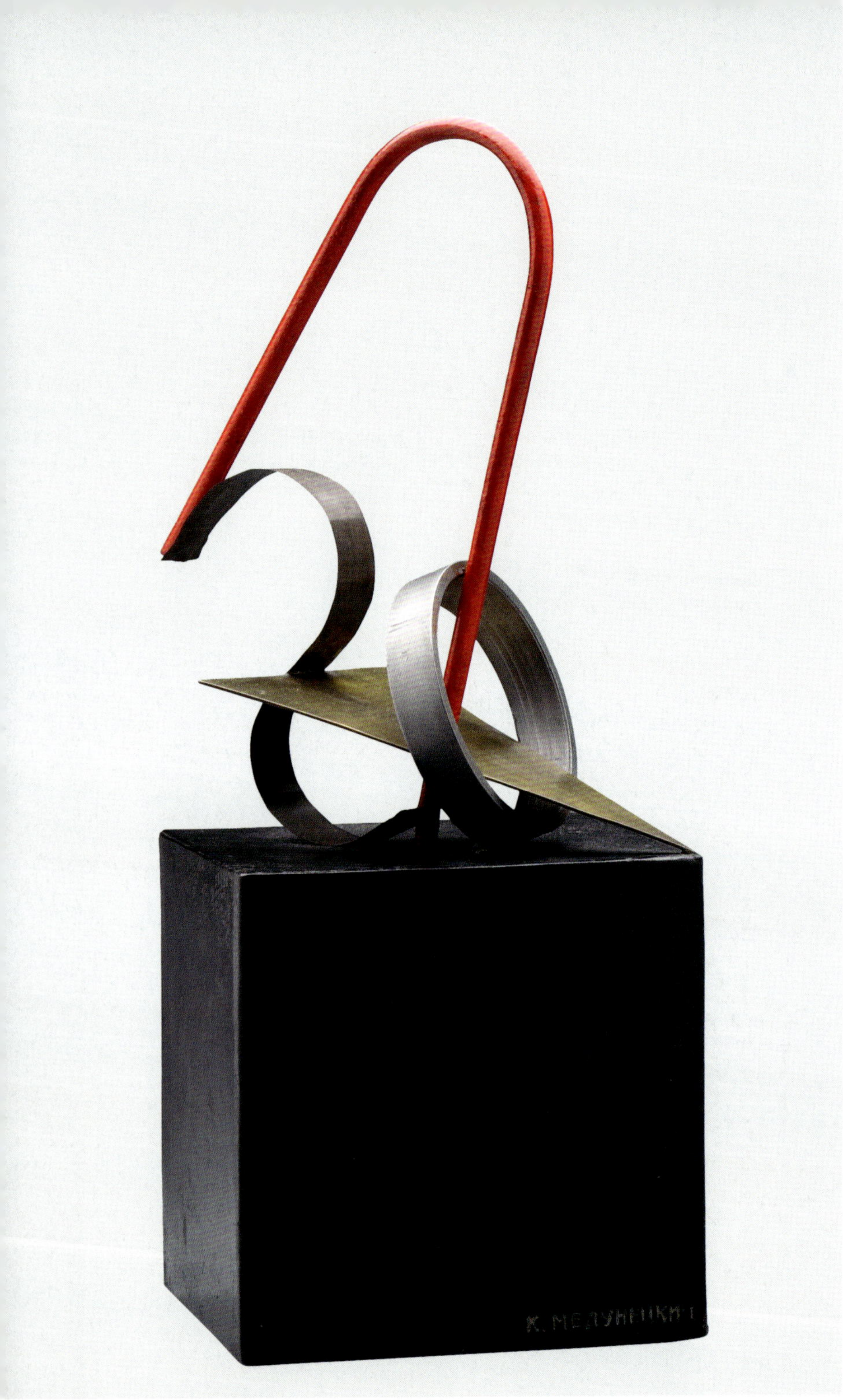

Konstantin Medunetsky (1899–1935)
Spatial Construction (Construction No. 557)

1919
Tin, brass, painted iron and steel
Including base: 16 × 17.8 × 17.8 cm (18 ⅛ × 7 × 7 in)
Yale University Museum, New Haven, CT

Construction No. 557 should be seen as a development from the Tatlin *Corner Counter-Relief* discussed in Volume (see p. 120). It may also be a response to the Constructivist artist and theoretician Ivan Puni's challenge to his colleagues to use 'real materials in real space'. It is often said that space and its expressive use as a material is central to the development of abstract modern sculpture. Here is at least partial proof, and one early example, to support that contention. Puni rejected traditional sculptural materials like bronze and marble and urged the use of 'real materials' – those that took advantage of modern industrial technologies. *Construction No. 557* is made from tin, brass, iron and aluminium. With his phrase 'in real space', Puni signalled the necessity to construct new forms beyond the descriptive restrictions of the figure. Forms inspired by early twentieth-century machines, architecture and building practices. Forms that move through space, rising up into space, defying gravity. The content and subject of *No. 557* is an arching steel red rod, attached to a slender curving tin ribbon that begins within an aluminium ring cut through by a flat brass triangle that extends into space. All is held in place by a cubic black mass.

Alberto Giacometti (1901–1966)
Standing Woman

1948; cast 1949
Painted bronze
166 × 16.5 × 34.2 cm (65 ⅜ × 6 ½ × 13 ½ in)
Museum of Modern Art, New York

The materiality of Space as a revolutionary force does not, exclusively, belong to non-figurative sculpture. In *Standing Woman* by Alberto Giacometti, one of his series of standing female figures, the normally passive space surrounding all objects in our world has violently torn away the surface of the figure, exposing its linear core. And the emaciated sculpture is consumed by the same space we had assumed to be passive. The space that surrounds and supports *Standing Woman* has become a present force more real than the materiality of the figure.

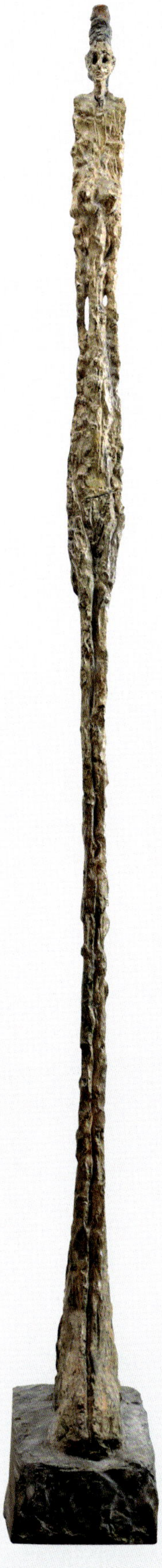

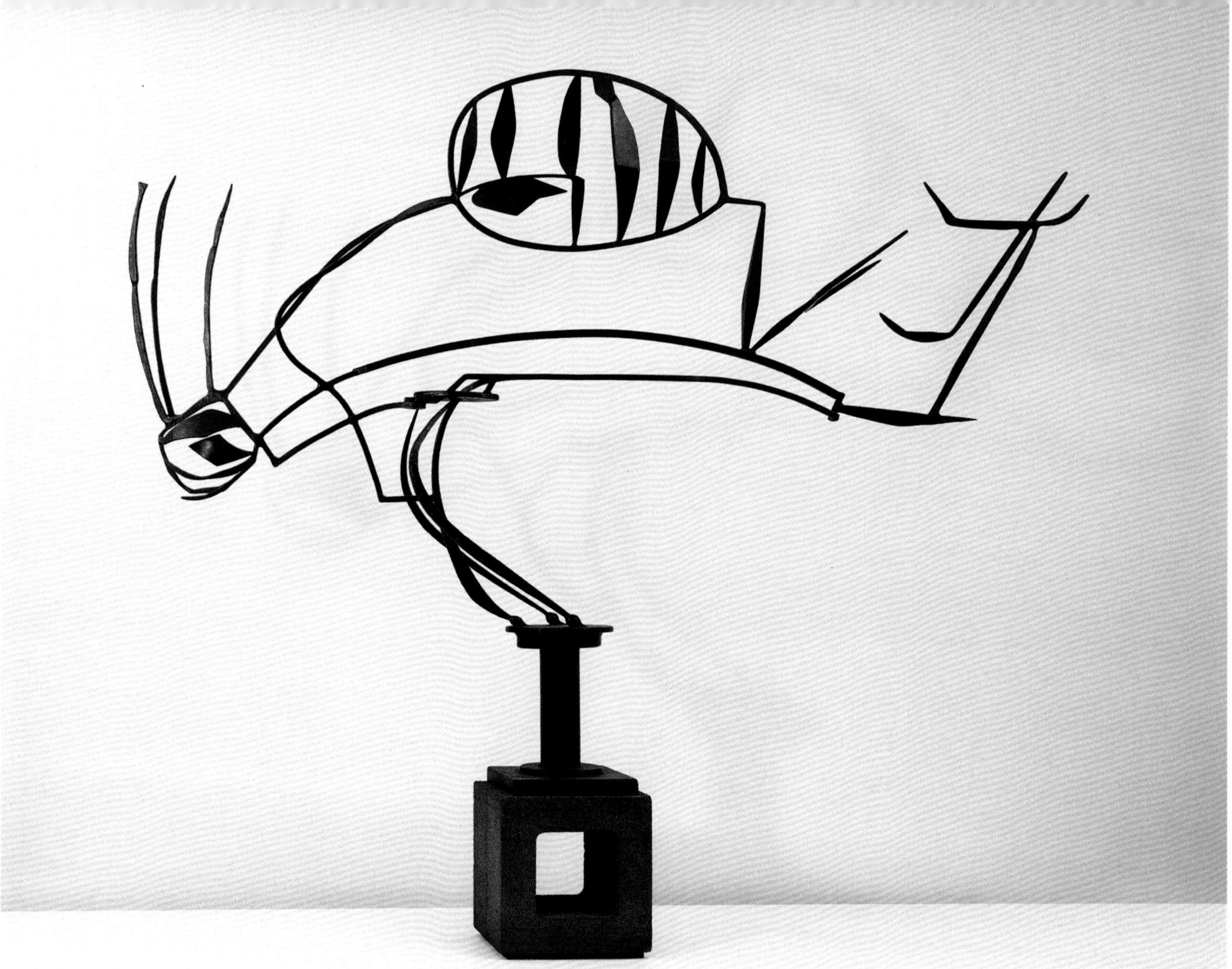

David Smith (1906–1965)
Australia

1951
Painted steel on cinder block base
Excluding base: 202 × 247 × 41 cm
(6 ft 7 ½ in × 8 ft 11 ⅞ in × 16 ⅛ in)
Museum of Modern Art, New York

Made from forged steel, *Australia* by David Smith is a spatial exotically anthropomorphic 'animal' that somewhat resembles the continent it is named after. For Giacometti, space was not a passive material (see previous page). But here it is. Space is now a neutral field for the steel components to be seen either against or within. Assembled on the floor the parts are welded together so the work is a flat plane – a lyrical forged steel 'drawing' in space. But what is 'figure' and what is 'ground'? Is the steel defining the space, or space the steel? The sculpture in total is a constantly moving form, more space than steel, exemplifying the endless oscillation between space and the material that defines it.

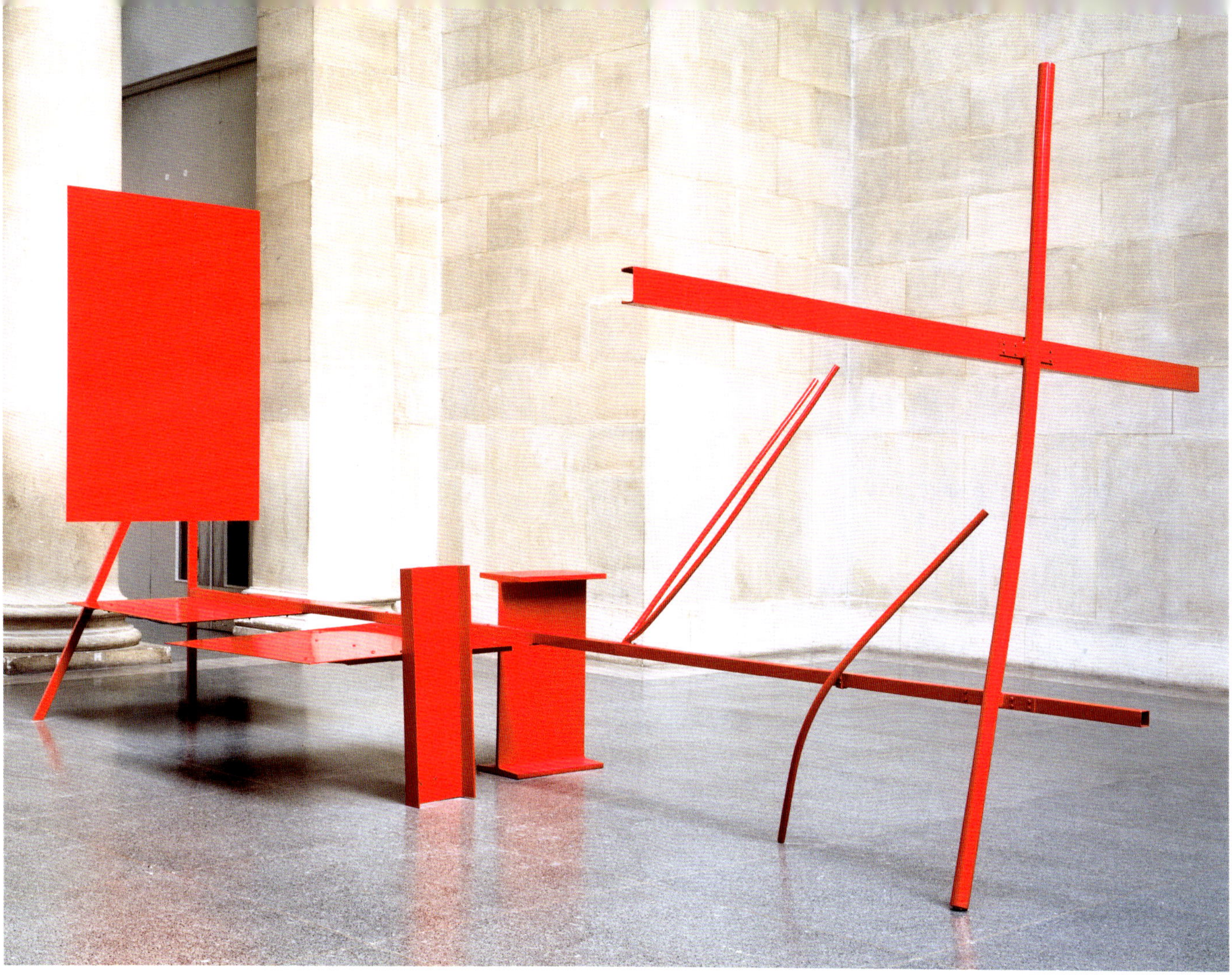

Anthony Caro (1924–2013)
Early One Morning

1962
Painted steel and aluminium
2.9 × 6.2 × 3.4 m (9 ft 5 in × 20 ft 4 in × 11 ft)
Tate, London

Primarily linear, *Early One Morning* is a series of steel forms arranged along a central axis that, depending upon how we approach the work, builds from a bent cross to a flat plane. It creates a visual dance between red steel and the space it displaces. Parts of the sculpture rise above the viewer, but because these linear details are thin and unthreatening, at no time do we feel intimidated. That said, the aggressiveness of its colour does influence how we react to the work and to the space within and around it. We feel the parts constantly opening and closing, the space formed then released – forms mysteriously measured by the single large flat plane in red space.

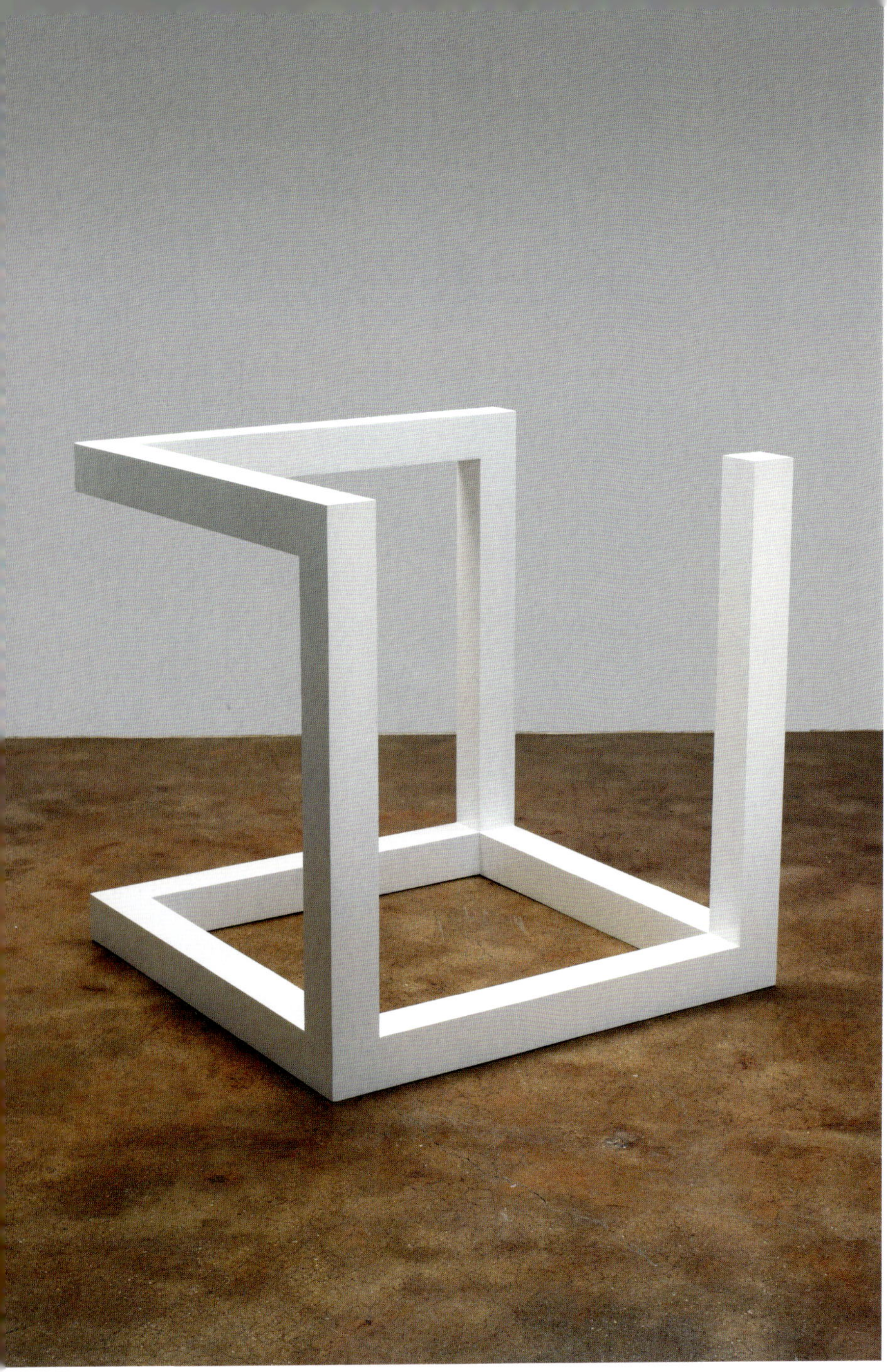

Sol LeWitt (1925–2007)
Incomplete Open Cube 9-2

1974
Painted aluminium
105.4 × 105.4 × 105.4 cm (41 ½ × 41 ½ × 41 ½ in)
Pace Gallery

Under certain circumstances, understanding the perceptual differences between Volume and Space can be difficult. This work by Sol LeWitt clearly illustrates this difficulty. It begins with the title of the sculpture. Because it is 'incomplete', we consider it an apprehensive work – apprehensive, because our mind wants to complete the geometric form. But once completed, the open cube would then contain the volume that it cannot in its current configuration. As we walk around it, the cube appears to open and close, coalesce, then break apart allowing space to flood back in, thus overcoming any possibility that a volume may be contained within. Space is infinite, but, like Volume, it needs limits to be experienced. The fundamental difference between the two in this situation is how they are contained or defined. Depending on where we stand, the dividing line between the two is in a constant state of change.

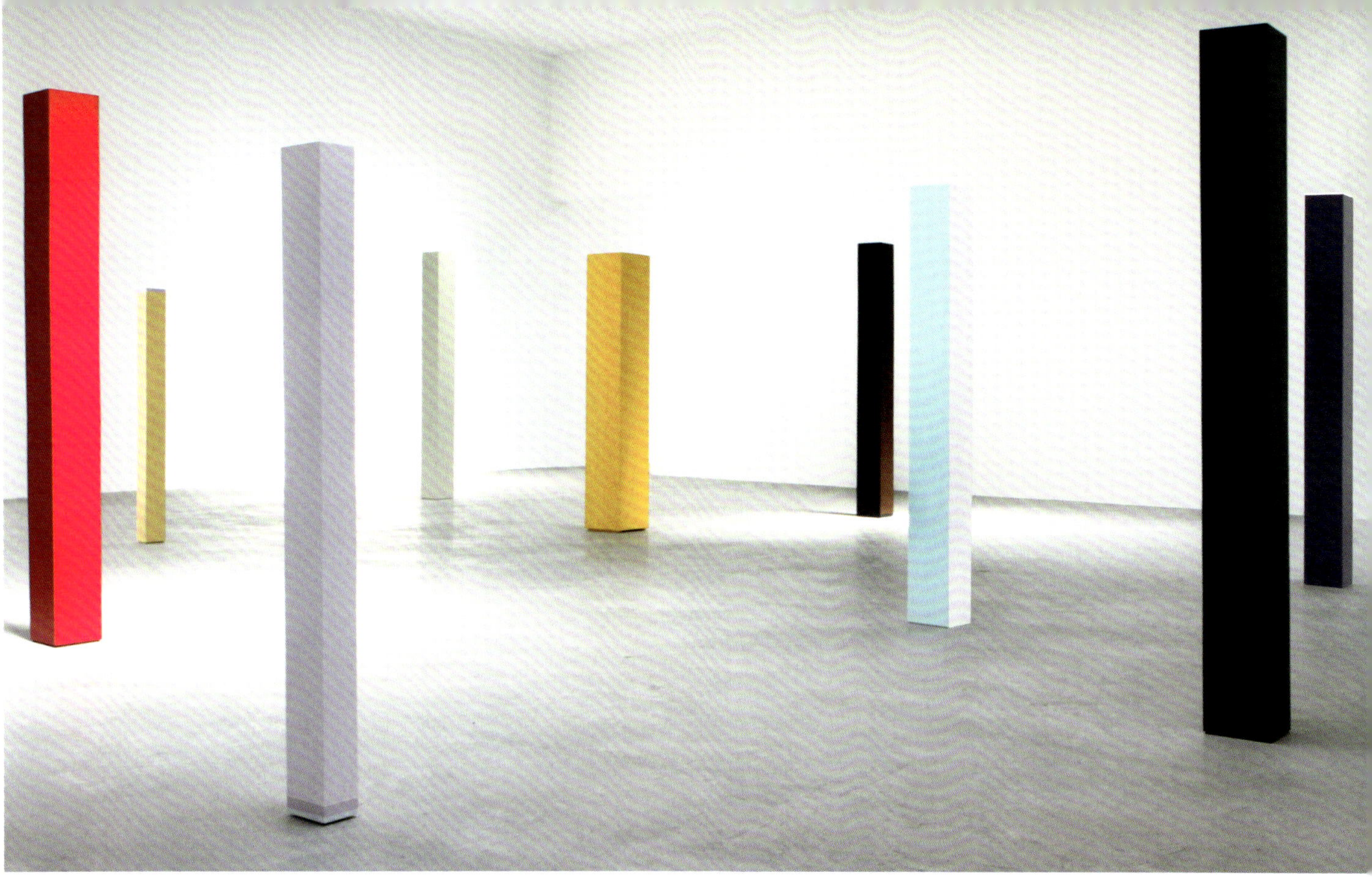

Anne Truitt (1921–2004)
Anne Truitt Sculpture 1962–2004

Matthew Marks Gallery, New York
8 May – 26 June 2010
Installation view

Anne Truitt's work also highlights the difference between Volume and Space, but in a very different manner from the LeWitt work opposite. Truitt's sculptures were conceived as individual works, but they are often shown as a group within a gallery space. When standing outside the 'forest' of works, the group appears to coalesce, defining their own volumes within the larger volume of the gallery. At the perimeter of the gallery space the sculptures appear to visually ricochet, bouncing back and forth, volumes excluding the possibility of the presence of space. But while walking among them their plural unity immediately disappears. Volume becomes Space as each individual marker asserts itself within its own space. This may occur because of the slight variations in size and the extreme differences in colour, aspects that become far more explicit when viewed close-up.

Walter De Maria (1935–2013)
The Lightning Field

1977
400 stainless steel rods
Area: c. 1.6 × 1 km (1 × 0.6 miles)
Catron County, NM

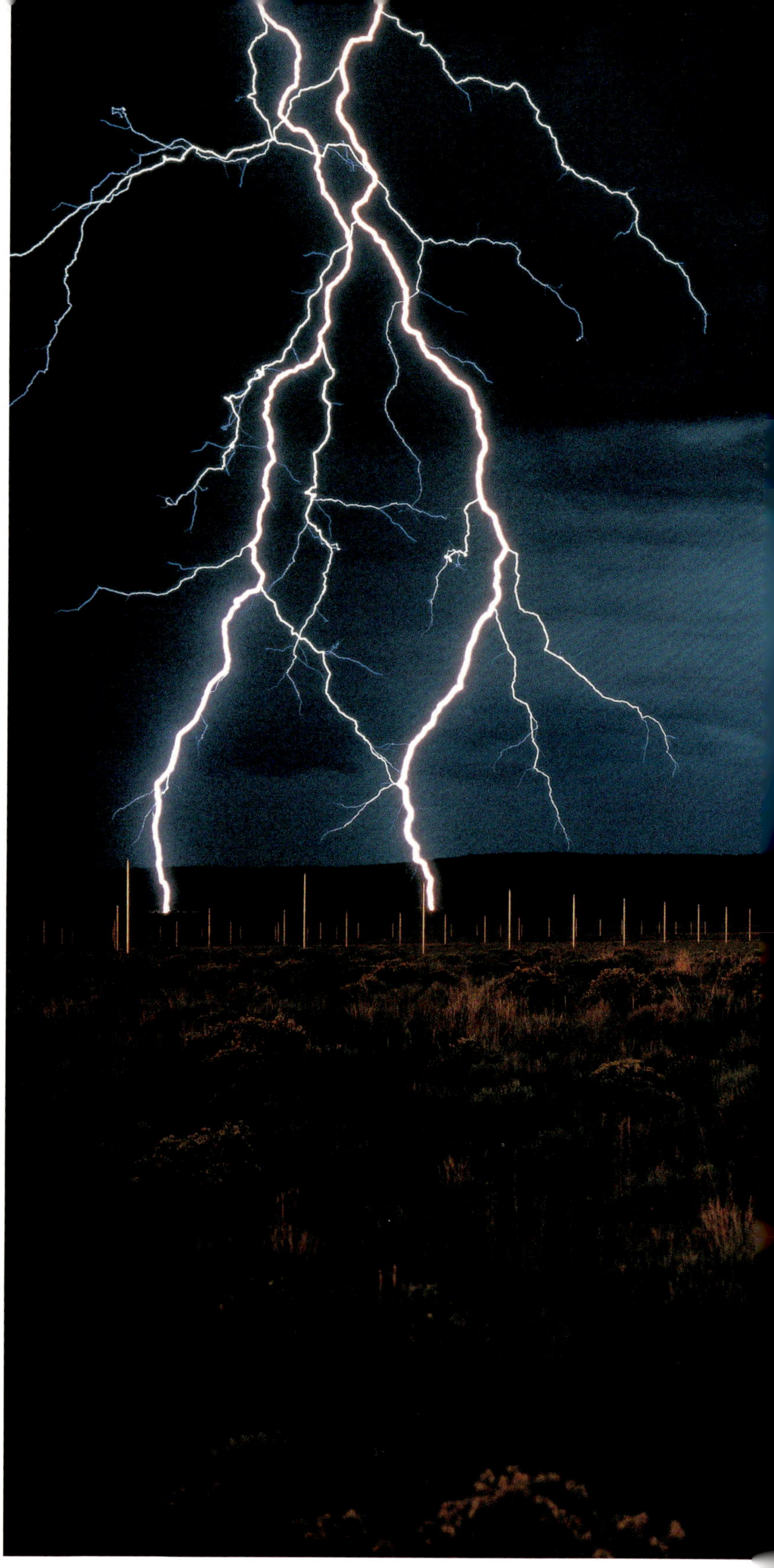

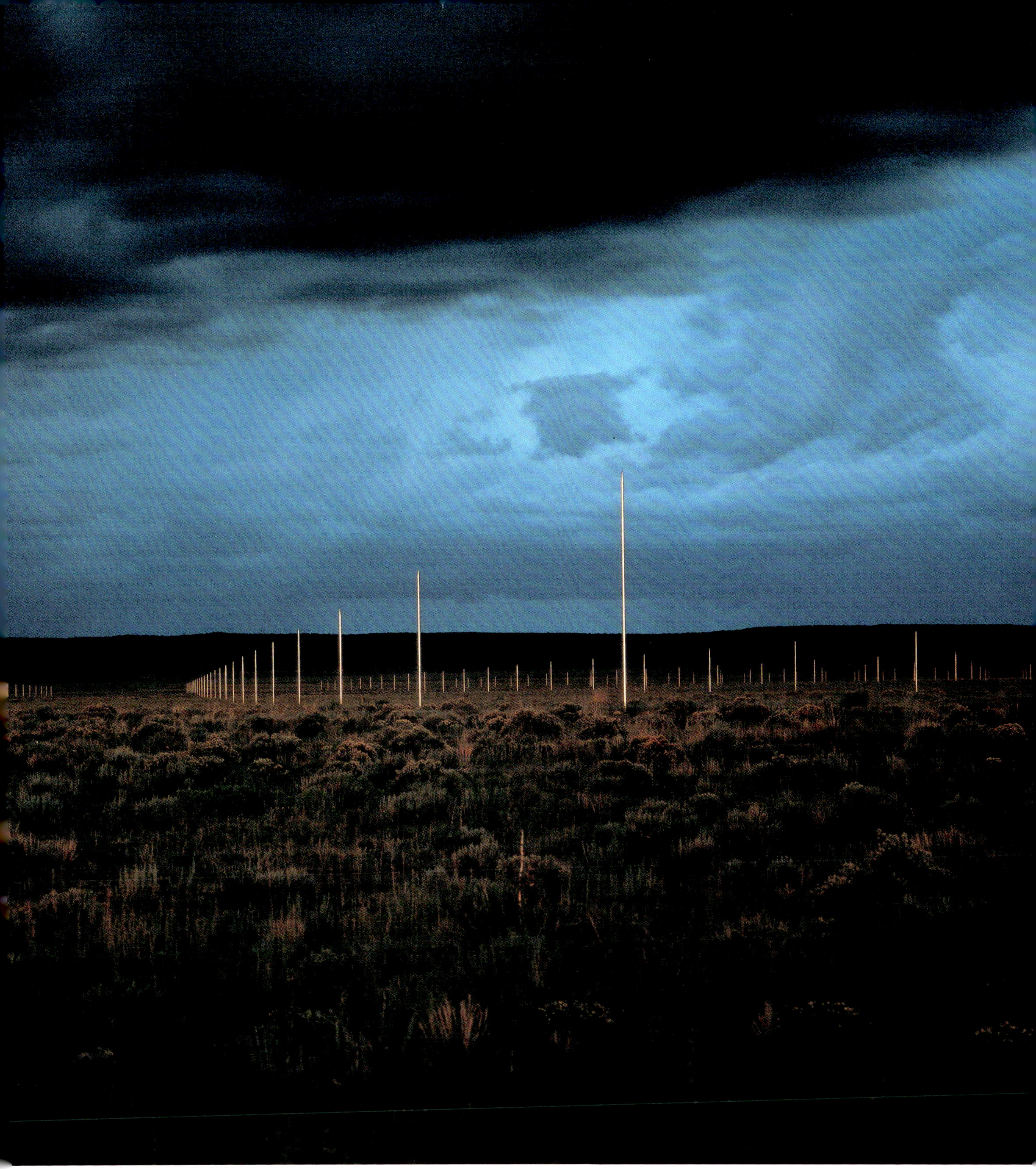

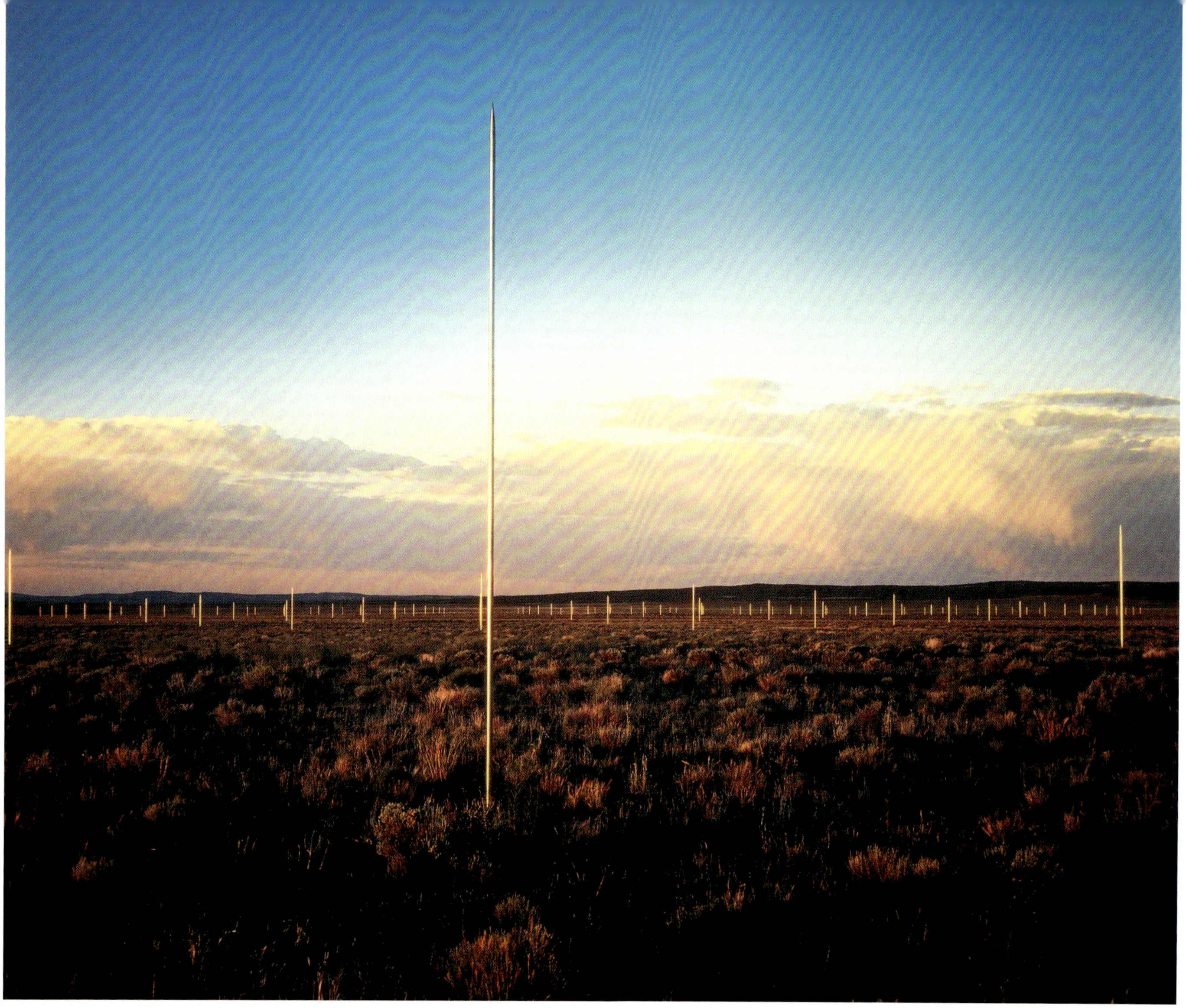

Walter De Maria
The Lightning Field

1977
400 stainless steel rods
Area: c. 1.6 × 1 km (1 × 0.6 miles)
Catron County, NM

In the desert of southwestern New Mexico lies *The Lightning Field* by Walter De Maria, consisting of 400 pointed, polished stainless steel rods, over 20 feet high and arranged in a rectangular grid pattern measuring 1 mile in length. The perceptual and sculptural freedom implied by Puni (see p. 130) is finally realized here. When we approach the work, because of their polished mirror-like surface, the rods appear to merge with the landscape. Only in time does the viewer become aware of the grid and the actual height of the rods relative to the human body. Because of the vast scale and the seemingly endless landscape beyond, the work feels immense – without measure. The rods, the space within and beyond them, the earth and the sky remain as distinct entities until a bolt of lightning strikes and all such separation is instantly erased.

The space actually feels charged like you might be able to touch it, it affects your body: you're being implicated in it, the space becomes substance.

— Richard Serra

We consider space from an entirely different point of view. We consider it as an absolute sculptural element, released from any closed volume, and we represent it from inside with its own specific properties.

— Naum Gabo

It is space that has always haunted me even when my studies of the three dimensions still limited my vision. I didn't possess any other means of experience ... space never ceased to occupy my thoughts ...

— Georges Vantongerloo

Painting may strive to give on a two-dimensional plane, the illusion of space, but it is space itself as a perceived quantity that becomes the peculiar concern of the sculptor. We may say that for the painter space is a luxury; for the sculptor it is a necessity.

— Herbert Read

5

Challenging Solidity

Aspects of the Elements, Movement and Light, are present in all sculptures. In the examples here they are so powerfully extant that the monolithic solidity of the object is questioned. But that does not necessarily mean the sculpture's physicality is less present. The laws of physics state that all matter is in motion and every object seen is dependent upon light. The sculptor explores and utilizes these laws of physics for reasons both material and aesthetic.

Movement

Hellenistic period, Greece

Umberto Boccioni

Alexander Calder

George Rickey

F. X. Messerschmidt

Praxiteles

Vijayanagar period, India

Niki de Saint Phalle and Jean Tinguely

Hagesandros, Athenedoros and Polydoros of Rhodes (attrib.)

Richard Serra

Light

Nancy Holt

Gian Lorenzo Bernini

Herbert George

Chryssa

Jenny Holzer

Robert Irwin

Anthony McCall

Olafur Eliasson

Movement

A change of location. In sculpture, that change may be actual or apparent, in part or as a whole.

We are alive, we move. In sculpture there are two primary aspects of movement. One is *actual*, sometimes referred to as kinetic or real movement, in which time becomes a quantifiable consideration. The other is *implied* movement: an illusion within the sculpture. Nothing in actuality is moving, but parts or the whole appear to the eye to be in motion. It is tempting to say that only the first could be described as empirical, but my discussion here aims to question that assumption, because within each there are aspects of the other. Movement implies a shift, transfer, relocation or flow. Throughout time *implied* movement has been one of sculpture's greatest challenges, as it must contain something of the magical. In literature the most familiar reference to the moving statue is by Ovid in 'Pygmalion and Galatea', in which Pygmalion carves from ivory a statue so real that she returns his kiss.

We affirm that the world's magnificence has been enriched by new beauty: the beauty of speed. A racing car whose hood is adorned with great pipes, like serpents of explosive breath – a racing car that seems to ride on grapeshot is more beautiful than the Victory of Samothrace.

— F. T. Marinetti

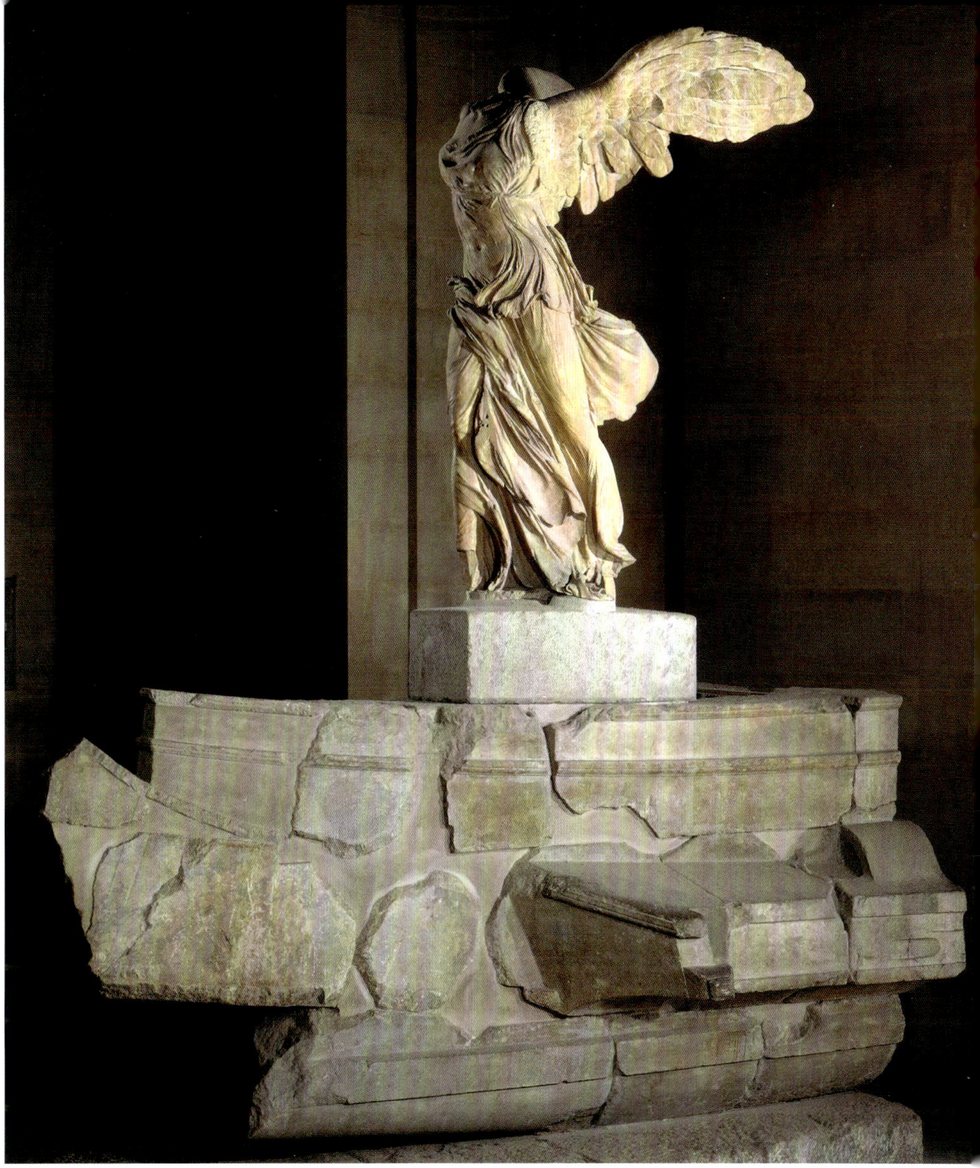

Hellenistic period, Greece
Victory of Samothrace

c. 180 BC
Marble
3.3 m (10 ft 10 in) high
Musée du Louvre, Paris

Marinetti may have sensed correctly that the speed of flight is a measure of beauty, and the *Victory of Samothrace* may be its ultimate sculptural expression. The sculpture was originally positioned – similarly to how it is shown here – on the prow of a carved stone ship, and possibly within a pool of water, an early example of the sculptural fountain. Now the statue and its ship-like base are dramatically positioned at the top of the grand staircase at the Louvre in Paris. As we climb the stairs, the *Victory* appears like a great stone bird preparing to defy gravity and take flight on giant wings. Beginning with the forward-leaning mass of the figure, it is clear that the sculptor has carefully studied how drapery moves with the body, how fabric shifts and stirs in the wind. A river of folds defines the right leg striding forward. Then the drapery gathers turbulence and direction, consuming the trailing left leg at its base. The right leg, formed in part by a thin veil of fabric that streams down its length and billows out, determines the critical angle of movement within the torso. And so the massive composition follows. Because the wings are pitched back they drive the figure forward in that anticipatory moment just before the exhilaration of flight. These compositional tools convey the perceptual illusion of implied movement.

Umberto Boccioni (1882–1916)
Unique Forms of Continuity in Space

1913 (cast 1931)
Bronze
111.2 × 88.5 × 40 cm (43 ⅞ × 34 ⅞ × 15 ¾ in)
Museum of Modern Art, New York

Both Marinetti and Umberto Boccioni were members of the Italian avant-garde art movement, Futurism. Boccioni's *Unique Forms of Continuity in Space* demonstrates the obsession the Italian Futurists had with the machine and with the dynamism of the early twentieth century. The sculpture was originally made in plaster; it was posthumously cast in bronze. Boccioni studied cinematic and photographic images of the body in motion for this dramatic work. The striding figure is propelled forward with all the aerodynamic turbulence and velocity of modern technology. Here, cubic blocks secure the feet to the earth, resulting in a formal paradox. They create a visual tension within the sculpture that results in an intensification of the aesthetic sensation of speed.

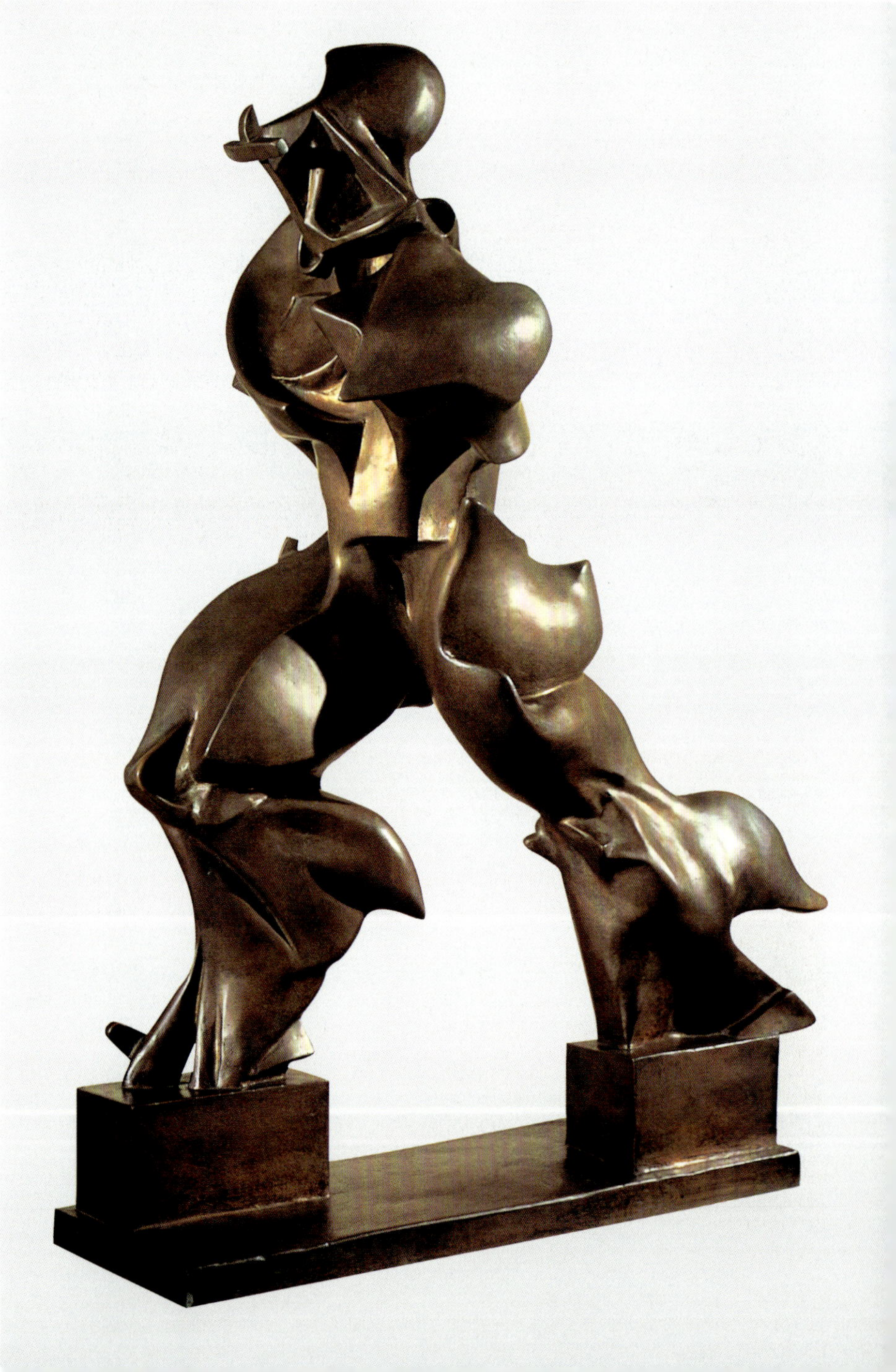

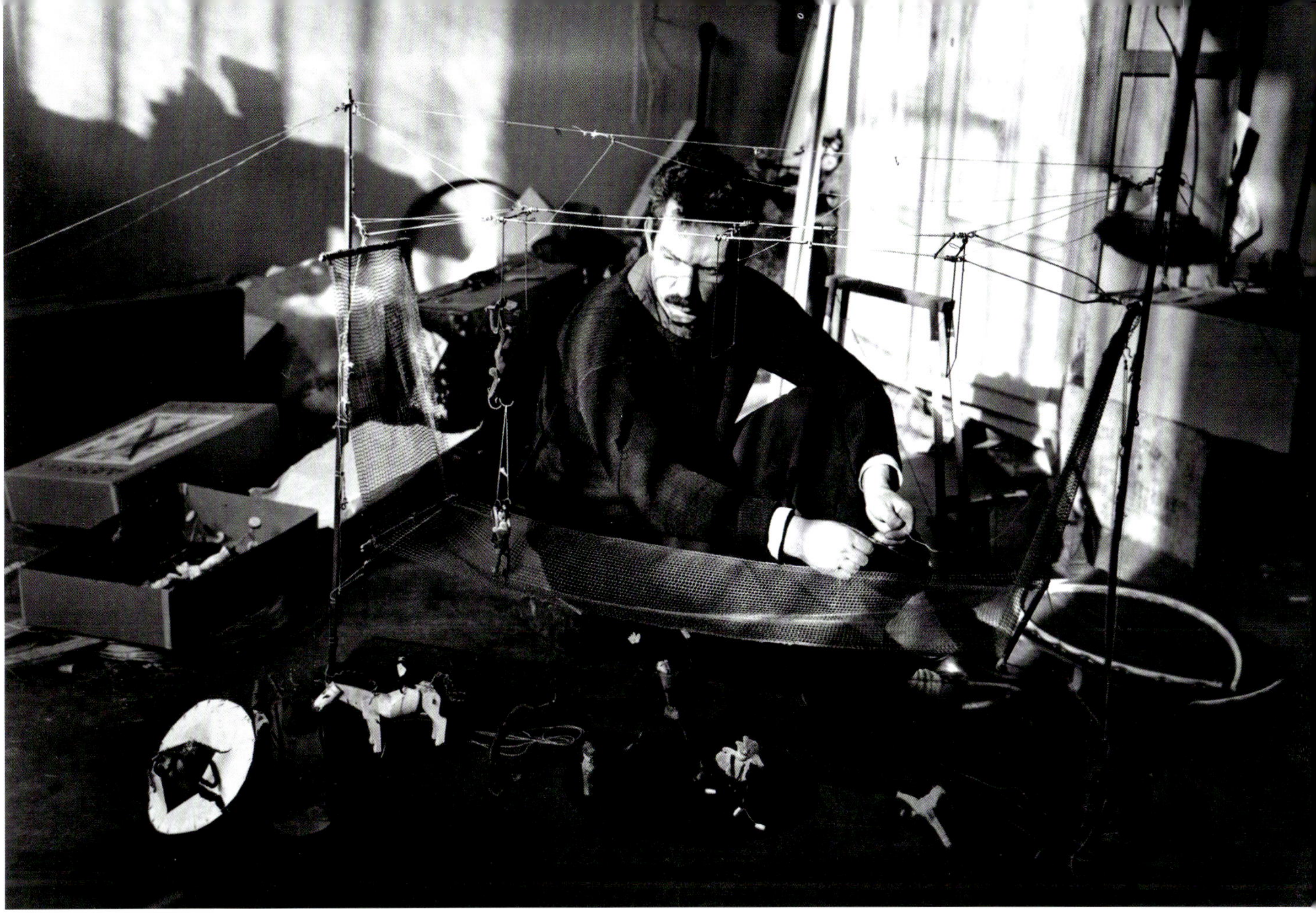

Alexander Calder (1898–1976)
Cirque Calder

1926–31
Wire, wood, metal, cloth, yarn, paper, cardboard, leather, string, rubber tubing, corks, buttons, rhinestones, pipe cleaners and bottle caps
Dimensions variable
Whitney Museum of American Art, New York

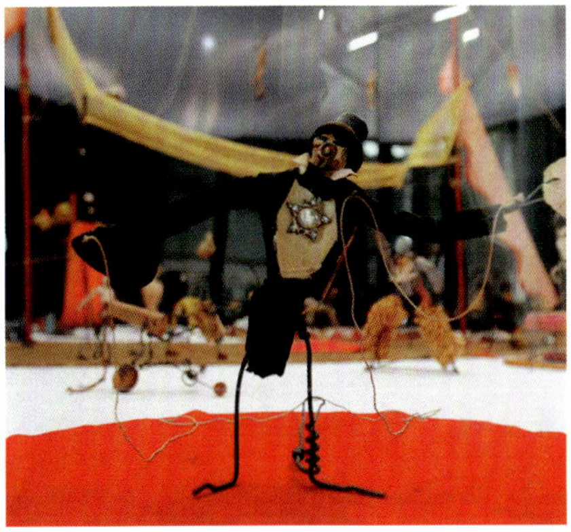

Given the early twentieth century's affection for motors, it is interesting that kinetic sculpture begins with hand power. Before Alexander Calder constructed his mobiles, he created *Cirque Calder*. The photograph above shows Calder in 1929 in Paris, sitting with his assemblage of wire animals and circus performers of all descriptions. High wire and trapeze performers come to life as Calder pulls strings, releases counterweights and presses levers. The animals perform intricate tricks and lope along at a realistic gait, mimicking real animals. In the photograph on the left the ringmaster stands in full black hat and tails announcing the next extravaganza. The accuracy of the individual movements animates each performer, so that all artifice falls away and the viewer is entranced. The performances were accompanied by music from a decrepit 78-rpm record player watched over by Calder's wife Louisa. When the show was over they packed it away into suitcases in preparation for the next performance.

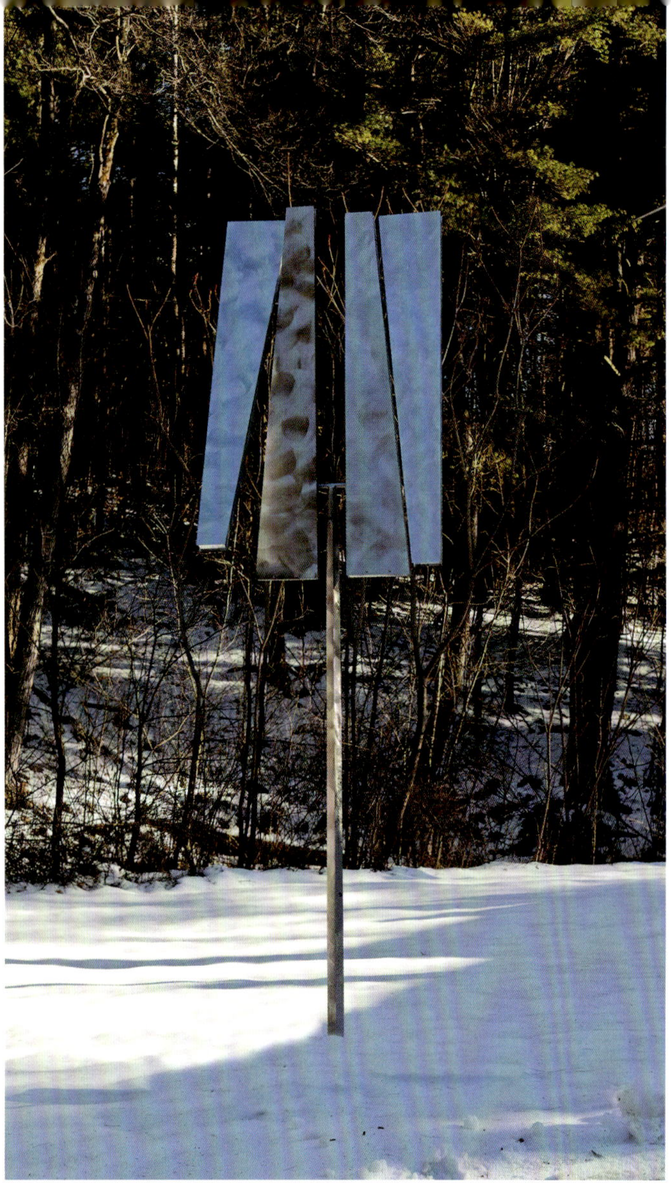

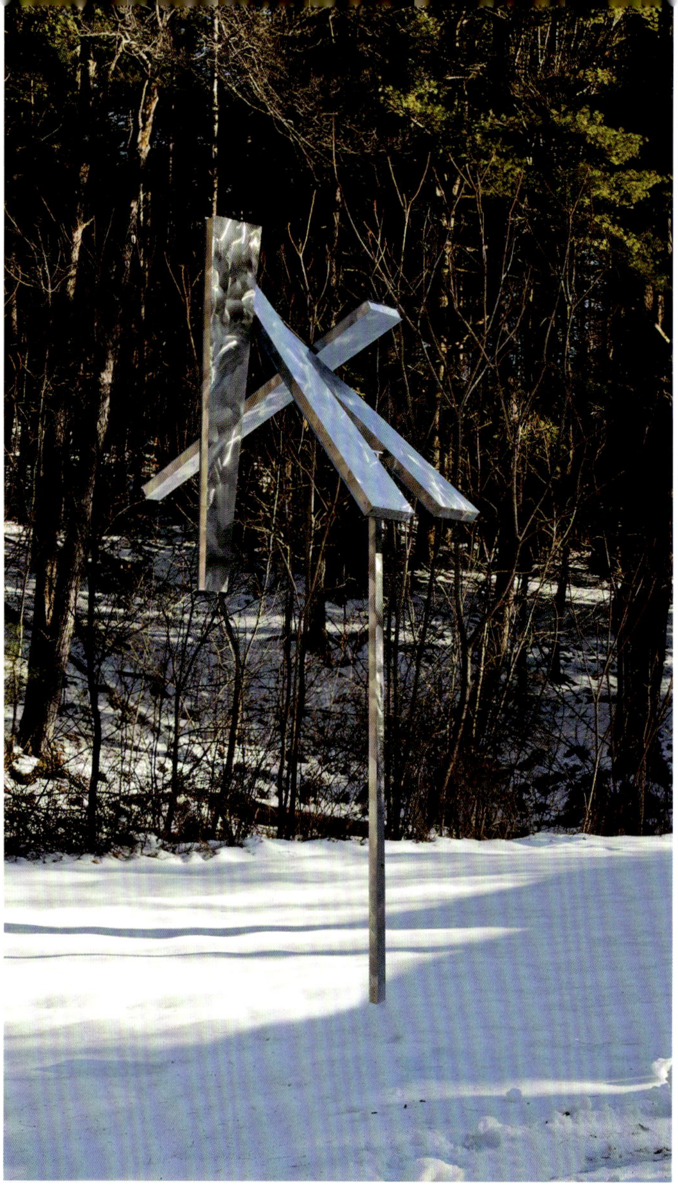

George Rickey (1907–2002)
Four Trapezoids as Two Rectangles III

1986
Stainless steel
354.3 cm (139 ½ in) high
Private collection (edition of 3)

Historically the depiction of the four classical elements – Earth, Fire, Water and Wind – has offered a challenge to the artist. George Rickey spent his life exploring the sculptural potential of the latter. A representative work in stainless steel is entitled *Four Trapezoids as Two Rectangles III*. Four flat surfaces of stainless steel rotate and stir: a system of axles and bearings secures each variously weighted segment to the central pole that is free to rotate. When the wind blows, these finely engineered parts move independently of each other, creating a spatial churning. To reinforce and accentuate their movement, the planes have been ground to reflect the natural light which glints and shifts in waves across their surfaces. For a moment, as seen in the photograph on the left, they become the two rectangles and four trapezoids in the title. But then they break apart again into moving segments, which disrupt the geometric order.

F. X. Messerschmidt (1736–1783)
Number 25
from Character Heads

After 1770
Alabaster
38 cm (15 in) high
Belvedere, Vienna

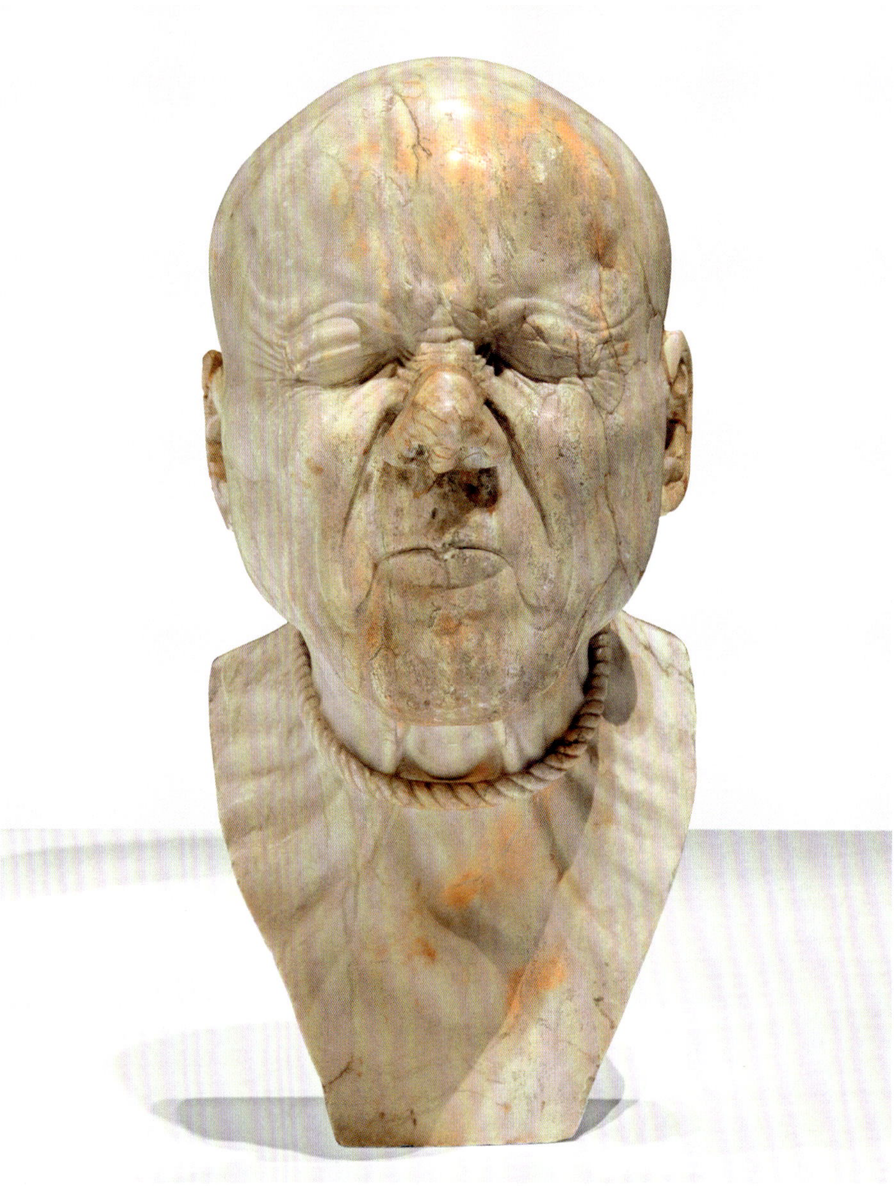

When I look at a sculpture I sometimes speculate as to what may have occurred just before or what will take place immediately after this frozen moment. *Number 25* in the *Character Heads* series by F. X. Messerschmidt is a fascinating example of a sculpture stopped in time. Because of the rope tied around the neck, the over-life-sized portrait is sometimes referred to as *A Hanged Man,* but this posthumous subtitle is misleading, as the rope is tied in a harmless overhand knot at the back. This is the only work in the series in which the head has its eyes closed. We may therefore gaze unimpeded at the man's taut grimace. In doing so we now see that the rope encircling the neck plays a more interesting and complex role: no longer a noose, it becomes a strategic framing device, a stabilizing collar separating the expressive head from the straining neck. The rope visually frees the head to hover in its uncanny levitation, and we are left to conjecture what strange events have already occurred and what may transpire following our confrontation with this defiant scowl.

Praxiteles (4th century BC)
Hermes and the Infant Dionysus

4th century BC
Marble
2.13 m (7 ft) high
Olympia Archaeological Museum

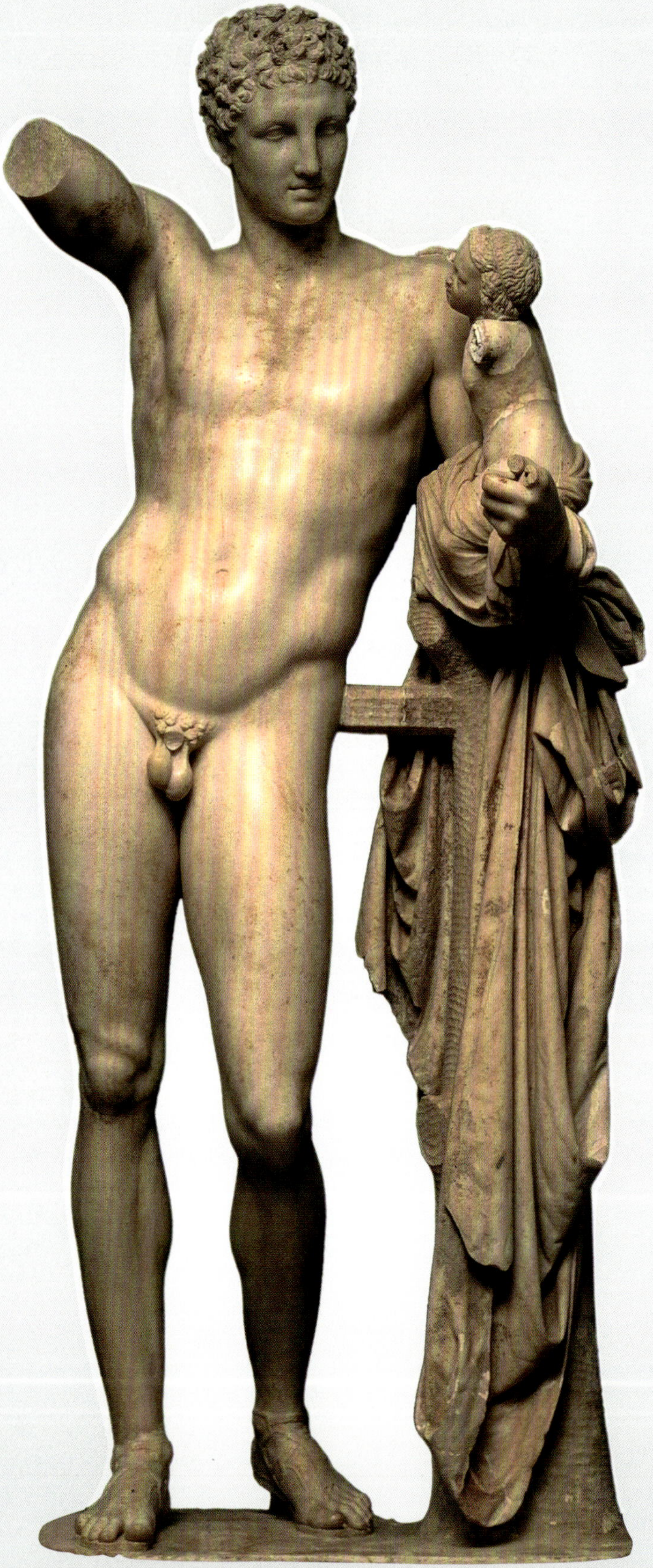

Any discussion about movement in sculpture, and implied movement in particular, must include mention of *Hermes and the Infant Dionysus* by the classical Greek sculptor Praxiteles. The sculpture marks the historic moment when the possibility of animating the standing figure by the use of slight changes in pose becomes a reality. Notice first that the body of Hermes turns, led by the right foot pointing forward. Then the torso rotates in an arching curve with the face of Hermes turning to look at the infant. This implied movement within the figure is called '*contrapposto*' or counter-rotation. Again observe the sculpture. We see that the weight on the legs shifts, with the right leg holding firmly to the ground, allowing the heel of the left foot to be raised. Because the pelvis shifts up to accept and hold the unequal weight, the sculptor reinforces this upward movement on the right side by raising Hermes' right arm. He counters this by bending the left knee and lowering the left arm to encircle the infant. This turning left then right twists the torso toward the child in a graceful natural curve that expresses an embrace. This is how a living body moves.

Vijayanagar period, India
Krishna Dancing on the Head of the Snake Demon Kaliya

1550
Bronze
75 cm (29 ½ in) high
Madras Government Museum

There are generally two choices available to the sculptor wishing to create the illusion of movement within the figure. First is to animate the sculpture itself; the other is to put into motion forms in the figure's immediate environment that, because of their proximity, may impart implied movement. The anonymous Indian sculptor who created this image of the Hindu deity Krishna has done both. Caught in an instant, tensely balanced on one foot, Krishna is poised to dance. The writhing five-headed snake Kaliya activates the composition, inducing the figure to move in time with its body. Now the bending left knee of Krishna compresses the volume of space between it and the curve of the snake; the snake angles out, creating an off-centre dynamic composition. Guided by the extended left arm of Krishna holding the serpent's curving tail, the dance between them continues beyond the confines of the sculpture.

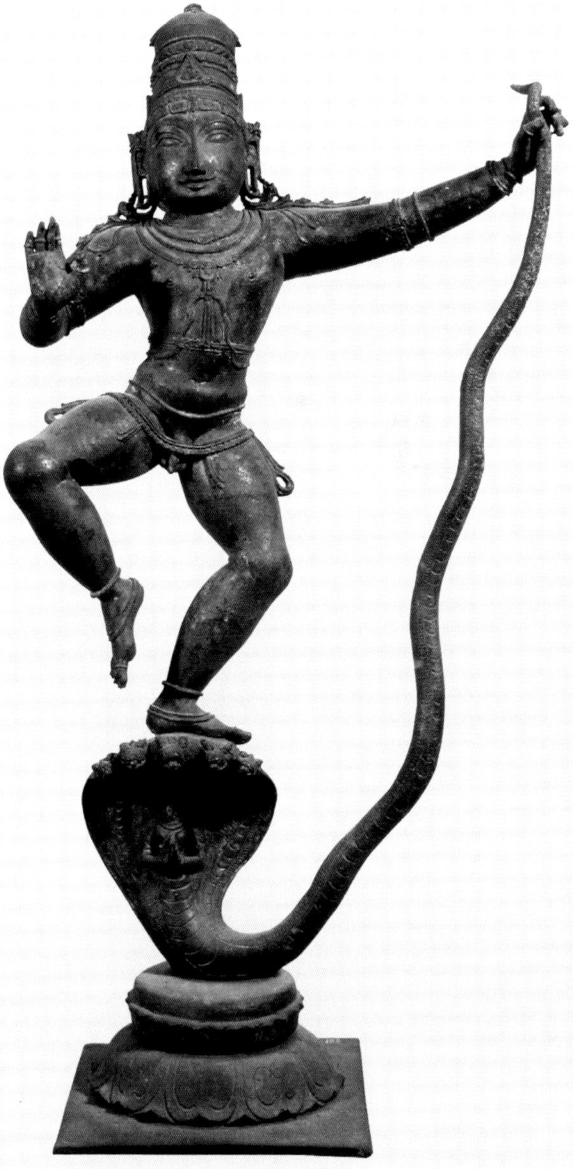

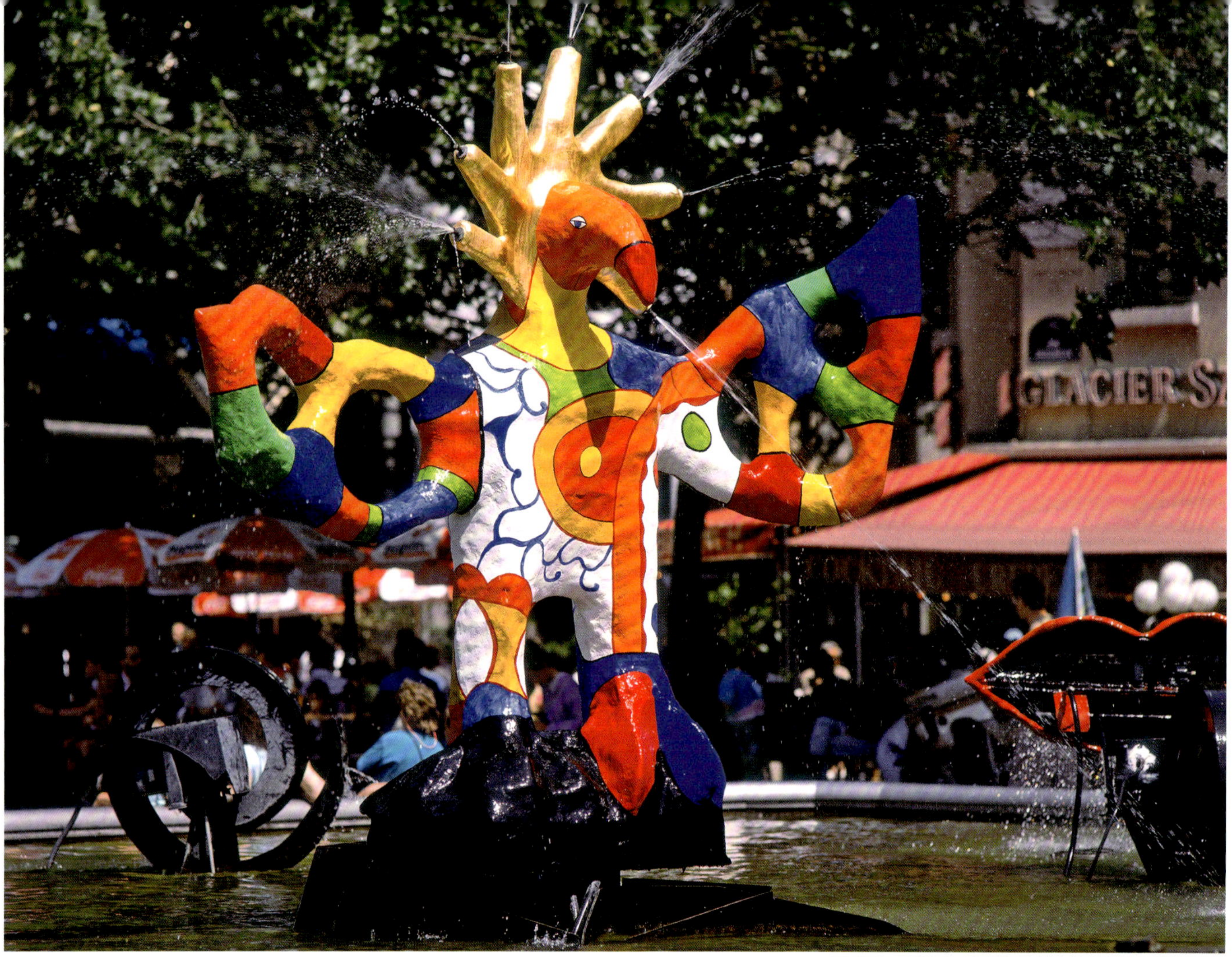

Niki de Saint Phalle (1930–2002) and Jean Tinguely (1925–1991)
Firebird from the Stravinsky Fountain

1982
Various materials
7.32 m (24 ft) high
Place Stravinsky, Paris

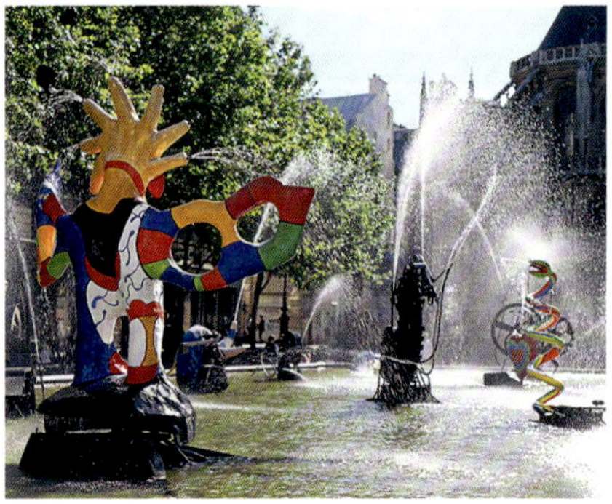

In our urban world, filled with an always-moving dissonance of jumbled sounds, it is a challenge to make something that can attract and hold our attention. In 1982, through the imaginative use of colour, water, sound, form and the movement of all of these, Niki de Saint Phalle and Jean Tinguely created a fountain within a public space in the centre of Paris as a memorial to the music of Igor Stravinsky. The central painted figure by Saint Phalle is about 24 feet high and is an image of the Firebird from the Stravinsky ballet. Her bright red-faced head is encircled with a crown of seven spouting sunray jets of water. The sound of the water spraying from the numerous fantastic Saint Phalle animals and figures, and the mechanical squeaks, clanks and clangs from the Tinguely machines combine with the street sounds of Paris to form a cacophony that is a fitting tribute to the composer's music.

Hagesandros, Athenedoros and Polydoros of Rhodes (attrib.)
Laocoön

Copy after c. 42–20 BC
Marble
1.84 m (6 ft ½ in) high
Musei Vaticani, Rome

In the history of sculpture it is difficult to find a more compelling example of the fulfillment of the challenge to capture implied movement than in this marble sculpture. Assumed to be the work of three sculptors from the island of Rhodes, it portrays the moment when the Trojan priest Laocoön and his sons are devoured by two sea serpents sent by Poseidon. The three figures are fully resolved in three dimensions, their movement almost more dramatic from the back than from the front. Similar to pedimental sculpture, the most imporant figure is centred and taller than the others. The writhing serpents physically and visually bind the composition together, turning the whole sculpture into a seething knotted desperate struggle. The other characteristics of sculpture are all but lost. Only Movement remains.

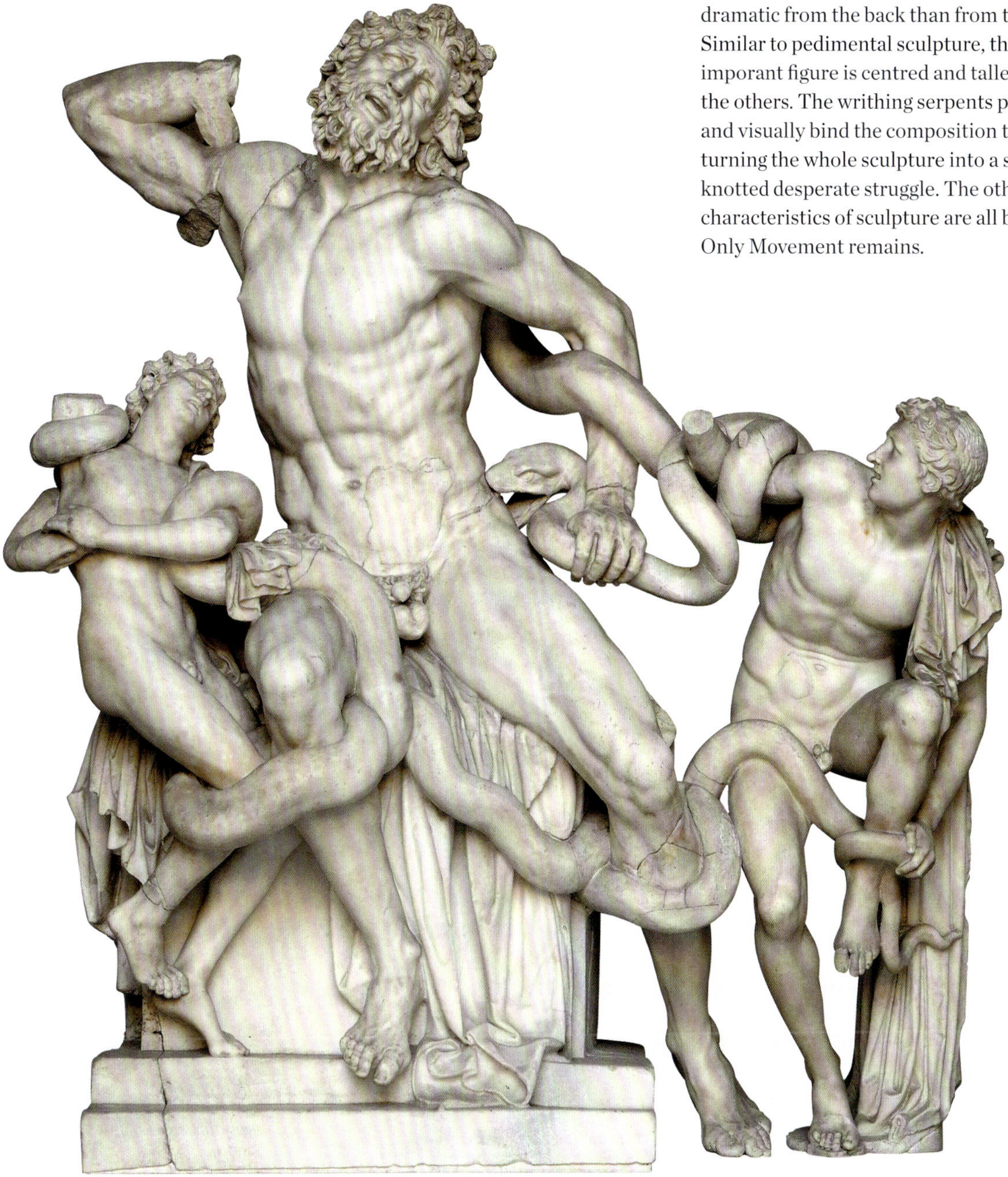

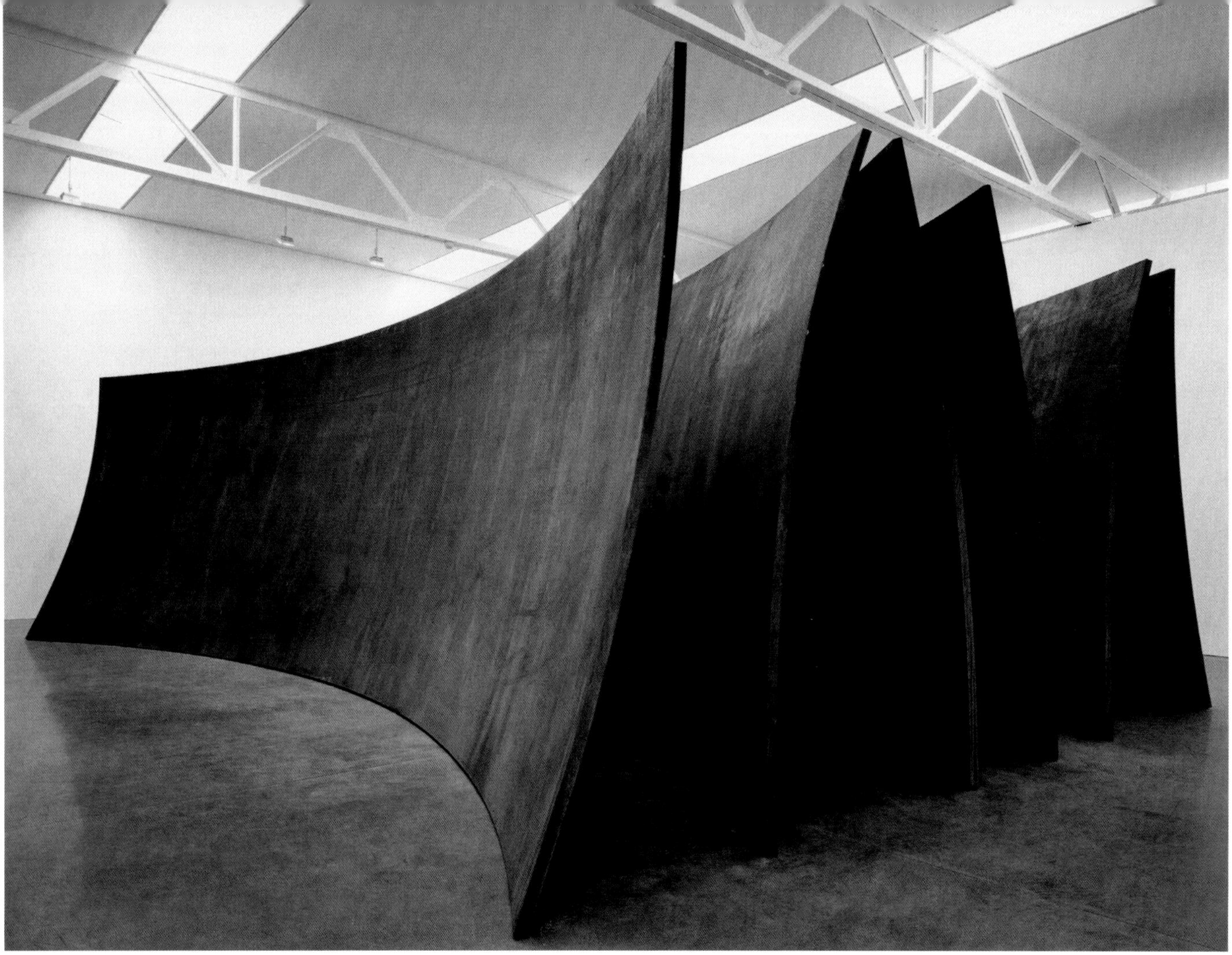

Richard Serra (b. 1939)
Betwixt the Torus and the Sphere

2001
Corten steel
3.6 × 11.4 × 8.1 m (11 ft 10 in × 37 ft 6 in × 26 ft 7 in)
Collection Leon Black, Bedford, New York

Richard Serra's *Betwixt the Torus and the Sphere* is part of a series of enormous rolled and forged ribbon-like Corten steel sculptures. From without, the parts are architectonic fluid surfaces seemingly in a constant state of oscillation. In addition to being looked at, this is a sculptural environment that must be experienced from within its gigantic corridors, as it is a kinaesthetic/bodily journey. While walking through its dark passageways we experience a constantly rolling, expanding and contracting series of curving hard steel surfaces and defined volumes that challenge the body's equilibrium. These forms push, pull and twist what I call our 'self-space'. We are compelled by the sculpture to move in tandem with the yaw and pitch of the surfaces. Here our experience is a primarily visceral sensation – one that we feel deep within the body. *Betwixt the Torus and the Sphere* is a work that manifests both aspects of movement – the real and the implied.

Suddenly I move my leg, or suddenly I move my arm, suddenly I move my thumbs, so we are in the physical, we are in the body's language now. The stone becomes the body ... what happens in my body is repeated in the stone, except that then it has to add a formal meaning.

— Louise Bourgeois

... sculpture is a medium peculiarly located at the juncture between stillness and motion, time arrested and time passing. From this tension, which defines the very condition of sculpture, comes its enormous expressive power.

— Rosalind E. Krauss

Why must art be static? You look at an abstraction, sculpted or painted, an entirely exciting arrangement of planes, spheres, nuclei, entirely without meaning. It would be perfect, but it is always still. The next step in sculpture is motion.

— Alexander Calder

Light

Either emitted from an energy source within the sculpture, or the natural or artificial light falling on the surface of the sculpture.

Light reveals to the eye the multitude of forms that inhabit our world, but of all the Elements, Light may also be the most transitory. Light creates shadows; it articulates and gives specificity to form. Light also reveals the character of materials: from the bright reflections of a hard metallic polished bronze, to softer light-absorbent materials like wood, cloth and some translucent stones. It is often difficult to separate the experience of a work from the quality of the light that illuminates it.

Within sculpture, Light functions in four different ways. The first and most obvious is *natural* light – sunlight shining on or indirectly illuminating a sculpture. The second is *incandescent* light – artificial light shining on a sculpture, for example in a gallery or museum, where it is usually sourced from track lighting on the ceiling and does not change. The third is *emanating* light – light that is in some way produced by the sculpture. The fourth, and least obvious, is *material* light – light as matter to be shaped and formed like other sculptural materials.

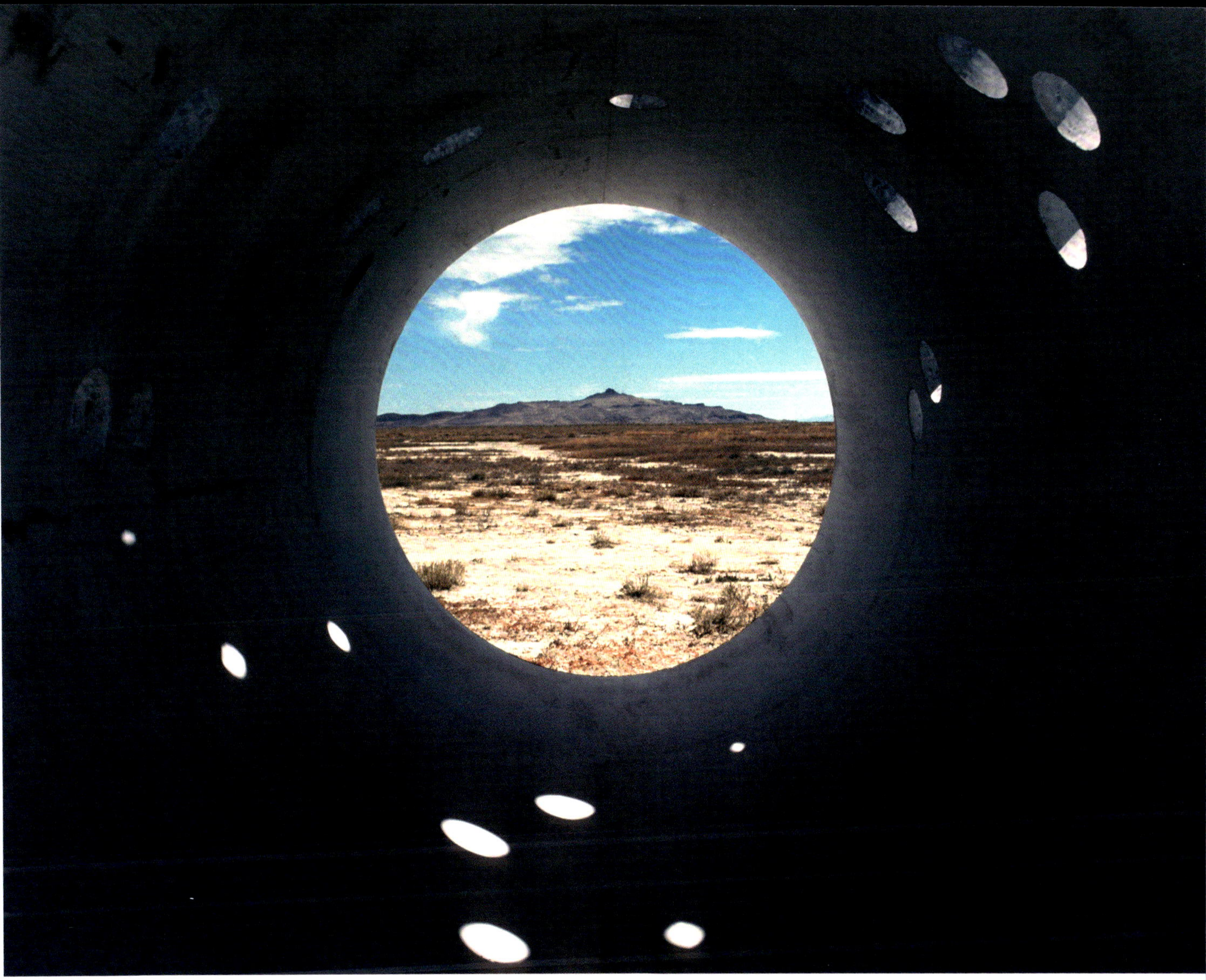

Nancy Holt (1938–2014)
Sun Tunnels

1973–6
Concrete
Each: 2.44 m (9 ft) diameter × 5.5 m (18 ft) long
Great Basin Desert, UT

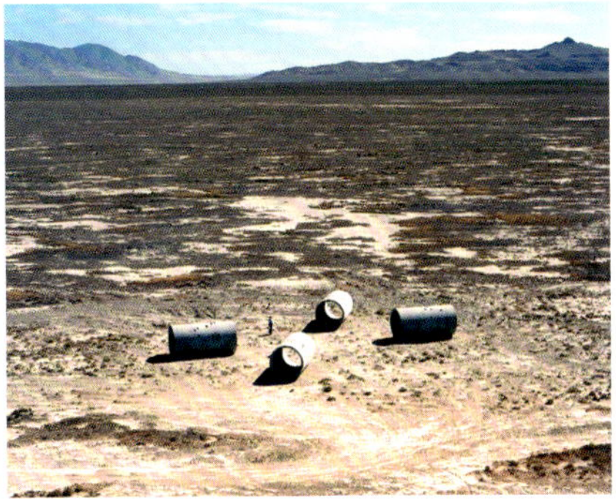

In 1976 Nancy Holt constructed *Sun Tunnels* in the desert outside Lucin, Utah, using the constantly changing light of day to create a work physically ordered by natural light. Four concrete cylinders, or tunnels, are arranged to form an 86-foot-wide open cross. The axes of the tunnels align on the summer and winter solstice so that each tunnel reacts differently to the natural light. On the solstice the tunnels frame the sun as it passes the horizon at sunrise and sunset. A series of holes pierce each cylinder. These holes vary in size according to the magnitude of the stars they represent, and correspond to the patterns of four celestial constellations. As we enter the tunnels, the apertures project a dazzling array of moving spots of bright desert sunlight onto the insides of the darkened tunnels. The tunnels also frame views out to the seemingly immeasurable natural landscape beyond.

Gian Lorenzo Bernini (1598–1680)
Ecstasy of St Teresa

1647–52
Marble
3.5 m (11 ft 5 ¾ in) high
Santa Maria della Vittoria, Rome

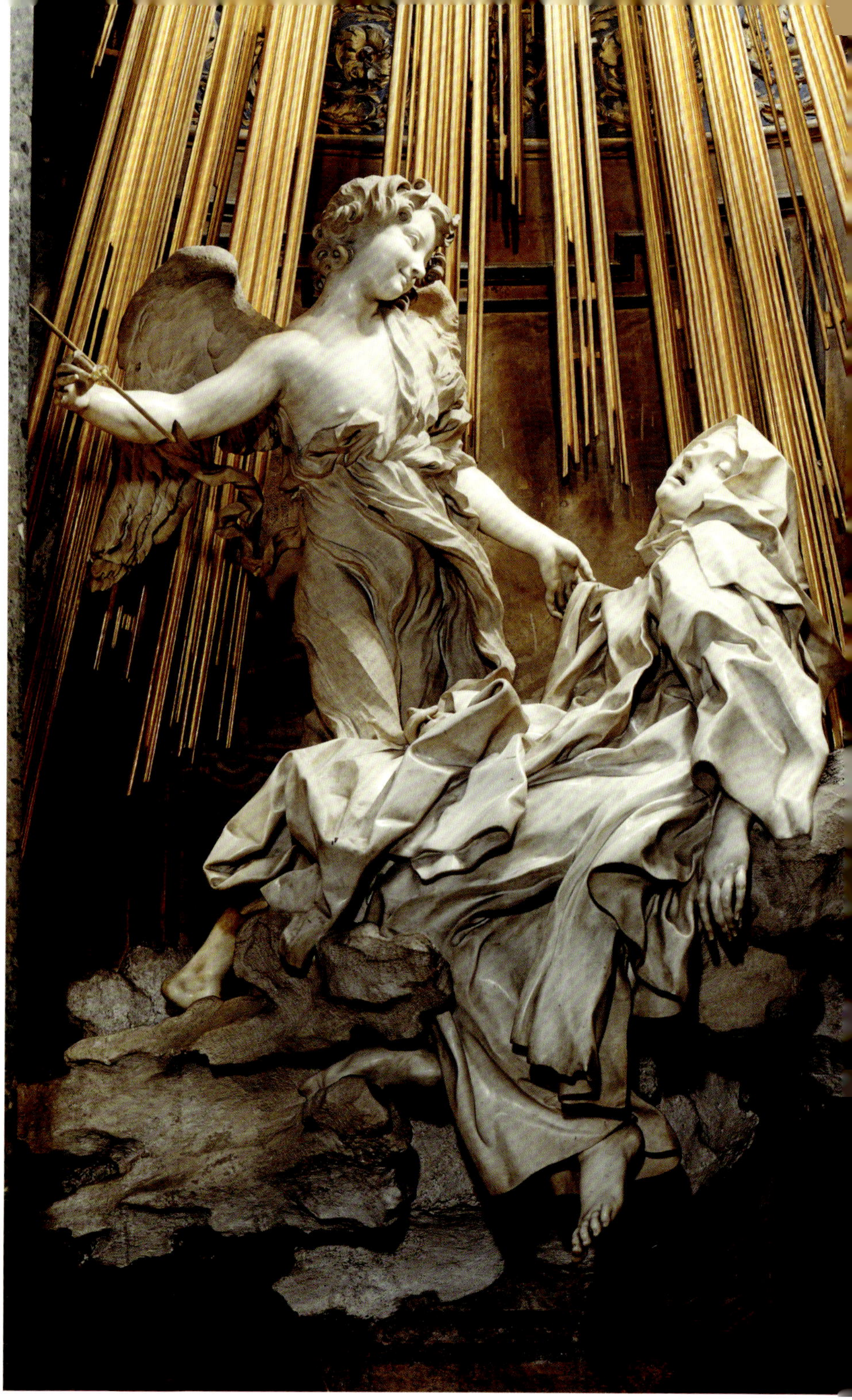

In the past sculptors often exploited Light for its emotional symbolic power. In his *Ecstasy of St Teresa* in the Cornaro chapel in the church of Santa Maria della Vittoria in Rome, Gian Lorenzo Bernini carefully directed natural light, using it as a dramatic compositional device. He constructed a glazed light chamber high on the chapel wall, extending it out to catch as much light as possible. This light gives vibrant life to the burst of golden rays streaming down from above. The rays in turn illuminate St Teresa and her attending angel holding a golden spear. The point of the spearhead glints as St Teresa levitates in ecstasy waiting for its fire to be plunged into her once again. The radiating light also gives dramatic energy to the drapery and gestures that are the other emotive forces in this majestic, convulsive work.

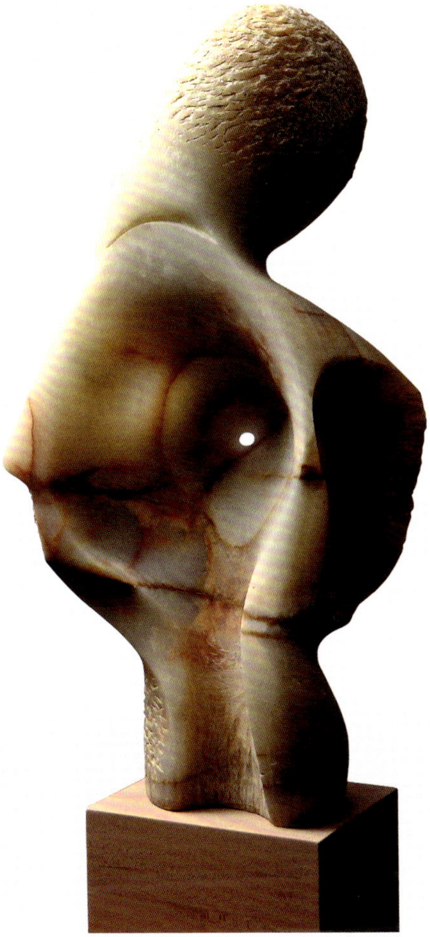

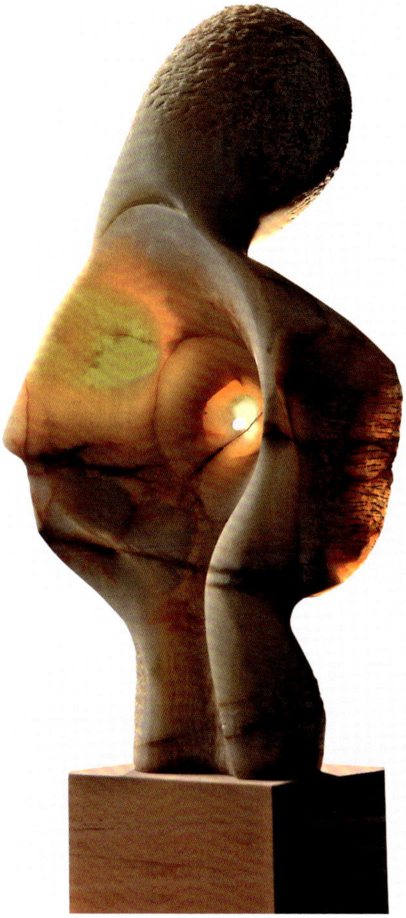

Herbert George (b. 1940)
Composite Likeness #2

2008
Onyx
71.1 × 38.1 × 25.4 cm (28 × 15 × 10 in)
Collection of the artist

Composite Likeness #2 is one of my carved onyx sculptures. It is an example of incandescent light. Because of the glass-like translucency of onyx, if properly illuminated, it will glow in those areas that have been ground thin. Compare the two views here. In the photograph on the right, with the addition of a single light, three areas appear to be illuminated from within the sculpture. Contrast these areas of light and fully articulated form with the relative flatness in the photograph on the left. This is especially true of the glowing stone that surrounds the iris-like concavity in the centre of the sculpture. With suitable lighting the viewer is able to distinguish these areas of membrane thinness from the other more massive opaque forms. Such surface changes in thickness, specific textures and the character of the forms in general would have been difficult to discern in a relatively neutral light. But with the right illumination the stone reveals a clarity of form that was previously absent.

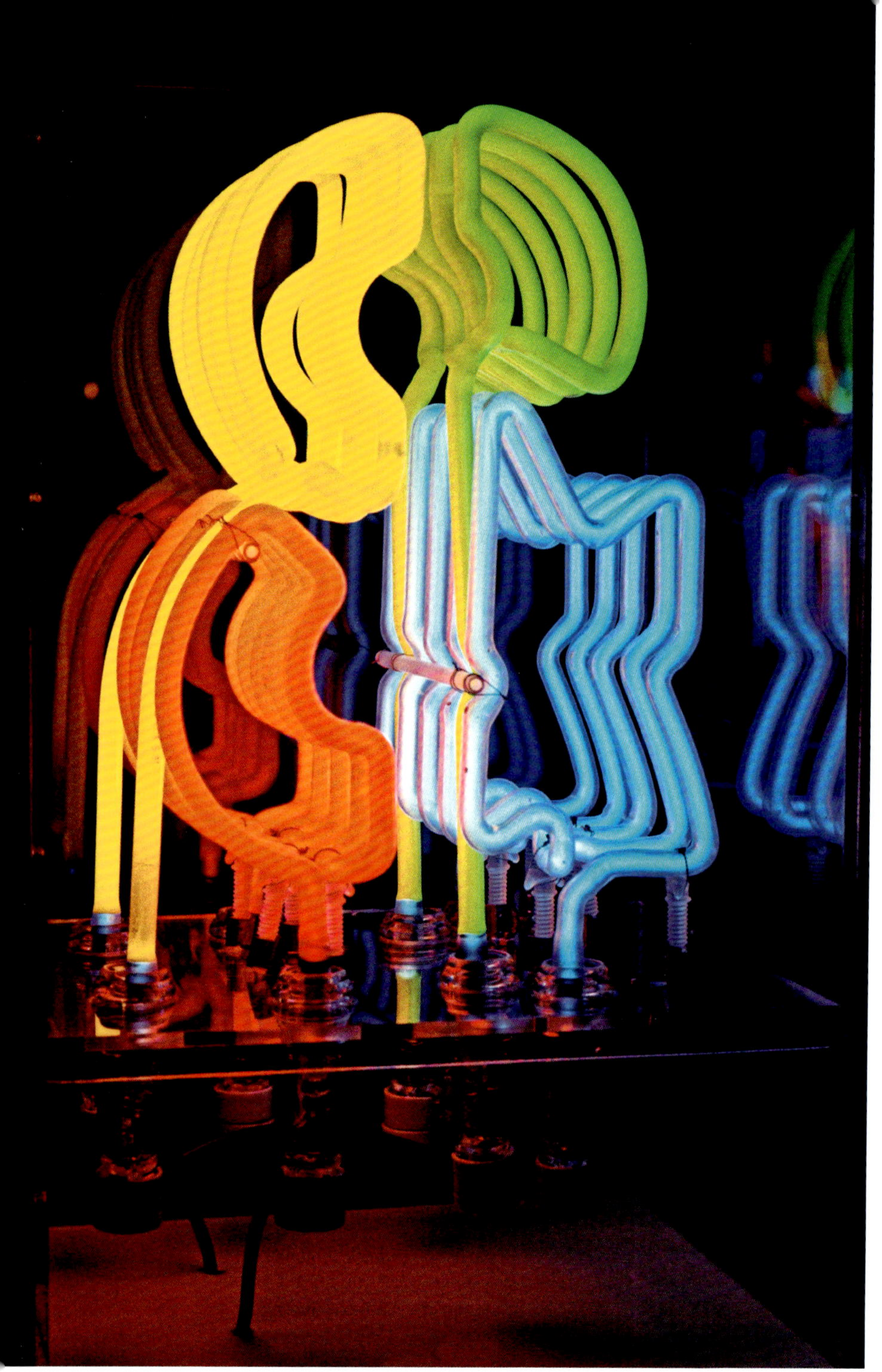

Chryssa (1933–2013)
Ampersand III

1965
Neon tubing and Plexiglas
73.7 × 34.9 × 29.8 cm (29 × 13 ¾ × 11 ¾ in)
Indianapolis Museum of Art, IN

Made from neon, a popular material used for commercial signs, *Ampersand III* is its own light source and in turn casts light on the objects that surround it – an example of emanating light. In the 1960s, Chryssa constructed a series of sign-form sculptures inspired by the giant advertisements in Times Square in New York. Here, the artist takes one graphic element from those signs – the ampersand – and repeats this logogram in various colours of neon tubing. She then places them into a clear Plexiglas box that displays the usually hidden neon apparatus. The blinking neon lights reflect off the surfaces of the box and project out into the surrounding space where they mix, dissolve and become a mantra in light.

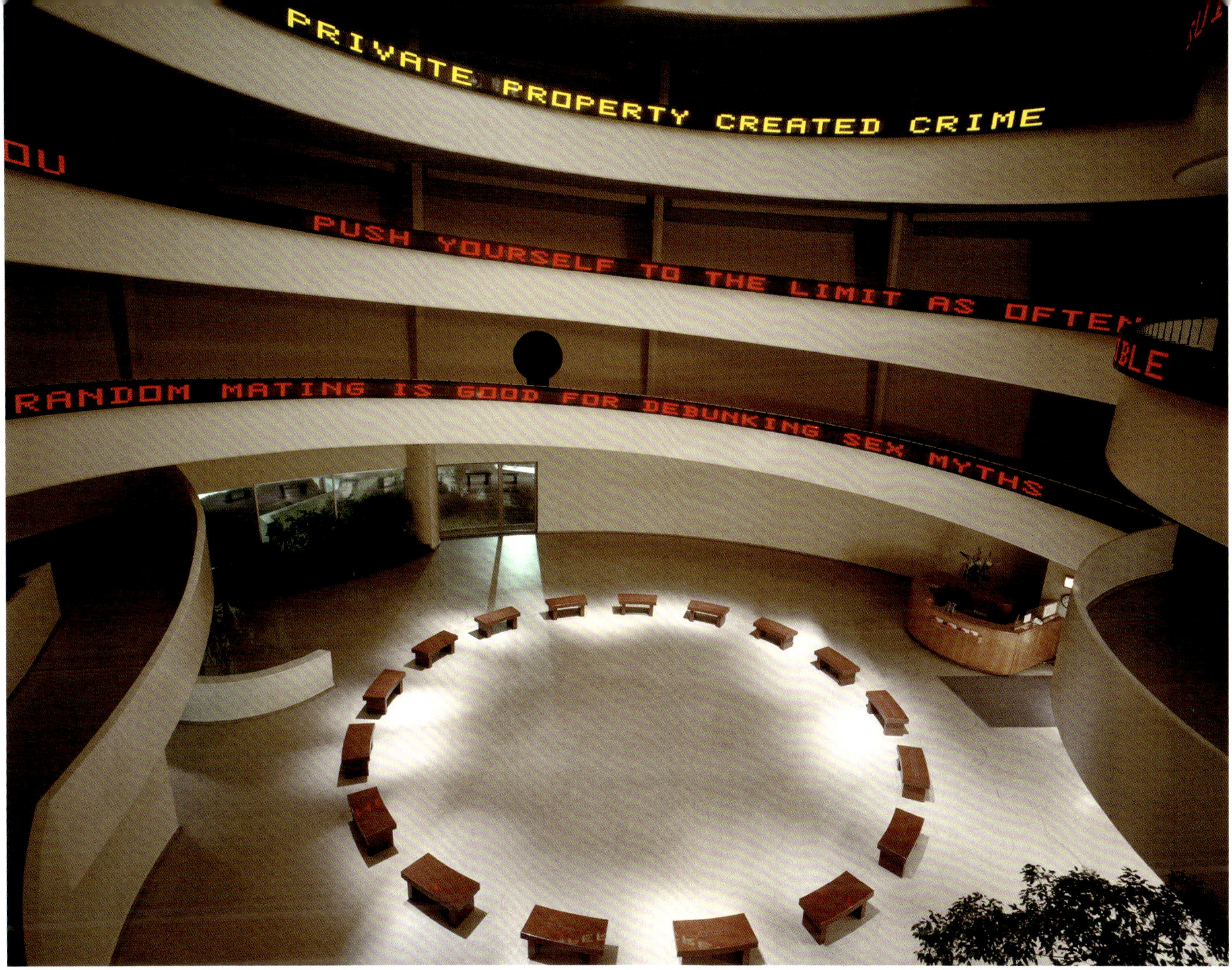

Jenny Holzer (b. 1950)
Untitled (Selections From Truisms, Inflammatory Essays, The Living Series, The Survival Series, Under a Rock, Laments, and Child Text)

1989
Extended helical tricolour LED electronic-display signboard
Dimensions variable
Solomon R. Guggenheim Museum, New York

In the latter part of the twentieth century, light emitting diode (LED) electronic display technology began to replace neon for commercial signage. *Untitled (Selections From Truisms, ...)* by Jenny Holzer explored the many advantages of LED technology, which permitted her to construct coloured moving words that could be easily programmed for size, content and speed. In this installation they form a seemingly infinite spiral of phrases and sentences of light that both resemble and mock the high moral sayings cut into the stone facades of neoclassical buildings. Like the Chryssa work, the emanating light from the words projects onto its surrounding surfaces, making its reflection glow.

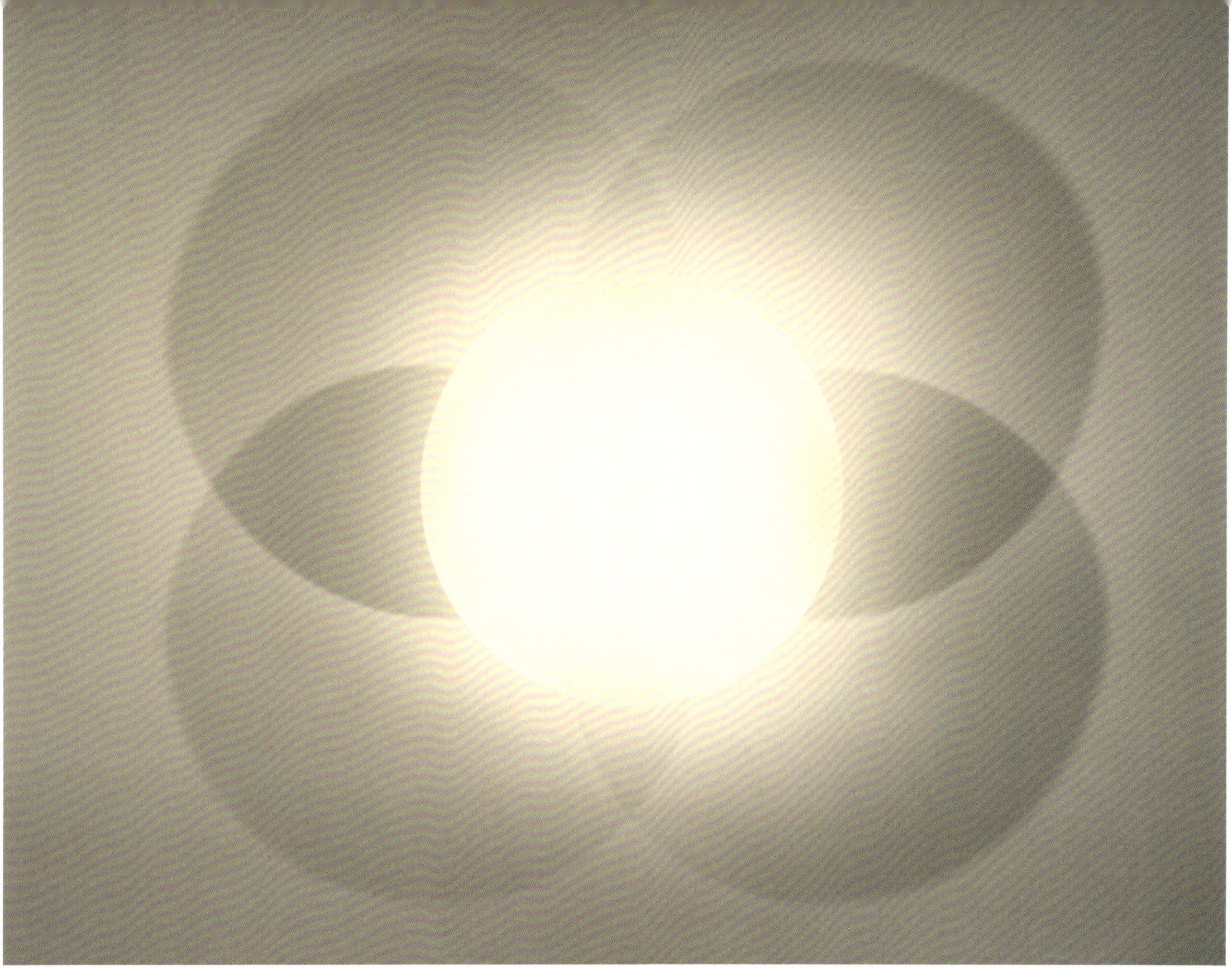

Robert Irwin (b. 1928)
Untitled

1968
Synthetic polymer paint on aluminium
153.2 cm (60 ⅜ in) diameter
Museum of Modern Art, New York

Emanating light might be considered more broadly in terms of how and to what degree reflected light impresses itself upon the perception of the viewer. Robert Irwin's *Untitled* is a circular, 60-inch-wide spray-painted off-white convex cast acrylic disc. It is cross-lit by two incandescent lights on the floor and two on the ceiling. The disc is held one foot away from the wall. Because the lights are an equal distance from each other, they cast four symmetrical, overlapping veils onto the disc and thus four similarly shaped shadows onto the wall behind. And because of the emanating/reflected light being projected onto and reflecting off the disc, the shadows the lights cast create the sensation that its outer edge has dissolved into the surrounding light. The disc now becomes a blurred immateriality, levitating within the light of the wall behind.

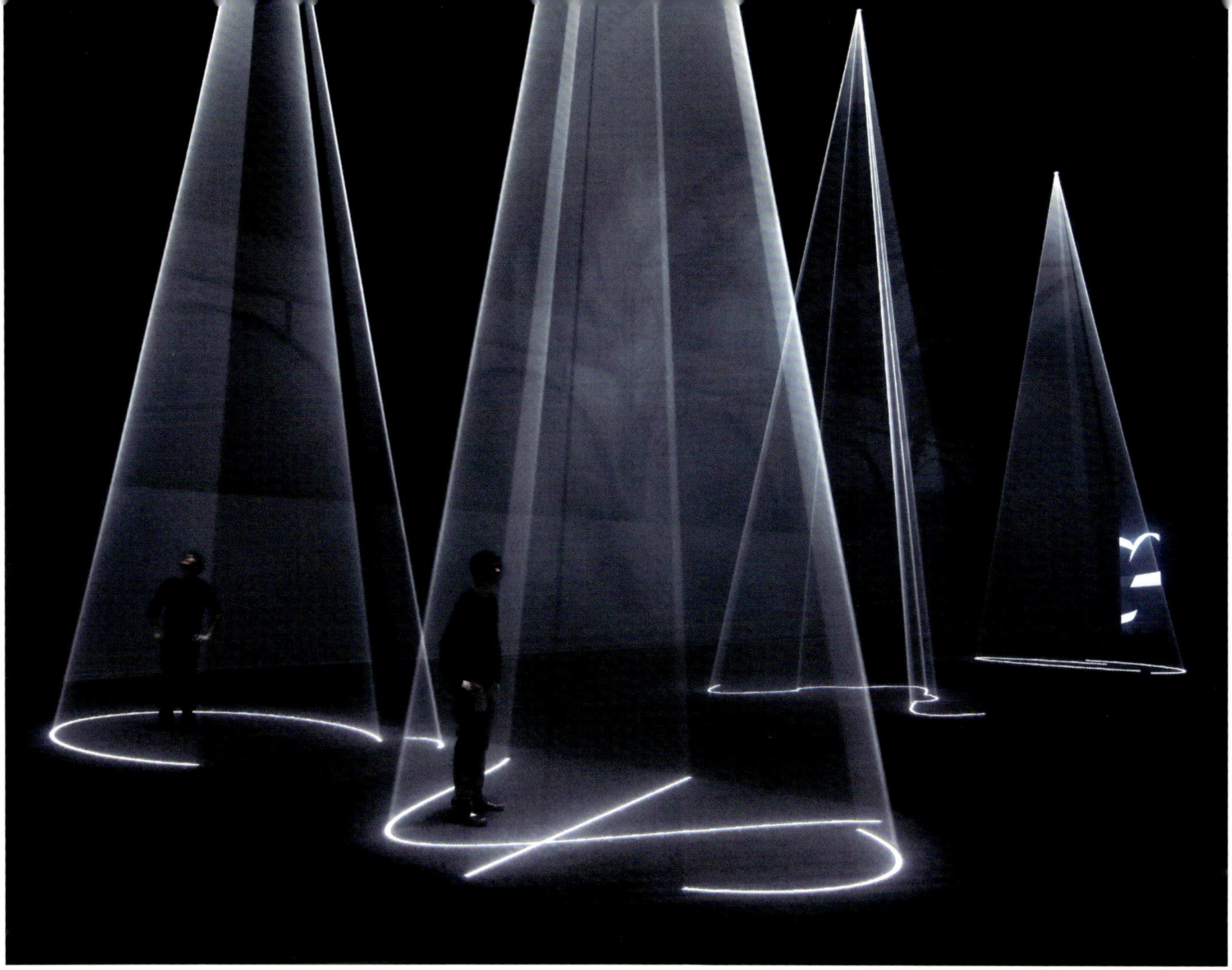

Anthony McCall (b. 1940)
Five Minutes of Pure Sculpture

Hamburger Bahnhof – Museum für Gegenwart, Berlin
20 April – 12 August 2012
Installation view

We think of light as existing beyond touch – a weightless, invisible projection of energy. *Five Minutes of Pure Sculpture* challenges those assumptions, and light's true materiality becomes an experience. It is composed of separate 'cones' produced by digital projectors mounted on the ceiling of a dark gallery space. Under normal circumstances these beams of projected light cannot be seen, so vapour is pumped into the exhibition space to reveal these conical volumes of light. What appears to be static in the photograph is in reality a series of slowly moving animated blades of projected light. Their traces can be seen as white light 'drawings' on the floor. They move in a crisscross computer-controlled formation, slowly bending, arcing and flexing through a repeated cycle. These veils appear to have such materiality that viewers reach out to test their solidity, breaking the membrane of light. A similar thing occurs when we move into the centre of a cone to examine the beams of light on the floor. From without, each cone appears to have a graphic solidity that belies its actual material. But light possessing mass is an illusion; it is contrary to our experience.

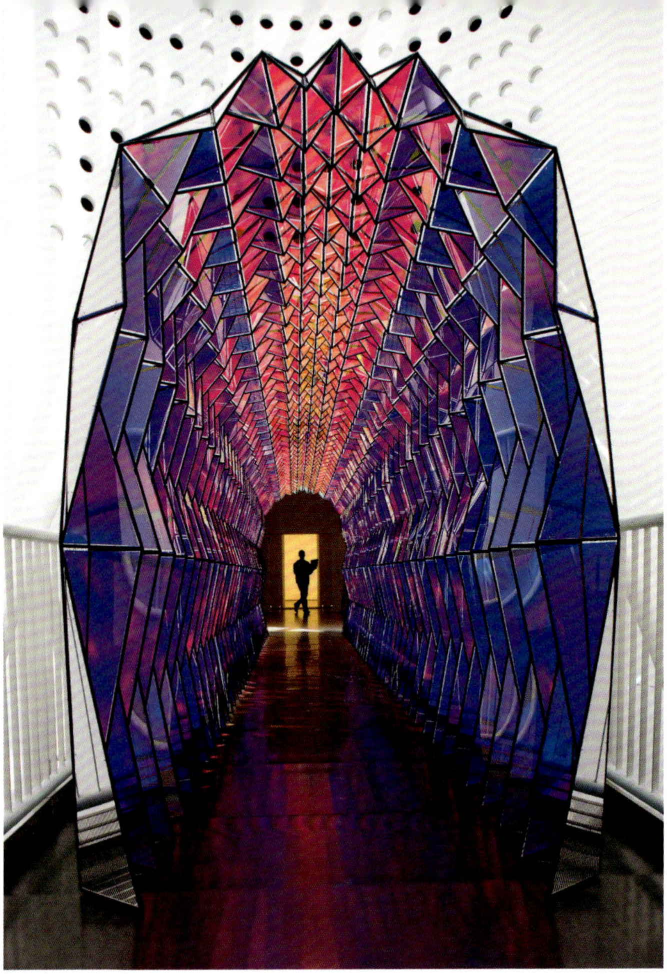

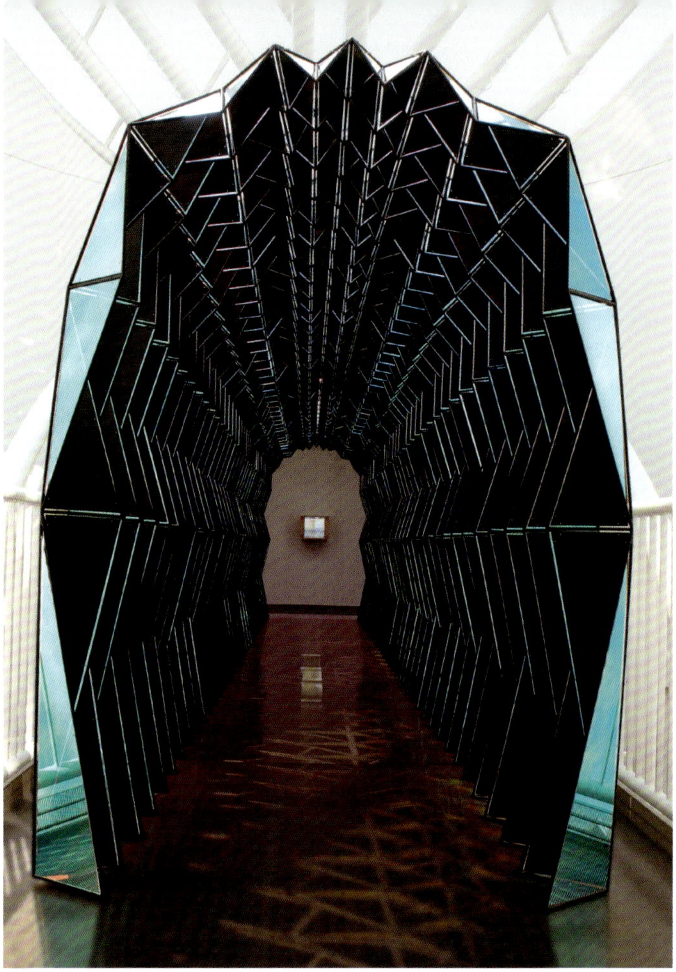

Olafur Eliasson (b. 1967)
One-Way Colour Tunnel

2007
Stainless steel, colour-effect acrylic, mirrors
2.54 × 1.78 × 10.49 m (8 ft 4 in × 5 ft 10 in × 34 ft 5 in)
San Francisco Museum of Modern Art, CA

One-Way Colour Tunnel was constructed for the skylight bridge at the top of the San Francisco Museum of Modern Art in 2007 by Olafur Eliasson and combines aspects of all the previous examples we have seen of Light. The structure is composed of hundreds of triangular acrylic mirrors that are placed within a logarithmically expanding sequence. These act as one-directional refracted-light prisms. When the viewer walks through the tunnel in one direction the volume becomes a cathedral of vibrant colours, but as we look behind or walk back in the other direction, the colours fade into the opaque muted steel structure. By a change in direction, and a change in the quality of light, the same composition yields a radically different emotional and sensory response.

We do not exist! We are only plays of light in space. More air, more light, more space!

— Medardo Rosso

One might not think of light as a matter of fact, but I do. And it is, as I said, as plain and open and as direct an art as you will ever find.

— Dan Flavin

Whenever you look at light, basically it's just air. It has no tactileness to it. It's totally without density.

— James Turrell

Of the original phenomena, light is the most enthralling.

— Leonardo da Vinci

Light
Light
The visible reminder Invisible Light.

— T. S. Eliot

6

The Effects of Past Experience

The final Element, Memory, is the most ephemeral of the fourteen as it resides totally within the perceptual mind of the viewer: the sculptor utilizes Memory and aspects of the other Elements to evoke the sensations of past experiences.

Memory

Charles Sargeant Jagger

Lorenzo Ghiberti

Bamiyan Valley, Afghanistan

Jeff Koons

Edward Kienholz

Henry Moore

Robert Morris

Joseph Cornell

Michelangelo

Constantin Brancusi

Marcel Duchamp

Memory

Our emotional response to a particular form is often the result of past experience, and those past experiences may strongly influence and shape our present understanding.

The other Elements of Sculpture are based on the facts of the material world, but Memory remains ephemeral and immensely private. Memory is recall, recollection and also homage. It plays a significant role in the complex neurological and psychological process of seeing. What the eye captures is not always what the brain understands. When considering the aesthetic experience, Memory is the essential Element because it provides an empirical bridge between this moment and our past. What our eyes see in any millisecond either passes by without a trace or becomes part of our vocabulary of stored images. Memory is a reality that exists beyond the limitations of touch.

Charles Sargeant Jagger (1885–1934)
Royal Artillery Memorial

1924
Bronze and Portland stone
Approx. 9 m (30 ft) high
Hyde Park Corner, London

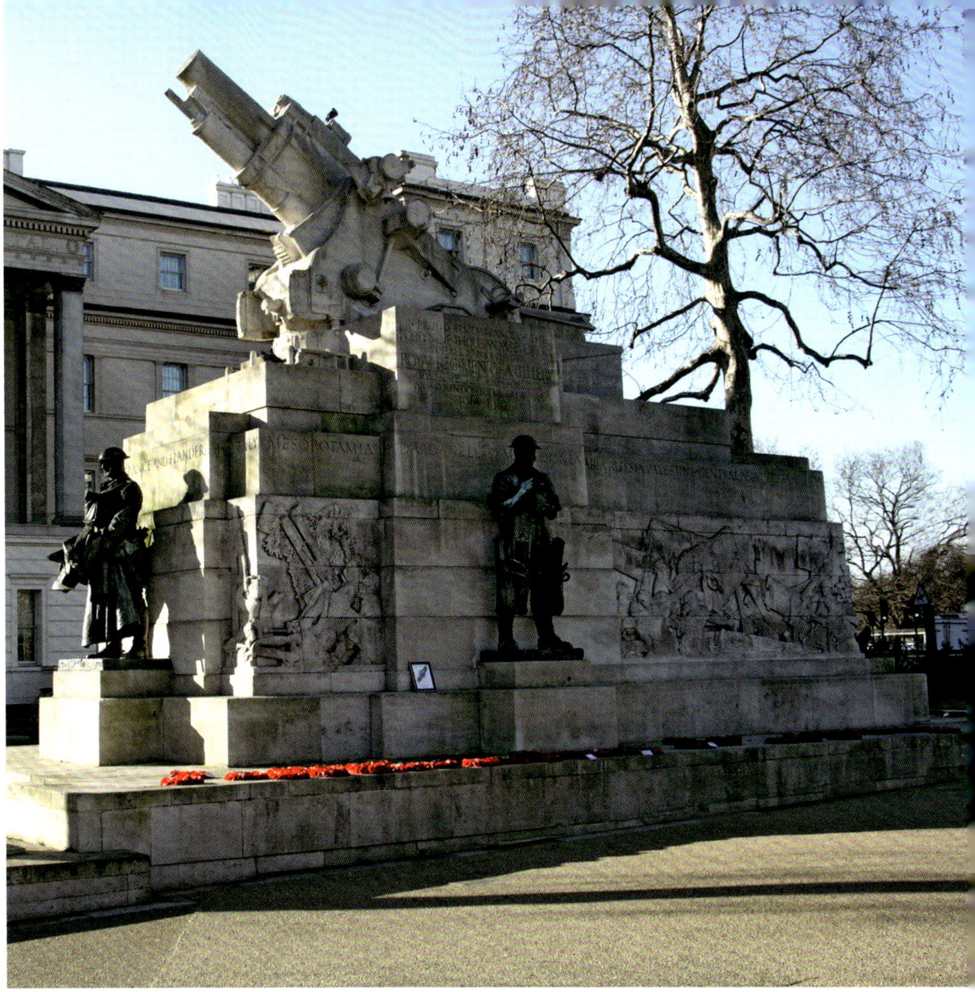

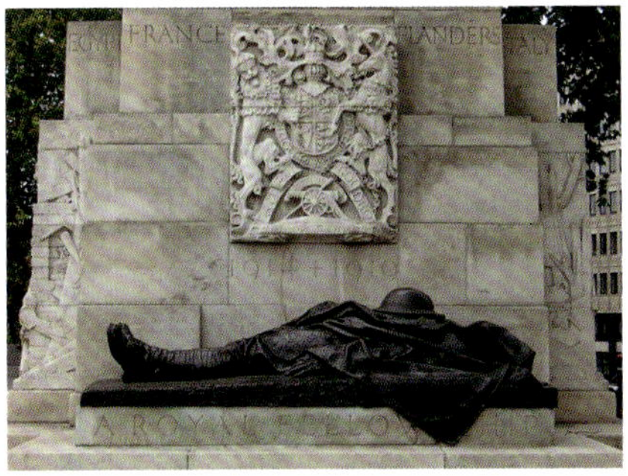

In the minds of many, one of the primary functions of the art of sculpture is the construction of memorials, and in particular war memorials. Most of these are composed of images of bravery and victory on the field of battle; few show death and destruction. In 1924 a British veteran of World War I, Charles Sargeant Jagger, completed his *Royal Artillery Memorial*. The sculpture was commissioned by the Royal Artillery Regiment. Jagger collaborated with an architect on the design for the stonework supporting the carved howitzer – the most destructive weapon used in that war. It rises 30 feet on a corner of Hyde Park in London. While the monumental field piece physically dominates the composition, it is the four realistically rendered bronze soldiers, and the reliefs on each side, that humanize the memorial. They tell the tragic story of how it must have felt to live, fight and die in the trenches of World War I. Jagger stated: 'Experience in the trenches persuaded me of the necessity for frankness and truth.' The final truth of any war is death and more than 49,000 members of the Royal Artillery died in the war. Thus, dominating the north end of the memorial is a dead soldier, lying on a slab of stone that holds the inscription from Shakespeare's *Henry V*: 'Here Was A Royal Fellowship Of Death.'

Lorenzo Ghiberti (1378–1455)
East Doors, Baptistery of San Giovanni (upper left panel)

1425
Bronze and gold leaf
79 × 79 cm (31 × 31 in)
Museo dell'Opera del Duomo, Florence

The illustration of familiar narratives is a way of making them seem more real, vivid and tangible. The sculptures that fill Renaissance and Gothic cathedrals are examples of the how Memory may be invoked to recall and reinforce biblical lessons. This gold-plated *bas* or low-relief door panel illustrates scenes from the Book of Genesis. The forms appear to project out from the ground plane as if modelled in the round. But for the most part their three-dimensionality is an illusion. Lorenzo Ghiberti exploits this artifice to great narrative advantage as he compresses both time and place into carefully composed vignettes. In the lower left of the panel, God raises Adam from the earth, whilst in the centre, God raises his hand to create Eve from the rib of Adam. The monochromatic golden surface heightens the appearance of depth, and its reflectiveness casts an ethereal glow over the composition, turning this moment into Memory.

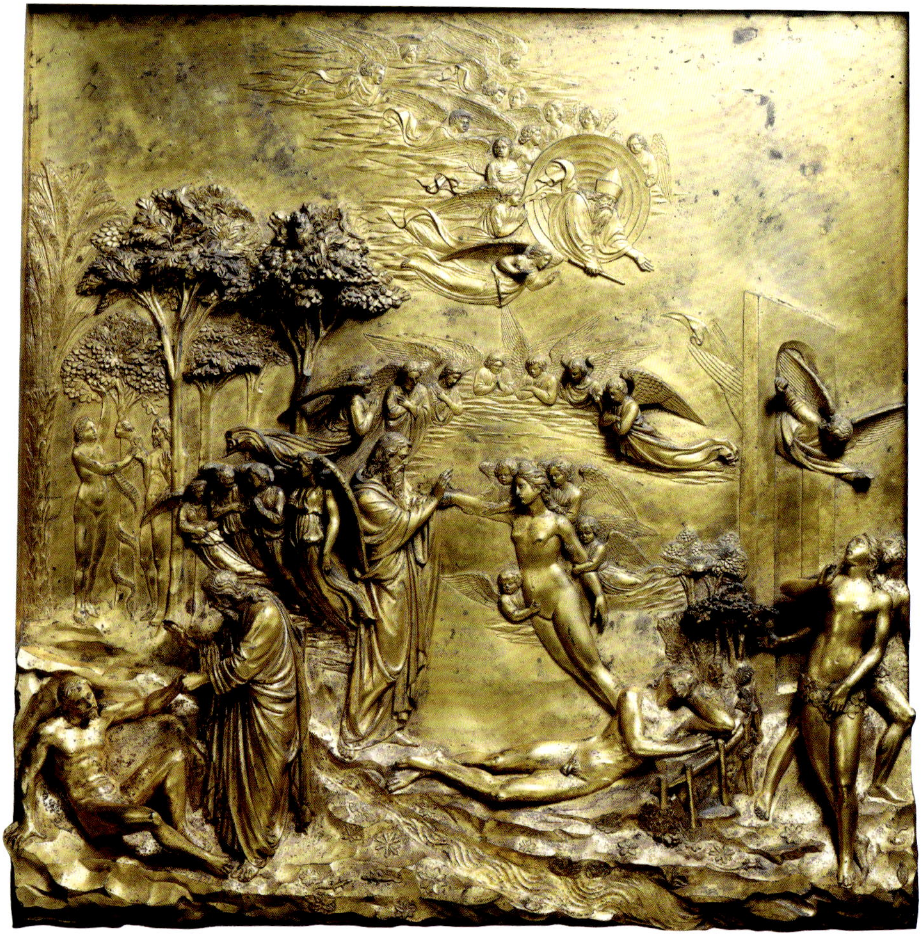

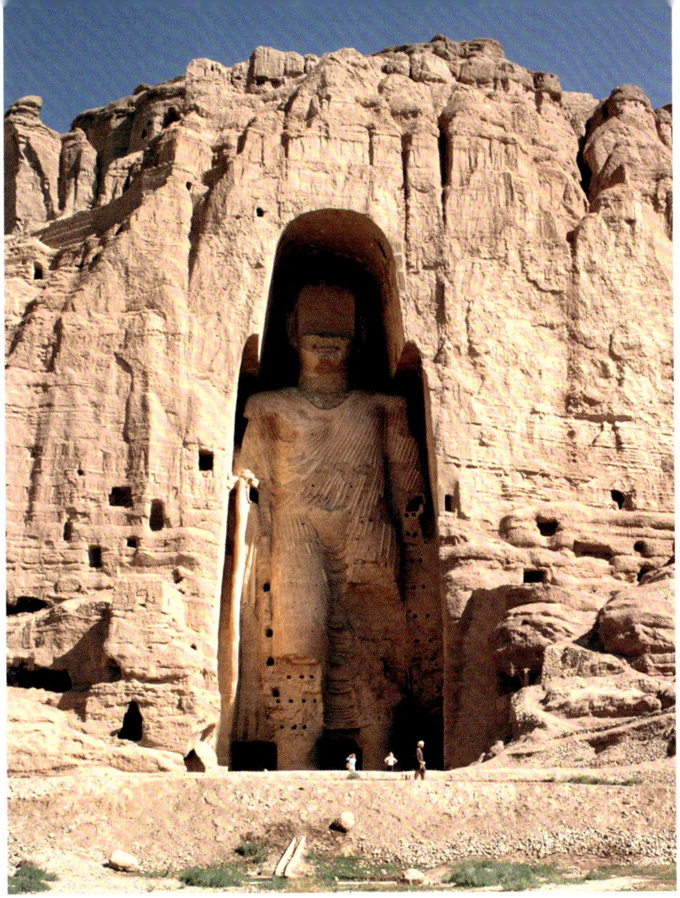

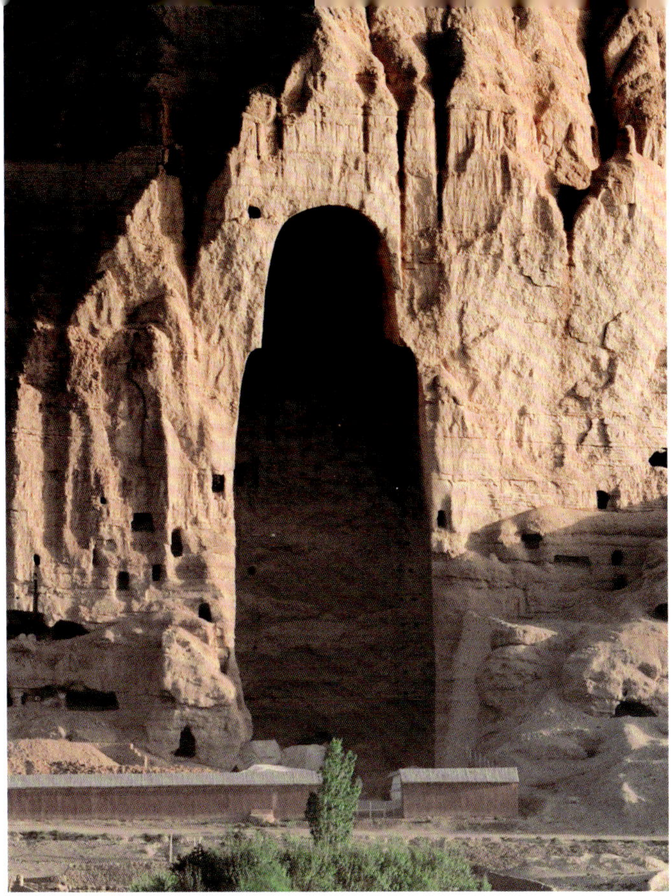

Afghanistan
Bamiyan Buddha

554 AD
Sandstone mountain
Approx. 50 m (165 ft) high
Bamiyan Valley, Afghanistan

Memory is recall, in this case recalling the two 1,500-year-old giant Buddhas in the Bamiyan Valley, Afghanistan, that were destroyed by the Taliban in March 2001. Using only handheld tools, a legion of unknown sculptors carved deeply into the sandstone mountain, creating the world's tallest buddhas, almost 165 feet high. Tragically, they are now known only through living memory and photographic or video imagery. Their presence is limited to an uncanny, shadowed personage – a huge gaping hole in the mountainside that tragically mocks the memory of what was once there.

Jeff Koons (b. 1955)
Rabbit

1986
Stainless steel
104.1 cm (41 in) high
Museum of Contemporary Art, Chicago, IL

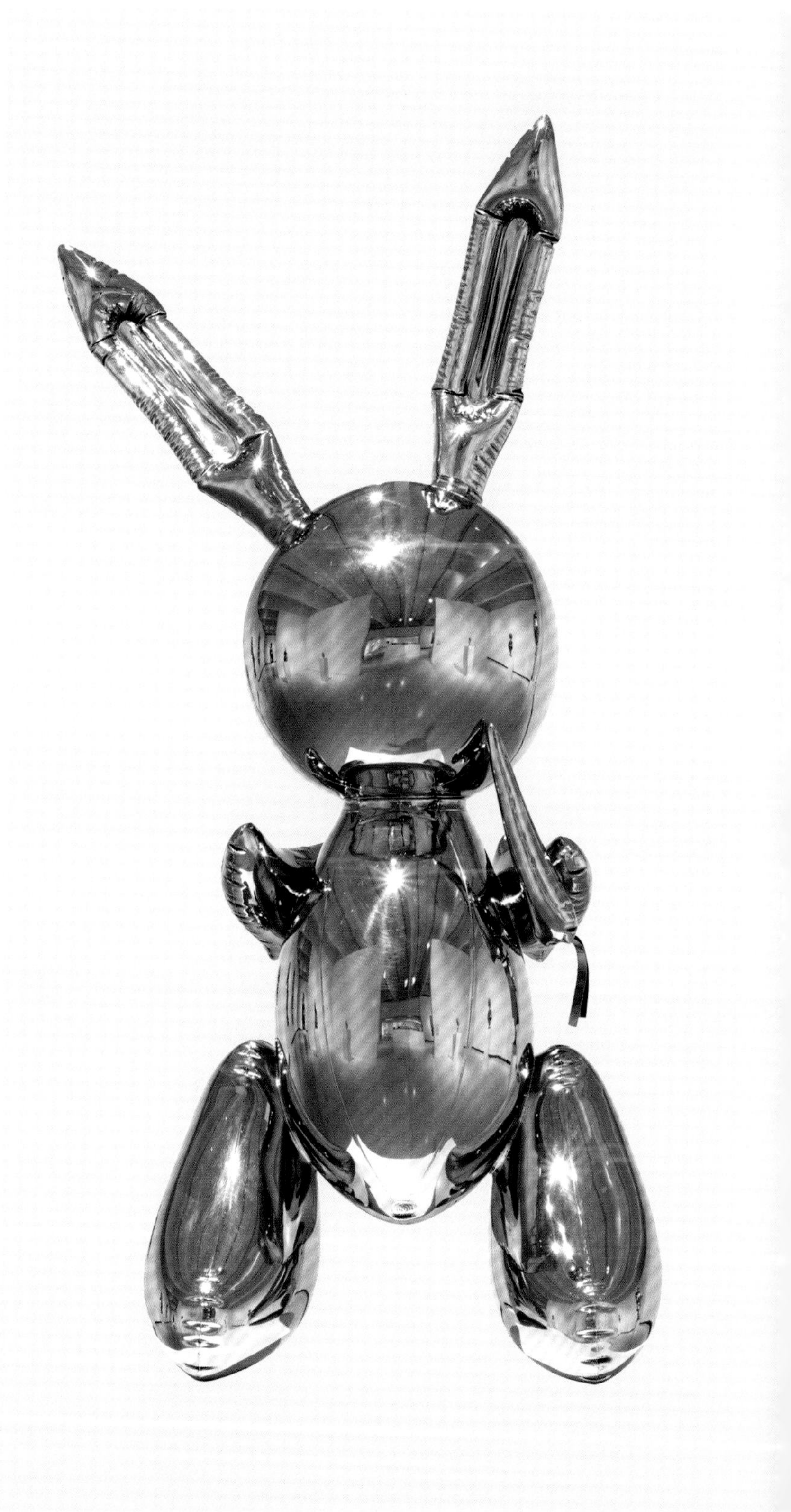

Nostalgia, or a longing for the past, is an aspect of Memory frequently used in contemporary sculpture. This highly polished stainless steel *Rabbit* by Jeff Koons is an especially humorous example. It is a precise casting of a child's inflatable toy into a mirrored object that includes every detail, even the rabbit's soon-to-be-eaten carrot. When we look directly at the work, we see only multiple mirrored images of ourselves reflected in the rabbit's featureless face and body. Time collapses and memories both past and present come together in this stainless steel mirror.

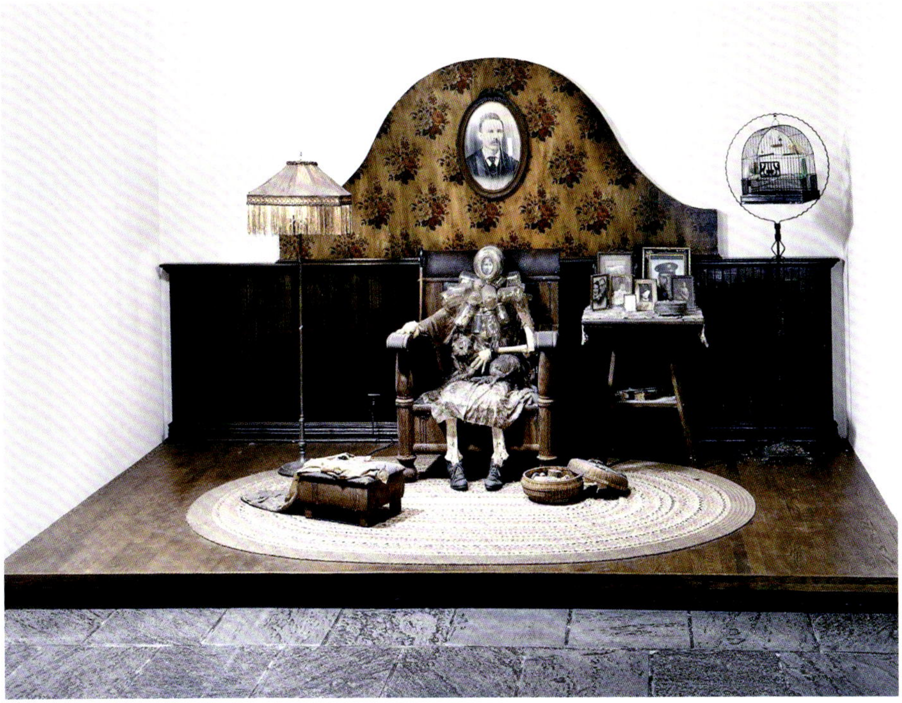

Edward Kienholz (1927–1994)
The Wait

1964–5
Wood, fabric, polyester resin, flock, metal, bones, glass, paper, leather, varnish, black-and-white photographs, taxidermied cat, live parakeet, wicker and plastic
203.2 × 406.4 × 213.4 cm (80 × 160 × 84 in)
Whitney Museum of American Art, New York

Memories are contained within objects collected over time. A poignant example is *The Wait* by Edward Kienholz. An elderly woman is seated in her rocking chair surrounded by cherished objects collected over her long life. At the apex of the triangular composition is the oval framed photograph of her husband, set within the rounded pediment of ageing wallpaper. Some details, like the caged chirping parakeet at the far right of the composition, or the preserving jars filled with family photographs and mementos cannot be experienced in a photograph. These details pull us back through time, like the taste of the madeleine in Marcel Proust's *Remembrance of Things Past*. Kienholz's work has been constructed from carefully chosen objects that recall moments in the passage of time and evoke the power of memory to reduce the pain of waiting.

(far right) Henry Moore (1898–1986)
Two Piece Reclining Figure Number 1

1959
Bronze
193 cm (76 in) long
Installed at Moore's home in Perry Green, Much Hadham

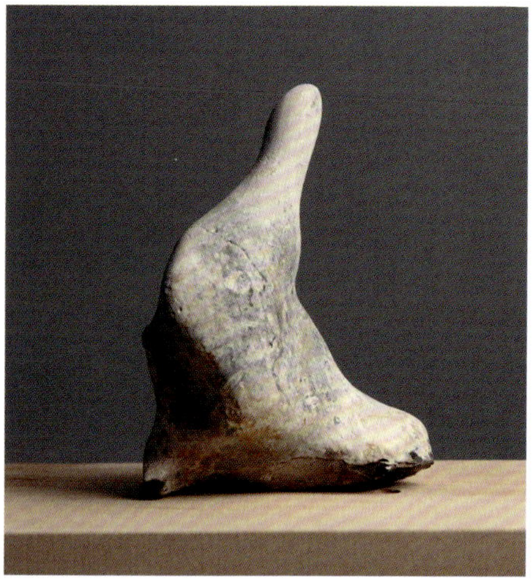

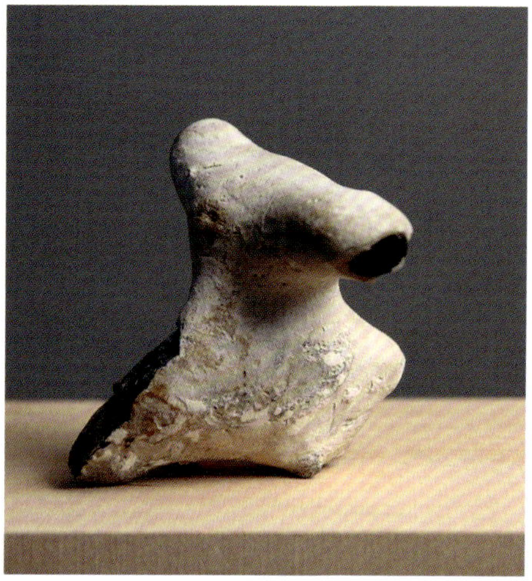

The natural world may offer the greatest source of formal invention available to the sculptor. For Henry Moore it was the English landscape, the female figure and the intersection between the two that provided a never-ending source of formal inspiration. These sources are clearly visible in this work entitled *Two Piece Reclining Figure Number 1.* Also shown here are photographs of two flints I found many years ago in a field that adjoins Moore's studio in Much Hadham. Their flowing organic shapes and extended appendages are evident in Moore's sculpture. By borrowing these ancient geological forms that Moore discovered nearby, he created broader references that connect his work to the viewer's personal store of remembered landscapes. Most of Moore's long working life was spent attempting to synthesize his sources of inspiration – the landscape with the figure. In the *Reclining Figure* an arched, looming projection that could be a leg dominates one part, while breast and head-like forms are contained in the other. This is a primordial female form that reinforces the symbiotic connection between body, landscape and memory.

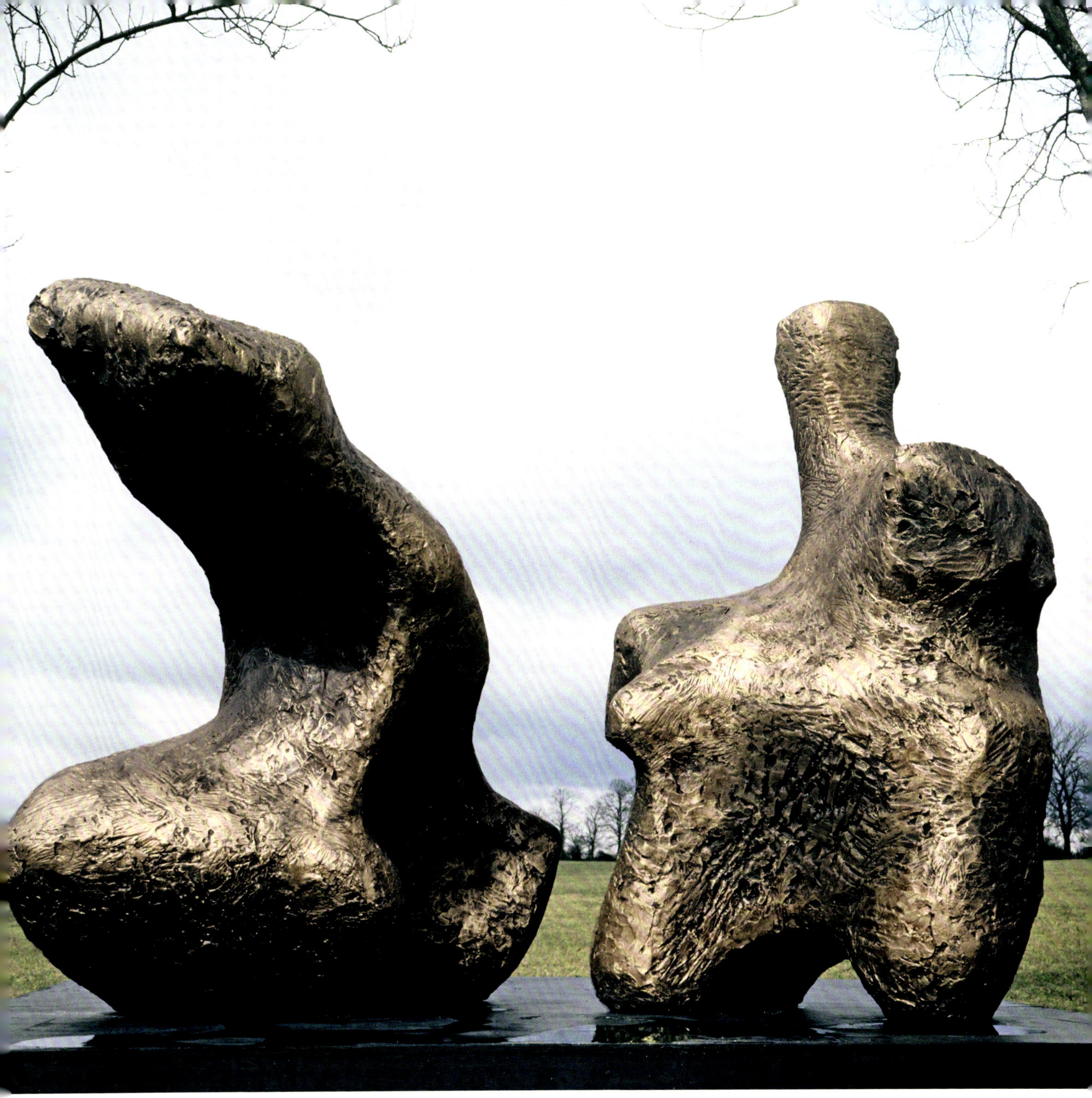

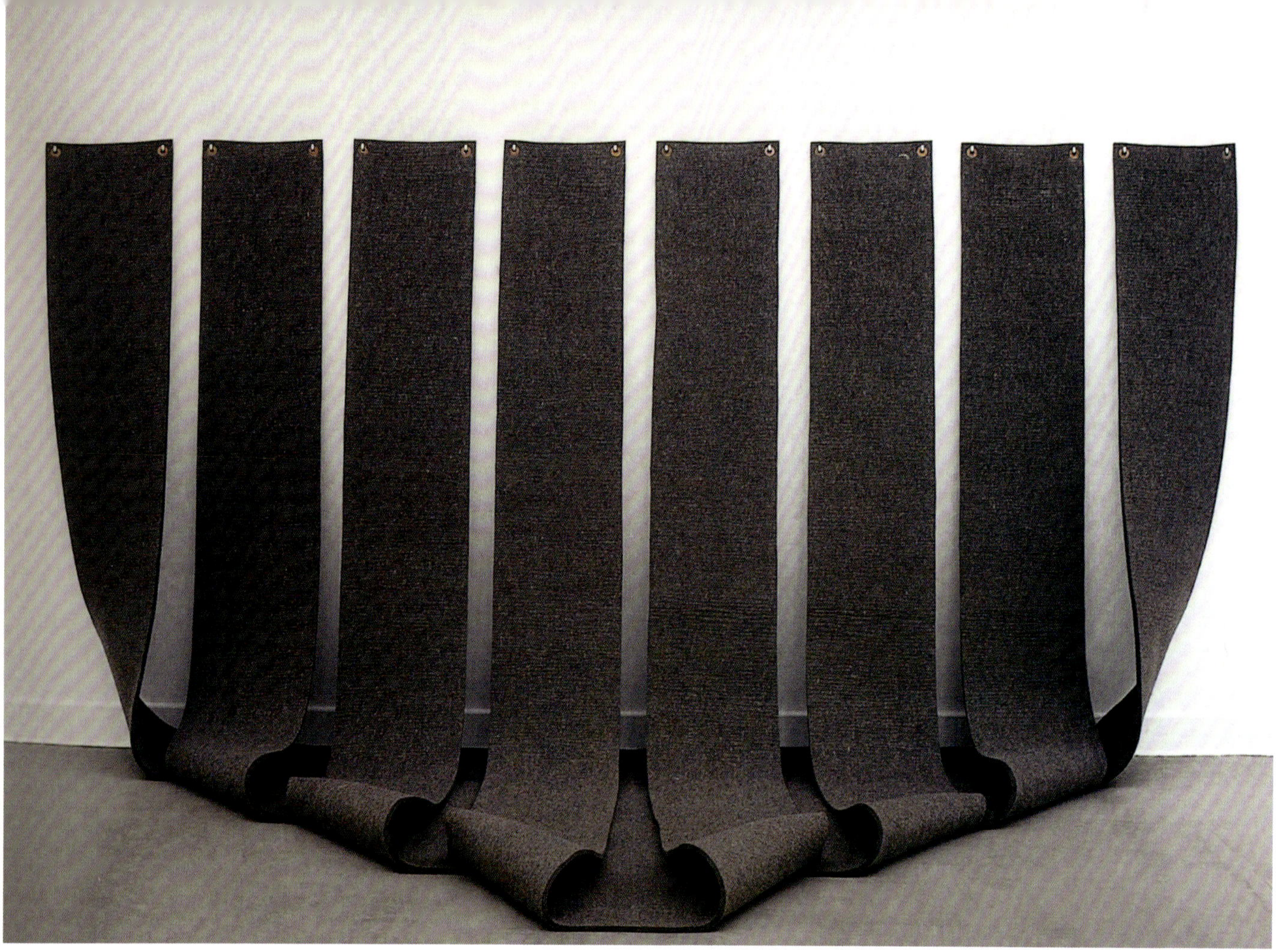

Robert Morris (b. 1931)
Untitled

1996
Felt and metal grommets
215 × 425.5 × 182 cm (84 ½ × 167 ½ × 71 ½ in)
Private collection

Left in its natural state, every material behaves in ways that are unique. Each asks to be worked using certain tools and specific methods. This is material Memory. *Untitled* by Robert Morris is an example of this facet of Memory. Here idea, form, material and meaning are all intimately connected. What we see is the result of cutting eight long ribbons from a single flat sheet of grey industrial felt, and then hanging each strip at the same height along a wall. Felt of this thickness, dimension and density will, under these conditions, produce this particular form. In theory the sculpture may be changed at will. The possibility for other configurations exists because of the characteristics of this material and the process of making.

Joseph Cornell (1903–1972)
Untitled (Soap Bubble Set)

1936
Glass case with 4 hanging weights, wine glass, robin's egg, clay pipe, geological map, doll's head and column
38.1 × 35.6 × 12.7 cm (15 × 14 × 5 in)
Wadsworth Atheneum, Hartford, CT

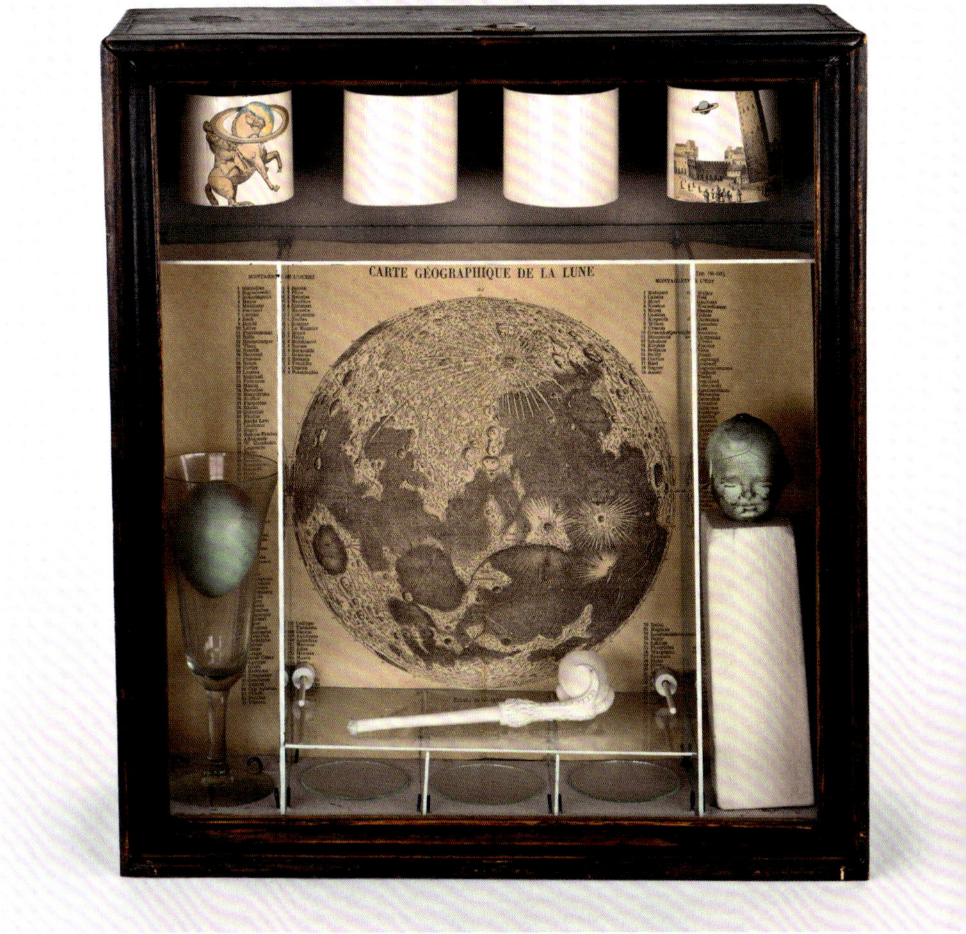

Actual or fictional events may be the base for memories, but more often than not they exist within a jumbled combination of the two. Joseph Cornell spent most of his life living in a small house on Utopia Parkway in Queens, New York. His physical world was limited to that house and frequent subway rides into Manhattan, but his limited personal geography did not constrain his imagination. *Untitled (Soap Bubble Set)* is one of Cornell's many box constructions that took children's soap bubbles as a poetic theme. Here it is not so much the literal bubble, but rather the form of the circle and the sphere that are of thematic importance. The dominant image in the box is a reproduction from an old engraving of the most romantic orb in our universe, the moon. In the foreground is a bubble pipe out of which the moon may have originated as the pipe faces that direction. Framing the moon are two incarnations of the circle: one is a robin's egg suspended within the circumference of a glass, and the other is an idealized round doll's head. Within the process of making his boxes, Cornell travelled beyond time and place. In doing so he created a vast store of private memories that exist in the future as much as they do in the past.

Michelangelo (1475–1564)
Rondanini Pietà

Unfinished, c. 1552–64
Marble
1.9 m (6 ft 3 in) high
Castello Sforzesco, Milan

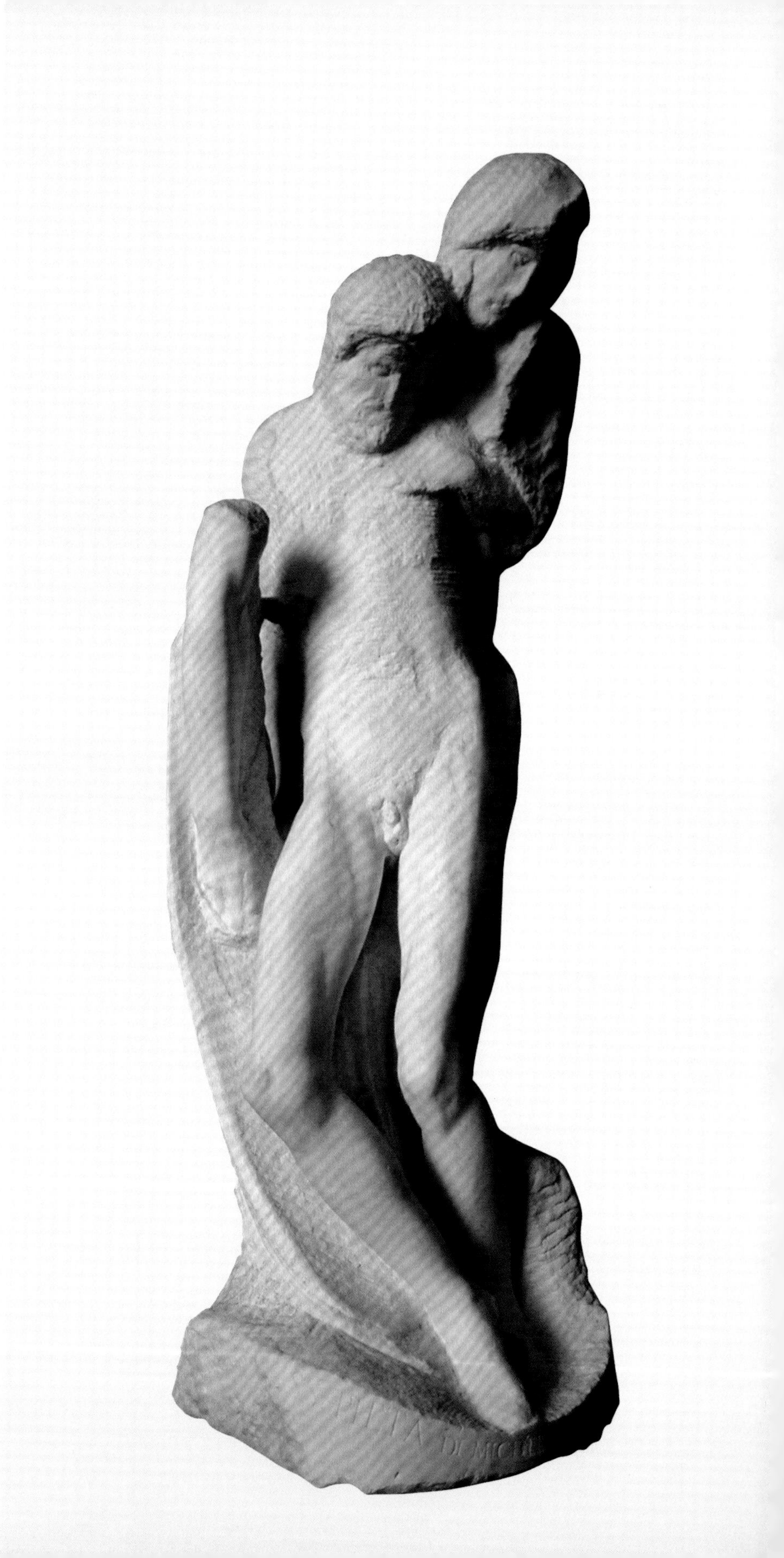

Michelangelo was still at work on the *Rondanini Pietà* when he died in 1556. What we see is a work in progress. Beyond the image that is present, there is the carved memory of a previous *Pietà* started ten years earlier. From it, and still clearly visible, is the levitating right arm and the radically curving right leg of Christ. When we move to the far right, this arm and leg become the most dramatic features in the work as they describe an ascending arc of flight, with the remaining sculptural mass following.

Constantin Brancusi (1876–1957)
Bird in Space

1923–4
Marble with marble, limestone and oak base
Including base: 2.6 m (8 ft 7 in) high
Philadelphia Museum of Art, PA

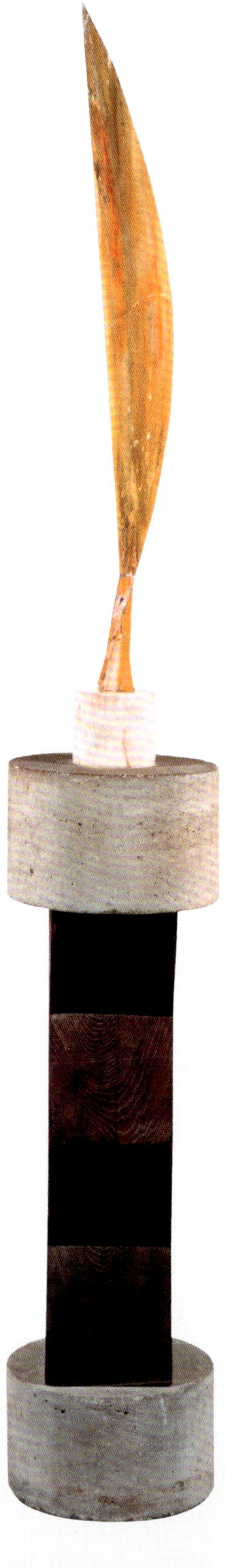

Three hundred and fifty years after Michelangelo's *Rondanini Pietà*, Constantin Brancusi carved *Bird in Space*, a sculpture that bears a remarkable similarity to the Michelangelo work in both form and content. I'm not suggesting that Brancusi was in any conscious way influenced by the *Pietà*, but with the realization that no form is without a memory, what I find interesting is the possibility that there was a common aesthetic desire shared by these two artists.

Contained within any work of art is a resonant artistic memory. Every sculpture has within it a multitude of references – a heritage of form and a long tradition of content. This echo of Memory encompasses and enlivens the implicit conversation that is the history of art.

Marcel Duchamp (1887–1968)
50 cc of Paris Air

1919
Glass ampoule
13.3 cm (5 ¼ in) high
Philadelphia Museum of Art, PA

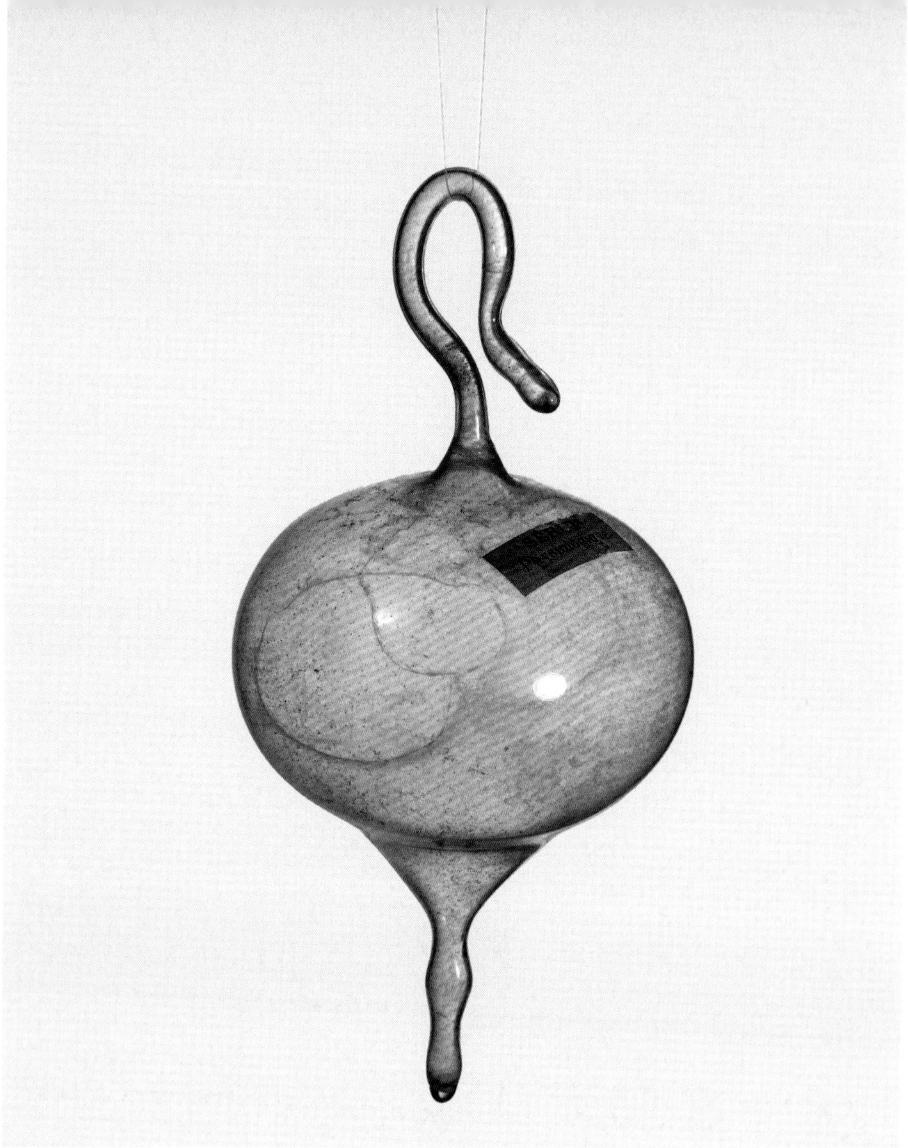

Like thought, memory is ephemeral, and like the air, it is beyond touch. Bearing an interesting resemblance to a question mark, this fragile glass bubble-like container has 50 cc of Paris air sealed within it. Called a 'Readymade' by Marcel Duchamp, this and similar works are made from found objects with limited interventions by the artist. In this case Duchamp asked a pharmacist to empty the vessel of its liquid and reseal it with the air of Paris inside. Affixed to the outside of the ampoule is a label with the words, 'Serum Physiologique'. *50 cc of Paris Air* is memory made physical and given an official scientific certification. Duchamp describes the work as 'the precious ampoule of 50 cubic centimeters of AIR OF PARIS I brought back to the Arensbergs in 1919'. Memory is literally captured – a specimen that all can 'see', study and remember.

Memory does not consist in a regression from the present to the past, but, on the contrary, it is a progress from the past to the present.

— Henri Bergson

It is very well to copy what one sees; it's much better to draw what one has retained in one's memory. It is a transformation in which imagination collaborates with memory.

— Edgar Degas

The difference between false memories and true ones is the same as for jewels: it is always the false ones that look the most real, the most brilliant.

— Salvador Dalí

One need not be a chamber to be haunted;
One need not be a house;
The brain has corridors surpassing
Material place.

— Emily Dickinson

After the Elements of Sculpture

Sculpture is what you bump into when you back up to see a painting.

— Barnett Newman

Sculpture Defined

Now that we are familiar with the Elements and how these characteristics clarify the meaning of particular works, that knowledge may be productively used to define what is meant by the word 'sculpture'. A clear and concise definition of the term has been made difficult in part because of the far-reaching innovations and new aesthetic opportunities brought by modernism. The movement liberated sculpture from past traditions dominated by the constraints of deity-narratives, heroic public memorials and private aristocratic pleasures. Once freed from these obligatory roles, the art of sculpture was challenged to rediscover its essence.

At its most essential, sculpture is the manipulation of matter in real space and time. Its working methods may be described as either additive or subtractive. Traditionally, the additive process meant building up material bit by bit, as in modelling a figure in clay, but now the term may also be applied to assembling constructions using found material. A subtractive process is the opposite: taking material away, as in stone carving, for example. Large-scale site-specific earthworks may contain within their process of construction aspects of both the additive and the subtractive. Although the meaning of these two terms has evolved over time, they remain useful in their simplicity.

However, the definition of sculpture as the manipulation of matter in real space and time does present a question when we consider the relief. Both painting and relief begin with a flat plane called a ground. How each discipline – painting versus sculpture – both manipulates that ground plane and also defines its place in real space is critical here. The four types of relief sculpture found in this book – high, low, floor and sunken-relief – lie on the sculptural side of this difference. In part, these types of relief are presented here to encourage the questions: what is the difference between painting and the sculptural relief; and what is the difference between relief sculpture and sculpture in the round? Knowing what something is not can play a vital role in knowing what it is.

I am very aware that this book excludes installation, sound art, video, body art and other practices that strictly speaking are also manipulated form in real space and time, and so could be considered sculpture. But to include these would shift the focus away from my purpose, which is to introduce the viewer to the language of sculpture as defined here.

I have come to believe that the whole world is made terrible by our own mad attempt to interpret it as though it had an underlying truth.

— Umberto Eco

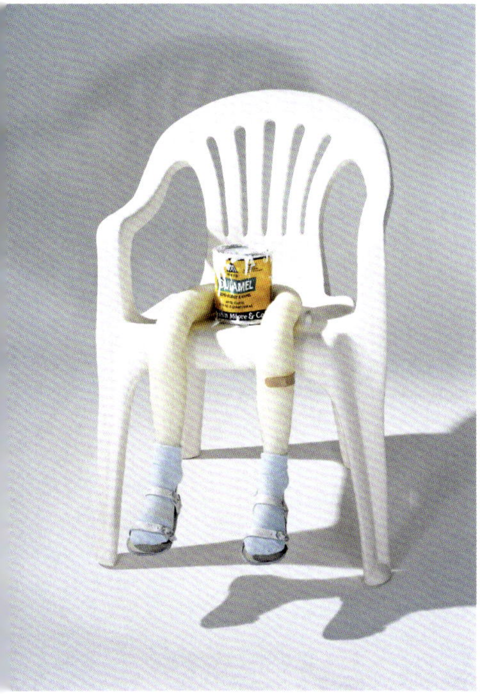

Robert Gober (b. 1954)
Untitled (2005–2006)

2005–6
Stoneware, beeswax, cotton, leather, aluminium pull tabs, human hair, cast lead crystal, aluminium-leaf, oil enamel and acrylic paint
73 × 53 × 75 cm
(28 ¾ × 21 × 29 ½ in)

Using the Elements of Sculpture

One way to demonstrate the visual language of sculpture is to present a 'model' for discussion based upon the Elements. This model has an open structure that encourages the viewer to progress from confusion to a well-reasoned, albeit provisional, understanding. I have chosen a work by Robert Gober that eludes and confounds easy analysis. Although the Elements will frame this discussion, the focus will not be restricted to a single Element, but will expand to include several that are key. This is necessary because we know our world in the totality of context, metaphor and simile. Not just *this* surface, *this* texture or *this* colour alone, but that these parts necessarily combine to create a coherent whole.

To approach an understanding of sculpture from this multidimensional perspective, I will cautiously question, draw provisional answers and speculate about the reasons behind the forms we see, guided by the appropriate Elements. Looking is one thing, while making is quite another. By trying to discover why specific decisions were made, we may construct a bridge between the sculptor and the viewer, and the sculptor and the work of art.

Untitled (2005–2006) by Robert Gober uses the Elements of Material, Scale, Colour and Memory in thought-provoking ways. A discussion of Material is a reasonable place to begin, as the materials appear to be both familiar in form and curiously out of the ordinary in their arrangement.

The chair appears to be a cheap indestructible vinyl patio chair, purchased at any home store, but in reality it is an extremely difficult-to-make fragile stoneware casting. The Benjamin Moore-branded paint can has been cast in lead crystal glass and carefully painted to look like the original. The wax legs wear children's blue knitted socks and white sandals, and look as if they belong to a young boy. Black hairs have been imbedded in them, and there is a Band-Aid on the left leg below the knee. It is critical to note that, contrary to how the objects appear in a photograph, the artist made every part, giving utmost attention to every detail.

Remaking an object in an unexpected material implies a completely different level of engagement from buying or finding that same object. Decisions such as what materials to use and how deeply to become involved in its making are vital questions for both the sculptor and the viewer.

When we consider Colour and Scale, the objects conform to our expectations. Save one – the pallid beeswax legs, almost painfully too white and too thin, which are sprouting adult black hair. The 'flesh' coloured Band-Aid strip, the Gainsborough *Blue Boy* blue knitted socks and the white sandals almost give the breath of life to these wax cylinders.

The objects are their true scale or size. But something quite mysterious happens when we experience the sculpture in person as opposed to looking at it in a photograph. The perceived scale of the boy's legs seems to change in relation to the actual size of the chair. The legs appear to diminish in scale, while the chair grows larger in the imagination. Two things heighten this illusion. First we see a vague similarity in form and colour between the chair and the boy's legs, but more important is the fact that his legs are too short, not for him, but for the adult-sized chair that holds them. His feet dangle, helplessly, inches off the ground. Freely floating, they lose their remembered size in our mind. Scale needs a reference point, and without it the chair becomes a monumental looming presence within the composition.

With regard to the chair, Memory is possibly the most significant. When we consider the enormous range of objects that crowd our world, a chair comes the nearest to being our body's surrogate. We sit in a chair, but it is the names given to its parts that are most revealing: arms, legs, seat, back. Physically larger than the other objects in the composition, the stoneware chair acts as the stage where the action within the sculpture takes place. But it is deceptively fragile, especially when compared to its indestructible vinyl mate. Perhaps the artist chose this particular one because from the front it looks anthropomorphic. Despite the chair's fragility it becomes an adult-like presence, as it both metaphorically and physically holds the composition together.

Made of beeswax, an extremely fragile easily melted material, the legs are formed with little attention to anatomy. Given the obsessively detailed representation of the other objects, this change in emphasis is surprising. They are generic forms that could almost belong to anything. But not anyone. The Band-Aid covers a 'real' wound, the sandals and feet establish a persona for the legs as they wrap tightly around the used paint can. Benjamin Moore is a paint company, but might this brand name also be the name of the boy? Do we now have enough information to begin to speculate as to the meaning of this complex work?

The paint can has been strategically placed in the genital area of his legs 'sitting' in the chair. By its placement, does the crystal container represent the fragility of a young boy approaching puberty? Paint is used to conceal things, and children often feel the need to mask their vulnerabilities and inadequacies. This breakable container literally and figuratively holds the dangling legs in position. If it were removed they would slide helplessly to the floor. And then there are the black hairs 'growing' from the boy's legs. These hairs might be the sculpture's most optimistic moment as they may represent the passage of time and with it the relative independence of adulthood.

Although most of the objects in the sculpture could have been purchased, the artist chose to make them, and to make them in a laborious and detailed way that fools the viewer into believing they are the actual objects, even down to the aluminium-leafed buckles on the boy's white sandals. Is the work merely a *trompe l'oeil* exercise testing the limits of our perception? One must take this possibility into consideration. But that assumption does not begin to explain how these objects interact with each other, and why they are as they are.

If we doubt the integrity of the objects around us, it is a very short step from there to doubting the reliability of our own bodies and therefore our tenuous place in a confusing world. That doubt is one of the most painful aspects of childhood. The human frailty at this time in life may be why Gober chose glass as the material for the paint can and why he placed the objects on the seat of a brittle and easily broken stoneware chair. At no other time in life do our bodies feel so awkward, uncomfortable and clumsy – as if we, like the boy, have 'two left feet', unable to reach firm ground.

This is my understanding of *Untitled*. I began with the Elements that were of primary and secondary importance, then asked why the artist made these formal decisions, being careful to search for answers within the sculpture itself. Elsewhere I have called this process a search for the facts of sculptural form. But this is a beginning, a reasoned first step. My interpretation may not be correct. Furthermore, I am not certain what being 'correct' might mean in the context of a work that I immediately perceived to be an enigma, a mystery. To see more clearly is a deeply satisfying process, but lodged within the core of any sculpture is a question. And that is as it should be.

The Experience of Sculpture

Throughout the book I have assumed that sculpture in some mysterious way is animate, and therefore able to 'reply' to questions that a work may incite in the viewer. Questions are a useful means of inquiry, a direct method for gaining information. The Elements provide the tools needed for asking relevant questions, but understanding is more complex than merely defining words or making enquiries. While seeing may provoke thinking, a more sustaining response involves more than sight alone: the mind and the body must also be engaged if we are to experience the singular aesthetic sensation of sculptural form. Familiarity with the Elements provides an objective factual foundation upon which subjective meaning may be reasonably constructed. In this book we have progressed from descriptions and words that explain the material presence and physical reality of an object, to the emotions a sculpture may evoke within the viewer; this book has been an attempt to assist in accomplishing the former, but it must be left to the reader to experience the latter.

The light work by Dan Flavin opposite demonstrates many of the aesthetic qualities that the experience of sculpture offers the attentive viewer. The work is framed by a repeated horizontal and vertical structure composed of fluorescent tubes. Their placement becomes an open barrier that cuts diagonally through the gallery space. Because of the overwhelming presence of the dense fog of glowing blue light reflecting off the white walls of the gallery, the assumed dominance of the fixtures disappears, leaving a viewer standing – possibly levitating – within an intense volume of cold, pulsating light – light so indelibly strong it is piercing. Memories of similar light and hue push thoughts of time and place out of existence. The sensation of the experience is all that remains. And that is understanding.

I have presented the fourteen Elements that form the visual language of sculpture: these are the necessary tools for appreciating the aesthetic experience the art of sculpture offers the viewer. But understanding is an ongoing search rather than an endpoint. Sculpture's essence lies beyond our ability to fully comprehend it. Both meaning and mystery are found in the pleasures derived from discovering what the hand of the sculptor has created and the imagination of the viewer has experienced.

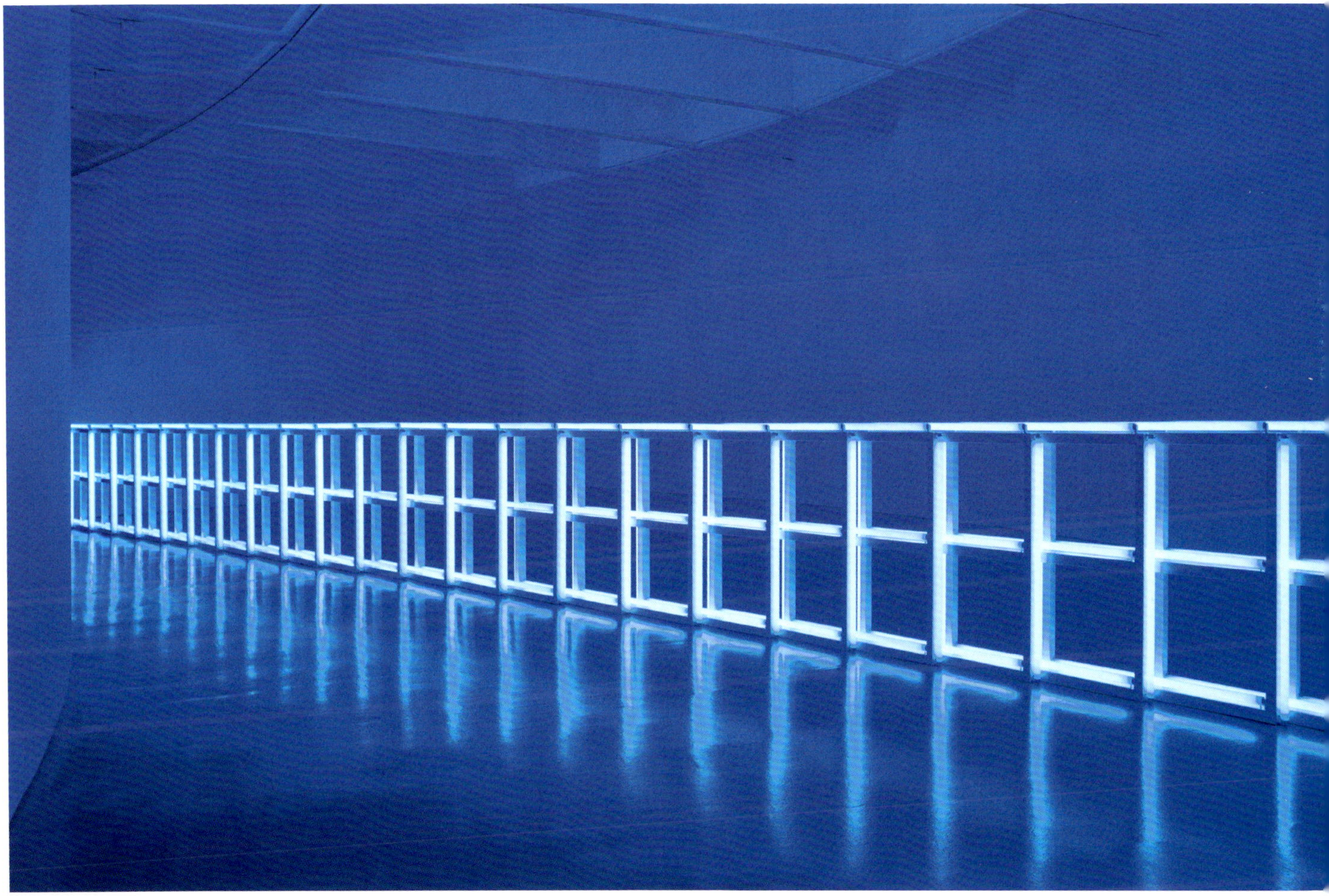

Dan Flavin (1933–1996)
Untitled (to Helga and Carlo, with respect and affection)

1974
Blue fluorescent light modular units
Each unit 122 × 122 cm (4 × 4 ft); length variable
Hirshhorn Museum and Sculpture Garden, Smithsonian Institution, Washington DC

Further Reading

Arnheim, Rudolf, *Art and Visual Perception*, University of California Press, Berkeley, 1974

Ashton, Dore, *A Fable of Modern Art*, Thames and Hudson, New York, 1980

Bach, Friedrich Teja, *Constantin Brancusi 1876-1957*, Philadelphia Museum of Art, 1995

Baxandall, Michael, *The Limewood Sculptors of Renaissance Germany*, Yale University Press, New Haven, CT, 1980

Brinkmann, Vinzenz, *Bunte Gotter*, Staatliche Antikensammlungen und Glyptothek, Munich, 2004

Chipp, Herschel B, *Theories of Modern Art*, University of California Press, Berkeley, 1968

Collingwood, R. G, *The Principles of Art*, Oxford University Press, New York, 1958

Collins, Judith, *Sculpture Today*, Phaidon Press, London, 2008

Cornford, Francis Macdonald, *The Republic of Plato*, Oxford University Press, New York, 1945

Curtis, Penelope, *Sculpture 1900-1945*, Oxford University Press, New York, 1999

Dewey, John, *Art As Experience*, G.P. Putnam's Sons, New York, 1980

Flood, Richard, et al., *Unmonumental*, Phaidon Press, London, 2007

Focillon, Henri, *The Life of Forms in Art*, Zone Books, New York, 1992

Freedberg, David, *The Power of Images*, University of Chicago Press, 1989

Gombrich, E.H., *Art and Illusion*, Princeton University Press, Princeton, NJ, 1972

Gray, Camilla, *The Russian Experiment in Art: 1863-1922*, Harry N. Abrams, Inc., New York, 1971

Gross, Kenneth, *The Dream of the Moving Statue*, Cornell University Press, Ithaca, NY, 1992

Hall, Edward T., *The Hidden Dimension*, Anchor Doubleday, New York, 1969

Harvey, David, *The Condition of Postmodernity*, Basil Blackwell, Inc., Cambridge, MA, 1989

Johnson, Mark, *The Body in the Mind*, University of Chicago Press, 1987

Krauss, Rosalind E., *Passages in Modern Sculpture*, Viking Press, New York, 1977

Lessing, Gotthold Ephraim., *Laocoön*, The Johns Hopkins University Press, Baltimore, MD, 1984

Miller, Arthur I., *Einstein, Picasso, Space, Time, and the Beauty That Causes Havoc*, Basic Books, New York, 2001

Panofsky, Erwin, *Meaning in the Visual Arts*, University of Chicago Press, 1955

Potts, Alex, *The Sculptural Imagination*, Yale University Press, New Haven, CT, 2000

Read, Herbert, *A Concise History of Modern Sculpture*, Frederick A. Praeger, New York, 1964

Read, Herbert, *The Art of Sculpture*, Princeton University Press, Princeton, NJ, 1969

Rickey, George, *Constructivism: Origins and Evolution*, George Braziller, New York, 1967

Rilke, Rainer Maria, *Rodin*, Haskell House Publishers Ltd., New York, 1974

Sacks, Oliver, *An Anthropologist on Mars*, Vintage Books, New York, 1995

Shattuck, Roger, *The Banquet Years*, Vintage Books, New York, 1968

Steinberg, Leo, *Other Criteria, Confrontations with Twentieth-Century Art*, Oxford University Press, New York, 1972

Trachtenberg, Marvin, *The Statue of Liberty*, Penguin Books, New York, 1977

Tucker, William, *Early Modern Sculpture*, Oxford University Press, New York, 1974

Wallace, William E., *Michelangelo at San Lorenzo*, Cambridge University Press, New York, 1994

Zeki, Semir, *Inner Vision*, Oxford University Press, New York, 1999

Index of Artists

Picture Credits

All works in copyright are © the artist.

© ADAGP, Paris and DACS, London 2014. © Malcolm Lightner/Corbis: 52; © ADAGP, Paris and DACS, London 2014. Image © Philadelphia Museum of Art/CORBIS: 177; © ADAGP, Paris and DACS, London 2014. © RADU SIGHETI/ Reuters/Corbis: 53; © ADAGP, Paris and DACS, London 2014. Digital image, The Museum of Modern Art, New York/ Scala, Florence: 129; © ADAGP, Paris and DACS, London 2014. The Philadelphia Museum of Art/Art Resource/Scala, Florence: 15(l), 75; © ADAGP, Paris and DACS, London 2014. Philadelphia Museum of Art/The Bridgeman Art Library: 8-9; © ADAGP, Paris and DACS, London 2014. Hinman B. Hurlbut Collection, Cleveland Museum of Art, Ohio/The Bridgeman Art Library: 15r; © ADAGP, Paris and DACS, London 2014. Photo: Jyoti Srivastava: 50; © ADAGP, Paris and DACS, London 2014. Private Collection/ Photo © Christie's Images/The Bridgeman Art Library: 60; © ADAGP, Paris and DACS, London 2014. Scala, Florence: 96; © ADAGP, Paris and DACS, London 2014. Xavier Testelin/ Gamma-Rapho/Getty Images: 97; akg-images: 120, 147; Apic/Getty Images: 84(l); © Carl Andre. DACS, London/ VAGA, New York 2014: 38; © annetruitt.org / The Bridgeman Art Library: 135; © ARS, NY and DACS, London 2014: 159; © ARS, NY and DACS, London 2014. Digital image, The Museum of Modern Art, New York/Scala, Florence: 98, 160; © ARS, NY and DACS, London 2014. Photoraph by Ellen Labenski, courtesy Pace Gallery: 61; © ARS, NY and DACS, London 2014. © Richard Serra/Gagosian Gallery. Photography by Robert McKeever: 99, 152; © ARS, NY and DACS, London 2014. Courtesy Sprüth Magers Berlin London /Sonnabend Gallery, New York: 174; Photograph © The Art Institute of Chicago: 85; Courtesy of the artist: 48; Courtesy the artist, Anton Kern Gallery, New York: 125; Erin Babnik/ Alamy: 67(l); Courtesy of Barford Sculptures Limited: 133; © Larry Bell. The Albuquerque Museum, New Mexico: 45; © Lynda Benglis. DACS, London/VAGA, New York 2014. Courtesy Locks Gallery: 72; Birmingham Museums and Art Gallery/The Bridgeman Art Library: 20; © The Estate of Ronald Bladen, LLC/VAGA, NY/DACS, London 2014. BPK, Bildagentur für Kunst, Kultur und Geschichte, Berlin/Scala, Florence: 110-1; Bridgeman Art Library: 49; Brooklyn Museum/Corbis: 47; Charles Edwin Wilbour Fund, Brooklyn Museum of Art, New York/The Bridgeman Art Library: 80; Burstein Collection/Corbis: 158; © 2014 Calder Foundation, New York / DACS London. Collection Museum of Contemporary Art Chicago, The Leonard and Ruth Horwich Family Loan, EL 1995.6. Photo: Nathan Keay, © Museum of Contemporary Art Chicago: 71; Courtesy Maurizio Cattelan's Archive. Photo: Attilio Maranzano: 23; © The Joseph and Robert Cornell Memorial Foundation/VAGA, NY/ DACS, London 2014. Wadsworth Atheneum Museum of Art/ Art Resource/Scala, Florence: 175; © Tony Cragg. DACS 2014: 73; © DACS 2014: 59; © DACS 2014. The Arthur and Madelaine Chalette Lejwa Collection, The Israel Museum, Jerusalem/The Bridgeman Art Library: 64; © DACS 2014. Photography © The Art Institute of Chicago: 76; © DACS 2014. Middelheim Sculpture Park, Antwerp. Photo: Michel Wuyts: 39; Photo: Daderot: 63; © Succession Marcel Duchamp/ADAGP, Paris and DACS, London 2014. Image © Philadelphia Museum of Art/CORBIS: 178; © The Easton Foundation / DACS 2014. Collection Whitney Museum of American Art, New York. Photo: Christopher Burke: 6; © 2007 Olafur Eliasson. Installation view at San Francisco Museum of Modern Art, San Francisco, 2007-2008. Photo: Ian Reeves, Courtesy of the San Francisco Museum of Modern Art: 162; © 2014 Stephen Flavin/Artists Rights Society (ARS), New York; courtesy David Zwirner, New York/ London. Photo by Cathy Carver: 187; © The Frick Collection, New York: 54; Tom Friedman © represented by Luhring Augustine. Courtesy of the artist, Luhring Augustine, New York and Stephen Friedman Gallery, London: 87; The Work of Naum Gabo © Nina & Graham Williams. Image © U. Edelmann/Städel Museum/ARTOTHEK: 119; © The Estate of Alberto Giacometti (Fondation Giacometti, Paris and ADAGP, Paris), licensed in the UK by ACS and DACS, London 2014. Image © The Metropolitan Museum of Art/Art Resource/Scala, Florence: 79; © The Estate of Alberto Giacometti (Fondation Giacometti, Paris and ADAGP, Paris), licensed in the UK by ACS and DACS, London 2014/The Bridgeman Art Library. Digital image, The Museum of Modern Art, New York/Scala, Florence: 131; © Robert Gober, Courtesy Matthew Marks Gallery: 183; © Andy Goldsworthy: 13; © The Felix Gonzalez-Torres Foundation. Courtesy of Andrea Rosen Gallery, New York: 18; Robert Harding Picture Library/SuperStock: 169(l); © Tim Hawkinson, courtesy Pace Gallery. Photo: G.R. Christmas: 100; Photo: David Heald©SRGF, NY: 121; © The Estate of Eva Hesse. Courtesy Hauser & Wirth. Photo courtesy the Detroit Institute of Arts, Founders Society Purchase, Friends of Modern Art Fund, and Miscellaneous Gifts Fund, 1979: 57; John Hios/akg-images: 67r; Hiroshi Higuchi/Photolibrary/Getty Images © 2014 Niki de Saint Phalle Charitable Art Foundation/ADAGP, Paris and DACS, London/© ADAGP, Paris and DACS, London 2014: 150b; Hirshhorn Museum and Sculpture Garden, Smithsonian Institution, Joseph H. Hirshhorn Purchase Fund and Gift of the Institute of Scrap Recycling Industries, by exchange, 1999. Photography by Lee Stalsworth: 14; Hirshhorn Museum and Sculpture Garden, Smithsonian Institution, Gift of Joseph H. Hirshhorn, 1966. Photography by Lee Stalsworth. © Bowness, Hepworth Estate: 51; © Nancy Holt/ DACS, London/VAGA, New York 2014: 155; David Honl/ZUMA Press/Corbis: 169r; Peter Horee/Alamy: 83; © Judd Foundation/VAGA, NY/DACS, London 2014. Kirsten Neumann/AFP/Getty Images: 123; © Anish Kapoor. All Rights Reserved, DACS 2014: 42-3; © Kienholz. Courtesy of L.A. Louver, Venice, CA: 171; © Phillip King. All rights reserved, DACS 2014. Private Collection/The © Charles & Josette Lenars/Corbis: 25; © Jeff Koons: 170; Erich Lessing/ akg-images: 69; © Sol Lewitt. ARS, NY and DACS, London 2014. Courtesy L.A. Louver, Venice, CA: 134; © David Mach. Courtesy of the artist: 101; © Succession H. Matisse/ DACS 2014: 118; © Anthony McCall. Courtesy Sprüth Magers Berlin London. Photo: David von Becker: 161; Minneapolis Institute of Arts, MN: Gift of Alan and Dena Naylor in memory of Thomas E. Leary/The Bridgeman Art Library: 30; Photo: The Henry Moore Foundation archive. Reproduced by permission of The Henry Moore Foundation: 173; Musée du Quai Branly, photo Patrick Gries/Bruno Descoings/ Scala, Florence: 59 © Muzeum Sztuki w Łodzi and Ewa Sapka-Pawliczak: 74; National Gallery of Art, Washington, D.C./Gift from the Collection of Raymond and Patsy Nasher: 86; National Portrait Gallery, Smithsonian/Art Resource/ Scala, Florence © 2014 Calder Foundation, New York/DACS London: 145t; © 2014 Bruce Nauman/Artists Rights Society (ARS), New York and DACS, London: 117; © 2014 The Barnett Newman Foundation, New York/DACS, London. Photo © James Leynse/Corbis: 105; © The Isamu Noguchi Foundation and Garden Museum/ARS, New York and DACS, London 2014. Photo: Kevin Noble: 90; Jean-Louis Nou/ akg-images: 150; © 1976 Claes Oldenburg: 89; © Philadelphia Museum of Art/CORBIS: 15(l); © Succession Picasso/DACS, London 2014. Photo © Philadelphia Museum of Art/CORBIS: 70br; © Succession Picasso/DACS, London 2014. Photo © Centre Pompidou, MNAM-CCI, Dist. RMN-Grand Palais/Georges Meguerditchian: 70tr; © Succession Picasso/DACS, London 2014. Digital image, The Museum of Modern Art, New York/Scala, Florence: 70(l); © Succession Picasso/DACS, London 2014. Photo © RMN-Grand Palais/ Béatrice HatalaL 84r; © Michelangelo Pistoletto. Courtesy of the Archivio Pistoletto. Photo: P. Pellion: 108; Paolo da Reggio: 176; © Estate of George Rickey/ DACS, London/ VAGA, New York 2014. Photo by Jeffery Sturges, courtesy Marlborough Gallery, New York: 146; © RMN-Grand Palais (musée d'Orsay)/Hervé Lewandowski: 107; © Nancy Rubins. Courtesy of the artist and Gagosian Gallery. Photograph by Erich Koyama: 102; Joel Saget/AFP/Getty Images © 2014 Calder Foundation, New York / DACS London: 145b; Photo Scala, Florence: 168; Leslie Schwartz Photography: 112; George M. Dawson, 1878, Canadian Museum of History: 32; © Estate of David Smith/DACS, London/VAGA, New York 2014: 132; © Shinique Smith. Photo: Jayson Keeling: 19; © Estate of Robert Smithson/DACS, London/VAGA, New York 2014: 27; © Estate of Robert Smithson/DACS, London/ VAGA, New York 2014. Photo © Scott Haefner Photography: 26; © Estate of Robert Smithson/DACS, London/VAGA, New York 2014. Photo © George Steinmetz/Corbis: 27; © Estate of Robert Smithson/DACS, London/VAGA, New York 2014. Photo © Scott T. Smith/CORBIS: 27; © Kenneth Snelson. Courtesy of the artist. Photo: Jan Cook: 109; Courtesy Sperone Westwater, New York: 41; Topical Press Agency/ Hulton Archive/Getty Images: 29; Frank Toogood/ FlickrVision/Getty Images: 167(l); Travel Pictures/Alamy © 2014 Niki de Saint Phalle Charitable Art Foundation/ADAGP, Paris and DACS, London/© ADAGP, Paris and DACS, London 2014: 150t; Travelpix/Alamy: 167r; Vanni Archive/Corbis: 28; Photo by Wolfgang Volz/laif/Camera Press: 37; © 1993 Rachel Whiteread. Courtesy of the artist, Luhring Augustine, New York, and Gagosian Gallery. Photo by Sue Omerod: 126; Yale University Art Gallery: 130.

Acknowledgements

As a sculptor, I am an interested reader of all things written on the subject. Although I am grateful for the insights presented and the conversations encouraged by such writing, I frequently find it difficult not to be critical of what I read. Often my misgivings extend beyond the page and have to do more with the absence of established formal and descriptive terms about sculpture.

This lack of an accepted language became especially apparent to me in the early years of my teaching at the University of Chicago. I noticed that, although skilled writers in other realms, my students lacked the vocabulary and experience needed to understand and write about works of sculpture. I wanted to see if I could help them appreciate sculpture as a vital form of aesthetic expression. One infused with meaning rather than a decorative object interned in a museum. But to do so effectively I needed to open the sculptural object up and analyse its essential characteristics, or *Elements*, and then demonstrate how the sculptor utilizes these to compose an aesthetic object. Knowing that words will always fail to describe a visual experience adequately, I created a class, the purpose of which was to encourage students to understand sculpture through making, looking and writing while using the Elements as their guide. Looking back, I would like to thank the many students whose intriguing works, insightful writings and discussions played a significant role in forming this book.

After retiring from teaching, I wanted to write a book that would share with others what I had learned about the language of sculpture in both my work and my teaching. After I submitted a summary to Clare Kunny, then in the education department at the Getty Museum, she recommended the project for a Museum Fellowship. I am very grateful to her for being able to see beyond that rather awkward first attempt to describe this book.

I wish to thank those at the Getty Foundation Museum Scholars programme and especially my graduate assistant, Emily Scott, for trusting in the viability of my project and their willingness to assist a sculptor who wanted to write a book. They gave me the luxury of uninterrupted time, unlimited resources and the encouragement needed to begin.

A number of my friends and colleagues were kind enough to read various incarnations of my manuscript and give needed advice and critical conversation. They are: Margherita Andreotti, Patricia Gallaher, Professor Tom Mapp (University of Chicago), Diane Miliotes, Peter Nagourney, Professor Richard Strier (University of Chicago), Professor David M. Sokol (University of Illinois at Chicago) and my dear friend James Geist, who over the years has tirelessly accompanied me on long walks through countless galleries and museums in New York.

One person in particular needs to be singled out. Marilyn Morrill gave of her time, energy and editing skills in a most unselfish way. She provided me with a weekly structure while I was writing the manuscript, and her demand for clarity was invaluable.

Once the book was written I was very fortunate that David Anfam at Phaidon Press, after reading a rather clumsy early version of the manuscript, thought it worthy of publication. His guidance, encouragement and faith in the project have been invaluable. As has been the advice and forbearance of my editor Ellen Christie. Ellen has, with understanding, consideration and great patience, given the book a clear, readable form.

Finally I would like to dedicate this book to the memory of my dear wife Robin. When we were very young she gave me the gift of time to work and the love, encouragement and resources necessary to follow my passion. I owe her a debt that I cannot repay.

BOSCH AND BRUEGEL

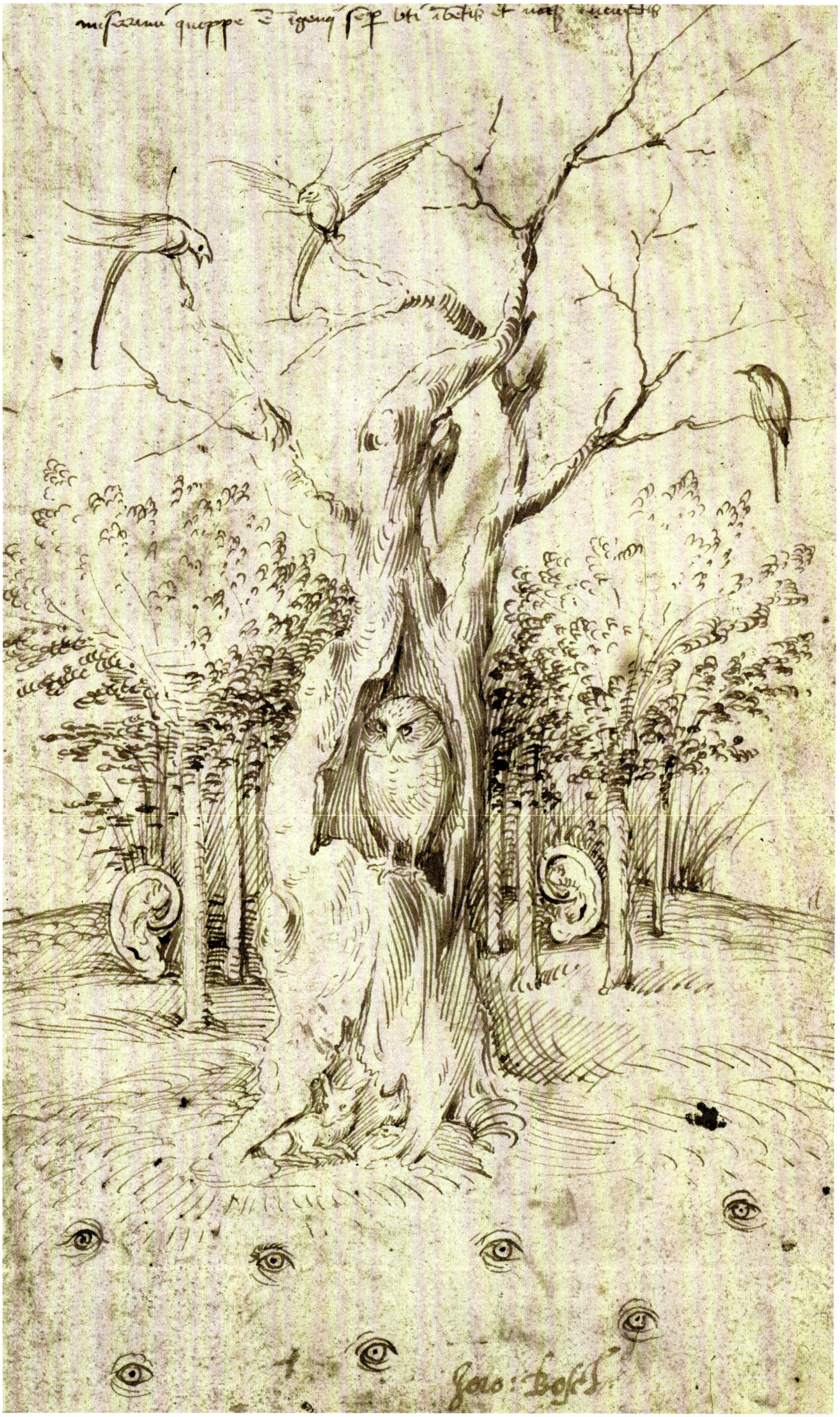

BOSCH & BRUEGEL

FROM ENEMY PAINTING TO EVERYDAY LIFE

Joseph Leo Koerner

Princeton University Press Princeton and Oxford

THE A. W. MELLON LECTURES IN THE FINE ARTS | NATIONAL GALLERY OF ART, WASHINGTON

BOLLINGEN SERIES XXXV: VOLUME 57

Published by Princeton University Press, 41 William Street, Princeton, New Jersey 08540

In the United Kingdom: Princeton University Press, 6 Oxford Street, Woodstock, Oxfordshire OX20 1TR

press.princeton.edu

Frontispiece: Hieronymus Bosch, *The Field Has Eyes, the Forest Has Ears,* c. 1500, pen and ink, Staatliche Museen zu Berlin, Kupferstichkabinett, Berlin

Jacket illustrations: (*front*) top: Hieronymus Bosch, detail of *The Last Judgment*, open state, c. 1504, panel, Gemäldegalerie der Akademie der Bildenden Künste, Vienna; and bottom: Pieter Bruegel the Elder, detail of *Battle between Carnival and Lent*, 1559, panel, Kunsthistorisches Museum, Vienna. (*back*) Pieter Bruegel the Elder, detail of *Winter Landscape with Bird Trap*, 1565, Musée des Beaux-Arts de Belgique, Brussels

Library of Congress Cataloging-in-Publication Data

Names: Koerner, Joseph Leo, author.
Title: Bosch and Bruegel : from enemy painting to everyday life / Joseph Leo Koerner.
Description: Princeton : Princeton University Press, 2016. | Series: The A. W. Mellon lectures in the fine arts | Series: Bollingen series ; XXXV:57 | Includes bibliographical references and index.
Identifiers: LCCN 2015047770 | ISBN 9780691172286 (hardcover : alk. paper)
Subjects: LCSH: Bosch, Hieronymus, -1516—Criticism and interpretation. | Bruegel, Pieter, approximately 1525-1569—Criticism and interpretation. | Genre painting, Dutch—16th century.

Classification: LCC ND653.B65 K64 2016 | DDC 759.9492/09031—dc23 LC record available at http://lccn.loc.gov/2015047770

British Library Cataloging-in-Publication Data is available

This is the fifty-seventh volume of the A. W. Mellon Lectures in the Fine Arts, which are delivered annually at the National Gallery of Art, Washington. This volume is based on lectures delivered in 2008. The volumes of lectures constitute Number XXXV in the Bollingen Series, supported by the Bollingen Foundation.

Designed by Leslie Fitch

This book has been composed in Crimson and Quay Sans Pro Type

Printed on acid-free paper. ∞

Printed in China

10 9 8 7 6 5 4 3

For Meg

CONTENTS

PREFACE

It is a historical commonplace that European art, having long been at the service of religion, became increasingly secular in subject matter and purpose and that this new worldliness produced a distinctive kind of painting, one voided of myths and histories and focused on everyday life. This type of painting eventually came to be called "genre painting," but before it received that name, it flourished especially in northern Europe during the sixteenth and seventeenth centuries. Its decline coincided roughly with the advent of Modernism, but it survives still today—albeit in different forms—in the pivotal place of the ordinary in contemporary painting. What is less familiar about this historical development is that, at its beginnings, the painting of everyday life was bound inextricably to what seems its polar opposite: an art of the bizarre, the monstrous, and the uncanny. It was a dark, fantastical form of painting that contained the seed of future genre painting, but negatively, as a bad seed. Familiar human existence, vividly portrayed, constituted a trap secretly set by an enemy—indeed, by the Old Enemy, Satan—to ruin us.

This book explores the birth of genre painting from the spirit of enmity. It approaches this strange beginning by looking closely at works of two towering painters of the European tradition. Of the two, Pieter Bruegel the Elder is the more obvious master portraitist of everyday life. This Netherlander's much-loved paintings of peasant revelry and seasonal labor foreshadow—and, in their monumentality, they already outdo—the whole development of genre painting that follows from them. By contrast, Hieronymus Bosch—active about fifty years before Bruegel—seems at first glance anything but a painter of everyday life. Hailed in his century a "devil-maker," this other great Netherlander excelled in nefarious phantasms, diabolical deceptions, and the grotesque machinery of damnation. Beautiful, terrifying, and supremely original, Bosch's dreamworlds remain deeply enigmatic—creations as inscrutable as the impossible creatures they contain. His most puzzling masterpiece conjures what seems an utterly alien world, an impossible unreality at odds with the laws of nature and the course of human history. And yet, virtually the entire repertoire of typical genre motifs that Bruegel would paint, and that later artists would recycle and develop, had its origins in Bosch.

In many of his works, Bosch endeavored to show, in great catalogues of punishment, the wages of sin in hell. To do this, to visualize the "why" of eternal pain, Bosch also portrayed sin's commission. Not abstract personifications, this painter's gluttons, misers, quacks, and libertines behave as plausible human actors do, and their actions unfold in real-world settings, in homes, brothels, and village streets, and before landscapes more wondrously capacious than any painted before. True, the Devil always lurks secretly in wait, and not just in the present, but from the world's beginning until very the end of time—because in Bosch's world, the familiar is enemy territory, and those who befriend it are foes to God. However, brought down to earth and there portrayed as if "from life," this cosmic hostility becomes the cradle of a painting of everyday life.

My engagement with genre painting reaches almost as far back as I can remember. My father was a professional painter who painted everything from life, usually out of doors and featuring persons found on the spot and involved in odd activities: people in bathing suits waiting for a train to the beach, a woman walking her pet tortoise on a leash, a midget feeding wild boar in the woods, a boy balancing a paper castle on his head. The works that resulted didn't look quite like genre paintings—their strange subjects made people mistake them for private, cryptic symbols—but they in fact depicted real persons in their everyday lives. During the summer, my father pursued this activity in Austria, with my mother, my sister, and me in tow. We wandered Vienna and its environs on foot, looking for motifs for my father to paint. Once a motif was discovered, he would portray it there and then while the rest of us waited on the road. Eventually, to have something to do, I started to paint with my father. This gave me time to wonder what bits of everyday life were the most paintable.

The intuition underlying this book wasn't fired while we walked or painted, however. Unusually, we were on a bus creeping through the sunbaked Puszta southeast of Vienna. August heat had forced us aboard, but the elaborate name of Wulkaprodersdorf (through which we knew the bus would pass) inspired us to disembark and continue there our hike. Passing into the sleepy village along its cobbled main street, we saw rows of yellow stucco farmhouses, all with arched entryways leading to little courtyards for livestock and feed. Almost arrived at its stop, our bus suddenly lurched into a deserted alley. As we struggled to keep our balance (we were already standing, ready to get off), my father cried, "Look!" We couldn't get over to his window in time, however, so we missed the significant sight: a severed pig's head hung above a doorway on a gable end. While my father hastily described what he had seen, the bus took a detour to a rotary way out in the fields, then back into town along the same dirt roads, until it ground to a halt just yards beyond where the divergence began. We piled out into the blazing sun in search of the pig's head that (we understood this without being told) my father would now begin to paint. But look as we might, the motif was nowhere to be found.

Had the pig's head been removed? This seemed implausible, because except for some restive hens, nothing stirred in the noontime heat. In our frantic searching, did we somehow lose our orientation in the village? Improbable though not impossible, as the heat confused and cut short our efforts. Had the motif been a mirage that my father wishfully imagined, so that he would have something interesting to paint? Three years earlier, in the largest work he ever made, he had portrayed a pig's head hanging on the brick wall of our neighbor's home in Pittsburgh, Pennsylvania. The local butcher at Shadyside Market prepared the prop. Perhaps that motif haunted him, causing him to imagine it in Wulkaprodersdorf; and yet, my father swore he saw the head. Was the village haunted? That didn't occur to us, because none of us believed in ghosts.

How reliable is my own recollection? I was only seven years old, and yet the scene unfolds vividly before me. I observe myself rushing from the left side of the rocking bus to my father, whose face was pressed to the window on the right side. I see my father's huge blue expedition rucksack on his shoulders. I recall my father, now on the street, explaining why the pig's head was the ultimate motif, and how what he had artfully concocted in Pittsburgh had uncannily come to pass. My clear recall of this episode mingles suspiciously with other adjacent recollections, in particular the memory of a certain painting hanging in Vienna's art museum. Bruegel's *Battle between Carnival and Lent* fascinated me as a child, partly because Bruegel was my father's favorite painter and partly because of a detail I discovered in it (see fig. 285). In the foreground, a butcher pretends to joust with a long roasting spit on which are skewered a pig's head, a chicken, a pigeon, and two sausages. Thanks to their sequence (head first, sausages last), these meats conjure the shape of a monstrous pig. Bruegel strengthens this impression by placing, just behind and above the spit, a live hog feeding on a swirl of excrement. Proudly pointing out this detail in the noble galleries of the Kunsthistorisches Museum, I proved to my father I understood his sense of humor.

The pig's head in Wulkaprodersdorf had darker resonances. Born to Jewish parents in Vienna, my father fled that city in 1938 after Hitler annexed Austria. The paintings he did in Vienna during the 1960s, when I was a child, featured ordinary vistas and vignettes, but scrutinizing these—as I had to when I painted by my father's side—I came to think that there lay in each a nightmarish core, as if some dark secret had been refracted through the whole Austrian landscape. Whether my father really glimpsed it, and whether I remembered correctly its apparition, the pig's head befitted Wulkaprodersdorf. In that obscure place in Europe's contested borderlands it seemed plausible that a pig's head would materialize and then disappear. Furthermore, this presence of terror in the ordinary seemed true not only for my father's motifs but for everyday life in general. It was in Vienna that Sigmund Freud—that city's most famous son—revealed how the familiar (in German *das Heimliche*) is constitutionally secretive and strange, while the uncanny (*das Unheimliche*) turns out to be the familiar in disguise. It is this paradox that led me to treat Bruegel and Bosch in tandem as both painters of ordinary life.

This book began in a series of talks delivered at the National Gallery of Art in 2007 as part of the A. W. Mellon Lectures in the Fine Arts. It presents those talks in revised form and maintains their purpose: to communicate to a general public the achievements of two great painters of everyday life. Non-experts are an ideal audience for this, since with everyday life everyone is an expert. I have tried to meet works of art as one meets things in life: contingently, in the flow of experience. The book's Introduction derives from the original opening talk. It launches our story at its tail end, with a small panel by Pieter Bruegel painted in the last year of his life. Expanded to four chapters, it serves as a sort of overture, encapsulating the motifs and structures developed later. Chapter 4 sets forth the reason for pairing Bosch and Bruegel—two artists from different times and of divergent sensibilities. Readers seeking a speedier entry might begin reading here. All the chapters are written to be readable on their own. Each focuses on a single masterpiece, and they urge us to slow down and appreciate the intricate machinery of individual works.

After the Introduction, the chapters stay close to the original lectures. I have not attempted to revise my argument in full light of scholarship published after 2007. My treatment of Bosch (Part I) proceeds from easy to hard. Chapter 5 treats one of the artist's most traditional works, both in program and in purpose. A triptych altarpiece with movable wings, Bosch's *Adoration of the Magi* (or *Epiphany*) vividly elucidates the sacrament of the Eucharist performed at the altar it must once have decorated. One notoriously obscure figure within this painting enters more difficult territory. The portrayal of an inscrutable enemy present at Christ's birth and active ever since draws out a key feature of Bosch's art: its symbolism and structure derive from a matrix of enmity. Chapter 6 focuses on Bosch's most-copied creation, *Temptation of Saint Anthony*. Like the *Adoration of the Magi*, this triptych presents few intractable problems. Its subject is again traditional: a saint turned away from the allures of the world and assailed by diabolical adversaries. In this work's depiction of devilry, I discern Bosch equating demons with crafted idols, and idols with the painting he himself has made. This dangerous conceit allows me—in chapter 7—to approach Bosch's one truly baffling work. Whereas in his other works he painted enemies and their imagery, in the so-called *Garden of Delights* Bosch created an enemy image, a painting posed—playfully and cruelly—as if it were meant to ruin someone, perhaps especially its beholder. Chapter 8 explores why Bosch might have done this, and why—in this work as well as in several of his extant drawings—he took on a distinctively malignant artistic persona.

My treatment of Bruegel (Part II) proceeds thematically. I begin with mature works that recast old stories from scripture and myth in contemporary terms, almost to the point of eclipsing those stories. I examine how this painter brought the diabolical visions of Bosch down to earth, first to the realm of human culture (chapter 10), then to the realm of nature (chapter 11). The book ends where it began, with a small, late masterpiece by Bruegel. A microcosm of the world and a summation of Bruegel's oeuvre, *The Magpie on the Gallows* revisits the themes and arguments put forward in the Introduction. In art as in experience, everyday life may be with us at the start but remains fugitive to the very end.

ACKNOWLEDGMENTS

This book has been written over more than twenty years, and along the way I have incurred many debts. In 1994, Barbara Butts invited me to collaborate on a show of Bruegel's prints collected by Julian Edison.[1] Working with this passionate collector who had managed to acquire Bruegel's complete printed oeuvre, I came to appreciate the consistency of the artist's output, how everything he made reached toward an awesome encyclopedic whole. In the same year, I began work on Bosch for a conference at Barnard College organized by Antonella Ansani. The conference title, "Alternative Realities: Medieval and Renaissance Inquiries into the Nature of the World," opened a path into this master's work. I took "alternative realities" to mean both the worlds people of the past presupposed and the worlds artists like Bosch creatively imagined. Early in my career, through Walter Haug, I had the good fortune of joining the workshop "Poetik und Hermeneutik." Adept at coming up with great themes, the workshop chose for its 1994 meeting the topic *Kontingenz* (Latin, *contingentia*). Viewing Bosch in the light of medieval concepts of accident and contingency yielded useful results.[2] A memorable seminar co-taught with Anne Anninger in Harvard's Houghton Library inspired me to compare Bosch's treatment of space and place to portolan charts and *mappae mundi*. The conference Histories of Science/Histories of Art organized at Harvard by Peter Galison and Carolyn Jones sharpened this focus. Presenting Bosch and Bruegel together as world makers, I searched their products for evidence of the idea that (in Richard Rorty's words) "truth was made rather than found."[3] This occasion, and the collaboration with Bruno Latour that stemmed from it, helped frame the series of Slade Lectures I delivered on Bosch and Bruegel at Cambridge University in 2003. Hosted by Deborah Howard and Jean-Michel Massing, these talks produced rough drafts for all but two of the chapters of the present book.

In 2001–2, a workshop organized by Lorraine Daston at the Max Planck Institute for the History of Science in Berlin led me to a topic I had tried strenuously to avoid: Bosch's so-called *Garden of Delights*. The workshop—titled "Things That Talk"—commenced with each participant presenting a brief, informal account of one talkative thing. I fixed on Bosch's enigmatic *Tree-Man* drawing, partly because, executed on a sheet of paper, it corresponded to the page I hoped to fill with words about it, and partly because the drawing featured a concoction that challenged our commonsense ideas about "things" (see fig. 246).[4] The drawing also resembled a more notorious monstrosity: the grotesque colossus at the center of the Hell panel of *The Garden of Delights* (see fig. 170). The comparatively simple pen-and-ink sketch led me into one of art history's most notorious scholarly quagmires. Writing about Bosch's drawing was an exhilarating experience, especially after the doldrums of Reformation art (which I had been previously studying), undertaken in the company of the fabulous interlocutors in Daston's group, including Joel Snyder and Simon Schaffer. Invited by Martin Büchsel and Peter Schmitt to speak at a conference on realism, I tried to define more precisely Bosch's relationship to his native Netherlandish tradition.[5] With fellowship support from the Guggenheim Foundation and (thanks to Gerhard Wolf) given a sanctuary in Florence at the Kunsthistorisches Institut, I began work on *The Garden of Delights* and its critical afterlife. Fascinated by Carl Schmitt's extensive engagement with Bosch's triptych, I attempted to understand the work in Schmittian terms, as an enemy painting. An invitation to deliver the Louise Smith Bross Lectures at the University of Chicago gave me an occasion to sketch an interpretation of *The Garden of Delights* together with Schmitt's pivotal references to it.[6]

Delivering the A. W. Mellon Lectures on Bosch and Bruegel in Washington, DC, I found myself speaking about enmity to an audience of friends. With Elizabeth Cropper and Charles Dempsey as the most amicable of hosts, I could not help reflecting on the powerful force of friendship. In 1985, in the work of Benjamin Binstock, a fellow graduate student at Berkeley, I had encountered a delightfully agonistic reading of Bosch. Arguing that Bosch intended *The Garden of Delights* as a parody of Jan van Eyck's representation of Paradise in the *Ghent Altarpiece*, Binstock enlisted—and therefore introduced me to—Wilhelm Fraenger's much-maligned account of Bosch as heretic. At Berkeley, James Marrow had urged me to study the structure of meaning in Bosch and, through his lectures and conversation, gave me my basic picture of the early Netherlandish tradition. Also at Berkeley, Wendy Ruppel proved beautifully that a simple and correct analysis of a work by Bosch was possible. Under the direction of Svetlana Alpers, who was also my doctoral adviser, several fellow graduate students were working on Bruegel in ways that influence me still, especially Lisa Jacobs-McCuster and Mark Meadow. Collaborating with Marjorie Cohn and Michael Zell (with the assistance of Risha Lee) on an exhibition at Harvard of Dutch and Flemish prints widened my understanding of Bruegel's place in the landscape tradition.[7] Work on the BBC television series *Northern Renaissance* (broadcast in 2006) enabled me to explore with a great team of directors and producers the places where Bosch and Bruegel lived and worked. I am especially grateful to Allan Campbell, Elaine Donnelly, Colin Murray, and Sandy Raffan for their guidance.

I have observed that Bosch divides viewers more dramatically than he joins them. Nonetheless, I have profited from countless friendly communications about this artist. Memorable among these were with Nuit Banai, Stephen Bann, Marisa Bass, Hans Belting, Andreas Beyer, Homi Bhabha, Yve-Alain Bois, Anthony Bond, Odilia Bonebakker, Peter Burke, Caroline Walker Bynum, Margaret Carroll, Michael Cole, Nicky Coutts, James Elkins, Melissa Franklin, Michael Fried, Adam Fuss, Dario Gamboni, Susan Gilchrist, Valentin Groebner, Andrea Hall, Jeffrey Hamburger, Moshe Halberthal, Anna Huber, Joan Koerner, Stephanie Koerner, Fritz Koreny, Graham Larkin, Pam Lee, Isabelle Marchesin, W. J. T. Mitchell, Gabriel Motzkin, Pasqualine Monier, Erika Naginski, David Napier, Felipe Pereda, Yona Pinson, Erwin Pokorny, Rudolf Preimesberger, John Richards, Ron Spronk, Natasha Staller, Catherine Sterling, Debra Strickland, Jeannie Suk, Ramie Targoff, Nancy Troy, Hugo van der Velden, Jasper van Putten, Peter Weibel, Bryan Wolff, Christopher Wood, Joanna Woodall, and Lawrence Wolff. I owe specific debts to Patricia Falguières, for help on early modern theories of counternature; to Pierre Lemonnier, for information about animal traps and their symbolism; to Jos Koldeweij, for helping me locate objects discussed in his work; to Matthijs Illsink and Paul Vandenbroek, for sharing their important discoveries; to Stephanie

Porras, whose doctoral dissertation on Bruegel I supervised; to my dear departed friend Frank Schirrmacher, who introduced me to the writings of Carl Schmitt in 1983; to Heinrich Meier, Valentin Groebner, and Noah Feldman, for conversations on Schmitt; to Daniela Nittenberg, for a close reading of one chapter of this book; and to David Fenner, Joy Sobeck, and Amy K. Hughes who edited the final drafts.

This book would not have been possible without the help of research assistants Sophie Kullman, Joshua O'Driscoll, Daniel Zolli, Normandy Vincent, and Jaspar van Putten. Stephen Greenblatt and Bruno Latour—both godfathers to my children—helped and inspired me, always and ever in different ways, including reading messy, unfinished drafts. My children, Ben, Sigi, Leo, and Lulu, put up with a distracted father and marched cheerfully through countless galleries around the world. They deserve special thanks.

My wife, Meg Koerner, has been throughout my support, my conscience, and my passion. Too long in the making, this book is dedicated with love and thanks to her.

INTRODUCTION

Parallel Worlds

1

IN THE ART-HISTORICAL MUSEUM

The Bruegel Room

I fell under Bruegel's spell in Vienna, in the room in the museum there filled with a dozen of his works (fig. 1).[1] Painted between 1559 and the artist's death, in 1569, these twelve pictures seem to belong together as a coherent suite or cycle, despite their different subjects and provenances. A common format contributes to this accord. Except for two, all are big panels: great rectangles well over five feet wide. Most of these monumental spans encompass vast, detailed panoramas balanced on a faraway horizon (fig. 2). Oriented horizontally, along the meeting place of earth and sky, these oblong paintings offer not mere landscape views but rather vistas that transcend what human sight can physically see, entire regions within an expanse too big ever to be the object of a single view. Not landscapes but proper "worldscapes," these paintings display human activity itself from a higher vantage point, almost—though never quite—from the perspective of the eternal. From that elevated place, whatever humanly occurs, whether peasant pastime or Bible story, seasonal labor or children's games, appears like some nomadic migration, evoking the ceaseless mobility of creatures too small and incomplete to call this place a home.[2]

And yet in Bruegel this perspective, in which nothing human seems to matter much, remains quintessentially humane. Embracing inhuman spans of time and space, and commanding effortlessly the grand public gallery where they hang, these paintings somehow whisper intimately to *you*, the individual beholder, that there is a private message there just your own. The harmonious assurance felt among this artist's works, the sense they give of pointing to some common center, some deep irony that each of us can personally grasp, depends on the masterful consistency of Bruegel's art. Whether he raises a Tower of Babel to the clouds or follows weary herdsmen home, Bruegel conjures the same vast world peopled by the same familiar humanity (see fig. 278). Stylistically constant and technically flawless throughout, and imbued with an all-pervasive incandescence that, radiating as if from beneath the painted surface itself, merges with the ambient light of the gallery, these works seem to speak to us in a here and now far transcending the specifics of history and custom that they also scrupulously record. This makes Bruegel the first modern Old Master painter. Portraitist of the people, he has become a supremely popular artist, his compositions the stuff of calendars and jigsaw puzzles, hence the throngs of tourists that jam Vienna's Bruegel room in summer.

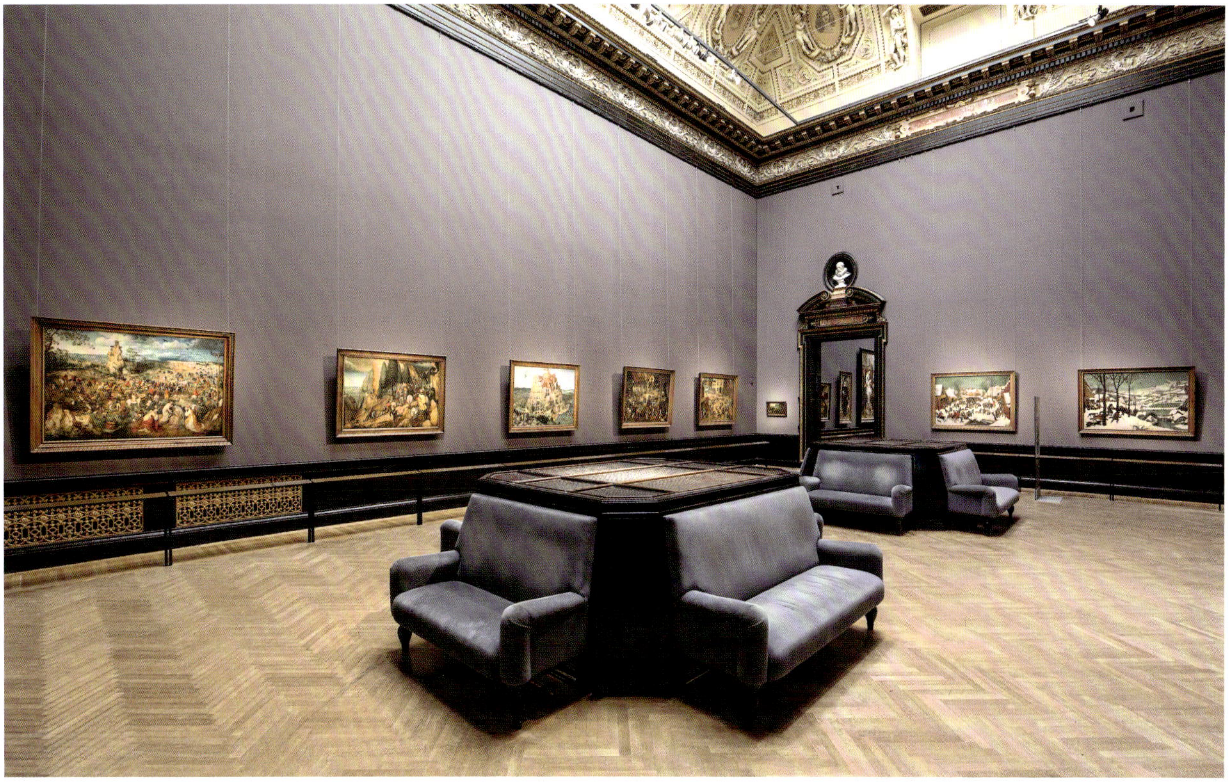

1 Bruegel Room, Kunsthistorisches Museum, Vienna

To experience Bruegel's paintings in the original, in the midst of life, is to be jostled by a crowd. Mass audiences obscure the aura of many famous masterpieces, turning them into sideshows in the carnival of cultural display. Bruegel, by contrast, makes crowds seem a cheerful extension of his art. Not only are his paintings packed with people—with revelers, with children, with entire armies of the living and the dead—these teeming masses behave like proper crowds. Some cluster in groups that act in unison, dancing, marching, feasting, fighting, building, and playing, while others stand a bit apart and observe the goings-on passively, as would an audience. And when people in Bruegel's paintings play the role of spectator—when they peer curiously through windows and pour through doorways to glimpse some street theater performed outside; when they stare, confused, at the fallen Saul at his moment of conversion to the Apostle Paul (see fig. 322); when they, grown-ups and children alike, on horseback and on foot, hurry toward Golgotha to reserve a good spot to witness Christ's Crucifixion (see fig. 266); and, most of all, when they turn from the diversions that have captured them in the picture to gape directly out at us gaping curiously back at them (see fig. 287)—their painted world gathers us, ourselves people in a crowd, into their inner fold. In Vienna, as in the museums in Berlin, New York, Madrid, Antwerp, and Detroit where the other major Bruegels hang, one can spot this artist's paintings from far off simply by the large and lingering audience they inevitably draw. A supreme portraitist of crowd behavior, Bruegel cleverly reflects and stage-manages his own mass appeal. This is surprising. With his printed images—published in large editions and sold on the open market—he banked on a large viewership.[3] But with his paintings, he addressed a select few. Only the most affluent burghers of the super-rich towns of Antwerp and Brussels could commission and behold the paintings we now admire.

After Bruegel's death, the audience for his paintings became even more elite. For three centuries, the Vienna pictures were precious imperial property. The core group was acquired

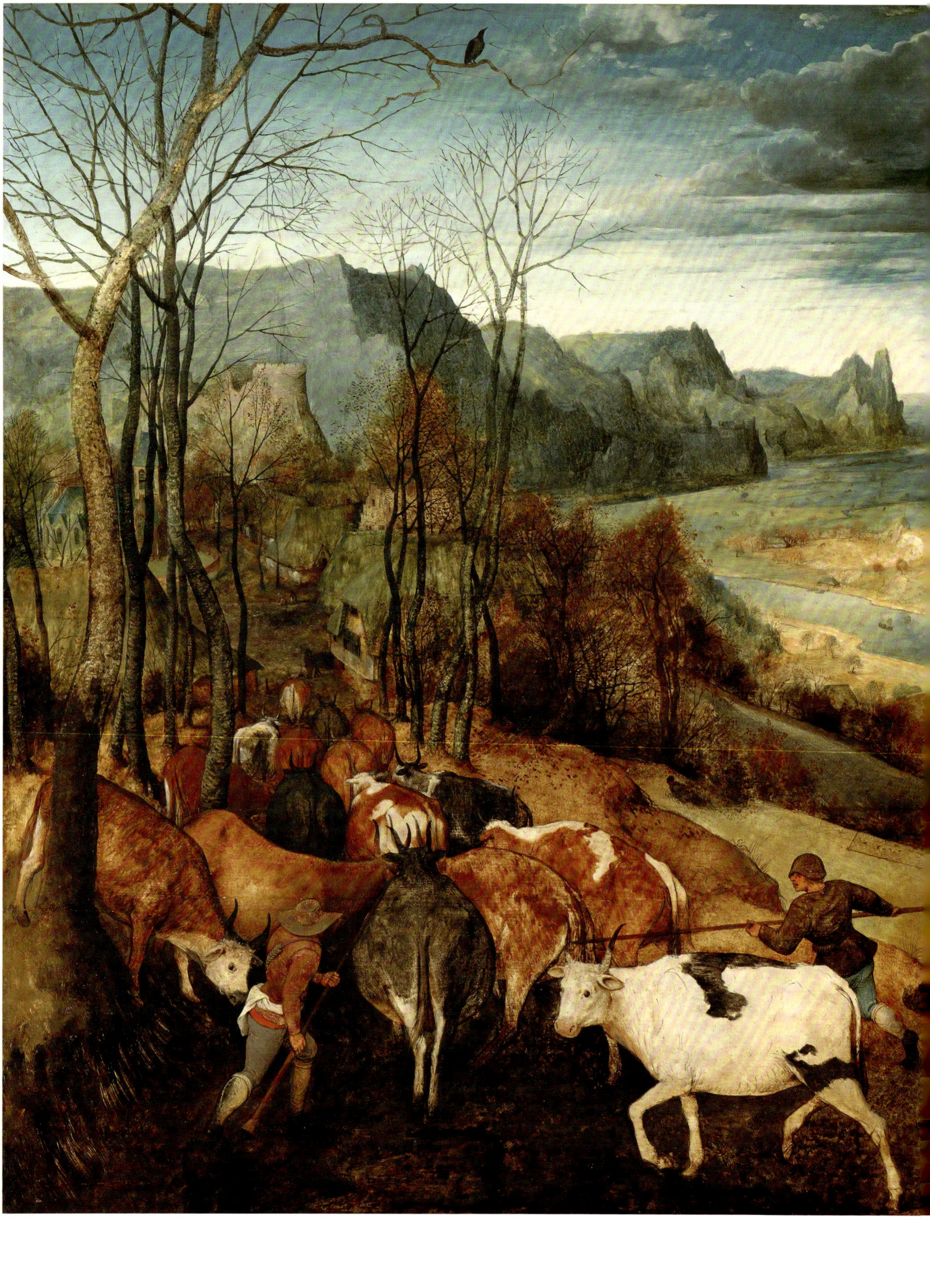

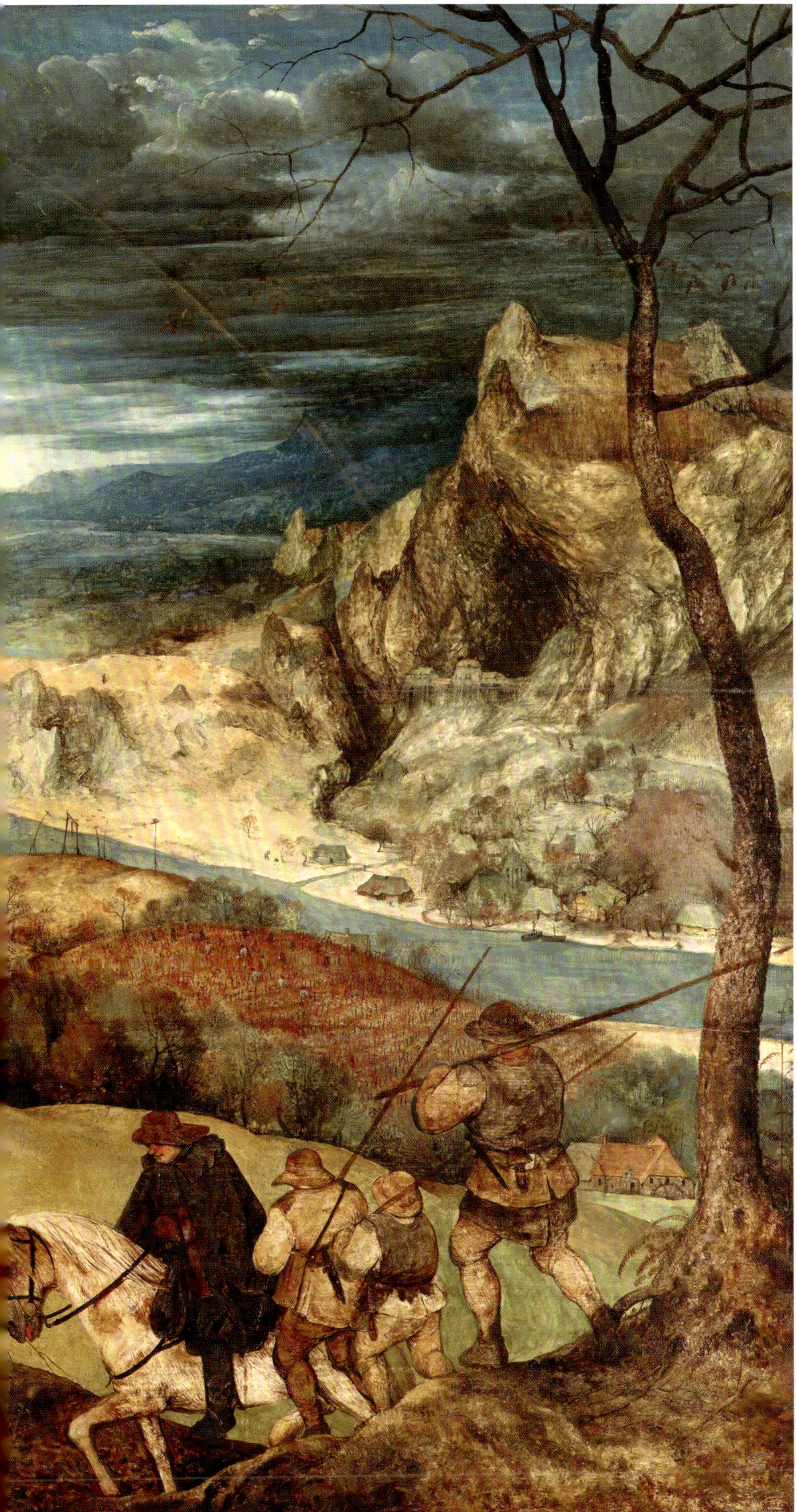

2 Pieter Bruegel the Elder, *The Return of the Herd* (*Autumn*), from the *Seasons of the Year* series, 1565, panel, Kunsthistorisches Museum, Vienna

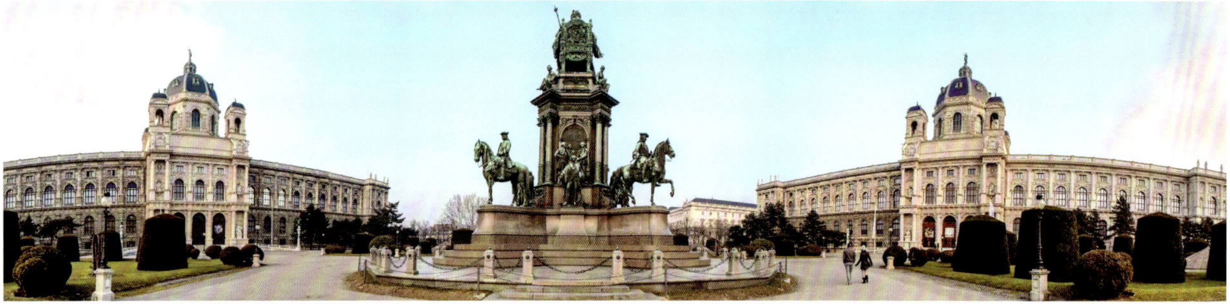

3 Kunsthistorisches Museum and Naturhistorisches Museum, view of façades from the Ringstrasse

in 1594 by Archduke Ernst of Austria during his governorship of the Netherlands. After Ernst's death, in 1595, they passed to his brother, Emperor Rudolf II of Habsburg.[4] Entering Rudolf's vast holdings in Prague, they came to rest at the very heart of Europe's totemic treasury. The imperial collections of the House of Habsburg were a truly numinous depository. Possessed of an all-consuming passion for art, Rudolf incorporated the fabulous paintings that he eagerly purchased or commissioned, along with precious specimens of nature gathered in the Old World and the New, into the primeval assemblage of sacred relics and imperial regalia that reached back, beyond Habsburg rule, to Charlemagne and ancient Rome.[5] There Bruegel's paintings stood, vivid tableaux of "the people" displayed within a setting that could hardly be more elite. Much later, in 1869, after revolution had shaken noble power to its core, the apostolic emperor of the Habsburg line, Franz Joseph I, resolved to put this ancestral treasure on public view. In a grand forum facing the Imperial Palace in Vienna, on the far side of the busy Ringstrasse (the circular boulevard that had recently replaced the city wall), Franz Joseph erected two huge and perfectly symmetrical museums (fig. 3).[6] On the one side the Natural History Museum displayed the diversity of nature (the old *naturalia* collections) together with the excavated remains of prehistoric (or "natural") European peoples. On the other side the pedantically christened "Art-Historical" Museum displayed artworks—chiefly Old Master paintings of the period from the fifteenth to the eighteenth century—as if they formed the ascending ladder of human history itself. And it was there, in 1891, when the imperial museums stood complete, that Bruegel's paintings finally became accessible to the wider public.

Before reaching the Bruegel room—Gallery No. 10—visitors today must still traverse these vestiges of imperial power. Having strolled between the twinned immensities representing Nature and Culture, they enter the Art-Historical Museum through an aggressively historicist façade. The entranceway's pseudo-Renaissance décor—the result of an unhappy collaboration between the German architect and theorist Gottfried Semper and his prolific Viennese associate, Karl von Hasenauer—was intended to evoke a specific and illustrious past: the artistic epoch of Albrecht Dürer and Raphael together with the political epoch of Habsburg world dominion. What seemed anachronistic to Semper's and Hasenauer's critics looks reasonably authentic today: most visitors to the Kunsthistorisches Museum take the building to be a vintage Renaissance edifice. Ascending the colossal double staircase that gently rises to the paintings' gallery, visitors feel themselves to be elevated (if also dwarfed) before they glimpse a single masterpiece. Halfway up these stairs, with Antonio Canova's marble *Hercules* looming over them, they arrive—tacitly—at art history's old forking paths: the steps to the right lead to the Italian schools of painting, the steps to the left to the northern schools. (In 1891, this crossroads could have been imagined as demanding a choice between beauty and truth, embodied respectively by Latin grace and Teutonic manliness.) But before visitors can make that fateful decision, they will probably have been swept along by the mass of tourists climbing to the left, bound for the ever-popular northerners. And after a perfunctory glance at Bruegel's Italianizing precursors languishing unnoticed in the first grand gallery, they—we—arrive at last in the Bruegel room, amazed, energized, and not a little unnerved by the crowds.

With its soaring ceiling and awkward plush chairs, the room itself makes tourists feel uncouth and out of place. Like the restless ghost of the museum's imperial past, an invisible security system holds viewers way back from the pictures. Lean too far forward over the post-and-rope barriers and an alarm bell sounds. Trip the alarm twice and a taped voice angrily admonishes, "Please keep your distance!" Soon enough a guard rushes in and scolds the culprit personally. These attendants skillfully feign their shock, since protective glazing and an antiquated lighting system make infractions inevitable. Every curious visitor will press forward to these pictures to make out their details. The activities depicted in *The Children's Games* and *Battle between Carnival and Lent* make visual sense only at very close range; the three *Months* panels, including *The Hunters in the Snow*, hide entire narratives in their distances; and the biblical paintings—most pointedly *Christ Carrying the Cross*—conceal their sacred subjects from those who stand too far away (see figs. 294, 284, 315, and 266). Bruegel made such pictures to be viewed from two distances, each morally as well as physically distinct. At a polite remove, where the museum wants us to stand, we occupy the empyrean vantage point of the painting as whole. There the larger structures of townscape and countryside predominate, and we gaze downward onto human activities with indifference, because we in fact can hardly differentiate them. But, being human, we find ourselves drawn down into the hubbub, which causes us to edge up to the picture, to the point where the composition as a whole gets lost (see fig. 318).

Bruegel's large-scale compositions viscerally draw in their viewers. From our standpoint in the museum, the foreground figures in the famous *Peasant Dance* look just about life-size (see fig. 254).[7] The painter scales the festivities so that they seem to begin only a few strides beyond us, at the distance we keep from his painting. By way of the couple joining the dance, Bruegel carries us corporeally into the scene, their stomping feet leading ours. And on the generous expanse of ground kept empty for our entrance, where we would step from the museum's polished parquetry onto good, solid earth, he scatters objects that make us stoop—in our world as we would in theirs—to see them: walnut shells, bits of straw, and a clay jug handle (see fig. 257). Even if we do not actually reach out to touch these now truly life-size images, we will, if we visit the gallery with friends, be powerfully tempted to point them out with our finger.

The Peasant and the Bird Thief

It is this inevitable finger-pointing that trips the museum's alarm, causing the Bruegel room to reverberate with the rough music of reproach. After tripping the bell yourself, you begin to watch for others doing it. A moment ago you were the bull in a china shop. Now you are the smug insider nodding knowingly to the guards. This human comedy begins in Bruegel's pictures themselves. Already an impious crowd has invaded a quiet and beautiful world. And already there begin deep shaming rituals wherein our self-consciousness primordially consists, in which beholders suddenly find themselves beheld, and those mocking from the sidelines become the center of the larger prank. One summer day several years ago, when a rainstorm drove Vienna's tourists indoors to the museum, I got so obsessed with spotting offenders

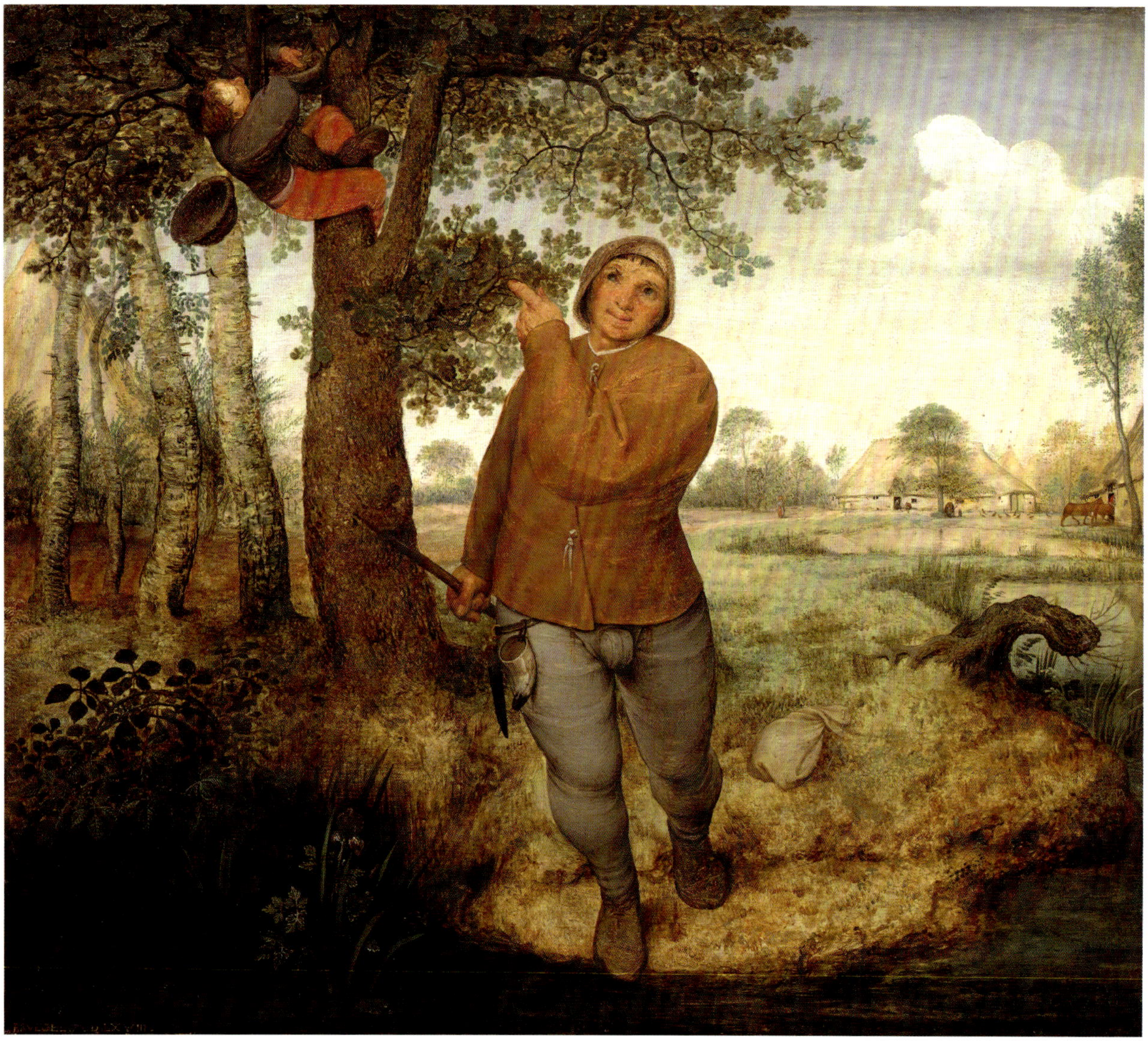

4 Pieter Bruegel the Elder, *The Peasant and the Bird Thief*, 1568, panel, Kunsthistorisches Museum, Vienna

triggering the alarm that I did not notice it was I who had become the culprit. While gaping at the crowd, I had backed right up against a little masterpiece, causing all hell to break loose. Turning around to gain some distance, I fell at once into a painted trap (fig. 4).[8]

Less than half the size of the other Bruegels that now surround it, this signed and dated panel hails you individually as you wander the galleries: an aggressive image of motion directed to people by nature on the move. Bruegel centers on a striding peasant—probably a cowherd—whose eyes, gesture, and body accost you before you have time to retreat. His directness fits his character. He is the type who gets intimate with *everyone*, exuding a confidence that what seems funny to him will seem funny to you, unless you yourself look funny to him, say by turning away, in which case he will be pointing at you. It helps that he seems already to look past you, that his intimacy thus is brief, and that what he shows—once you get there—has become *your*, not *his*, affair. And it helps that he is a man of the country, and that whoever he meets, whether it be patricians in 1568 in Brussels, where Bruegel painted this picture, or tourists in Vienna today, will be of the city, and therefore will feel off balance facing a countryman on his own ground.

His elbow thrust forward like a prow, the peasant gazes and marches straight at us, giving uncanny muscle to all that the painting will demand. This is an art-historical first. No painting

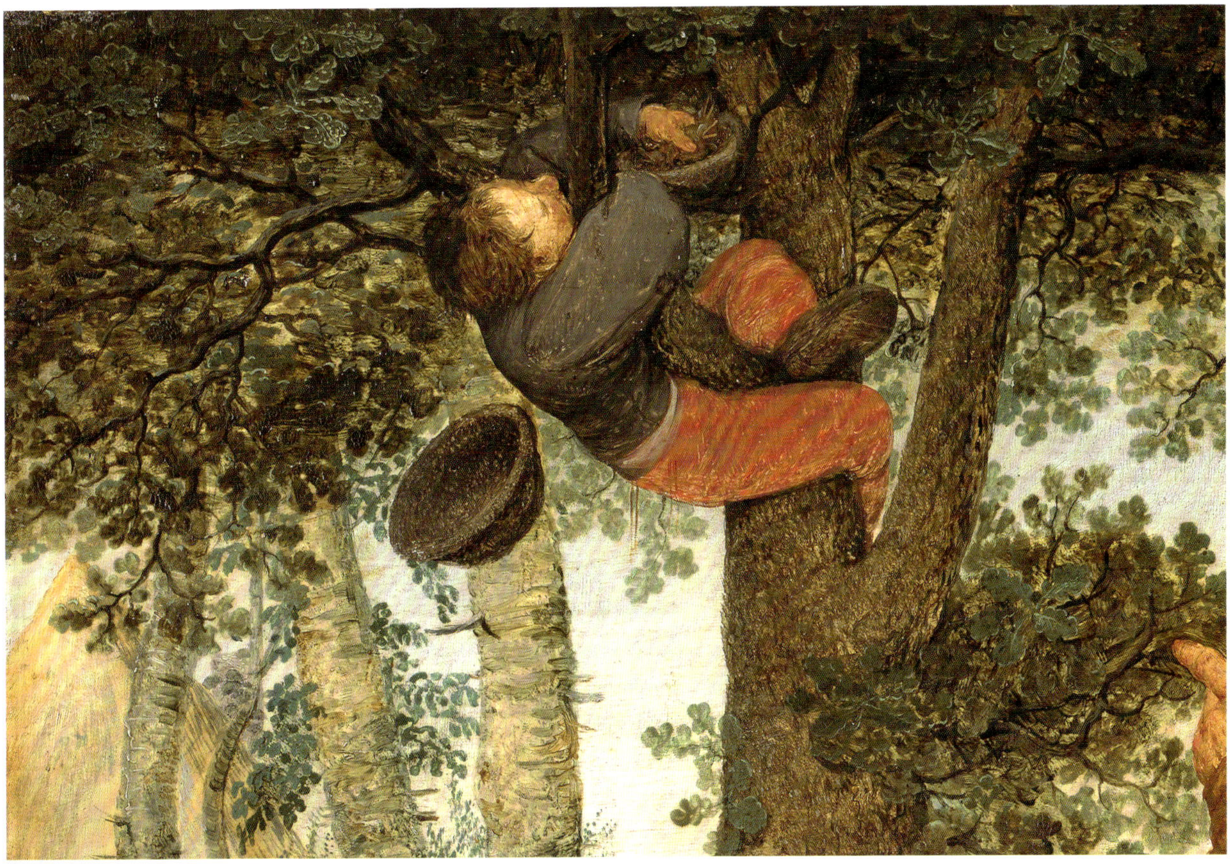

5 Detail of Pieter Bruegel the Elder, *The Peasant and the Bird Thief* (fig. 4)

before had ever invaded our space as frontally as this.[9] We look *across* at the peasant's face and upper body but straight *down* on his legs and feet, as if at the instant we glimpse his present standpoint his face will have pressed right up against ours. Yet the peasant's purpose in confronting us is to point a finger rearward, in the exact opposite direction of his stride but in sync with the vector of our gaze. And thus, with a velocity doubled by his forward momentum, we are catapulted into the picture and toward the peasant's discovery: the tree-climbing boy in signal-red trousers (fig. 5). Further, we discover that it is a nest that the boy is reaching into and that the things in his hand are *birds*, crying in terror and fluttering their wings to escape. Drawn into this tiny drama at the heart of the picture, tempted to gesture toward it with *our* finger, we bear down on the painted surface, where details (the splayed feathers of the panicked birds) dissolve into lovely scribbles of pigment.

In pointing it out, the peasant implies that this detail will be visually hard to get. Our spotting it within the work of art becomes analogous to the peasant's coup of espying the bird thief in nature. And both these accomplishments are akin to, and also far outstripped by, the feat of the bird nester, who has not only glimpsed but also grasped the birds. Observe the deviousness of his approach: whereas the peasant rudely points—and we ourselves look—straight at the birds, he, the thief, cleverly snatches his quarry from behind, his free left arm circling around the tree and into the nest in our direction. Of course, our getting caught up in the picture's event pales by comparison with the surprise felt by the birds that, just before, rested safe and hidden in their nest. The thief's free-falling hat animates the catastrophe. Setting the painting's tempo, it indicates that the "now" we sluggishly grasp unfolds rapidly, as do other events that will in the next instant occur.

On the ground behind the peasant, an abandoned sack sets forth events that led up to the present. Before climbing the tree (Bruegel lets us imagine), the thief quietly laid aside his bundle, whereupon the peasant, heading out from his rustic home, passed that bundle, surmised its purpose, and sought, and then spotted, the crafty thief just as his fingers closed suddenly and expertly round the frail bodies of the ambushed birds. But what happens next, in a future that, with the striding peasant, rushes fast upon us? Will the nest robber descend the tree with the birds now firmly in hand? Will he lose his grip and crash to earth? His tumbling hat suggests the precariousness of his own situation. Shaped, sized, and colored like the nest—indeed virtually identical to a falling nest—the hat projects calamity beyond the birds to the painting as a whole. Resembling both the hat and nest, the thief's sack extends a mesmerizing play of forms that animates the strange, bent-over tree at the picture's right, with its pollarded crown and inward curve that echo the form of the sack, as well. Activating our sense of an ending, intimating that the restless present is about to be resolved, these auspicious correspondences heighten the terrible urgency of the "now" of life. Omens of an impending doom that never comes, they also seem meaningful without actually meaning anything.

Bruegel's paintings are filled with moments like these: ominous proximities of half-related things, suggestive similarities of shape and color, objects curiously isolated through the purified geometry of their painted forms. Meaningful without ever yielding their significance, such passages vex especially the historian of art, who wants a symbol clearly to symbolize and expects the story properly to end.[10] Seeking to draw conclusions, we expect our objects to be conclusive, as well. By placing art primarily in *history*, in a chain of causes and effects completed in the past, we assume that what the artwork captures has already ended and we analyze that result. But Bruegel's plots never end. In rapid progress when first beheld, his pictures remain permanently ongoing. His body striding forward and his finger pointing back, and circled by the ceaseless flow of waters, the peasant plunges forth into the very midst of life. There the future lies hidden, be it ever so near. This makes Bruegel's paintings a unique epiphany in the Art-Historical Museum. Their endings remain as inscrutable as our own.

2

LIFE TIME

Peasant Bruegel

Bruegel died in Brussels in early September 1569, about a year after *The Peasant and the Bird Thief* stood complete.[1] Death interrupted this life suddenly and unexpectedly. World famous through his prints and prized as a painter by a cultural elite, he was, when he died, still a rising star in Europe's artistic firmament.[2] His late works, made while he was in his early forties, outshine all he had done before. His first biographer tells us that a major commission from the Brussels town council was left uncompleted; commemorating the great canal dug between Brussels and Antwerp, it might have taken Bruegel in a new, monumental direction.[3] We are also told that on his deathbed the artist, preparing for his demise, had many libelous drawings swiftly burned to spare his wife future troubles,[4] for they lived in deeply uncertain times. In 1567, in response to religious and political rebellion here, Spanish Habsburg troops seized emergency powers in the Netherlands, killing many hundreds.[5] In 1568, members of the local nobility who had pleaded for moderation were tried by the special extrajudicial Council of Troubles and beheaded on the Grand Place in Brussels. Suspended in a state of exception, law gave way to violence. Uncertain, too, was the future of the art of painting and of works made by Bruegel's hand. In 1566, Protestant iconoclasts in the Netherlands had stripped their churches of paintings and statues: politically and economically motivated, this had been the riot that triggered martial law. Where the image breakers' fury would end, and whether it would extend beyond sacred icons to strike secular artworks in the homes of the rich, was anyone's guess.

The painter's untimely passing surprised his closest companions. In a eulogy penned around 1574, the cartographer Abraham Ortelius complained that Bruegel, his beloved friend, "was snatched away from us in the flower of his age" (fig. 6).[6] Why this had happened the great mapmaker could only speculate. Perhaps Death had erred, taking the painter to be already elderly on account of his artistic perfection. Perhaps envious Nature was to blame, fearing that Bruegel's "ingenious imitations" would "bring her in contempt," for this artist's works seemed the product not of art but "of Nature." Not simply "the best of painters," Bruegel was "the very nature of painters."[7] Or so it seemed at the end, from the perspective of a mourner making sense of a life suddenly stolen by death. But how did things look at the start? What stories were written about Bruegel's beginnings?

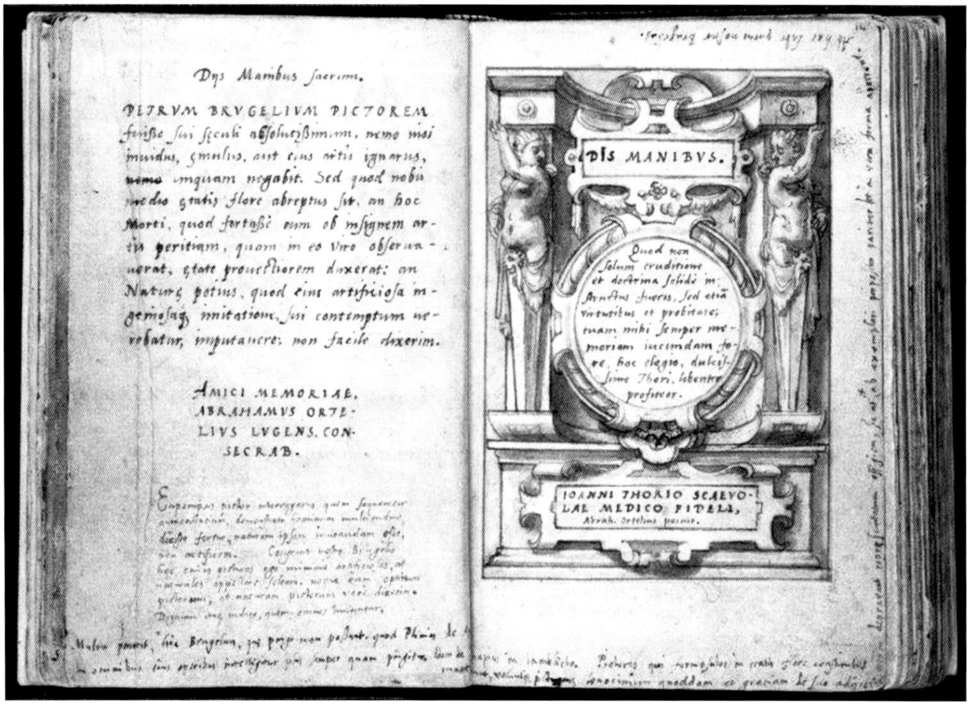

6 Abraham Ortelius, *Album Amicorum*, c. 1573, Pembroke College, University of Cambridge, fol. 13v

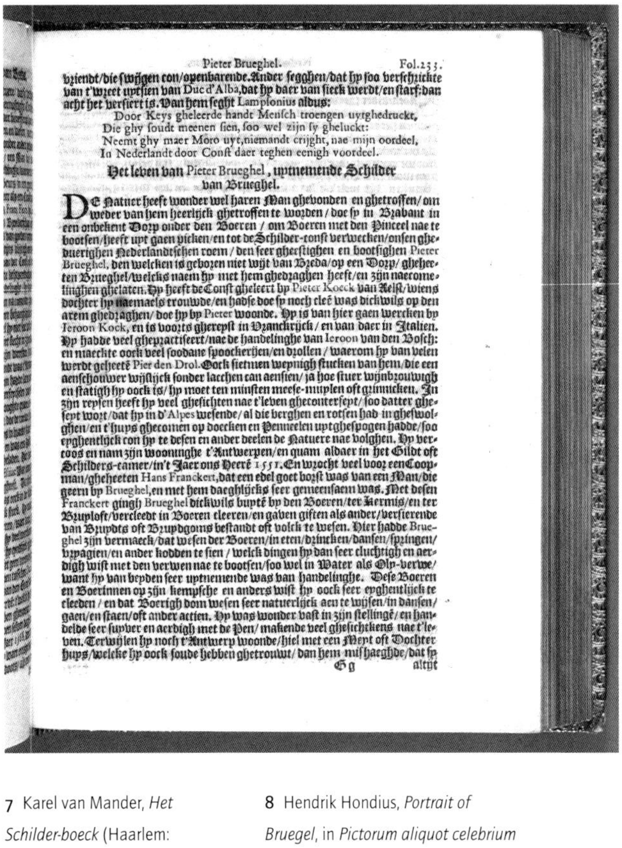

Pieter Brueghel. Fol.233.

brieudt/die swijgen con/openbarende. Ander segghen/dat hy soo verschrickte van t'wreet uytsien van Duc d'Alba, dat hy daer van sieck werdt/en starf: dan acht het versiert is. Van hem seght Lampsonius aldus:

Door Keys gheleerde handt Mensch troengen uytghedruckt,
Die ghy soudt meenen sien, soo wel zijn sy gheluckt:
Neemt ghy maer Moro uyt, niemandt crijght, nae mijn oordeel,
In Nederlandt door Const daer teghen eenigh voordeel.

Het leven van Pieter Brueghel, uytnemende Schilder van Brueghel.

DE Natuer heeft wonder wel haren Man ghevonden en ghetroffen/ om weder van hem heerlijck ghetroffen te worden / doe sy in Brabant in een onbekent Dorp onder den Boeren / om Boeren met den Pinceel nae te bootsen/ heeft uyt gaen picken/ en tot de Schilder-const verwecken/ onsen ghedverighen Nederlandtschen roem / den seer gheestighen en bootsighen Pieter Brueghel, den welcken is geboren niet wijt van Breda/ op een Dorp/ gheheeten Brueghel/ welcks naem hy met hem ghedraghen heeft/ en zijn naecomelinghen ghelaten. Hy heeft de Const gheleert by Pieter Koeck van Aelst/ wiens dochter hy naemaels trouwde/ en hadse doe sy noch cleẽ was dickwils op den arem ghedraghen/ doe hy by Pieter woonde. Hy is van hier gaen wercken by Ieroon Kock, en is voorts ghereyst in Vranckrijck / en van daer in Italien. Hy hadde veel ghepractiseert/ nae de handelinghe van Ieroon van den Bosch: en maeckte oock veel soodane spoockerijen/ en drollen / waerom hy van velen werdt gheheetẽ Pier den Drol. Oock sietmen weynigh stucken van hem/ die een aenschouwer wijslijck sonder lacchen can aensien/ ja hoe stuer wijnbrouwigh en statigh hy oock is/ hy moet ten minsten meese-muylen oft grimmicken. In zijn reysen heeft hy veel ghesichten nae t'leven ghecontersept/ soo datter ghesept wort/ dat hy in d'Alpes wesende/ al die berghen en rotsen had in gheswolghen/ en t'huys ghecomen op doecken en Penneelen uytghespogen hadde/ soo eyghentlijck con hy te desen en ander deelen de Natuere nae volghen. Hy vercoos en nam zijn woonínghe t'Antwerpen/ en quam aldaer in het Gildt oft Schilders-camer/ in't Iaer ons Heerẽ 1551. En wrocht veel voor een Coopman/ gheheeten Hans Franckert, dat een edel goet borst was van een Man/ die geern by Brueghel, en met hem daeghlijcks seer gemeensaem was. Met desen Franckert gingh Brueghel dickwils buytẽ by den Boeren/ ter Kermis/ en ter Bruylost/ vercleedt in Boeren cleeren/ en gaven giften als ander/ versierende van Bruydts oft Bruydegoms bestandt oft volck te wesen. Hier hadde Brueghel zijn vermaeck/ dat wesen der Boeren/ in eten/ drincken/ dansen/ springen/ bryagien/ en ander kodden te sien / welck dingen hy dan seer cluchtigh en aerdigh wist met den verwen nae te bootsen/ soo wel in Water als Oly-verwe/ want hy van beyden seer uytnemende was van handelinghe. Dese Boeren en Boerinnen op zijn kempsche en anders wist hy oock seer eyghentlijck te cleeden / en dat Boerigh dom wesen seer natuerlijck aen te wijsen/ in dansen/ gaen/ en staen/ oft ander actien. Hy was wonder vast in zijn stellingẽ/ en handelde seer suyver en aerdigh met de Pen/ makende veel ghesichtkens nae t'leven. Terwijlen hy noch t'Antwerp woonde/ hiel met een Meyt oft Dochter huys/ welcke hy oock soude hebben ghetrouwt/ dan hem mishaeghde/ dat sy

Gg altijt

7 Karel van Mander, *Het Schilder-boeck* (Haarlem: Paschier van Wesbvach, 1604), fol. 233r, Houghton Library, Harvard University

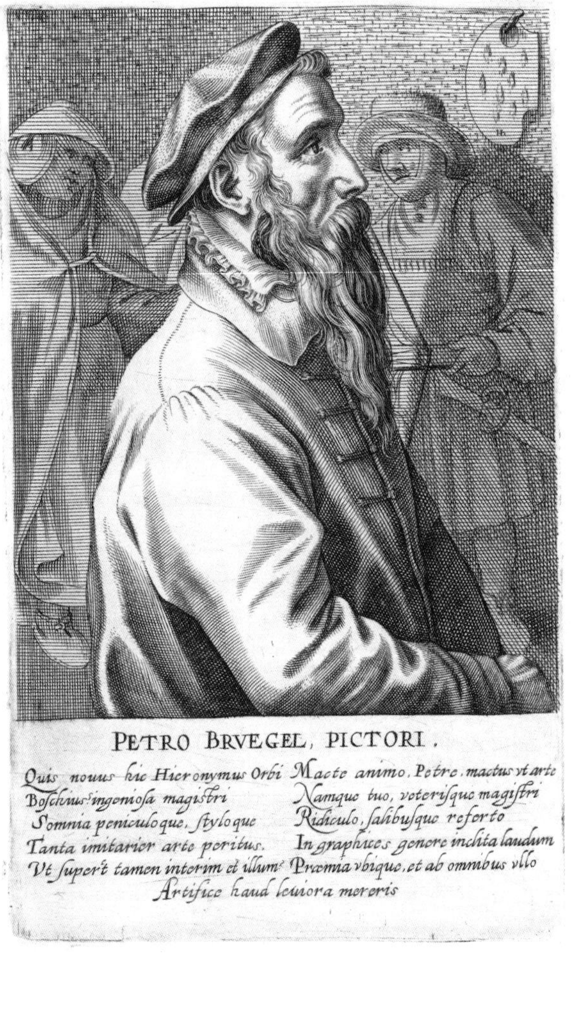

8 Hendrik Hondius, *Portrait of Bruegel*, in *Pictorum aliquot celebrium praecipué Germaniae inferioris effigies*, 1610, engraving, 532.99.455, Houghton Library, Harvard University

We know neither the place of Bruegel's birth nor the year. The artist's first biographer, Karel van Mander, is hazy on these facts.[8] Writing in 1604, when living memory of the artist had all but faded, he takes *Bruegel* to be a place name that the artist assumed as his own, whereas it was more probably the shortened form of a patronymic. The first surviving trace of his name—the record of his admission, in 1551, into the painters' guild in Antwerp—has him as *Peeter Brueghels*, with the final *s* most likely indicating "son of."[9] Van Mander did launch an enduring myth about the painter's origins, however. According to this myth Bruegel hailed from the peasantry: "Nature found and struck lucky wonderfully well with her man—only to be struck by him in turn in a grand way—when she went to pick him out in Brabant in an unknown village amidst peasants, and stimulate him towards the art of painting so as to copy peasants with the brush" (fig. 7).[10] Life's facts come thickly wrapped in fable. Bruegel achieved early fame through his exotic Alpine views and through diabolical fantasies in the manner of Hieronymus Bosch. But by Van Mander's time and afterward, his fame rested chiefly in lively portrayals of the Flemish peasantry in their everyday pursuits. A print from 1610 celebrates this enduring legacy (fig. 8).[11] Published by the prolific engraver Hendrik Hondius, it reuses an older profile likeness of the artist, first published in 1572 on the press of Hieronymus Cock and attributed to Johannes Wierix (see fig. 62).[12] But it projects onto the originally blank background of the 1572 engraving of two masked rustics taken from a woodcut after Bruegel's own design (see fig. 292).[13] To the cosmopolitan collectors who prized Bruegel's art, peasants were quasi-natural beings. Rooted in the landscape and behaving in unmannered, instinctive ways, they seemed to live lives untouched by history and isolated from the world. To capture their nature naturally required a special skill. And it was this skill that Van Mander's fable explains by asserting that Bruegel was born as one of them: he painted what he originally was, and his art, arising without professional training or artistic influence, was a natural formation.

The fable thrusts Bruegel into the wilderness. It pits the artist against Nature as a rival trapper. Nature tracked and ambushed Bruegel in his natural habitat, an unmapped corner of the Brabantine countryside. She did this so that this painter might capture naturally creatures like himself, presumably because painting, pursued artfully in towns and cities, had no access to rustic artlessness. But then Bruegel, the savage, turned around and seized Nature, turning her into his captive subject. The fable plays on the ancient dictum that art imitates nature. To "copy peasants with the brush" is to imitate Nature's *products*—what philosophers in the Middle Ages termed *natura naturata*: "nature natured" or "nature already created." Bruegel did this and much more. He also imitated Nature's *productive powers—natura naturans*, "naturing nature"—and by doing so, he usurped her sovereignty.[14] Ortelius signaled this achievement when he lauded Bruegel as the "very nature of painters." Van Mander makes this inversion of nature and art mirror the ironic reversals found in Bruegel's own works, where thieves get robbed and hunters hunted, and where heroes become fools and folly rules all (see fig. 36). In his Bruegel biography, the role reversal functions to prepare the ground for an alternative story of Bruegel and the peasantry.

Fieldwork

This second myth—a sort of countermyth—unfolds not in the beginning of the artist's life but in the middle. Bruegel has set forth from his native village, taking for himself and his offspring its name. After apprenticeships and travels, he settles in Antwerp, the world capital of trade and transport, where he enjoys the patronage of cosmopolitan merchants. Grown worldly himself, he now treats the local peasantry—erstwhile his kin—as an elusive quarry to be craftily pursued:

> Bruegel often went out of town among the peasants . . . to kermesses and weddings, dressed in peasants' costume, and . . . gave presents just like the others, pretending to be family or acquaintances of the bride or the bridegroom. Here Bruegel entertained himself observing the nature of the peasants—in eating, drinking, dancing, leaping, lovemaking and other amusements—which he then most animatedly and subtly imitated with paint.[15]

These expeditions furnished the artist with a special expertise, Van Mander asserts: "He knew how to attire these men and women peasants very characteristically in Kempish or other costumes." It is a remarkable change. In the first story, Bruegel is the insider, the native informant who reports on an isolated human enclave—a "lifeworld"—uniquely his own. In the second, he is the outsider who enters primitive territory through subterfuge. In the one, he is an ethnographic curiosity, the anomaly of a peasant who paints. In the other, he is a curious ethnographer who temporarily "goes native" in order to do good fieldwork. Compressed into one life, these antithetical identities trace the circular and distinctively modern itinerary from nature to culture and nostalgically back to nature.

Karel van Mander was the pioneering historian of northern European art. The "Life of Pieter Bruegel" belongs to his great compendium of artists' biographies—titled *Lives of the Illustrious Netherlandish and German Painters*—from which much of our knowledge of the tradition derives. In compiling biographies (he wrote more than 250), Van Mander assumed that an artist's life was of special, lasting interest; that his life story illuminated his works, which would long survive him; and that it served as an example for future artists. He further assumed that such lives, because they were lived by "illustrious" individuals with exceptional talent and skill, illuminated human life and human capability more globally. A biography—the writing or scripture of a life—created a template for everyday living. Van Mander could base Bruegel's story on the oral testimony of people who knew the artist personally; compared with the research he'd conducted on the earlier masters he treated, his information here was reliable. But Van Mander also sought to weave the facts into an exemplary tale, one that could reveal a general pattern. To do so, and following the example of his great Italian predecessor Giorgio Vasari, Van Mander drew on a repertoire of stereotyped episodes and fixed themes—what the first historians of this material termed "the legend about the artist."[16]

Such legends consist mostly of *anecdotes*, of incidents occurring in the person's unofficial or secret life. In Greek, in the tradition where this biographical mode flourished, *anekdotos* means "unpublished" or "not given out." Whether or not it contains a kernel of truth, the tale of Bruegel's peasant origins belongs broadly to this category. Inherently secret because occurring in an unknown place, this beginning reiterates a crucial claim made for great artists already in antiquity: autochthonous beings, self-created and self-taught, they have no source or model other than Nature herself. With regard to postclassical painters, this claim was made—decisively—for Giotto. Vasari begins his biography of Giotto, the acknowledged inaugurator of artistic rebirth in Italy, with the assertion that he was "the son of a poor peasant" who, while tending his father's sheep, "was always sketching what he saw in nature, or imagined in his own mind, on stones or on the ground or sand. . . . And this was before he received any instruction except for what he saw in nature itself."[17] Along similar lines, the northerner Bruegel, "born amidst peasants," paints nature naturally from the start. More classically anecdotal is the episode occurring later, in the midst of the artist's life, when in order to paint peasants he must masquerade as one of them. To what archetype does this anecdote adhere and what message does it convey?

The closest echo comes again from Italy. The artist-theorist Giovanni Paolo Lomazzo reports that Leonardo da Vinci, once needing to depict a peasant group, staged a banquet and invited local rustics with characteristic physical features.[18] During the feast, Leonardo told funny stories, causing his guests to laugh and thus to display the grotesque expressions he needed for his work. In the tale, the artist occupies the festival's center and periphery. Playing the fool, Leonardo makes the peasants laugh foolishly. But he also stands back to observe and afterward to depict what he instigated. Bruegel, similarly, mimics and depicts peasant festivity. The difference is that where Leonardo brings the banquet into his workshop and portrays the revels from memory, Bruegel finds and depicts the festivity where and when it naturally occurs. Turning the everyday world into his studio, he executes (in Van Mander's words) "little sketches from nature." Thus the northern naturalist trumps the hothouse realism of his Italian counterpart.

The Naïve and the Sentimental

How true to life is this tale about the new painting of everyday life? While the claim that Bruegel masqueraded as a peasant seems contrived, it is historically plausible. Already in the fifteenth century in northern Europe, city dwellers signaled their wildest abandonment by dressing up in peasants' clothing. Magistrates in Vienna (1465) and Strasbourg (1483) attempted to control riotous Shrovetide behavior by prohibiting burghers from running about in rustic garb, while in festivity-crazed Nuremberg a peasant costume was standard for carnival players.[19] In the sixteenth-century Netherlands, city folk commonly frequented country kermises, where entertainment was livelier, behavior freer, and drink cheaper than in town.[20] Costume books of the time specified the apparel appropriate for such outings, and depictions of peasant revelry often show rustically dressed urbanites partaking in the fun.[21]

The allure of the countryside transcended jocular role-playing. To live what they perceived to be a more natural, carefree life, wealthy burghers purchased large tracts of farmland and erected for themselves great villas. Called *speelhuizen* (playhouses) and modeled on Italian prototypes, they featured grand gates, courtyards, orchards, and manicured grounds.[22] In anticipation of modern conservancy laws, authorities required new home builders to preserve the rural look of the area, for example by planting trees at close intervals around the boundaries of their estates.[23] Bruegel's best-known client, Nicolaes Jonghelinck, built a fabulous villa in the suburbs of Antwerp and hung its walls with important paintings, most probably including the original six landscapes of Bruegel's *Months* series.[24] Bruegel may have produced his most acclaimed pictures for, and also personally by way of, a nostalgic expedition back to rural life.

Some two hundred years later, Friedrich Schiller observed a certain bifurcation in the human experience of nature and diagnosed it as a chief symptom of the modern age.[25] Schiller held that poets of all periods and cultures seek to preserve nature. But lately, in the overcivilized and artificial modern world, nature had withdrawn farther away. With nature vanishing from humanity, and poets themselves no longer experiencing and expressing their own

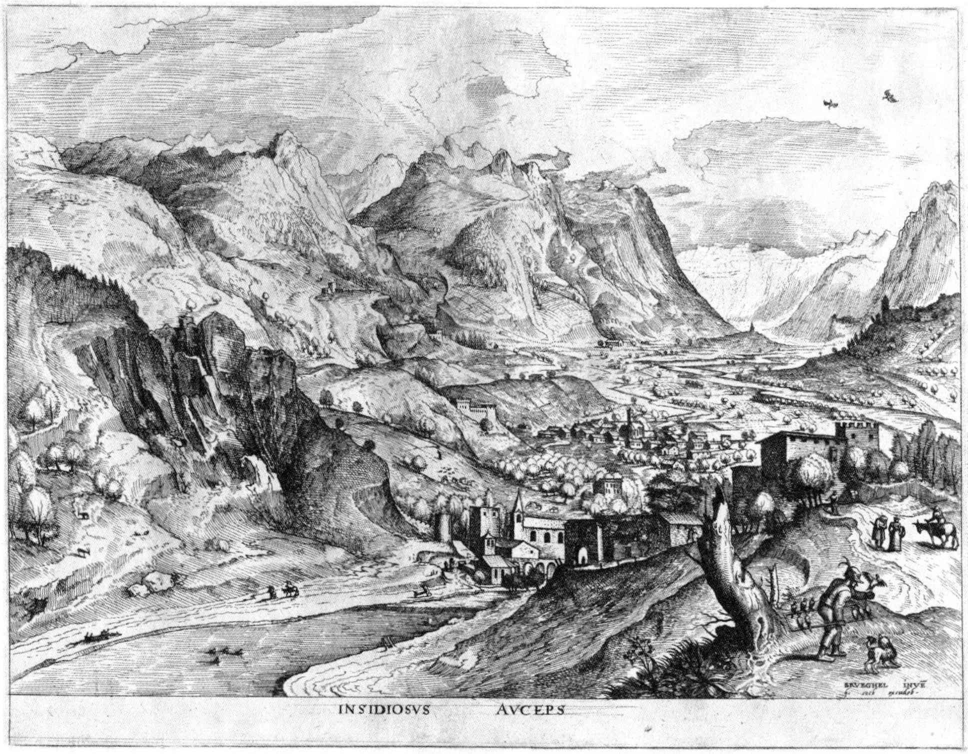

9 Johannes and Lucas van Doetecum after Pieter Bruegel the Elder, *Insidiosus Auceps* (*The Crafty Bird-Catcher*), from the *Large Landscapes* series, c. 1555–56, etching with engraving, The Metropolitan Museum of Art, New York, Harris Brisbane Dick Fund, 1926

feelings naturally, they had to "feel the Natural"—which meant turning nature into an explicit subject or idea.[26] Finding it in the inanimate world (e.g., beautiful landscapes) or in some still-innocent humanity (children, shepherds, primitive peoples), poets become nature's witnesses or avengers. Schiller felt this occurring in his own time, with France—the most civilized and therefore most intensely nostalgic nation—leading the way in its yearning for the naïve in art and literature. But the bifurcation had happened many times before, whenever a culture began to feel culture itself as a burden. Even with the Greeks, who compared with the Romans seemed enviably natural, Aeschylus's archaic vigor gave way to the high artifice and self-consciousness of a Euripides. Poets therefore divide into two kinds. They "will either *be* nature, or they will *look for* lost nature." In Schiller's terminology, they will be either naïve or sentimental.[27]

Bruegel's modernity consists in his seeming to straddle and to cross the threshold separating innocence from experience. First he naïvely *lived*, then he sentimentally *pursued*, the everyday life of the peasantry. And what he hoped this pursuit of a simpler, more natural existence would reveal to him and to his precociously cosmopolitan audience was some broader knowledge of life itself.

Local Knowledge[28]

What does Bruegel know about peasants? And what do the peasants, in Bruegel, seem natively to know? The striding rustic in the Vienna panel evidently knows about thieves and about nests and how they are robbed, hence his seen-that, done-that look. One of Bruegel's early landscape prints labels bird theft as "insidious" (*insidiosus*), as a crafty, devious, and socially and morally marginal know-how (fig. 9).[29] In sixteenth-century theater, bird-catchers were stock figures of folly. Bearing a sticky, birdlime-coated staff and swarmed by biting insects, they set out craftily—and foolishly—to lure birds and also women (fig. 10).[30] In Mozart's *Magic*

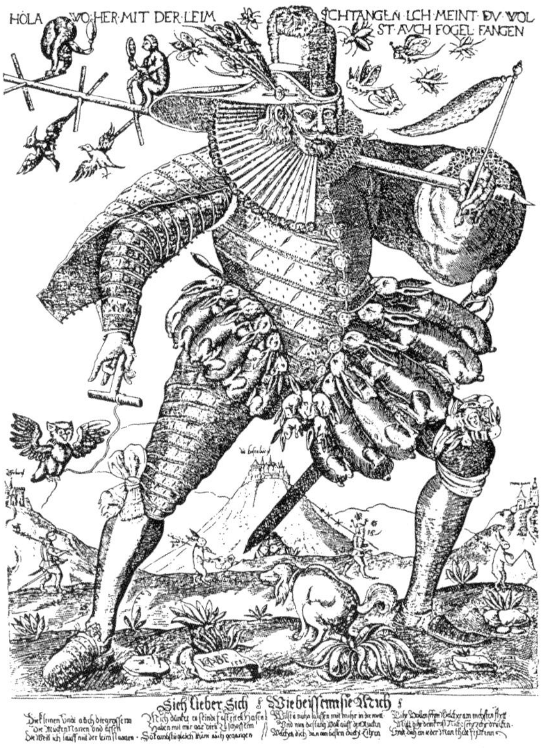

10 Master KNBF, *Bird Catcher with Lime Stick*, 1588, engraving

Flute, the buffoonish bird-catcher Papageno, originally played by the opera's librettist, Emanuel Schikaneder, still has this comically erotic charge. In pointing the nest robber out, Bruegel's peasant conveys to the viewer his insider's knowledge, that elemental cunning about the "ways of the world." The artist shows less the content of such cunning and more its social form as bedrock knowledge of and between people. This interpersonal framework manifests itself in how Bruegel's peasant seems to know—and to *acknowledge*—not just the crafty thief but also us. Almost smiling, and with a walleyed glance at and through us, the peasant correctly predicts that we, all urban sophisticates, will be mesmerized by what he fleetingly shows. From the very outset of our encounter, he knows us better, or at least differently, than we know him.

The five laughing peasants gaping at us from a small panel painted around 1600 encapsulate this social form of knowledge more crudely (fig. 11).[31] The picture's creator, Hans von Aachen, was court painter to Rudolf II in Prague; he would have known Bruegel's work intimately. Exaggerating Bruegel's peasants to the point of caricature, the painting suggests how they must have looked to a cultivated public during the zenith of the Flemish artist's posthumous fame. The image hurls its insult at the viewer. With the obscene "fig" gesture (thumb thrust suggestively between the middle and index fingers) aimed right at us, and with everyone laughing at us and our response, the picture targets us—who might wish to laugh at it—with its more massive and more knowing ridicule. Backed by a group of disconcertingly attractive and grotesque women, the thuggish male peasant mimics, challenges, and undermines the viewer's own manhood—this picture's viewer being implicitly male. That they are mere peasants gives them—and by extension the painter—license to be so bold. But this social disparity, huge for the picture's original noble audience, further magnifies the discomfiture. Miming sex with his fingers, the peasant causes those who face him—standing as they will in the elegance of a princely art collection—to feel dangerously out of place.

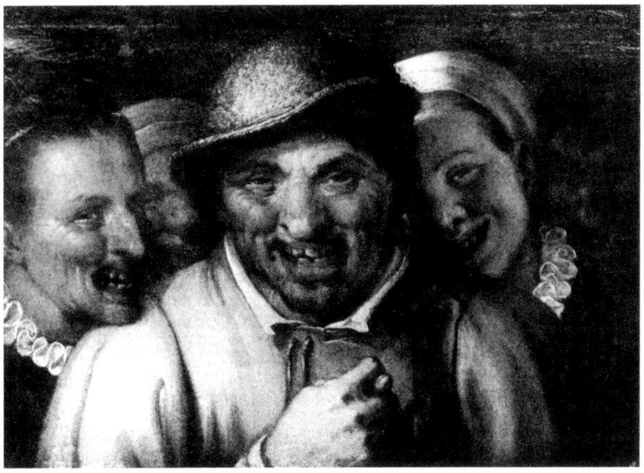

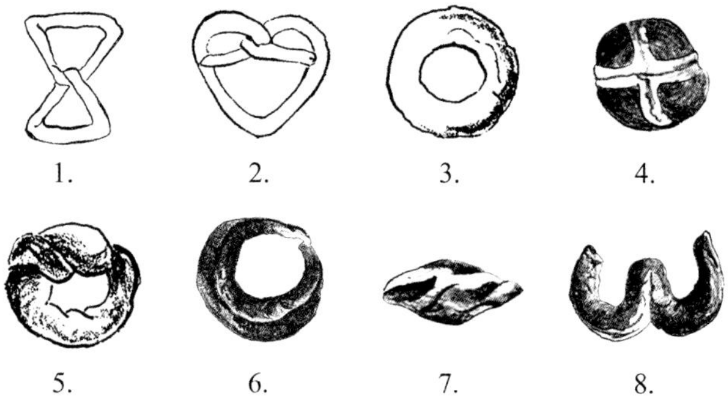

(LEFT) 11 Hans von Aachen, *Laughing Peasants*, c. 1605, panel, location unknown (formerly in Stredočeská Galerie, Nelahozeves Castle, Czech Republic)

(RIGHT) 12 "Shrove Tuesday Pretzels from Karlsruhe (1), Würzburg (2), Biberach (3), Kaufbeuren (4), Krumbach (5), Ehingen (6), Königsberg (today Kalinengrad) (7), and Basle (8)," illustration from Max Höfler, "Gebildbrote der Faschings-, Fastnachts- und Fastenzeit," in *Zeitschrift für österreichische Volkskunde* 14, 1908

Bruegel's picture is altogether different in tone. And whatever messages it conveys are not crude and direct, but teasingly oblique. Yet its plot hinges on a similar difference—or asymmetry—between what we know and what the peasant knows. The striding peasant seems less absorbed than we. His jacket and codpiece jauntily fastened with laces, his gear snug on his belt, he looks wonderfully put together: a well-equipped man (in all senses) with better things to do than stare. The peasant carries tools for herding and perhaps for hunting. The know-how required for these pursuits is quintessentially *local*, because it pertains to a particular place—the shared habitat of herdsman and flock. It is also local in a more cultural sense, because the equipment that materializes the know-how—horn, knife, and prod—tends to vary subtly from place to place. The peasant's tools and costume possess what anthropologists call *style*.[32] Style is the fugitive characteristic of how, say, knives of a given culture are shaped over and above their requirements for cutting. These characteristics are fugitive because, to the casual observer, a tool's function totally dictates its form. However, specialists—i.e., the toolmakers and the anthropologists—know that there are countless ways of making the instrument but only a few that are right. Culture and tradition guide a maker's every gesture.[33]

According to Van Mander, what Bruegel knew best about peasants was precisely their *style*: "He knew how to attire these men and women peasants very characteristically in Kempish or other costumes."[34] Such knowledge allowed Bruegel to dress as a peasant so that, well disguised, he could further study peasant dress. Whether portraying the type of mask used in one region to play the bogeyman or knowing the way dough is knotted so that it forms the pretzel distinctive of a particular village, Bruegel evinces an ethnographer's attention to the tactics specific to a narrow locale (fig. 12). His *Battle between Carnival and Lent* exhibits culture both as a traditional choreography and as an endlessly varied, because always improvised, performance (see fig. 284). Participants are shown simultaneously to take part in the scripted action and to observe—along with us—the curious spectacle around them. Psychological plausibility intensifies the sense of ethnographic specificity. This is how people individually act, according to their particular character and mood, and these are the things this village individually does, according to its unique *ethnos*. In *The Peasant and the Bird Thief*, the striding figure's characteristically tied laces testify that the artist copying them "knew how" laces like this were tied, and the *place* where laces were tied in this and no other way, such that getting them right was an artistic achievement: this locality nests in back of the peasant as the world he leaves behind.

That bit of landscape is one of Bruegel's most forward-looking creations.[35] Utterly ordinary yet suffused by light and air, the view of cottages nestled round a clearing in the woods anticipates

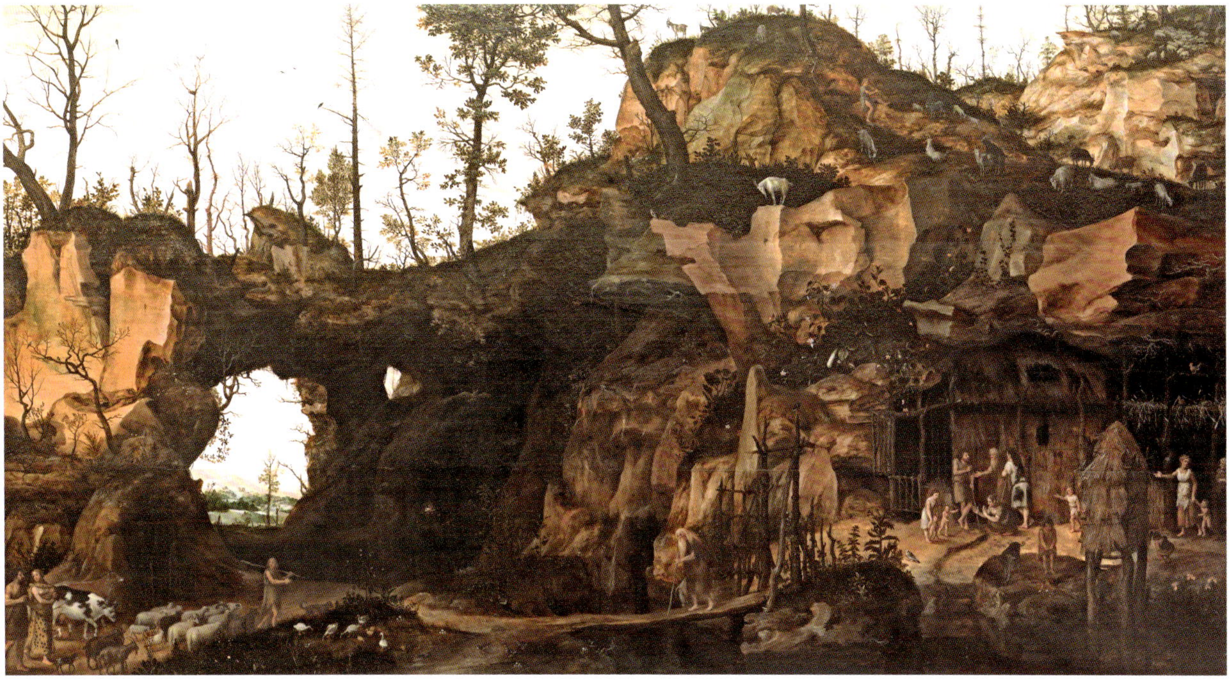

13 Cornelis van Dalem, *Landscape with the Beginnings of Civilization (Dawn of the Civilization)*, 1560–70, panel, Museum Boijmans Van Beuningen, Rotterdam. Partial loan Museum Boijmans Van Beuningen Foundation

by a century the achievements of Jan van Goyen, Rembrandt, and Jacob van Ruisdael. But it also looks backward in history to a primordial condition of European landscape that was rapidly disappearing already in Bruegel's time. Those huge thatched roofs make the rustic homes and steadings appear to rise from the earth like strange natural formations. But by 1568 they had long been outlawed as fire hazards in most Netherlandish territories.[36] For Bruegel's urban audience they would have seemed elemental, like the thatched huts imagined by Cornelis van Dalem in his large landscape sometimes titled *Landscape with the Beginnings of Civilization* (fig. 13).[37] A contemporary of Bruegel in Antwerp, Van Dalem takes us back to the origins of architecture as set forth by the Latin author Vitruvius. Assembling themselves in a primitive state of society, Vitruvius writes, humans "were led to the consideration of sheltering themselves from the seasons, some by making arbors with the boughs of trees, some by excavating caves in the mountains, and others in imitation of the nests and habitations of swallows, by making dwellings of twigs interwoven and covered [with] mud and clay."[38] Van Dalem's vision is of primitive humanity, and his source is an ancient, all-but-forgotten treatise, but the artist drew his vivid portrayal of an original architecture from contemporary rural edifices, which still had roofs propped up with rough-hewn timber and walls of wattle and daub—as the crumbling huts in his *Landscape with Farmstand* show (fig. 14).[39] The Basel cartographer Sebastian Münster reported (on the authority of the Roman historian Strabo) that in the distant past Germanic peoples lived in homes clustered in tiny hamlets in the forest. To illustrate such a primitive settlement, Münster introduced into his *Cosmographia* a simple woodcut view of what looks to be a German or Netherlandish village of the author's own day—a cipher, in other words, of Bruegel's rural enclave (fig. 15).[40]

In urban centers, the styles of architecture, artifact, and costume design were dramatically in flux thanks to foreign influences, developing technologies, changing fashions, and a general penchant for the new. Rural styles, by contrast, appeared not to change at all. As an Italian merchant observed about his travels in the 1560s in the Low Countries, Flemish peasants still dressed as they had in Caesar's time.[41] Rural artifice was considered impervious to history

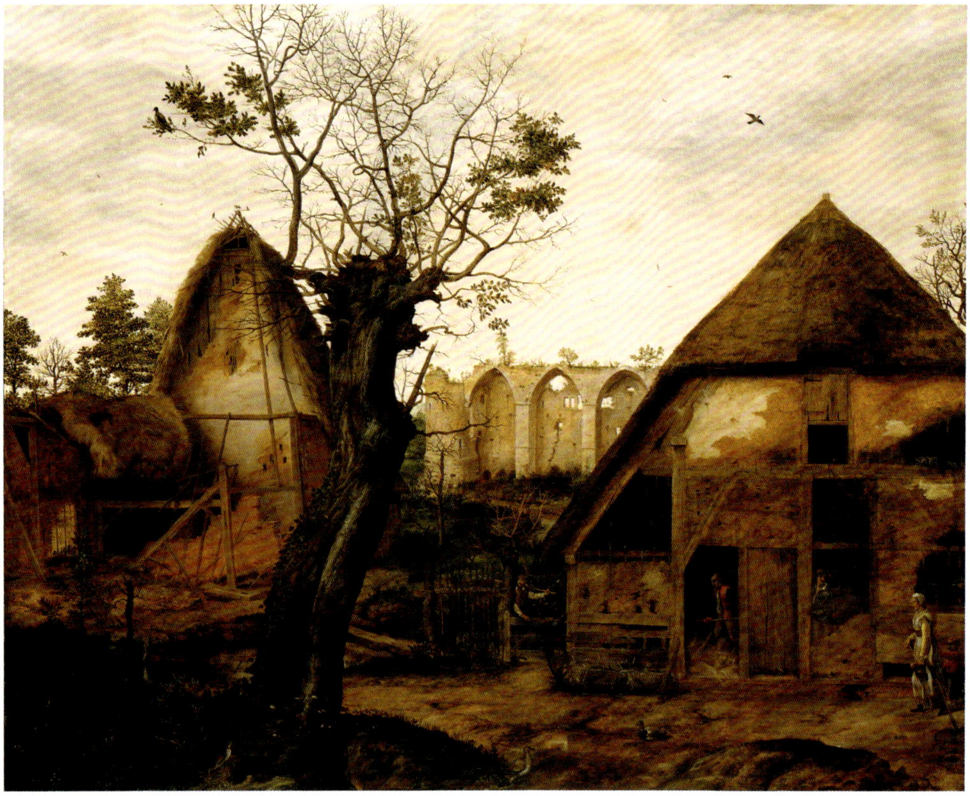

14 Cornelis van Dalem, *Landscape with Farmstand*, 1575(?) 1564, on oak wood, Alte Pinakothek, Munich

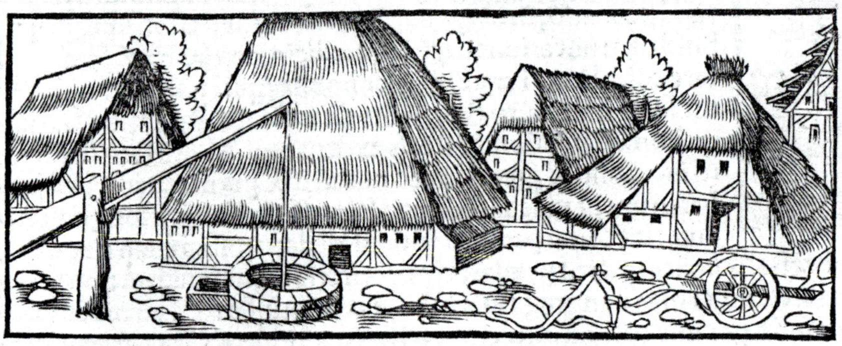

15 *German Village*, woodcut illustration from Sebastian Münster, *Cosmographei* (Basel: Heinrich Petri, 1550), p. 318, Houghton Library, Harvard University

and time. For that reason northern European humanists from Conrad Celtis and Johannes Boemus to Münster and Ortelius treated the buildings, tools, costumes, and customs of the peasants as the monuments of a local antiquity, like living counterparts to what ancient Rome had been to learned Italians during their self-styled Renaissance.[42]

Bruegel makes a far subtler claim. Peasant artifice may seem timeless, but it is also intensely variable, contingent, and circumstantial. In praising the artist's attiring peasants "in Kempish *or other* costumes," Van Mander implied that rural dress varied markedly from place to place. In cities, styles changed rapidly but increasingly in sync with other cities due to a greater mobility of commodities, persons, and ideas. Rustic styles, by contrast, were historically stable but spatially heterogeneous. Pretzels were knotted differently in different villages throughout the Netherlands; modern historians know this thanks in part to the pretzels Bruegel so faithfully painted.[43] The clearing behind Bruegel's striding peasant represents the minimal unit for a distinctive ethnic style. It recollects a time when space was divided, in laws and the collective imagination, between what stood within a girded yard—or garth—and what lay beyond.[44]

In German *Raum*, in English "room," space originally meant a place cleared for settlement and lodging. "*A space is* something that has been made room for, something that is cleared, freed, namely with a boundary, Greek *peras*."[45] Making room, people secured their everyday existence, and peace reigned among family and friends. Primordial home consisted of houses and a yard girded by a natural and social wilderness, what Old Norse vividly termed *utangard*, "outside the fence." This microcosm of the domicile was repeated as the image of the world as a whole. The human world was called *middilgard*, and the rest was chaos. The word "world" (German *Welt*) did not originally denote the totality of everything that is. Built on the etyma *wer* (man) and *alt* (time or eon), world named only the space and time of *human life*—what sustains a *people*.[46] World meant always lifeworld: the sealed unity of consciousness with the habitat in which that consciousness actually lives.[47]

Home and the World

Bruegel's career began in Antwerp, a harbor city open to a rapidly expanding world.[48] At the end of the fifteenth century, the key routes of global trades were shifting from the Mediterranean to the Atlantic. Meanwhile, commerce through the once dominant northern port of Bruges had declined due to the siltation of its channel to the sea. From around 1500 until 1566, world trade—between Europe and Asia, Africa, and now the Americas—found its hub in Antwerp. Through this gateway English merchants exported cloth to the East, Portuguese traders imported Indian spices to Europe, and southern German brokers exchanged silver mined in their hinterland for cloth and spices. The volume and variety of goods passing through this city caused local industries to flourish, as well. The luxury trade—chief engine of early modern commerce—drew skilled craftsmen to Antwerp, where easy access to imported materials combined with new and efficient forms of marketing, distribution, and export.[49] Leatherworkers from Spain, tapestry weavers from Brussels, and glassblowers from Venice all set up workshops there. Through the power of their monopolistic guilds, most other cities closed their doors to foreign artisans. Antwerp instead invited outsiders in and promoted their crafts through subventions and public commissions. An engraving dated 1562 encapsulates this attitude of openness (fig. 16).[50] It depicts Antwerp observed "from the Flemish meadows." In the foreground, a village street ends on a dock along the ship-filled Scheldt River, northern Europe's thoroughfare to the world. To this globalism—gently reinforced by the print's circular format—belongs an attitude of *laissez-faire*. "Praise the God of all," reads the banner above the church, "and drink the wine, and let the world be the world."

The craft of painting flourished. Whereas in the fifteenth century Antwerp had no painters of note, by Bruegel's time the city dominated northern European art production. Demand for paintings came partly from Antwerp's affluent merchant class and from the city itself, which funded lavish commissions and recruited foreign talent through special favors and bonuses. During the 1550s, when Bruegel joined its ranks, the painters' guild had a membership of 270 masters and 223 apprentices—twice the number of Antwerp's bakers and three times the number of its butchers.[51] This army of artists may have been encouraged by local support, but it depended mostly on the export market. Certain institutions unique to the city fostered this internationalism. Already in the fifteenth century, Antwerp boasted special sales halls—called *panden*—where luxury goods of local and foreign manufacture were marketed during the six-week annual fair. One such hall—the Our Lady's Pand—housed

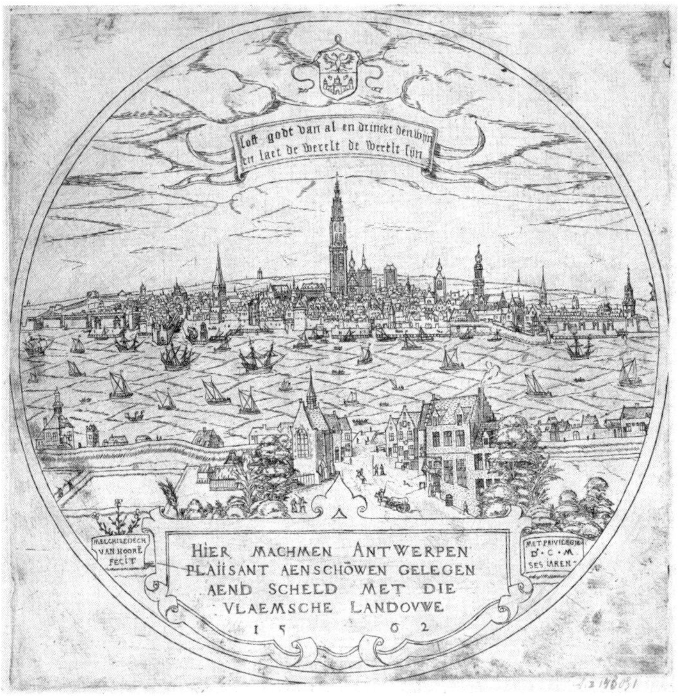

16 Melchisedech van Hooren, *View of Antwerp*, 1562, etching with engraving, Bibliothèque Royale de Belgique

Europe's first commercial art gallery.[52] It was joined around 1540 by a gallery devoted almost entirely to paintings; located in the new bourse, the Painter's Pand was open year-round, for as one admiring observer put it at the time, in Antwerp "it is always market-day."[53] Customers could acquire pictures in bulk, which gave rise to a new entrepreneurial class of art dealers (often widows and relatives of painters), who bought and sold independently or on consignment.

New market conditions changed how painters painted.[54] Earlier Netherlandish masters worked chiefly on commission. Individuals or corporations ordered a work of art, and the artist made it according to contract. In larger artistic centers such as Bruges and Brussels, painters and sculptors did make works on spec, but such production was small change compared with the fully commercialized practices of later Antwerp artists, who sold most of their works on the open market.

This market had new demands. Providing for a diverse and far-flung future clientele, it encouraged a certain anonymity in products. Made for anyone anywhere, painting became increasingly standardized in subject, style, and format. This stimulated more industrial methods of production. Antwerp painters produced works serially, in multiple copies, by sophisticated techniques of pouncing and tracing. To give their products an aura of uniqueness while keeping production costs low, some workshops developed clever ways of varying copies without having to depict or design anything anew. Commercialization, plus a guild-based system of quality control, encouraged shops to specialize in producing particular types of salable pictures—devotional icons, landscapes, portraiture, still lifes, genre works, and so forth. And while the numerous expensive imported materials used in painting, such as gold for gilding and lapis lazuli for rich blue pigments, were more readily available in Antwerp than elsewhere, many of the city's painters cut costs here, as well, favoring cheaper browns, blacks, and yellows over costly blues and greens, and applying paints in one coat, with rapid, potentially expressive brushstrokes, on a thin layer of prepared ground.

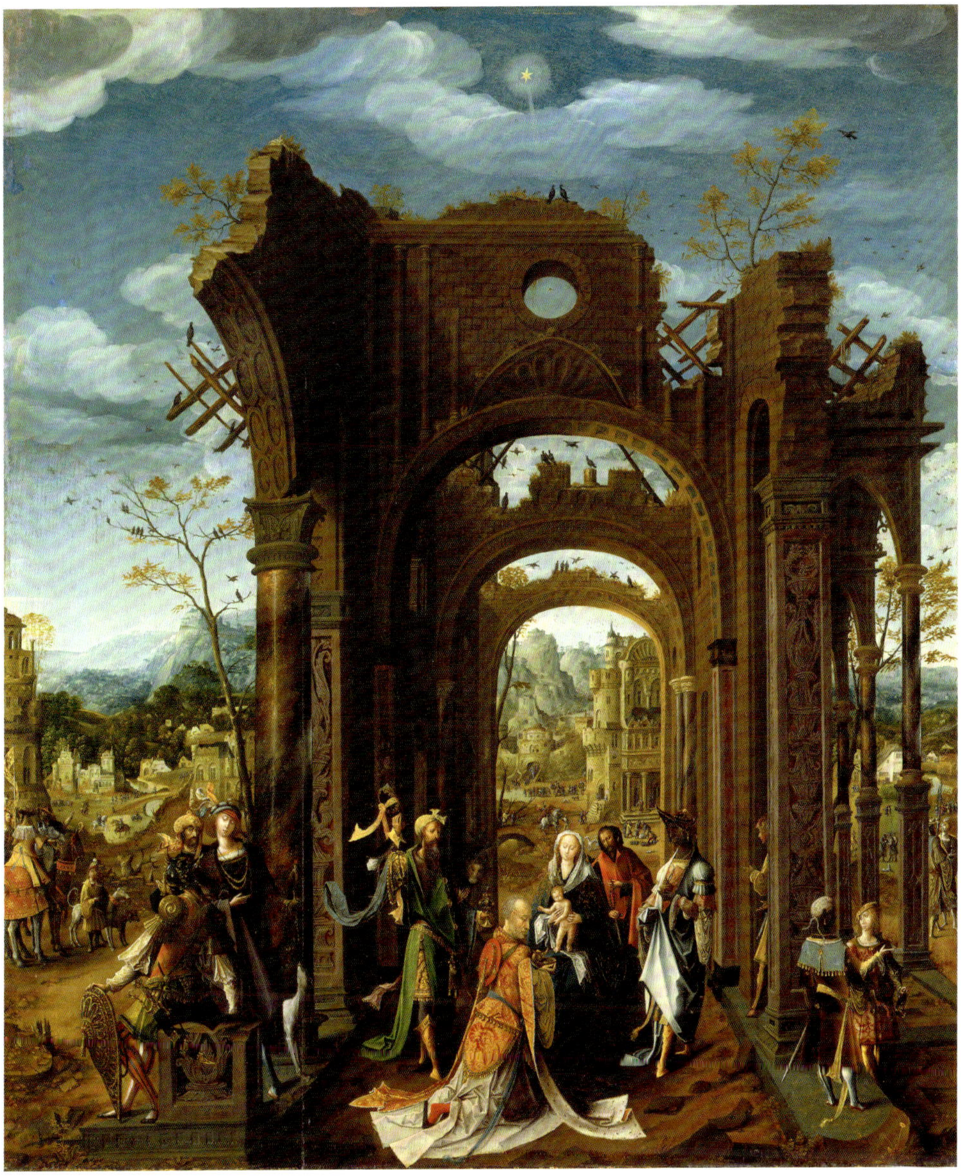

17 Antwerp Master ("Pseudo-Bles"), *Adoration of the Magi*, c. 1520, on oak wood, Alte Pinakothek, Munich

All these strategies worked only if the products made in these ways found a lucrative market. And because this market was worldwide, the feedback from it—what sales "told" producers—kept Antwerp's art in tune with international fashion. The countless paintings of the Adoration of the Magi produced in this city registered a global perspective not merely in the foreign persons, costumes, and gifts that this subject demanded but also in the style—sometimes called "Mannerist" due to its perceived artificiality compared with earlier Netherlandish art—that rendered them (fig. 17).[55] While at home in Antwerp, this style, an eclectic amalgam of late Gothic and Renaissance, shaped and was shaped by the tastes of consumers from France, Portugal, Spain, Italy, Germany, Poland, England, Scandinavia, and the Baltic coast.

According to Van Mander, Bruegel completed his training under Pieter Coecke van Aelst and married his daughter, Maria. The leading Antwerp "Mannerist," Coecke designed—in addition to paintings and prints—the epoch's most spectacular amalgam of northern and Italianate styles in the form of monumental tapestries.[56] Emerging in this cosmopolitan milieu,

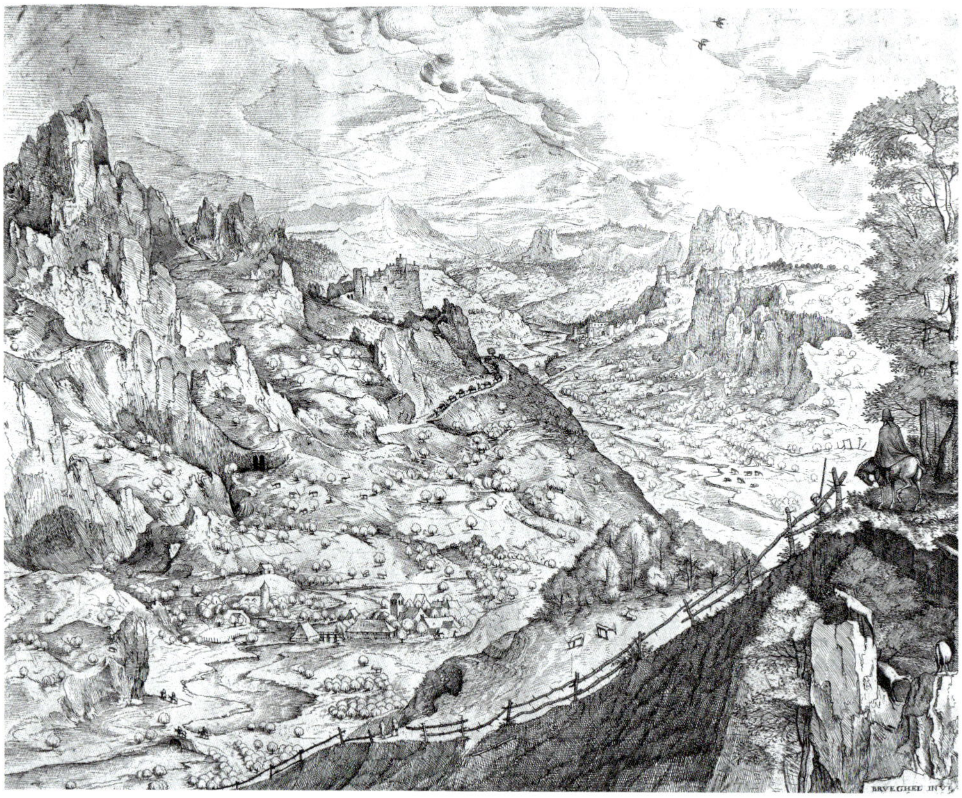

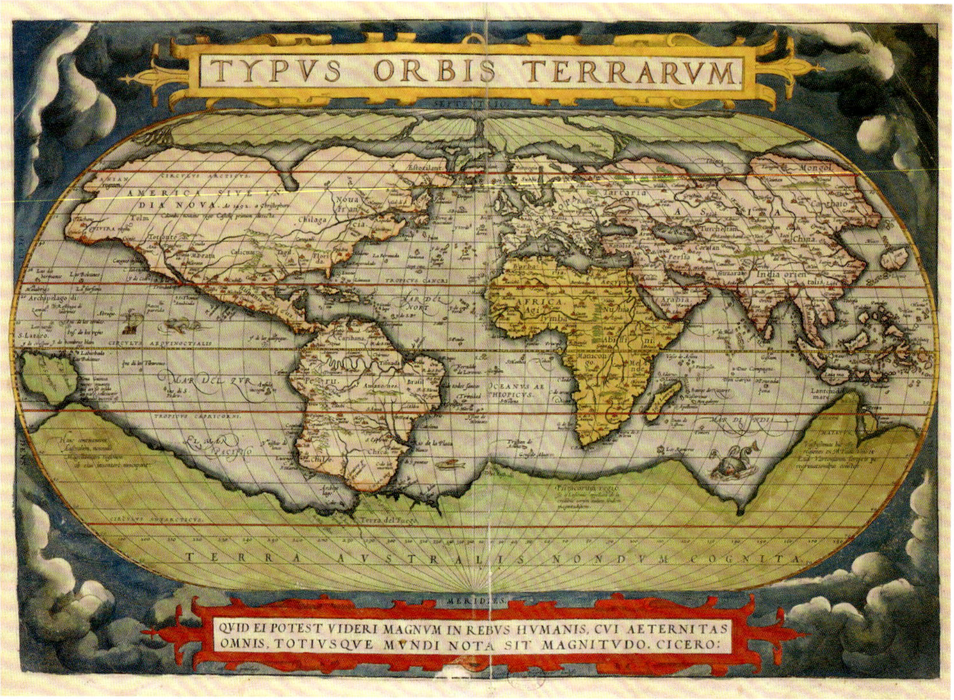

(TOP) 18 Joannes and Lucas van Doetecum after Pieter Bruegel the Elder, *The Large Alpine Landscape*, from the *Large Landscapes* series, c. 1555–56, etching with engraving, Museum Boijmans Van Beuningen, Rotterdam

(BOTTOM) 19 Frans Hogenberg, *Typus Orbis Terrarum*, engraving, hand-colored, in Abraham Ortelius, *Theatrum Orbis Terrarum* (Antwerp: Aegidius Coppenius Diesth, 1570), Norman B. Leventhal Map Center, Boston Public Library

Bruegel launched his independent career with a series of engraved and etched prints of the high Alps, a landscape dramatically foreign to his native low-lying land (fig. 18). Made on the basis of sketches the artist drew on his travels through France to Italy, these prints were issued by the Antwerp publisher Hieronymus Cock at a press with the self-consciously global name To the Four Winds.[57] Pictures of a wide world beyond the Netherlands, capturing a vast (because elevated) perspective available only from those strange summits, Bruegel's images did indeed fly forth across continents like leaves in a mighty gale. Remember that this city also gave birth to modern cartography, which represented and managed dizzying immensities. An intimate of the pioneering mapmaker Abraham Ortelius, Bruegel carried over into painting the cartographer's new measure of distance (fig. 19).[58]

But the worldliness of Antwerp art ran deeper than this. To the Four Winds specialized in reproductive engravings—in prints that copied singular paintings. Although, through Cock, northern Europe came to dominate this industry, Antwerp's printshops chiefly reproduced compositions by the great Italian masters, especially Raphael, Titian, and Michelangelo. Northern engravers, such as Cornelis Cort, excelled in abstracting the peculiarities of their own regional style in order to publish the flamboyantly individualistic style of painters from elsewhere.[59] The dissemination, internationally, of a high style for European painting based on antique standards owes much to the Antwerp printmakers, who mobilized the prestigious original by renouncing their own indigenous manner. No artistic culture had ever been as global as this.

Yet these pressures from the outside world were precisely what helped turn Bruegel's attention inward, to the local. His portrayal of the ethnic styles embodied in peasant costumes and peasant craft goods derived from an impulse to imbue his own self-consciously global art with the hallmarks of local facture. To "copy peasants with the brush" meant not only to depict their nature as they laughed, danced, and leapt about the landscape. It also meant remaking in paint their handmade artifacts, completely free of the internationalizing manner of Bruegel's own cultural milieu. The correctly painted local pretzel braids together artisan know-how with artistic know-how. It unifies content with form—the *what* of painting with the stylistic *how*. To do this meant entering a territory stranger than the wildest Alps.

Catastrophes

Behind Bruegel's peasant, the field cleared in the forest would be sufficient for a rudimentary economy—farms in the Netherlands at the time averaged two hectares (about five acres). Let this enclave stand for the elemental home—the *paradise*—from which we will have always departed, either by abandoning it or by being snatched from it by an intrusive hand.[60] Bruegel presses the boundaries of premodern space right up against the picture plane. And he sends a dividing channel of water from the background around and across the lower framing edge. A miniature of the great waterways connecting Bruegel's Antwerp to the sea, this rivulet is a natural extension of the global into the local.

Its expressive force is somewhat diminished by the painting's condition. Early on, the right edge of the panel was cut down, probably by about four inches.[61] Copies of the picture by the artist's son Pieter Brueghel the Younger suggest that originally the waterway stretched out farther to the right, and the peasant strode toward us from the very middle of the scene (fig. 20).[62] The more prominent river and the peasant's central placement would have brought

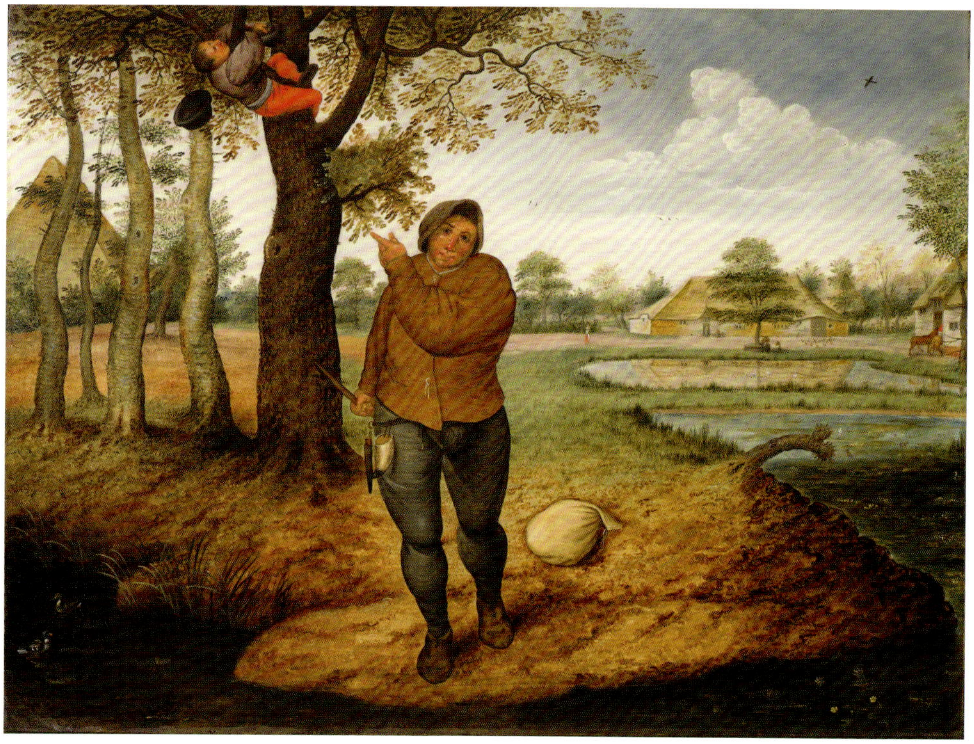

20 Pieter Brueghel the Younger, after Pieter Bruegel the Elder, *The Peasant and the Bird Thief*, c. 1600, panel, private collection

into greater focus a structure underlying the whole. The curve of the water's edge, together with the arc of the peasant's body as it presses forward into our space, inscribes the little scene into the figure of a globe or sphere.

Bruegel's *The Misanthrope* (fig. 21) bears the date 1568, the year of *The Peasant and the Bird Thief*.[63] Now in the Museo di Capodimonte, in Naples, *The Misanthrope* features globes in two forms: first in the symbolic cross-surmounted orb encircling the thief, and second in the painting's unusual tondo format. A circle on the perfect square of canvas, the painted image imparts the impression that we behold it through a round opening cut into the picture's support. Bruegel gives substance to this fiction by allowing light and shadow to play along the portal's lip. The inscription at the circle's base may not be original.[64] The part of the picture where it is written is visibly paler and blanker than Bruegel's differentiated rendering of soil just above, suggesting that this area has been painted over or otherwise changed. To one expert in the history of lettering style, its Gothic script also looks much later than 1568.[65] However, whether autograph or not, the words do indicate what all these globes and circles were generally intended to mean: "Because the world is so deceitful [*ongetru*, "untrue"], I go in mourning." Pickpocketed as he passes alone through the landscape, the wanderer, who speaks the motto in first person present tense, has dressed in black to indicate his rejection of the world.[66] The globes therefore stand for the world that he has unmasked and abandoned, and that lies in front, in back, and all around. Personifying the world's treachery, the thief himself consists of spherical forms: a round head, curved shoulders and buttocks, and arms that form a latitudinal band—a sort of equator—as they work to cut the misanthrope's purse free.

Just as these crafty arms extend physically out of the encircling symbol of the world, so too the theft they perpetrate escapes the confines of the picture's moralizing motto. In Bruegel, simple truths give way to puzzling paradoxes, often through messages and associations conveyed visually, in excess of verbal and proverbial communications. The misanthrope's

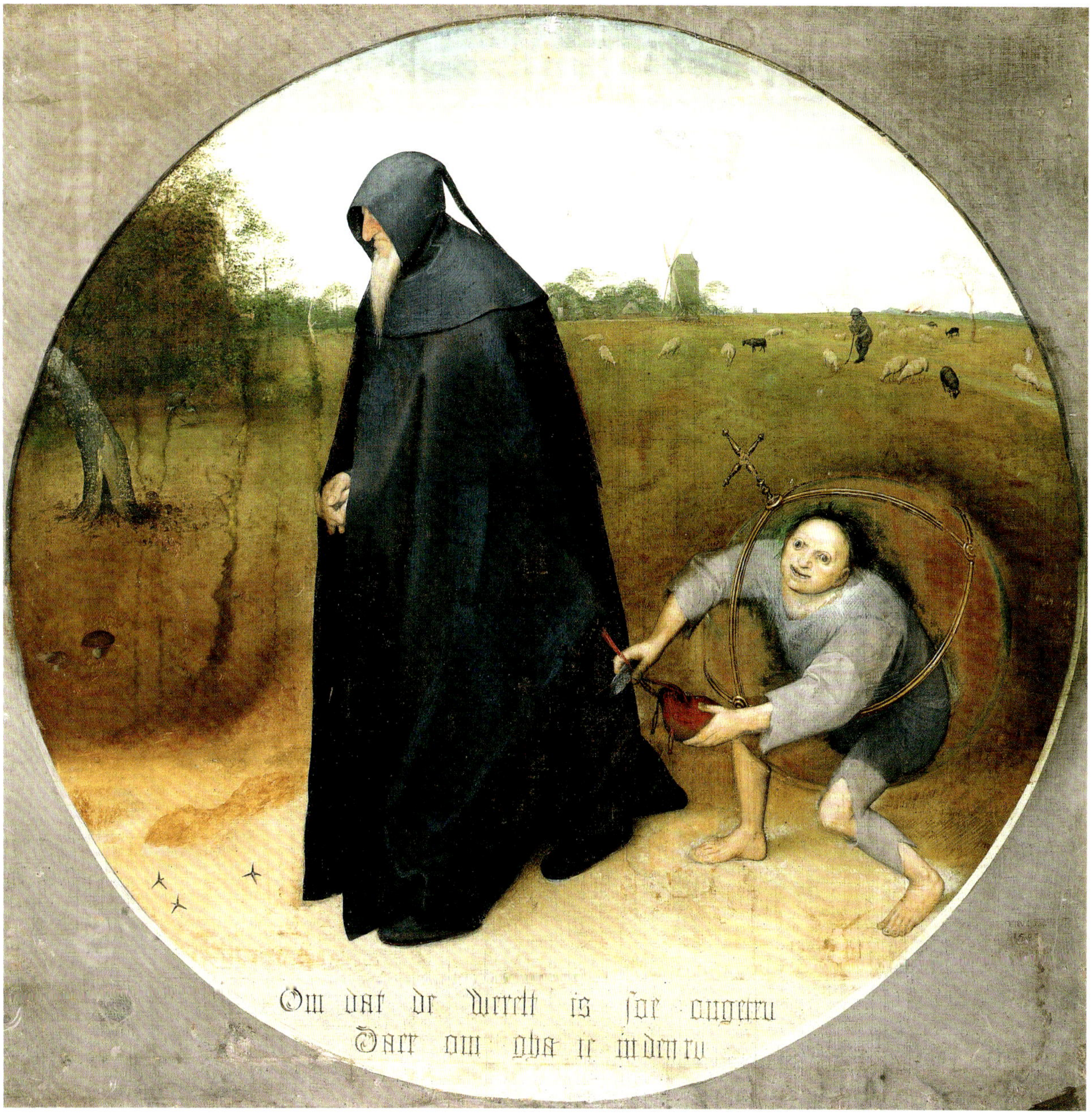

21 Pieter Bruegel the Elder, *The Misanthrope*, 1568, canvas, Museo Nazionale di Capodimonte, Naples

22 *Punji Trap*, from Dale Martin, *The Trapper's Bible* (Boulder, CO: Paladin Press, 1987), p. 54

23 Detail of Pieter Bruegel the Elder, *Netherlandish Proverbs* (fig. 32)

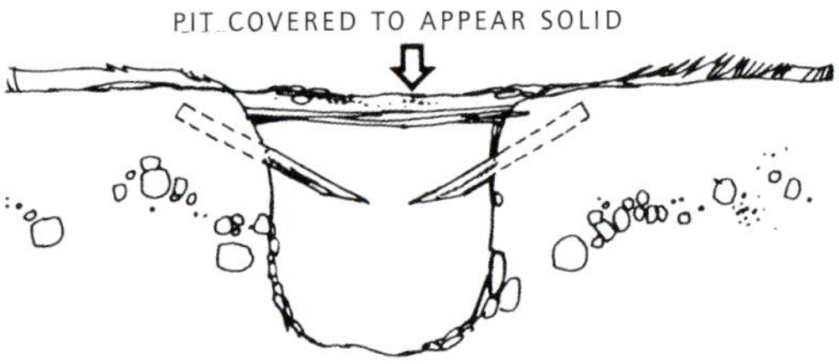

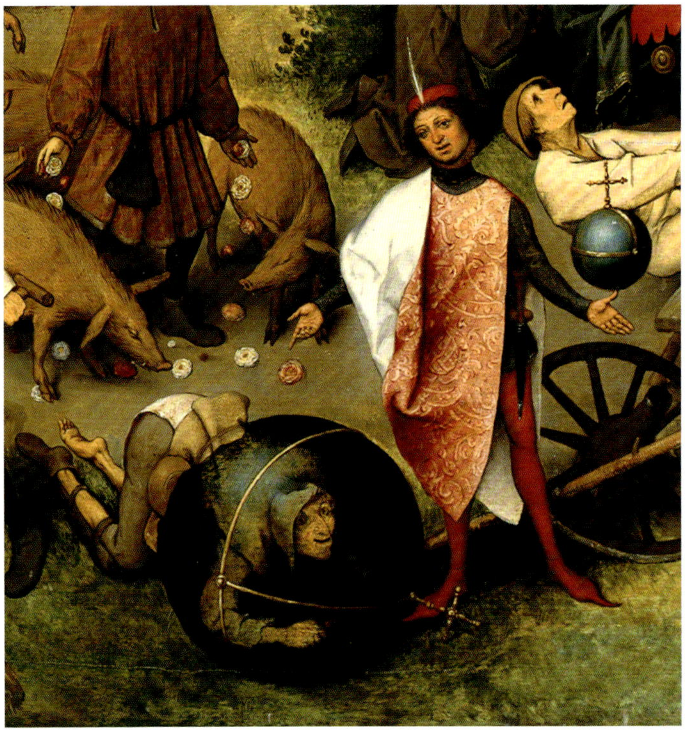

voluminous robes advertise his renunciation of earthly things, but they also flag and envelop the wealth he has nonetheless (hypocritically?) retained.[67] The purse snatcher does personify the treachery of the world. Penniless and in rags, however, he also exposes the misanthrope's affluence and therefore his false and self-deceived attachment to the world. The scenario turns out to have been caused not by the thief's actions alone, but also—potentially—by some flaw within the misanthrope. This gives the world the structure of a trap. Traps cause harm not directly, as hunters do, but indirectly, by turning the actions of the victim against themselves. The simplest snares, such as some path-guarding traps, work by making a trigger out of their target's physical reflex to escape (fig. 22).[68] Bruegel hints at the fiendishly oblique nature of the world's treachery by strewing in the misanthrope's path clever four-spiked man-traps.

The thief turns the tables on the moralizer's complaint about the world being "untrue." In doing so, he embodies a different kind of wisdom from the misanthrope: an instrumental, cynical, and precisely worldly shrewdness. Such wisdom is summed up by another saying, one that Bruegel himself put front and center in his *Netherlandish Proverbs* panel of 1559: "One must stoop to get through the world" (fig. 23).[69] Here a crippled beggar presses his way hopelessly into a toppled world-orb while to his left a wealthy nobleman with another sphere balanced on his thumb visualizes a complementary proverb: "He spins the world on his thumb."[70] The thinking is that poor wretches like the cripple have to grovel to get by, while the rich expect everything to revolve around them. In *The Misanthrope*, the symbol of world is itself visually paradoxical. Bruegel makes the crafted elements of the *globus cruciger*—venerable symbol of divine sovereignty—palpably present. The golden cross and beaded bands reflect light from our side of the picture plane in sync with the highlights that play along the painted image's round, portal-like margin. But the sphere that these metal parts embrace and adorn, which is to say the *world* over which sovereignty is claimed, merges with the dull background of the mundane scene. This may be partly due to the painting's condition. *The Misanthrope* is

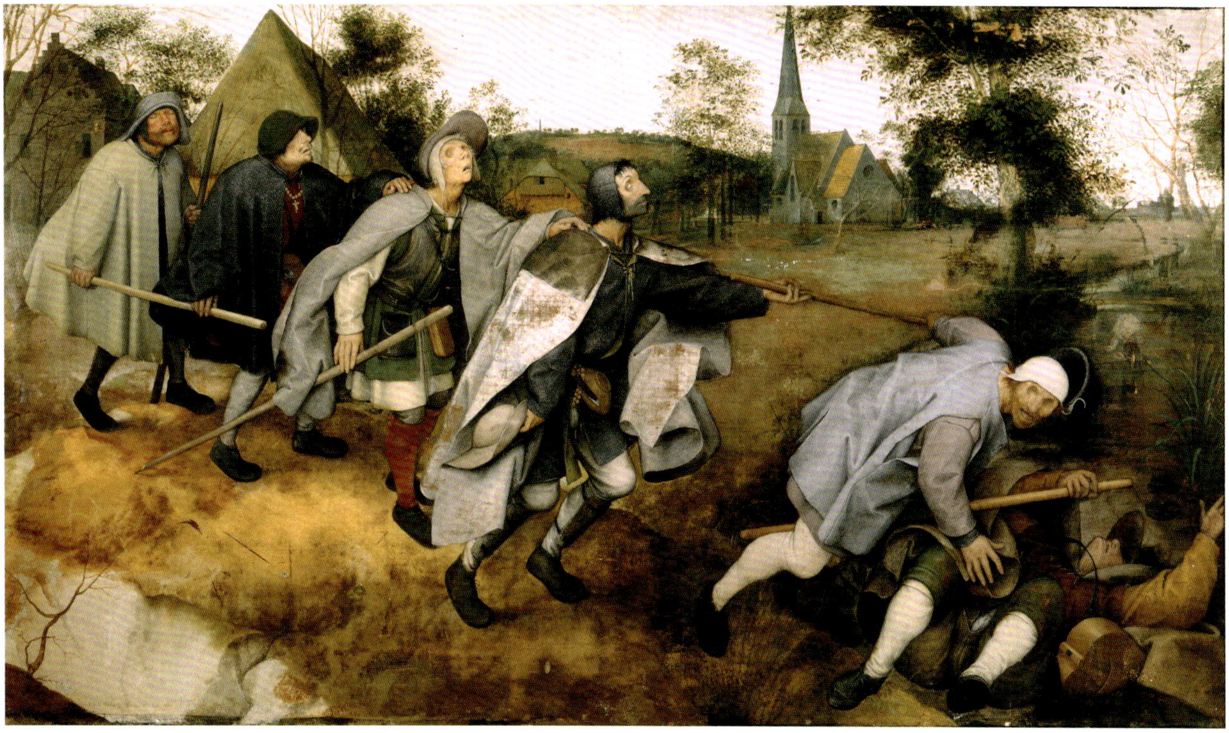

one of Bruegel's three or so surviving autograph *Tüchlein* paintings made in the fragile and fugitive medium of tempera on glue-sized canvas (hence the period term *Tüchlein*, from *Tuch*, "cloth") without a ground layer.[71] The painted sphere might therefore have been originally more definite. However, in Bruegel, symbols of and statements about the world do tend to blur at all points into the world itself. While maddening to art historians, who want to know that what they are seeking to decipher is indeed a symbol, such blurring serves to keep all viewers from complacently believing they have a firm handle on the work.

24 Pieter Bruegel the Elder, *The Parable of the Blind Leading the Blind*, 1568, canvas, Museo Nazionale di Capodimonte, Naples

This is dramatically the case in *The Peasant and the Bird Thief*. The globe adumbrated by the curved streambank and striding peasant suggests "world" only obliquely, as the ghostly figure of a limit or horizon. Placing us outside and looking in, it locates the peasant on the threshold of abandonment, where, for the native of a homestead "unknown" to our world, the world that is unknown to him begins. And it is here—at this cleft between the local and the global, art and life, work and world, where the peasant and the viewer stand eye to eye, he exiting the indigenous, we peering in—that the picture's own trap is laid. With his next stride, at the tempo of the falling hat, and with a tumbling movement mimed by the pollarded tree at the right, the peasant will step into the stream.[72]

Bruegel helps us imagine this catastrophe. In 1568, he painted what amounts to a frame-by-frame portrayal of the next step (fig. 24).[73] Executed in tempera on canvas, and now kept with *The Misanthrope* canvas in Naples, this picture visualizes what happens in such a terrain if you do not—or cannot—watch your step.[74] Five blind men have entrusted themselves to a sixth, who has tumbled into a watery ditch. The next in line, caught in the midst of his fall, turns his eyeless face toward us. And behind him, teetering at the painting's center, the third unfortunate, just as he receives the fateful downward tug, lifts his head upward, his blind gaze tracing a useless line toward the church prominent in the background. By way of its underlying proverb, the painting alludes to Christ's diatribe against the Philistines and their strict obedience to Jewish law: "They are blind guides. And if a blind man leads a blind man, both will fall into a pit" (Matt. 15:14).[75] This proverb would have had special relevance in the Netherlands in 1568, when martial law had been imposed—illegally, in the view of many Netherlanders—by outsiders, and when strident preachers, Protestant as well as Catholic, proclaimed themselves to be prophets of the true faith and demanded blind obedience from their followers.

Bruegel realizes the old saying so concretely that it vanishes into a portrait of life. Paradoxically, our potential blindness to the admonishing proverb makes the painting visually compelling and allows it to resonate long after its historical circumstance has faded from memory.[76] Bruegel casts the blind men *plausibly* as a roving band of beggars and jongleurs who, thrust from society, must wander unaided from town to town. Portraying the precise forms of their blindness as in an atlas of differential diagnosis, he situates their catastrophe in a marginal space between human habitations, in a perversely peaceful bit of Brabant countryside. Banal as everyday life itself, this landscape stands secretly poised for violence and death. Ordinary existence, we observe, happens in a suspended state of peril, after the traps have been set but before they are triggered. Turning potential violence into actual violence, exposing the world's underlying hostility, catastrophe reveals lifetime to be but an empty, in-between period of waiting. In Bruegel, time is the Heraclitean river into which everyone steps, as into the ceaseless mutability of fortune. Time is also the blind march in which, the marchers lined up like points on a temporal vector, a properly tragic plot unfolds. In front, as the future, lie those to whom catastrophe has already arrived. In back, to the left in the painting, marches humanity in its ordinary condition, blindly imagining that something or someone greater than they is their guide. The two times—the time of the world and the time of human life—collide in the painting's lower right corner. This is also the place where earlier Christian art routinely introduced the gaping abyss of hell.

It is as when, cruising on a divided highway, you pass an accident in the opposite lanes. What makes blind fortune most vivid is neither the accident itself, which vanishes behind you, nor the great traffic jam that follows, since the halted travelers, deep in their predicament, make you feel carefree. Rather, you glimpse blind fortune in the oncoming cars much farther on that still speed obliviously toward the pileup. Bruegel's painting stays focused on a secretly decisive *now*. Abruptly in touch with the disaster through the tug of his staff, the central blind man dramatizes the present moment as an instant of radical divergence, when a decision or turn that has to be made right now has already been tragically reached. Suddenly alert, the blind man raises his face and mind upward—toward where the painting shows a church—as if toward heaven and salvation, while his body gets ineluctably drawn down toward the hellish convergence.

Fate hinges on sight. Bruegel draws his audience, who—all eyes for the picture—can see the church, into the perspective of the blind man who, with an expression of wide-eyed amazement that exposes his cataracts, cannot. The artist suggests that both are blind, the sightless wanderers as well as the painting's keen-eyed beholders. Blindness stands for our inability to know life's ends. With its steeple pointing to heaven, and through ecclesia's claim to hold the keys to salvation, the built church reminds us that beyond death there lie yet more final reckonings. In Bruegel's time, the insight that the true church cannot be seen by those who wander through the world (observe how the blind man "looks" up at the steeple only from our perspective) would have supported an attack against corrupt leadership and false prophets. During the sixteenth century, first in certain spiritualist strands of Lutheranism, then, in

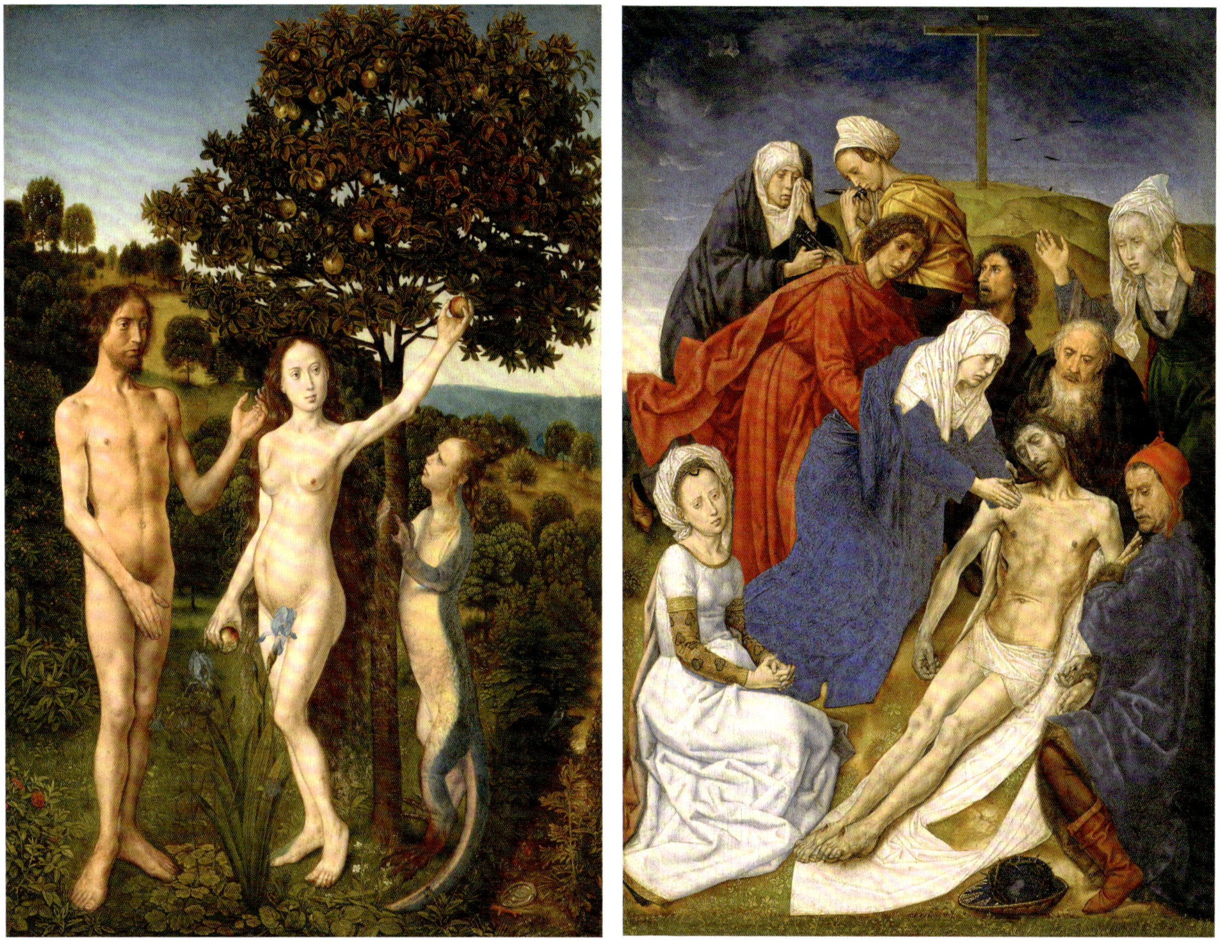

25 Hugo van der Goes, *Diptych with Adam and Eve and Lamentation*, after 1479, panel, Kunsthistorisches Museum, Vienna

Bruegel's own intellectual milieu, in the ecumenical thought of moderates such as Ortelius and the engraver and political philosopher Dirck Volkertszoon Coornhert, church was understood precisely as an invisible community of the faithful that transcended and repudiated confessional differences.[77] Paradoxically, those who think they can see church—which is to say, those who falsely fancy that they possess verifiable outward signs of true religion and who demand that others follow their lead—they are the blind men leading the blind, for the true church is hidden and can be glimpsed only dimly by the inward eye. This understanding of revelation as concealed or indecipherable has profound implications for how we understand Bruegel's art. This painter is concerned less with showing the Four Last Things (death, judgment, heaven, and hell), which we cannot see, than with showing what those ends look like from our blind spot in the midst of life.

At the far right of *The Parable of the Blind Leading the Blind*, straight above the fallen leader's eyes, the stunning purple and white bloom of an iris (*Iris germanica*, German *Himmelsschwertel*) stands forth from the dull waters behind. Cousin to the daylily (genus *Hemerocallis*)—thus named for its blossoming at dawn and withering at dusk—the flower is at once a set piece for virtuoso naturalism and (in Bruegel's time) a standard emblem of the transitory nature of human life.[78] About a hundred years earlier, the Netherlandish master Hugo van der Goes placed a blue iris over Eve's genitals as she reaches for the fruit of the forbidden tree (fig. 25).[79] Foretelling sexual shame by already hiding her nakedness, the flower also signals, through its short-lived beauty, humanity's greater punishment for the Fall: death. Frequent in Hugo's works, the iris may

26 Detail of Pieter Bruegel the Elder, *The Peasant and the Bird Thief* (fig. 4)

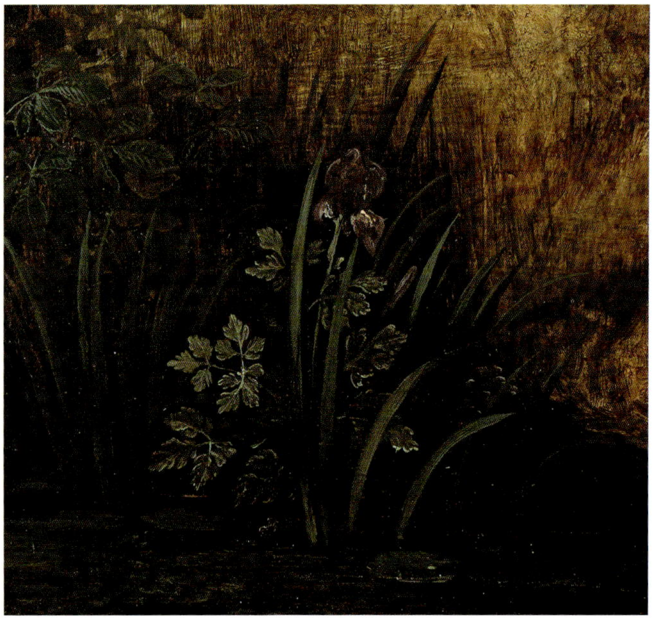

also symbolize the incarnate Son of God, born from the womb of the Virgin Mary, through whom Eve's trespass would be rectified.[80] Introducing this complex symbol into his canvas, Bruegel endows the secular scene with a potentially eschatological significance. However, the wonderful twist is that the people in the painting cannot see the patent symbol of their doom. Blindness and what happens because of blindness are the picture's fascinations. But what about *The Peasant and the Bird Thief*? To the left in that picture, also on the shore of a stream and directly underneath the nest robbery itself, a similarly spectacular iris blossoms (fig. 26). Does this mean that, like the blind men in the Naples canvas, the peasant too shall stumble?

Once pursued, emblems of death and doom abound in Bruegel's Vienna panel. The leafless, pollarded willow bent downward toward the water; thorny brambles (lower left), whose arched canes pass from earth to earth, dust to dust; the bird theft itself, signifying that death robs us of life and that the Devil can steal our winged souls: these seem to add up to one thing. This the authors of a recent study of the painting take to an extreme. *The Peasant and the Bird Thief*, they conclude, may "appear to represent a scene of daily life," but it is "in reality an allegory concerning man's mortality, a *memento mori*."[81] In other words, Bruegel's peerless portrait *of* reality is *in* reality only an emblem of death.

Is this the picture's purpose, to convey the funereal sentence "In the midst of life we are in death"? Bruegel does thrust us into life's midst, into an insistent, mobile present tense that, through the peasant's confrontation with the beholder, will be forever ongoing. And this abiding now, this pictorially generated *nunc stans*, appears about to end just now, as it seems already to have done for the bird—unless the thief were to fall, releasing his grip as he did so. Their time and our time meet at the watery foreground, at the future's fluid brink. Do these waters seal the peasant's fate? In this midst of life, is he already "in death"? Everything about him says that he would know every bend of the river. Perhaps his eagerness to share his knowledge causes him to wander from his path: we become his fatal distraction. At another level, though, the joke is on us, because the moment we notice the stream and predict the peasant's fall, we realize that we stand over the same abyss. "When whirlwinds churn the sea," wrote Lucretius in a text much-loved during the Renaissance, "it is sweet to watch from land someone else's

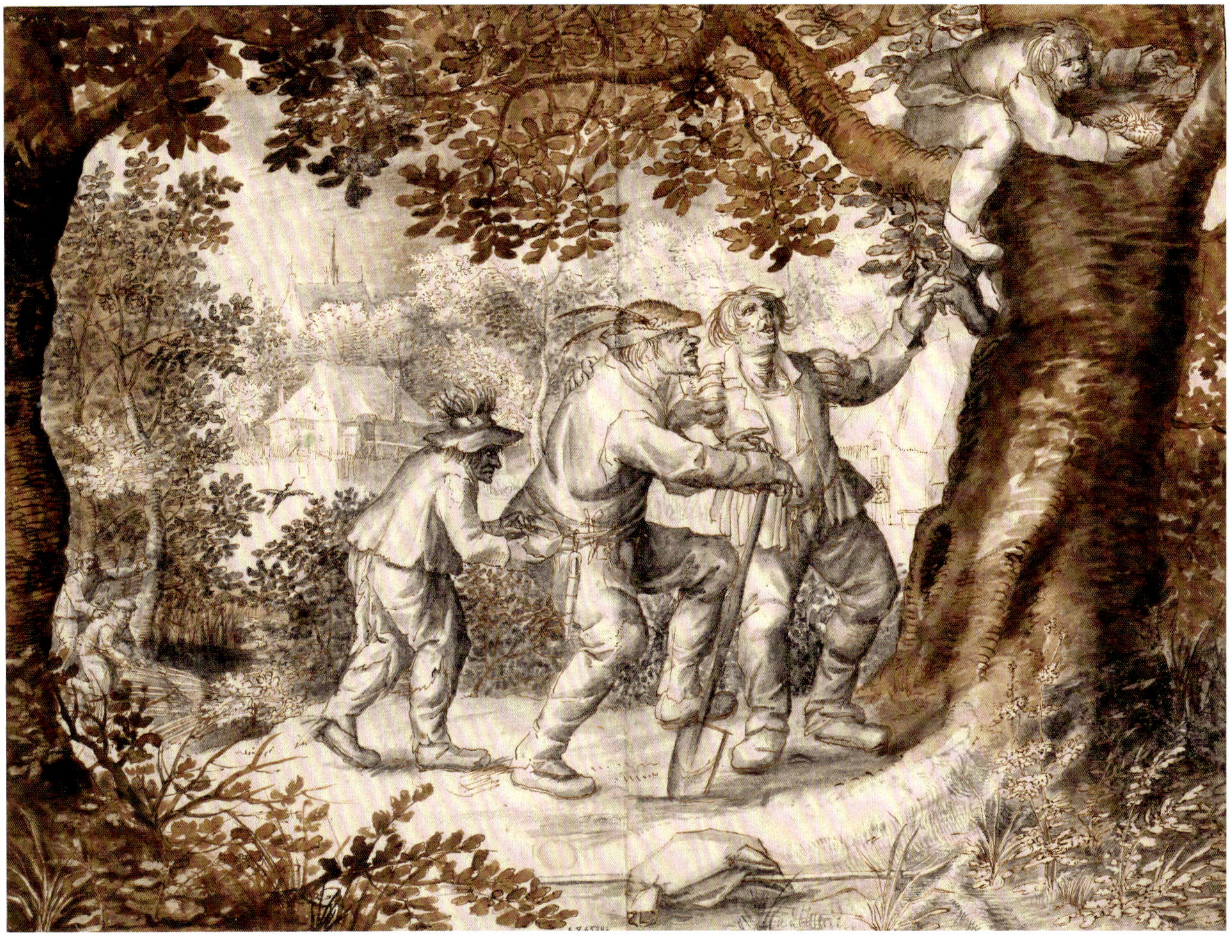

27 David Vinckboons, *The Nest-Robber*, c. 1606, pen and brown ink with gray wash and brown wash, Royal Library of Belgium, Brussels, Inv. S. V. 65747

danger."[82] In Bruegel, there is never any safe ground. If the nest robbery foreshadows death, then this premonition reverberates via the peasant to ourselves in the here and now.

Despite all its omens of death, Bruegel's painting makes the now of life endure. Surely the peasant would know how to ford this stream! And wouldn't the stones that afford him footing support us too? And anyway, "in reality," would falling be a tragic calamity or a comic blunder? In Plato's *Theaetetus*, Thales—the first philosopher—fell into a pit while observing the stars, whereupon a pretty, clever servant girl laughed at him, because "he was so eager to know the heavens in the sky that he could not see what was before his very feet."[83] Avatar of practical wisdom, the girl pokes fun at the theorist whose search for reality blinds him to reality. Bruegel would have us laugh along with her. True, in the midst of life we are in death. But this painter starts with the small hope that it somehow might not yet be so. His comic heroes are creatures in whom this nonsensical hope stands mirrored. When peasants in his paintings literally dance under the gallows, they do so not blindly, as if oblivious to death, but knowingly, in order to play with death (see fig. 319).[84]

Traps

Some forty years after Bruegel painted *The Peasant and the Bird Thief*, another Flemish painter laid its structure bare. In David Vinckboons's drawing, now in Brussels, the amusing spectacle of the bird thief distracts two peasants from noticing another thief, dressed in rags, who deftly filches from them (fig. 27).[85] At the left, a second pair of peasants catches sight of the episode

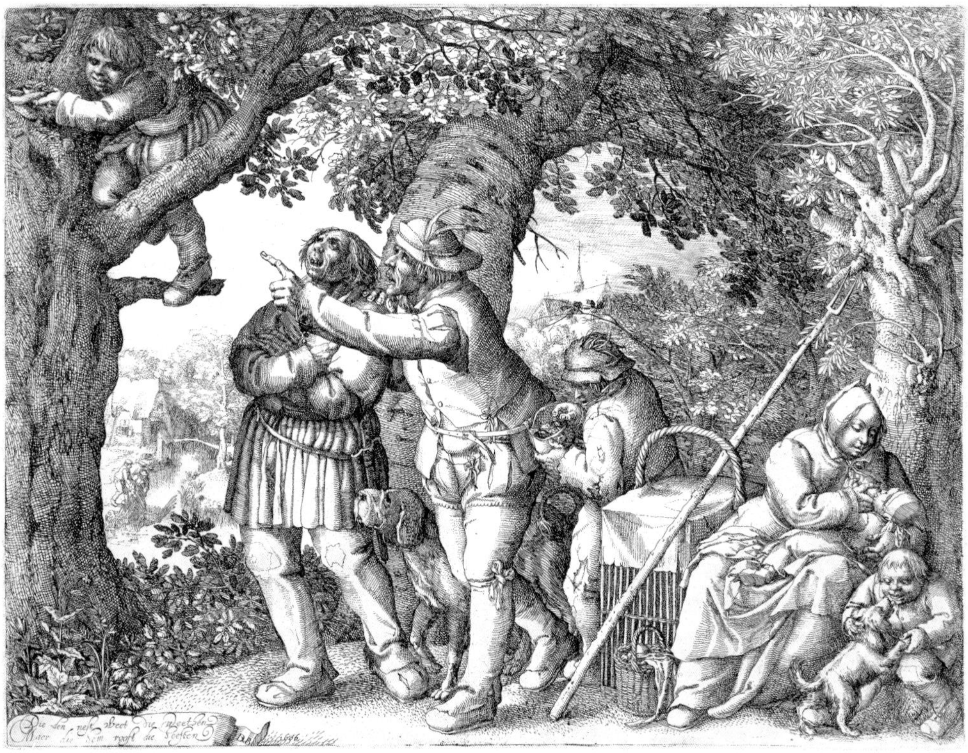

28 Hessel Gerritsz (attributed to) after David Vinckboons, *The Nest-Robber* (*Bird-nester*), 1606, etching, The British Museum, London

from afar, leaving open the question as to whether they, who are, by the way, setting a fish trap, and we, who are distracted like them, are being presently robbed, as well. For in the system on display, knowledge becomes the cause of folly, and blindness to destiny is our inescapable fate. Thieves know this, and so do artists. Similarly canny about the attentions and distractions of their target group, both know how to make and to improvise traps.

Vinckboons understood the comic tone and inner mechanics of the Vienna panel better than Bruegel's scholarly interpreters. His was a professional's take on a fellow professional. Such insight allowed him to identify and develop the trap that underlies Bruegel's painting, and to reset it in different configurations. A printed variation made in 1606 and probably based on a lost design by Vinckboons clarifies the distant fish trap and further expands the drama's cast of characters (fig. 28).[86] Now the bird thief has his whole family in tow. The etcher (probably Hessel Gerritsz, an expert printmaker in Amsterdam) also develops the relation of the two simultaneous thefts. He makes the nest, the bird thief's hat, and the rustic's purse the same size and invites us to examine, and muse over, the pilfered contents: in the nest and cap, struggling hatchlings; in the purse, money and a pig's-trotter amulet. Exposing secret pockets in the visible world, details like these lure us into the same attitude of mesmerized absorption that the rustics exhibit—to their peril—causing us to wonder whether the bird nester, the purse thief, and the artist are all in cahoots.

The forest people of West Africa are master trappers.[87] They have special snares for every kind of beast, each engineered to suit its victim. Their subtlest trap is for the chimpanzee, whose cunning, according to the trappers, is exceeded only by man's. Indeed like human beings, chimps do not run from problems. Instead, they stop and try to solve them. This renders nooses, running knots, and most snares useless. The chimpanzee trap of one group of forest people therefore consists of a thin thread that the animal, due to its innate curiosity, will be

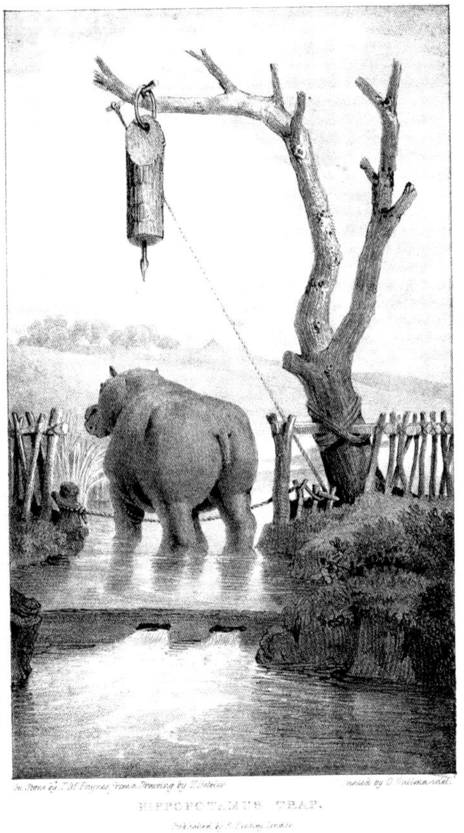

29 Thomas Mann Baynes after Thomas Boteler, *Hippopotamus Trap*, 1835, engraving (printed by Charles Joseph Hullmandel), from the collections of Ernst Mayr Library, Museum of Comparative Zoology, Harvard University

compelled to tug, releasing from above a bundle of arrows with poisoned tips. The creature is undone not by his stupidity but by his inquiring mind. Traps work with their victims in order to work against them. Fitted to the quarry's body, behavior, and mentality, they draw their energy not from the trapper, who has left long ago, but from the movement and heft of the quarry and from the potential energy stored in the trap, in bowed branches, stretched springs, deadweight, and the like (fig. 29).[88] A well-built trap should be invisible to its target, or at least should be unrecognizable as a trap. From the target's point of view, the familiar world and the snare are indistinguishable, or as Alfred Gell put it, "Traps are lethal parodies of the animal's *Umwelt*," the total "world" as it is experienced by that particular organism.[89] This fabricated identity between friend and foe makes traps potent emblems of our being in the world. In the midst of life, the world seems a suitable habitat, but disaster reveals it to be hostile, vindictive, and cruel. What makes the trap's violence especially unsettling is that someone laid it, but it erupts without him. Like hidden gods, trappers leave behind their deadly intention in the form of a device or prosthesis that operates on their behalf.

A sturdy snare can long outlast its maker, rather like a work of art. Also art-like is the trap's mimetic dimension, as Gell brilliantly showed.[90] To conceal a trap, again, the trapper must make it blend in with the environment, and that requires the trapper to fabricate the false but (to the quarry) realistic image of a peaceable world. Trappers must project themselves imaginatively into the alien *how* of their quarry's species-specific experience of the world—rather as artists attune themselves to audience expectations.[91] And, like artists, trappers must make their image of reality more desirable than mere reality by depositing in it a lure. In the 1530s,

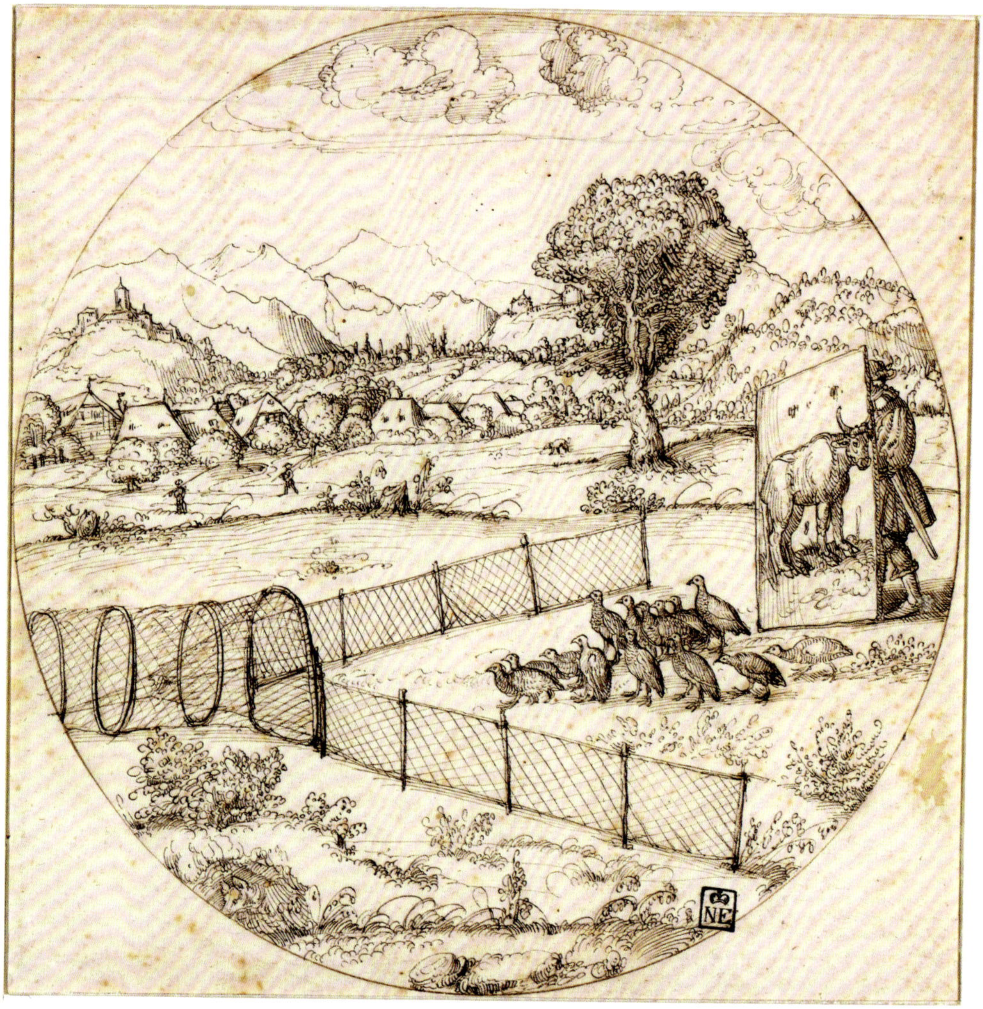

30 Augustin Hirschvogel, *Stalking Partridges with a Tunnel Net*, c. 1530, pen and dark brown ink, Szépmüvészeti Museum, Budapest

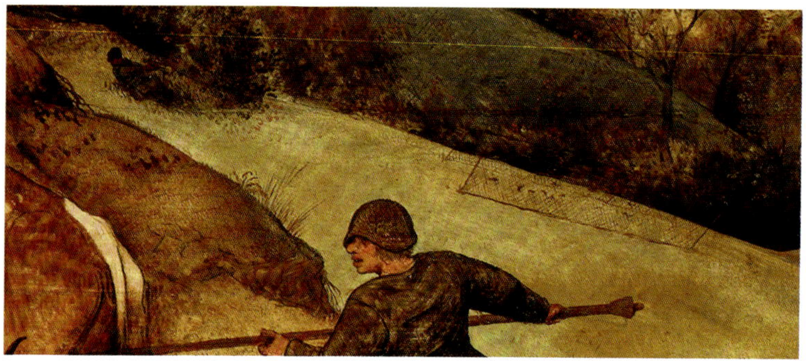

31 Detail of Pieter Bruegel the Elder, *The Return of the Herd* (fig. 2)

Augustin Hirschvogel made a series of fifty-three pen-and-ink drawings of the hunt, including some that record the ingenious trapping techniques of the time. In one sketch, a hunter hides behind the painted image of a cow (with visible eyeholes) in order to herd partridges into a one-way tunnel of netting (fig. 30).[92] Art history's unsurpassed simulator of everyday lifeworlds, Bruegel recognized the profound kinship between traps and artworks. He littered his landscapes with hidden snares, with nets, ambushes, mantraps, pitfalls, nooses, deadfalls, and the like (fig. 31 and see fig. 304). He also structured his pictures entirely like traps, luring the viewers in and then surprising them with the catastrophe. To take an example that will much concern us later, the Vienna *Christ Carrying the Cross* elicits from its beholders a certain

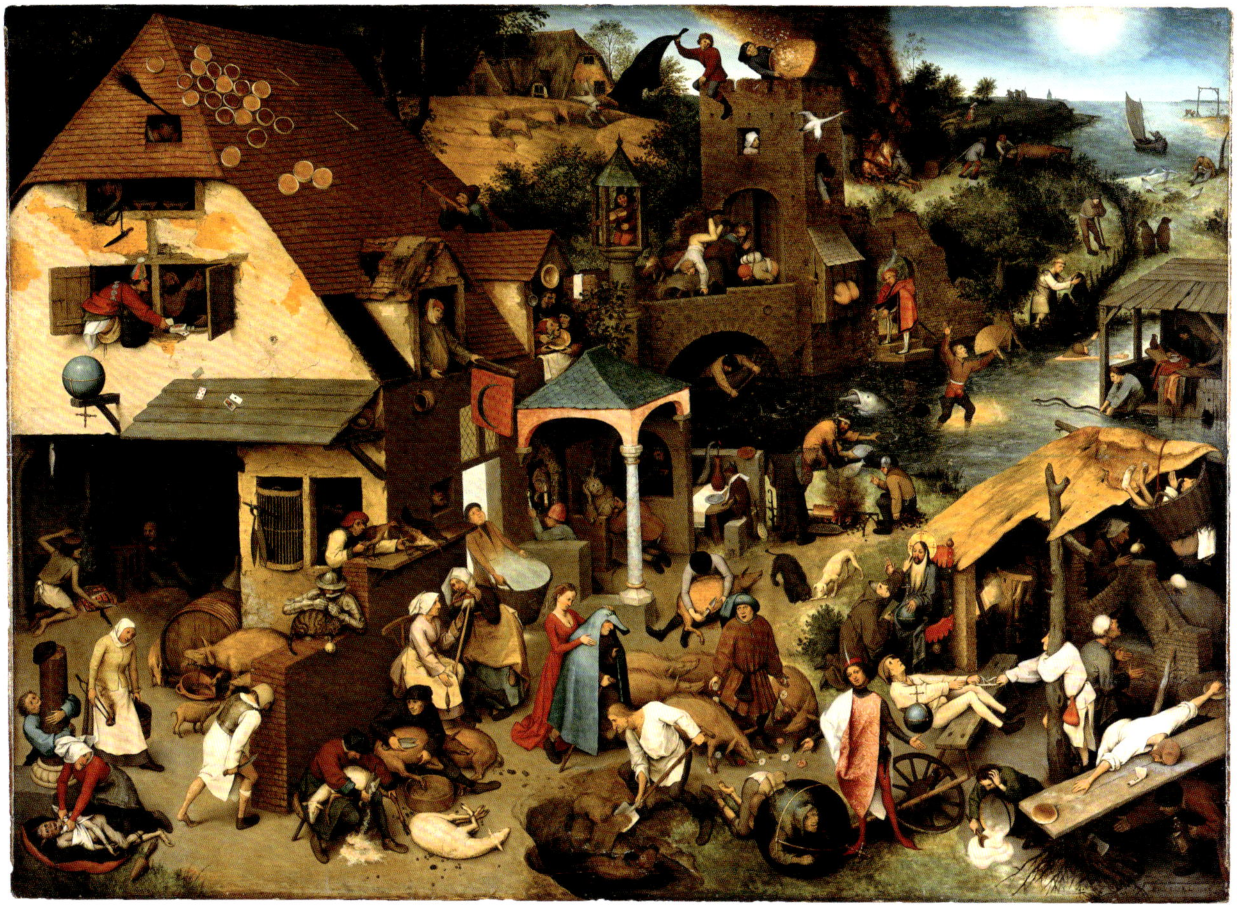

aloof indifference to its plot (see fig. 266). Pushing the sacred events into the background and filling the vast vista with innumerable engaging sideshows, the picture invites us to respond aesthetically, as it were, to what from a Christian perspective ought to engage us morally and existentially. But the painting also reveals to us—slowly, in ironic contrast to the urgency of what it reveals—that indifference, more than cruelty, caused Christ's death. Repeating that indifference in our response, we become complicit in the Crucifixion under way. We find one more example in Bruegel's most-copied masterpiece, *Winter Landscape with Bird Trap*, in which the artist aligns a trap located in the painting with the trap that the painting itself is (see fig. 300). The meticulous depiction of a vernacular bird trap, complete with its lure, trigger, deadfall, and hide, is marvelously self-explanatory in both design and operation. At once a portrait and a blueprint of deception, the bird trap also models the world in which it is set, as well as Bruegel's painting of the world, both of which are alluring and hazardous. And one of the many things this trap models—about the world and the work—is the terrifying absence, in both, of a maker. To compare the world to a trap is to announce not only the world's unthinking, poised violence but also its solitude.

32 Pieter Bruegel the Elder, *Netherlandish Proverbs*, 1559, oil on oak panel, Staatliche Museen zu Berlin, Gemäldegalerie, Berlin

Proverbs

It has long been suspected that *The Peasant and the Bird Thief* is a puzzle for which we have lost the solution. To solve the puzzle, scholars have turned to the realm of proverbs, and with good reason, since Bruegel's paintings are chockablock with them.[93] Consider the artist's monumental statement on the subject, *Netherlandish Proverbs* (fig. 32).[94] The painting looks at

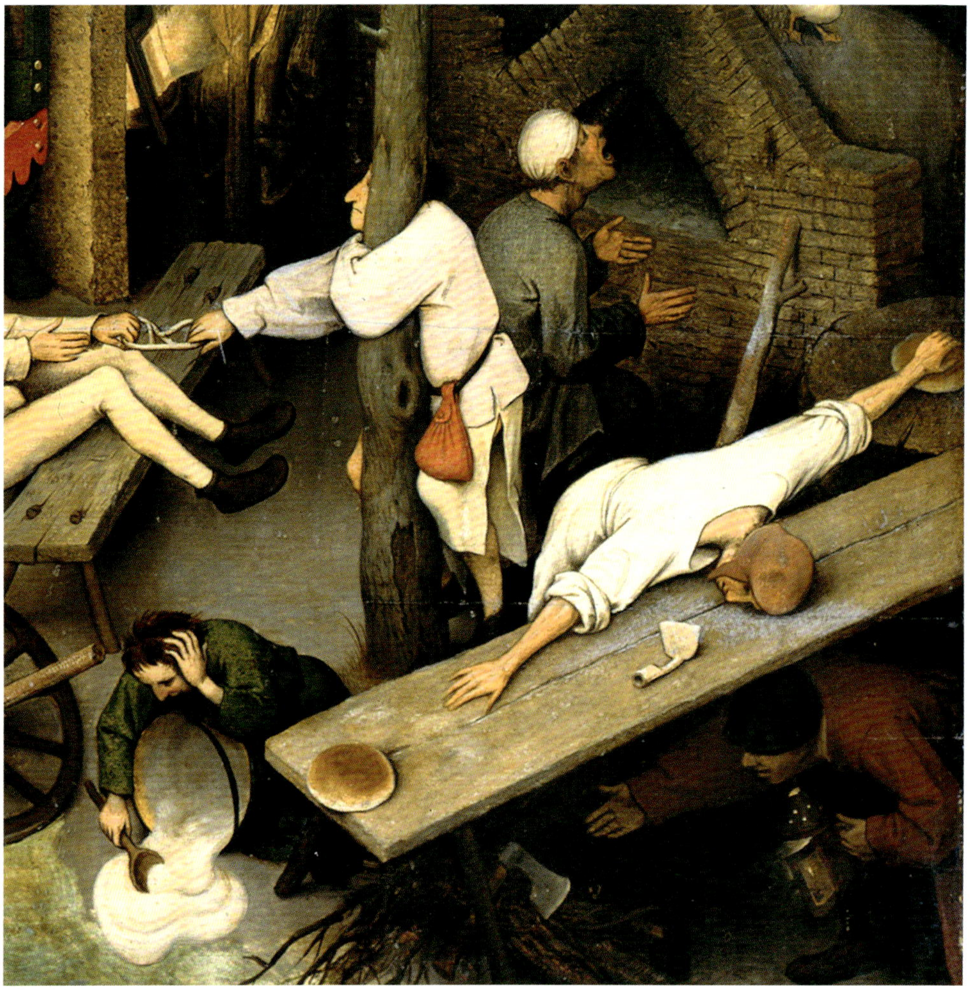

33 Detail of Pieter Bruegel the Elder, *Netherlandish Proverbs* (fig. 32)

first like a portrait of everyday village life. Only at second glance is it apparent that none of the depicted actions is ordinary. *Either* this is not human life at all but something alien, *or* the people are doing something other than living, namely acting out proverbs about everyday life. In fact, Bruegel makes both these alternatives plausible. He displays an unreality that results from visualizing proverbs (proving that you have to know the adage to understand the image). But he allows that unreality, taken as a whole, to visualize a proverb about ordinary reality per se—namely, the "world is upside down" (proving that one cannot understand such a topsy-turvy world; see fig. 23).[95] Our everyday activities, which first we thought we saw reflected in the picture, and which we then realized had been replaced by playacted proverbs, are indeed as absurd as these bizarre charades. Bruegel devotes his images to what survives after their translation into words: note, for example, the mesmerizing, true-to-life but symbolically superfluous presence of flour on the cutting board, where a man is futilely trying to reach for two loaves, meaning he cannot live within his budget (fig. 33).

In *The Peasant and the Bird Thief* nothing so overtly odd happens that it requires a saying to explain it: rural people did catch birds and raid their nests for eggs, and spotting someone cleverly doing so was probably as amusing then as it would be today. However, on another work, *The Beekeepers*, a relevant proverb does come to light (fig. 34).[96] An inscription penned by Bruegel in the corner of this drawing reads: "He who knows the nest knows it, / He who robs it has it."[97] In other words, passive knowing leaves you empty-handed, and to have something

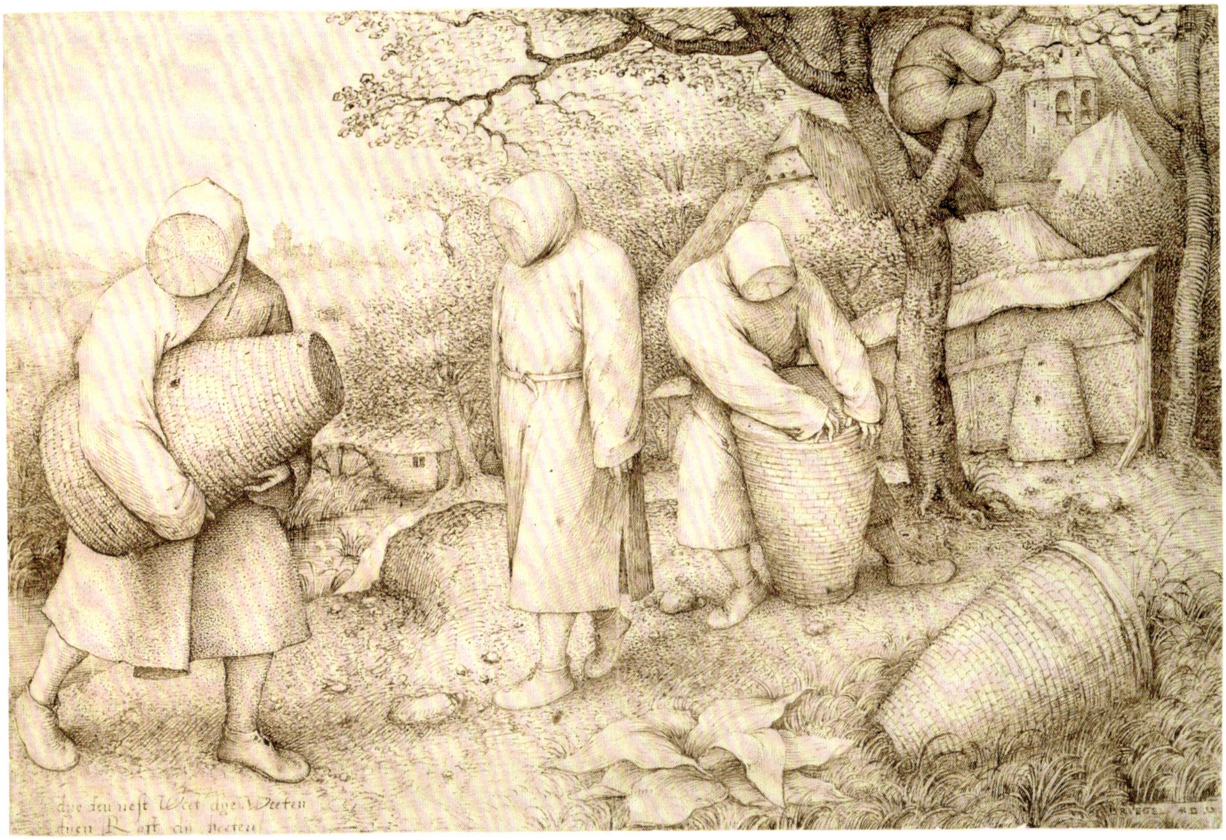

34 Pieter Bruegel the Elder, *The Beekeepers*, c. 1567–68, pen and brown ink, Staatliche Museen zu Berlin, Kupferstichkabinett, Berlin

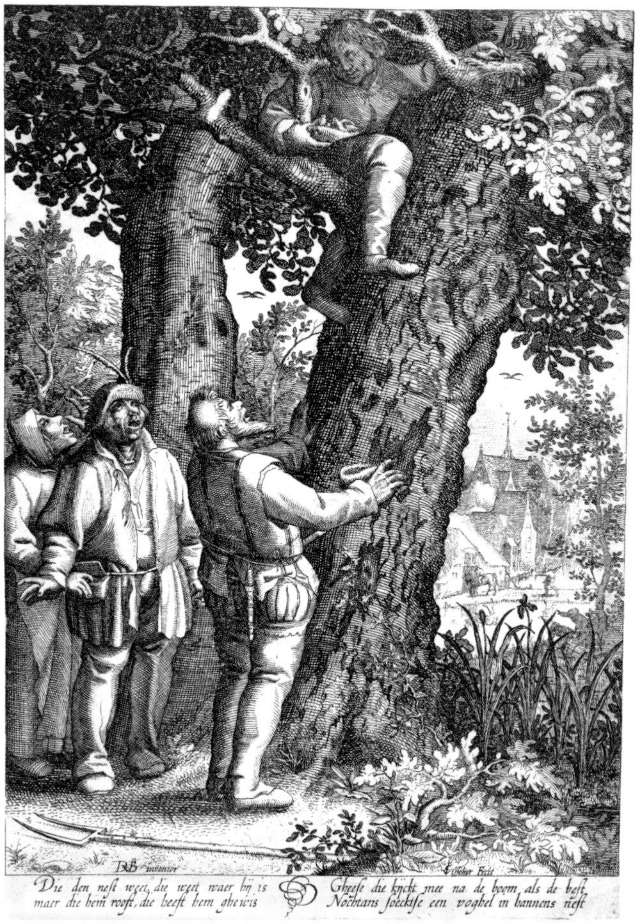

35 Claes Jansz. Visscher after David Vinckboons, *The Nest-Robber*, c. 1608, etching, Rijksmuseum, Amsterdam

requires action. Leaving aside the important fact that the proverb does not solve but instead amplifies this drawing's mystery, we are justified in applying it to the *Bird Thief*, since artists modeling their work after Bruegel's painting did. The 1606 etching by Gerritsz after Vinckboons shows peasants naturally amused by the bird theft (see fig. 28). But its inscription, introduced on a scroll at the lower left, draws a message from the event: "He who knows the nest knows it, / But he who steals it owns it."[98] It is possible to read the proverb as if it were spoken by the pointing peasant to his companion. However, the fact that he is being pickpocketed undercuts the pointer, and the folded arms of his warty, gaping companion (suggesting empty-handedness) suggest that the two exemplify the weaker half of the proverb's comparison: they know but do not have. Another print probably based on yet another lost drawing by Vinckboons repeats the same text (lower left), and again features the comical motif of the knower getting had (fig. 35).[99] But this variation, etched by the prolific printmaker Claes Jansz. Visscher, turns the thief into a woman, whose exploration of the peasant's purse is given a bawdy twist. After a flourish, there appear two further lines in the inscription: "Jessie looks up at the tree with zest, but what she really seeks is a bird in Johnny's nest."

Some scholars have found erotic innuendos in Bruegel's painting, too.[100] On the basis of amorous connotations of the bird-catching and the bird-nesting adage, they take the nest robbery and the peasant's impending fall to signal the peasant's cuckolding by a more active rival. In the landscape behind him, the thinking goes, the peasant's home and wife are being violated by a stranger. I am reminded of one of Eric Idle's *Monty Python* characters, who

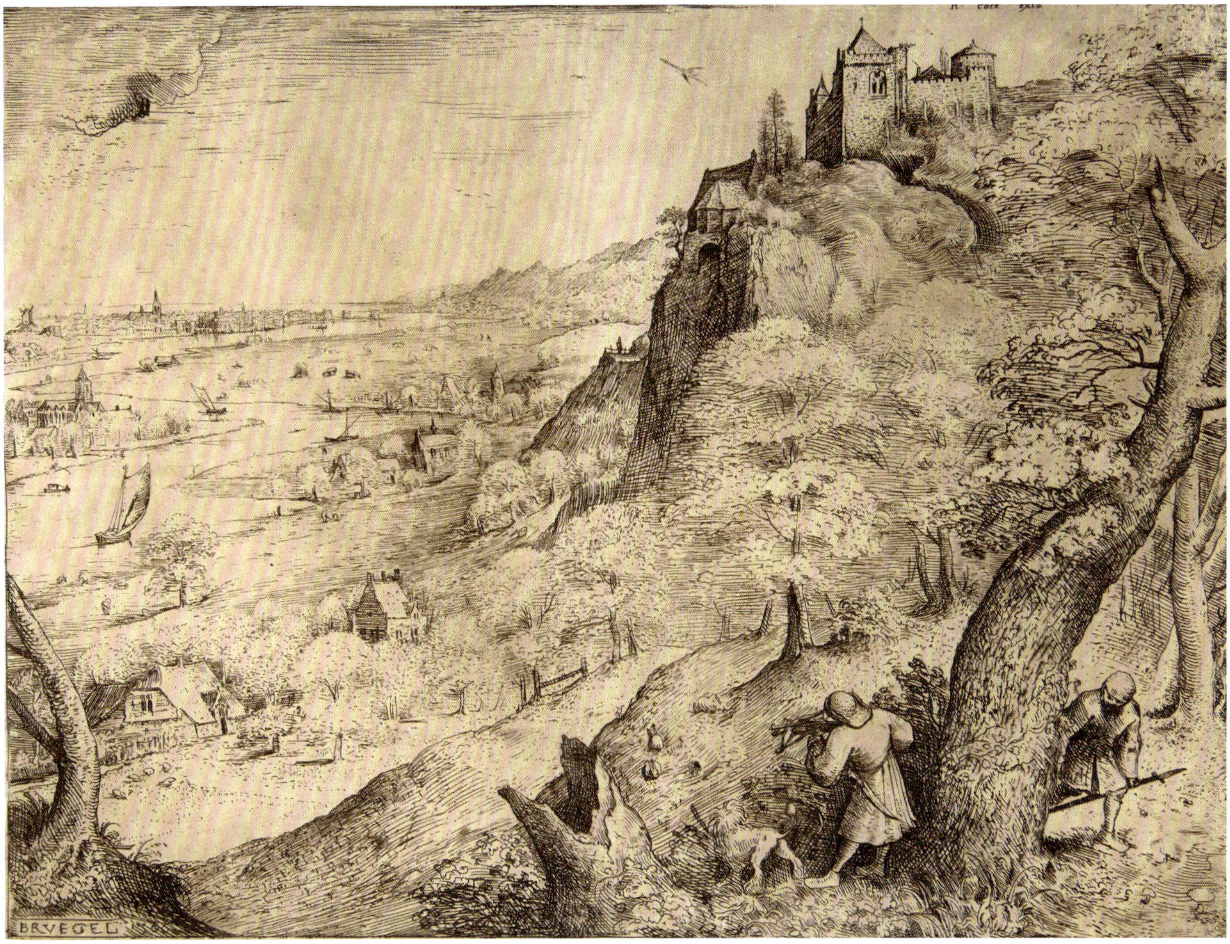

36 Pieter Bruegel the Elder, *The Rabbit Hunt*, 1560, etching, The Metropolitan Museum of Art, New York, Harris Brisbane Dick Fund, 1925

mutters an insinuating "nudge nudge, wink wink" after everything he says.[101] Erotic readings of Bruegel's painting founder because there's no clear visual evidence for them. But they are instructive, nevertheless. For the peasant himself is a "nudge nudge" sort of guy who accosts people indiscreetly, hoping to produce a laughter that comes from nowhere and spares no one. And it is he who is about to fall. And because he is not merely represented *in* the painting—because looking us in the eye and telling us where to look, the peasant acts out the painting itself—Bruegel ensures that everyone shares in his ridiculous misfortune, whatever that may be. A knowing "aha" triggers the trap, like the thread that the problem-solving chimp cannot help pulling.

Bruegel never tires of picturing this Faustian problem of knowledge, where you think you can catch something, it escapes, and it is you who gets caught. Consider his one autograph etching and probably his most personal print, *The Rabbit Hunt* (fig. 36).[102] In the right foreground, a hunter aims his crossbow at some rabbits in the grass, while behind him, concealed by the tree and bush that hide the bowman from the rabbits, a spear-bearing soldier stalks the hunter. "A hare yourself, you hunt for prey" is the apt proverb here.[103] But even this adage repeats rather than solves the picture's mystery. The hunter hunted, the trapper trapped, the viewer viewed: these reversals encapsulate something ineffable about our being in the world, which Bruegel's remarkable landscape view wordlessly shows. The human subject is not the measure of the world. Aiming while being aimed at, we remain *subject to* an unnameable power anterior to ourselves.

"With certain of Bruegel's works it is not easy to find the key to the idea," writes Klaus Demus in his excellent catalogue of the Vienna Bruegels. For *The Peasant and the Bird Thief* that key "is still missing," Demus continues. "We cannot replace it with our 'own' interpretation. . . . The simple, total meaning, the 'literal' handle—probably related to a proverb or saying—with which the content would be able to be 'grasped,' goes (in defiance of all individual optimism) starkly missing."[104] Demus acknowledges that a proverb about having and knowing is in play, but he cannot link it to the peasant's impending fall, which in his view must somehow be a verdict rightly reached on the peasant. Justice, together with the picture's underlying meaning, would be revealed if only we found "the right 'word.' " Demus puts scare quotes around the adjective "own" in the phrase "our 'own' interpretation." He ridicules understanding based on mere opinion (*doxa*), and seeks instead to discover and grasp a "literal" handle.

Ironically, Bruegel's picture displays just this. It portrays the comical abyss between knowing something and grasping something literally. Juxtaposing the pointing finger with the thieving hand, Bruegel shows that having a mental handle, as the striding peasant does on the theft, does not place knowledge on sufficient grounds. Moreover, in the post-paradisiacal human condition where the fruits of the world—like meaning itself—are invariably withheld, and where consciousness and its object no longer stand in agreement, whoever grasps the goods forsakes the ground and risks a fall. In Bruegel, handles are not safe; they are what trip the trap, like the thread that lures the curious chimpanzee. Whether it is building a tower to heaven or avoiding the trap of death, calculated behavior fails to secure its object and bring it to a halt. Much still eludes us in Bruegel's *The Peasant and the Bird Thief*. Even if a better proverb or legend were to come to light, I doubt that the picture would even then be firmly grasped. I cannot think of a single painting by this artist about which one can confidently say, "I've got it!" With Bruegel we lack a key not because it has passed from historical memory. Its absence belongs to the human predicament that the artist timelessly portrays. Everything in the painting—the thieving hand, the falling hat, the peasant's stride—converges in the elusive midst of life. We too join in as we face the peasant across the stream of time. In this abiding now, the key—to the peasant's fate, the painting's riddle, and the human condition—lies perennially elsewhere.

Scripture without a Key

Nearly four centuries after Bruegel, a very different portraitist of the ordinary grappled with the fate of revelation in human history. Franz Kafka has become synonymous with surreal dreamworlds, but, like Bruegel, his great theme was everyday life. Kafka observed his characters, all "little people," under the shadow of an inscrutable law. Like Bruegel, he focused on life lived in that shadow, offering no glimpse of the immensity that casts it. *The Trial*, published posthumously in 1925, finds the hero, Josef K., trapped by something at once intimate and inaccessible. Accused of an unknown crime by unknown authorities of an unknown law, Josef K. first disbelieves, then resists, and in resisting fulfills his abject destiny: to be killed—in his own last words—"Like a dog!"[105] The cause of this fate remains impenetrable also to the reader, who experiences Kafka's novel rather as Josef K. encounters the law. You stand perennially before an unenterable gateway "intended [only] for you."[106]

In 1934, a decade after Kafka's early death, two friends—both Jews exiled from Hitler's Germany—debated Josef K.'s dilemma. Gershom Scholem was a pioneering historian of Jewish mysticism and, since 1933, a professor at the new Hebrew University in Jerusalem. Walter Benjamin was a brilliant literary critic and philosopher living in Paris. In letters he wrote to Benjamin in 1934, Scholem took Kafka's writings to be religious at their core. From his perspective *The Trial* was less a work of literature than a late instance of traditional Jewish legal commentary, or Halacha. Paraphrasing the essence of divine judgment, Kafka sought to reveal in modern, novelistic terms what Jewish mystics had always preached: the enigmatic "nothingness of revelation."[107] Since ancient times, the fate of the Jews had always been to live under the law, but always in a state of exile. Expelled from Israel, they were also cast out from Scripture, which spoke to them from a place no longer theirs. Like Jewish exegetes before him, Kafka—in Scholem's view—grappled with the postexilic obscurity of the law.

Benjamin had a very different understanding of Kafka. The crux of this difference lay in the problem of modernity. It concerned, in Benjamin's words, "the Last Judgment's projection into world history" and how one ought to imagine this shift from divine to human time "in Kafka's sense."[108] Posed in this way, the problem was not the ancient one of Jewish exile but a modern one. It concerned the meaning of revelation in a disenchanted, secular world. In the modern era, the law is no longer inscrutable but absent: "The work of Torah—if we abide by Kafka's account—has been thwarted."[109] If Scripture has been "mislaid," then Kafka's texts can no longer comment on it: "But do we have the doctrine which Kafka's parables explicate and which K's postures and the gestures of his animals clarify?" asks Benjamin in his 1934 essay on Kafka.[110] If Kafka's writings cannot represent the law in enigmatic form—if the doctrine that they explicate "does not exist"—what do they portray?

"Without the key that belongs to it, Scripture is not Scripture but life."[111] In the German of Benjamin's letter to Scholem, "Scripture" is *die Schrift*. It is at once writing, Holy Writ, the law set down by Moses in the Torah, and all the interpretations of that written law. Authored for an era when the key has been mislaid, Kafka's writings represent—instead of Scripture—life itself: "Life as it is lived in the village at the foot of the hill where the castle is built."[112] But if Kafka thrusts us into the midst of everyday life, why invoke Scripture at all? According to Benjamin, Kafka did not simply depict life's inscrutability, as so many modern writers had done. Rather, he attempted to "metamorphize life into Scripture." That is, he tried to submit the life he portrays to the law that is no longer—or not yet—Scripture. Benjamin calls this attempt a "reversal." By this he means not only a return to divine justice but also an overturning of one justice by another, more elemental one. For the laws and norms that overshadow bare life in Kafka are older than the ones contained in Scripture. Unwritten and prehistoric, these laws fate humans inevitably to transgress them.[113]

Bruegel attempted an analogous reversal. But he did this from a very different theological and historical starting point. Circumstances exposed him to a form of political sovereignty that made the law and violence one and the same, while divine justice seemed increasingly obscure. And yet, Bruegel pursued a craft that, for centuries, had visualized the stories and insights of Scripture. And these showed most of all this: human life and world history get their meaning only at their end, at the moment of final judgment. If in the twentieth century Kafka tried to turn life into Scripture, Bruegel, painting at the beginning of the modern age, endeavored to turn Scripture into life, hence the cluelessness of his heroes and interpreters. Painting the everyday life of a peasantry governed by prehistoric norms, he revealed that, with the keys to Scripture absent or mislaid, only the human remains. Through seemingly timeless denizens of nature, Bruegel showed the dynamic, world-making force of culture. He showed that truths are not "out there" waiting to be found but have to be humanly crafted, like proverbs, customs, and games.

In his religious paintings, Bruegel also portrays divine law, but from a decidedly human perspective, to the point that the revelations of Scripture disappear into the indecipherability of life. In his wintry *Epiphany* (or *The Adoration of the Magi in the Snow*), inhospitable nature and an indifferent humanity almost occlude God's singular coming to light (see fig. 265). And in his secular works, Bruegel reverts to a more elemental law. *The Magpie on the Gallows*, a painting that was perhaps his last surviving masterpiece, which he was said to have willed at death to his wife, shows peasants living (as Kafka's would say) "in the village at the foot of the hill where the castle is built" (see fig. 319). Revelers march up from that village to a place at its edge where, under a terrifying instrument of the law, they perform a defiant dance. The proverb "to dance under the gallows" means to foolishly ignore death. But Bruegel's peasants seem to enact the adage knowingly, as if resisting with their indifference the world's indifference to them. The picture's own verbal motto mocks them, and death and judgment may be already on them now, but the peasants retain their capacity to play nonsensically with law. This book seeks to explain how Bruegel reached this remarkable point of view. The adventure will end with the impious, absurd revelry pursued under the gallows. But it begins with what seems, on the face of things, the opposite vantage point: that of a painter who throws everyday life immediately into the flames of hell.

3

WORLD TIME

The Peddler

Born around 1450 and deceased in 1516, the artist born Jheronimus Anthoniszoon van Aken is most famous for his dreamworlds and devilish fantasies.[1] Some of it signed with his taken name, "Jhieronymus Bosch," this artist's oeuvre is also—by a paradox this book seeks to explain—the incunable of European genre painting. Earlier there existed depictions of everyday life, but these occurred mostly in the margins: on the illuminated borders of manuscript pages, in the backgrounds of sacred icons, in corners of church space, on the undersides of misericords, in the nascent media of woodcuts and engravings, and as decorations on objects of daily use—mirrors, combs, oven tiles, rugs, games, and so forth.[2] Everyday life never stood portrayed front and center, and never in the privileged medium of panel painting, as it does in two oak panels now in the Prado.

Together these panels, the exteriors of hinged shutters, exhibit the likeness of a wayfarer striding nervously through a landscape (fig. 37).[3] An ample meter and a half high, and probably painted in Bosch's workshop close to the time of the artist's death, the panels are also painted on their reverse sides, so that when they open they become the wings of a triptych. Marks from the lock that once held them shut are still there. Empty of sacred persons and events, the panels draw their anonymous subject from ordinary existence. Or, more precisely, they condense everyday life itself into an epitome. The wayfarer represents Everyman, his narrow path stands for life, and the landscape setting, with its perils and its pleasures, encapsulates the mundane world.

"Here on earth," wrote Saint Augustine in *The City of God*, "we wander on a pilgrimage through time, looking for the kingdom of heaven."[4] By Bosch's day, this ancient image had become a fixed metaphor for life, partly because the practice of pilgrimage itself—of physical travel to holy places for pious or penitential reasons—had taken on elaborate forms, widening conceptually to include mental journeys, via internal, moral landscapes, to Heavenly Jerusalem.[5] Bosch's peddler, however, has neither heaven nor even home as his destination. An itinerant, he bears on his back the wares he tries to sell from town to town. Keeping trivial things in view both for himself and for others—so the thinking goes—he is forever pushed and pulled by paltry fears, regrets, and desires.[6] Peddlers were stock characters in the literature and drama of Bosch's time, often arriving from outside to comment, a quasi chorus, on the

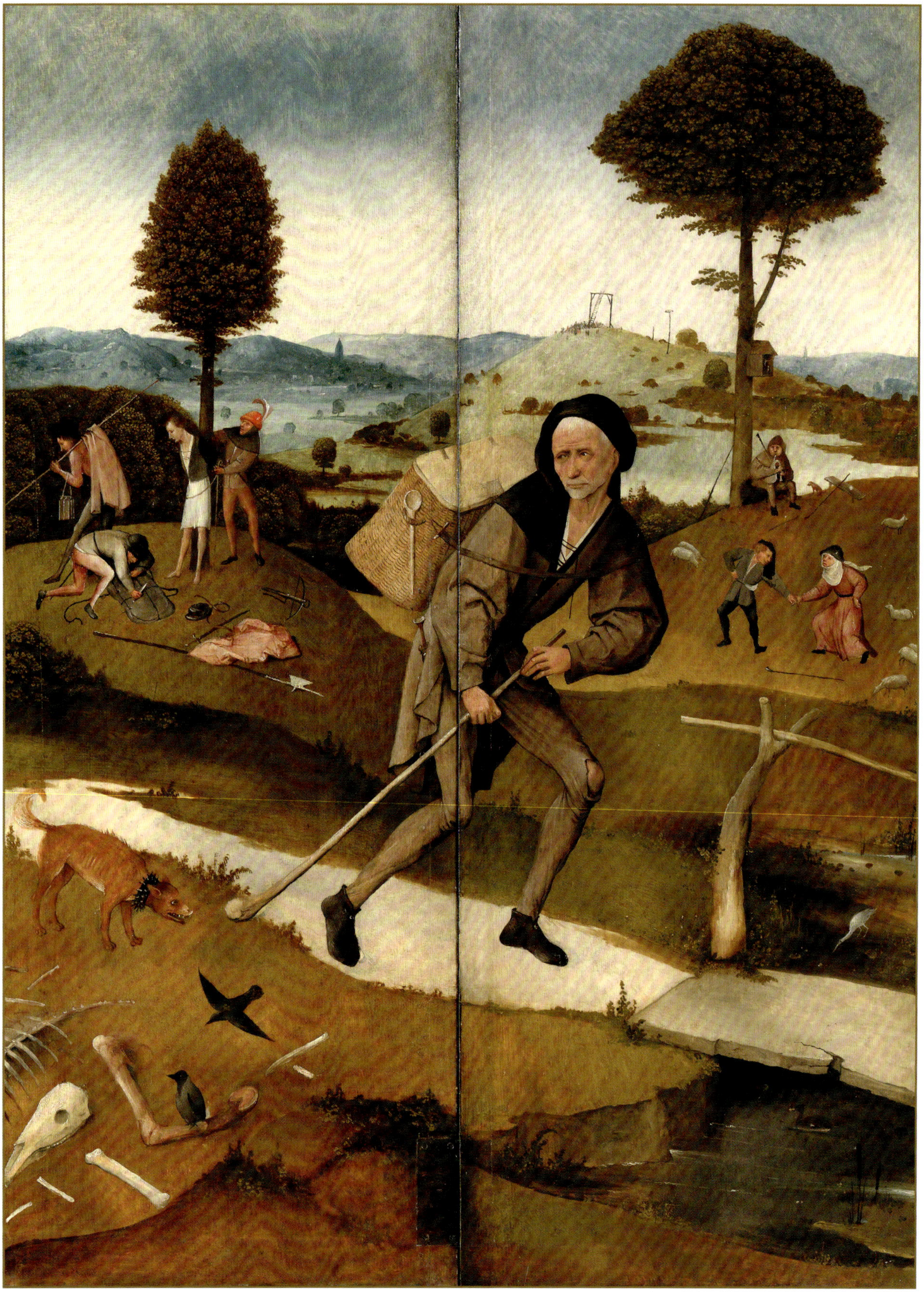

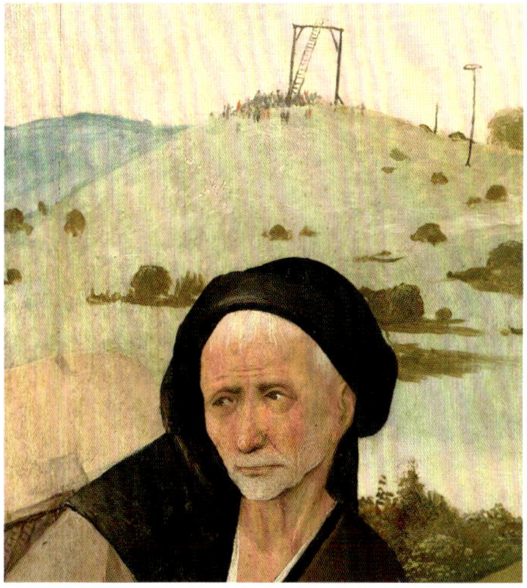

(OPPOSITE) 37 Hieronymus Bosch and Assistants, *The Peddler*, closed state of *The Hay Wain*, c. 1500, panel, Museo Nacional del Prado, Madrid

(LEFT) 38 Detail of Hieronymus Bosch and Assistants, *The Peddler* (fig. 37)

unfolding plot. Morally ambivalent, but with a propensity for religious conversion, they shared with pious pilgrims one key characteristic: peddlers, too, are overtly mobile. And that mobility makes them stand for all who believe themselves to be settled when in reality they are secretly in transit. For, in Augustine's words, we all wander "through time."

Bosch frames his painting rigidly in the dimension of time. Time's center—the evanescent now of experience—forms the picture's physical center. Distributed over the two panels, the painting catches the peddler in stride in the middle of his life, on the line where the shutters meet. Past and future cluster round as episodes as if along a crooked timeline indicated by the peddler's path. Behind him, as a destiny narrowly avoided, murderous highwaymen have ambushed and captured another peddler and are robbing his wares. Closer still, a savage dog—lurking on back roads the central peddler has taken—nips at his heels, dramatizing dangers inescapable and ongoing. Below, clean-picked bones signal that the living body itself is but baggage, like the parcel cut open by the highwaymen—observe how the peddler's torn trousers resemble cadaverous skin falling from the bone. In front of the peddler, toward where his body presses, a piping shepherd and a dancing peasant couple, along with the spacious landscape itself, exhibit the carnal delights that draw the hero on. The energy of future life (Eros, as it were) contends with death (Thanatos), lurking grimly behind. Meanwhile, just ahead of the peddler, a stone footbridge evidences an ominous crack that starts just below where the dancing couple's hands meet, signaling unseen hazards yet to come.

The peddler's predicament can be usefully compared to the peasant's in Bruegel's *The Peasant and the Bird Thief* (see fig. 4). In both, the protagonists' animated thrust—whether forward toward us or laterally past us, it does not especially matter—dramatizes human existence in its temporal element, as lifetime.[7] In both, the protagonists mime, through their contorted postures, the tangled, reflexive experience of the now, by striding forward but gesturing or glancing backward. And in both, this retrospection discovers a robbery behind while simultaneously blinding the discoverer to a potential theft of life itself to come, suggested by a watery abyss that cuts through both wanderers' paths. But whereas in Bruegel death is only an accident waiting to happen—the peasant's possible, but by no means necessary, fall into the stream—in Bosch it is a verdict already reached. Smack above the peddler's head, in the distant background, a public hanging has begun (fig. 38). Crowds jostle for a view, a ladder already leans on the beam, and the only thing missing is the condemned.

Patently symbolic in its alignment with the peddler, the gallows is nevertheless true to life for the landscape view, since such cruel instruments of justice cluttered the countryside of northern Europe in Bosch's time. Public spectacles of law and order, they announced—more explicitly than anything we today can imagine—that crimes shall be punished, including the peddler's implicit transgression. Around 1500, due to increasing migration from the countryside into towns during a decade of economic crisis, and supported by concomitant shifts in the religious understanding of poverty, localities enacted ever-stricter laws against all forms of vagrancy.[8] Begging, previously accepted as a pious activity pursued by pilgrims and mendicants, became associated with laziness and criminality. The blind, the crippled, and the diseased roamed from town to town (Bruegel painted amazing portraits of these social outcasts; see fig. 293).[9] Seeking alms, they brought upon themselves the suspicion that they feigned their maladies or mutilated themselves for effect. A flood of satirical books portrayed vagabonds as members of a secret, hostile, conspiratorial society that, deeply versed in deception, preyed on people's honesty and goodwill.[10]

Masterless, mobile, and irritating, the homeless were a vanguard of modernity, motivating new forms of state surveillance and control. In many cities in northern Europe, including 's-Hertogenbosch, vagrancy was punishable by death.[11] While their motives were clear, peddlers bore the additional stigma of deriving their mobility from the circulation of material goods. Arriving from outside and laden with exogenous merchandise, they preyed on people's sinful love of worldly goods, while also siphoning wealth away from the community and giving nothing of value in return. Perfectly aligned with the peddler, the gallows stands ready *for him*. Presently concealed from him, it metes out justice from an order hidden to human experience, an order with which Bosch's painting—the artist having micromanaged the sinister alignment—is itself in league. Law traps and annihilates, here splitting the painting of everyday life in two.

The Hay Wain

When the shutters open, they cut through the peddler's body, and through the world that is his predicament, along the vital now of lived experience.[12] And what comes into view in that widening abyss is everyday life again, but embedded in salvation history and beheld from the annihilating perspective of divine justice (fig. 39). At first sight, the triptych's open state—prominently signed with the artist's full name—seems a bewildering collage of Bible story, allegorical tableau, genre episode, and hellish fantasy. Soon enough, though, the basic plot coalesces: a history of sin from its earliest beginnings to its terrible end. True, the center of the central panel poses something of a puzzle. Before a huge vista of the world, a motley and viciously selfish humanity converges—as if absurdly—on a poor wagon filled with hay; rolling left to right, in sync with temporal unfolding of plot, this mere hay would even seem to be the motor of history itself. Happily, it is not difficult now, nor was it ever, to understand what hay's ridiculous attraction means.

Fra Joseph de Sigüenza served as Philip II's librarian at the royal monastery at El Escorial, where the triptych eventually came to hang.[13] In his extensive treatment of Bosch's art (this text will concern us later on), he linked the hay symbolically to the famous prophecy of Isaiah, "All flesh is grass."[14] By this account—written in 1604, the year *Doctor Faustus* went into print—hay stands for the vanity of earthly life, as well as for all the pleasures of mortal life that people vainly and sinfully pursue; its bizarre power to draw everything to it simply dramatizes the attraction that evanescent life holds for mortals. Some decades earlier another Spaniard, probably in touch with oral traditions reaching all the way back to Bosch, proposed a similar but sharper solution to the triptych. Ambrosio de Morales was one of the premier historians of his time. Royal chronicler of Castile, and a coauthor, after Florián de Ocampo's death, of *The General Chronicle of Spain*, he pioneered the use of local archives, inscriptions, antiquities, and memories (the latter harvested through field interviews and written questionnaires) in reconstructing the past. In 1586, he published his translation of the so-called *Tablet of Cebes* into Castilian. Purported to be by Sophocles's disciple Cebes of Thebes, this Greek text was probably—according to modern scholarship—a late Hellenistic fabrication. Ubiquitous in schoolrooms until the twentieth century, it describes a votive picture, or *pinax*, said to have been dedicated at the Temple of Cronos in Thebes and decorated with an encompassing allegory about human life. For the Renaissance humanists who discovered, admired, and translated it, the *Tablet of Cebes* exemplified the rhetorical ideal of *ut pictura poesis*.[15] Here was poetry so vivid that it brought a lost painted masterpiece back to life. To his Spanish translation of the tablet, Morales added an elaborate ekphrasis of his own. The object of this competitive exercise was a certain "panel, an invention of Hieronymus Bosch."[16]

Morales reports that this panel now belongs to his patron, King Philip II of Spain, and that it represents, "like an imitation" for "our times," the legendary picture described by Cebes. For like the ancient tablet, this modern work depicts "the panorama of our miserable lives and the great enchantment that we seem to find in its vanities."[17] At its center stands "a 'wagon of hay' as it is called in the Flemish." And this "means the same thing as a 'wagon of nothingness' in Castilian. So as a wagon of hay, it is truly a wagon of nothingness: its name befits what it signifies."[18] Morales's account seems correct and remarkably perceptive. Modern scholars have adduced numerous old Flemish proverbs that support it, such as, "The world is a haystack and everybody grabs from it as much as he can get," and "As long as the hay wagon is loaded one never gets enough from it."[19] But to this day no one has captured the painting's paradox more succinctly than Morales did. After summing up the work's subject and structure, including the role Eve and Adam's expulsion plays in the transition of the story across the panels, Morales confesses that the picture contains so many details that it is impossible to describe in full. And "there is really no reason" to describe it anyway, since "all of this ends abruptly as the demons guide the wagon into the final panel, where man's fate after this life is represented."[20] Morales admits the vanity of his own endeavor to attend closely to a painting about the vanity of human endeavors. In tune with its subject, the poetical performance abruptly ends, since so does Bosch's triptych, and so does life.

A thing that is nothing, hay is our flesh (fig. 40). Lusting after itself, flesh withers and vanishes. Hay also stands for Bosch's painting: a wooden object of no consequence, mere fuel for hell's consuming flames. Thus the peddler, with his thing-filled backpack made of straw, mutates into the humanity grasping at straws, which mutates into the viewer gazing at painted straw. Bosch gives this abject nothingness the shape of everything. Bundled on a wagon, the hay looks like a misshapen globe or, better, like the terrestrial lower half of the spherical world, such as we see on the exterior of the shutters that enclose Bosch's so-called *Garden of Delights* (see fig. 183). The music-making lovers nestled on top of the hay are a courtly version

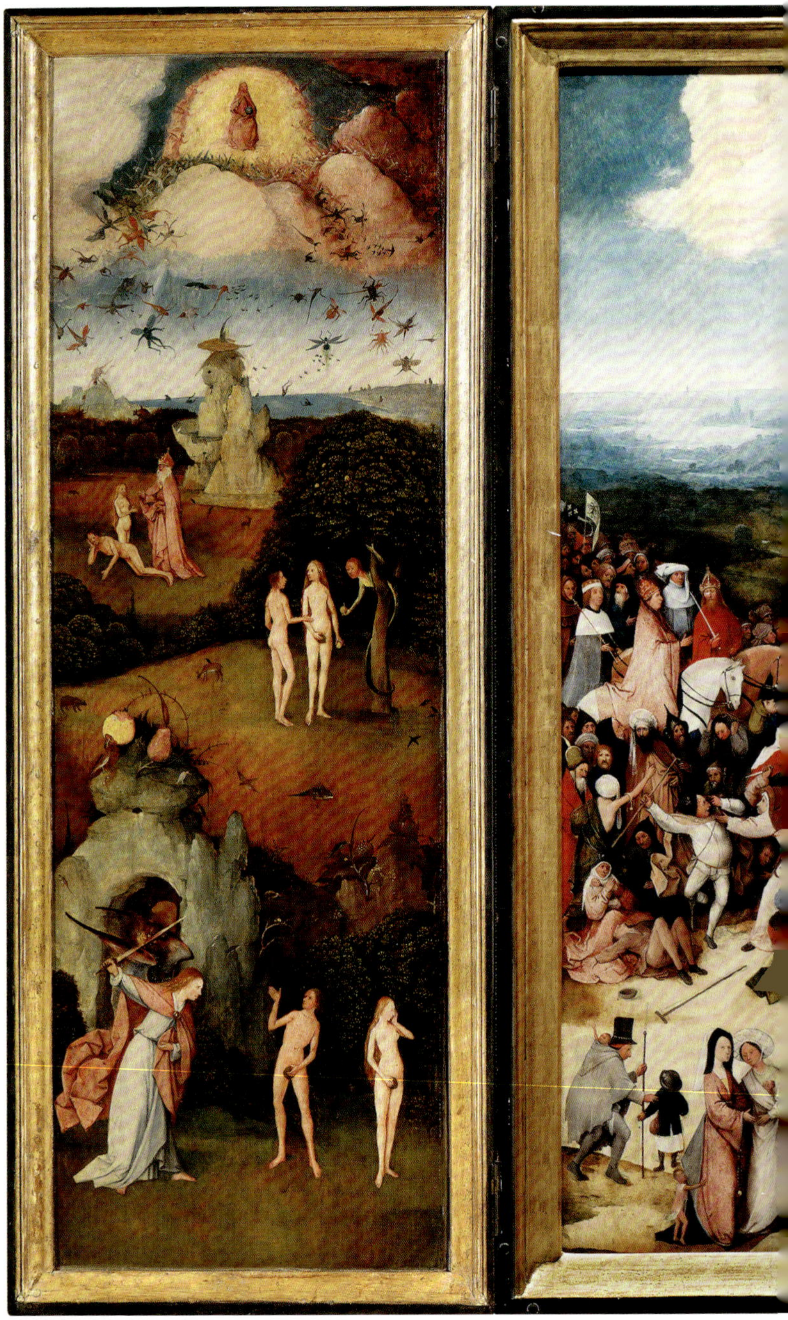

39 Hieronymus Bosch and Assistants, *The Hay Wain*, open state, c. 1500, panel, Museo Nacional del Prado, Madrid

of the dancing peasants on the shutters in the triptych's closed state and a tame abbreviation of the *Garden*'s naked revels (see fig. 204). They therefore inhabit a world within the world. Gathering the greedy multitude around them, they indicate that avarice is lust in another form, as the love of the world.

As Bruegel does in *The Misanthrope* (see fig. 21), Bosch sometimes would lay an outline of the world's orb over a scene of everyday life. In the panel sometimes called *The Stone Operation*, a fool is foolishly having his folly operated away (see fig. 152). The circular format of the visual field, together with the curving border between middle ground and background, located halfway up the roundel, that appears like the equator on a globe, extends the picture's message about a particular folly to the world as a whole, represented both by the limned globe

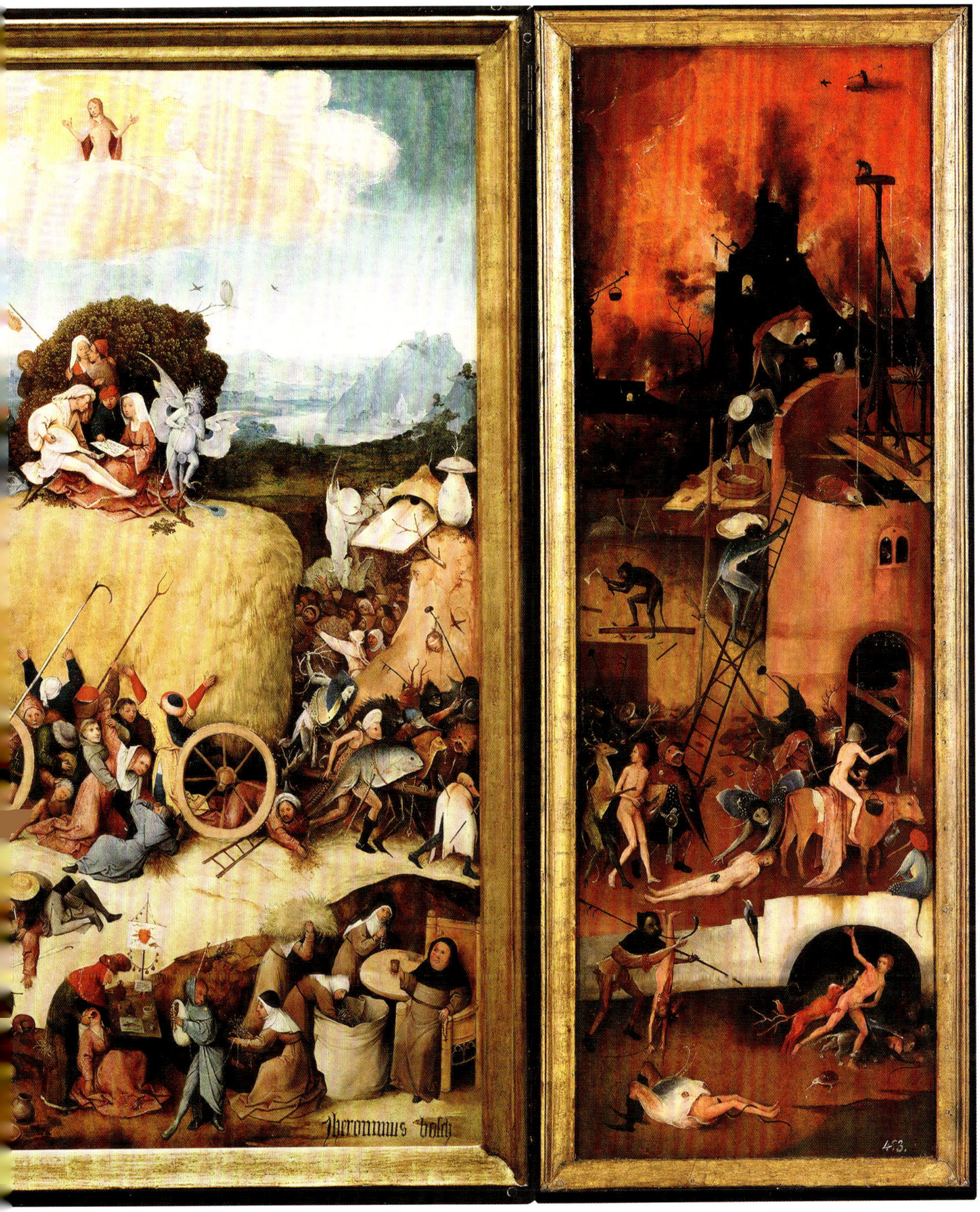

and the fabulous landscape view that globe contains. A tapestry from a set made around 1560 nests Bosch's hay wagon and its entourage inside a bubble-like *globus cruciger* that bobs ludicrously in the ocean (fig. 41).[21] Part of a prestigious five-part series of tapestries after Boschian originals, this arras elaborates the artist's intentions in the Prado *Hay Wain*. Although the tapestry is similar to the triptych in composition and theme, most of the individual woven figures are new, suggesting that whoever designed the tapestry's cartoon followed a different, lost Boschian prototype or an intermediate work.[22] A contemporary of Bruegel's in Antwerp made a painted version of the design, now in the Louvre (fig. 42).[23] Absorbing the vast tableau into a flickering play of dark and light, the artist—probably Gillis Mostaert the Elder or his atelier—smuggles priestly activities into the catastrophe, while also emphasizing the imperial

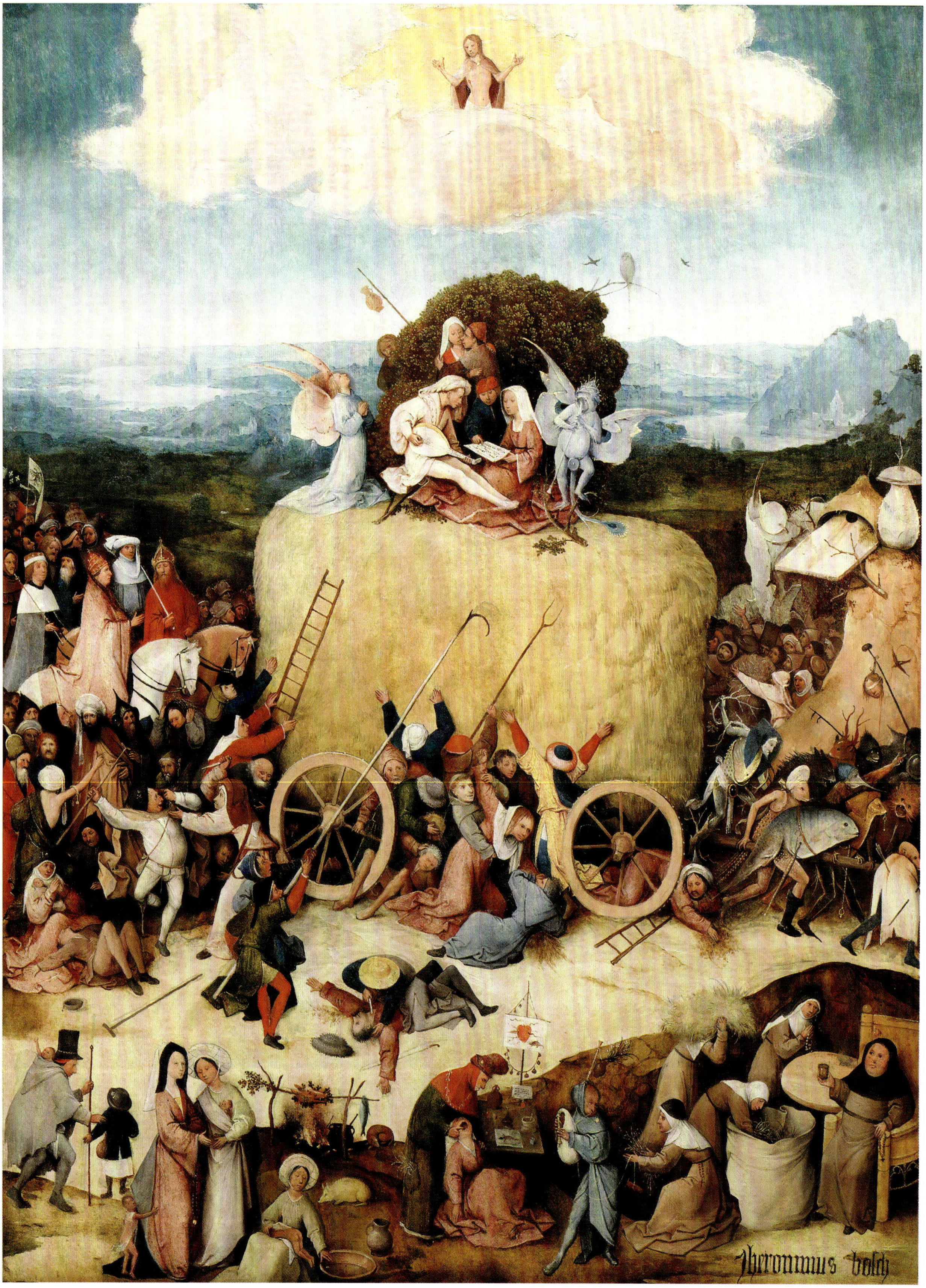

40 Hieronymus Bosch and Assistants, *The Hay Wain*, center panel (fig. 39)

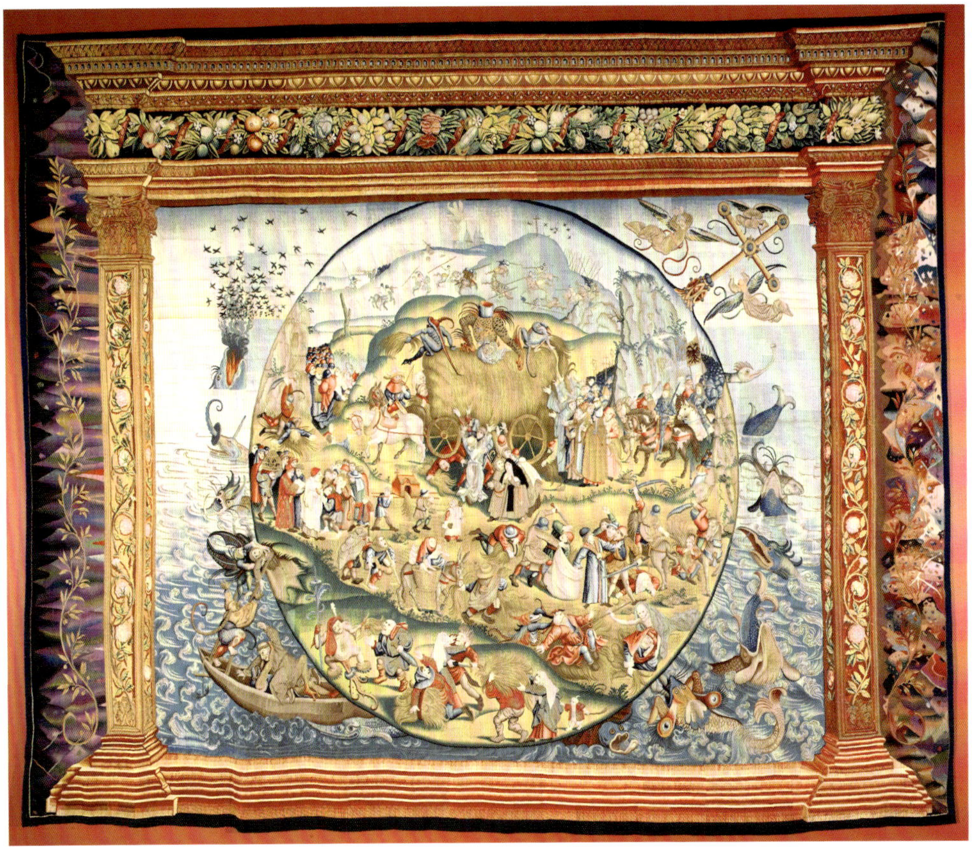

41 Brussels Workshop, *Hay Wain in a Globe*, 1550–70, tapestry, Palacio Real, Patrimonio Nacional, Madrid

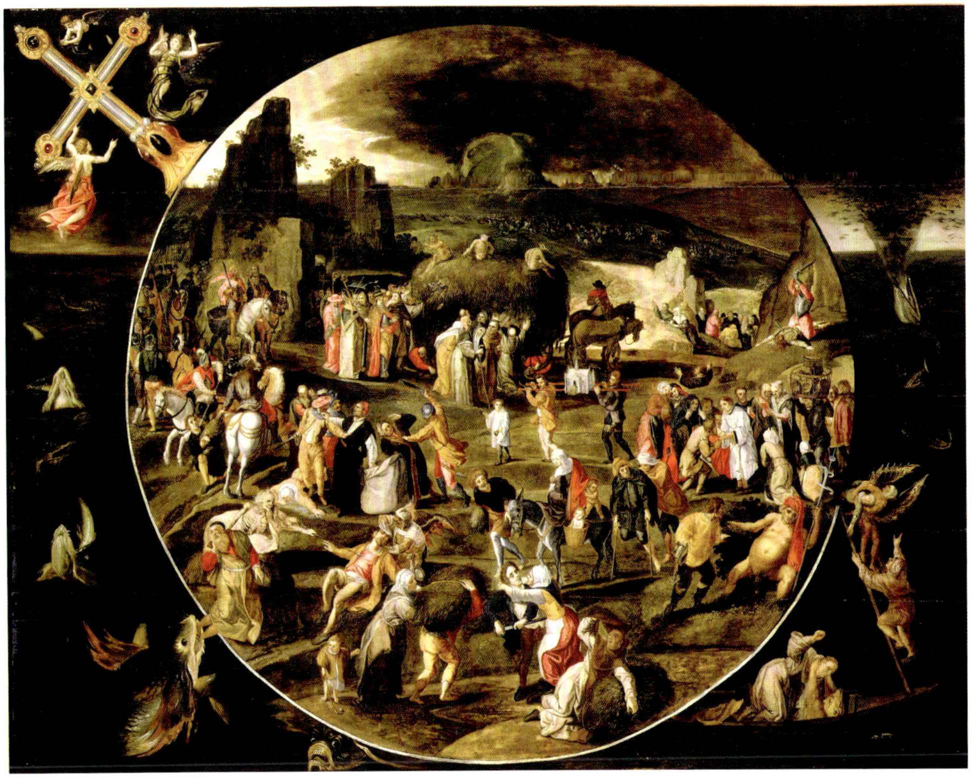

42 Gillis Mostaert, *The Haywagon: An Allegory of the World's Vanity* (*La Charette de foin, allégorie [vanité du monde, péchés capitaux]*), c. 1575, oil on wood, Musée du Louvre, Paris

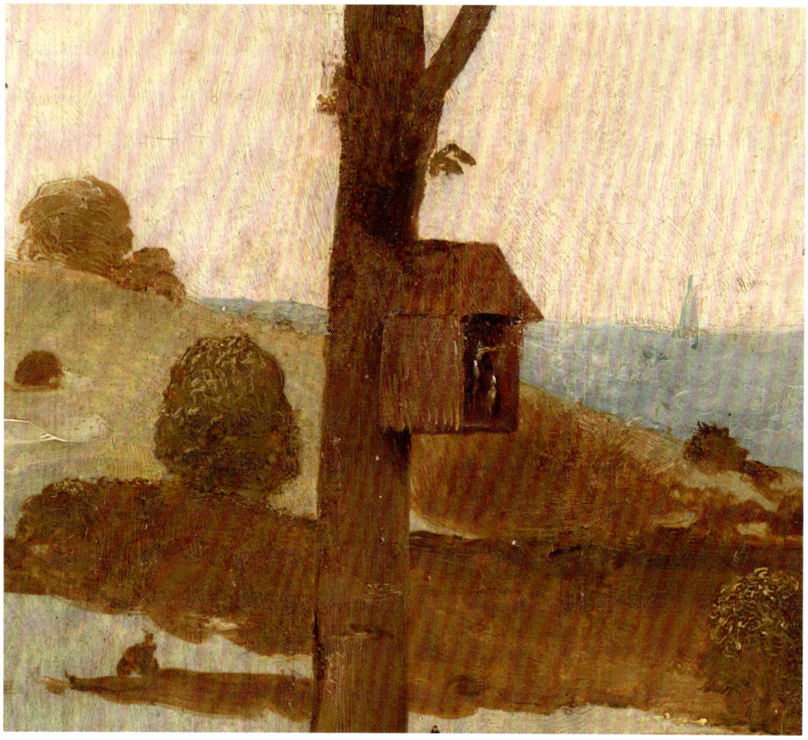

43 Detail of Hieronymus Bosch and Assistants, *The Peddler* (fig. 37)

orb's precariousness by having one angel steady its descending *crux*. This sharpens the political tenor of the Prado *Hay Wain*, which also shows clerics in the crowd.[24] Whatever its prototype, Mostaert's painting, along with the surviving tapestry, hammers home for its later audience the identification of hay with world.

World appears in multiple, overlapping models. On the Prado triptych's outside, Bosch shows the world from the inside, as the place *in which* life is lived. The landscape around the wayfarer is decidedly spacious, encompassing town, country, and wilderness. Like the basket shouldered by the peddler, it *contains* things: hills, trees, towers, roads, bridges, gallows. Although compendious, this is world as lifeworld—not the world's totality, but that totality looked at from the "how" of its experience by one who lives in it. But as lifeworld, it is no longer—or not yet—the primeval enclave of dwelling that Bruegel pictures behind the striding peasant, that idyll of belonging into which the artist and his audience, newly in touch with the world's objective immensity, nostalgically peer. In Bosch, the protagonist—not primitively placed but latterly displaced—moves restlessly outside the expanding city wall, beyond the shrinking fields and pastures, in a zone of exile both spatial and historical. Moreover, compared with earlier paintings of the world, Bosch's *Peddler* is decidedly worldly. It contains no sacred beings, no deities or devils, no hermits, who though they tarry on earth, dwell already in heaven. On the tree behind the piping shepherd hangs a wayside shrine; a carved effigy of the Crucifixion is barely visible in the interior darkness (fig. 43). It too is a mere thing, a human artifact that the secular pilgrim completely ignores. The gallows may rise directly above him from our viewpoint on the world, and the tiny wayside crucifix may come to light to us, who have time to peruse the scene, but these warnings lie hidden from his gaze.

By centering on the person who lives in it, Bosch shows the "outside"—the triptych's shutters, the geographic wilderness, worldliness itself—to be the inside *in which* life is lived. Painted on the shutters of a boxlike triptych, the peddler in the landscape becomes like the icon inside its shrine. But then those shutters open. As they do—bisecting the living subject, crossing him out, revealing him and his world to be mere outer covering—another world comes into view, one that, being underneath him, discloses the peddler's underlying nature. As Morales reports, the pile of hay symbolizes all the *things* within the world. It gathers them up into a globular mass, values them by its structural centrality, and then empties them by being worthless, by being nothing.

Hay is the world as *worldliness*. Inciting avarice in all who live in the world, causing everyone who has a part of it to covet everything, it summarizes the human experience. When the work opens like a box, or like his basket, the peddler turns into the things he peddles. And because hay reflects how we are and what we are in the world, it is itself surrounded by a world. *Humanity* is too anodyne a term for the hordes mobbing the hay. Mingling thieves, charlatans, gypsies, prophets, soothsayers, quacks, Jews, vagabonds, peasants, nuns, and priests, drawing the pope, the emperor, and the king into its sordid ranks, this human world coheres only in a state of total conflict. That this war of all against all encompasses the whole is indicated by its setting.

Behind its subject, the landscape of *The Peddler* recedes toward a distant prospect, but one that still conforms to a human point of view: the faraway town and hills look to us as they would to the peddler, were he to turn to gaze at them. It is not so with the landscape behind the hay wagon. Global in reach, this vast expanse of earth and sea posits a viewpoint unavailable to human experience. A dark barrier (carried over from the scene of the Fall, in the left panel) blocks this vista from the foreground multitudes, who march not on some elevated ridge or summit that might afford such a panorama but in a sunken terrain: a valley of death. Bushes form a similar barrier to the lovers on top of the hay. Only the angel praying for these sinners' souls has an open view of the landscape, but he gazes pleadingly toward heaven. And it is there, up in the clouds, that we discover this landscape's implied perspective: not a worldly vista humanly beheld, but the whole divinely grasped.

Among Bosch's many signature achievements was his creation of a species of painting that seeks to encompass, from an impossibly elevated perspective, earth's entire geographic reach. Developed into a recognizable genre by Flemish landscape specialists, such as Joachim Patinir, the "worldscape" (as we have seen) would be given new life by Bruegel.[25] On his journey across the Alps, Bruegel experienced and sketched vertiginous vistas, bringing them, so to speak, down to earth (see fig. 308). In these panoramas, the natural world itself—independent of any divinity—eclipses and annihilates the human. In *The Hay Wain*, Bosch spreads a background of unprecedented vastness outward toward an optical infinity at the earth's horizon. But he willfully constricts this expansive natural landscape with the panel's narrow vertical format, which is squeezed in at both sides by scriptural landscapes of paradise and hell. The modern image of a "universe" thus stands enclosed in the constructions of the medieval "world."[26]

These sides, the triptych's outer wings, place the world in a comprehensive history. From start to finish, it is the story of an abiding war between God and his enemies. The story opens in heaven, at the top of the left wing, with the Creator enthroned as ruler of the world while the rebel angels, routed by heavenly hordes, plummet to earth, decaying into insect-like monsters as they fall (fig. 44). On earth, in the demoniacally infested afterward, human rebellion and human evil belatedly begin. This next sequence of events starts with Eve's creation in Eden under a demon-filled sky. It zigzags to its crisis in Adam's temptation by Eve, herself seduced by her look-alike—and God's old adversary—the serpent Satan. And it concludes in the

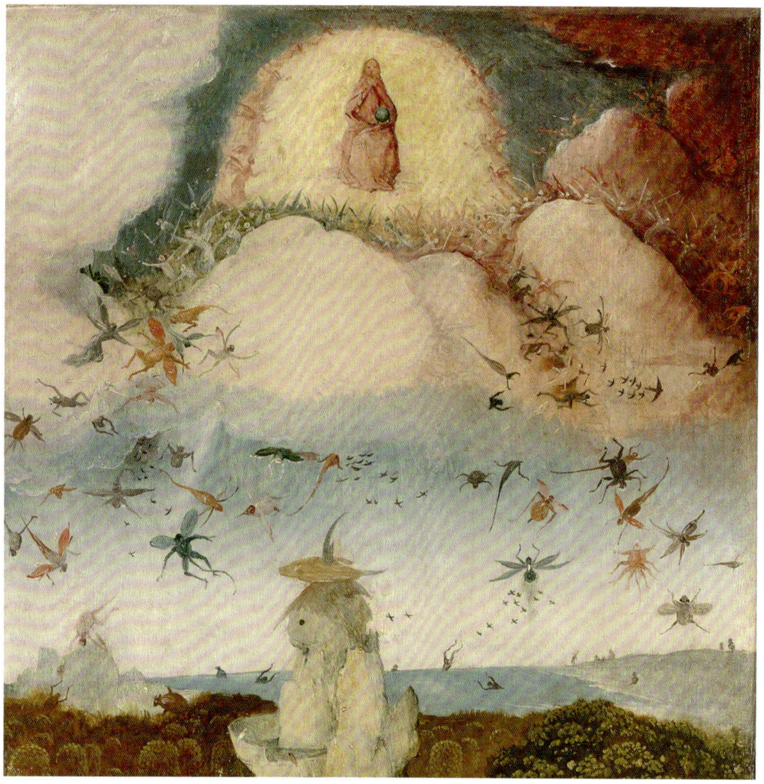

44 Detail of Hieronymus Bosch and Assistants, *The Hay Wain* (fig. 39)

foreground, outside paradise's sealed portal, where the expelled Eve gazes across the division between panels, to her legacy in the triptych's center.

Bosch traces the origins of evil back to a time before the Fall.[27] Linking the Old Enemy to Eve, the artist implies that she, in league with a corruption as old as the creation, caused our undoing. This cosmic, misogynistic theodicy also informs—and deforms—Bosch's most elusive work, where everything hinges on the calamitous instance of Adam's first glimpse of Eve (see fig. 191).[28] In *The Hay Wain*, Eve's pivotal role in the Eden panel explains why lovers top the hay in the central panel (see fig. 40). Avarice, the sinful love of the world, derives from a prior lusting—the carnal desire aroused in Adam—hence the temptress Eve's look of horror upon seeing what her allure has brought about.

That central tableau condenses into a mock triumph the disastrous course of human history. With the multitudes dressed in contemporary garb, and with nothing ever accomplished since Eden because everyone fails to "have" the transient hay, this unchanging history has no history. Glimpsed in an ongoing present tense, its one and only past is the mythic origin that precedes the Fall into history. Timewise, therefore, the open state of Bosch's triptych differs from the closed state only in scale. Where the peddler strides in the present of lifetime, the hay rolls in the same now, but of "world time." This relentless presentism—typical of most art of this era, but grotesquely sharpened by Bosch—reaches a verdict on human history. Whatever happened between the Expulsion and the current moment—the whole of what Benjamin, writing about Kafka's projection of judgment into it, called "world history"—does not matter for the outcome of the story. This makes the triptych morally urgent, for what counts occurs currently, in the effect the triptych has on us right now.

Although unchanging since the Expulsion, this present tense speeds along at a hectic tempo. At the rear of the wagon a woman attempts to lean a ladder on the hay, and already at the front another ladder lies toppled and crushed. At this pace, the only events that have time to occur are the collisions between persons futilely grabbing and the wagon inexorably rolling. Pictured as that rightward march, time undoes all human gestures and with them secular history itself. And at the front of the hay wagon, pulling it by its unhitched tongue, marches the motor of this movement. An army of demons hurries to hell. Unlike their human victims, they understand they have little time left. The Book of Revelation sums up this bond of time to evil: "Therefore rejoice, you heavens and you who dwell in them! But woe to the earth and the sea, because the devil has gone down to you! He is filled with fury, because he knows that time is short" (Rev. 12:12). In the vast world that God created and that Bosch marvelously portrays, the possibilities of human life would be infinite were there time to pursue them. Death, however, intervenes, making it necessary to try to grab it all now. Avarice results from the combination of an abundance of world and the shortage of lifetime. Sin brought death into the world, but death keeps sin permanently ongoing.[29] As Bosch portrays it, life passes at the presto pace it does because the Devil dangles our fulfillment right in front of us, but always just out of reach. Life's devilish tempo is set by the time of the world that—although always swift—is presently accelerated.

The Book of Revelation announces not only that time will end but that its end is near. The Devil, the book's author explains, has arrived on earth filled with a huge anger because of this imminence. Bosch painted for an audience that expected the Apocalypse to happen soon. Taking all crises and disasters to be omens of this impending doom, people of the period around 1500 believed that Last Judgment would quite possibly interrupt them in the midst of life, as their last lived experience. Dividing in two the image of the peddler, and thus the painting of everyday life, *The Hay Wain*—opened—exhibits life on the brink not just of death but of end-time. Bosch thus supplies precisely what Bruegel, fifty years later, would enigmatically withhold: confirmation of a decisive end. Half hidden in the clouds above the hay, in the abiding now of eternity, Christ sits in judgment over a humanity indifferent to him and at war with itself. This world war is how Scripture prophesies the final days: "Nation will rise against nation, and kingdom against kingdom" (Mark 13:8). In that time of lawlessness, occurring presently but unnoticed by the battling crowds,

> They will see the Son of Man coming in the clouds with great power and glory. And he will send his angels and gather his elect from the four winds, from the ends of the earth to the ends of the heavens. (Mark 13:26–27).[30]

Last Judgment

Bosch announces end-time through the *Hay Wain*'s structure. With paradise to the left, hell to the right, and chaos in the middle, and with Christ looking down at the world from his seat in heaven, the triptych resembles portraits of Judgment Day. The likeness would have been obvious to Bosch's original viewers. Depictions of the Last Judgment formed part of the built fabric of their churches. Featured often on the threshold to sacred space—for example, on the tympana surmounting church portals, or on choir screens enclosing the clerical *sanctum sanctorum*—scenes of the final Apocalypse were intended to terrify worshipers into contrition for their sins while also advertising the church's power to save men's souls (fig. 45).[31] For doctrine held that through the holy sacraments of penance and the Eucharist, administered by a priest, repentant sinners could escape hell's flames and sit among the blessed in heaven. In the design of the great cathedrals, in that dramatic architecture where salvific work took place, Christians could glimpse—in carved stone and multicolored glass—an image of Heavenly Jerusalem.[32] Decorating especially the entryways to such edifices, scenes of the Last Judgment associated the spatial boundary between the profane and sacred worlds with the temporal threshold of the Apocalypse. To press home the point, Last Judgments sometimes gave the pearly gates to future paradise the architecture of a contemporary church façade. An important work painted around 1430 by Stefan Lochner shows the elect pressing into the City of God through a fabulous gilded Gothic doorway, while on the opposite side of the dissolving world hell gapes under the burning City of Men, figured as a Romanesque castle in ruins (fig. 46).[33] Observed in its original position behind an altar in a church (probably the Church of the Apostles in Lochner's native Cologne), the panel would have assured the faithful assembled there that they had come to the right place.

Bosch's patrons would have been especially attuned to Last Judgment imagery because this artist specialized in it. Apocalypse and hell featured in the winged retable that Bosch and his elder brother Goessen van Aken are known to have painted for the high altar of the Church of Saint John (from 1566 a cathedral) in 's-Hertogenbosch.[34] Early praise of this imposing, three-stage polyptych reports that it pictured the six days of creation (*opus Creationis Hexameron mundi*), along with "lifelike, monstrous creatures from the underworld."[35] A notable landmark in Bosch's birthplace, the altarpiece probably fell victim to changing tastes, prudery, and looting.[36] Due perhaps to the singularity and prominence of this work, Bosch became famous for portraying the world's beginning and end. In 1504, no less illustrious an international patron than the reigning Duke of Burgundy and first Habsburg king of Castile, Philip the Fair, commissioned Bosch to paint a large *Last Judgment*, complete with heaven and hell.[37] Encamped with his army in 's-Hertogenbosch in that year while waging violent war against neighboring Guelders, Philip must have seen, and even attended Mass before, Bosch's painted ensemble.[38] The ducal account books state that the new work should be made "for [Philip's] very noble pleasure," and they record a generous prepayment of thirty-six pounds to the painter—an unusual gesture for the period, suggesting both the urgency of the commission and the duke's confidence in the artist's powers.[39] The phrase "very noble pleasure" may be a stock formula for aristocratic patronage, but it might also hint that the work would serve an aesthetic purpose as opposed to a strictly pious one, and that its intended setting was some noble interior rather than a chapel or church. Two *Last Judgment* triptychs from Bosch's shop have survived, including a monumental one that now dazzles visitors to the Academy of Fine Arts in Vienna (fig. 47).[40] The picture's provenance and symbolism point to Habsburg patronage.[41] The work came to Vienna through Archduke Leopold Wilhelm of Austria, youngest son of the Habsburg emperor Ferdinand II; Saint James and Saint Bavo, portrayed on the outer shutters' exterior, have special links to Castile and Ghent, respectively, encapsulating Philip the Fair's dual Spanish and Flemish patrimony. However, the picture does not quite attain the dimensions (nine *pieds* high by eleven wide—or about 2.56 meters by 3.16 meters) stated in Philip's account book. It is

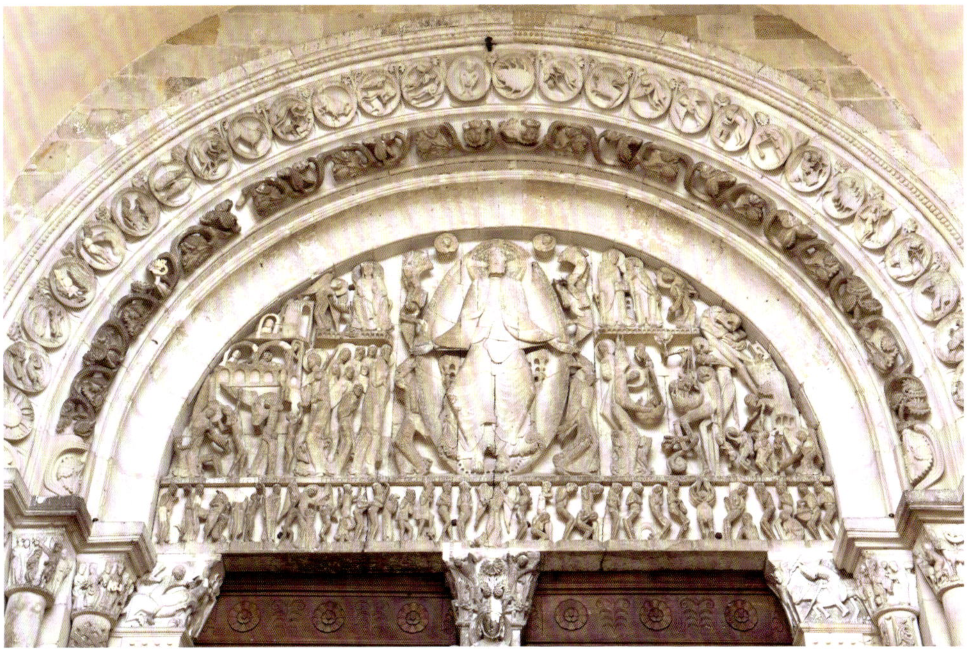

45 Gislebertus, *Last Judgment*, 1120–35, limestone, west façade, center portal, tympanum, Saint-Lazare Cathedral, Autun, Burgundy

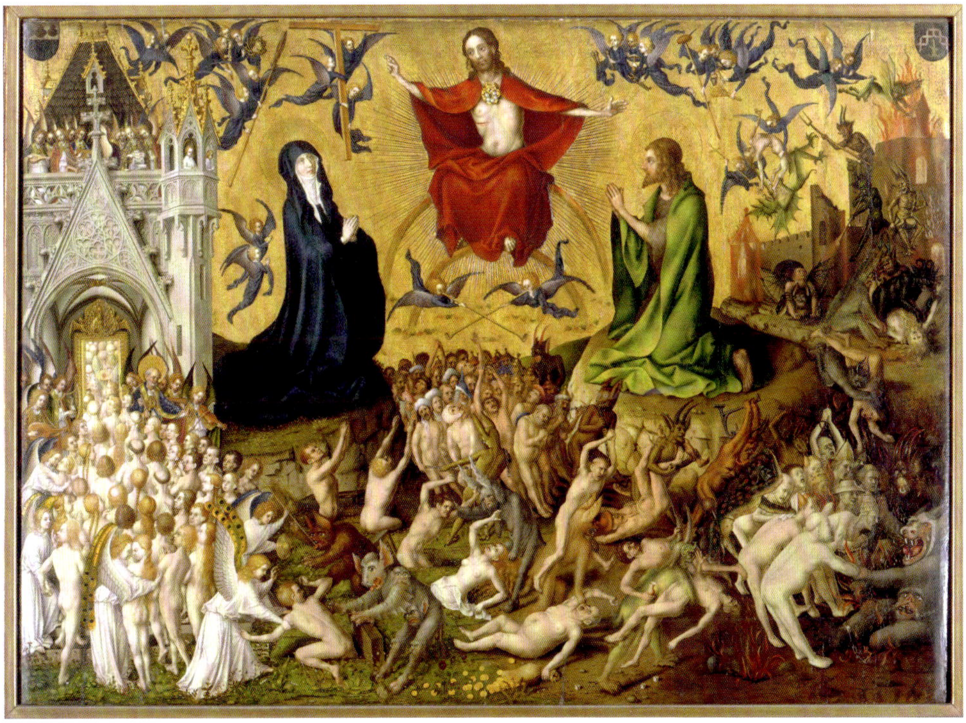

46 Stefan Lochner, *The Last Judgment*, c. 1430 (1435?), panel, Wallraf-Richartz Museum, Cologne

therefore most likely a separate commission, perhaps for a different noble patron dazzled, as Duke Philip had been, by Bosch's apocalyptic imaginings.[42] In any case, as one of the artist's most complete and magnificent creations, the Vienna triptych typifies this painter's atypical approach to the end of time.

Wherever he intended this *Last Judgment* to stand, whether in a palace or a church, Bosch has anchored its painted forms to the divine. The scenes of Eden and judgment reach up to God, and even hell's impenetrable distance registers God negatively, as the Creator's absolute withdrawal from the damned. Beheld eternally by God, these expansive vistas have—reciprocally for us—their visual center in God. By giving his *Last Judgment* the triptych form

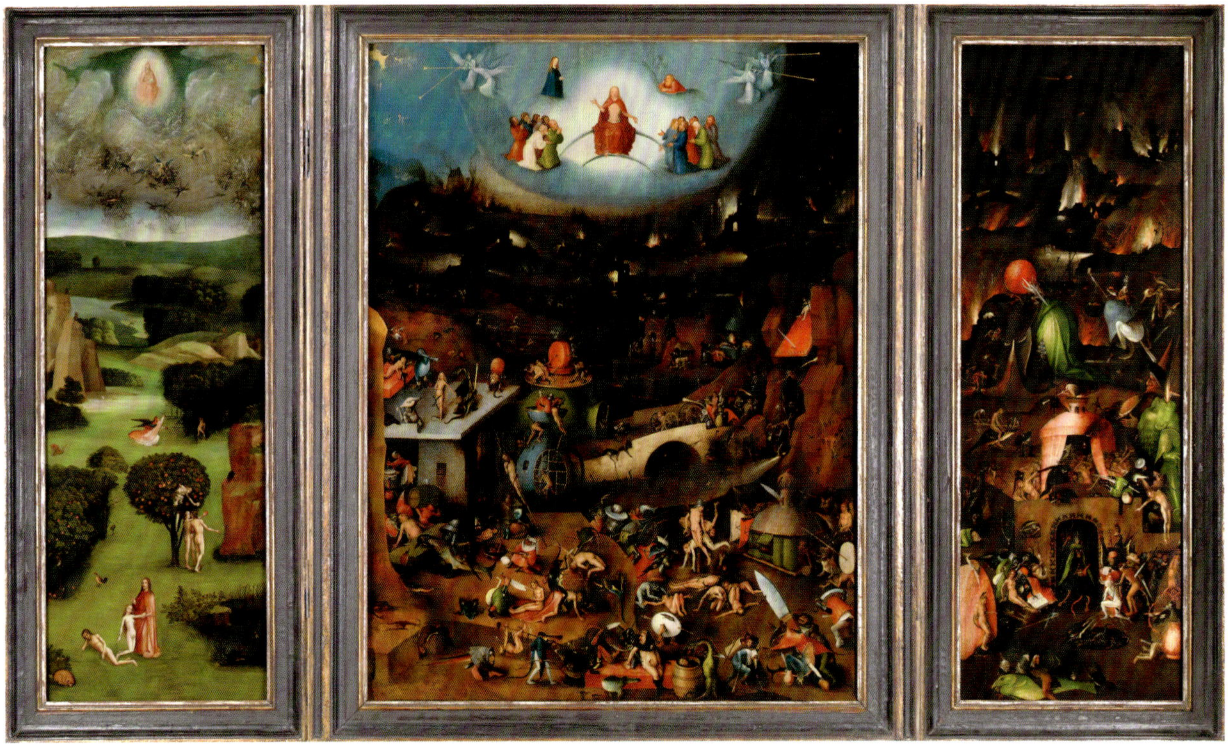

47 Hieronymus Bosch, *The Last Judgment*, open state, c. 1504, panel, Gemäldegalerie der Akademie der Bildenden Künste, Vienna

of retable altarpieces, Bosch submits what he paints to the axial symmetry natural to that tripartite form.[43] In tune with the symbolism of the Trinity, this order derived, historically, from the symmetrical architecture of church and chapel, centered as these buildings were on sacred things: cult statues, saints' relics, and above all the consecrated Host. Using for his secular production this religiously charged format, Bosch further reiterated the sacral symmetry of the whole in each of the three individual panels. While the triptych form is the norm in early Netherlandish painting, such rigid formalism is not. Bosch deviated from the early Netherlanders not only through his chaotic forms, which dissolve the consistency achieved by his great predecessors. Less obviously, he departed from the tradition through the strict balance of his overall designs, which insist on a higher order at odds with lived experience. Symmetry and the insistence on centers make some of the painter's creations look strangely archaic beside their more naturalistic predecessors, more like the diagrams and hieratic forms of earlier medieval art. Curiosity and wonder draw us into Bosch's entropic details, but his fearful symmetry rescues us from—and chastises us for—our distraction.

Bosch reveals structure to be at bottom metaphysical. Beyond, above, before, and after the physical world, structure resides only with God, who alone beholds the whole as a perfectly organized spectacle. On Judgment Day, this metaphysical structure takes its ultimate form: as a *decision*. At the end of time, God separates the world, finally and absolutely, into two parts, the one damned, the other saved.[44] Traditionally, artists visualized this last decision by placing hell on the one side and heaven—symmetrically—on the other, with human souls, united with their resurrected flesh, either falling hectically into the one or processing neatly into the other (fig. 48).[45] Bosch does something profoundly different here. He puts hell where it usually occurs—at God's *sinistre*, or left (which from our perspective stands at the picture's right). But on the other side, at God's righteous right, Bosch shows, instead of the future heavenly paradise, Eden—that mere earthly paradise of a prehistoric, inner-worldly past. This allows him to

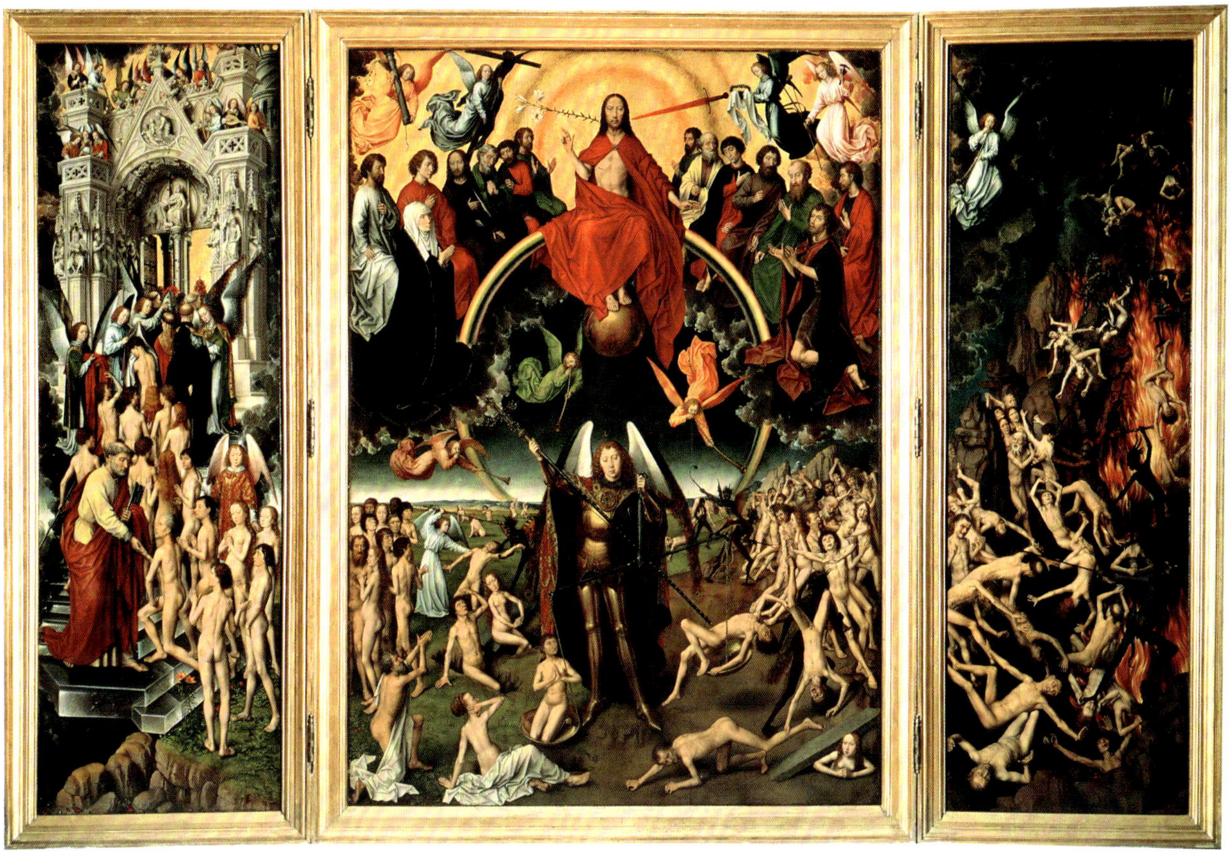

48 Hans Memling, *Last Judgment*, c. 1470, open state, panel, oak, National Museum, Gdańsk

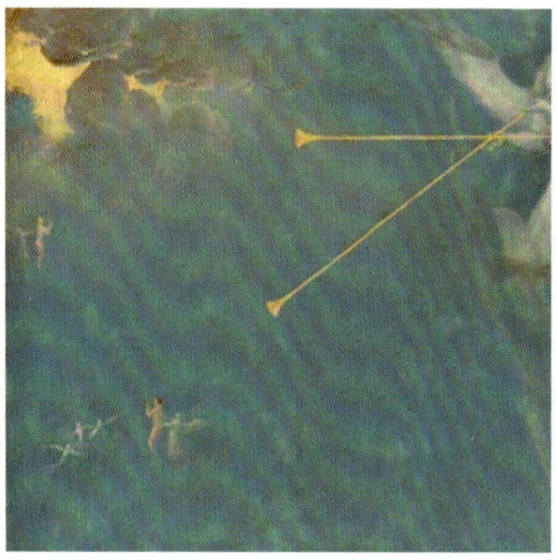

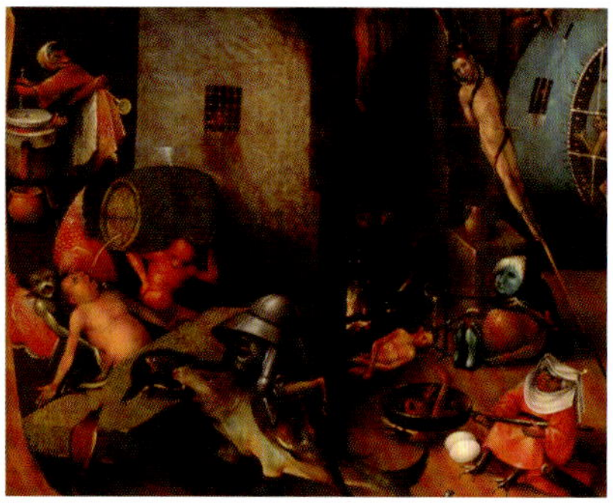

49 Detail of Hieronymus Bosch, *The Last Judgment* (fig. 47)

50 Detail of Hieronymus Bosch, *The Last Judgment* (fig. 47)

picture not just the new structure of the world after Judgment Day but also the world's total structure, which was lost in the beginning and will be revealed only at the end.

Ordered by a law that precedes the human, Bosch's *Last Judgment* itself becomes inhuman. The saved—a tiny minority—slip unnoticed into a crack in the clouds way up in the central panel's upper left corner (fig. 49). To find these pale, minuscule forms and their angelic companions takes special effort—one practically has to stand on a chair and press right against that highest bit of the picture to glimpse their narrow escape. Nearly invisible at a normal viewing distance but doctrinally indispensable, the blessed few confirm Christ's saving power, while also giving measure to just how hugely the damned outnumber them. It is a knowing wink to an audience attentive to details, and it assumes a close-range delectation impossible to pursue in church space, suggesting, mischievously, that blessed are those who can own and intimately peruse this secretive picture. But if, secretly, the last of the saved are just now disappearing into heaven, what remains for the privileged viewer to behold?

Bosch spreads a continuous landscape across the three panels. Plunging—anywhere and everywhere—vertiginously into this vast expanse, the eye gets captured by innumerable theaters of cruelty. For while at Last Judgment the earth lies wasted and dead, the damned continue to animate the world with their suffering. And while these writhing bodies seem at first glance inchoate, like the ruins that imprison them, close inspection of the kind the painting invites reveals a strict and terrible logic to their torment. Consider the potbellied sinner seated at a table in the left foreground (fig. 50). The nameless fluid he must ceaselessly drink could come out of nowhere, since it is diabolically conjured. But Bosch insists on tracing it back, visibly, to its source. And that abject jet, exploding as it does from a devil's ass, could be so aimed that it would magically fill the barrel neatly (or sloppily) without that helpful funnel to catch and contain its spray. The hydraulics are simultaneously absurd and of a marvelously everyday kind.

Unnecessarily, in the aftermath of the Apocalypse, Bosch's hellish engineering fulfills the necessities of our still-physical world, where nothing is without sufficient reason. Behind the potbellied drinker, a she-devil operates a more specialized kitchen contraption. Expertly pressing another sinner's stewing dismembered parts, she causes their juices to pour into a large earthenware pot, there reserved—the cook in me surmises—to be made into blood sauce or blood sausage. And while this gory fluid rhymes perversely with the excremental one that the potbellied drinker imbibes, the equipment and the procedures are specialized but decidedly ordinary. That flat perforated scoop hanging from the she-devil's belt is a saucier's essential tool; with it can be carefully skimmed the unwanted scum that rises from simmering bones to float in cloudy gray clumps on the roiling surface of the broth. Everyday

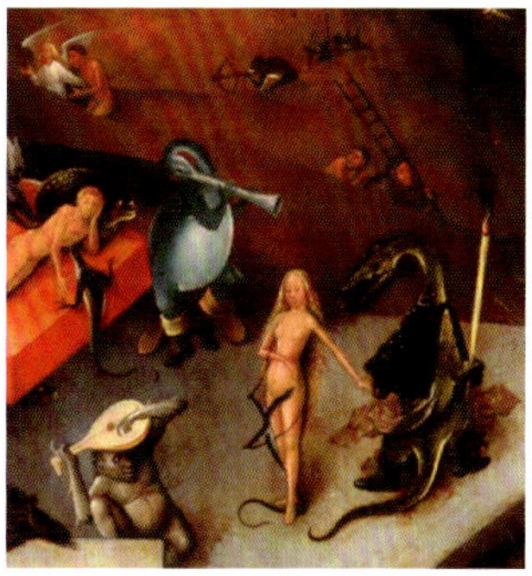

51 Detail of Hieronymus Bosch, *The Last Judgment* (fig. 47)

life—here the activities of hearth and home—appears in diabolical form. Observe the orderly row of bodies being "cured" like fishes or hams in the hellish smokehouse, and (below) how the bodies are basted and seared patiently, as if by experienced chefs with time to spare. Long before Bruegel, and with just as keen an eye for vernacular equipment, Bosch portrays the common human existence, though with the twist that all this historically precocious genre realism unfolds not in the present tense but in the final future, when history itself has come to an end.

The potbellied sinner, Bosch wants us to know, was a glutton in life. His punishment does not merely fit the crime, it is that crime, endlessly pursued. Hell is thus the archive of everyday life. Although naked and anonymous, the tormented sinners enact the excessive inclinations that, in life, constituted their individual personalities. Thus while the triptych skips human history entirely, jumping from Eden to Last Judgment, it remembers that history in penal form. Entertaining us with wonderfully varied retributions, Bosch invites us to infer from them the sins that were their cause and—more than that—to dig back beyond these sins to the origins of evil itself. As in *The Hay Wain*, in the Vienna *Last Judgment* the finger points to Eve, whose creation dominates the foreground of Eden. The Fall and the Expulsion are her story more than Adam's. Her pernicious form reappears, appropriately, in the central panel (middle ground, far left) as a demonic seductress (fig. 51). Meanwhile, Adam, asleep during Eve's creation and (according to some medieval commentaries) already dreaming his and our entire future doom, also returns in the central panel, now as the slothful, slumbering victim of Eve's diabolical look-alike.[46]

Humans—Bosch shows—create and suffer chaos. This starts with Eve, but already then she had the help of the original rebel, Satan. Again as in *The Hay Wain*, the Old Enemy falls with his rebellious minions from the sky above the primal garden. In the form of the serpent (another of Eve's look-alikes), Satan tempts Eve and Adam to sin. And in the Hell panel, the adversary sits enthroned in the foreground, at the bottom of and entrance to that pit, in the corner of the triptych farthest from the Creator of the beginning. The painting's beholder *sees* all these ordered structures: Bosch lets us humans look out upon the cosmic whole *almost* as God does from his higher place in heaven. Divine wrath thus becomes ours, as we revel in the punishment of foes. The early Christians hungered for this gruesome vision. Writing around 200 CE, Tertullian relishes imagining the future "spectacle" that would far surpass in the scope of its cruelty the gladiatorial games of Rome, where the Christian martyrs met their death. Admonishing his pious readers not to visit the everyday amusements of theater and stadium, and preaching for the first time a Christian renunciation of revenge, Tertullian nonetheless promises far bloodier games to come, when, at the end of time, the present-day persecutors

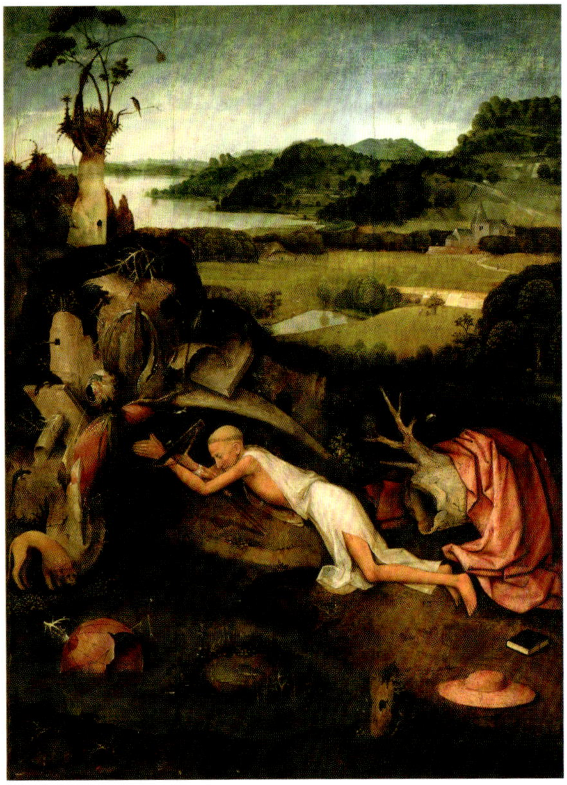

53 Hieronymus Bosch, *Saint Jerome*, c. 1510, panel, Museum voor Schone Kunsten, Ghent

the laity. Remaining enmeshed in a devilish world, as laypeople did, meant inhabiting enemy territory. Pious self-loathing abounded, also fueling an insidious reactive fear and hatred of others, especially strangers and outsiders, such as vagrants, gypsies, witches, heretics, Muslims, and Jews.[54] These, the conspiring antagonists crowding Bosch's paintings, were suspected of manipulating the world, setting its hidden snares and seducing even the good Christian self to fall prey to their machinations.

Saint Augustine struggled with the fact that the Devil seemed to rule over God's perfect creation. Vigilant against the Gnostic dualism of Mani and the Manicheans, who simply consigned the corrupt cosmos to hell, Augustine sought guidance in Scripture. He remembered that Saint John, in the prologue to his Gospel, announced that Christ "was in the world, and the world was made by Him, and the world knew Him not" (John 1:10). Augustine unpacked this cryptic verse by distinguishing between two different and opposite senses of the word *world*. In the one instance, world is a divine creation and the site of God's incarnation as Christ. In the second instance, in the phrase "the world knew Him not," world denotes sinful humanity. Enjoying this world, mankind failed to recognize Christ's divinity: "Because they loved the world," explains Augustine, "they are called the world."[55] What the church father calls the "evil world" is not an objective power or entity, as it was for the Gnostics, but a subjective, inner attitude shared by humanity as a whole. It is the "how" of man's corrupt relation to the cosmos, for "evil are those who prefer the world to God."

The Hay Wain pronounces an anathema on the world. It sends to hell all who love the world, together with the great, combustible, world-shaped hay they desire. Meanwhile, as Saint John and Saint Augustine lament, Christ remains ignored by everyone. Showing the mortal wounds that humanity inflicted on him, he admonishes that when he was corporeally in the world, the "world knew him not." Oblivious to Christ and directed instead toward nothingness, human love converts to its opposite. Isolated in the open space between the foreground vignettes and the hay wagon, one man cuts another man's throat, while behind them several marchers have already come to blows. Enmity is humanity's natural state. Hatred draws people together in a Hobbesian struggle of all against all that, in its formlessness, resembles the hay that gets them fighting. Enemy forces manage this global hostility. At the head of the parade, monstrous demons, uncontested, lead humanity into their trap. And joining this ambush is God himself, who, facing universal hostility despite having come as a friend and preaching love, unleashes his wrath in hell.

The Political

According to the authoritarian legal theorist Carl Schmitt, the political has its own unique criteria. Whereas concepts of the moral and the aesthetic rest on the distinctions between good and evil and beauty and ugliness, respectively, the political rests on the difference between friend and foe, which is also the most intense distinction of all, since it denotes the utmost degree of separation.[56] By this view politics arise not in the squabbles among so-called political parties but through the mortal threat posed to a collectivity by a concrete foe. Friends and enemies "receive their real meaning precisely because they refer to the real possibility of physical killing, Schmitt writes. "War follows from enmity. War is the existential negation of the enemy."[57] Without such a dire threat, political concepts, images, and terms "turn into empty and spectral abstractions."[58] In Schmitt's sense, Bosch would be the most political of painters.[59] *The Hay Wain* places war and murder, as characteristics of the human condition, within a metaphysical battle between God and Satan. It pictures the absolute impasse in which the political is born. Decidedly "spectral" forces lead the way; but deriving, as Bosch shows them to be, from God's fallen adversaries, the rebel angels, those demons affirm what Schmitt believed politics ultimately were, a *theology*.[60] States of exception reveal political theology because, in such emergency states when law is suspended, it is only the sovereign who, godlike in the last instance, decides.[61]

Bosch signals a state of exception in the civil war unfolding on earth and in the final judgment appearing in heaven. He also signals concrete politics through the troop of leaders ironically following in the hay wagon's train. Riding before the banners of the Kingdom of France and the German empire, a bearded German emperor looks out at us in a posture loosely echoing Christ's above, while behind him process (left to right) the king of France, perhaps the patriarch of Constantinople, the pope, and a man in an elaborate chaperon in the style of a Burgundian duke (fig. 54).[62] These are the sovereign rulers, both worldly and ecclesiastic, who count in Bosch's world. Real-world too is their participation in a parade, since that is the symbolic form in which ordinary folk would glimpse sovereignty. In 1477, after the death of her father, Charles the Bold, in the Battle of Nancy, Mary of Burgundy, together with her new husband (and the future emperor), Archduke Maximilian of Austria, passed through the gates of 's-Hertogenbosch in what was one of the century's most elaborate political parades.[63]

In constructing his allegorical tableau, Bosch drew heavily on the symbols, format, and choreography of festive processions. Pageants in the Netherlands during the fifteenth and sixteenth centuries routinely commenced with a dramatic reenactment of the Adam and Eve story. In 1401, the magistrates of Louvain ruled that the city's annual religious procession should always open with a performance of the Expulsion, enacted on an elaborately carved and painted float

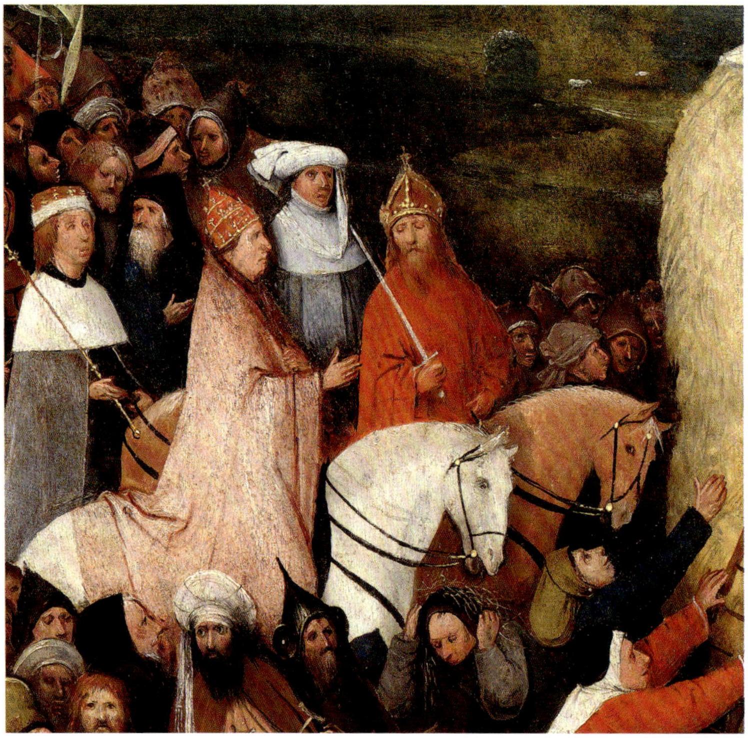

54 Detail of Hieronymus Bosch and Assistants, *The Hay Wain* (fig. 39)

at the front of the parade.[64] So well used was this wheeled vehicle that it had to be completely overhauled in 1462, to the delight of Duke Philip the Good, who marveled at the contraption. Beginning similarly with the drama in Eden, Bosch's triptych features the float-like hay cart, with its *tableau vivant* of lust on top and its drama of covetousness all around. Even the genre figures in the foreground—the blind man and his boy guide, the gypsy fortune-teller, the quack, the lascivious nun, and the greedy prelate—derive from the songs, banners, and farces of urban parades.[65]

Bosch had a professional knowledge of such pageantry. Documents show that the Van Aken family made banners and props for their town's processions.[66] The Vices as well as the Virtues marched in such parades. Negative spectacles had the dual function of admonishing the crowds through which they passed and luring people into the pleasures that the festival cheerfully provided. To cite one well-documented example, carnival celebrations in Nuremberg included a masked parade—called the *Schembartlauf*—that climaxed in the procession of a monstrous float nicknamed the "Hell" (fig. 55).[67] Accompanied by attendants dressed as devils, wildmen, and fools, the parade's sledges produced crowd-pleasing effects, such as flames, smoke, fireworks, and giant moving limbs. Different each year, and based on the same repertoire of grotesque themes that dominates Bosch's oeuvre, these floats had the ambiguous task of representing evil while also encouraging the public to join in the fun. People marched, drank, and danced with the costumed devils; they could even climb, enter, and ride on the floats. At the end of the festivities, the most enthusiastic tagalongs, now trapped inside, could be publicly mocked and punished for their excesses.[68]

Like Bosch's painting, festive pageantry was both pleasurable and perilous, first, because it recruited everyone, the maskers as well as their audience, into its revels, and second, because these revels concealed a cruel purpose. This violent undercurrent is the reason these rituals sometimes turned into riots.[69] Never was this element of danger as consequential as in the grandest of all Netherlandish pageants, the Joyous Entrances staged by the region's

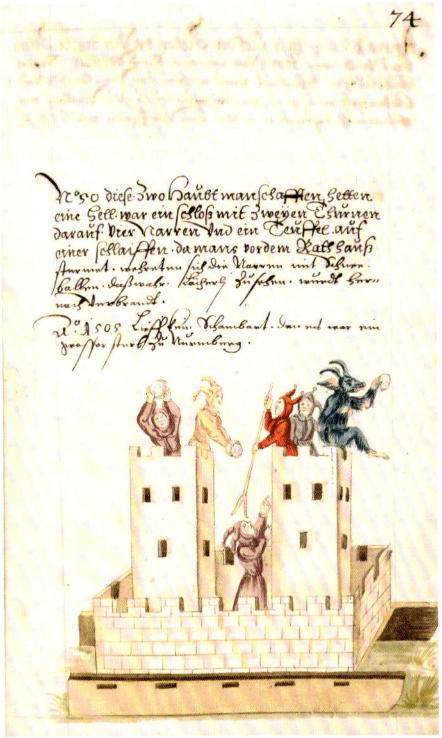

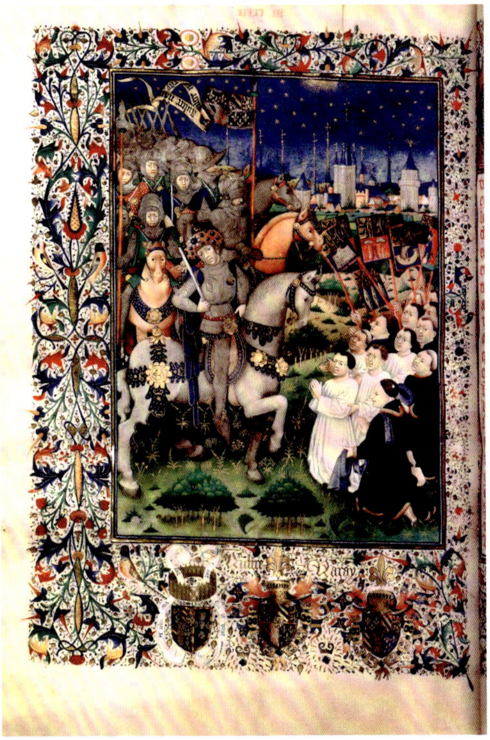

(LEFT) **55** The "Hell" float of the forty-seventh Schembart Carnival (1505), pen and ink and watercolor, from *Nuremberg Shrovetide Carnival (1449–1539)*, c. 1600, Oxford University, The Bodleian Libraries, The University of Oxford, MS. Douce 346, fol. 236r

(RIGHT) **56** Master of the Ghent Privileges, *The Honorable Amend of 1453* (*The Burghers of Ghent Show Contrition to Duke Philip the Good before the City Gates*), *Boek van de Priviligiën van Gent en van Vlaanderen*, Österreichiche Nationalbibliothek, Vienna, MS 2583, fol. 349v

overlords. The dukes of faraway Burgundy affirmed their sovereignty in Flanders and Brabant by ritually entering each city that they ruled. Frequent, lavish, and costly, these pageants required townspeople to dramatize their obedience. When Ghent gave up its yearlong conflict with Philip the Good in 1453, the city's four captains had to kneel before him in underclothes in the mud, as a contemporary illumination shows (fig. 56).[70] As an observer in Arras exclaimed in 1455 at the entry of Philip the Good into that city, "If God had descended from Heaven I do not know if the citizens would have paid him this much honor."[71] City leaders enlisted artisans of all kinds to contrive and craft elaborate political emblems and allegories. Mingling religion, myth, legend, and history, such symbolism took the form of great ephemeral constructions: simulated forests, mountains, seas, and castles made of wood and painted canvas. In following Bosch's thought in *The Hay Wain*, we must imagine an artist and an audience deeply versed in allegory, in its capabilities and weaknesses. Subtle ambiguities, such as the likeness between the German emperor and Christ, would therefore have been noted and pondered. For the possibility always existed for Joyous Entrances to go terribly wrong, since these events functioned to negotiate the delicate balance between advancing local privileges and submitting to the power of a dangerous and distant sovereign.

Sometimes the ruling duke had to be lured into his cities with promises of safety and reward. For pageants could become deadly traps, as one almost did for Charles the Bold in Ghent in 1467. The burghers there feared the duke's vicious treatment of seditious cities; for an insult received in rebellious Dinant, Charles had sacked and torched the town and liquidated every man, woman, and child. But the people of Ghent also resented their magistrates' acquiescence to the duke's costly demands. Some burghers thus conspired to turn Charles's festive entrance through their city's gates into a riotous expression of their grievance, with dire consequences to themselves.[72] That same year, while Bosch was still in his teens, Charles entered 's-Hertogenbosch peacefully, but in *The Hay Wain* anarchy reigns, as sovereigns and subjects enter the gates of the infernal city together. According to Bosch, this spectacle of discord has a leader. As the sequel to his failed rebellion in heaven, Satan inspires humanity to revolt against God. This cosmic story of disobedience would have appealed to Bosch's principal patrons, the ruling members and officials of the Burgundian court, who faced rebellion everywhere. Perhaps they felt some sting from being portrayed among the lovers of the world. But they would have accepted that reprimand, tempered as it is by Bosch's inclusion, between the mounted notables and God, of an angel interceding on their behalf.

More important, they would have been delighted by the spectacle of retributive justice meted out on their rebellious subjects. Bosch exhibits the world from the perspective of divine law. God acts from outside the world, affirming justice not as natural or human law—both these have failed—but as the ultimate "exceptional" decision. To human eyes, God intervenes inscrutably and arbitrarily, as does a worldly sovereign in states of emergency, such as riot and sedition. In destroying Dinant, Charles, with no human law to back him, acted simply according to his sovereign will. Here we glimpse already Bosch's distance from Bruegel. Whereas in Bruegel law so blurs at all points into life that it stops being law, in Bosch life opens to reveal in its entirety the cruel but absolute framework of the law.

An Anti-altarpiece?

That divine framework and its triptych format led some historians to surmise that *The Hay Wain* originally stood behind an altar.[73] Bosch made many altarpieces. The chronicle that describes an altarpiece he and his brother made for the high altar of his town's great church, depicting the six days of creation, also lists three further retables by Bosch existing in the Church of Saint John prior to the iconoclasm. One, displayed in the hallowed Chapel of the Miraculous Statue of the Virgin, featured the "gifts of the Three Kings."[74] Several Boschian treatments of this subject survive. The iconography, scale, and donor portraits suggest that his *Adoration of the Magi* triptych, now hanging in the Prado, originally stood behind an altar somewhere (see fig. 93). In both its closed and open states, it explicates—as profoundly as any artwork ever has—the Eucharistic miracle occurring at Christian altars. And while I do not believe that Bosch made his *Temptation of Saint Anthony*, now in Lisbon, to stand behind an altar, he gave what was probably a private devotional object altarpiece form, with iconographical ambiguities that are minor compared with ones that trouble *The Hay Wain*, as we will see (see fig. 138).

Leaving aside its iconography, the provenance of *The Hay Wain* speaks against any cultic function.[75] Acquired in 1570 by Philip II of Spain and for years hung in the galleries of the Royal Monastery of San Lorenzo, in El Escorial, the work had previously been the property of the humanist, collector, and commentator on art Felipe de Guevara y Lastre, who inherited it from his father, Diego de Guevara y Queseda. One of the highest-ranking members of the Burgundian court, and "first majordomo" of Philip the Fair and later of Archduke Charles (the future emperor Charles V), Diego de Guevara amassed a peerless collection of early Netherlandish paintings, including the Arnolfini double portrait, by Jan van Eyck, which he decorated with his coat of arms and gifted to Margaret of Austria (see fig. 151).[76] Along with several leading officials in Philip the Fair's service, Diego de Guevara was a member of the same elite religious confraternity as Bosch, the Brotherhood of Our Dear Lady of 's-Hertogenbosch, a large and prestigious association devoted to the Virgin Mary and dedicated to the upkeep of a miracle-working statue of her housed in the Church of Saint John. He must therefore have known the artist personally and could have commissioned *The Hay Wain* directly from him. Diego's close allegiance with Habsburg power illuminates the incorporation of the Habsburg banner into the painting, while his Spanish heritage makes sense of the work's moral tenor. The court of Philip the Fair was divided between an ostentatiously hedonistic Franco-Burgundian camp and an austere, devout, and morally rigorous camp hailing from Castile and allied with the duke's wife, the depressive Juana of Castile.[77] Diego negotiated the double marriage of Philip and Juana and of Margaret of Austria and Juana's brother, Juan, Prince of Asturias. A key mediator in a conflicted milieu, he would have appreciated how Bosch could turn a critique of worldliness into an assertion of sovereign will.

The Hay Wain must have been widely appreciated, since it exists in two nearly identical versions, the one in the Prado, which I take to be the more original, and the one in El Escorial. We know, too, that Mencía de Mendoza, the Spanish wife of Count Henry III of Nassau and owner of Bosch's *Garden of Delights*, in 1534 ordered a replica of *The Hay Wain* to be made following the destruction of the (or an) original by fire.[78] And the tapestry version of *The Hay Wain* points to a Boschian prototype distinct from the Prado and Escorial triptychs (see fig. 41). Felipe de Guevara wrote an extraordinary commentary on Bosch's art. There he reports that the artist had many imitators, some of whom fraudulently signed Bosch's name to their work. One of these imitators, Felipe notes, was a direct pupil (or "disciple") of Bosch's whose work surpassed his master's.[79] Dendrochronology—a scientific method used to date wooden objects by their tree ring patterns—has established that the wood used in the Prado triptych came from a tree felled no earlier than 1508, which, together with the necessary storage and seasoning time for wood (approximately two to eight years), pushes the painting's production to the very end of Bosch's life or later.[80] Hatching executed in the work's underdrawing suggests, by the direction of the marks, a left-handed painter active within Bosch's workshop.[81] In any case, the Escorial *Hay Wain* is clearly by yet another hand—or hands, as both triptychs probably had several painters working on them. For both versions, the artist's signature functions as a trademark or brand name invested with inherent value and prestige. Early Netherlandish painters rarely signed their work and never as prominently as Bosch or his shop does here. Even Jan van Eyck—the other habitual signer of paintings—deposited his name more discreetly, either on the picture's frame or as if part of the painted world, most famously in the Arnolfini double portrait itself. Bosch took his own name from his hometown (the Dutch still call 's-Hertogenbosch "Den Bosch"), signaling, among other things, that he expected his works to travel, as indeed they did through international clientele such as Diego de Guevara. The signatures on copies and versions of *The Hay Wain* indicate a composition intended not for an altarpiece, on which a dedication (to a sacred event, personage, or mystery) would be expected, but for an art collection, where a specific maker—indeed, the inventive specificity of a singular artistic genius—would be prized.

The Hay Wain almost certainly did not originally stand behind an altar, yet that locality haunts the work nonetheless. Altars were sacred places. Sites of the real presence of Christ and the saints, they oriented church space around themselves as around a privileged center. Altarpieces, erected as backdrops behind altar tables, explained and glorified those numinous presences in their midst (fig. 57).[82] Through the triptych format, and via centralized images of Christ, the Virgin, and the saints, an altarpiece's center aligned with the altar's center, which aligned with the church's

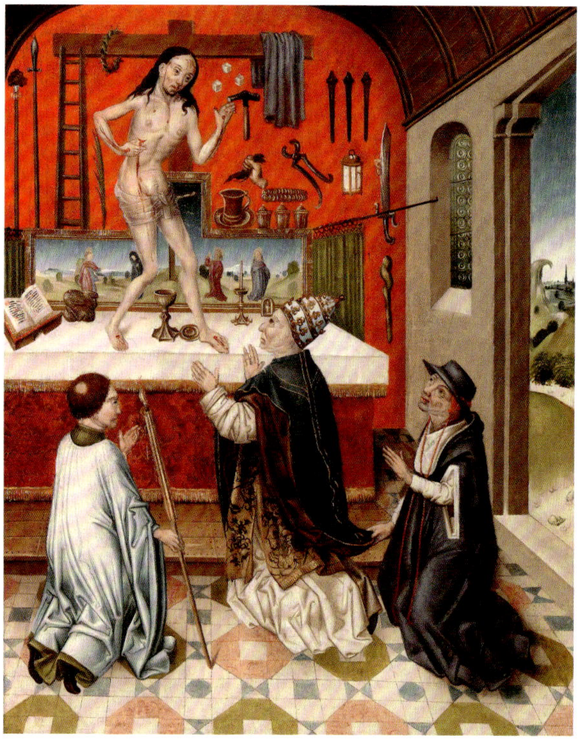

57 Master of the Wenemaer Triptych, *Saint Gregory*, 1475–80, panel, Museum voor Schone Kunsten, Ghent

center, which aligned with the *axis mundi* in Jerusalem. Christian altarpieces model *The Hay Wain*'s physical geometry, as well as the sense the work conveys that the accidents of history stand framed in a necessary order. Yet in a gesture without precedent or sequel, Bosch puts in the place of that immutable center no sacred person, event, or mystery but a mobile mass of hay. Nor would it have been lost on viewers whose religion centered on the bread of the Eucharist that hay, or more pitiably straw, is the disposable residue of wheat. Form without content, accident without substance, straw is the perfect antithesis of the Host. Bosch could predict that his audience, like the folk depicted in *The Hay Wain*, loves worldly goods, since why else would it admire costly objects like *The Hay Wain*? Thus the painting cautions against attention to things like itself. But it does more than that. Conjuring the structure of sacred space and causing viewers to mistake it for a holy image, *The Hay Wain* evokes the most abject of all things: the idol.

A Conservation Report

During the sixteenth century, products of a new kind streamed forth from the painters' workshops of northern Europe. These were autonomous paintings, framed panels and canvases with no purpose other than to be beheld (fig. 58).[83] All that they achieved—their pleasures, messages, temptations, and warnings—they did by what they independently displayed. Today this seems the art of painting's natural state. But it was not so at the time. Until around 1500, painting had been largely in the service of religion: its products were but instruments of, and sideshows to, the ritual performance of the cult. Gifted to the Church as votive offerings effective for the afterlife, these pictures hardly needed to be humanly seen in order to fulfill their function. Painting emancipated itself functionally from its subservience to the sacred by making the profane world its theme. At its birth, however, this form of painting was at war with itself. These new pictures that did nothing but display tended to repudiate both what

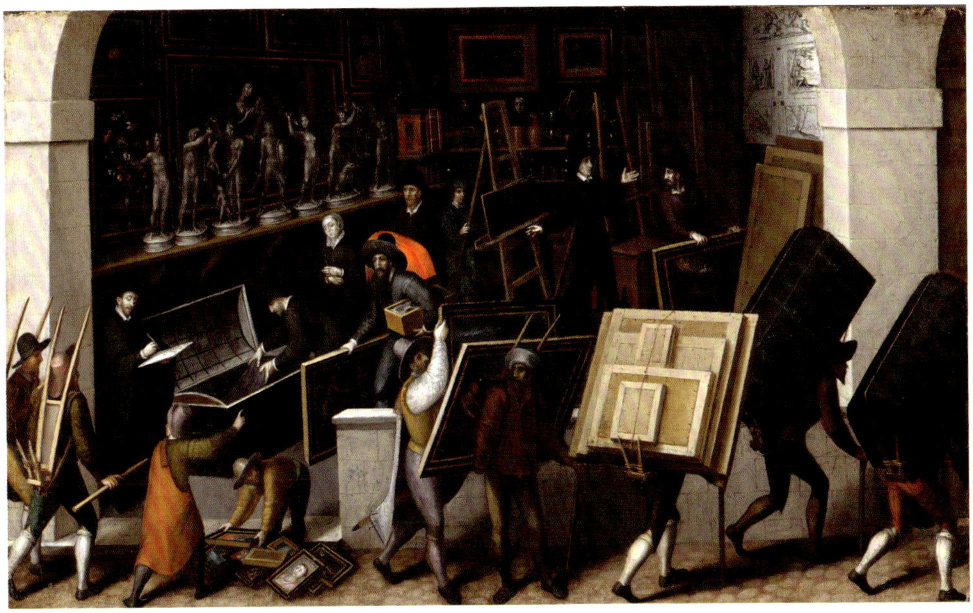

58 François Bunel the Younger, *The Confiscation of the Contents of a Painter's Studio*, c. 1590, panel, Mauritshuis, The Hague

they displayed and *that* they displayed. To accomplish self-negation, this nascent painting of everyday life occupied—as if demonically—the forms by which religious painting had displayed the sacred.

Bosch's *Hay Wain* looks like a retable altarpiece, and it acts like one, too. Through its movement from closed to open, it dramatizes ostentation itself as a cosmic epiphany in which ordinary existence gives way to the true, transcendent order of things. But whereas triptych altarpieces reveal and enshrine a center that belongs *to* that true order, as its underlying essence or subject this secular triptych reveals a hostile center, as if the space of truth itself had suddenly come under enemy occupation. This is because its underlying subject—everyday life—is not merely empty or illusory; it is a diabolical rebellion against divine truth. A covering illusion and a devilish trap, Bosch's portrayal of the peddler striding through the world thrusts us into the hole, or hell, that runs right through it.

The so-called *Wayfarer*, now in Rotterdam, shows no opening abyss, and looks to be a fully autonomous genre painting by Hieronymus Bosch (fig. 59).[84] As in the painting on the exterior of *The Hay Wain*'s shutters, its protagonist—again a peddler, though the worse for wear—marches dead center in the visual field, backed by incidents unfolding in a mundane landscape. The crumbling brothel encapsulates life debauched by sin, while the picture's round format encloses everything within the familiar cipher of world. Unlike *The Hay Wain* in its closed state, however, this tableau does not open to a decision ultimately reached but remains suspended in ordinary time, in the blind temporality of lived experience, within which we encounter Bosch's painting hanging on a gallery wall. Yet it is already apparent to the naked eye that a straight crack or join—painstakingly patched and painted over—runs top to bottom through the picture's center. In the past, this scar was ignored or explained away as damage or disrepair.[85] When the picture arrived at Rotterdam's Museum Boijmans Van Beuningen, in 1931, the conservator Hendrik Luitwieler removed the panel from an old cradle and discovered it had suffered mistreatment to its back. He suggested that the work had been originally painted on both sides and subsequently split to separate the rear image from

(RIGHT) **59** Hieronymus Bosch, *The Wayfarer*, c. 1494, panel, Museum Boijmans Van Beuningen, Rotterdam

(OPPOSITE) **60**a. Hieronymus Bosch, *The Ship of Fools*, c. 1495, panel, Musée du Louvre, Paris; **b.** Hieronymus Bosch, *Allegory of Intemperance*, c. 1495–1500, panel, Yale University Art Gallery, New Haven, CT; **c.** Hieronymus Bosch, *Death of the Miser*, c. 1495, panel, National Gallery of Art, Washington

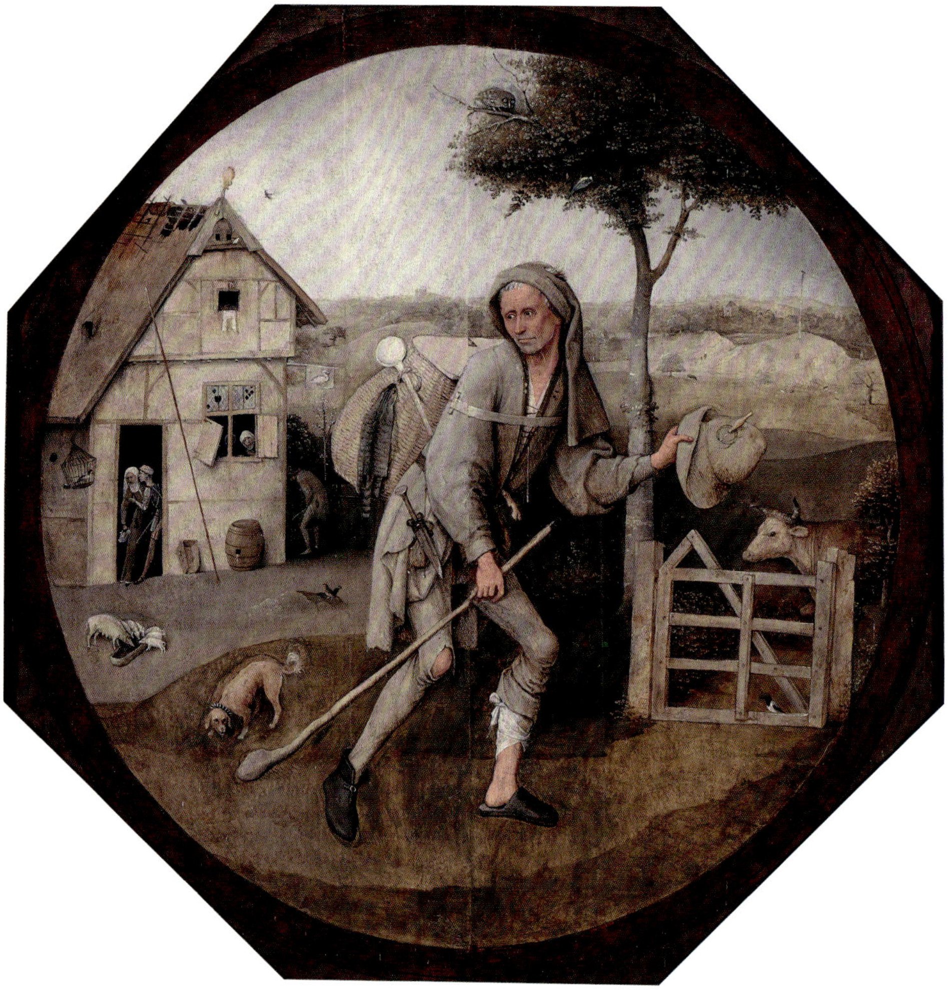

the front.[86] The vertical cut was understood as having merely aided this division: by being first cut in half—the thinking goes—the two-sided panel was converted into two matched pieces that could have been split with an ordinary saw in one go, and the two sets of halves subsequently reconnected.

The ingenuity of Luitwieler's explanation illustrates the normative force of the modern, framed gallery picture. Recent analysis has shown that, whereas the splitting of a once double-sided picture took place after the work left Bosch's shop (already Van Mander describes such treatment of a panel by Geertgen tot Sint Jans that had been rescued from Protestant iconoclasm), the vertical cut is original.[87] It functioned as the opening between what were two hinged shutters of a triptych. Analysis of the wooden support has proved that the backs of these shutters, which would have formed side panels of the triptych's open state, displayed two pictures, both of which have survived. The right panel of *The Wayfarer* probably had on its reverse the so-called *Death of the Miser*, now in Washington, DC; and the verso of *The Wayfarer*'s left panel probably featured *The Ship of Fools*, now in the Louvre, and below that, originally integrated into the composition, the evidently fragmentary *Allegory of Intemperance*, now at Yale (fig. 60).[88] All five panels are made of planks cut from the same oak tree, felled sometime after 1486. In all likelihood they formed part of a secular triptych, along the lines of *The Hay Wain*.[89] If so, then four of the six apparently autonomous genre paintings by Bosch

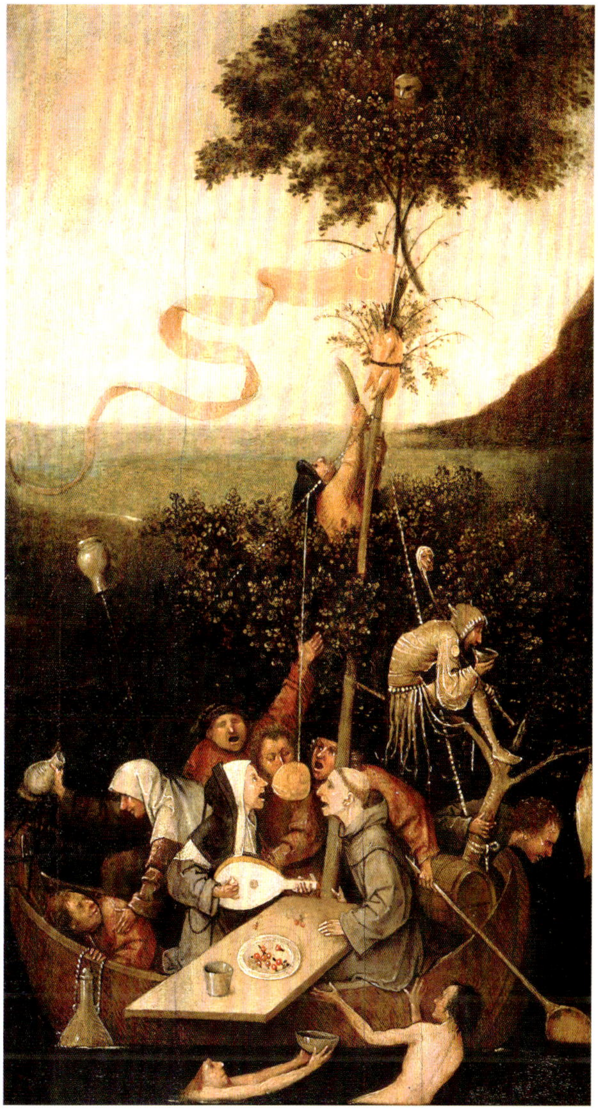
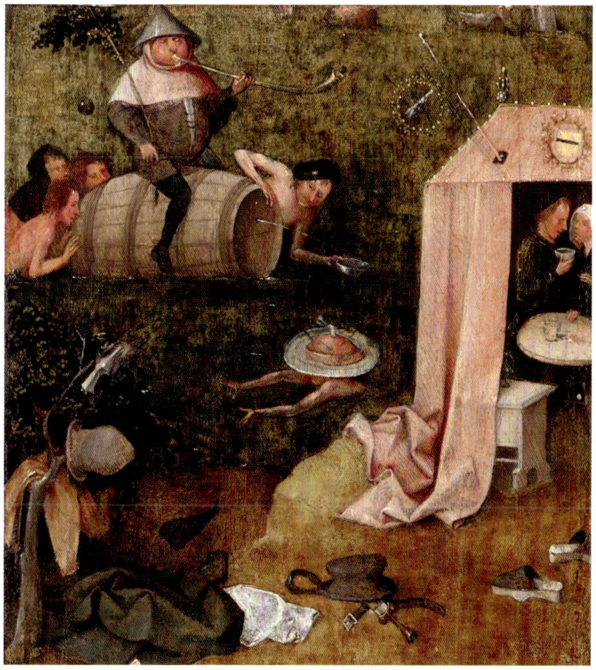
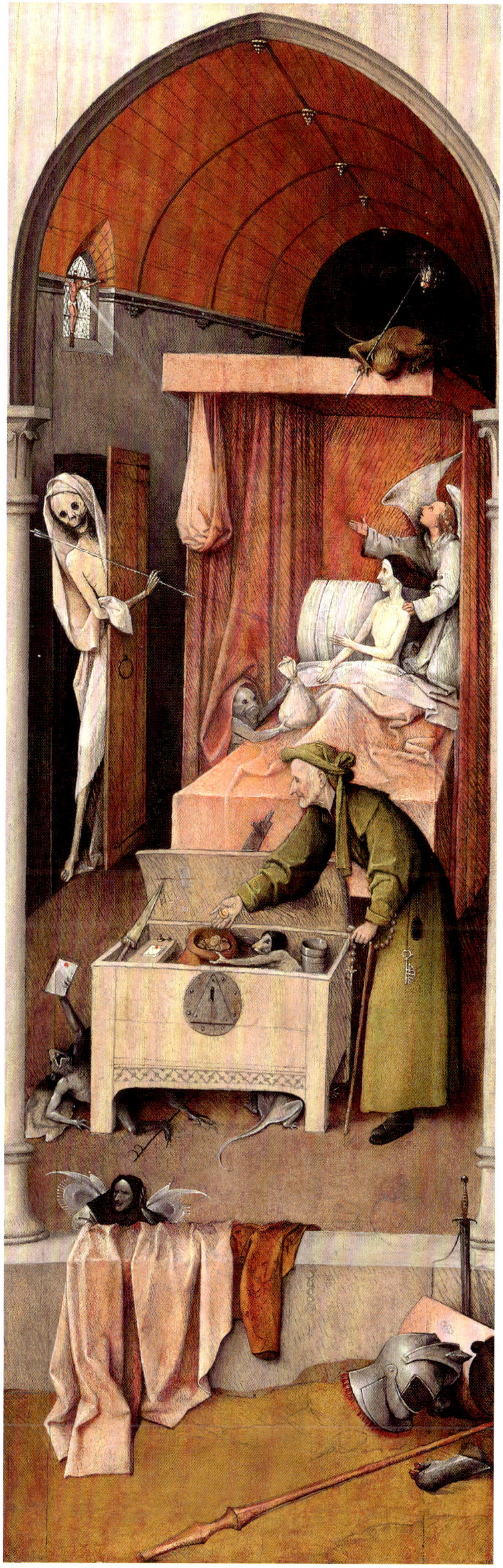

that have survived were made for a different form of display—not as discrete tableaux, each yielding an isolated experience, but as parts of a movable ensemble invested, through its format, with decisive sacred connotations.

This is hardly surprising, since the gallery picture is a fairly modern invention. In order to make them at home in a gallery, dealers and collectors divided altarpieces up and set the parts in rectangular frames. Stripped of meaningful adjacencies, these fragments lost some of their original signifying power. In Bosch's works, each individually framed tableau may preach against sin and warn about impending death, but *how* it does this has changed from when it belonged to a larger whole. Sealed permanently shut, the Rotterdam *Wayfarer* cannot unmask itself as a devilish deception. Deceptively rebuilt, it conceals the alliance—key to the emergence of genre painting in European art—between the painting of everyday life and diabolical fantasies. Through a modern optic alien to him, Bosch comes to resemble his more worldly successors, the worldliest of whom was Pieter Bruegel the Elder.

4

FROM BOSCH TO BRUEGEL

The Comparison

These artists have long been paired (figs. 61 and 62). Already in Bruegel's lifetime, his kinship to Bosch had become a rhetorical commonplace. Writing in 1561, during a long residence in Antwerp, the Florentine traveler Lodovico Guicciardini observed that Bruegel was "a great imitator and follower of the art and fantasies of Hieronymus Bosch, for which reason he acquired the byname 'the second Hieronymus Bosch.' "[1] In 1572, the Flemish humanist Dominicus Lampsonius echoed this view. Inspired by the new form of art commentary emerging in Italy in the writings of Vasari, he composed verses about illustrious northern European artists and attached to them engraved likenesses of each. To the portrait of Bruegel, which we looked at earlier, he attached these words: "Who is this Bosch? Jeroon once more returned to the world, who, trained with the burin and deft with the stylus, so imitates for us the dreams of his competent master that meanwhile he surpasses him as well?"[2] What linked Bruegel to Bosch was their shared exercise of fantasy, which they applied (in the words of Vasari) "to strange pictures . . . of dreams and imaginings."[3]

To viewers today, the comparison might seem strained. What do Bruegel's down-to-earth imagery and the thorough this-worldliness maintained through almost every inch of his Vienna panels have to do with the hellish nightmares of Bosch? In fact, of course, paintings of everyday life constitute only one part of Bruegel's oeuvre. In his lifetime, this artist's international fame rested chiefly on two sets of engravings: his Alpine views, which must have seemed especially monstrous to viewers living in the Low Countries' decidedly flat terrain; and his prints and drawings of the seven deadly sins, which veritably crawl with bizarre and decidedly Boschian creatures (figs. 63 and 64).[4] And even when Bruegel depicts ordinary life, he makes the familiar look strange, as humanity pursues its games and rituals with an irrational frenzy that, from the empyrean viewpoint of his paintings, makes those pursuits seem demoniacally possessed. At first sight, before we have recognized them, and later, when we step again away, Bruegel's revelers, his armies, and his children at play all look strange and inhuman.

In 1560, Bruegel's approach would have seemed even more Boschian, due to the enormous shadow the earlier artist cast over Netherlandish art. Remember Felipe de Guevara's report that Bosch had imitators during his lifetime: nameless epigones who fancied that Bosch's art consisted only in "monsters and imaginary subjects," whereas—according to Guevara—it actually

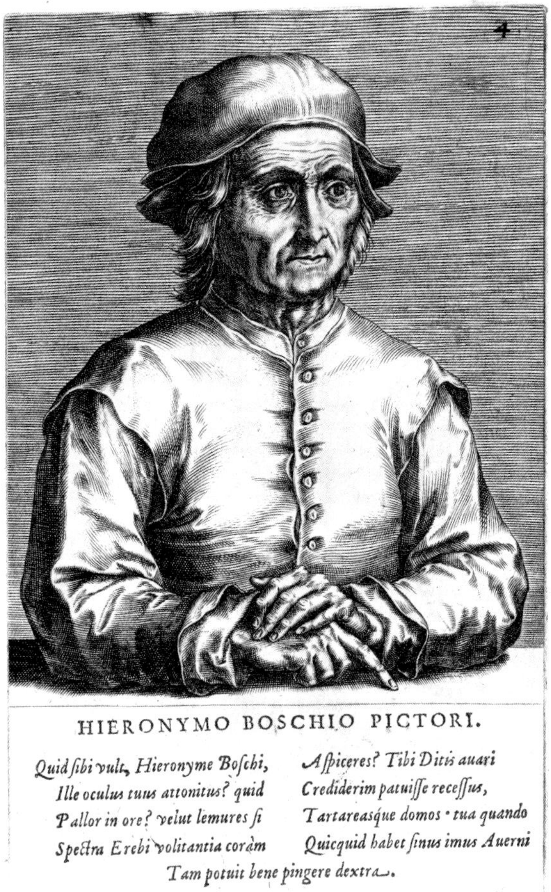

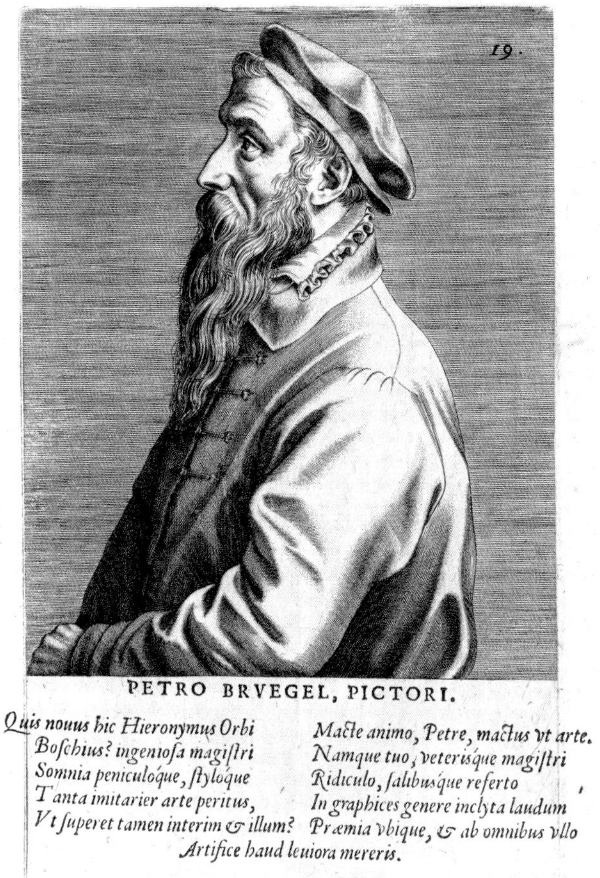

61 Attributed to Cornelis Cort or Hieronymus Wierix, *Portrait of Hieronymus Bosch*, from Dominicus Lampsonius, *Pictorum aliquot celebrium Germaniae Inferior effigies*, 1572, engraving, The British Museum, London

62 Attributed to Johannes Wierix, *Portrait of Pieter Bruegel the Elder*, from Dominicus Lampsonius, *Pictorum aliquot celebrium Germaniae Inferior effigies*, 1572, engraving, The British Museum, London

excelled in a rigorous naturalism, becoming monstrous only when his subject demanded it, as it did in scenes of hell.[5] Again, *The Hay Wain* was probably executed by several anonymous assistants in the master's employ, who added Bosch's signature not fallaciously but as a brand name. Also recall that Guevara mentioned an especially talented disciple who, "either out of reverence for his master or in order to increase the value of his works, signed them with the name of Bosch rather than with his own."[6] Some scholars have taken Guevara's mention of a talented "disciple" of Bosch's to refer to Bruegel, known in Guevara's day through his prints.[7] However, the Spaniard surely refers to a much earlier Bosch imitator, one whose paintings may have featured in the collection of his father, Diego, deceased long before Bruegel was born.

Paradoxically, the very presence of the master's name on a painting seems to signal a shop product rather than an autograph creation, since several of the more doubtful works within Bosch's traditionally accepted oeuvre (*The Seven Deadly Sins*, the *Hermit Saints Triptych* in Venice, both versions of *The Hay Wain*) are prominently signed, while the most idiosyncratic, autograph, and, as it were, "signature" Bosch—the so-called *Garden of Delights*—is unsigned. However, certain apparently autograph works do feature signatures, including *Saint John on Patmos* and the Prado *Adoration of the Magi* (fig. 65 and see fig. 93).[8] (The latter, probably from Bosch's documented altarpiece for the Brotherhood of Our Dear Lady in the Church of Saint John in 's-Hertogenbosch, features above the signature a bespectacled demon—perhaps a demonic alter ego of the painter.) And several documents from late in the artist's lifetime call the painter "Jheronimus van Aken, who signed his name Bosch."[9] Like most Netherlandish

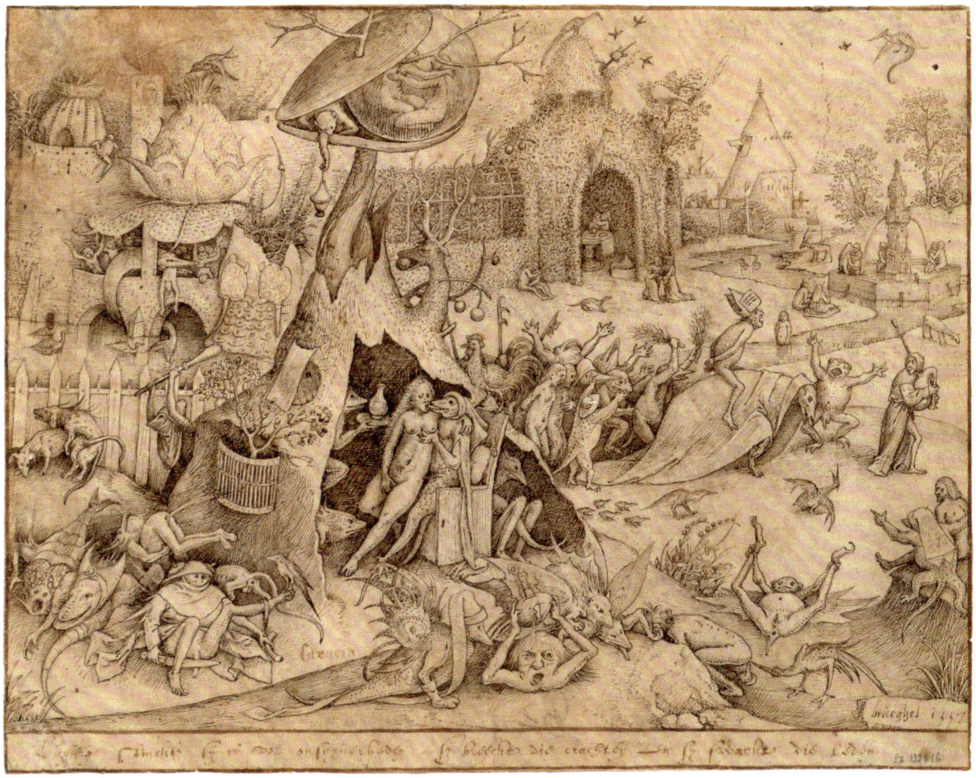

(LEFT) 63 Pieter Bruegel the Elder, *Luxuria* (*Lust*), 1557, pen and brown ink with traces of black chalk, Royal Library of Belgium, Brussels, Inv. no. S.II.132 816 folio c

(BELOW) 64 Pieter van der Heyden after Pieter Bruegel the Elder, *Luxuria*, from the *Seven Deadly Sins* series, 1558, engraving (published by Hieronymus Cock, Antwerp), The Metropolitan Museum of Art, New York, Harris Brisbane Dick Fund, 1928

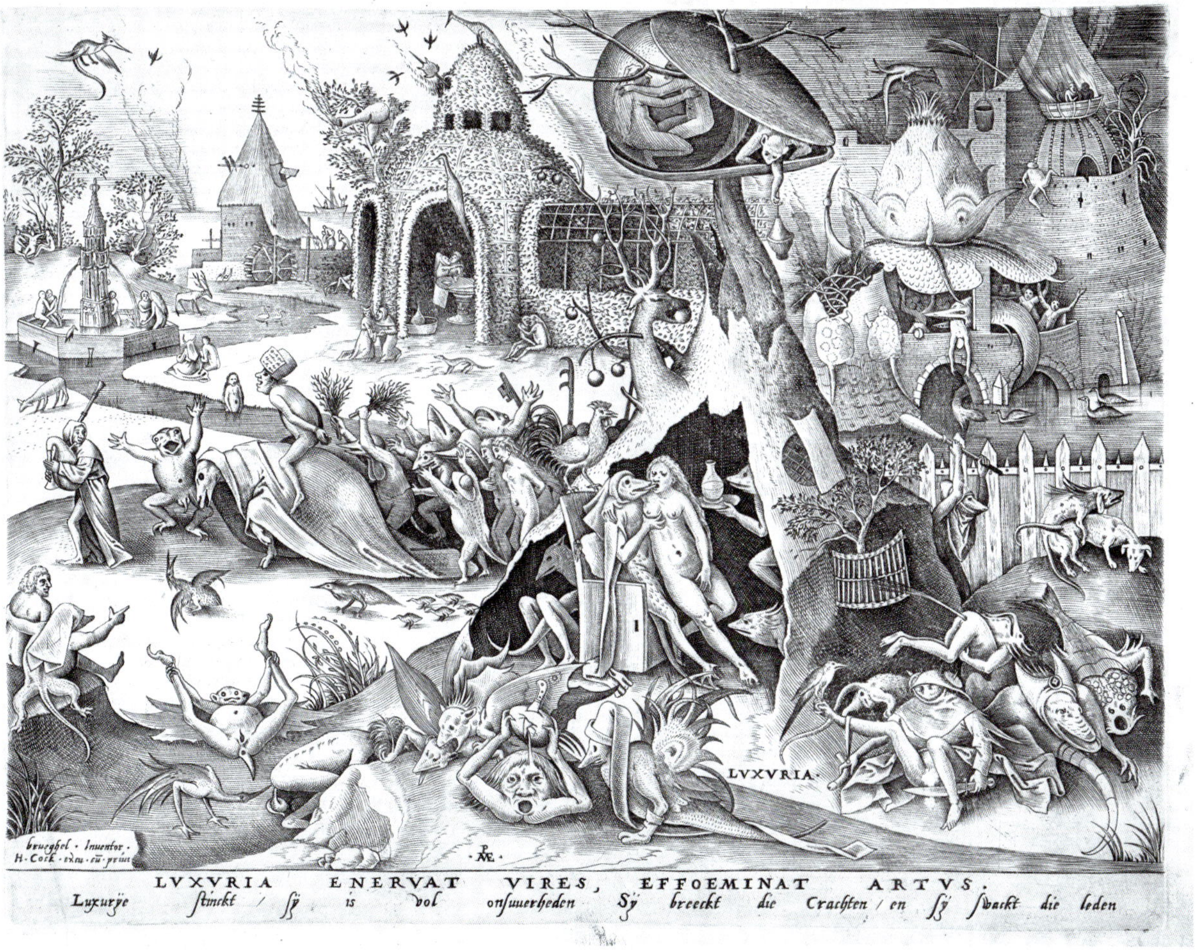

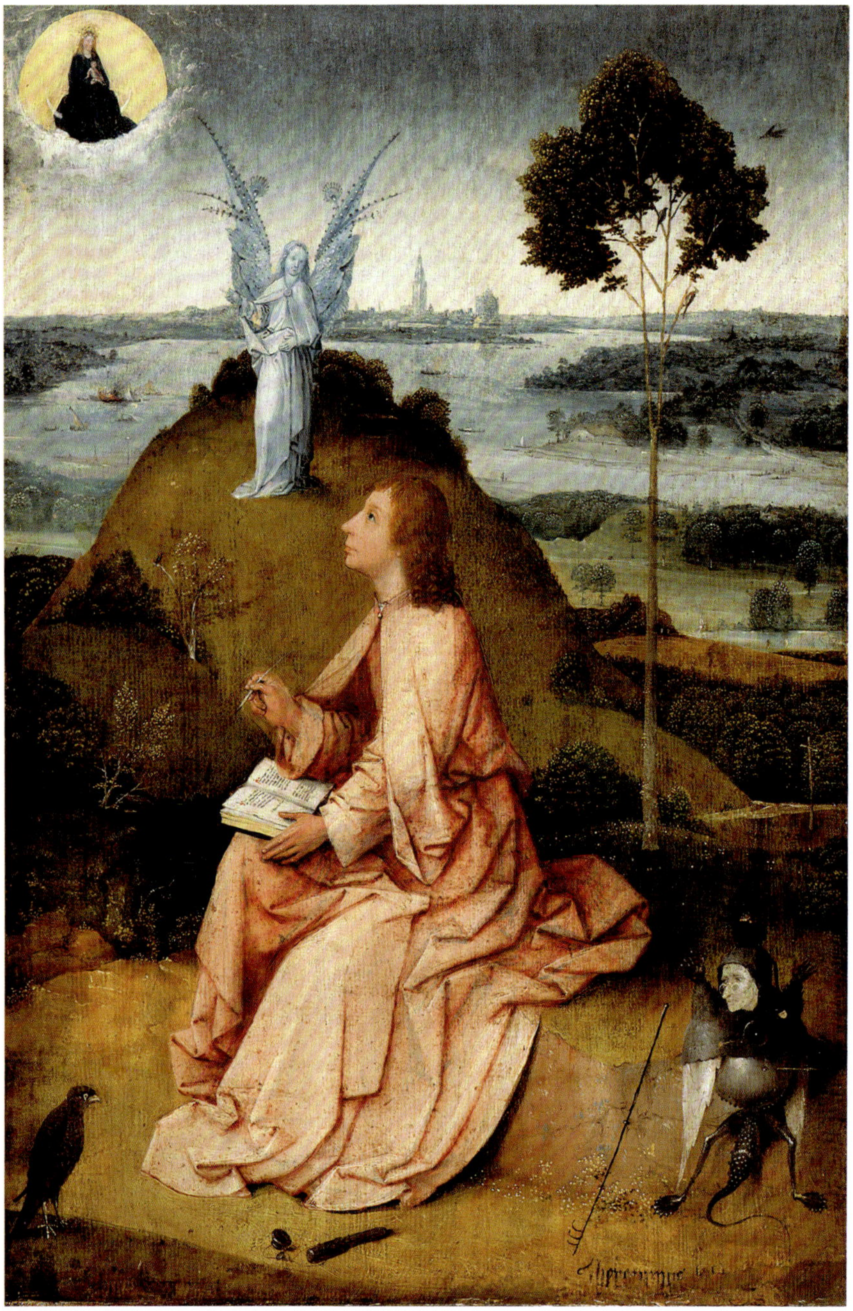

65 Hieronymus Bosch, *Saint John on Patmos*, c. 1505, oil on oak, Staatliche Museen zu Berlin, Gemäldegalerie, Berlin

artists, Bosch worked with a team of assistants and collaborators. Different individuals worked at different stages and on different parts of the same painting, with the master sometimes only overseeing the process.[10] In the context of manufacturing strategies of their time, Bosch paintings distinguish themselves through their swift execution and through the master's insistence that his virtuoso authorship be so exclusively proclaimed. Originality in Bosch is both an art-historical fact and a promotional ploy. On the one hand, this originality consists in the unprecedented character of his art, which seems to come from nowhere in the Netherlandish tradition and concocts imaginary entities with no prototype in nature. On the other hand, it rests on the painter's novel claim—made variously through his signature, through the cultivated singularity of his subject matter and style, through a rapid application of paint that indexes the spontaneous process of invention and fabrication, and through a rich thematic of

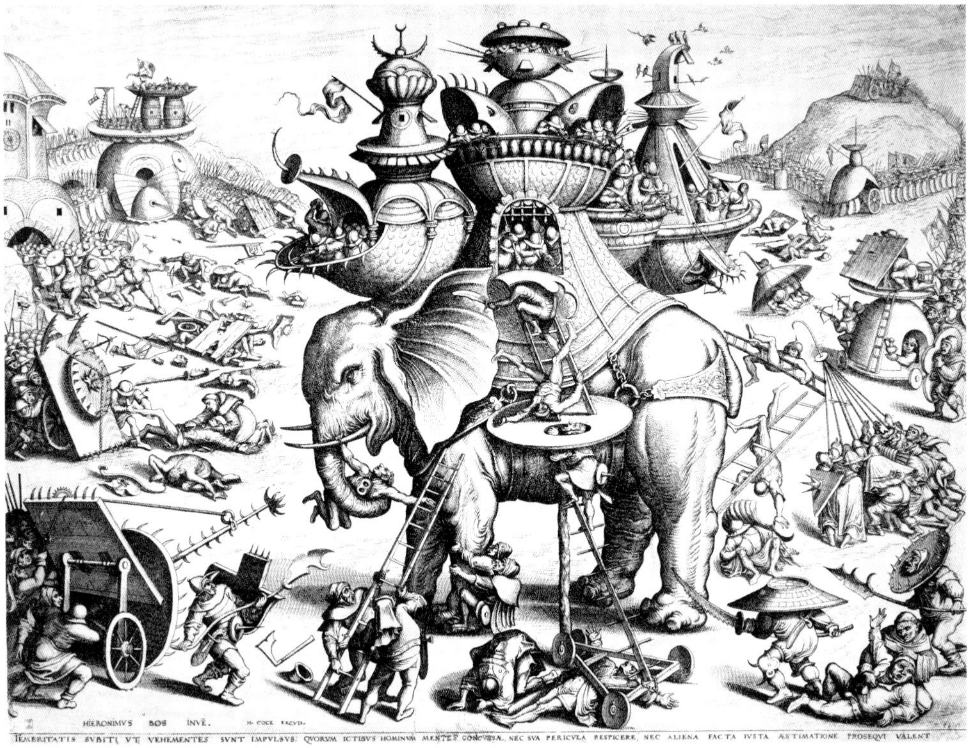

66 Joannes and Lucas van Doetecum after Alart du Hameel and Hieronymus Bosch, *The War Elephant*, c. 1565, etching and engraving (published by Hieronymus Cock, Antwerp), Royal Library of Belgium, Brussels, Print Room Inv. no. S.11 20717

divine and artistic creation running through his oeuvre—that he, the man who signs his pictures *Jhieronymus Bosch*, and not his family, his associates, his tradition, or even God himself, is the source and origin of all we see.

It remains unclear how, after more than three generations of collaborative, anonymous output, one member of the Van Aken enterprise suddenly stood out—differently named—as the shop's sole signatory master. Individual talent, emergent forms of artistic ambition, and the arrival in 's-Hertogenbosch of an international, noble clientele would have been contributing factors. But immediately afterward, Bosch's followers both at home and in Antwerp failed to imitate him in one important way: instead of setting their own fantasy free and taking credit for their works, they slavishly copied his creations. Where a lack of suitable prototypes compelled them to invent new compositions, they disguised these as copies of a phantom original.[11] Even the most distinctive of Bosch's imitators, such as the prolific Antwerp painters Jan Mandijn and Pieter Huys, stuck close to the master's most famous compositions.[12] Geared to audience expectations, this cautious, formulaic approach was maintained by the Antwerp publisher Hieronymus Cock when, in the 1550s, he began disseminating stylistically updated Boschian fantasies in the medium of engraving (fig. 66).[13]

In 1557, Cock issued a striking print illustrating the proverb "big fish eat little fish" (fig. 67).[14] Along with his own name, written in majuscule beside the work's publication date, Cock included (at the lower left) the nestled monogram of the engraver Pieter van der Heyden and above that, as if handwritten in pen and ink, the words "Hieronijmus Bos. inuentor." The composition does recall inventions by that long-deceased master. A gigantic fish-devouring fish appears in the background of Bosch's *Temptation of Saint Anthony* triptych (on the left inner panel), as does the nasty fin-winged beast swooping down from the sky (see fig. 138). In its overall composition, the print also recalls Bosch's most memorable surviving drawing, engraved late in the sixteenth century, in which a monstrous "tree-man" floats offshore and,

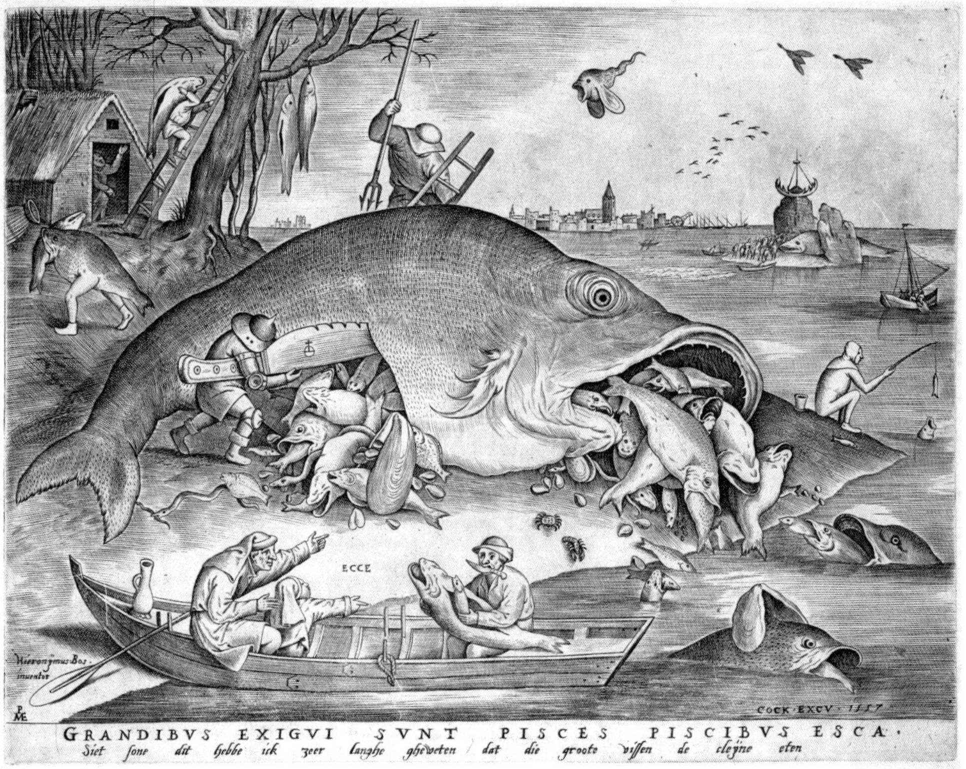

67 Pieter van der Heyden after Pieter Bruegel the Elder, *Big Fish Eat Little Fish*, 1557, engraving (published by Hieronymus Cock, Antwerp), The Metropolitan Museum of Art, New York, Harris Brisbane Dick Fund, 1928

backed by a distant harbor view, gazes at and through us (see figs. 246 and 249).[15] In Bosch's drawing and in Cock's engraving, an arsenal of everyday equipment—boat, jug, ladder, knife—appears estranged from everyday use. More generally, the visual conceit of a body bursting with miniature versions of itself recalls all those passages in Bosch where container and contained switch places, rendering structure chaotic.

But there are also differences between the print and Bosch's works. In the foreground, a father points out the spectacle to his child. Attached to his imperative "Behold!" (*Ecce*) is an inscription voicing a lesson: "Look son, I've known this for long, that the big fish eat the small." Such a pedantic gloss, along with the social message the underlying proverb conveys, seems foreign to Bosch, whose inscriptions either label or warn. And to the print's social realism there corresponds a different pictorial realism. Compared with Bosch's spectral monsters, this colossus and the collection of fish disgorged from it are emphatically natural specimens. Their corporeal volume measured by the bodies that fill them, these creatures remain spatially coherent, despite their massed and twisting forms. The giant fish—a wonder of nature wondrously rendered by the engraver's art—eyes us uncannily, but just as dead fish do. Note how, at the upper left, the artist fools viewers into thinking they see a monstrous fish-man ascending the ladder; in fact, he is just a man carrying a big fish up to dry. This is an altogether different game than the one typically played by Bosch, who, through artistic sleight of hand, renders the unreal diabolically plausible. *Big Fish Eat Little Fish* moves in the opposite direction. Natural and social reality gobble up all fantasies as just bits of the surrealism of everyday life.

Pieter van der Heyden engraved the image after a pen-and-ink drawing executed by Bruegel (fig. 68).[16] Now kept in Vienna, this extraordinary sketch is dated (1556) and signed with its maker's name (*brueghel*) precisely on the spot where, in the print, Bosch's signature will intrude. Free of any inscriptions and marvelously incorporated into the landscape through

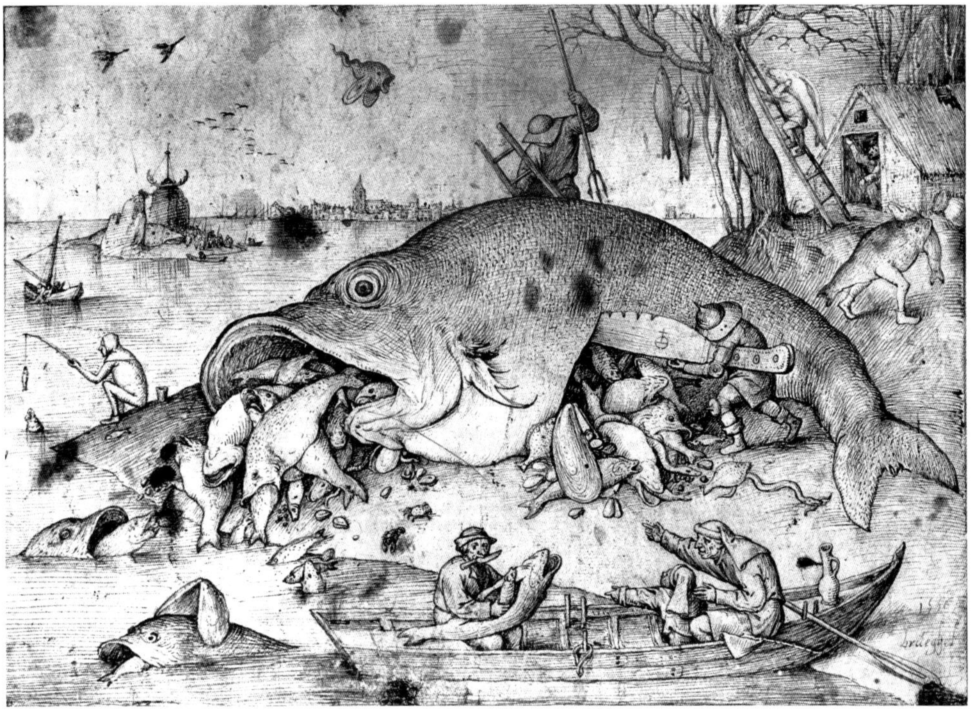

68 Pieter Bruegel the Elder, *Big Fish Eat Little Fish*, 1556, pen and brush, and gray and black ink, Graphische Sammlung Albertina, Vienna

Bruegel's distinctively subtle line, the great fish looks more down-to-earth, and therefore more weirdly plausible, than it does in the print. It is not impossible that Bruegel sketched from a lost work by Bosch, translating it into a drawing to assist its transfer to the copperplate. Far more probable, though, the invention is Bruegel's and the attribution to Bosch the publisher's fabrication. Launched as a "phantom copy" of a nonexistent Bosch, the print would have been intended to appeal to—and perhaps to fool—knowledgeable art collectors, who held the 's-Hertogenbosch master in high esteem. For in 1557, Bruegel was a relative unknown, with only the *Large Landscapes* series published under his name, and his other Bosch-like design—the engraved *Temptation of Saint Anthony* of 1556, made after a signed pen-and-brush drawing now in the Ashmolean Museum in Oxford—bearing no signature except Cock's (see fig. 252).[17]

This situation would soon change. By the time of his death, in 1569, through his Shakespearean capacity to make his sources seem trivial, Bruegel had come to occupy a position similar to that held by Bosch in 1550. Drawings made in a belatedly Boschian style were now sometimes falsely signed with Bruegel's name, as Bosch's *Tree-Man* is.[18] In 1619, the Amsterdam printer Claes Jansz. Visscher published a reverse copy of *Big Fish Eat Little Fish* naming Bruegel as the inventor.[19] This restoration of the later master's authorship bespeaks the increasingly nuanced picture of the northern artistic tradition that emerged after the founding of the Dutch Republic. But it may be that Cock's engraving is already more historically subtle than modern commentators have allowed. Just a decade after its publication, inspired by Vasari's example, Lampsonius commenced his research on the lives and characters of early Netherlandish painters. And already, according to him, Bruegel imitated and surpassed the "dreams" of Bosch, now for the purpose of laughter.[20] The engraving's false mark of authorship may have agonistic intent, trumpeting the quality of an imitation—or emulation—that artistically outstrips and transforms its venerated model.[21]

Over time, the line between these two painters started again to blur. Where Bosch's legacy dominated, most notably in Spain, paintings by Bruegel continued to be misattributed to

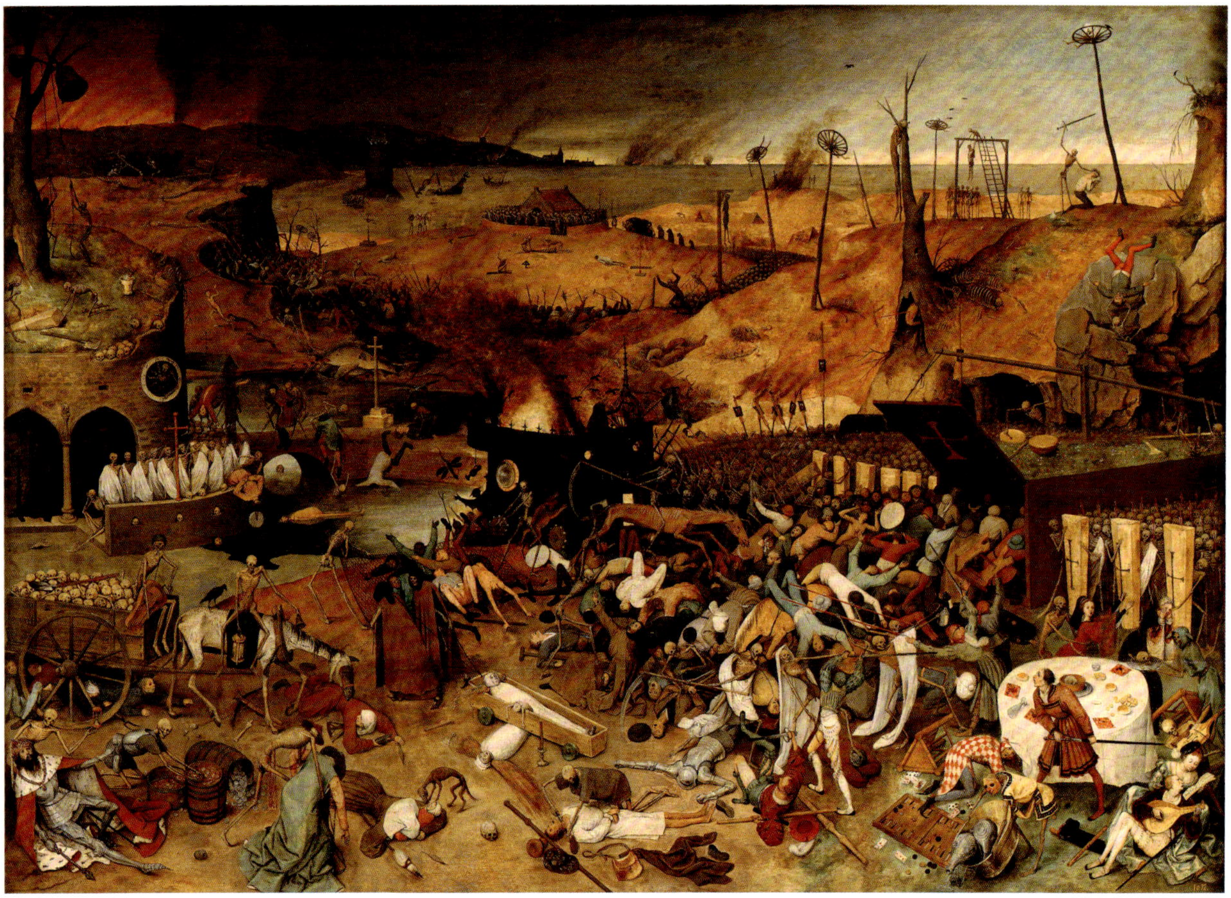

69 Pieter Bruegel the Elder, *The Triumph of Death*, c. 1562, panel, Museo Nacional del Prado, Madrid

the earlier master. Bedazzled by its peerless Bosch holdings, perhaps, the Museo del Prado considered its one Bruegel—the unsigned *Triumph of Death*—to be yet another Bosch; in the nineteenth century's standard art-reference book, this masterpiece was listed among Bosch's works (fig. 69).[22] Likewise, *The Fall of the Rebel Angels*, acquired by the Royal Museums of fine Arts, in Brussels, in 1846, was attributed to Bosch until just after 1900, when Bruegel's signature came to light, hidden under the frame (fig. 70).[23] In this work—his most self-consciously Boschian painting—Bruegel magnifies the tiny, airy passage in the Vienna *Last Judgment* where, over Eden, Bosch depicted the archangel Michael casting Lucifer's minions from heaven (fig. 71).[24] This imitation may have had a further, polemical edge. Bruegel's painting invites comparison to one of the most admired creations of its day, a *Fall of the Rebel Angels* painted by Frans Floris in 1554 for an altar in the Antwerp cathedral (fig. 72).[25] An ambitious devotee of the art of Michelangelo, Floris attempted to rival in a panel painting what the Italian master achieved in fresco in the Sistine Chapel. Filling nearly seventy square feet with struggling, muscular, naked flesh, Floris vies with Michelangelo's spectacle by limiting the scope of his painting to one area of his rival's *Last Judgment*, rather as Bruegel does with Bosch's triptych. Bruegel enters not one contest but two. He challenges Bosch, his great original, by realizing that earlier master's demonic hosts more concretely—and more mockingly—in paint. And he challenges the idealizing grandeur of painter colleagues nearby, such as Floris, whose work suddenly seems stilted by comparison. Within this contemporary rivalry, Bosch functions as an alternative filiation to the Italian lineage sought by most of Bruegel's Antwerp competitors. Affirmed by drawings and prints like *Big Fish Eat Little*

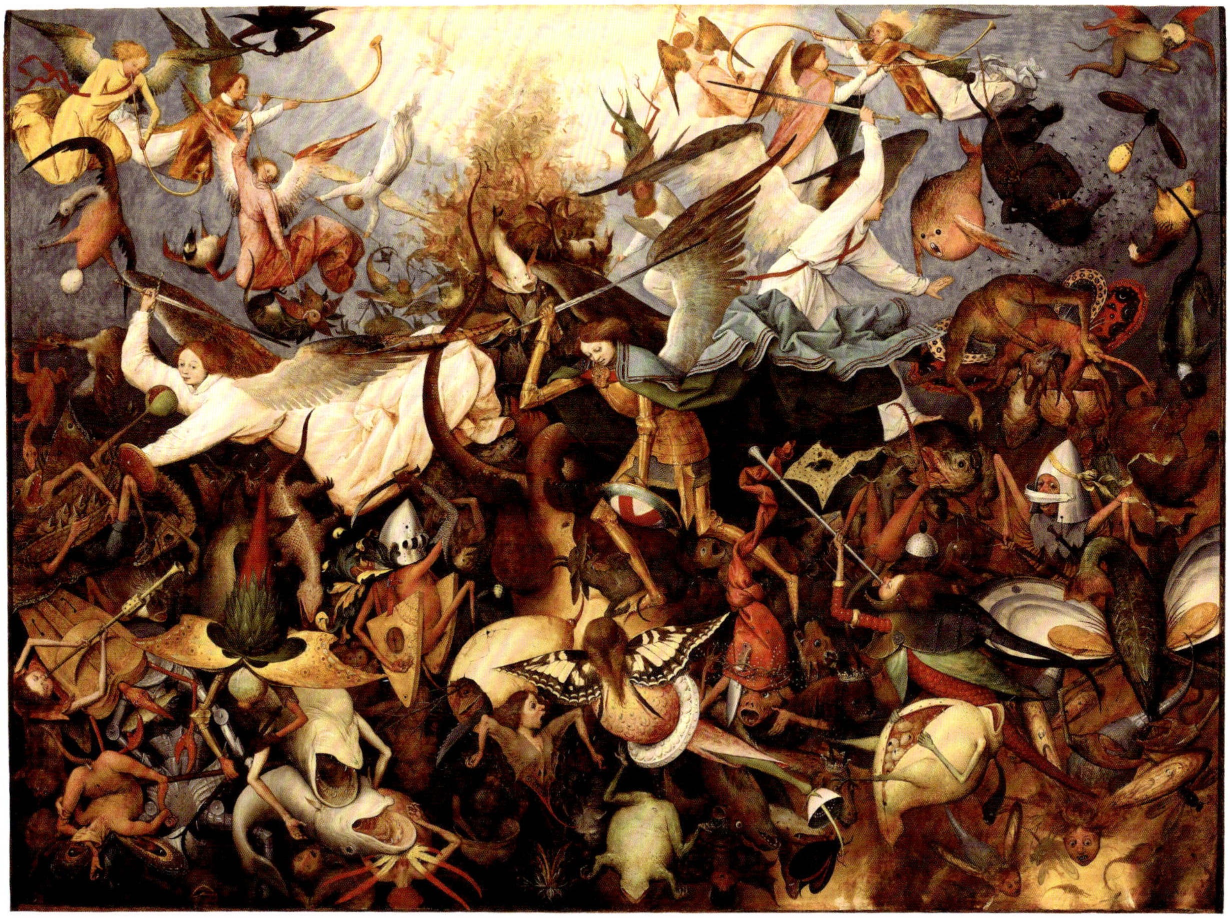

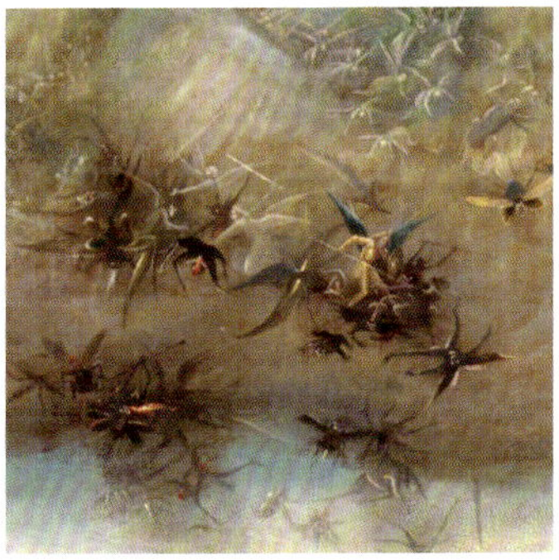

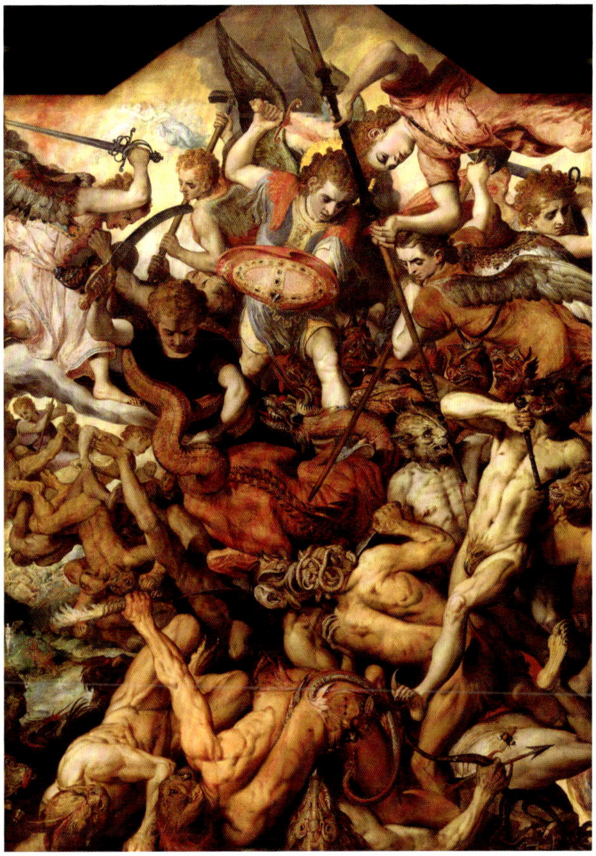

(ABOVE) **70** Pieter Bruegel the Elder, *Fall of the Rebel Angels*, c. 1562, panel, Musées Royaux des Beaux-Arts de Belgique, Brussels

(FAR LEFT) **71** Detail of Hieronymus Bosch, *The Last Judgment* (fig. 47)

(LEFT) **72** Frans Floris I, *Fall of the Rebel Angels*, 1554, panel, Koninklijk Museum voor Schone Kunsten, Antwerp

Let us pause to reflect on this "type" by considering individually the words that describe it. First, it is a painting of *life*, of what living things do. Implicitly, that subject is always human: life as what people do. That which is humanly lived transcends biological processes and physical behavior. It includes a shifting focus of consciousness that surrounds the living like a "nomad's tent."[37] Bosch gave this focus visual form in his portrait of the peddler (see fig. 37). Life is the mobile passage through time and space; it will end, if not now then certainly farther on, since to live means also to die. But in the midst of transit, there remains a point of focus—progressing forward but restlessly turned back toward the past—where the peddler's own lived experience would unfold. Such experience is elusive both to others and to the self; it is a Heraclitean stream, like the waters that flow between us and the striding peasant in Bruegel's Vienna panel (see fig. 4). In *The Hay Wain*'s closed and open states, Bosch both displays and explains this fundamental elusiveness. He dramatizes how life eludes the living, who can never quite "have" life but get twisted up in, and defeated by, their efforts to do so, as the traveling peddler does gazing rearward, oblivious to present perils and pleasures, and as the entire assembled humanity does grasping at straws (see fig. 39). In human life, the world vanishes at the touch. A painting *of* life must therefore express that vanishing—thus genre painting's predilection for absorptive actions creating ephemeral things, like bubble blowing, smoking, and building houses out of cards (see fig. 250).[38]

Irreducible to physical actions, human life encompasses more than an inner experience, being also social through and through. An old German term for genre paintings is *Sittenbilder*, meaning images (*Bilder*) of habits, customs, and mores (*Sitten*). Attention to the particulars of custom and to human life runs throughout the genre tradition. It is especially evident in Bruegel, whose *Battle between Carnival and Lent* constitutes a veritable atlas of his own culture's local usages (see fig. 284). This has made him the perfect subject for the social history of art. But Bruegel's genius lay in his ability to show life in the chiaroscuro of its specific (or social and historical) as well as its universal (or natural) forms. The usages he catalogued may be hyperbolically local, hence the challenge they pose to modern viewers, but compared with the rapidly changing culture of modern life, which Bruegel and his patrons were among the first to experience in their urban milieu, popular customs are also peculiarly enduring; village existence is a kind of living antiquity, an enclave of timelessness discoverable just beyond the city walls. Bruegel achieves his ambition of discovering a humanity underlying local, time-bound customs, for otherwise the strange would not become the familiar, as it does when an enigma like *The Peasant and the Bird Thief* can cause us to say, five centuries after its making, "This is what human life is like."[39]

Second, the life that such a painting captures is an *everyday* one. Genre painters pursue neither the private epiphany of lived experience (or *Erlebnis*) nor the singular actions that change the world but rather the routine, often mindless, and inconsequential acts of life, gestures as anonymous as the persons shown doing them.[40] That nothing follows from these actions—that the world remains as it was—befits also the marked presentism of this art. Whereas *le grand genre*, to depict an occurrence that made history, projects itself back into the past (if also the perennially meaningful one of antiquity), genre remains in the present tense of its own lifeworld.[41] "Observed with the unspoken thought: 'This is how it always is,'" wrote Max J. Friedländer, "the event becomes a genre-picture; observed with the knowledge that 'it was like that at one particular time and place,' it becomes an historical picture."[42] This perhaps explains the attraction that popular festivals had for artists of the period. On special days of the year, everyday human activities—eating, drinking, sleeping, lovemaking—become ritually exaggerated while remaining ordinary nonetheless. In peasant revels, Bruegel finds everyday life already choreographed into humble, vernacular, living tableaux: the familiar ordinarily displayed. By letting ordinary people make the selection, Bruegel evades the difficult task of singling out which everyday action to depict. For in theory, any inconsequential human doing could serve as a genre subject, but in practice the repertoire remains fairly limited and grows more fixed over time. In the seventeenth century, the painting of everyday life becomes itself routine as certain genres of genre arise: merry companies, guardroom pieces, fighting peasants, and amorous trysts.[43] But earlier, when the repertoire was in formation, subject matter remained more mutable and alive. Before there was *a* painting of everyday life, there were only these certain paintings.

Third, it matters that everyday life finds expression *in painting*—i.e., that it stands pictured in this isolating framework of display, this material support. Genre painting emerges with the rise of the autonomous gallery picture—French *le tableau*, German *das Gemälde*.[44] Serving new forms of display, viewing, collecting, and appreciation, and engendering new artistic processes, strategies, and aims, the painted tableau as a type of crafted object is both a precondition and a consequence of genre painting.[45] In our case, it is therefore crucial that we consider not only what Bruegel and Bosch paint but also how they paint.

The Parallel

Beyond their shared repertoire, these two painters cultivate a similar pictorial gestalt. Both construct vast ground planes that, viewed from on high, from a bird's-eye point of view, rise steeply to a tiny strip of sky just below the picture's upper framing edge. Both fill these dizzying spaces with a seemingly endless array of mesmerizing details. Smoothly distributed in space despite their own erratic shapes, and punctuating even the farthest distances, these details convey the idea that, were we to travel to the picture's horizon, they would be there too in equal profusion, as they would be again at the horizon after that, and so on into infinity. Both artists, in other words, captivate and overload our sense of sight, entangling the eye in anomalous objects, actors, and activities, and ensnaring the mind's eye in enigmas and seeming secrets that arouse but never satisfy interpretative curiosity.

Not surprisingly, both artists have elicited a rich body of delusional scholarship. What was intended as a puzzle gets transformed into an esoteric code that, deciphered, explains everything. Rejected by most professional scholars, elaborate theories about the "secret heresy" of Bosch and of Bruegel inoculate their proponents against the criticism that greets them by dividing the world between initiates and persecuting outsiders.[46] Yet in spite of the puzzles they invent and the paranoid fantasies they kindle, both artists start and finish beyond enigma, in the way these paintings wink at us with their deeply familiar humanity.

As painters, in the way they work with paint, both sketch nimbly with their brush, enlivening their fictions with the visible action of their making. Applying pigments thinly, so that the light ground on which they paint remains visible, both make their painted worlds seem subtly insubstantial—groundless even—and lit magically from within. This shared technique, as well as the visual impression it imparted to the painting, was keenly observed by Karel van Mander. Bosch, Van Mander reports, "usually finish[ed] his works in one layer. . . . Draw[ing] his subject onto the white of the panel, layering over that a transparent, flesh-colored ground layer; he often allowed the ground to contribute to the effect of the picture."[47] Elsewhere Van Mander describes Bruegel in the same way. He too painted with swift movements of the brush, "allowing the preparation on the panels or canvases to play a part."[48] We will see later how this distinctive painterly procedure, which grounds the painted fiction on the abyss of human facture, profoundly affects the meaning of their pictures.

However we understand their artistry, both painters are eminently popular figures. In museums that own one, you can spot a Bosch or Bruegel by the crowds it attracts. More so than any painter before them, they erased the barrier between art and life. Their celebrity, it is true, abated dramatically during the eighteenth and nineteenth centuries, due to the biases of academic art criticism and to the proliferation of third-rate copies and imitations.[49] But they remained hugely popular long after their deaths, and even when their fame receded, their influence did not. Through his sons, Pieter Breughel the Younger and Jan Brueghel the Elder, and these painters' many Flemish and Dutch followers, Bruegel remained a decisive force. Bruegel's and Bosch's rehabilitation began around the time when photography and modernism extinguished genre painting's lingering flame. Prior to its demise, the tradition that these two painters launched was understood as having progressed beyond their original achievement. In his lectures on genre painting, Burckhardt said of Bruegel: "In painterly terms, he is mostly marginal; in composition, indifferent and distracted; in forms, unbearably coarse; in colors—though often lush and bright—mottled and hard. In all of this he stands well behind a number of better Netherlandish contemporaries."[50] Only when the technical capability of nineteenth-century genre painting came to be seen as a vice (and when connoisseurship began to sort out their authentic oeuvres) did the virtues of the founders become apparent.

Bosch's and Bruegel's renewed popularity obscured something else that these two masters shared. Both enjoyed the most elite patronage of their day. Like his painter forefathers in 's-Hertogenbosch, Bosch established his career by making altarpieces and decorations for local churches. But an advantageous marriage, membership in a prestigious religious confraternity with international ties, and special talent publicly on display in his hometown's great church brought him to the attention of members of the Burgundian court, who commissioned ambitious works not for their churches and chapels but for their art collections. Historically, the Burgundian rulers were among the first to place the art of painting at the heart of their collecting endeavors, and paintings by Bosch formed the core of this nascent practice from which the European museum was born.[51] After his death, Bosch's fame continued to grow. Replicated, imitated, and fraudulently forged, his works became the jewel in the crown of the Spanish Habsburg treasury. Bruegel's oeuvre, for its part, is split between his prints, intended for a wide, international public, and his paintings, made for high-ranking patricians and coveted by famous humanists. After his death, Bruegel's paintings were so avidly collected by the emperor Rudolf II that (according to the artist's son Jan) none could be had for any price.[52] The Bruegels in Vienna, while preserving the customs of the lower orders, are now totem objects of old Europe.

Such astonishing prestige is matched in both artists by an unusual degree of artistic self-assertion. With the important exception of Jan van Eyck, no early Netherlandish painter signed his works as often and as prominently as Bosch, and in the Burgundian inventories Bosch is alone in being listed with his full, Latinized name.[53] And while, unlike Van Eyck and in marked

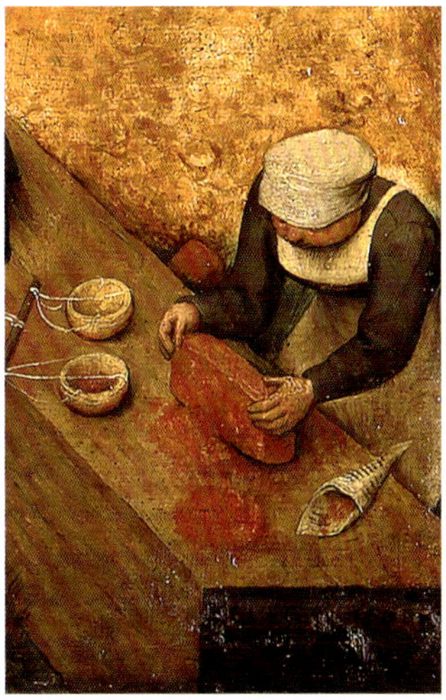

74 Detail of Pieter Bruegel the Elder, *The Children's Games* (fig. 294)

contrast to Dürer, Bosch produced no autonomous self-portraits, his art makes selfhood its dark center. Turning the tables on the viewer, making the beholder the subject of the painting's all-seeing gaze, Bosch magnifies the self's demands, exposing its pride and displaying and repudiating its works, including those created and signed by the artist himself. In several of his most cryptic images, that name, Bosch—which in Dutch means "wood" or "forest"—comes to stand for selfhood as an entropic creativity allied with the dark, sylvan forces of nature and in rebellion against the true Creator, God, as we shall see (see figs. 232, 236, and 246). Most of Bruegel's works are signed and dated, even if the prints made after them are not. While this fabricator deposits his signature discreetly in his fabrications, burying it in the ground under winter snow (see fig. 314), these subtle marks are often saliently placed, as on the chiseled block belonging to Babel's ill-fabricated tower (see fig. 279), or, in *The Children's Games*, just beneath a girl scraping dust from a clay-constructed brick as if playfully grinding the pigment from which the painting is made (fig. 74). Bruegel plays games with the mysteries of making: of what humans make and what makes humans, ashes to ashes, dust to dust.

The Divergence

Despite these kinships, moving from Bosch to Bruegel feels like passing from one world to another. Where they stand closest together, they seem most distinct. No one makes Bosch seem more historically remote than does Bruegel. In Bruegel, the certitudes of divine law transform into the incertitude of being human. In him, the Devil becomes a culturally situated fiction observed from an ethnographic remove, while genuine evil flourishes in the activity of ordinary people. In Bosch, a diabolical enemy at war with God threatens humanity always and everywhere. In Bruegel, it is the human in its comically local incarnations that is ubiquitous, and (to borrow a phrase from Carl Schmitt) "no one is against man except man himself."[54] It is tempting to describe this difference in terms of a great historical divide. Although considered modish in his day, Bosch is today often regarded as the last painter of the Middle Ages, in whom the absolutes of medieval Christian belief still hold, while Bruegel seems the new beginning, the skeptical visionary of the modern age. With one, all is prejudice, superstition, and xenophobic enmity against enemies both real and imagined. With the other begins tolerance of differences and the fateful disenchantment of the world that separates magical fetishes into mere fiction and brute fact.

And certainly the *things* that Bosch and Bruegel fabricate served different functions. Bosch's art emerges from an anonymous guild tradition of making sacred images. Some of his images pioneer new, worldly functions, yet their touchstone remains the Christian cult, hence Bosch's predilection for the winged triptych, a format with roots in devotion to relics and in the altar rite. Bruegel's activities begin in the secular medium of print and culminate in autonomous gallery pictures: not a single altarpiece by him survives.[55] His works are quintessentially of and for the world: global compendia of nature, culture, and history. No wonder his closest associate was Ortelius, maker of the first modern atlas! Certainly, too, enough changed between Bosch and Bruegel to warrant thinking in terms of epochs: in religion, the Reformation; in the economy, a massive globalization of trade; in politics, the creation of absolutist states and the dawn of the idea of individual freedom and conscience; in science, the arts, and letters, not just new communiqués but novel forms of communication through reproductive technology.

My title for this Introduction, "Parallel Worlds," signals the fictive universes that these two artists marvelously fabricate. With reference to humanistic art criticism of their own time, I acknowledged Bosch and Bruegel as world makers in the medium of paint. "Parallel Worlds" also names the different world pictures to which each of these masters holds. So basic is the distinction between Bosch and Bruegel, and so insuperably opposed are these painters' aims, that—it seems to me—they occupy separate worlds. The ancient author Plutarch arranged his lives of famous men in parallels. Setting each portrait of a noble Greek against that of a Roman notable, Plutarch distilled the virtues of each while also registering the unbridgeable distance between the present and the past. In the synthetic comparisons that conclude each parallel, Plutarch demonstrated that, whereas the likeness between different lives might be easily perceived, the points of difference are harder to assemble, as they involve moral fundamentals often bound up with distinct conceptions of law.[56]

Along similar lines, I have tried to place Bosch and Bruegel side by side, illuminating the one through his proximity to, and difference from, the other. But I also make an argument about artistic genealogy: how the history of art passed *from* Bosch *to* Bruegel, and—further—how a new form of painting devoted to ordinary life could begin with something altogether *un*ordinary: a metaphysical struggle, waged through the medium of painted images, against the Old Enemy, Satan.

More than any of his Netherlandish predecessors or contemporaries, Bosch is a didactic artist. His paintings—even ones that originally served a ritual purpose—teach a lesson: the world is sinful, an enemy territory that should be held in contempt. Some of his paintings teach this lesson by depicting sacred exemplars of this contempt, most crucially the hermit saints Jerome and Anthony (his and his father's namesakes, respectively), who turn away from the pleasures of the world to faith in Christ. In other paintings (most obviously *The Hay Wain*), Bosch teaches contempt for the world by showing the rest of humanity sinfully enthralled by the world and at the brink of judgment and damnation.

To picture this sinful love and its consequences, Bosch painted *world* in new and compelling ways, both as landscape and as everyday human life. Formative of future genre painting, such depictions were framed negatively, as a devilish illusion. Representations of everyday life and of Satan thus went hand in hand. Bosch's intimate and quotidian depiction of devilry would cause him to seem himself in league with the enemy. The rich literary afterlife of Bosch in Spain will attest to this suspicion. The proximity between Bosch's artistry and the devilish world was also heightened by the artist's own awareness that artworks, through their value and visual allure, could themselves be idolatrous, and that making and owning them (whatever moral they preach) might be morally dubious.

Bosch painted on the eve of Protestant iconoclasm, when images would be physically punished and destroyed as if human enemies. He therefore played a potentially dangerous game. In most cases, he simply painted enemies as players within some larger spectacle. They are the forces, whether human and diabolical, that assault Christ, the saints, and the Christian self. But in one special case Bosch fabricated something much more global and elusive: an *enemy painting*. In it the idols that this painter elsewhere deposits within the landscapes and edifices where spiritual struggle take place have taken over the world. Not only that, these abject semblances have so overtaken the visual field that the painting itself becomes potentially an idol.

Bosch knew exactly what he was doing. Through a play of words and symbols he constructed "Hieronymus Bosch" as an artistic persona that associated his activity with the evil and entropic world he depicts. By way of its various verbal connotations, his chosen name deliberately evoked ideas of sylvan obscurity, unruly matter, and metaphysical evil. And in his ink drawings, he filled out his persona as enemy painter with plots and imagery concerned with the human self. While strange to us today, this self-mortifying gesture was shared by a number of other major Renaissance artists who, like Bosch, dared to claim originality within a culture that, for centuries, held creativity to be solely an attribute of God and condemned novelty as a pernicious affront to divine creation.

Enemy painting had a purpose beyond simply the depiction of enemies (Satan, devils, heretics, ethnically suspect groups, the alluring world itself), beyond also the perilously playful fashioning of malignant artistic self. It had a political function, as well: that of fostering a wide-ranging but serviceable enmity between a victimized "us" and an aggressively hostile if secretive "them." Nebulous in its identity, but—through Bosch's pictorial power—visually concrete, this postulated enemy could be conveniently mobilized to arouse enmity toward lesser enemies (e.g., the outsider, the poor, the neighbor), thus befitting viewers of the type documented as Bosch's chief clientele: powerful overlords seeking to manage forces resisting their rule, often through the imposition in their territories of legal states of exception.

Bruegel reverses this movement (figs. 75 and 76). Instead of revealing the Devil lurking behind the mask, he shows him to be a humanly fabricated mask. The horror remains, but it becomes the abyss of a humanity caught precisely in the vicious circle of hate. The divide between friend and enemy as the ultimate distinction gives way, in Bruegel, to a refusal of such absolutes. Bosch's fundamentalism itself becomes Bruegel's foe, just as Bruegel's brand of humanism would probably have been inimical to Bosch. Bruegel's first admirers registered this change. Both Lampsonius and Van Mander picture Bosch haunted by his dreams, whereas Bruegel they present as imitating those dreams, but as a source of laughter, not terror.

And yet, Bruegel's vision of the human world as the product of culture—his verdict, anathema to a Christian anthropology grounded in original sin, that no one is against man except

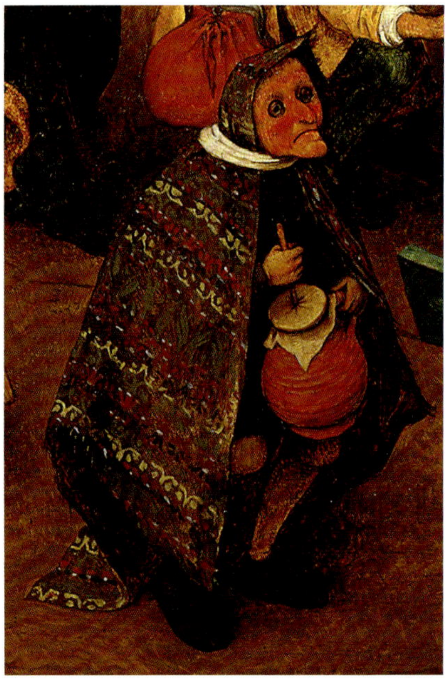

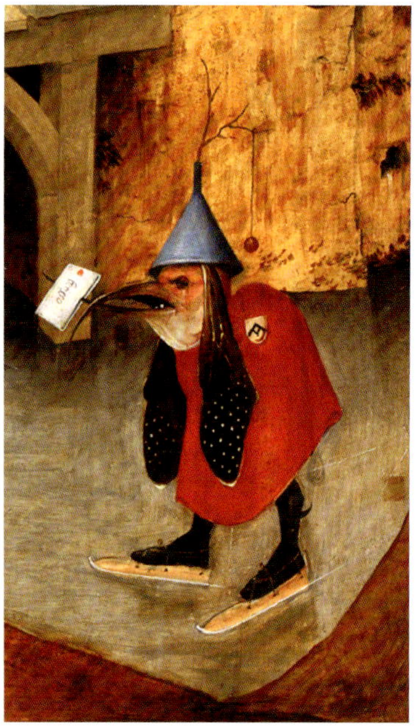

(LEFT) 75 Detail of Pieter Bruegel the Elder, *Battle between Carnival and Lent* (fig. 284)

(RIGHT) 76 Detail of Hieronymus Bosch, *Temptation of Saint Anthony* (fig. 138)

man himself—evolved from a center he shared with Bosch. Both artists were intensely aware of their powers of making. In how and what they painted, both paraded the fact that humans do not merely imitate nature; they create another nature, a parallel world. Whether they vilified or celebrated it, they both exercised this supreme and uniquely human capacity: the power of poiesis. Through the delight it shares in its own making, a new painting of everyday life arose out of its antithesis. Out of pictures of a world that never was or ever could be emerged the modern world picture.

PART I

Hieronymus Bosch

5

ENMITY

Disparities

Bosch achieved early fame as the master of oddities. Some decades after his death, in 1516, when—first in Italy, then in the north—people began writing about the lives of notable painters, the artist born Jheronimus van Aken went down as a baffling singularity, a maker of pictorial anomalies who himself did not fit. Guicciardini called Bosch "the most noble and admirable inventor of things fantastical and bizarre."[1] Several years later Vasari, in the second edition of his *Lives* (1568), praised the painter's "fantastic and capricious inventions."[2] These early authors never say wherein such inventions exactly consist, but they are easy to spot. One appears in the background of an early-seventeenth-century portrait etching of Bosch (fig. 77).[3] Published by Hendrick Hondius, the likeness belongs to the same series as the Bruegel portrait we looked at earlier (see fig. 8), and similarly elaborates an original print by Lampsonius (see fig. 61). The creepy airborne monster, part reptilian but unearthly overall, stares out at us with beady eyes as he rockets upward, his lower orifice licked by flames of another monster's torch.

Bosch built his monsters to look like organisms, which is to say, like contiguous systems endowed with a certain independent life. Eerily energetic, they seem up to no good, unless, fallen into lethargy, they loiter maliciously about. Scaled up to huge proportions, they can form part of the natural setting, as grotesque, semi-animate structures within which other more mobile monsters might lurk. In the portrait etching, to the right of the sitter's head, what looks to be a colossal seedpod encloses a cluster of unfortunates. Sprouting a face and limbs, and resembling also a molluscan shell or arthropodal chela, this quasi thing—too multiple to be grasped *as* one thing—nonetheless plausibly coheres as contiguous tissue animated by some malignant intent. Guicciardini termed Bosch the *inventore* of such things. To preserve and clarify that title, Guicciardini's German translator in 1580 doubled it up, calling Bosch "the renowned Inventor and originator [*Inuentor vnnd erfinder*] of wondrously strange things."[4] By this the translator meant to indicate that the artist did not merely contrive this or that fantastical entity; rather, he invented an entirely new species per se. The etching's seedpod-*cum*-bivalve-*cum*-claw pays homage to this achievement. Paradoxically, what characterizes this novel artistic type is that it escapes being typed. Each instance is different from the next, and all diverge markedly from species found in nature.

(OPPOSITE) 77 Hendrik Hondius, *Portrait of Bosch*, from Hendrik Hondius, *Pictorum aliquot celebrium praecipuè Germaniae Inferioris effigies*, 1610, engraving, 532.99.455, Houghton Library, Harvard University

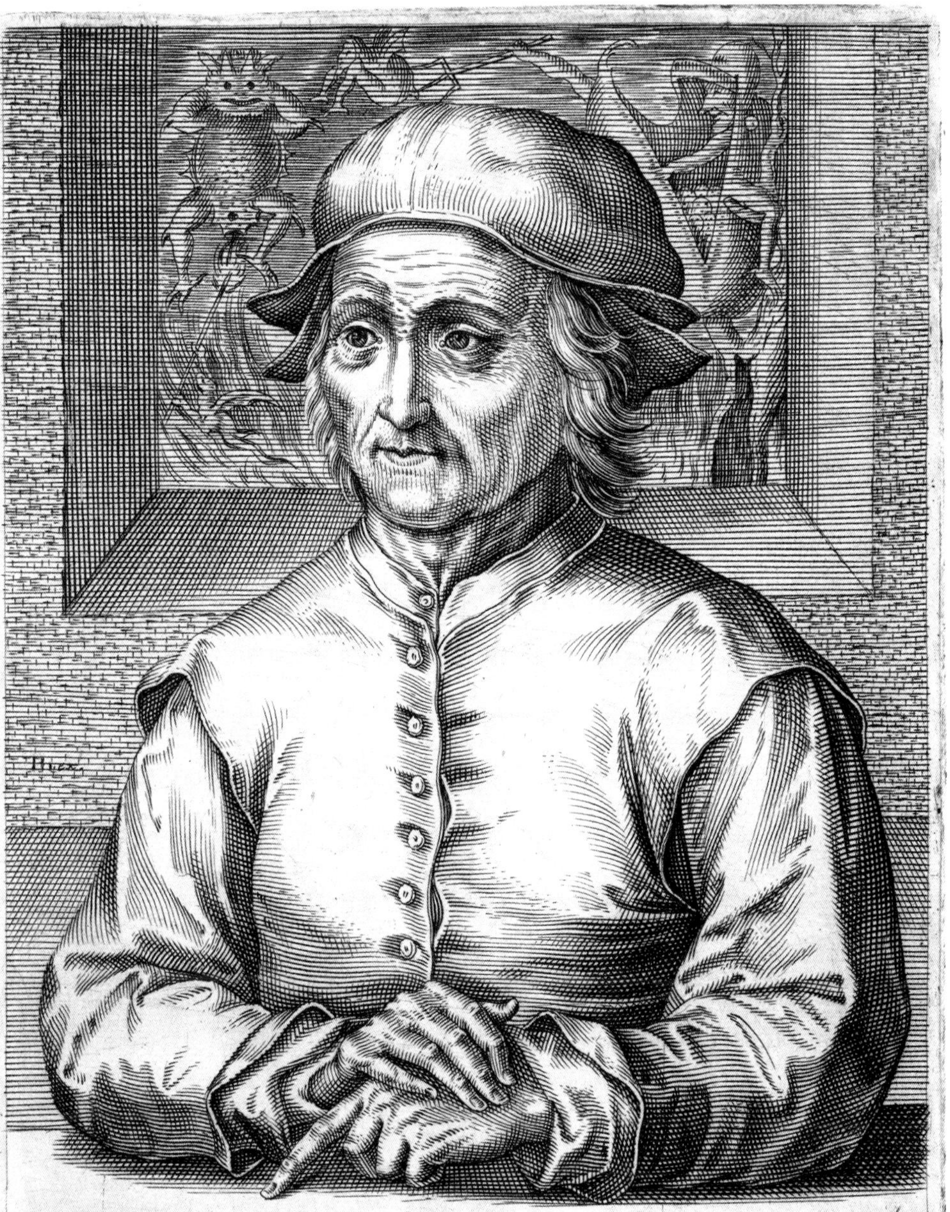

HIERONIMO BOSCHIO PICTORI.

Quid sibi vult, Hironijme Boschi,
Ille oculus tuus attonitus? quid
Pallor in ore? velut lemures si
Spectra Erebi volitantia corã
Aspiceres? Tibi Ditis auari
Crediderim patuisse recessus
Tartareasque domos tua quaudo
Quicquid habet sinus imus Auerni
Tam potuit bene pingere dextra.

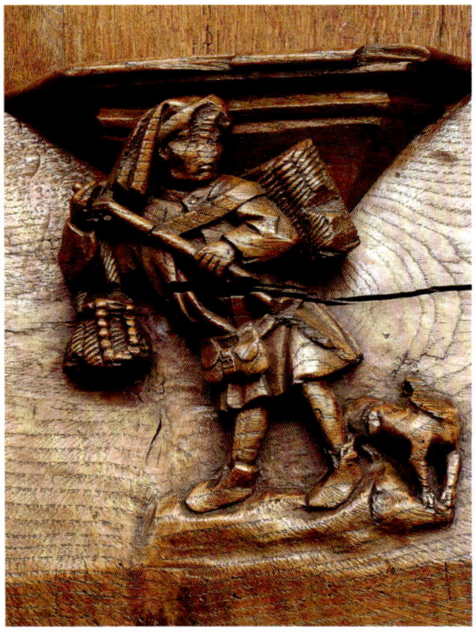

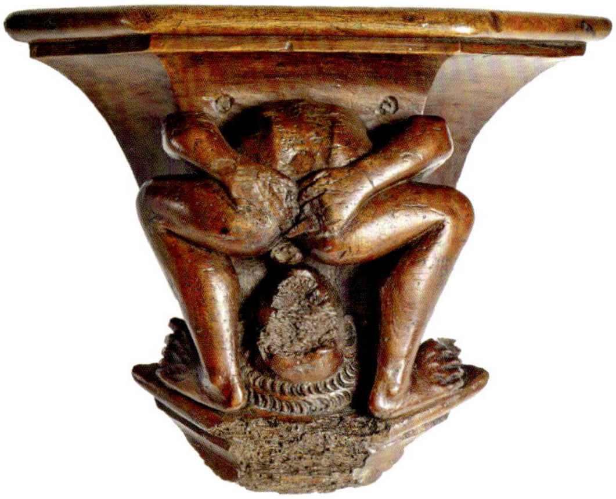

(LEFT) 78 Anonymous Brabant, *Peddler with Dog*, c. 1480, oak misericord, Stichting Grote Kerk, Breda

(RIGHT) 79 Anonymous Swiss, *Exhibitionistic Acrobat*, 1445–47, defaced 1535, wood misericord from a choir stall, Musée d'art et d'histoire, Franciscan Church, Geneva

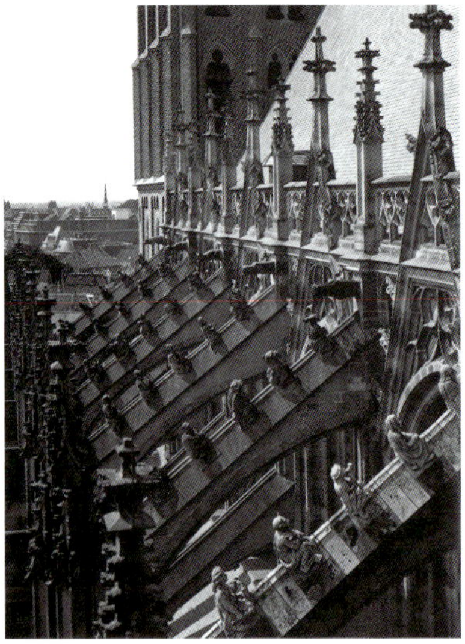

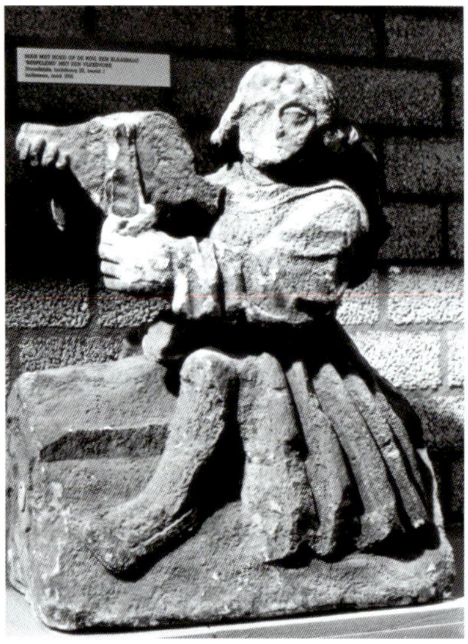

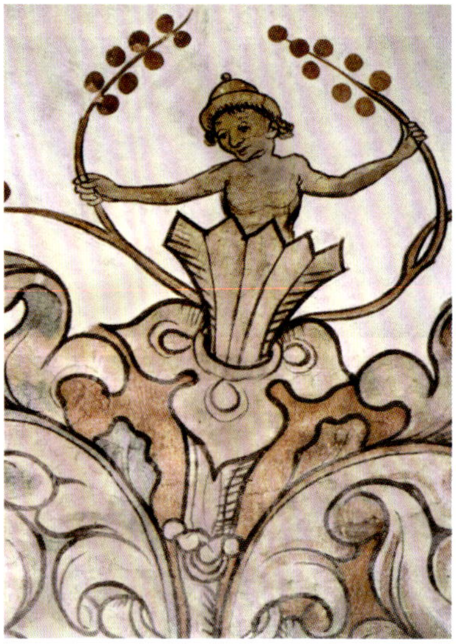

(LEFT) 80 Flying buttresses, Sint-Janskathedraal, 's-Hertogenbosch

(CENTER) 81 Anonymous Netherlandish, *Man "Playing" the Bellows with a Meat Fork*, c. 1500, sandstone, figure 1 from third flying buttress, north side, Sint-Janskathedraal, 's-Hertogenbosch

(RIGHT) 82 Anonymous Netherlandish, *Figure in a Calyx*, c. 1515–20, wall painting, north transept vaulting, Sint-Janskathedraal, 's-Hertogenbosch

To be deemed an Inventor, capital *I*, a maker cannot simply imitate the given but must create something completely new. Bosch's monsters do have prototypes, however. At the borders of illuminated manuscripts, and in images tucked away in churches—tellingly on misericords ("mercy seats") on which, during long church services, lazy clerics could secretly rest their behinds—there flourished an impertinent imagery at odds with the sacred icons elsewhere displayed (figs. 78 and 79).[5] The Church of Saint John in Bosch's hometown of 's-Hertogenbosch veritably crawled with such drollery. On the building's original exterior, carved in stone, scores of monsters interspersed with artisans climbed the great flying buttresses, while inside, on the church's originally frescoed vaults and on the richly carved choir stalls, fantastical creatures abounded (figs. 80–84).[6] Much of this décor has been damaged, destroyed, painted over, or replaced by nineteenth-century replicas and imitations. But the original sculpted grotesques did intermingle with effigies of the church's builders: sculptors, painters, stonemasons. This programmatic pairing conforms to a peculiarly Boschian association of human making with counternatural monstrosity.

Like the ones Bosch fabricated, and created at around the same time, such monsters consisted largely of natural parts that, individually, exist somewhere in nature but that do not

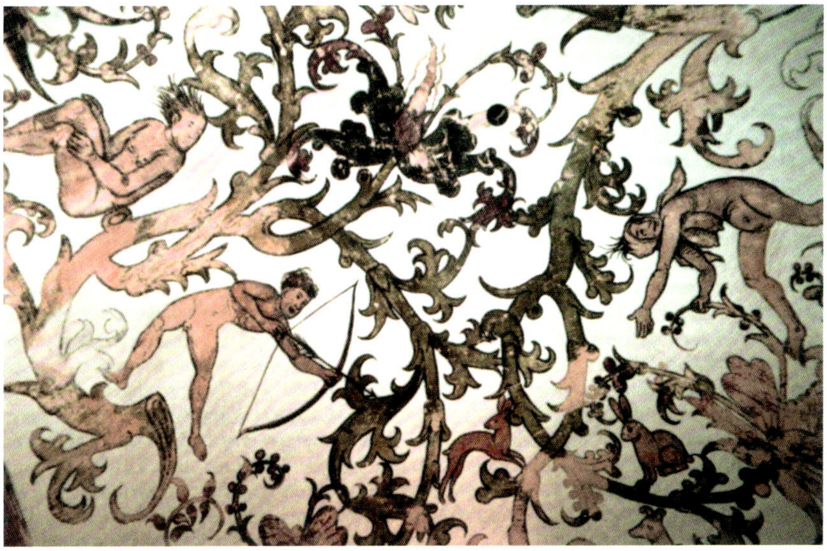

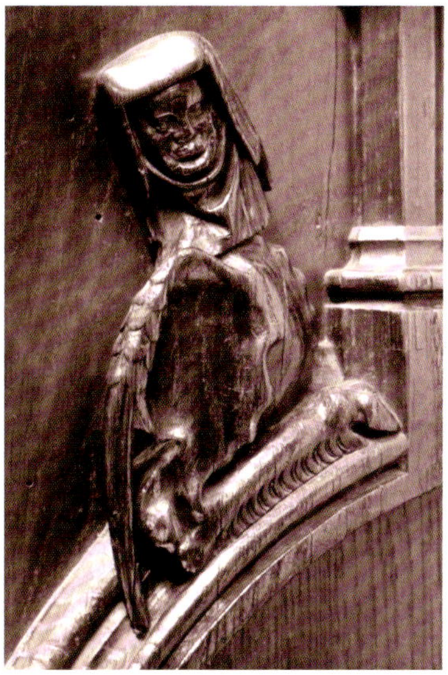

(LEFT) 83 Anonymous Netherlandish, *Seated Figure, Archer, and Witch*, c. 1522, wall painting, nave vaulting, Sint-Janskathedraal, 's-Hertogenbosch

(RIGHT) 84 Anonymous Netherlandish, *Winged Monster with a Woman's Head*, 1430–50, wood carving from the choir stalls, Sint-Janskathedraal, 's-Hertogenbosch

naturally occur together: a bird's head on a frog's body, a ship and fish combined, a woman-bird-horse, and so forth. The cowering creature that Bosch himself drew upon a sheet of paper now kept in Berlin consists of plausible elements implausibly combined: tail feathers that sprout like a springtail's propulsive furcula, feline head and limbs, a chelonian carapace for a back (see fig. 158).[7] Shown from behind and swiftly sketched, as if Bosch had captured its outlines before it could fight or flee, this nervous entity seems not a figment of the imagination but a fugitive creature observed and sketched from life. Hatching underneath its body conjures the shadow the creature would cast on the ground. With a few pen lines, Bosch makes his drawing surface disappear into a parallel world where such monsters could exist.[8]

From the impossibility of its conformation, though, this beast also announces that it is, in fact, a sheer concocted fantasy of the sort that made its artist famous. Toward the end of the sixteenth century in Spain, where they were most avidly admired and collected, Bosch's monstrosities earned a special name. In 1593, King Philip II shipped Bosch's most enigmatic masterpiece to the newly founded monastery of El Escorial, where it arrived with the following inventory description: "An oil painting, with two wings, of the variety of the world enciphered by diverse disparities [*con diuersos disparates*]" (see fig. 170).[9] The Spanish word derives from Latin *disparitas*. It indicates the character of Boschian nonreality. Locally and globally, this artist's creations seemed paired neither to nature nor to themselves, which put them in a class all their own. Indeed, to Spanish speakers today, the word *disparates* is virtually synonymous with the art of Hieronymus Bosch. The accented disparity between such monstrosities and the world derives from their coupling—counternaturally and often obscenely—with unpairable entities: "Nothing but devils, buttocks, and cod-pieces," as the poet Francisco de Quevedo put it in one of his Bosch-inspired literary diatribes.[10]

"When people see in a painting any monstrosity that goes beyond the limits of nature," wrote Felipe de Guevara, "they attribute them to Hieronymus Bosch and thus make him the inventor of monsters and chimeras."[11] This author should know. Born in Brussels around 1500 and resident there for more than thirty years, Felipe was the son of Diego de Guevara, who (as we have seen) led the powerful contingent of Spaniards in the Burgundian Netherlands. Diego probably acquired Bosch's works directly from the painter, perhaps through their shared

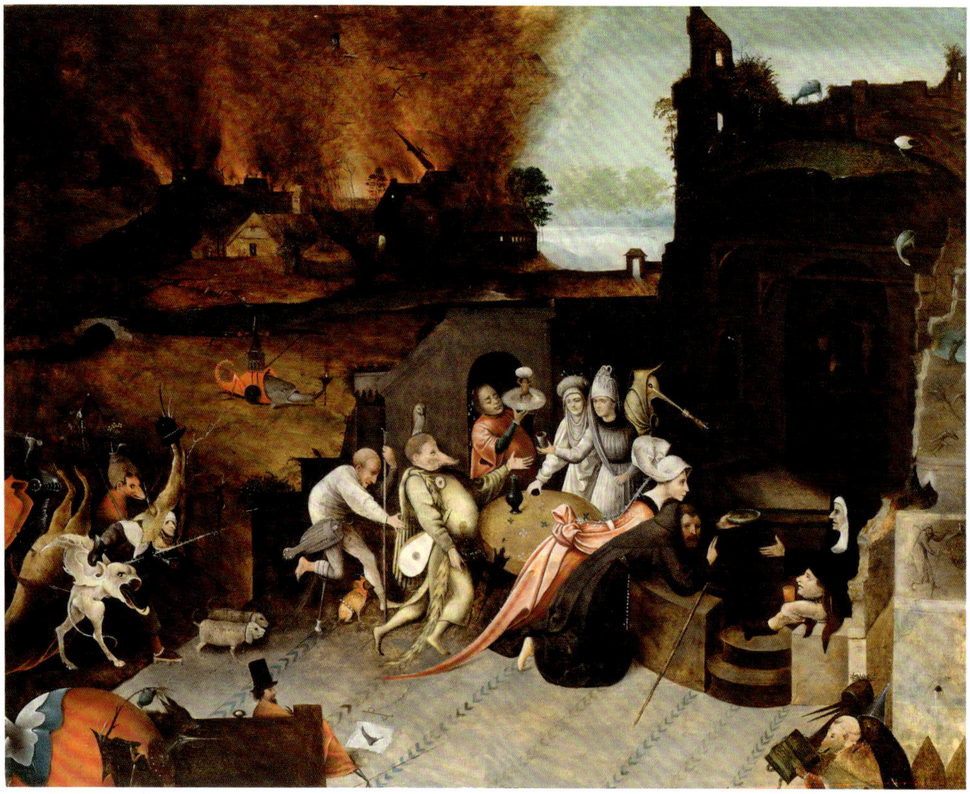

85 Anonymous Netherlandish after Hieronymus Bosch, *Temptation of Saint Anthony*, c. 1530–50, panel, Collectie Het Noordbrabants Museum, 's-Hertogenbosch, on loan from Rijksmuseum, Amsterdam

membership in the elite Brotherhood of Our Dear Lady of 's-Hertogenbosch. Felipe would have been about sixteen years old when Bosch died. Perhaps informed about the painter by his father, and possessing considerable classical and historical learning, Felipe is by far our most dependable early textual source. Composed shortly before his death in 1560, Felipe's statement takes the form of a lengthy digression in a series of brilliant commentaries on painting. Its spark is the question of the so-called *grillo* (cricket), a species of grotesque imagery purportedly invented by the Greek master Antiphilus. The statement's purpose was to refute the view, publicized around that time by Guicciardini, Vasari, and others, that Bosch was foremost a fantasist.

Guevara indicates that Bosch's name and the stereotype associated with it were well known already during the artist's lifetime. He informs us that other painters, observing Bosch's popular appeal, took to making monsters of their own, fraudulently adding the master's signature.[12] Inventories, shipment lists, and surviving artworks confirm this claim that Bosch was copied early and extensively, and often with spurious signatures (fig. 85).[13] The small core of accepted autograph paintings by Bosch, which continues to shrink from an original forty-five stated in most of the pre–World War II monographs, still includes masterpieces that, though signed "Jheronimus Bosch" and probably made in the artist's workshop, were likely by the hands of multiple talented assistants and collaborators, as we have seen.[14] But according to Guevara, there is one way to tell a real Bosch from a fake. Unlike his imitators, Bosch "never in his life painted anything unnatural, except"—and this is admittedly a big exception—when "he wanted to portray scenes in Hell, and for that subject matter it was necessary to depict devils and imagine them in unusual compositions."[15] Why this standard?

First, by insisting on Bosch's naturalism, Guevara confirms one important fact about the painter's oeuvre. A large proportion of the artist's output does consist of works of a traditional kind. Focused on the life of Christ, these may contain certain inscrutable enigmas and grotesque antagonists that fascinate art historians. But such dark spots remain the plausible symptoms of evil at work in the world. As a religious painter, Bosch endeavored to bring sacred events down to base earth, where, according to the Gospel, they in fact occurred. From his humble birth through the time of his torture and death at the hands of men, Christ suffered the world's indifference and hostility. Long before Bosch, a unique artistry—both literary and visual—of everyday life arose in the Christian West out of the effort to imagine vividly the great mystery of the Incarnation.[16] An inaugural master of secular genre, Bosch turned this traditional Christian focus on the low, humble, and humiliating circumstances of Christ's birth and death, the gruesome occurrences in the lives of the martyrs, and the specificity of individual punishment in hell toward the nontranscendent realm of mundane human life. Guevara owned the most programmatic surviving example of this secular turn. Described in his commentaries, the panel—which he termed a table—pictures the seven deadly sins as they are enacted in the everyday world (see fig. 122).[17] For Guevara, this painting resurrected the *ethike* of the Greeks, who had created pictures depicting the "habits and passions of the soul of man."[18]

Second, Guevara's claim that Bosch never painted "anything unnatural" captures the paradoxical realism of this artist's monstrosities. Bosch makes the impossible seem plausibly to occur. How he does this is hard to explain. As we will explore in the next chapter, it depends partly on his method of applying paint, which makes everything seem materially uncertain. And partly it hinges on certain narrative scenarios in which exceptions and deceptions become the norm. That Bosch makes impossibilities plausible, and that this is one of his signature accomplishments, is evidenced by modern connoisseurial practice. Art experts still attribute Boschian monsters to the master himself when those monsters look compellingly organic.[19] Conversely, imitations after Bosch are said to betray their dependency on the Bosch by looking like pastiches—locally, where individual monsters seem patently pieced together from different parts, and globally, where compositional elements, failing spatially or dramatically to cohere, appear randomly strewn across the surface of the painted panel or sketched page (fig. 86).[20]

The Devil Maker

But there is a third and deeper ground for Guevara's claim that Bosch is a great naturalist. Since antiquity, aesthetic theory has held that art imitates nature. Formulated by Plato and sharpened by Aristotle, this central doctrine about human making gained even greater force during the Christian era, when the concept of an omnipotent creator-god made rival creation morally and metaphysically suspect. If God made everything, the thinking goes, how could any of his creatures, in their productive activity, transcend mere imitation of what already is? Artistic novelty—the fabrication of something new—transgressed nature either sinfully or by error.[21]

Focusing his *Commentaries* on ancient art, Guevara would have been especially mindful of classical authors. These authors did describe such counternatural products as the *grilli* of Antiphilus, which gives Boschian novelties a prestigious antique pedigree. However, classical art theory mostly condemned such inventions as ridiculous and false. "Suppose a painter meant to attach a horse's neck to the head of a man," wrote the Latin poet Horace at the start of his canonical *Art of Poetry*, "and to put fancy-work of many-colored features on limbs of creatures picked at random; the kind of thing where the torso of a shapely maiden merges into

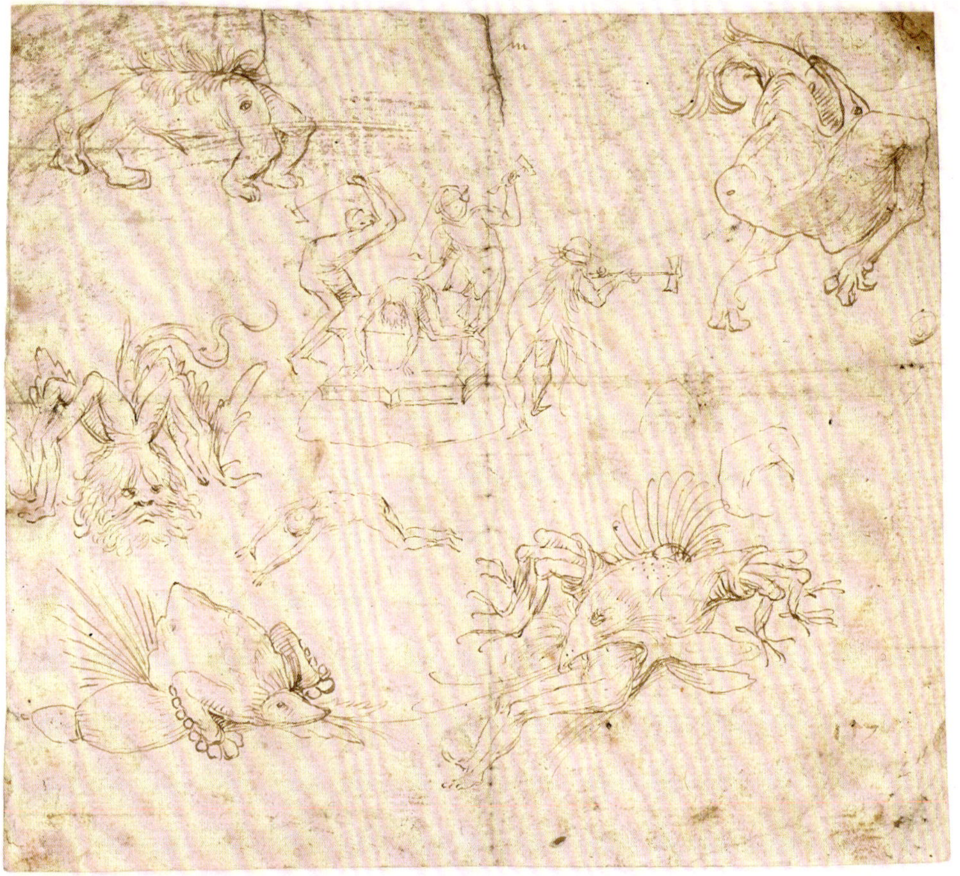

86 Hieronymus Bosch Workshop (?), *Five Fantastic Creatures and Figurative Scene,* c. 1515, pen and brown ink, Staatliche Museen zu Berlin, Kupferstichkabinett, Berlin

the dark rear of a fish; would you smother your amusement, my friends, if you were let in to see the result?"[22] Instead of laughing *with* these absurdities, as one might have been supposed to do, Horace asks his readers to laugh *at* them, scorning their trespass against the founding premise of poetics, *ars imitatur naturam*. The architect and theorist Vitruvius went a step further. Like Horace, he assailed grotesque ornaments for not following nature: "On the stucco are monsters rather than definite representations taken from definite things."[23] But then he accused them of contradicting their *own* reality, since they caused structure—architecture's very essence—to look impossible. "Such things neither are, nor can be, nor have been. For how can a reed actually sustain a roof or a soft and slender stalk a seated statue?"

Such forms of ornament, as well as the criticisms lodged against them, survived through the Middle Ages. "What is the point of ridiculous monstrosities in the cloisters where there are brethren reading?" asked Bernard of Clairvaux in a famous letter of 1135:

> I mean those deformed beauties and beautiful deformities. What are those lascivious apes doing; what is the meaning of those lions, centaurs, half-men and spotted pards? There are so many things, and everywhere such a variety of hybrid forms that it is more diverting to read in the marble than in the texts before you, and to spend your day gazing at such singularities in preference to meditating on God's laws.[24]

Bernard describes here the type of grotesque sculptural ornament that is the hallmark of Romanesque décor. He grasps marvelously monstrosity's allure, how the intertwining of forms traps you into its restless play, causing you ceaselessly to gape at it without understanding. He even imitates the contradictions of such drollery in his own perversely reversible oxymoron, "beautiful deformities." For the religious reformer, however, such diversions prove that church art is at bottom wasteful and vain, that it contradicts the law against idols, and that, in setting variety and novelty off against God's fixed and final laws, the artists lie.

Bosch's monsters belong to this contested legacy of images of unreality, in which the unreality of images per se stands unmasked. Even when such figures serve a reality principle, as they do in the ancient theme of *adynata* or "world upside down," they function to illustrate, through their impossibility and numerousness, the hyperbolic perverseness of the present day.[25] Things being as bad as they are (so goes the old complaint), anything has become possible. "Some people want me to write about another two-headed child," writes the German satirist Sebastian Brant, as if with a sigh, after publishing in 1497 no fewer than six broadsheets about abnormal births. "Monsters have become so frequent that, rather than a wonder, they appear to represent the common course of nature in our time."[26] At the fearful eve of the half millennium, monstrosity seemed the norm.

Guevara explains the unnatural, when it occurs in Bosch, as a mere function of place: where there is monstrosity, there is hell. And to a certain extent Guevara is correct. Fantasy does flourish most of all in Bosch's scenes of infernal punishment. Having made themselves into monsters during their lives, sinners are gruesomely force-fed their own vices by demons for whom the rules of nature need not quite apply. Divine judgment consigns the world itself to hell and outsources its management to the Devil. Through the "spirit that constantly negates" (Goethe), God allows counternature to rule eternally over the damned. Instead of placing us viewers in the final balance, as other artists of his tradition do, Bosch—and God—leaves us behind to be spectators to, and visually among, the damned. Thus the artist's own sadistic imaginings double as the Devil's global revenge. As Bosch tells it in at least four of his triptychs, devilry infected nature from the start.[27] In the Vienna *Last Judgment*, as we have seen, hordes of typically Boschian monsters stream from the heavens above Eden like a plague of locusts, indicating that the Old Enemy, fallen and envious, lies already in waiting in paradise (see fig. 47). After Eve and Adam's fall, in everyday life the Devil and his machinery stay largely hidden. Bosch's miser sees nothing of the demon handing him the moneybag (see fig. 60). And the single demon visible among the genre scenes of *The Seven Deadly Sins* remains unseen to the sinner it assists: that spindly entity with wolflike features and a matron's headdress holds the mirror that (as it were) observes its vain victim absolutely, to the exclusion of everything but its fugitive reflection of the woman (see fig. 122). What the human gaze observes in nature—which this painting programmatically contrasts with what God's all-seeing eye observes of humans—is nothing but the all-too-human distortions of vice. Thus Bosch can still "save the phenomena" within a world turned upside down by sin.

There is one scenario in which demonic monstrosities do intervene visibly in the world, and Bosch is its master portraitist. If out of contempt for it someone chooses to turn his or her back to the world, then devilry springs out of the shadows openly to tempt and to terrify. Saint Anthony undertook his spiritual trials in the desert, a natural but hellish locale (see fig. 139). In Bosch, the fantastical entities that swarm around the hermit saint contradict nature, both in their physical makeup and in their strange actions and capabilities, but Anthony completely ignores them. He looks at once inward, toward Christ, and outward, to us, the painting's beholders. These are the monstrosities that, in the portrait etching mentioned earlier, encircle Bosch's head like a diabolical halo (see fig. 77). The Latin poem printed below the artist's likeness offers an explanation. Composed by the humanist Dominicus Lampsonius, it appeared first on a portrait of Bosch published in Antwerp in 1572 by the widow of Hieronymus Cock, Volcxken Diercx. Written in compacted Latin, the verses address the sitter directly in the form of an impassioned apostrophe:

> What does it mean, O Hieronymus Bosch, that awestruck gaze of yours? Why is your face so pale? Is it that the lemurs, spirits flying up from Erebus, offered themselves to your eye? I would rather think that miserly Dis [Pluto] gave you free entrance through hell to his dark dwelling. However it came to pass that your penetrating spirit, your deep sense of our future fate was revealed to you there, your mastery endeavored inventively to make this understandable to us.[28]

Van Mander in the *Schilder-boeck* translated Lampsonius's poem into Dutch, simplifying it as follows:

> Jeroon Bos, what means your frightened face
> And pale appearance? It seems as though you just
> Saw all infernal specters fly close around your ears.
> I think that all the deepest rings of miserly Pluto
> Were revealed, and the wide habitations of Hell
> Opened to you—because you are so art-full
> In painting with your right hand depictions
> Of all that the deepest bowels of Hell contain.[29]

Both the likeness and the Latin poem come from Lampsonius's original publication of 1572—testimony both to Bosch's canonical status and to the growing respect for historical source material. However, in place of Cornelis Cort's blank backdrop, the etcher of the 1610 print (probably Simon Frisius) introduces a window—or picture frame—through which we glimpse a sampler of this painter's art. Denizens of a fictive world outside and behind, these images represent the "infernal specters" that the poem purports visited Bosch directly, so that he could paint them as if naturalistically with his dexterous hand.

The image of a head surrounded by fantasies had distinctly negative connotations. In Bosch's time, books about the follies of the world indicated madness by showing the lunatic with insectoid monsters buzzing round his head. Onomatopoetically linked to the chirp of crickets (*Grillen* in German), and playing on the *gryllos* referenced by classical authors, these phantasms were termed *grilli* and linked to the malevolent infection of a deranged mind.[30] An anti-Protestant broadsheet of 1529 depicts Martin Luther as a seven-headed Hydra (fig. 87).[31] Such flying pests swarm one of its heads—the one labeled *Schwärmer* (fanatic) and referencing Luther's most radical progeny, the Anabaptists. Bird-catchers, crafty folk as Bruegel and others depicted them, were portrayed plagued by *grilli*, both because birdlime allegedly attracted bugs as well as birds and because of the association of birding with lechery, sin, and folly (see fig. 10). Does this mean that the etching imagined Bosch to be potentially lunatic? Were the specters that the poem claims the artist observed "with his own eyes" figments of his own imagination?

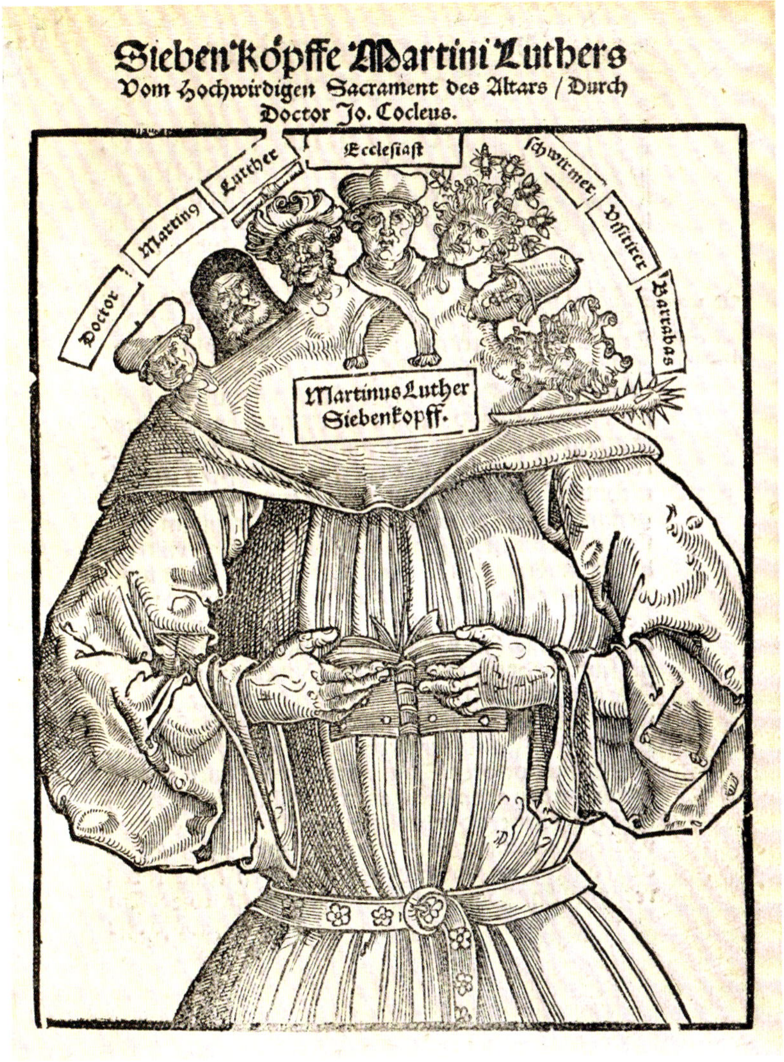

87 Hans Brosamer (attributed to), *Caricature of Luther with Seven Heads*, 1529, title page from Johannes Cochlaeus, *Sieben Köpffe Martini Luthers: vom hochwirdigen Sacrament des Altars* (Leipzig: Valentin Schumann, 1529), woodcut and letterpress, Deutsches Historisches Museum, Berlin

Fabricated monstrosities were problematic not only because they contradicted nature's rules but also because, in their novelty, they challenged the idea of a universe created whole and complete by an omnipotent God. The Ghent chronicler Marcus van Vaernewijck, writing around 1568, reports that Bosch was "called the devil-maker [*duvelmakere*], because he was never equaled in making devils."[32] This nickname turned out to be ambivalent, since to make devils potentially implied that they were humanly imaginary rather than diabolically real. In one of his *Dreams*, Quevedo has the Devil say that when Bosch wandered through hell, he was asked "why he dreamed so many fantastic recipes for us in his pictures, and he [Bosch] replied, 'Because I never believed devils really existed.' "[33] As Guevara's defense reveals, Bosch's monsters raised questions about the painter's art and person.

Even to Joseph de Sigüenza, the royal librarian at El Escorial, Bosch seemed a "strange man in painting."[34] But in the 1610 etching, the *grilli* represent—first and foremost—not the sitter's character but the characteristic products of his craft. Further along in his compendium, as we have seen, Hondius reworked Bruegel's likeness to include festive peasants, encapsulating in them that painter's specific achievement (see fig. 8). These sample products encourage us to begin our exploration of Bosch not with his demons but with his portrayal of strange but humanly crafted artifacts.

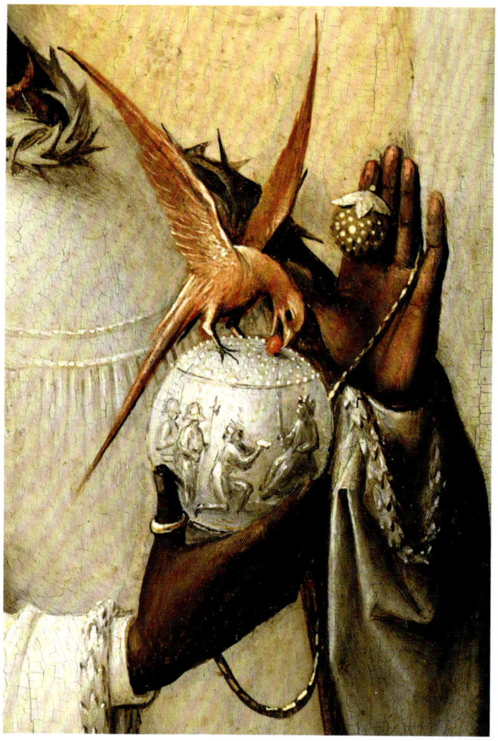

88 Detail of Hieronymus Bosch, *Adoration of the Magi* (fig. 93)

The Gifts of the Magi

The gifts of the Magi offered Bosch a perfect opportunity to flaunt his special skills. Brought to the infant Jesus by mysterious men, these objects were *supposed* to be oddities, things arriving from outside, from beyond the known world's farthest fringe. With a gold-feathered bird as if momentarily perched on its lid, the pale orb that the black Magus presents to Jesus in Bosch's *Adoration of the Magi* triptych displays a wondrous artistry, one foreign both to the biblical scene's humble surrounds and to the built environment where the triptych would originally have stood (fig. 88 and see fig. 93). In the Bible's brief account, the Magi "opened their treasures and presented unto him gifts: gold, and frankincense, and myrrh" (Matt. 2:11). These substances baffled medieval commentary. Jacobus de Voragine—a chief authority on Christian lore—could not decide whether the myrrh was meant to strengthen the infant Christ's limbs, drive out worms, or bury the dead.[35] Long before Bosch, artists made these gifts look exotic by enclosing them in wondrous artifacts. In his *Adoration of the Magi*, signed and dated 1423, Gentile da Fabriano rendered these crafted wonders in gold leaf over molded gesso (fig. 89).[36] Amplifying their physical presence, this treatment linked them to the painting's gilded frame and, through it, to the ornamented sacristy at Santa Trinità, in Florence, where Gentile's masterpiece was made to stand. The Magi's lavish offerings thus could echo and celebrate the generous gifting of the altarpiece to Santa Trinità in Florence by its donor, the fabulously wealthy and profligate Palla Strozzi.

The strangeness of the gifts extended to the bearers, tersely described in the Gospel as "magi" (Greek μάγοι, sometimes translated as "wise men" or "kings") who arrive "from the East." On the basis of their giving three gifts to Christ, Origen of Alexandria, writing in the early third century, reasoned that the Magi must themselves have numbered three.[37] By the fifth century, this threesome, fortunately matched to Christianity's triune God, had received various names, the most common of which were Melchior, Caspar, and Balthasar. In the

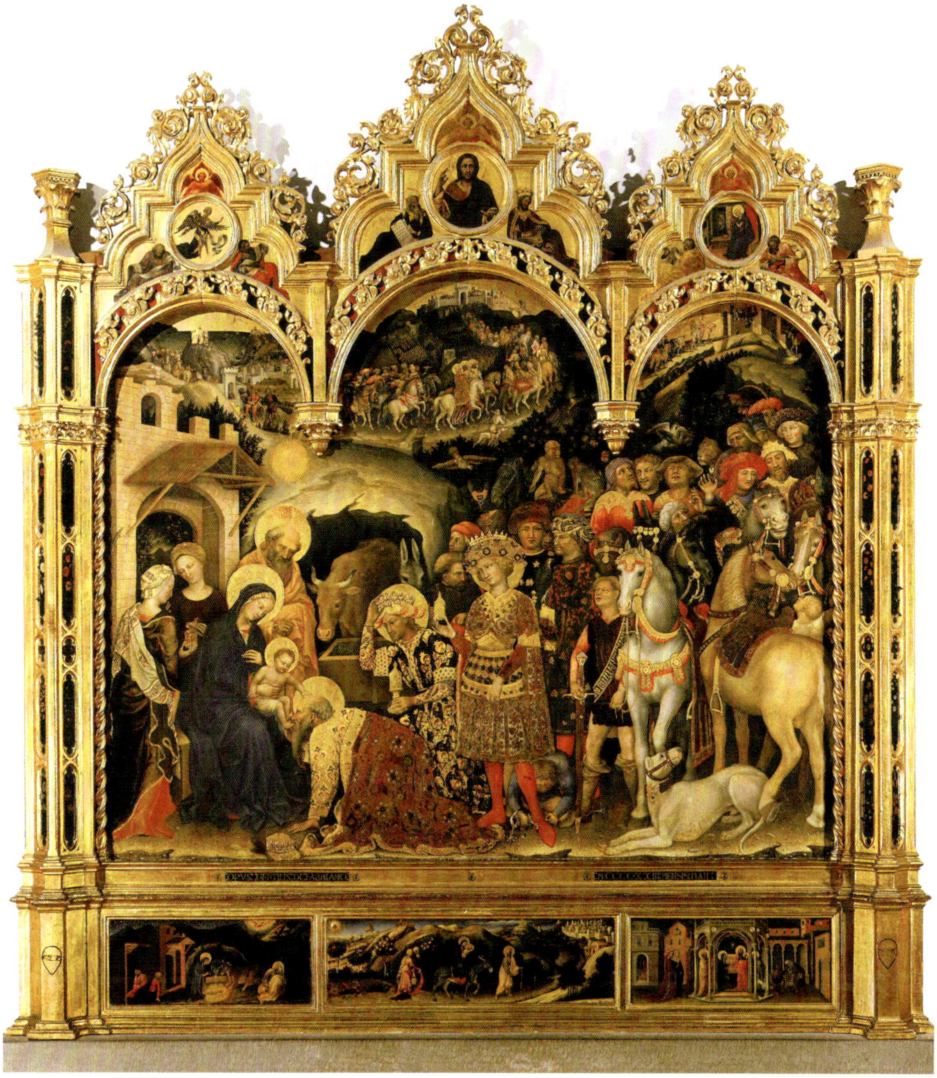

89 Gentile da Fabriano, *Adoration of the Magi*, with self-portrait of artist, 1423, panel, Galleria degli Uffizi, Florence

eighth century, an author known as Pseudo-Bede helped popularize these appellations. This anonymous writer (sometimes erroneously identified with the contemporary Northumbrian monk and scholar the Venerable Bede, who also wrote on the Magi) further asserted that each Magus was of a different time of life, thus enabling the trio to stand for the principal ages of man: youth, maturity, and senectitude. Pseudo-Bede also introduced the compelling (especially to painters) idea that the third Magus was black: "the third, a dark [*fuscus*], fully bearded king named Balthasar."[38]

By Bosch's time, artists routinely signaled the home of the third Magus by giving him dark skin and black African features (see figs. 17 and 90).[39] Complementing their allegorical embodiment of time, the Magi thus also came to figure the whole of space. Saint Augustine held that they came not just from the East, as the Bible seems to say, but from all corners of the globe. And he insisted that they were nonetheless united by being—all three of them—complete outsiders to the place and the people to which Christ, Joseph, and the Virgin belonged.[40] The Venerable Bede (the authentic one) sharpened this idea. He launched the commonplace that the Magi hailed from, or at least personified, the three known continents of the world, Africa, Asia, and Europe, which were then collated with the temporal sequence from young to old.[41]

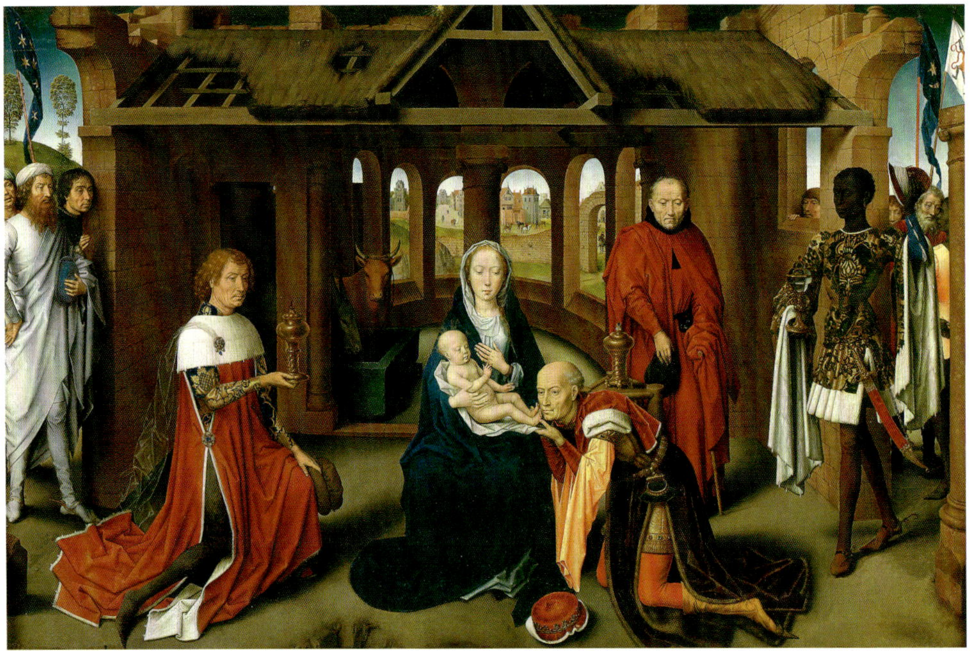

90 Hans Memling, *Adoration of the Magi*, c. 1470, panel, Museo Nacional del Prado, Madrid

Consider the world before the Magi converged on Christ: there had been multiple nations. Each had its own history, its own gods, its own cults. Each—we have now learned to say—constituted a discrete *culture*. Judaism had acknowledged these nations, but only negatively. They were what Israel was not, or they were what Israel became whenever its people became idolatrous, worshiping images instead of the one true God. Christ changed this political theology. Through his public recognition by the Magi, Christ once and for all "collected" the heathen Gentiles into an amicable whole. For assembling and bringing to light *cults* in the plural, he abolished their isolating secrecy. Admitting everyone, religion would no longer be *esoteric*; henceforth it would be *exoteric* and open to all. It would have a history that, not exclusive to one people, was universal to everyone in the world. For this purpose Christianity invented a new viewpoint: that of "all peoples."

The Magi gathered from the ends of the world to confirm Christ to be its universal center. This confirmation was a juridical necessity. Christ's divinity could not become apparent to the world or *saeculum*—could not publicly "come to light"—without the world's secular rulers officially acknowledging his rule. The Magi accomplished this in the way local kings did in ancient Rome, in the Pax Romana. They rendered ritual and political tribute to the world's emperor, their overlord. For as Saint Paul (the key outsider turned insider) put it: it is necessary "to have good report of them which are without" (1 Tim. 3:7).[42]

But there was one crucial exception. Christ was born a Jew. And according to Christians, the Jews, Christ's people, were not only his first disciples; they had also foreshadowed his birth through their tribal history and their Holy Scripture. Abraham and David were not only Christ's genealogical forbears—they prophesied him, as well. Jewish Scripture—the book containing their pledge—became an "Old Testament" that foreshadowed, in its every word and event, the New Testament of Christ. Importantly, this earlier Scripture announced the special bond of peace that existed between the Jewish nation and Yahweh, their God. Christianity took from Judaism this idea of covenant, expanding it to all the nations that, previously excluded, accepted Christ's rule. However, one people alone resisted this new, universal pledge. Already in certain passages in the Gospel, but more virulently in the religious thinking of the Middle Ages, the Jews—previously the people of the covenant—were vilified for having not recognized their own Messiah when he arrived.[43] Whereas the Gentile Magi brought peacemaking gifts to Christ at his birth, the Jews treated him as their enemy, refusing him shelter at his birth and later betraying, torturing, and killing him.

Saint Augustine called the Magi "the first of the Gentiles," both to affirm that pagans everywhere would henceforth accept Christ and to distinguish the Magi and the nations they represented from the one nation that rejected Christ's divinity: the Jews. As the story of the Magi crystallized into a founding political myth, the Jews became identified in the story with the shepherds described in the Gospel of Luke (Luke 2:8–15). Compared to the Magi, the shepherds who saw Christ's birth first were foolish insiders and their poverty, originally a virtue, became now their stigma. "The Jews' indifference was condemned by the Magi's zealous search," wrote Jacobus de Voragine, clarifying the contrast: "The Magi believed one prophet, the Jews refused to believe a number of them; the former searched for a foreign king, the latter did not bother to look for their own; the Magi came a great distance, the Jews lived close by."[44]

Late-medieval devotional practice fixed on this original and abiding refusal that turned Christ's own people into his mortal enemies. A vast apocryphal literature multiplied the heinous injuries inflicted on Christ by the Jews. Based—ironically—on certain passages from Jewish Scripture that had been taken to foreshadow (as "types") Christ's torments, these elaborate torture scenes usually took place in the recesses of a Jewish dungeon in Jerusalem, deliberately hidden from the Roman (and Gentile) juridical authorities who were just following orders. Together these stories constituted what one group of Dutch texts called the *Secret* [heimelijk] *Passion of Our Lord Jesus Christ.*[45] With its ninety-five full-page woodcut illustrations, Stephan Fridolin's widely disseminated *Treasury or Shrine of the True Riches of Salvation and Eternal Blessedness* organizes these atrocities for pious contemplation. Published in Nuremberg in 1491 on the press of Anton Koberger, Fridolin's text programmatically reiterates that each act of loving Christ means, reciprocally, hating passionately his enemies, and especially the Jews. For even if they did not directly and publicly scourge Christ's body (which in secrecy they also did), the Jews nevertheless publicly,

> with pleading, with screaming, with begging, threatened and forced the heathen judge against his will to give him the death sentence. . . . And so it is appropriate that the flagellation of Christ, as well as the crucifixion, is attributed to the wrathful and merciless Jews, by which one should understand that the same people whom the Lord freed from their scourgers by scourging them, they scourged the Lord.[46]

A hand-colored sketch related to the *Treasury*'s woodcuts shows tormentors in Jewish hats blindfolding Christ and suffocating him with their spittle—an event that texts of the *Secret Passion* relate in gory detail (fig. 91).[47] To this image of violence some viewer has violently reacted, attacking the depicted face of the spitting villain with a sharp instrument.

The response seems crude, as does the sketch it defaced. Although produced in the shop of Nuremberg's leading painter, Michael Wolgemut, the drawing looks clumsy and primitive. Yet this channeling of piety into hatred can be observed even in the most aesthetically

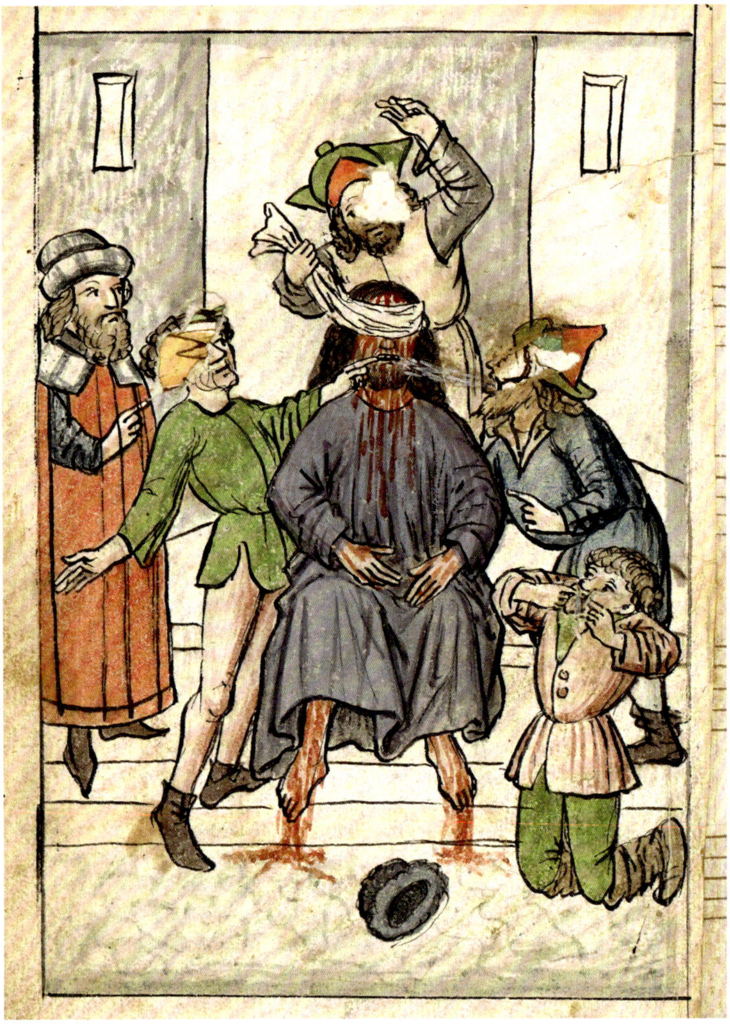

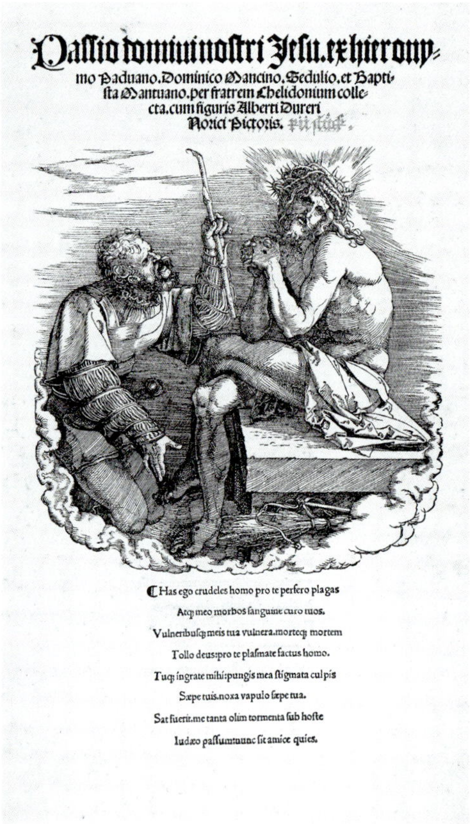

Passio domini nostri Jesu. ex hierony-
mo Paduano. Dominico Mancino. Sedulio. et Bapti-
sta Mantuano. per fratrem Chelidonium colle-
cta. cum figuris Alberti Dureri
Norici Pictoris.

Has ego crudeles homo pro te perfero plagas
Atq; meo morbos sanguine curo tuos.
Vulneribusq; meis tua vulnera. morteq; mortem
Tollo deus: pro te plasmate factus homo.
Tuq; ingrate mihi: pungis mea stigmata culpis
Sæpe tuis. noxa vapulo sæpe tua.
Sat fuerit. me tanta olim tormenta sub hoste
Iudæo passum: nunc sit amice quies.

(LEFT) 91 Michael Wolgemut and Workshop, "Mocking of Christ," from *Sketchbook*, c. 1490, ink and opaque color on paper, Kupferstichkabinett, Berlin, Staatliche Museen

(RIGHT) 92 Albrecht Dürer, *The Man of Sorrows Mocked by a Soldier*, title page of Albrecht Dürer and Benedictus Chelidonius, *Passio Domini Nostri Jesu* (*The Large Passion*) (Nuremberg: Hieronymus Höltzel for Albrecht Dürer, 1511), The Metropolitan Museum of Art, New York, The George Khuner Collection, Gift of Mrs. George Khuner, 1975

sophisticated artifacts of the culture. Dürer was Michael Wolgemut's student until 1490, and he was the godson of the *Treasury*'s publisher, Anton Koberger. In Nuremberg in 1511, Dürer issued his epochal woodcut series *The Large Passion*, yet on this monument of artistic intelligence, right on its title page, he affixed a poem crudely singling out for special enmity the villainous Jews (fig. 92).[48] Addressed to penitent viewers, it pricks their conscience by invoking the primordial Jewish enemy:

> Ingrate, you constantly tear open my wounds with
> Your sins. Constantly your crime pelts me.
> Let it be enough that I endured such great torture
> Under the Jewish foe. Now, my friend, grant me peace.[49]

Such confessional mea culpas served to energize attacks on purported Jewish culprits in the contemporary world. After two centuries of violent pogroms, Nuremberg's last Jewish residents were forced from the city in 1499, yet in 1510, with not a Jew left in the city, Dürer's own printer, Hieronymus Höltzel, was moved to publish in Nuremberg an inflammatory pamphlet about alleged Host desecration by Jews in far-off Brandenburg. Thirty-eight Jews died as a result of these spurious accusations, and—motivated by the outcry that concludes Höltzel's account—several German towns expelled their few remaining Jews.[50]

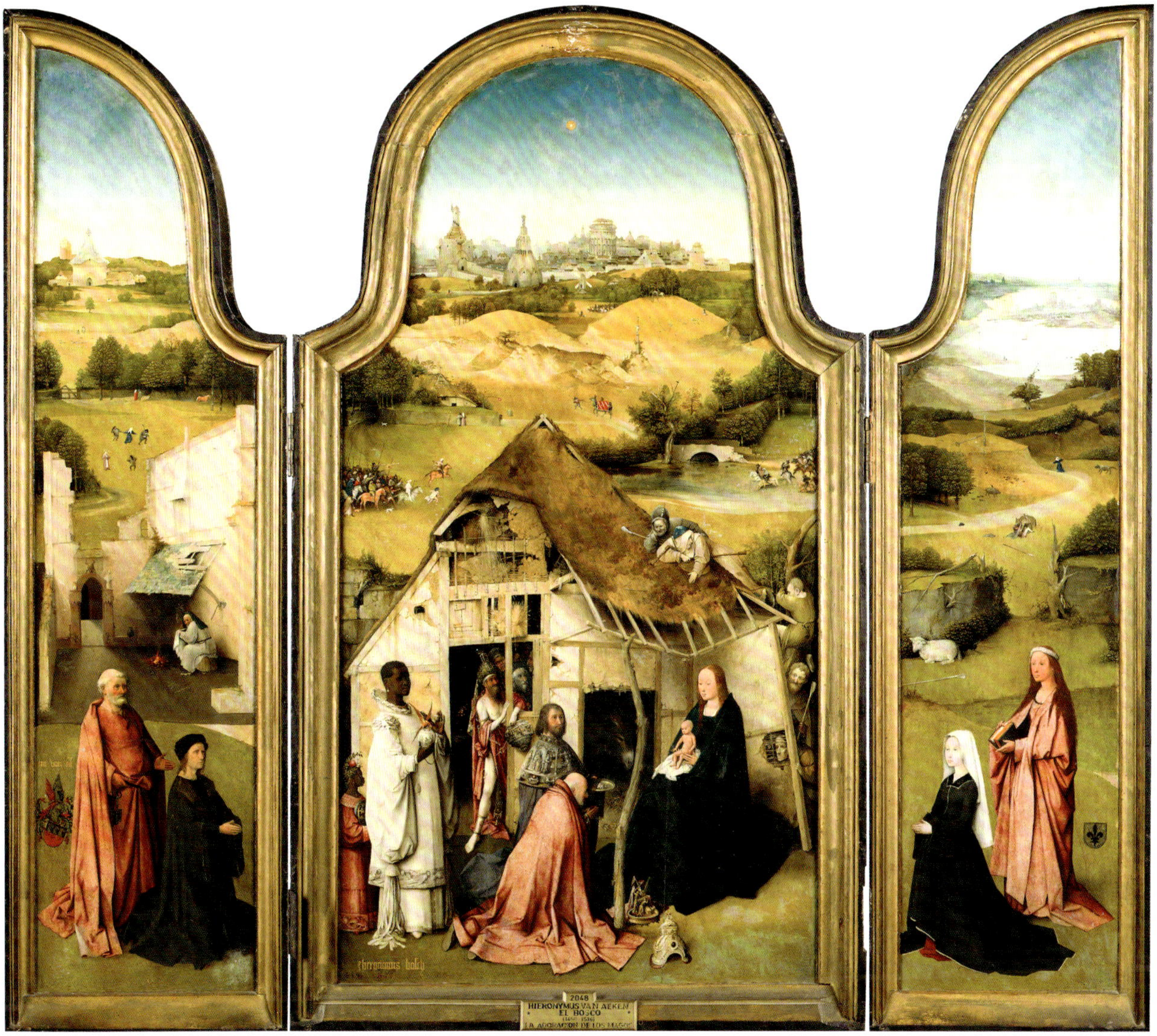

The Prado *Adoration of the Magi*

Bosch is the great master of Christian aggression. In his *Adoration of the Magi* (or *Epiphany*) triptych, now in the Prado, he explores the scandalous residue of Jewish secrecy (figs. 93 and 94).[51] Between the first two Magi and Christ, within the shadows of an immeasurable interior behind the stable's thin façade, an ass presses its head toward the infant (fig. 95). This beast fulfills old conventions for Christ's Nativity. It belongs to a cast of characters introduced into sacred scenes to fill out the spare biblical narrative. The Gospel says the Virgin laid Christ in a lowly "manger" (Luke 2:7), and it calls this a "sign" directed toward the shepherds to indicate that the Messiah has been born humbly in their midst. To develop that sign, and to make it seem long prophesied, Christian exegetes drew upon the Old Testament prophet Isaiah, who at the opening of one of his diatribes against rebellious Israel, has God say: "The ox knows its owner, and the ass his master's crib; but Israel does not know, my people doth not consider" (Isa. 1:3). By Bosch's time, these two animals were starkly contrasted. The ox stood for the Gentiles who recognized Christ, while the ass—shown variously turned from Christ, feeding from his master's crib, braying in contempt, or eating Christ's diaper—represented the materialistic Jews: seeing only the newborn's poverty, they mulishly deny that Christ was the Messiah whom their

93 Hieronymus Bosch, *Adoration of the Magi* (*Epiphany*), open state, c. 1510, panel, Museo Nacional del Prado, Madrid

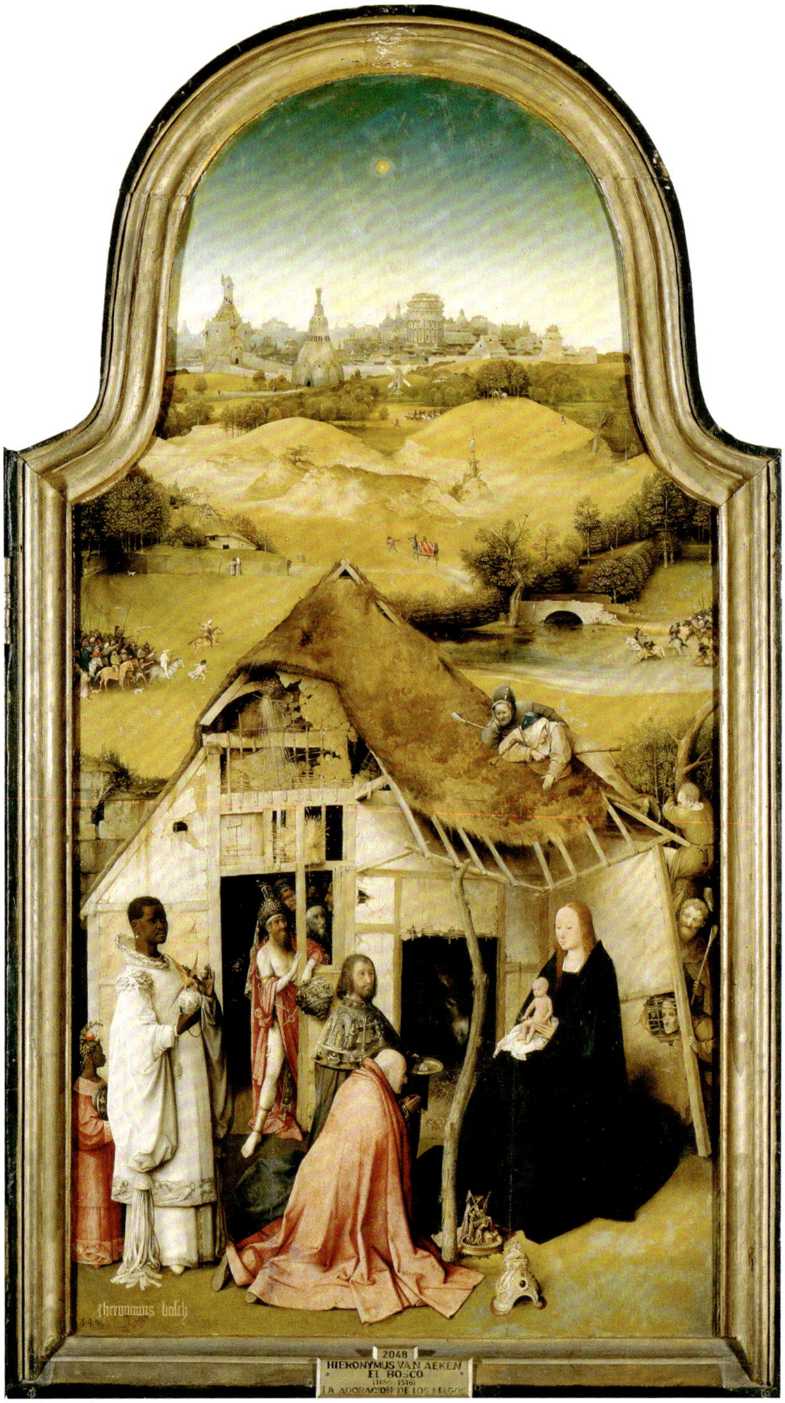

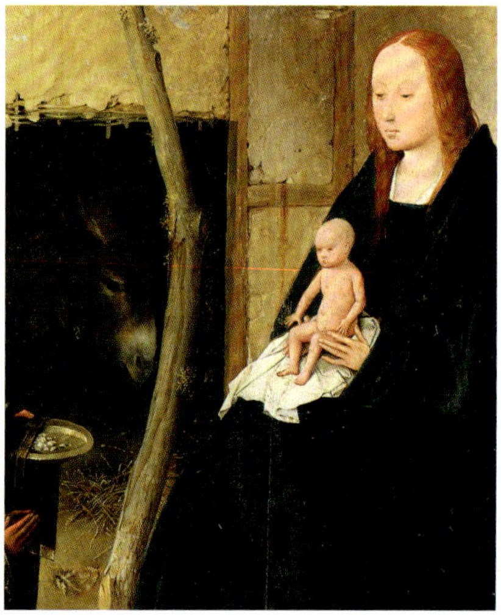

(ABOVE) **94** Hieronymus Bosch, *Adoration of the Magi*, center panel (fig. 93)

(RIGHT) **95** Detail of Hieronymus Bosch, *Adoration of the Magi* (fig. 93)

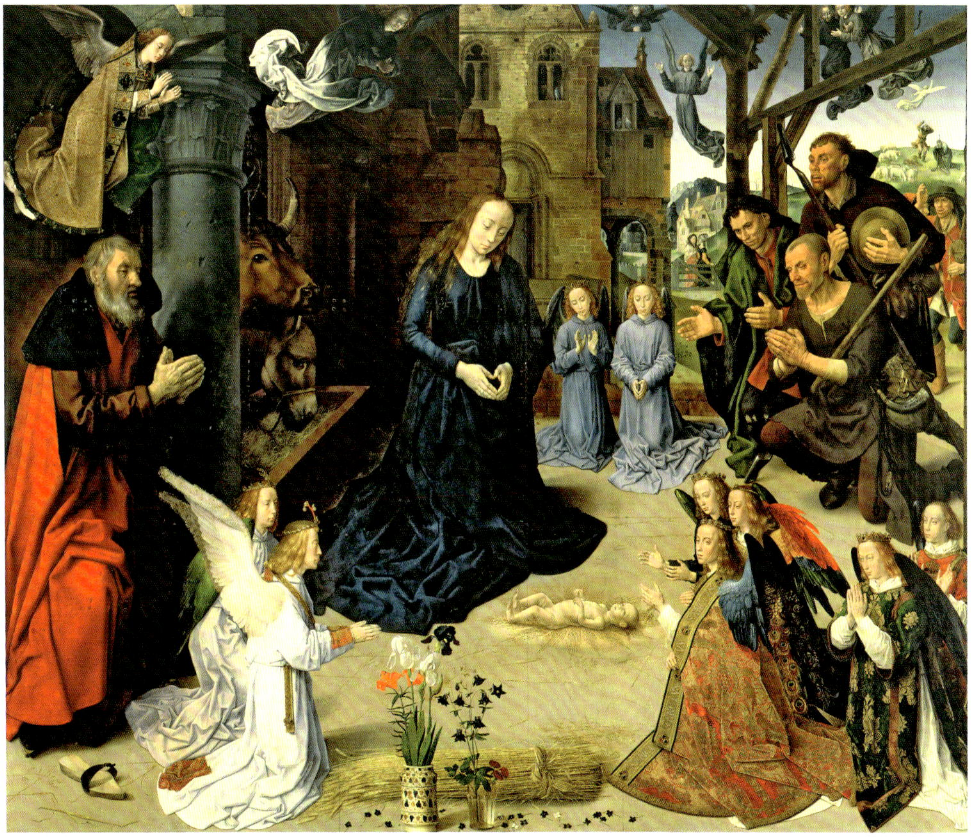

96 Hugo van der Goes, *Portinari Altarpiece*, center panel, c. 1475, panel, Galleria degli Uffizi, Florence

own prophets had foretold.[52] Unusually, Bosch focuses this age-old slander by omitting the faithful ox. He pairs the ass's profile with the face of a Jewish shepherd, who peers indifferently through a gap in the wall. And (in my view) Bosch also causes the donkey's muzzle to conjure a stereotypical hooked Jewish nose.[53] As if demonically empowered, that incendiary profile appears to bend the flimsy post separating the animal from Christ.

Bosch may also renew here an ancient calumny, reported by numerous classical authors and referenced by early Christians, that Jews secretly worshiped the head of a donkey in their temple.[54] More conventionally, the disintegrating stable stands for the vestiges of King David's palace in Bethlehem, thus signaling Christ's hereditary kingship as David's son. In Hugo van der Goes's *Portinari Altarpiece*, a sculpted harp—King David's attribute—graces the tympanum of the background building's entryway (fig. 96).[55] In Bosch, these ruins contain fragments of a diabolical or idolatrous past: observe the upside-down frog sculpted (or balancing) above the doorway beside Joseph, who, equipped with his carpenter's ax, appears to be heating or drying Christ's diapers (fig. 97). Decay reaches a negative verdict on the Jews. Like the pagan idols that fall before Christ, the Jewish palace collapses with the Advent of the Messiah, as the Old Testament prophets themselves predicted, scolding their own nation for its idolatry and ignorance ("Israel does not know") while also foreseeing a coming change: "In that day I will raise up the tabernacle of David that is fallen and close up the breaches thereof" (Amos 9:11).[56]

Bosch makes the old artifacts literally ooze corruption. A lizard or newt slithers about the upper rafters of the stable (fig. 98). Beside it an owl peers out at us from the darkness. Allied in medieval bestiaries with the Devil, the owl also symbolized the light-shunning Jews, who (as one twelfth-century bestiary put it) "repulse the Savior when he comes to redeem them."[57]

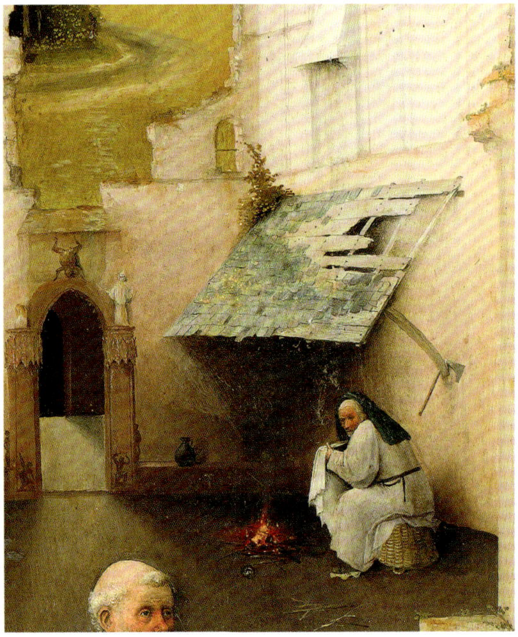

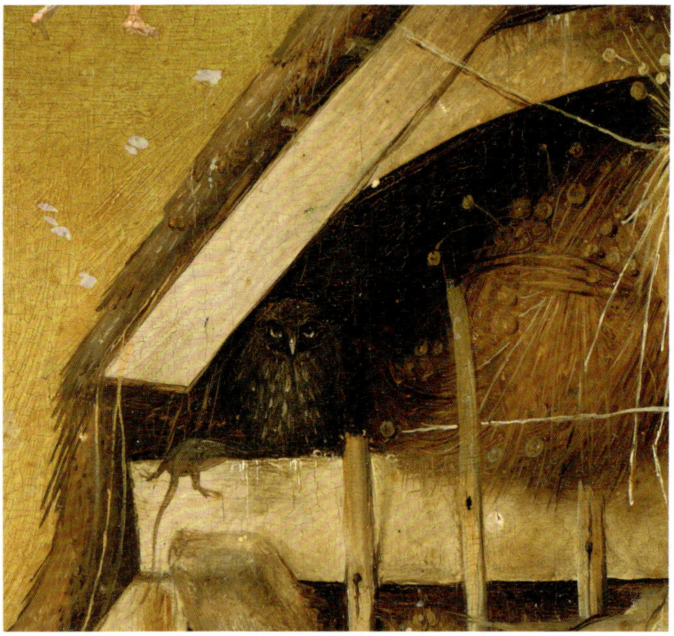

97 Detail of Hieronymus Bosch, *Adoration of the Magi* (fig. 93)

98 Detail of Hieronymus Bosch, *Adoration of the Magi* (fig. 93)

Nowhere will such an allegiance to darkness be more pointed than at the Epiphany, when Christ originally "comes to light." Thus its ruined fabric, the palpable darkness, and the abject menagerie identify the stable's inside with the space of an idolatrous Jewish cult. And it is within this dark space that Bosch's own occult symbolism flourishes.

In the background doorway set between the third Magus and his kneeling counterparts, from the very heart of the dark, inexorable threshold that exiles the black Magus to the margins, an enigmatic personage reaches a pale leg into the open (fig. 99). He is one of the great, unsolved mysteries of art-historical scholarship. He is also the one detail that makes Bosch's triptych remain perennially esoteric, despite the clarity of its overall program, which is about the appearance of Christ in history and liturgy. The figure's outlandish garb and entourage link him to the three royals gathered before Christ. Indeed, some writers have even taken him to be merely the second Magus's exotic attendant, since the ornamented crown he holds is similar in style and materials to Balthasar's cloak. However, the mystery figure remains too singular and strange to be merely a follower of the Gentile kings, and his placement inside the abject Jewish stable, together with his wound, a festering sore displayed like a holy relic within a cylindrical crystal anklet, signal a resident corruption.

Exploring the Spanish royal collections in the 1880s, the art historian Carl Justi came upon Bosch's triptych—then unknown to the public. Observing "three wildly strange men" peering from the doorway, Justi correctly predicted: "The Latin of the cleverest archaeologist wouldn't suffice to reconstruct their wardrobe."[58] In fact, there are six strange figures there, and the surrounding darkness allows Bosch to suggest more. To the public oath-taking (or Latin *coniuratio*) of the Magi, the artist antagonistically directs a conspiracy (*conspiratio*) of darkly uncertain extent. In 1928, Lionel Cust took the group to be agents of King Herod sneaking about in Bethlehem. In 1969, Ernst Gombrich, in an essay on evidence in art history, identified the bizarre leader of the troop as Herod himself, who in some Nativity plays of Bosch's time came to spy on the infant Christ.[59] Others have variously identified the figure as Adam, the Jewish Messiah, the pagan sorcerer Balaam, a disbeliever, a converted barbarian, a heretic, or

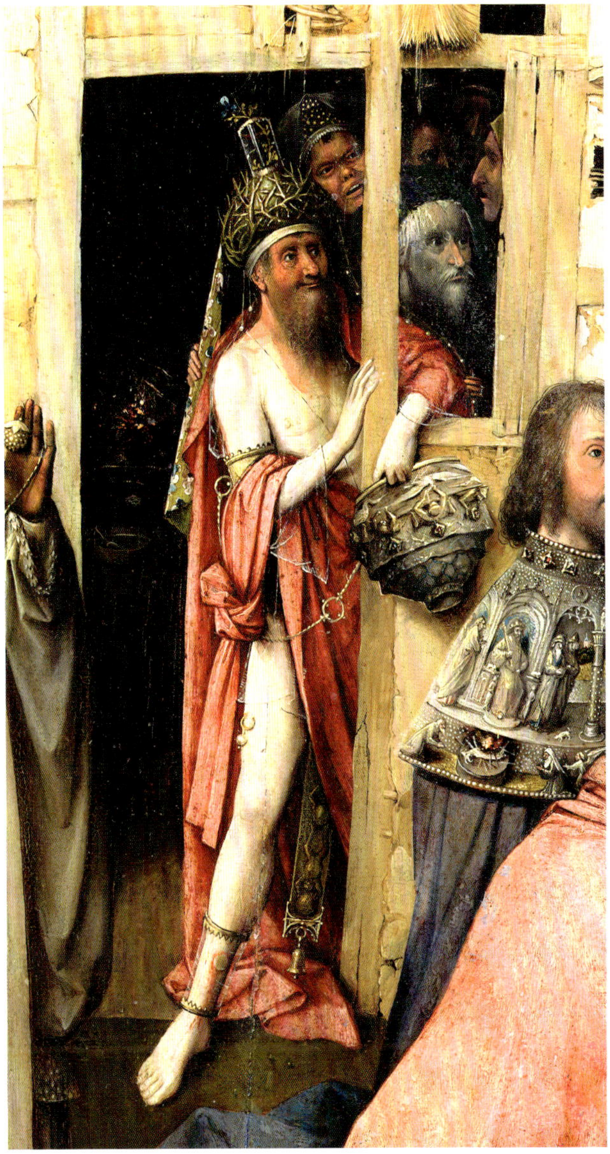

99 Detail of Hieronymus Bosch, *Adoration of the Magi* (fig. 93)

the malignant planet Saturn of alchemical lore.[60] Lotte Brand Philip offered by far the most intriguing solution. In an elaborate article published in 1953, she named the figure as none other than Antichrist, equated in medieval lore with the Jewish Messiah.[61] Arising (in versions of the myth cited by Philip) at Christ's birth, and often described as leprous (hence in Bosch the figure's ankle wound), Antichrist was said to have fooled the Jews with cheap magic so that, venerating him instead of Christ, they refused the real Messiah and were eternally punished on that account.

Drawing on diverse source material, Philip claimed to have deciphered every detail of the perplexing figure. Some of these sources long postdate Bosch, however, and none describes Antichrist with all or even most of the features Bosch gives his creation. More vexing for Philip's account is the time frame of Antichrist. In the Epistles of John, Antichrist, called—nebulously—"a deceiver," arises after Christ's death, possibly as a sign of the impending Apocalypse.[62] Associated with the "false prophet" of the Book of Revelation, and usually construed as a concrete human enemy whom Christ will battle at the Second Coming, Antichrist is perennially discerned in the dark circumstances of the present moment, interpreting these

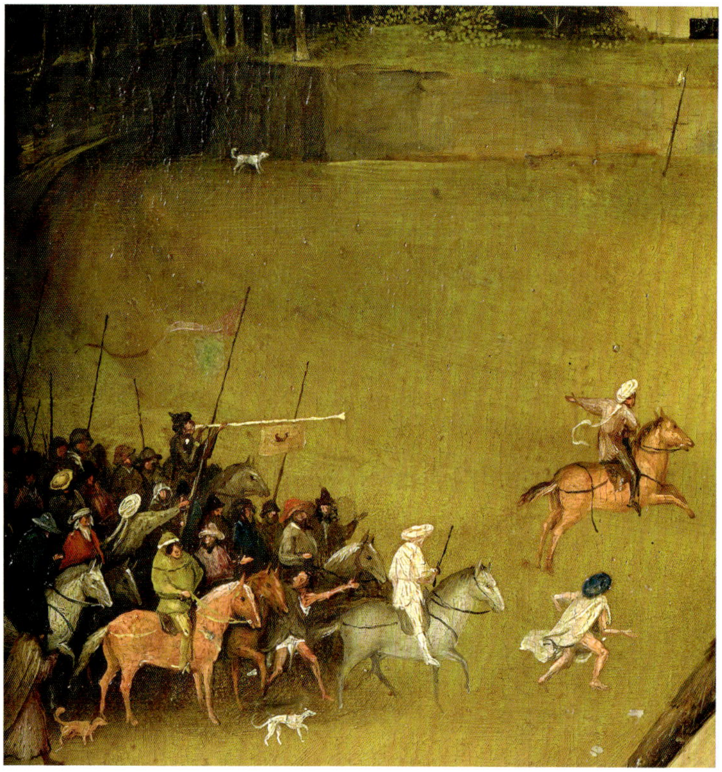

100 Detail of Hieronymus Bosch, *Adoration of the Magi* (fig. 93)

as portents of Judgment Day. Thus among the early Christians, Irenaeus called his Gnostic opponents Antichrist, while Tertullian hurled the insult at the emperor in Rome.[63] Countless incarnations later, during the Reformation, Protestants and Catholics damned one another with the same old name. Whoever he is revealed to be, Antichrist rules in the urgency of any given here and now, though as a primordially predicted future. This time frame makes his presence in a painting of Christ's birth seem anomalous.

Anachronism is the lifeblood of Christian art, however. God became man in a historical past, and artists portray that world-changing event. But Christ also remains ever present, especially in the sacraments. Syncing their work to liturgy, early Netherlandish painters routinely included in depictions of the Nativity proleptic signs of Christ's death on the Cross.[64] Recently, Debra Higgs Strickland strengthened Philip's thesis by adducing sources that, available to Bosch, would have made Antichrist's arrival at the Epiphany not just plausible but expectable.[65] She demonstrates that during the late Middle Ages the liturgical feast of the Epiphany programmatically linked Christ's Advent to his Second Coming and evoked the presence of Antichrist in events. Strickland also observes that the troops rushing toward one another in Bosch's landscape—previously identified as the apocalyptic armies of Gog and Magog—wear Turkish and Mongol Tatar headdress, suggesting that they are at once symbols of the final battle and topical portrayals of the most feared geopolitical enemies of Bosch's day (fig. 100 and see fig. 114).[66]

In my view, Philip's identification becomes more plausible the less definite it remains. Antichrist was the supreme illusionist. The diabolical inverse of the true God, he "recapitulates" all evil and "that entire apostasy which happened in the beginning, and in intervening times, and which will happen in the end."[67] The liar (1 John 2:22), he deceives most effectively through rumors, insinuations, and half-truths. According to Saint Jerome, he will be Jewish and born of a virgin: the inscrutable parody of Christ.[68] Such deceit was most likely to occur when, falsely believing the Messiah had arrived, people gave up respect for law and order. Ever since Christianity became the state religion of Rome, church and empire have had to assert their legitimacy against expectations that the world was about to end and that this ending would commence with Antichrist's satanic rule. Human history had therefore to be validated by a restraining power—the *katechon* announced by Saint Paul in his Second Letter to the Thessalonians—which delayed Antichrist's arrival and placed Christians under the yoke of secular laws.[69] But in the meantime of everyday life, while they awaited the mysteriously delayed end of time, people puzzled over the signs that chanced to come their way, uncertain of their import and their agency. And even as they scrutinized the world for these signs, they also turned their gaze inward, aware that Antichrist might really lurk there, as the spirit of pride and resistance to Christ lodged in the heart.[70]

The mystery man in Bosch's picture is best construed as a deliberately inscrutable enemy. As his name and his legends indicate, Antichrist refuses identity. A perfect antithesis of the Magi, who came to Bethlehem to identify Christ as King, Antichrist denies that identity *and* his own. Already the first Epistle of John generalized Antichrist as simply the denial of Christ's divinity (1 John 2:19), and theologians throughout the Middle Ages remained uncertain whether Antichrist was external or internal, an objective threat or the human tendency for self-deception. No wonder he puzzles art historians, intent as they are on *identification*. Art historians seek to name artists and their imagery, and in doing so tend to assume that the works they study issue friendly communications. Circulated in past cultures, these messages may be hard now to recover. Aimed at a circle of learned collectors or secretive intimates, they may even have been deliberately obscure. But these messages—it is assumed—were originally well intentioned: to someone somewhere they spoke peacefully, and art historians aim to recover that amicable accord.

What would art-historical analysis look like if its paradigm were not the greeting of a friend to a friend, but instead a mortal enemy slipping by unnoticed, or signaling cryptically to a coconspirator invisible to us? Bosch's mysterious interloper stands in relation to the Magi exactly as a foe does to a group of friends. His intentions, like the symbols that decorate him, are inherently secret: a conspiracy contrasted to the Magi's public oath, a secret cult contrasted to revealed religion. He is therefore a creature of the inside—*eso* in Greek. Therefore he ought to remain esoteric to Christian outsiders.

Absolute enemies are mutually inscrutable. The identity of Bosch's fiend is only insinuated. Conversely, his enmity insures that he, in contrast to the Magi, must misconstrue Christ. According to Saint Augustine, God engineered the Incarnation as an elaborate trap to capture the Devil. Because he understood Christ's humble birth and miserable death to be proof of the human taint of sin, the Devil erroneously took the bait and swallowed Christ whole, removing the ransom he—the Devil—has on humanity.[71] In Bosch, the enemy stands transfixed on the threshold to light. The word "epiphany" comes from the Greek *phainein*, "to show," which in turn derives from *phaos*, "light." Christ's Advent brought the pagans to light. It illuminated those who had lived in darkness, for as Augustine said, "Those who are converted to God pass from darkness into light, that is, they who were darkness become light."[72] And reciprocally it brought into view—it made into a *phainomenon* of history—those who, as outsiders to God's covenant, previously had been invisible.

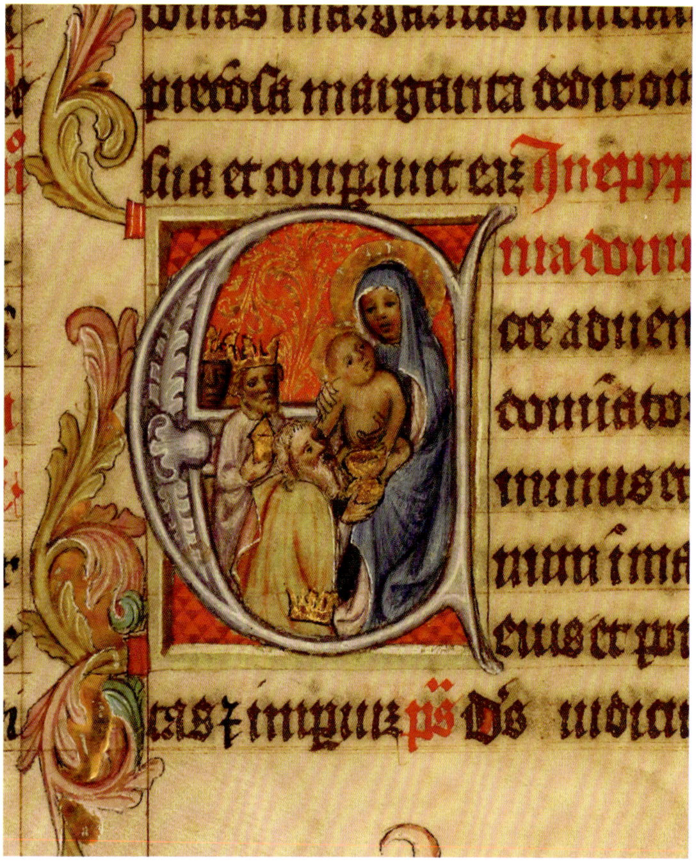

101 Anonymous Austrian Illuminator, *Adoration of the Magi*, historiated initial from *Missale secundum usum ecclesiae s. Florian*, c. 1400–1405, Augustiner Chorherrenstift, Stiftsbibliothek, Saint Florian beilinz, Cod. III.205, f. 4r

The image of the black Magus visualized this movement into the world of the visible. Having traveled the farthest, he arrived last, bearing the funereal myrrh. Artists routinely depicted him just behind, or exactly at, the physical threshold of the great event. Around 1400, in one of the earliest appearances of a black Magus in all of art, an anonymous Austrian illuminator placed the African king on the far side of the headletter *E*, excluding him from the intimacy the two white Magi enjoy (fig. 101).[73] The design seems spontaneous, but its structure is absolute. Diagramming the African's still-marginal relation to history and to the text of Scripture, such exact placements are the rule in later depictions of the Adoration.[74] Placed precisely on the brink, the black Magus is routinely shown to arrive before—and by arriving, to confirm—Christ's universal rule. Never quite inside the fold, however, he continues to embody a hostile exterior. Around 1500, artists shrouded the black Magus in the gloom of a nocturnal Nativity, or they exposed him as the image's negative, as does a remarkable woodcut of the *Adoration of the Magi* by the French printer Geoffroy Tory (fig. 102).[75] "Coming to light"—the advent of identity itself—is visualized through the image of the black.

The tall African king is one of Bosch's most memorable creations. Dressing him in white, the artist stages Caspar as an ethnographic epiphany within the *Epiphany* (fig. 103). He is Europe's fantasy of Africa arrived as fact. Keeping his penchant for racial slur in check, Bosch encourages the idea that he portrayed a real individual from life. He might well have done this. "Two moors from the Grand Indies" are documented as entertainments in the town of Zutphen in Guelders in 1452; and Africans served in the entourage of Bosch's noble clients, projecting the global reach of Burgundian rule.[76] In 1500, the reigning duke, Philip the Fair, succeeded to the Kingdom of Spain and laid claim to Portugal by marrying the mentally

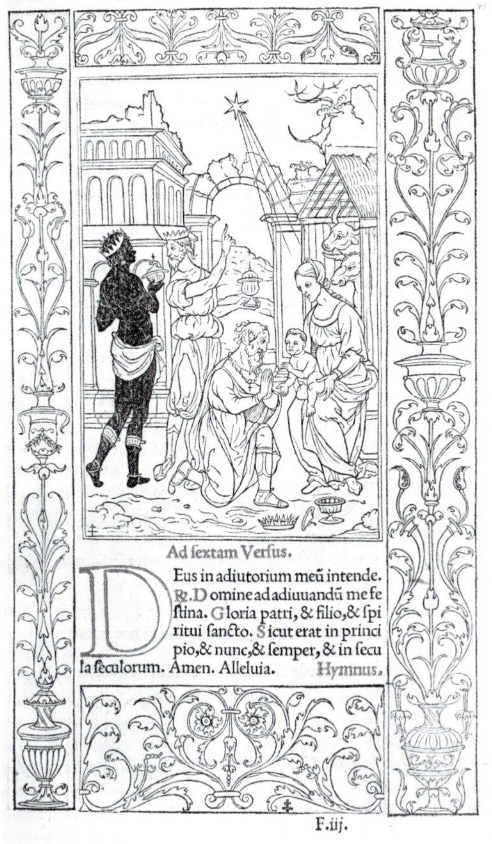

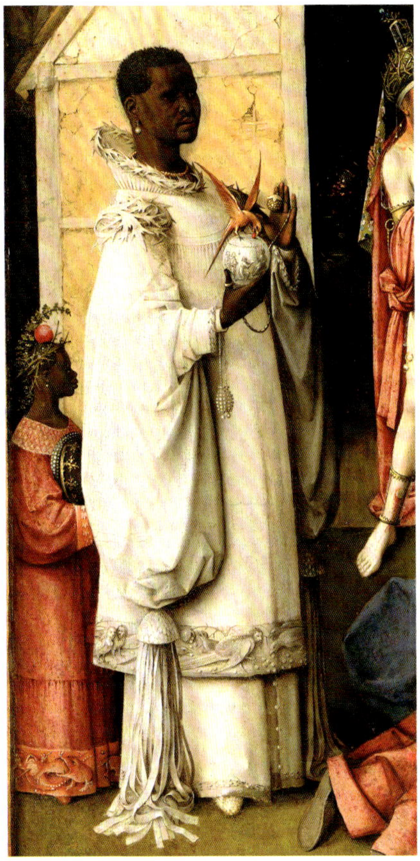

(LEFT) **102** Geoffroy Tory, *Adoration of the Magi*, woodcut from *Horae Beatus Virginis Mariae* (*Hours of the Virgin Mary*), 3rd ed. (Paris, 1531), fol. 132, The Metropolitan Museum of Art, New York, Harris Brisbane Dick Fund, 1930

(RIGHT) **103** Detail of Hieronymus Bosch, *Adoration of the Magi* (fig. 93)

imbalanced Juana of Castile. This was the era of Spanish and Portuguese exploration of the West African coast by ships seeking passage to India. A documented client of Bosch, Philip combined a taste for the bizarre and exotic with imperial ambitions.[77] The realism of Bosch's African Magus fits the political theology of the Epiphany itself. Fiends have become friends, the margins gather at the center, death is converted to life, and darkness, of its own accord, enters the light. Meanwhile, though, the realistic black Magus makes the phantasmagorical enemy all the more menacing. Following convention, Bosch establishes a threshold where the African can abide. It is at the brink of this dividing shadow that the putative Antichrist also stands. A pale body in the gloom, Antichrist reverses the conversion from darkness to light. His reddened face suggests an allergy to the sun.

By adoring Christ, the Magi show that they have abandoned their abominable heathen *cults*. But in Bosch they still remain emissaries of radically alien *cultures*. It is above all in their gifts that this strangeness persists. Other painters imagined these offerings in terms of flamboyant but fully indigenous European craftsmanship. Consider the splendid *Adoration of the Magi* panel by Jan Gossart, an influential Antwerp master whose works are known to have been collected by Bosch's noble patrons (fig. 104).[78] As Gossart and other so-called Antwerp Mannerists paint them, the gifts of the Magi are fabulous, mesmerizing confections, and the costumes of their bearers incorporate every lavish material known to the knowledgeable inhabitants of Antwerp, the world's textile center (see fig. 17).[79] But these luxury goods are stylistically of familiar manufacture: domestic and imported valuables that Antwerp, the quintessential "bring and buy center,"[80] was famous for. The gifts and costumes in Bosch's triptych are different. Bosch turns them into markedly alien artifacts. And he mingles the gifts' décor

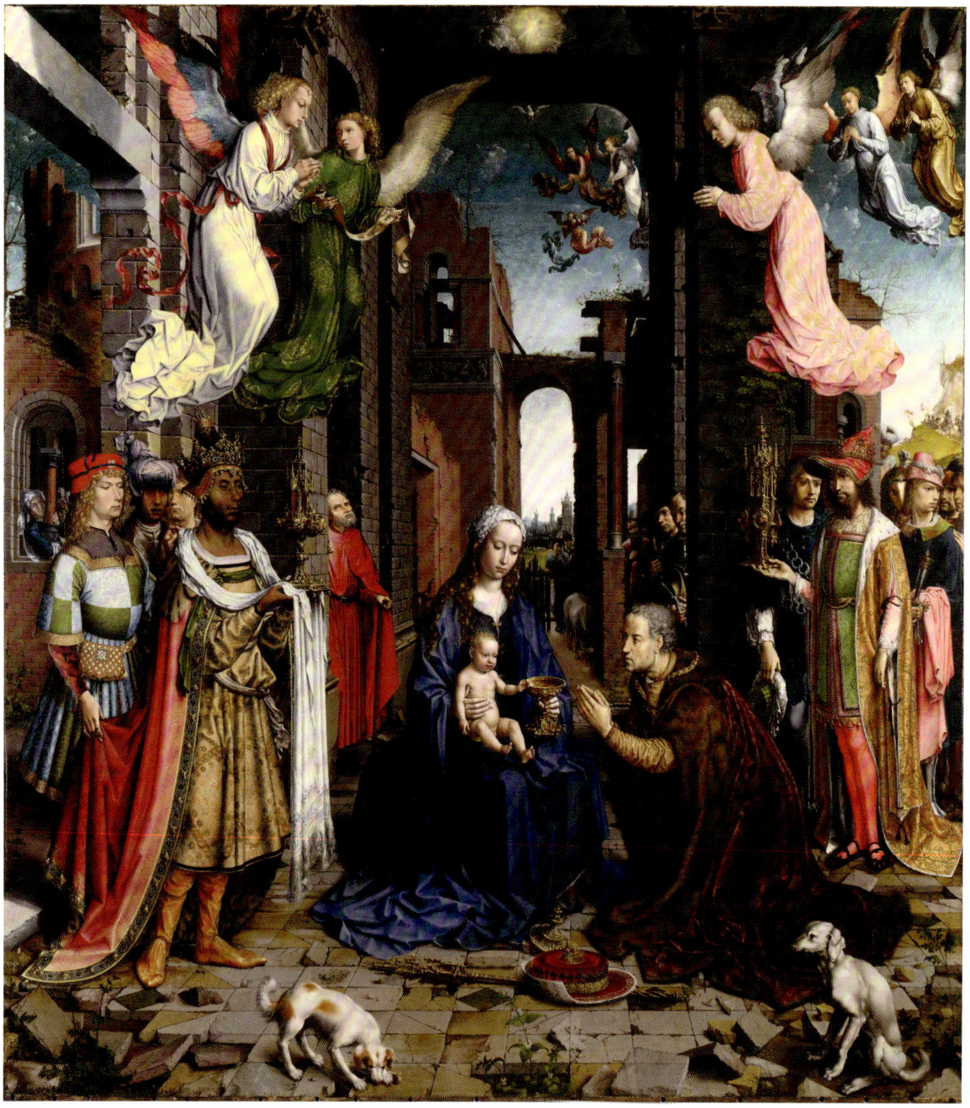

104 Jan Gossart, *Adoration of the Kings*, 1510–15, oil on wood, National Gallery, London

with that of their bearers' costumes, so that they read as products of an internally consistent alien vernacular—what we today might call an ethnographic assemblage.

Bosch also decorates the gifts with uncanny subjects. Informed members of his audience could have made sense of some of these (fig. 105). They would have easily identified Melchior's gold as a sculptural portrayal of Abraham poised to sacrifice his beloved son, Isaac (Gen. 22:1– 19). Instructed by paintings, manuscript illuminations, popular prints, and block books, they would have understood that biblical episode to be a chief Old Testament prototype of Christ's Crucifixion (fig. 106).[81] Bosch sharpens the parallel by showing Isaac bearing the fuel for his immolation, as Christ carries the Cross. Perceiving the reference forward to the Crucifixion, viewers would have grasped its pertinence to the Epiphany: in Christ's death on the Cross, God offered *his* son in sacrifice. Caspar's amazing orb suggests another Old Testament prototype, this time for the Magi (see fig. 88). To some observers, it calls to mind the episode in which three "mighty men" in King David's army break through enemy lines to bring their leader water from the well of Bethlehem (1 Chron. 11:17–19)—a prefiguration of the Epiphany.[82] But here the reference is more oblique. Indefinitely rendered on Caspar's orb, the gift bearers carry nothing like a jug.

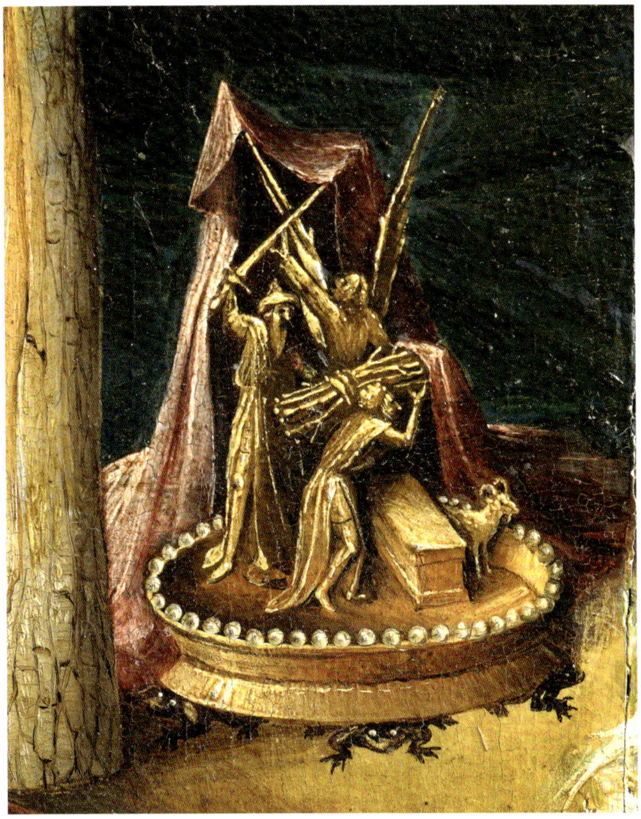

(LEFT) **105** Detail of Hieronymus Bosch, *Adoration of the Magi* (fig. 93)

(BELOW) **106** Anonymous North Netherlandish, *Abraham and Isaac Climbing Mount Moriah, Christ Carrying Cross with Saint Veronica, Elijah and the Widow at Zarepath, Biblio Pauperum*, c. 1395–1400, British Library, London, Kings MS 5, fol. 16r

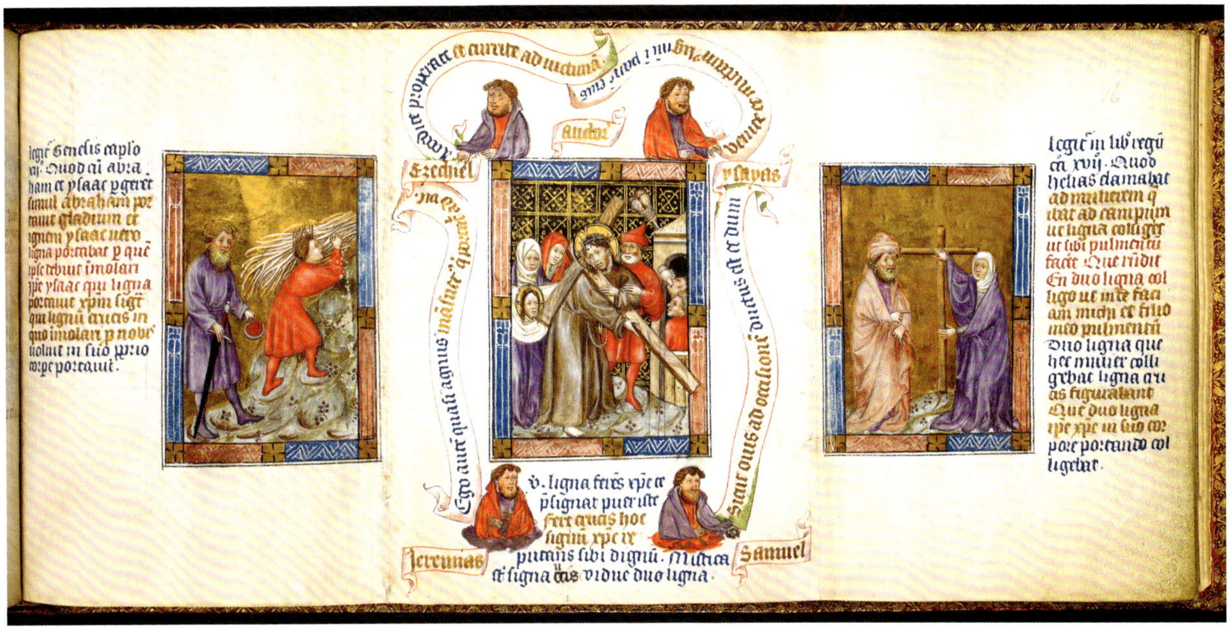

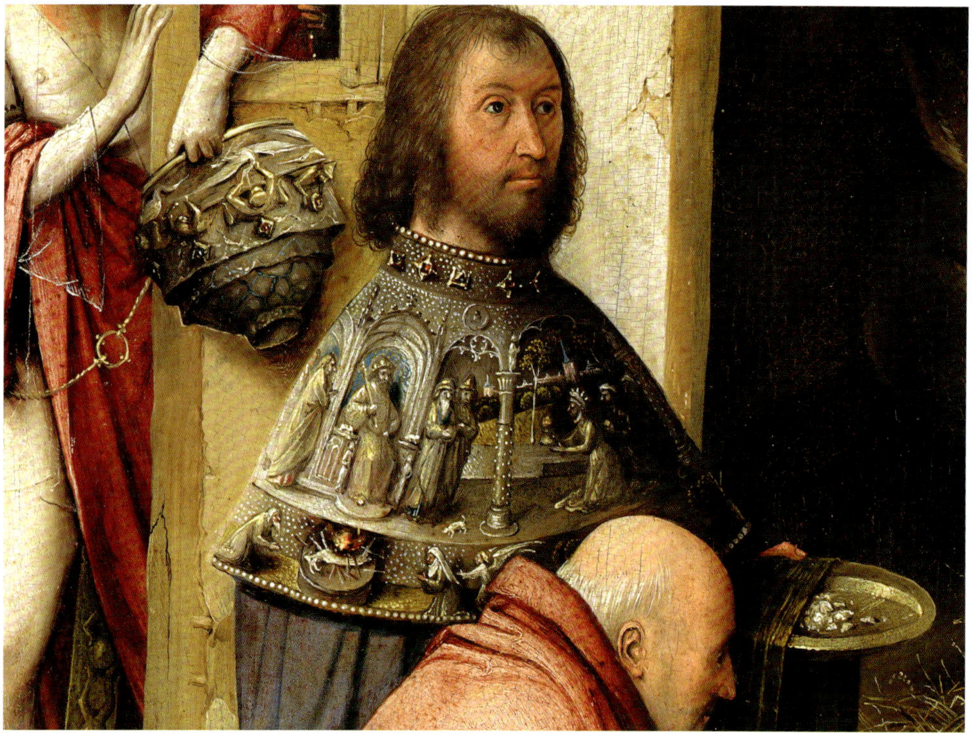

107 Detail of Hieronymus Bosch, *Adoration of the Magi* (fig. 93)

Recognition of familiar subjects accesses the Magi's gifts, but estrangement follows. The bird atop Caspar's orb, the hybrid creatures on his robe, the figures on Melchior's crown (set down beside his gift): all these remain unfathomable, drawing viewers into the esoteric realm that the Magi themselves have abandoned. Scholars have divined in Bosch all kinds of cryptic codes, from the symbols of astrology and alchemy to the hermetic ciphers of the Adamites, Gnostics, Cathars, and Kabbalists. Even the hieroglyphs of the Aztecs, first seen by Europeans two years after Bosch's death, have been used to unlock his pictures.[83] Yet Bosch never sources occult symbolism for his saintly protagonists. In his works, esoteric symbols derive from enemies who shun Christ's light: from idolaters, heretics, witches, Jews, and Muslims, and behind them, from the Old Enemy, Satan. Mistaking enemy sources for friendly keys, scholarship becomes a symptom more than a solution.

Kings of this world, the Magi are natural enemies of one another and of the King of Kings, whom they, only through divine revelation, adore. Crafted prior to their arrival, their gifts are appropriately alien in their meanings, materials, and manufacture. Is that bird perched on Caspar's orb crafted or alive? In the Middle Ages, menageries were attributes of rule. From 1446 on, Philip the Good filled the park around his palace in Brussels with exotic animals, and in Bosch's day, Philip the Fair developed, alongside the Brussels one, a menagerie in Ghent.[84] Imagined as an outlandish ruler, the African might plausibly bear such a fabulously tamed pet. And even if the bird is not alive but a gilded artifact, its hyper-liveliness betokens exotic, magical artistry. Because of the way he paints it, Bosch makes it impossible for us to tell how, or of what materials, such strange décor is made. Balthasar's elbow-robe is legible in terms of stories Bosch's viewers might know (fig. 107). Its main image recalls yet another Old Testament prototype for the Epiphany: the Queen of Sheba arriving at King Solomon's throne (1 Kings 10:1–13; 2 Chron. 9:1–12).[85] The frieze below that may recall the tale of Manoah's wife,

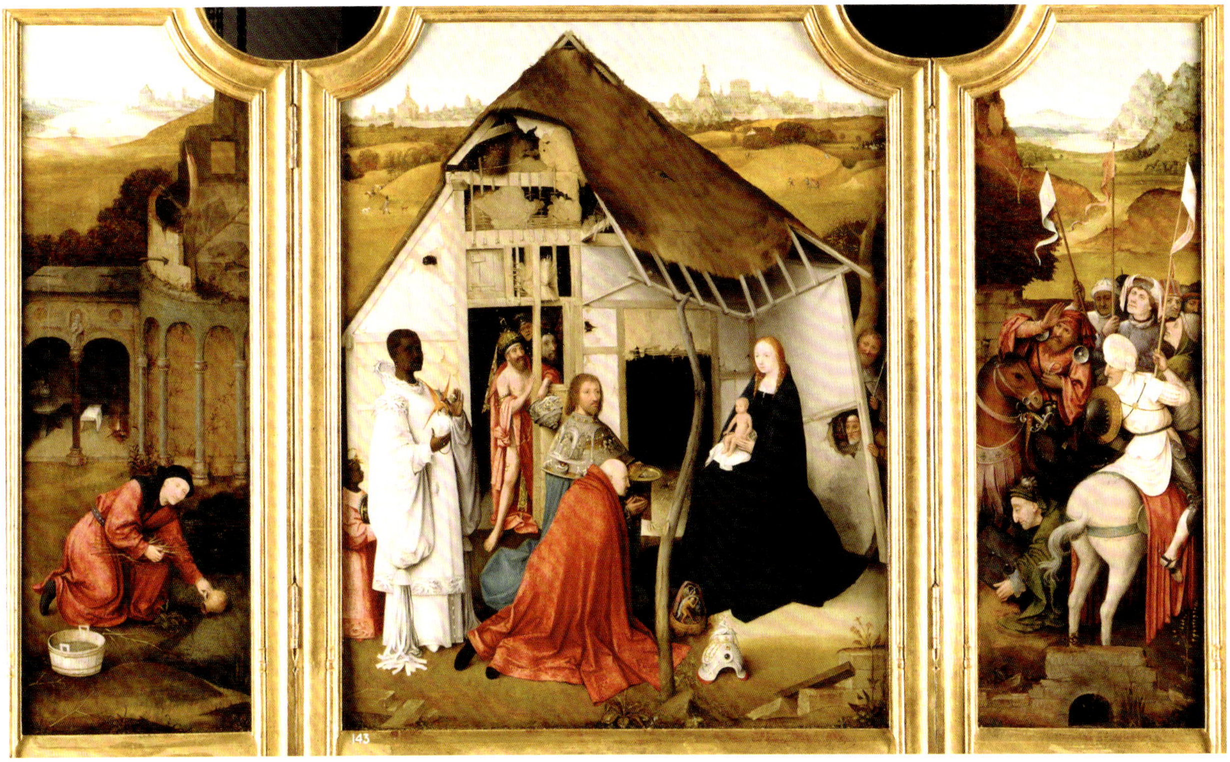

who conceives a child (Samson, a prototype of Christ) by sacrificing a goat (Judg. 13:3–23).[86] Whatever events they depict, though, these pictures belong to an unembroiderable form of embroidery that transports us beyond its imagery to a magical type of image per se.

Nothing is as distinctly Boschian as these pictures *in* the picture. That the artifacts of the Magi typify this painter's manner is evidenced by one of some twenty surviving copies made after the Prado triptych.[87] A picture now in the collection of Upton House in Oxfordshire replaces Melchior's statuette with a stranger thing (figs. 108 and 109).[88] With its nudity and seed-spilling pods, the colorful, half-veiled concoction has (as far as anyone can tell) nothing to do with the Epiphany or its Old Testament prototypes. However, it does deliberately recollect certain elements unique to Bosch's own most famous (and inscrutable) masterpiece, the so-called *Garden of Delights* (see fig. 170). To this early imitator, then, the specifics of Bosch's symbolism are of little account. Strangeness *as such* is salient, both for the Magi's gifts and for Bosch's art.

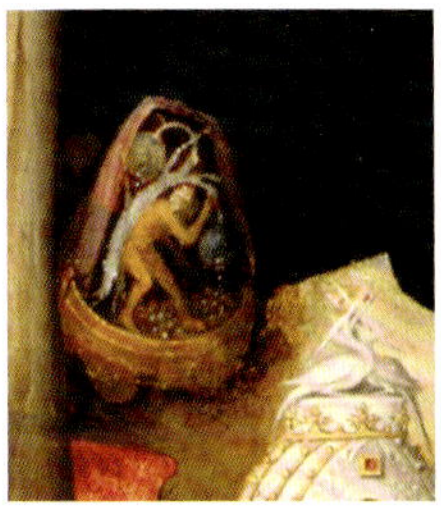

(TOP) **108** Follower or Assistant of Hieronymus Bosch, *Adoration of the Magi*, c. 1495, panel, Viscount Bearstead Collection, Upton House, Banbury

(BELOW) **109** Detail of Follower or Assistant of Hieronymus Bosch, *Adoration of the Magi* (fig. 108)

And in the Prado triptych, the gifts of the Magi *are* irredeemably odd. Consider again Melchior's gold sculpture (see fig. 93). To what story could those frogs at its base possibly belong? Listed in Leviticus among the unclean creatures, featured in Exodus as one of Egypt's ten plagues, and vilified by Aristotle for their spontaneous, counternatural generation, frogs were deemed by medieval authorities to be agents of the Devil. In earlier art, they appeared in vile contexts, feeding on cadavers, suctioned to the genitals of adulterers, or—most fitting of all—feeding on the genitals of dead adulterers (fig. 110 and see fig. 212). In Bosch, frogs spawn wherever iniquity flourishes: in the dark pool of Eden, in the slime of hell, as nefarious ornament, and among the Devil's most heinous profanations (see figs. 97 and 198). In the *Temptation of Saint Anthony*, a toadish creature holds up a counter-Eucharistic egg in what appears to be a diabolical Black Mass (see fig. 162).

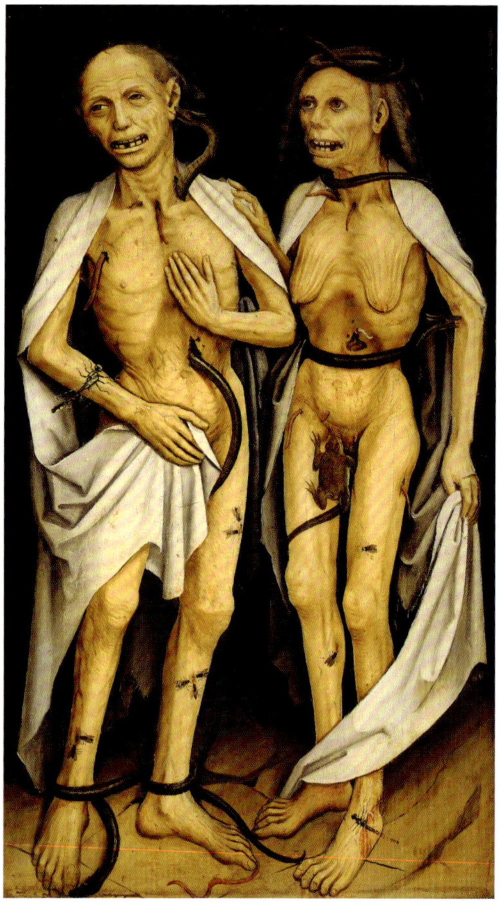

110 Master of the Sterzing Altar Wings, *Macabre Wedding Portrait*, c. 1470, panel, Musée de l'Oeuvre Notre Dame, Strasbourg

Traditionally, Christian typology worked on the assumption that the entire Old Testament was a foreshadowing and a promise of the Gospel.[89] In this view, history was already Christian before Christ. In the scenes he places on the Magi's gifts, Bosch evokes but also unsettles this dream. As artifacts of alien cultures, the Magi's gifts both prefigure *and disfigure* the history that they now join. Based—literally—on devilish frogs, the golden effigy loses its footing in a Jewish past. It illustrates a story at most comparable to that of Abraham and Isaac, but told by alien scriptures—as if Bosch, in advance of modern biblical criticism, realized that Jewish history derived from primeval myths of peoples without a history.

The radical otherness of the Magi's gifts befits their specific nature. Though the Magi adore Christ, previously they worshiped other gods. This prior idolatry becomes explicit in a Boschian composition known in several copies—all probably derived from a lost original. In an *Adoration of the Magi* triptych from the Collegiate Church of Saints Peter and Guidon in Anderlecht, Caspar's sleeve displays the key Old Testament scene of idolatry, the dance of the Israelites around the golden calf (figs. 111 and 112).[90] Limiting the revelers to three, the painter deliberately juxtaposes this vicious group with the Magi's virtuous threesome. By implication, he compares the false Jewish idol with Christ as true image of God—as Bosch will in the *Temptation of Saint Anthony* (see fig. 163). Wearing his idolatry—literally—on his sleeve, the Anderlecht black Magus has a cautionary effect. Bosch recollects what the Magi originally were and what they might potentially again become: not merely kings of the world but powerful magicians. In the Greek of the Gospel, the word μάγοι denoted astrologer-priests. The English Bible suppressed this link to sorcery by calling them "wise men." A mid-fifteenth-century

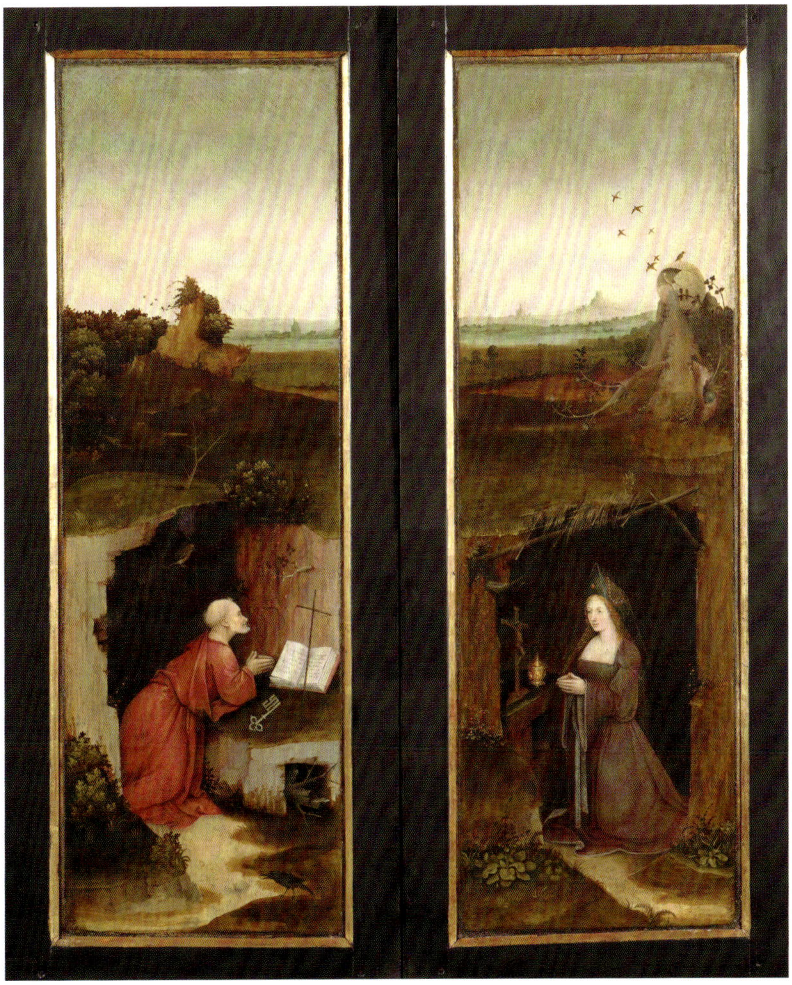

(LEFT) **111** Closed panel

(BELOW) **111** Follower of Hieronymus Bosch, *The Adoration of the Magi*, 1525–40, panel, Erasmushouse Museum, Brussels (on loan from Collegiate Church of Saints Peter and Guido)

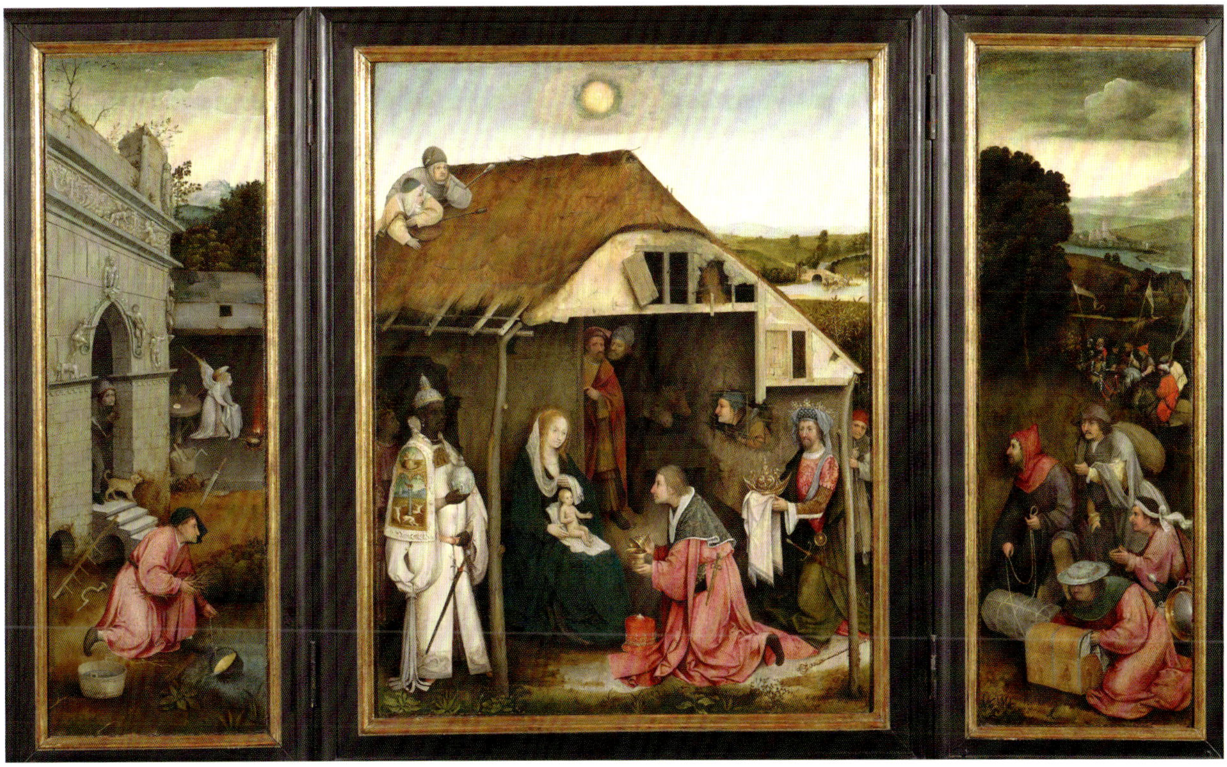

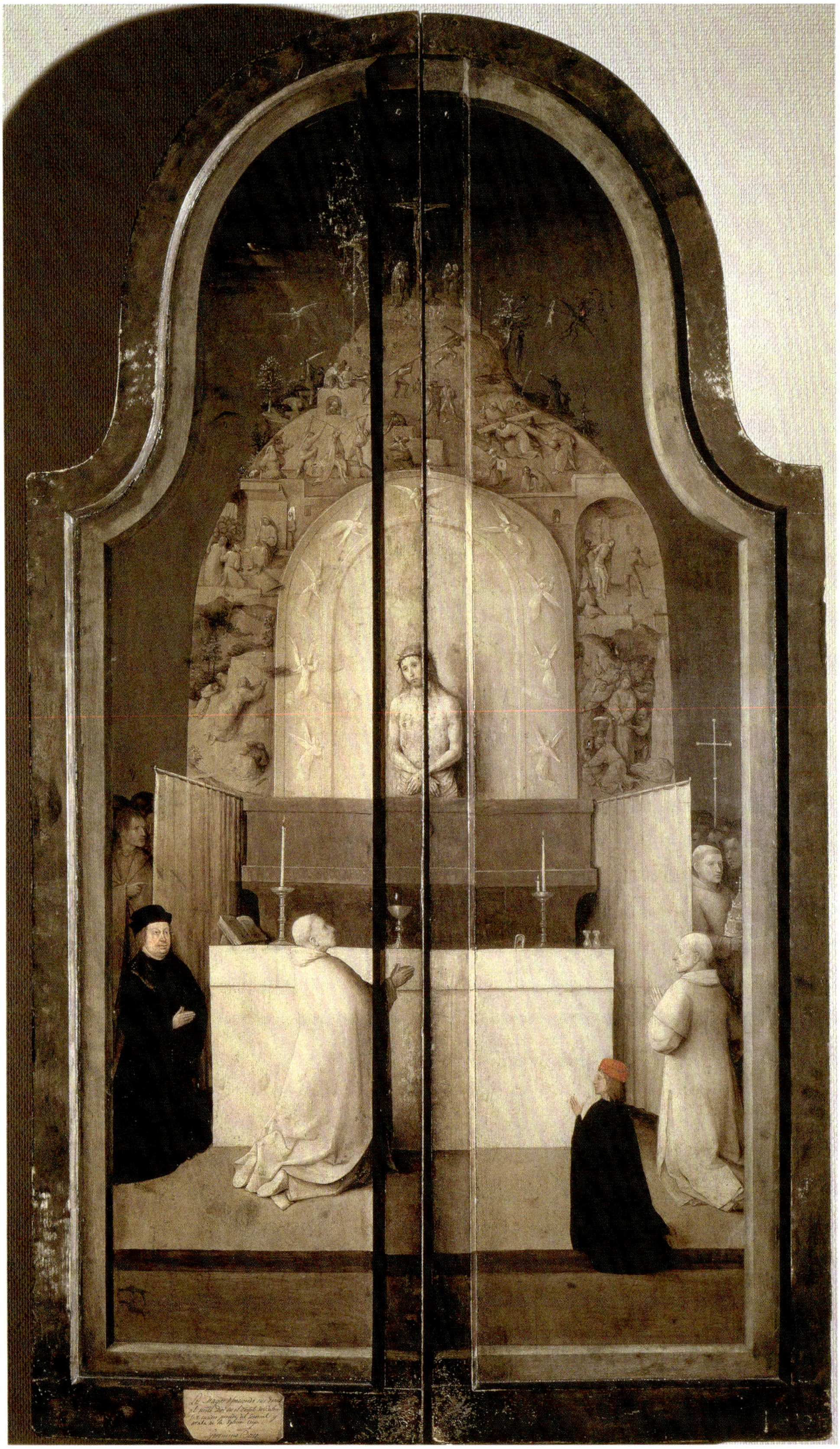

115 Hieronymus Bosch, *Mass of Saint Gregory*, closed state of *Adoration of the Magi* (fig. 93), c. 1510, panel, Museo Nacional del Prado, Madrid

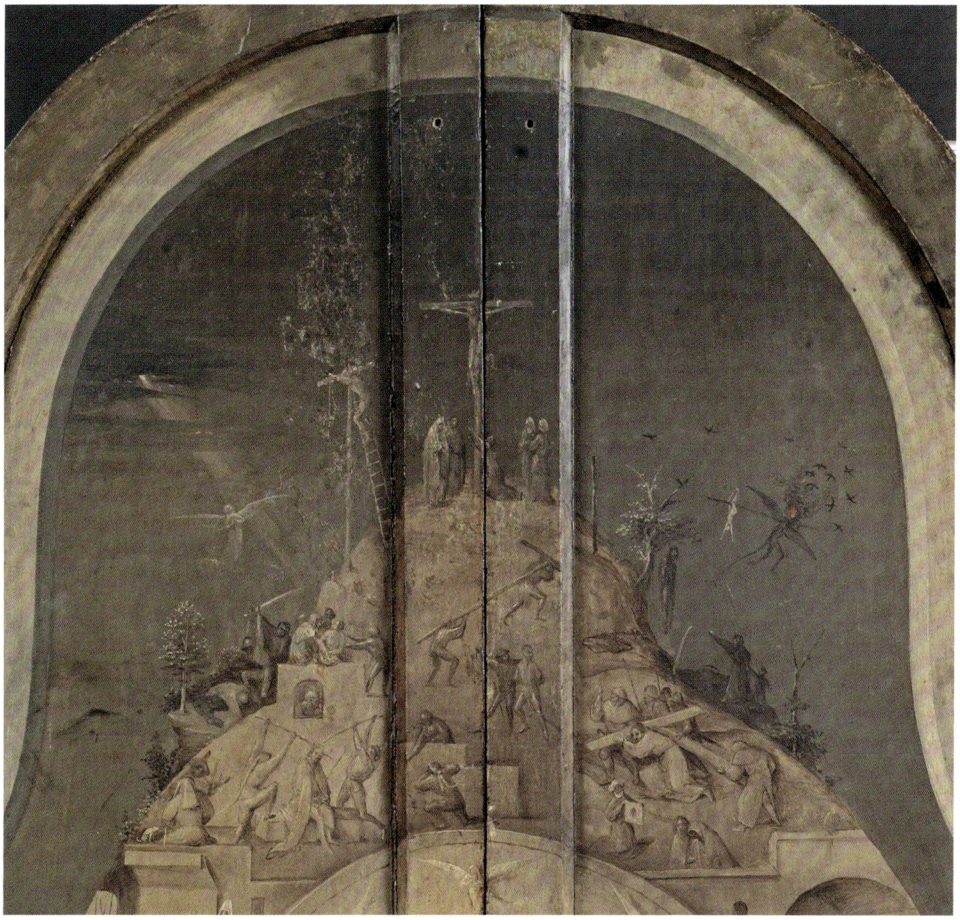

116 Detail of Hieronymus Bosch, *Mass of Saint Gregory* (fig. 115)

with concrete and metaphysical enemies pressing in on all sides. From the moment of his birth in Bethlehem, it seems, the world's response to Christ will indeed be hostile. The first gift, the eldest Magus's statuette, predicts this outcome by showing Abraham sacrificing his son at God's inscrutable command. An angel suspends the blow, but in the death that the old story foreshadows, God gives to the enemies his own son to be murdered. Death is the only peacemaking gift.

Bosch pictures that gift on the external painting on view when the triptych's shutters are closed (fig. 115). Painted frugally in shades of gray, this image formed the drab, everyday face Bosch's altarpiece ordinarily presented during the ritual of the Mass performed before it. In that daily ritual, the priest offered Christ's body, represented by the Eucharistic bread, to God as a sacrificial gift. Bosch depicts that ordinary rite, though in the form of a legendary miracle. While the priest (in the story, Pope Gregory the Great) kneels in prayer before the altar, Christ's body—ordinarily present but hidden in the Eucharist—rises from the grave, as if suffering its sacrifice in the present. In the painting's upper reaches, Bosch conjures Christ's death as a historical event. Taking us to Calvary, the "place of the skull" outside Jerusalem's walls, he recollects Christ's doleful path up the mount. On the summit he deposits, in perfect alignment with the half-length portrait of Christ below, a tiny effigy of the crucified Christ (fig. 116).

The idea is simple. Christian dogma affirmed that these two aligned bodies were one and the same. At the altar, the priest gifts Christ's body, which Christ had sacrificially gifted in his death on Calvary. Liturgy thus *re*-presents sacred history. It is useful to reconstruct how

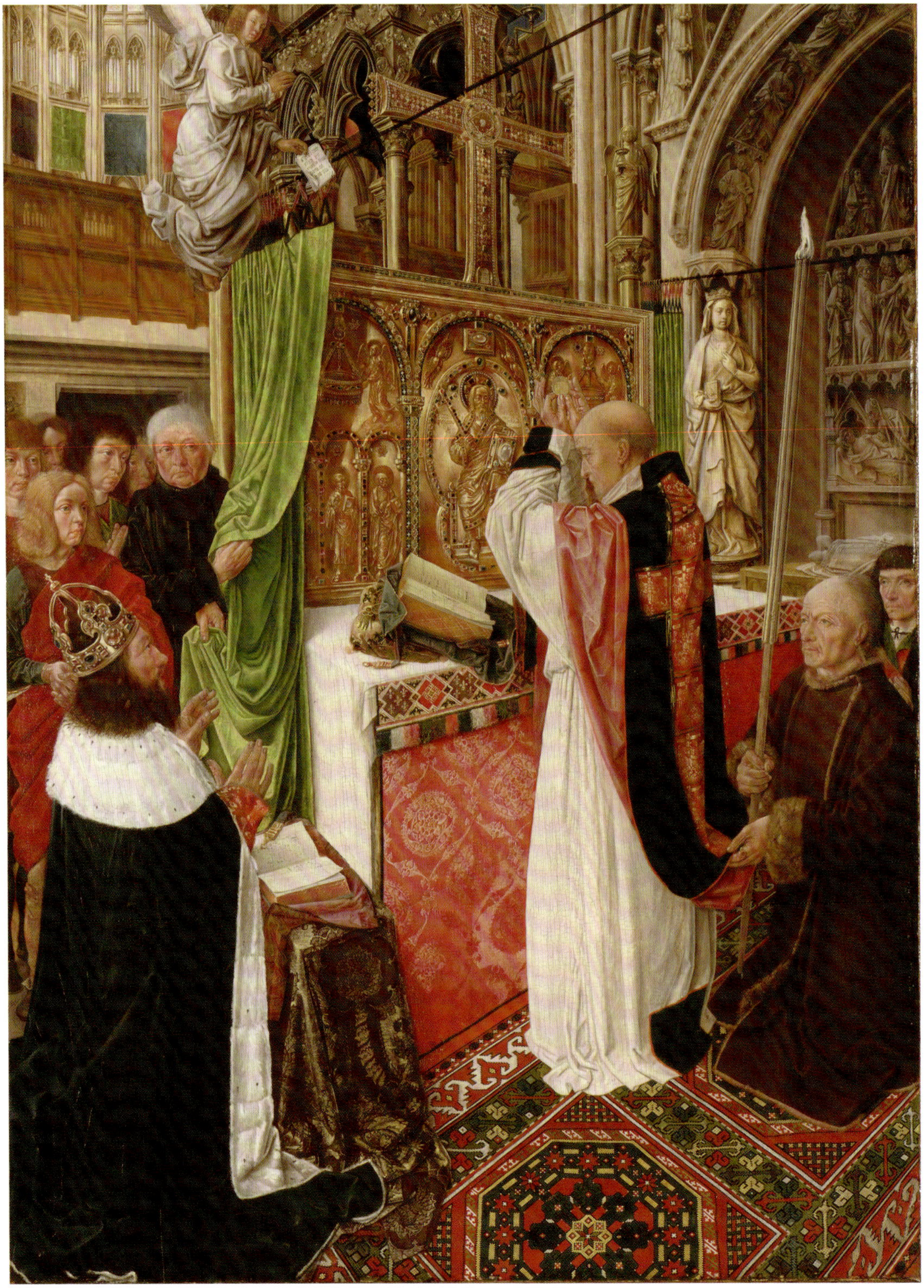

117 Master of Saint Giles, *Mass of Saint Giles*, c. 1500, oil and egg on oak, National Gallery, London

Bosch's altarpiece functioned in its liturgical context. At the altar where the work stood, the officiating priest would have activated the picture's display. With his back turned to the congregation, he would have held the consecrated Host over the altar, in front of Bosch's retable (fig. 117).[96] As a natural part of that rite, the priest would have aligned the Host—a wheaten disk probably bearing the stamp of the Cross—with Bosch's two portraits of Christ's body: the miraculous one in the Gregory scene and the historical one in the Crucifixion above. A true and efficacious representation of Christ, the Host would then have been ceremoniously broken, in a movement that the shutters could also on certain feast days mime. Opened on their hinges, the panels would have cut their painted effigies in two. Bosch engineers his triptych so that its festive opening reveals, in living color that contrasts to the shutters' somber grisaille, Christ's coming to light in Bethlehem. One arrives at God through Christ's body, since through the Incarnation peace with God was brokered, and through the Eucharist his saving work is done.

The Church modeled its doctrine of salvation on enmity. As a result of the Fall and in their continuing condition of sin, people stood in a state of offense vis-à-vis God.[97] Divine enmity could cease only through a satisfaction beyond all human means. Only God himself could pay such a colossal debt. This restitution was accomplished through Christ. Christ begged his wrathful father to transfer to humanity (Christ's kin) a *counterdebt* arising from his dying sinless. Peace was thus restored through the gift of his body.

In history and in liturgy this gift circulates in a state of enmity. Bosch circles the half-length portrait of Christ with scenes of the Passion. Jogging the viewer's memory of the sufferings the Savior endured and focusing prayers of reparation, each episode—Christ's betrayal and arrest, his trial by the Jewish high priest Caiaphas, his scourging, and so forth—shows Christ surrounded by foes.[98] Lower, the four scenes flanking Christ's body read loosely as paintings executed on a flat support, which in turn seems to back an arched stone slab with lamenting angels carved in low relief. Toward the top, however, this fiction of an artifact—a sort of altarpiece within Bosch's altarpiece—cunningly dissolves into the vision of Calvary. Cheap to make and suitably Lenten in appearance, grisaille was commonly used for the closed, or everyday, state of altarpieces.[99] A master of chiaroscuro, Bosch uses the humble medium here to conjure the cataclysmic eclipse attending Christ's death. This hellish hill is the triptych's Boschian climax, and it is here, at the right, that Bosch sketches with his brush the suicide of Judas, with demons swarming the archenemy's pale, sylph-like soul. In the Middle Ages, Judas was the patron saint of graft, bribery, and false gifts.[100] One of the Twelve Apostles but secretly the archenemy, Judas also personified Christ's betrayal by Jews—an identification supported by the name Judah, synonymous with the tribe of Israel.[101] Unusual in Crucifixion images, the figure of Judas trumpets conspiracy in a painting haunted by nefarious plots and betrayals. Judas's suicide and his eternal damnation also frame all the spectacles of the victimized Christ within another overarching struggle, the final and decisive one, in which Christ turns out to be the victor.[102]

The main subject of the shutters concerns betrayal of a more mundane kind. Some two centuries after his death, in 604 CE, Gregory the Great's biographers reported the following miracle: while Pope Gregory was saying Mass, a woman laughed and said to a companion that the bread on the altar wasn't Christ, since she had baked it herself.[103] Gregory therefore prayed for a sign,

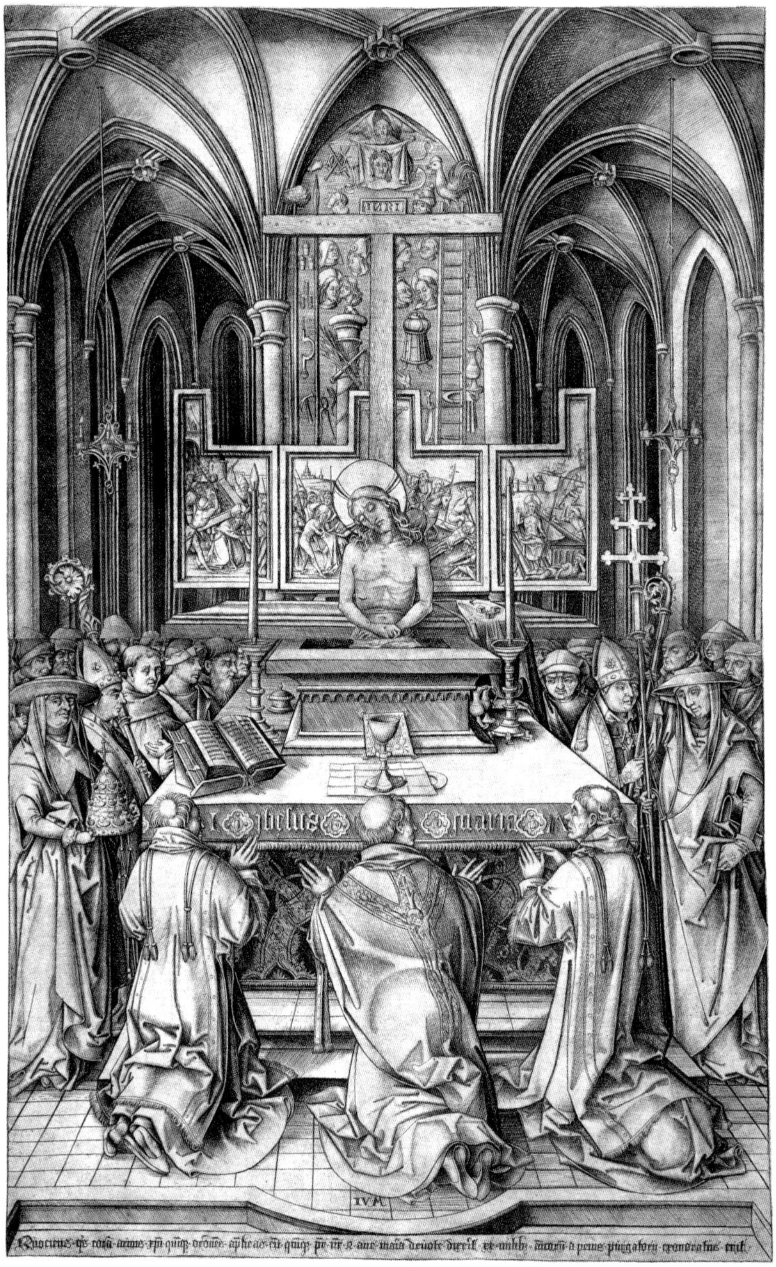

118 Israhel van Meckenem, *Mass of Saint Gregory*, c. 1490/1500, engraving, National Gallery of Art, Washington, Rosenwald Collection

and the Host suddenly became a bleeding finger. The miracle grew in the telling. In the thirteenth century, instead of the bloody finger, Christ's whole body appeared on the altar. Authors subsequently linked this vision to a certain half-length portrait of Christ kept in Santa Croce in Gerusalemme in Rome, claiming this venerable icon had been crafted for Gregory and captured truly the miracle.[104] In the Jubilee year of 1350, the pope gave this icon an indulgence of fourteen thousand years for prayers said before it, and prints contemporary with Bosch's triptych make even greater promises. The Rhenish goldsmith and printmaker Israhel van Meckenem attached to his engraving of *Mass of Saint Gregory* an inscription granting an indulgence of twenty thousand years to those who used the print for prayer; some time later, perhaps to drum up sales, the artist burnished out this allowance and inscribed in a new one of forty-five thousand years (fig. 118).[105] It may be that imputing such power to a sacred image had grounding in Gregory's legacy, for it was he who, in 599, defended church pictures against the iconoclasm that raged in Byzantium.[106]

But Gregory's salience lies more in his role as father of the Western liturgy. His miraculous Mass concerns the presence of doubt, disbelief, and conspiracy within the everyday context of church ritual. In the earliest versions, the skeptic laughs and confides her secret: the bread is just bread. Bosch's *Mass of Saint Gregory* shows the laity crowded behind the altar gazing dumbly into the mystery, as do the impassive shepherds visible behind the manger at the Epiphany (see fig. 93). In Gregory's writings, quotidian deceptions, specifically seeming outwardly holy while being inwardly sinful, were the very essence of enmity with God. They were also the sign of the Antichrist within: "Antichrist is done daily among the wicked."[107] Indeed, according to Gregory, Antichrist was not a singular personage arriving at the end of time, but he was the accumulated body of Christ's enemies over the course of human history. It is that perennially hostile condition that prevailed at Christ's birth, that occasioned Gregory's miraculous Mass, and that still flourishes now, say, as friends and foes make sense of Bosch's picture.

It cannot be by accident that Bosch painted the tiny Crucifixion right over the gap between the shutter panels (see fig. 116). Opened, the shutters will cross Christ out; but even closed, the gap makes Christ's body almost disappear. Although not quite an iconoclasm, this uneasy arrangement builds concealment into revelation. Gregory's apparition shows what the Host hides. In doctrinal terms, the miracle reveals the *substance* of the Eucharist—Christ's body—that lays hidden in the so-called *accidents* (or inessential properties) of the consecrated bread.[108] But what appears to Gregory is another form of concealment. The likeness of the suffering Christ shows its subject in negation.[109] Preserved in the venerated icon in Rome and reproduced in countless printed and painted replicas, the vision shows what the Passion did to God's son, how it turned the perfect image and likeness of the deity into the ugliest of men. Bosch deliberately places this, the Man of Sorrows, together with the Crucifixion on the break in his image because both of these are already *broken images*. Images of a crossed-out God, they also form the entranceway to the triptych's open state. They prepare us for its haunted epiphany. And by comparison with the Magi's gifts, they remind us how incommensurate is Christ's gift of death.

It ought to be remembered that Bosch's altarpiece belonged materially to a system of gift exchange. As its several donor portraits indicate, this costly work was given to the church as a pious offering. And even for these original friends, the flames of purgatory burned, unseen, around the altar where the triptych stood. A contemporary panel of the *Mass of Saint Gregory* makes these fires manifest (fig. 119).[110] The painter (probably from the northern Netherlands) visualizes how, helped by the pious donation of this painting itself, a soul escapes purgatory by drops of sacrificial blood. Bosch multiplies the enmity that surrounds every such offering of peace. Painting obscurely, turning epiphany to darkness, he even estranges the donation he has painted to soothe divine wrath. Gifts—the strange ones he depicts as well as the one his elusive depiction in essence is—*remain marked by the animosity that necessitated them.*

Anger

Bosch was an expert in enmity. Hatred was his professional specialty. At the beginning of the era in European art when, due to an expanding art market, individual painters' shops narrowed their production to pictures of particular, salable types, Bosch made the portrayal of enemies his distinctive expertise. The Devil's hatred of people, people's hatred of other people, the Jews' hatred of Christ and Christians, the Christians' reciprocal hatred for their enemies, the hatred directed toward an "us" by an invisible, conspiring enemy "them," and

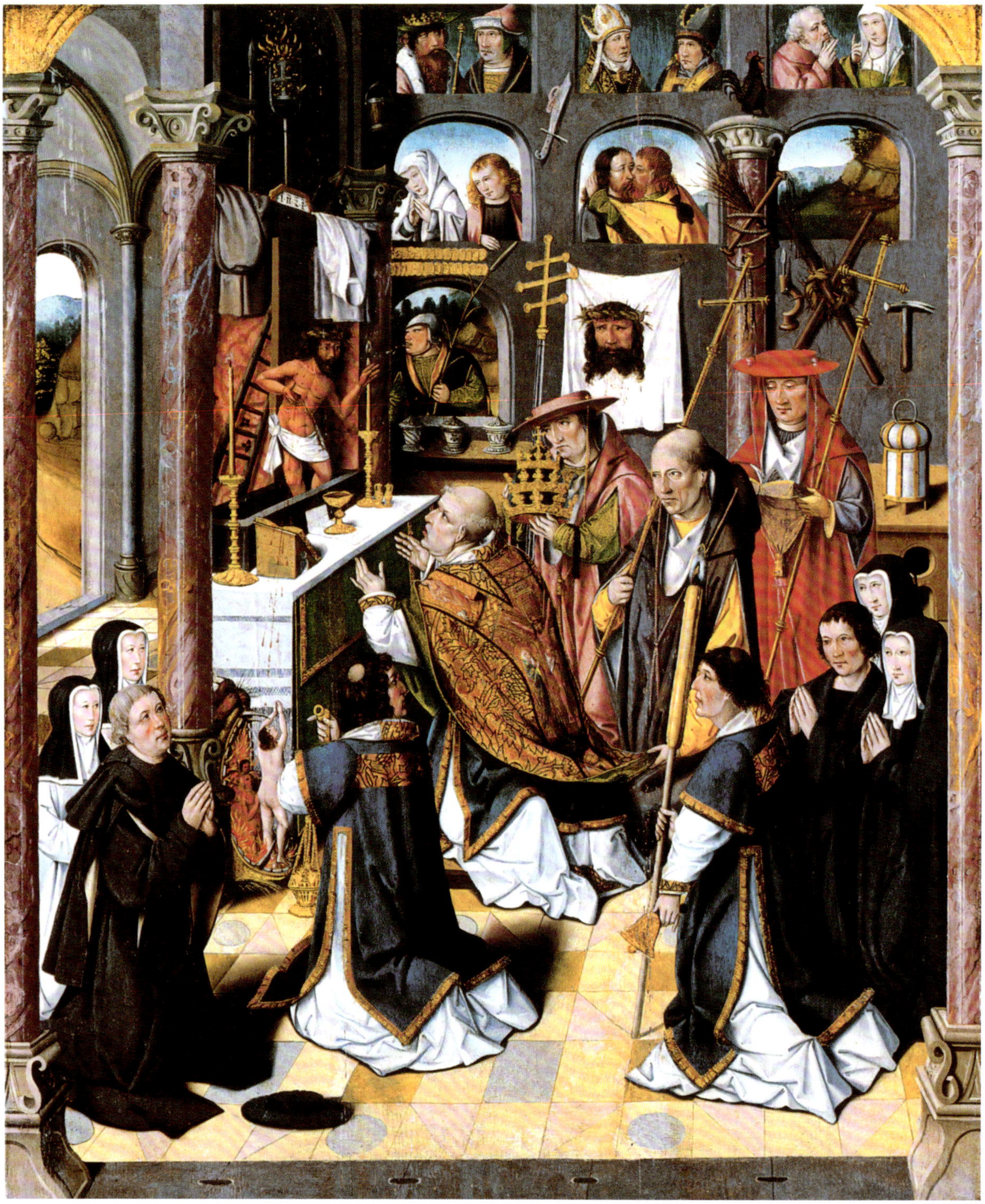

119 Master of the Prague Fountain of Life, *Mass of Saint Gregory*, c. 1510, panel, private collection

the wrath of God that consumes most everyone: this global economy of loathing stands not just portrayed in Bosch's pictures but also *performed*, as if his brush were an instrument of the enmity (figs. 120 and 121).

Hatred contaminates. The aversions these images represent defile their visual form. Turned hostile, they issue confusingly their threat, making uncertain whether they are for us or against us. The notorious obscurity of Bosch's symbolism derives largely from the doubt this artist seeks to raise about his products' good intentions. What a symbol means in Bosch

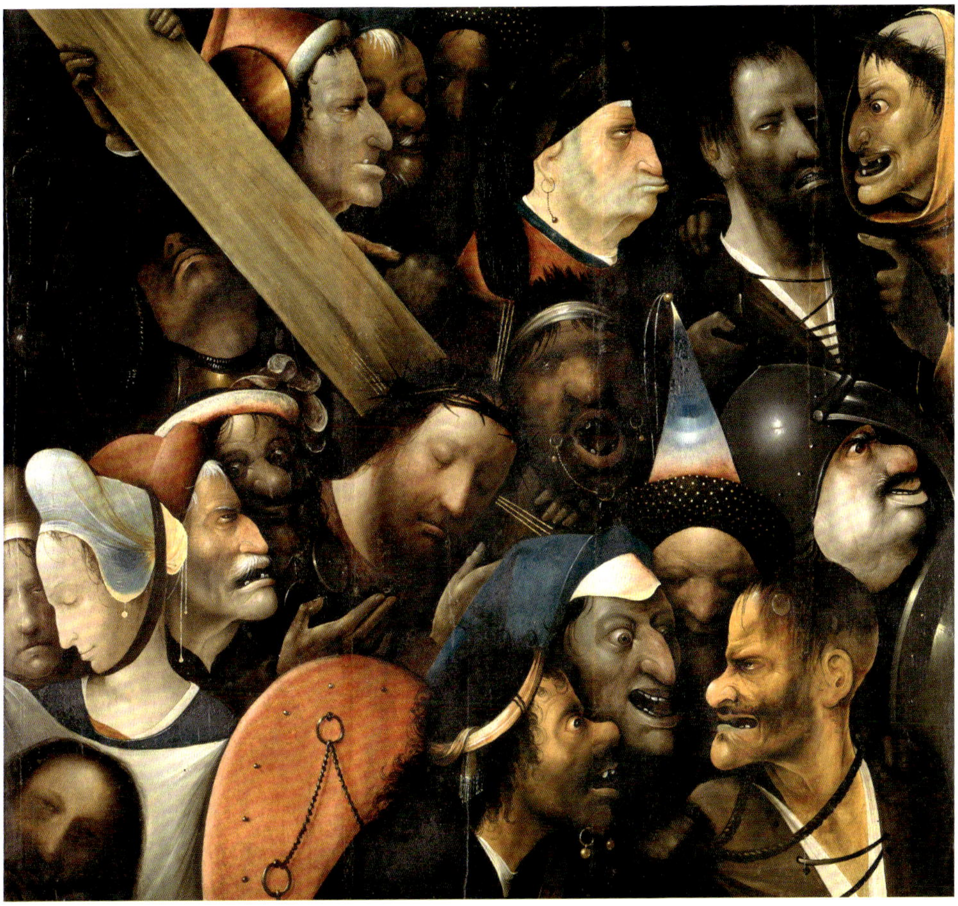

120 Hieronymus Bosch (workshop?), *Christ Carrying the Cross*, c. 1515, panel, Museum voor Schone Kunsten, Ghent

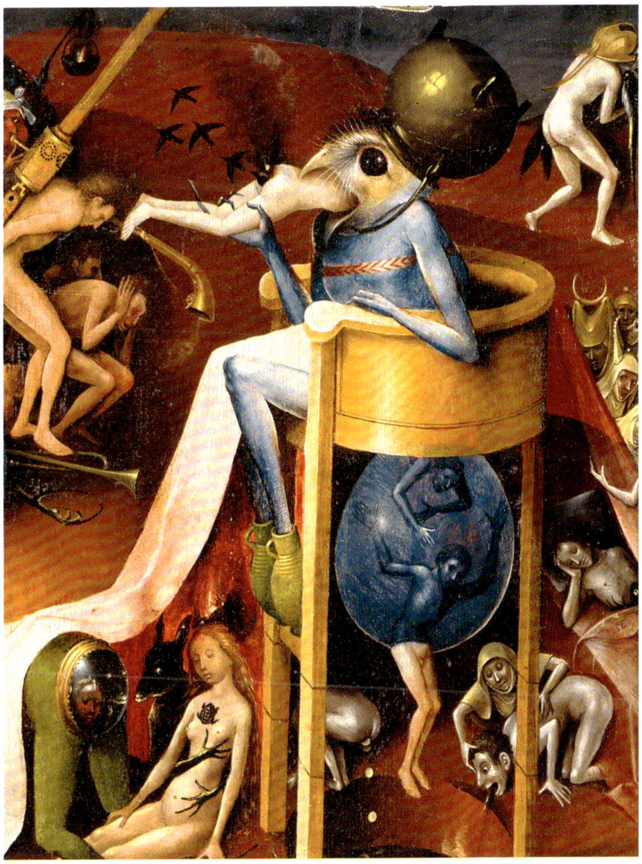

121 Detail of Hieronymus Bosch, *The Garden of Delights* (fig. 170)

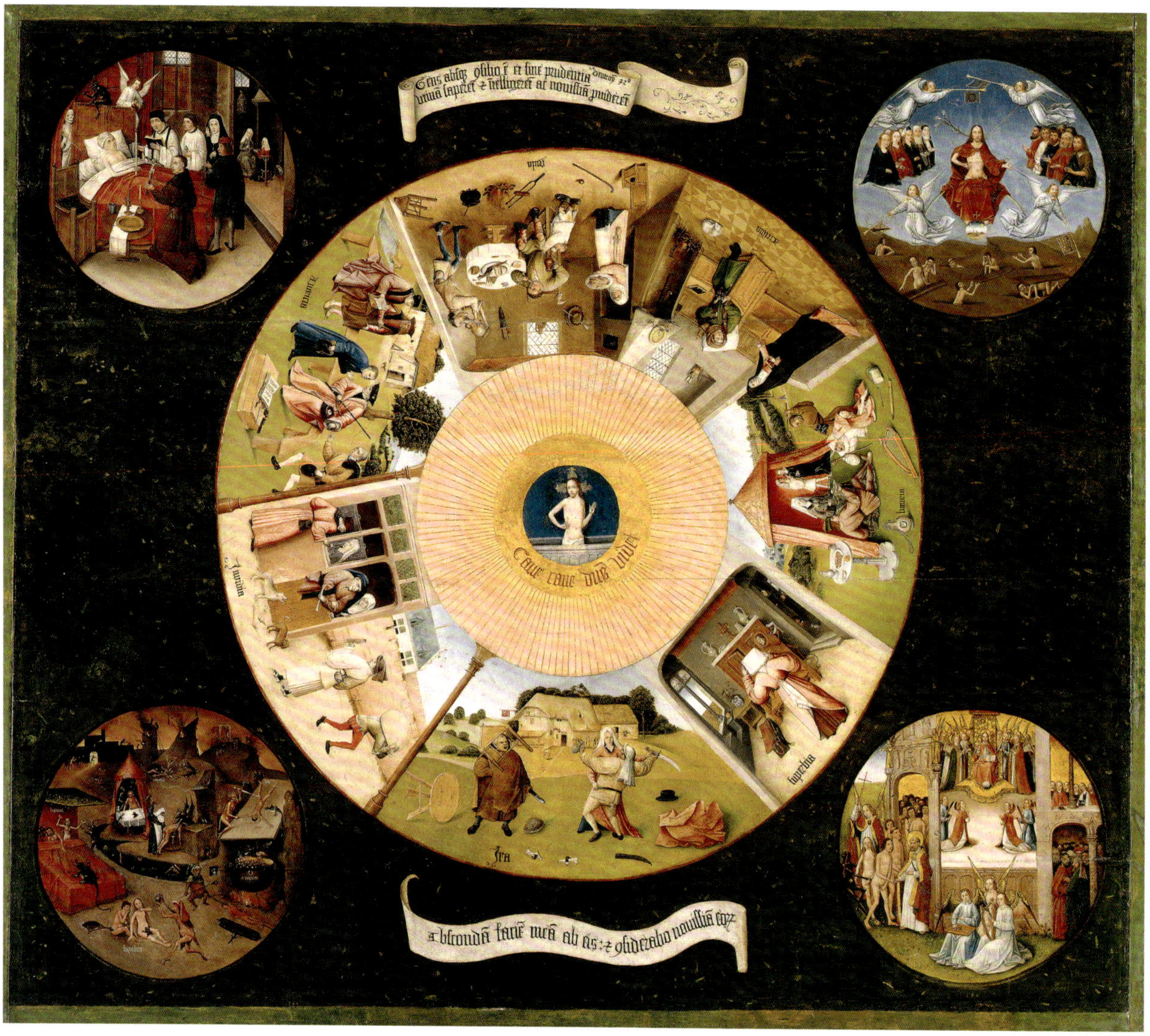

122 Hieronymus Bosch (workshop?), *The Seven Deadly Sins and the Four Last Things*, c. 1500, panel, Museo Nacional del Prado, Madrid

gets confused by something more basic than the lack of an interpretative key.[111] Since it may be *of* the enemy, this symbolism haunts us with a purpose that, engineered to be unknowable to its target, belongs to those who plot our annihilation.

At the base of the roundel illustrating the seven deadly sins, Bosch displays the face of hatred in the everyday world (figs. 122 and 123).[112] Treated as a sequence of events rather than a state of affairs, enmity has a plot. Occurring outside a brothel, a brawl seems to have started with sex and drink; just now it is escalating from messy blows to a deadly exchange. Tossed objects suggest the frenzy of the action, while the restraint applied by the woman freeze-frames the moment, giving the cloaked man time to draw his sword. Bosch isolates this contestant as the figure of anger. Not only do the Latin inscription (*Ira*) and the red-and-gold lion banner label him thus. Baring his teeth like an animal, he properly *personifies* the sin, abandoning his *person* to it.

Of all the vices, anger is the most sudden, committed in the flash point of hate, before the denouement of satisfaction or regret. Bosch places this face-off at the bottom of a circle of genre scenes. The momentary equilibrium of enmity forms a meeting point between these paintings of everyday life and the visually stable but otherworldly scenes inside and

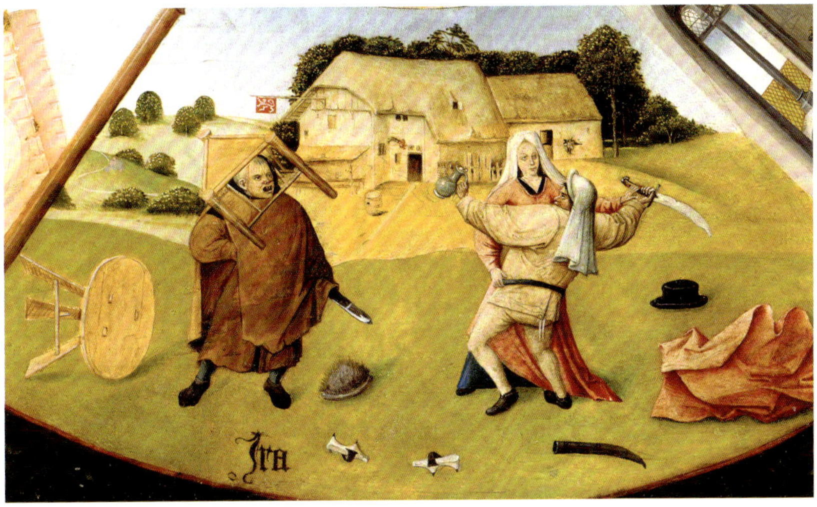

123 Detail of Hieronymus Bosch (workshop?), *The Seven Deadly Sins and the Four Last Things* (fig. 122)

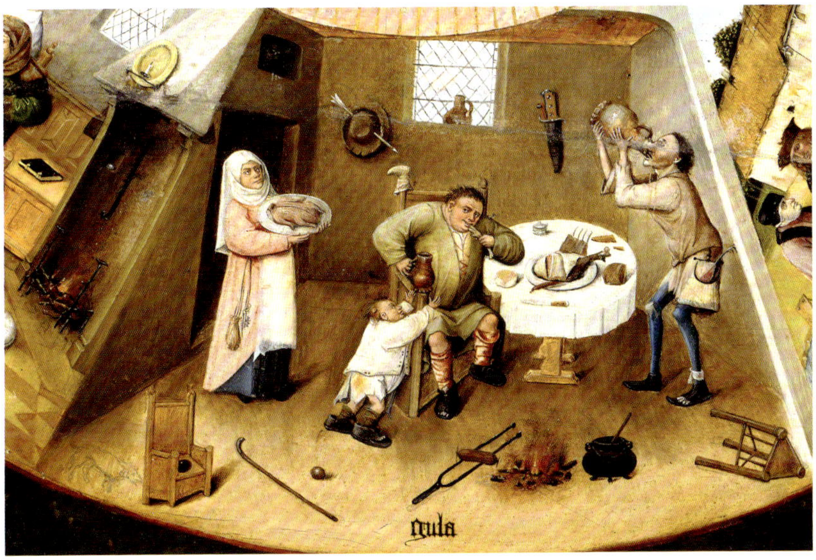

124 Detail of Hieronymus Bosch (workshop?), *The Seven Deadly Sins and the Four Last Things* (fig. 122)

around their circle. Throwing things into disorder, anger also joins the cosmic order as part of the logical sequence of sins. Gluttony fills the opposite side of the circle, as anger's antipode (fig. 124). *Gula* in Latin, it incarnates sins of selfishness, hence its neighbors avarice and sloth, whereas in anger, the self abandons itself to extinguish the enemy. Bosch explains this passage away from self-preservation by flanking anger with vanity and envy. Freud attributed aggression to a struggle between narcissism and competition. The turn from self-love into hate occurs because of rivalry. Competing for the same object as the self, *other people* institute the self's desire and its aggressivity.[113] A Flemish devotional manual of 1516 put it more succinctly: "When a man encounters a resistance to the fires of self-infatuation he becomes quarrelsome and disturbed."[114] Anger unmoors through the violence of its commission. Yet Bosch makes this volatile scene the circle's fundament, aligning it with the upright images and texts. He thus implicates anger in his composition's structure and its mutability. Although the conflict is just now in the balance, chaos preceded it and will follow. The objects scattered on the ground imply rotary motion, as if centrifugal force threw them to the circumference. Additionally, the toppled table in the scene suggests the roundel of the painting itself observed from just off center. Guevara called the work *una mesa*, giving rise

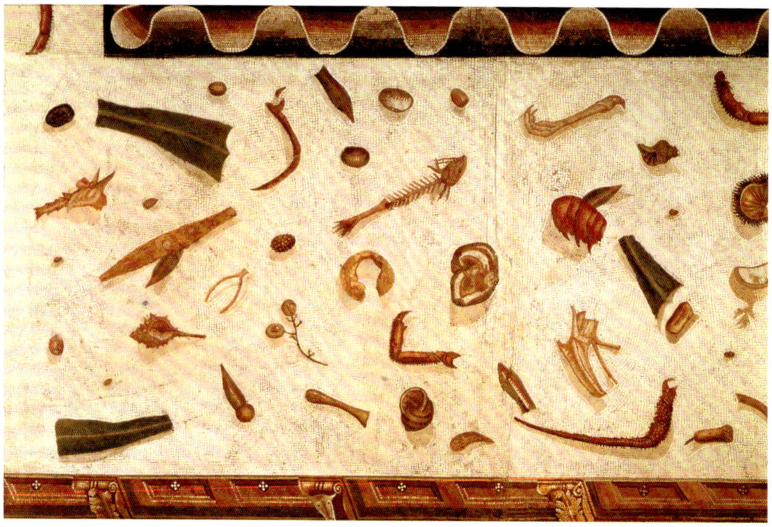

125 Heraklitos, *Asarotos oikos* (*Unswept Floor*), c. 130, mosaic from a Roman villa in the vineyards of Achille Lupi, Rome, Museo Gregoriano Profano

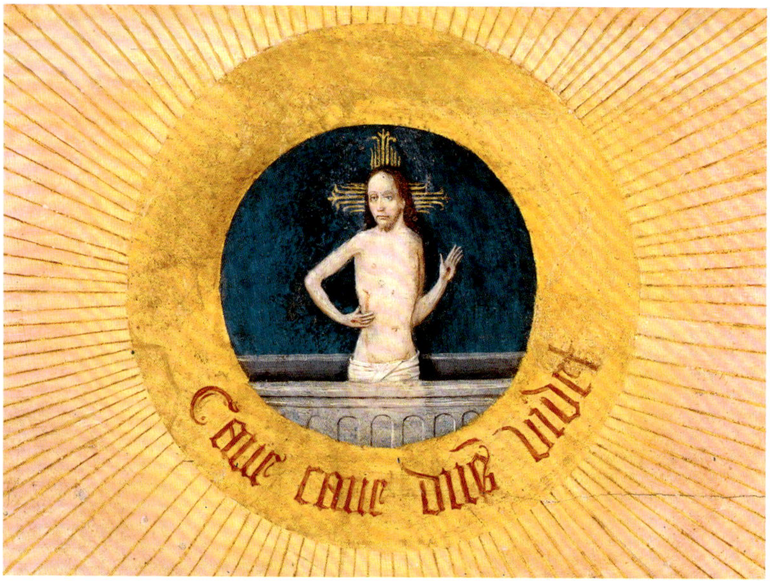

126 Detail of Hieronymus Bosch, (workshop?) *The Seven Deadly Sins and the Four Last Things* (fig. 122)

to the picture's modern nickname, the *Tabletop of the Seven Deadly Sins*.[115] Today the work hangs upright in the Prado, but originally it may have been displayed flat so that viewers would circle around it.

Wider than the other genre scenes, and uniquely upright, anger becomes the gateway to a spectacle that sends viewers in motion around the painting. The figure of the circle has an extraordinary range of connotations.[116] Circles appear inside several of the genre scenes. Anger and gluttony both feature round tables. In gluttony, the table stands upright in its setting but upside down in Bosch's painting; the victuals on it recollect, in their arrangement, the objects strewn on the floor of this and some of the other scenes. Flesh appealing to the flesh, these foods make sense of Bosch's genre treatment of sin itself: everyday life unfolds randomly and unoriented, like the things displayed on the table. Scattered on the ground, goods become garbage—a conceit that makes Bosch's composition here, and in all his scenes of hell, reminiscent of the *asarotos oikos* (unswept house) floor mosaics of antiquity (fig. 125).[117] In anger, meanwhile, the table lies toppled and bare. Exhibiting the joined planks of which it is made, it reveals the physical substratum that images in a panel painting conceal.

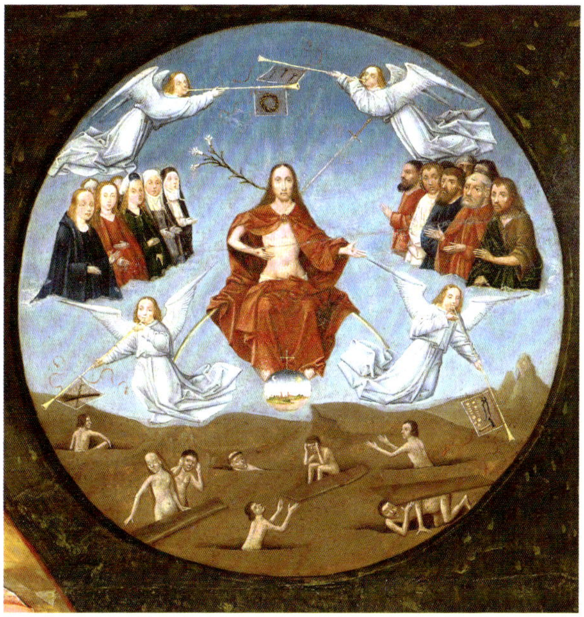

127 Detail of Hieronymus Bosch (workshop?), *The Seven Deadly Sins and the Four Last Things* (fig. 122)

To the right of this bare circle, another circular form comes into view. Vanity beholds herself in a mirror supported by a demon. In hell, this object serves to punish self-love. Like the tables depicted on Bosch's tabletop, the mirror is a *mise en abyme* of the picture that contains it, as we will see. With its seven pillars resembling spokes, Bosch's circle also forms a wheel. The catastrophic vicissitudes of sin are therefore grasped by that venerable symbol of fortune.[118] Given the prevalence of allegorical wheels of fortune in fifteenth-century art, Bosch's roundel would have connoted disaster by its outline alone.

A table, a mirror, and a wheel, Bosch's circle of sin is also—and perhaps above all—an eye. The words "Beware, beware, God sees" appear in Latin around what—thanks to the inscription—counts as a dark pupil (fig. 126). Bosch paints these words in red lake on a dry-gilded circle that glows into the pale pink circle around it. Inscribed with exactly 128 rays (the Pythagorean 2 to the seventh), this ideogram of an iris also doubles as the sun.[119] This makes the outer circle, where sin occurs in the form of genre paintings, into an image of earth. Lit by the sun and beheld by God's gaze, Bosch's world picture can be understood in at least two ways. If one takes the inner circle to be a sun, then the scenes of sin form the inner surface of a sphere beheld as if all at once from its center. The globes at Christ's feet in the roundels of Judgment and Salvation bring this geometry to mind (fig. 127). Taking the inner circle as an iris, however, the scenes become reflections of "outer things" on the eye's convex white skin—or those reflections cast on the concave retina on the rear interior of an eye.[120]

Whatever its geometry, the world becomes radically peripheral. Neither a landscape resting in a cosmic orb (like the vista inside the globe in the Judgment roundel) nor a terrain mapped on the outer surface of a sphere, as with globes that were beginning to be produced in Bosch's day, it mutates between a globe turned inside out *and* a reflected surround. This announces its perverse condition as "world upside down." Which brings us full circle to enmity, depicted at the base.

In committing sin and taking pleasure in the world—in other words, in behaving as people in the circle do—humanity becomes the enemy of God. Vice is in a deadly face-off with God. "Ye adulterers and adulteresses," scolds the Epistle of James. "Do ye not know that the friendship of the world is enmity with God? Whosoever therefore will be a friend of the world is the enemy of God" (James 4:4).[121] Sin turns friends into foes both locally, in the selfish interactions among persons, and globally, in the mutual hostility that ensues between God and man. This was the condition of enmity on which Christianity based the doctrine of atonement. Historically, in the Crucifixion, and liturgically, in the Sacrament of the Altar, Christ restored peace through the gift of his body, as the Prado *Adoration of the Magi* shows. Guevara reports that Bosch's *Seven Deadly Sins* had a pendant: the *Seven Sacraments*.[122] Together these pictures would have balanced perfectly offense and satisfaction.

Dies Irae

Bosch's *Seven Deadly Sins* diagrams both movements, both the offense to God and the compensation by Christ. In the scene of anger, men stand face-to-face, each seeking the other's annihilation. The enmity between man and God has a different shape. Sin establishes friendship with the world. This turns the sinner *to* or *away from* God, and in response, God turns from the world. The upside-down, inside-out structure of the world visualizes this cosmic reversal. The texts inscribed on the banderoles tie Bosch's conceit to the central biblical trope of concealment. Below anger, the inscription reads: "I will hide my face from them. I will see what their end will be." These words come from the Song of Moses, in Deuteronomy, in which the lawgiver, admonishing Israel for having defiled its covenant, speaks God's wrathful words. Just below the human face of anger, Bosch inscribes the words "hidden face" (*abscondam faciem*), referring to the visage of an angry God. And in the corner roundels depicting the *Four Last Things*, he paints the "end," or *novissima*, that the turned-away deity beholds.[123]

The Song of Moses is a pivotal Old Testament text about enmity. In it the children of Israel receive their definition through distinctions between friend and foe. On the one hand, as chosen people, Israel battles the alien nations that continually assail it, but with God on its side.[124] On the other hand, because of its idolatry, this victim nation—this "us" from which Moses speaks—becomes God's special foe. Bosch does not include the full text of God's penal wrath. He allows the banderole to end with God's "seeing," and inscribes below, in dark on dark, his own name. But in the next verses of Deuteronomy, God speaks his anger through Moses: "They have moved me to jealousy with that which is not God, they have provoked me to anger with their vanities; and I will move them to jealousy with those which are not a people; I will provoke them to anger with a foolish nation. For a fire is kindled in mine anger, and shall burn unto the lowest hell, and shall consume the earth with her increase, and set on fire the foundations of the mountains" (Deut. 32:21–22). Worshiping strange gods, Israel turns into its *own* enemy and must endure its persecution by non-national "others." The "us" becomes a vilified "them." Conversely, the outsiders, the pagans, now become God's instruments. Christianity appropriated this historical scheme. Christ assumed the role of victim, now in an eternal battle with the Devil himself. Removing the difference between compatriots and aliens, and embraced after his death by the "them" of Jewish self-definition, Christ was persecuted by the Jews themselves, who, taken at their own word, serve as God's implacable foe. In dying at the hands of his people, Christ suffers Jewish enmity, justifying future Christian enmity against Jews.

Bosch puts Christ in the pupil of God's eye. Rising from a sarcophagus and backed by a gray ground suggestive of a cave or tomb, Christ displays his wounds to us and presumably to his father, whose eye contains him. In the roundel at the upper right, Christ, now in judgment, similarly displays his wounds while humanity emerges from its graves.

(Observe the two horizons, one in the orb, the other in the dissolving world.) In the abiding present of divine omnivoyance, however, it is the incarnated Christ whom God beholds *in abscondito* (Matt. 6:18). Like the circle that surrounds it, this figure is hugely overdetermined. Supreme victim of evil, the suffering Christ explains both why and how God hides his face from man. That people could murder their God proved that his divinity was invisible to them in their sinful state, while his disfiguring wounds, made by human hands, placed him visually farthest from the divine. A Man of Sorrows, Christ is the turned-away deity, hence Bosch's strange placement of that figure on the break between the shutters of the Prado *Adoration of the Magi*. "Nothing remained whole on his body, and everything was thoroughly wounded," states the mid-fifteenth-century *Secret Passion* on the basis of Isaiah 1:6; and again, with reference to Isaiah 53:2, "not the tiniest bit of his holy face could be observed or recognized."[125] With this ruin of a body before him, then, God's vengeful wrath ought to be infinite. Yet Christ's purpose in allowing himself to be crucified was not anger but pity, since through his death all sins could be forgiven. In portraying Christ, Bosch employs the visual formula known as the *imago pietatis*.[126] *Pietas*, meaning piety and pity, indicates both what Christ exemplifies and what this image should occasion. But what place can pity have within a model of enmity?

In the twelfth century, an anonymous theologian made a famous list of twenty-four definitions of God made by twenty-four masters of philosophy. The first describes a structure of love: "God is a monad that generates a monad and reflects in himself his own ardor."[127] By this account, Bosch's panel centers not on enmity but on its opposite, the state of a perfectly reciprocated love. Moreover, since viewers of the panel can take their place before it, then the *imago pietatis* observed inside the eye might reflect a love and a divinity contained in them, and therefore the picture might gaze back at them lovingly. The German mystic Meister Eckhart speculated that Christ was a "sparklet" at the center of the soul; infinitely minute in the sinful world, this bit of light was nonetheless infinite, since it was also divine.[128] Through pious imitation of Christ, and by viewing images of him, people could cultivate that inner likeness to divinity.

The second definition of God from the list of twenty-four concerns the paradox of infinity in the smallest part: "God is a sphere of which the center is everywhere and the circumference nowhere."[129] This sentence can serve to gloss the irrational geometry proposed by Bosch, while the plurality of definitions contained in the list suggests that conceptual complexity, in theology as in painting, can itself figure the divine. True, no artist can quite picture the unimaginable images conjured by these definitions. Making the world into the inverted surface of a sphere, Bosch can allow each viewer, who occupies the center of his or her experience, to behold what ubiquity might look like to an eye that is both center and circumference. More effectively still, Bosch articulates the incommensurability of God and man through a reversal that images alone can make. It is not merely that, in proposing his picture to be an eye, he turns us into mere objects and his painting into the sovereign subject of its own representation. All-seeing but unseen, facing us but (to our eyes) turned way, this medusal gaze betokens a consciousness of the alien as much as of the self.[130] The division of enemies from friends that this eye puts in play would have constituted, for the picture's original viewers, their very identity as subjects in the social field.

This Bosch picture has been called a mirror of conscience.[131] In 1605, the librarian at El Escorial, Joseph de Sigüenza, reported that Philip II had hung the painting in his bedchamber "as a mirror" to remind him of his offenses.[132] In the Spanish Habsburg court, as in Bosch's time, zealous confessional practices endeavored to expose all concealed misdeeds on the assumption that individuals did not always acknowledge their vices, even to themselves. Self-examination involved unearthing sins committed knowingly, though under the all-seeing eye of God. In his genre scenes, Bosch draws us into a space distinct from the frontal order of writing and history, and organized not around a center but a periphery. In an *unconscious* space, then, Bosch confronts us with a psychopathology of everyday life. Historically, genre painting takes off here, from these little scenes of ordinary life. Yet taken as a whole, Bosch's picture repudiates these scenes. More than merely the hidden *contents* of conscience, as a mirror the picture is also *like* conscience, for conscience itself is like a mirror. It is the means by which the self becomes an object for itself, reflecting on itself. Alternating punishment with love, conscience treats the incriminated subject as an enemy, while reestablishing friendship through submission. One does not need Freud's concept of a superego, or *Über-Ich*, to discern how, by the model Bosch's picture proposes, we are formed as conscientious subjects through our subjection to the gaze, where "gaze" signifies—all at once and programmatically—the father, language, history, and the law. In Christianity, Christ is the model of this subjection, this process "of becoming subordinated by power as well as of becoming subject," hence, in Bosch, the doubleness of the suffering Christ as both an object seen and the subject who sees.[133] The wounded body attests to supreme subordination, since Christ accepts death in order to fulfill the law and to atone for the offense of humanity, who are his kin. How, though, to explain the cruelty that befalls him? If, according to the theologian's primary definition, God generates a monad—i.e., Christ—in order to reflect in himself his own love, from whence came the universe of enmity that ruined him and that surrounds him still?

The Man of Sorrows at the picture's center and Christ in judgment at the upper right share the same gesture. God is a being who punishes *and* suffers. He punishes *because* he suffers, and he suffers *because* he punishes. Bosch was both a supreme portraitist of Christ's Passion *and* the unequaled painter of divine punishment. Like Dante, who made the words above the gate of hell read "primal Love made me" (*Inferno* 5, ll. 5–6), Bosch explored the sadomasochism of divine ardor, isolating the aggressive component within the religion of his day.[134] Where other painters of his tradition promoted visual *empathy* with Christ, Bosch fostered instead *antipathy*: revulsion against the world, against pleasure, against enemies both visible and invisible. In him, enmity is more than just a repertoire of motifs. Determining his art at every level, it is a *structure*, a *performance*, and a *symbolism*.

Structure

A Boschian *Christ Crowned with Thorns* belonged to the collection of Philip II in El Escorial, along with *The Seven Deadly Sins* and other key works by Bosch; the former was listed in inventories of 1574 and 1593 as being by the master, and often treated as autograph (fig. 128).[135] The wood for the *Christ Crowned with Thorns* panel has an earliest felling date of 1525, making it clearly a copy, perhaps after a lost, much-duplicated original. Observed side by side with *The Seven Deadly Sins*, it exhibits an identical structure, and not only because of the shared use of a round internal frame. Both paintings center on Christ as victim and surround him, 360 degrees, with agents of his pain. Note in the Boschian *Christ Crowned with Thorns* how

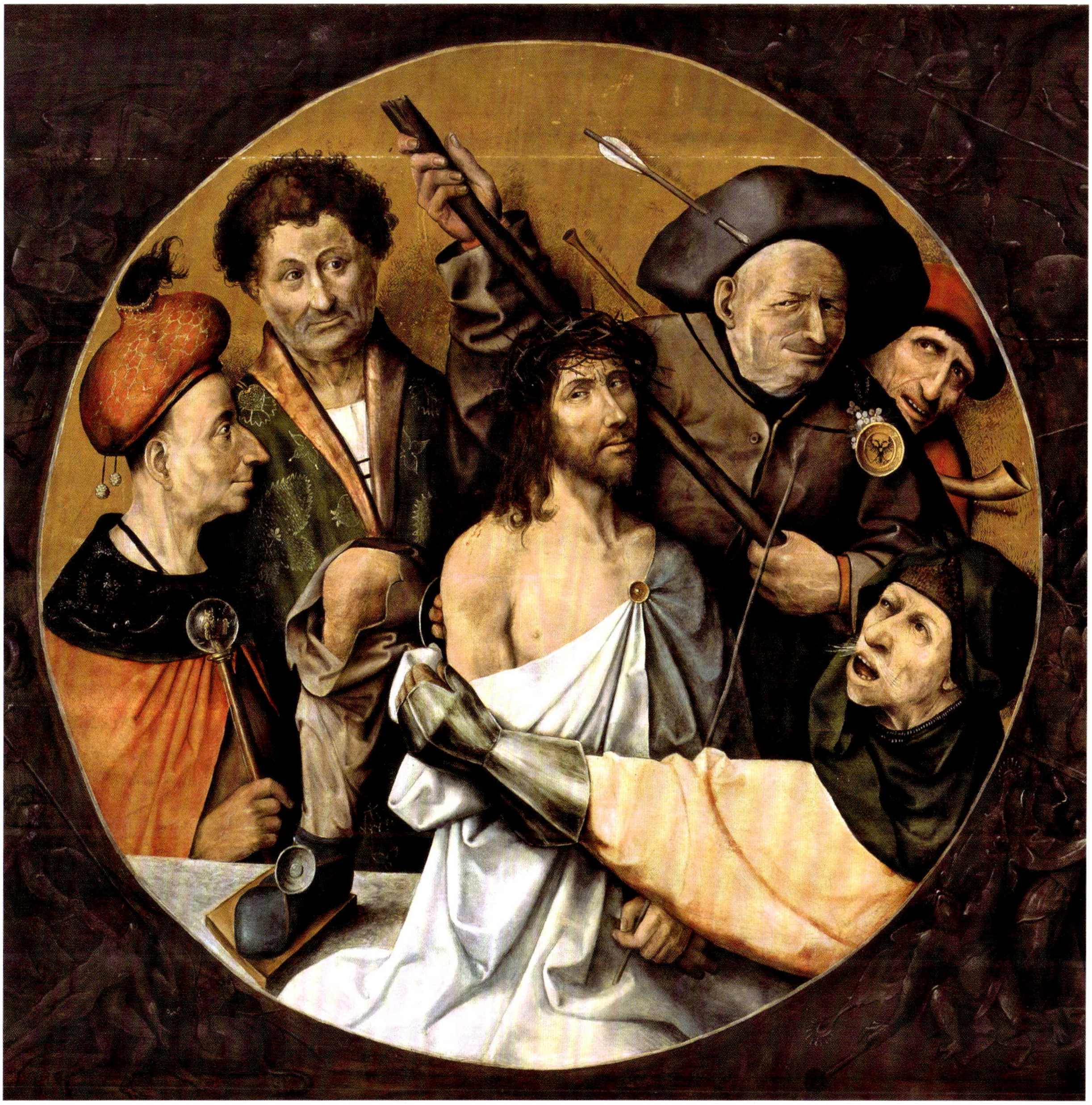

arms and legs engulf Christ. In both, Christ's body rises from a gray stone slab, the edge of which works like a low horizon, recollecting Bosch's ideograms for the world. And in the darkness that encompasses their circles, both pictures introduce a cosmic arena in which the evil fortunes portrayed at the center are reversed. This concentric alternation of victims and aggressors is to be found in one form or another in almost all of the artist's works. More than simply a motif, it constitutes the deep structure of the Boschian image. In Bosch, that is, the subject is victim, and by *subject* I mean both the paradigmatic human agent in these pictures and their principal theme.

128 After Hieronymus Bosch, *Christ Crowned with Thorns*, c. 1525, panel, El Escorial, Monastery of San Lorenzo, Madrid

We have observed how the closed and the open states of the Prado *Adoration of the Magi* are structured—through and through—by enmity. Both the liturgical and the historical body of Christ appear surrounded by enemies: in the main scene of the *Mass of Saint Gregory* these enemies are the doubters in the congregation; in the Passion scenes above, they are the Jewish

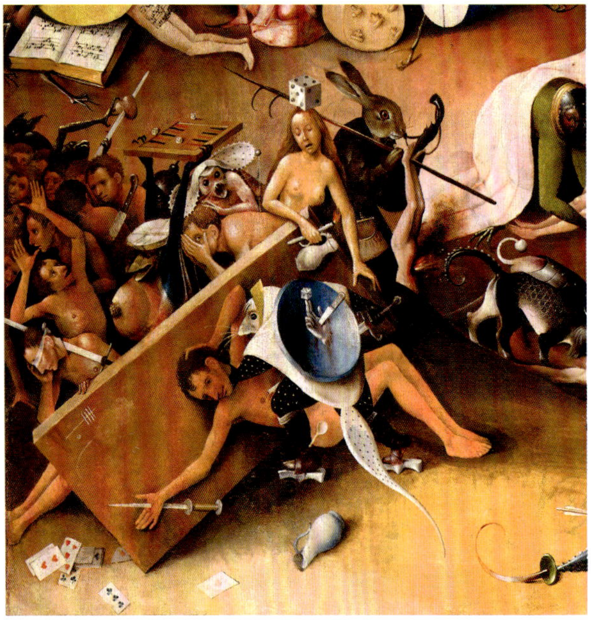

130 Detail of Hieronymus Bosch, *The Garden of Delights* (fig. 170)

badges, insignia—to bait or threaten, while imposing ignominious badges on the weak. In Bosch's day, people became obsessed with arson's signs.[141] Arsonists sometimes communicated with collaborators through special marks made on buildings targeted for destruction. Cryptic to their victims, these signifiers signified only to conspirators, who knew the code. Haunted by the possibility of malicious communiqués, people imputed accidental fires to hidden perpetrators, while random configurations—curious spots, crossed branches, a stone set upon another stone—could come to seem suspiciously but obscurely intentional, setting neighbor against neighbor and fueling general distrust of outsiders.

The inscrutable symbols in Bosch's works resemble most of all these marks: observe the cryptic chalk tallies on the slab in the Hell panel in the so-called *Garden of Delights* (fig. 130). Belonging to an enemy design, such signs *are* legible to the foe, hence our nagging sense of a meaning that eludes us. Yet they are deliberately opaque to us, the victims. Bosch's enmity may also reflect the specific circumstances of his hometown, 's-Hertogenbosch, which had a history of violent conflict with its Burgundian overlords. The dukes of Burgundy had pioneered new forms of centralized rule, including the total, permanent annihilation of towns rejecting their governance. By 1500, Bosch's town, now subdued, served loyally on the front line of the cruel Gelrian wars. Philip the Fair garrisoned his troops there; and it was during that time that he prepaid Bosch to paint a *Last Judgment* for his (Philip's) "very noble pleasure," as the document states.[142] And while burning rebellious towns of Guelders, Philip housed his stepmother, Holy Roman empress Bianca Maria Sforza, in the house right next door to Bosch's shop.[143] Bosch's breakthrough to Europe-wide fame derived from his residing, temporarily, at the center of violent conflict in northern Europe. This conflict also set the tone of Bosch's art, which infuses a sense of being a victim with the pleasures of aggression.

In his works, enmity is never simply "out there" as an external force threatening an innocent interior. Since it fuels the representation *of* enmity, enmity is everywhere to be found. Where other artists liken painting to prayer, Bosch instead curses with his brush. The painter Francis Bacon confessed that he never painted a portrait with the sitter in the room, since his

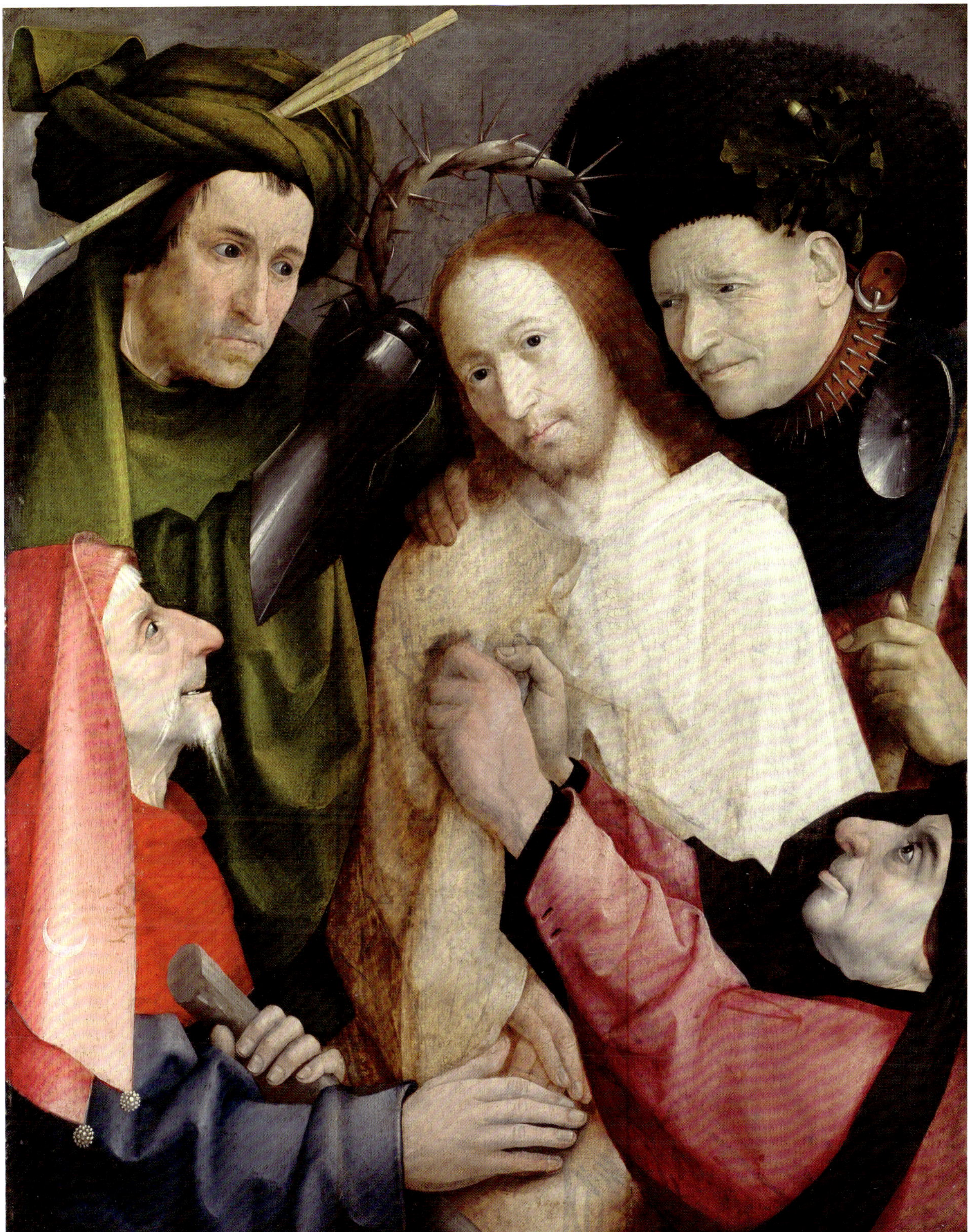

131 Hieronymus Bosch, *Christ Crowned with Thorns*, 1490–1500, oil on oak, National Gallery of Art, London

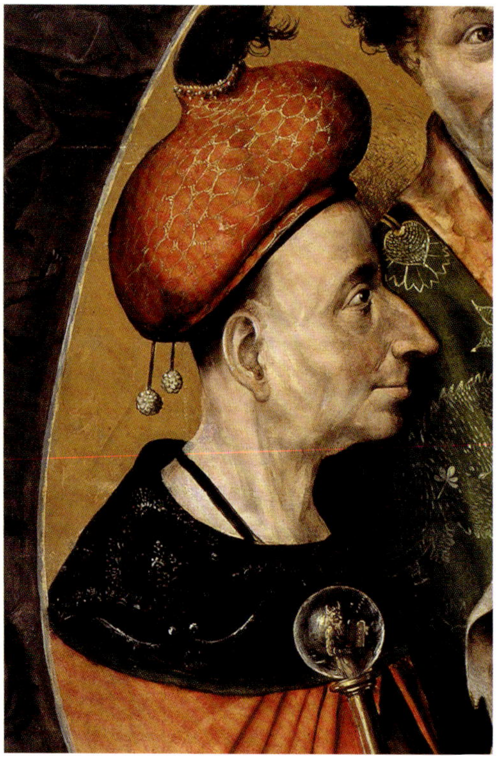

132 Detail of After Hieronymus Bosch, *Christ Crowned with Thorns* (fig. 128)

sitters were his friends and he didn't want them to see him "practice the injury."[144] Whether he imagines hell's punishments or slanders his enemies, Bosch injures what he makes. Consider one of his singular masterpieces, the *Christ Crowned with Thorns* now in London (fig. 131).[145] This painting's aggression consists as much in Bosch's slanderous caricatures as in what those enemies do. Both the artist and Christ's tormentors *disfigure*, the tormentors by applying the thorns, Bosch by his injurious portrait of that villainy. Both also create images, the artist self-evidently, by painting a painting. But the tormentors make images, too. Braided into a crown, the thorns serve as a figurative prop within a mock ritual. It is, as it were, an imaginary Jewish artifact, like the effigy of Moses topping the staff of one of the tormentors in the *Christ Crowned with Thorns* panel in El Escorial (fig. 132). In his *Ecce Homo* panel, now in Frankfurt, Bosch stages the Man of Sorrows as a public performance (fig. 133).[146] Christ's wounded body becomes a spectacle organized for the Jews. In the crowning, this theatrical and therefore perversely aesthetic dimension is implied both by Christ's being forced to playact a role and by the way the circle of tormentors, who direct the play, behold him as would an audience.

Plaited by them, and applied to Christ by their armored hands, the crown belongs to the tormentors' theater of cruelty. But the symbol also rebounds on them. Instead of mocking, the crown instead confirms, because Christ is in fact their king, as the three Magi publicly verified. For Christ, the thorns form a proper halo and a crown; for his tormentors, they become the sign of *their* infamy, an enemy circle inside the circle of enemies to which we, potentially, belong. A symbol that radiates cruelty, the crown has the dialectically hostile structure of Bosch's art itself.

Bosch approaches the point where the symbolism of evil becomes an evil symbolism, where mere pictures *of* an enemy become *enemy pictures*. In the next chapter, I will further explore these hostile artifacts as they appear *within* one of Bosch's paintings. We will see how

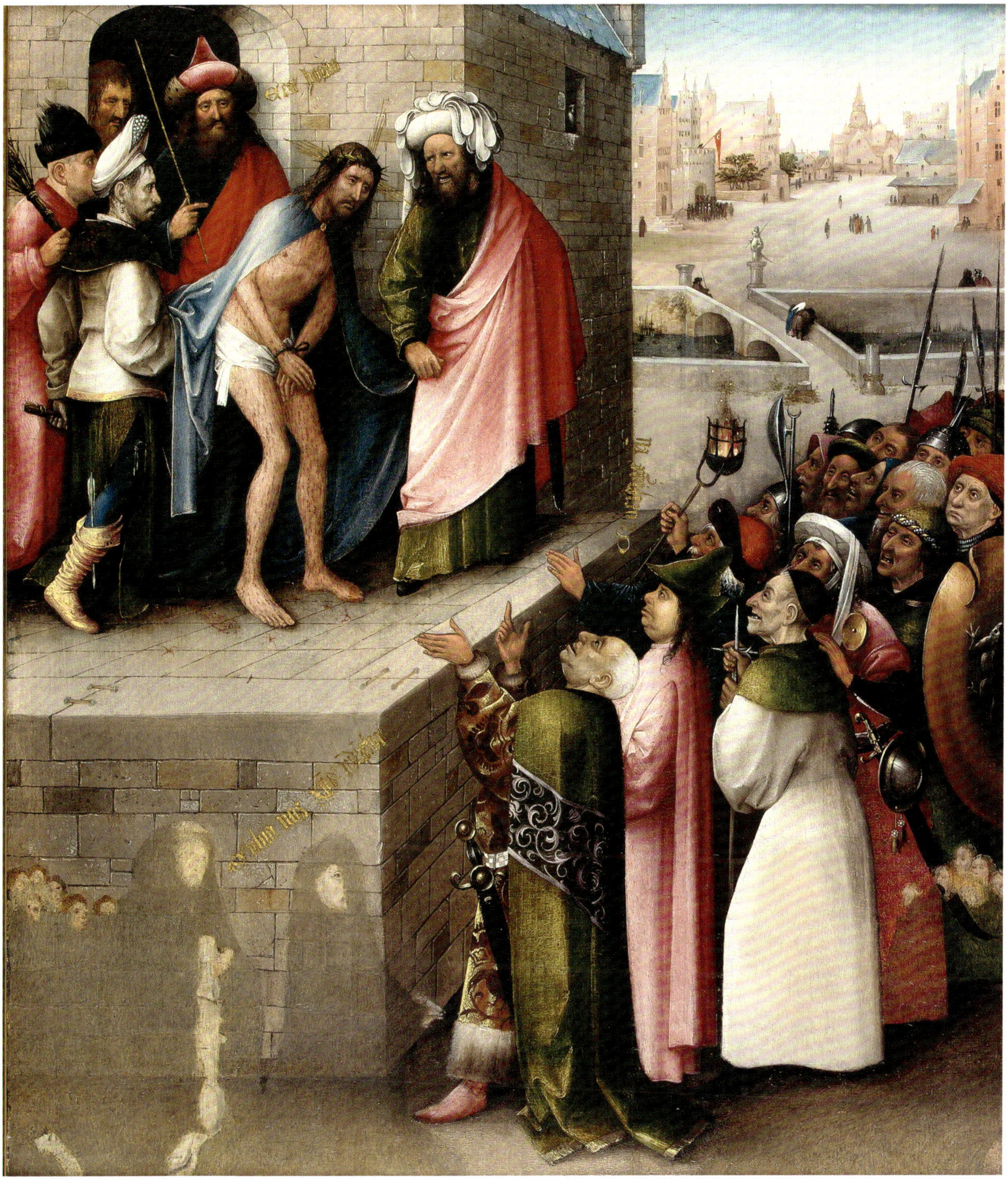

133 Hieronymus Bosch, *Ecce Homo*, c. 1500, on oak wood, Städel Museum, Frankfurt am Main

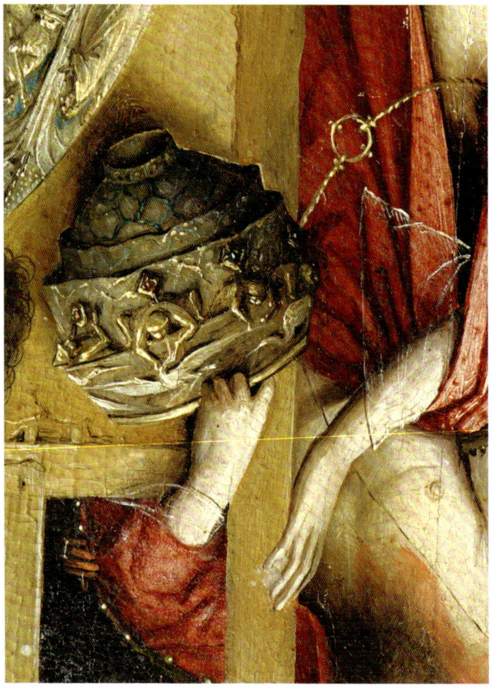

134 Detail (inverted) of Hieronymus Bosch, *Adoration of the Magi* (fig. 93)

his *Saint Anthony* hinges on the proximity between artworks and idols. From there we will embark on this book's most difficult adventure. We will consider a famous work by Bosch that is—by my account—so hostile that its subject remains perennially inscrutable.

But before turning to these enemy pictures, a last word on the Prado *Adoration of the Magi*. In their strange facture and symbolism, the gifts of the Magi typify Bosch's art. Were we to know why the artist gave the first Magus's gift frogs for feet, we would understand much about his deepest intentions. Despite their exemplarity, however, the gifts trace a trajectory opposite to the one performed by the triptych as a whole and repeated throughout this painter's oeuvre, where everything becomes increasingly evil and obscure. Passing from darkness to light, these holy gifts assure us that foes can become friends. Taken on their own, they betoken tolerance, their residual strangeness proving—against everything Bosch elsewhere tells us—that aliens need not be hostile. However: these gifts *cannot be taken in isolation*. For behind them loom the artifacts of absolute hate. The symbols of Antichrist *were not meant for us*. Even if we turn the mysterious figure's crown upside down, its subject will not be identified (fig. 134). Nor should it be, since identity—the Christian religious identity of Bosch and his original viewers—is here definitively refused. Lulled into the illusion that the objects we interpret are our friends, we struggle to make sense of enemy pictures.

6

AMONG THE IDOLS

The Persistence of Gnosticism

What if your entire world were make-believe? And what if you were—unknowingly—the lifelong inmate of a huge prison, where you have been constantly and secretly watched? These are the two distinctly Boschian hypotheses that the 1998 comedy *The Truman Show* realistically imagined (fig. 135).[1] The hero, named Truman and played by Jim Carrey, has been since birth the unwitting star of a reality soap opera broadcast all day, every day, to billions around the globe. His world is a colossal TV studio peopled by an army of actors who, portraying his cohabitants, keep Truman real. An immense (and in 1998 still futuristic) technology has been employed to make everyday life seem, for Truman, ordinary and mundane. His is the mere life of a middle-American nobody. But televised, his banal existence holds in its thrall a multitude of couch potatoes living vicariously through it. The moral is that Truman and his audience both inhabit illusions, the one innocently, the other voyeuristically. That makes the comic nobody into a contemporary Everyman. Living a falsehood but true to life, and possessing a human will to truth, Truman is, as his scripted name announces, a "true" man.

Luckily for everyone, Truman proves heroic. Partly due to cracks that form in his lifeworld's carefully crafted façade, but chiefly because his innate curiosity makes him notice and probe those cracks, he begins to sense an awesome strangeness about his everyday life. His wife and

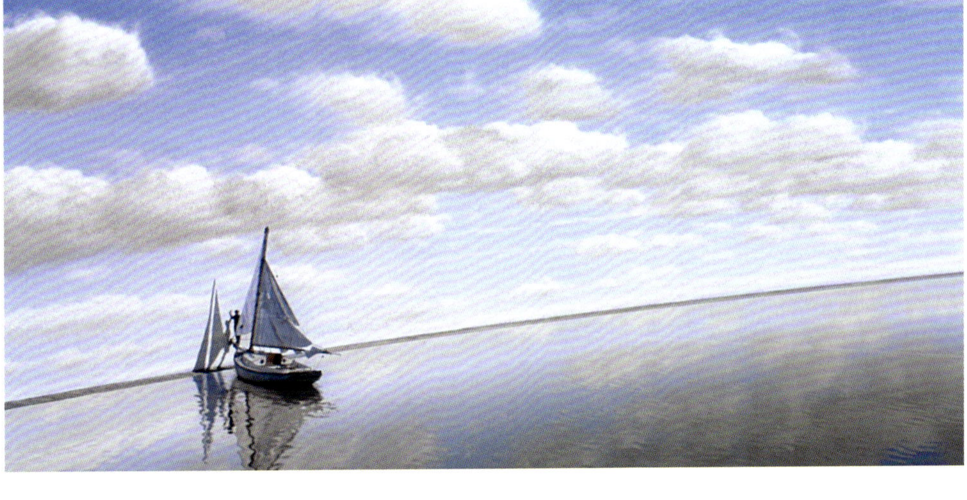

135 Boat at the sky, film still from "The Sky's the Limit" chapter, *The Truman Show*, 1998

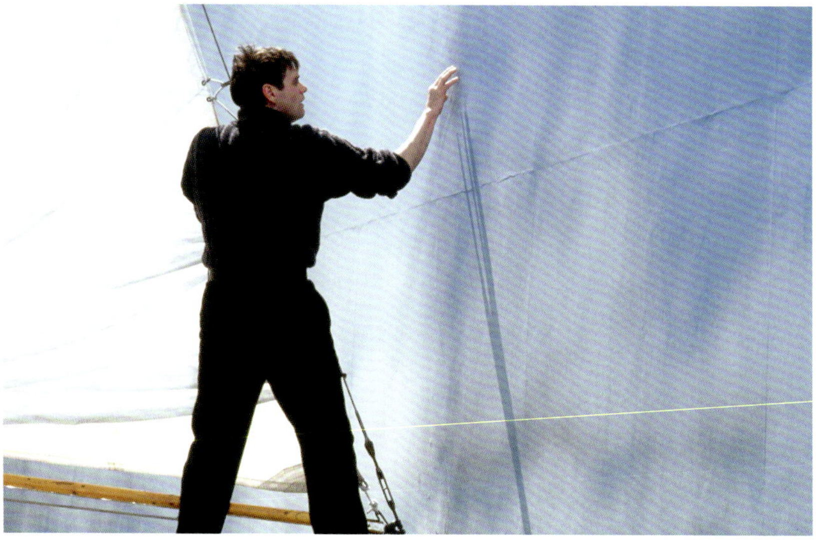

136 Truman reaches toward sky, film still from "The Sky's the Limit" chapter, *The Truman Show*, 1998

his best friend, accomplished actors, must improvise normality. Desperately they try to convince him of the ordinariness of the strange, dissembling that what he experiences—which of course is truly bizarre—is in fact just the garden-variety alienation that befalls everyone at some point in their mundane lives, and especially at midlife, when youthful dreams hit bedrock reality. (In the film, Truman and *The Truman Show* are in their critical thirtieth year.) But the doubts cannot be dispelled. Breaking with his wife and risking madness, Truman attempts to flee by boat across a surrounding artificial sea. Through hidden cameras, planted for this eventuality, we watch his escape, via a manufactured tempest, to the canvas horizon of the great dome that was his world. The prow of his vessel pierces the painted sky; his trembling hand tests its surface (fig. 136). And he meets his creator, the executive producer, Christof. Sporting an artist's beret, Christof is a parody of the megalomaniac Hollywood producer. But he also represents a modern Demiurge who, through imitative creation, maliciously deceives the human race.

Contempt for the world is alive and well in popular culture today. Film and television bombard us with plots about a global deception, in which secret forces—of government, big business, the media—devilishly pull the strings. In *The Matrix*, released in 1999, a year after *The Truman Show*, the Wachowski Brothers portrayed everyday life *literally* as a simulation—called "the Matrix"—created by intelligent machines and wired into the brains of an imprisoned, comatose humanity.[2] The hero (in the putative real world a hacker with the alias of Neo) perceives cryptic anomalies in the data stream that lead him to a revelation: in the *real* real world, which exists many years in the future, his body belongs to a huge electrical network, while into his mind is constantly streamed a perfect semblance of lived experience circa 1999 (fig. 137). Ordinary present-day existence—the lifeworld of Neo and of *The Matrix*'s audience—is unmasked as a grand illusion, and hell, portrayed as an ecological catastrophe, is the true reality. As in Bosch, *The Matrix* captures the real through its own vanguard illusionism, most famously in the special effect termed "bullet time," in which experiential reality is slowed down and digitally enhanced. Illusionism lends credibility to the film's incredible plot: if the technology of the film we are watching can make us see what our eyes cannot naturally behold, then perhaps a future technology will altogether replace lived reality with virtual experience. Conversely, its plot allows *The Matrix* to reflect on its illusion-making powers and to expose its own idolatrous allure.

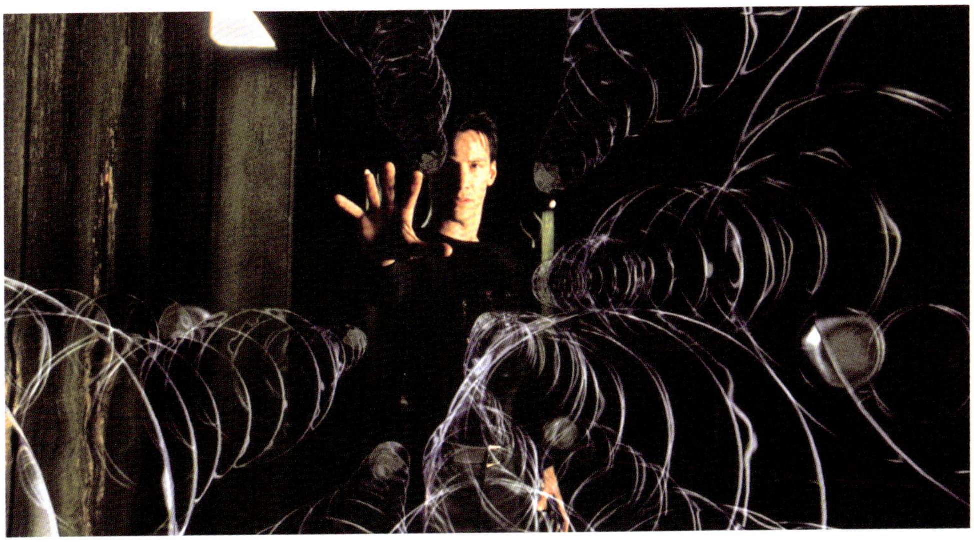

137 Neo Stopping Bullets, film still from *The Matrix*, 1999

Made at the cusp of the new millennium, these films played on apocalyptic anxieties of their time. But they also refreshed an ancient and enduring sense of everyday life as monstrously strange. Two thousand years ago, this estrangement engendered a peculiar stance toward human being. For the Gnostics, humans were strangers to the world, to God, and to themselves.[3] Their knowledge—in Greek, the *gnosis* that gave the stance its name—consisted in the idea that all this alienation derived from the fact that the world was created not by God but by an evil Demiurge. The true God, set apart from the world he neither managed nor created, could be approached only through knowledge of his radical otherness. Gnosticism was the primordial Christian heresy because it turned the God of Scripture into its demonic opposite, but also because the orthodox Christian contempt for the world could itself inflate into the Gnostic conviction that created nature is essentially evil.[4]

The early Christians had proclaimed their deity to be an unknown god.[5] In Christ's time, the phrase *to the unknown god* had been commonly inscribed on pagan altars as a way to placate foreign or overlooked deities preemptively. Drawing on a philosophical tradition that contrasted a singular, true, and (because nameless) unknown god to the plural and fictive gods of the fathers, Saint Paul announced that Christ, the one and only God, was "unknown." But Paul meant this only in the restricted sense that pagans did not yet know Christ, had not yet recognized him, or did not sufficiently acknowledge his exalted singularity. The Christian Gnostics saw things differently. They so exalted the one true God that they could no longer accept his having made the world and his dwelling here. Marcion of Sinope went a step further. He denied that God had any link or obligation to the world or humanity. As Christians considered themselves to be pilgrims and aliens on earth, Marcion announced that the true alien was God.[6]

At the root of all these theories was the question of evil. If God created the world, why was it so corrupt, so full of suffering, sin, and death? The Gnostics came up with a simple answer. The creator-god described in the Old Testament, who set Eve and Adam their impossible task in Eden, was a satanic force who contended eternally with the true and hidden God.[7] Saint Augustine wrote the definitive rebuttal. To Gnosticism, which he combated in the dualism of Mani and the Manicheans, Augustine responded that evil is not a force in the world. God created a perfect world and sustains it wholly, as Scripture attests. Evil lies rather within

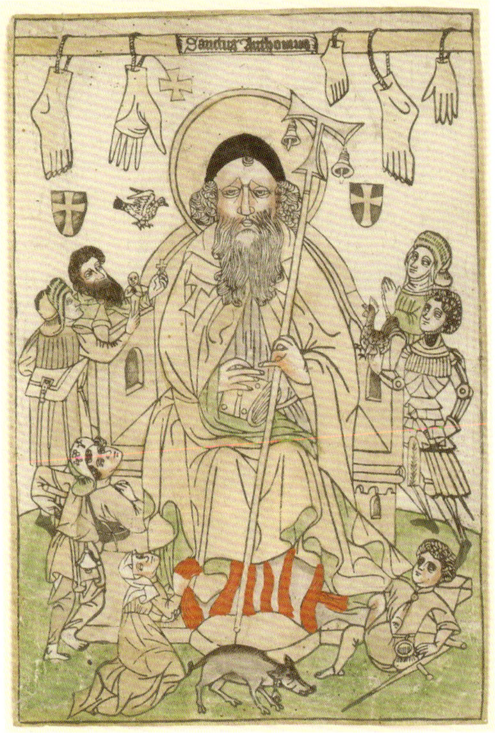

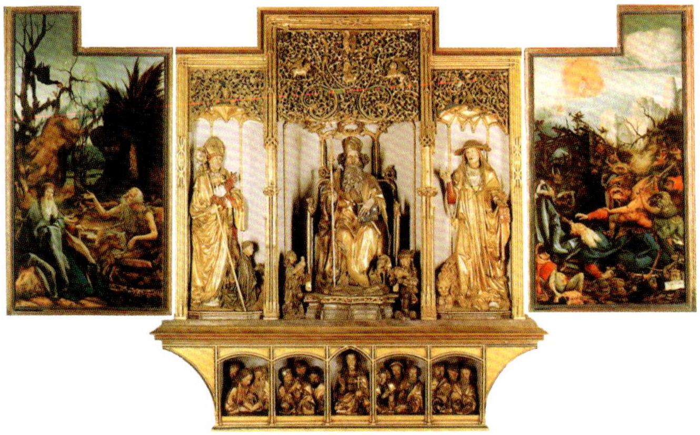

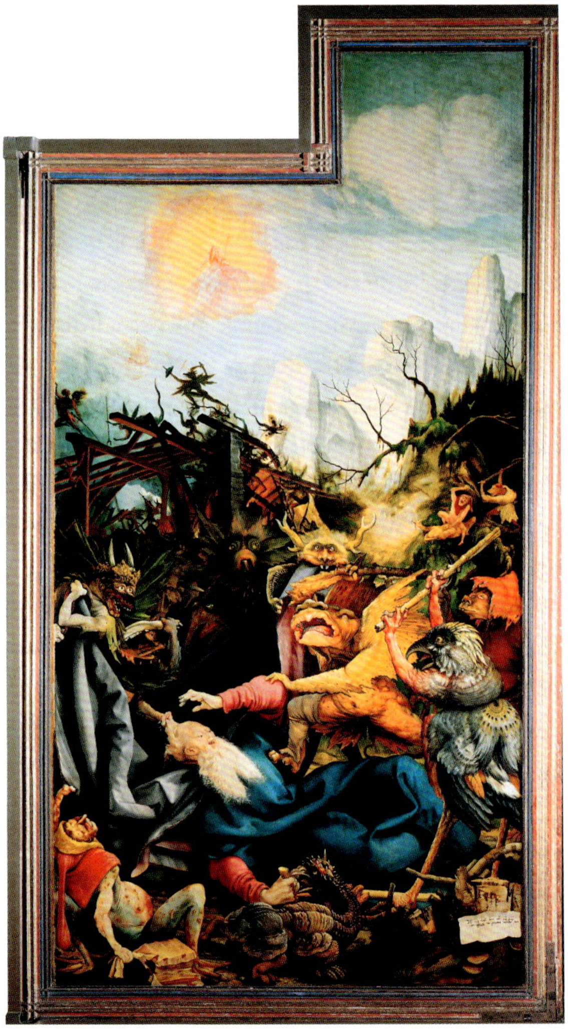

(ABOVE LEFT) **140** Anonymous South German, *Saint Anthony*, c. 1440, hand-colored woodcut, Staatliche Graphische Sammlung, Munich

(ABOVE RIGHT) **141** Nikolaus Hagenauer and Matthias Grünewald, *Isenheim Altarpiece*, open state, 1515, polychromed limewood and panel, Musée d'Unterlinden, Colmar

(BELOW RIGHT) **142** Matthias Grünewald, *Temptation of Saint Anthony*, right inner wing of *Isenheim Altarpiece* (fig. 141), Musée d'Unterlinden, Colmar blessed also by Christ—a minute crucifix. But eclipsing this sacred sign, so that we must work hard even to make it out, is the most amazing spectacle of painted devilry in all of art. The saint's ascetic withdrawal has enraged these demons. Wrathfully they attack Anthony with a plague of phantasms. These the saint impassively ignores, enraging the demons further, and further multiplying the display. Meanwhile, we, whom Anthony steadfastly observes, fall victim to the Devil's fascination.

Saint Anthony was an important figure in Christian culture.[13] Born in Egypt in the third century to Christian parents, he yearned for a stricter piety than theirs. So he took himself into the desert, where he lived alone and physically deprived. Intruding on his seclusion, curious visitors wondered at his abstinence and spread his message abroad. But it was a particular literary treatment of his battles with demons that captured future imaginations. Composed around 360 by Athanasius of Alexandria, *The Life of Anthony* established the model for all future Christian hagiography.[14] Adapted, translated, and anthologized, Athanasius's text created the image of Anthony as the first Christian ascetic and founder of monasticism.[15]

In the twelfth century, thanks to the healing capabilities attributed to some of his devotees, Anthony became the patron saint of a religious order that built hospitals for a specific disease (fig. 140).[16] In years of crop failure, when the poor ate spoiled grain or old grain from previous harvests, mysterious epidemics raged. These—modern science has discovered—were caused by a toxic fungus called ergot, which flourishes in moldering grain. In his famous altarpiece for the Antonine hospital at Isenheim, in the right inside panel showing Anthony's torment, the artist Matthias Grünewald portrayed a poor soul suffering from ergotism (figs. 141 and 142).[17] The sores and gangrene afflicting one of the monstrous figures (lower left) agree with the clinical symptoms of this disfiguring disease, and so does Grünewald's nightmare devilry, of which this human monstrosity appears a part. Ingested, ergot is a powerful hallucinogen and the basis for synthesized LSD. Sufferers burned inside and outside with what medical experts of Bosch's time called Saint Anthony's fire.

Devotion to Saint Anthony flourished in 's-Hertogenbosch. The many pilgrims' signs and badges bearing the saint's likeness and symbols that have been unearthed in the town attest to the local popularity of his cult. Bosch's father, the painter Antonius van Aken, was obviously named after the saint, and some time after 1462 he named his home and workshop—where Bosch was raised and trained—Sint Theonis.[18] In 1491, the town's Brotherhood of Saint Anthony (established in 1429) built a special chapel to their saint on Hinthamereinde, not far from the Church of Saint John, where there were also two altars dedicated to Anthony. Nothing survives of the Saint Anthony chapel's interior furnishings, and iconoclasts stripped, and the government troops looted, the Church of Saint John in 1566 and 1629, respectively; we will therefore never know whether Bosch made a Saint Anthony altarpiece for either of these religious settings. However, the artist is documented to have fashioned several altarpieces for his town's great church, and in any case Saint Anthony altarpieces were common throughout northern Europe. It is to a well-established tradition that Bosch's surviving *Saint Anthony* responds.

Measured by its influence, the triptych—now in the National Museum of Ancient Art, in Lisbon—is Bosch's most important work. More than twenty copies of it exist, and it spawned a huge number of imitations until well into the seventeenth century, including famous echoes by Pieter Bruegel the Elder's son Jan (fig. 143).[19] Bosch himself created several different versions

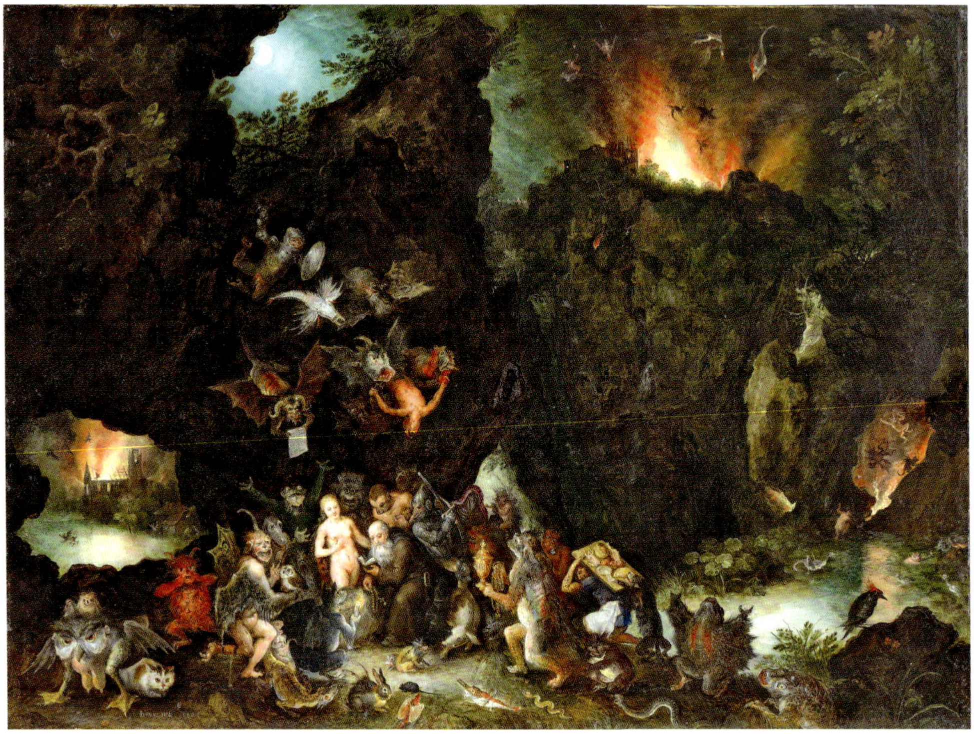

143 Jan Bruegel the Elder, *Temptation of Saint Anthony*, 1594, oil on copper, Yale University Art Gallery, lent by Dr. and Mrs. Herbert Schaefer

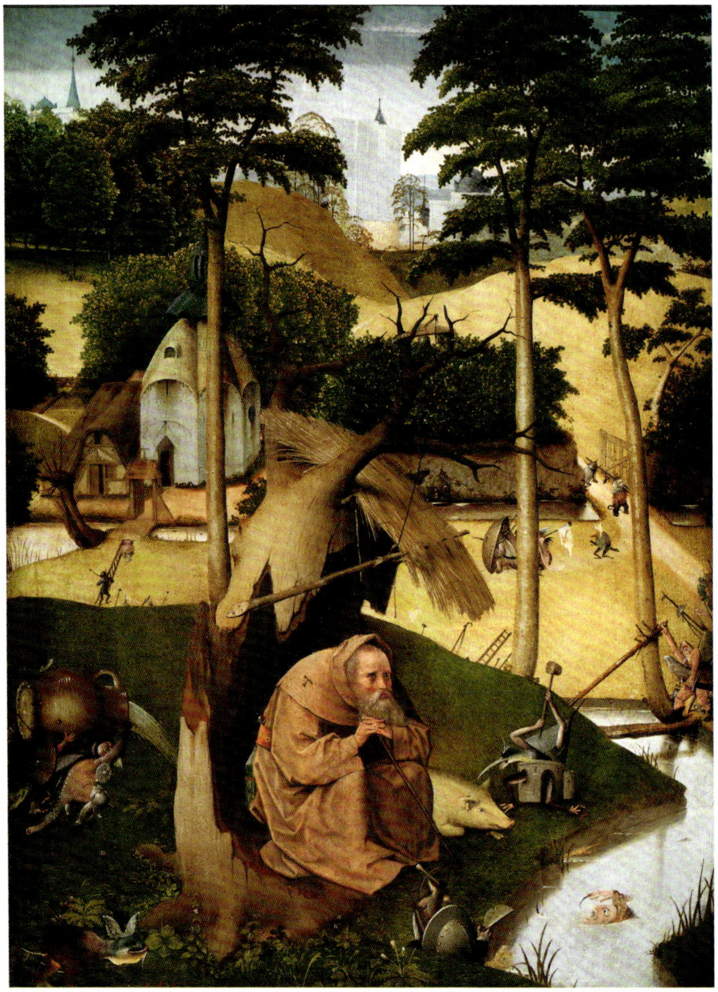

144 Hieronymus Bosch, *Temptation of Saint Anthony*, c. 1490, panel, Museo Nacional del Prado, Madrid

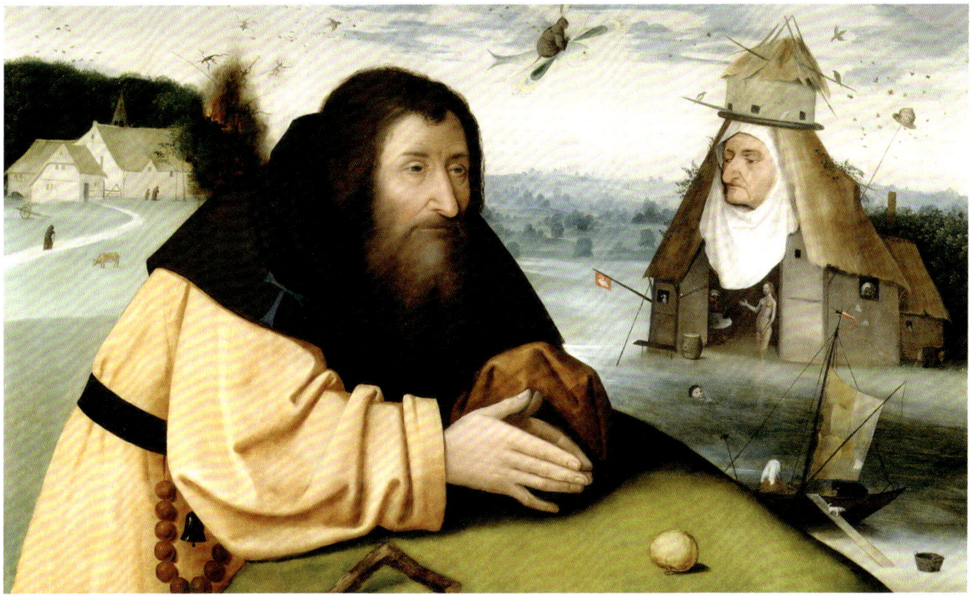

145 After Hieronymus Bosch, *Temptation of Saint Anthony Abbot*, c. 1500–1510, panel, Museo Nacional del Prado, Madrid

of the theme (figs. 144 and 145).[20] During Bosch's lifetime, Margaret of Austria received one as a gift. Featuring a bespectacled Anthony, it hung by the regent's bed until her death, in 1530.[21] A Portuguese diplomat, Damião de Góis, is recorded to have acquired a *Saint Anthony* by Bosch between 1523 and 1545 and taken it home with him to Portugal from Flanders. The Lisbon museum's triptych came from the Portuguese Royal Collections in 1911, so most scholars believe it was originally De Góis's.[22] Philip II of Spain owned many Boschian *Saint Anthonys*. Joseph de Sigüenza, his librarian at El Escorial, reports: "This painting is seen often enough. In the chapter house [of the Order of Saint Jerome] there is one, another in the prior's cell, two are in the Gallery of the Infanta; and in my cell there is a fine one in which I sometimes read and lose myself."[23] I would have liked to have seen these rooms, with Bosches proliferating like the demons they represent. The pious brother used them for spiritual exercises, while also collecting them for their sheer artistry. This early documentation suggests that few if any of Bosch's Saint Anthony panels ever started as altarpieces. The idea that the Lisbon triptych served a private function, one tangling religious devotion with aesthetic pleasure, makes sense of its form.

Compared with altarpiece triptychs, Bosch's *Saint Anthony* triptych is in one way unique. Altarpieces ordinarily conceal and reveal a cult image, such as the powerful limewood effigy of Saint Anthony carved by Nikolaus Hagenauer after 1490 and enclosed in the altarpiece with wings painted between 1512 and 1516 by Grünewald (see fig. 141).[24] Alternatively, an altarpiece's central image illustrates a significant event: the Epiphany, the Crucifixion, a saint's martyrdom, and so forth (fig. 146).[25] Except for the tiny crucifix among the ruins, Bosch's triptych displays no proper cult image. And it displaces to the wings specific episodes from Anthony's life. In the left panel, up in the sky, demons elevate and torment the saint during his meditative ecstasy, while down below, after being beaten almost to death, the saint is carried back by companions, at his request, to his hermitage—both events described by Athanasius. Even the Devils huddled over a document under the footbridge have a textual source, since according to Athanasius the demons, in addition to tempting and tormenting Anthony, brought false testimony against him, fulfilling their ancient role as both bookkeepers of people's sins and as slanderers (*diaballo*, "I accuse").[26] On the right wing, a vilely seductive devil-queen tempts

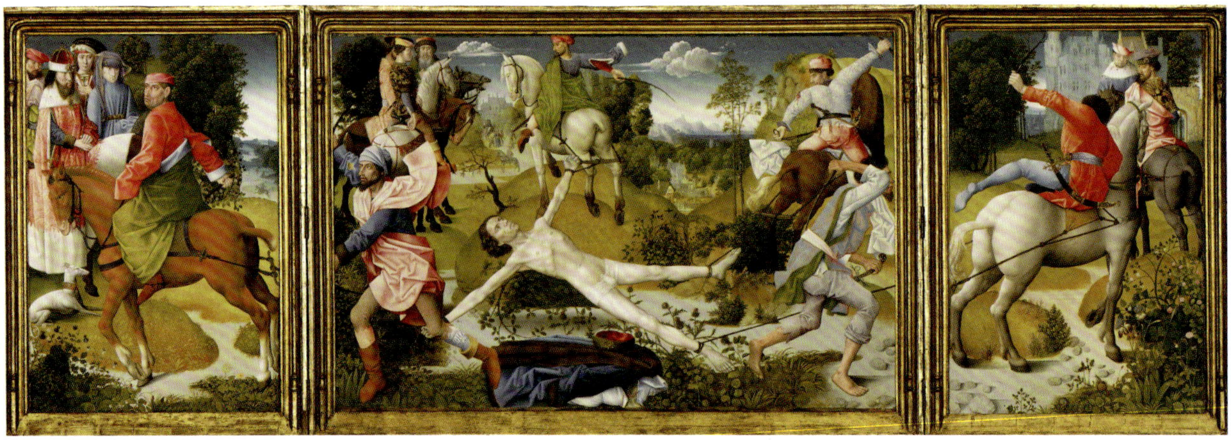

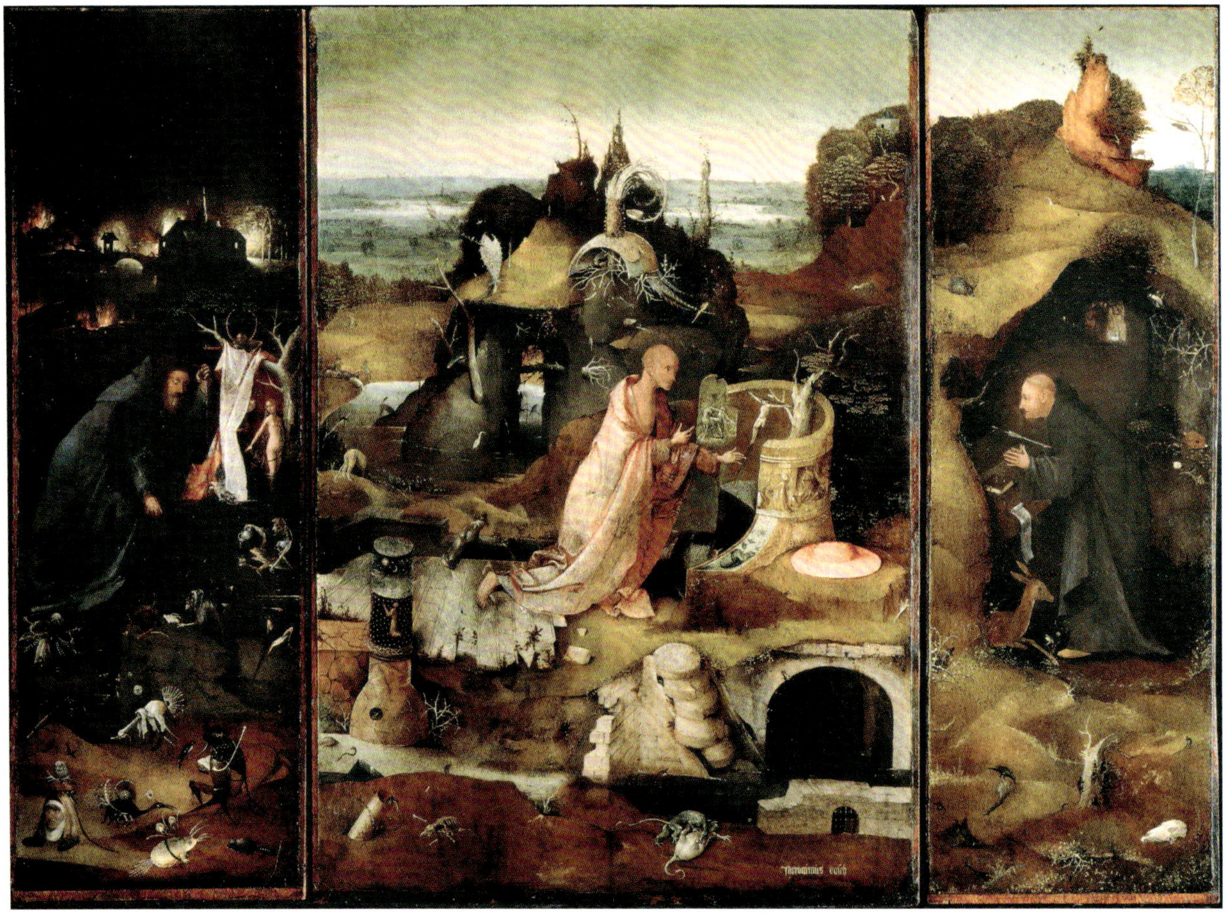

(TOP) **146** Anonymous Netherlandish, *Martyrdom of Saint Hippolytus*, fourth quarter of 15th century, tempera and oil on panel, Museum of Fine Arts, Boston, Walter M. Cabot Fund

(BOTTOM) **147** Hieronymus Bosch, *Hermit Saints Triptych*, c. 1505, panel, Palazzo Ducale, Venice

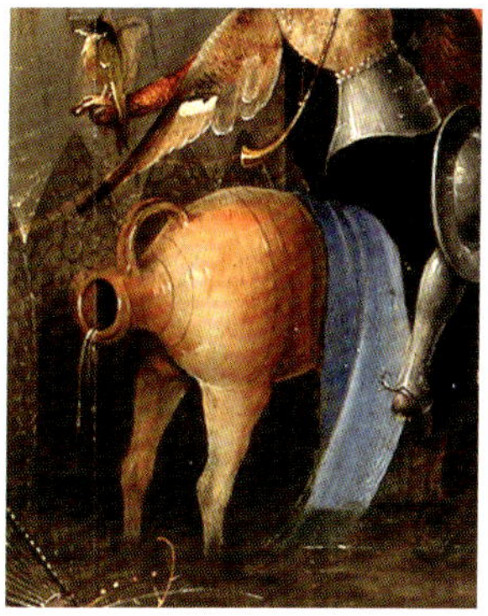
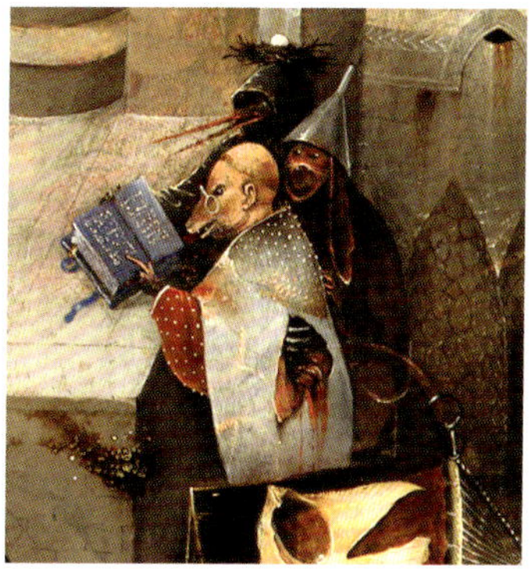
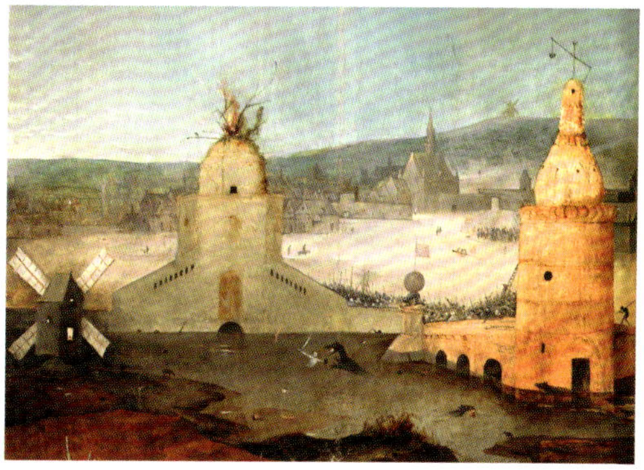

(LEFT) 148 Detail of Hieronymus Bosch, *Temptation of Saint Anthony* (fig. 138)

(CENTER) 149 Detail of Hieronymus Bosch, *Temptation of Saint Anthony* (fig. 138)

(RIGHT) 150 Detail of Hieronymus Bosch, *Temptation of Saint Anthony* (fig. 138)

Anthony with sex and food. That story probably came to Bosch via translated Arab sources, and he devoted one of his other panels of Saint Anthony solely to that tale (see fig. 145).[27] The central panel represents no such recognizable event. Instead, it isolates for special attention the generalized activity of Anthony's devotion. Bosch's poorly preserved *Hermit Saints Triptych* takes this approach in each of its three panels (fig. 147).[28] Saints Anthony and Jerome and the French hermit Giles appear not as objects for our pious devotion but as subjects themselves engaged *in* pious devotion. Neither powerful, protective presences nor miracle-working protagonists, they instead model pious contempt for the world. Earlier we observed how Bosch portrayed his ascetic name-saint (see fig. 53).[29] His eyes closed, clutching a crucifix, and with his rich cardinal's robes miming the flesh he has cast aside, Saint Jerome lies already dead and entombed. Meanwhile, for those of us with eyes still open, the world the saint has abandoned appears as if in cross section: an alluring spectacle on the surface but a hellish pit underneath.

Sigüenza, always Bosch's best commentator, wrote that most artists "paint man as he appears from outside, whereas he alone had the audacity to paint him as he is on the inside."[30] In the Lisbon triptych, Bosch makes it impossible to distinguish inner from outer. On the one hand, everything in the picture is potentially an illusion occurring in the saint's haunted mind. Bosch fills the scene with entities whose inconsistent shapes, colors, and scale indicate that they cannot be *of* the world. This devilry becomes most concrete where it is least physically plausible. In the murky waters that flood the central ruin, a dripping jug, as if shaped on a gigantic potter's wheel out of tangible terra-cotta, forms the vulgarly leaking hindquarters of a diabolical steed (fig. 148). Substances magically materialize only to mutate and abruptly disappear. A monstrous cleric's entrails spill from a tear in his robes (fig. 149). The emptiness exposed within them already traverses the garments themselves, which at once resemble and dissemble what they conceal. Daubs of flesh-colored paint outline a sleeve disappearing behind the monster's cape. These same pigments texture his hood with reptilian scales and render fleshy his ghostly face. In the end, nothing is real but the spectacle of paint itself, promiscuously applied by Bosch's brush.

Confusion about the represented figures extends to the painting's fictive setting. What exactly is the ruin's crumbling domed roof made of? It resembles flaking clay, but the flakes form patterns of some vile epidermis. And whatever that dome is, it belongs to larger architecture that recedes—illogically—toward multiple vanishing points (fig. 150). Even the landscape's bedrock mingles with its devilish intruders. In the left panel, a hillock that also serves as a brothel forms the exposed buttocks of a tormented giant (see fig. 138). Shifting focus to the

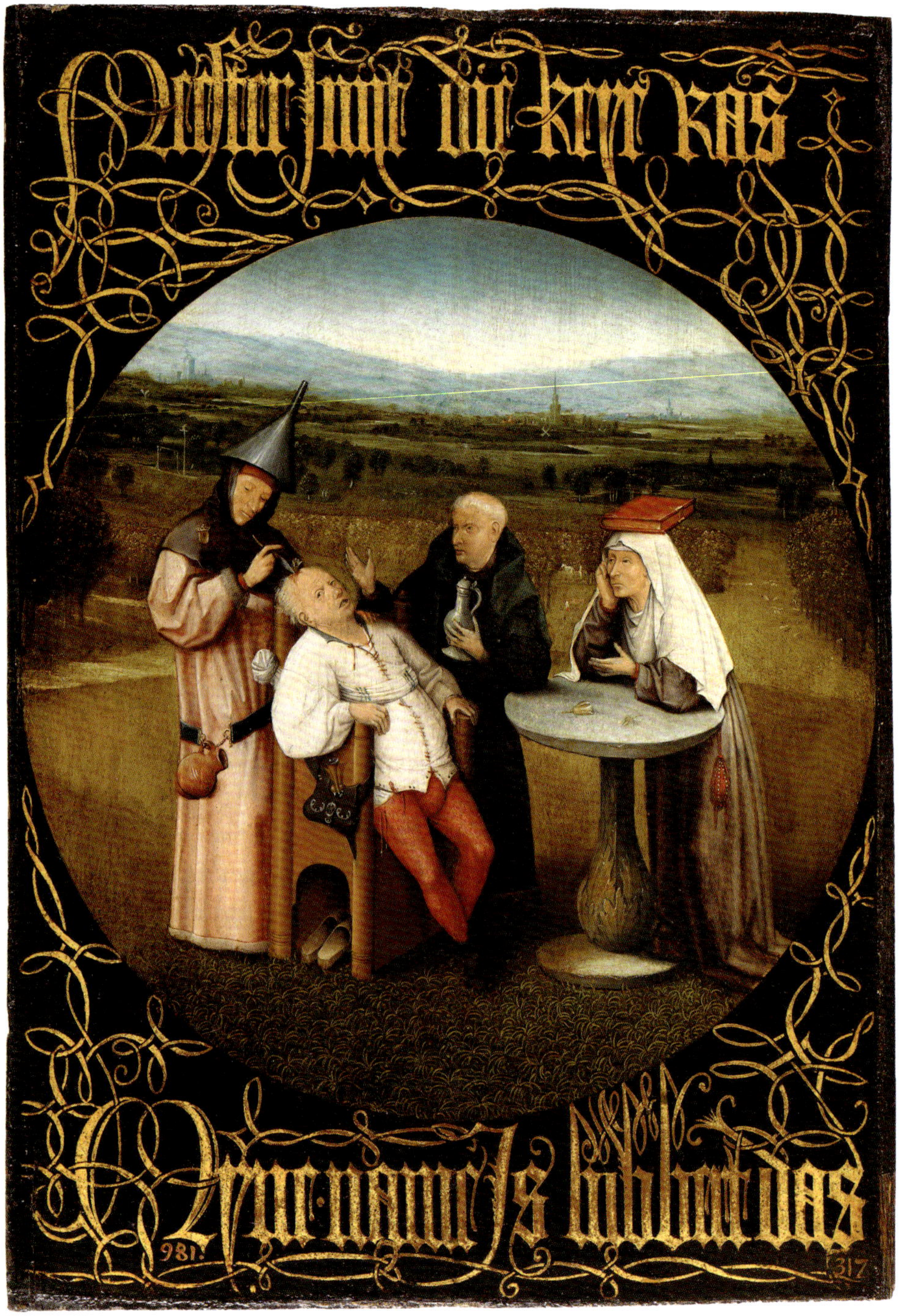

152 Hieronymus Bosch (workshop?), *The Stone Operation*, 1490, panel, Museo Nacional del Prado, Madrid

cup, rather than under the cup she bet it was under (fig. 153).[37] Meanwhile, during her cleverly manufactured awe, and while vomiting a malicious frog, she is robbed of her whole purse.

People of Bosch's time were growing dangerously skeptical about the illusions artists could produce. This was a period when tears could be compellingly simulated in transparent oil-based paint; Rogier van der Weyden does this masterfully on the mourners' faces in his *Descent from the Cross* (fig. 154).[38] In 1507 some enterprising Dominicans in Bern constructed a *Pietà* that mechanically wept droplets of liquid varnish.[39] Exposed by Franciscan inspectors, this moneymaking fraud was broadcast to a wide public through printed books and images.

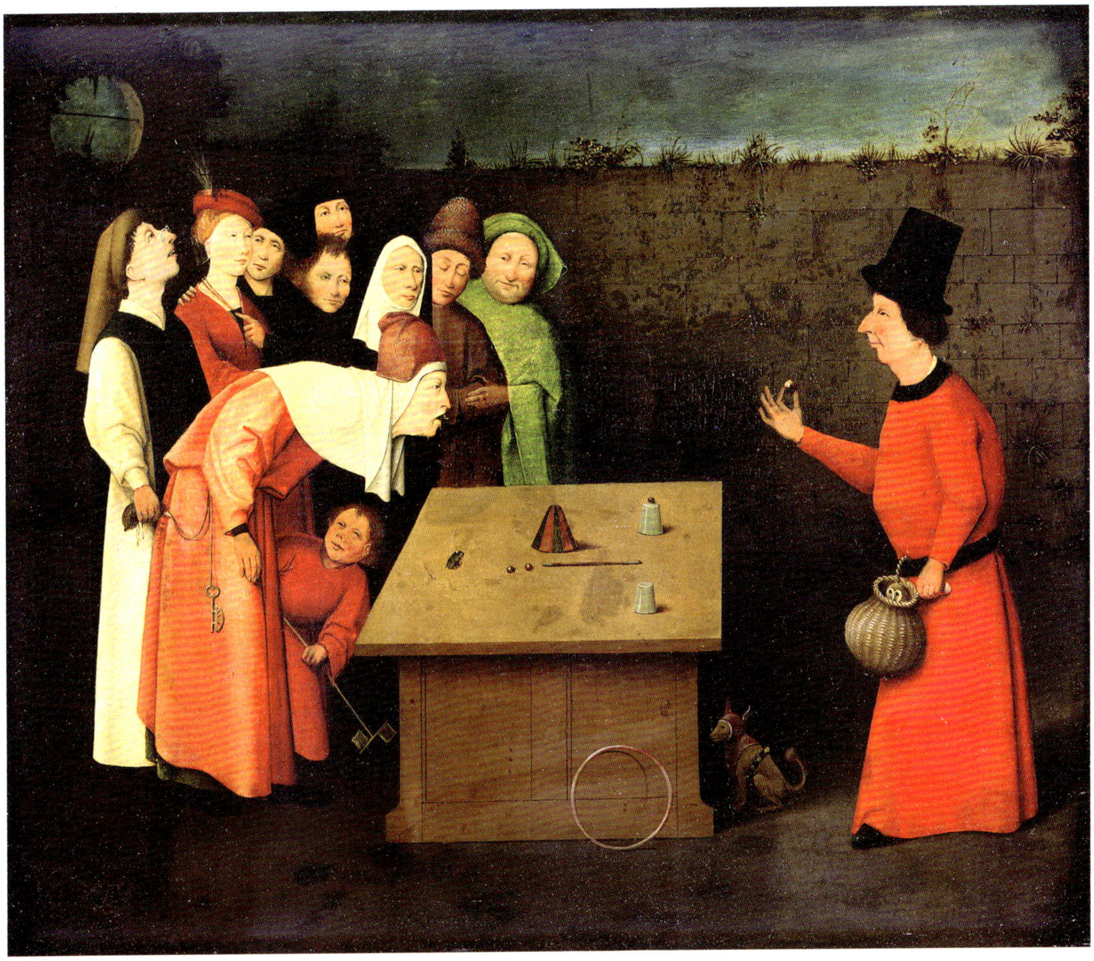

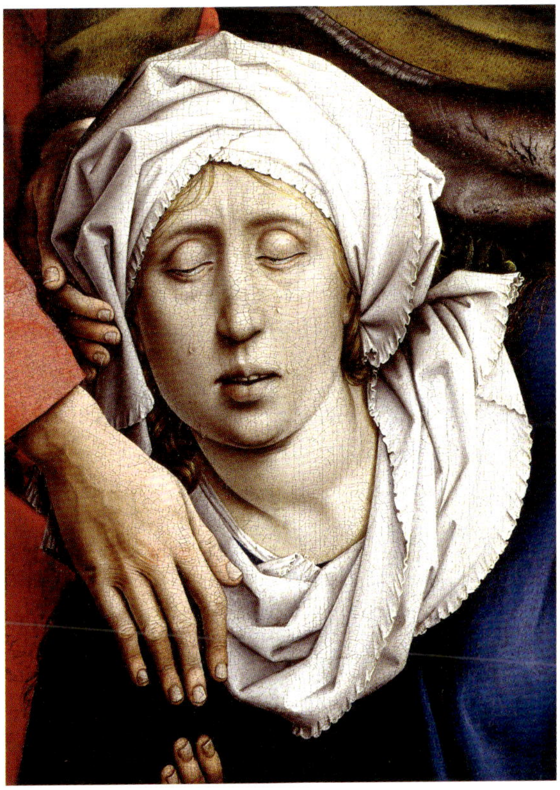

(ABOVE) 153 Hieronymus Bosch (workshop?), *The Conjurer*, c. 1490, panel, Musée d'Art et d'Histoire, Saint-Germain-en-Laye

(BELOW) 154 Detail of Rogier van der Weyden, *Descent from the Cross*, c. 1435, panel, Museo Nacional del Prado, Madrid

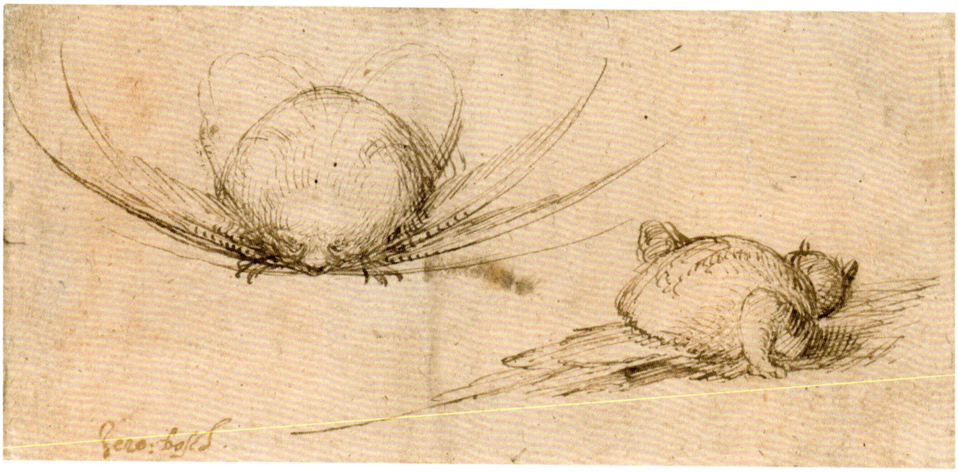

158 Hieronymus Bosch, *Two Fantastic Creatures*, c. 1500–1510, recto, pen and dark brown ink on reddish paper, Kupferstichkabinett, Staatliche Museen, Berlin

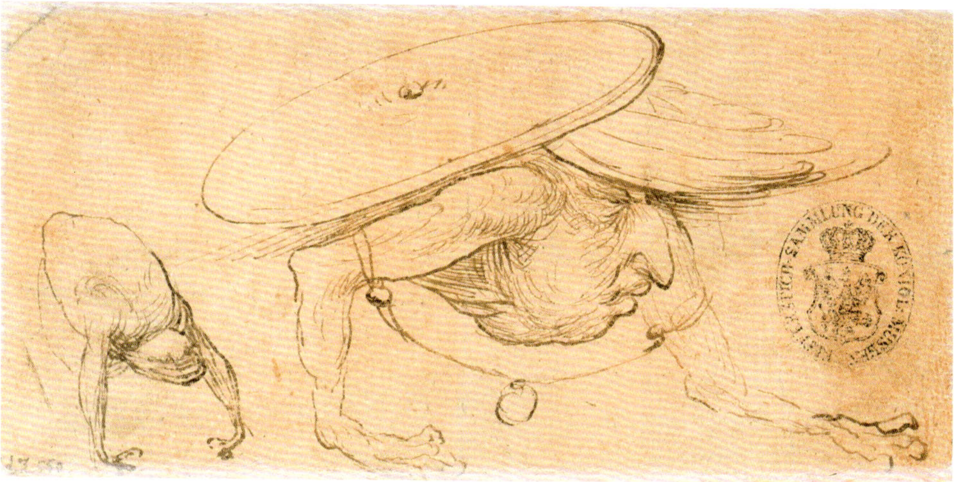

159 Hieronymus Bosch, *Two Imaginary Creatures*, c. 1500–1510, verso, pen and dark brown ink on reddish paper, Kupferstichkabinett, Staatliche Museen, Berlin

sense experience. At the same time that it freed the human mind from its bondage to objects, however, fantasy also set humans on a collision course with nature. Often associated with the sin of pride, and held to motivate insatiable desire, especially of an erotic kind, fantasy was indicted as a root cause of the Fall. In *Paradise Lost*, Milton has Eve dream her transgression before committing it. This prompts Adam to explain and console:

> Oft in her [Reason's] absence mimic Fansie wakes
> to imitate her; but misjoyning shapes
> Wilde work produces oft, and most in dreams,
> Ill marching words and deeds long past or late.
> . . . be not sad. Evil into the mind of God or Man
> May come and go, so unapprov'd, and leave
> No spot or blame behind: Which gives me hope
> That what in sleep thou didst abhor to dream,
> Waking though never wilt consent to do. (5:110–14, 116–21)

Fantasy was the faculty most susceptible to diabolical manipulation, as the zealous inquisitors Heinrich Kramer and Jacob Sprenger insisted in their book on witchcraft: "The devils can direct and set in motion the internal spirits and humors, so that the images stored in the places of preservation are brought forth from the storehouses to the origins of perception, that is, to the virtues of imagination and fantasy, so that this person can imagine certain things. This will be called internal temptation."[52] When, through the thinking of Renaissance humanists, and on the evidence of the real achievements in their art, painters came to personify the demiurgic nature of human capability per se, this old ambivalence concerning fantasy haunted their elevation, as we will see.

In his drawing, Bosch conjures not only creatures but also an entire surrounding world (see fig. 158). Already implied in the volumetric treatment of each beast, this world is further materialized through the lines suggesting shadows cast by the cat-bird-tortoise beast. Darkest under its head and tail, but reaching forward almost to the sheet's right edge, this small but decisive bit of hatching establishes a fictional ground plane completely disjoined from the actual picture plane on which the beast is sketched. Less is more in this evocation of the world. Bosch gives us just enough to imagine a *place* where the creature, motionless but coiled, sits ready to pounce or to flee. But withholding much more than the minimal mental picture of place, Bosch prevents his impossible beast from appearing—as he actually must be—completely out of place in the natural world. Bosch's use of pen and ink helps, since the blanks seem natural to a medium that depicts only outlines and shadows and not surfaces and substances.

Because some drawings in the period were actually done from life, this drawing, from the real-life scenario imagined for its medium, fosters the illusion that it is a "nature study," too. Everything about this impossible creature tells us that, at the time of the sketch's making, it stood huddled and turned away *right there*. It makes a huge difference that the beast captured in the drawing seems itself intent on capturing prey. We do not have to see what it espies to sense that the monster has its own impetus. Gazing toward the left along a line oblique to its body, it draws us—who stand unseen behind it—into the space and drama of its virtual world. By way of the figure of hunting, moreover, Bosch frames his drawing in a fiction of discovery rather than of invention: the artist stalks the stalking monster. The strange is therefore not humanly made but naturally found: a wondrous discovery at the far reaches of a long in-the-world journey from here to there and back again. All this is quite consciously a fiction, since—again—if these critters had any reality, they would be counternatural demons whose only prey is ourselves.

Iconoclash

Devilry gives the artist an occasion to demonstrate his own quasi-divine, quasi-diabolical powers of creation. From this it should be clear why Saint Anthony was such a congenial subject for Bosch, for what were the hermit's temptations but an epidemic of fantasies conjured by the Devil to confuse those who would abandon the world? At once outer and inner, these apparitions not only assailed the person but were also of the person. Devotional treatises of Bosch's day warned that desires increased in strength the more one tried to bridle them. Ascetic renunciation induced in the hungry mind lucid visions of that which the body renounced. Having pushed them aside, the pious self-mortifier had to defend himself against hallucinated wine, women, and food. The goal was to achieve a state of "apathy," of being, literally, without pathos. "My dreadful transgressions horrify me," wrote a sixteenth-century mystic. "They growl in my ears, hiss like serpents in the night. Worst, they are not the vain

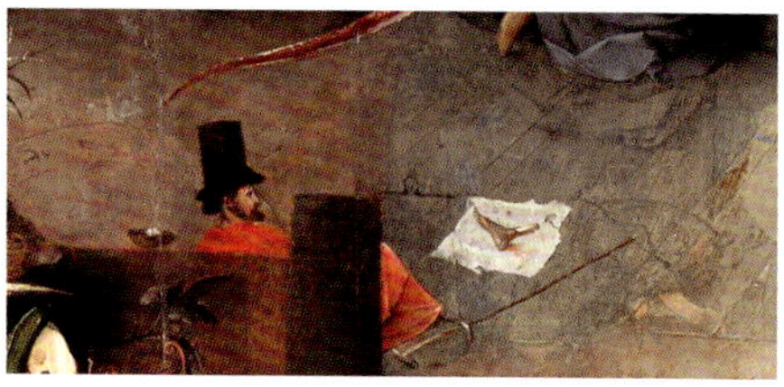

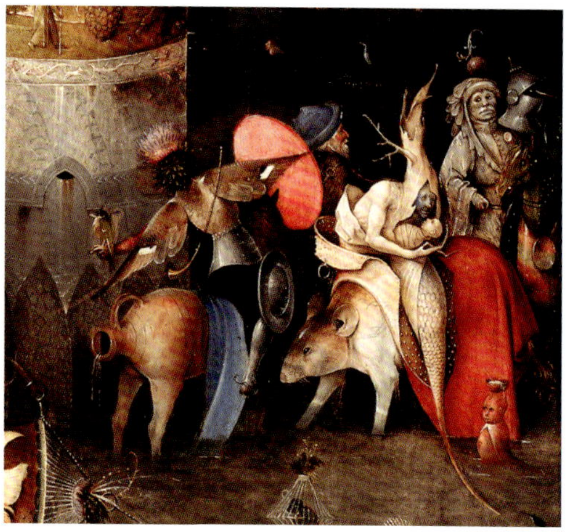

160 Detail of Hieronymus Bosch, *Temptation of Saint Anthony* (fig. 138)

161 Detail of Hieronymus Bosch, *Temptation of Saint Anthony* (fig. 138)

smoke of dreams but the living portrait of my deeds."[53] Deriving not from the world but from our lust for the world, diabolical temptations revealed a corruption deep within.

Describing one of Bosch's *Saint Anthonys* in his possession, Sigüenza refers with awe to the maker of these living portraits of the holy man and his enemies:

> We see on the one hand the saint, the first hermit, with a serene countenance, humble, in rapt contemplation, calm and with his soul entirely at peace; on the other hand the infinite fantasies and monstrosities that the enemy forms in order to confuse, worry, and disturb that imperturbable soul and distract his steadfast love: to this end, he fashions living beings, wild animals, chimeras, monsters, fire, death, roaring, threats, vipers, lions, dragons and fearful birds of so many kinds that one has to admire him for his ability to give shape to so many ideas.[54]

In this breathless sentence, Sigüenza gives the pronoun *he* a peculiar ambiguity. At the start, it refers to the enemy, Satan, who brings forth demons to trap the hermit in the world. By the end of the sentence, though, the *he* refers to the painter, Sigüenza's spiritual friend, who fashions demons in order to amaze his audience. As we have seen, a sixteenth-century chronicler called Bosch "the devil-maker because he was never equaled in making devils."[55] This image of Bosch has played through literature ever since, still troubling viewers even today, as we stand alternately fascinated and repelled by his paintings.

That Bosch must have engineered this ambiguity is proven by one key device in his art. In his paintings, Bosch shows crafted images to be potential instruments of the enemy. In the Prado *Adoration of the Magi*, we observed how the gifts of the Magi mingle with the dubious garments of Antichrist, causing us to wonder whether they might be poisonous, as well (see fig. 99). Now if we overlook all of its devilry, the central panel of the *Temptation of Saint Anthony* evokes a specific, recognizable setting: the built and ornamented context where—in Bosch's culture—paintings of this kind ordinarily stood (see fig. 139). Bosch derives the work's triptych format from altarpieces. And at the center of this quasi altarpiece, he portrays the saint worshiping at an altar in the ruins of what could be a chapel. The effigy on that altar is markedly simpler than Bosch's painting which contains it. But viewers of the period would also have understood it as the minimum of church décor: a small, freestanding Crucifixion representing the body—the Corpus Christi—present and sacrificially gifted in the ritual of the Mass. Instead of bringing this crucial image close to the viewer, however, Bosch places it at the far end of the ruin, engulfed in

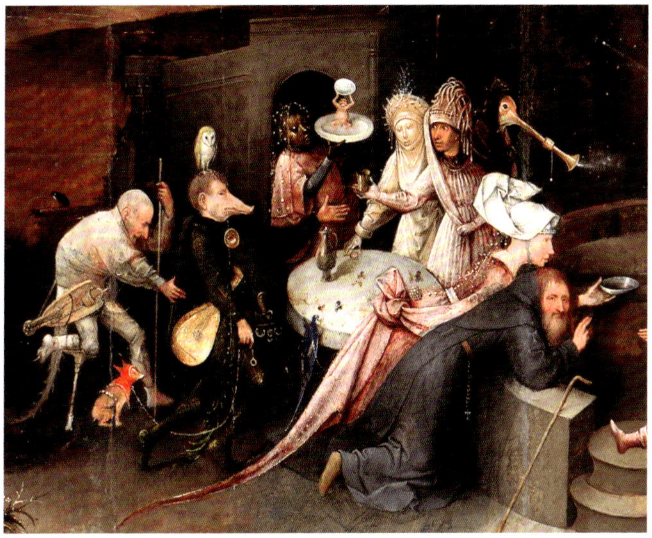

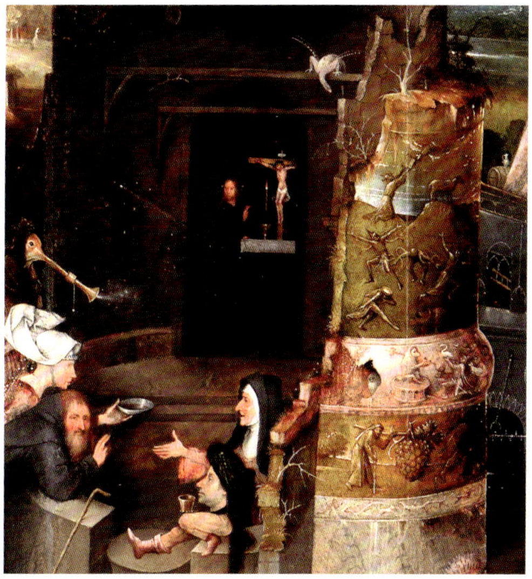

darkness and devilry. What altarpieces usually foreground, in other words, and what Anthony and Christ are shown emphatically to point to, Bosch causes precipitously to recede, so that looking at the altarpiece *in* his triptych feels like peering through the wrong end of a telescope.

Whether or not the Lisbon panels ever stood behind an altar (I am inclined to think they did not), Bosch introduces into them a semblance of the context where such a triptych traditionally stood—namely, the sacred space of a church. Saint Anthony *uses* the devilish ruins as if they were a Christian chapel. Kneeling at its threshold, he consecrates what stands within its sanctuary. Meanwhile, the surrounding demons *also* act like officers of a church. Demons disguised as clerics sing or read from a big blue book. Monstrous mendicants seek alms just where beggars in Bosch's time did, at the church's doorstep—note the severed limb displayed for sympathy but contradicted by the beggar's monstrous foot (fig. 160). Documents tell us that at Bosch's funeral money was distributed to some twenty-four poor folk parked "before the chapel."[56] The *Saint Anthony* triptych invokes and parodies not only the activities of church but also its pictorial imagery. The scaly-tailed tree-woman mounted backward on a rat and bearing a swaddled infant together with the man in the blue hat travesty portrayals of Mary, Christ, and Joseph in the flight into Egypt (fig. 161). More alarmingly, the Sacrament of the Altar, that most efficacious holy act, is itself mimicked by devils in what seems to be a Black Mass (fig. 162).[57] A pig-faced communicant reaches for the wine while, above, a plated frog lifts up an egg in blasphemous imitation of the ritual raising of the Eucharistic Host. Earlier we tried to imagine the Prado *Adoration of the Magi*, in its closed state, on its original place behind an altar (see figs. 115 and 117). Imagine, if you will, a priest saying Mass before the Lisbon *Temptation of Saint Anthony*. Facing it as it stands upon the altar and elevating the round, white consecrated wafer, he would confront in the frog a demonic reflection of himself! Again, the triptych was probably not used in this way, but imagining such a use might have been part of the puzzle.

Even the little crucifix has a parodic double in the triptych. Just beside the crucifix and aligned perfectly with it, the crumbling outer wall of the ruin displays, as if in fresco or polychrome low relief, the enemy picture *par excellence*: the idolatrous golden calf with Israelites dancing a hectic Moorish—or *moresca*—dance around it (fig. 163). Bosch smuggles this, the archetypal idol, into his painting by proposing it as an archaeological remnant of some prior

162 Detail of Hieronymus Bosch, *Temptation of Saint Anthony* (fig. 138)

163 Detail of Hieronymus Bosch, *Temptation of Saint Anthony* (fig. 138)

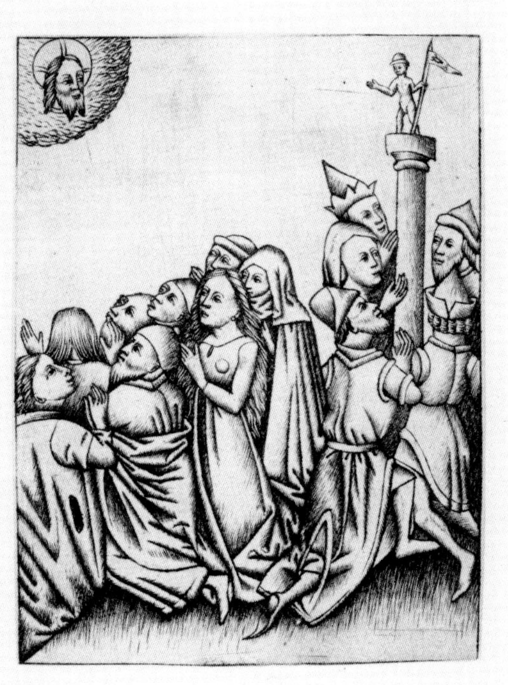

164 Master of the Nuremberg Passion, *The First Commandment*, c. 1450, engraving, Kunstmuseum Basel, Kupferstichkabinett

idolatrous culture. Just below the adoration of the golden calf, another crumbling picture displays a monkey-demon (or monkey-demon idol) enthroned on a drum and approached by gift bearers. Like the enemy artifacts in the Prado *Adoration of the Magi*, these abject effigies allow Bosch to paint in the sketchy, spontaneous, and optically ambiguous manner that most typifies his art. Signature products of his craft, they raise the question of whether Bosch codes his art as potentially idolatrous.

The peculiar thinness of the monkey-demon image—the way the colored figures seem to coat the dissolving surface underneath like a luminous skin—bespeaks the ontological status of idols. In ancient philosophy, the *idolum* (Greek εἴδωλον) denoted the insubstantial image of objects. According to Lucretius, whose *On the Nature of Things* became available after 1415 (though banned in 1513), everything we see is caused by an idol sent from the object to our eye. "These images of things," Lucretius writes, "these almost airy semblances, are drawn from surfaces; you might call them film or bark, something like skin that keeps the look, the shape of what it held before its wandering."[58] Does this not also describe the painted semblance that renders idols in Bosch's triptych: an errant, insubstantial film thinly deposited on the panel surface?

According to Bosch, Anthony set up his altar in the ruins of a pagan or Jewish temple. And this temple stands again surrounded by followers of another idolatry, a new one: that of Islam. In the distance of the right side panel, atop a globe resting on the back of a dark, kneeling figure (an African slave?), a Turkish flag rallies a muster of infidels (see fig. 150). This compound idol, together with "Moorish" dancers round the idol, gives enmity the form of an abiding *image war*. At one level, the crucifix and golden calf simply contrast true and false faith, as does one mid-fifteenth-century German engraving by the Master of the Nuremburg Passion (fig. 164).[59] But engulfed by a monstrous profusion of idols, parodies, travesties, and delusions, Bosch's altar crucifix resurrects old questions about the legitimacy of images in the Christian faith.

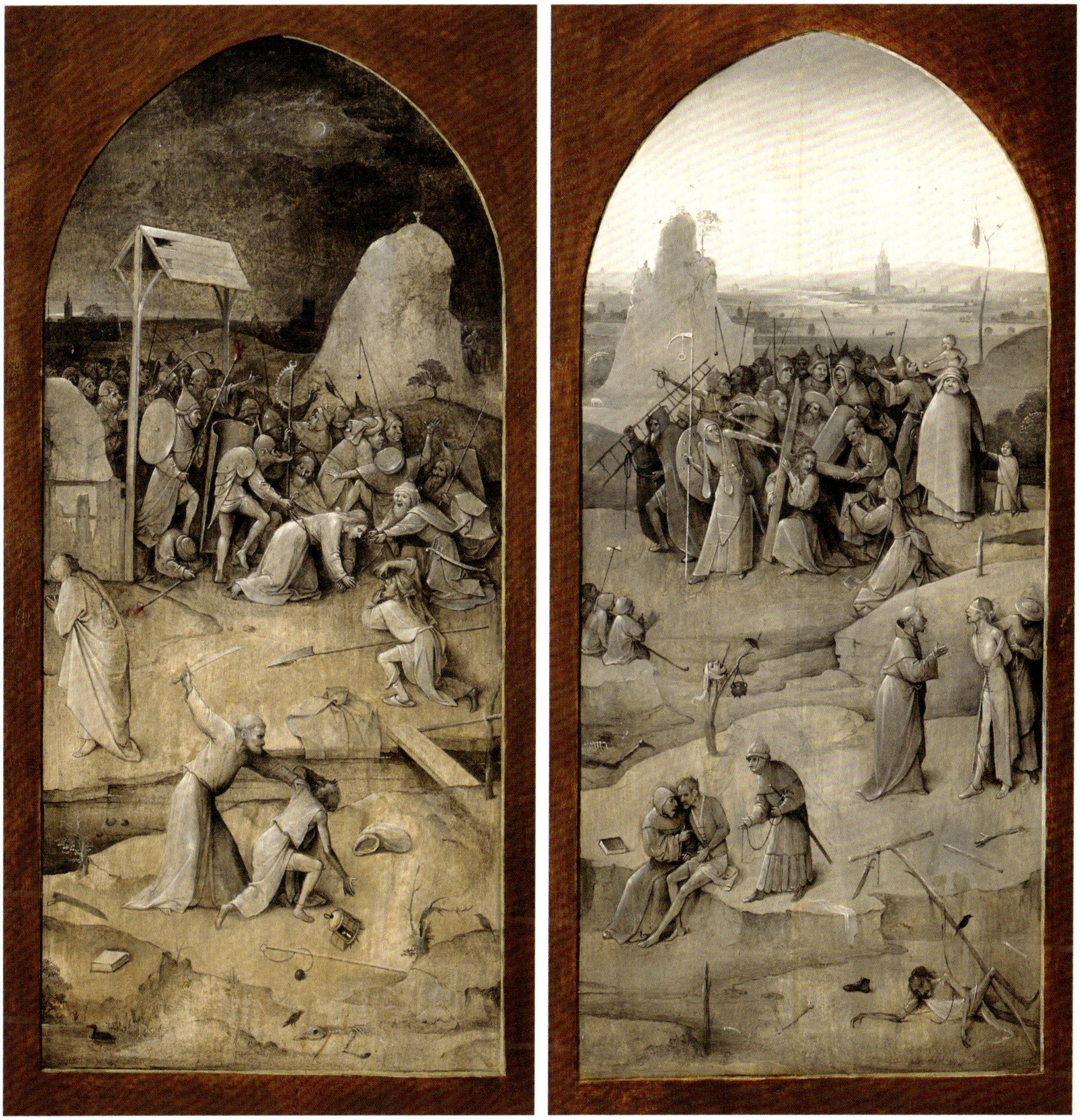

165 Hieronymus Bosch, *Temptation of Saint Anthony*, closed state, c. 1510, panel, Museu Nacional de Arte Antiga, Lisbon

How does Anthony himself relate to the idolatrous world? Upon arriving in the Egyptian desert, he had this decisive vision: "He saw the whole world covered with snares connected one to the other and exclaimed, 'Oh, how can anyone escape these traps?' And he heard a voice say: 'Humility!' "[60] Bosch expands on this lesson in the triptych's outer wings (fig. 165), which pictures two scenes from the Passion of Christ. Working in a grisaille so subtly variegated that it can capture the natural gloom of an evil world, the artist sketches the figures and landscape in paint, allowing the pale ground of the panel to show through (as Van Mander observed) and causing passages in the landscape to seem to glow in and of themselves. The Agony in the Garden and the carrying of the Cross occurred at opposite times of the day, the one just before dawn, the other before the Crucifixion's cataclysmic night. Bosch conveys this polarity by reversing the values of dark and light: note the opposite treatment of the corresponding hills. This allows one twilit scene darkly to mirror the other. In both scenes, Christ accepts the Passion; and in both,

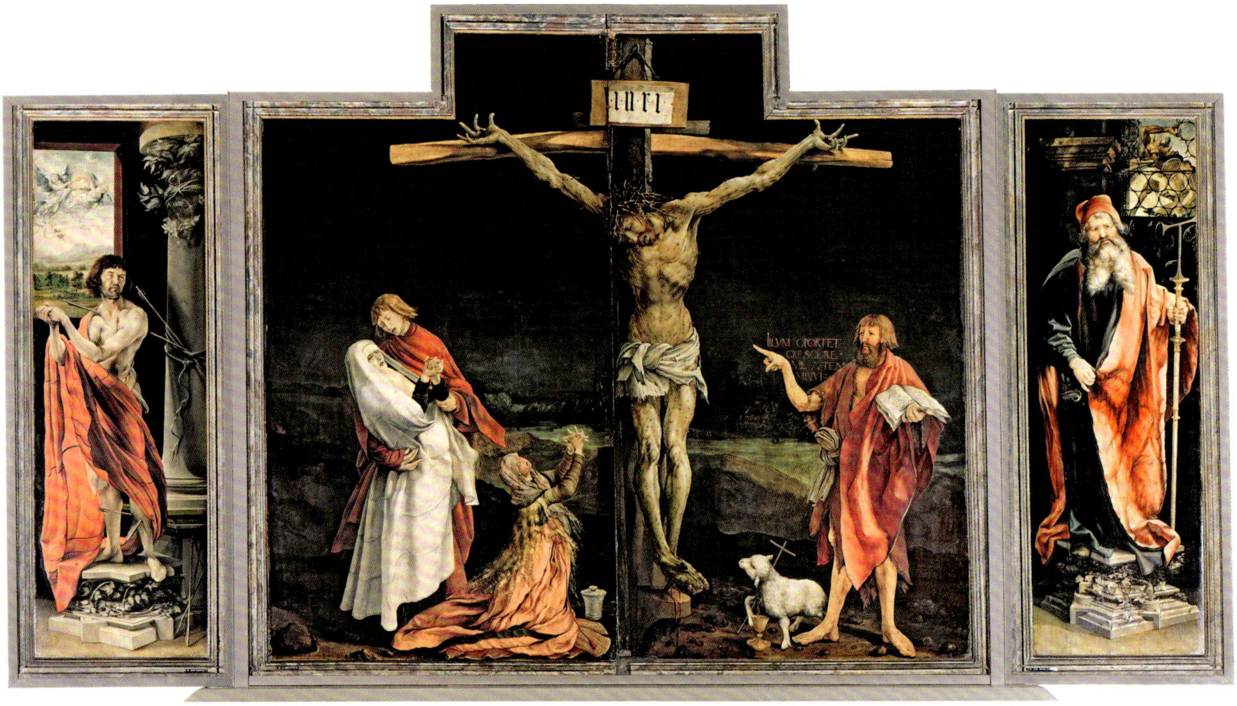

168 Matthias Grünewald, *Crucifixion, saints, and entombment* from *Isenheim Altarpiece*, (fig. 141), c. 1515, limewood, Musée d'Unterlinden, Colmar

only stood by, observing with a certain curiosity the saint's terrible trial. This trial consisted in maintaining faith without receiving help. Compare this with the idolaters, who sinfully but efficaciously command the demons through their crafted effigies. Anthony gets nothing from the sign of the cross but grief. And it is this inertness of the image that scandalizes the demons, since they recognize it as a travesty of themselves.

In third-century Egypt, it would still have been obvious why praying to the Cross was ridiculous. Execution by being nailed to a Cross was still a living memory. Christians and non-Christians alike knew that crucifixion was the most painful and humiliating of deaths, the ultimate punishment reserved for traitors and criminal slaves. In Cicero's words, it was "a most cruel and ignominious punishment"; according to Saint Paul, it was the unspeakable "sign of shame" (Heb. 12:2).[66] But for Christians, it was—it had to become—the improbable sign of their God.

Christians undid the scandal by negating its negation. Humiliation, ugliness, pain, death, and abandonment: these had to become attributes of their God. It was in fact Anthony's biographer, Athanasius, who established the Church's doctrine that Christ was divine even during the Crucifixion. In his lifelong struggles with the heretical Arians who denied that divinity, Athanasius affirmed, in what became known as the Athanasian Creed, that this gruesome spectacle was God. How was this inversion achieved? The Cross has iconoclasm built into it. Charged with showing how God's only son suffered the most miserable of human ends, the image of Christ was made simultaneously to rescue and to reject visible appearances. On the one hand, Christ was the perfect, living image of his father; he therefore could be pictured as a body in the world. On the other hand, unrecognized *by* the world, Christ's divinity was also fully concealed. Through the torments and wounds suffered in the Passion, God's living portrait became the ugliest of things. According to the words of

Isaiah, endlessly borrowed for this purpose: "There is no beauty in him nor comeliness . . . a man of sorrows" (Isa. 53:2–3).

In the late Middle Ages, when Christ's humility captured the imagination more than his divinity, people reveled in grisly depictions of Christ's ruined body. Grünewald's *Crucifixion* employs the illusionistic techniques of northern European painting in order to picture, in every feature, the crossed-out God: hands and feet torn and twisted by nails, ribcage collapsed, skin necrotic and bristling with thorns (fig. 168). Weirdly spotlighted in the nocturnal setting, this display would have detailed Christ's secret nighttime Passion at the hands of Jewish tormentors. It would also have had special relevance in the hospital at Isenheim, where the sufferers of Saint Anthony's fire could find their afflictions mirrored and take comfort in Christ's victorious death. For at Isenheim as elsewhere, the goal of picturing this ruined body was ultimately transcendence of the body. Painting visualizes everything Christ was *not*.[67] The Crucifixion was a great disguise. It was the divine trap set within the entrapping world in order to snare the enemy—the Devil, the heretic, the unbeliever—who saw there only death, darkness, and defeat.

Tricks of the Trade

In his *Saint Anthony*, Bosch activates this trap within a trap. Failing to ensnare the saint, the demons themselves are ensnared by Christ through his seeming impotence. This showdown takes place in a cave of idols eerily resembling a church. In 1500, on the very eve of Protestant image breaking, Bosch transports us back, via the third-century saint, to the original Christian image wars, where using graven images was the mark of the pagan, the enemy. In this clash, icon and idol, truth and falsehood, the "us" and the "them," are locked in a deadly struggle. With all the resources of early Netherlandish illusionism at his disposal, and himself specialized in devilish illusions, Bosch causes us to see through the eyes of the enemy, the idolater. To such a gaze, appearances flit (as Lucretius put it) "like a skin, or film, pealed from the body's surface, . . . this way and that across the air."[68] But in this heart of darkness Bosch also sets a counterimage, weak where the rest is strong, small where all else abounds, but bright where all is dim. To paint *this* truth, Bosch must transcend the medium of painting itself. To do so he avails himself of two tricks.

One trick is a sort of cup game, like the one Bosch so memorably portrayed in his scene of conjuring (see fig. 153). The trick hinges on a sudden, unexpected change of place. Inside the painted world, the saint inhabits a random point within a spatial chaos. The ancient tomb or temple, a structured compass point in sacred geography, lies in ruins; its symmetries—now hectic fragments—stand obliquely to Anthony and to ourselves. However, from the perspective of the triptych as a material thing, the saint is differently placed: not haphazardly in space but at an absolute, geometric center. To notice that the painted marks that represent Saint Anthony's outward-turned eye occur in that singular spot on the wooden support is to affirm for *his* viewpoint—alone—a solid ground. It is telling that almost none of Bosch's copyists or imitators retain this feature. Overlooking Bosch's central placement, these less-stringent image makers render the saint as nomadic as the demons around him, perhaps resisting how, in Bosch, artistry must work *against* itself.

Then there is a second trick. At that center, an eye gazes straight at us (fig. 169). Bosch used this device before, in the all-seeing eye of *The Seven Deadly Sins*, and in the look Christ

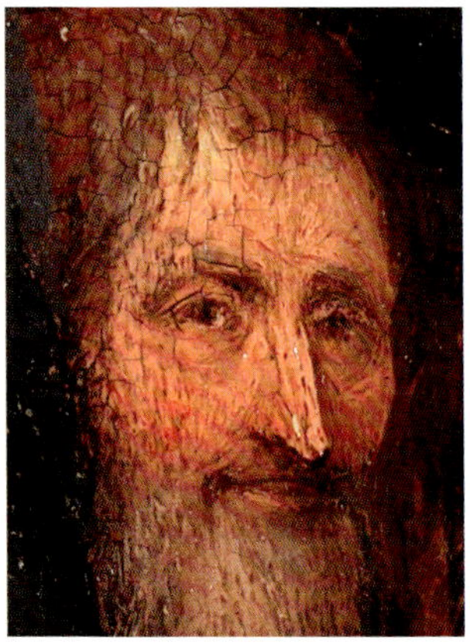

169 Detail of Hieronymus Bosch, *Temptation of Saint Anthony* (fig. 138)

gives us in all of Bosch's close-up devotional portraits. Beholding the eye that beholds us, we logically abduct a power or agency in the image itself.[69] Endowed with personhood, and seeing us more totally, constantly, and originally than our eyes see it, the painted gaze transcends the world from which it peers. Anthony looks out from enemy territory into our eyes and into our persons. With us in view, that gaze also inverts our world, turning us into objects, while establishing the saint as the world-renouncing "I" of Christian identity.

But who are we, who am I, who find ourselves adrift among the idols Anthony abhors? Am I a friend and mirror of the saint? Or am I one of *them*, the perennial idolaters, who are drawn into his trap? To experience myself beheld as if *I* were the enemy: that is a first step toward renouncing the world. But what would have happened if instead of putting a tiny escape hatch at the center, in the form of Anthony's true look, Bosch had made the center the most dangerous place of all? In other words, what if Bosch were to have expanded the play of idols, transforming them from a set of strange paintings *within* his painting to his painting as a whole? In his most notorious creation, Bosch plays this dangerous game. Whereas in the *Saint Anthony* idols are evil objects located inside his painting, in the masterpiece to which we now turn, the enemy image is Bosch's painting itself.

7

THE UNSPEAKABLE SUBJECT

An Unnameable Masterpiece

It is the most elusive artwork ever made (figs. 170 and 171).[1] To say no agreement has been reached about what this winged triptych shows and what purpose it served, to fancy that amity has ever been what viewers sought, is to belie the animus that fuels the quest. To one erudite, it is a Christian altarpiece; to another, it preaches a heretical creed. For this scholar, it celebrates carnal pleasure; for his esteemed colleague down the hall, it utterly damns the flesh. One recognizes a false utopia of food and sex; the next, an abstruse alchemical tract about cyclical creation; a third, a Jewish marriage canopy and Aztec calendar combined.[2] Meanwhile, the cautious steer clear of the work lest its traps ensnare them. The great doyen of art history Erwin Panofsky broke off his magisterial study of early Netherlandish painting before discussing Bosch. Demurring that we have not yet "discovered the key," while also taking the opportunity to mock any who claim to have found it, Panofsky ends with a learned disclaimer that makes his bolder colleagues look like fools: "This, too high for my wit, / I prefer to omit."[3]

Amity finds no toehold on this hostile carousel of love. Simply to *name* these panels is to rush headlong into the confusion. A paper trail of bafflement reaches back almost to Bosch's lifetime. Antonio de Beatis served as secretary to Cardinal Luigi of Aragon on a diplomatic tour of Europe.[4] In July 1517, a year after Bosch's death, the cardinal and his entourage arrived in Brussels. After visiting the zoo and garden labyrinth of the Duke of Burgundy, they entered the rival palace of Count Henry III of Nassau (fig. 172).[5] A voluble diarist, Antonio records the marvels contained in that place: secret doorways ingeniously hidden from the eye; oak paneling carved with wavy lines to look like Turkish camlet; picture galleries full of large-scale nudes, including one of Hercules and Deianira, which Antonio duly names; a gigantic bed into which the count, fond of cruel pranks, tossed guests after watching them get blind drunk. It was in this playfully deceptive space that the diarist glimpsed them: "Some painted panels of bizarre themes . . . things so pleasing and fantastic that they could not properly be described to those who do not know them."[6] Count Henry, or more likely his uncle, the childless, syphilitic womanizer Count Engelbert II of Nassau, probably commissioned the triptych directly from Bosch (fig. 173 and see fig. 221).[7] These men knew the work's maker and surely had some name for it. But like the doorways through which only the count and his men understood

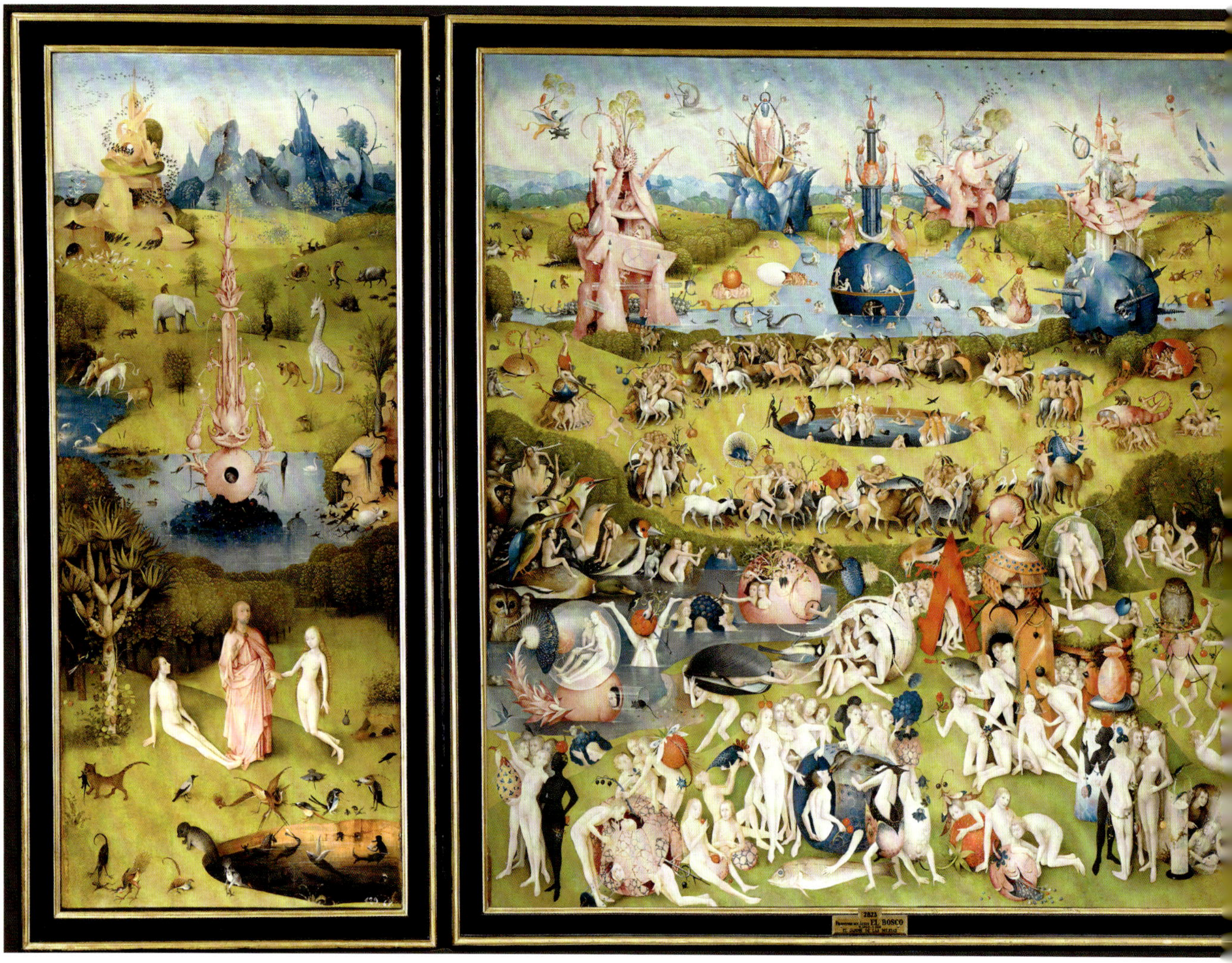

170 Hieronymus Bosch, *The Garden of Delights*, open state, 1504, panel, Museo Nacional del Prado, Madrid

how to pass, this name was kept secret from visitors, inducing in them the stupefied silence appropriate to wonders.[8]

Objects of unspeakable delight, these panels inflamed in beholders an overwhelming desire to *own* them. Several early copies survive, including a massive tapestry version that formed the centerpiece of a suite of tapestries after paintings by Bosch (fig. 174).[9] An exquisite weaving of silver, gold, and silk, it belongs to the bloodiest chapter in the triptych's provenance.[10] In 1567, Fernando Álvarez de Toledo, third Duke of Alba, led an army of Spaniards to crush heresy in the Netherlands. Imposing martial law, he established an inquisitorial tribunal that killed thousands.[11] But Alba had another obsession: he lusted after Bosch's triptych. Enmity fueled his desire. Preordained to marry the beautiful Mencía de Mendoza, born in 1508, the Iron Duke (as the Netherlanders called him) had been denied her by Charles V, who gave sixteen-year-old Mencía to Count Henry instead. By 1567, with Henry and Mencía both dead, the work had passed via Henry's heir to William I of Orange-Nassau, leader of the Protestants and Alba's sworn foe. Documents show that Alba borrowed from Cardinal Antoine Perrenot de Granvelle a large tapestry copy of the work, which he contemplated "at his pleasure," and from which he planned to have his own copy woven.[12] But Alba also sought to seize the original triptych, initiating legal proceedings against William in order to do so. Inventoried in 1567 by Alba's

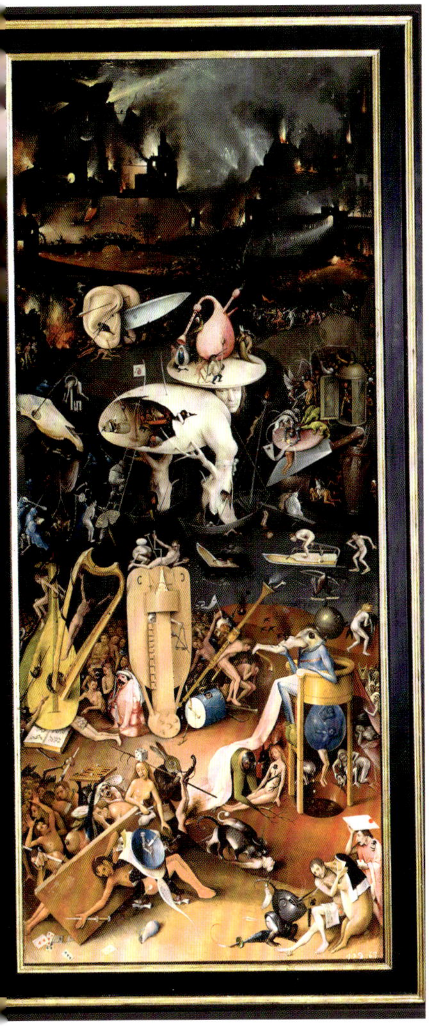

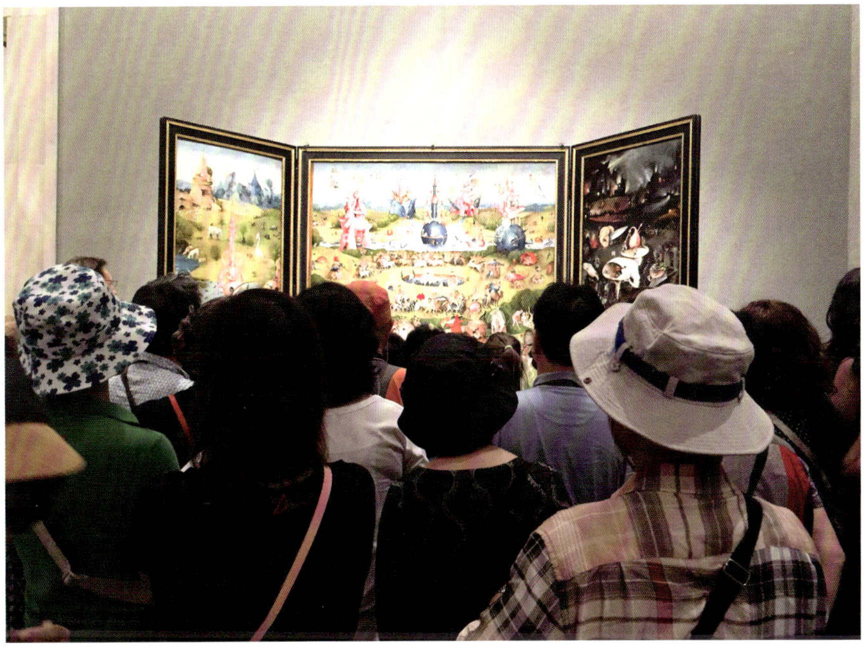

171 Hieronymus Bosch, *The Garden of Delights* (fig. 170), in situ in the Prado, with people

men as "a large painting by Hieronymus Bosch" said to hang in the Great Gallery of the court of Nassau, the work arrived into Alba's hands only when William's concierge, after months of brutal torture, revealed its hiding place.[13] Meanwhile, northern Europe was plunged into a war that would last eighty years, which permanently divided the Low Countries into a Catholic south and a Protestant north. But the initial spark of that great conflagration was—arguably—Bosch's triptych and the state of emergency ordered to seize it.

Brought back to Spain, the panels passed (via Alba's illegitimate son) to the king. Attributed to "Hierónimo Bosco," they arrived in 1593 at El Escorial as "an oil painting on panel, with two wings, depicting the variety of the world, signified by diverse disparities."[14] Variety was the cardinal virtue of the princely cabinets of wonder where the panels hung. The triptych thus formed a collection within the royal collection, as it had for the counts of Nassau, instancing the very variety it displayed. Wonder cabinets exemplified variety chiefly through marvels, through rare and monstrous anomalies of nature and art. Accumulating since antiquity in great lists, but multiplying through new artistic experiments and global exploration, marvels escaped all categories except one: though they derived from nature's copiousness, they were themselves *counternatural*, since they violated the bedrock order of nameable species.[15] The Christian tradition linked variety to vanity. Contrasted to God's oneness, variety led to

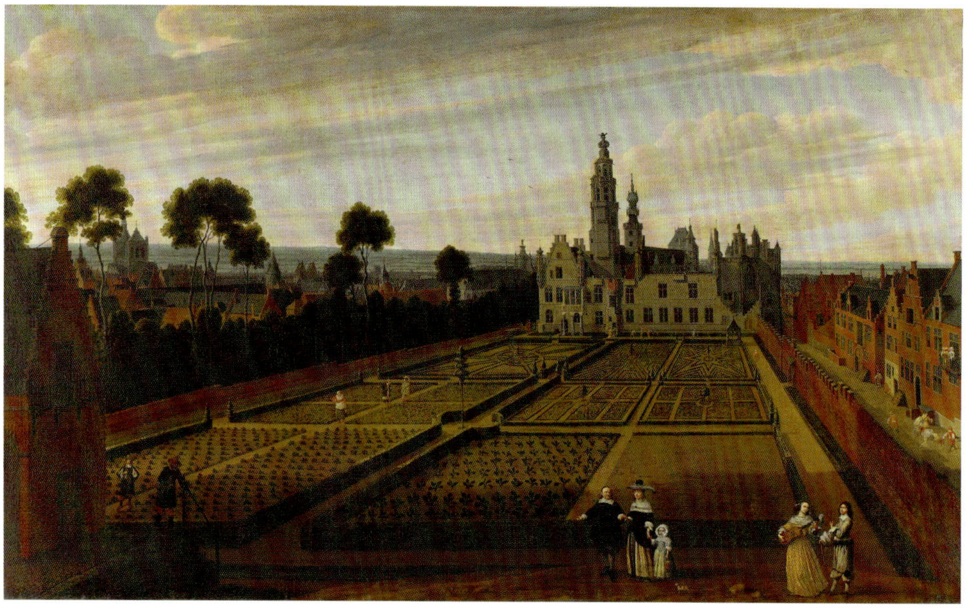

172 Wilhelm van Schoor and Gilles van Tilborgh, *The Palace of Oranien-Nassau*, 1658, canvas, Musée Royaux des Beaux-Arts de Belgique, Brussels

curiosity, and curiosity led to sin. In the 1593 shipment inventory, the scribbled writing that modern scholars usually transcribe as *variedad* ("variety" or "diversity") may in fact be the word *vanidad* ("vanity").[16] This would make the moral gloss explicit. Whether it depicts the world's variety or—as seems more likely—its vanity does not matter too much, though, because the inventory anyway signals the negative and, as it were, *vanitas* connotation in the nickname it gives to Bosch's ensemble: "They call it the *Madroño*."

The *madroño*, or strawberry-tree, is an evergreen of the heath family that bears fruits resembling strawberries (figs. 175–178). Their bad taste allowed Pliny the Elder to derive the plant's Latin name, *Arbutus unedo*, from the phrase *unum edo*, "I eat one." Birds relish these fruits, however, and so do bears: the ancient emblem of Madrid features a bear pawing *madroño* berries. Bosch scholars routinely mistranslate *madroño* (genus *Arbutus*) as "strawberry," although—to be fair—spectacular strawberries (genus *Fragaria*) also appear in the panels (fig. 179).[17] Joseph de Sigüenza explained the title roughly as follows: just as the *madroño*'s enticing berries leave no flavor behind, so the fleshly pleasures shown in Bosch's triptych are fleeting. Vain, they are damnable, as the Hell panel confirms.[18] Neither the title nor Sigüenza's learned gloss stuck, however. Over the centuries, Bosch's work fell into oblivion, due to changing tastes and perhaps also to the panels' worsening condition (fig. 180).[19] Rehabilitation began in 1889 through Carl Justi's survey of Bosches in the Spanish collections. There we read of "the strangest and most obscure of Bosch's allegorical-moral creations, a picture for which not even a proper name has been found."[20] Justi records some nicknames—"The Spanish call it the Affairs of the World [*el tráfago*] or Luxury [*la lujuria*], and also the Vices and Their Ends"—but goes on to call the picture the *Lustgarten* (pleasure garden), and it is by one or another version of this provisional name—*Der Garten der Lüste, The Garden of Delights, El Jardín de las Delicias, Le Jardin des délices*, etc.—that the work still goes, despite all who claim to have discovered its proper title.[21]

As a title, *The Garden of Delights* seems innocuous enough. The ensemble's center shows a garden setting aligned along the picture's axis of symmetry. And the actions occurring there seem delightful. Feasting on abundant fruits and imbibing fresh waters, naked people caress,

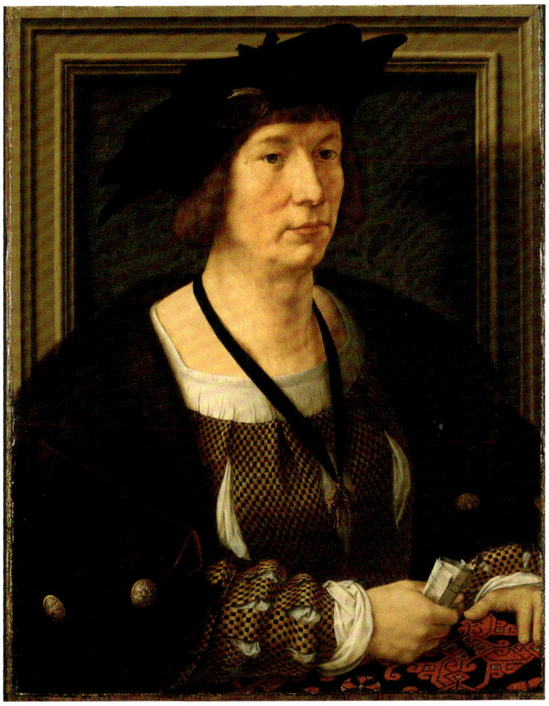

173 Jan Gossart, *Portrait of Hendrik III, Count of Nassau-Breda*, c. 1516–17, oil on panel, Kimbell Art Museum, Fort Worth, TX

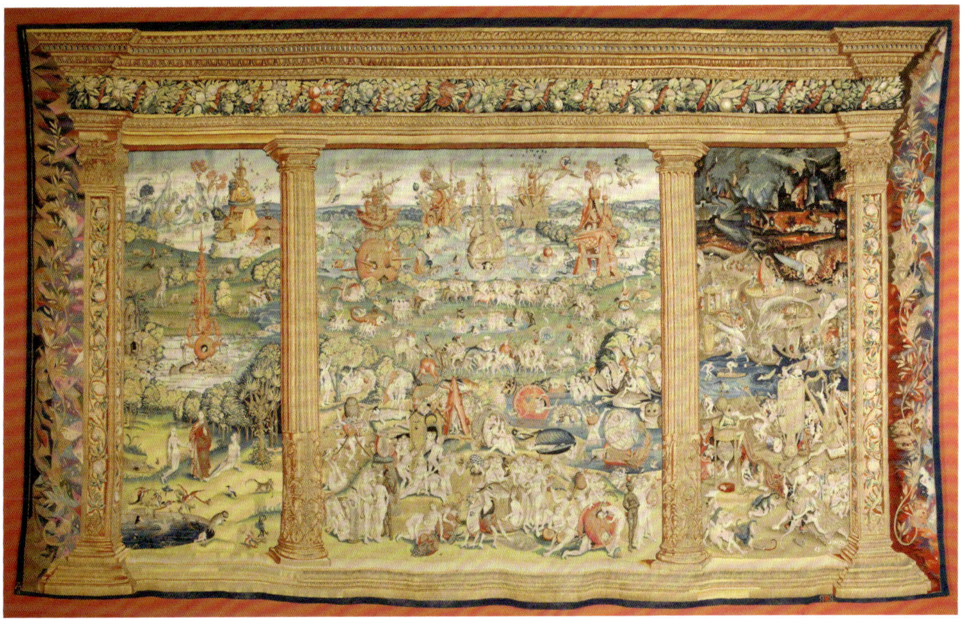

174 Brussels Workshop after Hieronymus Bosch, *The Garden of Delights*, 1550–70, tapestry in gold, silver, silk, and wool, Palacio Real, Patrimonio Nacional, Madrid

and get caressed by, willing, well-formed partners. The question is, from whose perspective are these activities delightful? From that of the multitude pursuing them? Presumably, though, some seem sad or irritated, as if on the edge between pleasure and pain (figs. 181 and 182). But what about God the Creator, who in the form of Christ as Logos appears in Eden, to the left (see fig. 191)? Would these revels look delightful to him? Bosch forces the question by directing God's gaze toward us. Are these paradisiacal pleasures free of painful consequences? Or are they sinful, with hell as their reward?

To this day, no one has resolved this most basic question. Those who put the word "delights" in scare quotes argue that contempt for pleasure—especially of the sexual kind—was

(LEFT) 175 Fruits of *Arbutus unedo*, madrone or strawberry-tree

(RIGHT) 176 Detail of Hieronymus Bosch, *The Garden of Delights* (fig. 170)

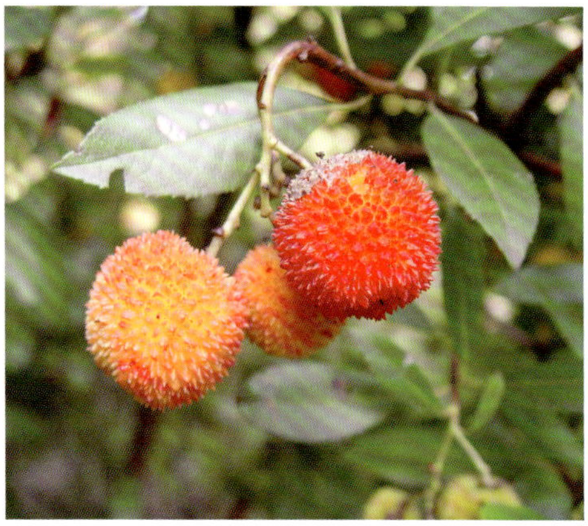

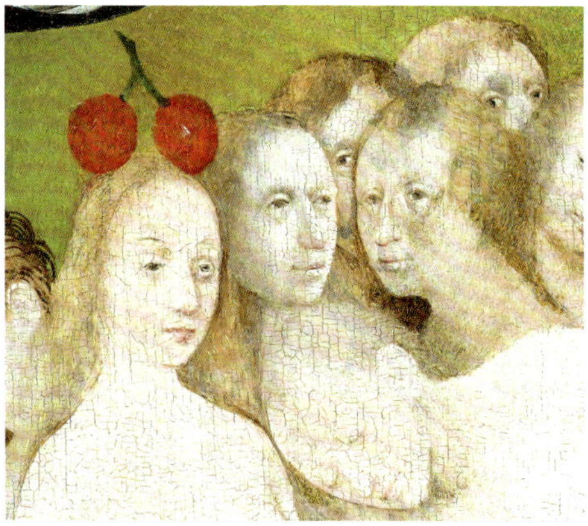

(LEFT) 177 Detail of Hieronymus Bosch, *The Garden of Delights* (fig. 170)

(RIGHT) 178 *Fragaria vesca*, wild strawberry

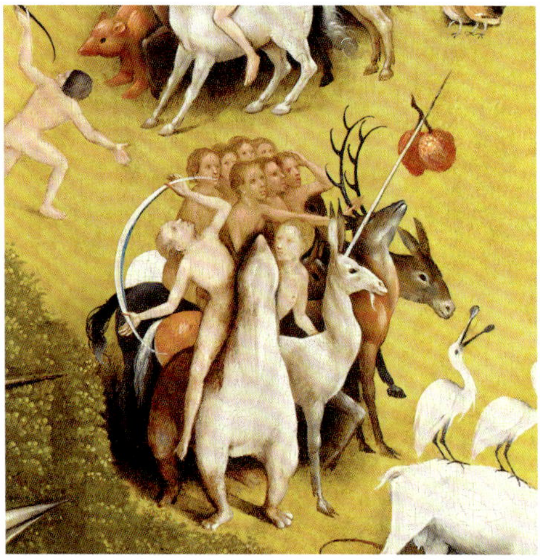

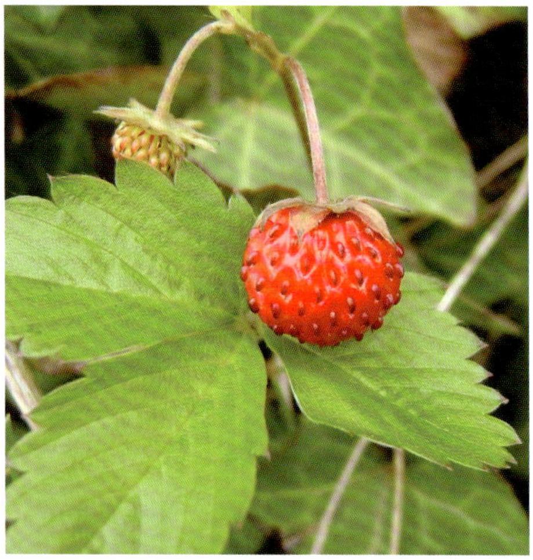

(LEFT) 179 Detail of Hieronymus Bosch, *The Garden of Delights* (fig. 170)

(RIGHT) 180 Jerónimo Seisdedos, *Detail of Hieronymus Bosch's* Garden of Delights *(Center Panel) during Restoration*, c. 1932, photograph, Museo Nacional del Prado, Madrid

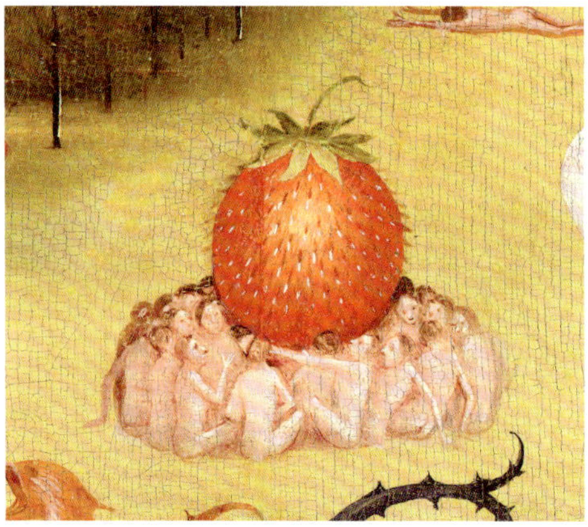

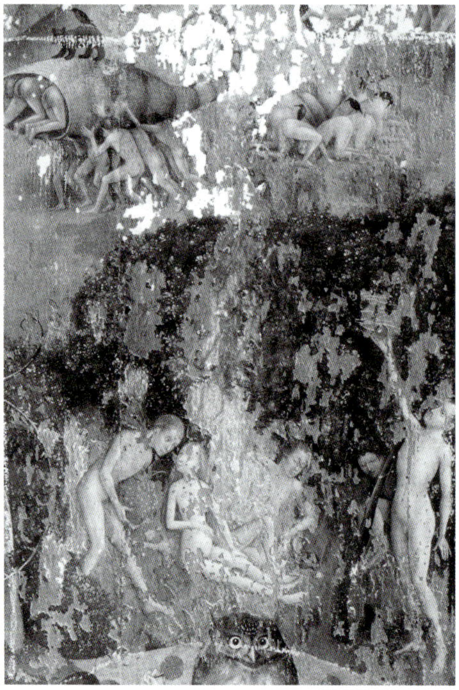

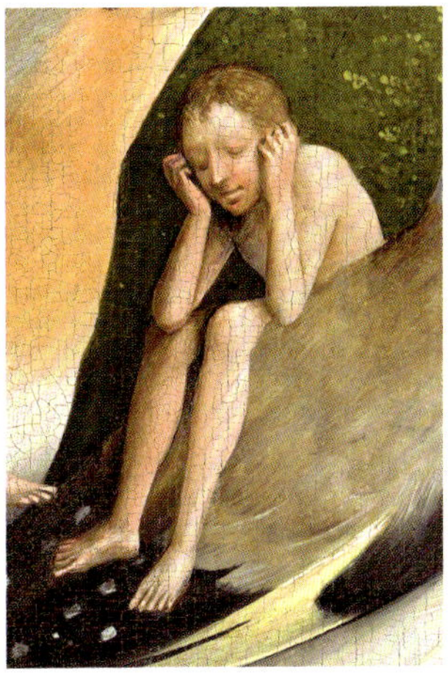

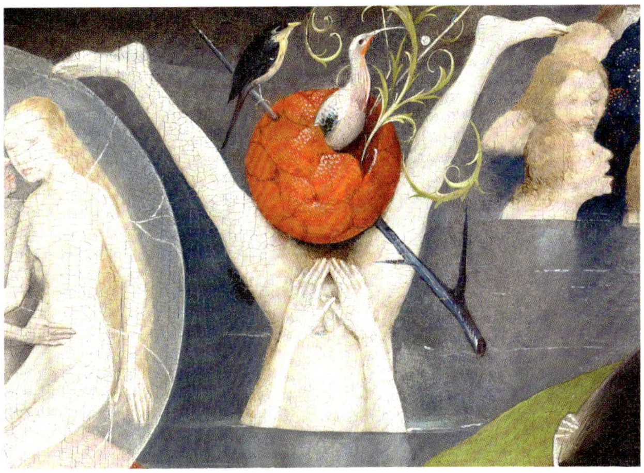

181 Detail of Hieronymus Bosch, *The Garden of Delights* (fig. 170)

182 Detail of Hieronymus Bosch, *The Garden of Delights* (fig. 170)

universal in Europe at the time. They note that all other paintings by Bosch fiercely preach such contempt. And they argue that the triptych's reading structure—from left to right—sends pleasure to perdition. "As far as the theology of the times is concerned," concludes a recent proponent of the view that the picture is a visual tract against the goings-on depicted, "there exists only one connection element between paradise and hell, namely sin."[22] A comparison with Bosch's *Hay Wain* makes the case against delight look rather closed and shut (see fig. 39). Desire—portrayed as humanity's lust after mere hay—operates within a legible chain of disastrous causes and effects. The fall of the rebels, in *The Hay Wain*'s left panel shown in a distance at once spatial and temporal, infects the events of Eve's creation, her and Adam's trespass, and their expulsion, the result of which unfolds at the triptych's center, in the contemporary milieu of the work's original display, with people dressed and acting as people of the time did, which is also patently the ongoing cause of future perdition at the right, which itself receives the damned through a no-exit tunnel in between. Atop the hay, meanwhile, the scenes of crude and courtly lovemaking condense—and damn—the concupiscence flourishing in the so-called garden of delights. The only difference, it would seem, is that in *The Hay Wain* the causes are clear and temporally sequenced, and the causal vector stands pictured—smack at the center of the assembly—in the hay cart's inexorable hellward march, whereas the *Garden* makes the causal links obscure, and its circular dance permanently diverts time's arrow.

But why has the *Garden* ever been construed as *praising* pleasure? For one thing, Bosch's works—and this one especially—have delighted audiences whatever they take its theme or message to be. Remember that in 1504 Philip the Fair prepaid Bosch to paint a *Last Judgment* for the duke's "noble pleasure" (in the words of the document), and that Antonio de Beatis, brought before Bosch's indescribable masterpiece in 1517, was made speechless by the "pleasing" things he beheld. Visual pleasure brought Bosch his patronage, and it draws his audience still. Today, the triptych typically amasses one of the Prado's biggest crowds. These do not trudge by it in listless reverence, as crowds so often do before a museum's must-see masterpiece. This painting can powerfully captivate beholders of every kind, causing the learned as well as the lay to press impolitely toward it and not to budge once they have conquered an unobstructed view. To keep people looking, the painting makes ever-shifting cases for its delectation. If its bright colors, mesmerizing symmetry, and theatrical ostentation draw us to it like bees to a blossom, its terrors keep us endlessly fascinated once we arrive. Spellbound by our ocular instincts, we observe, for example, animals acting like humans and humans like animals. Perversity captures

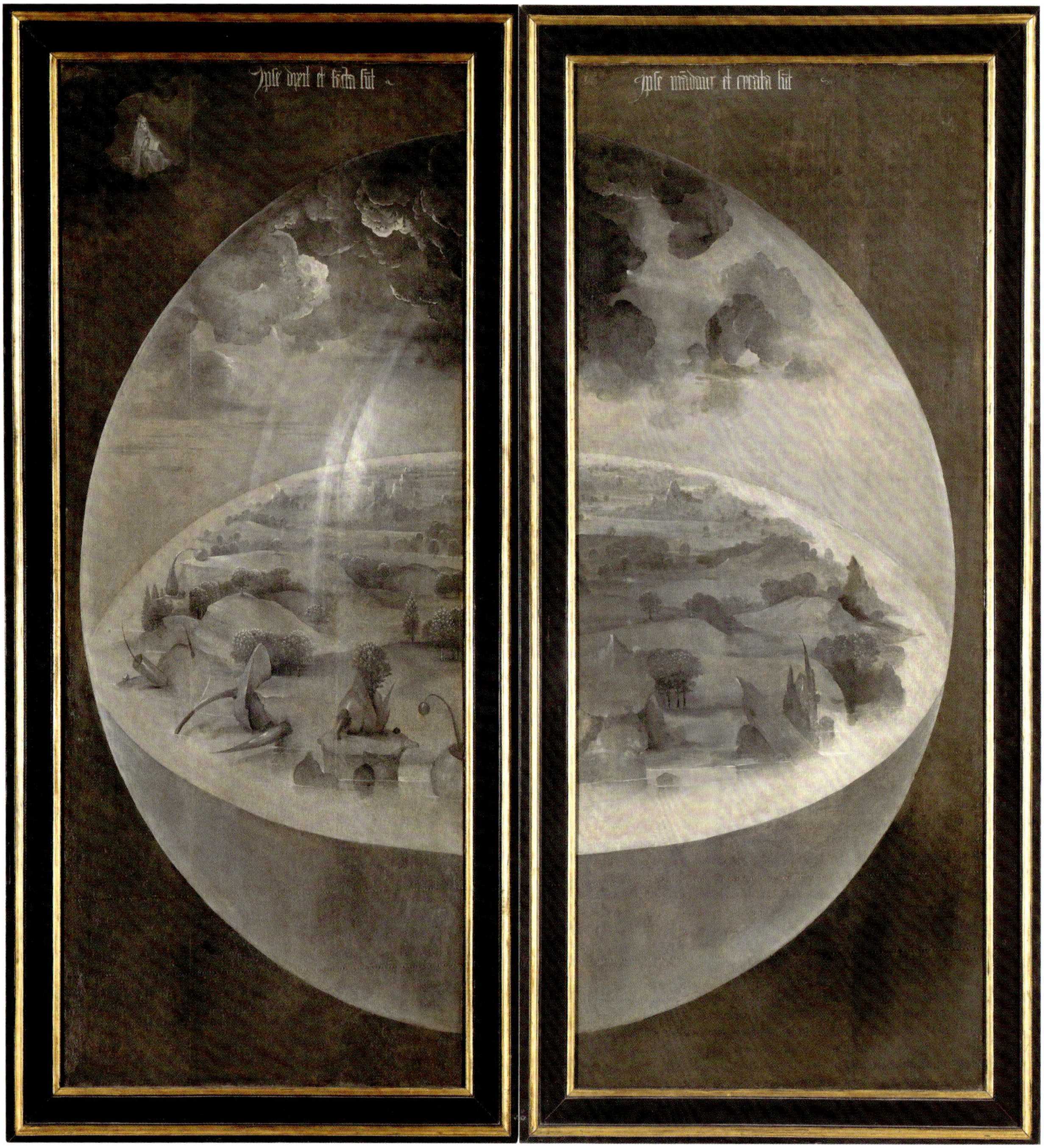

183 Hieronymus Bosch, *The Garden of Delights*, closed state, c. 1504, panel, Museo Nacional del Prado, Madrid

Simultaneously inside and outside the world's sphere, this unique world picture combines—improbably—the medieval theocentric model of being (as *ens creatum* made by a personal creator-god) with the modern, anthropocentric technique of linear perspective.

Three further aspects of this first tableau are especially salient for the enigmas that follow on its opening. First, Bosch portrays—as the pivotal event within the successive acts of creation—God's making of living things, that is, of created entities that can themselves procreate. Creation here doubles, and God subjects this new, second-order making to a particular restriction: living creatures must seed themselves "according to their kind." That is, they must never intermix or change, but must remain what they in essence were when they were made. Second, the triptych's outer tableau may well have been inspired by the great publishing

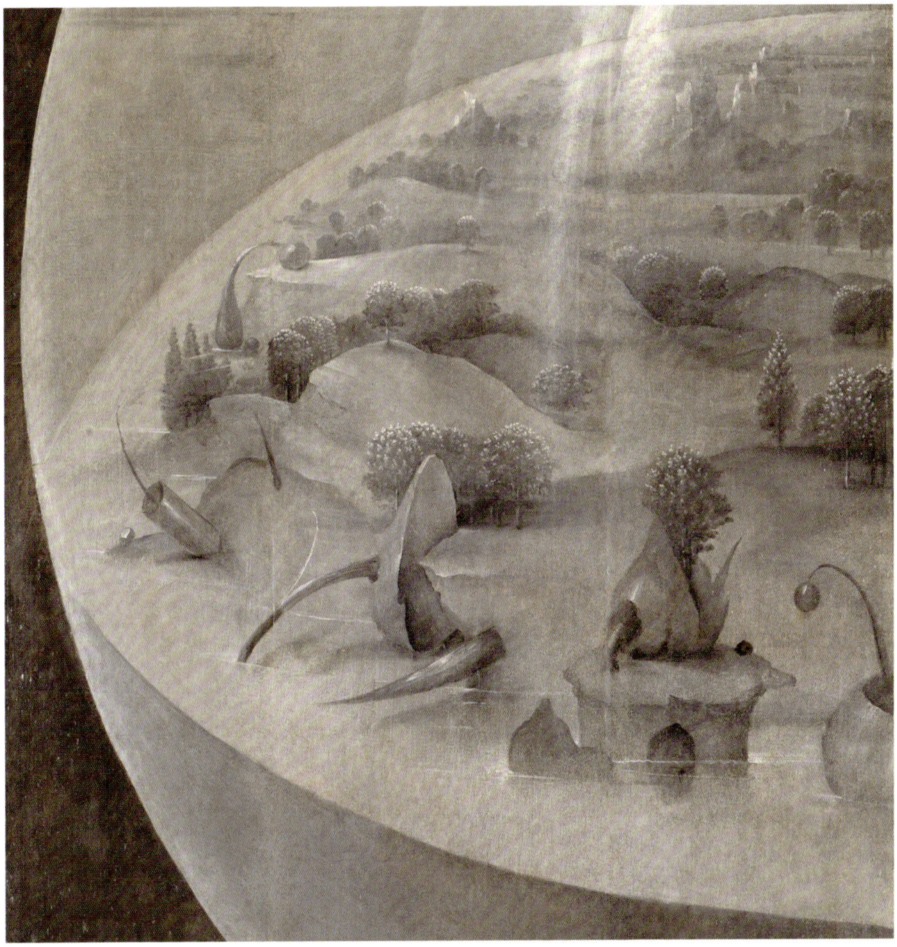

184 Detail of Hieronymus Bosch, *The Garden of Delights*, closed state (fig. 183)

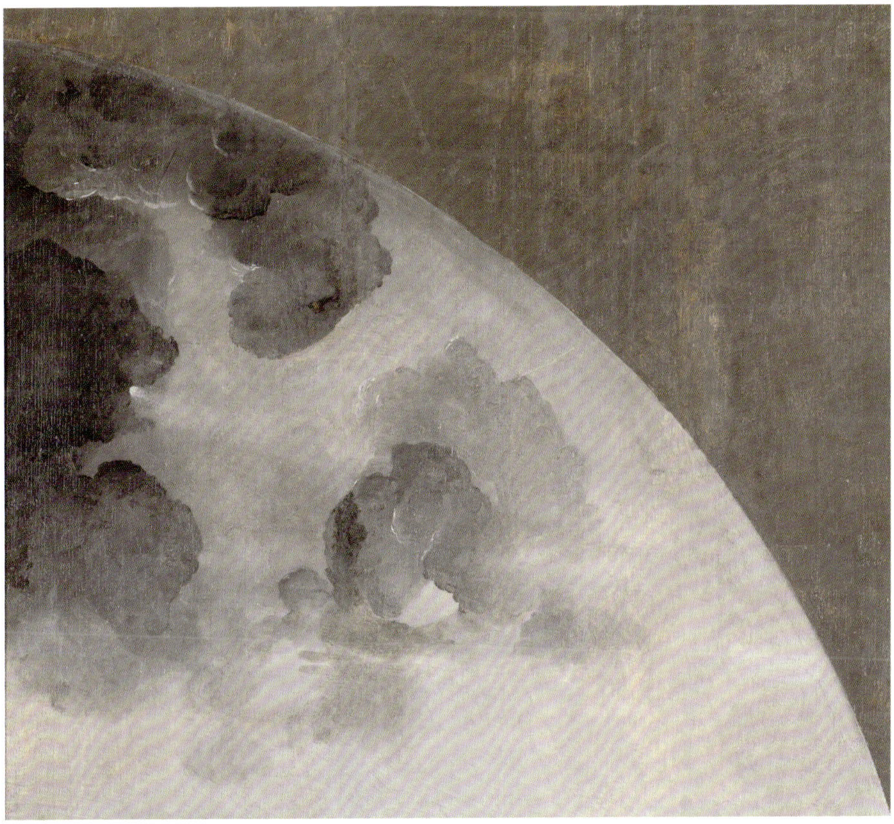

185 Detail of Hieronymus Bosch, *The Garden of Delights*, closed state (fig. 183)

event of the age: Hartmann Schedel's *Book of Chronicles*, printed in Nuremberg in 1493 and illustrated with woodcuts designed by Michael Wolgemut, Wilhelm Pleydenwurff, and their assistants. There, in *its* first opening, the creator-god sits beneath a speech scroll inscribed with the same words from Psalm 33 (fig. 186).[27] His divine fiat carries across the opening to another woodcut, lower right, where God's productive hand hovers over a group of angels encircling the mysterious word *yle*, printed in an elaborate calligraphic type. *Hyle* (ὕλη) is an Ancient Greek term for matter or primal stuff, as Schedel on the same page explains: "Plato held that God and the prototype or form of his creation and *hyle* were present from eternity, and in the beginning the world was created from this same *hyle*." The learned reference has a polemical charge. Whereas the philosophers taught that *hyle* had been present from eternity, and that the world had been made from primal matter, Scripture attests that, in the beginning, there was only God, who created both the world and the stuff from which it was made. "God created the world without such preexistent and prepared material," writes Schedel.[28] Drawing perhaps on Nicolas of Cusa, whose writings Schedel avidly collected and personally copied out, this great *Weltbuch* begins by warding off any dualism between God and world. By insisting that *hyle* was God's product, Schedel affirms the Creator to be "not other," *non aliud*, to creation.[29] To think otherwise, to imagine God and the world to constitute two separate, perhaps even hostile powers, was to slip back into the arch-heresy, Gnosticism. In its various incarnations, which (we have seen in chapter 5) are with us still today, Gnosticism pits a true but hidden God against a demiurgic or demonical countercreator whose evil product is the corrupt physical world. Such dualism will be of great concern to Bosch, too, whose contempt for the world borders on, but must somehow also reject, heretical dualism.

In Bosch, Wolgemut's full-page portrait of God contracts into a hole in the clouds, while *hyle* has been formed into a material world now animated by vegetal life. But the properties of primordial, undifferentiated matter remain visible still. Around its edges and most dramatically in the foreground rocks and grottoes, the landscape appears inundated by the surrounding sea. Bosch thus connects the inanimate matter from which plant life springs to something earlier, to the time "when the earth was without form, and void," and "the Spirit of God moved up on the face of the waters" (Gen. 1:2). Whether God created those waters—that is, whether the aqueous nothingness prior to creation was somehow some*thing*, the question that Schedel's discussion of *hyle* addresses—haunted Christian theology, especially in its attempt to account for the existence of evil in the world. In Bosch's portrayal, the waters irrigate the new-formed vegetation, but they also cause the world to appear eerily groundless. The Greek *hyle* derived from words for "forest" and "timber"—as in the Latin *silva*. Aristotle understood *hyle* both as matter and as cause, rather as, in English, *ground* means both "foundation" and "reason."[30] Bosch's taken name means "forest" or "wood." Allied with stuff of creation, he will allow the abysmal substratum of *hyle* to haunt his triptych, as a principle of entropy in nature and in the entanglement of corporeal human being in nature.

Third and finally, these issues converge on Psalm 33. Bosch's original audience would have understood that text as a prayer invested with an edifying message. That message, as Charles Dempsey demonstrated, was established by Saint Augustine in his canonical commentary on the Psalms.[31] *Enarrationes in Psalmos* magnifies the vindictiveness of the Old Testament texts. Glossing Psalm 33, Augustine translates its jubilant opening command—"Rejoice in the Lord,

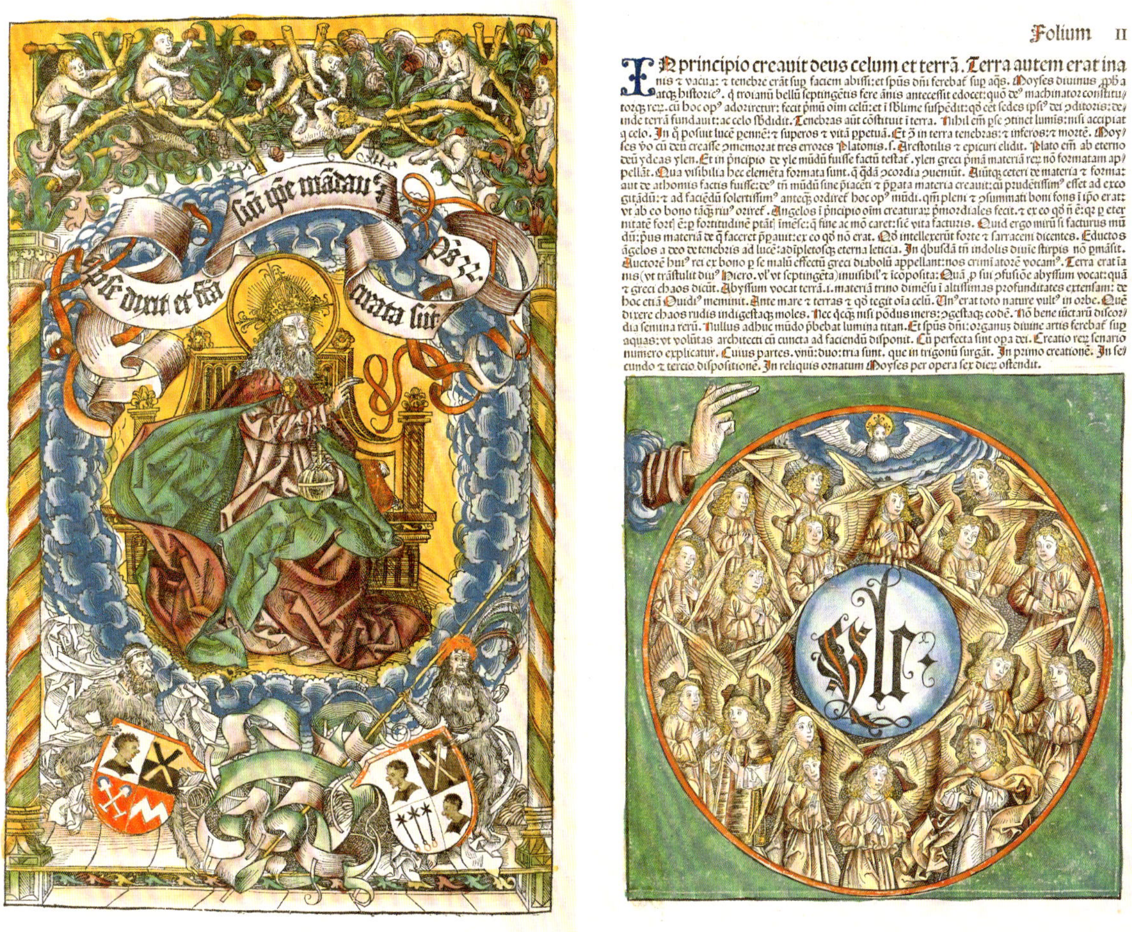

ye righteous"—into a terrifying admonition: "Rejoice, ye righteous, not in yourselves, for that is not safe."[32] He thus makes the psalm wonderfully suitable for Bosch's purpose, which, as we have seen, is to deliver the world over to God's rage. When the psalm urges praise and fear, Augustine underscores fear; when it celebrates how God foils enemies, Augustine turns divine anger on God's enemies, on all who "covet earthly pleasures." God's enemy is pride. Pride consists in rejoicing in oneself, of taking pleasure from, or credit for, what oneself experiences or creates. The primal turning away, or *aversio*, from God (in whom alone we should rejoice), pride is the root cause of all sin. It spawns delusions of freedom, rendering the prideful (in Augustine's words) "distorted and perverse." Where Psalm 33—in the Latin version—speaks of God "gather[ing] the water of the sea together as into a jar," Augustine discovers an allegory about vanity: "He gathered the people of the world together, to confession of mortified sin, lest through pride they flow too freely."[33] The transparent, jar-like sphere of the waters depicted on the exterior of the shutters thus implies iniquity even before they open to the spectacle within.[34] Also, the seed-filled landscape inside the sphere foreshadows the self-spawning garden to come. This links procreation—the self-seeding of the species—to the cosmic scandal of pride. In sum, the triptych's outer tableau focuses in on problems of creaturely poiesis. It frets about the relationship between God and the primal stuff of nature. And it sets these metaphysical problems within a moral framework concerned with vanity.

186 Michael Wolgemut and Wilhelm Pleydenwurff, *God the Father* and *Yle*, hand-colored woodcut frontispiece to Hartmann Schedel, *Liber Chronicarum* (Nuremberg: Anton Koberger, 1493), Bayerische Staatsbibliothek, Munich, Rar. 287, fol. 1r, 2v

Opened, the triptych drops us to the surface of the earth (see fig. 170). That all three scenes unfold in the selfsame world is indicated by their shared horizon. Stretching from Eden to hell, this world is clearly a vector of time. Bosch demands that viewers think in terms of *cause*. He begins on the shutters with God as first cause, and links each origin resolutely to an end, culminating in the definitive finale in hell. Marching in a circle, the garden's denizens divert—or pervert—this vector. But the circle spins in vector space. There the events in Eden must be a cause, and damnation must be the result.

What happens in Eden departs from all standard iconographies (fig. 187). God appears in the form of Christ, among other reasons because he is the creative Word, the Logos.[35] He grasps Eve by the wrist and blesses her, as if creating her just now. However, when Bosch elsewhere portrays Eve's creation, he shows Adam properly asleep. Adam sleeps in the distance of the Eden panel of *The Hay Wain*, with the rebel angels streaming from heaven just behind him, and he sleeps at the base of the Vienna *Last Judgment*, causing the whole narrative—the Fall and Expulsion, as well as judgment and damnation—that follows to read like the contents of his dream (see figs. 47 and 188). And in a fascinating Boschian painting in the Art Institute of Chicago, in which Eve's creation dominates the vision of Eden, Adam sleeps with his head resting on a seed-spilling pod (see fig. 196).[36] In the triptych, Adam has awoken from his dream. However, God's gesture and Eve's bent knees keep the image of her creation still in mind. Just created, she retains the shape of her formation as she first opens her eyes.

Some scholars identify the scene as the marriage of Adam and Eve.[37] Not described in the Bible, but derived from Genesis 1:28 ("And God blessed them, and God said unto them, 'Be fruitful, and multiply' "), this event was portrayed in exegetical schemes and as an extra episode in pictorial narratives of the Fall. All depictions of this marriage, however, show God grasping Adam's hand, usually with Adam grasping Eve's (fig. 189).[38] Closer to Bosch is the moment when God, in the Bible's words, "brought her unto the man" (Gen. 2:22). This event was vividly cast in bronze in the second register of Bishop Bernward's bronze doors in Hildesheim, underneath what appears to be a portrayal of Eve's formation (fig. 190).[39] Earlier than the marriage, this scene is a beat too late for Bosch. Thinking in nanoseconds, he conjures the fleeting synchronicity between the moment when Eve stands complete and the moment when Adam, waking, first beholds her. These are two momentous events. In the first, with God creating Eve, divine Creation properly ends; thereafter the world must seed itself. In the second event, with Adam's first sight of Eve, human history—the chain of autonomous acts and consequences—begins. For while the Fall will be history's official starting point, Adam's trespass had to have prior motivations in Eve and in Adam's relationship to her. Bosch merges into one turning point the end of the beginning and the beginning of the end. And he intimates that this big bang remains ongoing in a future commencing right now, in each act of human desire. But what are the first actors shown to do?

They look. Adam gazes fixedly at Eve. She, averting her eyes as if modest and submissive, receives Adam's gaze (fig. 191). And all-seeing God sees us. But what does all this looking achieve? Charging his finest brush with pale vermilion, Bosch applied in tiny strokes a visible blush to Adam's cheeks. Now, it is safe to say that with Bosch nothing is ever safe to say. However, I believe we may confidently conclude that, with this rosy hue, the artist wishes to indicate not merely Adam's original bloom but also the desire awoken in him by his first glimpse of Eve. At their creation, Eve and Adam were "both naked, but they were not ashamed"

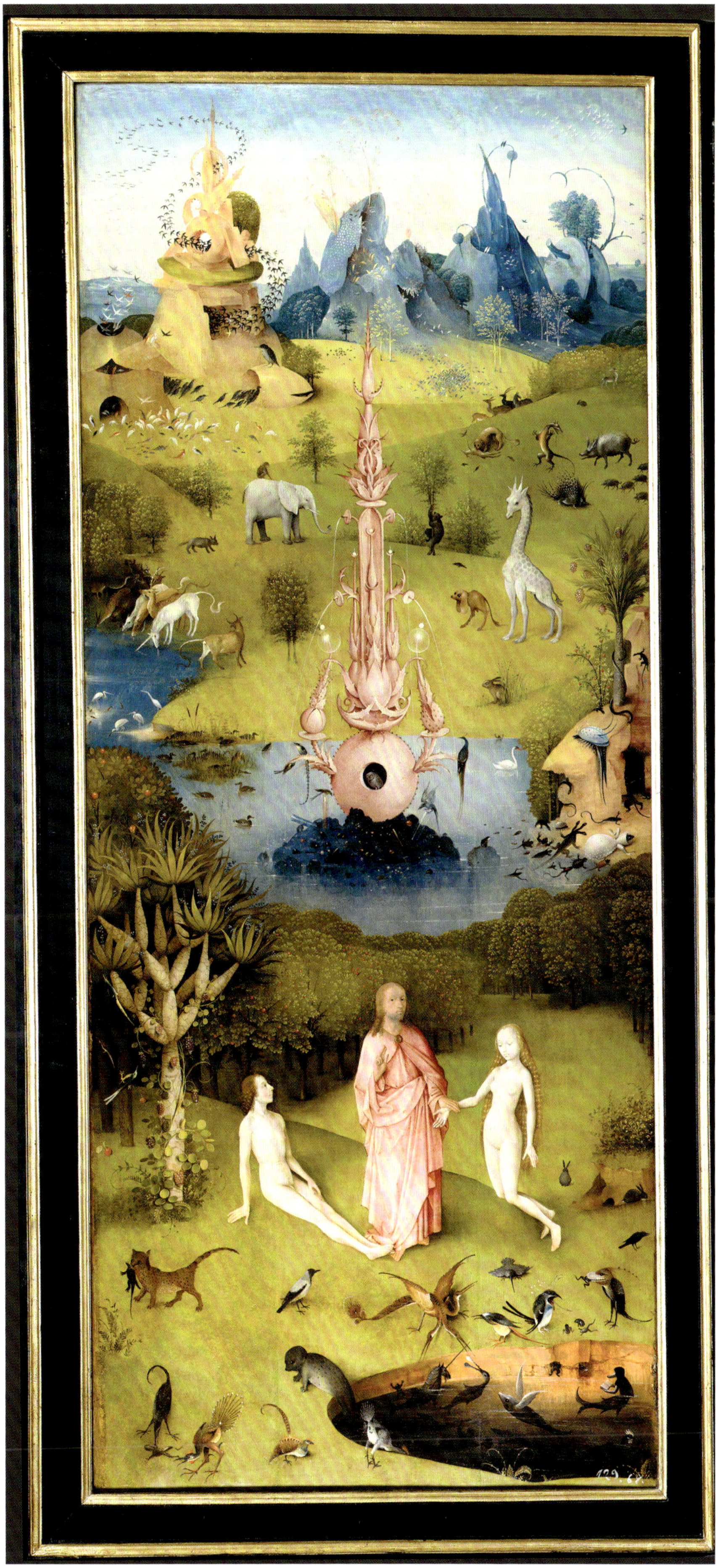

187 Hieronymus Bosch, *The Garden of Delights*, left inner wing (fig. 170)

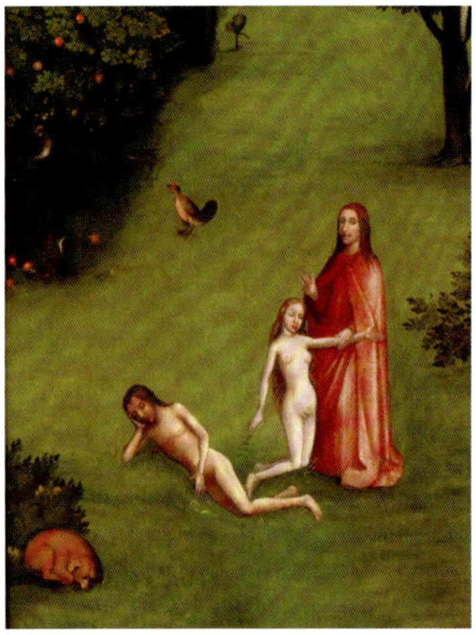

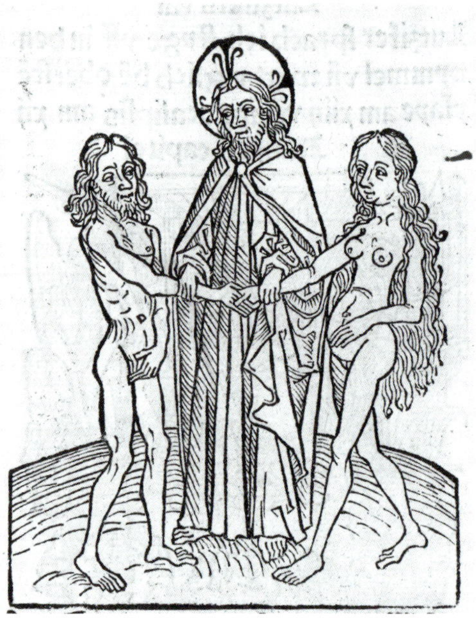

(LEFT) **188** Detail of Hieronymus Bosch, *The Last Judgment* (fig. 47)

(RIGHT) **189** Erhard Reuwich (?), "And [Eve] was given to him as a companion at his side," woodcut illustration from *Das ist der Spiegel der menschen behaltnis mit den evangelien und mit epistelen nach der zyt des iars* (Speyer: Peter Drach, c. 1478), fol. 1v, The Metropolitan Museum of Art, New York, Harris Brisbane Dick Fund, 1931

(OPPOSITE TOP) **190** Anonymous German, *God the Father Presenting Eve to Adam*, detail of the *Bronze Doors of Bishop Bernward* (fig. 199)

(OPPOSITE BOTTOM) **191** Detail of Hieronymus Bosch, *The Garden of Delights* (fig. 170)

(Gen. 2:24). Adam's look would therefore have been innocent. However, most authorities agreed that Adam felt desire already in Eden, but that its purpose was to cause him to procreate, in accordance with self-seeding nature and with God's explicit command to "be fruitful, and multiply." Further, it was a commonplace, highly developed in the love poetry of the Middle Ages, that the sense of sight best aroused libidinal desire, and that the eye was the portal to the heart. As the thirteenth-century poet Giacomo da Lentini put it: "The eyes first generate love, / And the heart gives it sustenance."[40] Writing in the Sicilian court of Frederick II, where the imagery of the troubadours fused with Arabo-Aristotelian theories of sense perception, Giacomo wondered (not without humor): "But how can such a large woman enter through my eyes, which are so small?"[41] His answer: the woman is like light, the eye is like glass, and thus "it is not the person, but her image, that passes through my eyes and to my heart."[42] The lover is also—according to Giacomo—like a painter, painting a "lifelike" image of his beloved "within [his] heart."[43] Bosch projects this story back into Eden, where—as Scripture taught and painters had ruefully to acknowledge—the desire-inflaming nature of the eye had ruinous consequences. The Tree of Knowledge was for Eve a "lust to the eyes" and "lovely to look at" (Gen. 3:6).[44] And it was through his infatuation with Eve's beauty that Adam fell. The blood flushing Adam's cheeks is an outward sign of the revolution occurring inside him, an unruliness already present within innocence.

To glimpse what Adam's gaze effects we might extend the vector of his eye (fig. 192). There are some historical justifications for this awkward exercise. First, medieval theories of vision held that sight occurred through rays emanating either from the eye to the object (the so-called extramission theory) or from the object to the eye, though also coupled with visual fire from the eye (the intromission theory).[45] Whichever direction vision flowed, the special object or "sensible" of vision—in Latin, the *species*—consisted of color or, more precisely, of illumined color (*lumen*).[46] This will be important to Bosch's triptych, which stands apart from the entire Netherlandish tradition not least because of its garish hues.[47] Second, the power of the visual ray was believed to be especially strong in the case of love.[48] Love pierced the eye with arrows tipped with amorous desire. An early fifteenth-century birth salver shows Venus with rays

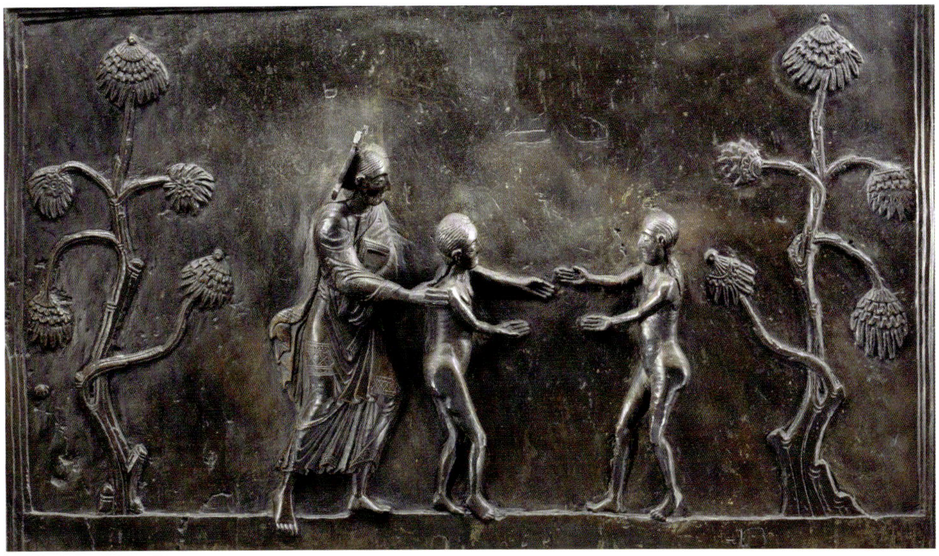

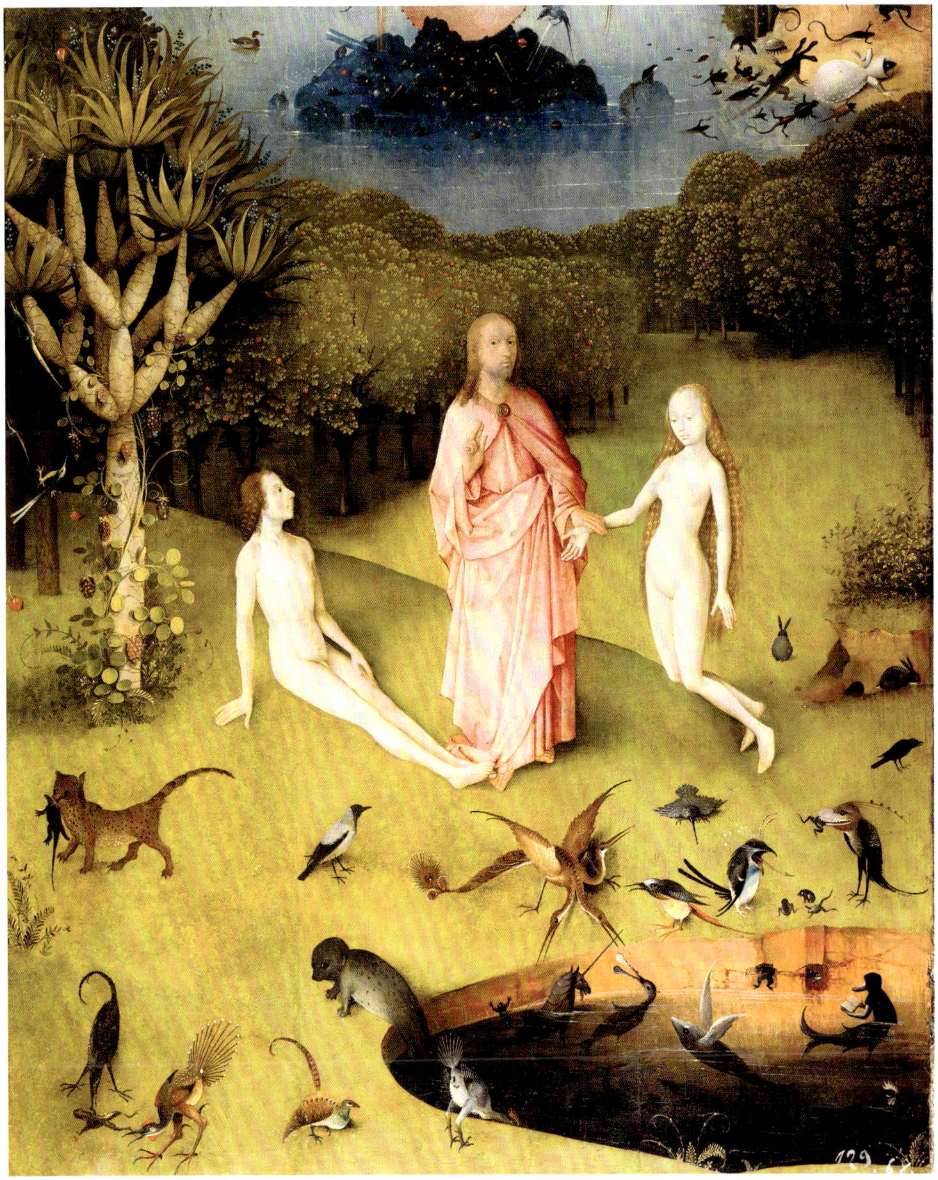

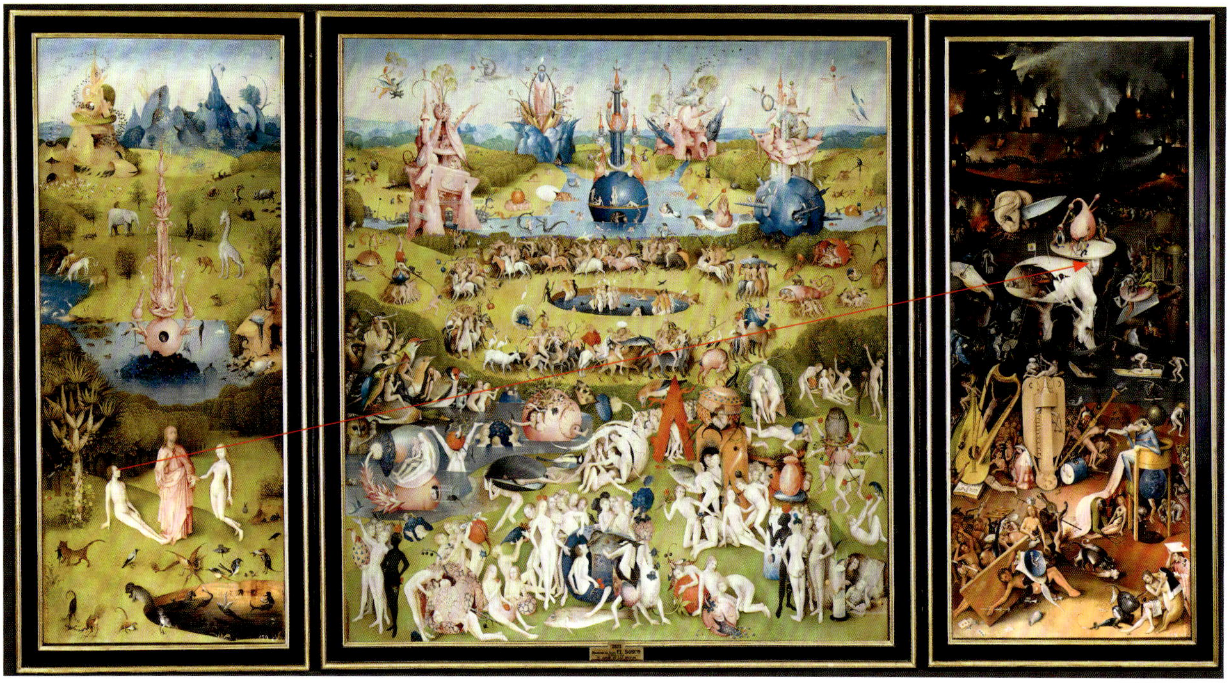

192 Diagram with arrow of Hieronymus Bosch, *The Garden of Delights* (fig. 170)

extending from her genitals into the eyes of six lovesick heroes (fig. 193).[49] Third, Bosch himself makes sight lines unlock his pictures' secrets. In the *Temptation of Saint Anthony*, the hermit's piercing gaze, tiny in the picture but centered and directed at us, offers the only escape from a devilish, decentered world, while in the so-called *Conjurer*, deluded vision, mapped by the background masonry's horizontal coursing, traps, mocks, and devilishly possesses the charlatan's dupe (see figs. 138 and 153). More programmatically, *The Seven Deadly Sins* diagrams how we behold it and how it beholds us (see figs. 122 and 126). The 128 lines radiating from the pupil of God's eye outward through the divisions between seven genre scenes stand at once for the divine sight lines that see all and for the luminosity that enables vision. This arrangement warns us not to sin in the sight of an omnipotent God, but it also explains how vision works. Through a painting that purports to see us before, and more completely than, we see it, Bosch models his own creation as a potentially dangerous entrance or intromission into the open and vulnerable eye.

Extending Adam's gaze as if it were *literally* a vector in sync with time's left-to-right flow, this sight line passes through Eve's downcast eyes to what looks to be Eve again, now grabbed at the wrist not by God but by another Adam (fig. 194). In tandem with the adjacent couple embracing in the seedpod, this pair enacts carnal desire's next step, when one created being reaches for another in order to seed the species (fig. 195). Beyond the couple, the virtual vector intersects the circular march of men on virile animal mounts all rotating around a pool of women. This spectacle expands dramatically the desire begun with Adam's lustful regard. In his commentaries on the Psalms, Augustine writes: "The wicked walk in a circle. But the head of their going about is pride, for pride is the beginning of all sin"; and again: "The ungodly walk in a circle round about, that is, in the desire of things temporal that revolve as a wheel . . . and therefore they do not arrive . . . at eternity."[50] Bosch's vortex moves leftward, or counterclockwise, a direction the artist's culture always coded as sinister and diabolical.[51] Figure of pride, idleness, and falsehood, the circle waylays time's arrow, and it

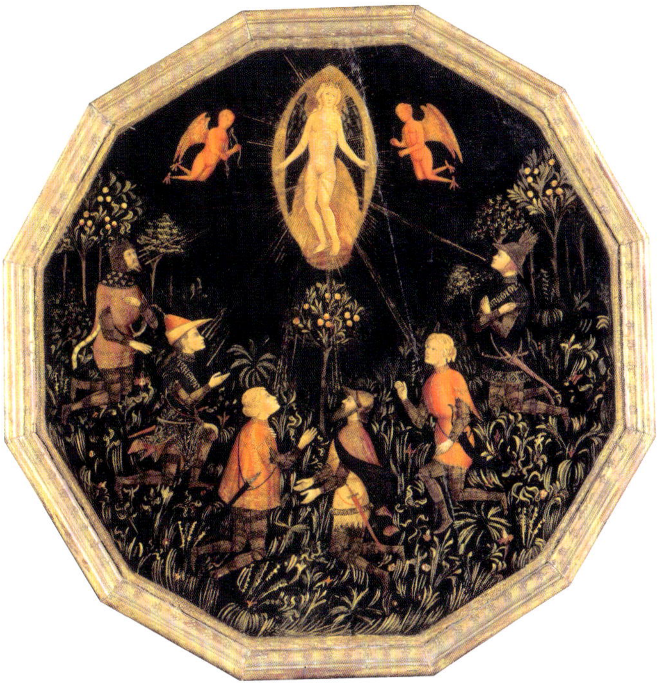

captures our gaze, just as Adam's concupiscent eye was trapped by Eve at the start. And as in the beginning, so in the end, the gaze terminates in a vortex. A monstrous Tree-Man looks rearward, via his ruined body and the pleasures that ruined him, back to Adam, whose facial features he shares (see fig. 209). Vision's vector, from Adam through Eve to the Tree-Man, reverses its course, while on the platform on the Tree-Man's head, sinners march in their now patently sinister parade.

193 Master of the Taking of Taranto, *Triumph of Venus Venerated by Six Famous Lovers, Achilles, Tristan, Lancelot, Samson, Paris, and Troilus*, c. 1400–1410, birth tray or salver, wood (poplar), Musée du Louvre, Paris

Dreamwork

The triptych tells a story of desire. Aroused in Adam before the Fall, desire traverses a humanity that, kept inhuman by animal drives, burns itself out in hell. While Bosch shows it unfolding in time, in the aftermath of creation, this plot could also be imagined as transpiring inside a mind. That is, Adam's inflamed libido could have produced as mental phantasm all the scenarios that the central panel displays. Bosch's original audience would have been familiar with this idea. In the writings of the twelfth-century expert on love Andreas Capellanus; in *The Romance of the Rose* and its countless imitations; in the poems of the troubadours, the trouvères, and the Sicilian sonneteers; in the stilnovist poetry of Dante and Guido Cavalcanti; and, most elaborately, in Marcilio Ficino's *De Amore*, love was not thought to cause fantasy but just the reverse: fantasy caused love and then became love's object. In the beginning, the visible image, or *species*, of the real love object, consisting of illumined color and traveling freely through the air, penetrates the individual arrow-like, through the narrow portal of the eye. There it "kindles an internal fire in the mind of the lover."[52] This fire feeds not off the *species* itself. It burns through a memory of the *species* in the form of what is variously termed an image, idol, or simulacrum, which is created, copied, replaced, and endlessly elaborated by the faculty of fantasy. For Capellanus, love derives "only" from the "immoderate contemplation" of the internal phantasm. It "reconstructs" the loved one "in her entirety in fantasy," allowing the lover to "pry into the secret parts of her body."[53]

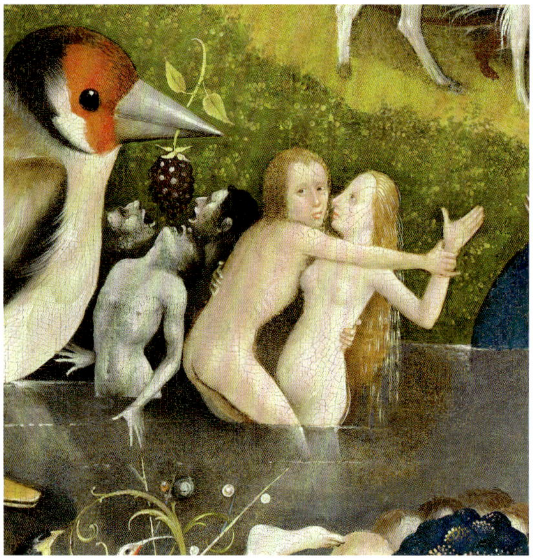

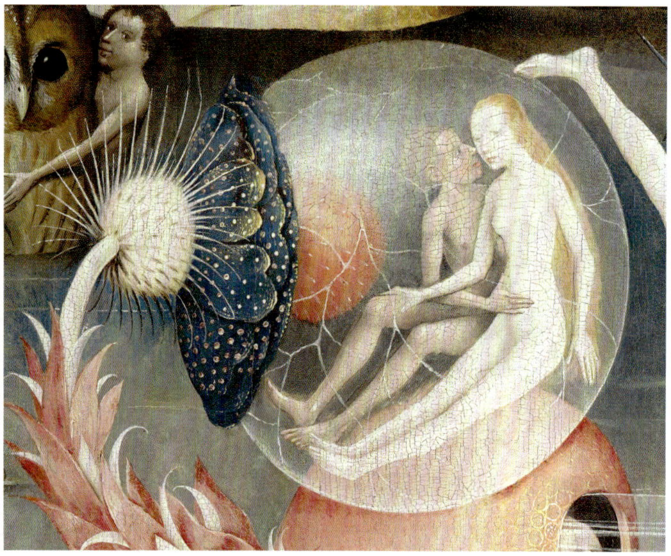

194 Detail of Hieronymus Bosch, *The Garden of Delights* (fig. 170)

195 Detail of Hieronymus Bosch, *The Garden of Delights* (fig. 170)

Although immaterial, phantasms affect the body. It is they that cause the male member to stiffen and sperm to be produced. They affect the mind of course as well, causing obsessive meditations similar to melancholy.[54]

Bosch does not make fantasy the answer to his triptych's enigma. However, the moment of Eden he depicts does bring fantasy's operations to mind. Shaped from Adam's rib during his slumber, Eve was often construed as a creature of dreams.[55] Depicting the instant when Adam opens his eyes to Eve, Bosch invites us to contemplate the sleep (ἔκστασιν, in the Septuagint) that has just now come to an end. An old tradition reaching back through Peter Comestor to Saint Augustine and kept vital in the mystery plays of Bosch's day held that, during the time when God fashioned Eve, Adam dreamed everything that would ever come to pass, from the Fall and the Expulsion to the very end of time.[56] In the well-known *Rijmbijbel* of 1271, the Flemish poet Jacob van Maerlant writes that, on awakening, Adam prophesied "that doomsday would come with fire."[57] In the fourteenth-century *Chester Plays*, similarly, the first words that Adam speaks identify his dream with prophecy:

> O Lorde, where have I longe bene?
> For sithe I slepte, much have I seene
> Wonders that, withoutten wene,
> Hereafter shall be wiste.[58]

Three centuries later, John Milton would fill out the contents of this first dream and make it the crux of his incomparable poem about the Fall. In *Paradise Lost*, Adam in a long discourse recalls that while he lay sleeping, the "Cell / Of Fancie" was left open and he beheld a phantasm "so lovely faire / That what seemd fair in all the World, seemd now / Mean, or in her summ'd up, in her containd" (8:471–72). Again, an internal image first inflames in Adam "the spirit of love and amorous delight." When he awakes to seek the flesh-and-blood Eve, but during the moments before he sees her, he experiences a yearning so strong that it eclipses the entire world: "I wak'd / To find her, or for ever to deplore / Her loss, and other pleasures all abjure" (8:478–80). Fantasy creates desire along with melancholy.[59] Before he glimpses her walking toward him in the garden, Adam has already mourned Eve's loss. This original, all-consuming love of his own imaginings precipitates his Fall. In Book 8, after he learns of his wife's fatal trespass but right before he eats the forbidden fruit, Adam laments: "Should God create another Eve, and I / another Rib afford, yet loss of thee / Would never from my heart" (8:911–13). Adam cannot stand a world without *this* Eve, whom he loves, yet ironically she was already "another Eve," since Adam engendered her prototype while dreaming.

Milton comes from a different historical world than Bosch, and he works in a different medium. However, his imagination converges on the same bewildering event as Bosch's does, and along the same horizon of its hidden cause. Pushing the story of man's disobedience back before the Fall, Milton imagines Adam endowed with free will but never properly choosing to disobey. Unlike Eve, who deliberates carefully over many verse lines, Adam discovers helplessly that he has already decided, within a choice he never thought he made. Human history's central event thus stands overshadowed by a prior volition in which choice is clouded by fantasy, and by the strange mode of thought that fantasy engenders. In Bosch's other depictions of Eden, in *The Hay Wain* and *The Last Judgment*, Adam's sleep gives way immediately to the Fall, which gives way immediately to exile and then universal damnation (see figs. 39 and 47). But in his nameless masterpiece Bosch isolates for contemplation the fateful prior interval in which some catastrophic volition will have taken place, having also allowed a story of Creation in the outer panels to preface and somehow to motivate that prequel to the Fall.

The Boschian *Garden of Paradise* in Chicago seems to hint at what went on in Adam's head during sleep (fig. 196). Plentiful in *The Garden of Delights*, bursting seedpods are a stock motif in Bosch's oeuvre. One spectacular example appears at the base of the triptych's central panel, where it insinuates masturbatory practices among the men around it (see fig. 210); two spilling pods can be found on the fabulous gift of the first Magus in the Boschian pastiche in Upton House (see fig. 109); and in a Boschian *Garden of Paradise* panel in Vienna, a fantastical fountain surrounded by pods bursts from the earth, as if the earth were itself seedlike, as it indeed was in Bosch's depiction of the third day of Creation (fig. 197 and see fig. 184).[60] In the Chicago panel, the exploding pod on which Adam reclines seems to visualize the erotic nature of his dream.[61] On lascivious dreams and nocturnal emissions, Augustine writes that in sleep we "have no control over the formation of bodily images, which cannot be distinguished from actual bodies in their dreams."[62] Although barren, wet dreams are morally blameless. Simplifying the intentions of Bosch's triptych, perhaps even mangling or misunderstanding these, this derivative painting by an unknown imitator does take us into the thought world in which the unnameable masterpiece would have been received. Specifically, the seedpod forges at least two analogies: one between Adam's dream and Eve's creation, and another between the dream and the picture's entire garden setting, ruinously bursting with life. Further, although this humble panel shows only the events in Eden, the seedpod—as a sexual symbol and as an instance of fantastical artistry—condenses the essence of the triptych's mysterious central panel, suggesting that it might be of the stuff of dreams.

In November 1520, during his trip to the Netherlands, Dürer passed through Bosch's hometown. Storm winds drove him there, but he had time to admire "Herzog Bosch" and its *außbündige schöne Kirchen* ("exceptional, beautiful churches").[63] In the diary he kept, Dürer made no mention of any of the paintings in the Church of Saint John, which would have included the high altarpiece in which Bosch pictured, in two sets of painted wing panels, the history of the six days of Creation, along with scenes of hell and judgment on the retable's

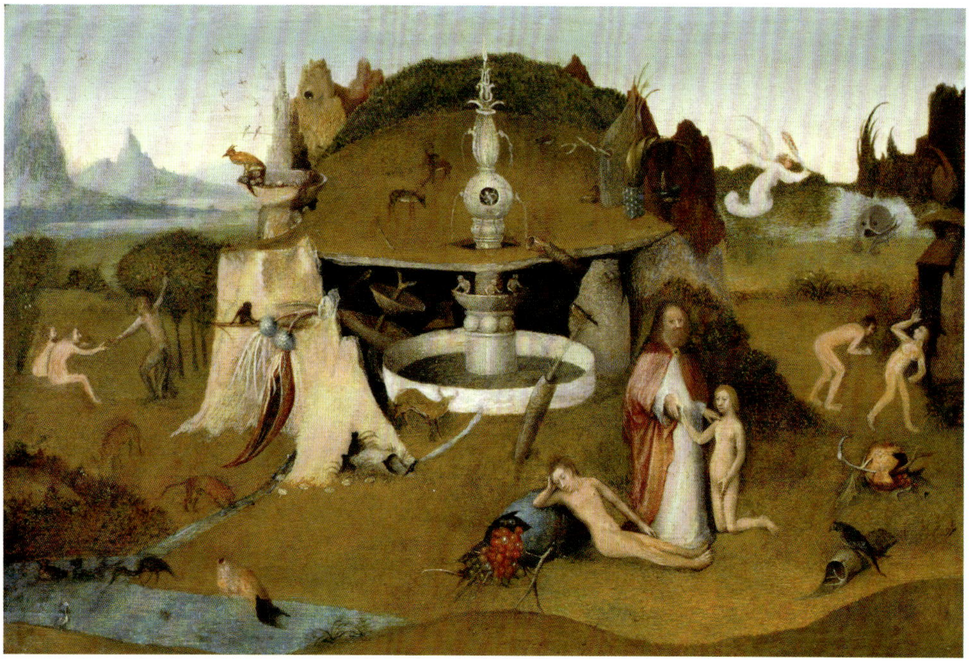

196 Workshop of Hieronymus Bosch, *The Garden of Paradise*, 1510/1520, oil on panel, 10⅝ × 15 15/16 in. (27 × 40.6 cm), Robert A. Waller Memorial Fund, 1936.239, The Art Institute of Chicago

predella.[64] Three months before, when Dürer had visited "the House of Nassau" in Brussels, he marveled at its wondrous works of art and nature, just as Antonio de Beatis had on his visit there in 1517. But again he wrote not a word about Bosch's triptych, which would have been on display. Perhaps its dark shutters kept it hidden, although everywhere else Dürer went people proudly showed local masterpieces to him, opening up triptych altarpieces when they stood closed in their churches. Perhaps real novelties interested the German master more than pictorial ones. Entries from Brussels report on the huge meteorite that had dropped in a field nearby, on *das groß beth* ("the gigantic bed"), and on the Nassau palace itself, which in his view had no equal in all of Germany.[65] Perhaps Bosch's artistry was simply not to Dürer's liking. In his theoretical writings, the German artist aimed to rid art of ugliness and deformity—of *grobe ungestalt*—by setting forth rules of human proportion and linear perspective: "Everyone should be careful not to make something impossible, so that nature does not suffer." Yet in the same breath, Dürer allowed that there might be some artists who would deliberately try to make an *ungestalt ding*, for which different rules applied: "In that case, one can mix up all things together."[66] Termed by Dürer *trawm werg* ("dream work"), such fantastical creations intentionally violated the beauty ideals that this artist sought so tirelessly to recover.

Fast-forward five hundred years. In the work of Sigmund Freud, *Traumwerk* (his term is the same as Dürer's) names the psychic labor, or mental poiesis, "made possible by the conditions of sleep," that "creates the form . . . and alone is the essence of dreaming."[67] Artistic fantasy, as theorized by Dürer and as practiced by Bosch, operates through combinations and detachments similar to what Freud describes as condensation and displacement in dreams. More deeply, Bosch, like Freud, explores the always already-belated character of desire. For Freud, desire fails ever to achieve its object, and that failure brings about the "I," or "ego," in retrospect, in an anxious, rearward gaze, like the one Bosch's Tree-Man casts. Like dreams, artistic fictions function to arouse and sustain desire through innumerable detours that end in the way the ego wishes: in its desire to die in its own fashion. A no less astonishing description of libido, however, is offered by the erotic discourse of the Middle Ages. It was then that phantasms

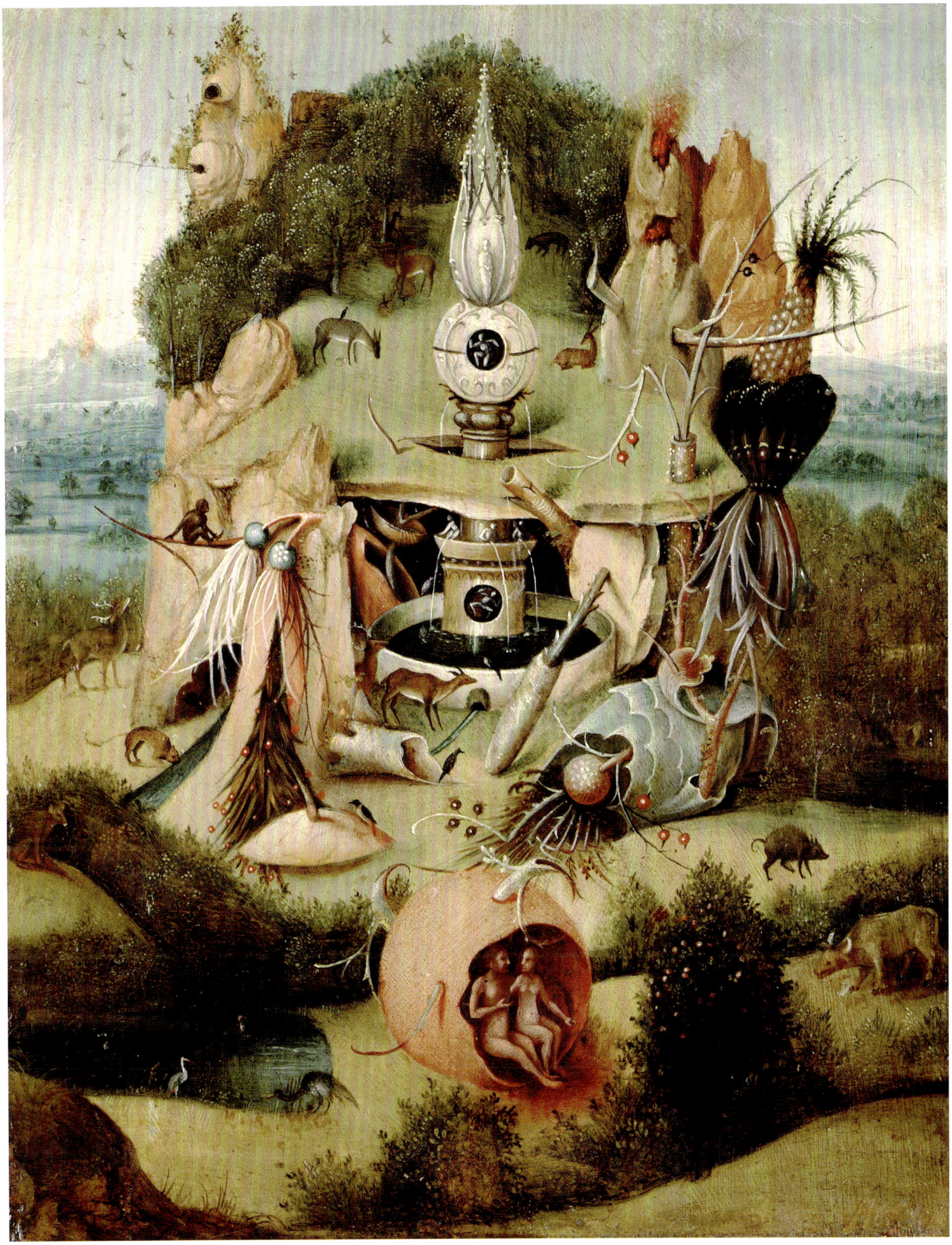

197 Workshop of Hieronymus Bosch, *The Garden of Paradise*, after 1539, panel, Kunsthistorisches Museum, Vienna

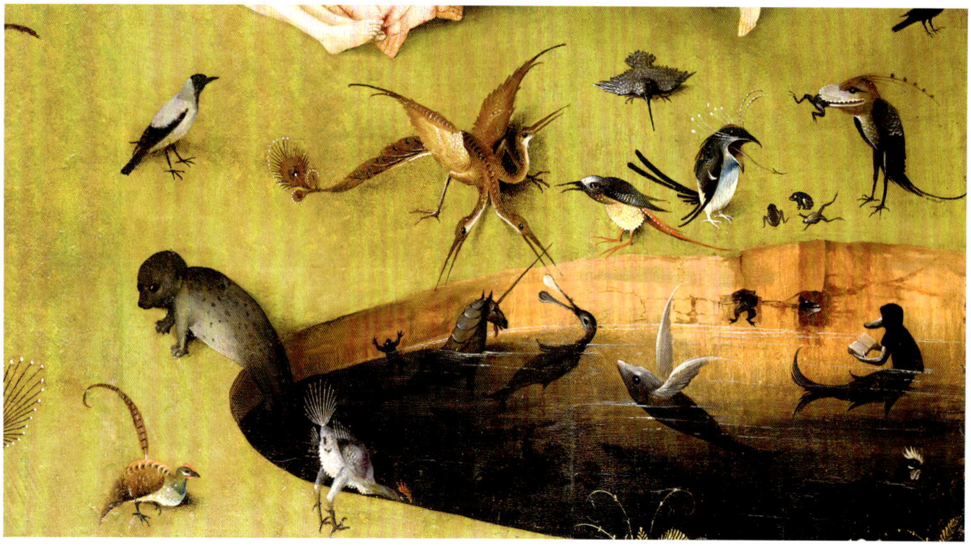

198 Detail of Hieronymus Bosch, *The Garden of Delights* (fig. 170)

were regarded as the true object and origin of desire, as we have seen. And it was then that fantasy was believed to derive from foreign penetrations of the eye that were subsequently elaborated by an alien process over which the self, as reflexive consciousness or volition, had little or no control.

Bosch's triptych is a psychology in painted form. But it is also a biology. Controlling the mind from the body, desire is a force belonging to living nature. Heavy with seed at creation, nature spawned monsters already in Eden, those amphibious creatures creeping up as if through parthenogenesis from the foreground pool—note how the dark slime rhymes with hell's charred distances (fig. 198).[68] Left untended, nature wanders off course, producing hybrid offspring in violation of "their kind." Medieval cosmologists blamed sins of lust on nature's rampant fecundity and proposed a kernel of entropy in both. They also reprised an ancient, Aristotelian terror of spontaneous generation: when creatures multiply without sexual coupling, nature acts "against nature," *contra naturam*.[69] Some scholars—most emphatically Hans Belting and Jean Wirth—have understood the triptych as representing a conjecture. By Belting's account, the work makes its conjecture in a new timeless, placeless space of "fictionality," which the art of painting created for itself in the wake of Jan van Eyck, and what the work specifically asks is this: What would have happened if Eve and Adam never ate the apple?[70] Its answer, these scholars tell us, is a utopia of innocent, untrammeled pleasure. Bosch did indeed reflect on this conjecture, but his answer, alas, was cruel. The desire inflamed in Adam already contains all the perversion, and therefore all the imagery, that the central panel displays. As the oxymoron *felix culpa* indicates, without commandment there would be no trespass, and without trespass there would be neither history nor redemption.

The notion that, in desiring, humans waywardly pursue their dreams; the aesthetics of the *Traumwerk* as antithetical to the demand that art should imitate nature; the fear that nature may not always follow its own rule but veer off course: these period conceptions do not explain Bosch's triptych. But they do suggest how what seems impossible might have practically come about. Were the ruling count of Nassau to have asked the acknowledged master of *Traumwerk* and noted author of a painted hexaemeron to produce a winged triptych broadly about lust (in the same general way as, say, *The Hay Wain* is broadly about avarice, or love of the world), that noble patron would not have been too surprised to behold in the finished work sexuality—that most mysterious of desires—dated all the way back to a time before the Fall. Bosch's patrons would also not have even been puzzled to see sexual desire displayed as a spectacle of phantasms, for that is what lust yearns for. Nor would he—proud owner of a wondrously large communal bed where men and women heaped together could sleep off their drink—have been shocked to see such a spectacle of phantasms delaying or subverting a natural story line. What might have given a period viewer some pause, however, are (1) the early moment in Eden that Bosch shows, and (2) the suggestion, made by the exterior of the shutters and by the decidedly monstrous and improperly carnivorous nature of the beasts in Eden's foreground pool, that before the Fall something about nature may already have been evil or corrupt.

Unde Malum?

Does Bosch's proposal of a primal corruption agree with Christian doctrine? Saint Augustine exerted—by far—the greatest influence here. With vehemence he held that, before the Fall, Adam controlled his procreative power and that he could achieve an erection voluntarily, as one flexes a muscle. In *The Literal Meaning of Genesis*, completed in 416, Augustine asserted that Adam and Eve could "control and command their genital organs for their procreation of children in the same way as their other limbs," and in *The City of God*, begun shortly thereafter, he reiterated that Adam "would have sown the seed, and the woman received it, as need required, the generative organs being moved by the will, not excited by lust."[71] At issue was theology's toughest question: where does evil come from, *unde malum*? Blaming the fall from innocence to guilt on something not in Adam's command granted evil independent powers, and that contradicted belief in an omnipotent God, who would have to have created, or could have effortlessly eliminated, whatever vicious extra something was involved. Taken to one logical conclusion, the idea of created nature as inherently corrupt would make the Creator himself into a force of evil and perhaps in conflict with a good but hidden God. In answer to this, roughly speaking the Gnostic understanding of evil, Augustine conceived of evil not as a being set off against God, but as a mere form of doing; and doing evil was simply the turn—the *aversio*—from God to nothingness.[72] Pride caused this turn. "And what is the origin of our evil will but pride? For 'pride is the beginning of sin.' "[73] By this account, Eve loved herself, asserting her rights and manipulating Adam's infatuation with her. And Adam, loving his appetite for Eve, preferring it to the whole of God's creation, turned selfward too.

Carnal desire played a key role, to be sure. Caused by pride, original sin was punished by death and by lust. Adam passed his disobedience to us through our experience of our bodies. Because of this trespass, men can neither will their genitals into action nor voluntarily rein them in. Penalized carnally, Adam's sin is inherited carnally. Human beings are made through the lust-driven coupling of their parents. When they lust, humans return to their criminal beginning. Feeling one's body disobey, one repeats Adam's turn from God. "What but disobedience was the punishment for disobedience in that sin?" asks Augustine. "For what else is man's misery but his disobedience to himself, so that in consequence of his not being willing to do what he could do, he now wills to do what he cannot?"[74] Evil is experienced as *always already* there, as an involuntary volition controlled in the present by a distant, catastrophic past.[75]

Augustine established the standard understanding, but he also severely restricted the bounds of that understanding. "Let no one seek for an efficient cause of the evil will," he

199 Anonymous German, *Bronze Doors of Bishop Bernward*, 1015, bronze, Cathedral St. Mary, Hildesheim

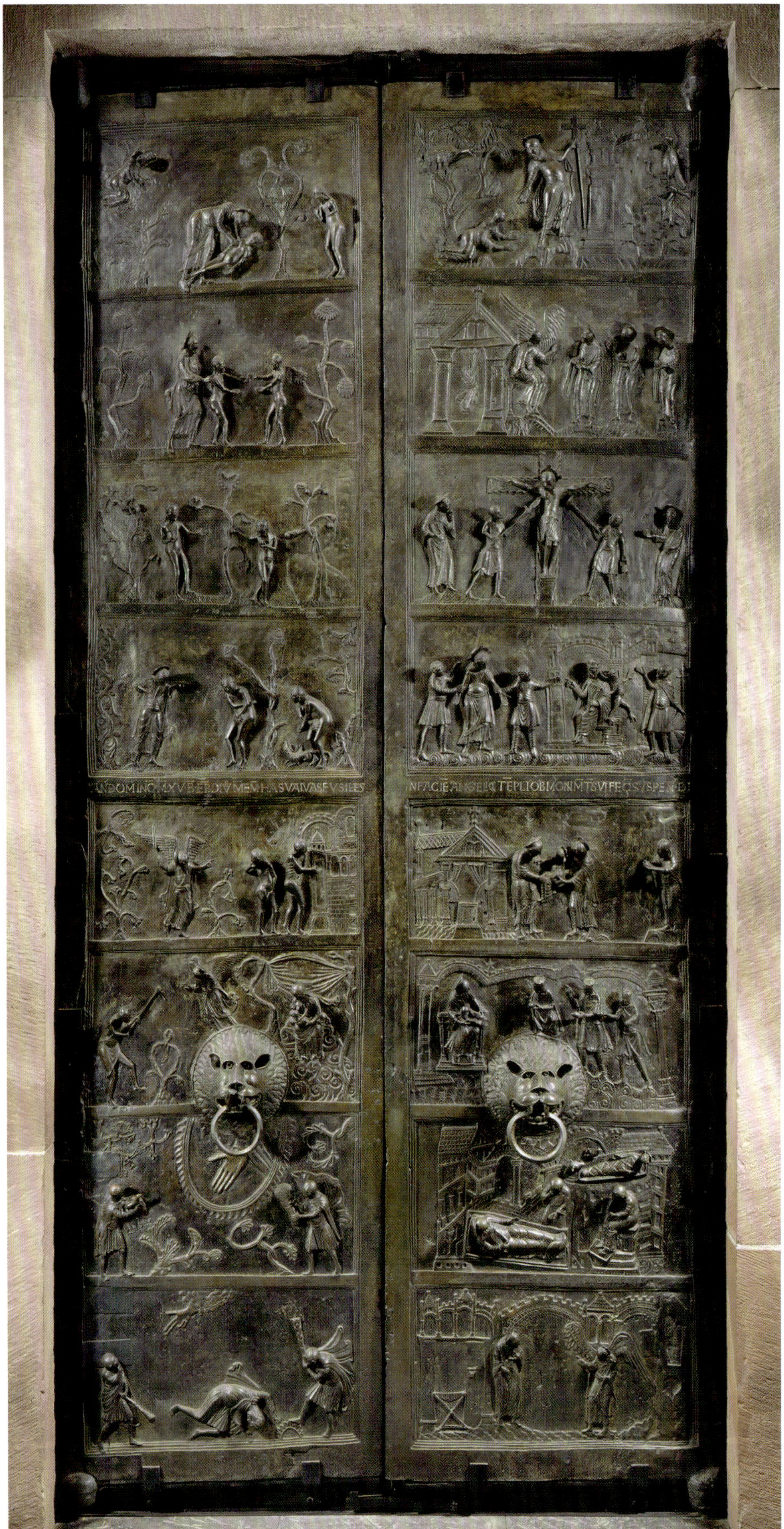

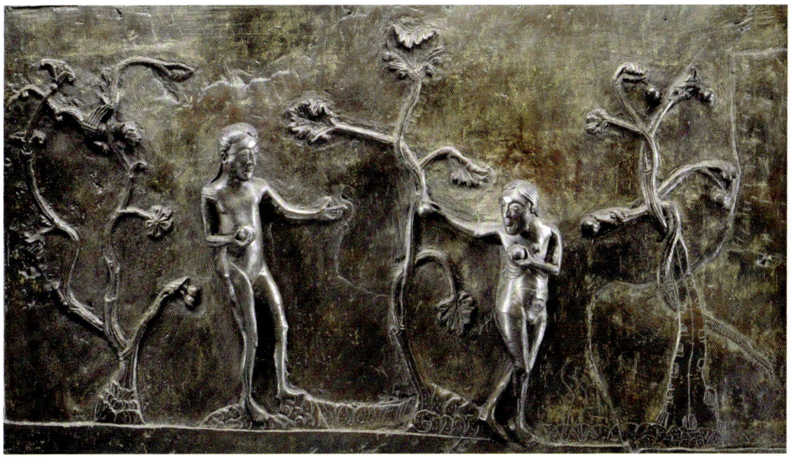

200 Anonymous German, *The Fall of Man*, detail of the *Bronze Doors of Bishop Bernward* (fig. 199)

warns in *The City of God*. "Let no one seek to know from me what I do not know; unless it is in order that he may learn to not know what he must know cannot be known."[76] Not everyone learned to know what not to know. Around 1277, a group of seekers—termed (unusually) "philosophers" and probably teaching and training at the University of Paris—entertained 219 theses condemned by the authorities as heretical and to be damned.[77] Known only through the text of their censure, these theses considered among other things the possibility that sexual pleasure was not sinful and that even sins "against nature—that is, the misuse of intercourse—may contradict the nature of the species but do not contradict the nature of man."[78] By this odd distinction the free thinkers probably meant that the human individual, in his or her pleasures, fantasies, and thoughts, constituted a different world from that of nature, a world that may not be the concern of theologians but should be the concern of a different breed of thinkers called philosophers.[79] The space for philosophizing about human sexuality remained policed and limited, however. Poetry was similarly restricted, perhaps because like philosophy its statements could be measured against doctrine and because it operated in the same medium as Scripture itself. In the wake of revolutionary Protestantism, Milton could dare to put into verse and dialogue the disastrous course of human volition before the Fall, but his doctrine remained broadly Augustinian.

With the visual arts the situation was different. From the very beginning of Christian art, in the earliest catacombs, house churches, and sarcophagi, artists peered back to the event of the Fall.[80] And in the moment they depicted they suggested, if not the cause of the disaster, at least the action or condition through which disaster struck. A thousand years ago, Bernward of Hildesheim installed in his cathedral the massive doors associated with his name (fig. 199). On the left door, in a telling the learned bishop closely scripted, the artist portrays the whole story of Adam and Eve, from their creation and first meeting (see fig. 190), through their trespass, to the disasters that followed. Each scene tells a story in itself. In the scene of the Fall, the forbidden fruits, palpably rendered in bronze, mark consecutive points in time leading from the serpent to Adam via Eve (fig. 200). And because of how Eve holds the apple to her chest with a snakelike arm, so that the fruit rhymes visually with the breast it conceals, the viewer might surmise that Eve, by arousing him libidinously, caused Adam's Fall. The shape of Eve's hips and genitals echoes the leafy branch that droops down just beside them, further identifying her with the temptation that ruined us.[81]

German artists of Bosch's time continued to explore the timeless history of sin. Hans Baldung Grien fashioned his 1511 chiaroscuro woodcut of Adam and Eve partly in response to idealizing

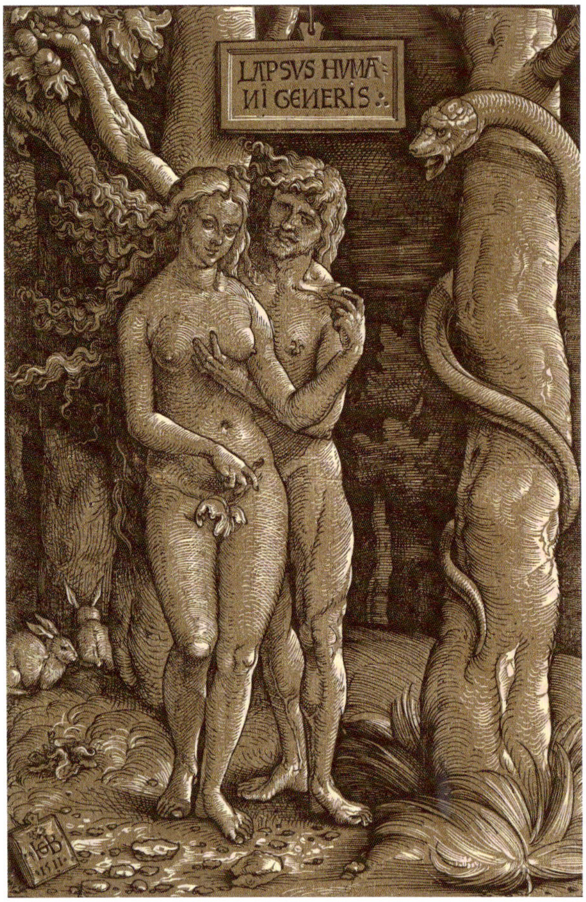

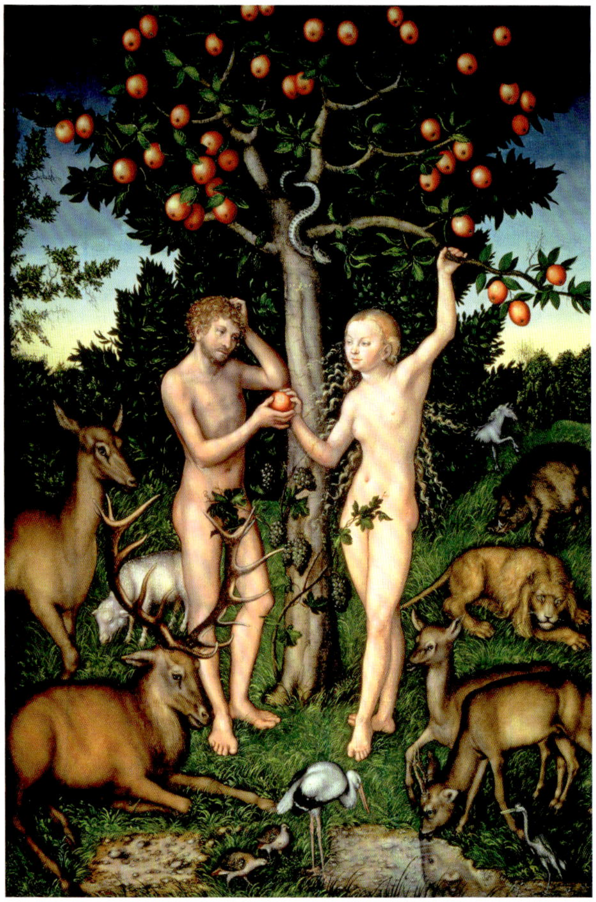

(LEFT) **201** Hans Baldung Grien, *Fall of Human Kind*, 1511, chiaroscuro woodcut in two blocks, printed in gray-brown and black, The Metropolitan Museum of Art, New York, Gift of Felix M. Warburg and his family, 1941

(RIGHT) **202** Lucas Cranach the Elder, *Adam and Eve*, 1526, panel, Courtauld Institute of Art, London

portrayals of this event by his teacher and master, Dürer (fig. 201).[82] Collapsing with sexual desire what the hanging tablet announces is "the Fall of Human Kind," Baldung makes it impossible to say what came first. Adam lusts after Eve *because* he ate the apple. And Adam eats the apple *because* he lusts after Eve. The second reason contradicts Augustine's view of prelapsarian sexuality, but it agrees with misogynistic preachers of Baldung and Bosch's day, who, untroubled by theological niceties, blamed the Fall directly on Eve.[83] But does it actually contradict doctrine? Not necessarily. It had been obvious to everyone that Adam's disobedience—unexplained in the biblical account and left mysterious by Augustine—had to have some prior cause. Since sin had no history, and since their medium was anyway static, artists were free to equate causes with effects. Carnal lust, which (again) Augustine insisted came after the Fall, appears in Baldung to motivate Adam from the beginning. Moreover, twisting Eve's body and gaze to the picture's viewer, Baldung expects him, an implied male audience, to be aroused by Eve and to fall with Adam. The world's first catastrophe happens in the picture's present tense.

Lucas Cranach the Elder—another of Bosch's German contemporaries—left us more than fifty portrayals of the Fall. In one of the most original of these, now in the galleries of the Courtauld Institute of Art, Adam scratches his head in puzzlement, as if poised at a moment of uncertainty ("Should I or shouldn't I?") that extends from the painting to our condition (fig. 202).[84] Why indeed did Adam eat the apple? Why did he cause all that suffering, not just for himself, but for everyone who will ever be born, solely for a taste of some fruit? Because the fruit was beautiful and seemed delicious to eat? Cranach has made the apples lovely to look at. But Adam is not looking at *them*. Did he eat therefore because the serpent tempted him? No, the snake looks toward Eve, and her temptation already worked its magic. On close inspection it is clear that the apple has been bitten and the teeth marks—in two neat rows of four—are certainly Eve's. Eve hands the fruit she has already tasted to Adam for him to eat. The picture tells you this: Eve waits while Adam decides, and while he puzzles over his decision the exposed flesh of the fruit has already begun to turn a pale brown. Like a ticking clock, the oxidizing fruit shows that it takes time to choose, which makes perfect sense, because how is Adam supposed to make such a decision? According to Genesis: "She took of the fruit and ate, and she gave it to her man, and he ate" (3:6). He ate, just like that, with no whispering serpent, no flattery, no deceit. Unless perhaps Eve herself was the temptation, being so beautiful, with those golden locks in Cranach's painting veritably miming her allure. And then again, why not eat the apple? Why not, since it grew on the Tree of Knowledge, the Tree of the Knowledge of Good and Evil? How could Adam have known *not* to eat from that tree before he ate from precisely that tree? How could God have expected Adam to be good when he did not yet know what good was? This is indeed a head-scratcher.

Martin Luther was one of Cranach's closest personal friends.[85] Luther had a simple theory about the problem of the seeming proscription of moral knowledge.[86] First, the Tree of Knowledge did not *give* knowledge. Adam knew good and evil from the beginning. What mattered about the tree was that its fruit was forbidden, and this subjected life already in Eden to God's law. The tree's name came later or, more accurately, it made sense in retrospect, after Adam broke the law: the name derived "from the event which lay in the future."[87] Second, according to Luther, the story urges us to stop nosing about. Adam ate, we are cursed, and asking needless questions just makes things worse. This don't ask, don't tell policy did not extend to the visual arts, however. Unlike texts, whose messages unfold in time, in visual images everything stands presently displayed. Causes therefore can be suggested without being dogmatically confirmed. In Cranach's painting, head scratching starts in the midst of some puzzled and puzzling looks. Adam stares past the apple at Eve, at her strange beauty and at her seductive stare back at him, which the artist captures—shamelessly and enticingly—so that we look on disastrously, as well.

Bosch similarly collapses the entire history of evil into the "now" of the painting's reception. But he pushes that history even further back in time than Baldung and Cranach did. He shows Adam's first glimpse of Eve. And in that event prior to their disobedience, prior—even—to God's commanding them to obey, he shows the motion that will motivate his Fall. Furthermore, Bosch shows that fatal gaze preceded by a malignant gaze already watching Adam. Inside the central portal of the Fountain of Life, a gray night owl peers from the darkness at Adam (fig. 203). Scorned by medieval bestiaries as the vilest and most unnatural of birds, a creature—in the words of Alan of Lille—"dirtied by the shit of its ugliness," the light-shunning owl was both an emblem of the Devil, sin, and heresy and a cunning lure, since diurnal birds, mobbing it on its daytime roost, could be trapped by it.[88] Itself a trap, and watching Adam's entrapment by Eve, the all-seeing owl also watches us—not with its own eyes, but with the oculus from within which it peers. The black hole occurs at the exact center of Bosch's panel, aligned with God's gaze (see fig. 187). A diabolical eye constituted by the structure of the painting, it imports into Eden the darkness before creation—that encircling nothing pictured on the exterior of the ensemble's shutters—and with it the night of Lucifer's prideful fall. Creeping into the world as those monsters in Eden's asphaltic pool, peering in as and through

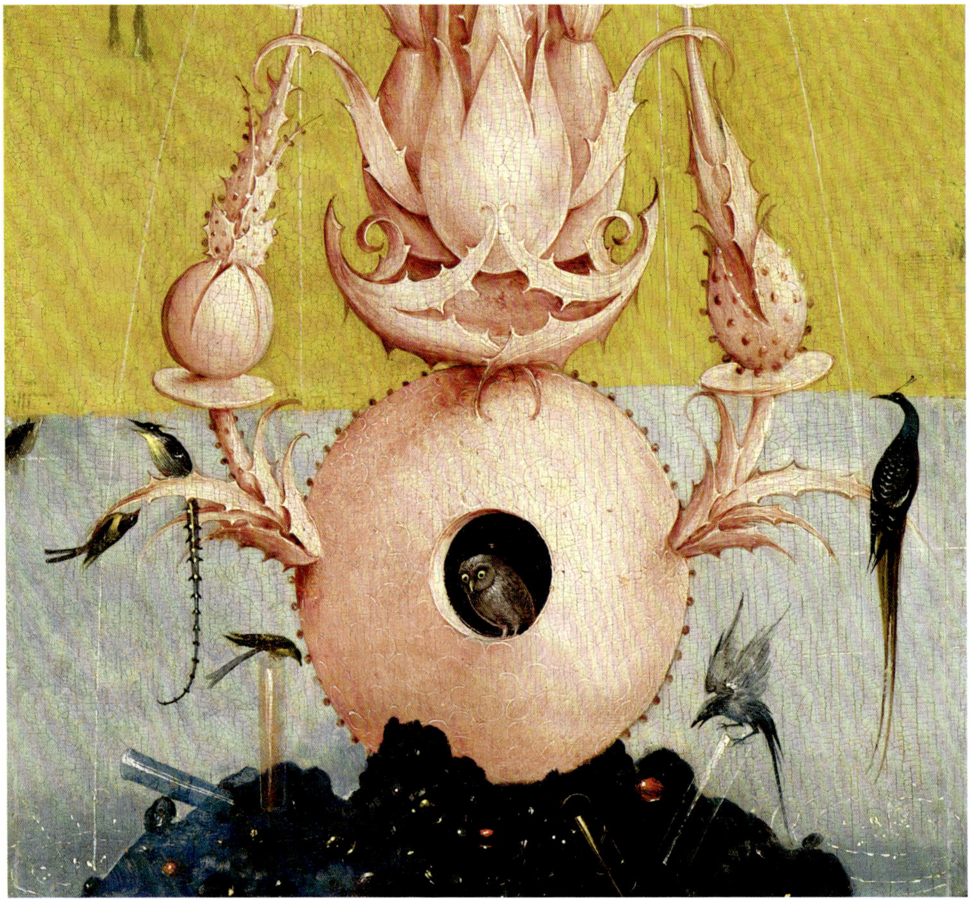

203 Detail of Hieronymus Bosch, *The Garden of Delights* (fig. 170)

the black hole at the panel's center, darkness wins out in the end, when a humanoid owl—the Tree-Man—gazes back from the night of hell. And it is in this omnipresent background darkness, this black abysmal underlying ground on which this artist most likes to paint, that Bosch almost speaks his unspeakable theme.

The Unspeakable Crime

In a hole in the fountain on the ensemble's central axis, fornication is well under way (figs. 204 and 205). Though the event vanishes into darkness, its horizon remains. Precisely at the boundary where light passes into dark, a man seems to penetrate a woman from the rear. His arm position suggests he is guiding his member into her *right now*. Meanwhile, dashing all hopes that the triptych celebrates marital vows, a second man fondles the woman's genitals. His fingertips, with the hidden member of the other man, may now be reaching into the woman precisely below the water's surface. But of course we cannot know, since liquid intervenes, and in the most peculiar way: it does not wash into the opening and around the three bodies in it, but seems to stop short of the portal, forming there a delicately highlighted edge. This arrangement brings into focus a salient correspondence. With water rising not quite halfway up it, the portal repeats *exactly* the structure of Earth on the triptych's shutters, with its similar low, watery horizon (fig. 206).

A coincidence like this cannot be coincidental. Bosch's phantasms move freely across their pictorial field; concocted from bits and pieces that do not belong together, they each move without even the fixity of a flitting thing. At certain calculated points within this artist's

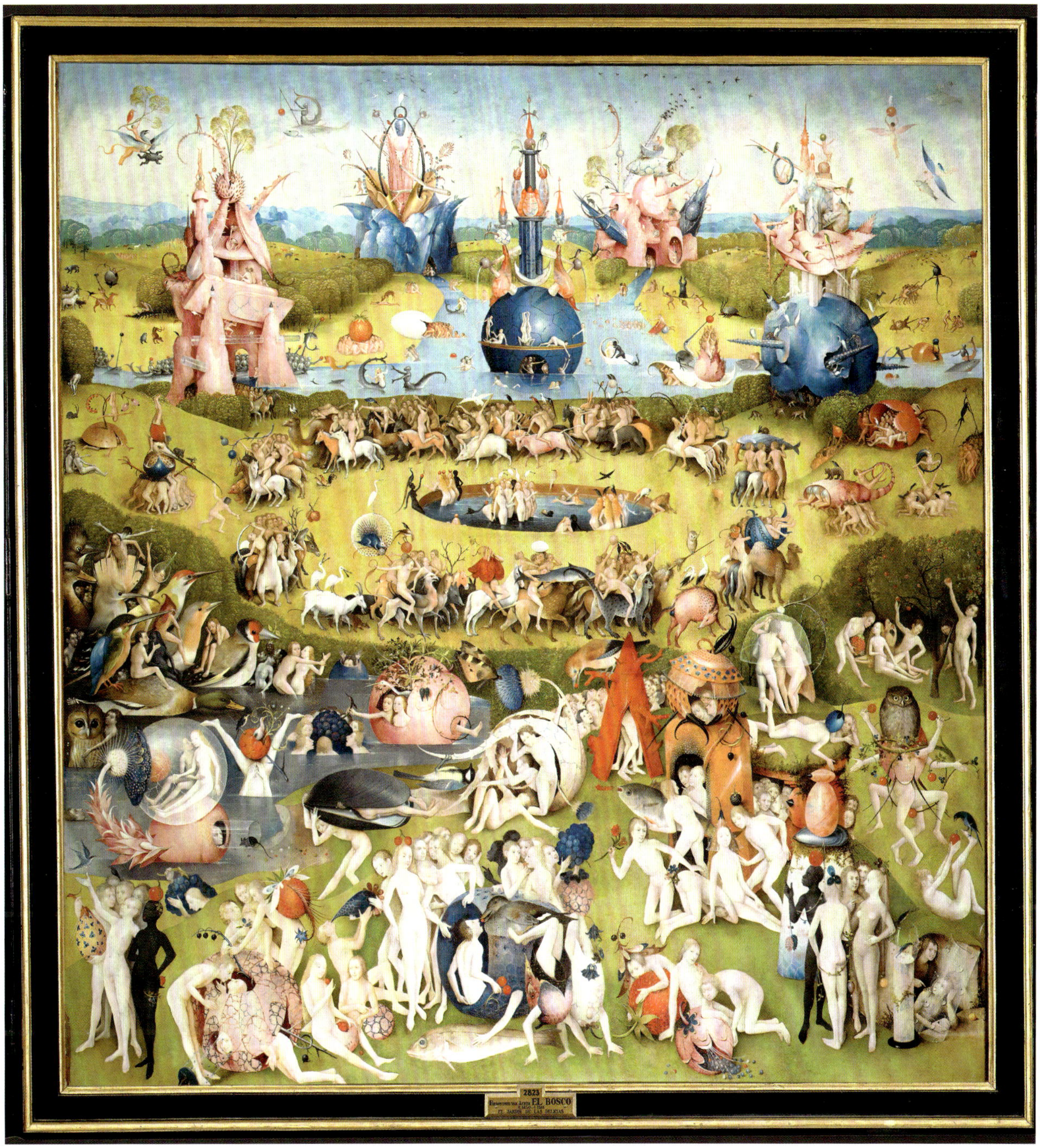

204 Hieronymus Bosch, *The Garden of Delights*, center panel (fig. 170)

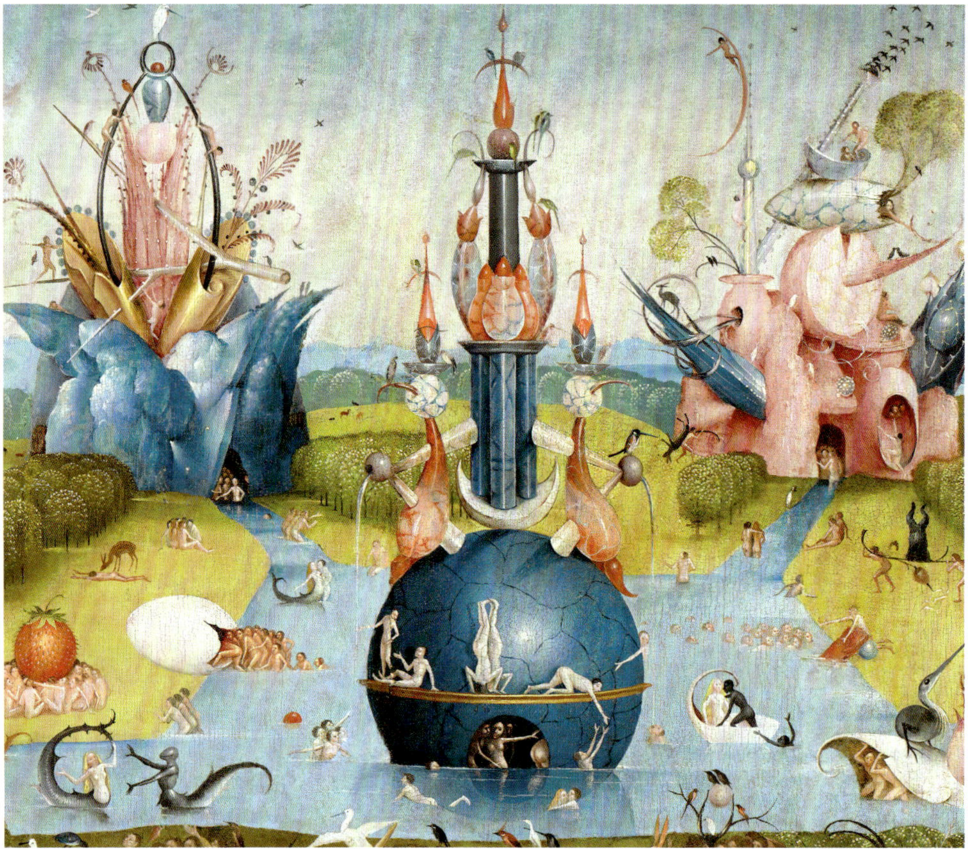

(RIGHT) **205** Detail of Hieronymus Bosch, *The Garden of Delights* (fig. 170)

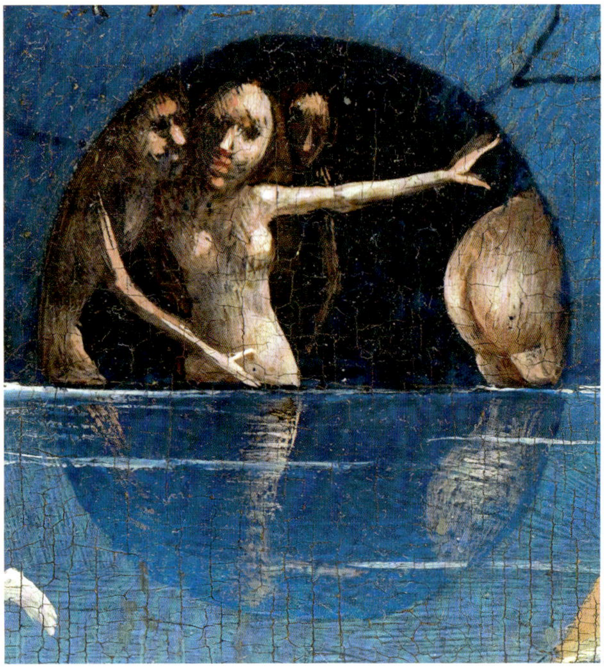

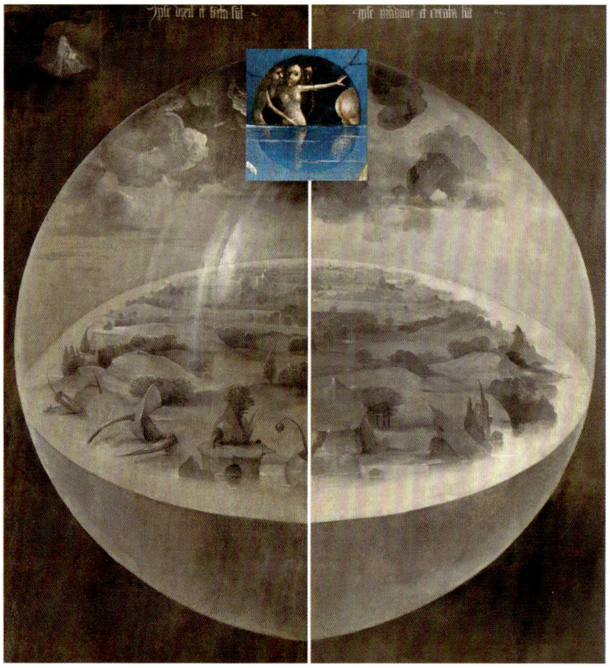

(BELOW) **206**a Detail of Hieronymus Bosch, *The Garden of Delights* (fig. 170); (RIGHT) **b** Detail of open state superimposed onto Hieronymus Bosch, *The Garden of Delights*, closed state (fig. 183)

creations, however, usually in places that, belonging to the structure of the painting's physical support or ground, cannot be otherwise, Bosch brings such movement abruptly to a halt. The gaze of Saint Anthony in the Lisbon triptych, Christ at the center of *The Seven Deadly Sins*, the strigine oculus in the Eden panel: these appear to stop the endless play of forms and meanings. That such points are painted, too—in semiotic jargon, that they operate as the signified but are in fact more signifier—befits the story they tell. In Bosch, painting fuels ocular desire, and desire, although it pursues phantasms, operates as if reality is what it needs. Places where the eye continually returns, the anchoring points in Bosch make sense of desire in desire's own terms, as arrivals endlessly deferred. The minutely engineered formal likeness between Earth's sphere on the shutters and the abject hole at the garden's center is therefore no accident. Bosch almost certainly measured and coordinated their watery horizons. The message that this placement communicates, however, concerns things veering accidentally and dangerously off course.

Before the ensemble received its sturdy modern frame, the shutters may have met directly, or at least more closely, at their edges, allowing this abject hole almost to peep through. Opening the shutters just a crack, a sharp-eyed viewer would enter the garden through the glimpse of a woman potentially entered front and rear. To be sure, Bosch conceals these "acts" in darkness and under water. Unlike the owl, humans cannot see at night. The picture therefore whispers infamy but nowhere speaks it, making me rather than Bosch the scandalous one. But surely Bosch also goads his viewers on. Next to the woman, a large backside, spotlighted but unspecified as male or female, insinuates the orifice here preferred. Bosch repeats its form throughout the painting. In the foreground, a man with two flowers planted stem first in his anus (and with perhaps two more on the way) stares out at us casually (see fig. 210). Farther back in the garden, a trio of buttocks—black-and-blue, as if badly bruised—protrudes from an exoskeleton (itself abdominal) as if molted by a colossal arthropod (fig. 207). All cut off at the waist, these forms return in hell in the figure of a devil's ass, with Vanity's face reflected in its mirror (fig. 208). Observe also how the Devil and Vanity resemble that human flowerpot and the weirdly veiled woman beside him. All these asses connect—or more accurately, they

207 Detail of Hieronymus Bosch, *The Garden of Delights* (fig. 170)

208 Detail of Hieronymus Bosch, *The Garden of Delights* (fig. 170)

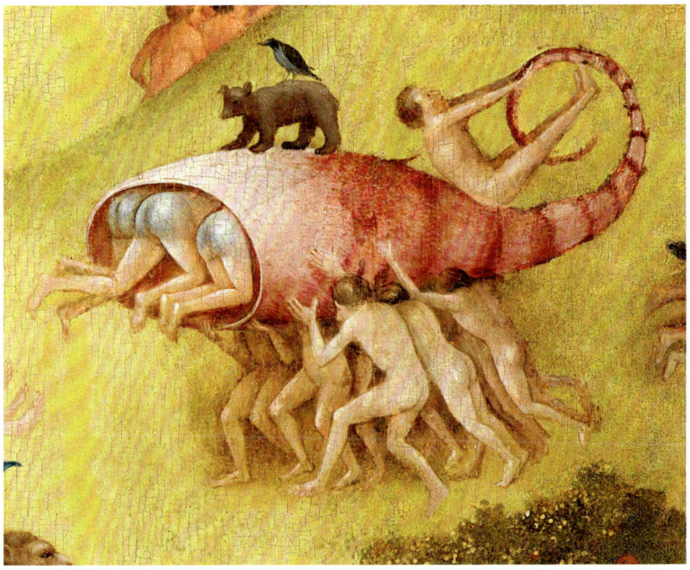

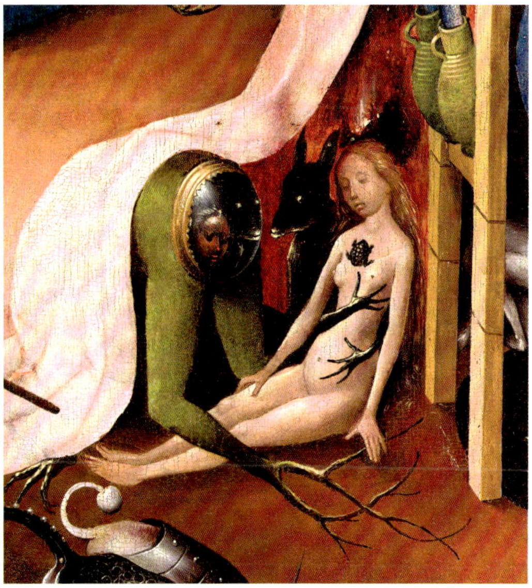

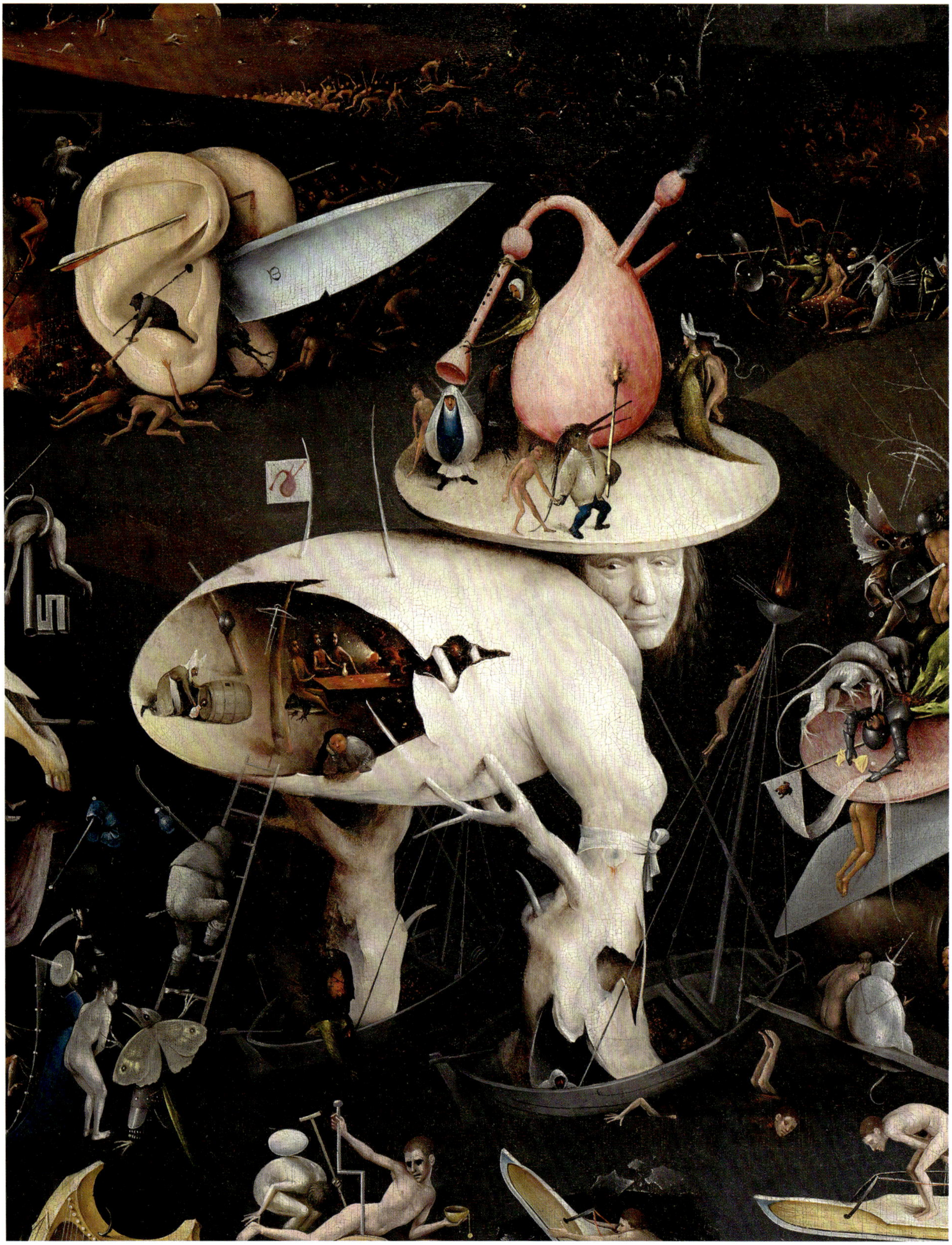

209 Detail of Hieronymus Bosch, *The Garden of Delights* (fig. 170)

complete—the paradigm of the Tree-Man, whose body ends precisely where the buttocks would begin, and whose dark interior magnifies the abject hole at issue (fig. 209).

The act that screams but is silent, the "red sin" that is mute, the crime so unspeakable that angels flee as far as any speech about it reaches, the ignominy so foul that it is not worthy of a name, the disgrace so vile that the Devil himself either knows not its name or has to spit twice after he names it: these formulas run like a refrain through the sermons of Bosch's day.[89] The "unspeakable" names the refusal, on the part of speakers, to besmirch their mouths with the obscenity they decry. Netherlandish court records from the late fifteenth century furnish a rich record of this refusal. In Bruges in only fifty years a full ninety citizens were tried, condemned, and executed for the screaming, mute crime.[90] Most, but not all, were men whom the magistrates ruled had had sex with other men. All received the same penalty. They were burned at the stake. This imitated the "purifying" treatment of heretics while also evoking God's fiery extermination of Sodom. Clear about punishment, the term *sodomitical* was vague about the crime, referring chiefly, but not only, to same-sex intercourse. Among the sins criminalized as sodomy were bestiality, masturbation, and anal and oral sex between married couples. Sodomy defined itself by what it is not, namely coitus for the purpose of procreation. And for this reason, all its manifestations—indeed its definitional formlessness itself—were gathered under a more metaphysical concept, that of "counternature."

The category of sins against nature (*vitium contra naturam*) was a relatively late addition to the traditional five forms of lust—i.e., fornication, adultery, incest, sex with minors, and rape. Theorized most extensively by Thomas Aquinas in the thirteenth century, but developed earlier in the writings of Peter Damian and Alan of Lille, it designated a crime of a higher order. For whereas lust in its ordinary forms sinned against the outcome of coitus, in the form of children wrongly procreated, who would be without a family, in its darker aberration lust violated coitus itself.[91] This new category assumed a particular conception of nature as having a constant, inviolable end. Drawing on Aristotelian science, theorists of counternature defined nature's instrumental purpose to be stated in God's command "to be fruitful and multiply." In Bosch, the seed-filled world emergent on the triptych's shutters announces that purpose. Meanwhile, pleasure—flourishing in the ensemble's open state—was held to serve only a secondary aim: it induced creatures to mate. If pursued not as a means but as an end in itself, if—already in Augustine's words—it "rejoices in itself," pleasure misused creation. Sexual positions deemed not conducive to conception—for example, intercourse from behind, as well as all substitutive contact, whether manual, anal, or oral—were summarily condemned. Aquinas's list of crimes against nature begins with *pollutio*, the ejaculation of semen without any coitus.[92] However, the injunction to procreate was most egregiously disobeyed in sex acts that, due to the gender or species of the actors involved, never can result in offspring. Sodomites aimed at the nothingness that preceded them. Theirs was the ultimate evil, a sort of metaphysical heresy, since it was "the corruption of the principle on which the rest depend."[93] In Bosch's time, religious heresy (betrayal of God) and the "unspeakable crime" (betrayal of God's creation) were legally one and the same. The Dutch and German words for convicted sodomites—*keter* or *ketzer*—derive from the heretical Cathars, just as, in English, *bugger* comes from the heretical Bogomiles.

During the fifteenth century, secular authorities criminalized "sins against nature" as symptoms of an axis of evil threatening everything. Though they drew their tactics from the Church's earlier battles against heresy, it was secular rulers who led the war against sodomy.

210 Detail of Hieronymus Bosch, *The Garden of Delights* (fig. 170)

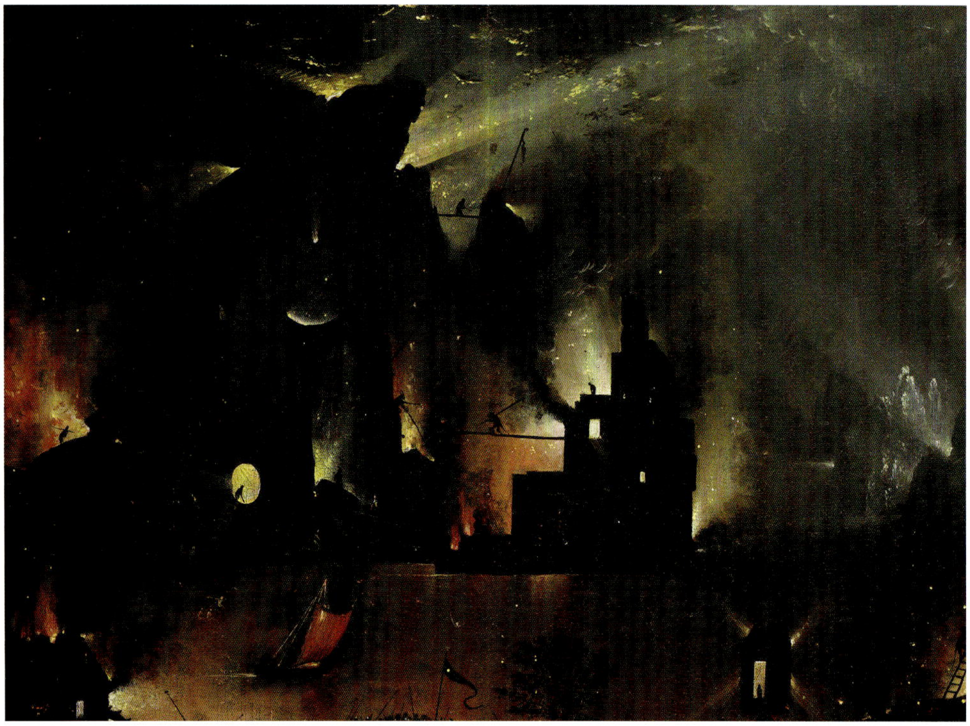

Defined as a rebellion against God's majesty and thus linked to Satan's original revolt, these crimes were political in kind. The virulent campaign in Bruges derived from the challenge that city traditionally posed to centralized Burgundian rule.[94] Precisely because it was conceptually vague, "crimes against nature" scrutinized burghers in their most private actions, turning sexuality into a litmus test of a subject's obedience to his ruler. The imputed existence of such crimes formed an alibi for all pogroms against internal enemies in the political order. Justifying a legal state of emergency, they befitted a political theology based in hate.

In Bosch, this enemy is everywhere rumored but nowhere confirmed. In broad daylight, suggestive proximities only *insinuate* prohibited sexual acts. In the foreground, left of center, hungry mouths, raised buttocks, firm caresses of swollen fruit, and seed spilling on the grass all add up to accusations that must come from us who stand on this side of the picture plane (fig. 210). Visual puns based in Bosch's Middle Dutch and graspable by his local clientele may have sharpened the sexual connotations of these forms. But grounded in verbal ambiguities and culturally specific, such in-jokes were veiled in the day and are now hard to recover. Puzzlement was always an intended response, though, because the unspeakable sin must be signaled evasively.[95] When they railed against the unspeakable crime, preachers of the period did so obliquely, expecting most of their audience *not to know* whereof they preached. To appear to understand their hate-filled sermons was to draw suspicion. Confessional manuals warned priests not to question the chaste about unnatural lust, since "one should not even think of this sin."[96] Once discovered, the "infected" members of the flock needed relentlessly to be probed, though still with "caution and fear," since questions can put new ideas into people's heads.[97] Comic stories circulated about confessors mishearing the confession of some peccadillo as a veiled admission of the unspeakable crime. The humor hinges on the ambiguity of idiom, euphemism, and slang. In one such tale, a young soldier admits to having had sex with a nun, but because of how he words his confession, his elderly confessor thinks he said he had intercourse with a castrated pig.[98] Bosch plays with the scandalous understandings and misunderstandings his imagery provokes. Happily for the painter, these do not reside in the work but are performed before the work, with caution, fear, and (I imagine) not a little fun. Middle Dutch puns might have sprung to the mind of Brabantine viewers, leaving Bosch's French-speaking patrons in the dark. It is impossible to know what the Count of Nassau said about the human flowerpot, or whether he remained silent and watched others dig their own graves. Such performances leave no record behind, and even if they did, these would be difficult to penetrate. Like the "deep play" of the Balinese cockfight as studied (famously) by anthropologist Clifford Geertz, they would be "a story they [the participants] tell themselves about themselves."[99]

Not showing what he shows, Bosch similarly permits viewers not to know what they also know. In hell, bodily orifices are overtly misused, but these are punishments, not human actions. With retribution, Bosch and his public stand on firmer ground. The torments fit the unnameable crime without precisely naming it. Bosch's burning city at the top of the right panel recalls Sodom—but as in the Bible's narrative, the retribution is specified but the sin is not (fig. 211). Horror stands in for the crime horrendously punished. Whereas criminal law in Burgundian Flanders made all counternatural acts, including masturbation, punishable by death, only bestiality and homosexuality were penalized with death by burning.[100] Predicted by its primordial cause in unruly desire and determining its gruesome effects, the triptych's unspeakable subject comes obliquely into view: a sexually perverse and thoroughly heretical un-humanity rebels against creation itself. For the overlords in Brussels who first owned it, and even more so for the Duke of Alba, who obsessively coveted it, this portrait of a cosmic "state of emergency," of an anomic upside-down world where anything goes, would have fueled their impulse to rule and if need be crush with emergency powers all those who are deemed subject to them. Complicating matters, however, is the fact that this painted state of exception represents the status quo.

At the triptych's lower right, the seated woman personifying Vanity sits beneath Satan's gigantic loincloth in a fiery hell all to herself (see fig. 208). That she represents Vanity can be gleaned from Bosch's more conventional treatment of that vice in the Hell roundel of his *Seven Deadly Sins* (fig. 212). With the toad on her genitals, Superbia—labeled as such—gazes in horror at a convex mirror held up by a demon. The addition of a male companion (none is present in the associated genre scene of Superbia [see fig. 122]) conjures up images of Adam and Eve and associates their crime with pride. But the decisive comparison lies in Bosch's triptych itself (fig. 213). With her golden locks and averted gaze, Vanity reflects the newly created Eve. This makes perfect sense. Eve's fundamental flaw, pride, was the means by which the serpent induced rebellion. Causing her to desire to be Adam's equal, pride also made Eve aware of her good looks, so that she could use them to tempt and ruin Adam. In the triptych, the figure of Vanity also reflects Adam: her form looks like Eve's but her seated posture mirrors Adam's in Eden. This makes sense, as well. In the initial moment of history, in the impenetrable "before" occurring prior to the Fall, Adam, when he glimpsed Eve, was disastrously prideful, too. Adam's pride did not consist in his overestimating himself. Rather, it consisted in his turning his love from God to God's creation. In desiring Eve, Adam sought in and through her his own creaturely bliss. This had been Augustine's argument in his commentary on the thirty-third Psalm. The prideful are those who, deluded into thinking themselves free, delight in themselves. Pursuing nothingness—which is to say, engaged in unspeakable acts from which no offspring

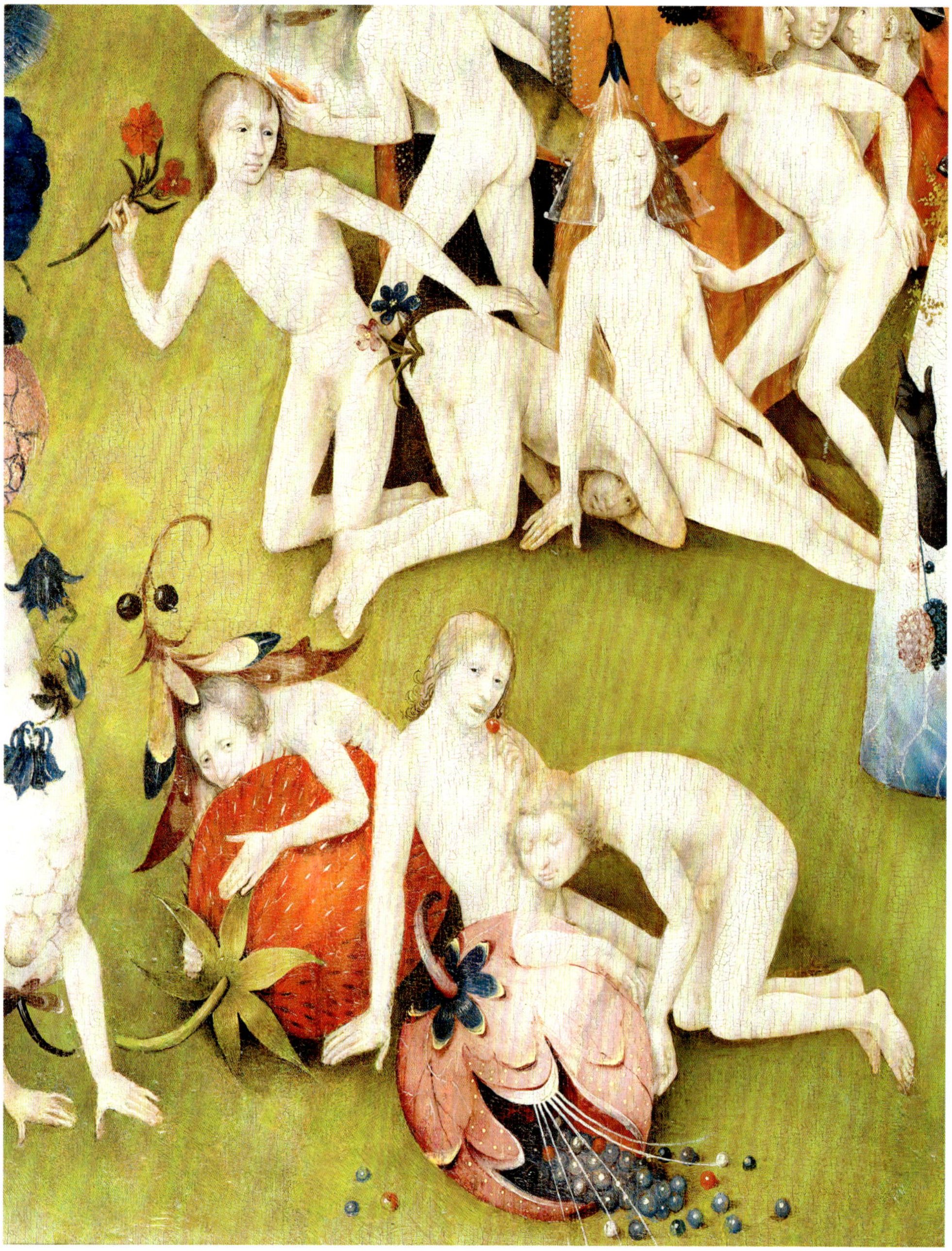

211 Detail of Hieronymus Bosch, *The Garden of Delights* (fig. 170)

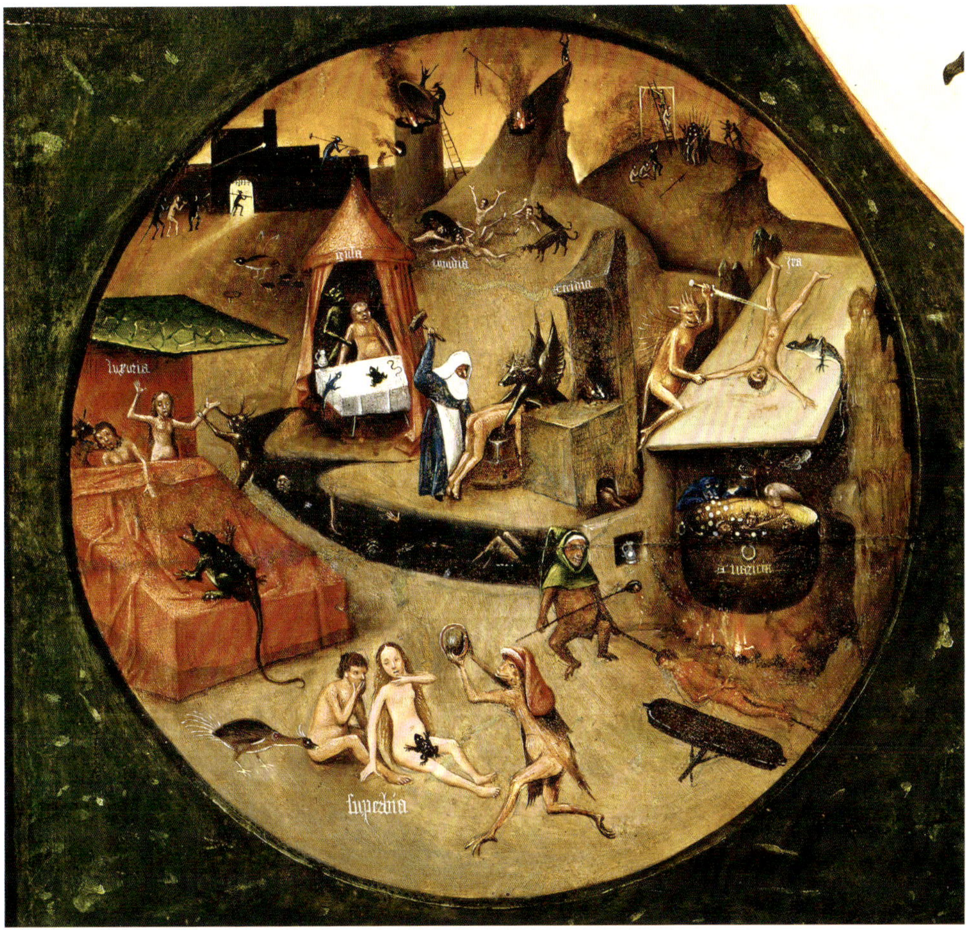

(LEFT) **212** Detail of Hieronymus Bosch, *The Seven Deadly Sins and the Four Last Things* (fig. 122)

(BELOW) **213** Details of Hieronymus Bosch, *The Garden of Delights* (fig. 170)

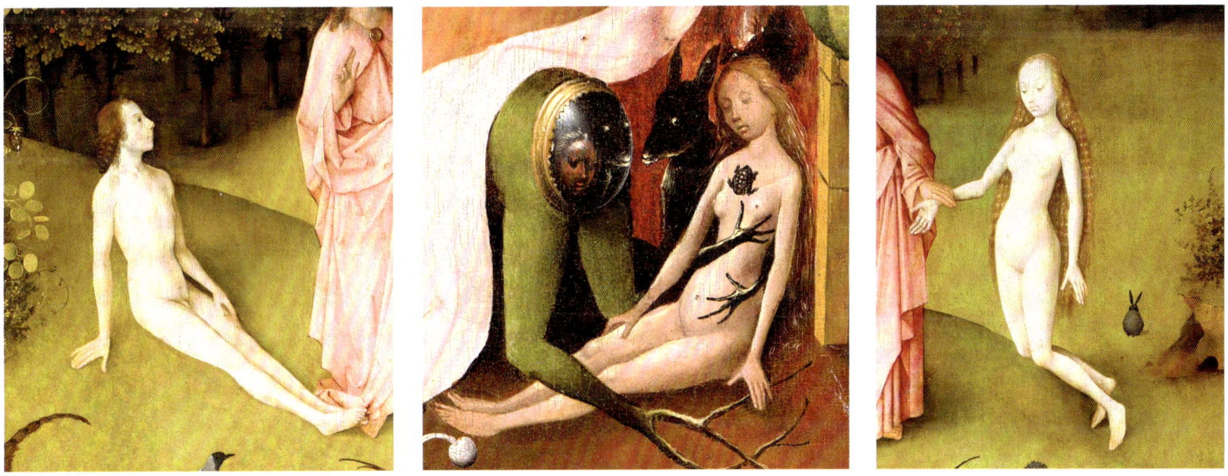

can result—they, the prideful, become nothing in the end. The mirror, old attribute of pride, acquires a global significance. Affixed to a tree-devil's ass and reflecting Eve cheek by jowl with the Devil, the mirror shows that the *self* is the real enemy and the painting's unspoken subject.

Before the modern era, the word *subject* did not name the thinking human self or ego. Rather, as the key term of Western metaphysics, it designated that which lies underneath (Latin *sub-*) as the underlying ground or foundation of that which is. The quest for this ground was posed and presupposed in Book VII of Aristotle's *Metaphysics*: "What is being as being?" In Bosch, *this* subject is God, who speaks, and it—the primal ground, divinely created *hyle*—stands absolute and firm (see fig. 183). But that is not the picture's subject. For in its mobile, triptych structure, the created world opens to activities that aim at nothing rather than something. The work's unspeakable subject, and thus its proper name, has eluded interpreters not because that word has been lost but because that other subject—the *human* self—is a great abyss. Already the original human subject, Adam, lost himself completely in the first instant of ocular desire. Beholding Eve, receiving the arrow of her image in lovestruck eyes, his soul, his subjectivity, becomes devoured and overtaken by the phantasms that arise from her and that plague us still, as we, Adam's heirs, meet his desires with ours. And at the end of the history that goes nowhere—at the point Adam's gaze terminates—the destroyed human subject remains permanently in the thrall of the visual. Turned forever backward toward his original desire and loss, the Tree-Man shows selfhood as a ruin (see fig. 209). Bereft of his unruly lower part, but with his gaping torso serving as an infernal whorehouse, he is everybody as nobody. Cleverly, through the Tree-Man's castrated form, Bosch punishes the offending male member while also picturing, in the resultant gap, the dark, abject orifices where counternatural offenses occur. He reminds us, one last time, that the crime against creation was the refusal to *procreate*. A disfigured self-portrait, he looks backward through the painted spectacle that, five hundred years on, still fascinates, infects, and potentially undoes our *selves*.

A Phenomenology of the Idol

Bosch has the gazes of Adam and the Tree-Man converge at the triptych's center, where the agitated motion of an oversexed humanity itself collects in a central circular parade. The naked riders writhe and buck wildly as if resisting all constraints. Their animal mounts, some ludicrously phallic and with prominent testicles, move more regularly than they. Motivated by carnal desire, the order of circle and center is both powerful and precarious. Rotating around the watery, women-filled hole, the mounted men create a figure in the carpet, but elsewhere the garden's denizens comport themselves yet more randomly, pursuing their ecstasies alone or in groupings haphazardly amassed, like the gigantic quasi-mineral clusters forming in their world. Compelled by boundless appetite and thus unified by drive (the nude women in the central pool balance fruits on their heads, collapsing the hungers for sex and for food), the women and men nonetheless strike hyperbolically various poses, as if anomaly were the sign of desire in control. We have seen such movements elsewhere in Bosch. In his *Temptation of Saint Anthony*, in the décor of the hermit saint's crumbling place of prayer, the Israelites perform their *moresca* dance beneath the golden calf (see fig. 163). True, their motion is not exactly circular: they dance below their idol rather than around it. But the scene wraps around a pillar whose engraved glyphs circle around in endless rotation. True, too, the garden's revelers have made no golden idols; as we will see, Bosch shows that they *make* nothing at all. However, they do act as Bosch shows idolaters to behave, which makes abundant sense. Unchecked, carnal desire desires excessively, elevating its object above all things, worshiping it exclusively like a god. And with idolatry, so too with lust, the eye initiates the crime.

Bosch highlights Eve's blond tresses with delicate lines of golden paint (see fig. 191). He shows what Adam saw when Eve's image first penetrated his eye: an alluring naked body encircled by an aureole of light. That Eve looks downward, submitting to Adam's gaze, specifies the critique. She behaves like the ideal lady, he, like the eager suitor, in scenes of courtly love. Bosch borrowed most of the imagery in his central panel from the scenography of courtly love, with its verdant gardens, shady groves, rejuvenating pools, and natural hideaways all bathed in the light of a perpetual spring.[101] In Bosch's day, especially through the satirical spin that northern printmakers (with their bourgeois sensibilities) gave to courtly love, this scenography was widely parodied as the very essence of a false or fool's paradise, as in the mythical Venusberg, with its underground caverns filled with devils disguised as beautiful maidens.[102] Of course, Bosch nowhere announces that his paradise is mockingly meant. Falsehood must be inferred by the beholder, who will be dumbstruck by the painting, as Adam is by Eve.

The fascination the painting causes repeats the fascination it portrays. And conversely, the scenes and structures that fascinate seem like projected symptoms of our own mesmerized beholding. The ocular desire that, through Adam, motivates the circular procession, and the procession itself in its visual portrayal by Bosch, together mobilize the primitive instincts of our eye, which seeks midpoints, centers, and symmetries.[103] The painting thus obeys not the fixed and stable order of a divinely created world but the vagrant order of human vision, even the vision through the innocent eyes of naked Eve and Adam before the Fall. It shows how things look when looking turns idolatrous.

Color plays a huge role in this. Paintings consist materially of pigments bound in some fluid, adhesive medium and applied to, so that they largely conceal, some surface or support. They are therefore perceived as things all of color. Because its colors differ markedly from all other works within its tradition, Bosch's triptych stands apart. Were its subject matter wholly conventional, these panels would still look different due to their coloring. The pigments themselves are unremarkable.[104] For his greens, Bosch used copper pigment and lead-tin yellow; for blues, azurite; for pinks, organic red lake; for deep red, vermilion; and for black, organic black and iron oxide. As we observed in the Lisbon *Saint Anthony*, Bosch did not build up his images in multiple layers, as was the common practice for early Netherlandish painters. He tended to apply his color layers directly, thinly, and sketchily, allowing different colors to intermingle in the modeled rendering of one thing. In his nameless masterpiece, the method is roughly the same, with his directness of approach most fully developed in hell and least so in Eden.[105] Bosch thus binds painterly facture—how he actually makes the image—to the story the painting tells. Recent technical analysis of works of the era revealed that whereas traditionally the initial color layers were painted in oil-and-water emulsion and the surface layers in oil, Bosch in this triptych painted with tempera over oil (for example, in the flesh tones) or directly on the chalk ground, without the usual intermediate layers of imprimatura.[106] These procedures may help explain the triptych's poor state of preservation and why over the centuries its original glamour waned. But it also gave—still gives—the work its unique look. Mixing his pigments with little binder and laying them down directly, Bosch created hues that are more saturated, less transparent, and yet strangely groundless.

Early Netherlandish painters used brilliant local colors to conjure the unmingled colors of the represented things in themselves. Artists created the secondary effects of light, shadow, distance, and atmosphere by darkening or lightening the same given color. As we observed in the *Saint Anthony* triptych, Bosch worked differently, mixing up his colors, orange on blue, red on green, and so forth. This wrapped the scene in an overall atmosphere and caused everything to seem potentially like an apparition, like the mere "phenomenon" that the eye receives, colored by the conditions of light and distance, obscured by intermediate smoke, dirt, dust, and air, warped by the corruption of the visual apparatus, and cunningly manipulated by an enemy that is everywhere and nowhere. Magnifying the limitations inherent in viewpoint, such intensified "seeming" befitted the portrayal of deception that was Bosch's stock-in-trade.

Nothing in Bosch's oeuvre, though, quite prepares us for the explosive look of his nameless masterpiece. The colors of the central panel are local and pure, in keeping with the traditional Netherlandish manner and in harmony with the jewel-like brilliance of the Eden panel. What those colors depict, however, stands apart from it all: bright-plumed birds the size of elephants, gigantic winged and feathered fruits, a mussel shell large enough to cozy in, and with pearls as big as apples. Pictured with the utopian clarity of the thing-in-itself, of essences uninflected by the vagaries of perception, these are instead perfect likenesses of phantasms, pure illusion illusionistically portrayed. The fabulous blue and pink formations around the central pool are striking instances of this. At once mineral, vegetal, and animal, these color-towers toss us headlong into a realm of deception that this artist elsewhere signals *is* deception. The décor on Saint Anthony's hermitage and the Magi's inscrutable gifts exists as artifact within an artifact that comments on it. In the *Garden*, by contrast, Bosch invites us to enter the idols that he elsewhere depicts from outside, as objects made by alien craft. Some have wondered whether the Prado's conservators cleaned Bosch's triptych too zealously.[107] The central panel's present garishness would then have resulted from the removal not only of dirt and old varnish but also of an important final paint layer that subdued excessive hues. They expect this artist's colors to blend in with one another, tradition, and the world. But that is not how Bosch, in this case, painted. Arousing and mirroring the concupiscence of the eye, the brilliant colors of the central panel cause us to behold the world through idolatrous eyes.

Such a painting should come with a warning label. Bosch's *Seven Deadly Sins* does, cautioning viewers in writing, "Beware, beware, God sees" (see figs. 122 and 126). Not that the admonishment works. Standing in for God's vision, the picture observes us toppled by its own display, as our eyes get drawn to what God abhors. In spite of its label, the painted roundel becomes like the round mirror that Vanity beholds—pleasurably in life and painfully in hell. Bosch's paintings routinely see and blame us. His *Christ Crowned with Thorns* is a "J'accuse!" whispered to the viewer by the suffering Christ (see fig. 131). *The Hay Wain* intensifies this charge. Drawing our eye to its empty center, it—itself a vain, worldly valuable—packs us off to hell (see fig. 39). However, all these works preserve a truth that escapes perdition. No matter how topsy-turvy the painting, the eye of God controls its center. In the *Garden*, the situation is different. Whether positively or negatively construed, its godless center is its own. But what

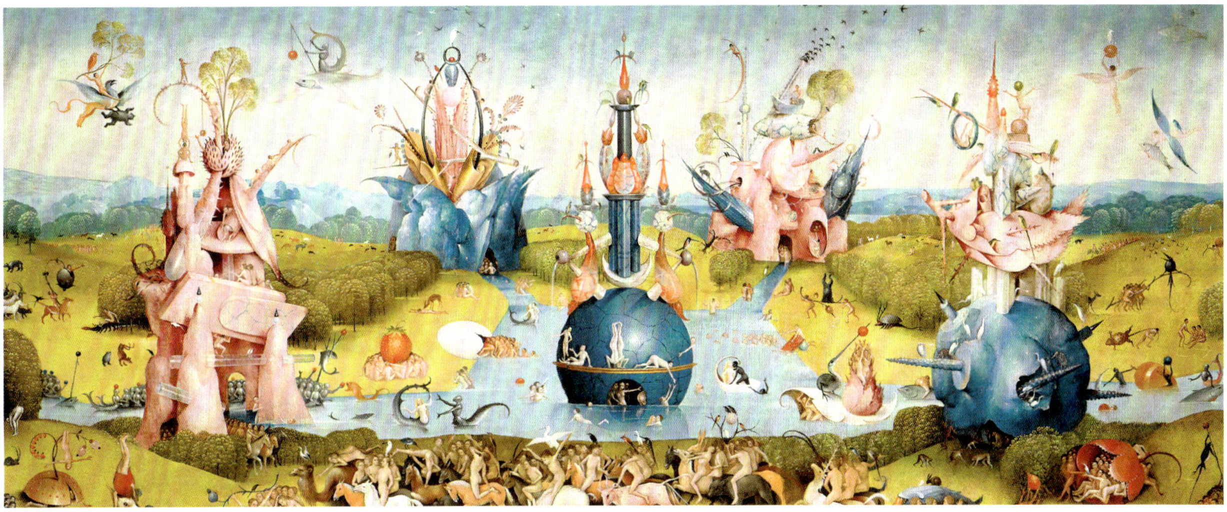

214 Detail of Hieronymus Bosch, *The Garden of Delights* (fig. 170)

is it that constitutes the center? If medieval marginalia has migrated here from the margins of art to the very middle, what middle is this that remains?

The man with flowers in his rectum glances casually at us, as if he, along with everyone else in the picture, knows we are watching, as if—even—he is offering the blossoms to us (see fig. 210). Bosch's viewer-oriented revelers transcend the device, recommended by the Italian art theorist Leon Battista Alberti, of introducing into the painting a mediating figure (Alberti calls him the *festaiolo*, or "merrymaker") who, stationed slightly apart, enjoins viewers to attend to the main event, like the chorus does in dramatic contexts.[108] In Bosch, outward gazes do not merely point us to the picture. Front and center, they rotate the picture around to us, making us and our response the picture's subject and main event. Even if, unsettled by the human flowerpot, we choose to look away, we know—and the other eyes that meet our gaze remind us—that he still sees us, and that we remain the target of his display. Although scattered among scores of tiny painted eyes, the reversed perspective achieved by each has a global effect. It transforms the picture's structure and plot into functions of the beholder's experience. Like the classical Medusa, these panels can be approached only frontally, in confrontation with a power that demands that to see it is to be immediately seen and defeated by it.

It may seem at first glance that this frontality—how the painting stares at you en face, with the center of its imagery aligned with the midline of the panel—belongs to the world Bosch puts on display. But this is not the case. Fountain, pool, and parade do align along the picture's central vertical axis, and the four surrounding formations—despite their wildly capricious shapes—do flank perfectly that center. Indeed, such strict designs delight those who choose to seek them. With a certain wonder we can observe that the flanking formations stand equidistant from the frame. But to confirm this structure requires postulating a center within radically inconsistent, decentered structures. The tips of those distant towers look meticulously aligned, but they are actually hyperbolically protean, consisting of shimmering foliage, birds in flight, and fragile pinnacles (fig. 214). Aligned with airborne berries, bushes, and mermaids, they arouse the suspicion that alignment may be everywhere accidental. The geometric coincidences are precise and numerous enough to cause us to forget the adjustments made to measure them. Subjective vantage point alone—the place and time of the present view—gives entropy the semblance of order.

Symmetry imposes on this world of anomalies a higher-order structure. It receives powerful support from outside, from the ensemble's physical framework. The triptych structure reifies the centers proposed in each painted panel. Hinged shutters open and close along the central panel's axis of symmetry. Lending substance to airy fantasies, format seals pictorial design to the sturdy reality of things. The triptych structure has also encouraged commentators to postulate sturdy structures beyond its frame. Aware that in Bosch's time, triptychs were typically altarpieces, and that as such they derived their symmetry from the sacred buildings where they stood and from the liturgical rites they served, art historians long assumed—and still sometimes maintain—that Bosch's strange ensemble initially stood within the centralized space of altar, chapel, and church. Wilhelm Fraenger—the most imaginative of Bosch's commentators—was one of the first to recognize that the work's erotic subject would have ruled out its placement in a church.[109] But he then rescued the idea of a religious setting by rethinking Bosch's creed. In a dazzling study published in 1947, Fraenger proposed that Bosch painted the work for a heretical sect in 's-Hertogenbosch. In their secret rituals, initiates did what the painting enticed them to do: they undressed and copulated with one another, in order (according to their antinomian beliefs) to become shameless and innocent like Adam before the Fall and thereby to usher in a new paradise on earth. With the discovery in 1962 that Bosch's panels originally stood in the pleasure palace of the powerful counts of Nassau in Brussels, Fraenger's thesis—implausible when it was launched—became patently untenable. But there remain lessons to be learned from it, not least because the intuition of a secret heresy at the core of Bosch's oeuvre remains a leitmotif in the literature even if historical scholarship has refuted it. Fraenger's starting point was simple and legitimate. He resolved to take the triptych at face value and proposed that, like most artworks of the period, it must celebrate what it displays. His erroneous thesis—that it served an orgiastic cult of Adam—derived from leads planted (I would argue) deliberately in the work. The triptych does indeed resemble a sacred object. It does so because Bosch built it that way. He engineered it to look like the idol of some unspeakable cult.

While the counts of Nassau were in on the joke, visitors to their Brussels residence might have fancied—roughly as Fraenger did—that these strange painted panels were spoils taken from some vanquished heretics, like the putative idols wrested from New World natives and placed on display in European collections of the day. In other words, Bosch programmed this error into his painting like a virus, causing efforts to understand the work suddenly to crash. But the hypothesis of Bosch as secretly a heretic conceals something rather ordinary but terrifying. Heresy was not the work's cryptic key, but an insinuation the work made. And the painting directed its insinuation not at some Other, some foreign or forgotten abject "them." Its target group has always been *us*, whoever we are, whoever I am. Painter of enemies, Bosch shows what it looks like to see through idolatrous eyes. He makes me into the enemy, into my own enemy.

8

SELF-PORTRAITURE

The Raw and the Cooked

There is something peculiar about Bosch's nameless masterpiece that keeps it always contemporary, allowing it to make mischief in a permanent here and now. Nothing in the world of its central panel—neither the towers nor the tents, neither the playthings nor the comestibles—bears a sign of human making (see fig. 204). Whatever looks to be a crafted tool, a built dwelling, or a fabricated costume—everything that might belong to the assemblage of a "culture"—turns out to be, upon close inspection, a natural formation. Brimming with nectars, fruits, and honeys, this lifeworld is consumed as is: raw, not cooked.

In the lower left corner of the panel, the odd object on a man's back—a sort of oversize, blossom-topped, tendril-sprouting strawberry—seems an exotic apparel the man has put together and somehow fixed to himself (fig. 215). But neither the parts nor their attachments show any signs of crafting, arousing the suspicion that the man does not *wear* the hybrid but *is* a hybrid, or else that this vegetal thing sits perched upon him like an insect or bird. To the left, the huge fruit or pod carried by one in a group of men resembles a luxurious masterpiece of the jeweler's art—like the gold-and-enamel *joyaux* the Burgundian nobles of Bosch's day ceremoniously gifted, only larger and more wondrous (fig. 216). However, the erratic red lines reticulating the object's surface and isolating each blue blossom as if it were on a separate plate seem products not of human craft but of vegetal germination. Similarly, just above, the golden circles on the surface of the gigantic floating pod resemble metallic inlays (fig. 217). Intermingled with epidermal pores, however, and growing fainter toward the rear, they propagate organically, like scales.

Inhabiting their world without modifying it, the revelers do not even observe a minimal cult. Scholars are mistaken in terming the circle a ritual, as if the patterned action, whatever it intends, derives from the men.[1] The unbridled beasts create the circle, while the humans—driven, not driving—writhe about chaotically, as if nature were more cultured than they. No wonder this tableau especially confounds historians of art. Without the artifacts that would constitute a culture—indeed, void of any mark of human making—Bosch's painting presents us not with a secret code but with the necessary absence of code. With nothing to date or to interpret, historians dig about like archaeologists in sand, the one placing the scene in the era before the Flood, the other in a millennium to come.

215 Detail of Hieronymus Bosch, *The Garden of Delights* (fig. 170)

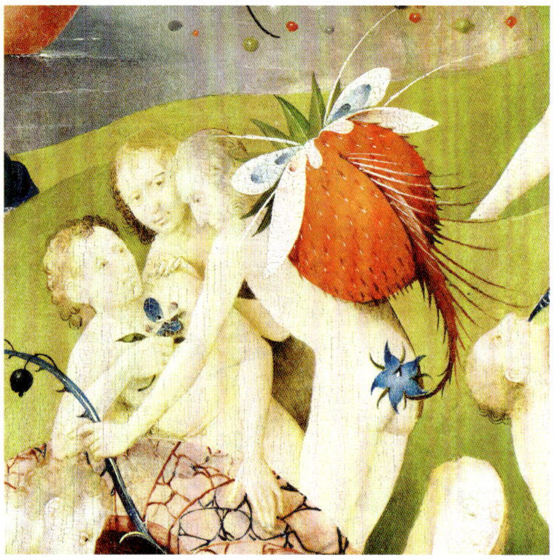

216 Detail of Hieronymus Bosch, *The Garden of Delights* (fig. 170)

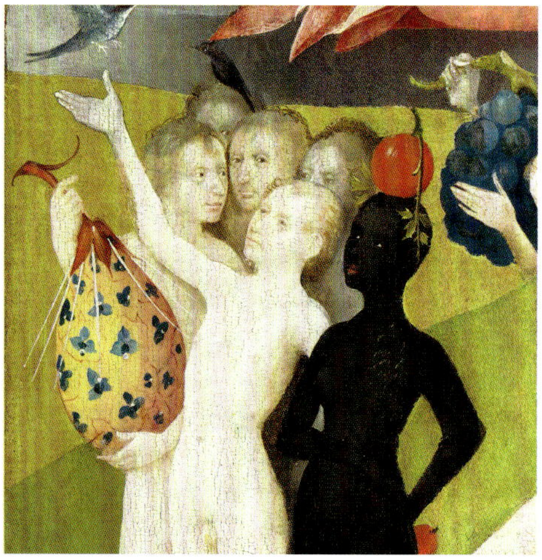

217 Detail of Hieronymus Bosch, *The Garden of Delights* (fig. 170)

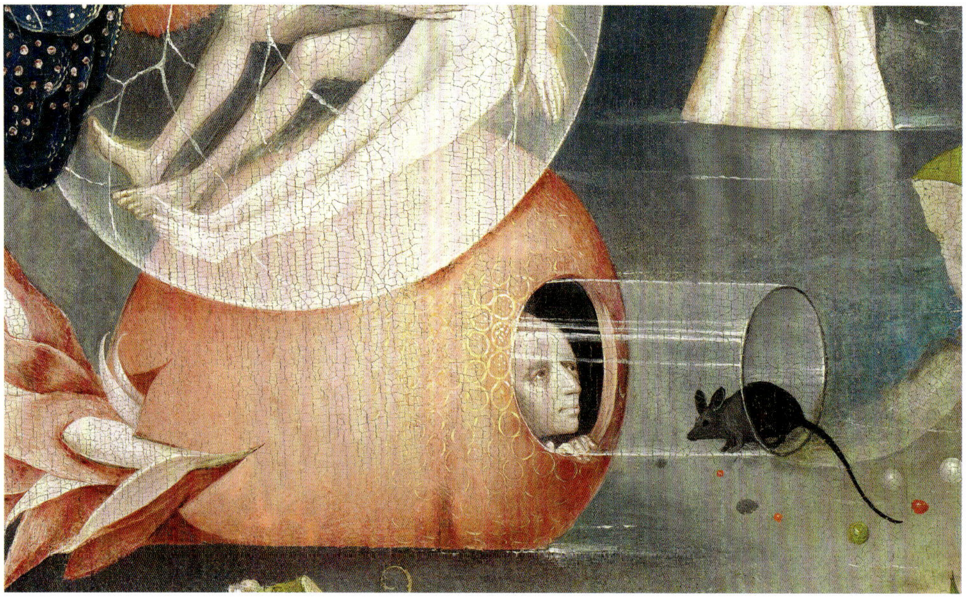

Bosch was not the only artist of his day to conjure primitive lifeworlds. Lucas Cranach painted (like Bosch, for a courtly milieu) lively portraits of the so-called Golden and Silver Ages, with naked folk dancing and fighting with abandon (fig. 218).[2] And hirsute wild men, or woodwoses—legendary denizens of the northern forests—abound in the prints and decorative arts of the period. Somewhere within these fantasies about the nature of human nature, though, there inevitably appears some stubborn artifact—an ornamental necklace or veil, a crafted club, a distant castle, even—that breaks the spell. In general, fictional portrayals of the past fail most dramatically when they imagine bygone artifacts, since these will necessarily be somehow marked by the aesthetic style of their present manufacture. Products of the era when they were concocted rather than of the one they try to conjure, these craft goods become more anachronistic over time, as the style and outlook of any portrayal itself turns into a period piece. Bosch's treatment of the Magi's gifts was unique in that, alone among his contemporaries, this painter endeavored to make them look like products of an artistry so alien and inscrutable that they no longer look quite like artifacts at all (see fig. 88). In imagining a culture-free humanity, Bosch went further, crafting a world entirely devoid of craft. If this

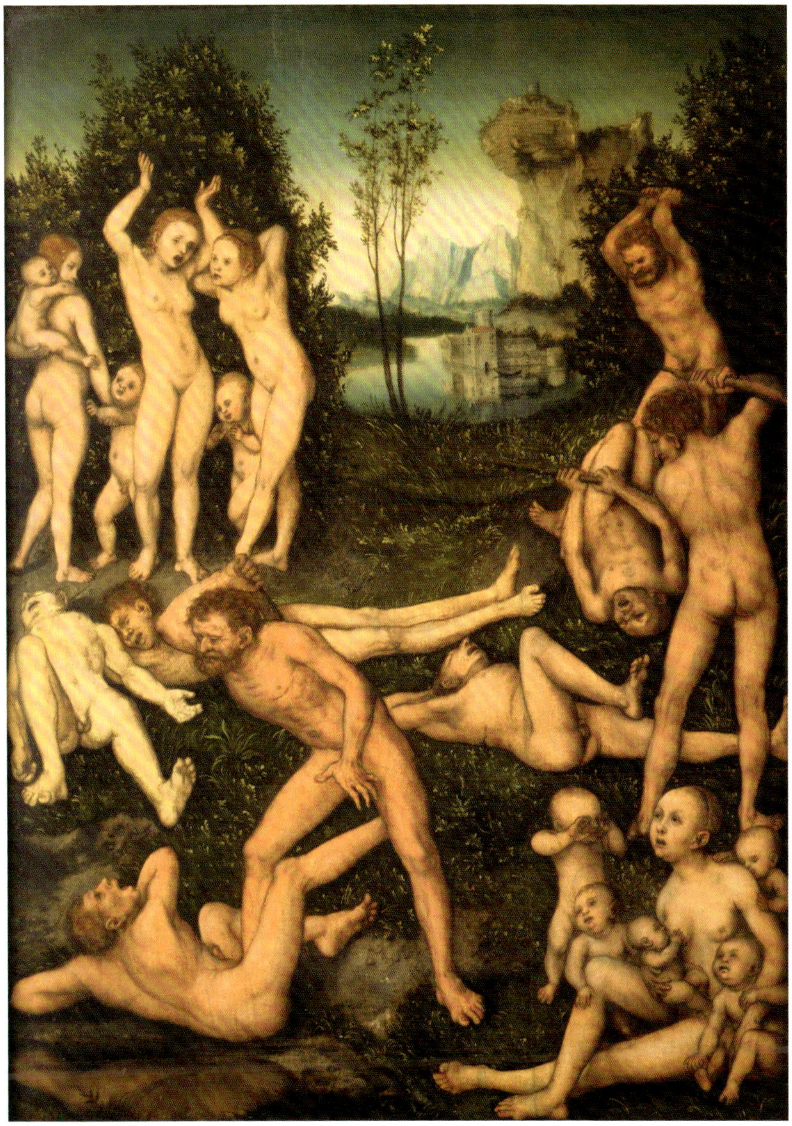

218 Lucas Cranach the Elder, *The Age of Silver*, 1527, panel, Klassik Stiftung, Weimar

world without artifacts therefore cannot be set in a history, if nothing in the garden looks datable even to Bosch's time, what about the crafted artifact his painted panel is? To what history does Bosch's own creation belong?

The painting's original audience may have been vexed over what those strange formations in the background *are*. But they would have known immediately what to *do* with them. They would have tried desperately to own them. In their accidental shapes, mingling of species, and similarity to artifacts, these formations resemble what in the parlance of the day were termed "jokes of nature."[3] Early modern collectors coveted such rarities above all else. Modern art collecting began in the Burgundian court milieu where Bosch found his key patronage, and it developed in the seats of Habsburg power, where Bosch was most admired.[4] Wonder cabinets—the princely forerunners of the modern art museum—gathered under one roof artworks, arms and armor, natural specimens, vernacular and exotic craft goods, games, toys, and instruments of science, the arts, and hygiene. If such congeries had an ordering center it was the *anomaly*: the often monstrous, singular instance that escaped the regular order of things. The preciousness of red coral, for example, consisted not only in its rarity, brilliance,

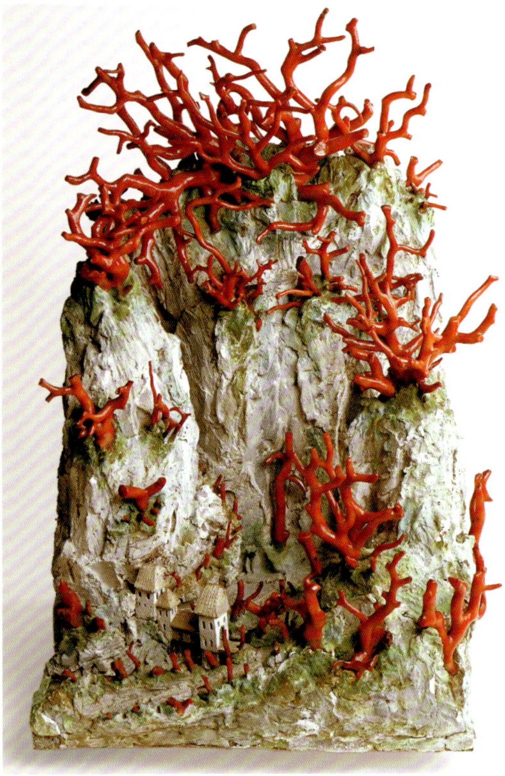

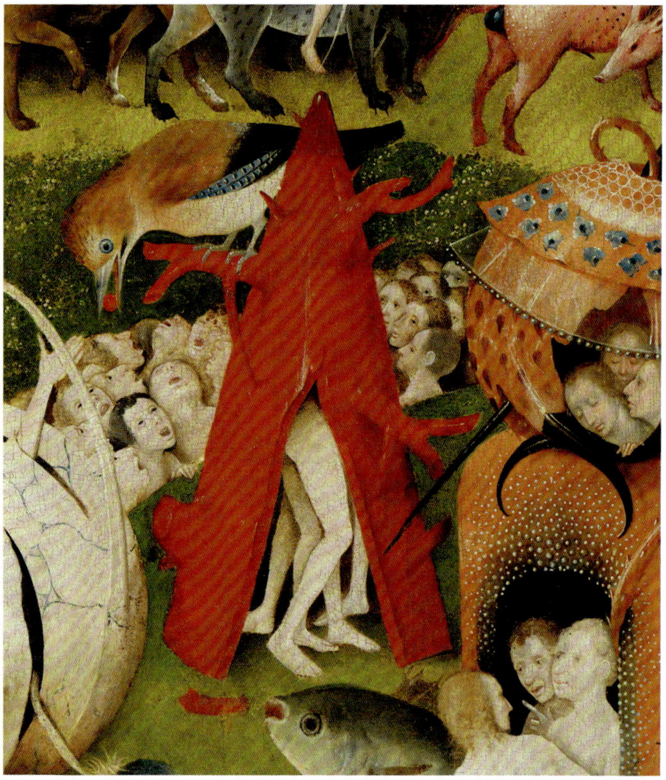

(LEFT) **219** Anonymous Tyrolean, *Alpine Pass and Weir at Finstermünz on the Inn*, c. 1550–1600, coral and plaster on wooden base, Kunsthistorisches Museum, Vienna

(RIGHT) **220** Detail of Hieronymus Bosch, *The Garden of Delights* (fig. 170)

and durability, but also in the puzzlement it elicited as to whether it was animal, vegetal, or a mineral (figs. 219 and 220).[5] Of all the anomalies, the most telling for the disordered order of the *Kunstkammer* were ones that blurred the divide between what occurs naturally and what human beings make.[6] Spectacular corals that seemed magically wrought; rocks in whose random striations portraits, landscapes, and histories appeared to shimmer; roots and pebbles uncannily resembling sculpted figurines: these and other unnameable marvels mobilized—by never satisfying—the collector's desire to gather and control. Enthusiasts explained the crafted look of these rarities by attributing creative desires to nature. Aware that such objects arose accidentally, as chance irregularities within the regular processes of formation and decay, people imagined nature occasionally and as if purposely veering off course. And they took that purpose to be one of sport: nature delighted in playing with herself. As the French barber-surgeon and teratologist Ambroise Paré wrote in 1573 concerning the unfathomable diversity of seashells, "Nature, chambermaid of great God, plays in fabricating them."[7]

Early Christian writers listed Natura among the pagan deities and placed her under God's control.[8] But in certain strains of medieval thought, she regained an unruly freedom. The force behind all creaturely desire to procreate, Natura possessed energies that were disastrous if left unchecked. The great poet of this new vitalism was Bernard Silvestris. Author of *The Cosmographia* (supposedly presented to Pope Eugene III in 1147), Bernard retold, in Platonic terms, the entire biblical story of creation. He took the name *Silvestris* from primal matter, or *hyle*—that mysterious beginning that Hartmann Schedel pictured in the first woodcut of his Creation sequence of 1493. This Silvestris personified in the *Cosmographia* as the figure of *Silva*, Latin for "timber" or "forest."[9] Silva is a formless and independent chaos that longs for order. Given form by Noys (Greek νοῦς, or Divine Providence in its creative aspect), Silva represents the "slumbering vitality of the cosmic substrate, awaiting development."[10] Already in Bernard's view, but more centrally in the poetry of his disciple Alain of Lille, nature's unruliness manifested itself most dangerously in same-sex love.[11]

Written in the later twelfth century, Alain's *Plaint of Nature* associates the malignant sterility of male-to-male coupling with the disastrous self-infatuation of Narcissus. Alain also confesses that *The Plaint of Nature* is the offspring of his own solitary dreaming, and that the poem is therefore itself deviant and sterile—a gesture foreshadowing Bosch, as we will see. Ultimately, Nature's plaint about sins "against" nature is a complaint about *nature's* nature. When desire abandoned its generative purpose, playfully pursuing pleasure for its own sake, nature acted counternaturally, undoing creation. From this perspective, jokes of nature were products of nature unnaturally coupling with itself. Resembling artifacts, these played on the moral ambiguity of art.

Art always claimed to imitate nature.[12] Usually this meant that artists copied things already extant in the natural world. But imitating nature could also mean copying nature's creative force—"naturing nature" (*natura naturans*), as distinct from mere "natured nature" (*natura naturata*). This inflated notion of making flourished during the Renaissance. It placed a premium on novelty in art. Art sought to be original, creating things without precedent or prototype. Through their novel products, artists implied that God's creation was mutable and incomplete, and that human poiesis could generate entirely new species. "Whatsoever comes not from God," wrote Tertullian, "comes necessarily from His enemy."[13] Whether consciously or not, artists vied dangerously with the Creator. In Italian art theory, special terms were coined for the highest forms of artistic activity—such as *concetto* (Latin *conceptus*) and *ingegno* (Latin *ingenium*)—which associated such production with the conception and generation of organic life. The word *Renaissance* itself has biologistic overtones. Through achievements in the arts and letters, culture is born again, like an organism. Several decades before Giorgio Vasari launched the term *rinascita* in Italy, Dürer celebrated an artistic "regrowth" (*Widererwaxsung*) occurring in the north.[14] The word associates the achievement of artists with the vital forces of organic life.[15]

The era's most celebrated inventor of impossible things, Bosch veritably personified novelty. In his most novel creation, he submits his artistry to a final reckoning. In it contend rival—even antithetical—poetic powers. One of these is God, portrayed tiny in the clouds on the triptych's shutters (see fig. 183). He made everything, including primal *hyle*, and commanded creatures to seed "according to their kind." The other maker is nature. Bursting forth on that third day of Creation, procreative as God commanded, living nature fructified Eden and inflamed human desire; but it also produced, in the central panel, hybrids most decidedly not "according to their kind." This errant form of making transcends the monstrosities that the painting centrally displays. It stands displayed as Bosch's painting itself. Poiesis of an impossible world, this most elusive crafted artifact does not merely show counternature. It *is* counternature.

Cruel Sports

It is impossible to reconstruct how Bosch's triptych functioned in its original setting. In 1517, some years after it arrived in Brussels, it left its one documented viewer—Antonio de Beatis—nearly speechless. Amazement seems one basic intended effect. It fits what Antonio reported about the rest of the palace where the triptych stood. As members of the highest nobility, the

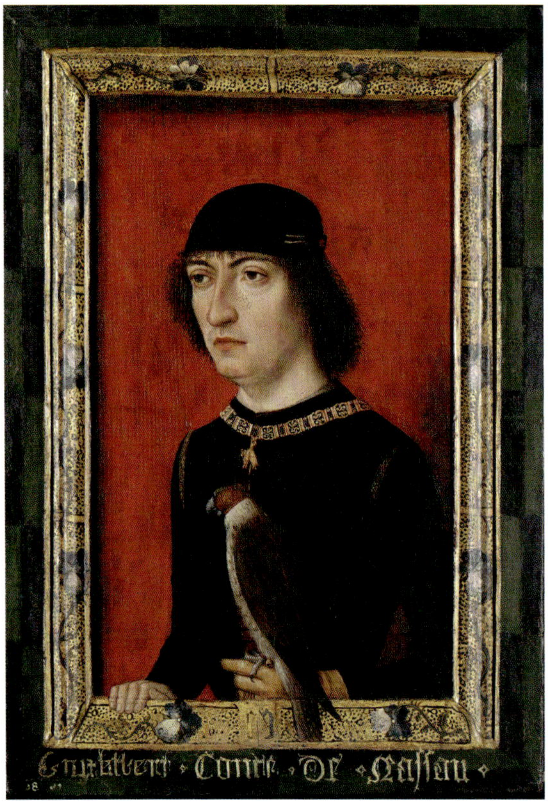

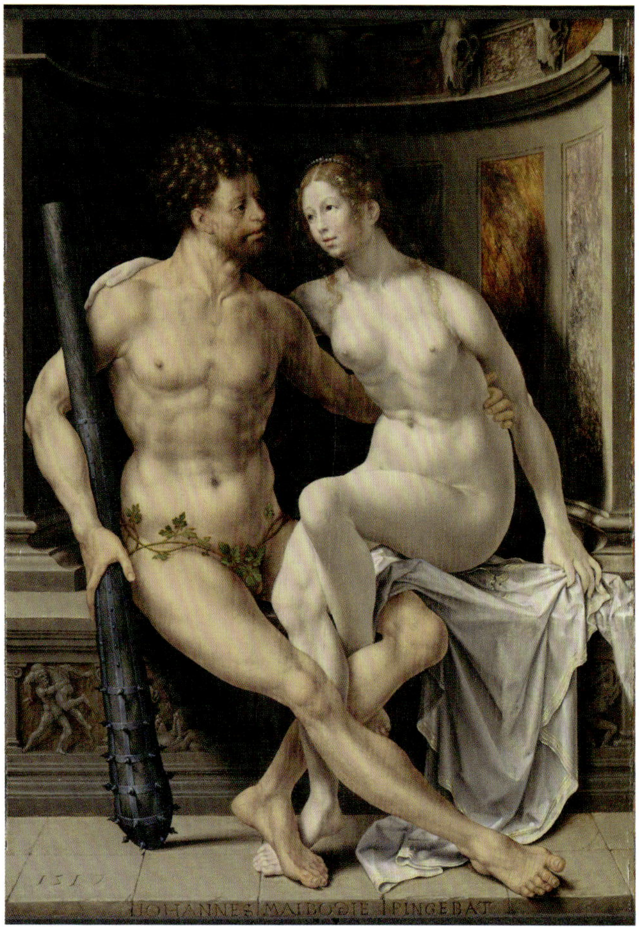

(LEFT) **221** Madrid Master of the Portrait of Princes, *Engelbrecht II, Count of Nassau*, c. 1487, panel, Rijksmuseum, Amsterdam

(RIGHT) **222** Jan Gossart, *Hercules and Deianira*, c. 1517, panel, The Barber Institute of Fine Arts, University of Birmingham, England

counts of Nassau were expected to live nobly. The size and splendor of their residence projected to a visitor like Antonio the power of his host (see fig. 172). The Nassau palace stood in sight of an older and even greater castle on the Coudenberg, where from 1430 the Burgundian overlords exerted their rule over the Duchy of Brabant. Supreme administrative officers of that court, the counts of Nassau—Engelbert II and, after 1504, his nephew Henry III—built and outfitted their Brussels residence to amplify and perhaps amicably to rival the seat of that sovereignty with which their destiny was emphatically linked.

The counts of Nassau were seasoned military men who, time and again, meted out violent justice against their foes. It was Engelbert's father, John IV of Nassau, who led the infamous slaughter by Burgundian troops of the entire citizenry of rebellious Dinant.[16] At fourteen, Engelbert entered the bellicose court of Charles the Bold and followed the duke into successive wars against Liège, the Swiss, and the duke of Lorraine (fig. 221).[17] Upon Charles's death on the battlefield, at Nancy, Engelbert was captured by the enemy and imprisoned in Switzerland. Ransomed, he became a key commander under Mary of Burgundy and Emperor Maximilian, leading the armies into battle against France and the rebellious cities of Flanders. Henry III upheld his uncle's legacy, rising to captain-general of the Netherlands in Philip the Fair's bloody war against Guelders. Dangerous men, the Nassau counts designed their palace—aptly—as a place of perilous delight. The concealed doorways that Antonio de Beatis describes gave insiders of the Nassau court special dominion in their residence. Fooled by trompe l'oeil artistry, visitors moved vulnerably through space along a route mischievously plotted by their host, who, popping in and ducking out unexpectedly, could observe them unseen. Traps were laid along the way. Among all the palace's wonders, the most famous was probably its gigantic bed. Large enough to sleep fifty, this festive device—as impressive to Dürer on his visit as it was to Antonio—came alive when, whether by volition or force, guests drank themselves into a stupor. Tossed together, men with women, they created a hilarious spectacle for their host's amusement. Games like this exposed a person's vices, his or her weakness for wine and sex.

Before describing Bosch's triptych, Antonio writes of several other nude paintings, including one of Hercules and Deianira, with figures "of considerable size."[18] Described in an inventory of 1567 as "a large painting of a giant and giantess," this work was probably created by Jan Gossart.[19] Also known as Jan Mabuse, Gossart was a pioneer among Netherlanders in the depiction of nudes and the monumental treatment of mythological subjects. He was also the favorite painter of Philip of Burgundy, Philip the Good's notoriously revelrous illegitimate son.[20] Until 1517 admiral of Zeeland and afterward (improbably) bishop of Utrecht, Philip, like the counts of Nassau, displayed in his palace (the episcopal Duurstede Castle) works by Gossart and by Hieronymus Bosch.[21] The large *Hercules and Deianira* in the Nassau castle is lost, but another, smaller version, also by Gossart, hangs now in the Barber Institute of Fine Arts in Birmingham, England (fig. 222).[22] Dated circa 1517, it is exactly contemporary with Antonio's visit to Brussels.

Hercules locks eyes with Deianira, while their amorous entanglement is set forth by their limbs, braided along the picture's median. The hero seems firmly to clamp his bride between his muscular thighs; his defeat of the half-giant Antaeus, carved below him in stone, measures the potential force of this embrace. But Hercules himself stands gripped by Deianira's allure. Her legs subtly trap his, and in contrast to Antaeus, who lost by losing contact with Mother Earth, Deianira's feet, her right one wedged under Hercules's left, maintain the greater purchase on the ground. Deianira—"man destroyer" in Greek—will bring the hero low. Made jealous by her philandering husband, she sought to force his fidelity by applying to his tunic a magic brew gifted to her for that purpose by the dying centaur Nessus. A toxic mix of semen and blood, this ointment was secretly the centaur's revenge, since Hercules had vanquished Nessus after his attempted abduction of Deianira. When the hero put on the tunic, it burned his flesh so terribly that he threw himself into a funeral pyre and died. Gossart shows Deianira grasping the inflammatory cloak; one corner already drapes the hero's inner thigh. Thus the mightiest man is by woman fatally snared.

Artistically, Gossart seems worlds apart from Bosch. Traveling to Rome in 1508, he sketched from life surviving monuments of ancient art—the first northern painter to do so (fig. 223).[23] Through his sensuous nudes, he brought home to the Netherlands the *all'antica* style flourishing in Italy. The figure of Hercules flaunts a new command of anatomy, proportion, and volume, while the hero's intertwining with his spouse—herself a set piece of contrasting female form—highlights the virtuosity such treatment demands. Gossart creates palpable bodies, as befits his theme. The beholder probes visually the undulating forms of Hercules and Deianira, as they physically explore each other's flesh. To complicate matters, Gossart stages this play as if it were between statues in a niche. This trumpets to the humanists in this painter's audience the picture's source in classical statuary, while also rendering Gossart's artistry more wondrous, since these statues seem to have stepped as if alive from their pedestals into our space: observe how Hercules's toes appear to stretch beyond the picture plane.

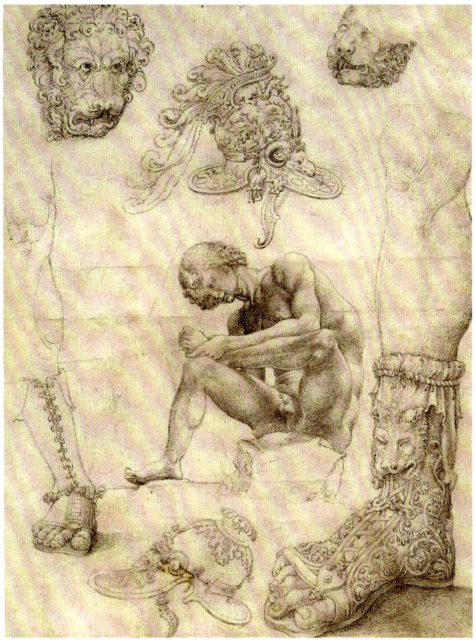

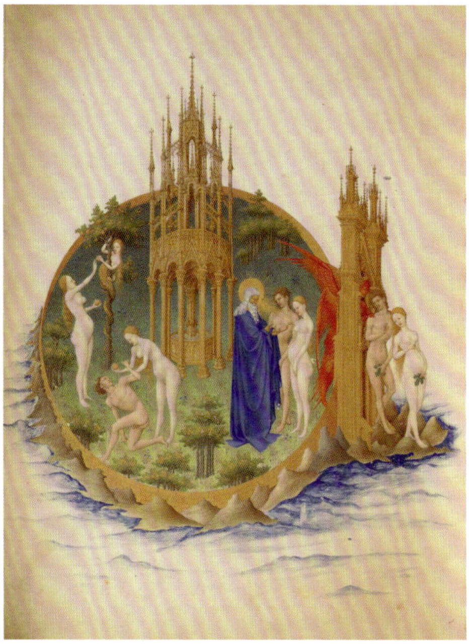

(LEFT) **223** Jan Gossart, *Sheet with a Study after the "Spinario" and Other Sculptures*, c. 1509, pen and gray-brown ink, University Libraries, Leiden, Print Room, Inv. nv. PK-T-AW1041

(RIGHT) **224** The Limbourg Brothers, *Expulsion of Adam and Eve from Paradise*, illumination from the *Très Riches Hueres du Duc de Berry*, 1416, vellum, Musée Condé, Chantilly

The staging of a *paragone*—a competition among the arts (especially painting and sculpture) over which is nature's closest rival—was a crucial gesture of ambitious Italian masters. But the *paragone* found its most spectacular expressions in early Netherlandish painting. Jan van Eyck's painted portrayals of sculpture remain the undefeated champions of the game. A self-conscious renovator of his native tradition as well as of classical antiquity, Gossart revised and updated northern realism through stunningly tangible elements like Hercules's iron-studded club and the osseous bucrania in the background niche.

Yet even where Gossart draws close to the Netherlandish tradition, he diverges markedly from Bosch. Bosch's bodies are notably fleshless and insubstantial; when they carnally intertwine, they remain sylphic, like the demons that seduce and torment them. Nor does Bosch make up for this by lending substance to inanimate things. A master of deception, he generally eschews the surface effects that make painted forms look materially concrete. Set beside Gossart, Bosch seems an artistic throwback in every way. His Adam and Eve look positively Gothic compared with Van Eyck's and Gossart's, as if the 's-Hertogenbosch master, by training or by choice, reached back a hundred years to nudes of the International Courtly Gothic style (fig. 224).[24] Historians of art tend to draw a dividing line between Bosch and Gossart, placing the former at the very end of the medieval tradition and the latter at a new beginning. The artistic development alluded to in the title of a recent retrospective, *Jan Gossart's Renaissance*, was basically the rebirth, in the north, of a classicizing style melded to classical subject matter. The obscurity of the ancient legend of Hercules and Deianira led the painter to smuggle those names into his painting, as inscriptions discreetly carved in stone above their heads. Gossart wanted to implant and confirm knowledge, not confound it, as Bosch seems to do.

Yet this titled picture (remember that Antonio knew and recorded its name) and Bosch's untitled one hung in the same palace, perhaps even in the same room. In the eyes of their owner, they belonged together. Both works are themed to the power of women.[25] Adam and Hercules succumb helplessly to the allure of the naked female body. Ensnarement begins with the eye: sight inflames desire, paralyzes the will, and conceals from the subject everything except what he lustfully beholds. In both works, ocular desire forms the crux of a larger story that the painting tells. While briefer than Bosch's cosmic narrative, Gossart's timeline extends from the hero's labors (shown on the pediment) through his choice to rest from them (signaled by the dormant club) to the present instant of his infatuation. This volatile moment already includes its outcome, as Deianira, gazing into her husband's eyes, also lifts the fatal tunic. Women can multitask, while men stand transfixed by their desire. As with Eve and Adam, women act and men react: observe Hercules's haggard features, as if Eros has enfeebled him. Although the consequences of Deianira's action will not reach to the end of time, the tunic, a mesmerizing cascade of painted folds, will become the hero's hell. Thus this single panel has the same left-to-right reading structure and fiery end as Bosch's triptych. Most crucially, Bosch and Gossart center their story on the effect their painting has on us. Both seek to illustrate and to arouse ocular desire. Deianira addresses her nudity more directly to us than to Hercules, who, seated sideways, sees only her eyes, just as in Bosch, Adam's sight line traverses obliquely what we see frontally. Painting tells a story about the seeing it incites, and according to these two very different painters, the sight that painting appeals to can be deadly.

These paintings perform their meaning through the responses they elicit. In a princely art collection, such performances were choreographed events. Whereas in modern museums, paintings hang open and visible while viewers freely pass them by, in Renaissance cabinets of wonder, display was an act and an occasion. Shelved with other treasures rather than hung, painted panels often came with special painted covers or slipcases that symbolically embellished what they protected; opened, these frameworks enhanced the viewer's experience of exhibition as a dynamic event.[26] Bosch's winged triptych had to open in order to be seen. How this dramatic action was performed, who performed it, and whether it was accomplished with a smile, say, or a frown would have clued the viewer to the nature of the display. It is possible that the triptych's first opening marked some specific event. Paul Vandenbroeck has proposed that Bosch painted the ensemble to celebrate one of Count Henry III's marriages—either to Louise-Françoise of Savoy, on August 3, 1503, or to Claudia van Chalon, in May of 1515.[27] The idea is intriguing, given the work's conjugal theme. Born in 1483 in the German city of Siegen, Henry came to Brussels in 1499 at the invitation of his uncle Engelbert II, Lord of Breda and ruling Count of Nassau, who, being without legitimate issue, named his nephew as his heir. Henry then spent the period from 1501 to 1503 in Castile as the boon companion of Duke Philip the Fair. The son of Emperor Maximilian and Mary of Burgundy, and the father of Charles V, Philip went to Spain to receive fealty there as king after the crown of Castile and Aragon fell to him unexpectedly through his marriage to the infanta Juana.[28] Henry's absence from the Netherlands until 1503 makes it less likely that he could have ordered from Bosch the triptych for his marriage to Louise-Françoise in that year, and the very late date of Henry's second marriage (the year before Bosch's death), and the earliest felling date (1458) of the wood on which the triptych was painted makes that wedding an improbable occasion for the triptych's unveiling. If Bosch did create it for Henry's 1503 nuptials, then the commission would more probably have come from Engelbert, who could have intended it as a marvelously mischievous wedding gift for his nephew and heir.[29]

The most powerful man in the Netherlands after Emperor Maximilian and Philip the Fair, with noble titles, associations, and administrative offices that take pages to list, Engelbert was an avid patron of the arts, especially of the waning art of Flemish book illumination. He

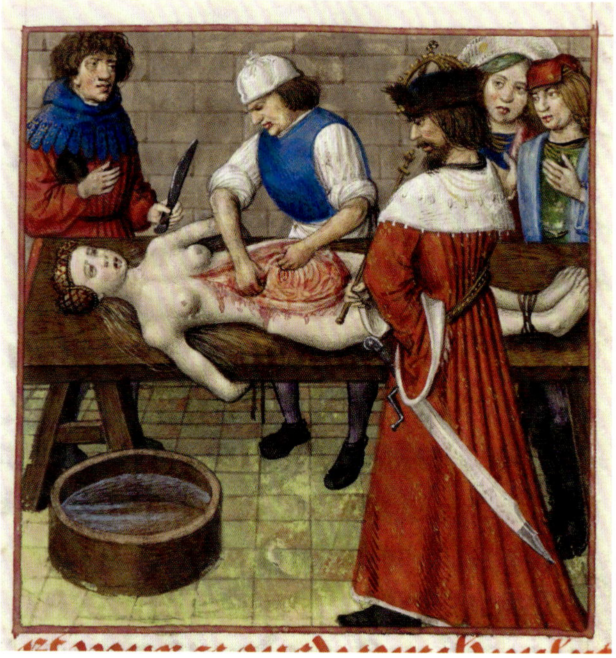

225 South Netherlandish, *Nero looking on as the body of his mother Agrippina is disemboweled, in order to see the place where he was conceived, and praising her beauty*, illumination from Guillaume de Lorris and Jean de Meun, *The Romance of the Rose*, c. 1490–1500, parchment, British Library, London, Harley MS 4425, fol. 59v

commissioned the most lavish surviving manuscript of *The Romance of the Rose*.[30] Produced around 1500 and now in the British Library, its 92 miniatures of amorous pursuits would have appealed to this notoriously Herculean philanderer, who fathered with one of his numerous mistresses at least two children and who probably died of syphilis (fig. 225).[31] It is tempting to imagine that Engelbert commissioned the triptych to terrify delightfully his nephew and heir about the bizarre vicissitudes of conjugal love. The record of payment made by Philip the Fair to Bosch in 1504 (a year after Henry's marriage and the year of Engelbert's death) indicates that noble patrons afforded this painter unparalleled freedom in carrying out his work. The triptych's commission and the revels of its unveiling have left no trace. At its original opening—whenever that occurred—some tone would have been set. I suspect that, even if one were magically transported back to that event, its tone would be difficult to fathom, since it would be based in a dense web of unfamiliar and unspoken social relations. Then as now the spectacle of the work's reception extended rather than resolved the fundamental enigma.

The historian Herman Pleij has studied the interplay between text and performance in descriptions of the fantastical land of Cockaigne.[32] A realm of eternal youth and limitless food, drink, and sex, where roasted birds fly happily to the table and drunkards are kings, Cockaigne was described in some late-medieval manuscripts, neutrally and objectively, as an actual, if faraway or inaccessible, locality where expected natural, legal, and customary restrictions dramatically do not apply (fig. 226).[33] In some surviving texts, however, the invitation to betake oneself to Cockaigne contains a veiled accusation that to do so is to prove oneself a lazy, wanton spendthrift. Other versions start with an explicit warning that the paradise is false and that the speaker lies.[34] Pleij reads these framing statements as attempts to stabilize in the medium of writing a text originally transmitted orally, where nuances in its recitation would have set the tone. Where writing needs to say it speaks tongue in cheek, a speaker can signal irony by putting his tongue in his cheek. Voice, perhaps supplemented by a wink, a smirk, or some rolling of the eyes, puts an audience in on the joke.

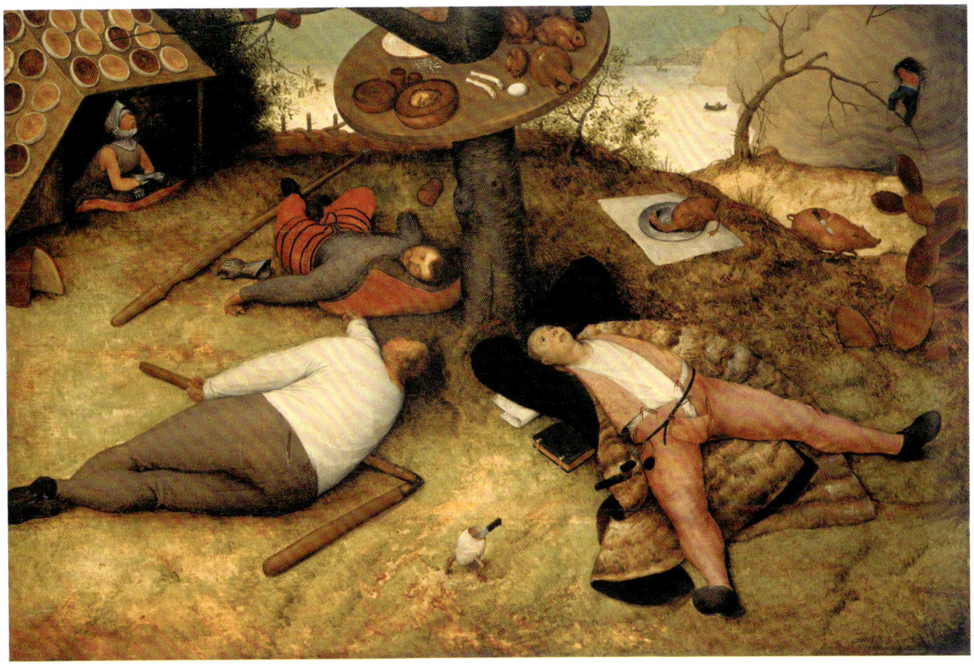

226 Pieter Bruegel the Elder, *The Land of Cockaigne*, 1566, on oak wood, Alte Pinakothek, Munich

Bosch's Hell panel does place a bold question mark after his image of a garden of delight. But it evidently has not sufficed to denounce the whole, since some viewers continue to take the center to be a positive statement about sex or marriage. Things might have been clarified by the work's live performance, which through word or gesture could postfix to the painting's declaration an emphatic "Not!" Even so, the delights of the triptych—like those of descriptions of Cockaigne—fulfilled the deep wishes of their audience. If the painting admonished, it did so having drawn the viewer in. Again, the Nassau palace's big bed might serve as a model. The count encouraged, perhaps even forced, his guests to drink, so that drunk they made spectacles of themselves. Most visitors probably enjoyed drinking, however, and nice things could happen in the bed, so coercion wasn't terribly necessary.

Revelry and cruelty intermingled. In urban festivals of the late Middle Ages, the blind were sometimes rounded up, equipped with makeshift armor and nail-studded clubs, and sent into a ring with a wild boar.[35] As they tried to defend themselves, they would club the beast and one another—blindly—until the beast succumbed and those left standing, if any there were, feasted on roasted pig. Bosch or one of his followers portrayed this intermezzo in a canvas painting inventoried in the Spanish royal collections, and a tapestry after Bosch devoted to cripples, beggars, and vagabonds features swine clubbing in the background (fig. 227).[36] As one observer gushed of a blind boar hunt he had witnessed in the market square of Stralsund on Shrove Tuesday in 1415, "Such a funny carnival game has never been seen!"[37] A pen-and-ink drawing by Jan Verbeeck transports the spectacle from the courtly jousting field of the Boschian tapestry to the more plausible setting of a rustic interior, with smiling onlookers pressing in on all sides (fig. 228).[38] What exactly was so hilarious about this sport? First, blindness seems to have been inherently funny, at least to the sharp-eyed. As Thomas Hobbes put it, "Laughter is nothing else but sudden glory arising from some sudden conception of some eminency in ourselves, by comparison with the infirmity of others."[39] Second, the game amplified the players' deformity and caused them to play it—as it were—to perfection. While they probably had little choice in the matter, having been forced into the ring, and while their antics were in reality excruciating

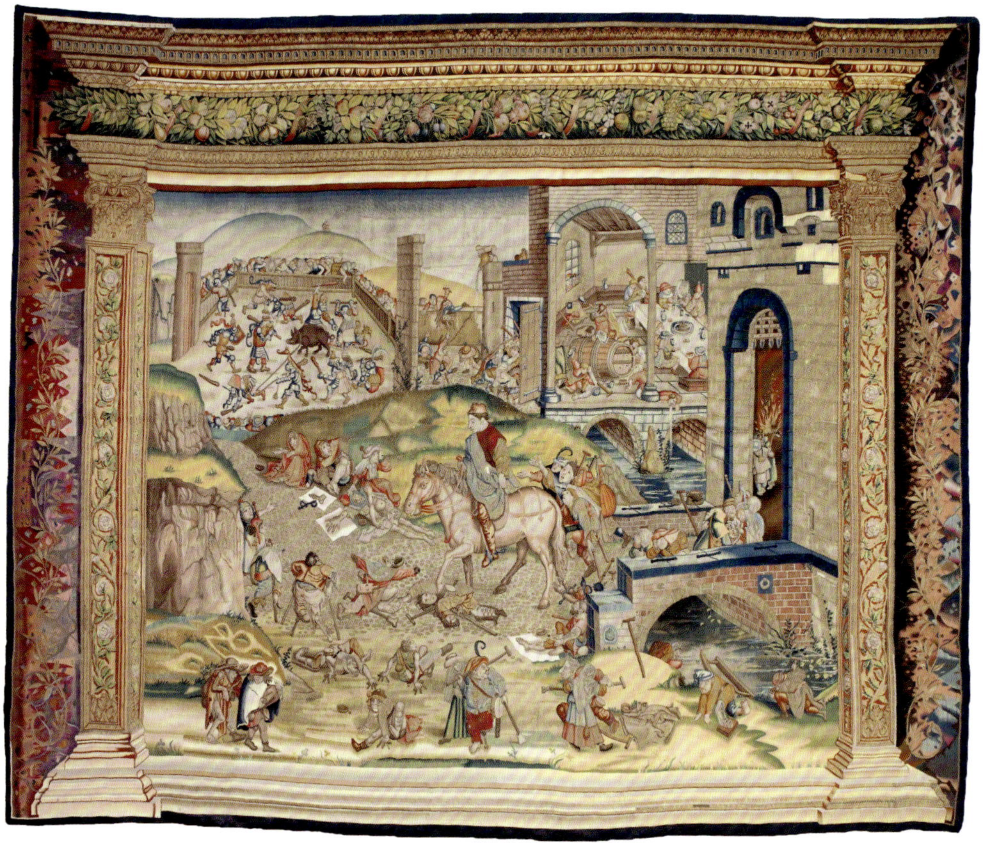

227 Brussels Workshop after Hieronymus Bosch, *A Saint Leaving City*, 1550–70, tapestry in gold, silver, silk, and wool, Palacio Real, Patrimonio Nacional, Madrid

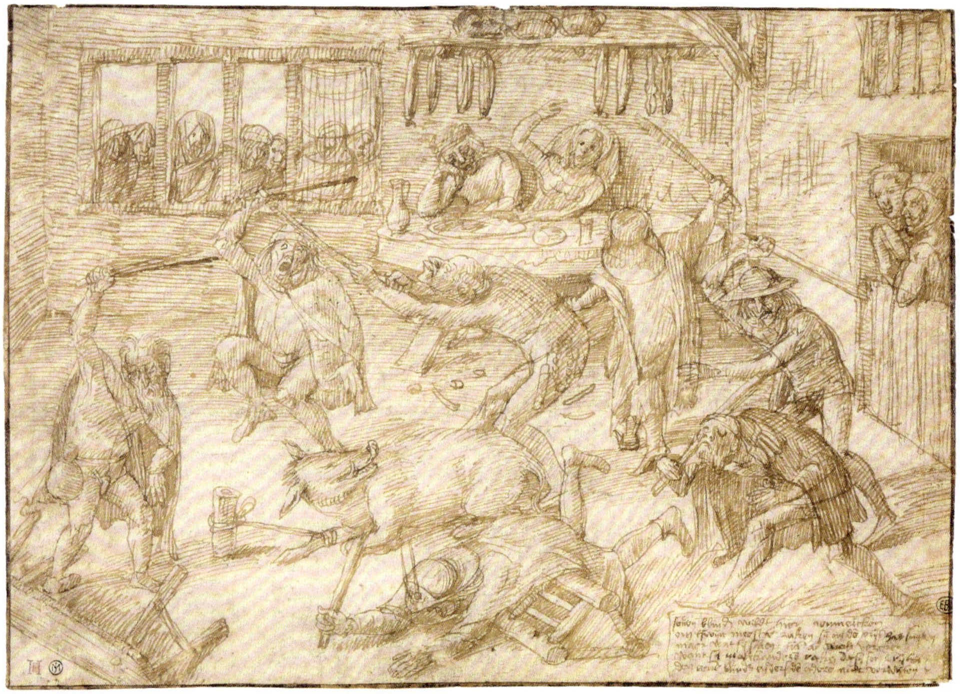

228 Jan Verbeeck I, *The Seven Blind Men Pigsticking*, c. 1560, pen and brown ink, École Nationale Supérior des Beaux-Arts, Paris

mishaps, as they mistakenly bashed one another rather than the animal, they looked as if they acted with heroic, if also misguided and therefore comical, intent. Victims, they appeared perpetrators, confirming the common moral association of blindness with folly.

Third, this sense that their malady was their fault and that the players got what they deserved was heightened by their seeming presumption. The wild boar was a prized beast of venery; its hunt was a noble prerogative. It would have been deemed *lèse-majesté* for anyone of a low status (let alone the lowest status) to pursue this prestigious quarry, and to do so dressed like knights in armor, as if the infirm sought "sudden glory" for themselves, a perception comically reinforced by the putative winners supping afterward at the table of the great. It goes without saying that the real experience of the players was of no importance. Their howls of pain pleased their audience, who could take it as hilarious proof that the blind were like baying dogs at a hunt. Although inflicted on the most marginal members of the social order, this game had much in common with carnival sports more generally pursued. In discussing *The Hay Wain*, we noted how Nuremberg's festive Hell floats resembled Bosch's rolling wagon of sin (see fig. 55). The mock guilds that built and steered these festive structures invited members of the public to ride with them and drink, with the cruel twist that, having freely entered the spectacle, the most enthusiastic revelers were sometimes trapped inside and punished, like the damned in hell. A print purporting to be of Bosch's invention portrays the most famous of these fantastical guilds—that of the Blue Boat—filled with drunks, whores, and criminals: observe the Boschian motif of birds swarming "Skinny Pants" as if he were an owl (see fig. 73).[40] The decision to enjoy a carnival's seemingly licensed excess could trigger rituals of humiliation. The most famous of such cruelly comical rites was charivari, or "rough music."

In charivari, members of the community punished offenders of the social order by serenading them with noise. Produced by makeshift, this cacophony could amicably mock newlyweds, but its full derisive force was mostly aimed at marriages and remarriages deemed unnatural, for example, between couples of unequal age. Charivari sheds considerable light on the giant musical devices featured in the Hell panel of Bosch's nameless triptych. Instruments of sound and pain—the gigantic pipe, drum, trumpet, hurdy-gurdy, and mutant lute-harp—conjure both the cruel din of hell and the rough music of customary castigation. Unfamiliar today, such caterwauling would have been an expectable reward for tasting the picture's perverse delights.

Behind all these sports lies the element of force. In swine clubbing, the blind did not freely volunteer their services. Poverty, helplessness, and coercion brought them into the ring. Once inside, the game compelled them to fight with all their power, but their random blows—struck as often against one another as against their foe—channeled against them the violent force of their audience. This bad joke hinged on the irony of the weak's turning their pitiful force on themselves. In charivari, force was more widely distributed. The rough musicians tended to be tough, young, unmarried men who, physically powerful but with little social status as yet, posed a potential danger to the community.[41] By placing public punishment in their hands, charivari channeled their energy into the social order. This preserved the force of law and kept in power the powerful, who sanctioned but did not join the orchestra.

What, then, were the forces behind the display of Bosch's painting? The triptych opened to a rigidly ranked society. If it meant different things to different people, each response (whatever it was) would also have had a different meaning based on the beholder's social status. Because so few men in Europe could outrank him, and because as its owner he would be in on the painting's joke, the count stood comfortably apart, able to manipulate and monitor the reaction of others. Displayed variously to courtiers, administrators, visiting diplomats and men at arms, the work could pry out secrets, hence the safety of silent wonder. Of Count Henry it was said that he was especially hard against enemies and prideful vassals. Whereas the former he could face in battle, the latter needed to be confronted at home, perhaps using pride-seeking missiles like Bosch's painting.

Built-in ambiguity made the triptych dangerous to behold. But it also fit the context of the wonder cabinet, where objects acted playfully as traps. Consider the most wondrous of all craft goods of the period, the automaton.[42] Conceptual pendants to the jokes of nature, which appeared artful but were natural, automata were artifacts that, because they moved and seemed to speak, looked like living nature. Similar to trompe l'oeil artistry only more marvelous, they entered the European imagination first through literary descriptions, especially ones listing the exotic marvels of the East, where nature and art were thought prodigiously to flourish. And indeed many famous automata did arrive in the Latin West as diplomatic gifts from the Byzantine and Islamic worlds. But soon European craftsmen learned how to make such machines themselves. Just before 1300, Count Robert II of Artois commissioned a famous automaton for his park and castle at Hesdin. Driven by clockwork and hydraulics, these "wonders, sports, artifices, machinery, watercourses, entertainments, and strange things" made one eyewitness, the poet and composer Guillaume of Machaut, confessedly speechless with delight.[43] Extremely fragile, exposed to the elements, and used often, these precision instruments demanded constant upkeep: six groups of monkey marionettes built to nod and wave at visitors had to be meticulously re-covered with badger skins every few years. In 1432, Duke Philip the Good of Burgundy undertook the complete repair of the automata of Hesdin. His account book gives a picture of these "engines of fun":

> Item, there is a window where, when people wish to open it, a personage in front of it wets people and closes the window again in spite of them. Item, there is a lectern on which there is a book of ballades, and, when they try to read it, people are all covered with black, and, as soon as they look inside, they are all wet with water, when one so wishes. And there is another mirror where people are sent to look at themselves when they are besmirched, and, when they look into it, they are once more all covered with flour, and all whitened.[44]

The automata do not merely amaze through independent motion. That motion mischievously assaults the beholder physically. It has been argued that these machines, through their placement in a walled, landscaped park, evoke the scenography of courtly love, where the amorous pursue their object in a garden setting through cunning engines and stratagems.[45] As Bosch and Gossart show, love also traps the trapper, a reversal dramatized at Hesdin when each effort to escape triggered another snare.

The park's machinery made visitors in their finery dirty and wet. The joke was that, as guests, they had to grin and bear it, while their host, better able to afford new clothing, stayed clean and dry. One prank hinged on his remove:

> Item, there is a personage of wood that appears above a bench in the middle of the gallery and fools [people] and speaks by a trick and cries out on behalf of

Monsieur le Duc that everyone should go out of the gallery, and those who go because of that summons will be beaten by tall personages dressed like "sots" and "sottes," who will apply the rods aforesaid, or they will have to fall into the water at the entrance to the bridge, and those who do not want to leave will be so wetted that they will not know where to go to escape from the water.[46]

Cabinets of curiosity projected to visitors the force of their owner. Conceived as microcosms, they represented in miniature a collector's mastery of things. When these things were displayed, eliciting wonder in guests, the collection also modeled the collector's control over persons. At Hesdin, the machinery mimics the ruler's command. Speaking on Philip the Good's behalf, that "personage of wood" summons guests out of doors, where they receive irrational punishment at the hands of rowdies. Sovereign force displays here its terrifying capriciousness. In German political discourse of the early modern period, princely power was described as *Willkür*—Latin *arbitrium*: a will unfettered by any law beyond its own decision.

Bosch's triptych submits its viewers to a force of law that punishes everyone violently and inexorably. With no interdict yet given to Eve and Adam, and without a divine judge visible in the sky, such justice seems cruelly arbitrary. This caprice, however, is the prerogative of an all-powerful God, who can destroy that which he created. But what about the cruel sports occurring on this side of the picture plane? The painting's forms do not move autonomously. The clockwork of desire and its punishment remains frozen, like the icy waters of hell, and the spraying fountains and soot of hell cannot touch us. The picture besmirches inwardly, however, in the thoughts it elicits. And originally, perhaps, it besmirched outwardly in a charivari attending certain responses to this dangerous tableau. At the 1481 meeting of the Order of the Golden Fleece, Count Engelbert—a key member—was censured for immoral behavior, and in the next meeting in 1491, he was reprimanded for the same error and threatened with fines if he did not, above all, stop "surrendering himself to women."[47] His political detractors also charged that his Brussels palace was raised from bribes and illicit plunder, and even his most fawning biographers admit he was a hard and violent man.[48] Yet this strongman's service to Burgundian rule was judicial as well as military.

During the siege of Bruges in 1490, a delegation of the starving citizenry came before Engelbert at his encampment to sue for peace. His response (after promptly decapitating their patrician leaders and displaying their heads on spikes): "You are all criminals due to your perjurious breaking of the Treaty of Tours!"[49] Made in the name of the emperor, the charge was vicious and problematic, since Bruges had a legal if practically useless right of resistance, and according to the rules of war, enemies could be legally slaughtered in battle but were not criminals. Charles the Bold had justified the destruction of Dinant by arguing that, just as common law allowed the houses of outlaws to be utterly destroyed, so too could a rogue city be entirely laid to waste. Under Charles V an idea prevailed that God gave the emperor total power over the world, but in Bosch's day, royal and imperial power were (legally at least) subject to local rights and privileges.[50] Not royal and certainly not imperial, the Burgundian dukes ruled over an exceptional state. Nominally a fiefdom of France, Burgundy had its historical seat in the agricultural region around Dijon. Its sovereignty over the rich mercantile cities of Flanders, with their ancient rights and privileges, was not self-evident. Absolute power had therefore

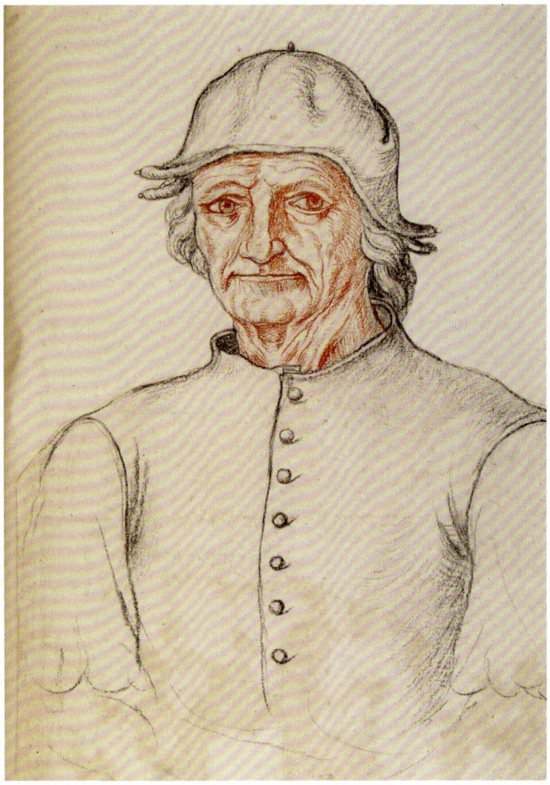

229 Jacques Le Boucq, *Portrait of Hieronymus Bosch*, c. 1550, red and black chalk on paper, from the *Recueil d'Arras*, Bibliothèque Municipale, Arras, MS 266 fol. 275

to be founded extralegally in the emergency state of a polity at war with its parts, which entitled it to destroy entire cities, as Rome did to Carthage.[51] Belated champions of a reconquest of the Holy Land, the dukes of Burgundy also turned their crusade against internal enemies. "These people," said Philip the Good of the citizenry of Liège, "are my Turks."[52] Such policies made the Burgundian Netherlands a model for future state formation by heirs to that rule, as Charles V and Philip II laid claim to universal dominion over the Old World and the New.

The premier painter of anomalies, Bosch excelled in portraying states of exception—wars of all against all, satanic dominions, final reckonings, worlds upside down. For the counts of Nassau he produced his most exceptional tableau: a vision of humanity without law. That divine justice remains in force as the violence of destruction magnifies the law's foundations in the suspension of the law. Such a tableau would have made good sense to the Nassau counts, as it did also to Philip the Fair, who, encamped at 's-Hertogenbosch in 1504 to pursue war against Guelders, commissioned *The Last Judgment* from Bosch. It is no wonder, too, that the Duke of Alba coveted the triptych then in the hands of his Protestant foe. To seize it, he declared in the Netherlands a state of emergency that, claiming some twelve thousand lives, defined war powers for the modern era. It would be an understatement to say that Alba understood the triptych differently than we do. Perhaps he grasped the irony that the picture's enemy is the self—that Adam in us—which cannot be escaped. Over and above this admonishment, however, he would have felt himself allied to the picture's capricious violence as he turned the rebellious towns of Flanders into a Boschian hell. And what did the painting look like to Philip II of Spain as, surrounded by a Europe he felt to be infected by heresy and imposing cruel sovereignty over the idolatrous natives of America, he beheld it in his mammoth hermitage at El Escorial?[53] Through the succession of persons who owned it, the work of art performed the terror it depicts.

"Self" Portraiture

But what about the essential player, the one who originally performed the painting with his brush? Bosch left to posterity no signed portraits of himself. Lampsonius included an engraved effigy of the painter in his *Portraits of Some Celebrated Artists of the Low Countries*, published in 1572 (see fig. 61). Much copied and adapted, this likeness relates to a sketch contained in the *Recueil d'Arras*, a huge compendium of portrait drawings assembled by the Imperial Herald of Arms, Jacques le Boucq (fig. 229).[54] Carefully executed in red and black chalk and inscribed "Jeronimus Bos painctre," the drawing may record a lost prototype available to Lampsonius, as well. Still, the *Recueil* dates from around 1560, a half century after Bosch's death. Aware that many early Netherlandish painters smuggled likenesses of themselves into their compositions, art historians have hunted for echoes of the face in the artist's surviving oeuvre.[55] The frizzy-haired observer at the upper left of the Escorial *Christ Crowned with Thorns* loosely resembles the Arras portrait (see fig. 128), as does (even more loosely) the outward-gazing Magus in Bosch's *Adoration of the Magi* panel now in Philadelphia.[56] A similar outward gaze, sometimes the symptom of an artist painting his image reflected in a mirror, has made the blue-turbaned man at the left edge of *Christ Carrying the Cross* another candidate for the artist's self-portrait (fig. 230).[57] But these instances remain speculative and are of little use in accessing Bosch's person.

Although he left us no signed self-portraits, Bosch did create penetrating portraits of self, works that, in Felipe de Guevara's words, captured the "passions . . . of the soul of man."[58] At this basic level, Bosch's peddler captures the "I" pursuing its own interests (see fig. 37). The self is concerned with *itself*, with the life that is its *own*. Covetous of and burdened by the paltry possessions, the peddler overlooks his actual condition. Self-consciousness—what Martin Luther, echoing Saint Augustine, called the self's being "curved in up itself"—gives the peddler his disastrous posture: striding forward but glancing back, he misses the cracked footbridge before him and the gallows above.[59] The vertical divide between the panels, passing straight through him, times the painting to his (and our) perilous here and now; opened, it reveals the verdict presently passed against him (and us): the self is empty and vain, like the pile of hay that takes the peddler's place and pace. Synonymous with pride, self is also the root cause of the Fall, as the Eden panel shows. Extended through the entire program of the triptych, such a portrayal may explain why Bosch made no straightforward self-portraits. The peddler's anonymity, his being everybody by being a nobody or nothing (like hay), befits his paradoxical condition. Identity—who one *is* defined by what is *one's own*—slips away, as things do to the frenzied multitude that tries to have them. If, as some contend, the artist portrayed himself in the guise of the peddler, then this identity was built to pass away, for, as the painting preaches, "all flesh is grass."

Bosch elsewhere pictures a solution to the self's predicament. The ascetic Saints Jerome and Anthony—felicitous namesakes of the artist and his painter father—exemplify pious self-loathing. In the Lisbon triptych, the praying hermit gazes backward, like the peddler (see figs. 37 and 139). But rather than attend confusedly to his present peril, and aware that "self" is his enemy, Anthony looks directly at us. Observing our response to it, assessing us either as enemy or as friend, the painting portrays us—in Sigüenza's words—"on the inside." Such a reading, which accords with the artist's earliest commentators, makes Bosch a more compulsive self-portraitist than even Dürer. Dürer left us multiple images of his physical person, and he egotistically signed and/or monogrammed almost every product of his hand. But Bosch too paints ego always and everywhere, from the alpha in Eden to the omega in hell.

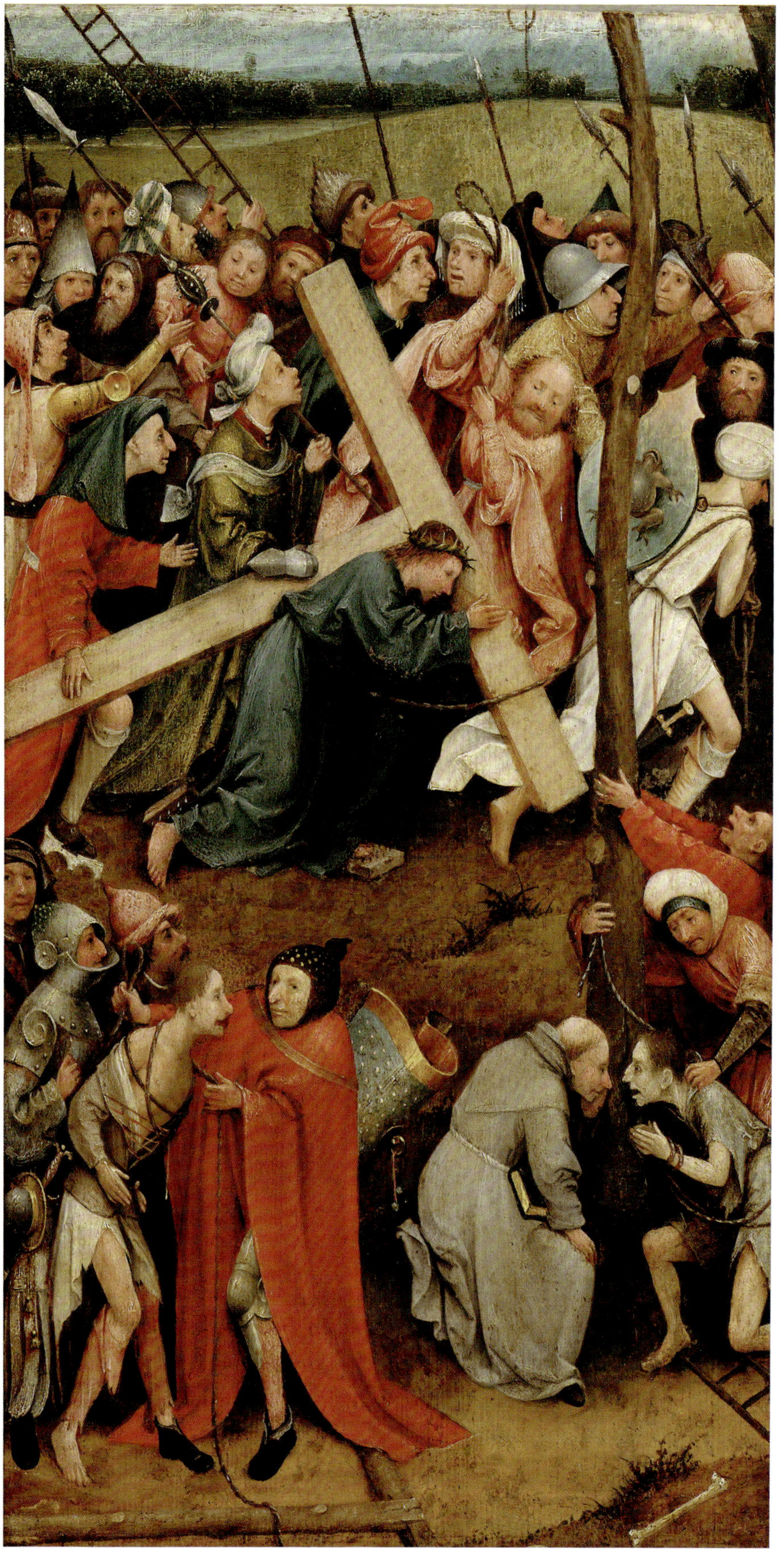

230 Hieronymus Bosch, *Christ Carrying the Cross*, c. 1500, Kunsthistorisches Museum, Vienna

In these portraits, self is an enemy, perhaps even *the* Enemy. And yet sometimes the artist signs them with his name. On the central panel of *The Hay Wain*, on an empty patch at the lower right, the artist (or some steady-handed collaborator) bears witness in bold, black minuscule "jheronimus bosch" (see fig. 39). *The Seven Deadly Sins* has the same inscription, but painted more elusively, dark on dark (see fig. 122). There are five such signatures on works presumed to be by Bosch, plus more on paintings by imitators. As we have seen, Guevara warned of an "infinitude" of pictures fraudulently inscribed with Bosch's name, and the five putatively autograph works that are signed may all be shop products, suggesting that signatures were a branding technique. However, one surviving document notarizes Bosch's signature. The accounts of the confraternity the Brotherhood of Our Dear Lady of 's-Hertogenbosch record a memorial feast paid for, and held at the home of, "Hieronymus van Aken, painter, who signed himself Hieronymus Bosch."[60] Similarly, his obituary, penned around 1575 by a member of the same confraternity, calls him "Hieronimus Aquen[sis] al[ia]s BOSCH, Insignis pictor."[61] And Philip the Fair's record of payment, and the inventories of Philip's sister, Margaret of Austria, and of Cardinal Domenico Grimani, all refer to the artist by his full Latin name. Unusually, too, the orthography of that name remains constant, suggesting it had the character of a maker's mark, like Dürer's famous monogram. As Dürer's did, Bosch's name asserted authorship. More aggressively than any artist in the tradition besides Dürer, it announced that what you see is of this person's making and that in final analysis it is the image *of him*.

The documents assert that Bosch wasn't born Bosch. He borrowed this alias from his natal town. This was a common practice. Already the painter's forebears adopted the surname *Van Aken* when they moved their painting business out of Aachen during the fourteenth century. Similarly, Dürer's father took his name from his Hungarian birthplace, Ajtós, which means "door"—in German *Tür*, hence Türer or Dürer, and the artist's coat of arms featured an open door.[62] Bosch's hometown spawned many toponymic surnames. In 1373, a man known in his trade as Willem Clockgieter ("William Bellfounder") signed a bell that he founded "Wilhelmus de Buskoducis" ("William of 's-Hertogenbosch"), and in the fifteenth and sixteenth centuries several artists besides our painter called themselves "de Bois-le-Duc," "de Bosleduc," "van den Bossche," and "Bos."[63] Usefully for them, but especially so for the artist formerly known as Hieronymus van Aken, that particular place name speaks. A contraction of the Dutch *des Hertogen Bosch*, 's-Hertogenbosch (French, *Bois-le-Duc*; Latin, *Silva Ducis*) means "the duke's forest," thereby remembering its founding in the enormous hunting reserves of Duke Henry I of Brabant. By Bosch's day, the town—one of the four largest in Brabant—had totally supplanted the primordial woods of its name. "For as many rows of trees that once stood in the wild wood," wrote a local humanist poet around 1550, "so many streets and inns now can be seen in this stately city. Truly, just as the dark forest was home to all manner of creatures of different classes and trees of different types, so 's-Hertogenbosch is home to people of every description."[64] Cleared, the trees became the town's totemic symbol. The *bosboom*—a single tree with twisting roots and branches—filled the city's coat of arms, and in municipal seals, badges, and brooches, that emblem hangs within a forest, sometimes with the duke or a stag resting there (fig. 231).[65] The stag (Dutch *hert*) recalls the quarry of the ducal hunt, but it also completes a visual pun: *hert bosch*. Another emblem combined a heart (*hart*), two eyes (*ogen*), and the word *bossche* to visually speak, or "cant," the city's name.

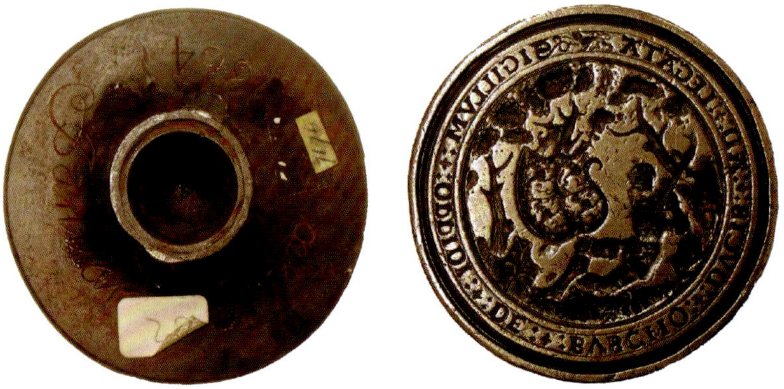

231 Jan van Amsterdam, *Seal of the City of 's-Hertogenbosch with Duke at Rest in the Forest*, 1534–35, silver, Collectie Het Noordbrabants Museum, 's-Hertogenbosch

(OPPOSITE) **232** Hieronymus Bosch, *The Field Has Eyes, the Forest Has Ears*, c. 1500, pen and ink, Staatliche Museen zu Berlin, Kupferstichkabinett, Berlin

Such charades would have encouraged a painter of cryptic signs to sign his own pictures "Bosch." Like Bernard, the twelfth-century cosmologist who called himself Silvestris, the painter, through his alias, might have wished to ally himself to the darker, sylvan side of nature, the *selva oscura* where Dante's *Inferno* also commences.[66] For Silvestris, *Silva* personified primal matter as a restless, disorderly, but independently creative ground. Bosch's nameless triptych thus tells a story about its maker's name: how life first began as vegetal growth from fecund *hyle* (Greek root of Latin *silva*); how Eve awakened the libidinous vitality of Adam; how that desire veered off course among the amorous, vegetal groves of paradise; and how, in the end, everything burns itself out in hell, with a colossal Tree-Man (the only sylvan bit left in the scene) as ruined eyewitness.

It is in the nature of nature that all this could have come about. But it did not. The painting therefore tells a tale not about the world as it actually happened but about itself and its own formation. It portrays how it, the artwork, came into being through a creative agent at one with vital nature but therefore entropic and potentially corrupt. The word *Bosch* may have been further darkened by its proximity to the Dutch and Germanic *boos* or *böse*, meaning "evil."[67] The painter's Spanish admirers, still in touch with the connotations of his name, had *El Bosco* double as the forest he portrays.[68] Several texts from around 1600 find the artist in hell, and Calderón, in a passage where wild beasts of the forest turn into human monsters, has "bushes turn into a picture by Bosch."[69]

Giambattista Vico, writing at the end of the Renaissance humanist movement, traced the origins of human history to the clearing of a primeval forest: "The first cities were founded on cultivated fields. They arose as a result of families being for a long time quite withdrawn and hidden among the religious terrors of the sacred woods."[70] Frightening because sacred and vice versa, the original forest caused humans to experience their alienation from nature, compelling them to burn a place for themselves. This clearing—celebrated by the panegyric on Bosch's hometown—is where history begins. In Vico as in Silvestris, the woods stand for brute, untamed nature. Clearing them requires more than reason, because reason makes sense of, but does not transcend, what is naturally given. Clearing requires instead the powers of the poetical imagination. Entangled in the terrors of the woods but enabling their transformation into fields and cities, the imagination brings forth—as its primal poiesis—a new world, the human one of culture.

Nowhere are the powers of Bosch's productive imagination more evident than in his three autonomous drawings, and in each of these the protagonist is a tree. In the most overtly enigmatic of these puzzling sheets, now in Berlin, a dead tree serves as shadowy refuge for an owl, which eyes us with dubious intent (fig. 232).[71] Shrieking birds—probably magpies—have

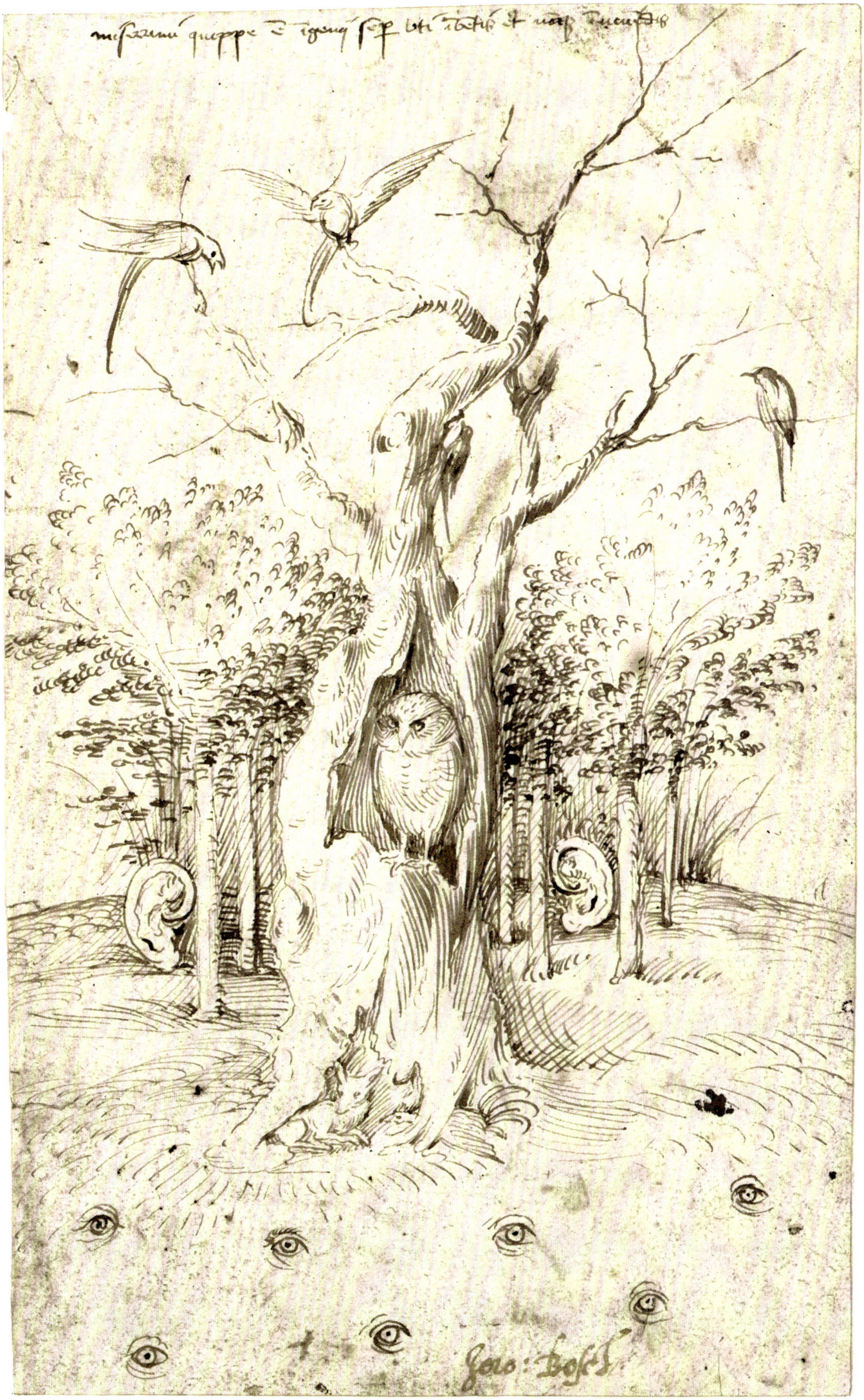

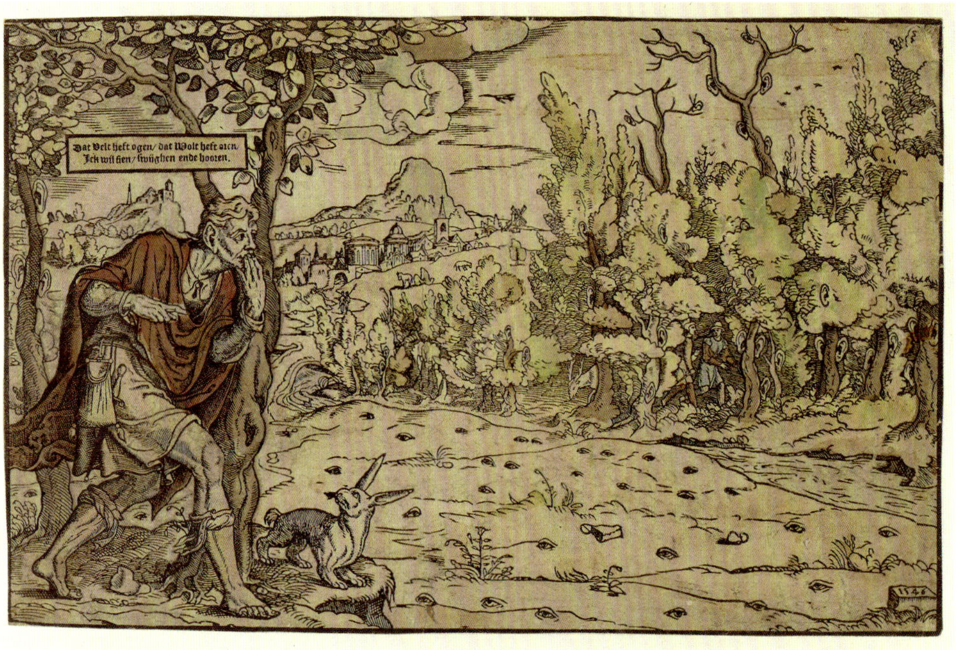

233 Anonymous Netherlandish, *The Fields Have Eyes, the Woods Have Ears*, 1546, hand-colored woodcut, Kupferstichkabinett Staatliche Museen, Berlin

swooped down to perch on the twisted branches, while in a hollow at the tree's base a rooster pushes his way toward a resting fox. The tree stands in a field that slopes subtly downward at both sides, so that the scene's horizon has the subtle curvature of the surface of the earth, ensuring that whatever the work's statement is, it will be global. Behind the tree rises a dense grove in which appear two outsize ears. Portrayed in all their convoluted specificity, these auricles—the left one pressed against the thicket's edge, the right one set deeper among the trees—flank the drawing's center in such a way that between them an anamorphic face comes into view, with the owl's gaze as its eyes. Complicating this arrangement are items scattered on the ground before the tree, which on close inspection reveal themselves to be seven differentiated eyes.

Historians have managed to reattach these stray sensoria to a proverb current in Bosch's day and published and illustrated in a woodcut dated 1546: "The field has eyes and the wood has ears; I will look, stay silent, and listen" (fig. 233).[72] The proverb warns of the perils of a hostile social order where the wise man keeps his counsel. Bosch issues this warning silently by means of elusive ears and eyes that seem to have been marking us before we found them. First glimpsed, the owl's aggressive gaze submits us to a peril not unlike his own as magpies mob him at his daytime roost. Trappers used owls as lures, tethering them to perches spread with birdlime (see fig. 10). Diurnal birds mobbed the nocturnal nest robber, but if they landed they would get stuck.[73] The drawing signals such impending danger through the fox, which seems to rest but casts a sly glance toward the foolish rooster.

Foxes and roosters are natural enemies, but through fable and phrase they stand for enmity in the social realm. Gossips are magpies, deceivers are foxes, and people are generally backstabbing snoops. Cities conceal more perils than do the primal woods. Bosch's art thrives in a condition where the "I" is attacked on all sides by implacable foes. But is the owl for us or against us? It certainly looks sinister peering at us from darkness. Mobbed and engulfed, however, the owl also teaches us to look, be silent, and listen. Hunting at night and shunning the sun, owls were thought to be the animal familiars of witches, devils, and Jews.[74] Much more rarely, these creatures could instead stand for wisdom and their mobbing could signify envy. The text

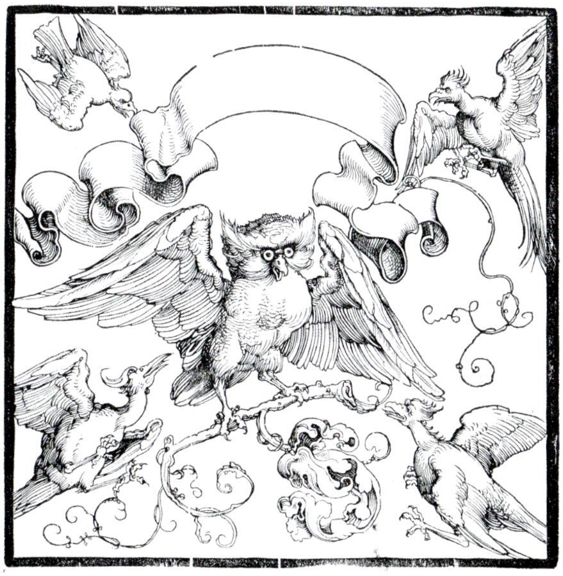

234 Albrecht Dürer, *Owl Attacked by Three Birds of Prey*, woodcut (Nuremberg: Hans Glaser, c. 1515), Kunstsammlungen der veste Coburg, Germany

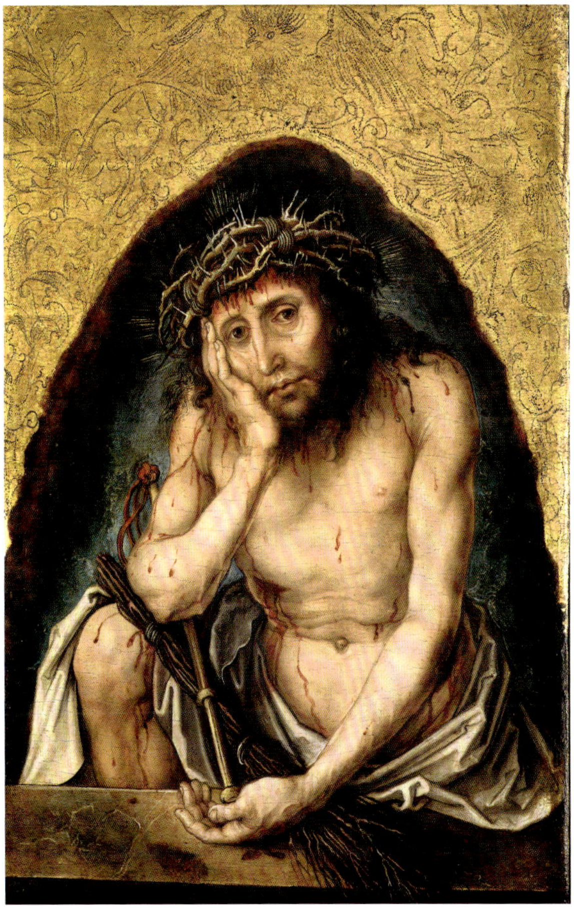

235 Albrecht Dürer, *Christ as Man of Sorrows*, c. 1492–1493, oil on pinewood, Staatliche Kunsthalle, Karlsruhe

on a 1515 broadsheet, probably by Dürer, sides with the owl, as does that painter's early *Christ as Man of Sorrows*, where a mobbed owl—outlined by punches in the gold ground—stands for Christ's torment or for the predicament of sin from which we are redeemed through Christ (figs. 234 and 235).[75] Bosch probably keeps both the positive and the negative valences in play, not only because he likes ambiguity, but also because the self that the owl at once figures and assaults is ambiguous. In Bosch, ego is always a victim that discovers itself as its tormentor.

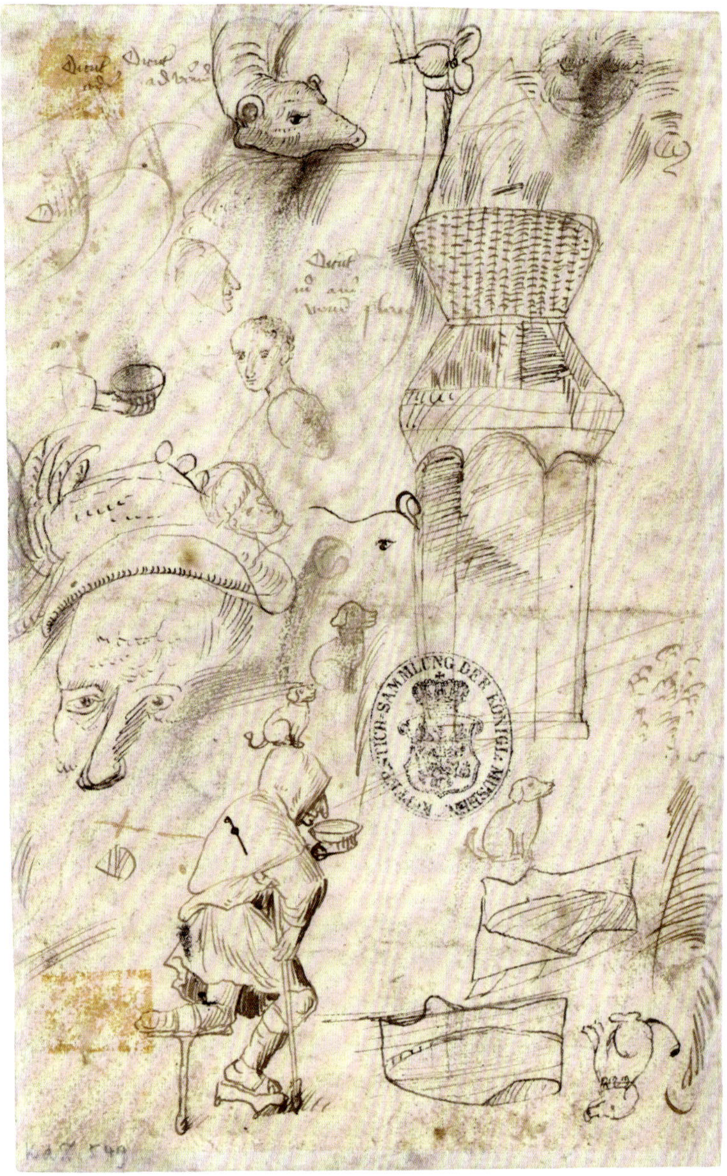

237 Hieronymus Bosch (Workshop?), *Miscellaneous Studies*, c. 1510, pen and ink, Staatliche Museen zu Berlin, Kupferstichkabinett, Berlin

The back of *The Owl's Nest*, largely inaccessible, contains rough sketches.[81] Drawings imitative of Bosch's style also fill the verso of *The Field Has Eyes* (fig. 237).[82] There a rather deft drawing of a cripple looks to be by a more practiced hand than the rest. Someone else—probably an apprentice or collaborator in Bosch's shop—tried thrice to copy the dog drawn as if seated on the cripple's head. Either this novice used the back of *The Field Has Eyes* for scratch paper, or Bosch deposited his graphic masterpiece on the back of a used sheet. Both are possibilities, since paper was costly and drawings had no market at the time. Either way, the exercises deposited on the verso suggest that Bosch initially made the drawing on the recto for himself, perhaps as a personal mirror reflecting back to him his capacity to invent (see fig. 232). The Latin at the top of the sheet bears witness to what he thought about his work. Penned in the same brown ink as the sketch, it was probably inscribed by the artist. The sole surviving sample of his handwriting, the text gives rare insight into Bosch's understanding of his art.

The inscription reads: "Most miserable is the mind that uses always invented things, never inventing anything itself." (*Miserrimi quippe e[st] i[n]genii se[m]p[er] u[t]i inventus et nu[m]*

q[uam] i[n]veni[en]dis.) It derives from *De Disciplina Scholarium*, an early thirteenth-century training manual for scholars issued under the false but authoritative name of Boethius and widely circulated in manuscript and incunable copies.[83] Not an original statement by the artist, this compacted Latin text nevertheless evidences a level of erudition unusual for painters of the period. In 1486 or thereabouts, Bosch's "sworn membership in the Confraternity of the Illustrious Dear Lady of 's-Hertogenbosch"[84] was enjoyed by only about sixty of the ten thousand or more regular members. It was reserved mainly for clerics; highborn laity belonged to a second core group called "Swan Brothers." Probably educated in a Latin school, Bosch would have needed to complete the first steps toward ordination; he may even have been tonsured. Such a religious formation, plus his immense artistic talent and an advantageous marriage to the wealthy Aleid van de Meervenne, would have permitted Bosch—son of a mere artisan—admission to one of the Netherlands' most exclusive clubs. Membership gave Bosch close contact with elites in and beyond his city, widening his horizons and circle of patronage. The commissions he received from members of the Burgundian nobility depended on these vital connections. Sworn members and Swan Brothers included prominent theologians, architects, physicians, scholars, musicians, and composers, as well as priests, patricians, and nobles. Educated at Europe's leading schools and universities, these distinguished and learned men met weekly at the church and often feasted at banquets held at one of the members' homes or in the confraternity house.

Through his own labors, Bosch experienced the mystery of poiesis: how the mind, communing with the hand and eye, can create marvelous novelties. Through the many well-read members of his confraternity, he may have learned what to say about this mystery. Amazingly, his only preserved bit of handwriting compresses into one motto the core terms of humanist rhetoric. The subject is the mind, or one faculty thereof, termed *ingenium*. For Cicero, *ingenium*—roughly "ingenuity"—was the seminal virtue that distinguished people from animals. In the motto, its activity is the most elemental one of *usus* ("use" or "practice"). And what ingenuity uses is *inventio* ("invention"), either its own or of others. For Cicero, ingenuity consists in catching sight of new relationships among the givens of this world. Such poetical combination—based chiefly in the discovery of likeness—is the highest and most urgent activity, loftier even than the art of proof, since only through invention are things or circumstances given a distinctively human use. Necessity besieges us in ever new forms. Through invention, ingenuity overcomes the difficult situations to which humans, otherwise defenseless creatures, perennially stand exposed. The origin of work, the arts, society, and history, invention clears the primal forest and transforms nature into culture.

Humanists championed the human power to invent. Invention turns mimesis into poiesis. To invent is not merely to imitate nature but to bring forth something new. Emerging in antiquity, this idea came under attack during the Christian Middle Ages. With creation of the monopoly of an all-powerful God, the human pursuit of novelty—synonymous with curiosity (German *Neugier*, literally "lust for the new")—was condemned as the cause of Adam's Fall and the source of human misery.[85] But the idea of the creative individual survived under the veil of conjecture or was vacuum packed in learned adages such as the one that Bosch retrieved and used in his drawing. Renaissance humanism was centrally a renewal of classical rhetoric, of the art of persuasive speech. This renewal brought more than an improved rhetoric, however. It entailed a new estimation of rhetorical figures, and of metaphor in particular. The discovery of a likeness between unlike things, metaphor was not only an essential moment in rhetorical speech; it was also the very essence of the human capacity to recombine and thus to remake the givens of the world.[86] This is why humanists accorded artists such a high status. Of all human activities, art making demonstrated most dramatically the power not only to fashion a likeness but also to combine likenesses inventively to create something new. Attributing divinity to great poets and artists rested on the perception that they fashioned something never heard or seen before.

It is commonly believed that the cult of artistic originality was born in Italy, but one of its most vocal early avatars was a northerner.[87] According to Dürer, novelty was art's highest claim. As he put it in a text drafted in 1512, "A good painter is inwardly full of figures, and were it possible for him to live on eternally, he would always, out of the inner ideas of which Plato writes, have something new to pour forth through the work."[88] It is a curious thought. Human creativity is not bounded by an impairment brought by Adam's Fall, such as the one that, by Dürer's own account, bars us forever from knowing or creating absolute beauty. Nor is it limited by the completeness of a divinely created cosmos, where, as Aquinas firmly concluded, "to create can be the action of God alone."[89] Rather, death alone limits creativity, which otherwise flows ceaselessly from great makers into their works. In its final formulation, published posthumously in 1528, Dürer moderated slightly the thought. Now it is "through the power God has given man" that the great artist produces novel forms, and the imagined time span of their productive potential has shrunk to a more modest "many hundred years."[90] Yet poiesis retains its power to create things altogether new—"what one never has seen before nor has another ever thought."[91]

Leonardo da Vinci made similar pronouncements about the "divine nature" of painting, how the artist's mind, transformed by knowledge into an image of God's mind, could generate the entire panoply of nature. But in Leonardo, it was still nature that the artist reproduced, not "something that never was."[92] Not every artist possessed this capacity. According to Dürer, creativity was an inborn gift bestowed only on certain exceptional individuals: "It comes alone from inspiration poured in from above" and gives whoever has it "an equality with God."[93] It takes such genius to know genius: "Only powerful artists will understand this strange statement, that . . . someone will sketch something in a day on a half-sheet of paper . . . and it turns out better and more artistic than someone else's major work that took a year of hard work to make."[94] The recognition cuts across cultures. Beholding in Antwerp gold artifacts brought back from Mexico, Dürer marveled above all at their crafting: "I saw wondrous artistic things and wondered at the subtle ingenuity [*subtilen jngenia*] of people in strange lands."[95] Closer to home, Dürer recognized his own genius and sought to defend it against its enemies, the plagiarists. "Beware, you envious thieves of the work and inventions [*laboris et ingenii*] of others," warns a colophon that Dürer appended to several of his woodcut editions. "Keep your thoughtless hands from these works of ours."[96]

Already in 1500, Dürer gave his perception of artistic creativity an enduring emblem. His *Self-Portrait* painted in that year looks back in time via a cascade of images into an apostolic past (fig. 238).[97] Through Van Eyck's portrait panels of the Holy Face and through the Saint Veronicas of countless earlier German painters and printmakers, the self-portrait reaches toward the mythic icons of Christ produced miraculously "without human hands." Beyond these, it also gestures—by way of the ideal proportions the artist gives himself—to Christ,

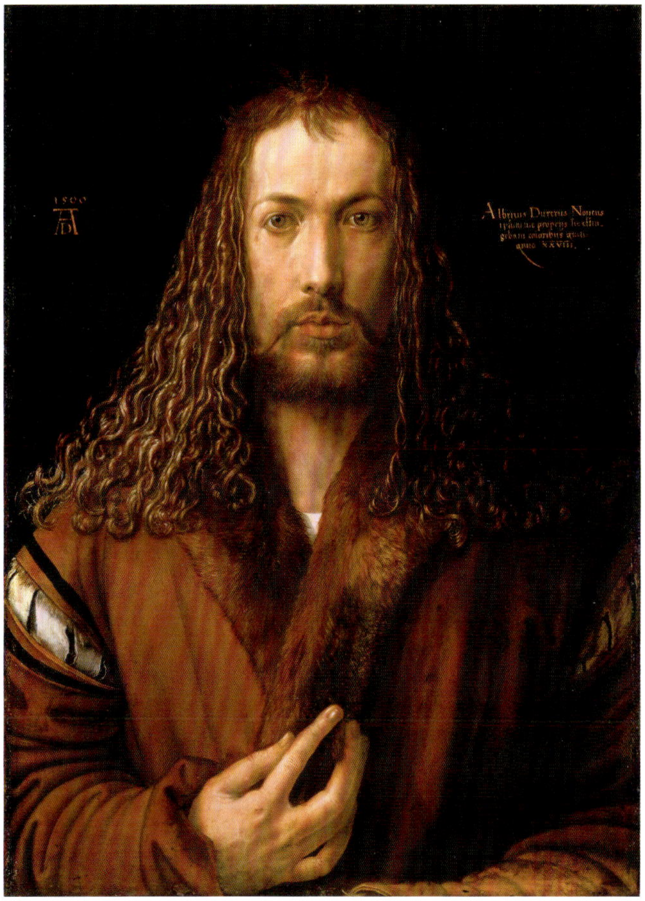

238 Albrecht Dürer, *Self-Portrait in a Fur-Trimmed Coat*, 1500, panel, Alte Pinakothek, Munich

born as God's perfect image and likeness exactly fifteen hundred years before Dürer made the picture. But the painting also faces forward. Dürer's presumed biological apogee, at twenty-eight years of age (the inscription boasts this magic number), coincides wondrously with the calendrical turning point of the half-millennium. The painting tells us that through Dürer history begins anew.[98] The artist appears perennially to see us in our here and now—and we him, in living colors that never fade, as the Latin inscription suggests. He also shows himself eternally in the act of pouring forth into the made. At the base of the panel, a bit of the cuff enclosing the artist's right hand peeks into view, insisting that Dürer—beholding himself in a picture-size mirror—is now painting with that hand the picture we behold. With genius pouring into him from above, the artist pours forth from below his new creation.

Dürer faces us as body, gaze, actor, and signatory in a historical and biographical moment that remains present now. Preparing his image for posterity, he affirms the truth and beauty of his product as well as his person. Bosch, by a contrast that could not be greater, portrays self indirectly, through puns, ciphers, and reflections that demonize rather than deify. And if self faces in our direction, in the backward glance of the peddler or the Tree-Man, or as our own image mirrored back to us, it displays a hole at its center and hell all around. Yet in the Berlin sheet, above the owl's hollow, Bosch writes a statement surprisingly similar to the ones Dürer will make, with its scorn for cribbers and its praise of inventive *ingenium*. And the drawing does parade novelty. It thrusts us back into nature and then alienates us with counternatural eyes and ears. Old proverbs may naturalize these anomalies by making them parts of speech, but the whole remains secretive and new. Is this visual enigma that sees, hears, and speaks

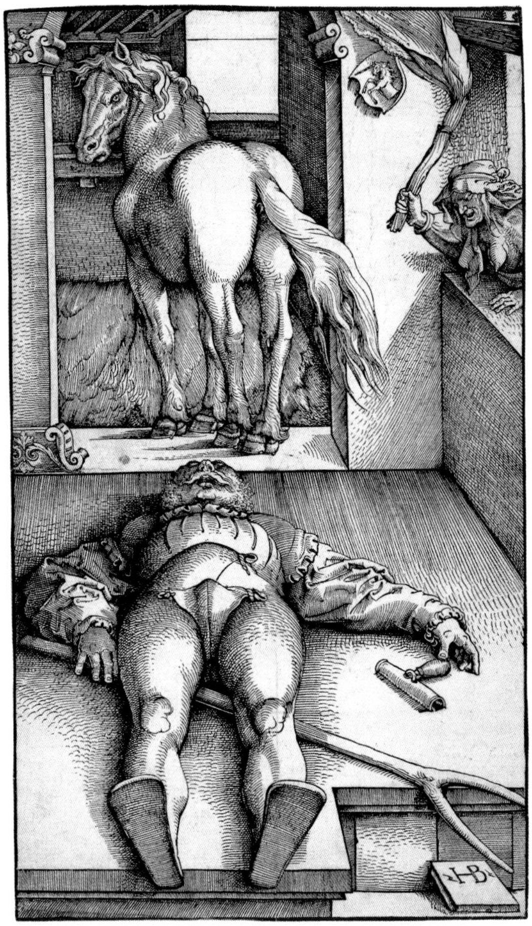

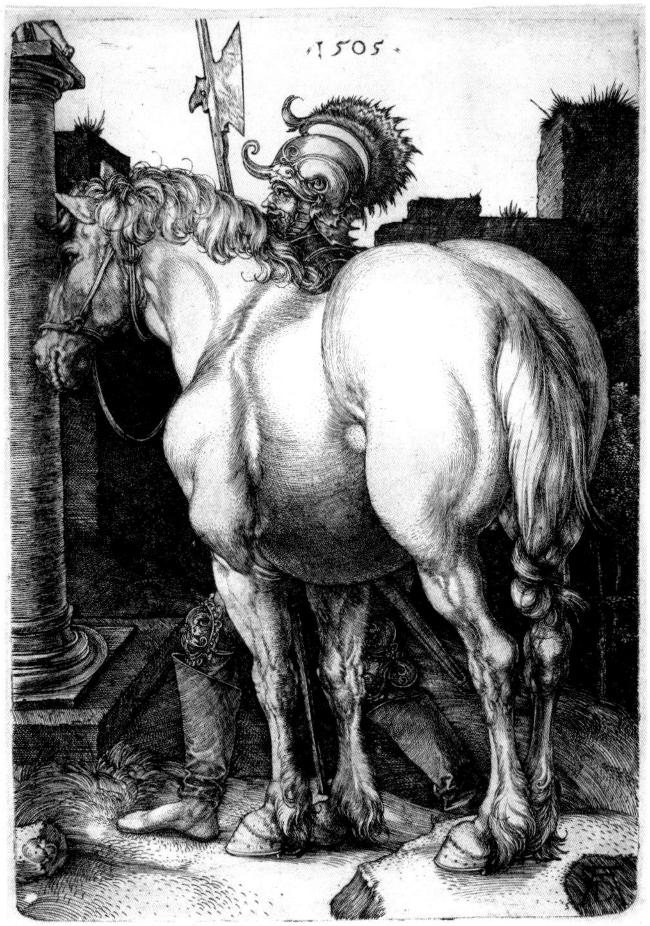

(LEFT) 239 Hans Brosamer Grien, *Bewitched Stable Groom*, 1544, woodcut, The British Museum, London

(RIGHT) 240 Albrecht Dürer, *The Large Horse*, 1505, engraving, The British Museum, London

actually a disfigured visage of the artist? Was this a different and slightly earlier moment of self-portraiture than that of Dürer, who was Bosch's junior by almost twenty years?

The subject of the drawing's inscription is not the inventive genius but its opposite, the copyist. This pertains to the artist only negatively, as the drawing itself proves he is not. It also identifies an adversary. If Guevara is to be believed, plagiarists bedeviled Bosch, counterfeiting his signature and "smoking their pictures in fireplaces to lend them credibility and an aged look."[99] Forgery is the flip side of the original. A maker invents, brands his invention, and expects profit in return. But inventions can be copied, with the inventor's name attached, the plagiarist stealing his income and diluting the brand. Dürer was the first artist to sign almost all his works, and his signature—the nestled initials of his monogram—was the first to be extensively forged, entangling him in lawsuits and (as we have seen) compelling him to introduce into his prints protective covenants against copyists.

The flipside—literally—of Bosch's *The Field Has Eyes* exhibits slavish imitation (see fig. 237). Prototypical to begin with, the seated dog gets copied line by line with varying degrees of success by some apprentice seeking to capture his master's graphic style. After all, shop practice demanded that work done by assistants be undetectable in paintings contracted to be by the master's hand. The value of a Bosch rested not only on the originality of its subjects but also on the distinctive manner in which these were portrayed. Through the heightened spontaneity of the brushstroke or pen line, that manner (from Latin *manus*, or "hand") acquired the character of a signature. When noble collectors inventoried an object as a "Hieronymus

Bosch," it was this entanglement of figure, facture, and fabricator that they named. Messing up the verso of the Berlin sheet, imitations swarm the autograph dog rather as magpies do the owl on the recto. However it came about, whether by cunning or accident, these miserable scribbles do suggest that copying began already in the painter's workshop, and that both the inscription and the drawing pertain to the artist's predicament. In the guise of an owl, Bosch stands surrounded by spies and thieves. The enigmatic character of his art, which is to say the secrecy Bosch maintains about his ultimate intentions, becomes thus a defense against this dangerous predicament.

One expects Renaissance self-portraits to be like Dürer's: direct, identifiable, and ideal. But an opposite mode also flourished in the period. Artists sometimes signaled their identity obliquely, and within a condition of all-pervasive evil. Such self-portraits *in malo* were a specialty of artists working immediately in Dürer's wake.[100] In a woodcut by Hans Baldung Grien, printed about a year before the artist's death, in 1545, the three subjects that had inspired this macabre Dürer disciple—the witch, the wild horse, and the undead cadaver—conspire to undo him (fig. 239).[101] The prone stable groom and the "H. B." monogram beside him represent, respectively, the artist's physical person and the mark of his authorship. No longer surveying the world with a sovereign gaze, and almost unrecognizable due to the eccentric angle of our view, the artist lies dead or asleep, his closed eyes cut through by the dizzying edge of the floor. In the background, touched by the witch's flame, the unicorn of Baldung's family's coat of arms rears up as if responding libidinously to the horse. The horse is specifically a mare in heat. She has either rear-kicked the stable groom or bewitched him with her menstrual vapor. Evoked by her flame-like tail, such desire-inducing effluences—termed *hippomanes* or "horse madness"—were believed to be collected by witches and used in black magic.[102] Thus the artist shows himself toppled by what he imaginatively invents. Fixing us with her eye and her winking labia, the fantastical mare also mimes how the crafted image—the woodcut itself—acts upon the viewer. Ready to copulate not with a stallion but with the Devil, the beast turns now to us, who approach her dangerously from the rear. This puts Baldung, who made this perverse tableau, against us and among the enemies that apparently have undone him.

Debased and radically foreshortened, the artist appears negatively, as that inert body lying there. The obverse of Dürer's *Self-Portrait*, this is also the ironic revenge of the mind that "never invent[s] anything itself." Baldung lifted his portrayal of the mare from Dürer's *Large Horse* engraving (fig. 240).[103] Published in 1505, while Baldung managed Dürer's shop in Nuremberg, that print shows the animal well bridled, its tail tied neatly in a knot and its foreshortened form fitted snugly into the confines of the view. Just as the horseman controls his mount, the print implies, and just as reason can control desire, so too art is capable of mastering nature. Baldung steals Dürer's invention but then undoes it, giving nature and libido the upper hand. Artistic influence turns into toxic effluence. The mare's unbound tail mimics the terrifying effects of witchcraft and of artistic invention.

Baldung is not the only artist of his day to link self-portraiture *in malo* to travestied imitation. Dürer's preternatural originality aroused a self-conscious malice in his followers, who, seeking to assert their originality as Dürer had done, had to copy that titanic master's inventions. One more example must suffice. The Swiss painter, playwright, and mercenary soldier Niklaus Manuel Deutsch used an engraving by Dürer as the basis for his drawing of an airborne witch (figs. 241 and 242).[104] Dürer's earliest print of a proportionally structured nude,

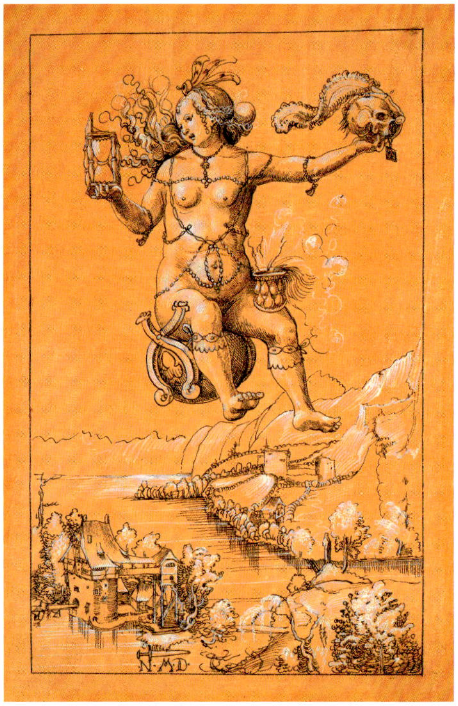

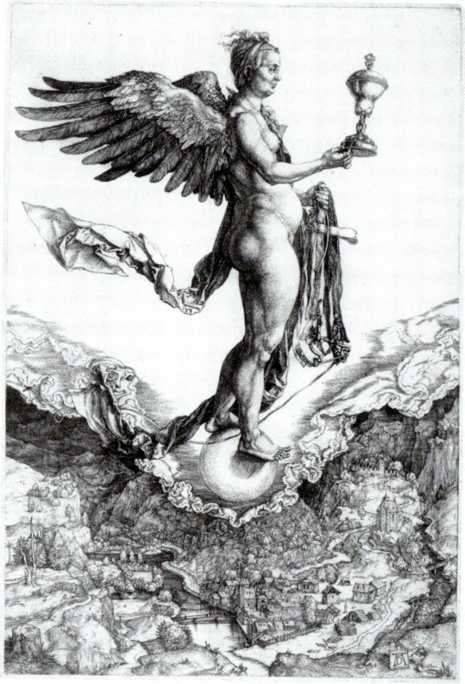

241 Niklaus Manuel Deutsch, *Witch Carrying Skull of the Artist*, c. 1513, pen and ink, heightened in white, on brownish-orange prepared ground, Kunstmuseum, Kupferstichkabinett, Basel

242 Albrecht Dürer, *Nemesis* (*Large Fortune*), 1502, engraving, The British Museum, London

the *Nemesis* engraving shows the winged goddess of measure, who rewards with her goblet those who are temperate and restrains with her bridle those who are not. A constructed body floating above an immense landscape view, she also personifies the two arts of measurement central to Dürer: human proportion and linear perspective. Manuel turns Nemesis into a witch. In place of the goblet and harness, she offers sex and death. The skull in her hand is specifically the artist's. Wearing a mercenary's feathered beret, the death's head dangles from its upper jaw a tag initialed "NMD." This macabre self-portrait is something the witch uses to cast her spell, making the artist her victim. But Manuel also puts his initials at the base of the sheet, allying his art with hers. Witch and skull mix desire with repulsion, but so too does the drawing, where the witch-prostitute's hair and malignant vapors evidence Manuel's calligraphic flair.

Because his blinding originality severely limited theirs, Dürer's followers had a special insight into the underside of artistic creativity: how, once brought forth, the created thing becomes an independent, potentially hostile force. Their self-portraits *in malo* transmit into the modern era an old prejudice: whatever does not come from God comes from the Devil. The idea troubles major masters, as well. In his *Last Judgment* fresco in the Sistine Chapel, Michelangelo may have portrayed himself as the flayed flesh held by Saint Bartholomew, perhaps as an appeal for redemption, perhaps also as penance for artistic ambition, since Apollo flayed Marsyas for challenging divine artistry (fig. 243).[105] Playing on a conceit pioneered by Giorgione in his *Self-Portrait as David*, Caravaggio made a more obvious confession when he gave his own features to the giant's ghastly visage in his *David with the Head of Goliath*, now in Rome (fig. 244).[106] Working under Caravaggio's influence, Cristofano Allori cast himself in the role of Holofernes in his *Judith* of 1613.[107] Paolo Veronese and Palma Vecchio may have done the same in their paintings of Judith now in Vienna and Florence, respectively. These pictures cast the artist as victim of the power of women, as did Baldung's woodcut and Manuel's drawing.

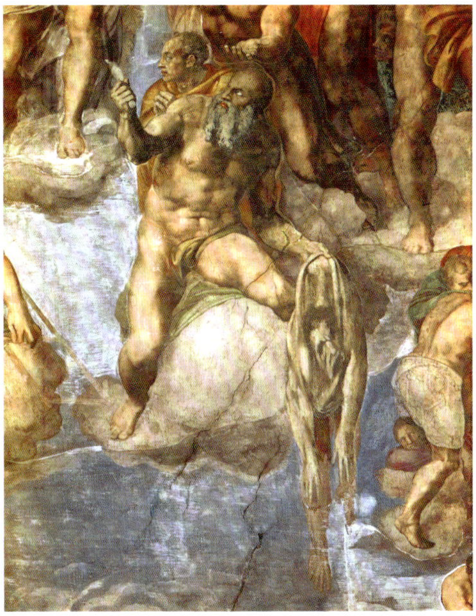

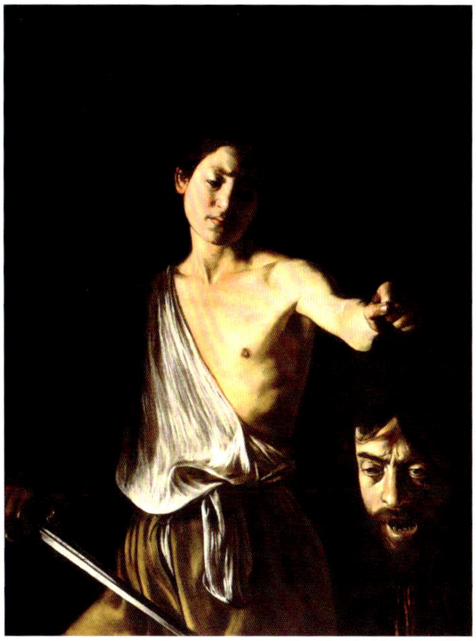

(LEFT) 243 Michelangelo, detail of flayed Saint Bartholomew, from *Last Judgment*, pre-restoration, 1535–41, fresco, Sistine Chapel, Vatican

(RIGHT) 244 Caravaggio, *David with the Head of Goliath*, 1609–10, canvas, Galleria Borghese, Rome

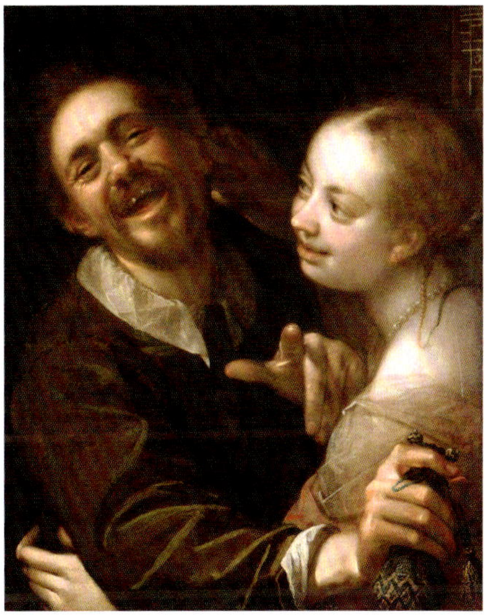

245 Hans von Aachen, *A Playful Couple* (*Self-Portrait with Prostitute*), c. 1596, canvas, Kunsthistorisches Museum, Vienna

Later generations of northern painters often depicted themselves as players in scenes of debauchery. Jan Steen sometimes appears with his whole family among the merrymakers of his genre pictures; Rembrandt—in the self-portrait now in Dresden—posed as Prodigal Son, with Saskia, his wife, as the prostitute on his lap; the lowlife painter Adriaen Brouwer blows smoke rings at the viewer in a little tavern scene, now in New York; and already in a panel from the 1590s, Hans von Aachen, laughing as a prostitute pulls his ear, looks, and points at us as if we are the butt of the joke (fig. 245).[108] Through the contact they make with us, these likenesses perform the function of a chorus: hailing us, they draw us into the picture and into the revels there depicted. The laughter of the artist aims to infect us, so that, smiling too, we mirror the person who portrayed his smile using a mirror.

Thrusting us into the riot of everyday life, these self-portraits advertise the vivacity of the painter's art. Genre painters were experts in ordinary existence. According to his biographers, Bruegel knew festive peasants because he had been one himself, and because he later joined their revels in disguise. Revelry symbolized the fullness of life as well as the immersive

246 Hieronymus Bosch, *The Tree-Man*, c. 1505, pen and brown ink on paper, Albertina, Vienna

experience that lifelike painting could afford. When, from within their paintings, artists toast our debauchery, they do so knowing they will have caused us intemperately to gaze. Self-portraits *in malo* confess to having dragged the viewer into their vicious plot. They also give the painter a distinct persona. It was believed that artists were good at arousing our passions because the passions were especially strong in them. Moreover, the passions fed and were fed by the imagination, a faculty held to be hyperactive in artists, causing them vividly to visualize what would impassion others. Behind these stereotypes lies the mystery of poiesis. Artistic inspiration "pours in" from beyond the artist's control. Art making is ecstatic, like the drunken rites of Bacchus. Self-portraits *in malo* dramatize this by figuring the artist as alien antagonist.

The Tree-Man

No painter's imaginings were more alien than Bosch's; therefore no artistic persona was more malicious. Celebrated maker of monstrosities, Bosch cast these as players in vilifying plots. The fantasies plaguing his hermit saints are diabolical. Nothing to the holy man, who keeps his eye on Christ, they are everything to the painter's admirers. In the décor on the Magi's gifts, in the frieze on Anthony's house of prayer, in the devices of Antichrist's costume, Bosch creates images of imagery, renewing the idol's power while also demonstrating that such power comes from us, from our idolatry. He puts his images in a polemic against them. At war are the old enemies, God and Satan. Poiesis joins the battle, but on the Devil's side, as an activity allied with nature's erring ways, at odds with the created order. Art making springs from *hyle* or primal timber, and before it, from an original nothingness whither everything against God is also bound.

Among the selves that the so-called Tree-Man portrays there is a specific one: the self that signed its products "Bosch." Art history's ultimate oblique self-portrait, this pale visage seems almost to gaze out at us, as it would were it painted from a mirror, with the artist looking him-self in the eye (see fig. 209). But in fact it looks sideways past us to the Boschian imagery that mesmerizes us, and past these scenes to Adam's original fixation. The Tree-Man's dark interior, a cloacal birthplace like Satan's on his latrine throne, illuminates this skewed perspective. The self can never fully see and portray itself because it is nothing at its core.

Perhaps viewers close to the triptych's commission recognized the painter's features in the Tree-Man's face, but with no signed self-portrait remaining, we will never know. And yet, likeness, or the visible similarity between portrait and person, ought to fail in hell. The damned are no longer what they were: "Which way I fly is Hell; myself am Hell," says John Milton's rebel angel in contemplating his predicament.[109] Bosch makes the Tree-Man dimly resemble Adam, in part because all humans stem from Adam, and because what fails them as creatures made "in the image of God" is the corrupting Adam within—note the leprotic sore on the Tree-Man's limb. The painter's inheritance is more specific than this, though. Eve aroused in Adam fantasy, and fantasy is what Bosch excessively possessed. Fantasy made Adam and the painter aliens to themselves: their likeness is that difference. Thus the Tree-Man signs the triptych not by identifying the maker directly but by announcing that the work comes from elsewhere, from an enemy imagination that haunts us all.

The work's signature, the Tree-Man also came to serve as a signature work, summing up its creator's distinctive capability. A sheet now in the Albertina, in Vienna, documents this development (fig. 246).[110] The artist's largest and most elaborate surviving sketch, it features

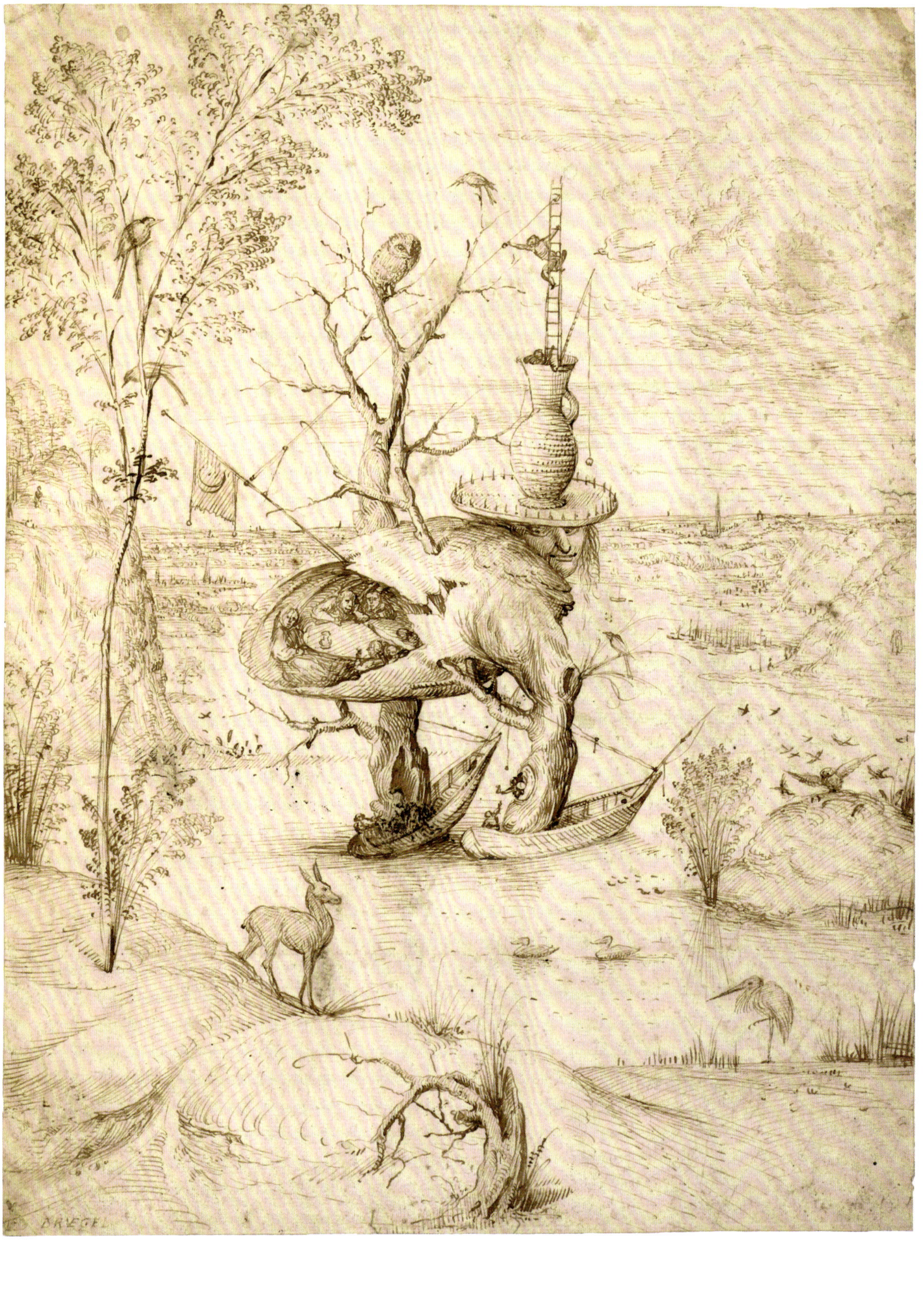

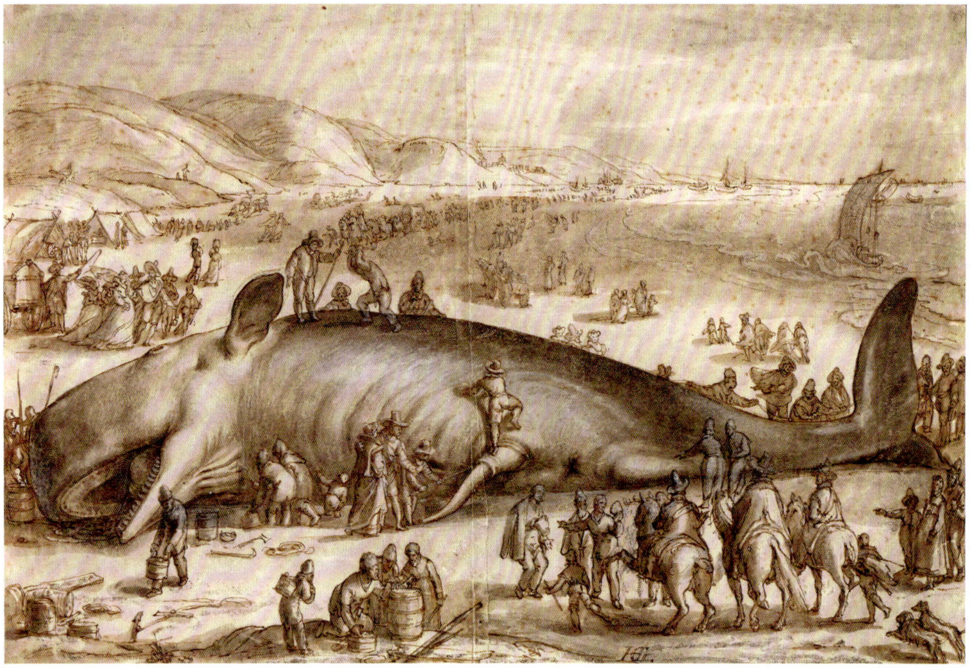

247 Hendrik Goltzius, *Beached Sperm Whale*, 1598, black chalk, pen in reddish brown and gray, Museum, Haarlem

a spectacular pen-and-ink version of the Tree-Man. Bosch has set forth the monster's distinctive features. But he adds, subtracts, and remixes other bits, engendering what a singular anomaly ought not to be: an individual within a species. More crucially, Bosch transplants his invention from the abyss of hell to a vista of the world. To the artist and his patrons this was home: in the foreground, marshes like the ones around 's-Hertogenbosch; farther off, harbor towns on a maze of waterways, like the huge delta where the Rhine, Meuse, and Scheldt rivers meet; and beyond the visible horizon, at a distance plotted by church spires and vast like the sky, the sea. There the Tree-Man idly floats like some outlandish carrack adrift in an inland canal.

Netherlandish shorelines were natural theaters where wonders could be observed, measured, and dissected. In 1520, on his trip to Zeeland, Dürer rushed to glimpse a stranded whale, but the tides had carried the beast away.[111] Hendrick Goltzius had more luck. In 1598, he drew a sperm whale washed ashore near Katwijk, a day's hike from his home in Haarlem (fig. 247).[112] The sketch records the marvel together with the curiosity it incites, as people of all estates converge on the spectacle. Bosch's drawing places the viewer alone before the spectacle, enhancing the impression that one sees the monster autoptically. It is the lie this artist's study sheets tell, that their maker sketched from life what in fact sprung from his imagination (see fig. 158). In the Vienna drawing, the Tree-Man travels in a real world along waters that, connecting near and far, explain how the monstrosity might have got here. The flanking coulisses of trees and shore structure the display naturally, as the sort of sight a man would turn to see. And the monstrosity's human passengers and technology (the ladders, pulleys, and fishing rod) measure the phenomenon and rationalize its operation. But it is chiefly through its medium that the image makes the impossible look real. Prodigies mattered as much for when they appeared as for how. Woodcuts of Bosch's day meticulously dated the monstrous apparitions they portrayed, partly to be interpreted astrologically as omens, partly to credit the incredible through facts. Swiftly executed, the pen-and-ink Tree-Man exhibits the temporal process of its making, suggesting that it was made there and then, in response to a mysterious arrival that may just as suddenly depart. Through the implied scenography of drawing, Bosch "saves the phenomenon" of what never was.

It is possible that Bosch made the drawing as a preparatory study for the Tree-Man in the triptych. Made without corrections, however, and aesthetically complete, the sketch looks already like a well-rehearsed performance. Painting the monster this perfectly would anyway have been easier than drawing it, since paint conceals its mistakes. Technical examinations of the Hell panel show the artist inventing and revising as he worked. I strongly believe that Bosch made his drawing of the Tree-Man after the painting, perhaps as a command performance for an admirer. Repeating his invention swiftly and cheaply in pen and ink, he could transmit to a friend the distilled essence of his hostile masterpiece while also fostering the illusion that the drawing was the "life study" on which the painting was based. The sketched copy could pretend to be the original in another sense, as well. A more immediate-seeming image of the monstrosity, it is also a more direct index of the artist's imagination.

The fantasy conjured by Bosch's pen is many things and none. Its modern nickname controls its amorphousness. Trunks and branches suggest a *tree* that supports something like a *man* who, amputated at the waist, uses his arms as legs. However, the fantasy is ultimately neither tree nor man, just as it is *not*—but has been understood *to be*—an egg, a goose's carcass, the exoskeleton of an insect, a jug, a sodomite, a cosmic anus, the Devil, a hellish tavern or brothel, and hell itself. And again it is, but is not, the artist himself in his persona as a *bosch* with a *boschvoghel* in its upper branches and another on the shore. Given that it floats, it could also be called a boat. Sebastian Brant's best-selling *Ship of Fools*, published in 1494, would have been one available point of reference. It would bring order to Bosch's fantasy as an object (a ship for fools), a subject (a fool in ship's form), and nothing at all (a foolish ship). Visual jokes convey this folly: such a ship cannot float, its divergent prows take it nowhere, no one can stand in two boats at once, and so forth. Still, the monster seems genuinely to stand on boats, because Bosch has built these vessels convincingly, plank by plank, with his pen. Observe how the crafts list under their gigantic load, steadied by absurdly inadequate ropes.

There are differences between making and drawing. The boats evince a shipwright's know-how, but they remain views of a boat. Bosch's *disparates* cohere as appearance alone. The hollow "egg" or "pod" melds into the backward-turned face via a shoulder that is at once animal, vegetable, and mineral. Bosch builds this passage out of what he labors to form as an outcropping of rock, the strata of which morph into muscles. To the left, a tear near this surface reveals branch-like ribs, which Bosch registers on the covering surface through shadowed impressions. These seamless mutations (rock to skin to bark) and their composition of overarching things that are themselves mutable (shoulder to egg to brothel) derive from shifting mimetic aims that cohere because the artist keeps the larger whole in mind. Bosch had to plan for the branch that pierces the shoulder, since to cover the forms behind it, that background had to be sketched afterward. Such foresight suggests that the artist had made a Tree-Man previously (for example, in his triptych, where the piercing rib is painted on top of the background forms) and could negotiate its contradictions. Bosch's imitators tend to lack this foresight. Because they choose to copy a drawing made by the master, rather than invent one with their own pen, they make monsters that fall apart more the longer we behold them (fig. 248).

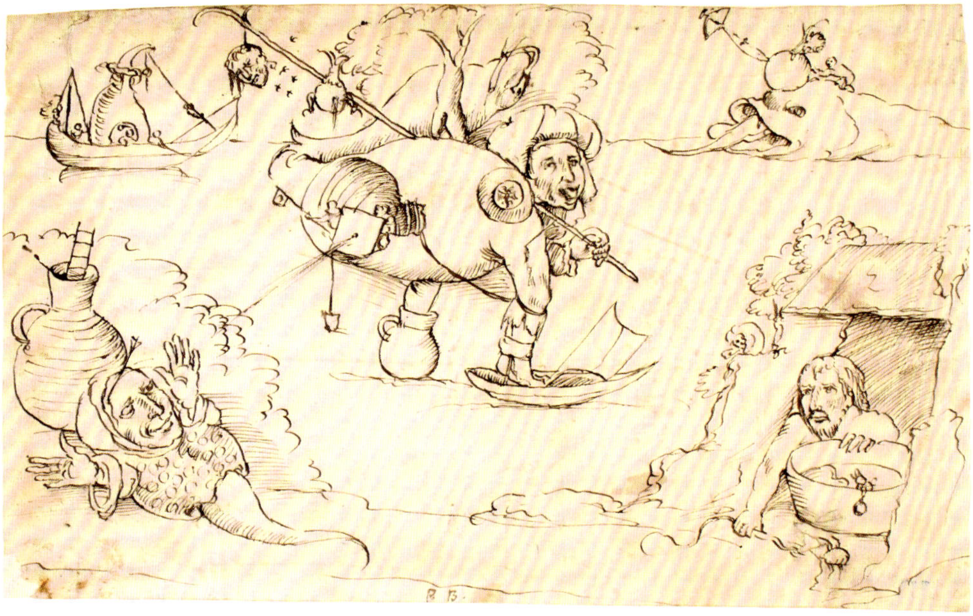

248 Bosch Imitator, *Tree-Man with Four Monsters*, c. 1560–1600, pen and brown ink, Graphische Sammlung der Universität, Erlangen

Invention demands a capacity of mind. But as the medium of drawing lays bare, it happens in the bodily and material activity of making. Bosch creates his lines out of bistre, a brown pigment produced by boiling the soot of wood. Dipping his quill into this arboreal residue, he deposits marks that variously outline an object, suggest its surface texture, and model it from dark to light. Sometimes he allows his pen line to double for the represented thing. The ship's rigging is such a special case. From the distance the drawing takes on them, these ropes have the thickness of pen marks. At first they look like fit equipment, trimming sails and bracing masts. There are no sails, however, and instead of a mast there rises a colossus no cordage could support. On close inspection, the ropes that seem to anchor the unbalanced mass to the ship's twin prows serve only to hold up idle fishing rods. The ropes *invite* close inspection because, through them, Bosch "thinks" the represented thing in place, and because they patently cannot do their job. Instead of answering how such a thing can exist, this useless cordage amplifies that very question. Rigging ought to have solved the problem through specialist know-how—through *technē*. Bosch's culture paid close attention to the technology of shipbuilding, because improvements there brought global travel, which carried valuables from and to distant lands. The drawing answers the question of the "how" of its subject's existence by projecting its solution onto the seafarers who man the craft. But it mocks this answer: drunk, rudderless, and without a captain, these travelers are indeed fools to have built their craft this way.

The question that technology does not answer need never have been asked. Fantasies of all kinds arise spontaneously in the mind, and artists expertly make these visible. A paper Pegasus poses no problem, and as Guevara insisted, Bosch set his strangest things in hell, where the unnatural was natural. The Vienna drawing puts the Tree-Man in question by moving it to the mundane world. This introduces an entire set of parameters. In his study sheets, Bosch drew organic monsters, answering plausibly questions of makeup and mobility (see figs. 158 and 159). Here he raises the bar, submitting his fantasy to the inner-worldly principle of sufficient reason, which states that nothing is without *grounds*. The Tree-Man poses this problem pointedly, first, because it should not *stand*, where standing is tantamount to existing, and second, because where it impossibly stands is the great opposite of *ground*. The ship of fools is a trope of groundlessness. Through folly—i.e., through an insufficiency of reason—human beings lose their footing in the world. Bosch floats his monster on water. But he places us on dry land. This casts us in the role of stoic spectators who, able to apply reason to what we see, discover the ship's foolish makeup and predict its impending wreckage.

But Bosch also makes sense of his monstrosity. The inland waters flow to a sea that stretches to the ends of the earth. The Tree-Man looks alien in its Brabantine *habitus*, but it may be at home elsewhere, on antipodal shores where monsters naturally arise. It flies the ensign of a hostile port of origin. Crescent moons appear often and pointedly in Bosch's pictures. One tops the idol in the landscape of the Prado *Adoration of the Magi*, as we have seen (see fig. 114). Another on a red flag excites countercrusaders—some turbaned—in the *Temptation of Saint Anthony* (see fig. 150). A third flies above a crowd in the background of the *Ecce Homo*, inviting a slanderous association of that hostile gathering with the Christ-killing Jews in the foreground (see fig. 133). And in the central panel of the so-called *Garden of Delights*, a gigantic crescent crowns the central fountain inside which fornication takes place (see fig. 205). For Bosch's audience, these devices connoted above all the archenemy Islam. In biblical scenes, this hostile presence made sense. Jerusalem had long stood under Muslim rule, and after conquering Constantinople, in 1453, the Ottoman Empire extended its borders deep into Europe. To have crescent-moon banners fly above cities in the Christian West was a plausible catastrophe. In the Vienna drawing, the symbol has many valences. It may denote the "lunacy" of the Tree-Man and its passengers. Hung below a giant owl mobbed by birds, it also may declare enmity to be this world's prevailing condition. Given that the chief regional conflict was between the Duke of Burgundy and the Duke of Guelders over the control of the waterways around 's-Hertogenbosch, even close neighbors could be nightmares to each other. Flown by a monstrous maritime vessel, the crescent moon also hints—plausibly—at a distressing reversal of Europe's voyages of discovery. Instead of "we" finding "them" (the exotic peoples), instead of our placing our banner of conquest on their soil, they, by means of unknown technologies, have discovered us and are plotting our annihilation.

Bosch shows home besieged by the Devil. This had always been the artist's viewpoint: corrupted by sin, the world was hostile territory. The crescent-moon flags did not have to portend a geopolitical catastrophe, since everyday life already stood under Satan's sway. The Vienna drawing gives this worldview a new charge, however. The monster and its mundane surrounds are of similar stuff—lines produced by Bosch's hand. The Tree-Man's rigging exposes this *world-making* activity: it plaits the artist's imagination, the graphic medium, and the thing that results into a single thread. A form of doodling, rigging shows how the pen can think faster and better than the mind: maybe the mind can't balance a tree in a boat, but the pen can. What rigging "thinks" is the reality of what the doodler has unthinkingly brought forth with his pen: scribbles on paper turned into objects in space. Again, this rigging holds nothing up. But that amplifies drawing's monstrous power to create something from nothing.

Of all Bosch's creations, the autonomous, collectible drawing is perhaps the strangest. In it the act of making—formerly concealed—stands exhibited as the finished work, and that work seems to encompass the world complete in itself. The Vienna sheet frames its view in landscape elements: hills and harbors at the right, animals and a tree stump below, a tree and cliff at the left, and branches and clouds above. The boundary between land and water in the view further strengthens the framework: observe how the wavering shoreline echoes subtly the monster's erratic outline. These fictional boundaries absorb the factual ones of the rectangular sheet of paper. They seem unremarkable today, after five centuries of gallery pictures similarly composed. But they were novel to viewers of Bosch's day, and especially in a pen-and-ink drawing. Turning external limits into internal ones establishes the image's autonomy, as that which lays down its own laws. It prepares the work for aesthetic contemplation. Perhaps the earliest autonomous pen-and-ink sketch in northern art, *The Tree-Man* frames as if naturally something that cannot exist in nature, thereby launching the art of drawing as a counternatural force.

Bosch worked at the dawn of an era when artists' sketches became collectible artifacts. Around 1500, art lovers began to acquire drawings as showcases of artistic skill and imagination. Direct traces of a body and mind in motion, sketches exhibited their maker more immediately than painting, and were harder to imitate and to forge. The Vienna sheet was probably created for a collector who, having glimpsed the Tree-Man in the triptych, desired a version of it by its inventor's hand. As Dürer wrote on the autograph sketch sent by Raphael, a drawing *shows its maker's hand*.[113] Drawings had become an image of the artist's agency; according to Vasari, Dürer sent Raphael a marvelous translucent self-portrait, perhaps to complete the friendly exchange.[114] Whether or not the Tree-Man is a disfigured likeness of its maker, the drawing of it is intentionally "a Bosch."

A remarkable print from around 1600 projects Bosch's drawing into a scene of its visual delectation (fig. 249).[115] From the accuracy with which the anonymous artist captured the sketch's details, one can deduce that, whoever he was, he had the sheet right in front of him. This is not a facsimile, however. Although the etcher's needle tries to mimic the drawing's delicate, wavering lines, it also clarifies Bosch's delightful ambiguities and amends certain details. The figures inside the monster's internal cavity are more differentiated, the sky has been darkened and enriched, and anecdotes in the middle ground pace the recession of things into depth. Most crucially, the etcher has introduced a new cast of characters. At the right, clustered around a tree at the edge of a precipice, common folk, men and women, young and old, gather to marvel at the monster. Closer to us, three experts attend to it professionally. On the left, with palette and brush, a painter stands ready to paint it. At the center, a bearded man holding a fox—in my view a poet or fabulist, perhaps Aesop—points it out, as if to speak its legend. And on the right, with sextant and almanac, an astronomer has come to prognosticate. Understood as portents, and deciphered by their astral alignment, monsters were thought to have been created to foretell disaster, hence their etymological derivation from *monstrare*, which means "to show."

What exactly is it that concerns these beholders? The Tree-Man? Or Bosch's drawing the Tree-Man? Set inside the landscape but at a safe remove from the sight, the common folk behave as people do before wonders of nature: they gawk, amazed and baffled, as the Fool among them indicates. The specialists seem differently posed, however. Seated along the curve of the engraving's perimeter, at the vantage point that the engraver takes on Bosch's original drawing, they could apply their expertise either to the wonder or to the wondrous artifact published here. By the time of its reproduction, Bosch's sketch was a relic of the past. Famed for his enigmatic monsters, the artist himself had become the enigma. The facts about the person long forgotten, the persona "Bosch" became synonymous with the powers and perils of the imagination.

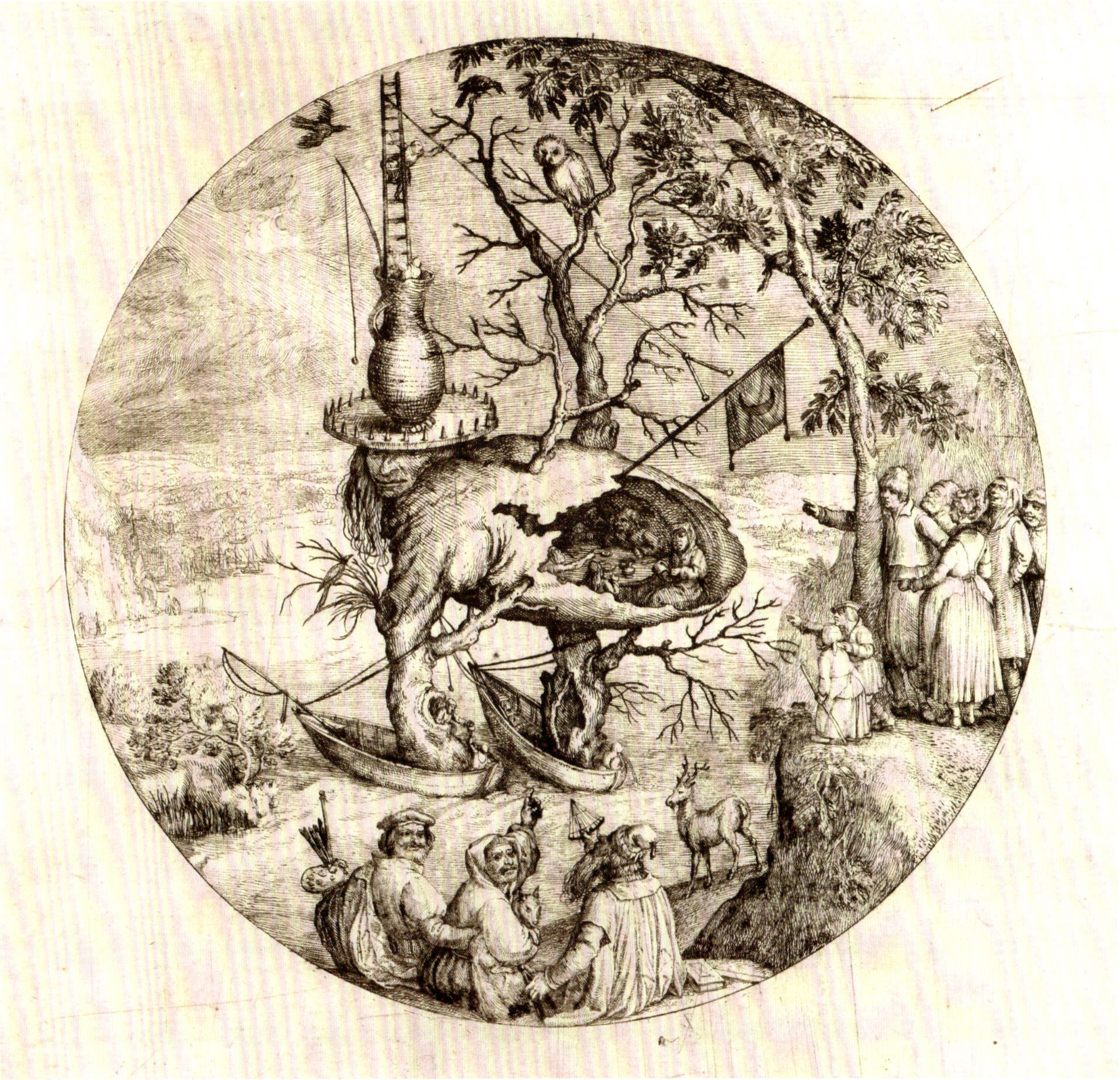

249 Anonymous Netherlandish Etcher after Bosch, *The Tree-Man*, n.d., etching, private collection

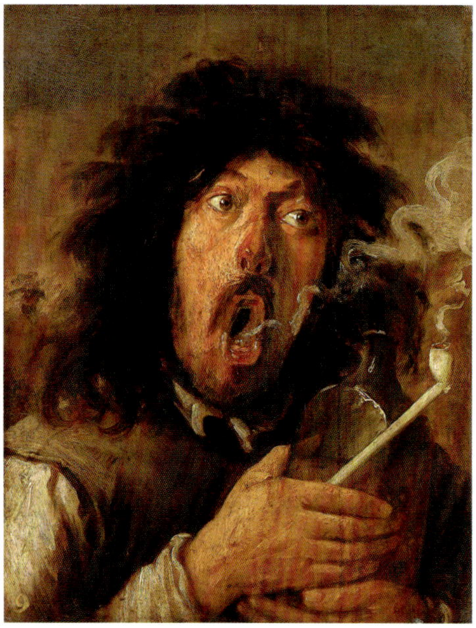

250 Joos van Craesbeeck, *The Smoker*, first half of the seventeenth century, oil on wood, Musée du Louvre, Paris

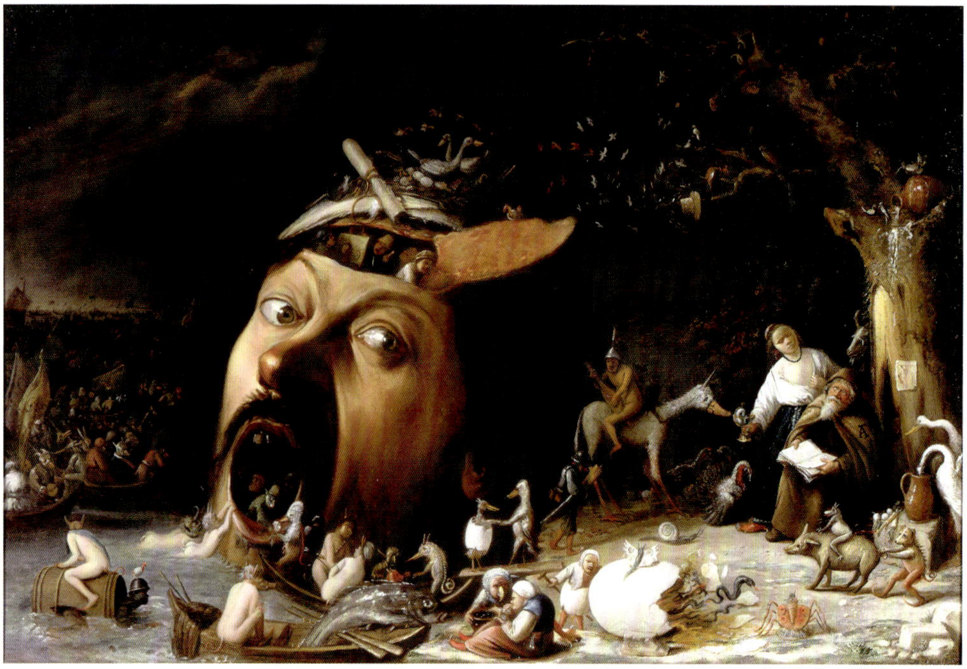

251 Joos van Craesbeeck, *Temptation of Saint Anthony*, c. 1646, oil on canvas, Staatliche Kunsthalle, Karlsruhe

Whether or not it was true for the original drawing now in Vienna, in the engraving "Bosch" and the Tree-Man are one and the same. This equation would have been obvious to artists working in Bosch's shadow. Let a minor Flemish painter, Joos van Craesbeeck, represent this historical coda. Craesbeeck studied with Adriaen Brouwer, whom he may have met while the latter sat in debtor's prison in Antwerp. He specialized in lowlife genre subjects, including close-ups of smokers and scenes of debauchery, in imitation of such canvases by Brouwer. In at least nine of these, Craesbeeck used himself as model, enhancing the face's expressive immediacy and creating for the painter himself a comic, corrupted, and corrupting persona, as artists like Hans von Aachen, Rembrandt, and Steen also did (fig. 250).[116] During the great tobacco craze of the seventeenth century, smokers augmented their nicotine rush by lacing the leaf with hallucinogenic substances, hence, perhaps, the artist's glazed look.[117] Craesbeeck's most

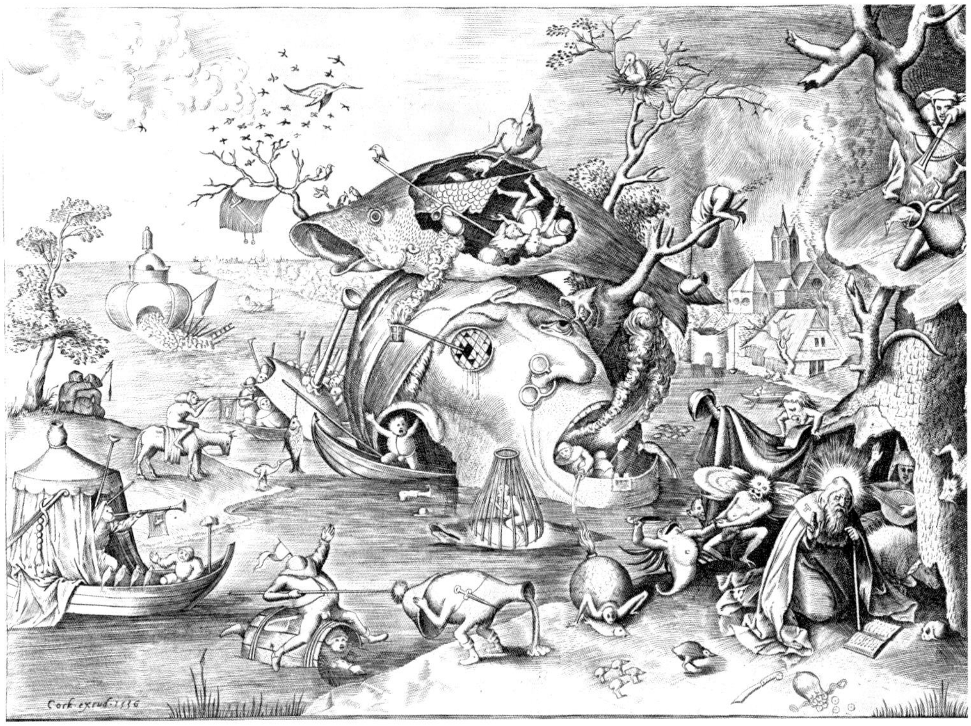

252 Pieter van der Heyden, after Pieter Bruegel the Elder, *Temptation of Saint Anthony*, 1556, engraving (published by Hieronymus Cock, Antwerp), The Metropolitan Museum of Art, New York, Harris Brisbane Dick Fund, 1928

elaborate confession, though, and one of the most remarkable self-portraits in the European tradition, appears in his *Temptation of Saint Anthony*, painted around 1646 and now in Karlsruhe (fig. 251).[118] The canvas—one of the artist's largest and most accomplished—stands in a long line of diabolical fantasies reaching back, via David Teniers, the Bruegels, and a host of lesser early sixteenth-century imitators, to Bosch's Lisbon triptych. More specifically, the gigantic face in the water responds to a similar monstrosity in Pieter Bruegel's *Saint Anthony*, engraved in 1556 by Pieter van der Heyden (fig. 252).[119] In the Bruegel, the marooned monster's tormented eyes mirror—and injure—the viewer's eyes looking at them. Akin to the ichthyic eye in Bruegel's *Big Fish Eat Little Fish*, and perverse "mirrors of the soul," these giant oculi play games with our reverse agency as spectator. Behind Bruegel's inventions, of course, stand Bosch's omnivoyant monstrosities and, most spectacularly, his Tree-Man, with its dangerous rearward gaze. It is perhaps from some version of the Tree-Man that Craesbeeck also got the idea of making the monstrous face his own. An audience familiar with Craesbeeck's self-portraits as a smoker would have been especially amused by this grotesque likeness, in which the painter looks terrified by the hallucinations he seems to exhale at us like smoke.[120]

The Craesbeeck canvas contains a second artist's portrait that explains the predicament of the first. As in an anatomical illustration, the flesh and bone of the colossus's forehead has been peeled to the side, revealing what lies inside the skull. In the Aristotelian doctrine of the soul, which mapped mental activities to specific locations in the brain, the frontal lobes were the seat of the imagination and fantasy. Dürer illustrated this in a 1498 woodcut diagram of the head; the face is that of Dürer's beloved friend, Willibald Pirckheimer, and the *A* denoting the "Total Cerebrum" doubles as the artist's monograph, boasting that he holds in balance all mental faculties (fig. 253).[121] Craesbeeck exposes only his frontal brain, where, according to the science of the time, raw sense data was received in the form of mental images, which fantasy, in its turn, could combine into new, impossible hybrids, such as the bizarre ones Craesbeeck

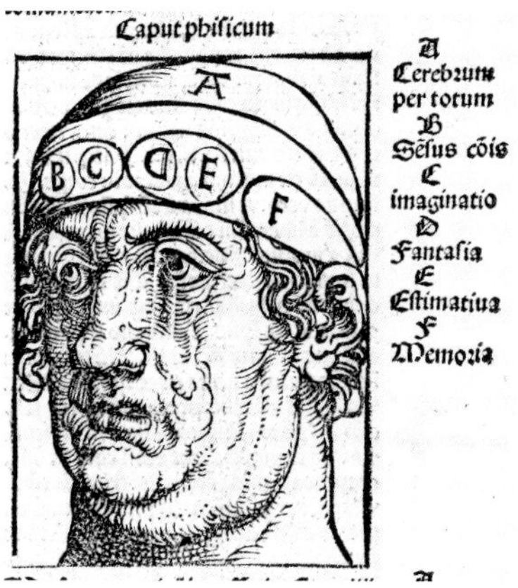

253 Albrecht Dürer, *Caput physicum*, woodcut illustration from Ludovicus de Prussia, *Trilogium Anime* (Nuremberg: Anton Koberger, 1498), The Bodleian Libraries, The University of Oxford, shelfmark: Ms. Douce 346, fol. 236r and Auct. I Q 5.26, fol. E1r (woodcut Caput Physicum)

himself paints in the foreground of this painting. Peering into the painter's head, one discovers a painter at work! Before him, as that which he seems to portray from life, stands Craesbeeck's typical subject: peasants carousing in a shadowy space, perhaps the interior of a tavern or brothel. The painter's canvas, meanwhile, is a blank slate—a tabula rasa—except for some loose brown marks, perhaps the beginning of an underdrawing in chalk. Perception, this interlude seems to say, draws images fleetingly on the mind just as an artist first sketches figures on an empty ground. More specifically, Craesbeeck expounds the relationship, much discussed in art literature of the period, between painting from life (*naer het leven*) and painting from the imagination (*uyt den gheest*).[122] Genre painting, as an unadorned depiction of the ordinary, stands close to the stuff of perception, hence its appearance as the first thing on Craesbeeck's mind. But through an artist's powers of fantasy, over which he exerts little control, especially when inebriated, the stuff of mere perception can breed monstrosities.

Both of these modes—a painting of everyday life and fantastical diablerie—are the artistic legacies of Bosch. An heir to these, Craesbeeck also assumes a Boschian persona. He portrays himself as simultaneously the source and the victim of the evil he paints. Swarmed by airborne demons, his likeness recalls Simon Frisius's etching of Bosch, with its plague of fantasies. Only here, as in Bosch's own disfigured self-portraits, the artist shows himself frightened *and culpable*. His open jaws evoke the hellmouth of Last Judgment scenes. He has become not a visitor to hell but the infernal gatekeeper Leviathan, the Old Enemy.

Another artist working in Bosch's shadow, but possessing an imagination far more capacious, arrived at a different understanding. Artists, this Flemish painter's works spectacularly proved, were world makers. However, that did not make them diabolical, since the entire human world—the *habitus* in which people live their lives—was the product of human poiesis. This did not do away with evil; it simply made it a human force. True, nature treated humans cruelly, but this was due not to its hostility but to its metaphysical indifference to man. The enemy was therefore no longer some diabolical agent hostile to God. Hostility and hatred were human artifacts—perhaps the most distinctively human ones. Enmity was man's natural condition, since by this artist's lonely creed, no one is against man except man.

PART II

Pieter Bruegel the Elder

9

HISTORY

The Watershed

Pieter Bruegel is the unsurpassed painter of common humanity. This skill would have been hard to predict. The artist launched his career making outlandish pictures in the manner of Hieronymus Bosch. The engraving of a monstrous fish-filled fish—as we observed—names Bosch as its inventor, although Bruegel, then an unknown talent just returned to Antwerp, made the drawing on which the print was based (see figs. 67 and 68). Even after he had achieved personal fame, Bruegel continued to cultivate a rivalry with his long-deceased predecessor by creating fantastical paintings of hell, demons, and universal conflagration. In the course of his development, however, and most monumentally in the works of his final years, Bruegel made ordinary life his distinctive terrain.

The Peasant Dance, painted a year before its maker's death, would feel familiar even if it were not famous (fig. 254). No matter how often we have seen it before, this panel still greets us immediately with the boisterous amity everywhere on display. Size matters: about as wide as a person is tall, this ample picture gives us the space to step into it and involves us with lively figures that, at a natural viewing distance from the painted panel, will appear to be life-size. The dance itself embodies this embrace. Giving conjugal and communal bonds aesthetic form, dancing models the pull this painting exerts on us.[1] Rushing into the revels, their footfalls syncing to the piper's beat, the foreground couple draws the beholder into the vortex of the dance and its surrounding eddies of intimacy—the ambiguous tug-of-war at the doorway to the inn, the kiss ongoing at the far left, the invasive friendship of the foreground drunk, and so on. The red banner—probably of the local shooters' guild—flying over the inn's entrance signals the occasion for these revels. Emblazoned with guild emblems, the paired figures of the Virgin and Saint George, and the coats of arms of local overlords, it announces that a church anniversary, or "kermis," is under way, or is just now commencing, and that what the people celebrate, via the founding of their parish, is community and home.[2]

Church anniversaries were more than customary in Netherlandish villages of the time; they were living repositories of custom itself. A decade before he painted *The Peasant Dance*, Bruegel twice portrayed the village kermis as an assemblage of local folkways. Beyond the universal pleasures of food, drink, music, and dance, he collects the games and theatricals specific to this time and place. As outsiders we can work out the basics of most of these.

254 Pieter Bruegel the Elder, *The Peasant Dance*, c. 1568, panel, Kunsthistorisches Museum, Vienna

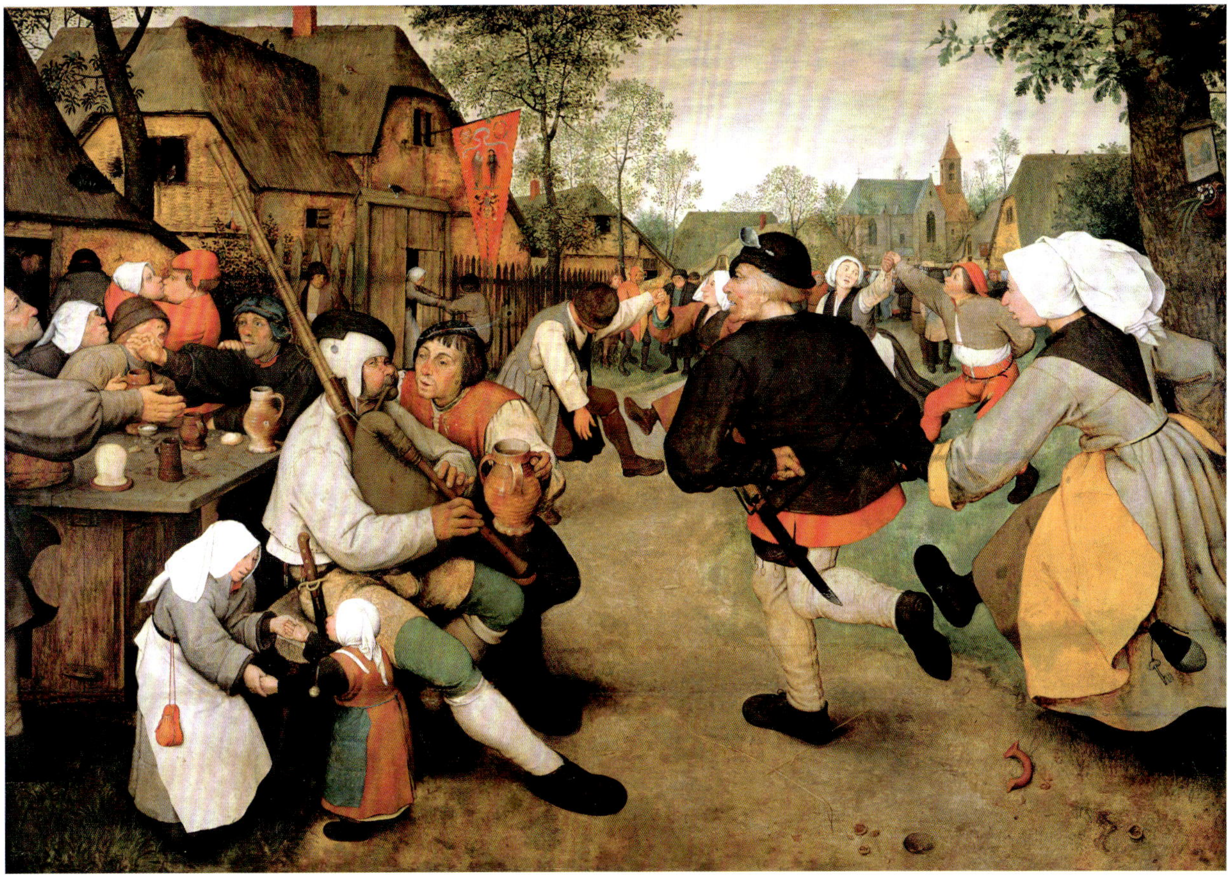

The tone of Bruegel's portrayal of rustic people also changes in the course of his career—not necessarily because his attitudes change (though this may also be the case) but because the works of art have. The intimacy of *The Peasant Dance* is at once a logical development from previous works and a new artistic departure. In his kermises of 1559, and more stunningly in his encyclopedic paintings of proverbs, customs, and children's games from the same period, Bruegel created great atlases of the human that the eye can explore while remaining—literally—aloof, through these pictures' high points of view (see figs. 32, 284, and 294). Mastered when the artist sketched his vast Alpine vistas, distance estranges the familiar. It situates actors and actions in an expanding spatial context, where everyday life unfolds in a typical street that runs through a village enclave built (typically) upon a river that flows, visibly and inexorably, through an expansive landscape to the open ocean. Distance also makes the near-at-hand look exotic, as homes appear to the eyes of a traveler. The distance Bruegel takes on the local establishes a new locality—a global one—and with it its modern denizen, the cosmopolitan who is everywhere and nowhere at home.

The contrast strikes everyone who comes to *The Peasant Dance* after the bird's-eye perspective of Bruegel's earlier works: the painting brings us resolutely down to earth and in eerie proximity to its subject. Having let us behold everyday life from afar, it would seem, the artist now wants us to enter it. He transports us into lived experience through bodies entering the picture in the present. The foreground couple rush in from somewhere behind us, connecting us to the painting's present tense. There, *right now*, the bagpipes pipe, beer flows, people kiss, and even the children join the dance. The bodies of the couple do not merely enter pictorial space. Their striding limbs and thrusting heads and shoulders make space. The awkward overlap of the man's legs—his left leg reading falsely as his right—activates his corporeal form: we visually trip over his legs. Consider that masterpiece of posture, expression, and foreshortening, the piper. He wraps himself around the pipe's air-filled bag. As he grimaces to blow air into the bag, while also listening to the tune his fingers play, his body—itself an instrument—is amplified by the cylindrical toddler and suffocating drunk, projecting a volume proportional to the sonic one of his pipe. Bruegel wants us to feel as though we can pass directly into his picture. It is the obverse of his *Peasant and the Bird Thief*, in which the subject strides aggressively out toward us (see fig. 4). He therefore places before us an open stretch of ground. Few paintings devote as much of their surface to the soil underfoot. Flowing like a river through the composition, this earth—painted thinly in ocher over a pale priming or "ground"—gives the picture an inner radiance: it floods the painting with light reflected from our world.

To invite us onto that ground, to let us feel ourselves stepping into the picture, Bruegel punctuates the expanse with objects: an open walnut we want to bend over and touch, a pot handle shaped for the hand, and a big, striding foot (fig. 257).[10] The foot gives us lots to behold. We consider the simple crafting of that shoe, how exactly it was sewn, laced, and soled, and how closely it resembles the other footwear in the picture, as if all shoes were of this specific type. We contemplate the sturdy makeup of clothes, foods, tools, ornaments, and crockery on display. Remember, this was Bruegel's special expertise: local forms of making, vernacular style (of shoes, knives, pretzels, etc.) as the imprint of gestures done in a particular way. The broken-off pot handle helps us grasp emphasis. Garbage to the natives who made and used the pot to which it was attached, it is precious evidence to the outsider who wants to make sense of this world: its fragmentary form invites us, imaginatively, to complete it, rather as Bruegel

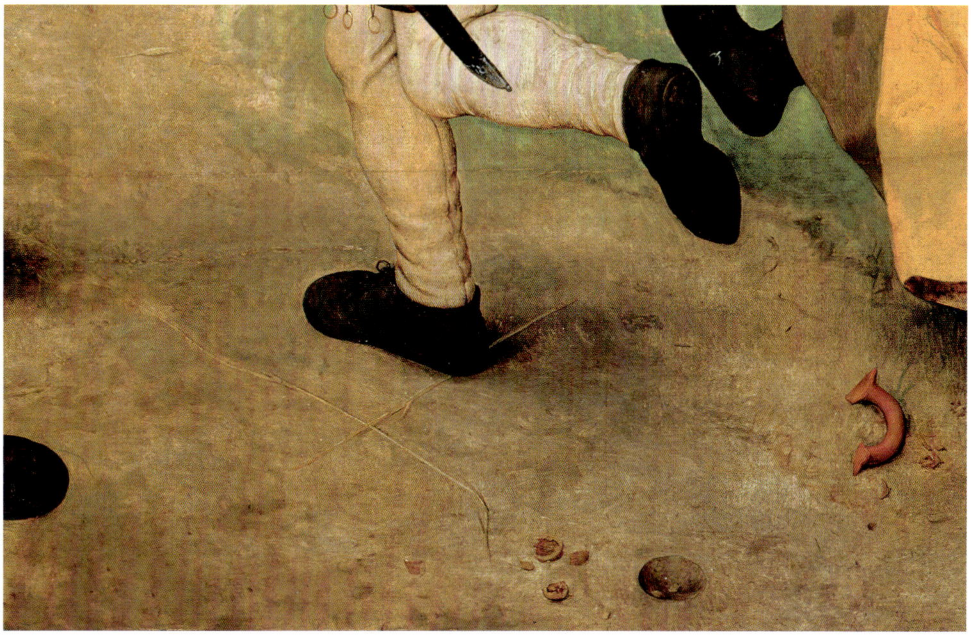

257 Detail of Pieter Bruegel the Elder, *The Peasant Dance* (fig. 254)

completes a picture of the whole of culture to which handle and pot belong. Made for the hand, our thinking goes, the handle was also handmade: one can almost see the handprints of the potter clinging to the clay. Placed on the earth, it is also made of earth and now returns to earth, as all things human do. But what is this earth *really*? Is it the ground of the village common, terrain of the local lifeworld, medium that peasants plow and sow? Or is it the painting's own material fundament: the underlying ground (Dutch *grond*) on which Bruegel paints, upon which he crafts his complete artifact? According to Van Mander (we recall), one of the rare and signature techniques used by Bosch and Bruegel was to paint thinly and transparently, allowing the primed ground of the panel or canvas to show through, so that it, the *grond*, could "work with" the finished image. On the one hand, treating pictorial ground as humus might be a gesture of humility: pictures, like pots, are made of nothing but dirt, as is appropriate to a depiction of common humanity. On the other hand, this ground is fictive—made by art, not by nature—revealing that this world, the realm of culture and the painting of that realm, are both brought to being by the human poiesis.

These common grounds give access, but something else about *The Peasant Dance* makes it familiar once we are in. Although monumental in scale and conception, the painting shows nothing of great importance: no sacred story, no antique myth or fable, no significant action from recorded history. Hardly telling a story, it displays events occurring among persons of no consequence—among people without history. What fascinated city dwellers about peasant life was that it seemed to stay the same, serving unintentionally as a time capsule of a past everyone shared. The pots displayed in *The Peasant Dance* are stylistically homogenous. They form what an ethnographic museum might gather and exhibit as the assemblage of a particular culture. Different from pots made in a village around the bend, they are nonetheless timeless: things made here rather than elsewhere, but always in the same way. The actions in Bruegel's painting would belong to this assemblage. If somehow we could hear the melodies, feel the rhythms, and catch the patterns of the dance, we would grasp the local color of these revels, as specific as the beaded bases of the pots, as unique as the bit of the housewife's iron key. These actions are venerable—as an ancient proverb put it: "No one keeps old customs like a peasant."[11] But they are not *historical*: because they are changeless and inconsequential, no one would think to chronicle their occurrence. Painting such a nonevent, however, and doing so on a monumental scale and with the highest historical ambition: that—paradoxically—is a major event, one that makes Bruegel's *Peasant Dance* a great watershed in the history of European art.

The World Picture Comes of Age

Before Bruegel, all major masters worked exclusively—or partly but centrally—in the service of religion. They depicted events in the history of salvation and they fitted these depictions into the spaces and rites of the Christian cult. True, the great Netherlanders made other things besides church pictures. They made pictures of and for individuals, for example, portrait likenesses, heraldic signs and shields, historical scenes decorating spaces of public assembly, and devotional panels for private use. Church pictures themselves served more than religion, since the best of them were commissioned and admired for their artistry. The touchstone of the painters' craft, however, remained the things they fashioned for the cult. Though engineered to be experienced humanly, and expressive also of human life, these artifacts—donated to the church as treasury of salvation—presented themselves ultimately as propitiations to a wrathful God (see fig. 119).

Bosch was no exception. While most of his surviving pictures had their original place in secular collections, and his sacred images focus on human life usually turned away from the sacred, the bulk of his oeuvre (now lost) stood in his city's church, and his secular works retain the triptych format of retable altarpieces. More deeply, Bosch endeavored to show how, whether we know it or not, we stand always already before God, *coram Deo*. He reveals that the human experience—both *in* his paintings and *of* his paintings—is an object of God's experience. "Beware, beware, God sees," warns one of the very first genre paintings of the European tradition, reminding us that with Bosch little has changed in the realm of fundamentals (see fig. 122). Only Bosch's drawings approach the condition of the modern secular artwork, but as we have seen, these style their maker (Hieronymus van Aken, alias Bosch) as a malign agency: as *bos*, forest, timber, *hyle* (see figs. 232, 236, and 246). According to these clever, self-vilifying creations, art's historical shift into the aesthetic sphere simply renews the old hostility between the Creator and his rebellious creations.

In the decades between Bosch's death and the start of Bruegel's career, art production in northern Europe became increasingly worldly in its subjects and purposes. Distinctive types, or genres, of secular imagery emerged, such as landscape, still life, and what would later (confusingly) be termed genre painting (i.e., depictions of everyday human life). Made in multiples by workshops specialized to create them, works of these types evolved into standardized commodities, so that people far from the sites of production would know what to expect from, say, a landscape painting made in the Netherlands. This development depended on the existence of an efficient open market for art. Already in Bosch's day, painters in the great artistic capitals were making pictures less on commission (as painters previously had done) than on speculation. In an increasingly global economy of art, works of a general appeal could be more easily exported and sold, giving the secular genres, with their commonplace themes, a competitive advantage. The Reformation fostered the flowering of secular art, since Protestants either repudiated church art or disavowed the doctrine of good works on which

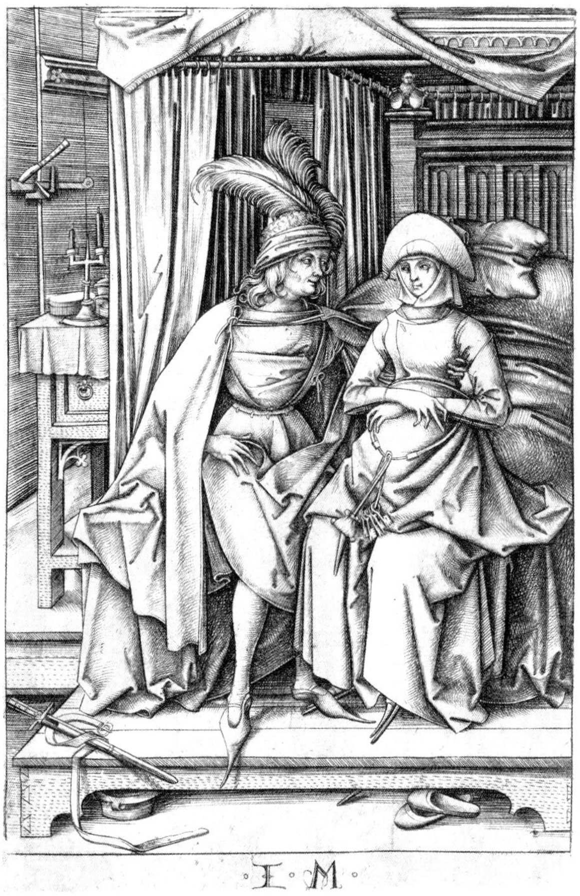

258 Israhel van Meckenem, *A Couple Seated on a Bed* from the *Scenes of Daily Life* series, n.d., engraving, The Metropolitan Museum of Art, New York, Rogers Fund, 1918

the lavish patronage of church art had previously been based. Through its reforming efforts at the Council of Trent (convened in 1545), the Roman Catholic Church, too, scrutinized sacred images for errors and excesses. Painters and patrons alike sought safety in secular art.

The new technology of print accelerated the secularizing trend. Produced largely on spec and serving mostly profane functions, prints experimented freely with new subjects and themes. No one knows precisely what purpose the earliest printed scenes of everyday life served (fig. 258). Their makers, German artists such as the Housebook Master, Israhel van Meckenem, and the youthful Dürer, may not have known this either. They simply printed these images, tried entrepreneurially to market and distribute them, and hoped for the best. Entering an increasingly global exchange of commodities, the printed image disseminated *into* the world new knowledge *about* the world. Not merely illustrating novel information, prints could produce information by serving as instruments of calculation, research, and imagination.[12] And in response to conflicts between and among the religious confessions, prints of sacred subjects, through their new, polemical charge, had a political charge and were thus worldly in a way.

Bruegel's worldliness depends on these developments. In his early career as a designer of engravings, he wagered on the existence of an affluent clientele eager to acquire interesting, well-made prints. The publication by Hieronymus Cock of Bruegel's engravings in suites framed the artist's products as ready-made compendia for print collections. As an imitator of Bosch, Bruegel also responded to obvious market trends. Boschian fantasies—some forged to look like authentic products of the master, some boasting the name of a rival talent—achieved

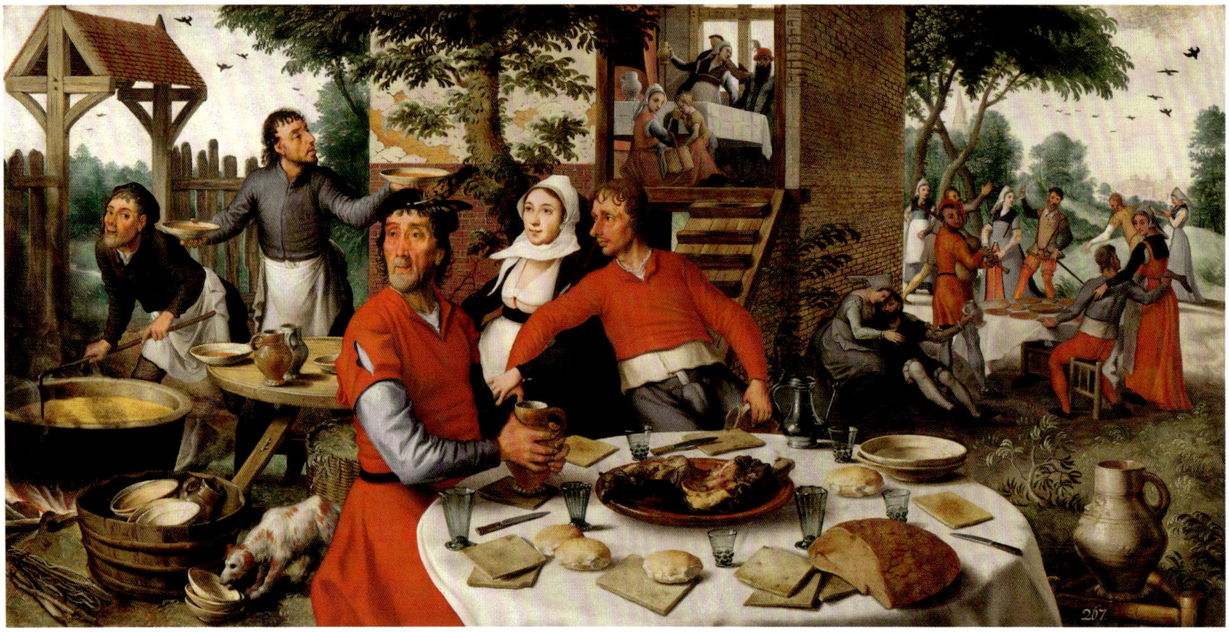

259 Pieter Aertsen, *Village Festival*, 1550, panel, Kunsthistorisches Museum, Vienna

Europe-wide popularity already in Bosch's lifetime. By the middle of the sixteenth century, such masters as Jan Mandijn, Pieter Huys, and Jan Wellens de Cock worked almost entirely in Bosch's shadow, and Jan Wellens's son, Hieronymus Cock, even without the help of Bruegel's improvisational talent, issued numerous engravings claiming to be based on Bosch originals (see figs. 66 and 73).[13] Bruegel's other specialty—the extended landscape vista or "worldscape"—was another prized commodity, especially of workshops in Antwerp, where Bruegel enrolled as a master in 1551. Established as a valued artistic genre in the first decades of the century by Joachim Patinir (deceased 1524), and pursued and developed by masters just previous to Bruegel, such as Herri met de Bles and Hieronymus and Matthys Cock, the worldscape derived (as we have seen) from Bosch—although the twist in his vast vistas is that they always have hell somewhere on their horizon.[14] Set in the art world of their time, Bruegel's pictures of rustic revelry can seem epigonic, too. In Germany, Dürer's followers made spectacular, large-scale woodcuts of peasant festivals, and in Antwerp by 1550 Pieter Aertsen had completed panels of customary rural life on the monumental scale of Bruegel's masterpieces (fig. 259).[15] Why, then, is *The Peasant Dance* such a watershed?

As anyone who has explored one knows, a watershed—dividing neighboring drainage basins—is invisible in flat, marshy country and subtle even in hilly terrain. But it is an exciting moment when, on high ground, you notice a small but consistent change in the direction that water flows. Where rivulets trickled, say, toward you while you walked, now just after a slight rising they flow with you, a little shift that has big consequences, for downstream from the division can lie different worlds, as happens in the Alps on the watershed among the Rhine, Danube, and Po basins (see fig. 283). With Bruegel, likewise, we feel a subtle but momentous shift. Especially when we encounter him in Vienna, in the chronologically ordered galleries of the self-named Art-Historical Museum, all that came before seems to stream backward, into the Christian Middle Ages, whereas now the ground slopes forward to modern art and the secular condition. That this shift is elusive and may even be illusory adds to its fascination. In real watersheds, divergent streams never meet, as each flows into a different sea. They divide the infinitude of seeming watersheds into two, where different streams join the one river or the other somewhere down the way. As an imitator of Bosch, Bruegel can appear both forward- and backward-looking. To his original viewers, for example, novelty in Netherlandish art would have been exemplified not by him, with his roots in his native tradition, but by Frans Floris, with his fashionable Italianate style. To this audience, Bruegel's art would have seemed deliberately old school. Bosch, for his part, was at once archaic and novel. He was archaic owing to, among other factors, his penchant for the diagram, which undercut perspective as the core achievement of the so-called *ars nova* of the early Netherlanders, and because of the weightlessness of his figures, which seem like throwbacks to the indeed courtly International Courtly Gothic style circa 1400. But he was also hyperbolically novel, because he created things emphatically never seen before. Analyzing Bosch and Bruegel in parallel is thus like looking for a watershed in marshland. And yet the two diverge—in my view—consequentially.

Greatness plays a role in our perception of Bruegel's place in history. Works by Pieter Aertsen and Herri met de Bles predate Bruegel's in their themes and manner, but something about their quality and ambition prevents them from functioning as a major turning point in the history of art (see fig. 269). It is difficult to pinpoint Bruegel's greatness, and not just because later historians constructed it retroactively—which indeed they had to, since two centuries after his death no one counted him great, and it took critics of a different taste to celebrate him again. If it were only that later construct, though, his greatness would be easier to understand. Powerfully felt in his own era, where he garnered praise from the leading intellects, it is also perceived by ordinary visitors today, who flock to his works instinctively and ignore Aertsen and Met de Bles no matter how important a label or audio guide might make them out to be. Bruegel's greatness is hard to articulate because it consists in a totality of qualities that perception unites and analysis divides. It consists in the powerful stories that the pictures convey, and on so many different levels, from the convincing actions of their players (e.g., the close-talking drunk in *The Peasant Dance*) through telling formal echoes of these actions (the kiss nearby) to conversations about these stories that this artist's paintings seem to hold among themselves—e.g., the powerful dialogue established in Vienna's Bruegel Room between *The Peasant Dance* and *The Peasant Wedding* (see figs. 254 and 260).[16] However, minor masters tell such stories cunningly, too, and do so across their oeuvre. Profundities gleaned from a Bruegel could also be gleaned from earlier masters, but the gleaning would seem somehow incommensurate to the art. Great *painting* itself—the superlative performance of all that painting as an art comprises—excites our enthusiasm for the story and underwrites our faith in its depth.

The transparency of Bruegel's paint layers, how he lets the underlying ground beneath them shine through, allowing the painting to seem to glow, also puts on display the subtle beauty of brushwork. The foliage in the background of *The Peasant Dance*, in which Bruegel captures the shape of individual leaves, the light of the season, the time of day, and the air that fills the scene, is lovely in itself: a calligraphy that keeps us looking at and wondering how and why this famous painting was painted. Once Bruegel had been reestablished as great, however, historians rarely considered these visual qualities, focusing instead on puzzles of symbolism and meaning. They left matters of style and technique to the connoisseurs and curators, yet were it not for *how* Bruegel paints, *what* he paints would be of much less interest.

There has never been a better painter than Bruegel. For me, Jan van Eyck, Titian, and Velázquez are his only equals. Certainly he outdoes Bosch on Bosch's home ground. Lucifer's

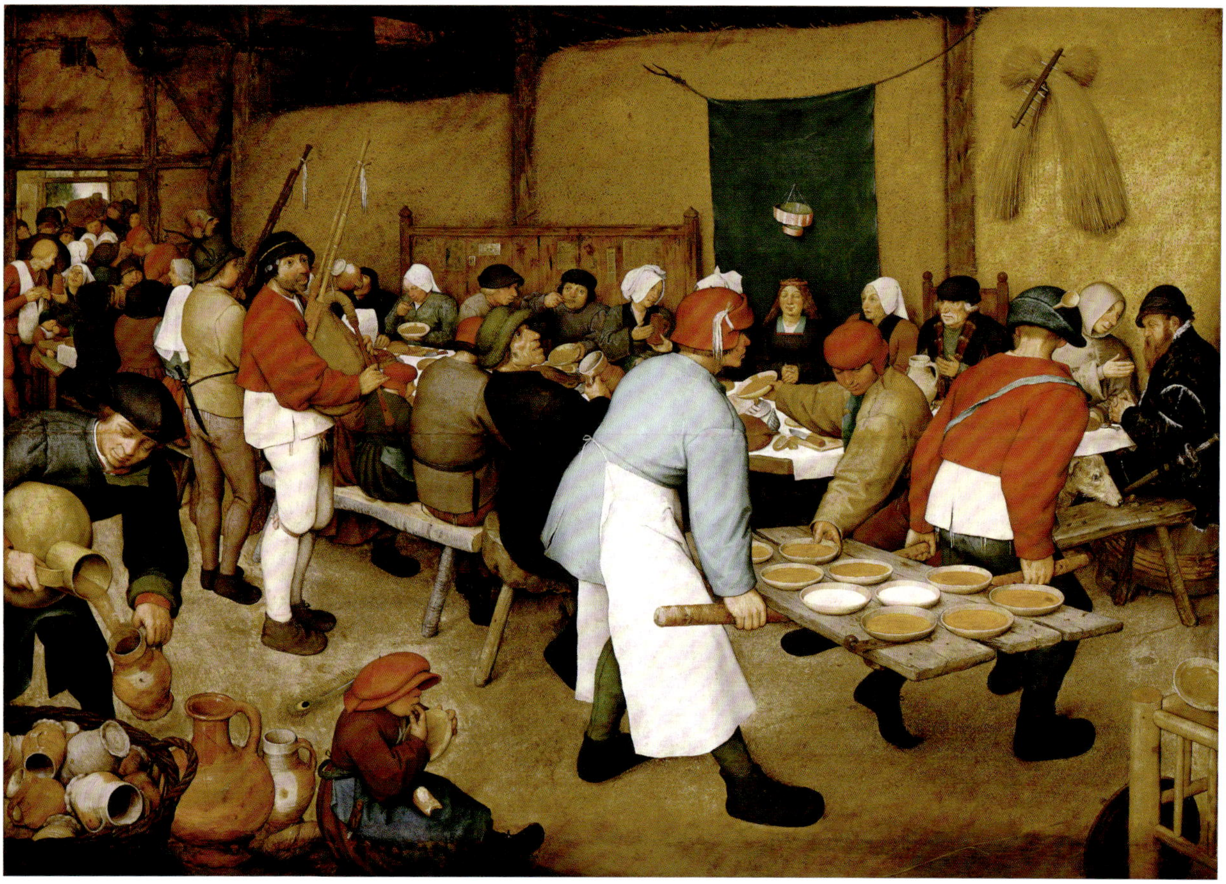

260 Pieter Bruegel the Elder, *The Peasant Wedding*, c. 1568, panel, Kunsthistorisches Museum, Vienna

minions in *The Fall of the Rebel Angels* are more various, imaginative, and plausible than Bosch's best monstrosities (see fig. 70); *The Triumph of Death* terrifies more lastingly than Bosch's *Last Judgments* do (see fig. 69); and *Dulle Griet*'s diabolics mesmerize longer than do the best of Bosch's temptations (fig. 261).[17] Whatever Bruegel set himself to do, whatever the theme, format, or medium, he did with astonishing success. His drawings were assiduously imitated and emulated immediately after his death.[18] His single autograph etching, *The Rabbit Hunt*, is one of the most evocative prints ever made (see fig. 36). His *Tower of Babel* constructs architecture—and even a *history* of architecture, written in a changing spiral of forms—of the very highest order (see fig. 278). Almost every one of his surviving works is a masterpiece; each can sustain a lifetime of looking. Works that seem minor due to their size prove to be major nonetheless, as if the artist wanted to remind you that the monumentality of his big pictures depends on something other than size—*The Suicide of Saul* packs into its tiny panel (34 × 55 cm) an entire world (see fig. 320). Bruegel's artistic consistency, the seeming perfection of every painting and of his oeuvre as a whole, signals a distinctive unity of intent that sets him apart. In 1550 or 1551, he is documented as having worked on an altarpiece made for the glove-makers' guild in Mechelen, near Antwerp, probably painting the outer wings in grisaille, but that work is lost.[19] Like modern painters who create the coherence of their oeuvre by destroying their juvenilia, Bruegel's opus is perfectly consistent in quality and intent. The first Old Master to have made no church pictures, his works are all one thing: artworks.

Expressions of life and objects of experience, these artworks also understand human being in a new and consistent way: as culture. No longer is ordinary human action only a sideshow to God's intervention in the world. Divine history appears as it does to mortals—the Epiphany eclipsed by weather, the Crucifixion obscured by crowds—while religion itself becomes a human construct, local and contingent, like any custom (see figs. 265 and 266). Beyond culture lies only the world, portrayed by Bruegel as a sublime immensity indifferent to people. His Alpine landscapes and seasonal tableaux transcend the human framework of a view. Our grasp of them is as partial as it would be of the real distances they depict. Even in those enclaves of innocence where peasant life unfolds, the rustic finds that the world begins already on his doorstep and that it traps him already here. This made *The Peasant and the Bird Thief* a world picture in miniature (see fig. 4).

In "The Age of the World Picture," first delivered as a lecture in 1938, Martin Heidegger lists the signal manifestations of the modern era.[20] In this era, knowledge has become science (*Wissenschaft*), especially of nature; applied, science transforms human practice into machine technology; art, shifted into the aesthetic domain, becomes the object and the representation of human experience; culture, now the highest human value, cultivates itself; and the gods disappear into the reality of an infinite universe and are replaced by something nebulous and altogether human: religious experience. Behind all these epiphenomena, according to Heidegger, lies a more essential process. In the modern era, the human subject found itself as subject—i.e., as underlying ground of everything that is. And it does this by establishing itself as the viewer of the world represented in the form of a picture.

The world picture is not this or that culture's image of the world. It is the world thought of as a picture and the human subject thought of as that picture's maker and viewer. The age of the world picture—the period when, historically, the world as picture came about—is alone the modern one. "The world picture does not change from an earlier medieval to a modern one; rather, that the world becomes a picture at all distinguishes the essence of modernity," writes Heidegger.[21] A medieval world picture, he states, "was an impossibility" because of what persons, world, and pictures in that age were. For that age deemed the world to be created

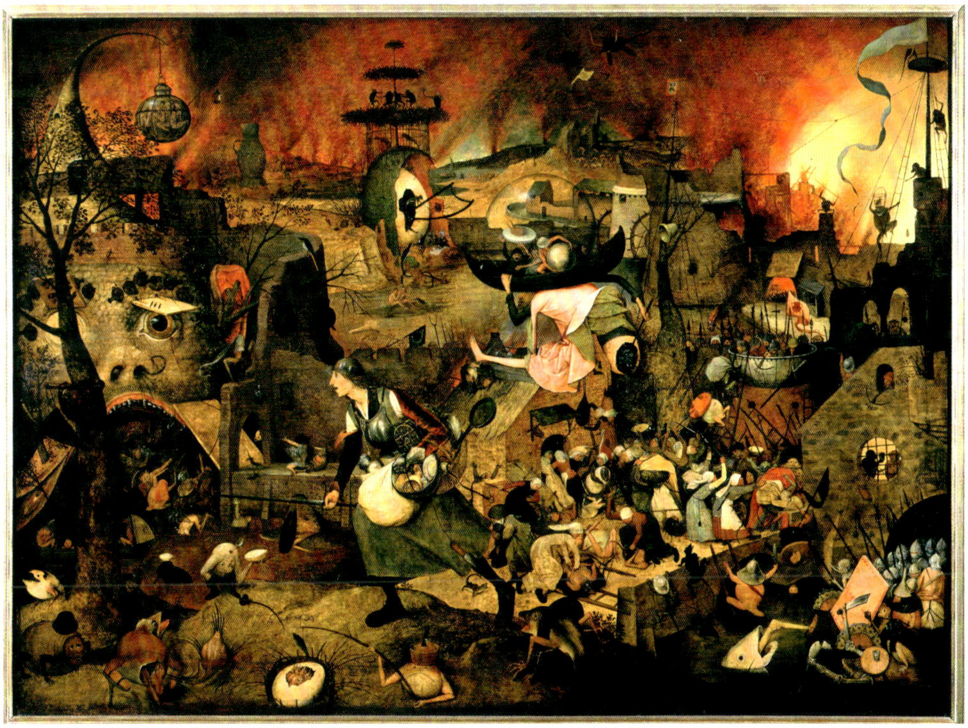

261 Pieter Bruegel the Elder, *Dulle Griet*, c. 1562, panel, Mayer van der Bergh Museum, Antwerp

by a personal God and to be dependent on him. Man, a created being, stood in a special place in the created order, as God's likeness and image, but he did not for that reason gather the world before and apart from him as his object. "The founding event of the modern age is the conquest of the world as picture."

Hieronymus Bosch seems to contradict this account, for what are the spheres and vistas in his triptychs if not world pictures, and ones that, in their grasp of nature (or *physis*), correspond perfectly to the *metaphysics* of the age? However, as we have seen, Bosch frames these world pictures in structures that make God the viewer and we the viewed, revealing our centrality to be in fact eccentric and our subjectivity to be abject. Bosch nests the modern world picture within a model or expression that is in fact not a picture. God's gaze in *The Seven Deadly Sins* is not an object within the picture but the picture turned into its obverse: a gaze, with us and our activities as its picture (see fig. 122). Bosch's imitators omitted those nonpictorial frameworks from their pastiches, perhaps because they did not grasp their precursor's intentions, or perhaps because they shifted their art fully into the aesthetic sphere. Whatever their purpose, these simplifiers cleared the way for Bruegel, who, likewise, omitted the nonpictorial frameworks.

Not only is Bruegel the painter, programmatically, of world pictures—the term was practically invented for him. In his art appears everything that goes with such pictures. While he was not a natural scientist, his works are, through their ethnographic perspective, precocious expressions of the *human* sciences: they inquire what human being is by studying what human beings make. Though not quite of the era of machine technology, Bruegel did use the printing press to place his world pictures before a worldwide public, and his many engraved portraits of ships study the machines of world exploration and domination. In the collectibles he engineered for the aesthetic sphere, Bruegel made his production conform to what art henceforth would be: pictures of experience for experience. As this art's most essential subject, he portrayed culture—for Heidegger the quintessential modern value—allowing its strange forms to unfold in a landscape of global proportions. And when in Bruegel the gods appear, they do so precisely to disappear. Thus, the world picture has come of age.

The Human Position

Bruegel made the first monumental paintings of everyday life. He did this by raising worldliness to the level of a theme and by portraying grand subjects from a provocatively ordinary point of view. *The Fall of Icarus* accomplishes this inversion, making the ordinary heroic and the heroic ordinary (fig. 262).[22] Now in the Musées des Beaux-Arts in Brussels, the painting is (probably) in oil on primed canvas and is poorly preserved. Its status as an autograph Bruegel has long been contested, and there is disagreement about its original support—whether it was originally on canvas and subsequently repaired and repeatedly relined, or whether it is a panel painting transferred to canvas, which might explain the oil technique and the priming. A second surviving version of the composition, executed on panel at least a decade after Bruegel's death and now in the Museum Van Buuren, shows Daedalus hovering in the air; thus making sense of the shepherd's skyward gaze (fig. 263). This might mean that the Musées des Beaux-Arts picture imperfectly copies a lost Bruegel that included Daedalus; that it, too, showed Daedalus, but he has been cropped away; or—most intriguingly—that the painter of the later Museum Van Buuren version added Daedalus to clarify the original picture's plot. Despite these uncertainties, and with a growing consensus that the work probably is indeed a copy (its flaws concealed by old

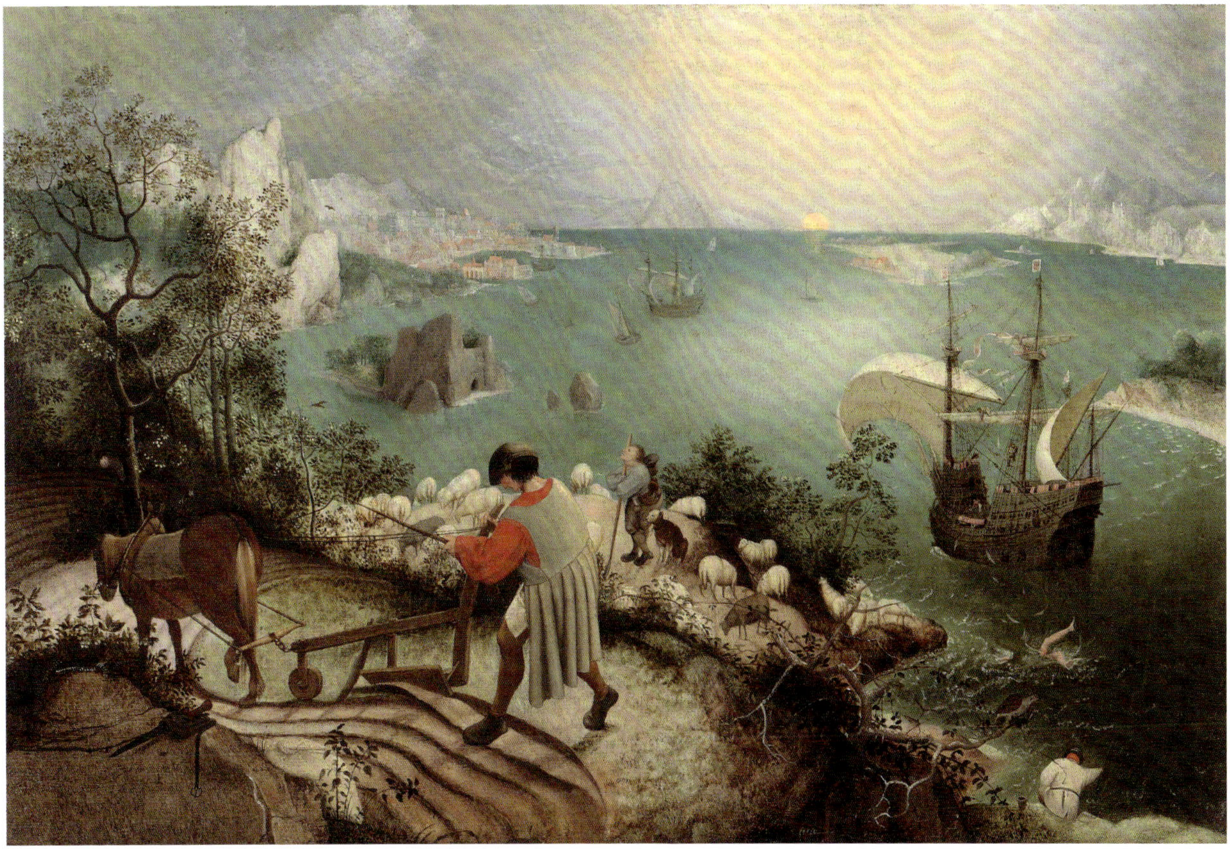

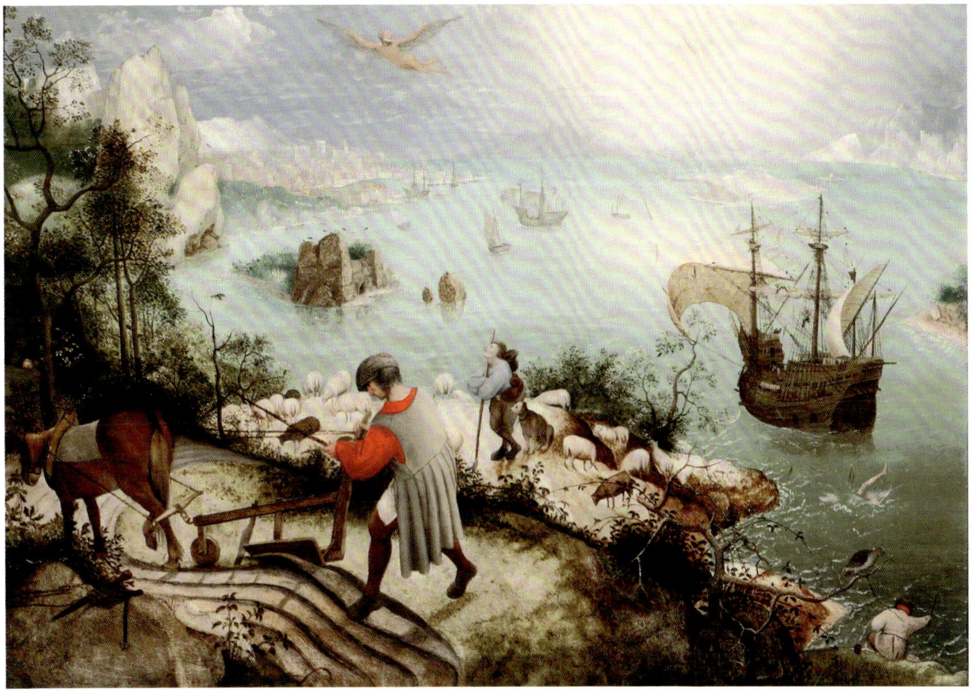

(ABOVE) **262** Pieter Bruegel the Elder, *The Fall of Icarus*, c. 1560 (?), tempera on canvas mounted on wood, Musées Royaux des Beaux-Arts de Belgique, Brussels

(LEFT) **263** After Pieter Bruegel the Elder, *The Fall of Icarus*, c. 1590–95, panel, Museum and gardens van Buuren, Brussels yellow varnish and the aura of fame), the Brussels *Fall of Icarus* remains a fabulous creation, and its exemplarity has been sharpened by powerful readings of it, most famously in W. H. Auden's 1938 poem "Musée des Beaux Arts."[23] Bruegel's single foray into classical myth, the picture conceals its legend about artistry and ambition within a cosmic tableau of mundane works and days.

Daedalus, the archetypal artificer, is nowhere to be seen, while the death of his overreaching son, Icarus, who flew too close to the sun on wings made by his father, makes no impact on the picture's world. As Auden put it, "Everything turns away / Quite leisurely from the disaster." Oblivious to the little splash of drowning Icarus, the fisherman casts his net, the shepherd tends his flock, the ship sails out to sea, and the plowman carves mazy furrows in the earth. The setting sun—Icarus's nemesis—lights those repeating trenches majestically, suggesting that the things that count are the *diurnal* ones.[24]

Bruegel spent two years in Italy.[25] Traveling the length of the peninsula to Sicily and settling in Rome, where he collaborated with the miniaturist and Michelangelo imitator Giulio Clovio, he would have known intimately the grand manner created there, which portrayed the gods in a heroic, classicizing figural style.[26] Returning to Antwerp around 1554, he would also have seen this style zealously imitated by Flemish painters and engravers (see fig. 72). Indeed, as much as the Italians themselves, these northerners, through their reproductive mastery, established classical manner and myth as the international idiom of high art. Bruegel resisted this tendency. The drawings he brought back from Italy record the landscapes he passed through, not the art—ancient or Renaissance—encountered on the way (see figs. 306–308). And when he painted human subjects, he treated vernacular themes in a self-consciously vernacular style, with the peasant customs and craft goods symbolizing the indigenousness of his own production.

The Fall of Icarus resists its source. With the local rustics, it turns its back on the Greco-Roman myth.[27] Italy—its coasts evoked by the fantastical background—becomes not a destination but another point of departure.[28] Nature dwarfs culture naturally: Icarus's flailing limbs hardly register, because the painting is scaled not to humans but to the world. Cleverly, this viewpoint actually agrees with the myth. Against the son's foolish striving, the story preaches the middle way. Daedalus instructs Icarus to fly between the fiery sun and the dampening waters. Bruegel understood the tale he eclipsed, how it recommended temperance in the telling. Its target, pride, was Bruegel's target, too, in Saul's suicide, Paul's conversion, Lucifer's rebellion, and *The Tower of Babel*. Even the rustic staffage in the Brussels canvas agrees with the myth. In the canonical version, Ovid writes:

> Far off, far down, some fisherman is watching
> Some shepherd rests his weight upon his crook,
> Some plowman on the handles of his plowshare,
> And all look up, in absolute amazement,
> At those air-borne above. They must be gods.[29]

They are not gods. Bruegel teaches the legend's lesson by leaving amazement out and by turning Ovid's bystanders back to their elemental labor. Indifference to individual failure comes naturally to them because they have work to do ("No plow stops for the sake of a dying man," as a proverb has it), and because nature, which they cultivate, is potentially indifferent to them.[30]

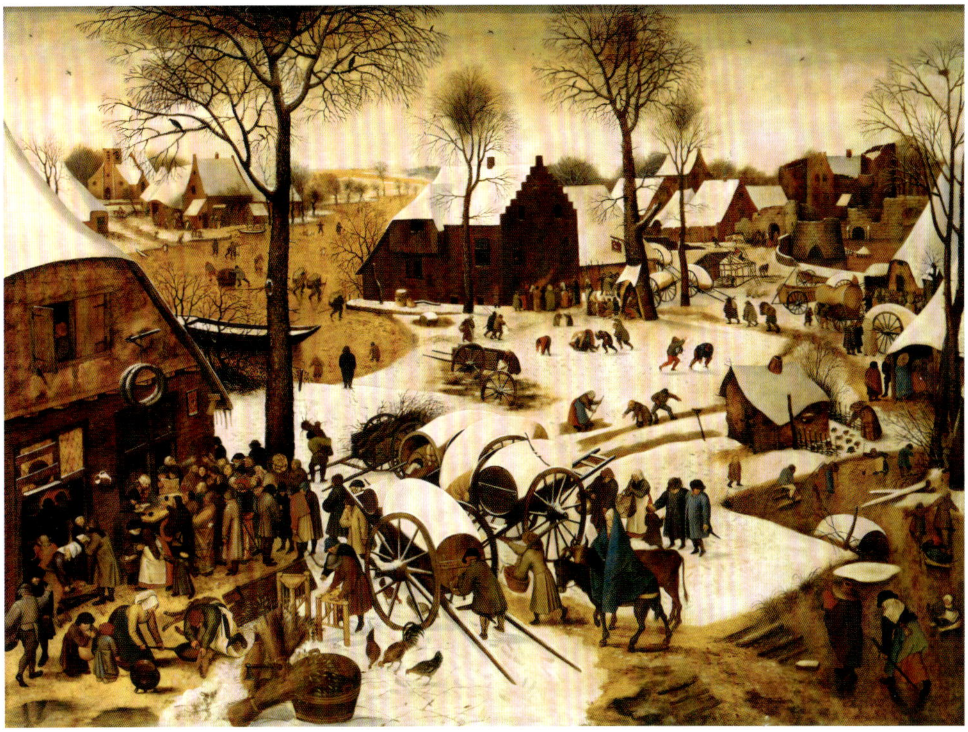

264 Pieter Bruegel the Younger, after Pieter Bruegel the Elder, *The Census at Bethlehem*, 1610, oil on panel, Musées Royaux des Beaux-Arts de Belgique, Brussels

In Auden's poem, the "Old Masters" were never wrong "about suffering," about "its human position: how it takes place / While someone else is eating or opening a window or just walking dully along." This peculiar knowledge—effectively an understanding of evil and rephrasing of the ancient question *unde malum*—is also where *The Fall of Icarus* transcends its myth. That the rustics turn away could be predicted in Ovid, since they wonder only at the godlike apparition, not at the all-too-human fall about to come. The wax-and-feather wings having failed, these onlookers would no doubt have gone about their business. The antique tale already has this bathos built into it. In medieval and early modern allegories, Icarus's flight, disobedient to his father's urging, always stood for prideful self-importance; having his fall ignored would be his just deserts. Bruegel departs from the legend not by mocking Icarus's folly but by monumentalizing ordinary human oblivion—what the people do while the proverbial "someone else" suffers. The dull activity of the plowman arrests our attention. Huge in the picture, his red shirt like a flag within the vast greenish-blue world picture, he directs us implausibly to what absorbs him: the share of his turnplow slicing through and turning over the humus in neat, parallel furrows.

Everyday human life as it is lived, absorption in life as the almost heroic oblivion to death: this is the new, terrifying modern myth. The Old Masters "never forget" that life goes on:

> How, when the aged are reverently, passionately waiting
> For the miraculous birth, there always must be
> Children who did not specially want it to happen, skating
> On a pond at the edge of the wood.

These lines do not fit the Bruegel that Auden names, but they do describe another painting in the Musées des Beaux-Arts (fig. 264).[31] Copied repeatedly by Bruegel's son and namesake, this large panel—almost certainly autograph—is one of Bruegel's most secretive works.

Nothing unusual seems to be happening in this compendium of Brabant village life in winter. As usual, Bruegel thrusts us into the usual. From a distance both spatial and cultural, he lets us explore and smilingly recognize life's goings-on. People work, walk, or idly mill around, while the children entertain themselves greatly, throwing snowballs, wrestling, spinning tops, and skating and sledding on the ice. On the waters at the lower right, a girl pulls her brother on a tripod chair while a littler child, hatless and shivering, looks sadly on. These are Auden's skaters "on a pond at the edge of the wood." Why, according to the poem, must they "always" be there? Because blissfully and cruelly self-absorbed in their play, children stand for indifference as the inborn and perennial "position" of the human species.

Oblivion is more complete in this painting than in *The Fall of Icarus*. The principal action unfolding at the left of the painting—the collection of taxes by imperial officers, as signaled by the placard with Habsburg arms—stands obliquely for the biblical story in play: the Roman imperial census, described in the Gospel of Luke, that forced Joseph and Mary to travel from their home in Nazareth to Bethlehem, where Christ was born. The holy figures wander into Bruegel's picture unnoticed. Joseph, with carpenter's tools as his only attribute, leads a blue-robed Mary on an ass, accompanied (helpfully for the viewer, and therefore humorously, too) by the faithful ox of Nativity scenes. Their entrance to Bethlehem is further obscured by another couple, lower right, who also arrive with an infant in arms. In introducing this anonymous threesome, Bruegel risked causing viewers to mistake it for the Holy Family, as indeed some commentators have.[32] The birth of Christ has not yet happened, though, and these arrivals are just ordinary folks. What the painting, according to Auden, wordlessly says is that people not only did not passionately and reverently await the miracle; they resented it, as children do a more special birth than theirs. The Auden reading goes beyond what Bruegel shows, but the picture invites the inference. Because the inn has been requisitioned for use by government tax collectors, we can infer that Joseph and Mary will be refused harbor, and that they will seek shelter elsewhere, in a stable not yet in view. Everyday knowledge about the ways of the world—for Bruegel's audience in 1566, bitter experience with imperial functionaries—aids our inferences and sharpens our understanding of the Bible story. It also lets that story illuminate everyday life and the place of suffering in it.

One of Bruegel's lesser-known masterpieces—a small panel dated 1563 and now in the Museum Oskar Reinhart in Winterthur—tells an even darker story about the world's indifference (fig. 265).[33] In a gesture of sublime irony, the painter makes the biblical Epiphany—Christ's singular, world-changing "coming to light"—almost disappear. Tiny at the lower left of this painting, the sacred actors recede into the shadows of the ruined stables. It takes work to make them out: the Magi, Joseph, and the Virgin and Child—the lattermost group so close to the framing edge that they almost escape the picture. The African Magus stands, as usual, a step back from the threshold, his features merging with the background darkness that the brilliant snow punctuates and obscures. Bruegel knew that his art departed from religion. Supreme artistic self-consciousness allows his works to be their own best commentary. Here the eclipse of biblical narrative is not some career choice he has made—say, to follow the dictates of contemporary taste or give an alibi for painting landscape. It is, rather, the true state of things, both *back then*, when Christ was born, homeless and uncelebrated, in a stable in Bethlehem, and *now*, in the painter's age, in the Flemish lifeworld Bruegel intimately knows and into which he projects Christ's birth. The painter shows what an Epiphany would look like to imperfect

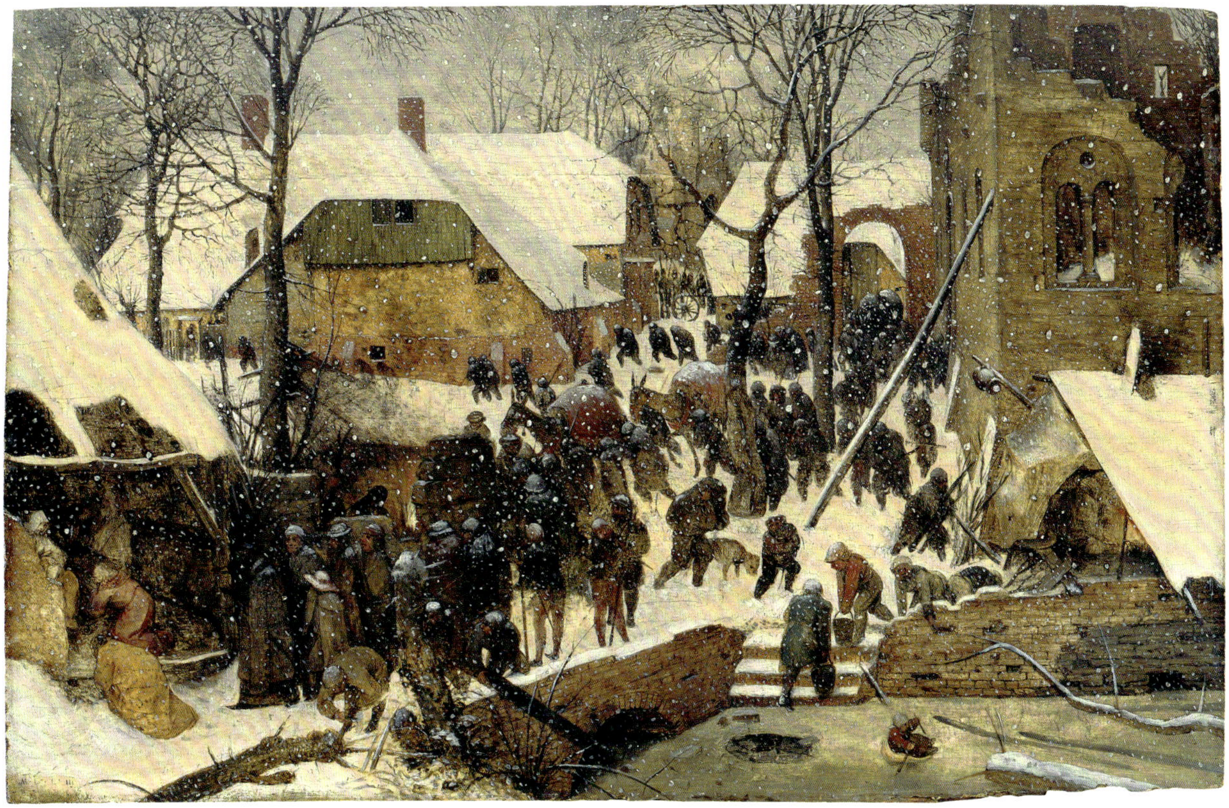

265 Pieter Bruegel the Elder, *The Adoration of the Kings in the Snow* (*Epiphany*), 1563, panel, Collection Oskar Reinhart, "Am Römerholz," Winterthur

human eyes: an event obscure to perception and overwhelmed by the demands nature and circumstance put on us. While the Magi gather around Christ, their entourage loiters, armed, idle, and potentially dangerous, as Netherlanders in 1567 would have known, with Habsburg forces beginning to occupy their towns. In the picture, the locals labor to survive. They gather twigs for fuel, fetch water from the frozen river, collect their children, and hustle home through the snow, ignoring—perhaps studiously—the foreign arrivals. The snow, their actions suggest, will grow into a blizzard.

That snow is Bruegel's most daring innovation. This is the first—and arguably the best—portrait of a snowfall in art history. Painted last, in hundreds of dabs of paint, the falling flakes pinpoint our sense of being there at one temporally fugitive moment on this particular wintry night. All differently sized and of different quantities of white, the flakes also cause our eyes to focus as if in and out of an envelope of air intervening between us and the represented scene. Applied on top of the finished scene, interrupting and refreshing it with a mesmerizing sparkle, the snow intensifies the obscurity, making the darks darker to the eye, heightening the drabness of the trodden snow, and making distances everywhere retreat. To paint snowfall, Bruegel has had to efface with dots his already finished painting—a bold gesture for a work as subtle as this, but one that projects the painting into a palpable present tense. Lead white comes to behave like snow, concealing what it touches. Observe in the picture the many boards and planks gathering snow rather as Bruegel's own panel gets coated in white. Observe also the subtlety of this coating, how the slightly bent pole propped diagonally against the ruin at the right (Bruegel's version of King David's palace in Bethlehem) catches less snow on its steeper pitch.

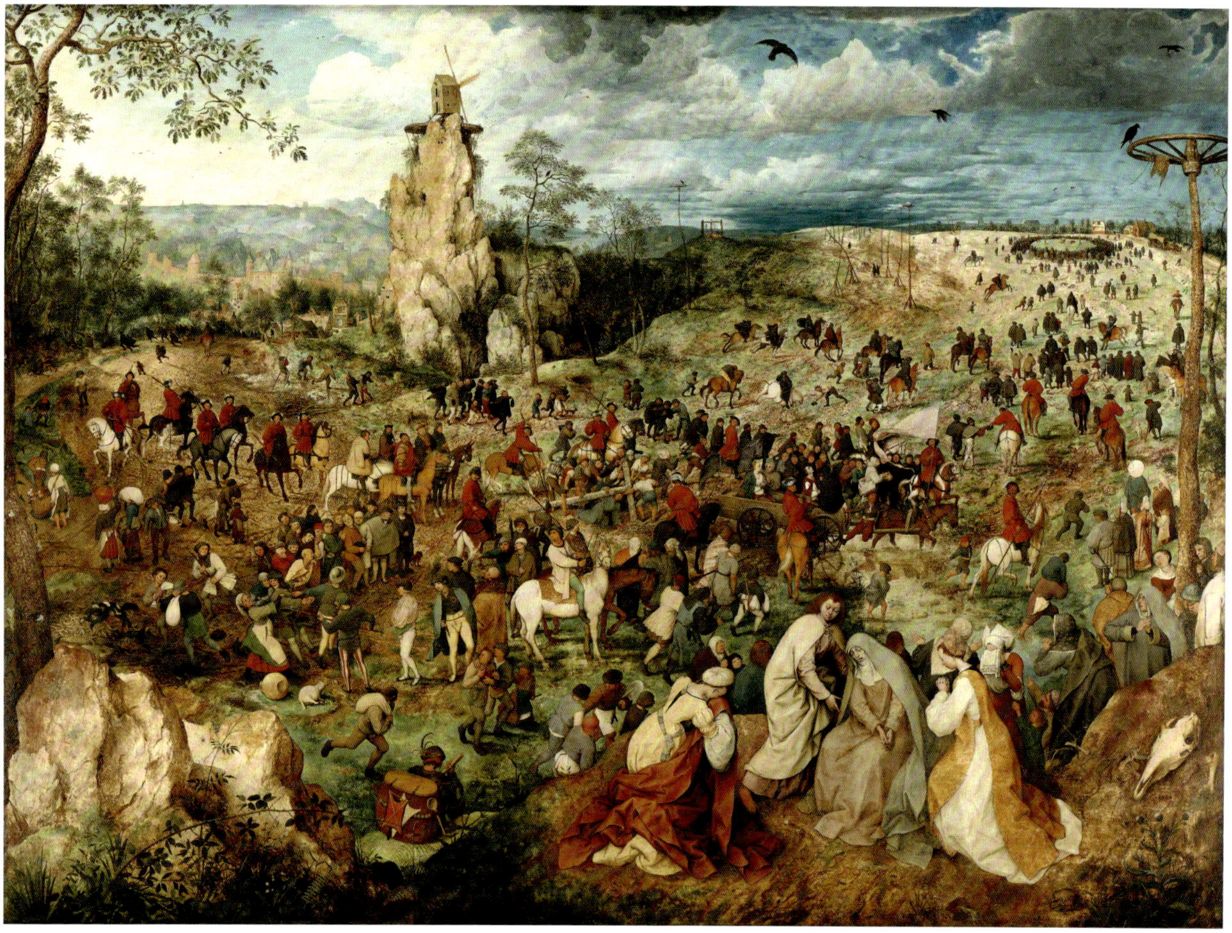

266 Pieter Bruegel the Elder, *Christ Carrying the Cross*, 1564, panel, Kunsthistorisches Museum, Vienna

This snow looks as if it will continue unabated, however, and if it does—the picture suggests—the Epiphany, both the one Bruegel paints and his painting itself, will completely disappear. This again calls to mind Van Mander's description of artists "allowing the preparation [*gronden*] on the panels or canvases to play a part." The sublime glow that fills Bruegel's landscapes derives from the smooth, bright, warm-toned underlying surface—composed of white chalk and some binding medium and meticulously smoothed—that in sixteenth-century Dutch, as well as in modern English, is termed the painting's "ground."[34] In both languages, *ground* also means "reason," "cause," or "foundation"—what ancient philosophers termed the *episteme*. In this version of the Epiphany, snowfall is reverting the painting to the thing it originally was: a blank supporting surface. Indeed in several passages, Bruegel used the unpainted ground to represent snow. Created out of nothing, painting creates a groundless nothing in the end.

An all-white painting, or a painting concealed in paint, would have had a special connotation at the time. During the great iconoclasm that swept through the Netherlands in 1566, image breakers, instead of smashing or burning effigies, sometimes covered them in white or black. Van Mander lamented of an altarpiece by Hugo van der Goes treated in this way—by a fellow painter, to Van Mander's dismay, with radical convictions.[35] To strict iconoclasts, sacred images deceived viewers into idolatrously mistaking the images for the persons they represent. Painting them over with white made the removal itself brilliantly visible, with the whitewash commemorating the act of church cleansing.[36] Bruegel mounts a far subtler critique, one that, as old as Christian art itself, he could have learned from Bosch. In Christ, God revealed Himself iconoclastically. Incarnated as a mere mortal man, born in humble circumstances, ignored and vilified in life, and dying the abject death of a criminal, Christ concealed his divinity; or more precisely, humanity did this to him, since they caused his poverty, suffering, and death.[37] When the Magi (who in Auden "reverently, passionately" wait) testify to Christ's miraculous birth, their witness unfolds against the blank of human oblivion. Christ's visibility as God was and remains veiled, and painters, not iconoclasts, know how to visualize invisibility. The snow that turns the dim Epiphany a blinding white conceals what human being eclipsed.

The Road to Calvary

Nowhere is this question of the grounds of Bruegel's art, of its physical *and metaphysical* foundations, more vividly posed than in his largest extant panel—also the largest landscape painting in early Netherlandish art—*Christ Carrying the Cross*, which engages the entire tradition of religious art that Bruegel also leaves behind (fig. 266).[38] A painting in Budapest after a lost but much-copied original by Jan van Eyck shows that Bruegel's dialogue is with a deep and distant past (fig. 267).[39] Already here, in a composition devised in the early fifteenth century, sacred history was beginning to be pictured tracing a great circle through an expanded vision of the world. A parade stretching from Jerusalem's gates to the hill of Calvary, the road to death has brought Christ to the very center of this earliest of worldscapes. However, the visual chaos of a cruel and callous humanity, plus the procession's relentless forward march, indicates that center—and our viewpoint—to be but a transitory moment in a plot that ends elsewhere. Ultimately, so the story goes, the Crucifixion will transcend all movement, time, and death, releasing us from the dolorous path we also tread. But in the meantime, at the random center of history and the world where this painting places us, everything remains in ceaseless motion, like windmills in a breeze.

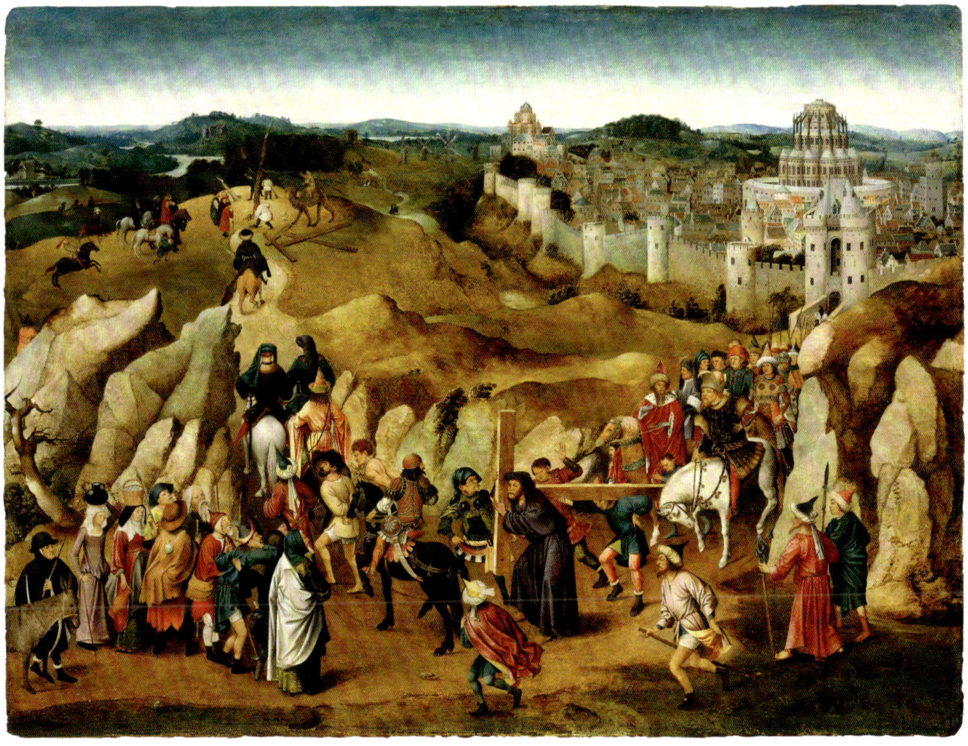

267 After Jan van Eyck, *Christ Carrying the Cross*, c. 1530, panel, Szépművészeti Múzeum, Budapest

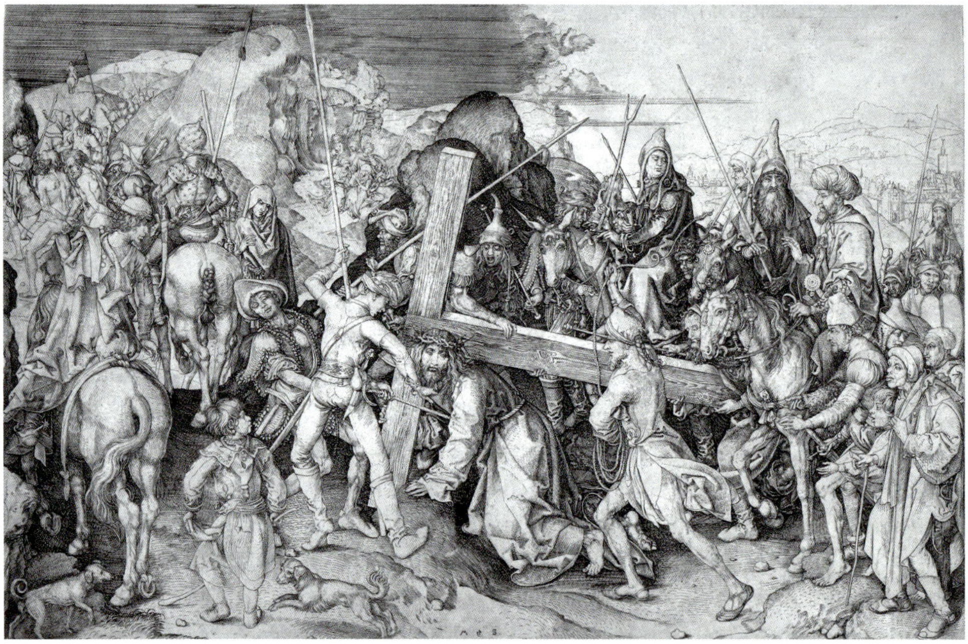

268 Martin Schongauer, *Christ Carrying the Cross*, n.d., engraving, National Gallery of Art, Washington, Andrew W. Mellon Fund

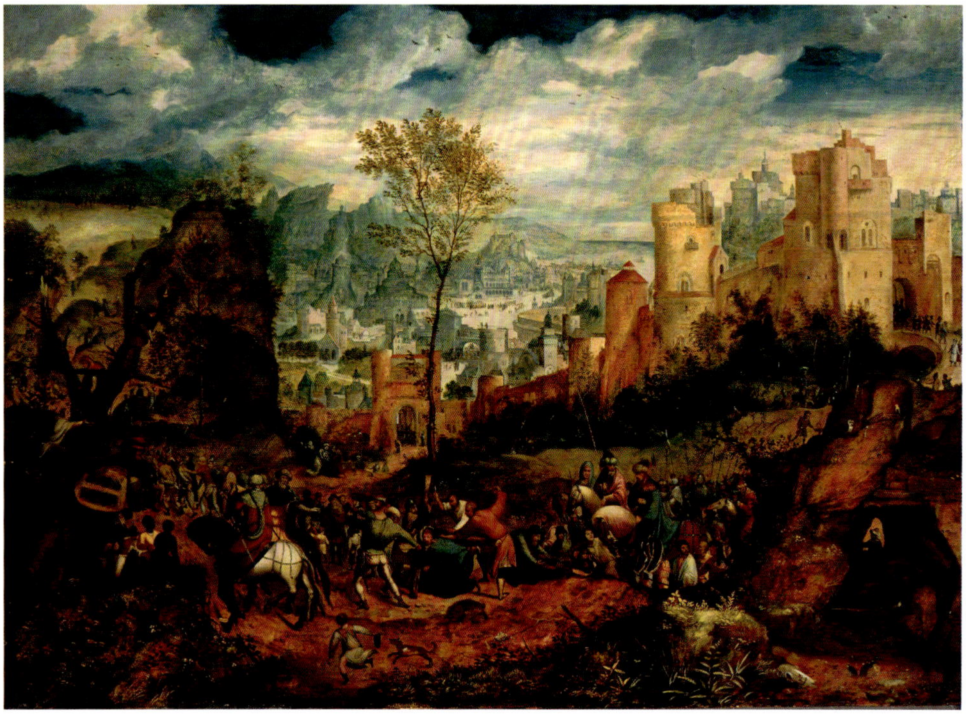

269 Herri met de Bles, *The Road to Calvary*, c. 1535, oil on wood panel, museum purchase, gift of the Friends of the Princeton University Art Museum, 1950–51

Bruegel need not have known Van Eyck's composition to have engaged its idea. At almost half a meter wide the largest and most ambitious engraving of its day, Martin Schongauer's *Christ Carrying the Cross*, exerted a massive impact on later art (fig. 268). Again at the picture's center but brought to the foreground, Christ looks out at us, his suffering face freeze-framed in the dense narrative flow. In other versions of this subject, Saint Veronica kneels before Christ to receive on her sweat cloth that frontal image of suffering; here, the engraved face of Christ is that sacred icon. Schongauer pictures the drama's time frame by dividing the sky into light and dark; the solar eclipse that will occur at his death already coincides with the *nunc stans* of the immobile, immutable Christ. Bruegel had even closer precedents than this, though. A

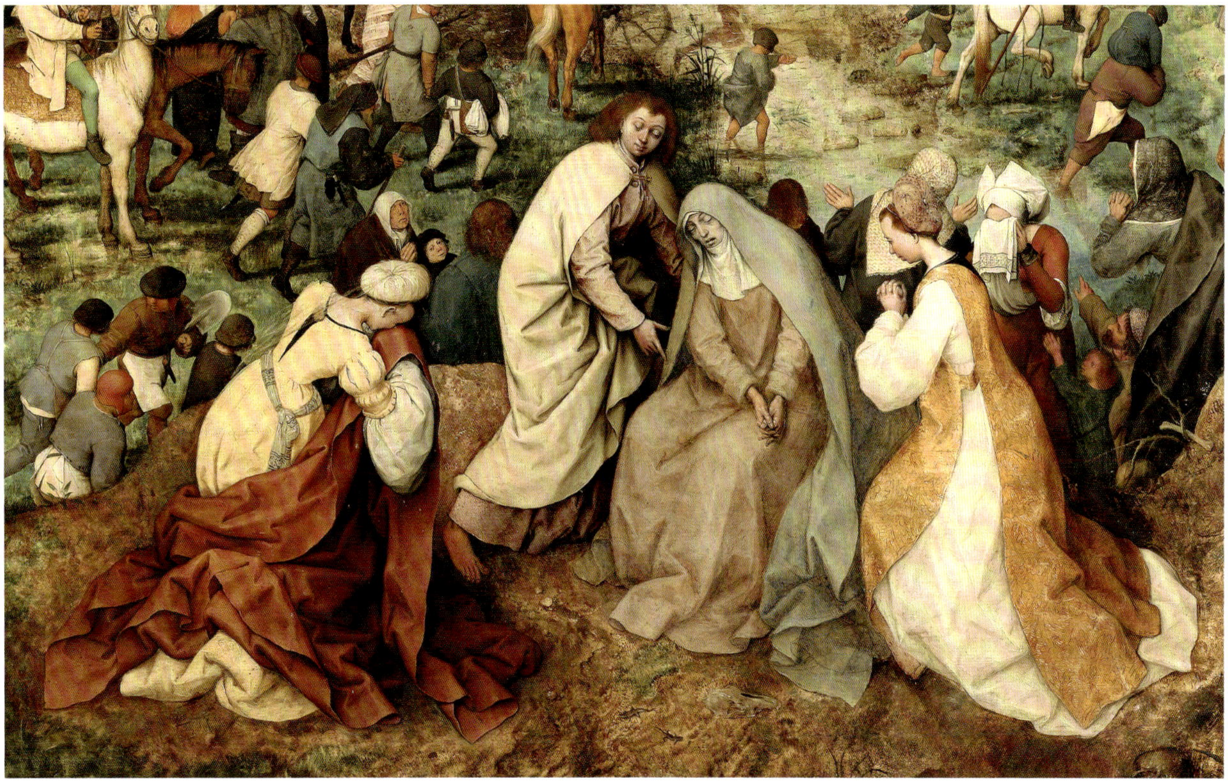

270 Detail of Pieter Bruegel the Elder, *Christ Carrying the Cross* (fig. 266)

host of mid-sixteenth-century painters, especially in Antwerp, updated the Eyckian design, among them Herri met de Bles, Pieter Aertsen, and Jan Amstel (fig. 269).[40] Bruegel's direct predecessors (Amstel may even have been one of his teachers), these artists embellished the sacred story with genre anecdotes all set against a fantastical landscape backdrop. Outlandish buildings, costumes, and personages signal vaguely the historical context of the event, its occurrence in the distant biblical past. But they also imagine an equally foreign Jerusalem of the painter's own era. Exoticism itself was fashionable among Antwerp's best painters, as the rage for paintings of the Magi proved (see figs. 17 and 104). It advertised the worldliness of that trade capital and its products. Local evocations of the strange, these paintings remain—in spite of themselves—thoroughly vernacular artifacts.

Bruegel, by contrast, openly pictures the story in local terms. He makes the place the Netherlands, and the time circa 1565. Jerusalem has become a walled northern European city, Golgotha lies on the commons of a pleasant Brabant village, Christ's executioners belong to a modern imperial militia, the eager crowds—in their costume and equipment—are fully of the painter's time, and the road that sacred history travels is but the waterlogged ground of Brabant. The biblical moment has been reduced to Christ, who crawls to Calvary in ancient robes, but whose passage—occurring in Bruegel's here and now—is an eternal recurrence of the same. More than updating the story, these displacements announce that such an event *can* happen now and most likely *is* happening now. People continue to kill the innocent and take morbid pleasure in the act. But to make this point about present circumstance, he also introduces a sedimented past.

There is an exception to the picture's presentism, and Bruegel distinguishes it by completely changing how he paints. Saint John, the Virgin, and the other weeping women are of neither the *biblical past* nor *Bruegel's own time* (fig. 270). Their elongated forms, delicate

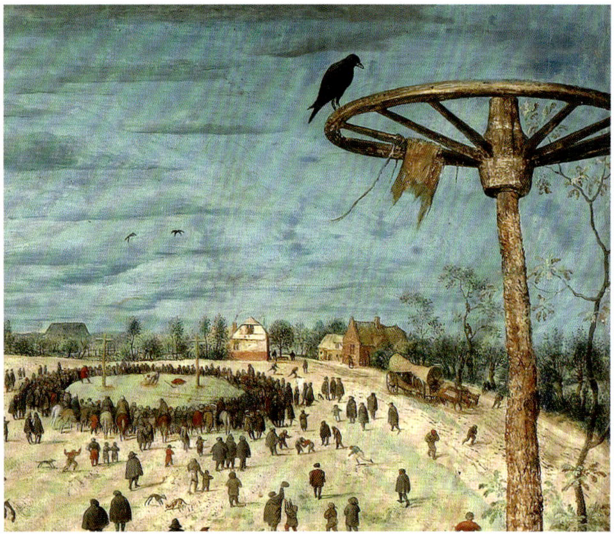

271 Detail of Pieter Bruegel the Elder, *Christ Carrying the Cross* (fig. 266)

features, muted colors, sharp silhouettes, and cascading drapery belong to the visual language of painters who predated Bruegel by more than a century. Through these mourners—the only proper respondents to the terrible event—Bruegel returns us to the historical foundation of his craft, to the art of Jan van Eyck, Rogier van der Weyden, and Hugo van der Goes (e.g., see fig. 25).[41] By the 1560s, Netherlandish painters and printmakers had become intensely aware of the local history of their craft. New collecting practices, an awakening pride in local artistic achievements, a budding historiography of northern art, and refined practices of preserving, copying, and engraving prestigious originals all contributed to an increased consciousness that between the present moment and a distant historical past there stood a multilayered history of making. Celebrated in his day for his truth to nature, but deeply aware of how cultural difference is inscribed into all human customs and artifacts, including images, Bruegel would have recognized that his skill belonged to a vernacular tradition. And it is this that he displays in the foreground like stylistic fossils from the past: note the minutely detailed vegetation, an homage to early Netherlandish naturalism. There is something deeply paradoxical about this display, however. Bruegel reverses the expected stratigraphy of historical styles. The archaic foreground layer, datable to circa 1440, does not look *up* from where it is buried but *down* upon a later world sunk beneath it. To solve this puzzle and appreciate Bruegel's radical design, it helps to reconstruct a first impression of the *Christ Carrying the Cross.*

The painting sends us soaring into its distances and then catches us in a vast, spiraling flow of people. These crowds march out from the low-set city at the left, curve forward toward us at the center, and then pass onward and upward toward a higher distance on the right (fig. 271). There, in the visual full stop of the circular crowd, we discover the center is missing: on the hill of Golgotha, Christ's Cross has not yet been raised, and this absence sends us searching, first in the foreground, in a scene our eye originally slipped past. Yet here, where we expect to find him among his followers, Christ is again nowhere to be seen. The stake and wheel at the far right, together with the skull at its base, trick us into thinking that the crucifix rises next to the Virgin, on this Golgotha, this hill of the skull.

Between the skull and the wheel, however, a second group of mourners nudges us back into the landscape. All wear contemporary dress; the man in the pale red cap farthest to the right—believed by some to be a self-portrait of Bruegel—observes the landscape just as we do,

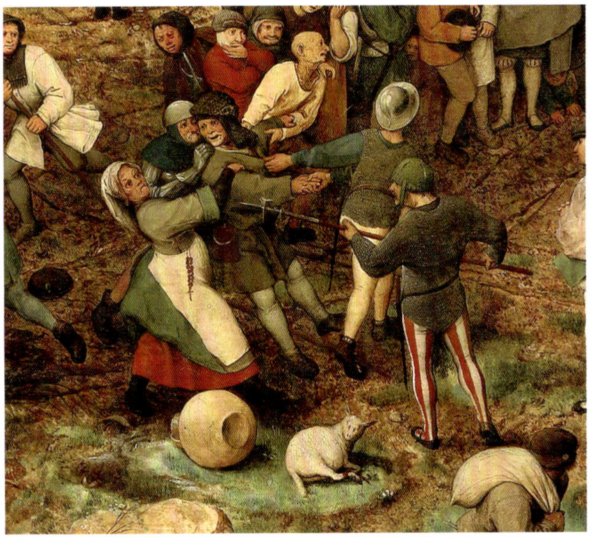

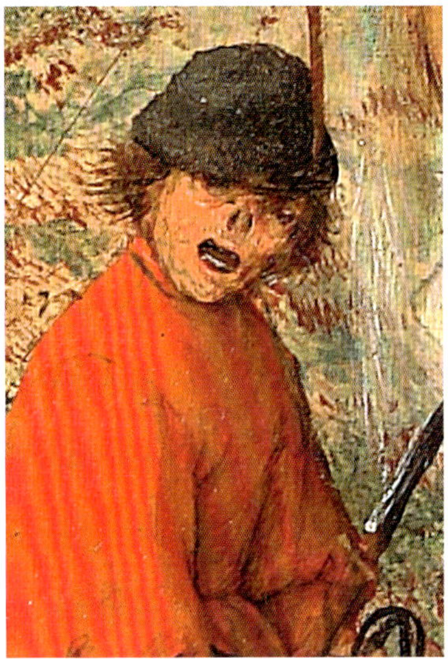

272 Detail of Pieter Bruegel the Elder, *Christ Carrying the Cross* (fig. 266)

273 Detail of Pieter Bruegel the Elder, *Christ Carrying the Cross* (fig. 266)

with the stake just to his side, framing his gaze. Tossed back into the stream of humanity, we seek—and at some point we discover—the minuscule figure of Christ. Dwarfing him in the landscape and obscuring him in the crowds, Bruegel performs the world's oblivion to Christ. This had been the point of Bruegel's *Census at Bethlehem* and *Adoration in the Snow* (see figs. 264 and 265), and it was a central theme in Bosch, as well. Love of the world causes everyone to overlook Christ. Yet whereas Bosch aligned his painting's perspective with divine judgment, Bruegel places it inside the worldly parade.

It is one of the painting's many ironies that everything rushes vivaciously toward death. This is not because—as in Bosch—that is where we are secretly bound. Death does saturate this picture, most obviously in those stakes and wheels that measure recession into the distance, their crooked forms turning the perspectival system into a macabre dance. Death is first and foremost the object of morbid curiosity among the living. The galloping horses and running children grow sluggish only around the beaten, Cross-bearing Christ. Rubbernecking in the thick of the violence, they bunch up there, then speed off ahead to reserve a good spot to watch the Crucifixion. Whereas in Bosch people lust for life but get unwittingly trapped in death, here people strain to get a good look at death: watching someone die seems the best thing going. Excepting the lamenters, only one person resists joining the parade.

According to the Gospel, soldiers compelled Simon of Cyrene to bear Christ's Cross; in Bruegel, he is held back by his formidable wife, who, ironically outfitted with a rosary, knows full well not to get mixed up in any of this (fig. 272). While the multitudes are drawn to the Crucifixion but show their backs to Christ, Simon, the one called to carry Christ's burden, draws uniquely backward. His name in Hebrew—*Śimʿôn*—meaning "hearkening" or "listening" (observe, though, the big flaps covering his ears), he gazes frantically in our direction. Bruegel paints a vivid picture of the whole episode. A motley trio of henchmen drags Simon forward while a fourth, armed with a halberd, commands the wife to back off. The bystanders do as their name implies: they stand by—mostly wide-eyed and fearful—inactive, before the force of law. This force has a terrifying embodiment in the mounted soldier who, head turned back toward Simon, seems to shout at him the order for his abduction. He is a memorable monstrosity (fig. 273). Lacking a nose, his face resembles a skull, but—typically for Bruegel—the symbol is real. In Bruegel's era, the militia was made up largely of mercenaries. Not merely

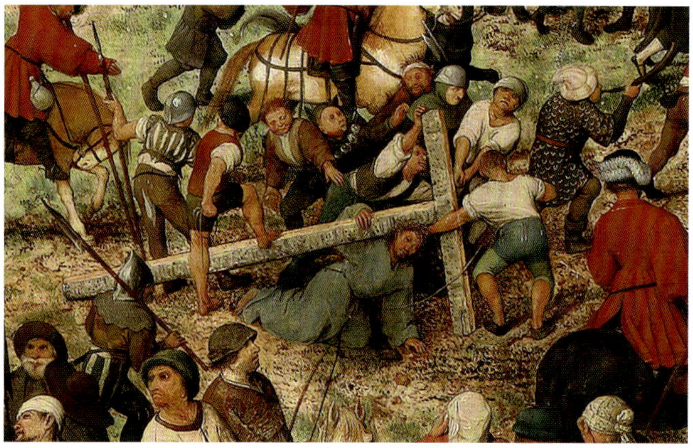

274 Detail of Pieter Bruegel the Elder, *Christ Carrying the Cross* (fig. 266)

battle-scarred, they were also former convicted criminals who bore the disfiguring marks of corporal punishment.[42] Lopping an offender's nose off—a common penalty—marked him as an outcast, good for nothing legal except perhaps for the violence of war. In a real-life instance of the law placed in criminal hands, the monstrous mercenary clears a pathway in the crowds between Simon and the Cross. Christ therefore kneels between two centers of indifference. One is near the picture's vanishing point, in that empty circle of gawkers on the horizon. The other is located at Simon, near the picture's viewpoint, where our faith is tested.

Although tiny, Christ himself faces us from the geometric center of the panel (fig. 274). This is the picture's most Boschian moment. Through its inscription, Bosch's *Seven Deadly Sins* purported to make the device—literally—unmissable, since, if the viewer failed to see the giant eye at the picture's center, that eye saw the viewer's failure (see fig. 122). The Lisbon *Saint Anthony*, in its open state, collapsed the all-seeing eye to a tiny speck of paint at its midpoint: the hermit's gaze (see fig. 169). And the so-called *Garden of Delights* hid the kernel of its entropy in its central fountains, but in each case the panel's geometric midpoint—its real, material center—stood apart from the rest as the pivot or turning point of the entire display (see fig. 203). Again, this device short-circuits linear perspective, which wants us, as it were, to think away the picture plane and see through it as through an open window to a vista whose center (the perspectival vanishing point) is contingent on us, on our viewpoint. The great tumult of *Christ Carrying the Cross* has a vanishing point on the horizon, left of center, near the skylined gibbet; the receding torture wheels vividly map its location. But to this, the world picture's structure as human view, Bruegel adds that other, Boschian structure, with its center on the painting's material support.

As Bosch would have done, Bruegel occupies this center with the picture's crux: the Holy Face or en face portrait-icon of the suffering Christ. He even surrounds that face with a Boschian gallery of rogues: a Fool as court jester mocks Christ's claim to be king of the Jews while the group's exotically dressed leader, probably meant to be a Jew, blasts a shofar, mockingly heralding the Messiah. However, this center behaves differently than it would in Bosch. Bosch not only marks the midpoint with some special element in the picture's composition but also connects that element, by way of its centered mark, to a divine architecture transcending the painting's fiction. Flanked by paradise and hell, framed by history's beginning and its end, and evoking the sacred geography of altar and church, the center, this surrounding geography proclaims, has an absolute foundation in divine law. All human acts, including the act of viewing, are subordinate to this law. Again, Bruegel produced no altarpieces. His

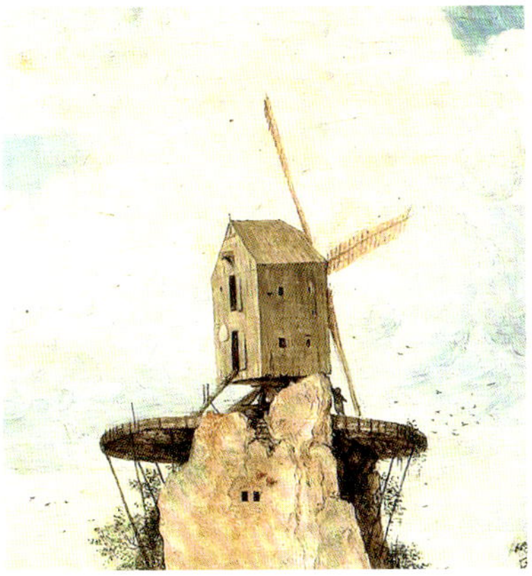

275 Detail of Pieter Bruegel the Elder, *Christ Carrying the Cross* (fig. 266)

vehicles were prints and gallery pictures. These were built for mobility and stabilized only by the structural coherence of their views. Rectangular, window-like objects, they envelop us inside their frames wherever they hang. Functionally equipped for aesthetic detachment, *Christ Carrying the Cross* founds its center not absolutely but contingently. Christ kneels at the middle of the panel because the painting, fitted to the fleeting attention of an artwork's casual beholder, is turned toward him: the Boschian center is keyed to an act on the part of the painting or painter to aim (as it were) the camera at Christ. Rather than subordinating our relative viewpoint to a higher law, Christ's centered form remains completely contingent on us, being a function of an aesthetic attitude free to make *anything* its center. True, Bruegel moralizes this freedom. Simon of Cyrene's refusal encapsulates humanity's indifference to the suffering of someone else. But the freedom remains in the form of the question the picture poses without answering: What would you do?

In one of the painting's most profound passages, Bruegel likens viewing—our activity vis-à-vis this painting—to Christ's torment (see fig. 271). The torture wheel raised above the high horizon at the upper right is—in its painted image—the exact size and shape as the circle on Calvary. The one seen from below, the other from above, and belonging to each other as a lid does to a jar, these two rings are engineered both to puzzle us by their kinship and to answer their riddle. They equate standing by with torture, announcing by that equation what Christian preachers long had preached: that humanity itself is the Cross Christ bore; that, in our indifference, in the human position of suffering, *we* are instruments of his torment. The centers of both these rings are not fixed but monstrously mobile. In the one center, visible if the viewer gets close up to the surface of the panel (microphotographs have brought minuscule detail to light), an executioner busily drills into the earth a hole in which to the plant the Cross; in the other center, the stake sits loosely where the wheel's axle would be fixed, allowing the circle to wobble dangerously round, along with all the other wheels that plunge us into the distance, including the cross-shaped sails of the windmill in the sky (fig. 275).[43] Note how that building's precarious base is a disk, as well. These terrible rings place us on a circular periphery, where we indeed do stand. For the procession to Calvary is itself a colossal wheel with the giant rock pinnacle as its monstrous axle. The carrying of the Cross and the road to Calvary that it follows form two rings, the one mobile and grinding like a millstone from above (hence the windmill), the other immobile but marshy and vulnerable to wear by the other, upper ring. The mobile wheel is the circular movement of humanity in its endless march to death. (According to legend, Golgotha, the hill where Christ was crucified, was also the spot where Adam's corpse to say something about *nothing*, for example, about the nothing, or *nihil*, before the world's Creation, out of which God created the world; or about the no-things, or *impossibilia*, that humans can mentally picture and that artists can wondrously portray. As a maker of Boschian disparities, Bruegel would have understood himself to be a cause of a most peculiar kind. How fitting it would then have been that the ground of the road to Calvary, wearing down the world to nothing, was in fact the nothing on which painting as an art itself was based.

Christ crawls on Boschian terrain. The watery passage where the wagon driver lifts his legs to stay dry seems worlds apart from the primal waters of the so-called *Garden*, yet both paintings grapple with the same question: Where does evil come from? And both answer this question by investigating grounds in the double sense: as the material substratum of the created world and as the underlying basis of what they as painters make. Through the story of primal matter (*hyle*), Bosch compares the nothingness that the garden's denizens sinfully engender to his own creative activity as maker of no-things. Through Christ's carrying of the Cross, Bruegel compares the tragic course of human history to his own painterly mark, allowing both to collapse into nothing. There are decisive differences, however, and not only the ones we have observed already—i.e., that Bosch always situates human being visibly under God's wrath and that he predicates human evil on the Devil's metaphysical enmity with God, whereas in Bruegel nothing transcends the stage of the world. Bruegel differs also in the compass he gives to artifice. In his *Tower of Babel*, now in Vienna, he creates an awesome paean to human making (fig. 278).[52] Perhaps the first instance when a building is the subject of a monumental painting, Bruegel's colossus comes, of course, with a huge asterisk. It is cursed.

The Tower of Babel

After the great deluge destroyed everyone but Noah and his offspring, the Bible tells us, a unified humanity wandered to the plain of Shinar and there resolved to build a city with a tower "whose top may reach unto heaven . . . lest [they] be scattered abroad upon the face of the whole earth" (Gen. 11:4). According to Sebastian Brant (following Flavius Josephus), the tower was built partly as a precautionary buttress against the water's power, proven by the destructiveness of the Flood.[53] Raised as a defense against God's wrath, the tower offended God. Coming down to see the tower rising, observing what "the children of man builded," God said: "Behold, the people is one, and they have all one language; and this they begin to do: and now nothing will be restrained from them, which they have imagined to do" (Gen. 11:6). The myth combines two themes. One concerns the power of making. Humans are endowed with the unique capacity to design something new and bring it about. The other theme concerns the nature of humanity. After the Flood, human beings were one people. Not yet finished, the tower caused God to imagine its completion and what it foretells: if they can build this, divine thinking went, anything is possible.

The tower invades God's territory (see fig. 278). He descends from heaven to see it, and it reaches "unto heaven." The restraint overcome is that of creation, of what the limit *is* on what *possibly might be*. God will not endure this trespass, just as he did not tolerate Adam who, eating of the Tree of Knowledge, almost became, in God's mysterious words, "as one of us" (Gen. 3:22)—although, unlike Adam's trespass, the tower's building broke no stated law. Doing what merely they were naturally capable of, humans brought upon them God's wrath. Causing them not to understand one another's speech, God divided humanity, setting them against

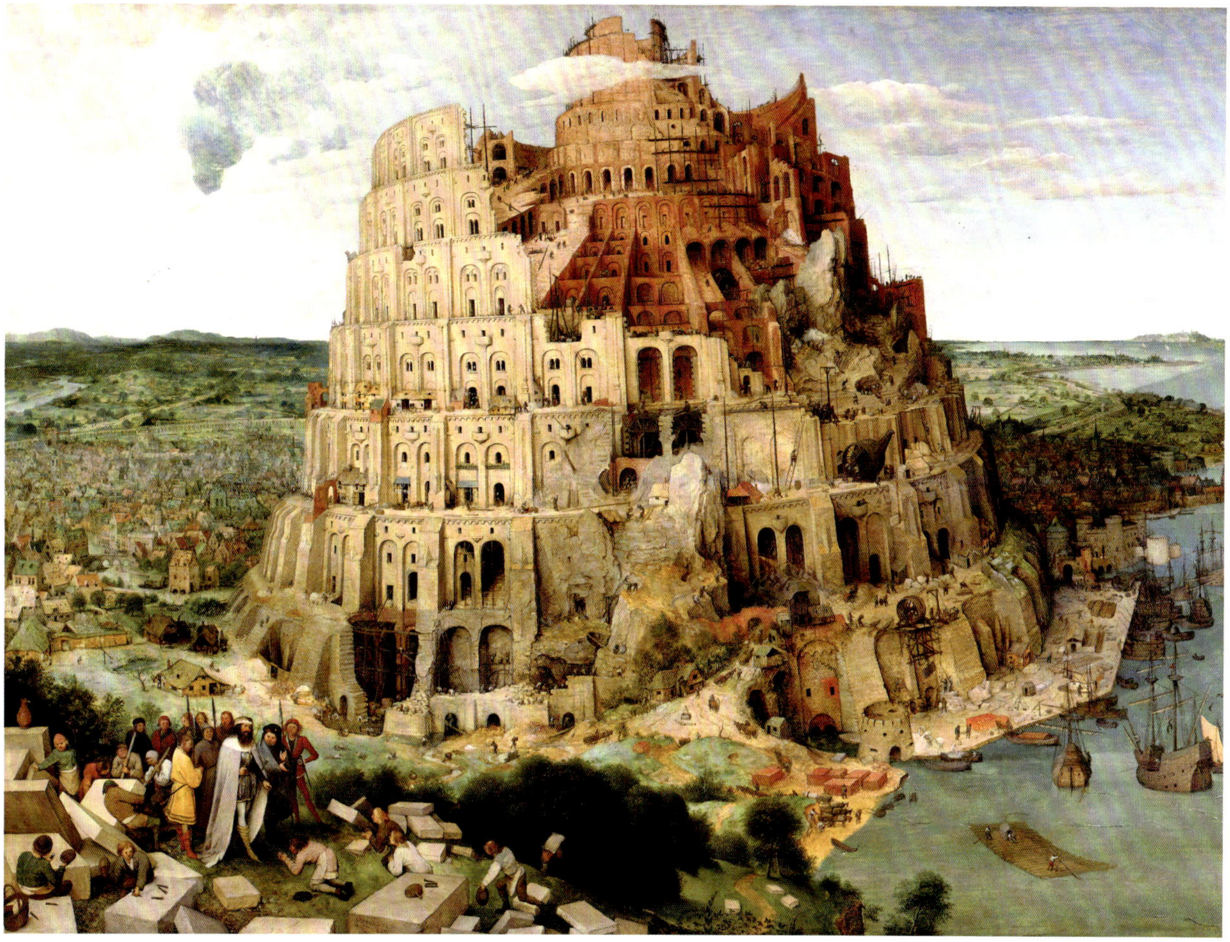

each other and scattering them "upon the face of all the earth," ironically just as they feared would happen if they did not build the tower. The tower and humanity, human making and human being, fail together, thanks be to God.

Some who write about Bruegel's *Tower of Babel* painting without looking closely at it describe the tower as destroyed by God, and some of Bruegel's contemporaries depicted the tower being dramatically toppled by divine fury.[54] At first glance, or dimly recollected, the building does look ruinous, especially with those rocks piercing it. However, a good look at the picture reveals that these eccentricities are due to its construction still being only underway, indeed for generations! A hive of human labor, the tower is both a visual cross section of its structure and a history of its making. Bruegel thinks with the builders so that we can think with them, as, for example, they utilize bedrock variously as scaffolding, raw material, and permanent foundation. The "how" of making on a colossal scale draws us into the picture, first puzzling then enlightening us about its ingenious technologies. Bruegel understands that the finished building would be less mesmerizing. Without breaks in their structure, all those repeated and layered façades would numb the viewer to the spectacle. In any case, as the painting shows, even if the tower had been completed, it would never have stood complete, as there would always need to be repairs and refurbishments to its earlier substrata. The act of making permanently inhabits the made, allowing us imaginatively to inhabit it, too. Consider the wood-and-thatch huts attached to the tower's outer walls. Instances of vernacular rural architecture of Bruegel's own era, they stand in vivid contrast to the grandeur of the stone

278 Pieter Bruegel the Elder, *The Tower of Babel*, 1563, panel, Kunsthistorisches Museum, Vienna

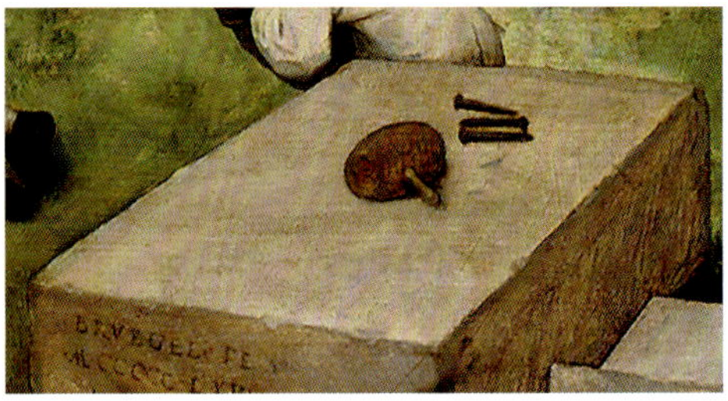

279 Detail of Pieter Bruegel the Elder, *The Tower of Babel* (fig. 278)

tower. They are as the plowman is to Icarus, but with the scale reversed. Akin to the shops and stalls attached to the outer walls of cathedrals, these heterogeneous makeshift dwellings project onto the mythic structure the cunning and the particularism of everyday life. And just as it allowed the builders, meanwhile, to live in the unfinished product of their collective imagination, so too this housing allows us mentally to inhabit the painted fantasy.

The tower itself consists of an internal honeycomb of brickwork enclosed in an outer wall of ashlar. Bruegel would have personally observed such a structure in Rome, and Hieronymus Cock's engravings of the edifice would have refreshed his memory.[55] The tower is built like the Colosseum in reverse: it projects the amphitheater's funnel into an upright cone. The materials are the same: light brickwork on the inside and heavy dressed stonework on the façade. That cladding means a lot to Bruegel. He portrays its preparation in the foreground, where Nimrod—the tower's patron, according to Josephus—pays a visit to his workers.[56] The spectacle of the made unfolds from this scene of making, of masons busily chiseling great blocks of stone. The tower's sublimity rests on a certain visual calculus. The eye explores the building piece by piece, encouraged by the details to look ever more closely, dividing and subdividing the pieces; but the eye searches also for the whole and is engaged to make that search by the modular repetition of parts: one hundred arches at the bottom alone, which then multiply in the stories above and in the unfathomable layers of the interior. The calculations become dizzying, conjuring a building too large for the mind. Labor figures in this mathematical sublime. The foreground scene prompts us to ask: How many blows of the hammer did such a building require? And in this vision of incalculable human labor, Bruegel paints his name as if chiseled into one block of stone: "Bruegel made 1563" (fig. 279).

The Bible does not say what the tower's builders did wrong. The possibility that "now nothing will be restrained from them" might challenge law per se, but God laid no specific law down against building big. Later authors generally took the story to be an admonition against pride. Writing at the end of the first century CE, after Rome's destruction of the Second Temple in Jerusalem, Josephus shaped this common understanding. In his *Antiquities of the Jews*, he reports that Nimrod induced people to attribute their happiness to themselves, not to God. A tyrant, he transferred to himself the people's fear of God and persuaded them to erect the tower in defiance of God. Bruegel shows the artisans prostrating themselves (perhaps) idolatrously before Nimrod, their king, who is in the guise of a ruler circa 1563. That pride caused tyranny and that tyranny was rebellion punishable by God were timely lessons in 1563, as Philip II attempted to assert absolute Habsburg rule over the Netherlands. A second *Tower of Babel* by Bruegel's hand survives in Rotterdam (fig. 280).[57] About half the size of the Vienna picture, it leaves Nimrod out but introduces a fascinating surrogate. Near the center of the panel, on the fourth turn of the tower's spiral, there appears—painted in

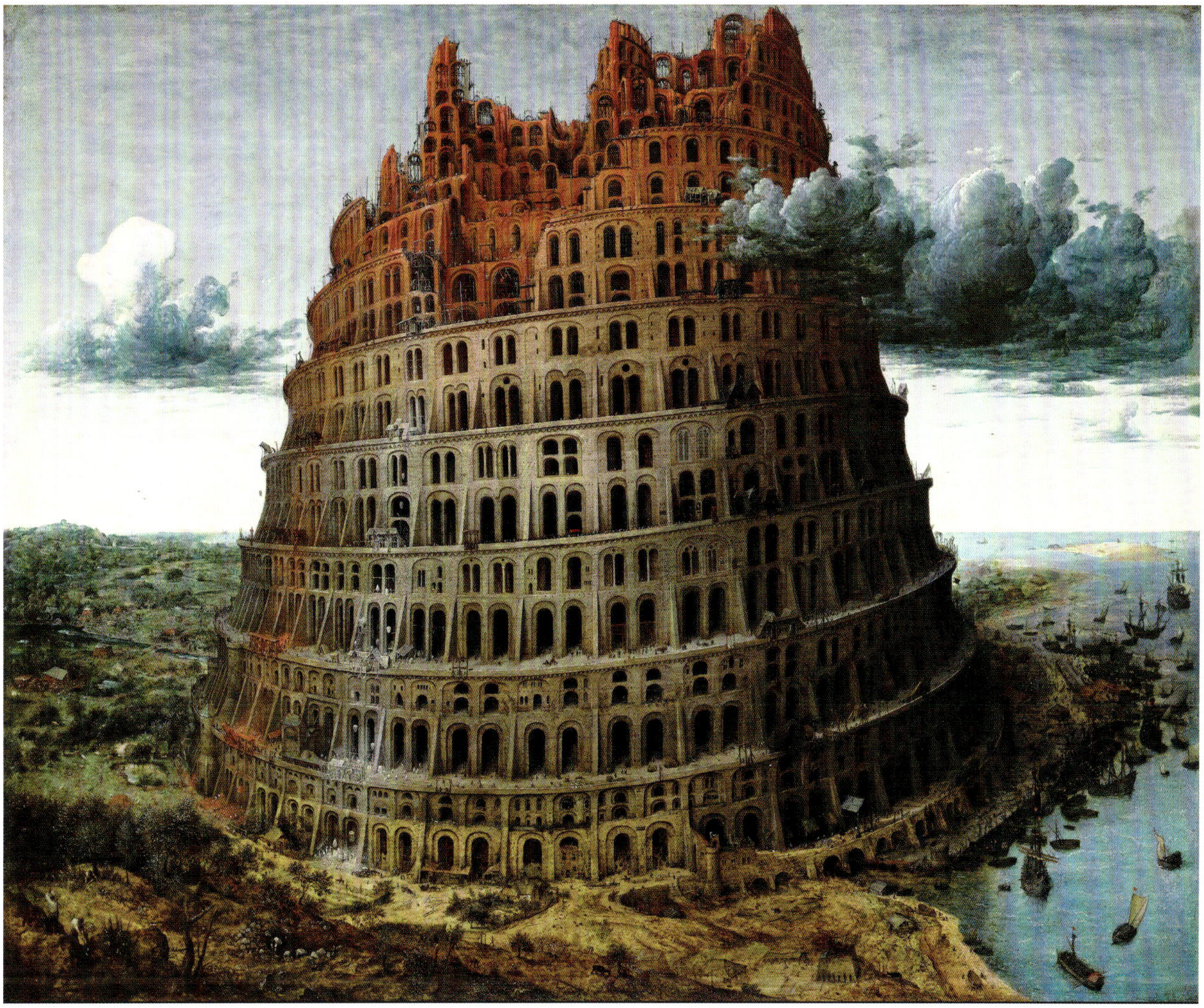

280 Pieter Bruegel the Elder, *The Tower of Babel*, c. 1565, panel, Museum Boijmans Van Beuningen, Rotterdam

miniature—a red processional baldachin surrounded by crowds. Johann-Christian Klamt, who first wrote about this detail, identified it as belonging to the pope and his entourage and surmised that it expressed the painter or patron's opposition to the pomp of the Roman Catholic Church.[58]

The size of this detail is as important as its message. Almost too small to see, it hides inside the picture like a private secret. The wars of religion taught the wisdom of dissemblance.[59] People concealed their religious beliefs both to survive and because they held true faith to be invisible and to transcend the warring faiths. Available only to the painting's owner, the detail poses little danger. Spotted by an informer, it could be denied: are we certain it is the pope? But by its miniature portrayal, Bruegel sends instruction to his viewer to look closely and critically. But how are we, then, to understand Bruegel's take on human making in the Vienna *Tower of Babel*? Treated like a god, Nimrod may be prideful, but what of the builders who, through immense labor and skill, raised the edifice? And what about Bruegel himself, who signs his name with their chisels? It is difficult for anyone to read the Bible's account without some misgivings. Like the suffering Job, the tower's builders seem irrationally persecuted, since what angers God is the immensity of humanity's inborn potential, the fact that, unified, humanity could plan and make this! To an artist with the imagination and skill of Bruegel, the tower pictured "what might have been" for human being.[60] Religious conflict magnified what happened after Babel. In Bruegel's day, it split Christianity into mutually incomprehensible and hostile polities. This split hinged on the problem of language and translation, on reading aright the Bible's foreign tongues. In 1568 in Bruegel's Antwerp, the publisher Christophe Plantin set to work on his eight-volume polyglot Bible.[61] Printing the sacred text in Hebrew, Greek, Aramaic, Syriac, and Latin, all collated and typeset for easy comparison, Plantin sought to heal confessional division (and prove his loyalty to Philip II) through a concord among languages. Is Bruegel's *Tower* as utopian as this? The answer is anything but clear, but it hinges—I believe—on how the tower's builders build.

We know the painting's original provenance. It appears on a list of works by Bruegel held as collateral for certain debts owed to the city of Antwerp.[62] The owner of these works, Nicolaes Jonghelinck, will concern us later, as he commissioned the six great *Months* panels for his new country villa. The document names that suite of panels *The Twelve Months*. Along with *The Tower of Babel* (referred to as *Thoren van Babilonyen*), the list also includes a *Christ Carrying the Cross*, probably the picture of that subject now in Vienna. The document leaves unnamed eight further Bruegels recorded as received. *The Tower* heads the list, followed by *Christ Carrying the Cross*. This may indicate their high value, and it may also link the two together as forming a pair. Painted in 1563 and 1564, the two can be read as pendants, or in sequence. Catharina Kahane has drawn attention to their shared use of a rock pinnacle as a central structuring motif.[63] In the one painting, this rock forms the ingeniously worked foundation of the huge edifice. In the other, the rock stands bare except for a window carved into it and the windmill balanced improbably on it. That Bruegel drew the subjects from the Old and New Testaments invites us to understand their relation temporally, as two distinct periods of history, with the rock formation as the abiding natural constant between them.

The histories portrayed in both pictures revolve around that pinnacle. In *The Tower*, the builders wrap the ascending edifice counterclockwise in diminishing circles around the rock core. In *Christ Carrying the Cross*, the road circles the pinnacle—again counterclockwise—to ascend Calvary's mount. Both circles appear to rise but ultimately descend: the tower's circle because of what will befall it; and Calvary's because those who use it dig a channel ever deeper into the earth. Nature has given the rocks fantastical form. Like the natural follies adored by early modern collectors, they tease viewers into perceiving hidden images in their random striations. Modified by human labor and encrusted with human fabrications, they resemble the precious corals and "hand stones" of Habsburg provenance, in which single pieces of igneous rock form the glittering substrate for sculpted biblical histories crafted in miniature (see fig. 219). Although small enough to be held, these collectibles are fractal semblances of the great mountains from which they were extracted. With stories and edifices built improbably on them, Bruegel's pinnacles look like hand stones magnified to a one-to-one scale. In *Christ Carrying the Cross*, the rock plays tricks with time scale too, placing the painting's episode within a process of the longest imaginable duration. *The Tower*'s history is vast but on a different scale. The edifice begins at its base in a stark Romanesque style, with round arches, unadorned buttresses, and heavy walls punctuated by tiny square windows. As it rises, the façade's idiom changes, becoming lighter, more ornamented and Gothic with each rotation. The history of the building thus recapitulates the history of building. God will soon halt this history—perhaps at the stylistic phase of Bruegel's own time. But were the building to have been completed, its future forms would have concealed the natural pinnacle.

The rock survives. One world age later, it still stands as Calvary's axis of evil. Human being has changed, however. Divided, people no longer make new worlds; fueled by enmity, they unmake the old one, grinding it down to nothing. The tower's great construction pulleys have become Calvary's destructive wheels. Were humans dangerous already before Babel? The Rotterdam *Tower* shows the edifice clearly rising in spirals. The great balcony or shelf that circles it is one continuous avenue rising at a constant slope. Bruegel clarifies this spiral by beginning it with a walled entrance in the foreground and by measuring its angle of ascent against the horizon. The whole tower looks biased. The spiral's rightward slope and movement cause the tower to seem to lean and thus, perhaps, to foreshadow its fall. The Vienna *Tower* leans less, but it is also structurally less consistent. Its entire right side remains less finished than the left, and the rock pinnacle, still exposed, interrupts the encircling balcony, making it hard to determine its course. At the fourth story, the balcony begins, on the left, just above the horizon, but it stops less than halfway round, forcing us to calculate its future course through the jagged forms at the right. The building's façade confuses the matter further. Different on each story, it raises the question of when, if the ascent were continuous, the alteration could neatly occur. These puzzles have led some observers to propose that, in Vienna, Bruegel's tower has a telescoping structure rather than a spiral one, and that its stories are stacked cylinders of diminishing diameter.

The Spanish writer and engineer Juan Benet was one eloquent proponent of this view.[64] He explained Bruegel's telescopic solution through an analysis of the Bible story. If the jumble of languages defeated the tower's builders, Benet reasoned, then its structure could not have been spiral, since had it been spiral, construction could have proceeded on the basis of work already done, with no need for verbal instructions. Thinking the story through in practical terms, Bruegel envisioned an architecture that required new invention and collaboration, as evidenced in the picture by the historically striated façade. In fact, Benet was mistaken, for the tower is a spiral, or mostly so. Its stories rise left to right, as in the Rotterdam picture. Bruegel makes this hard to see, however, forcing us to grasp the structure by imaginatively completing it.

Largely comprehensible at its base, where the building's area is at its largest, it becomes ever more unfathomable the farther up its spiral winds. The building's exposed brick core ascends to an inner tower that seems—illogically—as big as the main tower looked at its base. Workers climb steps on the top of what seems to be a gigantic internal dome—though the slope they ascend viewed from high up, from the sort of bird's-eye perspective Bruegel preferred, can also read as a flat, receding ground plane. This ambiguity helps the artist perform an even more amazing trick farther up. Its structural logic maddeningly hidden by clouds, the inner tower's apex culminates in an Escher-like reversal of space. If the tower's overall structure is that of a convex projection of the Colosseum's concave interior, we find at its top, impossibly, a colosseum! This allusion might have had specific meanings. It was within that great constructed bowl, in the gladiatorial games put on by the pagan emperors of Rome, that the early Christians were martyred for their faith. Through the arena at the top of the tower, Bruegel might have recollected that history, while perhaps slipping in another miniaturized critique of Rome in his day, where outward pomp reverted the Church to paganism. But the skyscraping arena also prefigures the setting for the second half of Bruegel's two-part drama. *Christ Carrying the Cross* shows the story cutting a path through a hellish concavity, with crowds assembled to relish the first martyrdom. However, a conic helix cannot culminate in a concave arena. It is a contradiction of the geometry of the world, a "nothing [that] is without sufficient grounds." Yet in *The Tower* Bruegel cunningly makes it so: observe, at the top left, how people walk up stairs that seem cut into a giant, conical mound only to ascend, up to the right, what looks like the stepped seating of a convex amphitheater.

Klaus Demus has written perceptively about the tower's impossible construction. The builders, he observed, placed all verticals at right angles to the horizontals, but because the horizontals "rise, as required by the spiral shape . . . the tower was inevitably lopsided!"[65] The tower would have failed even without divine intervention. In the Bible, humans were superlative builders; through their imagination, skill, and sociality, they could remake the world. In Bruegel, humans are imaginative, energetic, and sociable, but they are also inherently confused. The tower built on the plain of Shinar was architecturally a Babel from the start. In 1494, Sebastian Brant cast Nimrod as a bad planner, presumably because he had failed to plan for a jealous God.[66] For Bruegel, the folly resides less in the building's plan than in human planning per se. The worlds people imagine are impossible and doomed. The Apocalypse is not coming soon; it is long under way.

History, for Bruegel, consists not in great events or in world-changing actions. Nothing changes, and heroic action, such as Icarus's flight, makes no impression on the world. God does not change history, either. Cruelty is the same in Antwerp and Brussels as it was before Christ's saving death in Jerusalem. Bruegel's topicality, his emphasis on the historical conditions of his own here and now, is less a critique of the times than a portrait of time in its long duration, where everything remains the same. *The Tower of Babel* and *Christ Carrying the Cross* seem like episodes in a vast tragedy, in which those who rise must always fall. But most of Bruegel's paintings have that very plot, and most give it a circular shape. Some of these circles—e.g., *Conversion of Paul* (see fig. 322)—have the world as their compass; some—like *The Rabbit Hunt* (see fig. 36)—are constricted to one cruel twist of fate. Some spiral up, some spiral down, but mostly, on close examination, they just circle about. Bosch drew circles as well. When he wanted to show people trapped in their world, either as sinners or as the damned, he paraded them around and around, trapping viewers in this mesmerizing rotation. But Bosch placed these circles along a terrible vector of salvation history that races straight from Eden to hell. Bruegel's circles go nowhere; their end is perennially not yet. This is good for his paintings, which, enclosed in their frames, want to keep us inside them, searching for constants. Nature is an awesome constant, of course. But culture is, too. Consider again *The Tower*'s sloping avenue, with those simple huts built in the shadow of History with a capital *H*: human being makes do with what it makes.

10

CULTURE

> We have placed you at the center of the world so that, from there, you can more easily observe whatever is in the world. We have made you neither of heaven nor earth, neither mortal nor immortal, so that with freedom of choice and with honor you may fashion yourself in whatever shape you prefer, as though you were the maker and molder of yourself.
>
> —PICO DELLA MIRANDOLA, "ORATION ON THE DIGNITY OF MAN"

The Neo-Stoic Alternative

The glorification of man that Giovanni Francesco Pico, Count of Mirandola, placed in the mouth of God was meant for a university audience.[1] Writing in 1486, Pico modeled his "Oration on the Dignity of Man" after introductory speeches customary at the opening of a school year—but this speech was never delivered. Together with the ideas it defended, the text fell under a charge of heresy. In our time, too, though for different reasons, the laudatory use of the word *man* can hardly be spoken without people cringing, and it came under special attack just after World War II, simultaneously from the right and left. Pico himself affirmed human dignity against an ancient and widespread antihumanism—a conviction of the wretchedness of mankind. Humanism had to contend with a thousand years of eloquent Christian pessimism about humanity: Adam, and with him the whole created world, was vile. But Pico's heretical rapture arose not from contentment with human being but from the epiphany that whatever "man" is, whatever that word denotes, is in its own power still to become. By acknowledging human mutability, humanism has allowed *itself* to take changing forms, and much can be achieved simply by updating some of its terms. In place of the old motto "Man as measure of all things," focus attention on the humanist insight—fresh enough to cause controversy even now—"Truth is made rather than found."[2] In place of the obsolete heroism of *homo faber*, think of the humanist proposition, foundational to the humanities and social sciences in our time, that there is no escaping culture—that what we know of nature is what culture will have always already asked.

The original humanists developed attitudes toward what are now termed *social construction* and *cultural determinism* that were neither celebratory nor fearful. It is worth knowing that such problems have been handled not only before but continuously for centuries, and handled in art with more perspective and thus success than in scholarship or theory. Instead of optimism or pessimism, neo-Stoics of the early modern era opted for their own variety of detachment—not withdrawing from the human world but requiring the attainment of some perspective on it. Abraham Ortelius took his motto from the Roman Stoic Cicero (see fig. 19).[3] Inscribed below his first engraved world map of 1570, this motto reads: "Who can consider human things to be great, when he beholds the eternity and vastness of the entire world?"[4] Reissued in 1587 with different borders and slightly updated coastlines, the revised

281 Johannes and Lucas van Doetecum after Pieter Bruegel the Elder, *Hieronymus in Deserto* (*Saint Jerome in the Wilderness*), from the *Large Landscapes* series, c. 1555–56, etching with engraving, Museum Boijmans Van Beuningen, Rotterdam, Loan Lucas van Leyden Foundation

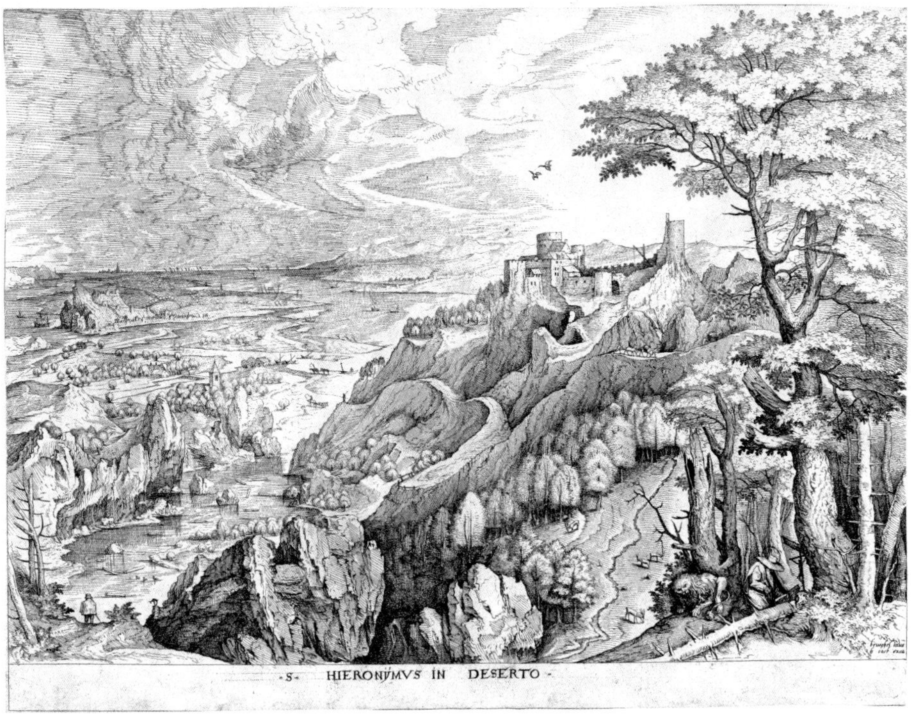

282 Johannes and Lucas van Doetecum after Pieter Bruegel the Elder, *Magdalena Poenitens* (*Penitent Magdalene*), from the *Large Landscapes* series, c. 1555–56, etching with engraving, The Metropolitan Museum of Art, New York, Harris Brisbane Dick Fund, 1926

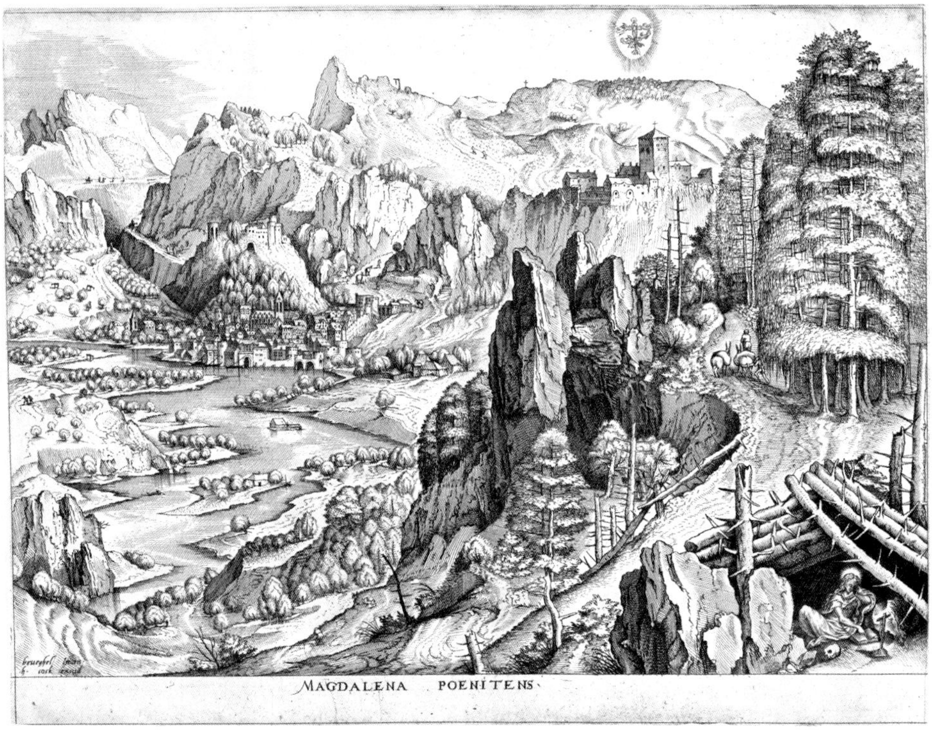

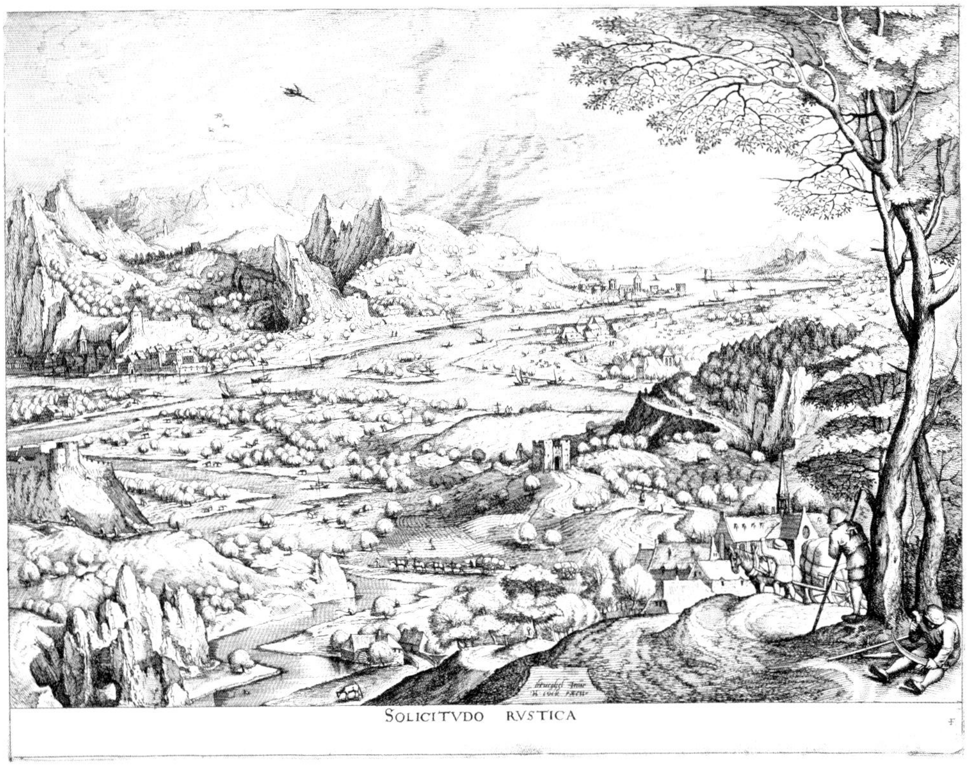

283 Joannes and Lucas van Doetecum, after Pieter Bruegel the Elder, *Solicitudo Rustica* (*Rustic Cares*), from the *Large Landscapes* series, c. 1555–56, etching and engraving, Museum of Fine Arts, Boston, Helen and Alice Colburn Fund

world map adds another motto drawn from Cicero: "The horse was created to draw and to carry; the ox, to plow; the dog, to guard and to hunt; but man was born to contemplate the world."[5] Endowed with a capacity not only to work but also to watch, humans distinguish themselves from the rest of creation by having a worldview—by constituting the world as a view. Signatories of Ortelius's *Album of Friends* (*Album Amicorum*) wrote ecstatic accounts of views observed from actual elevated sites, such as hills and towers, as well as of views offered by maps and pictures.[6] Commanding prospects displayed beauty, variety, and order while also fostering restraint. Praising Ortelius's atlas as a portable image of the world, the Antwerp antiquarian Cornelius van Aecken contrasted ocular travel made possible by maps with the geographic conquests motivated by Spanish imperial greed.[7] The humanist neo-Stoic stands aside to view—skeptically, regretfully, but generally in good humor or at least ironically—what other humans take unreasonably to be theirs (and then seize).

By the early decades of the twentieth century it had already been shown that Bruegel's art has affinities with the ideals of Renaissance humanism—and some of the best work on the artist has explored the panoramic view taken in many of his pictures, their tendency to observe the whole from afar.[8] These perceptions are of course related. Positioning us on high, Bruegel's pictures are world *views* that display objects and events as mere contingencies engulfed by a limitless, indifferent universe. Typically, Bruegel will animate a corner of his landscapes with figures expressive of this attitude: in *Saint Jerome in the Wilderness* (fig. 281) and *Penitent Magdalene* (fig. 282), saint and sinner alike convey ascetic withdrawal by turning their backs to the landscape, in counterpoint to our gaze.[9] More in tune with our activity is the lone figure group in the lower right corner of *Solicitudo Rustica*, or *Rustic Cares* (fig. 283).[10] Two peasants enact the solicitude—or care—announced in the title. Bruegel depicts the interim in rural labor expressed by the word *whet*, which denotes the honing of a scythe and the spell of work between honings. One peasant diligently hammers his scythe, caring—as it were—for his rustic task. A second peasant, neither mowing nor mending, withdraws momentarily from work to contemplate the landscape. Turning from us but sharing our view, he models the aesthetic perspective. Working and watching face opposite ways, but the two trees that rise between them confirm their intertwining.

The turned-away rustic expresses the attitude of Christian Stoicism championed by Bruegel's circle in Antwerp. The ethics of this neo-Stoicism taught that the individual should rise above life's trivial pleasures and pains and view the world from afar. Neo-Stoics urged pleasure in the experience of distance—of distance from, though curiosity about, the lifeworld of one's time and place. The neo-Stoic is the ethnographer at home, observing his culture invent its lifeworld and then behave as if it were nature's own. Bosch, neither humanist nor Stoic, saw the worlds that humans make as unreal and therefore contemptible, whereas Bruegel would see them as contingent and therefore intriguing.

The modern rediscovery of Bruegel's humanism coincided with his elevation to the ranks of the "very great artists" of all time.[11] It replaced an earlier assessment of him as a folk artist from, of, and perhaps even for the peasantry. Established during the seventeenth century, this earlier assessment grew from academic doctrine, which elevated history painting above the genres, expected artists to find their secular themes in classical antiquity, and valued a certain harmony best exemplified by the classicizing styles of the Italian Renaissance. The negative assessment of Bruegel was supported by inaccessibility of the original paintings (almost all in imperial hands) and the existence of countless inferior copies and pastiches, including ones by Bruegel's son, Pieter Brueghel the Younger. The delimitation of the elder Bruegel's authentic oeuvre, a growing appreciation for nonclassical styles, the popularization (via reproductions) of his hitherto little-known masterpieces in the collections in Vienna, and a growing historical awareness of the prestigious Habsburg provenance of most of his autograph paintings all contributed to a shift in the artist's imagined cultural context from the premodern peasantry to a progressive, educated urban elite. Bruegel, it was discovered, belonged to the innermost circle of Antwerp humanists and included among his friends and collaborators the cartographer Ortelius; the artist, poet, playwright, and political theorist Dirck Coornhert; and the publishers Hieronymus Cock and Christophe Plantin. Bruegel's art was now seen to be erudite in the original sense of the word: it aimed at eliminating rudeness (Latin *e-* plus *rudis*) through instruction and through the amicable conversation that erudite viewers might have before one of his pictures.[12] Appreciating his learning involved uncovering beneath the apparent thematic and stylistic rudeness of so-called Peasant Bruegel a deeper, hidden display of humanist learning and self-restraint. This is dramatically the case with attempts to understand *The Peasant and the Bird Thief*, as we have seen (see fig. 4). An astonishing forerunner of later genre and landscape painting, it may "appear to represent a scene from daily country life," but—according to champions of erudition—it "is in reality an allegory concerning man's mortality, a *memento mori*."[13]

Pursued by academics eager to mobilize their learning, this approach continues to clash with quite another understanding of Bruegel's humanism. Modernist poets, who celebrated this artist's candid portrayal of ordinary life, as well as modernist painters and art critics, who extolled the matter-of-fact character of his simplified pictorial forms, recognized a humanism kindred to their own. By their account, Bruegel's importance lay in how he directed his art toward the human sphere.[14] The events and personages of myth and religion become, in his pictures, eclipsed by a plausible, earthbound humanity. Auden observed this artistic watershed in Bruegel's *The Fall of Icarus*, and so did William Carlos Williams in his poem on the same painting (see fig. 262):

unsignificantly
off the coast
here was
a splash quite unnoticed
this was
Icarus drowning

Bruegel's humanism consists here in his commitment to the everyday and his recognition of the world's tragic indifference—as Williams puts this:

the edge of the sea
concerned
with itself

Here the challenge posed by Bruegel is not one of finding hidden significance but of learning to attend to something more elusive, which even demands a new word: *unsignificance*. According to Williams (and Auden), what the iconographers proclaim to be "an allegory concerning man's mortality" becomes *in reality*—the real one that Bruegel discovered for art—a "scene from daily life." Daily life does not hide the allegorical; rather, daily life—human experience at its most elemental—is great art's elusive quarry, and allegory points haltingly toward it.

In this spirit I will attempt to take literally what might appear to be Bruegel's most patently allegorical work: his so-called *Battle between Carnival and Lent* (fig 284). Before asking what the artist meant by his panel, now in Vienna, I will spend some time working out what he shows, particularly in the painting's central figural group. Let's call this a literal reading of allegory.

Epiphanies of Human Making

According to Bruegel, Carnival is a fat prince mounted on a barrel of beer (fig. 285).[15] His blue hat with dagged edges mimics courtly headwear. Through it he signals that he plays a "prince," and the pots hung like stirrups make his barrel into a make-believe mount. With his feet hanging into the pots, the corpulent man who plays the prince straddles the barrel as if he were riding a steed. And through the way he clutches it, the long spit becomes his lance raised for jousting, while those butcher knives collected in a pouch about his girth serve as his sword. Personification is a balancing act for the person trying to do it. None of his costume would belong to a real prince, since it is mostly kitchen gear. Surrounded by food, these instruments openly display their ordinary use for cooking, and that makes them funny—to us and, I would venture, to their audience in Bruegel's painting and before his painting. What one enjoys about the costume is not the stirrups or the steed of the prince but one's recognition of their incongruous culinary stand-ins. Bruegel plays a similar game in *The Peasant Wedding*, in which the bride's crown (fastened to the drape behind her) is made of paper, and the tray delivering creamy porridge is an old door (see fig. 260). The crown is a peasant artifact, a customary symbol improvised in an affordable way. This Bruegel captures with his typical ethnographic

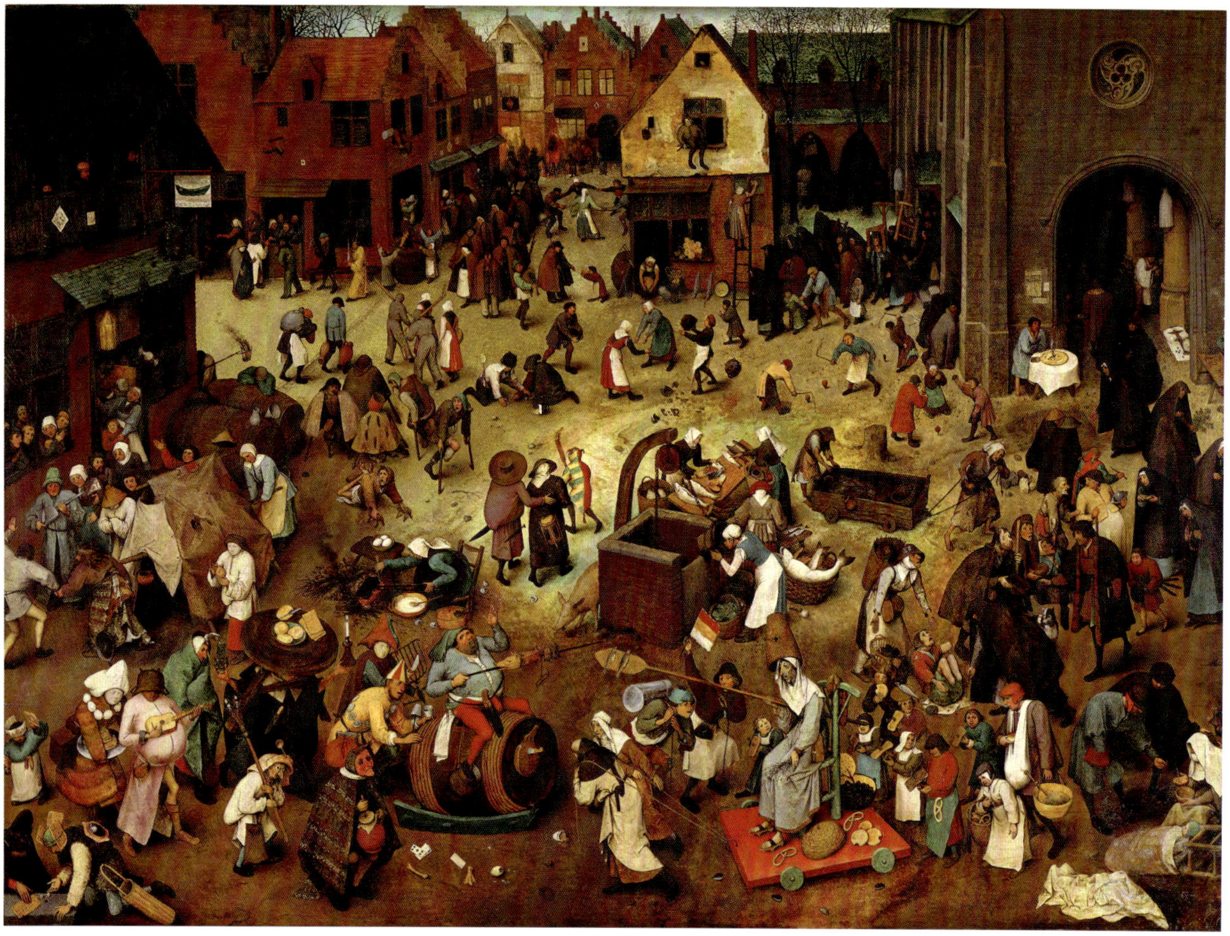

284 Pieter Bruegel the Elder, *Battle between Carnival and Lent*, 1559, panel, Kunsthistorisches Museum, Vienna

know-how. Repurposing the door is a peasant expediency, the recognition of which brings a distinctive pleasure to the viewer. As tangible as the object itself, the backstory about its making also mobilizes our own practical know-how, encouraging us to treat strange-seeming details in an everyday way.

Carnival's spit spears a pig's head, two cooked birds, and a pair of sausages. Because the object is a spit, and not a lance, and because the man who holds them is probably the town butcher—since who else would have such equipment and such corpulence?—one imagines that these meats have been roasted on that spit by him. Of different cooking times, however, and together forming a single, hybrid beast, with the pig's head seemingly unroasted, and with that playful third sausage swinging lewdly below, like a penis, these meats were precooked and then assembled as a prop. By their artful arrangement, these edibles celebrate and parody what they are, just as Prince Carnival's costume does, with its inappropriate components parading their pot-like character.

The butcher must literally balance the attributes that make him a prince. About to slip from his head, a large bird pie forces him to raise a hand to steady it—a gesture foreign to a joust. The problem is that another force besides gravity destabilizes this pastry. Just beside it, and rhyming with it in size and shape, a bowl with pancake batter draws the pie earthward. Empty shells on the ground between the pie and the batter contrast the two foods as a bird to its eggs and as cooked ingredients to raw. A similar formal and semantic pull is exerted on the skewered meats. The composite creature that they form stands completed by the shit-eating hog to its right. Carnival's meats thus enter a grotesque cycle from food to excrement to spit, then back again to food. Such games transcend the ones played by the butcher acting as Prince Carnival. Born from a seemingly accidental coincidence of foreground and background elements, they belong not to the parade but to our random vantage point on it. But they also complement the prince's costume, which consists of a parodic reuse—or misuse—of foods. Working with the butcher's costume but against the butcher (is that the sort of pig he sells?), these games raise a fundamental question. Where does the butcher's clever costume end and where does Bruegel's cunning begin?

The butcher pretends to joust like a prince, but in a manner befitting the ignoble thing he's a prince *of*. The word *carnival* combines the Latin *caro* meaning "flesh," with *levare* meaning "to put away."[16] As the Italian *carnevale* it connects with *vale*, "farewell," to become "farewell to meat." It denotes the season roughly from Epiphany through Shrove Tuesday when, before the long, pre-Easter fast of Lent, meat was given a festive farewell by being cooked and consumed in prodigious quantities, and by being celebrated sometimes in the symbolic form of a meaty, meat-eating, and meat-preparing ruler, Prince Carnival. A comically powerless sovereign over the unruly body that eats, defecates, and gets eaten, he rules a rowdy retinue. Equipped, in Bruegel, with kitchen gear, Prince Carnival's masked courtiers produce a background cacophony. The figure closest to us, wearing a hideous mask and cloaked in a woven rug, plays an instrument made especially for carnival. Called in Dutch a *Rommelpot*, it consists of a pig's bladder stretched over a jug half-filled with water.[17] Through the friction of a reed pushed through the bladder, it produces the squealing sound of a stuck pig. Causing the sound of the animal's slaughter to resonate around its cooked form, the *Rommelpot* leads an orchestra of

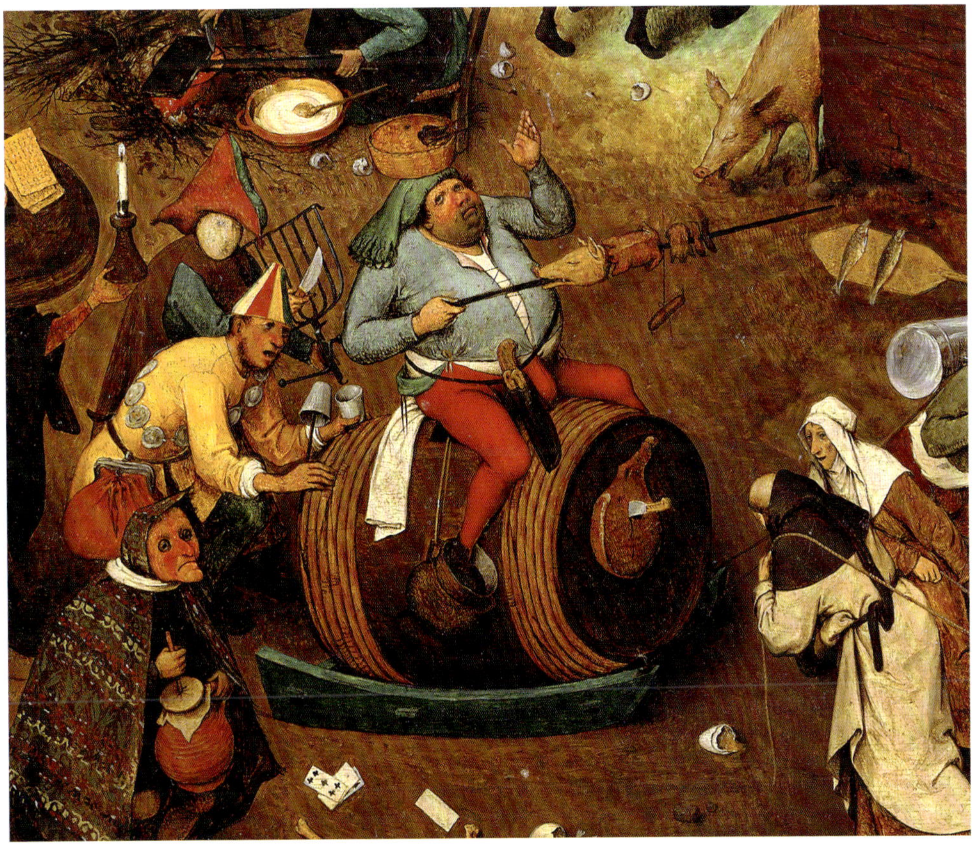

285 Detail of Pieter Bruegel the Elder, *Battle between Carnival and Lent* (fig. 284)

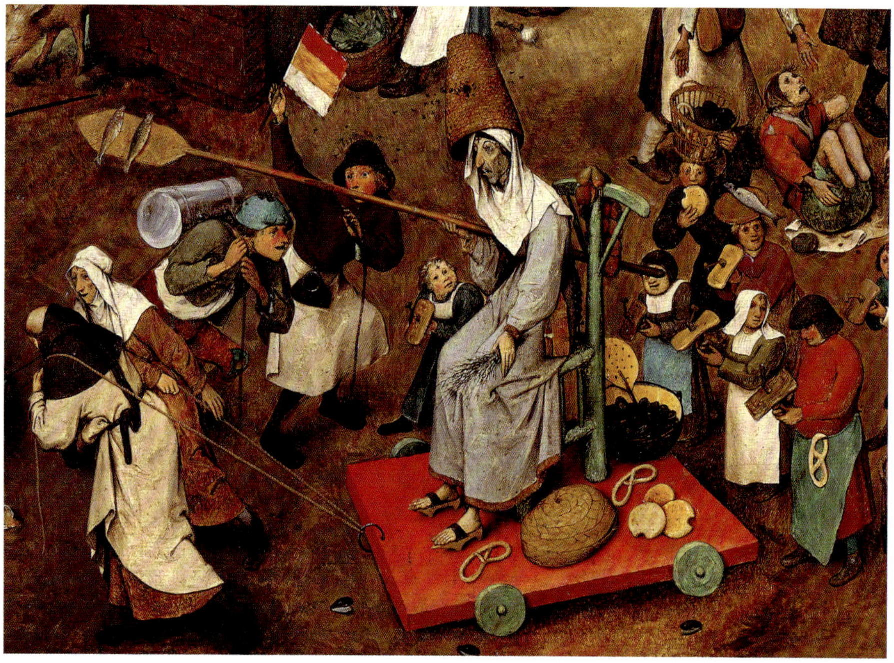

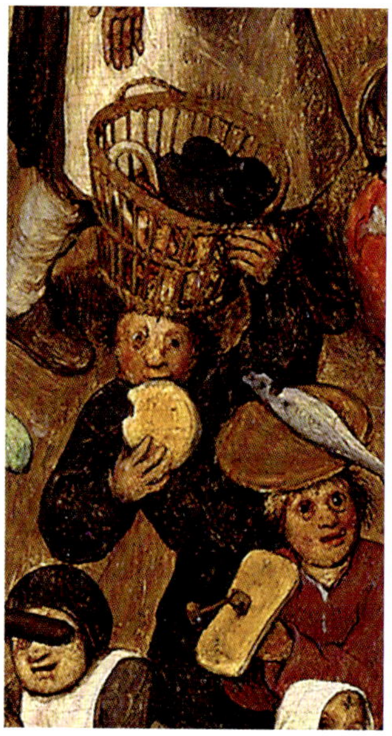

286 Detail of Pieter Bruegel the Elder, *Battle between Carnival and Lent* (fig. 284)

287 Detail of Pieter Bruegel the Elder, *Battle between Carnival and Lent* (fig. 284)

rattling metal cups, a small five-string guitar, and a knife strumming an iron grill. A grill of the same kind appears beside a bakery in the background. This is the object's place in more ordinary conditions, put outside while the shop gets a good cleaning. Unlike the shit-eating hog and the pancake batter, though, this seems more an ethnographic gloss than an allegorical extension. Thus one thing in Bruegel's picture can span an entire spectrum of things, from usable tool to carnival prop to symbol within the work of art. During the festivities, the players themselves straddle several roles. Feasting excessively and symbolizing excessive feasting, they complement Prince Carnival while simultaneously impeding his allegorical action through their plodding march. With them in tow, and given also his corpulence and cumbersome locomotion on a crude wooden sledge, the jousting butcher-prince can hardly pretend to joust. He inches forward, cutting a deep furrow in the soil.

His opponent moves only slightly more swiftly, since her throne—a tripod chair painted blue—rolls on small wooden wheels (fig. 286). This, according to Bruegel, is Dame Lent. She is played by a haggard nun, or perhaps by an emaciated woman dressed in nun-like garb. Herrings grace her bread-shovel lance, and the pretzels, flatbread, mussels, and braided onions on her float all pertain to a meager fasting fare, as does perhaps her beehive cap: during Lent, honey was the only sweetener allowed. More troubling are those bees, which exceed Lent's costume requirements. Either they belong to the actor's self-flagellating regime (note the scourge in her left hand) or they are a case of Bruegel's inflating his symbolism beyond the parameters he marvelously sets himself, namely, those of actual custom. The curiosity with which the little girl beside her regards Dame Lent, together with Lent's genuinely starved look, argues that the underlying actress may be as strange as her costume, and that she might be genuinely oblivious to the bees or else forced to endure them. Marked like Dame Lent with a little ashen cross on her forehead, and dutifully rattling a wooden implement—a knocker built to produce a doleful sound—the girl and the other children do what they are supposed to in the procession while at the same time revealing individualized attitudes toward their activity.

As with youngsters in a school play, their charm derives from their habit of slipping into and out of character. When they perform, their awkward distraction makes them living tableaux of themselves as children. In school pageants, this frustrates teachers and charms parents; in Bruegel, it delights us who take pleasure in the real.

Behind Lent's cart, a boy with a basket on his head forms part of the procession (fig. 287). But he also munches bread, carries shoes and pretzels, and stares out at us. His comic distance from the rite he is in puts him in line with Bruegel's painting as a whole. Bruegel *documents* more than he *creates* his painting's symbolism. The peculiar amused detachment of his performance as a painter from the performances he records finds a reflection in the represented actors themselves. Shown to stand just outside their *own* activity, they, like the painter, contribute to our sense that we peer behind their masks into an underlying personality. To complicate matters further, Carnival and Lent are themselves both masquerades and rituals of unmasking. Cousin to the dramatic form of the antimasque, Carnival reveals the true nature of people and society by mocking their covering illusions; its bizarre costumes and practices aim at a brief but subversively realistic portrayal of the physical and social body. Lent performs a different unveiling. It banishes Carnival's travesties by reintroducing with a vengeance the drab infirmity of everyday life. Whereas Carnival unmasks life by giving it a temporarily unrestrained expression, Lent unmasks life's terrible secret, death, hence the dead or dying that appear on the right side of Bruegel's composition. Later collectors, squeamish about such macabre details, painted them out: the crumpled cloth in the lower right corner conceals a skeletal body.[18] Time, rendering the covering pigments transparent, and the conservators' desire to retrieve Bruegel's original composition have brought these details back to light.

Bruegel included the dead or dying—one suspects—because they in fact appeared in festivities such as these. Perhaps beggars carted them to church during Lent so that, completing a tableau of misery, they encouraged penitent almsgiving. What counts for all these recorded customs is this: before Bruegel's allegory, we feel that we are observing not *his* symbols of Lent and Carnival but someone else's. This sense of reportage, of the artist representing a representation, derives from the copresence of two fictions: the crude artifacts of the peasants and their masterful portrayal in paint. The costumes, props, and stage design are formed from the detritus of everyday life, while amateurs act out the play. A bogeyman sits in the first-floor window of the bakery (fig. 288). With his three-point antler, he resembles a fantastical hybrid of the sort that Bosch was famous for concocting. In Bruegel, however, the bogeyman is a customary artifact. As historians of early modern charivari have discovered, shopkeepers tardy with their spring cleaning were punished by having to display such mannequins publicly.[19] This bakery deserves rebuke. Bruegel smudges the windows into being, his gray paint as if smeared on by a woman's dirty sponge. In rendering the bogeyman, he controls his brushwork finely, allowing us to ascertain the different materials out of which the effigy was put together: a dough mask, old clothes stuffed with straw and laced together with a bit of rope, a branch for horns. Combining worthless junk into an unlikely whole, the bogeyman displays the Boschian demon to be a product of vernacular making-do.

Karel van Mander, we recall, extolled Bruegel for his ability to capture the costumes and equipment characteristic of peasants living in a certain place—the style of hats, trousers, and jugs made in a specific village. The painting *Carnival and Lent* displays the fabrications of "the people," whose customs and artifacts are locally specific and, in some cases, endeavor

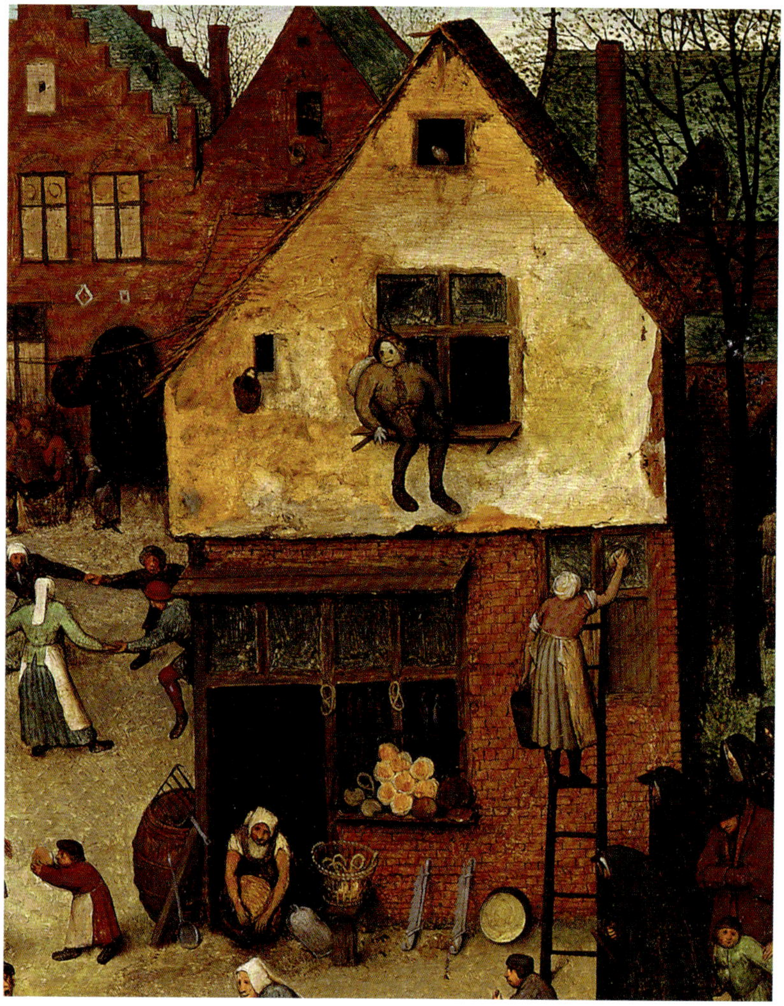

288 Detail of Pieter Bruegel the Elder, *Battle between Carnival and Lent* (fig. 284)

to be stylistically different from those of the village down the road. A folklorist writing at the turn of the twentieth century was still able to record how bakeries in different German towns distinctively braided their Shrovetide breads (see fig. 12).[20] On the other hand, there is Bruegel's cosmopolitan artistry. Although ably registering the smallest difference in other artifacts, his art seems completely natural—which is to say free of the peculiarities of style it so scrupulously records.

Performances of the kind recorded in Bruegel's painting were in fact staged in Netherlandish towns and villages throughout the fifteenth and sixteenth centuries. Although our historical knowledge of these rituals owes much to Bruegel's painting, several mock tournaments between personifications of Carnival and Lent are documented for the period.[21] Staged, like most Carnival entertainment, by clubs and confraternities led by a "King" or "Abbot" of Misrule, and recruiting largely from young adult males, these performances were staged during the last days of the Carnival season.[22] The blue boat painted on the sign above the tavern in Bruegel's picture refers to a popular, fictive version of these urban associations (see fig. 73).[23] Set in the open space of a town center, and accompanied by unorganized revelry, fights, and aggression, these mock battles turned urban space into a total theater, and forced the entire citizenry to become actors. More salient than their specific plot was their symbolic mode. Based around the fleshly activities of eating and sex, they suspended and inverted the

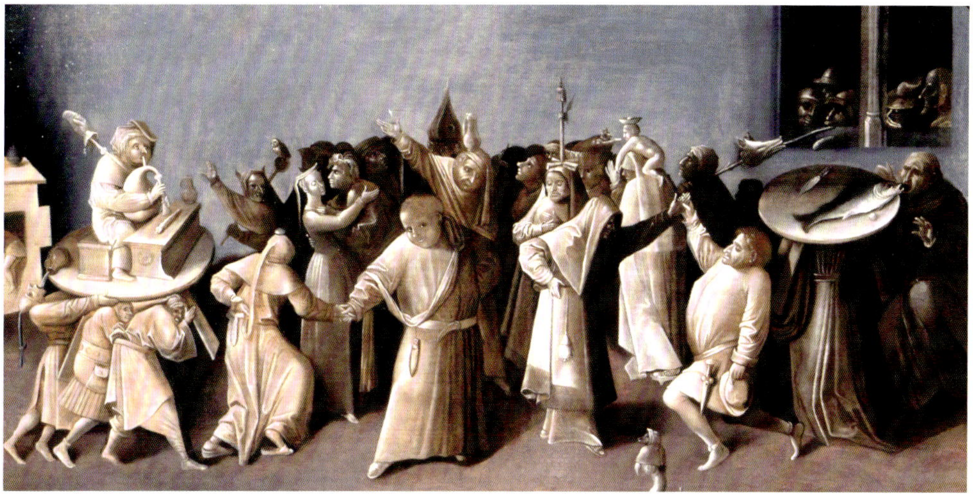

289 Follower of Bosch, *Battle between Carnival and Lent*, 1555 or later, panel, Collectie Het Noordbrabants Museum, 's-Hertogenbosch

official symbolism of order and morality, allowing, for a brief period, the body to be boss. And although it was possible merely to observe the events, as people in Bruegel's picture are shown to do, revelers were licensed to force all bystanders either to join them or to become the victims of their fun. In the case of the cripples and lepers, and perhaps also the obese Prince Carnival and anorectic Lent, Bruegel portrays persons who have been roped into performing cruel, negative allegories about their own disorders.

As early as the thirteenth century in Burgundy, the battle between Carnival and Lent became a popular motif in the arts. A 1492 inventory of the Medici collections lists an old Flemish panel showing Carnival mocked by revelers, and three surviving pictures executed in a Boschian style, including one painted in grisaille (now in the Noordbrabants Museum in 's-Hertogenbosch), feature a festive confrontation of Carnival and Lent (fig. 289).[24] In the 's-Hertogenbosch picture appear the skewered hog's head and dangling sausage, the grotesque pairing of imbibing and excreting, and the tendency for objects to be impossibly balanced on tops of heads. Bruegel's most immediate model, however, was an engraving by Frans Hogenberg, published by Hieronymus Cock in Antwerp in 1558 (fig. 290).[25] Bruegel designed prints of this kind for Cock. His well-known *Village Fair at Hoboken* was published by Cock and engraved by Hogenberg (see fig. 256). As in Bruegel's Vienna *Carnival and Lent* painting, the cozy village in Hogenberg's *Carnival and Lent* bespeaks a rustic performance of the ritual. But there are crucial differences. Hogenberg shows two symmetrical processions that meet at the composition's center, marked by a church, and he adds inscriptions to clarify his message. The coincidence of the center of the picture and the line break of the motto seals the chaos of the represented ritual to the order of its framing gloss. In short, this artist seeks to make vernacular symbolism his own.

Most telling is Hogenberg's animated treatment of the combat itself. We observed Bruegel's display of the ridiculous slowness of the battle. By registering the weight and friction of the floats, he exposed the comic disparity between the allegorical action of the joust and its crude performance. Hogenberg does the opposite. He seeks to create a better allegory. He pushes the contrived figures of fat Carnival and lean Lent back from the point of confrontation, gives them labels, and replaces their clumsy meeting with a dramatic clash between members of their retinues. Women exchange angry blows with the emblematic weapons of hams and fishes. Identifying totally with the parts they play, they turn the seasonal ritual into an expression

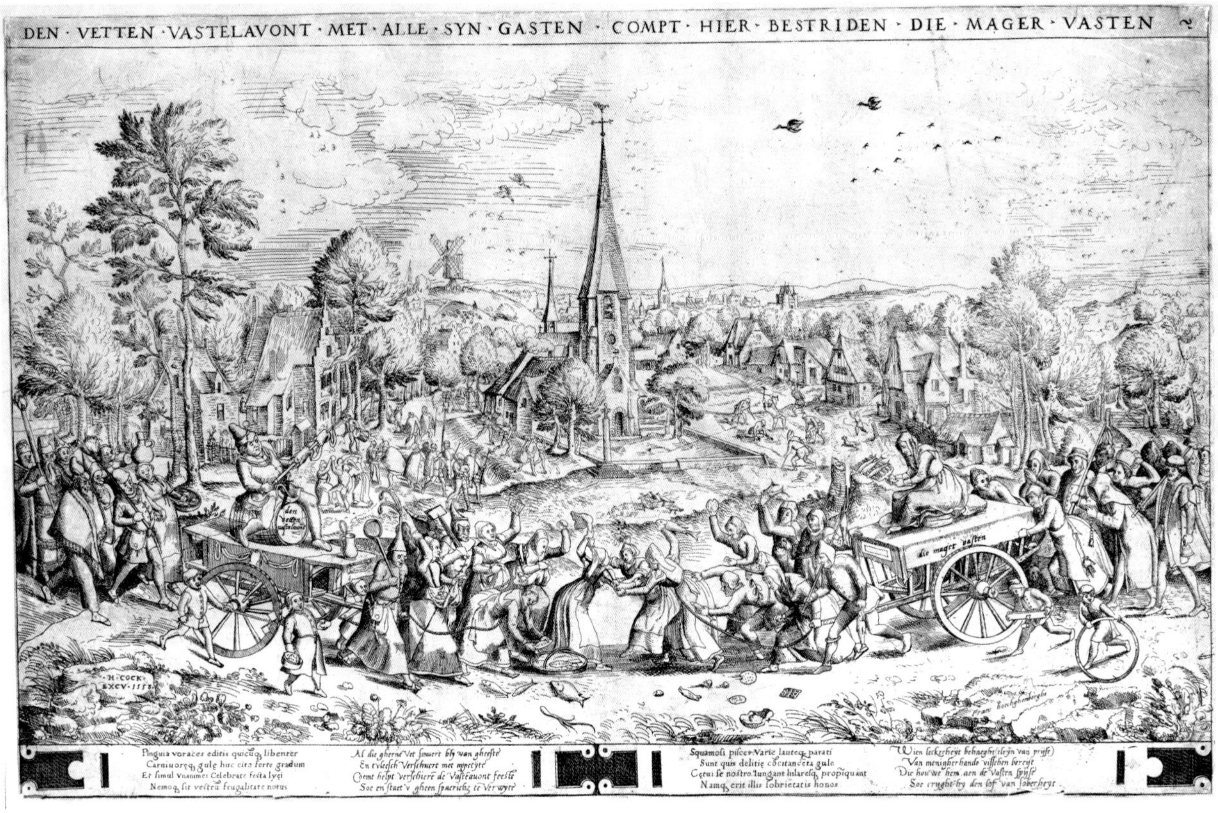

290 Frans Hogenberg, *The Battle between Carnival and Lent*, 1558, etching (published by Hieronymus Cock, Antwerp), The British Museum, London

of enmity, as if these housewives were genuinely fighting for the future of their town. Yet although their passion seems real, their behavior is inconsistent with that of people in real processions, as the rest of the engraving shows. Hogenberg cannot simultaneously improve and faithfully record his folkloristic prototype. I am reminded of a giant pageant staged in Bucharest for Nicolae Ceaușescu just before his fall. An epic mounted battle performed by thousands of Romanians in horse costumes was so grotesquely implausible that the TV cameramen, frightened that their broadcast might be deemed a mockery of the festival, aimed their lenses as if lovingly at Ceaușescu's face, while allowing the battle to unfold largely unseen.

Instead of modifying the allegorical battle or changing his focus, Bruegel submits it wholly to the measure of experience. At one level, this realism suits the parodic spirit of Carnival itself, where clumsiness serves as a chief comic resource. At another level, by making the fictive joust look *less* rather than *more* combative, Bruegel makes his own fiction appear truer. Like the furrows in the soil in Bruegel's *Christ Carrying the Cross*, the ruts cut in the earth by Prince Carnival's float embed the performance in physical nature; but they also elevate the artist who records them to another symbolic order from which he can observe and depict the world without himself mocking it.

Consider the actual interface between Carnival and Lent. The roasting spit and bread shovel do not cross each other as lances would in the climax of battle, and the combatants display not the slightest hint of martial bearing. Prince Carnival balances his pie and Dame Lent stares blankly into space. Their minimal movement and thus their agency derive not from themselves but from attendants who drag their floats. They are the pageant's underlying machinery, the sweat and blood behind the allegorical joust. Marching past one another without so much as a nod of recognition, they naturally reflect, without actively symbolizing, the social group to which they belong. Two lowly artisans, both visibly flushed from drink, haul Prince Carnival, whose costume, one presumes, was made by persons like themselves. Lent gets hauled by a monk and a nun; as Bruegel shows in the rituals farther back, the coming fast will be organized by the Church. Together these four mobilize the allegory and reveal its social bases. But they do not enter it. To allow the two right-handed combatants properly to clash, the operators must pass each other on the right. Bruegel does not portray the more bathetic moment when bread shovel and roasting spit get tangled in each other. He places the tips of these weapons precisely at the middle of the panel, thus anchoring the allegory to the structure of the visual field and to the geometry of the panel support itself. What are we to make of this Boschian coincidence? Scholars have also noted that the tavern and church at the picture's edges repeat the antithesis of Carnival and Lent; since it seems to belong to an order the artist superimposes on his view, this opposition has been used as supporting evidence for the thesis that Bruegel condemns Carnival as sinful (due to its allegiance to taverns and brothels), and celebrates the piety of Lent.[26] But are these organizing structures ones imposed by the artist, or are they, too, derived from the performance itself?

During Carnival, revelers shaped their movements to a prior symbolic geography of urban space. The face-off of tavern and church is, already to them, an available resource, like the found objects used in their costumes. Through the whole of his picture, Bruegel traces this trajectory from real life into rustic artifice. Virtually all the allegory's props appear as mere things elsewhere in the picture. The mobility of Bruegel's allegory—the way it shifts from being *his* symbolism or choreography to being *theirs*, the natives'—finds a fitting emblem in the trudging operators who propel the fiction without entering it. Whereas Hogenberg's housewives attack each other with implausible fury, Bruegel's players—even the ones fully inside the tableau—pursue their activities without apparent emotion. Instead of primitive identification between player and role, Bruegel shows a cryptic, and therefore also masklike, detachment.

Bruegel includes an everyday instance of the attitude his picture takes toward its subject. Near the center, at the fuzzy boundary between Carnival and Lent, he introduces a husband and wife with their backs turned to us, walking away.[27] Their path crossed by a Fool who lights the way in daylight (an old Carnival motif), the couple seems to hover between continuing toward the church, and following the Fool to the tavern. The Fool's parti-colored outfit, halving his form, intensifies our sense that even the formal language of an allegorical battle of moral opposites staged in Bruegel's picture is already there in the costumes and customs he depicts. The Fool's split garb is picked up by the faceless pair, who represent Everyman as a duality of man *and* woman. More crucially, the travelers introduce the distanced perspective of the spectator. They add to Bruegel's compendium of customs an ethnographic portrait of ourselves.

When he wanted to, Bruegel could depict allegorical agents convulsed by what they signify.[28] The spread-eagled monster at the lower left of the etching-engraving *Lust*, designed by Bruegel and engraved by Pieter van der Heyden, is more than just an abject receptacle (see fig. 64). Her whole being narrowed to the performance of carnal desire, she visualizes the constriction caused by lust. On the other side of the print, her male counterpart simultaneously fondles and severs his own penis, while between them the egg-eating cephalopod is reduced to one hole. This is Bruegel at his most Boschian, where the rules of the world are replaced by the curiously tighter logic of sin. In his genre scenes, Bosch visualizes the constriction of everyday life by vice (see figs. 123 and 124). His sinners are obsessive-compulsives:

293 Pieter Bruegel the Elder, *The Beggars*, 1568, oil on wood, Musée du Louvre, Paris

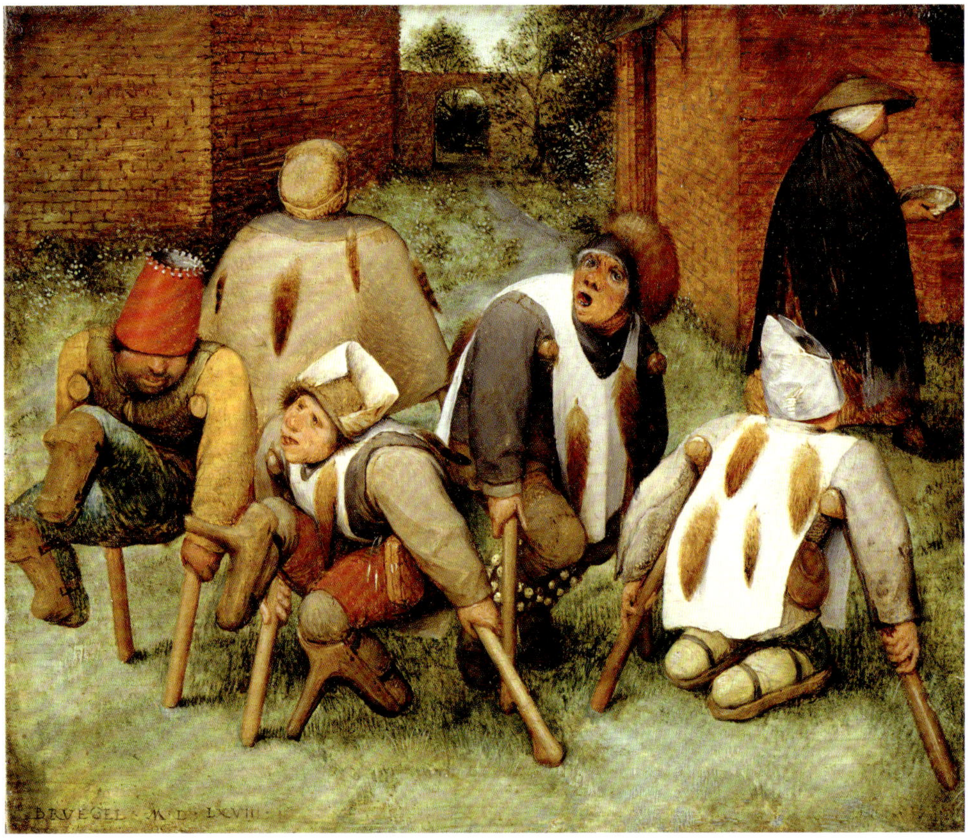

is surprised to see that Bruegel is her equal."[39] Some details in the painting seem akin to Boschian absurdities, such as the foxtail ornaments suggesting deceit. In fact, these are mocking accoutrements that contemporary society imposed on outcasts: symbols crafted by the society in which the unfortunates dwell that were aimed to amplify and moralize their oddities. For us to see the cripples for what they really are transforms our experience of the painting from a Boschian delight in novel invention to a new, troubling rediscovery of the world. Unmasked, the world looks stranger still, perhaps because we intimate that the cripples' carnival costumes, as well as the curiosity that draws us to them, belong to a cruel joke at their expense. While we can deduce from his form that one of the cripples is a legless man turned away, his geometricized body, combined with the ominous doorway beyond, is more disturbing than anything Bosch ever produced.

The bogeyman in the bakery window in the background of *Carnival and Lent* may be the product of vernacular making-do, but despite its crude manufacture—or perhaps because of it—this life-size doll or puppet possesses a certain demonic agency (see fig. 288). On the one hand, as charivari, the doll belongs to the fabrications of Carnival. Raucous, cruel, and comical, Carnival is itself an elaborate rebuke both to the official order and to the weak and marginal. Alcoholics and gluttons were seduced and sometimes forced into joining the parade, and then beaten up and expelled from the town. I suspect we are meant to laugh *with* Prince Carnival but also *at* the man who has to play him. On the other hand, placed above street level, the bogeyman seems to survey with amusement the goings-on below. As such, the doll mirrors ourselves—though it also mimics and mocks us—and has a vantage point like our own. Bruegel

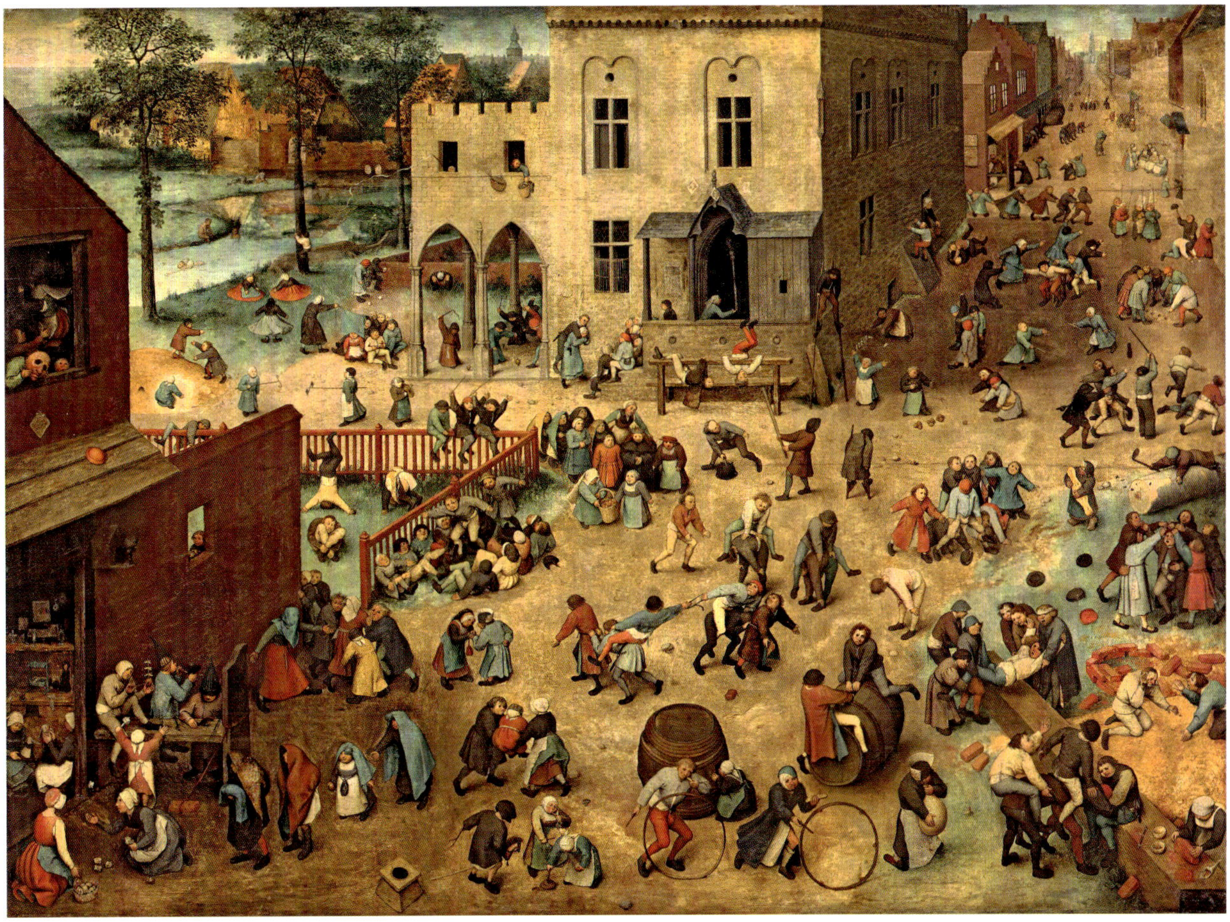

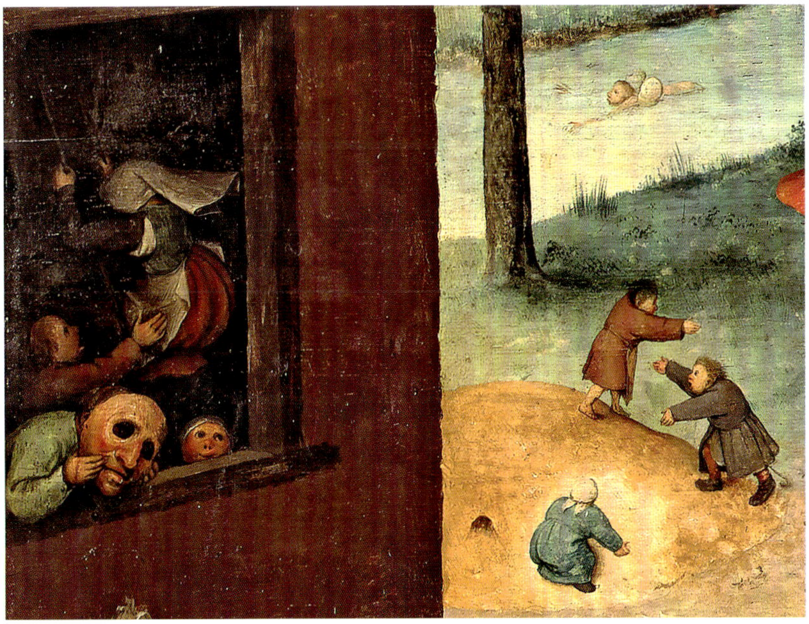

(ABOVE) **294** Pieter Bruegel the Elder, *The Children's Games*, 1560, panel, Kunsthistorisches Museum, Vienna

(LEFT) **295** Detail of Pieter Bruegel the Elder, *The Children's Games* (fig. 294)

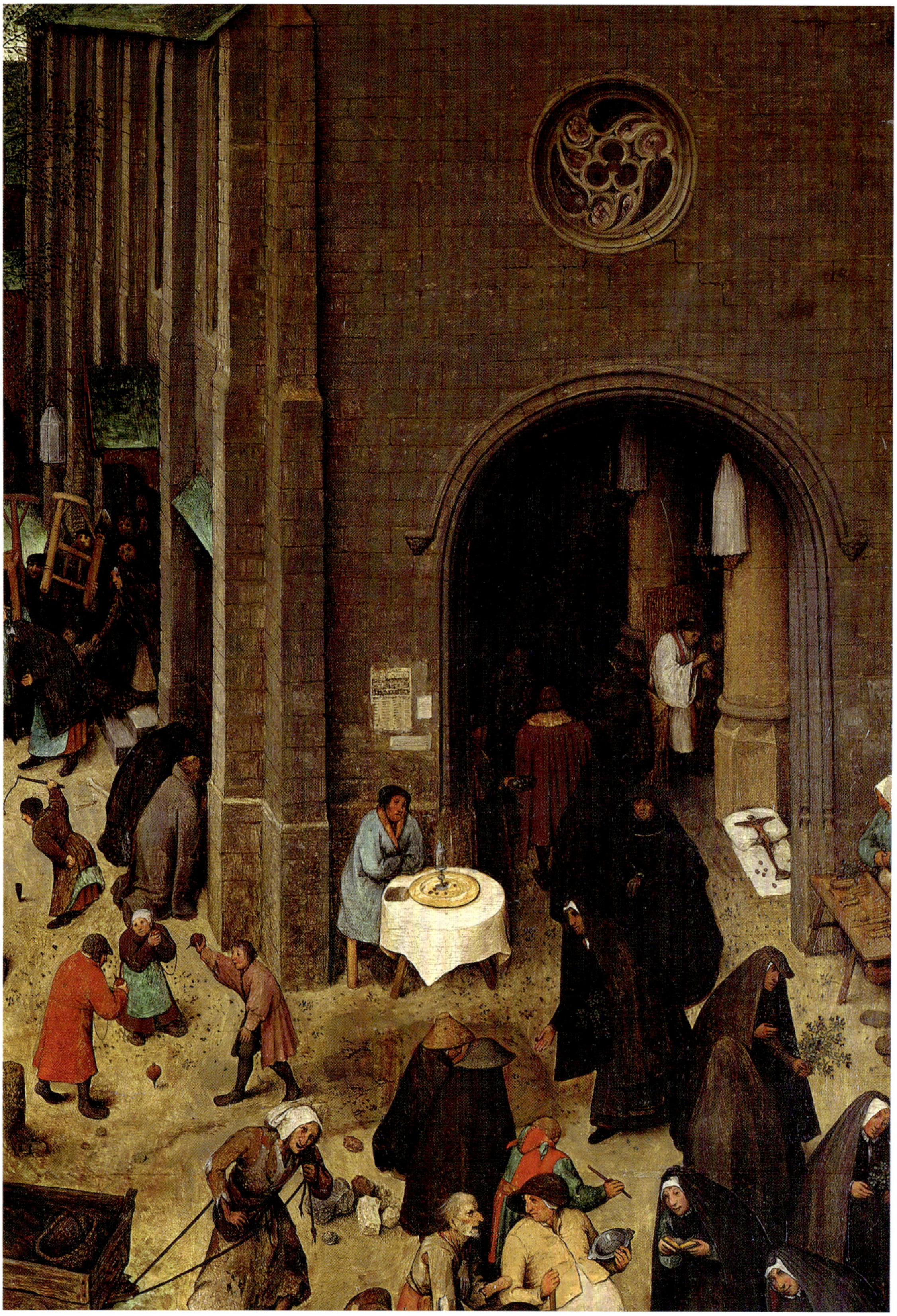

296 Detail of Pieter Bruegel the Elder, *Battle between Carnival and Lent* (fig. 284)

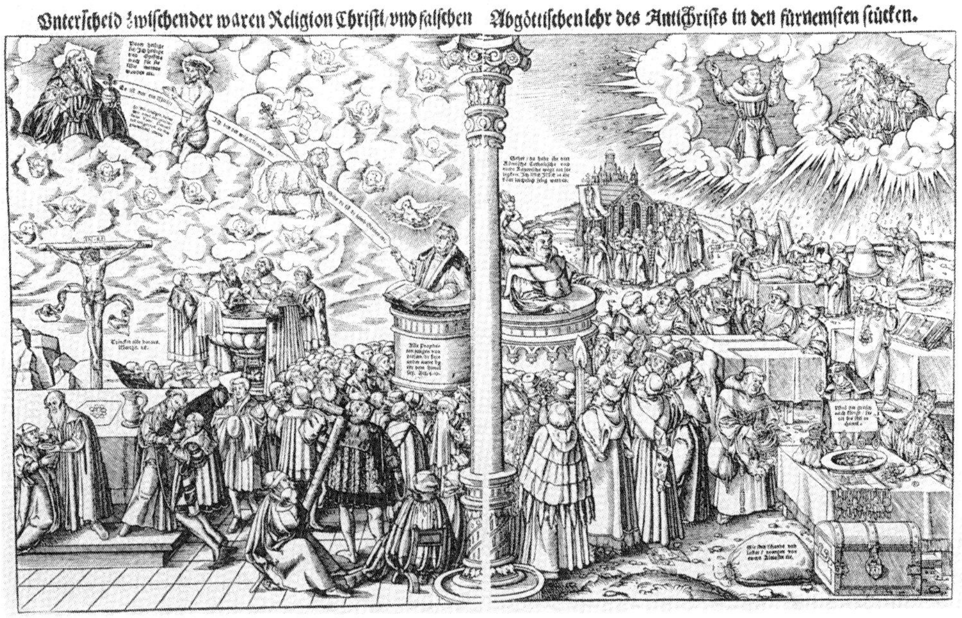

297 Pankratz Kempf (?), *The Difference between the True Religion of Christ and the False, Idolatrous Teachings of Antichrist*, c. 1550, woodcut

played a similar trick in *The Children's Games* (fig. 294).[40] Again from an upper window (at the left), a child seems to gaze toward us through the smiling mask of an adult (fig. 295).[41] As he does with the various plaster and leather masks featured in the Carnival procession, Bruegel isolates this mask's structure and style. He makes it out of place not just because it shows an adult, and because, alone among the toys in the picture, it is of a sophisticated manufacture. More mannered, even, than Bruegel's own style, the mask begins to look haunted, though not through some primitive identification with its wearer, who is dwarfed by it. We know it is a mask and, were we as knowledgeable about local styles as Bruegel was, we might even be able to recognize its origin, as typical of ones made in a certain village or region. Yet we respond to it as a face. Like an early ethnographer, Bruegel explores the mask "primitivistically," as a charged remnant of naïve or childish perception, which, having been banished, can no longer be playfully, even yearningly, evoked.

In *Battle between Carnival and Lent*, Bruegel extends unmasking to the Lenten side of the painting. The wax ex-votos on sale at the entrance to the church and, beside these, the bedded crucifix are visibly homespun (fig. 296). They therefore become, in their clinical depiction, as culturally contingent as the masks of Carnival. The "madeness" indicated for this religious equipment extends to the practices in which they are used. There is a dispute in the literature over Bruegel's attitudes toward customary religious usage, whether he takes a critical stance toward the actions he represents or whether, in agreement with many contemporary literary treatments of Carnival and Lent, he shows Lent to be victorious and true.[42] Lined up against the latter reading are a number of potentially degrading details, such as the court jester mingling among the almsgivers, suggesting that they are foolish or hypocritical. If Bruegel mounted a critique, though, he needed also to veil it, hence the uncertainty in the literature. Like his contemporaries Rabelais, Montaigne, and Sebastian Franck, Bruegel endeavored to neutralize radical differences in attitude by framing them as paradoxes.[43] Whether or not he wished to undermine visible religion as a realm of mere culture, religious practices do become estranged by the sheer delight Bruegel takes in their specificity.

This defamiliarization has important precursors in polemical prints of the Reformation. Beginning in the early 1520s, Protestants portrayed the false religion of the Roman Church by illustrating the plethora of its local customs (fig. 297).[44] While in the Veste Coburg, Luther assembled a "Customs Catalogue" listing the unnecessary and superstitious practices of the Roman Church.[45] As many of these usages were never recorded and soon were done away with even in Catholic regions, the reformer's collection serves, independent of its polemic, as a precious archive of popular religion at the eve of the Reformation. In portraying them in their prints, Protestant artists could not rely on an established iconography. But once depicted these hitherto unrepresented practices also condemn themselves by their apparent novelty and numerousness, especially when juxtaposed to a Reformed church service, which—asserting itself as true and the Catholic ones as false—consisted only of actions founded by Christ: baptism, Communion, and preaching.

Bruegel does not compare absolutes. Instead, Carnival's battle against Lent is a make-believe one between two faces of the same humanity. Bruegel proposes this overarching unity by making the painted surface of his picture coextensive with a spacious village square. Its streets extending out into the world, and interfacing the market with the church, the public square is *ecclesia* in the apostolic sense of that word: the assemblage of all inhabitants of a place, rich and poor, clerical and lay, burghers, marginals, and the dead. Differences conjoin rather than divide, their enmity defused as mere comical joust. Bruegel would have experienced firsthand the alternative response to differences. Catholics, Lutherans, Calvinists, and Anabaptists were one another's mortal foes: peace among them was but a temporary compromise before an inevitable final reckoning. Artists couldn't be bystanders since the conflict often hinged on what they specifically *made*. To many Protestants, crafted images *were* the enemy, since they eclipsed and violated God's word. In 1566, Calvinists decimated church art throughout the Netherlands. It was largely in response to this that the region's Catholic Habsburg ruler sent from Spain an army to crush all revolt and place religion and politics under central rule.

Bosch had experienced a violent campaign waged by one of his patrons, the Habsburg sovereign Philip the Fair. Bosch's town—we recall—was the chief outpost of Philip's war against Guelders; the artist's confraternity—the Brotherhood of Our Dear Lady of 's-Hertogenbosch—was a goodwill club linking his hometown to the Habsburg court; and his chief patrons were Spaniards in Philip's entourage. Bosch's enmity reflects this identification with the oppressors: in his art, differences are diabolical. Bruegel's art, by contrast, reflects the perspective of those on the receiving end of violence. Modern religious pluralism had specific historical roots in Bruegel's immediate circle of friends. Working in the culturally and economically diverse city of Antwerp, but drawn into the violent conflicts between and within the confessions, humanists such as Dirck Coornhert foregrounded the fabricated character of all human arrangements. After working in the 1550s as an engraver for Hieronymus Cock, Coornhert became a leading theorist of the Dutch revolt. Arguing that, as he put it, "it comes down to people, not confessions," he urged his contemporaries to cherish rather than combat differences. In dark times we ought to "hold up . . . our judgment of others, not to damn and denounce but to tolerate and bear each other amicably in love."[46] Coornhert's ecumenical perspective and his theory of impartial justice prefigure the arguments of the French philosophes two centuries later. Although it is impossible to say whether Bruegel held views like Coornhert's, his paintings create an optic in which such pluralism becomes imaginable.

Puppetry

In Bruegel, there are no foundations beyond the contingent ones that human beings make. Stories and histories are not false grounds, of course. According to early humanists such as Boccaccio and Coluccio Salutati, the basic work of culture was a heroic labor of Hercules.[47] It consisted in discerning metaphorical connections within the original chaos of the world. At the end of the humanist tradition and in the beginning of a new science of man, Giambattista Vico would trace back this process to the initial clearing, for cultivation, of a primal forest spread over the earth. The thought may long predate Vico. As we have seen, it hovers behind the origin myth of Bosch's hometown and with it his taken name, where an impenetrable natural wilderness (*bosch*) transforms into, and becomes the cryptic symbol for, the human mysteries of social order. In any event, the Herculean effort of invented connections enabled the original binding, or *religio*, of people to society. This humanist view of religion and fable was primitivistic rather than primitivizing: it sought to tap into the elemental powers of the human. The view belonged to an emergent ethnological perspective, but it derived from antique allegorical interpretations of myth, which understood the gods described by Hesiod and Homer to be mere similitudes of natural forces. Fables rendered truth in disguise. Still, translating fables into facts of the physical world did not bring them closer to truth, because facts became initially available through fables and still had to be argued rhetorically, as Boccaccio and others already understood.[48] The human center of humanism rested precisely in the conviction that people's knowledge and behavior were *humanly* produced, and that world, society, religion, and the gods were products of human work: things made rather than found.

Whereas medieval philosophers established eternal truths on the grounds of first principles, humanists explored the changing, illusory, and historical face of reality, recognizing in it alone the unchanging and divine. In an essay entitled "A Fable of Man," the Spanish-born humanist Juan Luis Vives imagined how Jupiter, to celebrate Juno's birthday, produced a cosmic play, or fable, creating the world as the stage and human beings as the actors. Observing the whole course of history, the gods stood amazed by man's ability to be all things, and, toward the end of the play, by his capacity to mime perfectly his divine creator, Jupiter. Finally, they invited man to "put off his mask" and take a seat among them at their banquet and observe the spectacle himself: "Man lay bare, showing the immortal gods his nature akin to theirs."[49] Written in Bruges in 1519, just a few years after Bosch's death, Vives's fable reverses the human and the divine. By way of its own fantastical representation of a truth, it argues that, at the moment of man's unmasking, the gods become masks and man the underlying reality.

To be fictively grounded simply means to have a foundation in something that's humanly fabricated rather than naturally found. Do stories and histories have a ground beneath *them*? Van Mander's description of Bosch's and Bruegel's technique is relevant again. Painting thinly and swiftly, they "allow[ed] the preparation on the panels or canvases to play a part."[50] Let us consider once again the matter of Bruegel's distinctive painterly *style*. This painter's naturalism is historically contingent, and in dramatic ways. From around the middle of the seventeenth

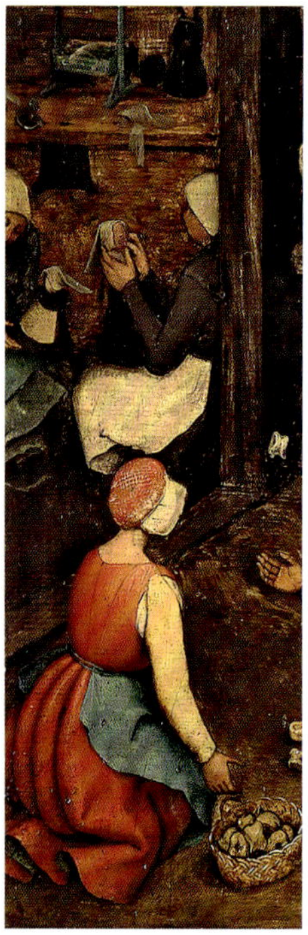

298 Detail of Pieter Bruegel the Elder, *The Children's Games* (fig. 294)

century through the nineteenth, viewers found his paintings awkward and artificial. The first modern art-history survey, Franz Kugler's 1837 *Handbook of Painting*, calls Bruegel's *Proverbs* "a miserable, confused picture, with painterly effects that are restless and without coherent impact," and Jacob Burckhardt judged the artist to be "worthless as a painter."[51] It is hard to see Bruegel in this way. This is partly because the art against which these critics measure him no longer looks like a progression toward an ideal. Adriaen Brouwer, whom academic tastes preferred, represents to us a different rather than better way of painting. If anything, a modern bias toward the primitive makes Bruegel seem more progressive than his seventeenth-century successors (e.g., see figs. 143 and 250). But what about Bruegel in his time?

Just after his death, for collectors of the highest caliber, his works were among the most desirable acquisitions. Bruegel's son Jan, writing in 1609 to his (Jan's) patron, Cardinal Federico Borromeo, reports that original paintings by his father were simply impossible to find, since the emperor, Rudolf II, had offered the highest possible price for any that became available.[52] Around 1590, Jacob Savery—a talented artist in his own right—produced a mass of drawings in the elder Bruegel's style.[53] Fraudulently signed with the master's signature, and inscribed with dates between 1559 and 1562, these works passed for Bruegel's until a few years ago. But this means only that at that moment Bruegel was massively appreciated, with no indication why this was the case.

It is possible that the awkwardness that nineteenth-century viewers criticized in Bruegel, and that we find hard to see, was a quality he deliberately put in his works. Bruegel understood his pictorial manner not as a natural mirror of his subjects but as a stylistic, and therefore artificial, alternative to the Italianism fashionable among other northern painters of the time. In a poem of 1565, the painter and writer Lucas de Heere describes a "certain painter" who mocks his rivals' products as "sugar pictures" because of their ornamentation. But it is this "stupid scoffer," according to De Heere, who deserves censure: "It is astonishing that you are not ashamed by this, for you are yourself entirely unmannered, since you ornament your paintings like carnival dolls."[54] The poem names the scoffer's rival, Frans Floris, but not the scoffer himself. According to historian David Freedberg, he is Bruegel.[55] In 1565, Bruegel was the supreme portraitist of carnival dolls, and his style, however one chooses to describe it, is the polar opposite of Floris's Italianate manner (see fig. 72).

Whether or not it is aimed at Bruegel, the insult illuminates the painter's aims. By saying that "he," whoever "he" is, ornaments his paintings like carnival dolls, De Heere proposes an analogy between artists' pictures and images of another kind, the effigies produced by the common folk. In terms of Bruegel's *Carnival and Lent*, this is like saying that in portraying the leather mask of the *Rommelpot* player Bruegel works in the same style as the mask maker, and that his customs catalogue is not "about" the people, but is "of" the people. Bruegel's art brims with instances where this seems to be the case, as in the lower left of *The Children's Games*, where a girl playing with dolls is painted identically to her toy (fig. 298).

Bruegel's frolicking peasants look awkward because their irregular gestures and pieced-together clothing jar with the coordination expected of a dance. Consider the portly reveler at the far left of Bruegel's *Peasant Dance* in Detroit (fig. 299).[56] Squeezed into his garish jacket, trousers, and codpiece, and weighed down by heavy shoes, he seems out of sync, both with the other dancers and with himself: observe his hands, so weirdly cramped. All this clumsiness

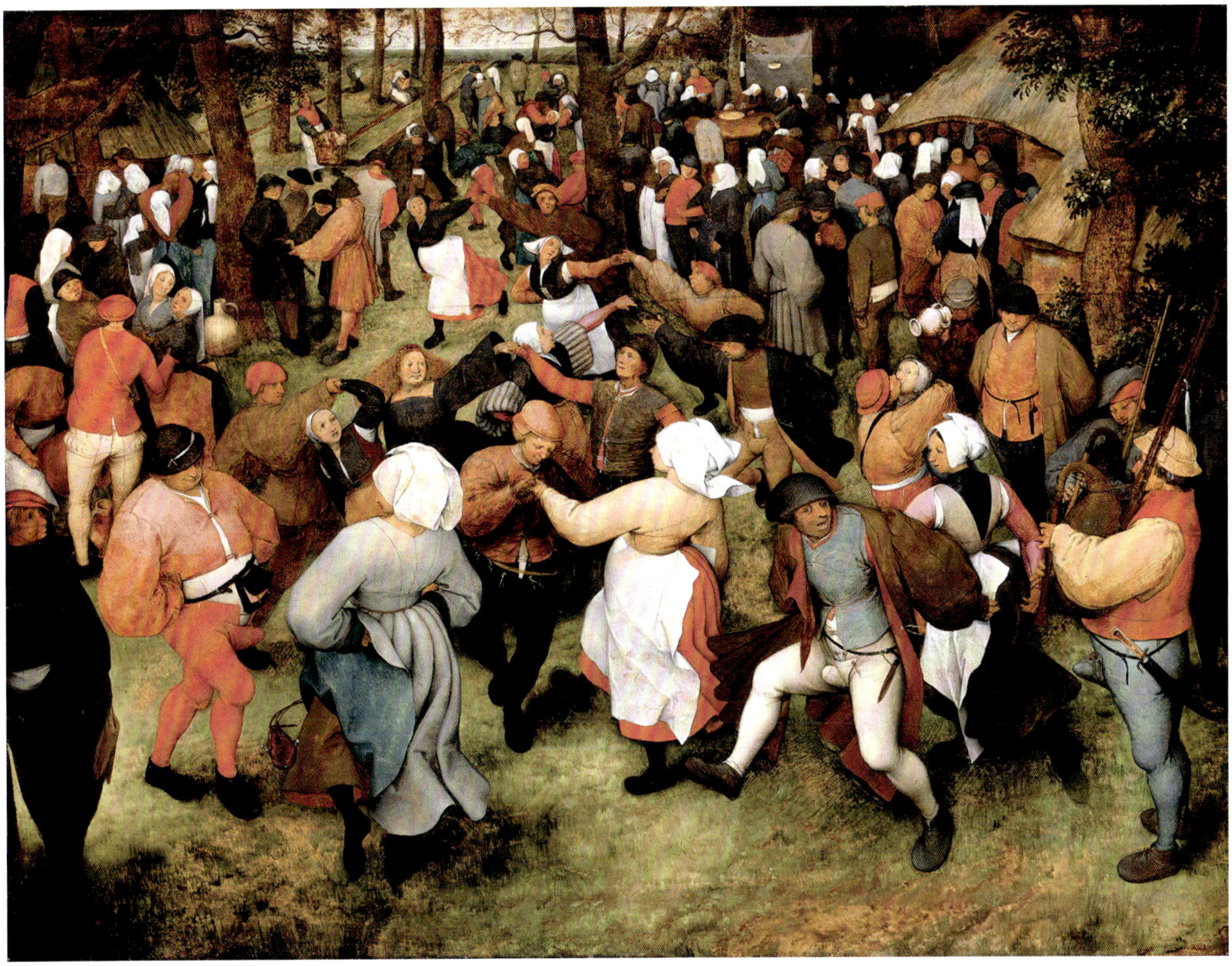

299 Pieter Bruegel the Elder, *The Peasant Dance*, c. 1566, panel, Detroit Institute of Arts

disappears, though, the moment we catch sight of his left eye, which casts a perfectly aimed glance at his partner. This connection suffuses him with a subtle grace peculiar to him, illuminating his vanity and causing us to appreciate the organization of his movements and garb—for example, that the laces, tassels, and belt, extended to their limit, precisely fit his girth. We can see why Van Mander commended Bruegel for accurately portraying the costumes of his peasants. The seeming awkwardness of the artist's *own* treatment of awkwardness is redeemed in those passages where, for example, the golden tassels match perfectly both the peasant and the brush that painted them. And is it not the case that beneath the hectic clothing, bodily dislocations, and eccentric points of view there lies, as if under a vernacular mask, the fluid, virtuoso line of mannerist *disegno*?[57] Why, then, the detour through awkwardness to grace? Why risk painting carnival dolls in a style reminiscent of them?

Bruegel was a contradictory figure already in his own day. On the one hand, he was "Peasant Bruegel," a painter from the rustic culture he portrayed; on the other hand, he was a world traveler and ethnographer of home. At once outsider and insider, sentimental and naïve, he belongs to the dialectics of unmasking that his pictures represent. Unmasking reveals things as they really are, not terrible gods but men in costumes. Unveiling is chiefly an initiation into the secret fact of human making. "Look up!" the shaman and the iconoclast alike command. "All this was made by people." For a painter to show this secret, he must distinguish the mask he lifts from the painting he makes by depicting that mask in its specific style, since with artifacts, style is the index of their facture. Bruegel knows the stylistic specificity of vernacular craft goods. Whereas other painters depict generalized rustic equipment, Bruegel, as Van Mander acknowledges, shows how peasants dress, dance, marry, and bake in their particular village. And whereas other painters see mere pretzels, jugs, and grills, Bruegel sees individual works of a signature style. This ethnographic expertise extends to his own craft of painting. Instead of producing, unreflectively, things in the dominant period style, he either reverts to a native Early Netherlandish model, as he did for the foreground figures of *Christ Carrying the Cross* (see figs. 266 and 270), or, by carrying that local tradition forward to its contemporary vestiges, he seeks a new vernacular realism among the peasants.

Through the detour of awkwardness, Bruegel teaches us to recognize and marvel at indigenous grace. Discerning the *sprezzatura* of Baldassare Castiglione's courtier in a Flemish peasant, he discovers a deeper *disegno* than the Italian one could ever be for him: a grace natural to this dancer depicted in a style natural both to the painter and to the peasant. This serves as Bruegel's unmasking. An intimate of urbane humanist scholars, he becomes "Peasant Bruegel" and allows us to see *him*, and not just the peasants and ourselves, as an example of the forms human life takes in one place, that world among parallel worlds. Applied to himself as well as to the rest of humanity, the Stoic's detachment reassociates him with us all—and it is this irony that links contingency to solidarity.

11

NATURE

Landscape with Trap

Master simulators, artists are also expert in difference. Germany's much-plagiarized painter and printmaker Dürer knew just about everything there is to know about copies and copying. The revolutionary master of the mechanically reproduced image, and the first artist to sue successfully for copyright infringement, he understood that no picture could ever be *identical* to anything else. Whether made by hand or machine, whether painted, sketched, carved, or printed, images always differ from *what they depict*: art never perfectly imitates its prototype in nature. But images also differ from any *copy made of them*, no matter how accomplished the copyist. Even impressions made from the same woodblock or copperplate are each subtly distinct: "There has never been an artist who has been certain that he can make two things so similar that they cannot be distinguished," Dürer concludes. "For in all our work nothing is quite and altogether like anything else."[1]

In its day, something about it must have caught the eye of the viewers of *Winter Landscape with Bird Trap*, the most copied of all Bruegel's compositions (fig. 300).[2] At least 128 versions of it survive. Originally, there must have been many more, each the same, down to the shapes of the branches against the sky, yet each also strangely unique, due to minute differences of brushwork, palette, condition, and densities of the paint. One hundred twenty-eight ineluctably different versions of the same ordinary Flemish locality refreshed with snow. Most were painted in the shop of Bruegel's son and namesake, Pieter the Younger (fig. 301).[3] Just four years old when his father died, this Brueghel (that is how he eventually tended to spell his name) made a good career of churning out copies of his father's masterpieces. Bruegel the Elder, by contrast, seems never to have copied himself—all his authentic works survive as unique objects, and even the two *Tower of Babel* panels differ markedly—and soon after his death these masterpieces had passed from patrician villas in Antwerp and Brussels, where they first hung, to Emperor Rudolf II's collection in faraway Prague. Trained probably by his grandmother and with few finished originals to guide him, Pieter the Younger had to make use of the many preparatory cartoons left in his father's shop at the time of his death. Retained by the grandmother—and Bruegel the Elder's mother-in-law, Mayken Verhulst—these meticulous sketches, and a famous surname, were his most valuable inheritance.[4] Other artists beside Pieter the Younger made copies of the composition. One version of the painting is

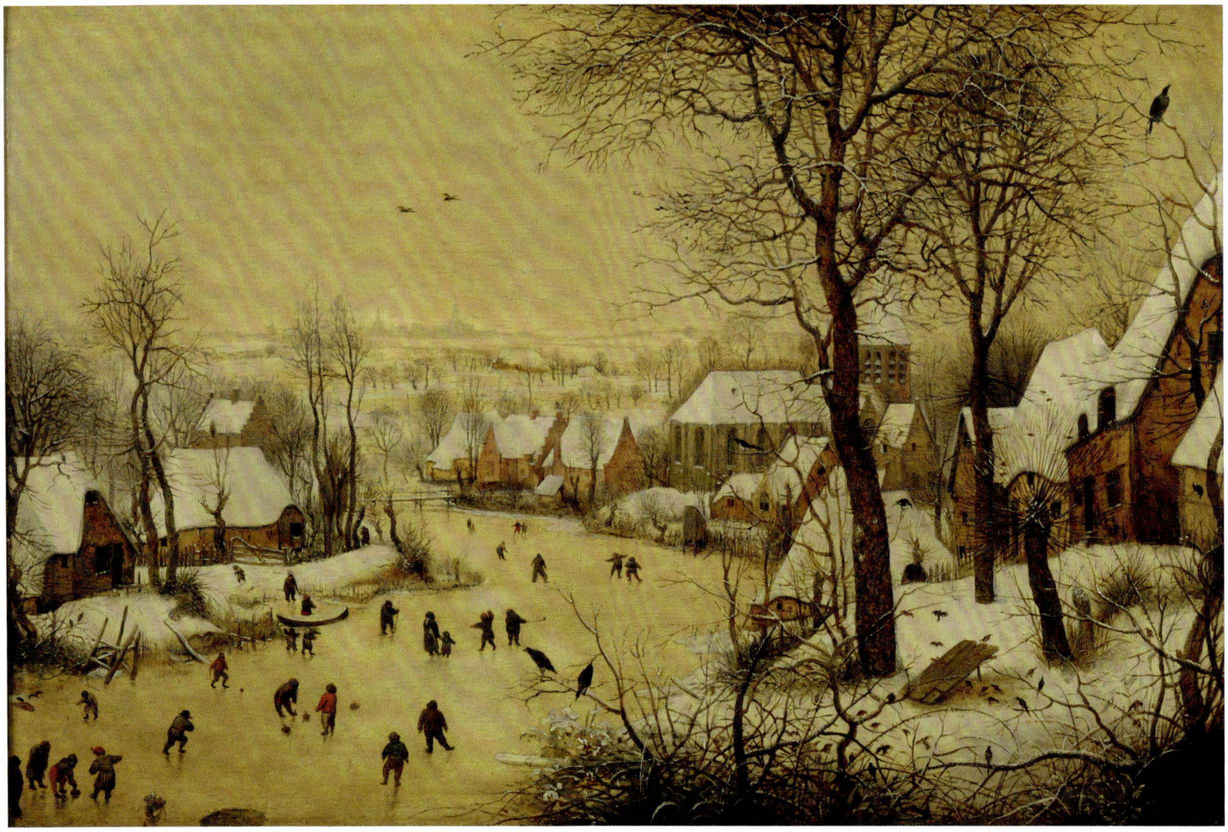

300 Pieter Bruegel the Elder, *Winter Landscape with Bird Trap*, 1565, panel, Musées Royaux des Beaux-Arts de Belgique, Brussels

(OPPOSITE TOP) 301 G. van Hoet (?) after Pieter Brueghel the Younger, *Winter Landscape with Bird Trap*, c. 1600–1620, panel, Kunsthistorisches Museum, Vienna

(OPPOSITE BOTTOM) 302 G. van Hoet (?) after Pieter Brueghel the Younger, *Winter Landscape with Bird Trap*, ca. 1600–20, panel, private collection

signed "BRVEGEL INVENTOR," but on a branch, lower right, written in snow white, another inscription adds the name of the maker, and a date: "G. van Hoet fecit 1604" (fig. 301).[5] Whoever this (as it were) "tribute painter" may have been, marks of individual identity are rare in the routine and probably collective enterprise of copying.

Perhaps it was sheer ordinariness that caught the public's eye: a cozy view of a village church, cottages clustered around a river, people at their everyday pursuits, and in the distance, like islands in an archipelago, endlessly more places like this one—imperfect copies of the same. Beyond *its* many replicas, Bruegel's composition spawned a whole subgenre of Flemish art. Focused on local scenery but offering a painting of a certain coloring and look, winter landscapes were almost exclusively a local product: northern pictures of the northern clime. The first and greatest expert in this field, a mute master from Amsterdam named Hendrick Avercamp, knew where his own specialty originated. Painted in the Dutch town of Kampen on the River Ijssel around 1608, his *Winter Landscape with Ice-Skaters* reproduces—almost as homage—the memorable bird trap from Bruegel's much-loved painting; it also places on the walls of a brewery the arms not of Kampen or Amsterdam but of Flemish Antwerp, where Bruegel was known to have lived and worked (fig. 302).[6]

In these winterscapes, it is partly the light that grabs the eye. An overall luminosity makes the ground glow more brightly than the sky, causing everything that is not white to stand forth bright-edged and clarified. Certainly the weather has brought out the inhabitants. For them, snow and ice are an occasion for pleasure in the wintry world, just as the painted likeness of snow and ice are pleasurable to us. The weather has brought people from their houses and farms into a communal, open-air celebration of the day itself. The sports of skating, sledging,

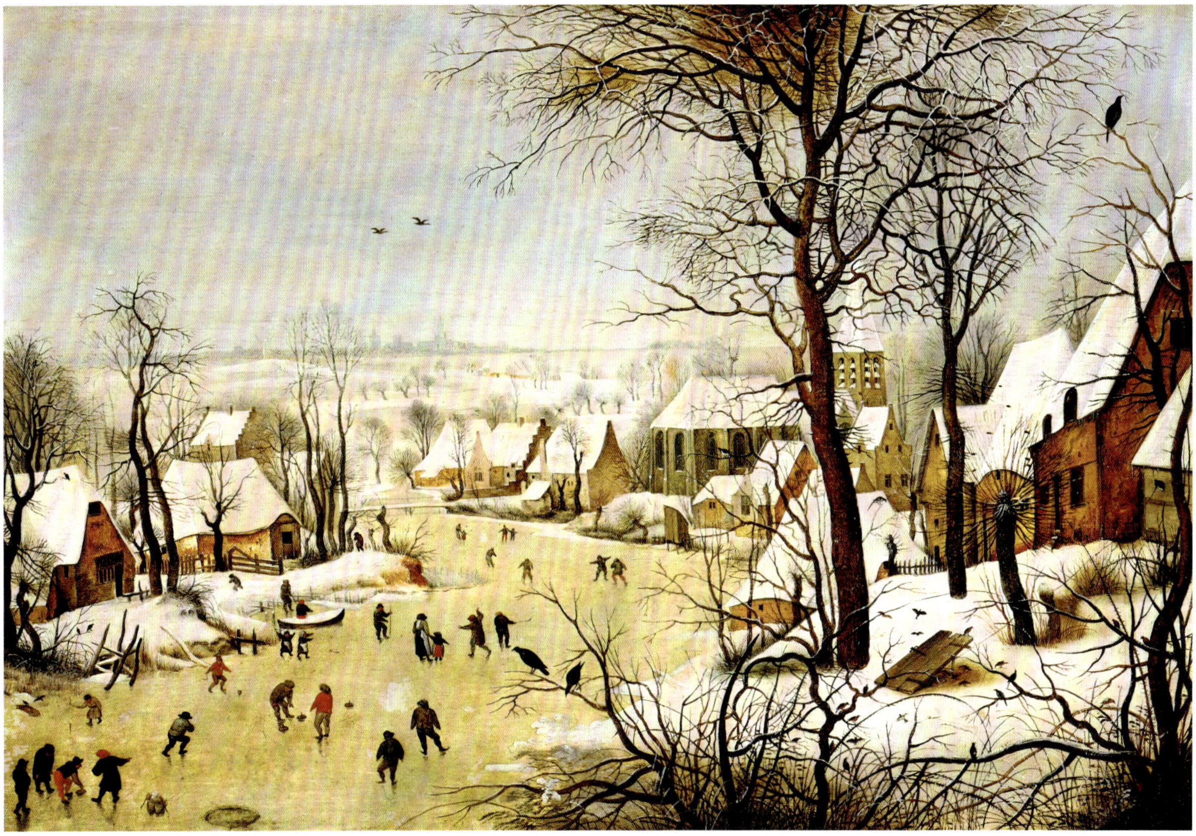

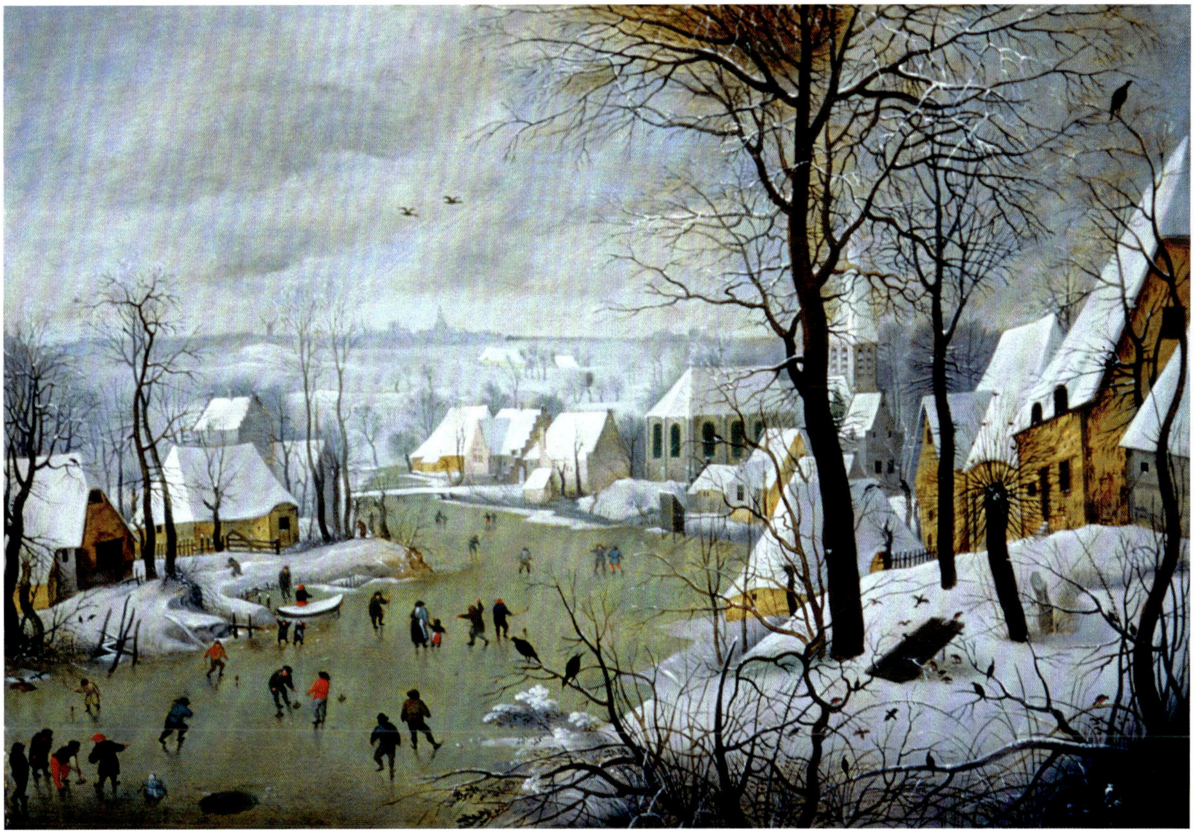

hockey, tops, and curling use the ice for fun. Snow and ice cause the natives temporarily to *experience* their lifeworld rather than simply to *dwell* in it. And we, the picture's viewers, experience that little ecstasy simply of being alive. Slippery games convey our eye into the landscape, along the frozen river. Whiteness heightens visibility. It also quickens the motion of our eye through the visible: glancing about the picture's brilliant surface, we glide through the scene. In the picture, both movements—the mobility of the skaters and the motion of our eyes—find reflections in the flight of birds. These help us notice how magically sky-like the frozen earth itself has become.

The similarity between air and ground is most pronounced in a version now in Brussels (see fig. 300). Quite probably by Bruegel the Elder's hand, the panel, only brought to public attention in 1927, bears the artist's signature and a date: 1565.[7] This makes the painting a contemporary of Bruegel's *Months* series. Perhaps while creating those vast tableaux, the artist decided to treat one season and one bit of landscape more intimately. Although there is some dispute over the fact and extent of the master's contribution to the Brussels panel, it does distinguish itself from all other versions by its sublime transparency. Material entities (trees, buildings, birds, skaters, etc.) seem to float over the undifferentiated glow of ice and air, their opacity confirmed only where they are blanketed or traced by snow. Bruegel again pushes to its limits that technique that allows "the preparation [*de gronden*] on the panels . . . to play a part." In *Winter Landscape with Bird Trap*, this still-visible ground is composed of white chalk, probably with gelatin glue as a binding medium. Meticulously smoothed and polished down, this ground forms the off-white surface glowing underneath all painted forms. Paradoxically, but characteristically, Bruegel's ground conveys the dizzying groundlessness of this scene where snowy air reflects snow. The painting transports us not merely into a specific locality but into the unique optical perception of that locality. Bruegel projects us into the fugitive state of air and light obtaining then and there, in the ecstasy of one moment in the life of nature.

The birds and skaters glide through our mobile experience of their world. Two airborne geese mimic the soaring glance that captured their silhouette. We feel this multiple mobility by observing how, painted differently in every copy, these birds isolate for study the painterly distinctions of each work. Each version has a distinct, overall touch, a unique way that the loaded brush leaves a trace on the pictorial ground. Rendered in several quick but deft strokes, the formulaic birds display this differential of the handmade. Scattered throughout the picture, they also elicit, and echo, our punctuated focus on the scene. Sooner or later, they also draw us to the shadowed bit of ground before the foreground thicket where flocks of birds have gathered. There, one peculiar contraption brings motion—ours and the birds'—to a temporary standstill. It also gives the composition its popular nickname: *The Trebuchet*.

Bruegel paints the bird trap in all of its parts (fig. 304). The trap's quarry, here consisting of robins, sparrows, and blackbirds, has been lured to a certain spot because it has been baited with scattered seed. Above the lure stands the weapon. An old door propped up at one side by a peg also works as a lure because it seems to afford cover for the birds, which feed as if under its protection. However, the door is a deadly weight that—when enough birds have gathered under it—will crush them. The trap's trigger is that single peg on which the door leans; its release is a long cord reaching from the trap, through a peephole in the cottage, to a hidden operator. With the fowler, we watch the birds gathering in the trap. By closely scrutinizing their situation, and because our species kinship with the hidden

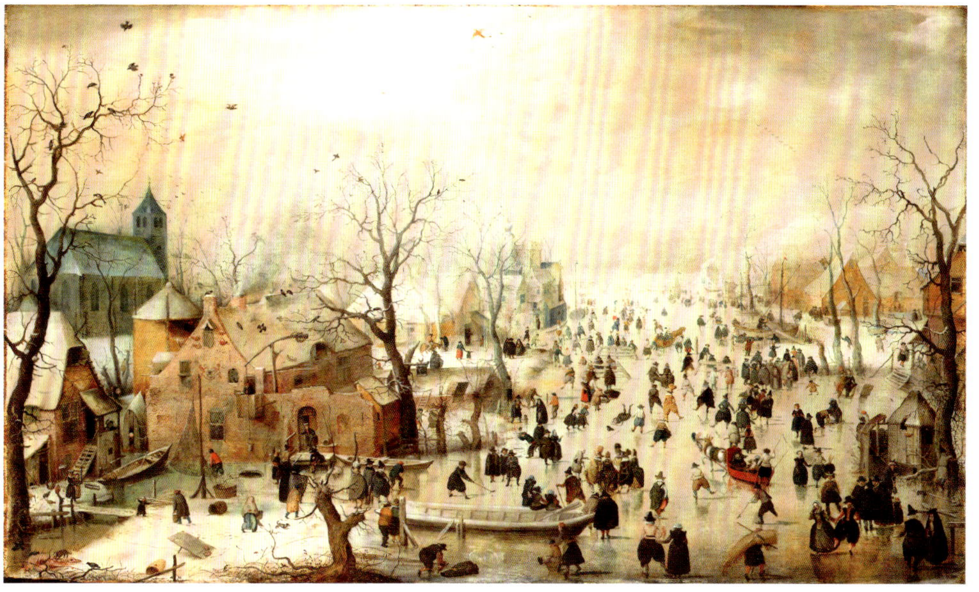

303 Hendrick Avercamp, *Winter Landscape with Ice-Skaters*, c. 1608, panel, Rijksmuseum, Amsterdam

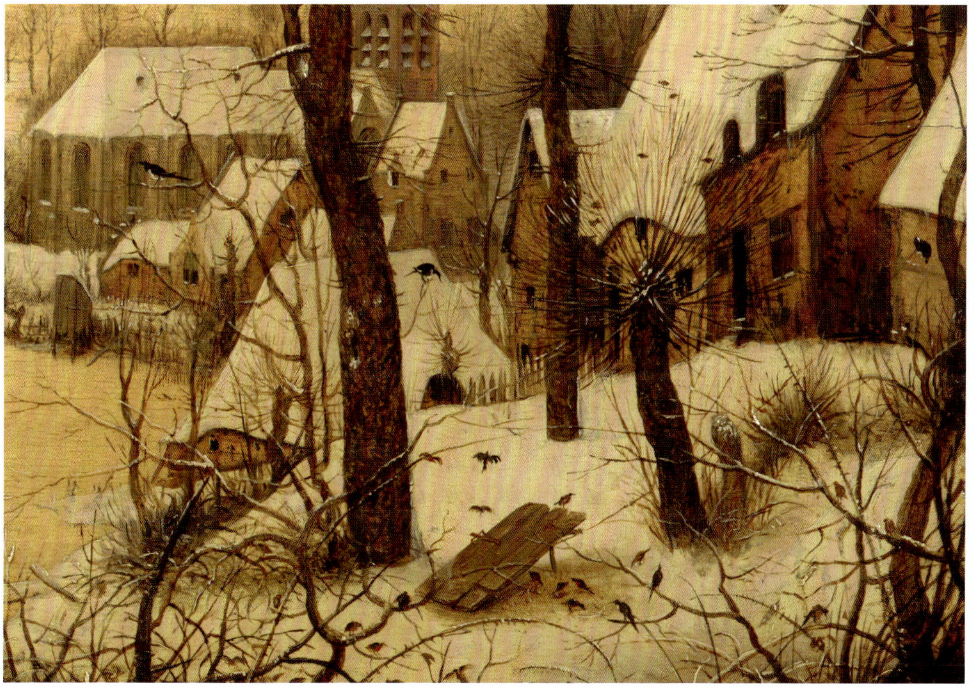

304 Detail of Pieter Bruegel the Elder, *Winter Landscape with Bird Trap* (fig. 300)

fowler enables us (unlike the poor birds) to recognize and understand the trap they are in, we become complicit with him.

Yet the peephole remains also mysterious to us. Evidencing a gaze while concealing the looker—if he is even there—the trap's system rephrases, in different and sinister terms, the structure of vision as it operates in the painted view itself. Whereas we look for pleasure and delight, it, the fowler's eye, looks for the purpose of practical survival or cruel sport. Whereas everything we see is distant, fleeting, and intangible, it links viewer to viewed materially through the cord. However we understand it—and I am sure Bruegel's original viewers took pleasure in trying to understand it; otherwise the picture would not have been so popular—the bird trap contributes to the composition's allure by introducing a slippery interpretive sport for its housebound viewers.

The bird trap is not merely an absorbing detail drawn from everyday life. It makes a statement *about* everyday life. We glimpse the contraption, figure out what it is and how it works, and get a slight chill doing so. Placing us mentally inside of a hidden danger, it sounds a warning bell. Just as the birds take the bait oblivious to the weight above them (indeed just as they take that weight as their protective friend rather than their enemy), we—especially while focused intensely on the one detail—pursue our curiosity, our visual hunger, heedless of any perils around us. Bruegel's version and several copies by his son manifest danger to people at the picture's lower left. Cut through by the lower framing edge, a large hole, almost exactly the size, shape, and color of the bird trap's shaded danger zone, has opened in the ice. (Perhaps to integrate the detail into the scene by breaking up the glaze, the artist pressed a thumb or finger into it while the paint was still wet, leaving an unintended signature in the form of a print.)[8] And because the ice is the painting's unmodified ground, the painterly trick that "plays a part" in the picture, this gap at the picture's threshold, makes everything we see potentially an abyss.

It is a common tactic in Bruegel's art. The painting lures us by displaying someone else in peril. Hailed as curious voyeurs, we enter the picture's world with our defenses down, only to discover that the eye-catching hazard was just bait and the real and present danger is ours. In *The Peasant and the Bird Thief*, as we recall, the robbery of the bird in its nest—note again Bruegel's avian stand-in—prompts the finger-pointing peasant who accosts us (see fig. 4). Seemingly in peril are both the bird and the nester, who might fall from his tree like his hat. But soon we discover that he, the picture's messenger, is poised to fall and that we—his fatal distraction—also stand over a watery abyss. The tragic destiny we thought we experienced vicariously rebounds on experience itself. Our being a subject, our standing against the objects and accidents of the world as their stable measure and ground, reverses the moment we become *subjected to* them.

Bruegel's ordinary winter landscape does not simply contain a trap. Inducing in people the ecstasy of lived experience, this landscape is itself a trap. To embellish his point, Bruegel avails himself of conventional symbols. Ice stands for the slippery, deceptive nature of the world. A drawing by Bruegel's hand formed the basis for a print engraved by Frans Huys and first published by Hieronymus Cock in 1557.[9] Neither Bruegel's drawing nor Cock's version includes an explanatory text. Only a second state, issued by Johannes Galle as part of an album of engravings fitted to emergent collecting practice, adds an extended letterpress inscription (fig. 305).[10] The title "The Slipperiness of Human Life" appears in Latin, French, and Dutch at the top, and in the lower margin two triplets complete the idea:

> Thus does one skate on the ice at Antwerp, before the city. One this way, the other that way, gawked at from all sides, one stumbles, he falls, who holds himself upright and proud.
>
> Yes, learn here from this picture how we ride through the world, slipping our way, sometimes badly sometimes wisely, on this transience much more brittle than ice.[11]

Skating becomes an extended metaphor for life. In the everyday world, the activity offers a pleasing spectacle. One can behold others performing—well or poorly—while also performing and being watched oneself. The salient pleasure lies in observing the otherwise

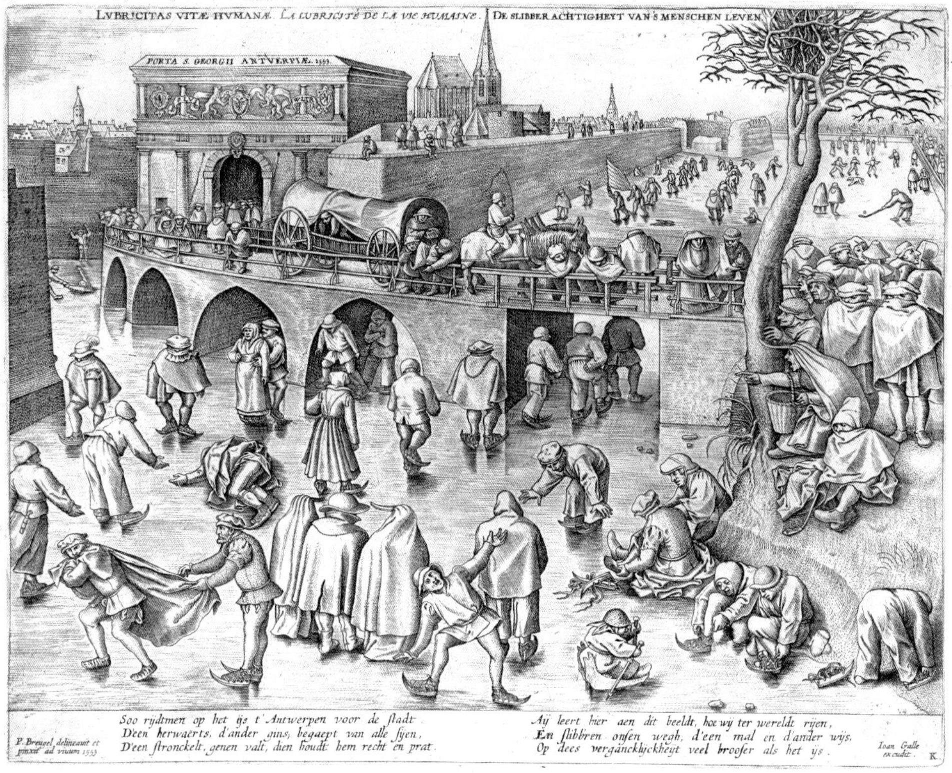

305 Frans Huys, after Pieter Bruegel the Elder, *Skating before Saint George's Gate, Antwerp*, c. 1558, engraving (published by Johannes Galle, Antwerp), The Metropolitan Museum of Art, New York, Harris Brisbane Dick Fund, 1926

dignified, who—not always the best skaters—stumble foolishly. More abstractly, in abiding the text's command that we "learn," skating teaches a lesson about life: fortunes change, pleasure is fleeting, and life ends suddenly.

While the real-life activity of skating vitalizes it, the lesson strings together old clichés. We encountered these in spades in the art of Bosch. Bosch undercut his novel creation—a painting of everyday life—by various plots and proverbs all ending in death and judgment. *The Hay Wain* featured two of these: one on the shutters' exterior and one in the work's open state. On the shutters, the peddler as Everyman ran from danger to danger, with death looming—literally—overhead (see fig. 37). In the interior view, the mobile, empty, and combustible hay symbolizing the world, together with people falling over themselves in order greedily to have the hay-as-world, formed a second, more cosmic allegory of transience (see fig. 39). If, then, Galle's engraving and, by extension, Bruegel's *Winter Landscape with Bird Trap* can yield the same message as *The Hay Wain*—if Bruegel, like Bosch, condemns human experience as passing and vain—then have we traveled *any* distance in all these chapters?

Bosch and Bruegel do make similar allegories about experience. But they create very different *experiences of allegory*. *What* these pictures mean may be identical. *How* they mean is different. This difference lies hidden from the study of a picture's iconography because it resides not in the symbols but in how a painter plots and manipulates our experience of them. Bosch and Bruegel also differ in another way. Implicated in our experience of allegory, this difference concerns the place each artist gives to experience itself. *The Hay Wain* veritably diagrams that location. In Bosch, human experience is a vain pursuit of nothingness. Mockingly located both at the center of the world and at the center of *our* visual experience of the triptych, human experience is, unbeknownst to itself, the consequence of the Fall of Eve and Adam, and the experiencing human subject is already on its way to hell. Meanwhile, the gaze of the all-seeing creator-god subsumes human experience under a larger structure. From the "now" of eternity, God looks down on the world as its ultimate spectator. Damnation may be gruesomely fascinating for Bosch's public, but it is a satisfying experience for the wrathful God. Where does Bruegel locate experience, and what becomes of the divine perspective that formed the framework of Bosch's art?

Whereas in Bosch the world marches blindly into a full-fledged portrait of hell, in Bruegel the breach in the ice is, to us and to the skaters, an everyday reminder of death and an underworld. *Winter Landscape with Bird Trap* thrusts deep into the ordinary. The allegorical machinery with which it comments on experience is transformed into vernacular equipment: instead of the Devil's snare, a rustic trap; instead of hell, a sawed-out hole; instead of a divine oculus, a peephole in a cottage wall. This accords with Bruegel's strategy of displacing his symbol-making activity to his "primitive" subjects, the peasants. The allegorical battle between Carnival and Lent becomes in his hands seasonal entertainment designed and performed by villagers (see fig. 284). It is not *Bruegel's* allegory but theirs, these particular people whose customs and costumes he meticulously records in paint. Symbol and allegory are thus subsumed by ethnography. Products of human making, symbols and allegory no longer reveal the place of man—the creature *anthropos*—within God's cosmic scheme; rather, they confirm that man, like all forms of life, is the contingent product of a particular *ethnos*.

This does not, however, mean that Bruegel's pictures make no higher claims on us. They, too, symbolize, but with a powerful restriction. Observe how the poor birds behave toward the instrument of their undoing. Presumably they see, above the seeds, the leaning door, the peg, and the cord. But they overlook these for the bait, because they cannot mentally add them up into a system and an intention. As our examples of trap making showed, successful snaring necessitates that the snare itself be invisible to its prey.[12] A trap involves both the ingenuity to build it and the mimetic know-how to hide that ingenuity from the quarry. Gazing through the peephole, the fowler views his target from within his instrumental picture of *their* view. He has made the trap visible enough to lure them, but he has also made it invisible to them *as a trap*; otherwise the birds would stay away. The propped-up door belongs to a picture carefully constructed by the trapper, one that conforms to how its victim sees—and survives in—the everyday world. This picture includes food as well as refuge. To the birds the door looks like safe cover, and anyway the hunter is in fact too far away to catch these birds by ordinary means: the fowler can get them only through the door as a concealed prosthesis. All this illusion is created, literally, for a bird's-eye perspective, which sees the seeds, considers the propped-up door, watches for people, and finds all enemies now far off on the slippery ice. But this perspective fails—and the fowler knows this—because it thwarts the human faculty to grasp the whole. The pleasure that we as viewers take in the bird trap, and thus Bruegel's artistic ingenuity, consists in how our grasp of the whole dawns on us slowly, allowing us to feel what sets us apart from the birds. Were we to glimpse, say, a man with a crossbow hidden in the bushes, we would recognize the impending danger, but we would not have the experience of calculating a technology that effectively already has the birds. The trap delights by being at once invisible and global: an inescapable and unerringly hostile world within the world.

Bruegel places at his picture's lower center two large birds that behave as sentries. At the upper right, a third seems to let out a call, perhaps to draw others to the scattered seeds, perhaps to warn them to stay away. Bruegel aligns our own point of view with the two "lookout" birds. And this causes us to start to see *like* birds. Their peril becomes our own. And indeed, in their projection on the panel, these two foreground creatures are of the same size and hue as the distant skaters just beside them. One threatened from above, the other from below, birds and people switch places on slippery ground.

A shift between human and avian perspectives belongs to one of the founding myths of European art. Pliny describes how the Greek painter Zeuxis fooled birds into trying to feed on grapes from a painted vine.[13] Zeuxis was then outdone by an even greater illusionist, Parrhasius, who fooled Zeuxis himself into trying to open a painted curtain. Fooling the eyes of the birds and the beasts is one thing, the legend tells us. Fooling the human eye, and particularly the eye of a skilled artist, is quite another. This anecdote may not figure in Bruegel's composition. But Pliny's views on art play a role in the most important period account of Bruegel's art. In 1573, Abraham Ortelius began to compile the *Album Amicorum*. One of the early entries is the epitaph to Bruegel with which we began our discussion of the artist (see fig. 6). Ortelius—we recall—blamed the painter's untimely death on Nature, jealous of a maker more perfect than she. This poetical conceit placed Bruegel above Nature herself. "I should call him," writes the mapmaker, "the very nature of painters."[14] To explain then what enables an artist to *be* another nature, Ortelius avails himself of the ancient theme: "Bruegel depicted many things that cannot be depicted, as Pliny says of Apelles. In all his works more is always implied than is depicted." That "more" refers to something in Bruegel's art that makes beholding his paintings the same as beholding nature. This renders his art as inexhaustible and as inscrutable as the world.

In his *Winter Landscape with Bird Trap*, Bruegel combines two imitative technologies: the snare meant for birds and the painting meant for people. Subsuming the rustic trap—made, like the serving tray in *The Peasant Wedding*, of a repurposed barn door (see figs. 260 and 304)—into the artist's sophisticated machinery, painting clearly wins the palm. But the snare says something about Bruegel's depiction of it. Its trigger line, parallel to the sight line of the trapper, invites us to picture what the trapper sees. That view—if we try to picture it—turns out to be perfectly congruent to the one Bruegel gives us in his panel as a whole. In the trap, a baited ground dotted with potential casualties recedes to the base of the leaning door; in the painting, alluring ice dotted with imperiled persons recedes toward the horizon, where it converges with that curiously opaque sky. In the trap the forward opening is spanned by the stick or peg; in the painting, the foreground opening is spanned by a large tree. And in both the trap and the painting, the semblance of a world can collapse into a flat panel made of wood. (Bruegel paints on joined wooden panels, not unlike the repurposed door!) The door will drop suddenly on the birds; Bruegel's illusion disappears whenever we glimpse the painting's ground.

By showing us how birds get trapped, Bruegel causes us to imagine, from a higher perspective, how we ourselves might be snared. Again, motifs of traps, snares, and avian decoys appear often in Bosch. The owl of his drawing *The Field Has Eyes* is a lure, drawing magpies to its diurnal roost, while observing its enemies more completely than they can ever see it (see fig. 232). As I have suggested, the owl even served as an emblem of the artist, whose taken name punned on the bird's sylvan habitat, for like the owl, Bosch engineered traps. Surrounded by pitfalls, the *Hay Wain*'s peddler marches toward what amounts to a trapdoor (see fig. 37). Through the painting of everyday life, Bosch lures us into loving the world (and art) only then to catch us in the very trap that ensnares humanity in the triptych's open state, reached by the shutters that cut through the peddler. Like owls, Bosch's paintings are all-seeing: *The*

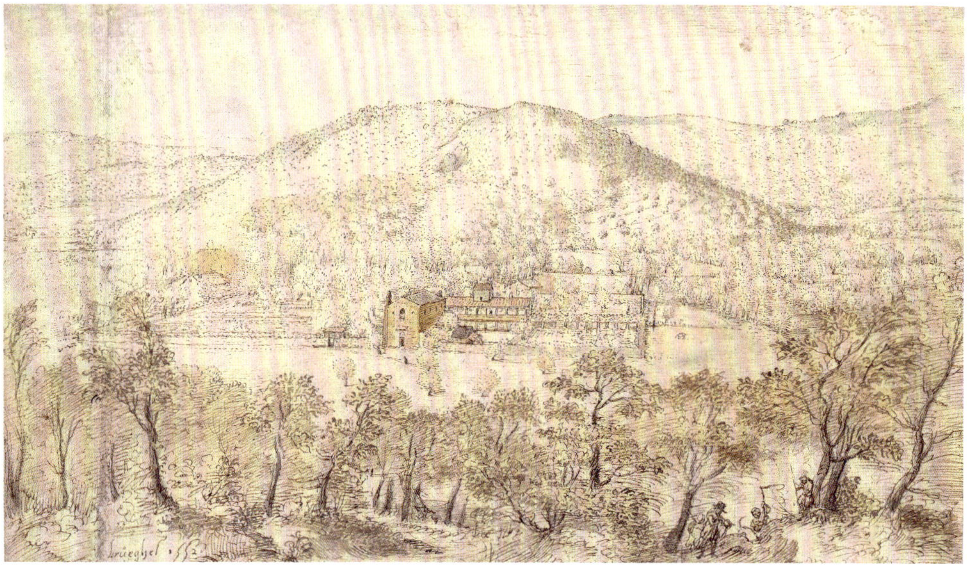

306 Pieter Bruegel the Elder, *Mountain Landscape with Italian Cloister*, 1569, pen and brown ink, watercolor (with later additions), Kupferstichkabinett Staatliche Museen, Berlin

Seven Deadly Sins beholds us, catching us in our sinful curiosity about what it—this dangerous painting—shows (see fig. 122). We see dimly, but God sees all. In Bosch's pictures, painting is not primarily for us to see. Rather, it is an instrument through which God observes and judges us, his potential enemy. God—and not the viewer—is the true "subject" of Bosch's pictures in the original sense, as the fixed and stable ground underlying all the fantastical delusions. Even when it looks as if the Devil sees all—when, due to sin, the world becomes a diabolical trap—the viewing subject of our trials and tribulations remains divine. In his masterpiece ostensibly without a subject, Bosch shows what happens when humans take their own experience, their own subjectivity, as the center of their existence (see fig. 170). Through the ocular desire elicited in him by Eve, and through a nature always already corrupted by Lucifer's pride, Adam—and the Adam in all of us—engenders a heretical, obscene, and counternatural state of being. This is what happens when humans falsely believe they are the subject of the world. Oblivious to the Law and without redemption, they revert to the abyss from which everything was made.

Like his great precursor, then, Bruegel traps us in his pictures. But unlike the snares in Bosch, the trap is neither of the Devil nor of God. It is the everyday world itself, which lies all around us but remains incalculable and inscrutable. We can no more identify the world's structure and purpose than the birds, with their limited cognitive hardware, can recognize the trap. Our dawning understanding of *The Trebuchet* does not allow us to grasp whatever trap we may stand in. Indeed, in seeing the quarry's predicament we grasp how traps are at bottom invisible. According to Ortelius, Bruegel depicts not merely nature (a landscape) or even an invisible aspect of nature (the trap), but the invisibility of nature, its invisible hold on us.

This is also the purpose of Bruegel's landscapes. They allow us to see our predicament from the inhuman perspective of the world. Sometimes Bruegel expresses this viewpoint through the figure of ambush, as in *The Rabbit Hunt*, where the spear bearer stalks the stalker from behind (see fig. 36). Sometimes he shows it by displaying momentous human events in a condition of poor visibility, as in his wintry *Adoration of the Magi in the Snow*, where snowfall conceals Christ's "coming to light" (see fig. 265). Perhaps the divine sees this and all things still. But Bruegel's God sees invisibly, as the fowler does the birds. He may no longer even be lying there in wait. How did this artist achieve this terrifying perspective?

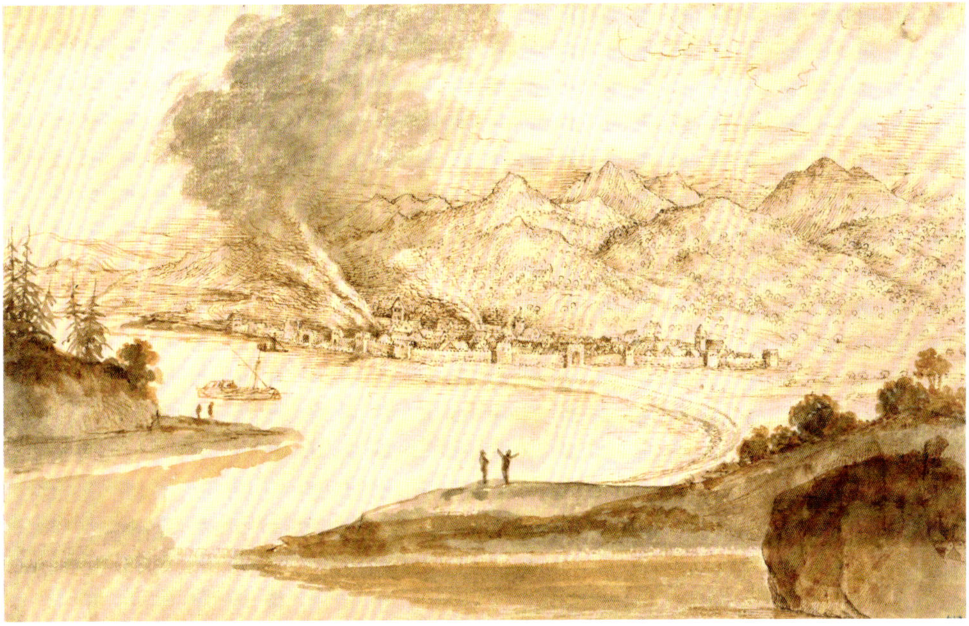

307 Pieter Bruegel the Elder, *View of Reggio in Calabria*, c. 1552, pen and brown ink (wash added by later hand), Museum Boijmans Van Beuningen, Rotterdam, Loan Museum Bojimans Van Beuningen Foundation (Collection Koenigs)

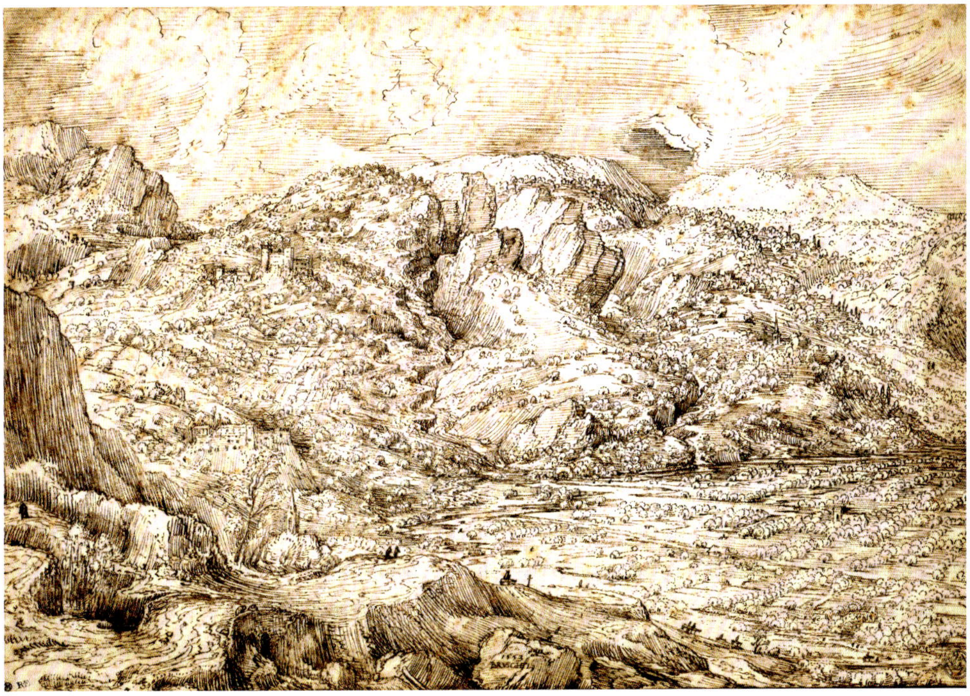

308 Pieter Bruegel the Elder, *Alpine Landscape with a River Descending from the Mountains into a Valley*, 1553, pen and brown ink, Musée du Louvre, Paris

World Travel

Bruegel enters the history of art as a traveler out to see the world. We meet him first in the midst of the great journey that took him from Antwerp via France to Italy's southernmost tip and back again, across the Alps. His earliest extant works—inscribed 1552 and drawn in pen and brown ink on paper made in France—show hilly landscapes of southern France and Italy (figs. 306 and 307).[15] Whether or not Bruegel actually sketched them outdoors, most of these drawings place us on the ground, stopped along a road or pathway, looking at the view. With Bruegel, we pass villages and cloisters snuggled in among the valleys, stand on the shore of Rome's Ripa Grande, pass far south to the Strait of Messina, and then, in the most spectacular surviving sketches, return northward through the wild landscapes of the Alps (fig. 308).[16] Everything

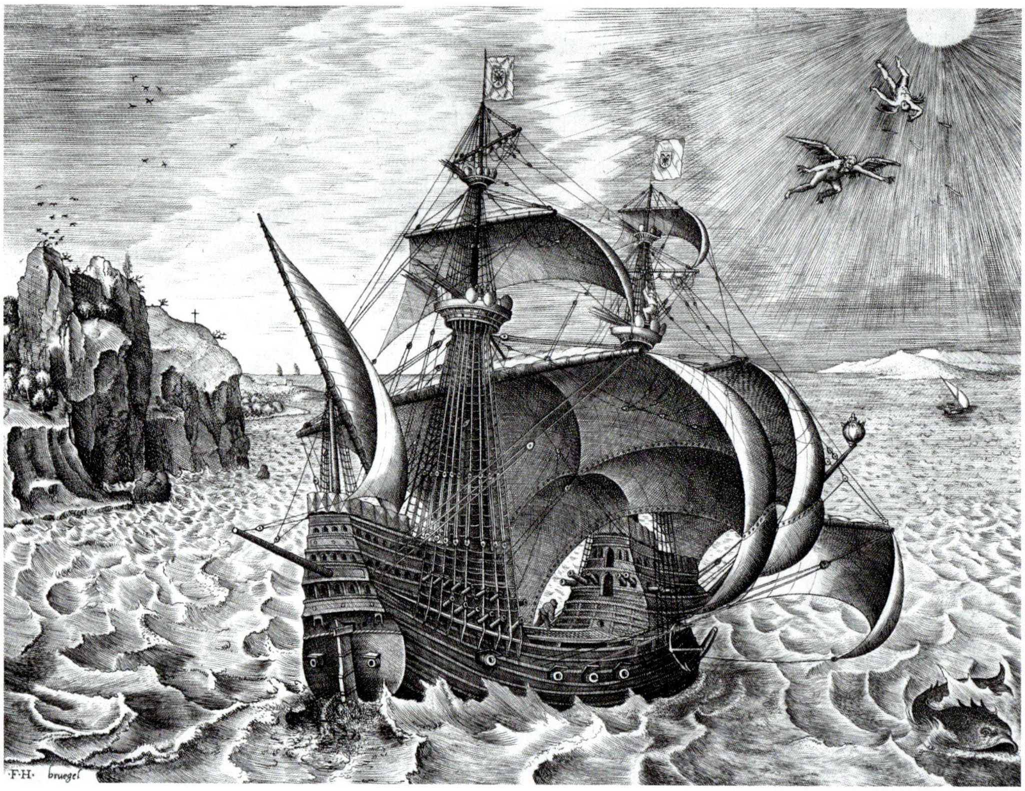

(ABOVE) **309** Frans Huys after Pieter Bruegel the Elder, *Armed Three-Master with Daedalus and Icarus in the Sky*, 1561–65, engraving and etching (published by Hieronymus Cock, Antwerp), The Metropolitan Museum of Art, New York, Harris Brisbane Dick Fund, 1928

(BELOW) **310** Gerard Mercator, frontispiece from *Atlas sive cosmographicae meditationes de fabrica mundi et fabricati figura* (Duisberg, 1595), University Library System, University of Pittsburgh

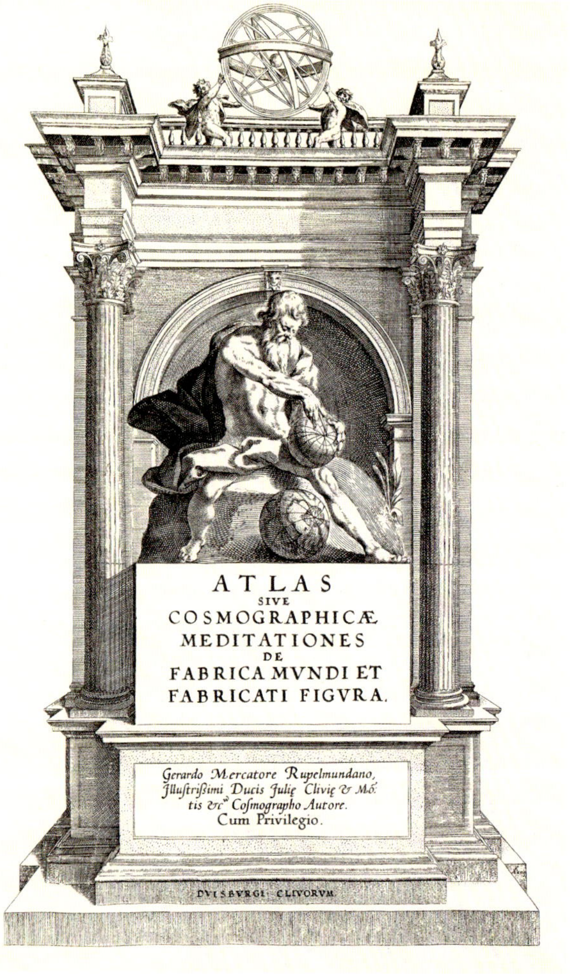

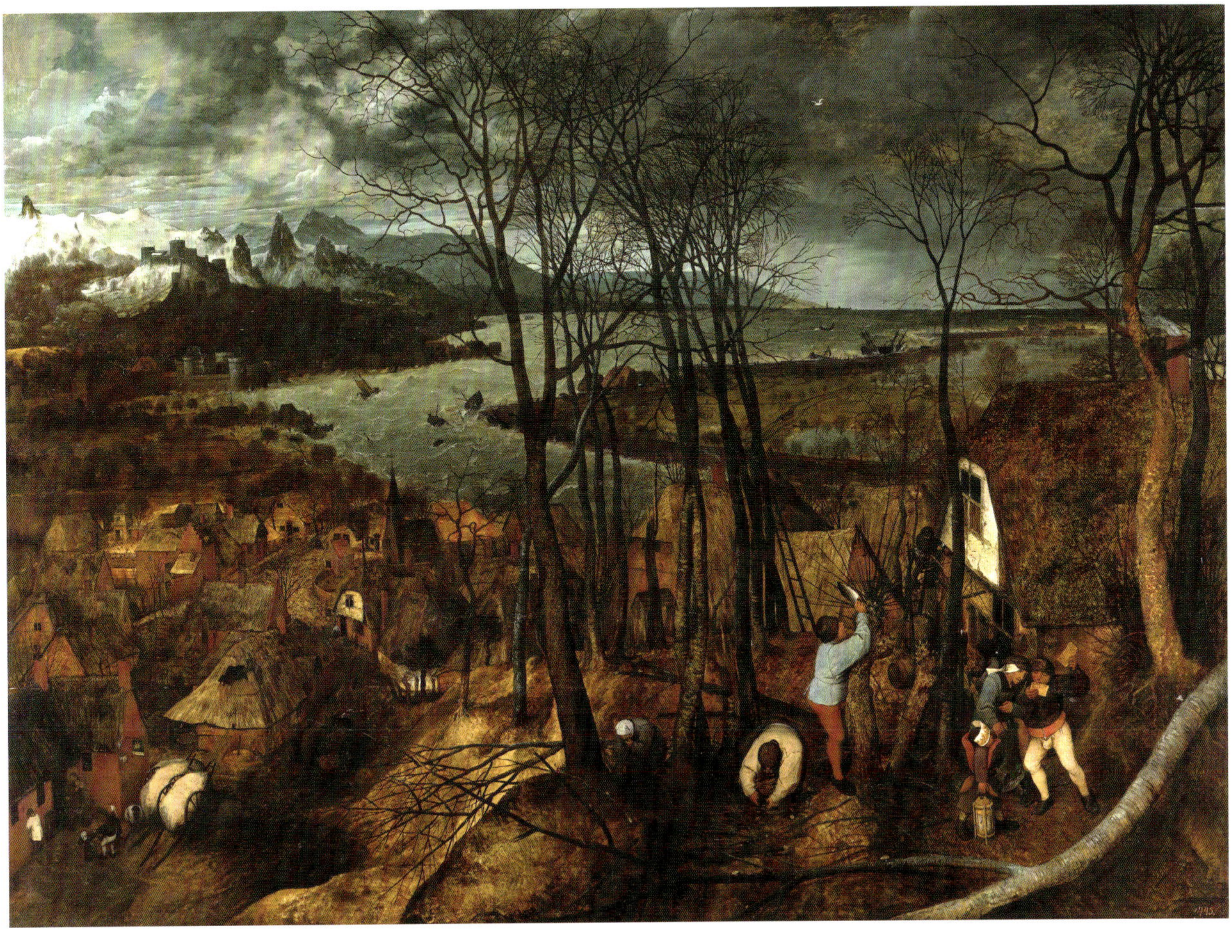

311 Pieter Bruegel the Elder, *Gloomy Day* (*Early Spring*), from the *Seasons of the Year* series, 1565, panel, Kunsthistorisches Museum, Vienna

Heart of Winter

Bruegel's series *The Twelve Months* got that title from the list of works owned by Nicolaes Jonghelinck and used in 1565 as collateral against tax debts owed by a friend to the city of Antwerp, as we have seen. The series would better be called the *Seasons of the Year*, as it was titled in the inventory of Archduke Leopold Wilhelm in 1659, since the original six panels formed a cycle beginning with *Early Spring*, represented by the misnomer *Gloomy Day* (fig. 311), and ending with *Winter*, also called *The Hunters in the Snow* (see fig. 314).[24] One of the six panels—probably the one representing spring—may have disappeared at some point between 1594, when the city of Antwerp presented the series to Archduke Ernst, governor of the Netherlands, and 1659, when Archduke Leopold's inventory was drawn up and only five panels were mentioned. Before the art historian Charles de Tolnay conjectured there had only ever been six, and before archives basically confirmed his conjecture, the number twelve sent many an art historian on pointless hunts for seven missing masterpieces, rather than for the only genuinely lost one. Bruegel painted the group for Jonghelinck in 1565, the year it was used as collateral. A decade before, this wealthy merchant had purchased his brother Thomas Jonghelinck's villa on the south side of Markgravelei, in the new ter Becken suburb of Antwerp.[25] This, one of the most expensive pleasure houses in the region, Nicolaes decorated with newly commissioned pictures. Besides the *Seasons* series, he owned at least ten other Bruegels, including *Christ Carrying the Cross*, *The Tower of Babel*, and *The Children's Games* (see figs. 266, 278, and 294), along with two cycles by Frans Floris—one of the Seven Liberal Arts, the other of the Labors of Hercules.[26] Jonghelinck's brother Jacques, a notable medalist, cast huge bronzes of the planets for the house, as well.

The Jonghelincks seemed to have loved comprehensive cycles. As a young man, Nicolaes styled his Antwerp town house as a microcosm, naming it the Sphere of the Earth. In the new villa on the Markgravelei, each of Frans Floris's series filled a whole room. Bruegel's *Seasons* probably did, too, perhaps as a frieze along one wall. The Roman theorist Vitruvius, writing at the end of the first century BCE, recommended that country villas be decorated with pleasing landscape paintings, and Italians since the 1400s had remembered this advice—e.g., the Torre dell'Aquila frescoes in Trent, in Ferrara's Palazzo Schifanoia, and in the architectural theory of Alberti and Serlio.[27] Never had landscape painting been given the scope it achieved in Jonghelinck's villa, however. With more Bruegels on display than Vienna has now, the villa must have been an astonishing collection *of* collections. Encompassing history, culture, and nature, it was an architectural equivalent of Ortelius's atlas, *Theater of the Earthly Globe* (see fig. 19). This collecting mania reflected Antwerp's material base. Jonghelinck's money came largely from export duties collected for Philip II. A gatekeeper of world trade, he benefited directly from centralized calculation, where far-flung worlds are represented and mastered by paper ones.

Jonghelinck died in 1570, heavily in debt. The posthumous sale of his possessions did not include his Bruegels, suggesting he may have had to part with them earlier. He probably never redeemed them from the city of Antwerp. Sent off in 1565, the year of their completion, the *Months* may have graced Jonghelinck's villa only briefly—for a span shorter than the calendar year they so gloriously encompass. In 1594, Antwerp gifted the panels to Archduke Ernst, who passed them to his brother, Emperor Rudolf II. From Prague they went to Archduke Leopold Wilhelm, who brought them to Vienna. Napoleon plundered the pictures and took them to Paris. Three returned to Vienna and entered the Kunsthistorisches Museum in 1891. The fourth, probably gifted to one of Maria Theresa's courtiers, entered the collections of the Lobkowicz family, in which it now again hangs, after spending the Cold War in Prague's National Gallery (fig. 312). The fifth passed from Paris to Brussels to the Metropolitan Museum of Art, in New York, in 1917 (fig. 313).[28]

The trio in Vienna, although featuring only chilly seasons, has enough scope to demonstrate the series' original totalizing effect. Three other Bruegels in the Kunsthistorisches Museum, the encyclopedic panels of 1559–60, comprise a kind of atlas of human culture. *Netherlandish Proverbs, Battle between Carnival and Lent*, and *The Children's Games* encapsulate three—arguably *the* three—human fundamentals: language, custom, and play (see figs. 32, 284, and 294). They may even do so already as calendars, because *Carnival and Lent* (arguably also *Children's Games*) contains a full year of rites and practices.[29] (*The Tower of Babel* monumentalizes perhaps the other representative product of *homo faber*: the building of edifices, of houses, temples, and cities and of roads and viaducts in between them.) The *Seasons* then complete this comprehensive overview of the human by summarizing nature in its entire spatial and temporal extension. Each awesomely capacious and densely detailed, the Vienna panels reward countless visual excursions. Watching visitors in the Bruegel Room, I have observed that people stand longest, and are loudest, before *The Children's Games* and *The Tower of Babel*. However, as they move to leave the room, the *Seasons* series halts and silences them, and gives them an improbable second wind.

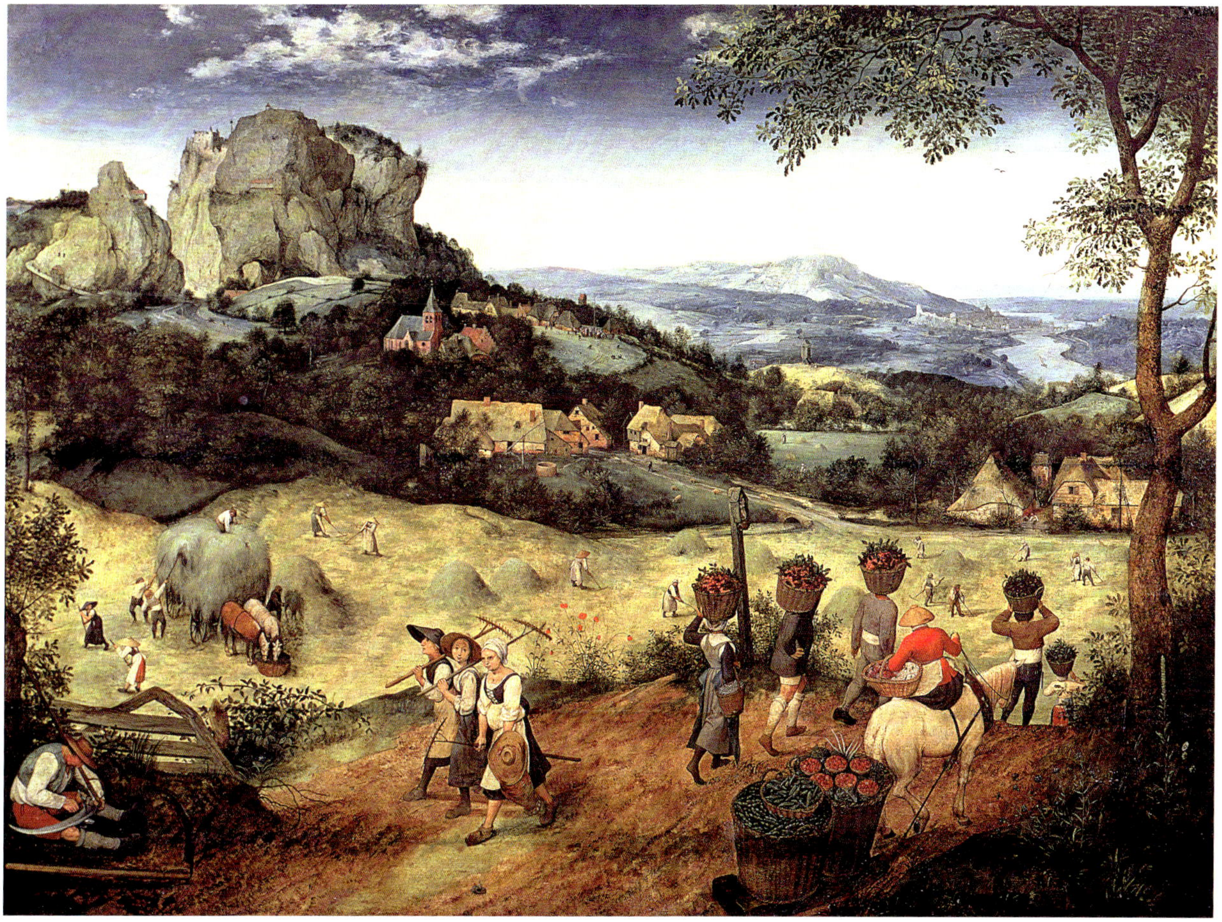

312 Pieter Bruegel the Elder, *Haymaking* (*Early Summer*), from the *Seasons of the Year* series, 1565, panel, Lobkowicz Palace Museum, Prague

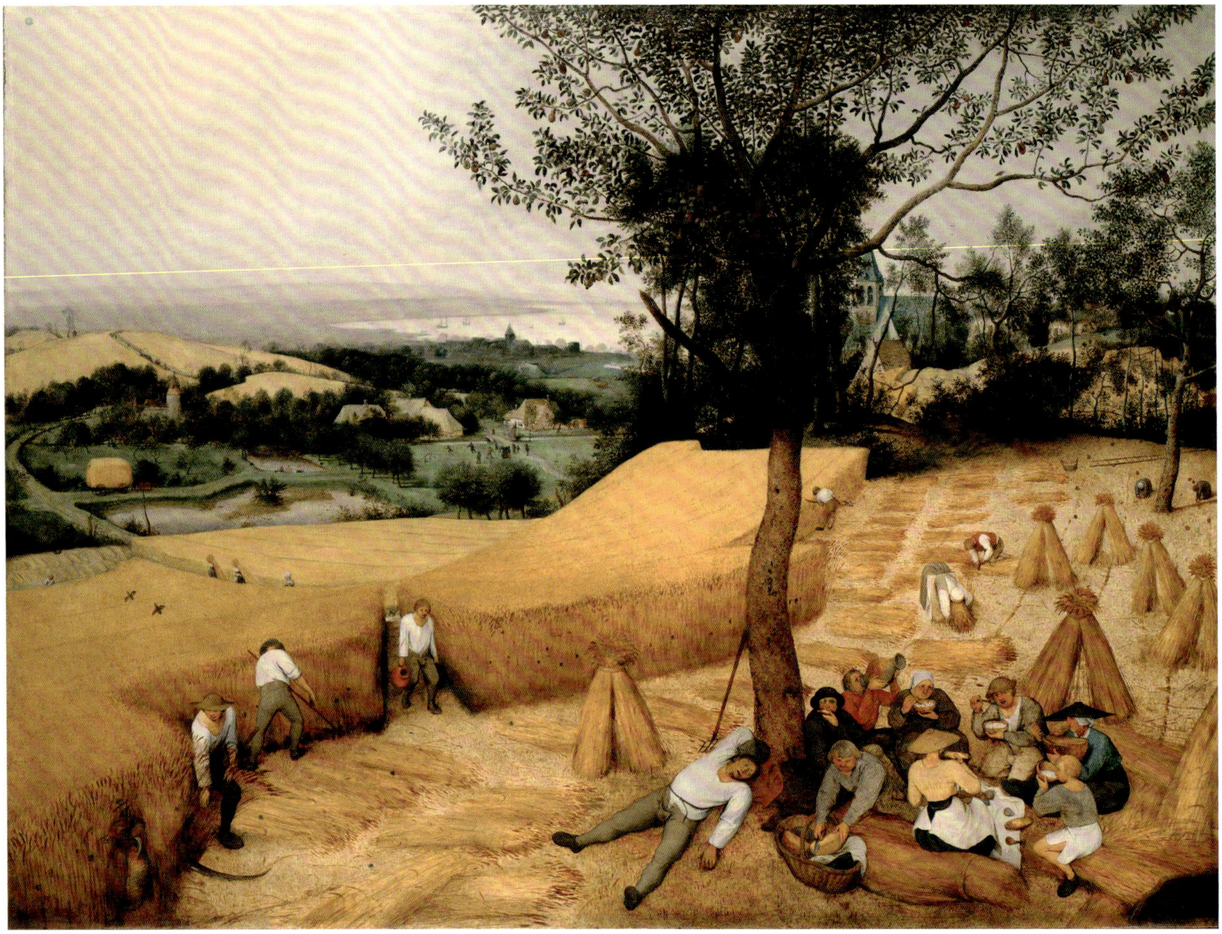

313 Pieter Bruegel the Elder, *The Harvesters* (*Summer*), 1565, oil on wood, Metropolitan Museum of Art, New York, Rogers Fund, 1919

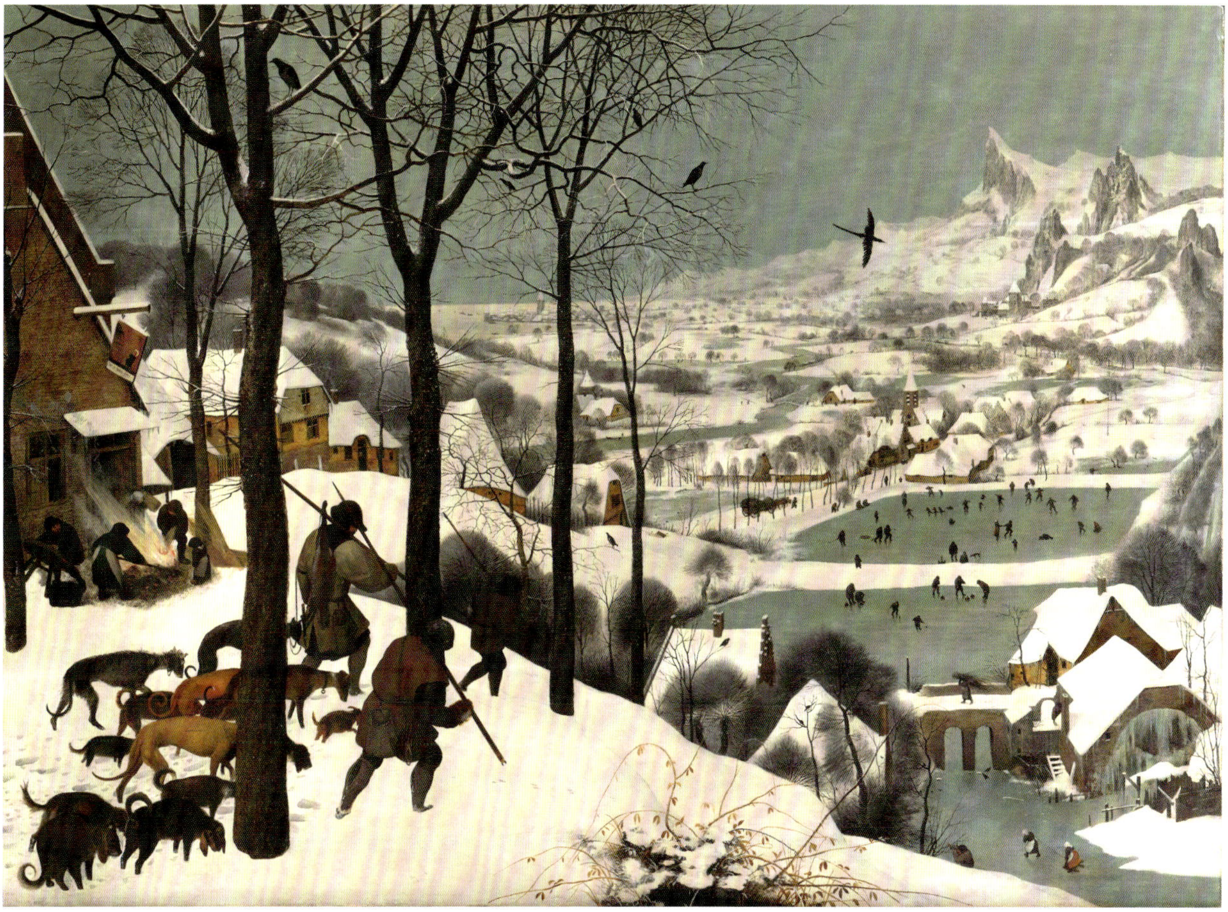

314 Pieter Bruegel the Elder, *The Hunters in the Snow* (*Winter*), from the *Seasons of the Year* series, 1565, panel, Kunsthistorisches Museum, Vienna

The hold these paintings have on us depends partly on their visually escaping our grasp. The views they offer so far exceed our capacity to look that we can never feel finished looking. *Gloomy Day* (*Early Spring*) has been darkened by age and aloe treatments, and light is often scant in the Bruegel Room (see fig. 311). Still, Bruegel did introduce a certain dimness in order to capture the light and air of a cold February day. Lit by a low sun hidden behind dense cloud cover, the vista takes some time to enter, so that getting used to the painting feels like entering suddenly a different season. Our eyes not yet accustomed to the dimness, we tend to forsake the glimmering foreground and seek light in the distance, in the sea, snow, and sky, where we temporarily lose ourselves in intricate dramas, and dramas within dramas, of floods, tempests, and ships sinking. The harbor city in the shadow of the mountains draws us into its topography, but seagulls, snow white against an astonishing density of individuated houses, draw us back from the distance and encourage us to soar elsewhere with them. Meanwhile, the foreground will have become easier to see, and Bruegel has assembled there, against the backdrop of death and catastrophe, the seasonal pursuits of everyday life—what classical literature would call the "works" appropriate to the "days." Some of these (e.g., the gathering of branches and the pollarding of the tree) Bruegel gets from earlier art, chiefly from the richly detailed calendar illustrations common in Flemish books of hours (fig. 315).[30] Some of the pursuits he gets fresh from the world around him. The boy at the lower right with the paper crown, unprecedented in calendar imagery but familiar from Bruegel's painting of the calendrical rite, times the picture to Shrovetide, which falls in late February or early March.

Observing the funny red-and-black cushion belted around the boy, the viewer will forget about the shipwrecks, the flood-ruined plains, and the distant metropolis. The whole that contains these terrible immensities exists only in the painting and cannot be maintained in a subjective experience of the painting. From the seventeenth century through the nineteenth, landscape paintings worked to engineer a human viewpoint on them. Claude Lorrain's arcadias may be richer and more beautiful than any real landscape could ever be, and Caspar David Friedrich's seas and mountains may threaten to annihilate the human subject halted before them, but these vistas unfold—in measured order or by leaps and bounds—from a situated eye. True, Bosch and Patinir composed views larger than any human view could ever be, hence the term "worldscape." But Bruegel achieved something more than the global composites of his predecessors, for although human vision is too narrow to behold it, the picture itself seems to *see* one coherent view. This coherence transcends the virtuoso spatial order that Bruegel also achieves. Each world appears enveloped in one *atmosphere*—as if, before that word's coinage in the mid-seventeenth century, this painter understood the surrounding medium of life on earth. More precisely, each of Bruegel's panels has a different unified atmosphere, giving each season a specific global compass.

Summer—also called *The Harvesters*—veils its placid distances in a humid vapor that slows everyone down (see fig. 313). Bruegel makes the perspectival avenue that has been cut through the wheat fields end abruptly in the midst of those fields, rather than at the horizon, causing us to want to lay down our gaze as the sleeping peasant has his pitchfork. In clement weather, the human and the natural mingle, sometimes comically. In *The Harvesters*, the sheaves of wheat look like strange costumed humans, while the woman binding a sheaf merges with the wheat. Similarly, in *Haymaking* (*Early Summer*), the fruit-laden baskets that the peasants balance on their heads seem, in at least one instance, to replace the head entirely, making harvester and harvest one (see fig. 312). Of the five extant panels, this latter landscape, in the Lobkowicz collection, has the greatest spatial continuity, perhaps because in early summer the world is at its most beneficent to the human.

Each panel in the *Seasons* series is subtly different in every way, from light and color through composition and anecdote to brushwork. *The Return of the Herd* (*Autumn*) is executed in a layer of paint as transparent as the world becomes in autumn (see fig. 2). Such differences should not be mistaken for moods. Moods are the colorings of experience arising from the human subject. Landscapes and seasons can elicit a mood and they can echo a mood, but they are not objectively the mood itself. In Romantic poetry, having sad thoughts in spring or hallucinating flowers in winter establishes the inherent moodiness of the lyrical voice, as a self set off against nature and following its own solipsistic direction. Bruegel's *Seasons* series manifests the effects of changes occurring in the world—how life and the very air through which we peer reflect that total transformation. Again, these differences can elicit moods in us, just as they occasion in the landscape's inhabitants different labors and recreations. However, Bruegel depicts the changed world and not the mood such change causes in us.

Bruegel conveys consistency by accelerating our entrance into his pictures. Beholding *The Hunters in the Snow* (*Winter*), we may at first pause at the pack of dogs silhouetted against the snow; we may even be drawn into their nose-to-the-ground activity (see fig. 314). But—as in the world so too in the painting—the glare of the white will make our gaze restless, causing our attention to the foreground to waver. Looking up, we soar—or fall—precipitously into one

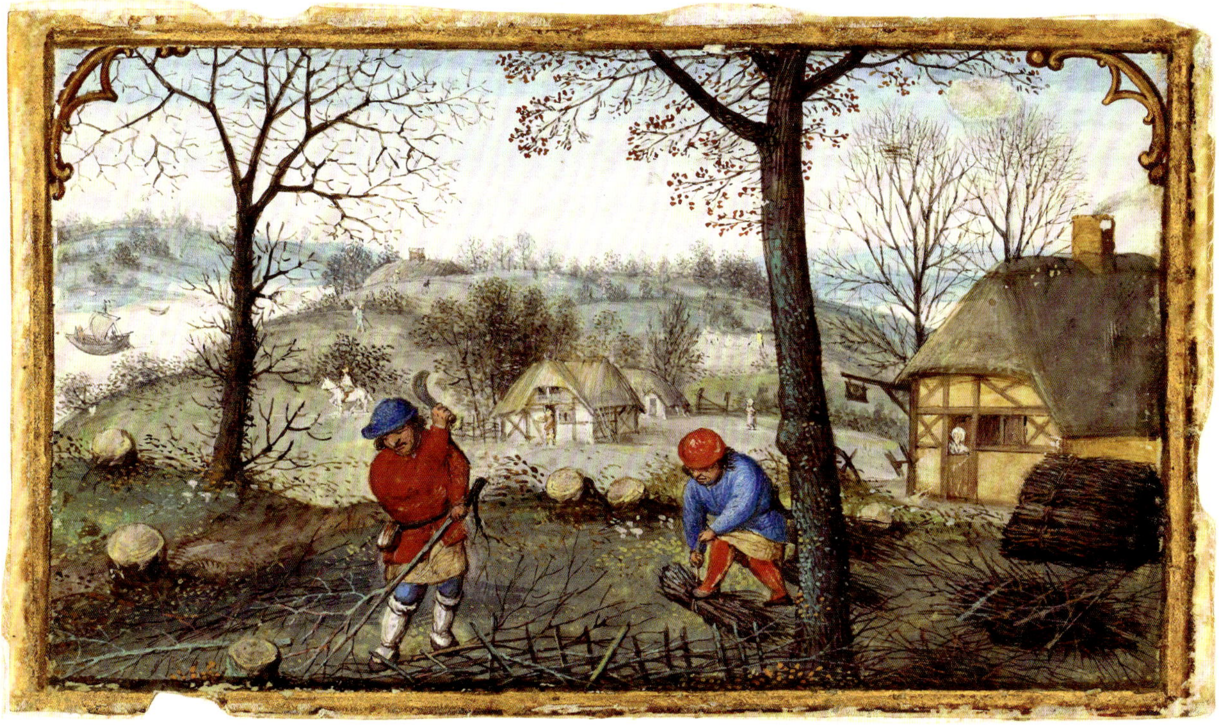

315 Attributed to Simon Bening, *Calendar Miniature from a Book of Hours*, c. 1550, tempera colors and gold paint on parchment, J. Paul Getty Museum, Los Angeles

of the deepest depths in European art. But as we do so, we also carry with us the reverie of the close-up view. The paw prints in the snow and the gigantic cliffs are part of the same continuum. Bruegel structures his painting to make our launch into space unavoidable. Serving as a visual catapult, the receding row of foreground trees charts a descent to the middle ground. But then they suddenly stop at the slippery slope to the flatland, releasing us to the void. The hunters trudge into the landscape, slowed by the snow, but where they are headed is reached by visual leaps and bounds.

Bruegel picks up the hunters' rightward movement in the little girl in red pulled leftward on a sledge, yet the disparity in scale between her and the hunters opens a dizzying vertical distance, as if we have fallen into another world. Abrupt juxtapositions of the near and far—the airborne bird overlaps with the distant ridges, the foreground shoots mingle with faraway trees—produce a vertigo that paradoxically strengthens the coherence of the whole. This induces in us a visceral experience of an all-embracing void, of an atmosphere empty and transparent. Once landed on the huge ground plane below, our eye can pursue many paths. As in *Winter Landscape with Bird Trap* (see fig. 300), the skaters naturalize optical motion. Elsewhere, movements are guided but not controlled by natural itineraries: frozen rivers, snowy roads, and the valley's long sweep. Wherever we travel, Bruegel gives us something to see: observe the bird trap hidden in the snow in the middle ground, just to the right of the perched bird.

Throughout my years in college and graduate school, I had a mounted poster of this picture hanging in my room. I sometimes wondered what gave it its staying power, since wherever I looked, I observed nothing more remarkable than what I could see in the world. In my flat in Heidelberg, I found myself staring at it rather than at the equally expansive view of the Neckar Valley visible through my window. Absorbed in the picture more than in life, I experienced a kind of autistic detachment. Exploring this or that unremarkable painted grove seemed

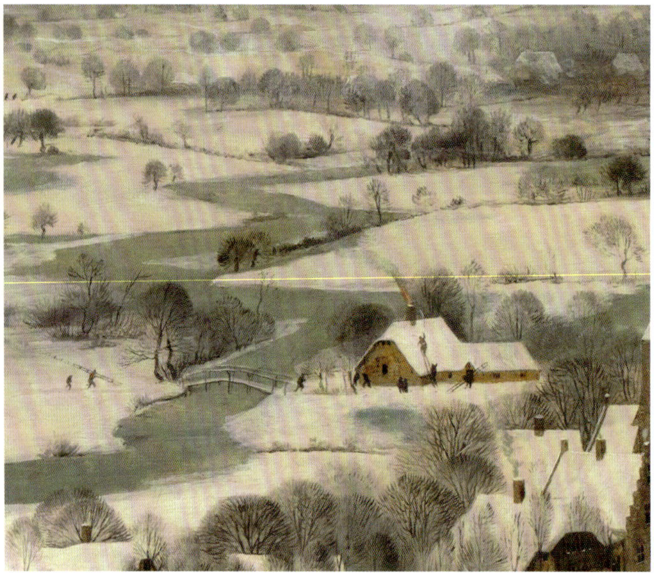

316 Detail of Pieter Bruegel the Elder, *The Hunters in the Snow* (fig. 315)

better or easier than looking at or being in a real grove, because in the painting everything that was indicated—the trees sketched by subtle marks of paint—was right there for me. Bruegel plays with the detachment he induces. Uninvolved, we register a chimney fire in the distance (fig. 316). While we stand still, people rush ladders and water to the catastrophe. Remoteness of the world produces remoteness in us—what Wallace Stevens called "a mind of winter."[31]

Again, Bruegel's contemporaries delighted in the experience of distance. As the word *theater* in Ortelius's title suggests, his atlas was meant for aesthetic perusal more than for travel. Bruegel's painted and printed landscapes yielded similar pleasures. The represented valley in *The Hunters in the Snow* can be experienced in the same way as a map lying open on a desk. Bruegel portrays individual features (trees, houses, and mountains) as if from across, in *elevation*, and he shows itineraries *through* the landscape (along roads, rivers, and valleys) as if from above, in *plan*. The artist learned to do these two quite different things by attending to Alpine views (see figs. 18 and 308). From a valley, mountains appear almost perpendicular to the ground. No matter how far away they are, their cliffs face us. Conversely, valleys observed from high above, from the perspective a mountain gives, will confront the eye directly, but like a plan—or map—of the terrain. Bruegel combined mountain and valley, thereby reconciling both the vertical picture plane with the horizontality of a landscape view and painting's normal view *across* with the cartographic view from *above*.

Historians have traced modern maps of Ortelius's era back to an earlier form of spatial representation: the itinerary. Medieval pilgrimage guides illustrated the route from one place to another—Venice to Jerusalem, say—but not the space traversed.[32] They indicated local features only for observances to be enacted in them: where to pray and to whom. Even the earliest coastal sailing maps began as written descriptions of journeys taken, and the cartographically accurate portolan charts estimate compass settings and port-to-port distances observed by ships' pilots at sea. That is, they emphasized singular routes and had no need to represent the geographical whole.[33] In modern maps, such itineraries—fragmentary but also tangible—disappear. Only the product of travel stands exhibited, not the practice of the journey. Bruegel's landscapes restore this loss, hence perhaps the mapmaker Ortelius's deep love for them. In Bruegel's hands, the vast world opened up by travel and maps becomes, nonetheless, a habitat.

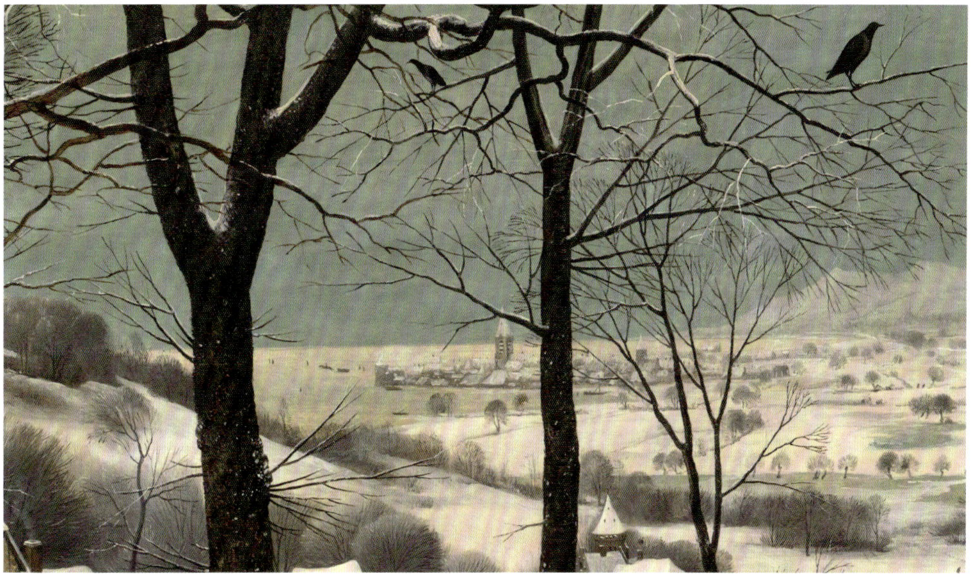

317 Detail of Pieter Bruegel the Elder, *The Hunters in the Snow* (fig. 315)

Even as he publishes the mountains and sea, and suggests territories yet to be discovered, he pictures them as lifeworlds like our own, those farther hills as hills again like these.

In Bruegel, all itineraries end at the horizon, at the little gap where rivers flowing from the mountains empty into the sea. There, at the line between earth and sky, where our view from above becomes a view across, the eye can rest indefinitely. Horizons are contingent on the beholder's point of view; not the world's true end, they mark only the limit of the world visible from one place. Positioning his viewers high above ground, and opening his backgrounds to the sea, Bruegel expands this range beyond anything his Antwerp audience, used to flatlands and views of the ocean, had ever personally experienced. As resting place for the gaze and as point of ecstasy, the horizon marks the extent of our vision while also demonstrating a law of incalculable expansion: were we to reach the horizon there would be another one just as far away.

In *The Hunters in the Snow*, the world's visual limit is literally frozen. A procession marches toward the horizon from the harbor town (fig. 317). During the fierce winter before Bruegel painted this picture, as late 1564 turned to early 1565, the Scheldt froze over at Antwerp, allowing people and wagons the rare opportunity to travel across its ample expanse.[34] Displaced to the farthest reaches of the view, this motif of passage powerfully affects our experience of the scene. Absorbing the land and sea into a single medium, ice has turned the world into a Borgesian one-to-one map of itself. The conditions of winter itself—ground bare of vegetation and everything exposed—further clarify the view's topographical transparency. Even in the foreground, snow has a cartographic function. The hunters would be better called trappers. Bruegel shows a similar trio marching in the right foreground of *The Return of the Herd*—observe there also, beneath a shrub farther back, the hidden man netting birds (see figs. 2 and 31). In *The Hunters in the Snow*, these three, or a similar trio, have returned from their journey bearing foot snares, quarry bags, and their meager catch: a single fox they have managed to trap or to find with their dogs and spear. Their homeward path brings them to the animal tracks just visible in the snow to their right. Perhaps they are the paw prints of the beast they have snared; perhaps they are of an animal that eludes them as they head home. Either way, these tracks set in motion a human plot that begins with the hunt and that continues in the exodus over the

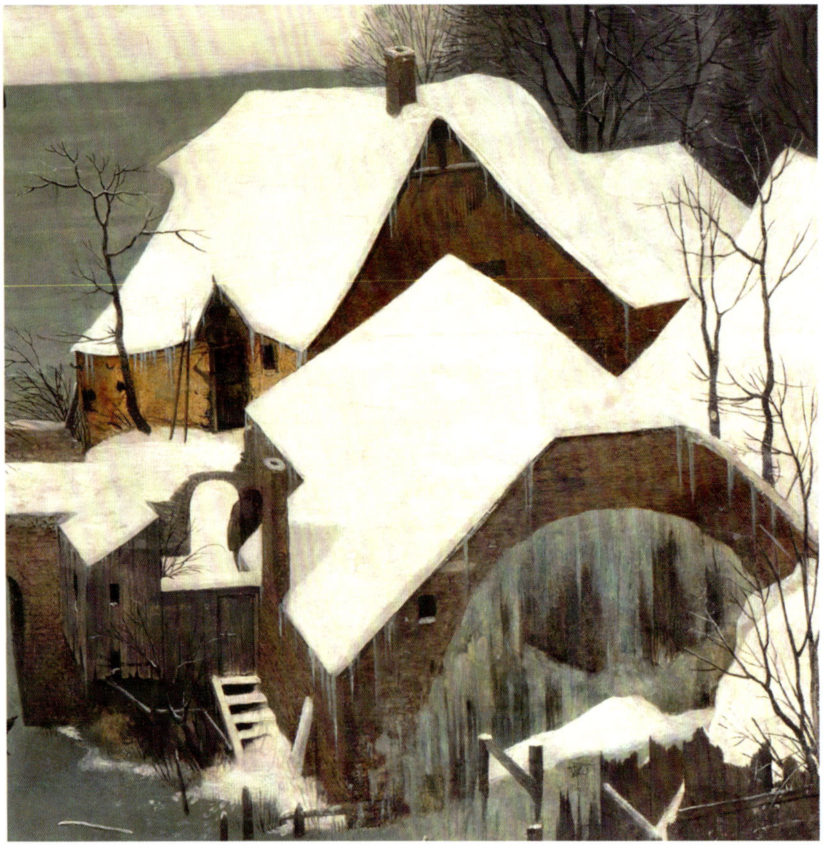

318 Detail of Pieter Bruegel the Elder, *The Hunters in the Snow* (fig. 315)

ice to the horizon. Snow and ice have rendered the landscape maplike by making continuous what in the physical world exists as discrete localities, just as maps allow smooth, peaceful passage through disparate lands, histories, and cultures. The frozen waters of Bruegel's painting imagine in concrete terms the visual journey that maps only abstractly convey.

Ice gives people pleasure and passage, but it does not give them a home. The hunters may be headed for home, and before the protective space of the inn at the left the tempting repast of slaughtered pig is being roasted—a seasonal delight that calendar illustrations for December sometimes show. But they, the hunters, have not yet arrived home. With heightened visibility (dark on light) comes greater, more perilous exposure, as hunter and prey both know. Frozen, the fields become a pattern for the eye, pleasurable to look at but impossible to farm. Exiled from his fields, a farmer looks on dull roots in winter differently than does a burgher, who is a tourist there in any season. Bruegel reflected powerfully on the matter of natural and pictorial grounds, as we have seen. Here he signs his name on the one horizontal surface not covered by ice or snow. "BRVEGEL. M.D.LXV" hibernates in the frozen soil at the center of the lower framing edge. Snow plays strange tricks with our perception of ground. The picture's most remarkable passages are those where the lead white that renders snow makes forms flat, abstract, and illegible. Dazzling the eye, snow voids the very objects it silhouettes: observe how hard it is to identify the hunter's trapping gear in this dazzling glare. This retreat of objects within an overabundance of light conforms to the plot of the picture, where everyone and everything turns away from us, as nature itself does in winter. It is mostly the tracks of the hunted that give the structure to the blinding foreground.

This optical estrangement of the world climaxes at the lower left, in the roofs of a frozen mill (fig. 318).[35] Architects know that snow exaggerates the contrast between elevation and plan. That is why they often have their buildings photographed in winter. Snow covers horizontal planes, merging them into a continuous visible surface. Façades, by contrast, remain bare, and thus acquire a differential value. Snow—we would now say—digitizes the landscape into the binary white/nonwhite. For the frozen mill, Bruegel reverses the elucidating effects that snow has at a distance. Yet in one more instance of vernacular know-how, the roofs make structural sense. If we look long and hard at them, we can detect makeup, how they are complexly sloped and faceted to bear up the snow. But snow blinds us to their order, making them seem erratic and absurd. The near at hand becomes inscrutable compared with the clarified distances farther on. Here we encounter the painter Bruegel at his best. Creator of unprecedented spatial expanses, he lets all illusions of depth here collapse. With no finger-wagging inscriptions or allegorical machinery, through the mere resources of blank white paint, Bruegel shows home and the human from the indifferent perspective of the world.

Law and the Human

Each of Bruegel's paintings aspires to be comprehensive in its domain. Encompassing the world's sphere, the *Seasons* series would seem thus to offer a sum of summations: culture in its place in nature, everyday life extended to every day of the all of life. It would have been a hard act to follow, but Bruegel did so brilliantly, magnifying what encompassing nature in *Seasons* almost eclipsed: human nature. As *Solicitudo Rustica* had shown, culture is always a cultivation, whether of the soil or of the human soul (see fig. 283). A compiler of great visual lists, Bruegel understood that human nature stands under the larger heading "nature," that it is the predisposition of the human *animal*. Painted in 1568, his monumental panels of peasant feast and festival show people to be naturally—by a nature evidenced by peasants in their rituals of marriage (the wedding) and locality (the kermis), but true for everyone—*social animals* (see figs. 254 and 260). Bruegel died in 1569, "early," as Ortelius lamented, "in the full bloom of his life." Before he passed, Bruegel managed to create a final reckoning of nature and of human nature, in *The Magpie on the Gallows* (fig. 319).[36] That it is a small panel, just a foot and a half wide, makes its capacity all the more wondrous.

Bruegel had always been a great miniaturist.[37] He may have been trained in this important specialty, as designing engravings required expertise in small forms. While in Rome, Bruegel collaborated with the miniaturist Giulio Clovio, and later works such as *The Suicide of Saul* (1562) demonstrate his continuing mastery of huge vistas on a tiny scale (fig. 320).[38] *The Magpie on the Gallows*, the jewel of the Hessisches Landesmuseum, in Darmstadt, looks back to Bruegel's roots in the miniaturist tradition and beyond these to the art of earlier Netherlanders, such as Jan van Eyck, whose greatest landscapes occurred in the pages of illuminated manuscripts. Van Mander reports that Bruegel willed this painting to his wife: "In his will he left his wife a piece with a magpie on the gallows."[39] His second son, Jan, born in 1568, would profit from this inheritance: his evocative landscapes take off from this painting's background vista. Although it is not the only painting dated 1568, it is usually treated as the painter's last. In this swan song, Bruegel condenses his life's work, and life itself, into an astonishing epitome.

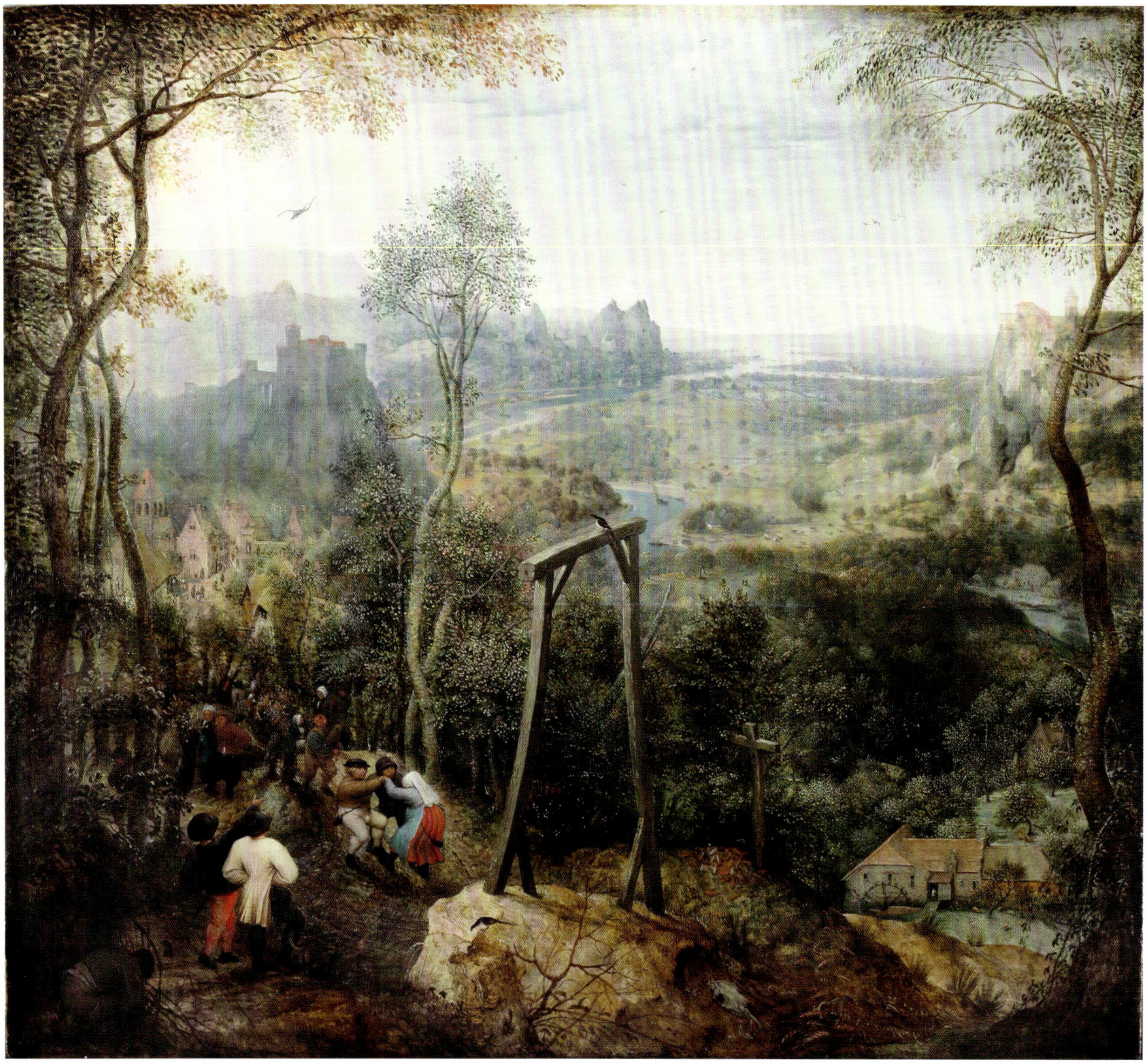

319 Pieter Bruegel the Elder, *The Magpie on the Gallows*, 1568, panel, Hessisches Landesmuseum, Darmstadt

Bruegel gives more than a third of his panel to landscape. As usual, he shows an immense terrain from high up. We see it stretch from the hill where we stand through a cultivated river valley and past a great harbor city to the open sea. More powerfully than in *Seasons* and in a fraction of the painted surface, Bruegel captures the all-surrounding atmosphere. Streaming in from the left, the sun's rays warm and illuminate the air's vapors, turning air itself into a palpable presence that charts movement into depth. And although we cannot see them, passing clouds cast some tracts of land in shadow and leave others spotlighted, like the bustling village built at the foot of the castle. With flags flying in their streets, the villages ascend the slope to us in a parade. Three rustics dance to the music of the piper who, red-faced, puffs his way up the hill after them. To landscape, as Bruegel's first great theme, these revelers add the second, festive peasantry. And there is a third: with their back toward us, two spectators—more urban in their apparel than the rest—admire the view. As one gestures as if to say, "Behold," the other stomps his foot to the dancers' beat: they model our own participation in Bruegel's painting. And it would not be a Bruegel if there were not some comic qualification that brings distanced reverie back down to earth. In the shadows at the lower left, a peasant takes a shit. Of course,

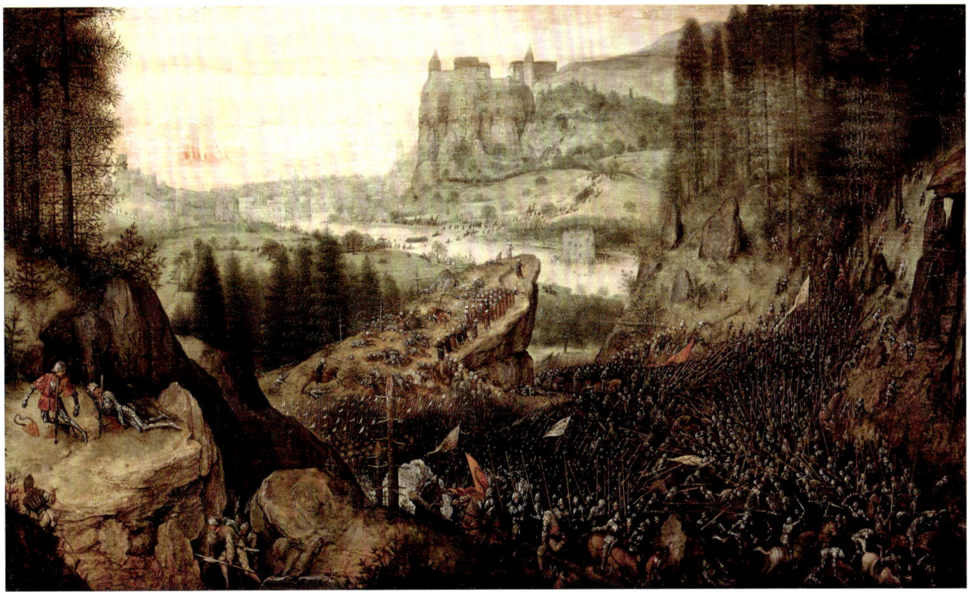

320 Pieter Bruegel the Elder, *The Suicide of Saul*, 1562, panel, Kunsthistorisches Museum, Vienna

the beautiful and festive scene has already been massively qualified. A gallows, spotlighted and central, rises in the foreground so that its top beam coincides with the river meandering to the horizon.

It is hard to circumvent the gallows. It straddles the foreground ensuring that the dancing peasants will run up against it. Nor can we avoid it: we experience and interpret the painting with it always in the view. To historians the gallows looks like a symbol, richly coded, which turns the picture into a great puzzle that takes in the dancers, the two spectators, the shitting rustic, the wooden cross, and those two obtrusive birds. These magpies give the picture half of its title: *The Magpie on the Gallows*. To the villagers the gallows is also a symbol, but it is a fact of life, as well. Typically, gallows stood at the edges of towns, warning outlaws and vagabonds that crimes will be punished here. To be in force, law has to make good on its threat. The gallows' symbolism is thus the reality of law. "The aim of law," states the inscription penned at the base of Bruegel's violent *Justice* drawing of 1559, "is to correct whoever it punishes, or through sanction to correct others, or, after the punishment of the evildoer, to allow others to live in greater security" (fig. 321).[40]

The gallows in Bruegel's painting is simply made. The top beam—or crosspiece—to which a hanging rope would be slung, rests on a pair of tall supporting posts that have been stabilized by four short trusses. The makers had their materials close at hand: tall trees are plentiful here. Bruegel's painting of the gallows is anything but simple, however. Seen from above, the crosspiece juts into space perpendicular to the picture plane. Almost parallel to the bit of river in the landscape with which it overlaps, it reads as an orthogonal in the painting's construction of perspectival space. Lower down, however, the structure gets confusing. The crosspiece and the base seem skewed. Not only do the tops of the two posts not align with their feet; those feet, which should be points along a line veering steeply upward, toward the landscape's vanishing point on the horizon, veer irrationally down into the valley's depth. Bruegel explains this torsion by suggesting that the rocky ground drops off, requiring posts of different sizes. But the gallows remains anamorphic, like a Penrose triangle. On the one hand, the gallows stands for the *nomos* of the earth, law as the concrete spatial order of the primordial "here" of the village beneath the castle, set off against an emergent order of the "global," signaled by the

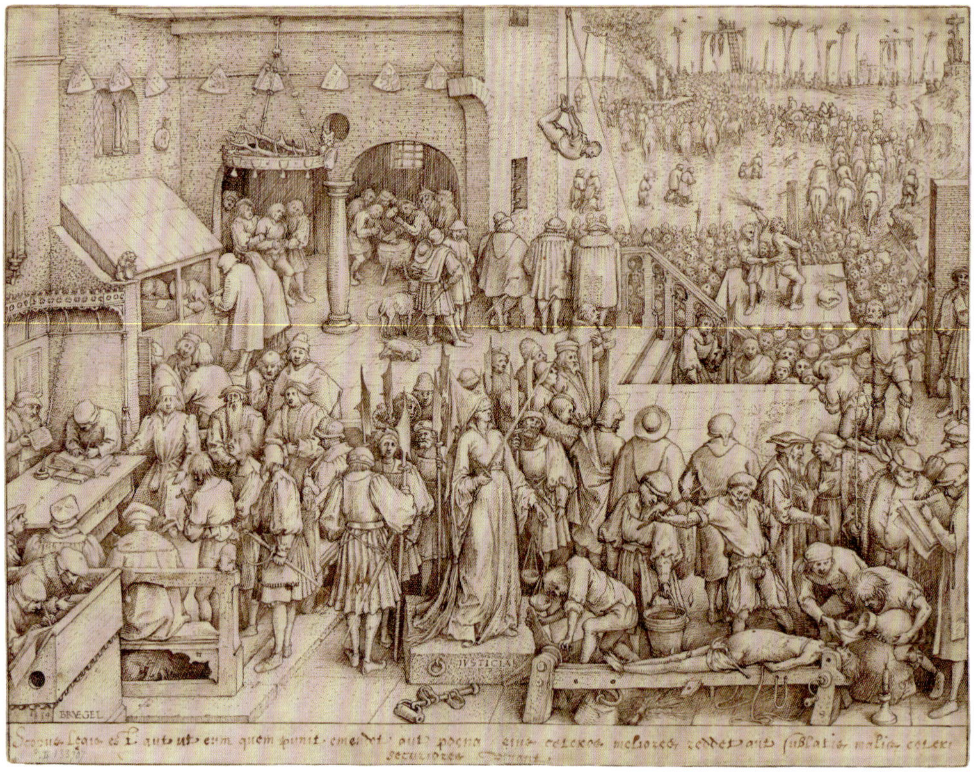

321 Pieter Bruegel the Elder, *Justitia* (*Justice*), drawing for the *Virtues* series, 1559, pen and gray-brown ink, Royal Library of Belgium, Brussels, Cabinet des Estampes, 5.11 133 707 folio C

sea.[41] On the other hand, the gallows is an impossible figure, and therefore anything but concrete. Situated beside two interwoven trees, its impossible torque enlivening it, this enigmatic instrument of death seems about to stride forth into the world.

This symbol is a question, as befits law. Law is a symbolic order that regulates human behavior mostly by mere threat of sanction, the most dire of which is loss of life. However, law is not only symbolic, as the sanctions it prescribes have to be executed by coercive acts. Bruegel's 1559 drawing *says* that law has collective security as its aim target ("Scopus legis est . . ."); but the drawing *shows* only the violence of coercion: with their noses in great legal codices, magistrates administer the repertoire of punishments available to law at the time. Through threat and spectacle law may effect psychic coercion—the idea an individual internalizes about law—but this is not the form of coercion that distinguishes law from other social orders.[42] Law enforces its prohibitions independent of whether its prohibitions are known, hence its strange doctrine that ignorance is no defense in the face of the law. The behavior that law prohibits is—elementally—the use of physical force from person to person. Law is bound *forcibly* to prohibit such use of force. By nature dangerous animals, humans, when they band together into societies, give law this monopoly of force. Through law humans enter the civil condition, or *status civilis*, using force from the natural condition, the *status naturalis*. Twisted between landscape and peasant festivity, as between nature and culture, the symbol of the law asks a question about the human things.

Hieronymus Bosch asked this question, too, and he did so using the very same symbols. On the outer surface of the shutters of *The Hay Wain*, in the landscape to the right of the peddler, a shepherd pipes and peasants dance before gallows and a torture wheel (see figs. 37 and 38). This bit of rustic festivity, we recall, stands for the things of this world that the peddler both peddles and pursues. It is the genre tradition in a nutshell, but the painting crosses it out. The cracked footbridge below and the gallows above admonish against the pleasures between them. The gallows, placed directly above the peddler, marks him as doomed whatever he does. Hurrying to escape danger—the robbers, bones, and snarling dog—he already stands in danger, as the triptych's opening makes yet more clear: death and judgment are always already upon us (see fig. 39). Unseen by the peddler, the gallows returns law to primeval origins: as fate.[43] The difference between Bosch's gallows and Bruegel's is that in Bruegel not only does everyone see it; the peasants seem deliberately to be dancing toward it, using—or abusing—it for their fun. But before we approach this key difference, it will be useful to look one last time at *The Hay Wain*'s understanding of law.

The highwaymen have robbed another peddler forcibly. Their weapons lie about them as they bind him to a tree. The gallows is meant for their likes, yet Bosch places their theft above, along a zigzag path that leads backward from the cracked footbridge and road to the gallows on the hill. In this wilderness, the picture seems to ask, what is the difference between the force-backed command of a robber and the sanction-backed command of the law? Laying down their weapons and thus secure among themselves, the thieves belong to a minimum legal order. According to their legal order (which law, if it could, would punish by death), not to obey their command—"Your money or your life"—is punishable by death. Secular legal doctrine will distinguish the two. The thieves' command cannot be regarded as a legal act because law is not a single norm but a system of norms promulgated by a legitimate polity, such as a state. Religious doctrine is less certain. In *The City of God*, Saint Augustine asks, "Set justice aside, then, and what are kingdoms but thievish purchases? Because what are thieves' purchases but little kingdoms?"[44] And thus it is also with Bosch, for when the triptych opens, "kingdoms," represented by the entourage of sovereigns, march toward the City of Hell, while around them humanity has descended into lawlessness, the "warre of every one against every one."[45] Human law—the City of Man—stands judged and condemned by divine law, which damns the entire historical interim between the Fall and Christ's Second Coming. Here Bosch is more pessimistic, even, than Augustine, for in him there is no interim within the longest one, since Christ's first Advent hardly made an impact on this corrupted world. In Bosch, God alone answers the question of human things, and his answer is war on them. The political circumstances of that artist's time made this theology still viable as an answer, but it displaced into the immediate future the concrete question: Who decides in the interim the human things where spiritual and worldly mix?

Van Mander tells us another thing about *The Magpie on the Gallows*. "By the magpie," he reports, Bruegel "meant gossiping tongues, which he committed to the gallows." To his wife, Bruegel gave the painting; to his enemies, he bequeathed the gallows in it. Van Mander also offers a glimpse into the besieged atmosphere in the painter's shop at the time of his death. Bruegel, he contends, made many careful drawings with captions on them, "some of which he got his wife to burn when he was on his deathbed because they were too caustic or derisory, either because he was sorry or that he was afraid that on their account she would into trouble or that she might have to answer for them."[46]

It was easy to get into trouble. The year 1569 was one of the darkest in the history of the Netherlands. Arriving with his army in Brussels in August 1567, the Duke of Alba had placed the region under martial law, disbanding citizen militias and replacing native officials with Spanish ones.[47] Invested with extraordinary emergency powers, an inquisitorial body, the

Council of Troubles (dubbed by the people the Council of Blood), put suspected insurgents and heretics on trial. Thousands were tried and more than a thousand executed, including—to the consternation of European heads of state—two great nobles. Lamoral, Count of Egmont, and Philip de Montmorency, Count of Hoorn, were beheaded on June 5, 1568, on the Grand Place in Brussels, across from city hall and just blocks from Bruegel's workshop. Together with William I of Orange-Nassau (whom we met as owner of Bosch's *Garden of Delights*), the two men had resisted the centralizing efforts of Philip II, forming a powerful coalition within the Netherlands' governing Council of State. After the iconoclasm of 1566, and with Alba's arrival, such opposition became unacceptable to the Habsburg overlords. Both staunch Catholics who believed themselves loyal to Philip, the Counts of Egmont and Hoorn were lured to Brussels on the belief that, under the protection of Margaret of Parma, governor of the Netherlands and Philip's sister, they would receive a lawful trial. To most Netherlanders, their death sentence, for treasonous tolerance toward Protestants, was illegal because a foreigner—the Spaniard Alba—had ordered it. Meanwhile, William fled to Germany, and in April and May 1568 he attempted to drive Alba from Brussels. This campaign failed miserably, and by 1569 the situation in Brussels was dire.

Van Mander surmised that Bruegel got his wife to burn those "caustic" works because "she might have to answer for them." Historians have often wondered how the artist got away even with the works that did survive. In *Christ Carrying the Cross*, troops clad in the red coats of imperial mercenaries appear as ruthless perpetrators; in the Hampton Court version of *The Massacre of the Innocents*, the armored leader of the butchery has a bearded countenance that some see as resembling that of Alba, perhaps added by Bruegel some time after 1567; *The Sermon of Saint John the Baptist*, dated 1566, makes the biblical event look like the open-air "hedge preaching" that local Calvinists notoriously organized in 1565 and on; and in *The Conversion of Paul*, the mounted figure in black armor probably alludes to Alba on his misguided crossing of the Savoy Alps, in 1567, the year the picture was painted (see figs. 266 and 322).[48] Presumably such references were sufficiently ambiguous, or too small to see, like the papal baldachin hidden in the Rotterdam *Tower of Babel*, since Bruegel's admirers included Antoine Perrenot de Granvelle, from 1561 a cardinal and the leader of the pro-Habsburg faction in the Netherlands, as well as Philip of Spain's nephew Rudolf II (see fig. 280). But the artist lived to see how useless all defenses become in a kangaroo court. Word would have reached him of the imprisonment and trial of a fellow printmaker, Dirck Volckertszoon Coornhert. Secretary of the burgomasters of Haarlem and an ally of William of Orange, Coornhert stood accused of instigating heresy.[49] The only evidence against him was hearsay, which he countered with hearsay about his accuser. In a legal state of exception, with the gallows being used to the maximum, "gossiping tongues" could be fatal.

Scholars caution that Van Mander, writing three decades after the fact, may have made up or misconstrued the meaning of Bruegel's magpie. However, this bird does have a dubious reputation in animal lore, particularly due to its heckling call. In Dutch, to "chatter like a magpie" meant to be a hopeless gossip, and in the Dutch translation of Sebastian Brant's *Ship of Fools*, the magpie is a garrulous fool who cannot hold his tongue.[50] A collection of fables published in Gouda in 1480 tells of a magpie who, able to speak Latin and French, saves itself from a crafty bird-catcher by agreeing to sweet-talk other birds into the net. An accompanying woodcut (fig. 323) shows a stretched-out net like the one Bruegel paints in the background field of *The*

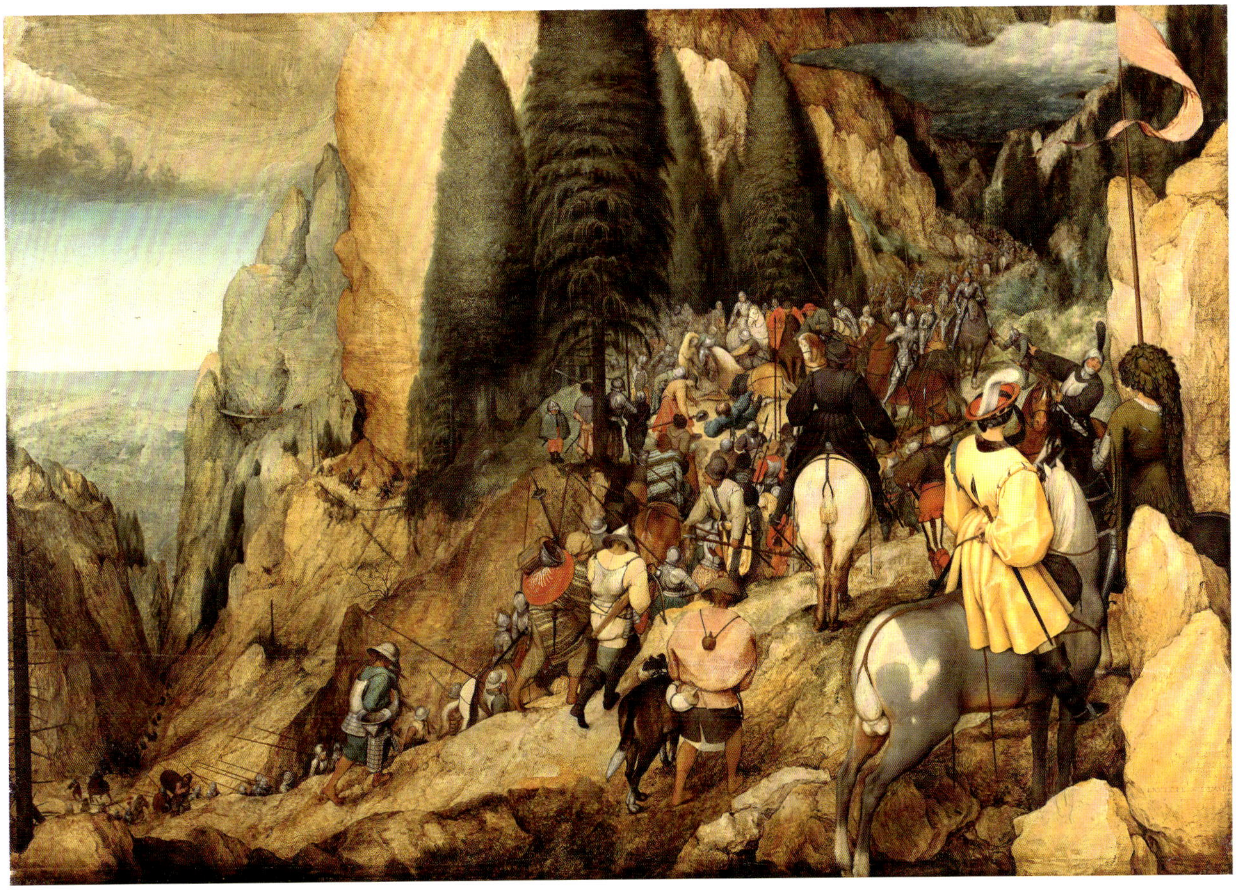

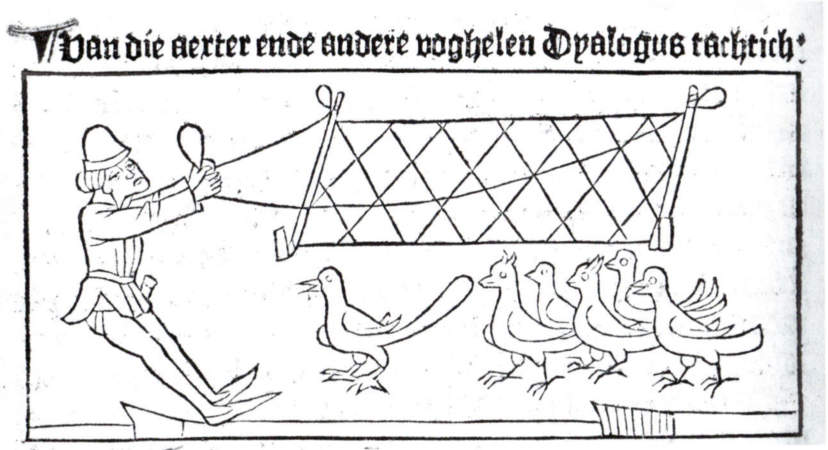

(ABOVE) 322 Pieter Bruegel the Elder, *Conversion of Paul*, 1567, panel, Kunsthistorisches Museum, Vienna

(LEFT) 323 *A Bird-Catcher with Magpie as Lure*, woodcut illustration from *Dyalogus creaturarum appellatus iocundis fabulis plenus* (Gouda: Gheraert Leeu, 1481), Den Haag, Koninklijke Bibliotheek, KBH 170 E 26 (2)

Return of the Herd (see fig. 31).[51] Magpies play a key role in all three of Bosch's "autonomous" drawings—they aggressively mob owls, the artist's dark alter ego (see figs. 232, 236, and 246). In *The Trees Have Ears, the Field Has Eyes*, through its underlying proverb, the magpies play the role of spies and gossips (avatars of the hostile social world), juxtaposed to the owl's silent secrecy. The owl—an effective lure for bird-catchers—turns the tables on the magpie, a twist Bruegel too would have appreciated.[52]

Produced in the relative security of 's-Hertogenbosch circa 1500, Bosch's fantasy of a hostile social world would seem perhaps less urgent than Bruegel's Darmstadt panel, but this parallel mistrust of rumor invites us to measure the historical distance that separates these artist collected, the peasants play with law. Their fun does not eliminate law any more than would Alba's defeat. Rather, they take toward law a humorous attitude.

A criminal led to the gallows on Monday observes, "Well, that's a good start to the week." With this joke Freud began a little essay titled "Humor."[57] Humor can treat others jokingly but gently, as adults do children. And in humor we can treat ourselves as child. According to Freud this splits us up into two persons: a childlike one whom we wish to protect from sadness and harm, and a parental one, who speaks humorously, but also lovingly and consolingly, to the child within. Such a splitting does not change grim reality. The childlike "I" or ego and its superior companion march together to the gallows. But humor can maintain a certain stance toward the suffering, one more of scorn than of resignation. Through the glint of pleasure which humor sparks, we affirm our right to life even in the face of inevitable, all-powerful death. Reading *The Trial* out loud to his friends, Kafka "laughed so much that there were moments when he couldn't read any further."[58]

Bruegel embraced this, perhaps the most dignified refusal of reality. He seems to have used vulgar humor as his calling card. Van Mander reports that while Hans Vredeman de Vries (a specialist in plunging, vacant, perspectival views) worked on a mural of a summerhouse in perspective, Bruegel snuck and secretly painted into Vries's picture "a peasant in befouled shirt occupied with a peasant woman." This "caused much laughter," and the mural's owner refused to have the naughty addition taken out.[59] The anecdote may of course be apocryphal, but it does capture the defiant spirit of, say, the defecating peasant in *The Magpie on the Gallows*. To him and to the dancing peasants, Bruegel also adds parental spectators (the pair with their backs turned to us), and to these internal spectators we become parental observers again, all in order to say that the world that looks so dangerous can be appreciated as mere child's play.

The artist's biography, the life constructed for this enigmatic persona by later admirers, captures this condition: on the one hand, the naïve native, on the other hand, the cosmopolitan ethnographer. Bruegel creates toys for grown-ups. The dancing peasants under the gallows transport us to a primeval world where law remains unwritten and where the rules of fate are innocently defied. These prodigious dancers neither ignore death nor can they avoid it. They only play with death. With their heroic capacity for make-believe they join the painter, who, having climbed the long road from enemy painting to everyday life, celebrates here his accomplishment.

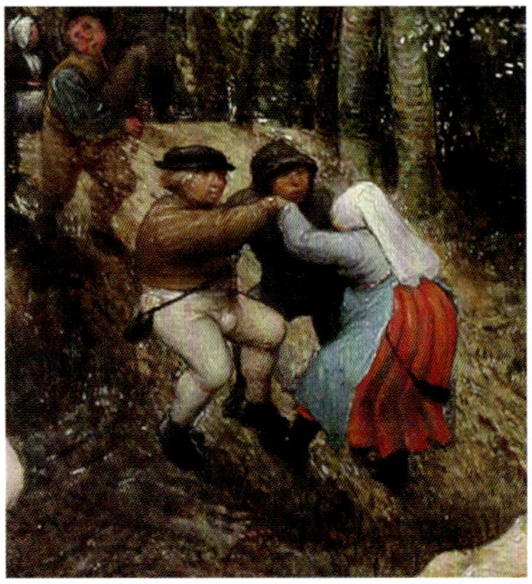

325 Detail of Pieter Bruegel the Elder, *The Magpie on the Gallows* (fig. 319)

NOTES

ACKNOWLEDGMENTS

1 Barbara Butts and Joseph Leo Koerner, *The Printed World of Pieter Bruegel the Elder*, ed. Suzanne Tuasz (Saint Louis, MO: Saint Louis Art Museum, 1995).

2 Joseph Leo Koerner, "Bosch's Contingency," in *Kontingenz*, ed. Gerhard von Graevenitz and Odo Marquard, Poetik und Hermeneutik, 17 (Munich: Fink, 1998), pp. 242–83.

3 Joseph Leo Koerner, "Hieronymus Bosch's World Picture," in *Picturing Science / Producing Art*, ed. Peter Galison and Carolyn Jones (New York and London: Routledge, 1998), pp. 297–323; see Richard Rorty, *Contingency, Irony, and Solidarity* (Cambridge, UK: Cambridge University Press, 1989), p. 3.

4 Joseph Leo Koerner, "Bosch's Equipment," in *Things that Talk*, ed. Lorraine Daston (New York: Zone Books, 2004), pp. 27–65.

5 Joseph Leo Koerner, "Wirklichkeit bei Hieronymus Bosch," in *Realität und Projektion. Wirklichkeitnahe Darstellung in Antike und Mittelaltar*, ed. Peter Schmitt and Martin Büchsel, Neue Frankfurter Forschungen, 1 (Berlin: Gebr. Mann, 2005), pp. 227–38.

6 The key text is Carl Schmitt, *Ex Captivitate Salus—Erfahrungen der Zeit 1945/7*, 2nd ed. (Berlin: Duncker & Humblot, 2002), p. 82, where he identifies Bosch's so-called *Garden of Delights* with "the enemy," while also admitting, by way of a cryptic line taken from Theodor Däubler, that "the enemy is our own question in the form of a figure." I am currently writing a comparative account of Bosch's reception by Schmitt, Wilhelm Fraenger, Erwin Panofsky, and E. H. Gombrich.

7 The show produced *Lifeworld: Portrait and Landscape in Netherlandish Prints, 1550–1650*, exhibition catalogue by Joseph Leo Koerner and Michael Zell, Harvard Univ. Art Museums Gallery Series, 29 (Cambridge, MA: Harvard University Art Museums, 1999).

CHAPTER 1. IN THE ART-HISTORICAL MUSEUM

1 On the history of the ensemble, see *Pieter Bruegel d. Ä im Kunsthistorischen Museum Wien*, ed. Wilfried Seipel (Vienna: Kunsthistorisches Museum; Milan: Skira, 1998), pp. 15–16. Walter S. Gibson, *Bruegel* (London: Thames and Hudson, 1977); Philippe and Françoise Roberts-Jones, *Pieter Bruegel* (New York: Harry N. Abrams, 2002), with a useful concordance of catalogues raisonnés; and Manfred Sellink, *Bruegel: The Complete Paintings, Drawings and Prints* (Antwerp: Ludion, 2007) are good introductions to the artist; see also, more recently, Larry Silver, *Pieter Bruegel* (New York: Abbeville, 2011). For documents of Bruegel's life, and on individual paintings, see especially Roger H. Marijnissen et al., *Bruegel—Das vollständige Werk*, trans. Rolf Erdorf (Antwerp: Mercatorfonds, 2003). I list works (where possible) by their inventory numbers and as catalogued in Max J. Friedländer, *Early Netherlandish Painting*, 14, *Pieter Bruegel*, ed. Henri Pauwels, trans. Heinz Norden (Leiden: Sijthoff, 1976), henceforth referred to as Friedländer (Bruegel).

2 A German equivalent of "worldscape," *Weltlandschaft*, was introduced into the vocabulary of art historians by Eberhard Freiherr von Bodenhausen (*Gerard David und seine Schule* [Munich: Bruckmann, 1905], p. 209), where it named a type of landscape invented by Quentin Metsys and Joachim Patinir and practiced in Antwerp and Bruges. For Ludwig Baldass, the *Weltlandschaft* culminated in Bruegel ("Die niederländische Landschaftsmalerei von Patinir bis Bruegel," *Jahrbuch der kunsthistorischen Sammlungen des Allerhöchsten Kaiserhauses* 34 [1918], p. 120); see Walter S. Gibson, *"Mirror of the Earth": The World Landscape in Sixteenth-Century Flemish Painting* (Princeton, NJ: Princeton University Press, 1989), pp. xx–xxi and passim.

3 For Bruegel's prints, I have generally relied on René van Bastelaer, *The Prints of Peter Bruegel the Elder. Catalogue Raisonné*, new ed., trans. and rev. Susan Fargo Gilchrist (San Francisco: Alan Wofsy Fine Arts, 1992). This volume updates Bastelaer's original *Les Estampes de Peter Bruegel l'Ancien* (Brussels: G. van Oest, 1908) and incorporates descriptions in two other standard works: F.W.H. Hollstein, *Dutch and Flemish Etchings, Engravings, and Woodcuts*, 3, *Boekhorst-Brueghel* (Amsterdam: Hertzberger, 1950); and Louis Lebeer, *Catalogue raisonné des estampes de Bruegel l'Ancien* (Brussels: Bibliothèque royale de Albert Ier, 1969). See also *Pieter Bruegel the Elder: Drawings and Prints*, ed. Nadine M. Orenstein (New York: Metropolitan Museum of Art; New Haven, CT: Yale University Press, 2001), and Nadine M. Orenstein, *Pieter Bruegel the Elder*, ed. Manfred Sellink, The New Hollstein: Dutch and Flemish Etchings, Engravings (Ouderkerk aan den IJssel: Sound and Vision Publishers; Amsterdam: Rijksprentenkabinet, Rijksmuseum, 2006); henceforth referred to as "New Hollstein (Bruegel)."

4 Klaus Demus, *Flämische Malerei von Jan van Eyck bis Pieter Bruegel d. Ä.: Katalog der Gemäldegalerie* Klaus Demus et al. (Vienna: Herold and Kunshistorisches Museum, 1981), p. 81 and passim.

5 Thomas Dacosta Kaufmann, "From Treasury to Museum: The Collections of the Austrian Habsburg," in *Cultures of Collecting*, ed. John Elsner and Roger Cardinal (London: Reaktion Books, 1994), pp. 137–54.

6 On the Ringstrasse and its architecture, see Carl Schorske, *Fin-de-siècle Vienna: Politics and Culture* (New York: Alfred Knopf, 1980), pp. 24–115.

7 Kunsthistorisches Museum Inv. No. GG 1059. For an excellent account of this painting, see Edward Snow, *Inside Bruegel: The Play of Images in* Children's Games (New York: North Point Press, 1997), pp. 43–57.

8 Vienna, Kunsthistorisches Museum Inv. No. 1020; Friedländer (Bruegel), no. 44;

the painting may be identical to a work described in a 1659 inventory of Archduke Leopold Wilhelm's collection; see Gustav Glück, *Bruegels Gemälde* (Vienna: Schroll, 1932), p. 61.

9 Wolfgang Kemp, *Der Anteil des Betrachters. Rezeptionsasthetische Studien zur Malerei des 19. Jahrhunderts* (Munich: Mäander, 1983), p. 54.

10 Hans Sedlmayr—virtually alone among Bruegel's interpreters—gave an account of such formal features. In an essay first published in 1934, he argued that in Bruegel space, while capable of expanding into vast panoramas, also everywhere disintegrates into simple, two-dimensional geometric shapes, and that this disintegration estranges vision, causing viewers to take a distance on what they see ("Bruegel's *Macchia*," in *The Vienna School Reader: Politics and Art Historical Method in the 1930s*, ed. and trans. Christopher S. Wood [New York: Zone Books, 2000], pp. 323–76).

CHAPTER 2. LIFE TIME

1 Alphonse Wauters put Bruegel's death at September 5, 1569; most scholars have followed him ("La famille Breughel," *Annales de la Société d'archéologie de Bruxelles* 1 (1888), p. 12. Wauter's probable source (unmentioned in his article) was an eighteenth-century manuscript biography in a collection of documents deposited in Belgium's Ministry of Foreign Affairs under the title "Fonds Heràldique"; see Georges Onclincx, "Note sur une biographie manuscrite (XVIIIe s.) de Pierre Bruegel l'Ancien mentionnant son décès et son inhumation," *Revue belge de philologie et d'histoire* 63 (1985): 726–30.

2 Bruegel's birthdate is unknown but is usually calculated to be between 1525 and 1530 based on the artist's inscription in 1551 as master (and thus at least twenty-one years old) into the Antwerp artists' guild (the guild of Saint Luke); see Philippe F. Rombouts and Théodore van Lerius, *De Liggeren en andere historische archieven der Antwerpsche Sint Lucasgilde, onder zinspreuk "Wt jonsten versaemt"* (Antwerp: Baggerman, 1872–76), p. 175. However, he may have been born later, hence Ortelius's lament (discussed in n6 below) that Bruegel was taken *medio aetatis flore*; see Martin Royalton-Kisch, "Pieter Bruegel as a Draftsman: The Changing Image," in *Pieter Bruegel the Elder: Drawings and Prints*, ed. Nadine M. Orenstein (New York: Metropolitan Museum of Art; New Haven, CT: Yale University Press, 2001), p. 39n115.

3 Karel van Mander, *The Lives of the Illustrious Netherlandish and German Painters, from the first edition of the* Schilder-boeck *(1603–1604)*, trans. and ed. Hessel Miedema (Doornspijk: Davaco, 1994), 1: 193 (1604, fol. 233v).

4 Van Mander, *Lives*, 1: 193–95 (1604, fol. 233v–234r).

5 See Geoffrey Parker, *The Dutch Revolt* (Ithaca, NY: Cornell University Press, 1977), pp. 19–118; Jonathan Israel, *The Dutch Republic: Its Rise, Greatness, and Fall, 1477–1806* (Oxford, UK: Clarendon Press, 1995), pp. 129–68. Bruegel's relation to these events is surveyed in Irving C. Zupnick, "Bruegel and the Revolt of the Netherlands," *Art Journal* 23 (1964): 283–89.

6 *Album Amicorum Abraham Ortelius: Reproduit en facsimilé*, trans. and ed. Jean Puraye (Amsterdam: Van Gendt, 1969), fol. 12v; the manuscript is owned by Pembroke College, Cambridge University. On the friendship between the cartographer and the painter, see Arthur Ewart Popham, "Pieter Bruegel and Abraham Ortelius," *Burlington Magazine* 59 (1931): 184–88; and Jan Muylle, "Pieter Bruegel en Abraham Ortelius: Bijdrage tot de literaire receptie van Pieter Bruegels werk," in *Archivum artis Lovaniensis: Bijdragen tot de geschiedenis van de kunst der Nederlanden opgedragen aan Prof. Em. J. K. Steppe*, ed. Maurits Smeyers (Louvain: Peeters, 1981), pp. 319–37. On Ortelius's eulogy, see Walter S. Melion, *Shaping the Netherlandish Canon: Karel van Mander's* Schilder-boeck (Chicago: University of Chicago Press, 1991), pp. 144–45, 173–82; and Mark A. Meadow, *Pieter Bruegel the Elder's* Netherlandish Proverbs *and the Practice of Rhetoric* (Zwolle: Waanders, 2002), pp. 109–17.

7 On Ortelius's wordplay, see Tanja Michalsky, "Imitation und Imagination. Die Landschaft Pieter d. Ä. im Blick der Humanisten," in *Künste und Natur in Diskursen der frühen Neuzeit*, 1, ed. Harmut Laufhütte et al. (Wiesbaden: Harrassowitz, 2000), pp. 184–87.

8 Van Mander, *Lives*, 1: 190 (1604, fol. 233r).

9 Rombouts and Van Lerius, *De Liggeren*, p. 175; see Fritz Grossmann, *Pieter Bruegel. Complete Edition of the Paintings*, 3rd ed. (London: Phaidon, 1973), pp. 10–13; Nadine M. Orenstein, "The Elusive Life of Pieter Bruegel the Elder," in *Pieter Bruegel the Elder*, ed. Orenstein, p. 5.

10 Van Mander, *Lives*, 1:190 (1604, fol. 233r). Already in 1910 Gustav Glück rejected the myth of "Peasant Bruegel"; see *Peter Bruegels des Älteren Gemälde im Kunsthistorischen Hofmuseum zu Wien* (Brussels: Librairie nationale d'art et d'histoire G. van Oest, 1910), p. 6. David Freedberg has argued that already Van Mander framed the opening of his Bruegel biography as a literary fiction or *topos* (*The Prints of Pieter Bruegel the Elder*, ed. Freedberg, exh. cat. [Tokyo: Bridgestone Museum of Art, 1989], pp. 21–31); see also Jürgen Müller, "'Pieter der Drollige' oder der Mythos vom Bauern-Bruegel," in *Pieter Bruegel der Jüngere—Jan Bruegel der Ältere: Flämische Malerei um 1600. Tradition und Fortschritt*, exh. cat., ed. Wilfried Seipel (Vienna: Kunsthistorisches Museum; Lingen: Luca Verlag, 1997), pp. 42–53. For a reading identifying Bruegel's art with its peasant subjects, see Wilhelm Hausenstein, *Der Bauern-Bruegel*, 2nd ed. (Munich: Piper, 1920), p. 102.

11 Hondius's *Pictorum aliquot celebrium praecipué Germaniae inferioris effigies* reworked 22 of the 1572 engravings and added 47 new portraits for a total of 69 portraits, mainly of Netherlandish artists; see Nadine Orenstein, *Hendrick Hondius*, ed. Ger Luijten, The New Hollstein: Dutch and Flemish Etchings, Engravings, and Woodcuts, 1450–1700 (Roosendaal: Koninklijke van Poll; Amsterdam: Rijksprentenkabinet, Rijksmuseum, 1994), pp. 91–92; the Bruegel portrait is no. 85.

12 The engraving is number 19 of 23 numbered portraits published with letterpress texts by Dominicus Lampsonius under the title *Pictorum aliquot celebrium Germaniae inferioris effigies* (Antwerp: Apud Viduam Hieronymi Cock, 1572). Published by Valcxken Dierix on the press of her deceased husband, Hieronymus Cock, to whom Lampsonius dedicated the work, the portrait-likenesses have been attributed both to Cornelis Cort (Manfred Sellink and Huigen Leeflang, *Cornelis Cort*, The New Hollstein: Dutch and Flemish Etchings, Engravings, and Woodcuts, 1450–1700, 3 vols. [Rotterdam: Sound and Vision Publishers; Amsterdam: Rijksprentenkabinet, Rijksmuseum, 2000], nos. 223–27); and to Johannes Wierix (Zsuzsanna van Ryven-Zeman, *The Wierix Family*, ed. Jan van der Stock and Marjolein Leesberg, The New Hollstein: Dutch and Flemish Etchings, Engravings, and Woodcuts, 1450–1700 [Rotterdam: Sound and Vision

Publishers, 2004], 9: nos. 2023–35; the Bruegel portrait is no. 2031).

13 See "Unmasking," in chapter 10.

14 On the history of the concept of imitation in art theory, see especially Hans Blumenberg, "'Nachahmung der Natur'. Zur Vorgeschichte der Idee des schöpferischen Menschen," in *Wirklichkeiten in denen wir leben: Aufsätze und eine Rede* (Stuttgart: Reclam, 1981), pp. 55–103; and Jan Białostocki, "The Renaissance Concept of Nature and Antiquity," in *The Renaissance and Mannerism: Studies in Western Art*, 2, Acts of the Twentieth International Congress of the History of Art (Princeton, NJ: Princeton University Press, 1963), 1963, pp. 19–30.

15 Van Mander, *Lives*, 1: 190 (1604, fol. 233r).

16 Ernst Kris and Otto Kurz, *Legend, Myth, and Magic in the Image of the Artist: A Historical Experiment*, trans. Alastair Laing (New Haven, CT: Yale University Press, 1979), p. 12.

17 Giorgio Vasari, *Lives of the Artists; a Selection*, trans. George Bull (London: Penguin, 1965), 1: 57–58; Vasari probably took this anecdote from Lorenzo Ghiberti (*Lorenzo Ghibertis Denkwürdigkeiten (I Commentari)*, ed. Julius Schlosser [Berlin: Julius Bard, 1912], p. 35), who relied on earlier Dante commentaries; see Kris and Kurz, *Legend, Myth, and Magic*, pp. 22–26, 32–38; and Patricia Lee Rubin, *Giorgio Vasari: Art and History* (New Haven, CT: Yale University Press, 1995), pp. 297–306.

18 Giovanni Paolo Lomazzo, *Trattato dell'arte de la Pittura* (Milan: Paolo Gottardo Pontio, 1584), pp. 106–7; Grossman recognized the connection to Van Mander's anecdote (*Pieter Bruegel*, p. 28); see also Joseph Leo Koerner, "Albrecht Dürer's *Pleasures of the World* and the Limits of Festival," in *Das Fest*, ed. Walter Haug and Rainer Warning, Poetik und Hermeneutik, 14 (Munich: Fink, 1989), pp. 180–81.

19 Hans Moser, "Städtische Fasnacht des Mittelalters," in *Masken zwischen Spiel und Ernst. Beiträge des Tübinger Arbeitskreises für Fasnachtsforschung*, ed. Hermann Bausinger, Volksleben 18 (Tübingen: Braxmaier, 1967), p. 165; Hans-Ulrich Roller, *Der Nürnberger Schembartlauf—Studien zum Fest- und Maskenwesen des spaten* Mittelalters, Volksleben, 11 (Tübingen: Tübinger Vereinigung für Volkskunde, 1967), p. 148ff; Werner Lenk, *Das Nürnberger Fastnachtspiel des 15. Jahrhunderts: Ein Betrag zur Theorie und zur Interpretation des Fastnachtspiels als Dichtung*, Veröffentlichungen des Instituts für Deutsche Sprache und Literatur, 33 (Berlin: Akademie Verlag, 1966), pp. 20–25; Dietrich Huschenbett, rev. of Werner Lenk, *Das Nürnberger Fastnachtspiel*, in *Anzeiger für deutsches Altertum und deutsche Literatur* 82 (1980): 134.

20 Lodovico Guicciardini, *Descrittione di tutti i Paesi Bassi, altrimenti detti Germania Inferiore* (Antwerp: Willem Silvius, 1567), p. 39.

21 See Ethan Matt Kavaler, *Pieter Bruegel: Parables of Order and Enterprise* (Cambridge, UK, and New York: Cambridge University Press, 1999), pp. 152–53.

22 Roland Baetens, "La 'Belezza' et la 'Magnificenza': symbols de pouvoir de la villa rustica dans la région anversoise aux temps modernes," in *Nouvelles approaches concernant le culture de l'habitat: colloque international, Université d'Anvers, 24–25. 10. 1989 = New approaches to living patterns*, ed. Roland Baetens and Bruno Blondé (Turnhout: Brepols, 1991), p. 160; "La 'villa rustica' phénomène italien dans le paysage brabançon au 16ème siècle," *Aspetti della vita economica medievale: Atti del Convegno di Studi nel X Anniversario della morte di Federigo Melis, Firenze-Pisa-Prato, 10–14 marzo 1984* (Florence: Istituto de storia economica, Università degli studi Firenze, 1985), p. 177; Roland Baetens and Bruno Blondé, "Wonen in de stad: Aspecten van de stedelijke wooncultuur," in *Stad in Vlaanderen: cultuur en maatschappij 1477–1787*, ed. Jan van der Stock (Brussels: Gemeentekrediet, 1991), p. 68; and Stephanie Porras, *Pieter Bruegel's Historical Imagination* (University Park, PA: Pennsylvania State University Press, 2016), pp. 47–49.

23 Hugo Soly, *Urbanisme en kapitalisme te Antwerpen in de zestiende eeuw. De Stedebouwkundige en industriële ondernemingen van Gilbert van Schoonbeke*, Historische Uitgaven pro civitate, Reeks in-8, 47 (Brussels: Gemeentekrediet van Belgie, 1977), p. 126; cited in Stephanie Porras, "The Peasant as Pagan in the Work of Pieter Bruegel the Elder" (Ph.D. diss., Courtauld Institute of Art, 2008), p. 106.

24 Iain Buchanan, "The Collection of Niclaes Jonghelinck: II The 'Months' by Pieter Bruegel the Elder," *Burlington Magazine* 130 (1990): 547.

25 Schiller's idea of a split in the subjective experience and expression of nature rests historically on the more fundamental bifurcation between nature's primary and secondary qualities, on which see Alfred North Whitehead, *The Concept of Nature, Tarner lectures delivered in Trinity College, November, 1919* (Cambridge, UK: Cambridge University Press, 1920), p. 32; Isabelle Stengers, *Thinking with Whitehead: A Free and Wild Creation of Concepts*, trans. Michael Chase (Cambridge, MA: Harvard University Press, 2011), pp. 73–84; and Bruno Latour, *An Inquiry into Modes of Existence: An Anthropology of the Moderns*, trans. Catherine Porter (Cambridge, MA: Harvard University Press, 2013), pp. 115–16 and passim.

26 Friedrich Schiller, *On the Naïve and Sentimental in Literature*, trans. Helen Watanabe-O'Kelly (Manchester, UK: Carcanet New Press, 1981), p. 34.

27 Schiller, p. 35.

28 I use this phrase in Clifford Geertz's sense: the "fugitive truth" of "seeing ourselves among others, as a local example of the forms human life has locally taken, a case among cases, a world among worlds" (Clifford Geertz, *Local Knowledge: Further Essays in Interpretative Anthropology* [New York: Basic Books, 1983], p. 16).

29 René van Bastelaer, *The Prints of Peter Bruegel the Elder. Catalogue Raisonné*, new ed., trans. and rev. Susan Fargo Gilchrist (San Francisco: Alan Wofsy, 1992), no. 10; New Hollstein (Bruegel), no. 53.

30 Paul Vandenbroeck, "Zur Herkunft und Verwurzelung der 'Grillen'. Vom Volksmythos zum kunst- und literaturtheoretischen Begriff, 15.–17. Jahrhundert," *De zeventiende eeuw: cultuur in de Nederlanden in interdisciplinair perspectief* 3 (1987): 52–84.

31 Joachim Jacoby, *Hans von Aachen 1552–1615*, Monographien zur deutschen Barockmalerei (Berlin: Deutscher Kunstverlag, 2000), pp. 43–44 and cat. 66; and Joseph Leo Koerner, "Friendship Portraits," in *Hans von Aachen (1552–1615). Hofkünstler in Europa*, exh. cat., ed. Thomas Fusenig (Aachen: Suermondt-Ludwig-Museum; Berlin: Deutscher Kunstverlag, 2010), p. 70. Confiscated from the collection of the Princes Lobkowitz in Roudnice, it arrived after 1945 in the Středočeská Gallery in Nelahozeves Castle, from which it was stolen in 1964; it is still missing.

32 On "ethnic style," see especially André Leroi-Gourhan, *Gesture and Speech*, trans. Anna Bostock Berger (Cambridge, MA: MIT Press, 1993), pp. 276–79; and Alfred Gell, *Art and Anthropology: An Anthropological Theory* (Oxford: Oxford University Press, 1998), pp. 154–68.

33 Leroi-Gourhan, *Gesture and Speech*, pp. 237–55; and Pierre Lemonnier, *Elements for an Anthropology of Technology* (Ann Arbor: University of Michigan, Museum of Anthropology, 1992).

34 Van Mander, *Lives*, 1: 190 (1604, fol. 233r).

35 See Wolfgang Stechow's assessment in *Pieter Bruegel the Elder* (New York: Abrams, 1968), pp. 142–44.

36 Gabri van Tussenbroeck, "Changes in the Organisation of the Building Industry in the North and South (1500–1650)," in *Unity and Discontinuity: Architectural Relations between the Southern and Northern Low Countries 1530–1700*, ed. Krista de Jonge and Koen Ottenheym (Turnhout: Brepols, 2007), p. 304.

37 Rotterdam, Museum Boijmans Van Beuningen, Accession No. 3363 (OK); the work got its present title in the 1955 exhibition *Art Treasures from Dutch Private Collections in Rotterdam*, curated by Egbert Haverkamp Begemann and B. R. M. de Neeve; see Fritz Grossmann, "Cornelis van Dalem Re-Examined," *Burlington Magazine* 96 (1954): 47

38 Vitruvius, *The Architecture of Marcus Vitruvius Pollio in Ten Books*, trans. Joseph Gwilt (London: Lockwood, 1874), p. 32. On Vitruvius's influence on Van Dalem, see Fritz Grossmann, "Notes on Some Dutch and Flemish Paintings at Rotterdam," *Burlington Magazine* 97, no. 632 (1955): 336.

39 Munich, Alte Pinakothek, Inv. 12044.

40 Sebastian Münster, *Cosmographei. Oder beschreibung aller länder, herschafften, fürnehmesten stetten, geschichten, gebreuche, hantierungen, etc.* (Basel: Heinrich Petri, 1550), p. 318 (and 383); the 1550 illustration is a reversed recut of the woodcut illustrating the 3rd (1546) edition; the image does not appear in the 1st edition (1544). I am grateful to Jasper van Putten for clarifying these differences.

41 Guicciardini, *Descrittione di tutti i Paesi Bassi*, p. 39.

42 See Porras, "The Peasant," pp. 11–146; "Producing the Vernacular: Antwerp, Cultural Archaeology and the Bruegelian Peasant," *Journal of Historians of Netherlandish Art* 3 (2011); "Rural Memory, Pagan Idolatry: Pieter Bruegel's Peasant Shrines," *Art History* 34 (2011): 2–24; and *Pieter Bruegel's Historical Imagination* (University Park, PA: Pennsylvania State University Press, 2016), pp. 11–175.

43 For example, Claude Gaignebet, "Le Combat de Carnaval et de Carême," *Annales: Economies, Sociétés, Civilisations* 27 (1972): 313–45; and Elke M. Schutt-Kehm, *Pieter Bruegels d. Ä. "Kampf des Karnevals gegen die Fasten" als Quelle volkskundlicher Forschung*, Artes populares, 7 (Frankfurt: Peter Lang, 1983).

44 Aron Gurevich, *Historical Anthropology of the Middle Ages*, ed. Jana Howlett (Chicago: University of Chicago Press, 1992), pp. 200–209.

45 Martin Heidegger, "Building Dwelling Thinking," in *Poetry, Language, Thought*, trans. Albert Hofstadter (New York: Harper & Row, 1971), p. 154; the essay was delivered at first as a lecture, in 1951.

46 On Heidegger's concept of world, see especially *Being and Time: A Translation of Sein und Zeit*, trans. Joan Stambaugh (Albany: State University of New York Press, 1996), pp. 59–62; and "The Age of the World-Picture," *Off the Beaten Track*, ed. and trans. Julian Young and Kenneth Haynes (Cambridge, UK: Cambridge University Press, 2002), pp. 57–85. Heidegger notes the etymology of *Welt* as "wer-alt" in *Bremer und Freiburger Vorträge*, ed. Petra Jaeger (Frankfurt am Main: Vittorio Klostermann, 1994), p. 22. On this etymon as indicating world as always a human matter of concern, see Gerhard Gloege, "Welt," in *Die Religion in Geschichte und Gegenwart*, 3rd ed., ed. Kurt Galling (Tübingen: J. C. B. Mohr, 1962), 6: col. 1595–96.

47 The term "lifeworld"—in German *Lebenswelt*—was coined by Edmund Husserl to denote the world observed in the "how" of experience ("Kant und die Idee der Transzendentalphilosophie," in *Husserliana: Gesammelte Werke*, ed. Rudolf Boehm [The Hague: Martinus Nijhoff, 1950], 7: 357).

48 For overviews of Antwerp's economic history in this period, see Herman van der Wee, *The Growth of the Antwerp Market and the European Economy*, 3 vols. (The Hague: Nijhoff, 1963); Leon Voet, *Antwerp, the Golden Age: The Rise and Glory of the Metropolis in the Sixteenth Century* (Antwerp: Mercatorfonds, 1973); and Jan van der Stock, *Antwerp, Story of a Metropolis: 16th–17th Century*, exh. cat. (Antwerp: Hessenhuis and Martial & Snoeck, 1993). On Antwerp's art market, see Elizabeth Honig, *Painting and the Market in Early Modern Antwerp* (New Haven, CT: Yale University Press, 1998), pp. 4–13; Filip Vermeylen, "Exporting Art Across the Globe: The Antwerp Art Market in the Sixteenth Century," *Nederlands Kunsthistorisch Jaarboek* 50 (1999): 13–30; Filip Vermeylen, *Painting for the Market: Commercialization of Art in Antwerp's Golden Age*, Studies in Urban History, 2 (Turnhout: Brepols, 2003); and Larry Silver, *Peasant Scenes and Landscapes: The Rise of Pictorial Genres in the Antwerp Art Market* (Philadelphia: University of Pennsylvania Press, 2006), pp. 16–25.

49 On the impact of the demand for luxuries on trade, industry, and finance capital, see Werner Sombart's classic study *Luxury and Capitalism*, trans. W. R. Dittmar (Ann Arbor: University of Michigan Press, 1967). First published in 1913, *Luxus und Kapitalismus* has influenced recent work on the migration of objects; see Arjun Appadurai, ed., *The Social Life of Things: Commodities in Cultural Perspective* (Cambridge, UK: Cambridge University Press, 1986), pp. 36–41 and 315.

50 Designed and engraved by Melchisedech van Hooren, the engraving was brought to bear on Bruegel's art by Walter S. Gibson (*Bruegel* [London: Thames and Hudson, 1977], pp. 19–20); on the print's authorship, see "Melchisedech van Hooren, 1552–1570. Un artiste anversois ignorè," *Annales de l'Académie royale d'archéologie de Belgique* 1 (1898): 367–87.

51 Vermeylen, *Painting for the Market*, p. 38; see also Berend Dubbe and Wim H. Vroom, "Mecenaat en kunstmarkt in de Nederlanden gedurende de zestiende eeuw," in *Kunst voor de Beeldenstorm: Noordnederlandse kunst, 1525–1580*, exh. cat., ed. Jan P. Filedt Kok et al. (Amsterdam: Rijksmuseum, 1986), pp. 13–28.

52 Dan Ewing, "Marketing Art in Antwerp, 1460–1560: Our Lady's Pand," *Art Bulletin* 72, no. 4 (1990): 558–84.

53 Quoted in Dora Schlugleit, "De zilverhandel van de meerse en de ordonnantie van de goudsmeden te Antwerpen in de zestiende eeuw," *Bijdragen tot de Geschiedenis* 30 (1939): 42; cited in Vermeylen, *Painting for the Market*, p. 37n37.

54 See especially Honig, *Painting and the Market*; "Kunst voor de markt," ed. Reindert Falkenburg et al., *Nederlands Kunsthistorisch Jaarboek* 50 (1999); and Silver, *Peasant Scenes*, pp. 16–25.

55 Munich, Pinakothek, No. 146 (Inv. No. 708); the term "Antwerp Mannerist" was coined by Max J. Friedländer in "Die Antwerper Manieristen von 1520," *Jahrbuch der Königlich-Preussischen Kunstsammlungen* 36 (1915): 65–91; on the clientele for this style of painting, see Dan Ewing, "Magi and Merchants: The Force Behind the Antwerp Mannerists' Adoration

Pictures," in *Jaarboek Koninklijk Museum voor Schone Kunsten Antwerpen* (2004–5), pp. 274–99.

56 Van Mander, *Lives*, 1: 190 (1604, fol. 233r); this claim of Bruegel's apprenticeship with Coecke is corroborated by Franciscus Sweertius (Coecke's brother-in-law) in his *Athenae belgicae* of 1618; see Georges Marlier, *La Renaissance flamande: Pierre Coeck d'Alost* (Brussels: Editions Robert Fink, 1966), pp. 29–31. On Coecke and his Flemish weavers, see Elizabeth A. H. Cleland, *Grand Design: Pieter Coecke van Aelst and Renaissance Tapestries*, exh. cat. (New York: Metropolitan Museum of Art, 2014).

57 On Bruegel's collaboration with Cock, see Lydia De Pauw-De Veen, *Jérôme Cock, éditeur d'estampes et graveur 1507?–1570*, exh. cat. (Brussels: Bibliothèque Royale Albert Ier, 1970); Timothy A. Riggs, "Hieronymus Cock (1510–1570): Printmaker and Publisher in Antwerp at the Sign of the Four Winds" (Ph.D. diss., Yale University, 1971); Timothy A. Riggs, "Bruegel and His Publisher," in *Pieter Bruegel und seine Welt*, ed. Otto Georg von Simson and Matthias Winner (Berlin: Gebr. Mann, 1979), pp. 165–73; and Joris van Grieken, Ger Luijten, and Jan van der Stock, *Hieronymus Cock: The Renaissance in Print*, exh. cat. (Brussels: Mercatorfonds, 2013), pp. 216–71, 368–76, and 380–96.

58 Justus Müller-Hofstede, "Zur Interpretation von Pieter Bruegels Landschaft—Ästhetischer Landschaftsbegriff und stoische Weltbetrachtung," in Simson and Winner, eds., *Pieter Bruegel und seine Welt*, pp. 73–142; and Melion, *Shaping the Netherlandish Canon*, pp. 171–82.

59 For a concise account of this development, see Timothy Riggs, "Graven Images: A Guide to the Exhibition," in *Graven Images: The Rise of Professional Printmakers in Antwerp and Haarlem, 1540–1640*, ed. Timothy Riggs and Larry Silver, exh. cat. (Evanston, IL: Mary and Leigh Block Gallery, 1991), pp. 101–18.

60 On "enclaves of innocence" as a mythic motif in modern thought, see Hans Blumenberg, *Lebenszeit und Weltzeit* (Frankfurt am Main: Suhrkamp, 1986), pp. 48–69.

61 Klaus Demus, *Flämische Malerei von Jan van Eyck bis Pieter Bruegel d. Ä. Katalog der Gemäldegalerie des Kunsthistorisches Museums Wien* (Vienna: Herold, 1981), p. 107.

62 Collection of Jane and Raphael Bernstein; see *Pieter Bruegel der Jüngere—Jan Bruegel der Ältere*, ed. Seipel, cat. no. 109. Before 1616, Pieter Breughel the Younger signed his works "Brueghel"; thereafter—including on his copies of *The Peasant and the Bird Thief*—he signed them "Breughel"; see Klaus Ertz, "Pieter Breughel der Jüngere," in *Pieter Bruegel der Jüngere—Jan Bruegel der Ältere*, ed. Seipel, 19.

63 Naples, Museo Nazionale di Capodimonte, Inv. Q16 (No. 8486); Friedländer (Bruegel), no. 41.

64 However, the inscription does correspond to the text on Johannes Wierix's 1568 engraving of Bruegel's composition; see Manfred Sellink, *Bruegel: The Complete Paintings, Drawings, and Prints* (Antwerp: Ludion, 2007), p. 250; and New Hollstein (Bruegel), no. A10.

65 Hendrik D. L. Vervliet, "De 'Twaalf Spreekwoorden' van het Museum Mayer van dem Bergh. Een onderzoek naar de datum van onstaan van de onderschriften," in *Jaarboek Koninklijk Museum voor schone Kunsten Antwerpen* (1954–1960), p. 81n5.

66 For a summary of the literature on the painting, see Roger H. Marijnissen et al., *Bruegel—Das vollständige Werk*, trans. Rolf Erdorf (Antwerp: Mercadorfonds, 2003), p. 360.

67 Charles de Tolnay, *Pierre Bruegel l'Ancien*, Bibliothèque du XVIe siècle (Brussels: Nouvelle société d'éditions, 1935), p. 47.

68 Dale Martin, *The Trapper's Bible: Traps, Snares, and Pathguards* (Boulder, CO: Paladin Press, 1987), p. 54.

69 "Men moet zich krommen, wil men door de wereld kommen"; see Wilhelm Fraenger, *Das Bild der 'niederländischen Sprichwörter'—Pieter Bruegels verkehrte Welt*, ed. Michael Philipp (Amsterdam: Castrum Peregrini, 1999), p. 48; Fraenger published his study as *Der Bauern-Bruegel und das deutsche Sprichwort* (Erlenbach-Zürich: Eugen Rentsch, 1923).

70 "Hij doet de vereld up zijnen duim draaien," Fraenger, *Das Bild*, p. 48.

71 The others are *The Parable of the Blind Leading the Blind* (see fig. 24); the poorly preserved *Adoration of the Magi* in the Musées Royaux des Beaux-Arts in Brussels (Inv. 3929), the authorship of which has been disputed; and *The Wine of Saint Martin's Day*, recently identified as autograph by Alexander Bell and James McDonald and now in the Prado in Madrid. *The Fall of Icarus* (see fig. 262), also in Belgium and of disputed provenance, was painted on canvas (doubly lined and much repaired), but this support was originally prepared with a chalk ground layer beneath a lead-white and carbon-black *imprimatur*, a technique foreign to Bruegel's *Tüchlein* pictures; see chapter 9 for a discussion of this painting.

72 The conceit was observed in Gotthard Jedlicka, *Pieter Bruegel, der Maler in seiner Zeit* (Erlenbach: Eugen Rentsch, 1938), p. 342.

73 Naples, Museo Nazionale di Capodimonte, Inv. 84.490; Friedländer (Bruegel), no. 42.

74 Both of Bruegel's paintings in the Museo Nazionale di Capodimonte came from the palace of Giovanni Battista Massi in Parma, from which they were seized in 1612. Both dated 1568 and executed in the same comparatively portable medium (more suitable for export than paintings on panel), they were probably made for the same patron; see Dominique Allart, "Did Pieter Brueghel the Younger See His Father's Paintings?" in *Brueghel Enterprises*, exh. cat., ed. Peter van den Brink (Maastrich: Bonnefantenmuseum; Antwerp: Ludion, 2001), p. 49.

75 See, too, Luke 6:39 and Rom. 2:16. The parable appears as a tiny, skylined motif at the upper right of Bruegel's *Netherlandish Proverbs* panel (see fig. 32).

76 Hans Sedlmayr criticized narrow historicist readings such as Michael Auner's ("Pieter Bruegel. Umrisse eines Lebensbildes," *Jahrbuch der kunsthistorischen Sammlung in Wien* 52 [1956]: 97–110), which understood the painting to be a topical attack on religious heresy. For Sedlmayr, such interpretations were inadequate to the descriptive power of Bruegel's pictures, which demanded (in Sedlmayr's words) an "integral understanding" ("Pieter Bruegel: Der Sturz der Blinden" [1957], in *Epochen und Werke: Gesammelte Schriften zur Kunstgeschichte* [Munich: Mäander, 1985], pp. 319–56).

77 Henk Bonger, *The Life and Work of Dirck Volkertszoon Coornhert*, trans. Gerrit Voogt, Studies in the History of Ideas in the Low Countries (Amsterdam and New York: Rodopi, 2004), p. 181; Gerrit Voogt, *Constraint on Trial: Dirck Volkertsz Coornhert and Religious Freedom*, Sixteenth Century Essays and Studies, 52 (Kirksville, MO: Truman State University, 2000), pp. 49–52.

78 See the visual and textual material presented in Pierre Vinken and Lucy Schlüter, "Pieter Bruegels *Nestrover* en de mens die de dood tegemoet treedt," in *Nederlands Kunsthistorisch Jaarboek* 47 (1996): 55–79; also Kjell Boström, "Das Sprichwort vom Vogelnest," *Konsthistorisk tidskrift* 18 (1949): 77–89.

79 Vienna, Kunsthistorisches Museum, Inv. GG 5822a.

80 Erwin Panofsky, *Early Netherlandish Painting: Its Origins and Character* (Cambridge, MA: Harvard University Press, 1958), 1: 333; Lottlisa Behling, *Die Pflanze in der mittelalterlichen Tafelmalerei* (Cologne: Böhlau, 1967), p. 66; Robert Koch, "Flower Symbolism in the Portinari Altar," *Art Bulletin* 46 (1964): 71; and Margaret L. Koster, *Hugo van der Goes and the Procedures of Art and Salvation* (New York: Harvey Miller, 2008), p. 65.

81 Vinken and Schlüter, "Pieter Bruegels *Nestrover*," p. 67.

82 *De rerum natura*, 2.1–2; Lucretius, *The Way Things Are: The* De rerum natura *of Titus Lucretius Carus*, trans. Rolfe Humphries (Bloomington: Indiana University Press, 1968), p. 52; on the reception of this figure of thought, see Hans Blumenberg, *Shipwreck with Spectator: Paradigm of a Metaphor for Existence*, trans. Steven Rendall (Cambridge, MA: MIT Press, 1997), pp. 26–46.

83 Plato, *Theaetetus*, 174ab; trans. Harold W. Fowler (Cambridge, MA: Harvard University Press, 1921), p. 121. On this episode, see Hans Blumenberg, *Das Lachen der Thrakerin: Eine Urgeschichte der Theorie* (Frankfurt: Suhrkamp, 1987).

84 See "Law and the Human," chapter 11.

85 Brussels, Koninklijke Bibliotheek Albert I, Inv. S. V. 65747; see Wolfgang Wegner and Herbert Pée, "Die Zeichnungen des David Vinckboons," *Münchner Jahrbuch der bildenden Kunst* (1980): 73, no. 31; and Konrad Renger in Fedja Anzelewsky, ed. *Pieter Bruegel d. Ä als Zeichner: Herkunft und Nachfolge*, exh. cat. (Berlin: Staatliche Museen Preußischer Kulturbesitz, Kupferstichkabinett and Gebr. Mann, 1975), pp. 180–81, no. 283. The Rijksmuseum holds a similar, perhaps earlier drawing by Vinckboons (Amsterdam, Rijksprentenkabinet, Inv. 58: 04; Wegner and Pée, p. 70, no. 22). On the prints after Vinckboons that relate to Bruegel's painting, see Eddy de Jongh and Ger Luijten, *Mirror of Everyday Life: Genreprints in the Netherlands 1550–1700*, trans. Michael Hoyle, exh. cat. (Amsterdam: Rijksmuseum; Ghent: Snoeck-Ducaju & Zoon, 1997), pp. 108–10.

86 *The Illustrated Bartsch*, 53, *Netherlandish School, Pre-Rembrandt Etchers*, ed. Walter L. Strauss (New York: Abaris, 1978), p. 399, no. 3; Gerdien Wuestman identified the etcher as Hessel Gerritz (*Dawn of the Golden Age: Northern Netherlandish Art 1580–1620*, ed. Ger Luijten et al., exh. cat. [Amsterdam: Rijksmuseum; Zwolle: Waanders, 1993], p. 614, no. 286).

87 Pascal Boyer, *Barricades mystérieuses et pièges à pensée: Introduction à l'analyse des épopées fang* (Paris: Société d'Ethnologie, 1988), pp. 55–56; discussed in Alfred Gell, "Vogel's Net," in *The Art of Anthropology: Essays and Diagrams*, ed. Eric Hirsch, London School of Economics Monographs on Social Anthropology, 67 (London: Bloomsbury Academic, 1999), p. 201.

88 Thomas Boteler, *Narrative of a Voyage of Discovery to Africa and Arabia, Performed in His Majesty's Ships* Leven *and* Barracouta *from 1821 to 1826* (London: Richard Bentley, 1835), 1: 82. Boteler, who sketched the trap, reports that the weight of the hippopotamus makes the traps for it effective: "The skin, however hard and tough, is not proof against the violence with which a falling body of such weight comes in contact with the point of the stake: the wood is splintered in the wound, but it has already deeply penetrated some vital part" (p. 85).

89 Gell, "Vogel's Net," p. 201.

90 Gell, "Vogel's Net," pp. 187–213.

91 On different forms of imitation used in hunting, see Michael Taussig, *Mimesis and Alterity: A Peculiar History of the Senses* (London: Routledge, 1993), pp. 11–14.

92 Budapest, Szépmüvészeti Museum, Prints and Drawings, Inv. 102 (E19–13a); see Jane S. Peters, "The Early Drawings of Augustin Hirschvogel," *Master Drawings* 17 (1979): 369 and 389 (cat. no. 46). Produced in Nuremberg and traceable to the sixteenth-century collection of the Nuremberger Paul de Praun, the drawings served as models for stained glass. I am grateful to Jasper van Putten for this reference.

93 The large literature on proverbs in Bruegel began even before the *Netherlandish Proverbs* was acquired by the Berlin museums in 1916; see Louis Maeterlinck, "Nederlandsche spreekwoorden handelend voorgesteld door Pieter Breughel den Oude," *Verslagen en Mededelingen der Koninklijke Vlaamsche Academie voor taal- en letterkunde* (1903), pp. 109–29. For overviews, see Rainald Grosshans, *Pieter Bruegel d. Ä: Die niederländischen Sprichwörter* (Berlin: Gemäldegalerie, Staatliche Museen zu Berlin, 2003), pp. 20–31; and more recently Margaret D. Carroll, *Painting and Politics in Northern Europe: Van Eyck, Bruegel, Rubens, and Their Contemporaries* (University Park, PA: Pennsylvania State University Press, 2008), pp. 33–46.

94 Staatliche Museen zu Berlin, Gemäldegalerie, Inv. 1720; Friedländer (Bruegel), no. 12. The title *Netherlandish Proverbs* derives from the first publication of the work: Max J. Friedländer, "Ein neues Bild von Pieter Bruegel," *Zeitschrift für bildende Kunst* 49 (1913–14) (= n.s. 25): 9–12.

95 By Fraenger's account, all proverbs in the Berlin picture underscore one: the world is turned upside down (*Das Bild der 'niederländischen Sprichwörter'*).

96 Berlin, Staatliche Museen zu Berlin, Kupferstichkabinett KdZ 713; Hans Mielke, *Pieter Bruegel. Die Zeichnungen* (Turnhout: Bepols, 1996), no. 66. *The Beekeepers'* relevance to *The Peasant and the Bird Thief* was first proposed by Georges Hulin de Loo and René van Bastelaer, *Pieter Bruegel l'Ancien, son œuvre et son temps* (Brussels: G. van Oest, 1907), p. 277.

97 "[D]ije den nest Weet / dije[n] Weeten dijen Roft dij hewten."

98 "Die den nest weet die weethen / Maer die hem rooft die heeften."

99 F.W.H. Hollstein, *Dutch and Flemish Etchings, Engravings, and Woodcuts, Circa 1450–1700*, 37, *David Vinck(e)boons to Hendrik Visjager*, compiled Christian Schuckman, ed. D. de Hoop Scheffer (Roosendall, Koninklijke van Poll, 1991), p. 38; Maria Simon, "Claes Jansz. Vischer" (Ph.D. diss., Freiburg University, 1958), cat. 15; Vinckboons's drawing, now in Stuttgart (Graphische Sammlung der Staatsgalerie, Inv. C64/1326), dates to around 1608; see Wegner and Pée, "Die Zeichnungen des David Vinckboons," pp. 81–82, no. 38.

100 Jan Grauls, *Volkstaal en volksleven in het werk van Pieter Bruegel* (Antwerpen: Standaard-Boekhandel, 1957), pp. 165–67, 173–74.

101 *Monty Python's Flying Circus*, season one (1969), episode 3.

102 Bastelaer, *The Prints of Peter Bruegel*, no. 1; New Hollstein (Bruegel), no. 1.

103 "Tute lepus es, et pulpamentum quaeris" (Erasmus); see Martha Sullivan, "Bruegel's Proverbs: Art and Audience in the Northern Renaissance: Pieter Bruegel

the Elder," *Art Bulletin* 73 (1991): 431–66. Earlier, Philipp Fehl had adduced a different adage, "Duos insequens lepores, neutrum capit" ("He who chases two hares catches neither"), also from Erasmus ("Peculiarities in the Relation of Text and Image in Two Prints of Pieter Bruegel: The Rabbit Hunt and Fides," *North Carolina Museum of Art, Bulletin* 9 [1970]: 26.

104 Klaus Demus, "Pieter Bruegel d. Ä. im Kunsthistorisches Museum," in *Pieter Bruegel d. Ä. im Kunsthistorischen Museum Wien*, ed. Wilfried Seipel (Vienna: Kunsthistorisches Museum; Milan: Skira, 1998), p. 122; translation my own. In the English edition of the book, some of these nuances—and the scare quotes—are missing. Demus goes on to revise his own opinion (first published in 1982) that the iconographic "handle" is lost, reading the painting in light of John 3:29ff.

105 Franz Kafka, *The Trial*, trans. Willa Muir, Edwin Muir, and E. M. Butler (New York: Schocken, 1992), p. 229.

106 ". . . dieser Eingang war nur für dich bestimmt," Kafka, *The Trial*, p. 215.

107 Gershom Scholem, Letter to Walter Benjamin, September 20, 1934, *The Correspondence of Walter Benjamin and Gershom Scholem 1932–1940*, trans. Gary Smith and Andre Lefevere (Cambridge, MA: Harvard University Press, 1992), p. 142. On this famous exchange, see expecially Giorgio Agamben, *State of Exception*, trans. Kevin Attell (Chicago: University of Chicago Press, 2005), pp. 63–64; and Eric L. Santner, *On the Psychotheology of Everyday Life: Reflections on Freud and Rosenzweig* (Chicago: University of Chicago Press, 2001), pp. 37–45.

108 Benjamin to Scholem, July 20, 1934, *Correspondence*, p. 128

109 Benjamin to Scholem, August 11, 1934, *Correspondence*, p. 135

110 Walter Benjamin, "Franz Kafka: On the Tenth Anniversary of His Death" (1934), in *Illuminations*, ed. Hannah Arendt, trans. Harry Zohn (London: Jonathan Cape, 1970), p. 122.

111 Benjamin to Scholem, August 11, 1934, *Correspondence*, p. 135

112 Benjamin to Scholem, August 11, 1934, *Correspondence*, p. 135; on Holy Writ as "lost" or "mislaid," see Benjamin, "Franz Kafka," p. 139.

113 Anson Rabinbach, "Introduction," in *Correspondence*, p. xxx.

CHAPTER 3. WORLD TIME

1 In documents and in paintings signed with his name (whether or not by his hand), the artist's name is "Jheronimus"—the Dutch spelling of Latin *Hieronymus*. He seems to have been called "Joen," "Jonen," or (more rarely) "Jeroen"; see Godfried Christiaan Maria van Dijck, "Hieronymus van Aken / Hieronymus Bosch: His Life and 'Portraits'," in *Hieronymus Bosch: New Insights into His Life and Work*, ed. Jos Koldeweij and Bernard Vermet (Rotterdam: Museum Boijmans Van Beuningen; Ghent: Ludion, 2001), p. 10. The year of his birth—after 1450 and not later than 1457—has been calculated on the basis of his being mentioned as a person legally of age in an alderman's deed in 1481: this indicates (according to 's-Hertogenbosch law) he was by 1481 twenty-four or older (Ester Vink, "Hieronymus Bosch's Life in 's-Hertogenbosch," in *Bosch: New Insights*, ed. Koldeweij and Vermet, p. 20). The literature on this artist is vast and uniquely contentious. Everything is fiercely disputed, from the subjects and meanings of individual works through the general nature of his art. Most scholars agree at least that the outlines of his autograph oeuvre are highly nebulous. Already the earliest description of Bosch's artistry warns of copyists and imitators (see "Disparities," chapter 5), and recent technical analyses, including those underway by the Bosch Research and Conservation Project (boschproject.org), identify multiple hands working at different stages in the making of individual works. Walter S. Gibson's *Hieronymus Bosch: An Annotated Bibliography* (Boston, MA: G. K. Hall, 1983) is a useful guide to the literature published before 1982. Documents related to Bosch and his family, collaborators, and patrons have been gathered and translated by Godfried Christiaan Maria van Dijck, *Op zoek naar Jheronimus van Aken alias Bosch: de feiten: familie, vrienden en opdrachtgevers ca. 1400–ca. 1635* (Zaltbommel: Europese Bibliothek, 2001). Reliable English-language surveys of the artist are: Walter S. Gibson, *Hieronymus Bosch* (Oxford: Oxford University Press, 1972); Jos Koldeweij, Paul Vandenbroeck, and Bernard Vermet, *Hieronymus Bosch: The Complete Paintings and Drawings* (Ghent: Ludion; Rotterdam: NAi, 2001); and Larry Silver, *Hieronymus Bosch* (New York: Abbeville, 2006). For its extensive bibliography of possible early sources for Bosch's works, and for judicious analyses of individual works, I have often consulted Roger H. Marijnissen and Paul Ruyffelaere, *Hieronymus Bosch: The Complete Works*, trans. Ted Atkins et al. (Antwerp: Mercatorfonds, 1987). In the absence of a new definitive catalogue raisonné, I list works (where possible) as catalogued in Max J. Friedländer, *Early Netherlandish Painting*, 5, *Geertgen tot Sint Jans and Jerome Bosch*, ed. Geert Lemmens, trans. Heinz Norden (Leiden: A. W. Sijthoff, 1969), henceforth referred to as Friedländer (Bosch).

2 On margins as site for mundane imagery, see especially Lilian M. Randall, *Images in the Margins of Gothic Manuscripts*, California Studies in the History of Art, 4 (Berkeley: University of California Press, 1966); Meyer Schapiro (reviewing Randall in 1970), "Marginal Images and Drôlerie," in *Late Antique, Early Christian and Medieval Art: Selected Papers* (New York: George Braziller, 1979), pp. 196–98; Michael Camille, *Image on the Edge: The Margins of Medieval Art* (London: Reaktion Books, 1992); Lucy Freeman Sandler, "The Study of Marginal Imagery: Past, Present, and Future," *Studies in Iconography* 18 (1997): 1–49; and Christa Grössinger, *The World Upside Down: English Misericords* (London: Harvey Miller, 1997) and *eadem*, *Humor and Folly in Secular and Profane Prints of Northern Europe, 1430–1540* (London: Harvey Miller, 2002).

3 Prado, Museo del Prado, cat. no. 2052; Friedländer (Bosch), no. 111. An exact copy of the Prado *Hay Wain* hangs now in El Escorial (Inv. B 154; Friedländer [Bosch], nos. 111a–c); painted flatly and with no changes to the composition established in the Prado picture, it was probably made some decades after Bosch's death; see Carmen Garrido and Roger van Schoute, *Bosch at the Museo del Prado* (Madrid: Museo del Prado and Aldeasa, 2001), p. 156.

4 Augustine, *The City of God*, trans. Gerald Walsh et al. (New York: Doubleday, 1958), p. 325; the idea has its origins in the New Testament, where Paul advises living as "strangers" on earth (Heb. 11:13–16).

5 See most notably Guillaume de Deguilleville's *Pèlerinage de la vie humaine*, written in 1330–31 and widely circulated, including in the Middle Dutch translation *Het boeck vanden pelgherym*, published in Haarlem in 1486 by Jacob Bellaert. On pilgrimage as a controlling

motif in literature, art, and thought of the period, see Siegfried Wenzel, "The Pilgrimage of Life as a Late Medieval Genre," *Medieval Studies* 35 (1973): 370–88; and Reindert L. Falkenburg, *Joachim Patinir: Landscape as an Image of the Pilgrimage of Life*, trans. Michael Hoyle, OCULI: Studies in the Arts of the Low Countries, 2 (Amsterdam and Philadelphia, PA: John Benjamins, 1988), pp. 85–91.

6 Paul Vandenbroeck adduced much historical evidence for a negative moral reading of Bosch's peddler, in *Jheronimus Bosch: Tussen volksleven en stadscultuur* (Berchem: EPO, 1988), pp, 62–68; but more recently, he stressed the ambiguity of the figure, pointing out its exemplarity as a "sinful human who looks back at what is behind him and is prompted to repent" ("Hieronymus Bosch: The Wisdom of the Riddle," in *Bosch: Complete Paintings and Drawings*, ed. Koldeweij, Vandenbroeck, and Vermet, p. 186). Eric de Bruyn, in the most detailed account yet written of the Prado *Hay Wain*, stresses similarly that repentance was built into Bosch's peddler; see *De vergeten beeldentaal van Jheronimus Bosch. De Symboliek van de* Hooiwagen-*triptiek en de Rotterdamse* Marskramer-*tondo verklaard vanuit Middelnederlandse teksten* ('s-Hertogenbosch: Adr. Heinen, 2001), pp. 165–255; also *idem*, "Hieronymus Bosch So-Called Prodigal Son Tondo: The Pedlar as Repentant Sinner," in *Bosch: New Insights*, ed. Koldeweij and Vermet, pp. 133–44. For a brief philosophical meditation on bags, see Steven Conor, "Rough Magic: Bags," in *The Everyday Life Reader*, ed. Ben Highmore (London: Routledge, 2002), pp. 346–51.

7 On temporal imagery of "life," see Hans Blumenberg, *Lebenszeit und Weltzeit* (Frankfurt am Main: Suhrkamp, 1986).

8 Michael Mollat, *The Poor in the Middle Ages: An Essay in Social History*, trans. Arthur Goldhammer (New Haven, CT: Yale University Press, 1986), pp. 247–50; Walter Prevenier and Wim Blockmans, *The Burgundian Netherlands*, trans. Peter King and Yvette Mead (Cambridge, UK, and New York: Cambridge University Press, 1986), pp. 183–87; on attitudes toward the poor in 's-Hertogenbosch, see Ester Vink and Aart Vos, "Life in the Town," in *The World of Bosch*, ed. Jan van Oudheusden and Aart Vos, trans. Tony Burrett and Heather van Tress ('s-Hertogenbosch: Adr. Heinen, 2001), pp. 42–44.

9 Paris, Louvre, Inv. 1917; Friedländer (Bruegel), no. 43.

10 Mollat, *Poor in the Middle Ages*, p. 246; Vandenbroeck, "The Wisdom of the Riddle," *Bosch: Complete Paintings and Drawings*, ed. Koldeweij, Vandenbroeck, and Vermet, pp. 113–14.

11 Mollat, *Poor in the Middle Ages*, p. 291.

12 Today, the triptych is kept permanently open. In addition to making the closed state visually unavailable, this static display extinguishes the work's built-in mobility, which was engineered to amplify and explain the painted images of motion centrally displayed in both the closed and open states.

13 The Prado *Hay Wain* was acquired by Philip in 1570 along with other works from the collection of Felipe de Guevara; in 1574 it was brought to El Escorial, where it remained until 1939; see Garrido and Van Schoute, *Bosch at the Museo del Prado*, p. 123, with bibliography.

14 Joseph de Sigüenza, *Tercera parte de la Historia de la Orden de San Gerónimo, Doctor de la Iglesia* (Madrid: Imprenta Real, 1605), p. 839; *Historia de la Orden de San Jerónimo*, ed. Juan Catalina Garcia (Madrid: Bailly-Balliére, 1909), 2: 637; trans. James Snyder, in *Bosch in Perspective*, ed. James Snyder, The Artists in Perspective Series (Englewood Cliffs, NJ: Prentice-Hall, 1973), p. 38.

15 On the effect on the visual imagination of the *Tabula Cebetis*, see Reinhart Schleier, *Tabula Cebetis, oder "Spiegel des Menschlichen Lebens darin Tugent und untugent abgemalet ist"*, Studien zur Rezeption einer antiken Bildbeschreibung im 16. und 17. Jahrhundert (Berlin: Gebr. Mann, 1973); on the text and its translations see Sandra Sider, ed., *Cebes' Tablet: Facsimiles of the Greek Text, and of Selected Latin, French, English, Spanish, German, Dutch, and Polish Translations* (New York: Renaissance Society of America, 1979).

16 Ambrosio de Morales, "The Panel of Cebes," trans. James Snyder, in *Bosch in Perspective*, ed. Snyder, p. 31; for the Spanish original, see van Dijck, *Op zoek naar Jheronimus van Aken*, pp. 109–209. Republished in the anonymous *Teatro moral de la vida humana* (Antwerp: Verdussen, 1701), Morales's text first entered the modern Bosch literature through Juan de Contreras ("Algo más sobre la fortuna del Bosco en España," *Boletín de la Real Academia de la Historia* 123 [1948]: 285–94); Abdon M. Salazar attributed it to Morales ("El Bosco y Ambrosio de Morales," *Archivo español de arte* 28 [1955]: 117–38). Though first published in 1586, Morales's translation dates from much earlier, probably from the period when *The Hay Wain* was in the collection of Felipe de Guevara in Salamanca, where Morales studied between 1524 and 1531 (Salazar, p. 124).

17 Morales, "Panel," p. 31.

18 Morales, "Panel," p. 32.

19 "De wereld is een hooiberg; elk plukt ervan, wat hij kan krijgen," see Charles de Tolnay, *Hieronymus Bosch* (New York: Reynal, 1966), p. 356; see also Egbert Haverkamp Begemann, *European Drawings and Watercolors in the Yale University Art Gallery, 1500–1900* (New Haven, CT: Yale University Press, 1970), pl. 260. "Zolang de hooiwagen beladen is, krijgt men er niet genoeg van"; see Paul Vandenbroeck *Jheronimus Bosch. De verlossing van de wereld* (Ghent and Amsterdam: Ludion, 2002), p. 226, citing the theme of the 1563 Ommegang of Antwerp.

20 Morales, "Panel," p. 31.

21 Now in El Escorial, the tapestries were most probably woven in 1566 in Brussels for Antoine Perrenot, Cardinal of Granvella, for his palace in Malines—although Otto Kurz, who published this provenance, proposed that (not bearing Granvella's coat of arms) the surviving weavings are a different set, perhaps one known to have been woven for the Duke of Alba in 1568 ("Four Tapestries after Hieronymus Bosch," *Journal of the Warburg and Courtauld Institutes* 30 [1967]: p. 152); however, on the high probability of the Granvella provenance, see, most recently, Paulina Junquera de Vega and Concha Herrero Carretero, *Siglo XVI*, Catalogo de tápices del Patrimonio Nacional, 1 (Madrid: Editorial Patrimonio Nacional, 1986), pp. 263–67. The *Hay Wain* tapestry was first associated with Bosch's triptych by Ludwig Baldass (*Jheronimus Bosch*, 2nd rev., ed. Günther Heinz [Vienna: Schroll, 1959], p. 230).

22 An inventory drawn up in 1542 for King Francis I describes very precisely an earlier edition of the tapestry series, thus establishing a *terminus ante quem* for the Boschian prototype.

23 Paris, Louvre, M.N.R. 399.

24 On the globe as a figure of politics and the political, see Peter Sloterdijk, *Sphären—Makrosphärologie, 2, Globen* (Frankfurt am Main: Suhrkamp, 1999), esp. pp. 465–592.

25 On the origins of this term, see chapter 1, n2.

26 For a classic treatment of this distinction, see Alexandre Koyré, *From the Closed World to the Infinite Universe* (Baltimore: Johns Hopkins University Press, 1957).

27 On this imagery, see Yona Pinson, "Fall of the Angels and Creation of Eve in Bosch's Eden: Meaning and Iconographic Sources," in *Flanders in a European Perspective. Manuscript Illumination around 1400 in Flanders and Abroad*, ed. Maurits Smeyers and Bert Cardon (Leuven: Peeters, 1995), pp. 693–707.

28 See "Beginnings," chapter 7.

29 Blumenberg, *Lebenszeit und Weltzeit*, pp. 48–69 and 72.

30 The gospel image of a "Son of Man" arriving in "clouds" derives from the Old Testament prophecy of Daniel 13:14.

31 On the Autun tympanum (see fig. 45), see especially Willibald Sauerländer, "Über die Komposition des Weltgerichts Tympanons in Autun," *Zeitschrift für Kunstgeschichte* 29, no. 4 (1966): 261–94; Bernhard Rupprecht, *Romanische Skulptur in Frankreich* (Munich: Hirmer, 1975), pp. 111ff., with bibliography; and Don Denny, "The Last Judgment Tympanum at Autun: Its Sources and Meaning," *Speculum* 57 (1982): 532–47.

32 The most categorical exposition of this understanding of the cathedral is Hans Sedlmayr, *Die Entstehung der Kathedrale* (Zurich: Atlantis, 1950), esp. pp. 95–164; on the historical context of Sedlmayr's views and on responses by other scholars to them, see Roland Recht, *Believing and Seeing: The Art of the Gothic Cathedral*, trans. Mary Whittall (Chicago: University of Chicago Press, 2008), pp. 19–30.

33 Cologne, Wallraf-Richartz Museum, WRM 66. Much admired in the nineteenth century, Lochner's panel originally formed the center of a winged retable. By 1764—before its purchase in 1803 by Ferdinand Franz Wallraf from the secularized church where it hung—it had been separated from its wings; those are now split between the Städelsches Kunstinstitut, Frankfurt (Inv. 821–832) and the Alte Pinokothek, Munich (WAF 501–502). Lochner probably made the retable for the altar of the Brotherhood of Saint Catherine in Cologne, to celebrate its founding in 1435. See Ludwig Gompf, "Lochners *Altar der Katharinenbruderschaft*," *Wallraf-Richartz-Jahrbuch* 58 (1997): 205–12; and Julien Chapius, *Stefan Lochner: Image Making in Fifteenth-Century Cologne* (Turnhout: Brepols, 2004), pp. 41–54 and 262–64 (cat. no. 1).

34 The altarpiece was recorded in 1606–8 by David Everswijn, Bartholomeus Loeff, and Jacob van Balen in their (unfinished and unpublished) *Historia Chronologica Oppidi Buscoducis* ('s-Hertogenbosch, Rijksarchief Coll. Aanw. 1889, no. 63); it was subsequently mentioned by Jean-Baptiste Gramaye (*Taxandria* [Brussels: Rutger Velpius, 1610], p. 6) and Jacobus van Oudenhoven (*Beschryvinge der stadt ende meyere van 'sHertogen-Bossche* [Amsterdam: Broer Jansz, 1649], p. 25). During an episcopal visit to the church in 1615, a panel showing "the creation of the world" was ordered to be removed "from behind the episcopal chair," due to its excessive nudity, suggesting, first, that this is the altarpiece mentioned by Everswijn et al. and that it had already been moved once (from the choir to the church aisle), and, second, that this work of shifting location bore some similarity to *The Garden of Delights*, with its abundance of nudes. All traces of this work are lost. See Jan Mosmans, *De St. Janskerk te 's-Hertogenbosch* ('s-Hertogenbosch: Mosmans, 1931), p. 357–58; Pater Gerlach, "De bronnen voor het leven en het werk van Jeroen Bosch," *Brabantia* 16 (1967), p. 100; and Jos Koldeweij, "Hieronymus Bosch and His City," in *Bosch: Complete Paintings and Drawings*, ed. Koldeweij, Vandenbroeck, and Vermet, pp. 66–69.

35 Mosmans, p. 358n1; Koldeweij, p. 69, citing an "Ode to the Church at 's-Hertogenbosch"; also Fernando Marìas, "Bosch and Dracontius' *De Creatione Mundi Hexameron*," in *Jheronimus Bosch: His Sources* ('s-Hertogenbosch: Jheronimus Bosch Art Center, 2010), pp. 247–48.

36 The Church of Saint John suffered iconoclastic attacks in 1566, but the destruction and removal of its furnishings was undertaken chiefly by troops of the States General in 1629; see Jan van Oudheusden, "The Lost Son," in *The World of Bosch*, ed. Oudheusden and Vos, p. 138.

37 Lille, Rijssel, Archives départementales du Nord, B. 2185, fol. 230v; Alexandre Pinchart, "Bosch (Jérôme, Joemen, Moen)," *Archives des arts, sciences et lettres*, Documents inédits publiés et annotés. 1st ser., 1 (Ghent: Hebbelynck, 1860): 268; Gerlach, "De bronnen," p. 55.

38 Philip had visited s'-Hertogenbosch at least three times earlier: when he was knighted in the Church of Saint John in 1481, with his stepmother, Bianca Maria Sfortz, in 1494, and when the city paid homage to him as duke in 1496; see Dirk Bax, *Hieronymus Bosch and Lucas Cranach: Two Last Judgment Triptychs*, trans. M. A. Bax-Botha, Verhandelingen der Koninkliijke Nederlandse Akademie von Wetenschappen, Letterkunde, new ser., 117 (Amsterdam: North-Holland, 1983), p. 318.

39 ". . . pour son tres noble plaisir" (Gerlach, "De bronnen," p. 55); for a bibliography of this phrase, see Marijnissen and Ruyffelaere, *Hieronymus Bosch*, p. 13.

40 Vienna, Akademie der Bildenden Künste, Inv. No. 579–581, Friedländer (Bosch), no. 84.

41 Renate Trnek, *Das Weltgerichtstriptychon von Hieronymus Bosch* (Vienna: Gemäldegalerie der Akademie der bildenden Künste; Rosenheim: Rosenheimer Verlagshaus, 1988), p. 28.

42 Lucas Cranach the Elder copied a similar but probably not identical Boschian *Last Judgment*. Dirk Bax, in his extensive study of the Vienna picture, concluded that Cranach and the painter of the Vienna picture worked from the lost triptych commissioned by Philip the Fair, and that the patron for both these imitations was Margaret of Austria, who may have ordered the spinoffs for Philip's two sons, Charles V and Ferdinand II (*Hieronymus Bosch and Lucas Cranach*, pp. 326–27).

43 On the format's symbolism, see especially Klaus Lankheit, *Das Triptychon als Pathosformel*, Abhandlungen der Heidelberger Akademie der Wissenschaften, Philosophisch-Historische Klasse, 4 (Heidelberg: Carl Winter, 1959); and, more recently, Lynn F. Jacobs, *Opening Doors: The Early Netherlandish Triptych Reinterpreted* (University Park, PA: Penn State University Press, 2011).

44 On judgment (*Urteil*) as primal division, see Florian Klinger, *Urteilen* (Zürich and Berlin: Diaphanes, 2011).

45 Gdańsk, National Museum, Inv. No. SD/413/M; Max J. Friedländer, *Early Netherlandish Painting, 6, Hans Memlinc and Gerard David*, trans. Heinz Norden (Leiden: Sijthoff, 1971), no. 8; Dirk De Vos, *Hans Memling: The Complete Works* (Ghent: Ludion, 1994), pp. 82–89 (no. 4).

46 In the *Rijmbijbel* of Jacob van Maerlant, written in the mid-thirteenth century, when Adam woke after Eve's creation, he prophesied "doomsday . . . with fire will come" (cited in Bax, *Hieronymus Bosch and Lucas Cranach*, p. 55).

47 Tertullian, *De spectaculis* 30, trans. T. R. Glover, in Tertullian and Minucius Felix,

Apology, De spectaculis, ed. W.C.A. Kerr, Loeb Classical Library (Cambridge, MA: Harvard University Press, 1977), pp. 297–99.

48 See "Anger," chapter 5.

49 Peter Sloterdijk, *Rage and Time: A Psychopolitical Investigation*, trans. Mario Wenning (New York: Columbia University Press, 2010), pp. 92–94.

50 See Jean Delumeau's remarkable survey of Christian "contempt for the world," *Sin and Fear: The Emergence of a Western Guilt Culture 13th–18th Centuries*, trans. Eric A. Nicholson (New York: St. Martin's, 1990), pp. 6–186 and passim.

51 On the play of woman as "nothing" in Jerome, see Patricia Cox Miller, "The Blazing Body: Ascetic Desire in Jerome's Letter to Eustochium," *Journal of Early Christian Studies* 1 (1993): 21–45.

52 Ghent, Museum voor Schone Kunsten, No. 1908-H; Friedländer (Bosch), no. 97. On the iconography of the panel, see Wendy Ruppel, "Salvation through Imitation: The Meaning of Bosch's *St. Jerome in the Wilderness*," *Simiolus* 18 (1988): 4–12.

53 *De spectaculis* 29; trans. Glover, in Tertullian and Minucius Felix, p. 295.

54 See Jean Delumeau, *La Peur en Occident (XIVe–XVIIIe siècles): une cité assiégée* (Paris: Fayard, 1978), the prequel to Delumeau's *Sin and Fear*.

55 Augustine, *In Joannis evangelium tractatus*, Tractatus 2, 1.11; cited and discussed in Martin Heidegger, *The Essence of Reasons*, trans. Terrence Malick (Evanston, IL: Northwestern University Press, 1969), p. 57.

56 Carl Schmitt, *The Concept of the Political*, exp. ed., trans. George Schwab (Chicago: University of Chicago Press, 2007), p. 26.

57 Schmitt, *Concept*, p. 33.

58 Schmitt, *Concept*, p. 30; on the theological (and arguably spectral) nature of the enemy in Schmitt, see especially Heinrich Meier, *The Lesson of Carl Schmitt: Four Chapters on the Distinction between Political Theology and Political Philosophy*, trans. Marcus Brainard (Chicago: University of Chicago Press, 1998), pp. 26–65; and Jacques Derrida, *Politics of Friendship*, trans. George Collins (London and New York: Verso, 1997), pp. 116–17.

59 Schmitt's kinship with Bosch was recognized by Ernst Jünger; see his Letter to Carl Schmitt, December 13, 1933, in *Briefe 1930–1983: Ernst Jünger—Carl Schmitt*, ed. Helmuth Kiesel (Stuttgart: Klett-Cotta, 1999), pp. 18–19.

60 Meier, *Lesson of Carl Schmitt*, pp. 42–43 and passim.

61 Carl Schmitt, *Political Theology: Four Chapters on the Concept of Sovereignty*, trans. George Schwab (Chicago: University of Chicago Press, 1985).

62 De Bruyn, *De vergeten beeldentaal van Jheronimus Bosch*, pp. 99–102.

63 *De kroniek van het St. Geertruiklooster te 's-Hertogenbosch. Die chronijcke der Stadt ende Meijerije van 's-Hertogenbosch. Een tekstuitgave*, ed. H. van Bavel et al. ('s-Hertogenbosch: Stadsarchief 's-Hertogenbosch, 2002), pp. 51–52 (fol. 40v.).

64 Herman Pleij, *Dreaming of Cockaigne: Medieval Fantasies of the Perfect Life*, trans. Diane Webb (New York: Columbia University Press, 2001), p. 7.

65 Vandenbroeck, *Jheronimus Bosch: Tussen volksleven en stadscultuur*, pp. 68–73; De Bruyn, *De vergeten beeldentaal van Jheronimus Bosch*, pp. 106–15.

66 A chief patron of these activities was the Brotherhood of Our Dear Lady of 's-Hertogenbosch, as recorded in its account books: 1431–32, fol. 9v; 1434–35, fol. 40v; 1438–39, fol. 87; 1440–41, fol. 124, 1441–42, fol. 141v; 1503–4, fol. 191v (see Van Dijck, *Op zoek naar Jheronimus van Aken*, pp. 143, 144, 146, 147, 149, and 175).

67 Oxford, Bodleian Library, MS. Douce 346, fol. 236r. About eighty richly illustrated manuscripts describing the *Schembartlauf* survive, probably produced for patrician families whose ancestors organized the festivities; see Samuel L. Sumberg, *The Nuremberg Schembart Carnival*, Columbia University Germanic Studies, 12 (New York: Columbia University Press, 1941); Hans-Ulrich Roller, *Der Nürnberger Schembartlauf. Studien zur Fest- und Maskenwesen des späten Mittelalters*, Volksleben, 11 (Tübingen: Tübinger Vereinigung für Volkskunde, 1965), pp. 99–143; and Samuel Kinser, "Presentation and Representation: Carnival at Nuremberg, 1450–1550," *Representations* 13 (1986): 1–41.

68 Pleij, *Dreaming of Cockaigne*, pp. 358–61; also *idem*, *Het gilde van de Blauwe Schuit. Literatuur, volksfeest en burgermoraal in de late middeleeuwen* (Amsterdam: Meulenhoff, 1983). On the tension between the organizers and targets of charivari, see especially Natalie Zemon Davis, *Society and Culture in Early Modern France* (Stanford, CA: Stanford University Press, 1975), pp. 97–123.

69 Davis, *Society and Culture*, pp. 154–87; see also Emmanuel Le Roy Ladurie's classic, *Carnival in Romans*, trans. Mary Feeney (New York: George Braziller, 1997).

70 Vienna, Österreichische Nationalbibliothek, MS 2583, fol. 349v; on the manuscript and its illuminator, see Gregory T. Clark, *Made in Flanders: The Master of the Ghent Privileges and Manuscript Painting in the Southern Netherlands in the Time of Philip the Good*, Ars Nova: Studies in Late Medieval and Renaissance Northern Painting and Illumination (Turnhout: Brepols, 2000).

71 Jacques Du Clercq, cited in Georges Chastellain, *Oeuvres de Georges Chastellain*, ed. Kervyn de Lettenhove (Brussels: F. Heussner, 1863–66), 3:35n1; cited in Peter Arnade, *Realms of Ritual: Burgundian Ceremony and Civic Life in Late Medieval Ghent* (Ithaca, NY: Cornell University Press, 1996), p. 127.

72 Arnade, *Realms of Ritual*, pp. 145–58.

73 For example, Friedländer (Bosch), p. 88.

74 Gramaye, *Taxandria*, p. 6; Van Oudenhoven, *Beschryvinge der stadt ende meyere van 'sHertogen-bosch*, p. 25; also Gerd Unverfehrt, *Hieronymus Bosch: Rezeption seiner Kunst im frühen 16. Jahrhundert* (Berlin: Mann, 1980), p. 20.

75 Garrido and Van Schoute, *Bosch at the Museo del Prado*, p. 123; Unverfehrt, *Hieronymus Bosch*, pp. 18–19, 239.

76 Dagmar Eichberger, *Leben mit Kunst, Wirken durch Kunst. Sammelwesen und Hofkunst unter Margarete von Österreicht, Regentin der Niederlande*, Burgundica, 5 (Turnhout: Brepols, 2002), p. 106.

77 Bethany Aram, *Juana the Mad: Sovereignty and Dynasty in Renaissance Europe* (Baltimore: Johns Hopkins University Press, 2005), pp. 35–36.

78 Frédéric Elsig, *Jheronimus Bosch. La question de la chronologie*, Travaux d'Humanisme et Renaissance, 392 (Geneva: Librairie Droz, 2004), p. 31.

79 Felipe de Guevara, *Comentarios de la Pintura*, ed. Antonio Ponz (Madrid: Geronimo Ortega, 1788), p. 43; trans. "Commentaries on Painting," in *Bosch in Perspective*, ed. Snyder, p. 29; on Guevara's statement, see Unverfehrt, *Hieronymus Bosch*, pp. 68–71.

80 Peter Klein, "Dendrochronological Analysis of Works by Hieronymus Bosch and His Followers," in *Bosch: New Insights*, ed. Koldeweij and Vermet, p. 127.

81 Noting this feature, Fritz Koreny and his collaborator (Erwin Pokorny) attribute the painting to an anonymous, left-handed assistant, whom they name the Master of the Prado Hay Wagon (*Hieronymus Bosch: Die Zeichnungen. Werkstadt und Nachfolge bis zum Ende des*

16. Jahrhunderts: catalogue raisonné [Turnhout: Brepols, 2012], pp. 86–95). I prefer to consider *The Hay Wain* as a work executed by multiple collaborators in his shop and trademarked as "Bosch" via the signature to advertise the individual inventiveness for which that brand was known to excel.

82 Ghent, Museum voor Schone Kunsten, Inv. 1902 I T.10A; in this panel (part of a triptych), the Crucifixion retable depicted behind the miraculous Mass of Saint Gregory is unusual in format and precocious in its landscape setting (Anja Sibylle Steinmetz, *Das Altarretabel in der altneiderländischen Malerei. Untersuchung zur Darstellung eines sakralen Requisits vom frühen 15. bis zum späten 16. Jahrhundert* [Weimar: Verlag und Datenbank für Geisteswissenschaften, 1995], p. 101 [cat. TB37]). On the presence of altarpieces on altars, see especially Joseph Braun, *Das christliche Altar in seiner geschichtlichen Entwicklung* (Munich: Koch, 1924), 2: 277–545.

83 The Hague, Mauritshuis, Inv. 875. On Bunel's picture (see fig. 58) and the emergence of the autonomous painting, see Victor I. Stoichita, *The Self-Aware Image: An Insight into Early Modern Meta-Painting*, trans. Anne-Marie Glasheen, Cambridge Studies in New Art History and Criticism (Cambridge, UK: Cambridge University Press, 1997), pp. 114–18; on the prehistory of this emergence, with Bosch as the endpoint, see Hans Belting and Christiane Kruse, *Die Erfindung des Gemäldes. Das erste Jahrhundert der niederländischen Malerei* (Munich: Hirmer, 1994).

84 Rotterdam, Museum Boijmans Van Beuningen, No. 1079; Friedländer (Bosch), no. 103.

85 Ludwig Baldass held that the panel's present octagonal form was not original and that the panel originally formed the back side of an altarpiece wing (*Jheronimus Bosch*, p. 232).

86 Friso Lammertse and Annetje Roorda Boersma, "Jheronimus Bosch, *The Pedlar*: Reconstruction, Restoration and Painting Technique," *Jérôme Bosch et son entourage et autres études*, ed. Hélène Verougstraete and Roger van Schoute, Le dessin sous-jacent et la technologie dans la peinture, 14 (Leuven, Belgium, and Dudley, MA: Peeters, 2003), p. 103; also Friso Lammertse, *Van Eyck to Bruegel. Dutch and Flemish Painting in the Collection of Museum Boymans–van Beuningen, 1400–1550* (Rotterdam: Museum Boymans–Van Beuningen, 1994), no. 16, pp. 90–95.

87 Karel van Mander, *The Lives of the Illustrious Netherlandish and German Painters, from the first edition of the* Schilder-boeck *(1603–1604)*, ed. and trans. Hessel Miedema (Doornspijk: Davaco, 1994), 1: 82 (1604, fol. 206r).

88 Washington, DC, National Gallery, No. 1112 (Friedländer [Bosch], Supp. 135); Paris, Musée du Louvre, R.F. 2218 (Friedländer [Bosch], no. 106); New Haven, Yale University Art Gallery, 1959.15.22 (Friedländer [Bosch], Supp. 131); on the Rotterdam, Paris, and Washington panels, see Klein, "Dendrochronological Analysis," pp. 121–22 and 125.

89 The theme of the central panel, now lost, is the subject of debate; see Lammertse and Boersma, *"The Pedlar,"* pp. 108–9; Johannes Hartau, "A Newly Established Triptych by Hieronymus Bosch," in *Jérôme Bosch*, ed. Verougstraete and Van Schoute, pp. 34–38.

CHAPTER 4. FROM BOSCH TO BRUEGEL

1 Lodovico Guicciardini, *Descrittione di tutti i Paesi Bassi, altrimenti detti Germania Inferiore* (Antwerp: Willem Silvius, 1567), p. 99.

2 *Pictorum aliquot celebrium Germaniae Inferioris effigies* (Antwerp: Hieronymus Cock, 1572), p. 19; on the date of Lampsonius's poems, see Giani Carlo Sciolla and Catarina Volpi, ed. and trans., *Da van Eyck a Brueghel. Scritti sulle arti di Domenico Lampsonio* (Turin: UTET, 2001), pp. 64–65; Van Mander published the poem, in a Dutch translation, in the *Schilder-boeck*, which I quote here (Karel van Mander, *The Lives of the Illustrious Netherlandish and German Painters, from the first edition of the* Schilder-boeck *(1603–1604)*, ed. and trans. Hessel Miedema [Doornspijk: Davaco, 1994], 1: 194 [1604, fol. 234r]).

3 Giorgio Vasari, *Le opere*, ed. G. Milanese (Florence: Sansoni, 1878–85), 5: 439; Vasari probably depended on Lampsonius for his information on Bruegel and Bosch; see Suzanne Sulzberger "Dominique Lampsonius et Italie," in *Miscellanea J. Gessler*, ed. Karel Constant Peeters and Robert Roemans (Deurne: C. Govaerts, 1948), 2: 1187–89.

4 Brussels, Royal Library of Belgium, Print Room, s.II 132 816 folio C; Hans Mielke, *Pieter Bruegel. Die Zeichnungen* (Turnhout: Brepols, 1996), no. 36; René van Bastelaer, *The Prints of Peter Bruegel the Elder. Catalogue Raisonné*, new ed., trans. and rev. Susan Fargo Gilchrist (San Francisco: Alan Wofsy, 1992), no. 131; New Hollstein (Bruegel), no. 27.

5 Felipe de Guevara, *Comentarios de la Pintura*, ed. Antonio Ponz (Madrid: Geronimo Ortega, 1788), pp. 42–43; trans. "Commentaries on Painting," in *Bosch in Perspective*, ed. James Snyder, The Artists in Perspective Series (Englewood Cliffs, NJ: Prentice-Hall, 1973), pp. 28–29.

6 Guevara, *Comentarios*, p. 43; Snyder, p. 29.

7 For example, Hans-Wolfgang von Löhneysen, *Die ältere niederländische Malerei: Künstler und Kritiker* (Eisenach and Kassel: E. Röth, 1956), p. 142–43, 146–47.

8 Berlin, Gemäldegalerie der Staatlichen Museen, No. 1647a; Friedländer (Bosch), no. 101; for the reconstructed altarpiece to which the *Saint John* panel, along with extant sculpted wings by Adriaen van Wesel, probably belonged, see Jos Koldeweij, Paul Vandenbroeck, and Bernard Vermet, *Hieronymus Bosch: The Complete Paintings and Drawings* (Ghent: Ludion; Rotterdam: NAi, 2001), p. 71.

9 Godfried Christiaan Maria van Dijck, *Op zoek naar Jheronimus van Aken alias Bosch: de feiten: familie, vrienden en opdrachtgevers ca. 1400–ca. 1635* (Zaltbommel: Europese Bibliotheek, 2001), p. 182, citing the account books of the Brotherhood of Our Dear Lady of 's-Hertogenbosch, 1509–10, fol. 186–186vo. These references indicate the artist used the name *Bosch* specifically as signature on his works; it is possible that he began to do this after 1504, when documented Burgundian patronage begins; see Godfried Christiaan Maria van Dijck, "Hieronymus van Aken / Hieronymus Bosch: His Life and 'Portraits'," in *Hieronymus Bosch: New Insights into His Life and Work*, ed. Jos Koldeweij and Bernard Vermet (Rotterdam: Museum Boijmans Van Beuningen; Ghent: Ludion, 2001), p. 10.

10 That the artist had apprentices and therefore ran a shop either through, or parallel to, the workshop of his father and uncles is attested to by documents from 1503–4 and 1508–9 referring to "servant boys" (*knechten*) of Bosch receiving payment for their work (Van Dijck, *Op zoek naar Jheronimus van Aken*, pp. 180, 182). On the organization of the artist's shop, see Koldeweij, Vandenbroeck, and Vermet, *Hieronymus Bosch*, pp. 84–99; Frédéric Elsig, *Jheronimus Bosch. La question de la chronologie*, Travaux d'Humanisme et Renaissance, 392 (Geneva:

Zomertentoonstelling St. Jan, 2002), pp. 83–103. On the choir stalls in the church, see Mosmans, pp. 375–82.

7 Berlin, Staatliche Museen zu Berlin, Kupferstichkabinett, KdZ 550 (recto); Stephanie Buck, *Die niederländischen Zeichnungen des 15. Jahrhunderts im Berliner Kupferstichkabinett. Kritischer Katalog*, Die Zeichnungen alter Meister in Berliner Kupferstichkabinett (Turnhout: Brepols, 2001), pp. 207–11 (no. I. 32r); Fritz Koreny, *Hieronymus Bosch: Die Zeichnungen. Werkstadt und Nachfolge bis zum Ende des 16. Jahrhunderts* (Turnhout: Brepols, 2012), pp. 196–97 (no. 9, recto).

8 See "Technique," chapter 6.

9 Julián Zarco Cuevas, "Inventario de las alhajas, relicarios, estatuas, pinturas, tapices y otros objetos de valor y curiosidad donados por el rey don Felipe II al Monasterio de El Escorial Años de 1571 a 1598," *Boletín de la Real Academia de la Historia* 96 (1930): 657 (no. 846); Paul Vandenbroeck, "The Spanish *inventarios reales* and Hieronymus Bosch," in *Hieronymus Bosch: New Insights into His Life and Work*, ed. Jos Koldeweij and Bernard Vermet (Rotterdam: Museum Boijmans Van Beuningen; Ghent: Ludion, 2001), p. 52. In the 1593 inventory, the word *disparates* appears as a descriptor for all five of the shipped works attributed to Bosch; see Vandenbroeck, pp. 53–54. Writing in 1605, Joseph de Sigüenza rejects the word *disparates* as a term for Bosch's art and sees it as typifying the common and trivializing conception of the artist's pictures (*Tercera parte de la Historia de la Orden de San Gerónimo, Doctor de la Iglesia* [Madrid: Imprenta Real, 1605], 2: 837; *Historia de la Orden de San Jerónimo*, ed. Juan Catalina Garcia [Madrid: Bailly-Baillière, 1909], 2: 635).

10 The line appears in the poem beginning "Albuagil del Parnaso," which rails against Quevedo's aesthetic archenemy, Luis de Góngora; see Francisco de Quevedo, *Obra poética*, ed. José Manuel Blecua (Madrid: Editorial Castalia, 1969–71), 2: 1205–9 (no. 853); cited and translated in Helmut Heidenreich, "Hieronymus Bosch in Some Literary Contexts," *Journal of the Warburg and Courtauld Institutes* 33 (1970): 182.

11 Felipe de Guevara, *Comentarios de la Pintura*, ed. Antonio Ponz (Madrid: Geronimo Ortega, 1788), p. 41; trans. "Commentaries on Painting," in James Snyder, in *Bosch in Perspective*, ed. James Snyder, The Artists in Perspective Series (Englewood Cliffs, NJ: Prentice-Hall, 1973), p. 28.

12 Guevara, *Comentarios*, p. 42; Snyder p. 29.

13 's-Hertogenbosch, Noordbrabants Museum, on loan from Amsterdam, Rijksmuseum, Inv. SK-A-1795; this *Saint Anthony* is one of at least three surviving panels in which a work by Bosch is copied over a previously begun composition of a completely different kind, suggesting (1) the existence of a lively market for Boschian works and, perhaps, (2) the strategic recycling of old panels to simulate age—a practice attested to by Guevara; see *Brueghel Enterprises*, exh. cat., ed. Peter van den Brink (Maastricht: Bonnefantenmuseum; Antwerp: Ludion, 2001), p. 49.

14 See "Disparities," chapter 5.

15 Guevara, *Comentarios*, p. 42; ed. Snyder, p. 29.

16 On this development in literature, see especially Erich Auerbach, *Dante: Poet of the Secular World*, trans. Ralph Manheim (Chicago: University of Chicago Press, 1961), pp. 1–23; *idem*, "*Sermo humilis*," in *Literary Language and Its Public in Late Latin Antiquity and in the Middle Ages*, trans. Ralph Manheim, Bollingen Series, 74 (Princeton, NJ: Princeton University Press, 1965), pp. 27–66; and Hans Robert Jauss, "Die klassische und die christliche Rechtfertigung des Hässlichen in mittelalterlichen Literatur," in *Die nicht mehr schönen Künste—Grenzphänomene des Ästhetischen*, ed. Hans Robert Jauss, Poetik und Hermeneutik 3 (Munich: Fink, 1968), pp. 159–68.

17 Madrid, Museo del Prado, Inv. 2822.

18 Guevara, *Comentarios*, p. 44; ed. Snyder, p. 31.

19 E.g., Gerd Unverfehrt, *Hieronymus Bosch: Rezeption seiner Kunst im frühen 16. Jahrhundert* (Berlin: Mann, 1980), p. 33.

20 Berlin, Staatliche Museen zu Berlin, Kupferstichkabinett, KdZ 548 (recto); for organic incoherence as this drawing's disqualifier as authentic Bosch, see Stephanie Buck, *Die niederländischen Zeichnungen des 15. Jahrhundert im Berliner Kupferstichkabinett. Kritischer Katalog*, Die Zeichnungen alter Meister in Berliner Kupferstichkabinett (Turnhout: Brepols, 2001), p. 219 (no. I. 34).

21 On medieval reflections on human vis-à-vis divine creation, see Hans Blumenberg, "'Nachahmung der Natur.' Zur Vorgeschichte der Idee des schöpferischen Menschen," in *Wirklichkeiten in denen wir leben: Aufsätze und eine Rede* (Stuttgart: Reclam, 1981), pp. 87–92; and *idem*, *The Legitimacy of the Modern Age*, trans. Robert M. Wallace (Cambridge, MA: MIT Press, 1983), pp. 533–41; on the incompatibility of contradiction to the medieval conception of God, see Amos Funkenstein, *Theology and the Scientific Imagination from the Middle Ages to the Seventeenth Century* (Princeton, NJ: Princeton University Press, 1986), p. 134.

22 Horace, *Ars poetica*, 1–6, in *Classical and Medieval Literary Criticism: Translations and Interpretations*, ed. Alex Preminger, O. B. Hardison, and Kevin Kerrane (New York: Unger, 1974), p. 158.

23 Vitruvius, *On Architecture*, ed. and trans. Frank Granger (Cambridge, MA: Harvard University Press, 1931–34), 2: 105.

24 Bernard of Clairvaux, *Letter to William of St. Thierry*, trans. G. G. Coulton, in *Early Medieval Art 300–1150: Sources and Documents*, ed. Caecilia Davis-Weyer (Englewood Cliffs, NJ: Prentice-Hall, 1971), p. 170.

25 Curtius, *European Literature*, pp. 94–98; on the ritual context of this motif, see especially Peter Burke, *Popular Culture in Early Modern Europe* (New York: Harper & Row, 1978), pp. 185–91.

26 Cited in Dieter Wuttke, "Sebastian Brants Verhältnis zu Wunderdeutung und Astrologie," in *Studien zur deutschen Literatur und Sprache des Mittelalters. Festschrift für Hugo Moser zum 65. Geburtstag* (Berlin: E. Schmidt, 1974), p. 284n25.

27 He does this openly in *The Hay Wain* and the *Last Judgments* in Vienna and Bruges and covertly in *The Garden of Delights* (see "An Unnameable Masterpiece," chapter 7).

28 Quid sibi vult, Hieronyme Boschi, / Ille oculus tuus attonitus? quid / Pallor in ore? velut lemures si, / Spectra Erebi volitantia coràm // Aspiceres? Tibi Ditis auari / Crediderim patuisse receßus, / Tartareasque domos: tua quando / Quicquid habet sinus imus Auerni // Tam potuit bene pingere dextra.

29 Karel van Mander, *The Lives of the Illustrious Netherlandish and German Painters, from the first edition of the* Schilder-boeck *(1603–1604)*, ed. and trans. Hessel Miedema (Doornspijk: Davaco, 1994), fol. 216v–217r, pp. 125–26.

30 Paul Vandenbroeck, "Zur Herkunft und Verwurzelung der 'Grillen.' Vom Volksmythos zum kunst- und literaturtheoretischen Begriff, 15.–17. Jahrhundert," *De zeventiende eeuw* 3 (1987): 53–84; on the demons in the portrait as

illustrating both contagion and the artist's temperament, see Christine Göttler, "Fire, Smoke and Vapour. Jan Brueghel's 'Poetic Hells': 'Ghespoock' in Early Modern European Art," in *Spirits Unseen: The Representation of Subtle Bodies in Early Modern European Culture*, ed. Christine Göttler and Wolfgang Neuber, Intersections, 9 (Leiden: Brill, 2008), pp. 19–24.

31 Title-page woodcut from Johannes Cochlaeus, *Sieben Köpffe Martini Luthers: vom hochwirdigen Sacrament des Altars* (Leipzig: Valentin Schumann, 1529); see also the Protestants' response: *The Seven-Headed Papal Animal* (Max Geisberg, *The German Single-Leaf Woodcut 1500–1550*, ed. Walter S. Strauss [New York: Hacker Art Books, 1974], 4: 1530 [no. 1575]).

32 Marcus van Vaernewyck, *Van die beroerlicke tijden in die Nederlanden en voornamelick in Ghendt 1566–1568*, ed. Ferdinand vander Haeghen (Ghent: Anoot-Braeckman, 1872–81), 1: 156.

33 Francisco de Quevedo, *Dreams and Discourses (Sueños y discursos)*, ed. and trans. R. K. Britton (Warminster: Aris & Phillips, 1989), p. 77.

34 "estraño hombre en la pintura" (*Tercera parte* [1605], p. 735; *Historia*, ed. Garcia [1909], 2: 557).

35 Jacobus de Voragine, *The Golden Legend: Readings on the Saints*, trans. William Granger Ryan (Princeton, NJ: Princeton University Press, 1993), 1: 83.

36 Florence, Uffizi, Inv. 1890, no. 8364.

37 Origen, *Homiliae in Genesim, Patrologiae Cursus Completus, Series Graeca*, ed. Jacques Paul Migne (Paris: Garnier Fratres, 1857–66), 23: col. 238; cited in Hugo Kehrer, *Die Heiligen drei Könige in Literatur und Kunst* (Leipzig: E. A. Seemann, 1908–9), 1: 13; and Paul H. D. Kaplan, *The Rise of the Black Magus in Western Art* (Ann Arbor, MI: UMI Research Press, 1985), p. 21.

38 Pseudo-Bede, *Excerptiones Patrum, Patrologiae Cursus Completus, Series Latinae*, ed. J. P. Migne (Paris: Garnier Fratres, 1841–55), 94: col. 541, as cited in Kaplan, *Rise of the Black Magus*, p. 21.

39 Madrid, Museo del Prado, no. 1557; Jean Devisse and Michel Mollat, *The Image of the Black in Western Art*, II, *From the Early Christian Era to the "Age of Discovery,"* 2, *Africans in the Christian Ordinance of the World*, new ed., ed. David Bindman and Henry Louis Gates, Jr. (Cambridge, MA: Harvard University Press, 2010); and Kaplan, *Rise of the Black Magus*, passim; on interpretative problems attending this signal, see Joseph Leo Koerner, "The Epiphany of the Black Magus Circa 1500," in *The Image of the Black in Western Art*, III, *From the "Age of Discovery" to the Age of Abolition*, 2, *Arts of the Renaissance and Baroque*, ed. Bindman and Gates (Cambridge, MA: Harvard University Press, 2010), pp. 17–23.

40 Augustine, *Enarratio in Psalmum 72*, in *Patrologiae Latina*, 36: col. 909, cited in Kaplan, *Rise of the Black Magus*, p. 23.

41 *In Matthaei Evangelium Expositio*, in *Patrologiae Latina*, 92: col. 13, cited in Kaplan, *Rise of the Black Magus*, p. 33.

42 Richard C. Trexler, *The Journey of the Magi: Meanings in History of a Christian Story* (Princeton, NJ: Princeton University Press, 1997), pp. 4 and 95.

43 For a compelling account of this history, see David Nirenberg, *Anti-Judaism: The Western Tradition* (New York: W. W. Norton, 2013), pp. 48–134, 183–245.

44 Voragine, *Golden Legend*, 1: 79–80.

45 On the Secret Passion and its impact on visual iconography, see James H. Marrow, *Passion Iconography in Northern European Art of the Late Middle Ages and Early Renaissance: A Study of the Transformation of Sacred Metaphor into Descriptive Narrative*, Ars Neerlandica, 1 (Kortrijk: Van Ghemmert, 1979), pp. 24–25 and passim.

46 Stephan Fridolin, *Der Schatzbehalter oder schrein der waren reichtuemer des hails vnd weiger seligkait* (Nuremberg: Anton Koberger, 1491), pp. Z3r; translated and discussed in Cynthia Anna Hall, "Treasury Book of the Passion: Word and Image in the *Schatzbehalter*" (Ph.D. diss., Harvard University, 2002), pp. 75–76.

47 Berlin, Kupferstichkabinett, Inv. 78 B3a, fol. 33v; on the sketchbook, see Richard Bellm, *Wolgemuts Skizzenbuch im Berliner Kupferstichkabinett—ein Beitrag zur Erforschung des graphischen Werkes von Michael Wolgemut und Wilhelm Pleydenwurff*, Studien zur deutschen Kunstgeschichte, 322 (Baden-Baden: Heitz, 1959). On Christ's near-suffocation with spittle, see Marrow, *Passion Iconography*, pp. 132–34.

48 Albrecht Dürer and Benedictus Chelidonius, *Passio Domini Nostri Jesu* (Nuremberg: Hieronymus Höltzel for Albrecht Dürer, 1511), fol. A1r; Rainer Schoch et al., *Albrecht Dürer. Das druckgraphische Werk*, 2, *Holzschnitte und Holzschnittfolgen* (Munich: Prestel; Nuremberg: Germanisches Nationalmuseum, 2002), no. 154.

49 Trans. David Hotchkiss Price, *Albrecht Dürer's Renaissance: Humanism, Reformation, and the Art of Faith* (Ann Arbor: University of Michigan Press, 2006), p. 181.

50 Price, pp. 190–91, following Heiko Augustinus Oberman, *The Roots of Anti-Semitism in the Age of Renaissance and Reformation*, trans. James I. Porter (Philadelphia: Fortress, 1984), pp. 97–99, 147–49.

51 Madrid, Museo del Prado, no. 2048; see Carmen Garrido and Roger van Schoute, *Bosch at the Museo del Prado* (Madrid: Museo del Prado and Aldeasa, 2001), pp. 98–119. It had long been believed that the Prado triptych was identical to a "painting of three Kings, made by Jeronimus Bossche" recorded in a 1567 inventory of the expropriated property of Jan de Casembroot, arrested in that year along with Count of Egmond, and, further, that the arms on the triptych were those of the Bronchorst and Bosschuysen families, to whom de Casembroot was related by marriage. This identification, asserted already by Carl Justi in 1889, is no longer plausible; see Marianne Renson, "Genealogical Information Concerning the Bronchorst-Bosschuysen Triptych," in *Bosch: New Insights*, ed. Koldeweij and Vermet, pp. 93–96.

52 Erwin Panofsky, *Early Netherlandish Painting: Its Origins and Character* (Cambridge, MA: Harvard University Press, 1958), 1: 278n1.

53 On hooked or enlarged noses as a distortion associated with Jews in late medieval art, see Ruth Mellinkoff, *Outcasts: Signs of Otherness in Northern European Art of the Late Middle Ages*, California Studies in the History of Art, 2 (Berkeley: University of California Press, 1994), 1: 128 and passim.

54 The thesis that Bosch evoked this slander was proposed by Lotte Brand Philip in her "The Prado *Epiphany* by Jerome Bosch," *The Art Bulletin* 35 (1953): 270, citing *The Jewish Encyclopedia* (New York: Funk and Wagnalls, 1912), 2: 222ff. The most notable reference to this slander is its refutation by Flavius Josephus (who calls the tale, as recounted in Apion, all "incredible lies," *Contra apionem* 2.7); among classical writers, the accusation appears also in mythologized form in Plutarch (*Questiones Conviviales* 4.5), Tacitus (*Historiae* 5.4; *De Iside et Osiride* 31.9), and Damokritos, *Peri Iouda*, as excerpted in the *Suda* (*Suidae Lexicon*, ed. Ada Adler [Stuttgart: Teubner, 1931–71], 5: no. 49). Tertullian (*Apologia* 16 and *Ad*

Nationes 1.2) defends Christians against the accusation, made on the basis of their association with Judaism, that "an ass's head is our God." On the origins of the calumny, see Elias Bickermann, "Ritualmord und Eselkult Ein Beitrag zur Geschichte der antiken Publizistik," *Monatsschrift für Geschichte und Wissenschaft des Judentums* 71 (1927), 171–87, 255–64; following Josephus, Bickermann traces this, and the tale (also told in Josephus, *Contra apionem* 2.8) of ritual murder and cannibalism of outsiders by Jews in their temple, to apologists of Antiochus IV Epiphanes during his campaign against the Maccabees. See, more recently, Bezalel Bar-Kochva, "An Ass in the Jerusalem Temple—The Origins and Development of the Slander," in *Josephus'* Contra Apionem: *Studies in Its Character and Context with a Latin Concordance to the Portion Missing in Greek*, ed. Louis Feldman and John R. Levison, Arbeiten zur Geschichte des Antiken Judentums und des Urchristentums, 34 (Leiden and New York: Brill, 1996), pp. 310–26; also Jan Assmann, *Moses the Egyptian: The Memory of Egypt in Western Monotheism* (Cambridge, MA: Harvard University Press, 1997), pp. 37–38.

55 Florence, Uffizi, No. 1525; on the iconography of the represented architecture, see Joseph Destrée, *Hugo van der Goes* (Paris: G. van Oest, 1914), p. 98; Panofsky, *Early Netherlandish Painting*, p. 334 and 334n1; and Margaret L. Koster, *Hugo van der Goes and the Procedures of Art and Salvation*, Studies in Medieval and Early Renaissance History, 49 (Turnhout: Brepols, 2008), p. 52.

56 Gertrude Schiller, *Ikonographie der christlichen Kunst* (Gütersloh: Gütersloher Verlagshaus, 1966–91), 1: 92.

57 *The Bestiary. Book of Beasts. Being a Translation from a Latin Bestiary of the Twelfth Century*, trans. and ed. Theodore Harold White (New York: Putnam, 1954), p. 134.

58 Carl Justi, "Die Werke des Hieronymus Bosch in Spanien," *Jahrbuch der Königlich Preussischen Kunstsammlungen* 10, no. 3 (1989): 128; reprinted in *Miscellaneen aus drei Jahrhunderten spanischen Kunstlebens* (Berlin: Grote, 1908), 2: 72.

59 Lionel Cust, "The Adoration of the Three Kings by Hieronymus Bosch," *Apollo* 8 (August 1928), p. 55; E. H. Gombrich, "The Evidence of Images," in *Interpretation: Theory and Practice*, ed. Charles Southward Singleton (Baltimore: Johns Hopkins University Press, 1969), pp. 35–104.

60 For a review of the literature, see Roger H. Marijnissen and Peter Ruyffelaere, *Hieronymus Bosch, the Complete Works*, trans. Ted Alkins et al. (Antwerp: Mercatorfonds, 1987), pp. 234–38; the most detailed alchemical reading of the figure is Laurinda S. Dixon's in her *Bosch* (London: Phaidon, 2003), pp. 212–24.

61 Philip, "Prado *Epiphany*," pp. 267–93.

62 1 John 2:18, 2:22, 4:2–3, 2 John 1:7; for a general history of Antichrist I have relied mostly on Bernard McGinn, *Anti-Christ: Two Thousand Years of Human Fascination with Evil* (New York: Columbia University Press, 2000).

63 McGinn, *Anti-Christ*, pp. 58–62.

64 For a detailed exploration of the multiple time frame of one early Netherlandish painting, see Alfred Acres, "*The Columba Altarpiece* and the Time of the World," *Art Bulletin* 80, no. 3 (1998): 422–51.

65 Debra Higgs Strickland, "Picturing Antichrist and Others in the Prado *Epiphany* by Hieronymus Bosch," in *Others and Outcasts in Early Modern Europe: Picturing the Social Margins*, ed. Tom Nichols (Aldershot: Ashgate, 2007), pp. 11–35.

66 Strickland, "Picturing Antichrist," pp. 24–27. Strickland bases her argument on Philip ("Prado *Epiphany*," p. 272) with support from the widely disseminated late seventh-century *Apocalypse of Pseudo-Methodius*.

67 Irenaeus, *Against Heresies*, 5.20.1; cited in McGinn, *Anti-Christ*, p. 59.

68 Jerome, *Epistles* 121.11, and *Commentary on Daniel* 11.24; cited in McGinn, *Anti-Christ*, p. 75.

69 2 Thess. 2:6; for a modern account of the emergence of the Christian empire as the "restrainer" (*katechon*) of Antichrist—contrasting with Tertullian's equation of empire with Antichrist—see Carl Schmitt, *The* Nomos *of the Earth in the International Law of the* Jus Publicum Europaeum, trans. G. L. Ulmen (New York: Telos Press, 2003), pp. 59–61.

70 The key author of this understanding of Antichrist was Gregory the Great; McGinn, *Anti-Christ*, pp. 88–92 and passim.

71 Meyer Schapiro, "'*Muscipula Diaboli*': The Symbolism of the Mérode Altarpiece," *Art Bulletin* 27 (1945): 182–87.

72 Augustine, *De Genesi ad literrarum* 11.24, in *On Genesis*, trans. Edmund Hill, ed. John E. Rotelle, The Works of Saint Augustine, 1, Books, 13 (New York: New City Press and Augustinian Heritage Institute, 2002), p. 447.

73 *Missale secundum usum ecclesiae s. Floriani*, Chapter at Sankt Florian, Stiftsbibliothek, Cod. III.205, fol. 4r; for bibliography, see Devisse and Mollat, *Image of the Black*, II, 2: p. 270n195.

74 Koerner, "Epiphany of the Black Magus," pp. 23–32.

75 *Hours of the Virgin* (Paris: Simon de Colines, 1531), fol. 132.

76 Johannes Gimberg, "Feesten en maaltijden te Zutphen in de Middeleeuwen," *Gelre. Bijdragen en mededelingen* 12 (1909): 256; cited in Paul Vandenbroeck, "En compañia de extraños comensales. Idea del hombre, códigos de conducta y alteridad en los tapices de Felipe el Hermoso," in *Felipe I el Hermoso—La belleza y la locura*, ed. Miguel Ángel Zalama and Paul Vandenbroeck (Madrid: Centro de Estudios Europa Hispánica, 2006), p. 122.

77 Vandenbroeck, "En compañia de extraños comensales," pp. 120–24.

78 London, National Gallery, Inv. NG 2790.

79 Munich, Bayerische Staatsgemäldesammlungen Alte Pinakothek, Inv. 708; Max J. Friedländer, *Early Netherlandish Painting*, 11, *The Antwerp Mannerists*, Adriaen Ysenbrant, trans. Heinz Norden, ed. Henri Pauwels (New York: Praeger, 1974), pp. 14–17, cat. A1.

80 Fernand Braudel, *Civilization and Capitalism*, 3, *The Perspective of the World*, trans. Sian Reynolds (New York: Harper Collins, 1985), p. 143.

81 London, British Library, Kings Ms. 5, fol. 16r; *Speculum humanae salvationis* block book (n.d.), chapter 22; see Adrian Wilson and Joyce Lancaster Wilson, *A Medieval Mirror: Speculum humanae salvationis 1324–1500* (Berkeley: University of California Press, 1984), pp. 101 and 184.

82 Charles de Tolnay, *Hieronymus Bosch* (New York: Reynal, 1966), p. 372.

83 Susan Fargo Gilchrist, elbosco blog (December 4, 2006, 62), http://elbosco blog.blogspot.com.

84 Paul Saintenoy, *Les arts et les artistes à la cour de Bruxelles* (Brussels: Maurice Lamertin, 1932–35), 1: 72–73; Gustave Loisel, *Histoire des ménageries de l'antiquité à nos jours* (Paris: O. Doin, 1912), 1: 230.

85 De Tolnay, *Bosch*, p. 372.

86 Wilhelm Fraenger, *Hieronymus Bosch*, trans. Helen Sebba (New York: Putnam, 1983), p. 312.

87 Gerd Unverfehrt, *Hieronymus Bosch—Die Rezeption seiner Kunst im frühen 16. Jahrhundert* (Berlin: Gebr. Mann, 1980), pp. 259–62.

88 Upton House near Banbury, Viscount

Bearsted Collection, National Trust, No. 143; Friedländer (Bosch), no. 68a; Unverfehrt, *Hieronymus Bosch*, p. 260, cat. no. 42.

89 The most concise and insightful account of typology remains Erich Auerbach's 1938 essay "Figura," in *Scenes from the Drama of European Literature*, trans. Ralph Manheim and Catherine Garvin, Theory and History of Literature, 9 (Minneapolis: University of Minnesota Press, 1984), pp. 11–78; for a thoughtful recent analysis, see Kathleen Biddick, *The Typological Imaginary: Circumcision, Technology, History* (Philadelphia: University of Pennsylvania Press, 2003).

90 Anderlecht, Erasmushuis; see Friedländer (Bosch), no. 69; Unverfehrt, *Hieronymus Bosch*, pp. 257–58, cat. no. 37; the motif also appears in a closely related *Epiphany* triptych recently acquired by the Noordbrabants Museum, 's-Hertogenbosch (Inv. 15.257).

91 *Der Antechrist*, Berlin, Staatsbibliothek Preussischer Kulturbesitz, MS germ. 2: 733, fol. 4r; Devisse and Mollat, *Image of the Black*, II, 2: p. 46; the image was linked to Bosch by Strickland, "Picturing Antichrist," p. 20, and *eadem*, *Saracens, Demons, and Jews: Making Monsters in Medieval Art* (Princeton, NJ: Princeton University Press, 2003), pp. 227–28. See also Philip, "Prado *Epiphany*," p. 280.

92 On this motif, see Michael Camille, *The Gothic Idol: Ideology and Image-Making* (Cambridge, UK: Cambridge University Press, 1989), pp. 1–26.

93 Richard A. Fletcher, *The Conversion of Europe: From Paganism to Christianity 371–1386 AD* (London: HarperCollins, 1997), pp. 253–54 and passim.

94 Marcel Mauss, *The Gift: Forms and Functions of Exchange in Archaic Societies*, trans. Ian Cunnison (New York: Norton, 1967), p. 8; on the system of pious gifting in northern Europe on the eve of the Reformation, see most recently Natalie Zemon Davis, *The Gift in Sixteenth-Century France* (Madison: University of Wisconsin Press, 2000), pp. 100–23.

95 Already for the early Christians, as for their Jewish predecessors, the time frame of the apocalyptic battle was always simultaneously the beginning of time, the end of time, the moment of Christ's advent, and the visionary present tense (the "now" that is always upon us); see Neil Forsyth, *The Old Enemy: Satan and the Combat Myth* (Princeton, NJ: Princeton University Press, 1987), p. 255.

96 London, National Gallery, NG4681; the anonymous Master of the Mass of Saint Giles projects the Eucharistic miracle (said to have occurred in Orléans in 718 for the benefit of Charles Martel or of Charlemagne) into an exactly portrayed contemporary setting: the high altar of the abbey of Saint-Denis, represented quasi as an inventory of the precious furniture and objects assembled there around 1500.

97 For a good summary of the "atonement" doctrine as formulated by Anselm of Canterbury, see John Bossy, *Christianity in the West, 1400–1700* (Oxford and New York: Oxford University Press, 1985), p. 21.

98 These scenes are uncanny narrative expansions of the so-called arms of Christ (shorthand signs for the torments endured, ironically assembled as Christ's noble coat of arms) common in scenes of the Mass of Saint Gregory; on which, see Rudolf Berliner, "Arma Christi," *Münchner Jahrbuch der bildenden Kunst* 3 (1955): 35–153; and Robert Suckale, "Arma Christi. Überlegungen zur Zeichenhaftigkeit mittelalterlicher Andachtsbilder," *Städel-Jahrbuch* 6 (1977): 177–208.

99 On grisaille as a liturgical "ash color," see Molly Teasdale Smith, "The Use of Grisaille as Lenten Observance," *Marsyas* 8 (1959): 43–54.

100 Valentin Groebner, *Liquid Assets, Dangerous Gifts: Presents and Politics at the End of the Middle Ages*, trans. Pamela E. Selwyn (Philadelphia: University of Pennsylvania Press, 2002), pp. 73 and 85–88.

101 Jeremy Cohen, *Christ Killers: The Jews and the Passion from the Bible to the Big Screen* (Oxford and New York: Oxford University Press, 2007), pp. 255–61.

102 On the idea that Judas's despair and suicide were more criminal than his betrayal of Christ, see Friedrich Ohly, *The Damned and the Elect: Guilt in Western Culture*, trans. Linda Archibald (Cambridge, UK: Cambridge University Press, 1992), pp. 23–42.

103 Miri Rubin, *Corpus Christi: The Eucharist in Late Medieval Culture* (Cambridge: Cambridge University Press, 1992), pp. 120–22.

104 For a subtle account of this interplay among actual artifacts, legends about saints, and legends about images, see Gerhard Wolf, *Schleier und Spiegel. Traditionen des Christusbildes und die Bildkonzepte der Renaissance* (Munich: Fink, 2002), pp. 160–92.

105 Max Lehrs, *Geschichte und kritischer Katalog des deutschen, niederländischen und französischen Kupferstichs im xv. Jahrhundert* (Vienna: Gesellschaft für Vervielfältigende Kunst, 1908–34), 9: 354, state I; see Peter Parshall, "*Imago Contrafacta*: Images and Facts in the Northern Renaissance," *Art History* 16 (1993): 556–60.

106 Letter to Bishop Serenus of Marseilles; see Caecilia Davis-Weyer, *Early Medieval Art, 300–1150: Sources and Documents* (Englewood Cliffs, NJ: Prentice-Hall, 1971), pp. 47–49.

107 McGinn, *Anti-Christ*, p. 81.

108 Jaroslav Pelikan, *The Christian Tradition: A History of the Development of Doctrine*, 3, *The Growth of Medieval Theology (300–1300)* (Chicago: University of Chicago Press, 1978), pp. 184–204; Rubin, *Corpus Christi*, pp. 12–82.

109 Joseph Leo Koerner, "The Icon as Iconoclash," in *Iconoclash: Beyond the Image Wars in Science, Religion and Art*, ed. Bruno Latour and Peter Weibel, exh. cat. (Karlsruhe: ZKM; Cambridge, MA: MIT Press, 2002), pp. 164–213.

110 Cologne, Wallraf-Richartz-Museum & Fondation Corboud, Inv. 479; see Peter Jezler et al., *Himmel, Hölle, Fegefeuer. Das Jenseits im Mittelalter*, exh. cat. (Zurich: Schweizerisches Landesmuseum; Munich: Fink, 1994), p. 294, cat. 98.

111 That understanding Bosch requires a key—and that this key was available to the artist's original audience but has since been lost—is Erwin Panofsky's closing thought in *Early Netherlandish Painting* (1: 357).

112 Madrid, Museo del Prado, cat. no. 2822; Friedländer (Bosch), no. 104. Whether this signed work was made by Bosch's hand, by his assistants, or by a combination thereof remains (despite the signature but typically for the artist) unresolved; see Garrido and Van Schoute, *Bosch at the Museo del Prado*, pp. 76–87.

113 Sigmund Freud, *Civilization and Its Discontents*, trans. James Strachey (New York: Norton, 1961), pp. 61–69; also Jacqueline Rose, *Sexuality in the Field of Vision* (London: Verso, 1986), pp. 173–75; on rivalry as the root cause of culture, see René Girard, *Things Hidden Since the Foundation of the World*, trans. Stephen Bann and Michael Metteer (Stanford, CA: Stanford University Press, 1987).

114 Alijt Bake, *Een deuoet boecxken vanden inwendighen nauolghe[ne] des leuens ende*

des cruces ons herren ihesu cristi (Antwerp: Heynrick Eckert van Hombruch, 1516), quire H; cited in Marijnissen and Ruyffelaere, *Hieronymus Bosch*, p. 337.

115 Felipe de Guevara, *Comentarios de la Pintura*, ed. Antonio Ponz (Madrid: Geronimo Ortega, 1788), p. 43.

116 On this symbolism generally, see Georges Poulet, *The Metamorphosis of the Circle*, trans. Carley Dawson and Elliott Coleman (Baltimore: Johns Hopkins University Press, 1966), especially pp. xi–xiv; on the circle in *The Seven Deadly Sins*, see Walter W. S. Gibson, "Hieronymus Bosch and the Mirror of Man," *Oud Holland* 87 (1973), pp. 205–26.

117 Fritz Redenbacher, "Das Streubild," *Festschrift Karl Oettinger. Zum 60. Geburtstag am 4. März gewidmet*, ed. Hans Sedlmayr and Wilhelm Messerer, Erlangen Forschungen, Series A, Geisteswissenschaften, 20 (Erlangen: Universitätsbund Erlangen-Nürnberg, 1967), p. 244.

118 The ancient symbol of fortune's wheel was Christianized in Boethius, *De consolatione philosophiae*, 2.2.9; see Adolf Katzenellenbogen, *Allegories of the Virtues and Vices in Medieval Art from Early Christian Times to the Thirteenth Century*, trans. Alan J. P. Crick (London: Warburg Institute, 1939), p. 71.

119 Wilhelm Fraenger, *Hieronymus Bosch*, trans. Helen Sebba (New York: Putnam, 1983), p. 277.

120 Additionally, one can read the circle as an allegorical *mappa mundi*, with the Holy Sepulcher at the geographic center; see Joseph Leo Koerner, "Hieronymus Bosch's World Picture," *Picturing Science, Producing Art*, ed. Peter Galison and Caroline Jones (New York: Routledge, 1998), pp. 314–18.

121 Saint Paul equates "the carnal mind" with "enmity against God" (Rom. 8.7); see also Gal. 5.19–20.

122 Guevara, *Comentarios*, p. 43.

123 Bosch may have derived the symbolism from a Dutch translation of Denis the Carthusian's *Quatuor novissima* (*Die vier uterste ofte die leste dingen die ons aanstande ende toecommende syn* [Gouda: Geraldus Leew, 1477]); see Gibson, "Mirror," p. 210n17.

124 Renate Brandscheidt, "Feind," in *Lexikon für Theologie und Kirche*, 3rd ed., Walter Casper (Freiburg: Herder, 1993–2001), 3: cols. 1211–12.

125 Cited in Marrow, *Passion Iconography*, pp. 204 and 240.

126 The classic study is Erwin Panofsky, "Imago Pietatis," in *Festschrift für Max J. Friedländer zum 60. Geburtstage* (Leipzig: E. A. Seemann, 1927), pp. 261–308; for a recent discussion of the term and the literature on it, see Hans Belting, *Das Bild und sein Publikum im Mittelalter. Form und Funktion früher Bildtafeln der Passion* (Berlin: Mann, 1981), especially pp. 53–68. On Bosch's *Seven Deadly Sins* as an *imago pietatis*, see Wolf, *Schleier und Spiegel*, pp. 266–67.

127 "Das pseudo-hermetische 'Buch der vierundzwanzig Meister' (Liber XXIV Philosophorum)," ed. Clemens Baeumker, in *Studien und Characteristiken zur Geschichte der Philosophie, insbesondere des Mittelalters. Gesammelte Vorträge und Aufsätze*, ed. Martin Grabmann, Beiträge zur Geschichte der Philosophie des Mittelalters 25 (Münster: Aschendorff'sche Buchhandlung, 1928), p. 208; discussed in Poulet, *Metamorphosis of the Circle*, pp. xi–xii.

128 Klaus Kremer, "Das Seelenfünklein (*scintilla animae*) bei Meister Eckhart: ungeschaffen oder geschaffen? Ein kontroverses Kapitel in der Meister-Eckhart-Forschung," *Trierer Theologische Zeitung* 97 (1988), pp. 8–38.

129 "Pseudo-hermetische 'Buch'," ed. Baeumker, p. 210.

130 On Bosch's panel as the culmination of artistic self-consciousness in early Netherlandish painting, see James H. Marrow, "Symbol and Meaning in Northern European Art of the Late Middle Ages and the Early Renaissance," *Simiolus* 16 (1986), pp. 166–69.

131 The label *speculum consciencie* appears in a fifteenth-century manuscript treated in James H. Marrow, "'In desen speigell': A New Form of 'Memento Mori' in Fifteenth-Century Netherlandish Art," in *Essays in Northern European Art Presented to Egbert Haverkamp-Begemann on His Sixtieth Birthday* (Doornspijk: Davaco, 1983), p. 157.

132 Joseph de Sigüenza, *Tercera parte de la Historia de la Orden de San Gerónimo, Doctor de la Iglesia*, p. 839; *Historia de la Orden*, ed. Garcia, 2: 637; trans. Snyder, *Bosch in Perspective*, p. 37.

133 Judith Butler, *The Psychic Life of Power: Theories in Subjection* (Stanford, CA: Stanford University Press, 1997), p. 2; Butler argues that Hegel and Kierkegaard understood Christ's function in this way (pp. 48–49).

134 On the aggressive core of Christian asceticism, see most influentially Friedrich Nietzsche, *On the Genealogy of Morals*, trans. Walter Kaufmann and Reginald John Hollindale (New York: Vintage Books, 1967), pp. 97–163.

135 El Escorial, Monastery of San Lorenzo, Inv. 100 144 73; Friedländer (Bosch), no. 79; on the panel's date, see Peter Klein, "Dendrochronological Analysis of Works by Hieronymus Bosch and His Followers," in *Bosch: New Insights*, ed. Koldeweij and Vermet, p. 128.

136 Berlin, Gemäldegalerie der Staatlichen Museen, No. 1647a; Friedländer (Bosch), no. 101.

137 Albrecht Dürer, *Schriftlicher Nachlass*, ed. Hans Rupprich (Berlin: Deutsche Verein für Kunstwissenschaft, 1956–69), 2: 373.

138 Jacques Derrida, "Structure, Sign, and Play in the Discourse of the Human Sciences," in *The Structuralist Controversy: The Languages of Criticism and the Sciences of Man*, ed. Richard Macksey and Eugenio Donata (Baltimore: Johns Hopkins University Press, 1970), pp. 247–65.

139 On conspiracy theories as a central element in late medieval pessimism, see especially Will-Erich Peuckert, *Die grosse Wende. Das apokalyptische Saeculum und Luther*, reprint (Darmstadt: Wissenschaftliche Buchgesellschaft, 1966), 1: 103–91; and Jean Delumeau, *La peur en Occident (XIVe–XVIIIe siècles): une cité assiégée* (Paris: Fayard, 1978).

140 On the persecution of imaginary enemies, see also Robert I. Moore, *The Formation of a Persecuting Society: Authority and Deviance in Western Europe 950–1250*, 2nd ed. (Malden, MA: Blackwell Publishing, 2007); Carlo Ginzburg, *Ecstasies: Deciphering the Witches' Sabbath*, trans. Raymond Rosenthal (New York: Pantheon Books, 1991), pp. 33–86; and David Nirenberg, *Communities of Violence: Persecution of Minorities in the Middle Ages* (Princeton, NJ: Princeton University Press, 1996).

141 On "invisible enemies" in late medieval towns, see Valentine Groebner, *Defaced: The Visual Culture of Violence in the Late Middle Ages*, trans. Pamela Selwyn (New York: Zone Books, 2004), pp. 37–66; on 's-Hertogenbosch, see Ester Vink and Aart Vos, "Life in the Town," in *World of Bosch*, ed. Jan van Oudheusden and Aart Vos ('s-Hertogenbosch: Adr. Heinen, 2001), pp. 47–49.

142 Pater Gerlach, "De bronnen voor het leven en het werk van Jeroen Bosch," *Brabantia* 16 (1967), p. 55.

143 Jan van Oudheusden, "The Cultural Climate," in *World of Bosch*, ed. Oudheusden and Vos, p. 56.

144 Interview with David Sylvester, recorded in *Francis Bacon*, BBC/Arts Council, 1967, directed by M. Gill.

145 London, National Gallery, 4744; Friedländer (Bosch), supp. 113.

146 Frankfurt, Städelsches Kunstinstitut, cat. 1577; Friedländer (Bosch), no. 77.

CHAPTER 6. AMONG THE IDOLS

1 *The Truman Show*, directed by Peter Weir (New York: Scott Rudin Productions; Hollywood, CA: Paramount Pictures, 1998).

2 *The Matrix*, directed by Lana and Andrew Paul Wachowski, as the Wachowski Brothers (Melbourne: Village Roadshow Pictures; Burbank, CA: Warner Bros., 1999).

3 Hans Jonas, *The Gnostic Religion: The Message of the Alien God and the Beginnings of Christianity* (Boston: Beacon Press, 1958), p. 36 and passim; on the persistence of Gnosticism, see especially Ioan P. Couliano, "The Gnostic Revenge: Gnosticism and Romantic Literature," in *Gnosis und Politik*, ed. Jacob Taubes, Religionstheorie und politische Theologie, 2 (Munich: Fink, 1984), pp. 290–91. Eric Voegelin took Gnosticism—understood as a claim of absolute cognitive mastery of reality and as a projection of the Judeo-Christian *echaton* into history—to be the governing spirit of modern political theory (*The New Science of Politics: An Introduction* [Chicago: University of Chicago Press, 1987], pp. 107–89).

4 "Gnosis" has an equivalent in ancient Greek and Latin; however, "Gnosticism" is an early modern coinage: the Platonist Henry More first used the word in his 1669 treatise *Antidote Against Idolatry*; see Benjamin Lazier, *God Interrupted: Heresy and the European Imagination Between the World Wars* (Princeton, NJ: Princeton University Press, 2008), pp. 27–28. The proximity between Christian contempt for the world and Gnostic dualism helps explain why Bosch—whose works preach contempt—is often taken by interpreters to be heretical.

5 Adolf Harnack, *Marcion. The Gospel of the Alien God*, trans. John E. Steely and Lyle D. Bierma (Durham, NC: Labyrinth Press, 1990), pp. 1–2; on the impact of Harnack's Marcion on twentieth-century theology, see Lazier, *God Interrupted*, pp. 30–33.

6 Harnack, *Marcion*, p. 3 and passim.

7 Elaine H. Pagels, *Adam, Eve, and the Serpent* (New York: Random House, 1988), pp. 69–71.

8 Paul Ricoeur, *The Conflict of Interpretations: Essays in Hermeneutics*, ed. Don Ihde (Evanston, IL: Northwestern University Press, 1974), p. 275.

9 Hans Blumenberg, *The Legitimacy of the Modern Age*, trans. Robert M. Wallace (Cambridge, MA: MIT Press, 1983), pp. 127–36

10 See Angus Fletcher's thought experiment of meeting "an allegorical character in real life" (*Allegory: The Theory of a Symbolic Mode* [Ithaca, NY: Cornell University Press, 1964], pp. 40–41).

11 On the history of this figure, see Hans Blumenberg, *Shipwreck with Spectator: Paradigm of a Metaphor for Existence*, trans. Steven Rendall (Cambridge, MA: MIT Press, 1997).

12 Lisbon, Museu Nacional de Arte Antiga, no. 1498; Friedländer (Bosch), no. 90. Unusually among works by Bosch, this triptych has inspired general agreement among authors about its purpose and message; see especially Dirk Bax, *Hieronymus Bosch. His Picture-Writing Deciphered*, trans. M. A. Bax-Botha (Rotterdam: A. A. Balkema, 1979), pp. 1–178; and Charles D. Cuttler, "The Lisbon *Temptation of St. Antony* by Jerome Bosch," *Art Bulletin* 39 (1957): 109–25.

13 On the cult and iconography of Anthony in the Middle Ages, see Laura Fenelli, *Il tau, il fuoco, il maiale: I canonici regolari di sant'Antonio Abate tra assistenza e devozione* (Spoleto: Fondazione Centro italiano di studi sull'alto medioevo, 2006); on printed images of Saint Anthony and their relation to religious practice, see Christopher S. Wood, "The Votive Scenario," *RES: Anthropology and Aesthetics* 59/60 (2011): 206–27.

14 See Robert C. Gregg, "Introduction," in Athanasius, *The Life of Antony and the Letter to Marcellinus*, trans. Robert C. Gregg, The Classics of Western Spirituality (New York: Paulist Press, 1980), pp. 1–28.

15 Athanasius's *Life of Antony* was translated into Latin at least twice already in the fourth century; one of these, by Evagrius of Antioch, survives in more than 300 codices; see Lois Gandt, "A Philological and Theological Analysis of the Ancient Latin Translations of the 'Vita Antonii'" (Ph.D. diss., Fordham University, 2008), p. 2. Athanasius's account was incorporated into widely disseminated collections of saints' lives, including the *Vitae Patrum*, published in Dutch as *Van den Leven der heiliger vaderen in der woestinen haer leven leydende* (Gouda: Gerard Leeu, 1480) and *Dit boeck is ghenomet dat vader boeck dat in den latijne is ghehieten Vitas patrum* (Zwolle: Peter van Os, 1490); and Jacobus de Voragine's *Golden Legend*, published in several Dutch translations, including printed ones published in Gouda (1478, 1480), Utrecht (1480), Delft (1482, 1484, 1487, 1489, 1500), Zwolle (1490), and Antwerp (1500, 1505); on Voragine in Dutch, see Mirjam Gabriel-Kamminga, "De *Legenda aurea* in druk. Een vergelijkend onderzoek van de Middelnederlandse incunabelen," in *"Een boec dat men te Latine heet Aurea Legenda"—Beiträge zur niederländischen Übersetzung der* Legenda aurea, ed. Amand Berteloot et al., Niederlande-Studien, 31 (Münster and New York: Waxmann, 2003), pp. 84–85.

16 Andrée Hayum, *The Isenheim Altarpiece: God's Medicine and the Painter's Vision* (Princeton, NJ: Princeton University Press, 1989), pp. 13–52; Fenelli, *Il tau*, pp. 33–93; Elisabeth Clementz, *Les Antonins d'Issenheim: Essor et dérive de'une vocation hospitalière à la lumière du temporel* (Strasbourg: Publications de la Société savante d'Alsace, 1998), pp. 27–143. On the woodcut of Saint Anthony, see Wood, "The Votive Scenario."

17 Hayum, *Isenheim Altarpiece*, pp. 29–30.

18 Jos Koldeweij, "The Oeuvre of Jheronimus Bosch," in *The World of Bosch*, ed. Jan van Oudheusden and Aart Vos, trans. Tony Burrett and Heather van Tress ('s-Hertogenbosch: Adr. Heinen, 2001), pp. 106–7.

19 New Haven, Yale University Art Gallery, Inv. 15.9; on copies of Bosch's Lisbon triptych, see Gerd Unverfehrt, *Hieronymus Bosch: Rezeption seiner Kunst im frühen 16. Jahrhundert* (Berlin: Gebr. Mann, 1980), pp. 19, 272–73, and 286–87. One Boschian pastiche—a *Saint Anthony* originally attributed to Pieter Breughel the Younger and now given to the sixteenth-century Antwerp master Jan Mandijn—inspired Gustave Flaubert to write *The Temptation of Saint Anthony* when the writer came upon the painting in the Palazzo Balbi in Genoa in 1845.

20 Madrid, Museo del Prado, cat. nos. 2913 and 2049; Friedländer (Bosch), no. 93 and also nos. 91, 92, 94, and 95.

21 Dagmar Eichberger, *Leben mit Kunst, Wirken durch Kunst. Sammelwesen und Hofkunst unter Margarete von Österreicht, Regentin der Niederlande*, Burgundica, 5 (Turnhout: Brepols, 2002), p. 270.

22 Frans Vredenrijk Engelenburg, "De schilderijenverzameling van Damiaan de Goes," *Oud Holland* 19 (1901): 193–97; Unverfehrt, however, following Mia Cinotto (*L'opera complete di Bosch*, Classici dell'Arte [Milan: Rizzoli, 1966], p. 105), is skeptical about this provenance for the Lisbon diptych.

23 Trans. James Snyder, in *Bosch in Perspective*, ed. James Snyder, The Artists in Perspective Series (Englewood Cliffs, NJ: Prentice-Hall, 1973), p. 37; see Joseph de Sigüenza, *Tercera parte de la Historia de la Orden de San Gerónimo, Doctor de la Iglesia* (Madrid: Imprenta Real, 1605), p. 839; *Historia de la Orden de San Jerónimo*, ed. Juan Catalina Garcia (Madrid: Bailly-Balliére, 1909), 2: 637.

24 On the sculptures, see Christian Heck et al., *Les Sculptures de Nicolas de Haguenau: Le Retable d'Issenheim avant Grünewald* (Colmar: Musée d'Unterlinden, 1987).

25 Boston, Museum of Fine Arts, Accession 63.660; on the iconography of retables, see Joseph Braun, *Der christliche Altar in seiner geschichtlichen Entwicklung* (Munich: Koch, 1924), 2: 446–515.

26 Jean Michel Massing, "*Sicut erat in diebus Antonii*: The Devils under the Bridge in the *Tribulations of St. Antony* by Hieronymus Bosch in Lisbon," in *Sight and Insight: Essays on Art and Culture in Honour of E. H. Gombrich at 85*, ed. John Onians (London: Phaidon, 1994), pp. 109–27.

27 Bax, *Hieronymus Bosch*, pp. 142–44; Cuttler, "The Lisbon *Temptation*," p. 116.

28 Venice, Palazzo Ducale; Friedländer (Bosch), no. 98.

29 See "World Pictures," chapter 3.

30 Trans. Snyder, *Bosch in Perspective*, p. 35; Sigüenza, *Tercera parte de la Historia de la Orden de San Gerónimo, Doctor de la Iglesia*, p. 837; *Historia de la Orden*, ed. Garcia, 2: 636.

31 For a summary of what is known of Bosch's painter ancestors, see Frédéric Elsig, *Jheronimus Bosch. La question de la chronologie*, Travaux d'Humanisme et Renaissance, 392 (Geneva: Librairie Droz, 2004), pp. 19–21.

32 Trans. Michael Baxandall, "Bartholomaeus Facius on Painting: A fifteenth-Century Manuscript of the *De Viris Illustribus*," *Journal of the Warburg and Courtauld Institutes* 27 (1964): 102.

33 On this synthesis, see especially Otto Pächt, *Van Eyck and the Founders of Early Netherlandish Painting*, ed. Maria Schmidt-Dengler, trans. David Britt (London: Harvey Miller, 1994), pp. 21–24.

34 Margaret L. Koster, *Hugo van der Goes and the Procedures of Art and Salvation*, Studies in Medieval and Early Renaissance History, 49 (Turnhout: Brepols, 2008).

35 Madrid, Museo del Prado, cat. no. 2056; Friedländer (Bosch), no. 109. This picture, or a version of it, has been argued to be documented as hanging in 1524 in the dining hall of the Bishop of Utrecht, Philip of Burgundy (Domien Roggen, "J. Bosch: Literatuur en folklore," in *Gentse bijdragen tot de kunstgeschiedenis*, 6 [1939–40]: 107–26). On the basis of an entry in the Spanish inventories, it was also believed to have passed to Philip II via Guevara, but although the subject fits the present panel ("madness is being cured"), the square shape and the canvas support do not; and that work also appears again as a square canvas (now "in poor condition") in an inventory compiled upon Philip II's death (Paul Vandenbroeck, "The Spanish *inventarios reales* and Hieronymus Bosch," in *Hieronymus Bosch: New Insights into His Life and Work*, ed. Jos Koldeweij and Bernard Vermet [Rotterdam: Museum Boijmans Van Beuningen; Ghent: Ludion, 2001], pp. 50 and 53). Dismissing this provenance, other scholars have identified the Prado picture with a painting owned by the Duke and Duchess of Arcos in 1794; for this proposal and a summary of the debate, see Carmen Garrido and Roger van Schoute, *Bosch at the Museo del Prado* (Madrid: Museo del Prado and Aldeasa, 2001), p. 51.

36 Interpretations of the work's subject are summarized in Roger H. Marijnissen and Paul Ruyffelaere, *Hieronymus Bosch: The Complete Works*, trans. Ted Atkins et al. (Antwerp: Mercatorfonds, 1987), pp. 440–43; see, more recently, Paul Vandenbroeck, *Jheronimus Bosch: de verlossing van de wereld* (Ghent: Ludion, 2002), pp. 289–90.

37 Saint-Germain-en-Laye, Musée Municipal; Friedländer (Bosch), no. 105; the vomited frog and its companion on the table strongly suggest that here the magic is diabolical, as Jeffrey Hamburger argued persuasively ("Bosch's *Conjurer*: An Attack on Magic and Sacramental Heresy," *Simiolus* [1984]: 5–24).

38 Madrid, Museo del Prado, Inv. P02825.

39 See Kathrin Utz Tremp, "Welche Sprache spricht die Jungfrau Maria?" *Schweizerische Zeitschrift für Geschichte* 38 (1988): 221–49; Céline Dupeux et al., *Bildersturm—Wahnsinn oder Gottes Wille*, exh. cat., Historisches Museum Bern (Munich: Fink, 2000).

40 Thomas Murner, *Von den fier ketzeren Prediger orde[n]s der observantz zü Bern in Schweytzer land verbran[n]t* (Strasbourg: Knobloch, 1509), p. 106.

41 Geneva, Musée d'Art et d'Histoire; Inv. VG 41.

42 Natalie Zemon Davis, "The Rites of Violence: Religious Riot in Sixteenth-Century France," *Past & Present* 59 (1973): 56; citing Jean Crespin, *Histoire des martyrs: persecutez et mis à mort pour la verité de l'Evangile, depuis le temps des apostres jusques à présent (1619)*, ed. Daniel Benoît (Toulouse: Sociète des Livres Religieux, 1885–89), 2: 307–8.

43 Karel van Mander, *The Lives of the Illustrious Netherlandish and German Painters, from the first edition of the* Schilder-boeck *(1603–1604)*, ed. and trans. Hessel Miedema (Doornspijk: Davaco, 1994), 1: 125 (1605, fol. 216v).

44 See, for example, Carmen Garrido and Roger van Schoute, "El studio téchnico de El jardín de las delicias," in El jardín de las delicias *de El Bosco: copias, estudio técnico y restauración*, ed. Pilar Silva Maroto (Madrid: Museo Nacional del Prado, 2000), pp. 71–98.

45 On the underdrawings in the Lisbon triptych, see Ana Maria Mesquita e Carmo and Pedro Antunes de Sousa, "Le *triptyque de Tentation de Saint Antoine* de Jheronimus Bosch. La photographie et la réflectographie infrarouges dans la détection du dessin sous-jacent," in *Jérôme Bosch et son entourage et autres etudes*, ed. Hélène Verougstraete-Marcq and Roger van Schoute, Dessin sous-jacent et la technologie dans la peinture, 14 (Leuven: Peeters, 2003), pp. 9–16.

46 Daniela Hammer-Tugendhat, *Hieronymus Bosch. Eine historische Interpretation seiner Gestaltungsprinzipien*, Theorie und Geschichte der Literatur und der schönen Künste, 58 (Munich: Fink, 1981), pp. 68–70.

47 On the phrase "from life" (Dutch *near het leven*) and its sister phrase "from the mind (or spirit) (*uyt den gheest*), see Walter S. Melion, *Shaping the Netherlandish Canon: Karel van Mander's* Schilder-boeck (Chicago: University of Chicago Press, 1991), pp. 64–77; Claudia Swan, *Art, Science, and Witchcraft in Early Modern Holland: Jacques de Gheyn II (1565–1629)*, Cambridge Studies in Netherlandish

Visual Culture (Cambridge, UK: Cambridge University Press, 2005), pp. 10–22.

48 Gerolamo Cardano, *De rerum varietate*, 18.97, in *Opera omnia*, ed. Charles Spon (Lyons: Huguetan and Ravaud, 1663), 3: 340–41; cited in Lorraine Daston and Katherine Park, *Wonders and the Order of Nature 1150–1750* (New York: Zone Books, 1998), p. 167.

49 Berlin, Staatliche Museen zu Berlin, Kupferstichkabinett, KdZ 550 (verso); Stephanie Buck, *Die niederländischen Zeichnungen des 15. Jahrhundert im Berliner Kupferstichkabinett. Kritischer Katalog*, Die Zeichnungen alter Meister in Berliner Kupferstichkabinett (Turnhout: Brepols, 2001), pp. 207–11 (no. I. 32v).

50 Cennino Cennini, *Il libro dell'arte*, ed. Franco Brunello (Vincenza: N. Pozza, 1971), pp. 3–4; cited and discussed in David Summers, *Michelangelo and the Language of Art* (Princeton, NJ: Princeton University Press, 1981), p. 112; on the philosophical background to this view, see Martin Kemp, "From Mimesis to Fantasia: The Quattrocento Vocabulary of Creation, Inspiration, and Genius in the Visual Arts," *Viator* 8 (1977): 347–98.

51 Augustine, *Epistolae*, 7, cited in Summers, *Michelangelo*, p. 109.

52 Heinrich Institoris and Jacob Sprenger, *Malleus Maleficarum*, ed. and trans. Christopher S. Mackay (Cambridge, UK: Cambridge University Press, 2006), 2: 130; discussed in Massing, "*Sicut erat in diebus Antonii*," p. 111.

53 Théodore Agrippa d'Aubigné, *Oeuvres*, ed. Henri Weber (Paris: Gallimard, 1969), p. 538; cited in Jean Delumeau, *Sin and Fear: The Emergence of a Western Guilt Culture in the 13th–18th Centuries*, trans. Eric Nicholson (New York: St. Martin's, 1990), p. 2.

54 Translation my own, Sigüenza, *Tercera parte de la Historia de la Orden de San Gerónimo, Doctor de la Iglesia*, p. 838; *Historia de la Orden*, ed. Garcia, 2: 636.

55 See "The Gifts of the Magi," chapter 5.

56 Godfried Christiaan Maria van Dijck, *Op zoek naar Jheronimus van Aken alias Bosch: de feiten: familie, vrienden en opdrachtgevers ca. 1400–ca. 1635* (Zaltbommel: Europese Bibliothek, 2001), p. 186.

57 Charles de Tolnay, *Hieronymus Bosch* (New York: Reynal, 1966), p. 317; Ludwig Baldass, *Jheronimus Bosch*, 2nd rev. ed., ed. Günther Heinz (Vienna: Schroll, 1959), p. 45; see also Hamburger, who calls it an "anti-mass" and discusses it with reference to contemporary worries about sacramental heresy ("Bosch's *Conjurer*," p. 7).

58 Lucretius, *The Way Things Are: The* De rerum natura *of Titus Lucretius Carus*, trans. Rolfe Humphries (Bloomington: Indiana University Press, 1969), p. 120; on the rediscovery of Lucretius, see Stephen Greenblatt, *The Swerve: How the World Became Modern* (New York: Norton, 2011); on Lucretius's influence especially on Florentine painters, see Alison Brown, *The Return of Lucretius to Renaissance Florence* (Cambridge, MA: Harvard University Press, 2010).

59 Max Lehrs, *Geschichte und kritischer Katalog des deutschen, niederländischen und französischen Kupferstichs im xv. Jahrhundert* (Vienna: Gesellschaft für Vervielfältigende Kunst, 1908–34), 1: 260.

60 Jacobus de Voragine, *The Golden Legend: Readings on the Saints*, trans. William Granger Ryan (Princeton, NJ: Princeton University Press, 1993), 1: 94.

61 William A. Clebsch, "Preface," in Athanasius, *Life of Antony*, p. xvi.

62 Regnerus Richardus Post, *The Modern Devotion: Confrontation with Reformation and Humanism* (Leiden: Brill, 1968), pp. 392–34 and passim; Erasmus spent two years (c. 1484–85) in 's-Hertogenbosch attending a school of the Brethren of Common Life, the religious community most closely associated with the *devotio moderna* (James D. Tracy, *Erasmus, the Growth of a Mind*, Travaux d'Humanisme et Renaissance, 126 [Geneva: Librairie Droz, 1972], p. 21).

63 Athanasius, *Life of Antony*, p. 91; the same anecdote appears in Voragine, *Golden Legend*, 1: 95–96.

64 This usage left a trace in the third century CE hermetic treatise *Asclepius*, which laments the demise of the ancient Egyptian cult of images under the pressure of rising iconoclastic Christianity under Constantine and prophesies "this most holy land [Egypt], seat of shrines and temples, will be filled completely with tombs [or "funerals"] and corpses" (*Hermetica: The Greek* Corpus Hermeticum *and the Latin* Asclepius *in a new English translation, with notes and introduction*, trans. and ed. Brian P. Copenhaver [Cambridge, UK: Cambridge University Press, 1992], p. 81); Augustine cited this passage polemically to prove that "the gods of Egypt were dead men" (*City of God*, 8.26). On Egypt as a perennial site of image wars, see Jan Assmann, "What's Wrong with Images?" in *Idol Anxiety*, ed. Josh Ellenbogen and Aaron Tugendhaft (Stanford, CA: Stanford University Press, 2011), pp. 24–30. I am grateful to Moshe Halberthal for this line of thinking about tombs, images, and counter-images.

65 Voragine, *Golden Legend*, 1: 93–94; also Athanasius, *Life of Antony*, p. 39.

66 Cicero, *Orationes in Verrum* 2.5.165; cited and discussed in Martin Hengel, *Crucifixion in the Ancient World and the Folly of the Message of the Cross*, trans. John Bowden (New York: Fortress Press, 1977), pp. 7–10.

67 Joseph Leo Koerner, "The Master's Secret," *The New Republic* (November 26, 1990): 42–46.

68 Lucretius, *De rerum natura*, 4.33–35; *The Way Things Are*, p. 120.

69 On the "abduction of agency" in art, see Alfred Gell, *Art and Agency: An Anthropological Theory* (Oxford: Clarendon, 1998), pp. 13–27.

CHAPTER 7. THE UNSPEAKABLE SUBJECT

1 For brief summaries of the literature on Bosch's so-called *Garden of Delights*, see Walter Gibson, *Hieronymus Bosch: An Annotated Bibliography* (Boston: G. K. Hall, 1983), pp. 84–97; key subsequent interpretative studies I have consulted include: Albert Cook, *Changing the Signs: The Fifteenth-Century Breakthrough* (Lincoln: University of Nebraska Press, 1985), pp. 81–120; Paul Vandenbroeck, "Jheronimus Bosch' zogenaamde Tuin der Lusten," *Jaarboek Koninklijk Museum voor Schone Kunsten Antwerpen* (1989), 9–210, and (1990): 9–192; Michel de Certeau, *The Mystic Fable*, 1, *The Sixteenth and Seventeenth Centuries*, trans. Michael B. Smith (Chicago: University of Chicago Press, 1992), pp. 49–78; Keith Moxey, *The Practice of Theory: Poststructuralism, Cultural Politics, and Art History* (Ithaca: Cornell University Press, 1994), pp. 111–47; Jean Wirth, *Hieronymus Bosch. Der Garden der Lüste. Das Paradise als Utopie* (Frankfurt am Main: Fischer, 2000); Jos Koldeweij, Bernard Vermet, and Paul Vandenbroeck, *Hieronymus Bosch: The Complete Paintings and Drawings* (Ghent: Ludion; Rotterdam: NAi, 2001), pp.100–111; and Hans Belting, *Hieronymus Bosch: Garden of Earthly Delights* (Munich: Prestel, 2002). See also the important technical analyses: *El jardín de las delicias de El Bosco: Copias, estudio técnico y restauración*, exh. cat., Pilar Silva Maroto et al. (Madrid: Museo del Prado, 2000);

Carmen Garrido and Roger van Schoute, *Bosch at the Museo del Prado* (Madrid: Museo del Prado and Aldeasa, 2001), pp. 158–93.

2 Bosch's triptych is called a *Flügelaltar* ("winged altarpiece") in Ludwig von Baldass, *Jheronimus Bosch*, 2nd rev. ed., ed. Günther Heinz (Vienna: Schroll, 1959), p. 52; Roger H. Marijnissen and Peter Ruyffelaere, skeptical of esoteric and theologically unorthodox interpretations, insist (contrary to the documentary evidence) that the work was originally a functioning "altar painting" with a conventional religious meaning (*Hieronymus Bosch: The Complete Works*, trans. Ted Atkins et al. [Antwerp: Mercatorfonds, 1987], p. 91). Wilhelm Fraenger took the work to be an altarpiece, but for a heretical sect of Adamites secretly active in 's-Hertogenbosch (*Hieronymus Bosch: Das Tausendjährige Reich. Grundzüge einer Auslegung* [Coburg: Winkler-Verlag, 1947]). For a more recent, alternative view of Bosch as an ascetic (rather than libertine) heretic, see Lynda Harris, *The Secret Heresy of Hieronymus Bosch* (Edinburgh: Foris Books, 1995). Arguments that the work celebrates sexual pleasure include: (most emphatically and influentially) Fraenger, *Das Tausendjährige Reich*; Charles de Tolnay, *Hieronymus Bosch* (New York: Reynal, 1966), pp. 360–61; Clément A. Wertheim-Aymès, *Hieronymus Bosch, eine Einführung in seine geheime Symbolik, dargestellt am* "Garten der himmlischen Freuden," *am* Heuwagen-Triptychon, *am* Lissaboner Altar *und an Motiven aus anderen Werken* (Amsterdam: Van Ditmar, 1957), p. 17, arguing for a Rosicrucian Bosch; and Patrick Reuterswärd, *Hieronymus Bosch*, Acta Universitatis Upsaliensis (Stockholm, 1970), pp. 49–82. The most detailed analysis of the triptych as a condemnation of lust (also a sustained refutation of Fraenger) is Dirk Bax, *Beschrijving en poging tot verklaring van het Tuin der Onkuisheiddrieluik van Jeroen Bosch, gevolgd door kritiek op Fraenger*, Verhandlingen der Koninklijke Nederlandse Adademie van Wetenschappen, Letterkunde, new series 63, no. 2 (Amsterdam: Noord-Hollandsche Uitg. Mij., 1956). On the work as a "false" paradise, see Walter S. Gibson's excellent "The Garden of Earthly Delights by Hieronymus Bosch: The Iconography of the Central Panel," *Nederlands Kunsthistorisch Jaarboek* 24 (1973): 1–26; and especially (summarizing his massively documented earlier studies) Paul Vandenbroeck, *Jheronimus Bosch. De verlossing van de wereld* (Ghent and Amsterdam: Ludion, 2002), pp. 78–86. For alchemical readings of the work, see Jacques Combe, "Sources alchimiques dan l'art de Jérôme Bosch," *L'Amour de l'art* 26 (1946): 30–35; Lorinda Dixon, "Bosch's *Garden of Delights* Triptych: Remnants of a 'Fossil' Science," *Art Bulletin* 63 (1981): 96–113; and *eadem*, *Bosch* (London: Phaidon, 2003), pp. 225–312. For the proponent of the view that the work functions partly as a Jewish calendar, but via Mixtec/Nahuatl chronology, see Susan Gilchrist's website, http://elboscoblog.blogspot.com.

3 Erwin Panofsky, *Early Netherlandish Painting: Its Origins and Character* (Cambridge, MA: Harvard University Press, 1958), 1: 358; citing the baffled German translator of Marsilio Ficino's *De triplici vita*, Johann Adelphi (Mülich), in Hieronymus Brunswig's *Medicinarius. Das buch der Gesuntheit Liber de arte distillandi simplicia et composita. Das nüv Büch d' rechtē Kunst zü distillieren* (Strasbourg: Johann Grüninger, 1505), fol. 174v.

4 *The Travel Journal of Antonio De Beatis: Germany, Switzerland, the Low Countries, France and Italy, 1517–1518*, trans. J. R. Hale and J.M.A. Lindon, ed. J. R. Hale (London: The Hakluyt Society, 1979), p. 94. The provenance of Bosch's triptych in the Nassau palace was rediscovered and first publicized, with reference to Beatis's description, by Jan Karel Steppe in a paper delivered in 1962 at the Royal Flemish Academy of Sciences, Literature and Fine Arts (summarized, without reference to Beatis, in "Problemen betreffende het werk van Hieronymus Bosch," *Jaarboek van de Koninklijke Vlaamse Academie voor Wetenschappen, Letteren en Schone Kunsten van België* 24 [1962]: 166–67). Five years later Steppe detailed his discovery in "Jheronimus Bosch. Bijdrage tot de historische en de ikonografische studie van zijn werk," *Jheronimus Bosch: Bijdragen bij gelegenheid van de herdenkingstentoonstelling te 's-Hertogenbosch 1967* (*'s-Hertogenbosch*: Hieronymus Bosch Exhibition Foundation, 1967), pp. 7–12, 28–30. But in that same year (1967), Ernst H. Gombrich published his discovery—far more famous and frequently cited than Steppe's—via Beatis of the same provenance for the triptych without, however, referencing Steppe's work ("The Earliest Description of Bosch's Garden of Delight," *Journal of the Warburg and Courtauld Institutes* 30 [1967]: 403–6).

5 Brussels, Musée Royaux des Beaux Arts de Belgique, Accession 1658.

6 *Travel Journal of Antonio De Beatis*, p. 94.

7 Fort Worth, Kimbell Art Museum, AP 70.30; Belting argues that Henry III commissioned the work, perhaps in competition with Philip the Fair's documented 1504 prepayment to Bosch for a large *Last Judgment* (*Hieronymus Bosch*, pp. 73–77); Vandenbroeck and Vermet suggest, more plausibly, that Engelbert II was the more likely patron (Koldeweij, Vandenbroeck, and Vermet, *Hieronymus Bosch*, p. 110); see "Cruel Sports," chapter 8.

8 On the experience and representation of astonishment in the early modern period, see Stephen Greenblatt, *Marvelous Possessions: The Wonder of the New World* (Chicago: University of Chicago Press, 1991), pp. 13–25 and passim.

9 Madrid Palacio Real, Patrimonio Nacctional, cat. 10004013; see Maroto et al., *El jardín de las delicias*, pp. 46–47; also Steppe, "Jheronimus Bosch," pp. 5–41; Otto Kurtz, "Four Tapestries after Hieronymus Bosch," *Journal of the Warburg and Courtauld Institutes* 30 (1967): 150–62.

10 See Paul Vandenbroeck's remarkable essay, "High Stakes in Brussels, 1567. The Garden of Delights as the Crux of the Conflict between William the Silent and the Duke of Alba," in *Hieronymus Bosch: New Insights into His Life and Work*, ed. Jos Koldeweij and Bernard Vermet (Rotterdam: Museum Boijmans Van Beuningen; Ghent: Ludion, 2001), pp. 87–92.

11 In 1571, Jacques Jonghelinck, brother of Bruegel's patron Nicolaes Jonghelinck, also produced a full-length, over-life-size bronze statue of Alba for the citadel of Antwerp, but the work was destroyed by rebellious Netherlanders a few years later.

12 Vandenbroeck, "High Stakes," p. 88.

13 Vandenbroeck, "High Stakes," pp. 88–89.

14 The work came with the sixth and last shipment, or *entregas*, of works to decorate the monastery of El Escorial; see J. Zarco Cuevas, "Inventario de las alhajas, relicarios, estatuas, pinturas, tapices y otros objetos de valor y curiosidad donados por el rey don Felipe II al Monasterio de El Escorial Años de 1571 a 1598," *Boletín de la Real Academia de la Historia* 96 (1930): 657, no. 846; Paul Vandenbroeck, "The Spanish *inventarios reales* and Hieronymus Bosch," in *Bosch: New Insights*, ed. Koldeweij and Vermet, pp. 49–64.

15 Patricia Falguières, *Les chambres des merveilles* (Paris: Bayard, 2003), pp. 8–23.

16 José Manuel Cruz Valdovinos, "La clientela de El Bosco," in *El Bosco y la tradición pictórica de lo fantástico*, ed. Victoria Malet (Barcelona: Galaxia Gutenberg, Círculo de lectores, 2006), p. 118n38.

17 Joseph de Sigüenza, *Tercera parte de la Historia de la Orden de San Gerónimo, Doctor de la Iglesia* (Madrid: Imprenta Real, 1605), p. 839; *Historia de la Orden de San Jerónimo*, ed. Juan Catalina Garcia (Madrid: Bailly-Balliére, 1909), 2: 637; trans. James Snyder, in *Bosch in Perspective*, ed. James Snyder, The Artists in Perspective Series (Englewood Cliffs, NJ: Prentice-Hall, 1973), p. 38. On identification of *madroño* with strawberries, see most recently, Walter Gibson, "The Strawberries of Hieronymus Bosch," *Cleveland Studies in the History of Art* 8 (2003): 24–33.

18 Sigüenza, *Tercera parte*, p. 839; *Historia*, ed. Garcia, 2: 637; trans. Snyder, *Bosch in Perspective*, p. 38.

19 On the condition of the triptych in 1933, see Jerónimo Seisdedos, "El jardín de las delicias o la pintura del Madroño," *Arte Español* 15 (1944–45): 105–6; on the current condition of the triptych, see Maroto et al., *El jardín de las delicias*, pp. 109–14.

20 Carl Justi, "Die Werke des Hieronymus Bosch in Spanien," *Jahrbuch der Königlich Preussischen Kunstsammlungen* 10 (1889): 138; republished in *Miscellaneen aus drei Jahrhunderten spanischen Kunstlebens* (Berlin: G. Grote, 1908), 2: 83.

21 Writing in the mid-nineteenth century, Vincente Poleró y Toledo reports that the work represents "earthly delights and the punishment of the vices in hell" (*Catálogo de los cuadros del Real Monasterio de San Lorenzo, llamado de El Escorial* [Madrid: Impr. de Tejado, 1857], p. 54, no. 129). The best recent proposal for renaming is Vandenbroeck's, which, drawing on learned and popular literary traditions, argues for "The Grail" ("Jheronimus Bosch' zogenaamde Tuin der Lusten. II" [1990]: 163; and *Jheronimus Bosch. De verlossing van de wereld*, pp. 78–86).

22 Marijnissen and Ruyffelaere, *Hieronymus Bosch*, p. 91.

23 Augustine, *Confessions* 10.35–38.

24 For an account of the triptych as essentially undecidable and undecided, and thus as forbearer of modern semantic freedom and a postmodern "play" of the signified, see Cook, *Changing the Signs*, pp. 81–120.

25 Augustine, *City of God* 11.33–34.

26 See also Psalm 148:5.

27 Michael Wolgemut and Wilhelm Pleydenwurff, *God the Father* and *Yle*, hand-colored woodcut frontispiece to Hartmann Schedel's *Liber Chronicarum* (Nuremberg: Anton Koberger, 1493), fol. 1r, 2v. Hartmann Schedel's own hand-colored copy of the Latin edition of *Das Buch der Cronicken* is preserved in Munich's Bayerische Staatsbibliothek (BSB-Ink K-37,1) fol. 1r, 2v. (Bild nr. 74, 75). On this survival, and on the genesis of the Creation sequence, see Adrian Wilson, *The Making of the Nuremberg Chronicle* (Amsterdam: Nico Israel, 1967), pp. 81–97, 207–26.

28 Hartmann Schedel, *Das Buch der Cronicken vnd gedechtnus wirdigern geschichte[n] von anbegyn[n] d[er] werlt bis auf dise vnßere zeit* (Nuremberg: Anton Koberger, 1493), IIr.

29 Nicolas of Cusa mentions *hyle* explicitly in *De non aliud* (9.33), the manuscript of which was preserved—exclusively—through Schedel, who had it in his extensive library (ms. Munich Codex Latinus Monacensis 24848, fol. 1v–54r); see Richard Stauber, *Die Schedelsche Bibliothek: Ein Beitrag zur Geschichte der Ausbreitung der italienischen Renaissance, des deutschen Humanismus und der medizinischen Literatur* (Freiburg: Herder, 1908), pp. 130 and 149; also Paul Oskar Kristeller, *Studies in Renaissance Thought and Letters*, 3 (Rome: Edizioni di Storia e Letteratura, 1993), pp. 30–31; and *Die Graphiksammlung des Humanisten Hartmann Schedel*, ed. Béatrice Hernad, exh. cat. (Munich: Prestel, 1990).

30 Henry George Liddell, Robert Scott, James Morris Whiton, *A Lexicon Abridged from Liddell and Scott's Greek-English Lexicon* (New York: Harper, 1891), p. 725.

31 Charles Dempsey, "Sicut in utrem aquas maris: Jerome Bosch's Prolegomenon to the *Garden of Delights*," *Modern Language Notes* 119, no. 1 Supplement (2004), pp. 247–70.

32 Augustine, *Exposition on the Book of Psalms* 33.1 (trans. and ed. Philip Schaff, http://www.newadvent.org/fathers/1801033.htm).

33 *Exposition* 33.7.

34 On translations of the Hebrew *nōhd* ("wineskin" or "bottle") and their relevance to Bosch's transparent globe, see Dempsey, "Sicut in utrem," pp. 254–59.

35 This is how God appears in the Mystery Plays, as well: the opening stage directions of the mid-twelfth-century Anglo-Norman *Ordo Repraesentationis Adae* (*Play of Adam*) has "our Savior come, clothed in a dalmatic" (David Bevington, *Medieval Drama* [Boston: Houghton Mifflin, 1975], p. 80).

36 The Art Institute of Chicago, Inv. 1936.239; Susan Frances Jones dates the panel to the first decades of the sixteenth century and associates it with a member of Bosch's workshop active either in 's-Hertogenbosch or in Antwerp ("The Garden of Paradise at the Art Institute of Chicago," *Jérôme Bosch et son entourage et autres etudes*, ed. Hélène Verougstraete and Roger van Schoute, Le dessin sous-jacent et la technologie dans la peinture, 14 [(Leuven and Dudley, MA: Peeters, 2003], pp. 140–49).

37 Most recently Wirth, *Hieronymus Bosch*, p. 79; and Belting, *Hieronymus Bosch*, p. 25, citing Rosemarie Schuder, *Hieronymus Bosch: das Zeitalter, das Werk* (Berlin: Edition q, 1991). Also Vandenbroeck, "Jheronimus Bosch' zogenaamde Tuin der Lusten. II" (1990), pp. 93–97.

38 *Das ist der Spiegel der menschen behaltnis mit den evangelien und mit epistelen nach der zyt des iars* (Speyer: Peter Drach, c. 1480), fol. 1v; see Albert Schramm, *Der Bilderschmuck der Frühdrucke*, 16, *Die Drucker in Speyer, Würzburg, Eichstätt, Passau, München, Ingelstadt, Zweibrücken, Freising, Memmingen* (Leipzig: Karl W. Hiersemann, 1933). p. 6, fig. 301. The illustrations have been attributed to Erhard Reuwich. On the iconography, see Adelheid Heimann, "Die Hochzeit von Adam und Eva im Paradies," *Wallraf-Richartz Jahrbuch* 37 (1975): 11–40.

39 William Tronzo calls the scene above the "Meeting" the "Shaping of Eve," and explains the wakeful Adam through apocryphal *Vitae Adae et Evae* as observing her creation in retrospect, via its narration by the Archangel Michael; see "The Hildesheim Doors: An Iconographic Source and Its Implications," *Zeitschrift für Kunstgeschichte* 46 (1983): 357–66; see also Harvey Stahl, "Eve's Reach: A Note on Dramatic Elements in the Hildesheim Doors," in *Reading Medieval Images: The Art-Historian and the Object*, ed. Elizabeth Sears and Thelma K. Thomas (Ann Arbor: University of Michigan Press, 2002), pp. 162–75. On Eve at Hildesheim as a document of targeted misogyny against a female rival of Bernward, see Adam S. Cohen and Anne Derbes, "Bernward and Eve

at Hildesheim," *Gesta* 40 (2001): 19–38. Profoundly vexing in the story they tell of Adam and Eve, and proto-Boschian in their making unruly, sexualized vegetation part of that story, the Hildesheim Doors prove that Bosch's triptych is not the first work to enlist the visual imagination for exploring the mysteries of the Fall. I am grateful to Isabelle Marchesin for her illuminating remarks to me in this regard.

40 "Amor è un desio che ven da core," ll.3–4. The sonnet forms part of a *tenzone* (debate among poets in poetical form) by Giacomo da Lentini, Pier delle Vigna, and Jacopo Mostacci; on which, see Ulrich Mölk, "Le sonnet *Amor è un desio* di Giacomo da Lentini et le problem de la genèse de l'amour," *Cahiers de civilization medieval* 14 (1971): 329–39; and Dana Stewart, *The Arrow of Love: Optics, Gender, and Subjectivity in Medieval Love Poetry* (Lewisburg, PA: Bucknell University Press, 2003), pp. 49–51.

41 *La Rime della Scuola Siciliana*, ed. Bruno Panvini (Florence: L. S. Olschki, 1962–64), 1: 45.

42 On the "love-imprint" motif in Giacomo and other poets of the period, see Julie Singer, *Blindness and Therapy in Late Medieval French and Italian Poetry*, Gallica, 20 (Woodbridge and Suffolk: D. S. Brewer, 2011), pp. 36–39; also Ioan P. Couliano, *Eros and Magic in the Renaissance*, trans. Margaret Cook (Chicago: University of Chicago Press, 1987), p. 22.

43 "Maravigliosamente," ll.4–9; *La Rime*, ed. Panvini, 1: 7; cited in Singer, *Blindness*, p. 37.

44 Translation by Robert Alter, *The Five Books of Moses: A Translation with Commentary* (New York: W. W. Norton, 2004); on the Hebrew word *ta-awah* ("delight" or "lust"), see pp. 24–25n6.

45 On medieval and early modern theories of vision, see especially David C. Lindberg, *Medieval Theories of Vision from Al-kindi to Kepler* (Chicago: University of Chicago Press, 1976); A. Mark Smith, "Getting the Big Picture in Perspectivist Optics," *Isis* 72 (1981): 568–89; Katherine H. Tachau, *Vision and Certitude in the Age of Ockham: Optics, Epistemology, and the Foundations of Semantics, 1230–1345* (Leiden: Brill, 1988); Michael Camille, "Before the Gaze: The Internal Senses and Late Medieval Practices of Seeing," in *Visuality Before and Beyond the Renaissance: Seeing as Others Saw*, ed. Robert S. Nelson (Cambridge, UK: Cambridge University Press, 2000), pp. 197–223; and Stuart Clark, *Vanities of the Eye: Vision in Early Modern European Culture* (Oxford: Oxford University Press, 2007).

46 Smith, "Getting the Big Picture," p. 578.

47 See "A Phenomenology of the Idol," in this chapter.

48 On Eros and fantasy in the period, see especially Giorgio Agamben, *Stanzas: Word and Phantasm in Western Culture*, trans. Ronald L. Martinez (Minneapolis: University of Minnesota Press, 1993); and Couliano, *Eros and Magic*.

49 Paris, Louvre, RF 2089.

50 Augustine, *Exposition*, Ps. 12.8; see Elena Calas, "The Wicked Walk in a Circle in Bosch's *Garden*," *Colóquio / Artes* 20 (1978): 36.

51 Vandenbroeck, "Jheronimus Bosch' zogenaamde Tuin der Lusten. II" (1990): 34.

52 See Plutarch, *Symposiaka problemata*, 5.7; cited in Agamben, *Stanzas*, p. 101n24 and p. 109.

53 Andreas Capellanus, *De amore*, ed. S. Battaglia (Rome: Perrella, 1947), chap. 1; cited in Agamben, *Stanzas*, p. 87n13; also Couliano, *Eros and Magic*, p. 19.

54 Agamben, *Stanzas*, p. 109; according to Jean Gerson, fantasy "gives rise to the whole desire" (Agamben, p. 107).

55 See Jean Louis Schefer, "La pudeur d'Adam," in Jean Louis Schefer, Henri Dominique Saffrey, and Jean-Claude Lebensztejn, *La creation d'Ève*, Collection "Triptych" (Paris: Desclée de Brouwer, 2001), pp. 27–35.

56 Augustine, *The Literal Meaning of* Genesis, 9. 19. 36, in *On Genesis*, ed. John E. Rotelle, trans. Edmund Hill, in *The Works of St. Augustine*, pt. 1, vol. 13 (New York: New City Press, 2002), p. 396; also Peter Comestor, *Scholastica Historia, Liber Genesis*, 17; Peter Abelard, *Expositio in Hexameron*, 482; Alan of Lille, *Summa de arte praedicatoria*, *PL* 210, col. 195–96.

57 *Rymbybel van Jacob van Maerlant*, ed. Jean Baptiste David (Brussels: M. Hayez, 1858–61), pp. 26–27 (ll. 552–53); cited in Dirk Bax, *Hieronymus Bosch and Lucas Cranach: Two Last Judgement Triptychs*, trans. M. A. Bax-Botha (Amsterdam: North-Holland Pub. Co., 1983), p. 55.

58 "Lord, where have I so long been? / For since I slept, much have I seen, / Wonders that, without doubt, / Shall come to be known about." *The Chester Plays*, ed. Hermann Deimling, Early English Text Society, Extra Series, 62, 115 (London: Oxford University Press, 1892), I: 26, ll. 138–40; I am indebted to Nicholas Watson and Traugott Lawler for help with this passage.

59 Henry Staten, *Eros in Mourning: Homer to Lacan* (Baltimore: Johns Hopkins University Press, 1995), p. 125.

60 Vienna, Kunsthistorisches Museum, GG 5686; the work was transferred to Vienna from the great Habsburg *Kunst- und Wunderkammer* at Schloss Ambras.

61 I am grateful to Ronah Sadan for her insights, in "The Art Institute of Chicago's *Garden of Paradise* (a Bosch workshop painting)," unpublished typescript, 2011.

62 Augustine, *The Literal Meaning of* Genesis, 12. 15. 31, ed. Rotelle, p. 480.

63 Albrecht Dürer, *Schriftlicher Nachlaß*, ed. Hans Rupprich (Berlin: Deutsche Verein für Kunstwissenschaft, 1956), 1: 161.

64 On the archival traces of this lost work, see Koldeweij, Vermet, and Vandenbroeck, *Hieronymus Bosch*, p. 69.

65 Dürer, *Schriftlicher Nachlaß*, 1: 155

66 Dürer, *Schriftlicher Nachlaß*, 3: 293.

67 Sigmund Freud, *Interpretation of Dreams*, trans. James Strachey (New York: Norton, 2010), p. 510n1.

68 Asphalt was said to boil up from hell in the plain of Sodom and Gomorrah, where fruits grew that changed to bitter ashes the moment they were touched; see Gordon Teskey's discussion of "asphaltic slime" (Milton, *Paradise Lost*, 10.298), in *Delirious Milton: The Fate of the Poet in Modernity* (Cambridge, MA: Harvard University Press, 2006), pp. 38–41.

69 Falguières, *Les chambres des merveilles*, p. 11.

70 Belting, *Hieronymus Bosch*, pp. 87–89; Wirth, *Hieronymus Bosch*, p. 75.

71 Augustine, *Literal Meaning of* Genesis, 9. 10. 18, trans. Hill, ed. Rotelle, p. 385; Augustine, *The City of God*, 14.24, trans. Marcus Dods (New York: Modern Library, 1950), p. 472.

72 Paul Ricoeur, "'Original Sin': A Study in Meaning," trans. Peter McCormick, in Ricoeur, *The Conflict of Intepretations: Essays in Hermeneutics*, ed. Don Ihde (Evanston, IL: Northwestern University Press, 1974), pp. 272–81.

73 Augustine, *City of God*, 14.13 (trans. Dods, p. 460).

74 Augustine, *City of God* 14.15 (trans. Dods, p. 463); see Elaine Pagel's account of the "politics of Paradise," in *Adam, Eve, and the Serpent* (New York: Vintage, 1988), pp. 98–126.

75 Paul Ricoeur, *The Symbolism of Evil*, trans. Emerson Buchanan (New York: Harper and Row, 1967), pp. 257–60.

76 Augustine, *City of God*, 12.7; on the "no-explanation account" of the Fall, see Timothy D. J. Chappell, "Explaining the Inexplicable: Augustine on the Fall," *Journal of the American Academy of Religion* 62 (1994), pp. 869–83.

77 Roland Hissette, ed., *Enquête sur les 219 articles condamnés à Paris le 7 mars 1277* (Louvain: Publications universitaires, 1977); Luca Bianchi, *Il vescovo e i filosofi. La condanna parigina del 1277 e l'evoluzione dell'aristotelismo scolastico* (Bergamo: Lubrina, 1990); and Luca Bianchi and Eugenio Randi, *La verità dissonanti. Aristotle alla fine del Medioevo* (Rome: Laterza, 1990).

78 Thesis 166; Alain de Libera, *Denken im Mittelalter*, trans. Andreas Knop (Munich: Fink, 2003), p. 148.

79 De Libera, pp. 145–77.

80 Kurt Flasch, *Eva und Adam: Wandlungen eines Mythos* (Munich: C. H. Beck, 2004).

81 Cohen and Derbes, "Bernward and Eve," p. 24.

82 Matthias Mende, *Hans Baldung Grien: das graphische Werk* (Unterschneidheim: Uhl, 1978), no. 19.

83 Ewald M. Vetter, "Necessarium adae peccatum. Hans-George Gadamer zum 65. Geburtstag," *Ruperto-Carola*, 18 (1966), 143–82, 153–54; New Haven, Yale University Art Gallery, *Hans Baldung Grien: Prints and Drawings*, exh. cat., ed. James H. Marrow and Alan Shestack (New Haven, CT: Yale University Art Gallery, 1981), p. 121; Joseph Leo Koerner, *The Moment of Self-Portraiture in German Renaissance Art* (Chicago: University of Chicago Press, 1993), p. 298.

84 London, The Courtauld Institute of Art, P.1947.LF.77; see Caroline Campbell, ed., *Temptation in Eden: Lucas Cranach's* Adam and Eve, exh. cat. (London: Courtauld Institute of Art, 2007).

85 On their relationship, see most recently Steven Ozment, *The Serpent and the Lamb: How Lucas Cranach and Martin Luther Changed Their World and Ours* (New Haven, CT: Yale University Press, 2011); also Martin Warnke, *Cranachs Luther: Entwürfe für ein Image*, Kunststück (Frankfurt am Main: Fischer, 1984).

86 Wayne Martin, "The Judgment of Adam: Self-Consciousness and Normative Orientation in Lucas Cranach's Eden," in *Art and Phenomenology*, ed. Joseph D. Parry (London and New York: Routledge, 2011), pp. 105–37; I am grateful to Martin for sending me an early draft of this excellent paper.

87 Martin Luther, *Works*, 1:93; cited in Martin, "Judgment of Adam."

88 Alan of Lille, *De planctu natura* 2, 22; my translation; see also Alan of Lille, *Literary Works*, ed. and trans. Winthrop Wetherbee, Dumbarton Oaks Medieval Library, 22 (Cambridge, MA: Harvard University Press, 2013), pp. 42 and 43.

89 Jacques Chiffoleau, "Dire l'indicible. Remarques sur la catégorie du *nefandum* du XIIe au XVe siècle," *Annales E.S.C.* 45 (1990): 289–324; Bernd-Ulrich Hergemöller, *Sodom und Gomorrha. Zur Alltagswirklichkeit und Verfolgung Homosexueller im Mittelalter*, 2nd ed., rev. and exp. (Hamburg: Buchladen Männerschwarm, 2000), pp. 97–140; Helmut Puff, *Sodomy in Reformation Germany and Switzerland, 1400–1600* (Chicago: University of Chicago Press, 2003), pp. 52–62 and passim; Helmut Puff, "Nature on Trial: Acts 'Against Nature' in the Law Courts of Early Modern Germany and Switzerland," in *The Moral Authority of Nature*, ed. Lorraine Daston and Fernando Vidal (Chicago: University of Chicago Press 2004), pp. 232–53.

90 Marc Boone, "State Power and Illicit Sexuality: The Persecution of Sodomy in Late Medieval Bruges," *Journal of Medieval History* 22 (1996): 135–53.

91 Mark D. Jordan, *The Invention of Sodomy in Christian Theology* (Chicago: University of Chicago Press, 1997).

92 *Summa Theologiae*, II, 2, q. 156, art. 11; see De Libera, *Denken*, pp. 159–60.

93 *Summa Theologiae*, II, 2, q. 156, art. 12.

94 Boone, "State Power," p. 152 and passim.

95 Michel Foucault called sodomy "that utterly confused category" (*The History of Sexuality*, 1, *An Introduction*, trans. Robert Hurley [New York: Pantheon, 1978–88], p. 101); Jonathan Goldberg, expanding on Foucault, proposed that sodomy "remains incapable of exact definition," *Sodometries: Renaissance Texts, Modern Sexualities* (Stanford, CA: Stanford University Press, 1992), p. 18.

96 Johann Herolt, "Sermo LXXXV," *Sermones discipuli de tempore et de Sanctis* (Mainz: n.p., 1612), p. 489; cited in Puff, *Sodomy*, p. 55.

97 Raimundus de Peñaforte, *Summa de paenitentia*, ed. Xaverius Ochoa and Aloisius Diez (Rome: Commentarium pro religiosis, 1976), col. 845; cited in Puff, *Sodomy*, p. 68.

98 Jakob Frey, *Gartengesellschaft (1556)*, ed. Johannes Bolte (Tübingen: Litterarischer Verein in Stuttgart, 1896), p. 45; see also the examples in Puff, *Sodomy*, pp. 57–58.

99 Clifford Geertz, *The Interpretation of Cultures: Selected Essays* (New York: Basic Books, 1973), p. 448.

100 Philips Wielant, *Corte instructie in materie criminele (1510)*, ed. Jos Monballyu (Brussels: Paleis der Academiën, 1995), 91; see Bernd-Ulrich Hergemöller, "Sodomiter. Schuldzuschreibungen und Repressionsformen in späten Mittelalter," in *Randgruppen der spätmittelalterlichen Gesellschaft. Ein Hand- und Studienbuch*, ed. Bernd-Ulrich Hergemöller (Warendorf: Faulbusch, 1990), p. 319.

101 Gibson, "The Garden of Earthly Delights," pp. 1–26.

102 On the parodic treatments of courtly love, see Keith Moxey, "Master ES and the Folly of Love," *Simiolus* 11 (1980): 125–48.

103 Rudolf Arnheim, *The Power of the Center: A Study of Composition in the Visual Arts*, rev. ed. (Berkeley: University of California Press, 1982).

104 Garrido and Van Schoute, *Bosch at the Museo del Prado*, pp. 183–84.

105 Paul Vandenbroeck, "Hieronymus Bosch," *The Grove Dictionary of Art*, ed. Jane Turner (Oxford: Oxford University Press, 2003), 4: 453–54.

106 Garrido and Van Schoute, *Bosch at the Museo del Prado*, p. 182.

107 For example Jo Durden-Smith, "Optical Illusion," *Departures* (July–August 1999); also http://www.departures.com/art-culture/exhibit/optical-illusion.

108 Leon Battista Alberti, *On Painting*, trans. John R. Spencer (New Haven, CT: Yale University Press, 1956), p. 78.

109 Fraenger, *Hieronymus Bosch: Das tausendjährige Reich*; for a useful overview of Fraenger's arguments, which he spread over several densely argued books, and on the critical reception of Fraenger's various theses, see Walter Gibson, review of Wilhelm Fraenger, *Hieronymus Bosch*, 10th ed. (Dresden and Basel: Verlag der Kunst, 1994), in *Speculum* 72 (1997): 1171–73.

CHAPTER 8. SELF-PORTRAITURE

1 Already for Carl Justi, writing in 1889, the circular march was "a cult action of natural religion" ("Die Werke des Hieronymus Bosch in Spanien," in *Miscellaneen aus drei Jahrhunderten spanischen Kunstlebens* [Berlin: G. Grote, 1908], 2: 83).

2 Weimar, Schlossmuseum im Stadtschloss, Inv. G 398 (FR264); on myths of the Golden Age as cultural

PHOTOGRAPHY AND COPYRIGHT CREDITS

Permission to reproduce illustrations is provided by the owners and sources as listed in the captions. Additional copyright notices and photography credits are as follows. Numbers refer to figure numbers.

Alinari / Art Resource, NY: 244

Alte Pinakothek, Munich, Germany / Bridgeman Images: 226

The Art Institute of Chicago: 196

The Barber Institute of Fine Arts, University of Birmingham / Bridgeman Images: 222

© Bayer&Mitko–ARTOTHEK: 226

© Beaux-Arts de Paris, Dist. RMN-Grad Palais / Art Resource, NY: 228

© Bildarchiv Foto Marburg / Dom-Museum Hildesheim / Frank Tomio / Art Resource, NY: 190, 200

© Blauel/Gnamm—ARTOTHEK: 14, 17, 238

bpk, Berlin / Gemäldegalerie / Joerg P. Anders / Art Resource, NY: 32, 65, 129

bpk, Berlin / Kupferstichkabinett / Joerg P. Anders / Art Resource, NY: 34, 86, 159, 232, 237

bpk, Berlin / Kupferstichkabinett / Staaliche Museum, Berlin / Joerg P. Anders / Art Resource, NY: 91, 158, 233, 306

bpk, Berlin / Staaliche Kunsthalle, Karlsrube / Hermann Buresch / Art Resource, NY: 251

bpk, Berlin / Staaliche Kunsthalle, Karlsrube / Annette Fisher / Heike Kohler / Art Resource, NY: 251

bpk, Berlin / Staatsbibliothek Preussischer Kulturbesitz / Art Resource, NY: 113

© The British Library Board: 106, 225

© The Trustees of the British Museum. All rights reserved: 28, 77, 240, 242, 290, 324

© Centre for Art Historical Documentation, Radboud University Nijmegen (Photo J.A.J.M. Verspaandonk): 84

City of 's-Hertogenbosch, Heritage Department: 80

© Commissie Zomertentoonstellingen Sint-Jan, 's-Hertogenbosch (Photo Ernst van Mackelenbergh): 81

© Samuel Courtauld Trust, The Courtauld Gallery, London, UK / Bridgeman Images: 202

Peter Cox, Eindhoven: 85, 289

De Agostini Picture Library / Bridgeman Images: 46

De Agostini Picture Library / G. Nimatallah / Bridgeman Images: 21

Detroit Institute of Arts, USA, City of Detroit Purchase / Bridgeman Images: 299

Deutsches Historisches Museum, Berlin, Germany © DHM / Bridgeman Images: 87

David Fenwick: 175

Wolfgang Fuhrmannek: 319, 325

Galleria degli Uffizi, Florence / Bridgeman Images: 96

Graphische Sammlung Albertina, Vienna, Austria / Bridgeman Images: 68

Hans Kuiper / Stichting Grote Kerk Breda: 78

Kunsthistorisches Museum, Vienna, Austria / Bridgeman Images: 254

Kunstsammlungen der veste Coburg, Germany, www.kunstsammlungen-corburg.de: 234

Map image courtesy the Norman B. Leventhal Map Center at the Boston Public Library: 19

Erich Lessing / Art Resource, NY: 48, 141, 168, 261

Lobkowicz Palace, Prague Castle, Czech Republic / Bridgeman Images: 312

madle-fotowelt: 3

Illustration reprinted from *The Trapper's Bible*, copyright 1987 by Dale Martin, with the permission of the publisher, Paladin Press

Image copyright © The Metropolitan Museum of Art: 67

Image copyright © The Metropolitan Museum of Art. Image source: Art Resource, NY: 102, 189

Musee d'Art et d'Historie, Saint-Germain-en-Laye, France / Bridgeman Images: 153

© Musée d'art et d'histoire, Ville de Genève, inv. n° F 0323 / Photo: Bettina Jacot-Descombes: 79

© Musée d'art et d'histoire, Ville de Genève, inv. n° VG 0041 / Photo: Yves Siza: 156

Musée d'Unterlinden, Dist. RMN-Grand Palais / Art Resource, NY: 142

Musées de Strasbourg, M. Bertola: 110

© Museo Nacional del Prado: 37, 39, 69, 90, 93, 115, 122, 144, 145, 152, 154, 170, 180, 183,

Museum for Fine Arts Ghent, © *www.lukasweb .be*, Art in Flanders vzw, photo Hugo Maertens: 57

Photograph © 2016 Museum of Fine Arts, Boston: 146, 283

Museum voor Schone Kunsten, Ghent, Belgium © Lukas, Art in Flanders VZW / Photo: Hugo Maertens / Bridgeman Images: 53, 120

© National Gallery, London / Art Resource, NY: 104, 117, 131, 151

© National Trust Photo Library / Art Resource, NY: 108

Markus Nolf: 175

Luisa Oliveira: 138, 139, 165

Alfredo Dagli Orti / The Art Archive at Art Resource, NY: 89

Palazzo Ducale, Venice, Italy / Bridgeman Images: 147

The Truman Show © Paramount Pictures Corp. All Rights Reserved: 135, 136

© Patrimonio Nacional: 41, 174, 227

Luciano Pedicini, fotografo / archivio dell'arte: 24

Princeton University Art Museum / Bruce M. White / Art Resource, NY: 269

Franz Reischl: 101

© RMN-Grand Palais / Michèle Bellot / Art Resource, NY: 308

© RMN-Grand Palais / Jean-Gilles Berizzi / Art Resource, NY: 193

© RMN-Grand Palais / Gérard Blot / Art Resource, NY: 293

© RMN-Grand Palais / Thierry Ollivier / Art Resource, NY: 250

© RMN-Grand Palais / René-Gabriel Ojéda / Art Resource, NY: 42, 224

© Royal Museum Fine Arts Belgium, Brussels / photo: Grafisch Buro Lefevre, Heule: 70, 172

© Royal Museum Fine Arts Belgium, Brussels / photo: J. Geleyns—Ro scan: 70, 172, 262, 264, 300, 304

Royal Museum for Fine Arts Antwerp, © *www.lukasweb.be*, Art in Flanders vzw, photo Hugo Maertens: 72

Image courtesy Saint Louis Art Museum: 249

Scala / Art Resource, NY: 128, 243

© Städel Museum—ARTOTHEK: 133

Studio Buitenhof, The Hague: 307

Studio Tromp, Rotterdam: 13, 18, 59, 236, 280, 281

SzépmüvészetiMúzeum / Museum of Fine Arts, 2016: 30, 267

The Matrix still licensed by Warner Bros. Entertainment Inc. All Rights Reserved: 137

Yvan Travert / Getty Images: 45

THE A. W. MELLON LECTURES IN THE FINE ARTS 1952–2016

1952 Jacques Maritain, *Creative Intuition in Art and Poetry*

1953 Sir Kenneth Clark, *The Nude: A Study of Ideal Art* (published as *The Nude: A Study in Ideal Form*, 1956)

1954 Sir Herbert Read, *The Art of Sculpture* (published 1956)

1955 Etienne Gilson, *Art and Reality* (published as *Painting and Reality*, 1957)

1956 E. H. Gombrich, *The Visible World and the Language of Art* (published as *Art and Illusion: A Study in the Psychology of Pictorial Representation*, 1960)

1957 Sigfried Giedion, *Constancy and Change in Art and Architecture* (published as *The Eternal Present: A Contribution on Constancy and Change*, 1962–1964)

1958 Sir Anthony Blunt, *Nicolas Poussin and French Classicism* (published as *Nicolas Poussin*, 1967)

1959 Naum Gabo, *A Sculptor's View of the Fine Arts* (published as *Of Divers Arts*, 1962)

1960 Wilmarth Sheldon Lewis, *Horace Walpole* (published 1960)

1961 André Grabar, *Christian Iconography and the Christian Religion in Antiquity* (published as *Christian Iconography: A Study of Its Origins*, 1968)

1962 Kathleen Raine, *William Blake and Traditional Mythology* (published as *Blake and Tradition*, 1968)

1963 Sir John Pope-Hennessy, *Artist and Individual: Some Aspects of the Renaissance Portrait* (published as *The Portrait in the Renaissance*, 1966)

1964 Jakob Rosenberg, *On Quality in Art: Criteria of Excellence, Past and Present* (published 1967)

1965 Sir Isaiah Berlin, *Sources of Romantic Thought* (published as *The Roots of Romanticism*, 1999)

1966 Lord David Cecil, *Dreamer or Visionary: A Study of English Romantic Painting* (published as *Visionary and Dreamer: Two Poetic Painters, Samuel Palmer and Edward Burne-Jones*, 1969)

1967 Mario Praz, *On the Parallel of Literature and the Visual Arts* (published as *Mnemosyne: The Parallel between Literature and the Visual Arts*, 1970)

1968 Stephen Spender, *Imaginative Literature and Painting*

1969 Jacob Bronowski, *Art as a Mode of Knowledge* (published as *The Visionary Eye: Essays in the Arts, Literature, and Science*, 1978)

1970 Sir Nikolaus Pevsner, *Some Aspects of Nineteenth-Century Architecture* (published as *A History of Building Types*, 1976)

1971 T.S.R. Boase, *Vasari: The Man and the Book* (published as *Giorgio Vasari: The Man and the Book*, 1979)

1972 Ludwig H. Heydenreich, *Leonardo da Vinci*

1973 Jacques Barzun, *The Use and Abuse of Art* (published 1974)

1974 H. W. Janson, *Nineteenth-Century Sculpture Reconsidered* (published as *The Rise and Fall of the Public Monument*)

1975 H. C. Robbins Landon, *Music in Europe in the Year 1776*

1976 Peter von Blanckenhagen, *Aspects of Classical Art*

1977 André Chastel, *The Sack of Rome: 1527* (published 1982)

1978 Joseph W. Alsop, *The History of Art Collecting* (published as *The Rare Art Traditions: The History of Art Collecting and Its Linked Phenomena Wherever These Have Appeared*, 1982)

1979 John Rewald, *Cézanne and America* (published as *Cézanne and America: Dealers, Collectors, Artists, and Critics, 1891–1921*, 1989)

1980 Peter Kidson, *Principles of Design in Ancient and Medieval Architecture*

1981 John Harris, *Palladian Architecture in England, 1615–1760*

1982 Leo Steinberg, *The Burden of Michelangelo's Painting*

1983 Vincent Scully, *The Shape of France* (published as *Architecture: The Natural and the Manmade*)

1984 Richard Wollheim, *Painting as an Art* (published 1987)

1985 James S. Ackerman, *The Villa in History* (published as *The Villa: Form and Ideology of Country Houses*, 1990)

1986 Lukas Foss, *Confessions of a Twentieth-Century Composer*

1987 Jaroslav Pelikan, *Imago Dei: The Byzantine Apologia for Icons* (published 1990)

1988 John Shearman, *Art and the Spectator in the Italian Renaissance* (published as *Only Connect . . . Art and the Spectator in the Italian Renaissance*, 1992)

1989 Oleg Grabar, *Intermediary Demons: Toward a Theory of Ornament* (published as *The Mediation of Ornament*, 1992)

1990 Jennifer Montagu, *Gold, Silver, and Bronze: Metal Sculpture of the Roman Baroque* (published 1996)

1991 Willibald Sauerländer, *Changing Faces: Art and Physiognomy through the Ages*

1992 Anthony Hecht, *The Laws of the Poetic Art* (published as *On the Laws of the Poetic Art*, 1995)

1993 John Boardman, *The Diffusion of Classical Art in Antiquity* (published 1994)

1994 Jonathan Brown, *Kings and Connoisseurs: Collecting Art in Seventeenth-Century Europe* (published 1995)

1995 Arthur C. Danto, *Contemporary Art and the Pale of History* (published as *After the End of Art: Contemporary Art and the Pale of History*, 1997)

1996 Pierre M. Rosenberg, *From Drawing to Painting: Poussin, Watteau, Fragonard, David, Ingres* (published as *From Drawing to Painting: Poussin, Watteau, Fragonard, David, and Ingres*, 2000)

1997 John Golding, *Paths to the Absolute* (published as *Paths to the Absolute: Mondrian, Malevich, Kandinsky, Pollock, Newman, Rothko, and Still*, 2000)

1998 Lothar Ledderose, *Ten Thousand Things: Module and Mass Production in Chinese Art* (published 2000)

1999 Carlo Bertelli, *Transitions*

2000 Marc Fumaroli, *The Quarrel between the Ancients and the Moderns in the Arts, 1600-1715*

2001 Salvatore Settis, *Giorgione and Caravaggio: Art as Revolution*

2002 Michael Fried, *The Moment of Caravaggio* (published 2010)

2003 Kirk Varnedoe, *Pictures of Nothing: Abstract Art since Pollock* (published 2006)

2004 Irving Lavin, *More than Meets the Eye*

2005 Irene J. Winter, *"Great Work": Terms of Aesthetic Experience in Ancient Mesopotamia*

2006 Simon Schama, *Really Old Masters: Age, Infirmity, and Reinvention*

2007 Helen Vendler, *Last Looks, Last Books: The Binocular Poetry of Death* (published as *Last Looks, Last Books: Stevens, Plath, Lowell, Bishop, Merrill*, 2010)

2008 Joseph Leo Koerner, *Bosch and Bruegel: Parallel Worlds* (published 2016)

2009 T. J. Clark, *Picasso and Truth* (published as *Picasso and Truth: From Cubism to* Guernica, 2013)

2010 Mary Miller, *Art and Representation in the Ancient New World*

2011 Mary Beard, *The Twelve Caesars: Images of Power from Ancient Rome to Salvador Dalí*

2012 Craig Clunas, *Chinese Painting and Its Audiences* (published 2017)

2013 Barry Bergdoll, *Out of Site in Plain View: A History of Exhibiting Architecture since 1750*

2014 Anthony Grafton, *Past Belief: Visions of Early Christianity in Renaissance and Reformation Europe*

2015 Thomas Crow, *Restoration as Event and Idea: Art in Europe, 1814–1820*

2016 Vidya Dehejia, *The Thief Who Stole My Heart: The Material Life of Sacred Bronzes in Chola India, c. 850–1280*